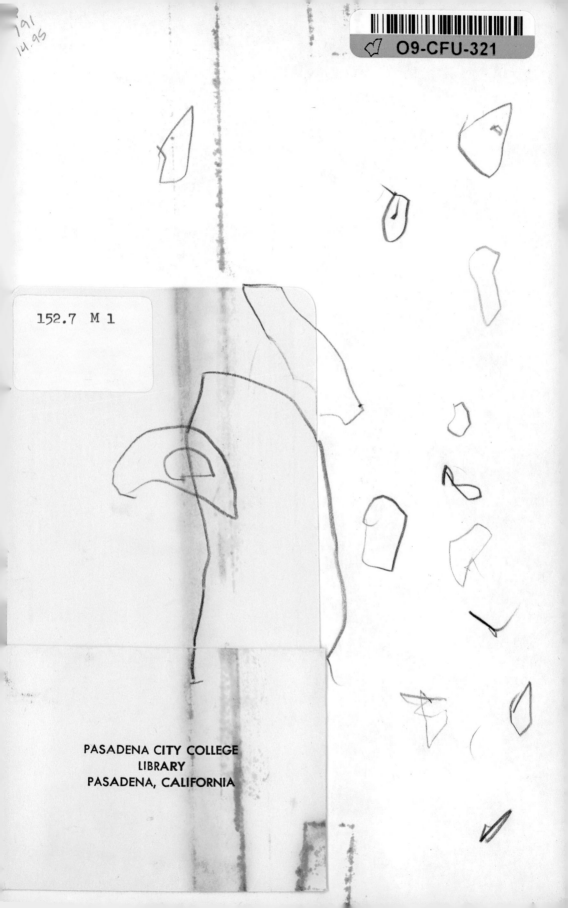

LANGUAGE and PERCEPTION

LANGUAGE
and
PERCEPTION

George A. Miller
Philip N. Johnson-Laird

The Belknap Press of
Harvard University Press
Cambridge, Massachusetts   1976

Library of Congress Cataloging in Publication Data

Miller, George Armitage, 1920-
  Language and perception.

  Bibliography: p.
  Includes index.
  1. Languages—Psychology. 2. Perception
I. Johnson-Laird, Philip Nicholas, joint author.
II. Title. [DNLM: 1. Psycholinguistics.
BF455 M648p]
BF455.M59   153   75-30605
ISBN 0-674-50947-1

Preface

"Take care of the sense," the Duchess said, "and the sounds will take care of themselves." If students of language have often ignored her advice, they can be excused. The sounds are much easier to take care of; how to take care of the sense raises questions no one can answer. To take the Duchess's advice seriously would require a much firmer theory of meaning than psychology has yet provided. If students of psychology—like ourselves—had done their work better, students of language might have done their work differently.

But perhaps the psychologists can be forgiven, too. According to one recent survey of the psychology of language,

> it is hardly surprising that psychology has thus far failed to produce theories of any importance in the area of semantics. We cannot ask pertinent or insightful (to say nothing of experimentally resolvable) questions about how the semantic system of a speaker-hearer is used, or about how it is learned, until something substantial is known about the properties of that system. The part of theory construction which consists in conceptual analysis is, in this sense, methodologically prior to the part which considers questions about application or assimilation of concepts. It is highly probable, though doubtless depressing, that specifically psychological work on semantics will continue to be largely impertinent until a great deal more theoretical insight has been gained about the structure of formal semantic theory than is currently available. (Fodor, Bever, and Garrett, 1974, p. 220)

In short, there can be no psychological theory of meaning until formal semanticists tell psychologists what such a theory would be a theory *of*.

The nature of meaning is too important a problem for psychology to set aside until formal semanticists have reached a consensus. Judging by what they have accomplished to date, it seems highly improbable that formal semanticists are going to solve any of psychology's problems in the near future or, unless they learn more about what psychology's problems are, in the distant future. At the considerable risk of impertinence, therefore, the following pages try to fill this gap in psychological theory—if not for meaning in general, then at least for that part of it most relevant to the English language. If we have not succeeded in filling it, certainly we have diligently explored the gap's psychological dimensions, which should be an important preliminary to filling it. We suspect that a collaborative effort will be required; here we have tried to set forth what psychology might be able to contribute.

This book attempts to lay the foundations for a new field of language study, a field that we sometimes hear ourselves calling psycholexicology, the psychological study of the lexical component of language. Lexicology is the theory that underlies lexicography; pyscholexicology is lexicology based on psychology, on how a language user's mind works. Or, psychology is the theory of mental and behavioral phenomena; psycholexicology is psychology based on lexicology, on how a language user's words work. Either way, psycholexicology tries to take care of the sense.

"Sense" has two senses, one perceptual and the other linguistic. We have tried to take care of them both, for we feel the two are not as different as they are sometimes made out to be. Saying how we believe they are related has turned into a major project.

The project began in 1971 with a study by Miller of motion verbs in English; some two hundred motion verbs were identified, classified, and their meanings related according to a list of twelve semantic components. Johnson-Laird, who came to the Institute for Advanced Study in the fall of 1971, became interested and offered suggestions as to how Miller's analysis might be deepened. Several of the semantic components seemed to have perceptual foundations: motion, change of motion, velocity, path, direction, instrumentality, deixis. W. J. M. Levelt, who was also at the Institute during the academic year 1971–72, noted that A. Michotte's work could provide a perceptual base even for the causative component. It seemed an intriguing possibility that the cognitive structure relating these verbs reflected basic mechanisms that had evolved for the perception of motion. We decided to explore the relation and to write a short sequel to Miller's paper.

Once launched, however, the project quickly grew in scope. For comparative purposes it was important to explore other verb domains in a similar fashion; Aravind Joshi, who also spent 1971–72 at the Institute, encouraged us in this direction by undertaking an analysis of English verbs of seeing. Since both of these domains feature locative and directional information, an analysis of spatial prepositions and adverbs was necessary; when that requirement was combined with the need for an analysis of deixis of place, a general discussion of English resources for expressing spatial relations was indicated. A deeper analysis of motion also revealed a similar need for an analysis of temporal relations. The causative component that distinguishes such motion verbs as "rise" and "raise" also demanded treatment. And in the background was always a commitment to say something about the relation of these analyses to the syntactic rules and social conventions of linguistic communication.

It soon became obvious that the correlations we had noted between perceptual and linguistic structures were mediated by an enormously complex conceptual structure. Space, time, and causation are concepts. Percepts and words are merely avenues into and out of this conceptual structure. Any theory of the relation between perception and language must necessarily be a theory of conceptual thought.

In order to do justice to these topics, a book was outlined. Not until it was well along did we remember that the relation between perception and language is one of the oldest and most tortured subjects in the history of Western thought. When Johnson-Laird had to return to England in 1972 there were still doubts whether the hundreds of pages that had been written would ever crystallize into a coherent manuscript. As our horizons expanded to include more ambitious sub-projects, we recognized more and more work in psychology, social anthropology, linguistics, philosophy, logic, and artificial intelligence that was directly relevant to our concerns. It was not merely that we had to assimilate a great variety of related thought and discussion but that excellent new work of critical importance to us was suddenly appearing in books and journals at an exponentially increasing rate. It seemed impossible to digest it all, yet the excitement of seeing ourselves as part of this intellectual adventure and incorporating diverse findings into our own point of view made it equally impossible not to try. But compromises were obviously necessary.

Large parts of the original plan had to be shrunk or abandoned. What remains is the core we regard as indispensable. Syntax is reduced to a few programmatic pages; developmental aspects are scattered as brief asides; relations to the sociolinguistic context are acknowledged but not explored; the possibility of a deeper logical structure underlying the domains we treat is scarcely alluded to. We have tried to leave our analysis open to further developments in these directions, but we could not do justice to them all in a single volume.

Thanks to the interest and patience of Carl Kaysen, director of the Institute for Advanced Study, and to support from the Sloan Foundation to the Institute, Johnson-Laird was able to visit each spring for a month of intensive collaboration. During this period Miller was also supported in part by Public Health Service Grants to The Rockefeller University and Johnson-Laird by a grant for scientific assistance from the Social Science Research Council (Great Britain) to the Laboratory of Experimental Psychology, University of Sussex. Johnson-Laird is also indebted to G. C. Drew and to University College London for a leave of absence in 1971–72. For their skillful typing and patient retyping of the manuscript, we are gratefully indebted to Elisabeth Balsa and Donna Kwilosz Lyons. Ballantine Books, a Division of Random House, Inc., kindly granted us permission to use illustrations from Jacques Carelman's *Catalog of Fantastic Things* (1971).

A list of those with whom we discussed our concerns between 1971 and 1975 would be too long, but some of our friends took the time to read, to criticize, and to educate us in important ways. It is a pleasure to take this opportunity to express our gratitude to Mark Altom, Elsa Bartlett, Catherine Bayliss, Jerome S. Bruner, Susan Carey, Harold Conklin, Clifford Geertz, Tarow Indow, Stephen Isard, Robert Jarvella, Aravind Joshi, Gerard Kempen, W. J. M. Levelt, Katherine Miller, Stanley Peters, Mark Steedman, Keith Stenning, N. S. Sutherland, Pamela Sutherland, Eric Wanner, and Joyce Weil. They are not responsible for mistakes we may have made in spite of their advice, but they are responsible for preventing many more mistakes we would certainly have made without it.

Contents

LANGUAGE and PERCEPTION

Introduction

A repeated lament of those who would understand human nature is that everything is related to everything else. A psychologist cannot speak of one mental function without considering others. If the ability to learn is to be the subject of inquiry, we are quickly forced to recognize that perception is an indispensable step in receiving the information to be learned, that little is learned by a student who has no motivation to remember it, that previous experience may facilitate or impede the learning process, that native intelligence sets the pace of learning, that boundaries between learning and thinking are vague to the point of indeterminacy, and that language provides the vessels for most of higher learning. If we take attention as our prime interest, we quickly find ourselves obliged to talk about perception, discrimination, motivation, learning, imagery, language—about all the chapter headings of general psychology. And so on. It is almost impossible to carve out a subset of psychological phenomena that interact tightly with one another yet are only loosely connected to everything else.

It is not uncommon, therefore, for psychologists to attack problems two or more at a time: learning *and* motivation, sensation *and* perception, language *and* thought, motivation *and* emotion. Such is the strategy we will follow here: language *and* perception define the double focus of our interest. Selection of this particular pair follows a tradition whose origin dates back to the earliest insight that what is seen and what is said are somehow related. The nature of that relation has fascinated philosophers for centuries; no doubt the British empiricists said most about it, but it certainly has not been ignored in more recent times.

Because philosophers have been so interested in the relation of perception to language, it is impossible to treat the subject seriously without taking account of their extensive investigations and disagreements. Our approach, though, is psychological. That is to say, our goal is to formulate a general theory relating language and perception, a theory adequate to support empirical and experimental investigations of scientific merit. To the extent that we are successful in so ambitious an enterprise our results should have some philosophical implications, even if only to show more clearly a proper division of labor between philosophers and psychologists in this domain. But our central concern is psychological, not philosophical.

Perception and language are related in many ways. The acoustic stimulus provided by the voice must itself be perceived if linguistic communication is to succeed; speech perception has been studied extensively by psychologists, linguists, and communication engineers. At a subtler level, there are reasons to believe that how people perceive the world is affected by the way they talk about it, a possibility that has interested many anthropologists, linguists, psychologists, and philosophers. We will be concerned here, however, primarily with how perception of the world affects communication about it.

We take it to be reasonably obvious that much of what people say—but certainly not all of it—depends directly or indirectly on their perception of the situation they are in. It is the nature of this dependency that we wish to explore. We assume that perceptual processes are, up to some point that we would like to determine, relatively independent of linguistic processes. Linguistic skills are acquired later than perceptual skills; people rely on perception as one way to attach meaning to their linguistic symbols. We will begin our exploration, therefore, with a consideration of perception. Once we have surveyed the perceptual resources that language can draw on, we will turn to a consideration of how perceptual judgments might be incorporated in the meanings of English words. We hope our survey will help us to see human perceptual processes in a new light, but our major aim is to formulate a psychological theory of lexical knowledge.

Someone educated in the intellectual climate of Anglo-American empiricism might approach our question in the following way: the central problem is to explain how words become associated with objects. For example, how does the word "lamp" become associated with lamps? Presumably, one hears it spoken while one is perceiving a lamp, and after this pairing has been repeated sufficiently often the association is established. This process would be taken as fundamental; the theoretical problem would be to reduce all linguistic knowledge to associating words with percepts.

Before one undertakes to solve this theoretical problem, one should be convinced that the general approach is sound. Is the central problem of relating perception and language really that of explaining word-percept associations? Or are such associations merely a superficial aspect of a much more complex psychological process? It is possible to raise objections in principle against the plausibility of an associationistic approach, but it is also possible to reformulate the approach in a variety of more sophisticated disguises and to introduce complications that would seem to avoid the more obvious objections. The fact that a scientific theory is wrong seldom suffices to overthrow it; lacking a better alternative, a scientist must live in the best theoretical edifice he has been able to construct.

If one finds associationistic accounts superficial, he should undertake to replace them by something less superficial. That, in a word, is the task we have set ourselves here. In order to undertake it, however, we have adopted a strategy that could lead to misunderstandings, and so it should be stated as clearly as possible in this introduction and not left as something for a reader to induce for himself. Our strategy might be called theoretical revisionism. Given the empiricist tradition in which relations between perception and language have been formulated, we have little alternative but to begin by taking seriously the claim that word-percept associations are fundamental. In this way we can discover some of the difficulties with this approach and suggest revisions that seem more adequate to the facts as we understand them. To borrow a familiar metaphor, we hope to rebuild our theoretical ship while we are voyaging on it; we need something to embark in, but we plan to remodel extensively as we go.

For example, what are the implications of taking seriously the claim that speakers of English learn what "lamp" means by hearing it spoken while perceiving lamps? Let us set aside for the moment (but never forget) the fact that "lamp" plays a role in an enormously complex combinatorial system that serves a bewildering variety of human purposes, and look at it merely as a label. What does "lamp" label? For speakers of English, it labels a certain class of physical objects people recognize as lamps. So the first task is to formulate some plausible account of the perceptual processes underlying such recognitions. Chapters 1 and 2 will review the psychology of perception with this task in mind, that is, with the idea of abstracting from what we know of human sensation and perception those attributes that might best serve as criteria for object recognition.

In chapter 3 we will try to sketch a conceptual system adequate to deal with language, and in chapter 4 we will put this system together with what we have abstracted from perceptual theory. At each step we will encounter problems that require us to revise and complicate our initial assumptions. In chapters 5, 6, and 7 we will apply our revised theory to groups of English words and will discover further necessary revisions. In the end we will have built a very different theory from the one with which we began. By then, if we are successful, the question of whether the associationistic hypothesis is correct will have faded from view—not answered, but replaced by a variety of other, deeper questions. A reader impatient to learn the course and direction of all this revisionary theorizing might jump to the Conclusion, where it is briefly summarized.

Throughout this revisionary pilgrimage one aspect that will remain constant is our interest in words and how people's knowledge of words should be characterized. In many respects words are rather dubious linguistic units. An objective definition of "word" might be "a textual unit consisting of consecutive letters bounded at both ends by spaces." One would scarcely expect a concept that depends on such accidental and transient matters as conventions of typography to lead into the important psychological processes underlying language. We could, of course, substitute some more sophisticated concept—the linguists' "morpheme" would be an obvious candidate—that would be less likely to limit our attention to literate adults. But the danger is more general than could be avoided by choosing morphemes over words. In either case, these are merely elements analyzed out of the flow of language, pieces with which the language game is played. Just as there is far more to perception than object recognition, so there is far more to language than knowing words.

Nevertheless we will focus our attention on words (or morphemes). We make no pretense that an account of word meanings is all we require for an adequate theory of language. We do believe, however, that any adequate theory will necessarily have a lexical component. And we suspect that the lexicon offers a convenient point of entry for psychological theory; certainly it is at this level that the most explicit psychological claims have been made about the relations between perception and language. Here, it would seem, is a theoretical toehold from which to begin.

To focus on words does not mean that the discussion can be limited to word units. No serious study of words could afford to ignore the contexts in which words are used. So the discussion will be much broader than the central theme. Consider some of the ways it will ramify.

A person's knowledge of the words in his language is not an easy thing to describe. The knowledge itself is most diverse, and the uses to which it can be put are far too various to catalog. What might be feasible, and what we will try to do, is to place certain limits on the range and variety of possible descriptions. We will try to do this by considering what we know about cognitive systems that support and exploit such knowledge. Insofar as words are involved in various cognitive systems, what we know of those systems can be used to constrain our psychological hypotheses about the organization and use of lexical knowledge.

This line of argument will be developed in detail later; it is nothing we can do justice to in a brief introduction. We can, however, illustrate the kinds of considerations that we believe are relevant to the argument and so perhaps prepare the reader for the variety of facts and inferences that we will try to marshal. That is to say, some of the issues that we will have to deal with can be anticipated even before the ground has been prepared to discuss them in detail.

For example, what constraints on the organization of the mental lexicon can be inferred from the requirements of grammar? When a linguist formulates a grammar for some language, what assumptions can he make about the types of information to be included in the lexical component of his grammar? Fillmore (1971c) tells us that each item in the lexicon must include information about:

—the phonological (or orthographic) shapes of the item
—its meaning

—the syntactic environments into which it can be inserted

—properties of the item to which grammatical rules are sensitive

—if the item is a predicate, the number of arguments it can take and the role of each argument

—conditions that must be satisfied for the item to be used "aptly"

—the conceptual or morphological relations of the item to other items in the lexicon

This list suggests some of the linguistic complications that distinguish a word-percept association from other, simpler kinds of association that psychologists have investigated.

It should be obvious that if linguists were in firm and incontrovertible agreement as to exactly how all this information should be characterized, the requirements of grammar would place very strong constraints on any psychological hypotheses about the organization of lexical memory. Unfortunately, such agreement is lacking. At present linguists are not even agreed as to where the lexical component of a linguistic description leaves off and the syntactic component begins; facts that one linguist would characterize lexically some other linguist might with equal plausibility characterize syntactically. For instance, one feels there is something wrong with the utterance "He frightens sincerity." All linguists would probably agree that a rule has been violated, but whether they would say it was a lexical or a syntactic rule would depend on their general theory of grammar. Or, to take another instance, if Oscar has refused to go, then it is acceptable to talk about either "Oscar's refusing to go" or "Oscar's refusal to go." The question thus arises as to how best to characterize these relations among "refuse," "refusing," and "refusal." It seems reasonable to assume that these three words are simply different shapes of a single lexical entry, but should the relations among these shapes be stated as syntactic or lexical rules? Chomsky (1970) claims that "Oscar refused to go" is syntactically related to "Oscar's refusing to go" but lexically related to "Oscar's refusal to go." Chomsky's reasons for this distinction are complicated and not above dispute, but the issues they raise are important in deciding what information should be included in the lexicon. Although the proper assignment of responsibilities to syntax or to lexicon is presumably an empirical issue, our bias here will be to lighten the explanatory load on syntactic theory wherever possible by putting as much information as we can into the lexicon.

Even without reviewing all the types of information that Fillmore lists, it should be clear that we can profitably join forces with linguistic theorists in a common effort to characterize people's knowledge of words. But linguists are not the only allies we will have.

At least one of the types of information on Fillmore's list—the conceptual relations of one lexical item to other items in the lexicon—has received considerable attention from social anthropologists. Some ethnologists believe that socially shared assumptions about the universe are reflected in the language that a social group uses to discuss them; analysis of the relations among their words can, in this view, provide valuable evidence about their assumptions.

This approach has been most extensively elaborated for kinship terminology, but it is usually assumed that it could be applied equally well to other lexical domains. Analyses generally take the form of decomposing word meanings into "semantic components." The representation of those components could impose additional constraints on any psychological hypotheses we might entertain about processes of lexical or sentential comprehension and the organization of lexical memory. Unfortunately, however, this field of inquiry is also something of an intellectual battleground. Componential analyses are seldom unique, and, given two or more plausible analyses, what criteria will enable us to determine which gives the better representation of the true psychological state of the people who speak the language? Or whether there is any single correct representation? No obvious or compelling answers have presented themselves.

Moreover, psychologists interested in the processes of verbal learning and memory have their own special brand of controversy and confusion to contribute. They would argue that a psychological theory of lexical memory should not be limited to a catalog of information that such a memory must contain. In addition to *what* is remembered, psychologists would like to say something about *how* it is remembered. A variety of theories of "semantic memory" have been put forward by psychologists in an attempt to characterize the cognitive processes that must be involved.

Probably the most general accounts of memory organization are to be found not in psychology but in the field of artificial intelligence, where attempts to organize computer memories for efficient information processing have taught us a great deal about what memory systems can be and do. In the case of lexical memory, anyone whose theoretical imagination is limited to the sort of inert, alphabetical lists that are printed in dictionaries will find these active memory systems a revelation. Indeed, the wide range of theoretical possibilities that modern computers suggest provides much of our present motivation to search for psychological, linguistic, anthropological, or other substantive boundary conditions on hypotheses about lexical memory. The computer metaphor can also help shape our hypotheses by directing our attention to what the system is expected to *do*—to the processes, operations, procedures, computations to be performed.

The relation of lexicon to syntax, the analysis of lexical items into semantic components, the organization of memory for lexical storage, are all matters of relating words to other words. They have to do with the internal relations of the system: the word "lamp" must be recognizable as a noun; it must be decomposable into semantic components like Inanimate or Human Artifact; it must be retrievable from memory. But even if we had a plausible theory that integrated all these diverse requirements, it would still not be an adequate theory of the lexicon. We must also consider the external relations of the system: if there were no way to relate "lamp" to concrete, objective instances of lamps, the word could hardly serve the purposes it does. If linguistic communication is to be of any practical value, words must not only be related to one another through grammatical, conceptual, or memorial systems; they must also be related to what is "out there," to what people want to talk about, to the things and events people perceive around them. The external relations of the system must be incorporated along with the internal relations. In our haste to point out how much more than word-percept relations a psychological theory must account for, we should not overlook the need to account for word-percept relations.

These external relations of the lexicon come into focus most sharply when we ask what the linguistic system is supposed to do. Consider, for example, what use a hearer might make of a particular sentence uttered on some particular occasion. Given that the hearer can assign a syntactic structure to the sentence, that he knows all the words, and that he can form some conception of their combined meaning, we are still interested to know what he might try to do about it: if a question has been asked, he may try to answer; if a request has been issued, he may try to comply; if information has been provided, he may try to remember; and so on. What a person may decide to do about any words he hears places strong constraints on the kind of information that must be lexically accessible to him.

One thing a person might try to do when he hears a declarative sentence is to verify it. This possibility has received almost as much attention from philosophers of language as grammaticality has received from linguists. Verification is related to our lexical interests in the following way.

Suppose a hearer decides to verify "This is a lamp" when accompanied by an ostensive gesture to some concrete object. In order to verify that the ostended object is indeed the kind of thing that speakers of English conventionally call lamp, he must have in memory some description of lamps that he can use to test the ostended object. Philosophers have been little interested in the mechanisms of such tests, but they have been very interested in the consequences of being able to perform them. That is what semantics, in a philosophical sense of the word, is all about. We will explore some psychological implications of their theories, but for the moment the important point to note is that the active *use* of words like "lamp" depends critically on one's ability to identify instances. The word must be associated somehow with a perceptual procedure capable of deciding which objects are and which objects are not instances of the appropriate kind.

Although verification is merely one of many procedures a hearer may try to carry out as a consequence of hearing a sentence, it illustrates the critical need for some way to link words and percepts. In formulating hypotheses about this link, one must deal with such questions as: What perceptual tests are available? How are they related? How does language control which tests will be performed? Is the availability of particular tests reflected in the lexical organization of particular words? And, in particular, how much of the lexicon depends on perceptual tests?

Our concern with relations between perception and language is obviously a concern for these "external relations" of the lexicon—for reference, rather than meaning. Our reasons are various. On the one hand, American psychology has been strongly influenced by empiricist philosophy—by the theory that perception is the only source of valid knowledge about the world. If this theory is correct, studies of perception should show us rather directly the foundations of human language in general and the meanings of human words in particular. This approach, in spite of its a priori plausibility, will fail, and we believe that it is important for psycholinguists to recognize its failure. On the other hand, most recent attempts by psychologists to characterize what is variously called long-term verbal memory, semantic memory, the subjective lexicon, the dictionary in your head, or lexical memory have been concerned almost exclusively with internal relations of the lexicon. We are convinced that this approach, too, must fail. And the two failures are related: each approach has too much of just what the other lacks. That is to say, one approach overemphasizes the dependence of language on perception and the other approach neglects it.

Our own goal is to achieve a theoretical synthesis of the external and the internal: to deal with problems of reference without ignoring the complexities of lexical memory, and also to deal with problems of meaning without ignoring the complexities of language use. Given this goal, our expository strategy develops as follows. First we will explore the inadequacies of any psycholexicology based solely on perception. In the course of that exploration we hope both to gain a new perspective toward perceptual processes by viewing them in terms of their contribution to human language and also to collect some ideas about the kind of externally related system that is needed to buttress current psychological theories of lexical memory. Thus, the initial exploration of perception, introduced to deprecate a predominantly external lexical theory, will subsequently undergo revisions intended to rescue a predominantly internal lexical theory. If all goes well, in the end we will have constructed a theory in which words and percepts are not linked directly to each other but in which both provide avenues into a conceptual realm that is itself the central concern of cognitive psychology.

These introductory remarks have anticipated many issues to be considered in depth as our argument develops, but at this point we are less concerned to defend our position on those issues than to foreshadow the general nature of the enterprise. It would be easier to indicate what lies ahead if we had an explicit, formal, psychological theory of lexical memory organization from which we could deduce direct consequences suitable for experimental test. Lacking such a formal theory, we must synthesize some general principles from a variety of disjoint sources and try to use them to characterize what an explicit theory might look like. The nature of this enterprise is intrinsically untidy. Discursive paths will often provide the only way through theoretical difficulties. But if we seldom seem to reach the ultimate, veridical, formalized revision of our theory, at least we will seldom underestimate the complexity of the cognitive system we are trying to understand.

1

The Sensory Field

There are good reasons to believe that the semantic markers in an adequate description of a natural language do not represent properties of the surrounding world in the broadest sense, but rather certain deep seated, innate properties of the human organism and the perceptual apparatus, properties which determine the way in which the universe is conceived, adapted, and worked on.
—*Manfred Bierwisch (1967)*

Those who believe in the psychological primacy of sensory processes normally distinguish between the physical world and the world of experience, with a third world—one of uninterpreted sensations—standing somewhere between physical and phenomenal reality. People live in a psychological world of everyday experience, a world very different from the abstract world of the physical sciences. The sensory field reflects more closely the pattern of physical stimulations impinging on the receptor organs, but it too differs drastically from the world in which people daily live and work and communicate. According to this view, the sensory field must face in two directions. On the one hand it requires a psychophysiological theory to explain how sensation is related to physical stimulation. On the other hand it requires a psychological theory to explain how the world of perceptual experience is related to, or derived from, the direct sensory consequences of physical stimulation.

Whether one poses this question in the terms of Helmholtz, who distinguished between sensation and perception, or in the terms of some more modern theorist like J. J. Gibson, who distinguishes between the visual field and the visual world, the theoretical problem has always been to explain how organisms can construct a stable world of tangible objects out of the flux of stimuli playing on receptor surfaces.

If we consider only the visual field (Gibson, 1950), we are presented with a continuous surface or an array of adjoining colored surfaces. From these elementary impressions of surfaces and edges we create for ourselves a visual world with depth and distances, including solid objects that lie in front of or behind one another. The visual world we construct contains objects and spaces between objects that do not change their dimensions as we move about, even though the pattern of stimulation or sensation we receive from the physical environment may change drastically. We tilt our heads, but the ground remains horizontal; we move our eyes, but the direction from ourselves to any object does not change; the world we live in is boundless, although our visual field is always bounded. The traditional psychological problem has been to relate this visual world to the tiny, blurred, wiggling, jerking, upside-down images that fall on our retinas.

There is, however, another psychological problem implicit in these observations, a problem that has received less attention than it deserves. Not only must a psychologist account for the generation of a visual world in terms of sensory qualia, geometry, stimuli, optics, learning, and so forth, but he must also develop some coherent way to characterize the visual world itself. Although psychologists have usually taken as their problem to explain how the visual world of experience is generated, an additional psychological problem is to characterize the contents of that perceptual world in such a manner that we can use it to account for *other* psychological phenomena. This second, related but distinct, problem for perceptual theory is critically important for discussions of the relation between perception and language.

Perhaps this aspect of the problem has been neglected because the answer was considered too obvious to merit serious study. After all, one can talk about the contents of the perceptual world well enough in ordinary language. If anything more is needed, one can fall back on the world of common sense and stale physics, with its precise locations in an infinite euclidean box. Or if that solution takes too little account of how the world looks to an observer located somewhere inside it, perhaps an answer could be phrased in terms of photographs and projective geometry. Or perhaps the problem has been neglected because it seems insolvable. Whatever the reason, too little attention has been paid to the question of how the visual world—a stable world of objects, regions, motions, distances, gradients, directions, events—might best be characterized for psychological purposes other than the study of perceptual processes. In order to relate perception and language, it is necessary to describe the *contents* of the world of perceptual experience. In the heyday of sensationistic psychology, this task was explicitly rejected; anyone who undertook it was accused of committing the "stimulus error."

In order to provide such a description it is necessary to give serious attention to the actual, mundane, familiar contents of the perceptual world. One who is interested only in perceptual processes can concentrate on those perceptual objects that reveal most clearly the nature of the particular processes he wishes to investigate—on points of light, contours, line drawings, uniform visual fields, monochromatic lights, pure tones, texture gradients, or whatever else seems most convenient for generation and manipulation in experiments. The fact that such perceptual contents are not representative of ordinary experience is irrelevant to a study of perceptual processes. In order to explore the perceptual bases for linguistic communication, however, it is necessary to devise some way to characterize *what* is perceived, not merely *how* it is perceived; people usually talk about what they perceive, not how they perceive it. The question is: How should the objects and situations that people talk about be characterized perceptually?

Psychologists interested in molar descriptions of behavior generally take the answer as given and speak (with little comment) about objects, situations, or events to which a behaving organism responds. Aspects of an organism's environment that are considered relevant to its behavior can usually be specified with great precision in centimeters, grams, and seconds, so the experimental situation can be replicated by other experimenters. But the psychological leap from physical description to subjective experience is usually left to the anthropocentric imagination of the reader. It is as if the problem were to analyze the relation between language and the physical world rather than between language and our perception of that world. In approaching the problem of characterizing the contents of perceptual experience, therefore, there is little established psychological theory to rely on. Consequently, our strategy must be to shape a plausible account and to hope that appropriate procedures for testing and correcting it will emerge after we see more clearly what is needed.

Although they are often ill suited to our purposes, distinctions among sensation, perception, and cognition organize the following pages; they serve to indicate which familiar bodies of psychological knowledge are being exploited. No doubt a theory of perception better suited to the present enterprise would enable us to approach our subject more directly. Lacking such a theory, we will take the opportunity to criticize the traditional distinctions even as we follow them.

1.1   FORMAL THEORIES OF SENSATION

The physical world can be characterized in terms of spatial coordinates, time, mass, velocity. What is a corresponding characterization of the world of experience? What are the sensory correlates of space and time, mass and energy? There are various informal and discursive answers that psychologists have offered to this question. If we look for formal theories of sensation, however, stated in a calculus appropriate to the phenomena and of comparable dignity to physical theories, there are few contenders. In the words of some experienced workers in this field, "The reader familiar with the visual literature knows that this is an area of many laws and little order" (Hurvich, Jameson, and Krantz, 1965, p. 101).

Consider a rough outline of the territory a comprehensive theory should cover. A theory of cognition should have two aspects. On the one hand, there should be a formal characterization of the functions or transformations performed by the cognitive system; on the other hand, there should be a description of the psychophysiological mechanisms whereby such a system could be realized. Although there is considerable information about neural mechanisms underlying afferent processes, and a picture of some of the mechanisms underlying sensation and perception is beginning to emerge, the possibility of saying anything definitive about the conceptual mechanisms of the nervous system is sufficiently remote at the present time to justify omitting this aspect of a comprehensive theory from our considerations. At the level of sensation, however, enough work has been done, both in the formulation of laws relating sensory attributes to physical stimulation and in the analysis of processes in the sensory receptors and nerves, that we might expect to find the beginnings of a comprehensive theory.

The fact that such a general theory of sensation does not exist should probably be counted as evidence that there is something artificial about the division of these input processes into sensory and perceptual components. Many psychologists have argued, and we tend to agree, that perceptual experience takes priority over sensory experience, that immediate apprehension of the sensory field is difficult if not impossible to achieve, that elementary sensations exist only by virtue of abstraction from the perceptual world, and, therefore, that any proposed division into sensation and perception must be artificial and misleading. A psychological attack on the plausibility of beginning an analysis of perception with elementary sensations can be found in the work of such gestalt theorists as Köhler (1929) and Koffka (1935); philosophical attacks have been made from widely differing sides—compare Austin (1962a) and Pitcher (1971). Whatever its faults or virtues, however, the distinction is deeply embedded in the history of the subject, and we have inherited interesting hypotheses at both levels of analysis. For the present exposition we will bow to historical precedent and begin the discussion of the perceptual world with a discussion of sensory experience. As theoretical revisionists we reserve the right to modify our initial assumptions as we proceed.

Attempts by Carnap and by Goodman can serve to suggest what some philosophers have thought a formal theory of sensory qualities might look like. Carnap viewed the problem as analytic: How are sensations abstracted out of the full panorama of subjective experience? Goodman viewed the problem as synthetic: How are experiences of concrete objects built up from sensory qualities?

Carnap (1928), using the methods of symbolic logic, took as the primitive, indivisible experiential elements of his system units he called Elementarerlebnisse—hereafter "erlebs"—which were full momentary cross sections of the total stream of experience. (We rely on the account of Carnap's system given by Goodman, 1951, chap. 5.) The formal problem was to describe how universal qualities can be abstracted from these concrete particulars. The primitive relation of Carnap's system was similarity, which could hold between any two erlebs possessing similar sense qualities. Classes of similar erlebs could be constructed, and these classes themselves could be members of classes defining sensory qualities (such as colors). Sense modalities were defined in terms of connecting chains of similar qualities. The visual modality was distinguished as being five-dimensional. Temporal order was denoted by a precedence relation among erlebs. A visual-field place (not a physical or perceptual place) was a quality distinguishable from the color quality in that one color can occur at two places but two colors cannot occur at one place; thus a "place" was a small part of the visual field in which the whole range of colors can occur. Spatial order was said to be derivable from a nearness relation defined in terms of similar colors occurring in places near each other. A "sensation" was defined as the ordered couple of an erleb and a quality class to which the erleb belongs.

Goodman (1951) also used symbolic logic to formulate his ideas. He began by dividing the stream of experience into qualia: times, visual-field places, and colors. For Goodman, the problem was to construct concrete particulars from these universal qualities. The qualia were the basic atoms of the system, and the primitive relation of the system denoted the occurrence of these qualia together in a color-spot-moment. Thus, Goodman rejected Carnap's attempt to define sensory qualities in terms of abstractions based on classes of similar erlebs. Moreover, he tried to construct the particularities of experience without resort to the calculus of classes. Categories of qualia were defined in terms of a primitive matching relation; the qualia in a category could not be divided into two parts such that no quale in one matched any quale in the other; this relation separated the color, space, and time categories of qualia. With "is a place" so defined, size was introduced in terms of a relation of equality—two individuals are of equal size if and only if they contain the same number of places—and one individual is bigger than another if it contains a proper part that is equal in size to the smaller individual. Shapes were to be characterized in terms of arrays of places related by nextness. With "is a time" so defined, moments could be linearly ordered by a relation of precedence, intervals could be defined, and qualia could be characterized as persisting through intervals.

Both of these approaches were empiricistic, in the sense made familiar by British philosophy from Locke to Hume. Both started with sensory experience, and both assumed as little as possible by way of primitive elements or logical predicates that might have to be attributed to some innate (and therefore suspect) propensities of the mind. Both were, in the general sense of the word, inductive, since they assumed that occurrences of the elements in a variety of combinations would provide evidence about the properties and relations that hold among sensory elements. Neither achieved an explanation of one's impression that the world is populated by things, but both left their systems open for further development in that direction.

Although neither Carnap nor Goodman thought of his work as providing a psychological theory of sensation, such formal systems can serve to set criteria that a psychological solution should satisfy. Thus, just-noticeable differences provide a psychological counterpart to Carnap's similarity predicate or Goodman's matching relation. Classification of sensations by modality and category must be psychologically explained, and scaling thories are the psychological counterpart to problems of temporal, spatial, and qualitative order within a formal system. (Goodman's incomplete attempts to account for shape can be considered more properly a perceptual problem.) The formal system organizes the theory of sensation into primitive atoms and relations and, by keeping these primitives as simple as possible, forces a theorist to define other elements and relations in terms of them, in the course of which the structural properties and implications of the system are explored and clarified.

Few psychologists accept either of these formal systems as an adequate basis for empirical investigations of sensory processes. There is, however, an informal version of sensory theory that once played a central role in psychology and still serves to provide a loose frame of reference for research on these problems. We shall refer to it as the theory of sensory attributes.

1.2   ATTRIBUTES OF SENSATION

Philosophers of the British empiricist school analyzed conscious experience into sensations and feelings. These were the atoms, the simplest possible contents of the mind, which, by a kind of mental chemistry called association, combined to form the compound particulars of consciousness. Some early psychologists believed that, by carefully controlled introspection, they could isolate and identify these sensory atoms, and methods of subjective measurement were developed to investigate their dependence on the conditions of stimulation that gave rise to them. The results of those researches were, in turn, related to the growing body of information about neurophysiological processes in the receptor organs and afferent nerves. This work constitutes a chapter in the history of scientific psychology too extensive for review here. (The reader interested in pursuing it might well begin with Boring's *Sensation and Perception in the History of Experimental Psychology,* 1942.) For our present purposes it will suffice merely to summarize the general conception of sensory attributes that emerged from this historical development.

Aristotle summarized the basic distinctions among the sensory modalities: visual, auditory, tactual, olfactory, and gustatory. In the nineteenth century Helmholtz defined a modality by the fact that it is possible for any sensation in a given modality to be continuously transformed through some sequence of intervening sensations into any other sensation in that modality. When continuous transformation from one sensation into another is not possible, the two sensations are in different modalities; it is not possible, for example, to transform a red visual sensation into a sour taste sensation. Given this definition of a sensory modality, it was possible to add to Aristotle's original five:

the sensations of bodily movement form a kinesthetic modality, and some have claimed that touch should be considered as consisting of four discrete modalities—warmth, cold, pressure, and pain (but see below). For each sensory modality, moreover, there is a specific receptor organ capable of transducing physical stimuli into neural activity and hence, presumably, into subjective experience. Moreover, each receptor reports to a particular area in the cortex of the brain, so the subjective discreteness of the modalities is paralleled by spatial discreteness in the nervous system.

In the theory of sensory attributes the modalities compose the first level of analysis. A perception of a meal, for example, consists of visual, tactual, gustatory, and olfactory sensations. The second level of analysis is a catalog of the sensory attributes within each modality. Four sensory attributes are distinguished: quality, intensity, extension, and duration. It is assumed that attributes are characterized by independent variation, or, in more operational terms, that two sensations in the same modality can be judged the same with respect to one attribute while other attributes vary. If the value of any attribute falls to zero, there is no sensation at all; thus, every sensation should have a value on every attribute.

In the visual modality, the quality of a sensation is its hue, the intensity is its lightness, the extension is its apparent area, and the duration is its apparent duration. In the auditory modality the corresponding attributes are pitch, loudness, volume (apparent size of the sound), and duration. In taste the qualities are said to be sweet, sour, bitter, and salt, which can vary in intensity and duration but do not seem to have an extension. In olfaction the qualities are said to be putrid, ethereal, fragrant, burned, resinous, and spicy, which can vary in intensity and duration but also lack extension. For touch, some argue that warmth, cold, pressure, and pain are qualities, not distinct modalities; touch sensations can also vary in intensity, duration, and extension. Much research was devoted to isolating and measuring each of these various attributes of sensation, and rival theories were advanced concerning how these attributes were transmitted by the nervous system to the brain.

If this analysis into modalities and attributes seems artificial, attempts to explain how these sensations were synthesized into perception were even worse. The general mechanism of synthesis was "association," but it was obvious even in the nineteenth century that some rather wonderful mental chemistry was required to knit a pattern of color-spot-moments together into our perception of a face or a tree. The catalyst required for this synthetic miracle was thought by many to be "meaning," although a better name for it would have been "familiarity." Sensations are uninterpreted and meaningless; perceptions are interpreted as meaningful (familiar) objects. E. B. Titchener (1910) proposed what he called a context theory of meaning whereby meaning emerged when a sensory or affective context "accrued" to a sensory core. The gist of his account was that it takes at least two sensations to make a meaning. This notion is at least relational, but it is far from an adequate solution to the problem of perceptual integration.

Originally, of course, many psychologists hoped that this research would lead to some mental equivalent to the periodic table of chemical elements. Such elementalism was effectively attacked by gestalt psychologists, who argued that the perception of an integral whole against a background is the primary phenomenal fact of experience and that sensations are artificial abstractions from that organized percept which only psychologists trained in the mysteries of introspection can ever experience directly. Thus the psychological reality of sensations came to be doubted, and attributes were left with nothing to be attributes of. In response to this anomalous situation, Boring (1933) suggested that instead of talking about the attributes of sensation, psychologists should regard these phenomena as dimensions of conscious experience; indeed, inasmuch as these dimensions could be correlated with processes observed in the brain, Boring called them the physical dimensions of consciousness.

Subsequent work on the sensory processes has accepted the spirit of Boring's suggestion if not the terminological details. A psychologist today might investigate the relations among, say, the physical amplitude of an acoustic stimulus, the subjective judgment of its loudness, and the rate of firing of the auditory nerve or the magnitude of the evoked potential in the auditory projection area of the brain; but he might speak of loudness as a subjective dimension, or as a sensory attribute, or as a dependent variable, or even, in some contexts, as an aspect, characteristic, feature, magnitude, or value. Moreover, once the tie between "attribute" and "sensation" is cut, these alternative terms can be generalized to refer to almost anything that people can reliably discriminate. Although the attributes are still studied, they are no longer seen narrowly as attributes of sensations.

Why, then, have we exhumed these sensory attributes from the graveyard of history? Certainly not with any intention of reviving the elementalistic philosophy from which they sprang. Our reason is much simpler and grows out of the nature of our present project. "Red," "loud," "sour," "fragrant" are English words; similar words are found in other languages. If we are to discuss the relation between language and perception, we cannot neglect these linguistic symbols simply because perceptual theorists no longer regard their referents as the basic atoms of the mind. As it happens, the classification of these words by modality and attribute still represents the best psychological insight we have into the perceptual basis for their use.

Philosophical discussion of such terms frequently raises the question as to whether attributes really exist in the same sense that three-dimensional objects exist. A physical object cannot be in two places at the same time, but a sensory attribute can: two different objects, for example, can have the same color. A nominalist would explain this difference by talking about the use of general words to describe particular objects but would deny that these general words label anything that exists independent of the particular objects that exhibit them. A realist would argue that such attributes do have an existence independent of the words used to refer to them. These competing metaphysical positions have their parallels among psychologists. Those who argue that psychological hypotheses must be evaluated solely in terms of behavioral evidence generally find the nominalist position more comfortable; those who argue that subjective experience can provide data for the evaluation of psychological hypotheses generally prefer the realist's approach. The ontological status of sensory attributes—or universals, as philosophers call them—is not a matter that we can hope to settle to anyone's satisfaction, but we should probably warn the reader that our own biases are realistic. That is to say, we assume that there are real physiological and psychological processes correlated with the use of such general words and that the meanings of these words cannot be explained satisfactorily on any other basis.

For the present, however, we will assume merely that the ability to use such words consistently derives from an ability to pay attention to different aspects of perceptual experiences. We will accept the criticisms of elementalism based on the claim that such attributes must be self-consciously abstracted after the perceptual fact. In order to account for linguistic usage, we will assume that sensation is a special kind of perception—constitutes a special suburb of perception—that results from an abstractive act of attention, and that this special kind of perception can be studied experimentally under conditions in which the perceptual world is deliberately simplified and attributes are varied one or two at a time. By simplifying the conditions of stimulation and controlling precisely the nature of the variations in that stimulation, psychologists and physiologists have accumulated considerable information about the relations among the physical, physiological, and psychological dimensions of this kind of conscious experience.

Sensory attributes can be divided into qualitative and quantitative ones. The ability to judge that some stimulus x has the subjective quality y can be thought of as an ability to verify (within determinable limits of error) such predicates as $\text{Qual}(x, y)$, where the quality may be color, pitch, odor, taste, or tactual feel in particular instances. Similarly, people can test such predicates as $\text{Magn}(x, y)$, that is, that stimulus x has the subjective quantity y, where y might be an intensive magnitude such as loudness or brightness or an extensive magnitude such as size or volume or a temporal magnitude such as duration in particular instances. Moreover, if y is the quality of x and y' is the quality of x', people can, by an abstractive act of attention, test such predicates as $\text{Simlr}(y, y')$, that is, that y is similar to y'; and if z is the magnitude of x and z' is the magnitude of x', they can test $\text{Greater}(z, z')$, that is, that z is greater than z'.* The ability to abstract attributes and to make such judgments of them is the foundation on which psychophysics is built.

*It is obvious that the range of values an argument can take will depend critically on the predicate itself. "Greater," for example, is defined for magnitudes, not qualities. Some theoretical machinery would be required to ensure that the requirements of the predicate were satisfied. We might write $\text{Greater}(z$ such that $\text{Magn}(x, z)$, z' such that $\text{Magn}(x', z'))$. Such explicit specifications would be needed for most of the predicates to be introduced below. We will omit them, however, in the interests of readability, and rely on the reader's intuitive understanding to impose the appropriate selection restrictions.

We will review some of the basic facts about these attributes—or dimensions —before proceeding to consider more complex perceptual judgments.

1.3 QUALITY

Qualitative changes within any given modality are usually defined in a negative way: they are changes that are not quantitative. This definition is peculiarly unsatisfying, since it is the quality that individuates one simple sensory experience from another—red from green, high pitch from low, sweet from sour. Some theorists have proposed a more positive definition: qualitative changes occur when the stimulus affects different receptor cells, and quantitative changes occur when the stimulus affects the same receptor cells more or less intensely. This is an empirical claim, whose merits we need not explore here. The phenomenal fact remains that variations in quality are somehow different from quantitative variations in intensity, extension, or duration.

The two modalities of greatest importance in the present context are vision and audition. The importance of vision is obvious; as someone has remarked, we are all children of the sun. The importance of audition is magnified in the present context by the fact that speech itself involves an auditory stimulus. In order to keep our discussion within reasonable bounds, therefore, but with no intent to undervalue the contributions of the other senses (life would be dull indeed without tastes or smells, motility would be precarious without kinesthesis, and survival itself depends on touch), we will confine ourselves here primarily to these two modalities. Vision and audition have been studied far more intensively than the so-called minor senses, so we are in a much better position to understand the processes involved.

Thus, our subject in this section is narrowed to the qualities of visual and auditory experience; in short, to hue and pitch. This narrowing is more apparent than real, however, for the amount of research and theory devoted to these two attributes is enormous. We must content ourselves with a brief summary of some basic facts.

1.3.1   Hue

If you adopt an analytic attitude toward your visual experience, you can describe the visual field as if it were a mosaic of colored surfaces. It is impossible to *see* it as a mosaic of colored surfaces, however, unless you look at it through a reduction screen. A reduction screen is a device—a small hole or tube—that blocks out all the surround and enables you to look at relatively uniform patches of color in limited areas of the visual field. Under these conditions of reduced stimulation, with a dark homogeneous surround provided by the screen, the colors do not look the same as they do under normal viewing.

In the older, elementalistic accounts of perception, it was assumed that a normal visual scene could be synthesized out of many individual patches of color resembling the patches one sees through a reduction screen. The color-spot-moment was the basic element of visual experience. But the fact that colors do *not* look the same through a reduction screen as they do under normal viewing is sufficient to refute any simple version of this elementalistic theory. Still, if you wish to simplify and control the conditions of stimulation for the purposes of scientific investigation, the small homogeneous patches of color that you see through a reduction screen are a great deal more convenient for research than the usual viewing situation.

When a reduction screen enables you to ignore familiar objects located in three-dimensional space, you can see patches of color that differ from one another in various ways. The variations can be described in terms of just three dimensions: hue, saturation, and lightness. Hue varies primarily with the wavelength of the light—from blue at the short wavelengths to red at the long —although the correlation is not perfect. Lightness varies with the energy level of the light stimulus, although black is probably produced only by contrast effects (for example, by contrast with a white background). And saturation is estimated on a scale ranging from gray to the purest hue; saturation is reduced by mixing two or more lights of different wavelengths, leaving hue constant. Without a reduction screen, however, color has many more subjective attributes; it can look transparent or opaque, luminous or nonluminous, lustrous or nonlustrous, two-dimensional or three-dimensional (D. Katz, 1935).

In laboratory studies of color, of course, it is not necessary to use reduction screens in order to produce homogeneous spots of color for experimental purposes. The viewer generally sees a circle of light against a neutral, usually dark, surround. In one technique, half the spot will be some fixed color and the other half will vary in color until it is judged identical with the first. In this way it is possible to explore all the physical distributions of energy density over the visible electromagnetic spectrum that will produce the same color experience for a human observer. These color-matching experiments provide the basic data about the perceptual effects of mixing different colors,* and the theoretical problem is to predict the perceptual results of such physical mixtures and to characterize the mechanisms in the retina (the sensitive surface of receptor cells at the back of the eye on which the visual image is focused) and the visual nervous system that underlie these perceptual judgments.

Krantz (1972) has provided a convenient summary of the measurement structures involved in color matching. Any particular light can be specified physically by giving its distribution of energy over the visible spectrum. When two lights, *a* and *b*, are mixed, their energies at each wavelength add to produce a new light, $a \oplus b$. Any given light *a* can have its energy at every wavelength

---

*The laws of color mixture for lights are, of course, not the same as the laws of color mixture for paints or dyes. Lights add; pigments absorb, and so subtract. Mixing all colors of light produces white; mixing all colors of pigments produces black. Moreover, it is very difficult to match a colored surface and a light source in hue, saturation, and brightness because their modes of appearance are so different.

multiplied by a nonnegative constant k, to give the light $k * a$. Both $\oplus$ and $*$ are physical operations. However, the judgment that two lights look identical, $a \equiv b$, depends on a human observer. Qualitative laws involving $\equiv$ were first stated by Grassman in 1854. Krantz reformulates them as follows:

(1)   Transitivity: If $a \equiv b$ and $b \equiv c$, then $a \equiv c$
          Reflexivity: $a \equiv a$
          Symmetry: $a \equiv b$ if and only if $b \equiv a$

The typical example of a transitive, reflexive, symmetric relation is the relation of identity. The conditions stated in (1) are usually considered a test of the adequacy of the empirical operations used to define $\equiv$. Grassman's laws also specify:

(2) $a \equiv b$ if and only if $a \oplus c \equiv b \oplus c$
          If $a \equiv b$, then $k * a \equiv k * b$

Condition (2) is usually taken to mean that $\equiv$ is determined at the level of the retina, before any nonlinearities are introduced by neural transduction. Finally, Grassman's formulation of Thomas Young's insight that only three colors are needed to specify all the others can be stated:

(3)   For any four lights, a positive linear combination of two of them
          or three of them matches a positive linear combination of the re-
          maining two or one, respectively; and there are three lights such
          that no positive linear combinations of any two of them matches
          the remaining one.

That is, for any four lights a, b, c, and d there is some set of nonnegative constants k, k', and k'' such that either

(4) $a \equiv (k * b) \oplus (k' * c) \oplus (k'' * d)$

or

(5) $a \oplus (k * b) \equiv (k' * c) \oplus (k'' * d)$;

and for any two lights a and b there is a third light c such that for no nonnegative constants k and k' is it the case that

(6) $(k * a) \oplus (k' * b) \equiv c$.

Krantz calls a measurement structure that satisfies (1) and (2) a Grassman structure; if (3) also holds, it is a trichromatic Grassman structure.

The practical significance of Grassman's laws is that it is possible to choose three convenient monochromatic lights (having energy only in a very narrow band of wavelengths) and to match any fourth light by some positive linear combinations of those three. For example, in 1947 W. D. Wright (revising an earlier choice) selected three lights having their energy at the wavelengths of

460 nanometers (nm), 530 nm, and 650 nm, which speakers of English would call blue, green, and red, respectively. Thus, any sample light s could be matched either according to (4), which would become

$$(4') \qquad s \equiv (k * b) \oplus (k' * g) \oplus (k'' * r),$$

or, since mixtures are of lower saturation than monochromatic lights, by adding one of the three primaries to s according to (5), which amounts to subtracting it from the trichromatic compound. The results of the color-matching experiment are the determinations of the values of k, k', and k'' required to make the match. Since it is necessary to know only the relative amounts of these three standard lights, it can be assumed that k, k', and k'' must sum to 1, in which case the proportion of the third is known when either of the other two is given. It is thus possible to represent all possible mixtures in the form of a two-dimensional chromaticity chart; the coordinates of the chart are standardly taken to be the proportions of red (650 nm) and green (530 nm) required to make the match. This method provides a precise system for describing any desired color, and international standards have been adopted for this trichromatic method of color specification.

The next question, of course, concerns the nature of the mechanisms in the eye and visual nervous system that achieve this lawful result. The history of psychophysiological research on color vision revolves largely around a controversy between those who believe that there are only three generic colors, each with its own channel to the brain, and those who believe that there are four, working as two sets of opponent pairs. The former view is usually called the Young-Helmholtz trichromatic theory; the latter is Hering's theory of opponent colors.

Apparently both theories have their domains of applicability. The receptor cells in the retina that respond to differences in wavelength are called cones, and it has been reasonably conclusively shown (see Rushton, 1962) that the human eye contains three kinds of cones: those primarily responsive to red, those primarily responsive to green, and those primarily responsive to blue. At the neural level, however, opponent processes are found. De Valois (1965), for example, found individual neurons in the lateral geniculate of the monkey that were quite sensitive to changes in wavelength but relatively insensitive to changes in stimulus intensity; some of these cells achieved their maximum and minimum rates of firing for red and green wavelengths, others for blue and yellow wavelengths, thus supporting the red-green and yellow-blue opposition assumed in Hering's theory. According to De Valois and Abramov (1966) these opponent cells "have connections with two (or more) cone types of different, though overlapping, spectral sensitivities. They receive an excitatory input from one cone type and an inhibitory input from the other; these inputs are subtracted from each other so that the opponent unit's firing rates reflect the extent to which light affects one cone pigment more than the other" (p. 345).

Currently, therefore, the two theories are combined into one, which can be called a trichromatic opponent theory of color vision. The general idea behind several different versions of this theory is that light is absorbed by three different kinds of pigments in the three kinds of cones, and that this information is then recoded neurally into opponent processes in two channels, one coding the red-green opposition, the other blue-yellow. This general view has been argued in detail in a series of experimental and theoretical papers by Hurvich and Jameson (1957).

Hering (1920) based his theory of opponent colors on the fact that redness and greenness are never perceived in the same place at the same time, and similarly for yellow and blue. He reasoned that the physiological processes underlying these two pairs must be opposite, or antagonistic. Jameson and Hurvich (1955) devised a method to determine the spectral distributions of these paired responses in the following way. As one varies the wavelength of monochromatic light, the color of the light changes. Some of the colors are reddish, some are greenish, and some are neither reddish nor greenish, but none is both reddish and greenish. The colors that are neither reddish nor greenish include yellow and blue. Similarly, some of the colors are yellowish, some are blueish, and none is both, but some are neither yellowish nor blueish —these include green and red. Jameson and Hurvich measured the redness of a light by the intensity of a standard green that was needed to cancel out the red and leave the resulting mixture in either the yellow-blue or achromatic (white-gray-black) class. In the same way they could measure the greenness of a light by the intensity of standard red needed to cancel the green. The same procedure was used to determine the yellowness and blueness of different wavelengths—by canceling the yellow with blue and the blue with yellow. They found that the measures of the red-green and yellow-blue processes they obtained by this cancellation procedure could be expressed as linear combinations of the trichromatic color-matching functions. As Krantz (1972) points out, this is equivalent to the assertion that these opponent processes yield unichromatic Grassman structures (conditions (1) and (2), with unichromacy replacing trichromacy in (3)).

Although the trichromatic theory gives an accurate and parsimonious account of the results of color-mixing experiments, and there is evidence that it describes the behavior of the visual pigments in the retinal cones, the color-mixing results are also compatible with the opponent-process theory, which seems to give a better description of the processes in the visual nervous system. Since the sort of color-naming conventions that are of central interest to our examination of the interface between perception and language presumably depend on the neural processes in the brain, not on the photochemical processes in the retina, we can take the opponent-process theory as the preferred description for our purposes. That is to say, when someone says that "object x has color y" we can assume that y is a term denoting some combination of values for the three opponent processes, for example, y_1 for the white-black process, y_2 for the red-green process, and y_3 for the yellow-blue process.

How these triples might be mapped into the color terms of English will be discussed further in section 5.1.

1.3.2   Pitch

The color mechanism is synthetic; the pitch mechanism is analytic. When two lights of different wavelength are added, you no longer see the color corresponding to those wavelengths but rather a color intermediate between them. But when two sinusoidal tones of different frequency (not harmonically related) are added, the ear (under most conditions) does not synthesize some tone of intermediate pitch; it is possible to hear both of the component pitches separately. The fact that the ear acts as an analyzer was first noted by Ohm in 1843; Ohm's acoustic law says that it is possible to pay attention selectively to the components of any compound acoustic stimulus. Whereas research on color vision emphasizes the laws of color mixture, research on audition has emphasized the analysis of complex sounds into their simple components.

The basic theory derives from a mathematical technique known as Fourier analysis, which makes it possible to analyze any complex periodic waveform into the sum of a series of sinusoidal waves of determinable amplitude and phase. According to Ohm's acoustic law, the ear performs such an analysis on the waveform of an acoustic stimulus, so that you hear each of the simple sinusoidal components individually. There are limits to the accuracy of the ear's analysis, of course; if two sinusoidal waves are too close in frequency, you hear beats (one pitch varying periodically in loudness); if some component sinusoids are much more intense, they may mask others; if two components are harmonically related, the overtone is harder to hear. But as a general characterization of the auditory mechanism, Ohm's acoustic law is still generally accepted.

There are names for colors but no similar names for pitches. In order to specify the pitch of a particular sound, we give the frequency of vibration of its fundamental sinusoidal component in hertz (cycles per second) or, since musical notation can be defined in terms of physical frequency, in terms of the musical scale (standard A is 440 hertz). This is a physical specification, however, not a psychological one. Although it is certainly true that the subjective impression of pitch is more closely correlated with frequency of vibration than with any other physical dimension of the stimulus, the correlation is not perfect; as intensity is increased, high tones sound slightly higher, low tones slightly lower (Stevens and Davis, 1938). It is possible to develop psychological scales of subjective pitch (Stevens and Volkmann, 1940) and to show that perceived pitch does not vary logarithmically with frequency, but this subjective scale is little known outside the field of auditory research. It certainly does not provide a terminology for pitches comparable to the names for colors. There is nothing about pitch perception that selects certain pitches as "primary."

When lights of different wavelengths are mixed, the mixture has a single hue, but the complexity of the stimulus will be reflected in a reduced saturation (a grayish tinge) compared to a monochromatic light of that hue. Thus, color-mixture studies necessarily work with the subjective variables of hue and saturation simultaneously. When sinusoidal tones of different frequencies are mixed, each pitch can be heard separately, but the complexity of the unanalyzed compound is perceived as a richer timbre; thus auditory studies work with the subjective variables of pitch and timbre (or, to confound our terminology, "quality") simultaneously.

English has far more words for denoting the timbre (or quality) of a sound than it has for denoting pitches. Pitches are simply called high, medium, or low, and these terms cannot be calibrated on the pitch scale because they vary from one context to another; a low-pitched voice is usually lower than a low-pitched whistle, for example. But for timbre there is a host of ill-defined terms: shrill, melodious, noisy, pure, brassy, rasping, harmonious, dissonant, piercing, booming, resonant, thin, harsh, rough, squeaky and so on. From a linguistic point of view, it might seem that timbre is the true qualitative attribute, not pitch. Certainly, sounds of the same pitch can have very different timbres; compare, say, a trumpet and a human voice sounding the same pitch. It is timbre that individuates sounds and provides information about the source of the sound. And timbre enables people to distinguish different speech sounds—particularly different vowels. Psychophysical tradition has it, however, that pitch is the qualitative attribute in audition and that timbre is to be understood as derivative from the perception of many pitches simultaneously.

Thus, Fourier analysis by the ear fits well into an elementalistic theory of perception. The perception of a complex sound is supposed to be built up from our perception of the individual sinusoids into which it can be analyzed. In fact, though, the elementalistic theory is as inadequate here as elsewhere. Its failures are most noticeable when we consider studies of speech perception, for speech is certainly not heard as the sum of a series of component pure tones. Speech is a rapidly changing pattern, coming in bursts and spurts, constantly varying in timbre; speech does not seem to rely on the same mode of hearing as music does (see Liberman, Cooper, Shankweiler, and Studdert-Kennedy, 1967). It is not possible to predict how people will perceive speech signals in terms of any studies of their ability to hear pure sinusoidal tones. Pitch, along with loudness, contributes to the perception of intonation, but its contribution to phonetic discrimination is minimal.

At low frequencies—up to, say, 1,000 hertz—the firing of the auditory nerve is known to remain synchronized with the envelope of the acoustic signal, that is, with fluctuations in the amplitude of the signal. Above that frequency, analysis is performed by detecting the place of maximum vibration on the cochlea, and pitch is presumably determined according to which neural fibers in the auditory nerve are stimulated. But at lower frequencies the ear is capable of analyzing the time patterns of stimulation (Miller and Taylor, 1948)—a capacity that is of critical importance for speech perception—in terms of overall rate of firing in the auditory nerve. The precise relation between this synchronization mechanism at low frequencies and the place mechanism at high frequencies is still a matter for theoretical dispute, however.

The relation of perception to language in the realm of audition is very different from the relation in the realm of vision (Miller, 1974b). It is ironic that people use vocal sounds to name everything else yet have such a limited vocabulary of names for sounds themselves; it is only a slight exaggeration to say that audition is used primarily to serve the other sense modalities.

1.4 INTENSITY

Intensity is the generic name psychologists give to the subjective attribute that in vision is called lightness or brightness and in audition is called loudness. The intensive dimension applies to every modality. Subjective intensity depends, other things being equal, on the energy in the physical stimulus. It is usually assumed that intensity is mediated neurally in terms of the number and rate of fire of the afferent neurons. It is possible to measure people's absolute thresholds (the minimal energy they can detect) or their differential sensitivity to small changes in intensity and to construct subjective scales of brightness and loudness that can be correlated with physical measurements of light or sound energy. In general terms, the magnitude of a just-detectable increment in intensity is a constant fraction of the intensity to which it is added (Weber's law), and equal ratios of stimulus intensity are perceived as equal ratios of subjective intensity (Steven's law). Details can be found in appropriate handbooks (see, for example, Kling and Riggs, 1971; Stevens, 1975).

There is little more that needs to be said about the psychophysics of intensity in the present context, but perhaps a word about black and white as visual phenomena would be helpful, because it is not entirely clear whether black and white should be regarded as qualities or intensities. Are "brightness" and "whiteness" two names for the same thing?

As the energy in a light is increased, it approaches white; the saturation of any chromatic component decreases as the intensity becomes great enough to stimulate all color receptors. Conversely, as the energy is decreased, the light approaches black. Thus it is possible to think of black and white as the extremes on an intensive continuum. This view, however, might lead us to think of black as the subjective experience associated with the total absence of stimulation—which would be incorrect. Black is a sensation, not the absence of a sensation. If a person is left in a totally dark room for an hour or more, he reports that he no longer sees black and that his whole visual field is a neutral gray, presumably attributable to the resting level of activity in the neural tissues. He sees black by contrast, by having seen something white shortly before or closely adjacent to it. This fact was well known in the nineteenth century and was hotly debated in the days when it seemed important to make sharp distinctions between qualitative and intensive attributes of sensation.

Hering believed that black and white are an opponent process, just as red-green and yellow-blue are, and Hurvich and Jameson (1957) concur. According to this view, brightness is simply the net response, $w - bl$, in the achromatic, black-white system. It is assumed that some higher-order neurons (those in the black-white system) receive information from all three kinds of retinal cones, and that these cells are particularly important in visual acuity and the detection of contours and edges.

In his studies of the monkey's visual system, however, De Valois (1965) found nonopponent cells in the lateral geniculate that seemed to carry brightness information; they were relatively insensitive to changes in the wavelength of the stimulus but quite sensitive to changes in brightness. The discovery of nonopponent cells for brightness suggests that a nonspecific system may exist side by side with the opponent system, in which case brightness and whiteness might be registered independently. Since the experts are still divided concerning the underlying neural mechanism, though, it seems advisable to await further research that may settle the question. The subjective evidence would seem to favor an opponent interpretation of black and white, so we will simply consider them on a par with chromatic opponents when we discuss color naming.

Functionally, intensity can have the effect of controlling attention (unexpected changes in intensity are hard to ignore) and, conversely, attention can have the effect of modulating intensity. Titchener, a main proponent of an attributive analysis of sensation, believed that the special clearness of a sensation when it is in the center of attention was itself an independent attribute on which observers could report, but his "attensive" attribute did not gain general acceptance.

The neurophysiological mechanisms underlying selective attention are complex, but some progress has been made in analyzing them. For example, if a person is asked to count the number of faint clicks embedded infrequently in a regular, one-per-second train of louder clicks, his subjective act of attention can be detected in his brain waves by comparing them to the brain waves recorded when he ignores the clicks (by, say, reading a book). In particular (Galambos, 1974), a person who is attending shows a large positive wave between 300 and 600 milliseconds after the target (the faint click) occurs. The occurrence and magnitude of this response seem to depend on the resolution of uncertainty, not on the physical properties of the stimulus.

1.5   DURATION AND EXTENSION

In order to distinguish between the objectively measured time and space of physical science and the subjectively experienced time and space of conscious experience, psychologists sometimes use Titchener's terms "protensity" and "extensity" instead of "duration" and "extension." Moreover, protensity and extensity, originally defined as attributes of sensations, must also be distinguished from the perception of time and the perception of size as these are normally experienced in the everyday perceptual world outside the psychological laboratory. These terminological niceties are not wholly arbitrary; they reflect the psychologist's attempt to maintain a consistent distinction between the physical world, the sensory field, and the perceptual world. They serve to mark putative boundaries for our discussion of time and space in the context of sensory processes.

In research on visual and auditory processes it is always necessary to specify the temporal conditions of stimulation, and in visual research it is also necessary to specify size (usually in degrees of visual angle). For example, the absolute thresholds of seeing and hearing are defined as the minimum amounts of energy in the stimulus needed for detection. This energy can be applied either at a high intensity for a very brief interval or at a low intensity for a more extended interval. Up to intervals of about a quarter of a second it makes little difference; the important point is that the product of intensity and time must be large enough to be detectable. Moreover, for the visual threshold, it makes little difference (up to about 20 minutes of arc) how this energy is distributed spatially. In such experiments, intensity, duration, and extension are intimately related. It should be noted, though, that these experiments demand nothing more than a judgment of "present" or "absent"; an observer or listener is not asked to judge these separate dimensions of the physical stimulus independently. The ability to report the inner workings of the sensory system by a deliberate act of attention is not unlimited.

The reason for regarding duration and extension as sensory attributes is that we know people *can* make judgments about them, independent of other attributes, just as they can judge quality or intensity. The accuracy of duration estimates has been measured, as has the ability to tell which of two intervals is longer (see Woodrow, 1951). The psychophysics of extension is considerably more complex. In vision, size and distance are complexly related in our perception of three-dimensional space, so the major psychological problem has been to understand why the apparent size of an object is not better correlated with the size of the image it projects on the retina of the eye. In touch, although it is possible to judge extension, major interest in the spatial attribute has concerned accuracy of localization rather than spatial extent. In audition, there has been considerable debate as to whether sounds have any extensive attribute at all; however, Stevens (1934) was able to get consistent judgments of "volume" (extensity, not loudness) indicating that the apparent size of a tone increases as its intensity increases and decreases as its frequency increases; and Thomas (1949) showed that for complex sounds apparent volume increases as their bandwidth increases. In the olfactory and gustatory modalities, extension does not seem to be an attribute. In short, extension has been studied primarily in vision, whereas duration is so universal an attribute that sensory content is not even necessary.

The ability to make judgments of size and of spatial relations presupposes an ability to recognize and isolate the shapes or objects whose sizes or relations one is judging. During the 1890s an attempt was made to treat form—both visual shape and auditory melodies—as an independent quality or attribute of sensation (see Boring, 1929, pp. 433–440), but shape is so clearly relational that this suggestion could not be integrated into the elementalistic sensationism of the day. Subsequently, of course, gestalt psychologists used form as one of their major arguments for the primacy of perceptual wholes over sensory atoms; a line is perceived as a whole, not as a string of elementary dots. In order to make judgments of extension, therefore, it is necessary to abstract it out of the perception of a figure. Extension is an attribute of percepts, not of sensations—a clear demonstration of the artificiality of any attempt to derive principles of perceptual organization from the study of sensory elements.

According to elementalistic theory, the perception of motion should be a compound synthesized from the independent attributes of duration and extent of motion. In fact, however, motion is perceptually given. Ontogenetically, the ability to analyze it into spatial and temporal dimensions is acquired only after a child has achieved considerable conceptual sophistication. Further discussion of the perception of motion must be postponed as more appropriate to chapter 2.

Temporal aspects of experience are expressed in language by a great variety of devices: tense and aspect attach to the verb; auxiliary verbs modulate the main verb; nouns denote dates or units of time; prepositions, adjectives, and adverbs can denote temporal relations. Spatial aspects are similarly the subject of many linguistic constructions indicating places and relations between places. And the complex interactions of space and time that are required to describe the apparent properties of motion are elaborately analyzed and represented linguistically. Time and space provide the basic coordinate system within which all experience can be located, and much of the machinery of language is devoted to making such localizations communicable. We will, therefore, return to these matters repeatedly.

2

The Perceptual World

Suppose that I look through a telescope and you ask me, 'What do you see?'. I may answer (1) 'A bright speck'; (2) 'A star'; (3) 'Sirius'; (4) 'The image in the fourteenth mirror of the telescope.' All these answers may be perfectly correct. Have we then different senses of 'see'? Four different senses? Of course not. The image in the fourteenth mirror of the telescope is a bright speck, this bright speck is a star, and the star is Sirius; I can say, quite correctly and with no ambiguity whatever, that I see any of these. Which way of saying what I see I actually choose will depend on the particular circumstances of the case—for instance, on what sort of answer I expect you to be interested in, on how much I know, or on how far I am prepared to stick my neck out. —J. L. Austin (1962a)

Now that we have surveyed some facts and theories historically allocated to the study of sensation, we can better understand the failure of attempts to reduce perception to elementary sensations. Sensations are not psychic atoms in perceptual compounds; they are abstracted from percepts by a highly skilled act of attention. Describing sensations is merely one of many ways to talk about perceptual experience—a way to speak with the neck out very little.

In the context of an inquiry into relations between perception and language, an important lesson to learn from sensations is that such acts of attention are possible. Not only do people pay attention to some attributes or dimensions of experience and ignore others, but they are able to make judgments of them— to say which particular quality, or what relative magnitude, duration, or extension, characterizes the experience they are attending to. A natural way to represent such acts of attention and judgment is in a predicate notation:

Red(spot), for example, might mean that a person who can perceive a spot can attend to its color, and judge that the hue is what he calls red. Similarly, Small(spot) might mean that attention is directed to the size of the spot and it is judged to be small. We will make extensive use of such predicate notations in our discussion of perception. Chapter 1 provided a partial catalog of predicates needed to characterize perception: Qual, Magn, Simlr, Greater, and various specific forms for specific attributes—Red, Small, and so on. In this chapter we will develop a list of properties and relations that people can pay attention to and make judgments of, and we will represent them in the form of simple predicates.

Expressions like Red(spot) and Small(spot) will be used to make formal statements about something. About what? Two answers seem possible. Either they are statements about the physical object, the spot itself that gives rise to the perception, or they are statements about some perceptual representation that the physical spot has produced. If we consider them to be statements about the stimulating object, we face problems in explaining nonveridical perception: the spot may look red, but it is really white, as would be seen if, say, its green surround were removed. In this case, we would have to consider Red(spot) to be false. But if the object is really white, then what was being judged when it looked red? Presumably the observer was judging not the spot itself but some perceptual impression that the spot created under those conditions of viewing. If we consider our predicates to be statements about a perceptual process, we could accept Red(spot) as true under these conditions. But now we face problems in explaining veridical perception—if a statement can be true about perception and false about the world, how can anyone know which percepts to trust? To say "I judge my perception of the spot to be red" is not merely excessively cautious and stylistically awkward; it seems to create a ghostly world of perceptual representations between the person who is perceiving and the world he perceives.

The pitfalls in either answer are well known to philosophers, of course, for they are central issues in the continuing debate about the perceptual bases of empirical knowledge. We will assume that when one English-speaking person utters to another English-speaking person such sentences as "The spot is red" or "The spot is small," he is making statements about the physical spot. But note that such utterances need not involve perception at all; they can be based on information gained at some earlier time in some unspecified way. The formal expressions Red(spot) or Small(spot), on the other hand, we will assume to denote subjective judgments about perceptual representations. That is, the subjective predication Red(spot) and the sentence "The spot is red" are not equivalent, because either can be true while the other is false. The predicates Red and Small are intended to denote attentional-judgmental processes which have some unknown neurophysiological correlates. If Red(spot) were to be expressed as an English sentence, it would be something like: "A person perceives the spot, and attention to its color leads to the judgment that it is red." This is clearly a theoretical sentence about a perceptual-judgmental process, not an ordinary sentence about the physical spot.

In order to translate the predication Red(spot) into a sentence in English, however, we introduced a presupposition, namely, that "a person perceives the spot." That is to say, if such predicates are used to make statements about perceptual representations, then there must be a further predicate to denote those processes whereby that representation is formed. We will use *Perceive* (x, y) to denote this relation between the person x and his perception y. Then the full theoretical statement corresponding to "a person perceives the spot, and attention to its color leads to the judgment that it is red" would be *Perceive* (person, y) & Red(y). Several comments should be made on this formulation.

First, *Perceive* is a different kind of predicate from Red. *Perceive* has to do with whatever processes are involved when an internal representation of an external object is constructed out of information from the receptors. Red has to do with whatever processes are involved when judgments are made of this internal representation. *Perceive* presupposes a person to do the perceiving; Red presupposes a perceptual content to be judged. By writing *Perceive* in italics, we hope to keep this difference in mind.

Second, we have used "person" as the first argument of *Perceive*. In some contexts this argument should be defined more broadly, in others more narrowly. Psychologists who study the perceptual capacities of animals, for example, might wish to interpret this argument as "living organism," and workers in the field of artificial intelligence might wish to extend it even to machines having certain capacities for sensing the environment. On the other hand, given the present state of neurophysiology, the only perceptions to which you have direct access are your own, so in those cases where you wish to stick your neck out very little you might wish to limit this argument to yourself, to "ego." We have used "person" to denote the perceiving system because that will surely be a primitive term in any psychological theory and because we will eventually be interested in relating *Perceive* to language, a relation best studied for persons.

Third, "the spot" has mysteriously disappeared, replaced by the non-committal symbol y as the second argument of *Perceive*. If we used "spot" as the second argument, it would suggest that shape judgments had already been made, whereas the purpose of our notation is to separate the construction of a perceptual representation from the judgments we can make about it. We prefer to use y as an index or pointer to the percept, since this makes y available as an argument for other predicates without committing us to any premature description or characterization of the percept. If we were to use "spot" as our index, we would be in constant danger of forgetting it was only a pointer, not a semantic category.

Suppose that y indexes the perception of a small, red spot: What determines whether the perceiver will attend to its size, or to its color, or to both attributes? There is clearly an intentional aspect to attentional-judgmental predicates; a person can exploit the same percept *y* in very different ways on different occasions by attending to and judging different attributes of it. If we think of a perceiving-behaving organism as a kind of negative feedback system, then we can view the behavior of the organism at any given moment as an attempt to maintain some perceptual feedback invariant. That is to say, the system provides an internal criterion that characterizes what it intends to perceive, and the actions it takes (both overtly and covertly) are those it calculates will best serve to achieve and sustain a perception that meets that criterion. What the system intends to perceive may be anything from a specific degree of tension in a muscle group to a particular face across the room. Thus, the system *x* must be able to change the value of the argument *y* in *Perceive*(*x*, *y*) until *y* satisfies some attentional-judgmental predicate that characterizes the system's goal. To say that the system can adopt Red(*y*) as a criterion is to say that it can attend to *y*'s color; to say it can recognize when Red(*y*) is satisfied is to say it can judge the color to be red. If we had a complete catalog of all the perceptual criteria the system is able to adopt, it would include all the attentional-judgmental predicates we would need in order to characterize the perceptual objects, properties, states, and events with which linguistic labels can be associated. Lacking such a catalog, we are forced to speculate about the criteria that the system can attend to and judge.

Our major concern in this chapter is to introduce further attentional-judgmental predicates—predicates similar to Red and Small, to take two examples for which groundwork was laid in chapter 1. Only cursory attempts will be made to describe mechanisms whereby the system is able to construct perceptual representations or to vary them until certain criteria are satisfied, although it is assumed that such mechanisms exist and that their description is a central task of perceptual theory. Since it is redundant, the predicate *Perceive* will be suppressed; imagine that it is implicitly present in invisible ink. Further discussion of intentional aspects of perception will be postponed to section 2.6.

Although the attentional-judgmental predicates of chapter 1 are special by virtue of their generality and, in some cases, by virtue of our understanding of neurophysiological mechanisms underlying them, people are capable of making many other attentional-judgmental abstractions. Moreover, few if any of the additional predicates needed to characterize perception can be reduced to those special predicates of greatest historical interest to students of the sensory processes. They involve relations, often highly intricate relations, that cannot be inferred from the particular predicates considered in chapter 1. And such complex perceptual relations are often difficult to distinguish from conceptual relations. As will become clear, the boundaries of perception within cognitive theory are as vague and arbitrary as the boundaries of sensation within perceptual theory. Attention and judgment, after all, are processes of conceptual thought as well as of perception. Indeed, the recognition of an object as, say, a table or a person is so very complicated and requires such elaborate conceptual support that we will not be able to consider it in any detail until chapter 4. For the present we will proceed as if perception could be isolated and treated independently from the rest of cognitive psychology. The limitations of this approach will emerge as the argument develops.

The most salient fact about the perceptual world, of course, is that it is filled with recognizable objects located or moving about in space and persisting through time. The task is to characterize judgments of those perceptual objects and events in such a way that they can be related to the words and sentences used to identify them. Before undertaking that task, however, we should pause to see what formal theories of perception are available to guide us.

2.1   FORMAL THEORIES OF PERCEPTION

As in our discussion of theories of sensation, here again we must report that there are many informal points of view adequate to guide and relate studies of particular aspects of perception, but nothing that qualifies as a formal theory of perception. Informal theories are valuable—indeed, lacking any comprehensive formal theory, they are indispensable—but they come in a distressing variety of shapes and sizes. Allport provided a useful survey that organized the theories existing in 1955 into rough groups: the classical empiricistic theories of sensations and associations; the configurational approach of gestalt theory; the topological theory of life spaces with their vectors, valences, tensions, and equilibriums; a neuropsychological approach through cell assemblies and phase sequences; motor theories involving sensory-tonic systems and set; adaptation-level theories emphasizing perceptual norms and frames of reference; functionalistic theories based on probabilistic weighting of cues or on transactions with the environment; motivational theories of directive states and perceptual defenses; theories that perception is determined by the relative strengths of the perceiver's hypotheses about the world; stimulus-response theories of the role of learning in perception; cybernetic theories involving coding, negative feedback, information processing; Allport's own outline of a general theory of event structure. This catalog is a reminder both of the complexity of the problem and of the variety of approaches to it that one might take.

Since Allport's review, workers in the field of artificial intelligence have entered the picture, and some of their formulations have begun to approach the level of analysis one should expect from a rigorous theory, at least in certain well-defined domains related to pattern recognition. In particular, it has been possible to formulate with some rigor the inadequacies of at least one version of the elementalistic approach. For example, we might imagine that the sensory field at any given moment consists of a spatial array of color sensations (the sensory output) representing an object to be recognized, and imagine a set of functions $f_i(x)$, where x is some subset of places (either adjacent or dispersed) in the array. The values of these f_i might be computed in parallel and delivered to another function, $g(x)$, such that $g = 1$ if the weighted sum of the f_i is greater than a predetermined threshold value. Then we might try to adjust the weights assigned to the various f_i (perhaps by a learning process involving feedback) in such a way that $g = 1$ if and only if the object is a member of a particular class of objects. Such two-stage schemes, where stage two is some linear combination of the functions at stage one, are known as perceptrons (Rosenblatt, 1962).

Minsky and Papert (1969) have proved numerous theorems about perceptrons, one of the more interesting being that no perceptron can distinguish between figures that are connected and figures that are not (see fig. 2.1). Since

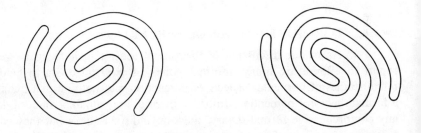

Figure 2.1 Connected and unconnected figures. (From Minsky and Papert, 1969.)

connectedness is central to topology, this failure represents a serious limitation in the formal properties of such devices. The central result established by their work, however, is the group-invariance theorem. As the eyes move about, the location of a pattern in the sensory field will be translated across the retinas. Thus it is necessary to ask what it means for a predicate g to be unaffected by such a group of transformations. The predicate g will be invariant just in case all the functions f_i that are equivalent under the group of transformations receive the same weighting in the computation of g. (Two f_i are equivalent under a group of transformations if there is a transformation h such that $f_1(hx)$ and $f_2(x)$ are the same for every pattern x.) Minsky and Papert also show that if it is possible for a perceptron to distinguish between two classes of patterns, then a simple feedback procedure exists for teaching it a set of weightings that will distinguish between them. Most of the theorems are negative, however, indicating that linear devices of this simple type are insufficient as a basis for any adequate theory of the perceptual world.

The hypothesis that object recognition is accomplished by "analyzers" or "feature detectors" (devices that scan the retinal array for particular, arbitrary configurations of stimulation) has enjoyed some popularity among theoretical psychologists since the discovery by Hubel and Wiesel (1962, 1965, 1968) that there are single nerve cells in the mammalian brain that respond maximally to light or dark edges or bars in particular orientations ending at particular points on the retina. Sutherland (1968, 1976), for example, extrapolating from theoretical work by Clowes (1967) on pictorial identification by computers, has proposed that shapes are described in the brain in a "language" for which the alphabet is given by such nerve cells; recognition occurs when this description matches a description stored previously. Sutherland argues that a variety of perceptual phenomena—invariances, confusions, segmentations, learning—can be explained in these terms.

The observations by Hubel and Wiesel are indeed suggestive, but the conceptual difficulties in understanding how such analyzers can work together to achieve object recognition are still forbidding. As Sutherland and Mackintosh (1971) remark, "It is clear that the notion of an analyzer does not begin to capture the complexity of what is going on when a representation of an object in the external world is formed in the brain" (p. 54). Until we understand these mechanisms better, it will remain difficult to incorporate them into any general theory of our perception of the visual world.

Minsky and Papert (1969) outline briefly what a machine would have to be able to do in order to find objects in a two-dimensional picture of a three-dimensional scene, although no formal theory of such a device is attempted. This object-recognizing machine would have to detect edges, infer connected surfaces from the edges and vertexes outlining them, cluster the faces into objects, recognize shadows and other artifacts, make each of its decisions on a tentative basis subject to revision, and submit to organization by some supervisory executive program. In a subsequent review, Minsky and Papert (1972) describe some components of such a machine in more detail. Although computers can be programmed to achieve many of these results, any formal theory of such a device, at a depth of analysis comparable to the theory of perceptrons, seems well out of reach at the present time.

If we try to imagine a completed perceptual theory, we think of a set of basic laws that can be given mathematical expression in such a way as to enable us to calculate, given appropriate parameters for the stimulus situation and the state of the perceiving organism, the nature of the perceptual representation that would result and the range of alternative responses that the organism might, with different probabilities, be expected to exhibit. Such a theory would describe a set of possible transformations that could be applied to the input stimuli in order to determine the output to the conceptual system. Moreover, the laws would have direct application to the perceptual nervous system—to neurophysiology as well as to psychology.

Such a theory may never be possible. "Nobody," according to von Neumann (1951), "would attempt to describe and define within any practical amount of space the general concept of analogy which dominates our interpretation of vision. There is no basis for saying whether such an enterprise would require thousands or millions or altogether impractical numbers of volumes" (p. 24). He argued that vision involves parts of logics with which we have no past experience, whose complexity is out of all proportion to anything we have ever known, and that we have no right to assume that logical notations and procedures used in the past are suitable. "It is not at all certain," he suggested, "that in this domain a real object might not constitute the simplest description of itself." Attempts to describe it by literary or formal-logical methods may lead to something less manageable and more involved. In any case, we have no such theory yet.

We have few perceptual laws that can be expressed mathematically for any but the simplest perceptual situations, and those we have are not integrated in any comprehensive theory. Moreover, the relation of our psychological results to the electrical and biochemical events that we can observe in the brain is so obscure that many philosophers suspect a fundamental conceptual error in the way most psychologists and neurophysiologists think about the relation. Rather than attempt to construct a formal theory, therefore, we will adopt a much weaker approach: we will try to imagine what the output of a perceptual theory might be if we had it. To the extent that this exercise is successful, of course, it will define goals that a perceptual theory would be expected to achieve. Our present interest in such imaginings, however, has more to do with what the conceptual system might assume as input than with what perceptual theory might provide as output.

Since the complexity of the brain, the unpredictability of the environment, and the variety of internal states of the organism are so forbidding, it seems plausible to suppose that any formal theory able to deal comprehensively with this system would have a probabilistic formulation at some if not all levels of description, supplemented, perhaps, by a formal theory of computation. We assume that an appropriate calculus for such a theory would evolve from current work on decision processes and computation. That is to say, we assume that the perceptual mechanism can be characterized—in part, if not totally— as a probabilistic decision-computing system.

This assumption enables us to proceed as if knowledge of the laws and mechanisms underlying these perceptual decisions were of less functional importance than knowledge of the decisions themselves. On this basis, therefore, we can ask ourselves what kinds of decisions—or judgments, as we shall call them—the perceptual system can make, without trying to explain how they are made. These decisions will be the output of the perceptual theory.

It may sound odd to speak of the "output" of a theory, so it is necessary to say how we understand this term. The conceptual system depends on the perceptual system for judgments about the world. These judgments—not the essence of redness, or the raw experience of a landscape, or the immediate existential apprehension of an experiential world—must be enumerated and characterized. Perceptual theory should explain how it is possible to make such judgments, but it is only the fact that certain judgments can be made, not how they are made, that is critical for linguistic communication. The input assumed by the conceptual system, therefore, refers to the outcomes of perceptual judgments about the contents of experience—outcomes that can be made available for purposes determined by the conceptual system.

We adopt the term "judgment" with some apprehension, since it seems to lend an intellectual dignity and formality to the outputs of perception that we do not intend. In general, the judgments we have in mind are unconscious, although they may, under appropriate circumstances, become the basis for conscious judgments in a more formal sense. In order to discuss these judgments we must be able to formulate them as statements, and in that context they look like judgments. So that is what we will call them, even though we recognize that they have this status only in our theory language, seldom in conscious experience.

As we have already suggested, a perceptual judgment can be represented in theoretical language by a statement that some property of a percept has a particular value, or that some relation holds between perceptual entities or properties. We will represent these judgments by such expressions as "Percept x has property P" or "The relation R holds between percepts x and y," or, more briefly, $P(x)$ and $R(x, y)$. Given such expressions, of course, a natural way to use them would be as statements in the first-order predicate calculus, thus bringing to bear the logical machinery of conjunction, disjunction, negation, implication, quantification. Such was the approach described by Kirsch (1963, 1964) as the basis of a "Picture Language Machine," PLM. The machine had available such atomic predications as "x is black," "x is bigger than y," "x is between y and z," and so on. A scanning device attempted to decide which predicates described a picture and then formulated a compound predication expressing that information. PLM also accepted English sentences that described the picture, parsed them, and translated the parsed sentence into another compound predication constructed out of the atomic predicates of the system. Then it attempted, by logical argument, to determine whether the sentence was true, that is, whether the logical translation of the sentence could be derived from the logical description of the picture.

A major limitation of PLM was that the input sentences had to be translated into the first-order predicate calculus. Once the translation was achieved, of course, the deductive system was quite powerful, but many natural-language expressions are difficult to express unambiguously in this logical form, and consequently PLM was quite limited in the variety of sentences it could handle. In an effort to avoid this limitation, we will use a procedural rather than a logical language to combine perceptual predicates. Moreover, we will not attempt to represent everything the perceptual system knows about the "picture" in predicate notation; a percept is formed and is available for description, but the decision to apply some particular predicate as a descriptor must come from the conceptual system. Only those perceptual predicates are transmitted from the perceptual to the conceptual system that the conceptual system asks for.

To say that such statements can be transmitted from the perceptual to the conceptual system entails (a) that perceptual mechanisms exist for making such judgments and (b) that the conceptual system can call on the perceptual system to make them. We will represent the judgments (a) by predicate expressions, as in PLM. But we will indicate (b), that the conceptual system has called on the perceptual system to test such a predicate, by making the predicate an argument of a control instruction to "test"; for example, test $(P(x))$ or test$(R(x, y))$. The complete statement of a test instruction must, of course, specify what to do next: test$(P(x))$ and, if it is true, proceed to the next instruction; otherwise go next to instruction a. Moreover, since few predicates describing the perceptual world are timeless, we will also include as one argument of "test" the time when the predicate is supposed to be realized: test (time, $P(x)$). In direct perception the time will usually be "right now," so this argument would seem to be redundant, and thus dispensable. Later, however, we will want to use "test" for changing or remembered percepts, where the temporal argument will be significant, so we wish to leave a place for it in order to indicate what particular state of affairs is to be tested.

How perceptual predicates might be exploited by control instructions from the conceptual system is discussed more fully in chapter 3. For the present, our concern is to characterize a representative sample of the perceptual predicates that are available.

When judgments are expressed as predicates, it becomes obvious that some are closely related to others; that if such-and-such tests can be performed, then so can others. We will, therefore, suggest various ways in which these judgments might be related. Lacking a formal theory of perception, these putative relations among perceptual judgments can be no more than suggestions, but we will support them with whatever information and intelligence we can muster.

Not having an explicit perceptual theory means that we cannot be sure what the primitives of the system are. It is intuitively obvious that some judgments are simpler than others—the judgment that a surface is red is somehow simpler than the judgment that an object is a table, for example. To whatever extent our judgment that some object is the sort of thing speakers of English call tables depends on perceptual information about the object, the judgment can be analyzed into simpler judgments: that it is a three-dimensional object, that it has a flat surface, that the flat surface is horizontal, that the flat surface is supported by vertical extensions, and so forth. No similar decomposition of a judgment of redness seems possible. In such cases we will trust our intuition that judgments of redness are more primitive than judgments of tablehood. In other cases, however, intuition provides little guidance. For example, it can happen that if we assume predicates P and Q to be primitive, then R is a consequence, but if we had assumed instead that P and R were primitive, then Q would have been a consequence. In order to decide which predicates are atomic and which are derivative in such situations, we require the kind of information that the missing perceptual theory would presumably provide. The best we can do, therefore, is to limit ourselves in this chapter to perceptual judgments that seem to be likely candidates as primitives and to postpone until chapter 4 those perceptual judgments that seem to us to be compound. In a sense, we are building on sand, but it is better to build on sand than on nothing at all.

In order to organize our discussion of the perceptual world, we will rely on

traditional categories: objects, space, time, change, causation.* The most compelling fact of perception is that people see objects. But object recognition is
not the sole end of perception. Objects are perceived as related in space and
time. It is difficult to imagine a satisfactory psychological characterization of
the world that did not begin with spatial and temporal aspects of experience.

Psychological space and time provide the coordinate system within which
phenomenal things are experienced and reacted to. And things change. In
particular, things move from one region to another from one moment to the
next. So we must have some way to describe these changes and motions in the
world of perceptual experience. Motions, of course, occur over distances in
various directions and with various causes. These we will take as basic terms
for judgments about the contents of the visual world, that is, as terms to be
defined by perceptual theory and taken as primitives for cognitive theory.

2.2   OBJECTS, SURFACES, AND COLORS

One of the most impressive accomplishments of the perceptual
mechanism is its organization of experience into substantial things, tangibly
and temporally connected, located in spatial relation with other things. Things
are characterized by surfaces and edges and vertexes, colors and textures,
shapes and sizes and weights, and coherent movement as units through space.
Things maintain their perceived shapes, colors, weights, and sizes independently of movement or orientation relative to the receptors. Most important,
things maintain their identity, so it is usually possible to recognize a subsequent exposure to a similar thing. If objects did not maintain their identity,
people would have little use for labels to identify them.

A basic component of this perceptual accomplishment is the isolation of
one object from another. The perceptual mechanism is able to differentiate an
object from the background against which it appears. The same object that is
a perceptual figure at one moment may become part of the background when
attention shifts to the perception of another thing nearby, yet people assume
its continued existence and stability even when they are not looking at it. Thus,
the simplest perception of a concrete object seems to depend on a prior concept of object permanence.

Although we will concentrate here on processes that are traditionally regarded as purely perceptual, the considerable conceptual contribution they
entail must not be underestimated. The perceptual mechanism can integrate
several diverse exposures to a thing into a coherent psychological entity;
people can usually recognize a familiar object even when stimulated by it in
some novel way. The ontological assumptions built into the thing recognizer
are sufficiently robust that people can discard the specific patterns of stimulus

---

*A comprehensive attempt to cover much of this ground is contained in Aristotle's
Physics (especially books 3–8), where the ideas of change, motion, place, space, time,
and causation are defined and discussed in terms close to the perceptual level.

information they have received in favor of some deeper conceptualization of the object that gave rise to them. Thus, they may be able to recognize that they have seen a particular thing before, even though they would not be able to distinguish the particular perceptions they have actually received from it from all the other perceptual patterns they might have received. Their conception of a stable world around them rests on some poorly understood but highly complex process that must have great survival value in spite of its vulnerability to error and illusion.

2.2.1   Objects

One type of judgment people make, therefore, is that some percept x is indeed a concrete, three-dimensional object, a judgment we will represent as Obj(x, 3d). The reason for including 3d in the object predicate is not only that it makes explicit the fact that x is a perception of a concrete object; it acknowledges that there are some concrete objects one perceives as two-dimensional. Two-dimensional objects are not limited to figures inscribed on smooth surfaces. Bierwisch (1967) gives "Strasse" and "Fenster" as examples of objects having only two dimensions: streets can be long and wide, windows can be tall and wide, but neither is thick (the asphalt or the casement can be thick). Since there is probably a strong effect of linguistic conventions on judgments of the dimensionality of such objects, for convenience we have made the number of dimensions an argument of Obj.

The mechanisms involved in separating an object from its surround are not well understood; even preliminary attempts to analyze them attest to their considerable complexity. For example, Minsky and Papert (1972) have reviewed attempts by themselves and their colleagues to characterize how we can see static, two-dimensional line drawings of blocks as representations of three-dimensional objects. The task can become quite complicated when several blocks are present in the scene, some behind or on top of others; the theoretical problem is to formulate a set of rules that will divide a scene into the separate objects that constitute it and to specify relations between objects. Minsky and Papert assume that each intersection of lines in the two-dimensional drawing can be used to infer which surfaces belong to the same three-dimensional object. For example, if an intersection is formed by three lines coming together in the shape of an arrow, it will usually represent an exterior corner of an object, so the two surfaces inside the arrow can be linked as belonging to the same object. If an intersection is a fork having the shape of a Y, it usually represents a corner formed by three surfaces of the same object, so all three surfaces can be linked. An intersection in the shape of a T, on the other hand, usually signifies that an edge of one object has disappeared under the edge of another, which provides evidence against linking the adjacent surfaces. And so on. By exploiting such evidence as this it is usually possible to represent each perceptual object by an abstract graph where the nodes, which represent surfaces, are connected by lines indicating which surfaces are linked together in the same object; in a correct analysis, each object has its own connected graph, and there are no links between graphs of different objects. This method of analyzing a scene into component objects was implemented in a computer program by Guzmán (1968) and subsequently was refined and extended by Martin Rattner and others. The computer can be fooled by some patterns, but so can a human observer.

Although there is little evidence that human viewers always put so much reliance on intersections, vertexes, and edges, it is unlikely that such relations could be totally ignored by the nervous system. If we accept the suggestion that a human observer draws similar inferences, however, it becomes difficult to see any sharp distinction between perception and conception. That is to say, without a reasonably definite conception of what objects should look like, it would be impossible to exploit the evidence provided by edges and corners in order to separate such a scene into objects. Even at this relatively simple level of analysis—where only the separation of an object from its background in a well-defined drawing is involved and questions of shape or recognition are ignored—any sharp division between perception and conception seems questionable. Indeed, when a person views complicated line drawings, shorn of all the information normally provided by color, texture, shadows, movement, or prior knowledge, his object-forming mechanisms may fail; several seconds may be needed before objects can be "seen." The deliberate search for objects in such a scene (the eyes moving along the edges to successive vertexes) must be guided by operations of thought that could only be characterized as conceptual, not perceptual.

When such computer programs are used to analyze photographs of actual three-dimensional scenes, they are far less successful than in analyzing line drawings. The various shades of gray, the shadows, the textures of surfaces in the photograph provide valuable information for the human perceptual system, but little progress has yet been made in incorporating such information into mechanical scene analyses. A detailed review of the current state of the art would take us far afield; fortunately, Sutherland (1976) has provided such a review written in the context of psychological theories of perception, and the reader interested in pursuing the topic further could well begin there.

The predicate Obj will be used extensively (in combination with other predicates) to characterize percepts to which linguistic labels can be applied. So we must assume that it is available to the conceptual system even though we cannot presently specify the mechanisms it might involve. Whatever they are, they must be able to do more than extract a coherent pattern from the general scene; they must also be able to hold that pattern through variations in spatial orientation over time. The simplest way to think about it is that any x satisfying the predicate Obj(x, 3d) has associated with it in some way a conceptual object that has individuality and permanence. The particular object that is seen may be assigned to some class of objects all taking the same label in some language, but that categorization does not mean that we perceive a category. We perceive a particular instance of the category, and it is that individual object that is indexed by x.

The permanence attributed to individual objects is so obvious to anyone capable of understanding a description of it that its importance—in particular, its importance for the way we talk about things—is easily overlooked. At the risk of seeming banal, therefore, we will attempt to analyze the object concept in more detail.

An observer stands watching a scene. He sees a man and hears the man call to a friend. At that point the observer turns away momentarily. When he turns back, he sees the man again, and again hears the man call to a friend. The observer believes that he saw the same man both times, but he does not believe that he heard the same call both times. The man is perceived as an object persisting through time, but the call is perceived as an event that occurs and is gone. Piaget argues that an observer's ability to recognize objects as persisting entities—his mastery of the object concept—must be acquired during the first two years of life; Piaget (1937; but cf. T. G. R. Bower, 1974) has given a detailed account of the developmental stages he believes the object concept goes through.

What is involved here is more than the ability to recognize that a percept is an instance of a particular kind—that the object seen was, in this example, an instance of the type "man." The observer sees the *same* man, the same instance he saw before. Before an infant acquires the object concept, he presumably does not see successive reappearances of mother as a succession of different mothers, since "different" means "not the same" and "same" is not part of the cognitive equipment of someone who lacks the object concept; the infant may recognize mother as an instance of a familiar kind, but the question of individual persistence through time has, if Piaget is correct, no relevance to what he recognizes.

The adult, on the other hand, has acquired, in addition to recognition functions for kinds of things, certain individuating functions for particular things. Suppose that A is the set of things an observer sees at one time and B is the set he sees at another time, and let a be a member of A and b a member of B. In order to perceive that $a = b$, the observer must have some individuating function f associated with a particular individual, so that f will select that individual from both A and B. That is to say, if $f(A) = a$ and $f(B) = b$, then a $= b$. But such a function, by itself, does not ensure that the particular individual persists even when he is unobserved. That is, f must have conceptual as well as perceptual status: if C is the observer's conception of all the things that exist in the world (or in that part of the world with which he is locally concerned), then it must be possible to apply f to C, and if $f(C) = c$, then $a = b = c$. If, when the observer turned back to the scene, the particular individual associated with f had departed, the observer would not conclude that the individual had ceased to exist, since he would exist conceptually in C even when $f(B)$ had no value (did not select the individual from the perceptual scene B). Individuating functions will be more detailed for some things than for others—the more similar a set of individuals are, the more information one needs to distinguish among them without error (Miller, 1953; Attneave, 1959; Garner, 1962).

Individuating functions are essential not only for the use of proper names but for any kind of reference to particular, individual objects. "My car," for example, selects one object from all others, although it may select a different object today from what it would select some other time—the verbal phrase may be associated with f_1 today and with f_2 at another time. And at some particular time "the car in the driveway" may select one object from all others. "My car is in the driveway" expresses the assertion that the object selected by the individuating function presently associated with the phrase "my car" and the object selected by the individuating function presently associated with the phrase "the car in the driveway" are identical at the time of utterance. Of course, if the speaker has a car and if it is not in the driveway, then it must be somewhere else—his car persists through time and space as an enduring object—but the phrases that can be associated with its individuating function change from one situation to another. The point is that if there were no individuating function for that particular object, there would be nothing for a definite description to be associated with. The object concept is fundamental for all our talk about individual objects.

In ordinary language we talk a great deal about concrete objects and seldom stop to question the implicit ontological assumption that if $Obj(x, 3d)$ applies, then x exists. The existential quantifier $(\exists x)$ is said by some logicians to make this assumption explicit. As long as physical existence is the only point at issue, ordinary linguistic constructions based on this implicit ontological assumption work quite well—so well, in fact, that they are freely generalized in ordinary language to abstract "objects." The philosophical problems that arise from this generalization, of course, are extremely complex (see, for example, Quine, 1960). If, in order to reflect conventional usage, we use quantifiers to range over abstract variables—attributes, for instance, or classes—we seem to impute to them the same kind of existence we assume for concrete objects. On the other hand, if we refuse to quantify over anything but concrete objects, we seem to be required to show how all our abstract talk, insofar as it is meaningful, can be reduced to or paraphrased in terms of talk about concrete objects. Since neither alternative is attractive, we are left in something of a dilemma.

It is certainly true that although ordinary language may be careless about its ontology, the scientific language in which we discuss ordinary language should not be. On the other hand, the fact that logical languages require a theorist to make his ontological assumptions explicit does not give him license to impose this convention on the ordinary language he is attempting to characterize. Threading one's theoretical way between the scientific requirement for precision and the natural language's easy neglect of ontological niceties is no simple matter.

We assume that the conceptual system has available a control instruction to find things; when this "find" instruction is executed, the receptors are moved systematically to vary the percept x in *Perceive*(ego, x) until the desired x is discovered. The arguments of the "find" instruction should include whatever information (if any) is available about the domain to be searched and some description of the entity that is the target of the search. When a "find" instruction is successfully executed, the result will be a centered perception of the target. We assume that the target "exists" only insofar as we assume that some neurophysiological process corresponding to the target exists.

In order to use the result of a successful "find," the conceptual system must also have available a control instruction to "assign" this underlying process as the value of some index. That is, once the system has found a target, it is called x (or T165, or arthur, or whatever). Whenever assign($x =$ percept) is executed, the variable x becomes an index or pointer to the percept in question, and this pointer can then be used as an argument in perceptual predicates like Red (x). For example, the conceptual system might set up a routine like this:

> (i) find(search domain, a three-dimensional object) and assign it to x; if none is found, exit
>
> (ii) test(now, Red(x)); if test succeeds, exit; if not, go to (i)

We assume that the "find" instruction will continue the search through the indicated domain for percepts satisfying Obj(x, 3d) until one is found that also satisfies (ii), at which point the routine will deliver x to whatever conceptual enterprise called it into action, or until the search domain is exhausted. If the instruction succeeds, the higher-order routine will then have a pointer that can be used in any subsequent routines involving that object.

The search routine we have imagined can fail either because the "find" instruction fails to produce an object percept or because no object that it finds satisfies subsequent tests. The former we will regard as a presuppositional failure; the preconditions of the test are not satisfied, so the test simply does not apply. The latter we will regard as a verificational failure; the test can be applied, but nothing satisfies it. If the routine succeeds on both counts, the higher-order routines that called it would have gathered the information normally sufficient to support the utterance of some such sentence as "There is a red object."

If we were to propose some theoretical sentence of the form "There exists an x such that x is an object and x is red," we would put the judgment that x is an object and the judgment that x is red on an equal footing. That is to say, if there were no object at all, the sentence would be false, whereas in the procedural formulation we have tried to capture the fact that the perception of the object is a precondition for judgments of its color—if there is no object, the sentence is vacuous. "There exists an object x such that x is red" comes closer to expressing the priority of object perception, but the difference is not easily captured in the notations of quantificational logic. When we are trying to characterize what people do when they talk about their perceptions, therefore, we will use procedural formulations. When we are trying to characterize relations among perceptual predicates, however, a logical formulation of those relations is often extremely convenient. We will therefore freely use notations of the predicate calculus and quantification theory whenever they seem to clarify relations among perceptual predicates.* For example, if a percept x that satisfies predicate P must also satisfy predicate Q, then we can write $(x)[P(x) \supset Q(x)]$. But it must be understood that this notation does not represent the procedures that we assume a person must execute when he runs routines involving the predicates P or Q.

Since the object percept indexed by x is embedded in the rest of the visual scene, it must have a location; since it is big enough to see, it must have a size; since it is bounded from its surround, it must have a shape. These attributes of any object percept can be represented:

(1) $(x)[\text{Obj}(x, 3\text{d}) \supset (\exists w)\text{Place}(x, w)$ & $(\exists y)\text{Size}(x, y)$ &
           $(\exists z)\text{Shap}(x, z)]$.

That is to say, for all x, if x is a three-dimensional object, then x has a location w, a size y, and a shape z. In order to say how object x differs from some other object, we can say how it differs in place, size, and shape.

The pointers w, y, and z deserve comment. First, they have unique values. An object cannot be in two locations at once, for example. A more precise formulation of (1) would also include uniqueness conditions—something like: $(v)[\text{Place}(x, v) \supset (v = w)]$. Second, instead of pointing to an object, as x does, w, y, and z point to properties. The location w is a different kind of hypothetical entity from the object x to which it is related in (1) by $\text{Place}(x, w)$. The idea to be expressed is that there is exactly one place w that is attributed to x. In the predicate calculus this might be written: (there is one w)[$w(x)$ & $\text{Place}(w)$], where $w(x)$ means w is a property of x and $\text{Place}(w)$ means that w is a place. Since $\text{Place}(w)$ attributes a property to a property, it is a predicate of the second order, or type two in the theory of types. And since $w(x)$ is a first-order predicate, its conjunction with $\text{Place}(w)$ forms a heterogeneous predicate. The convenience of such predicates is that they let us say that something has a location without saying where it is, or that something has a unique size without saying how big it is, and so on. Place, Size, and Shap are all defined as heterogeneous predicates in this manner.

Thus, (1) says that if a pointer x has been created to a percept of some object, then it is possible to assign other pointers to its location, size, or shape. So, given $\text{Obj}(x, 3\text{d})$, any conceptual routine also has available to it without further search such instructions as test(now, $\text{Place}(x, v)$), which will be affirm-

---

* The knowledge of symbolic logic that will be assumed here can be acquired from any good introductory textbook. Both Reichenbach (1947) and Strawson (1952), although not recent, contain important discussions of natural language in addition to clear presentations of the fundamental ideas of logic.

ative if $v = w$ (if the expected location v and the perceived location w are the same) and negative otherwise.

The direction of implication in (1) should not be understood to assign any kind of procedural priority to the object percept. It merely leaves open the possibility that there might be some x that had a location, size, and shape but that was not perceived as an object. We would like to think that the formation of an object percept occurs first, and that place, size, and shape are attributes of the object that, by attentional-judgmental acts, we can abstract from the object percept and talk about independently. But such sequential aspects are not expressed in the timeless logical notation of (1).

The question of what happens first has been much discussed by students of perception. In order to perceive that something is, say, a table, it would seem necessary to use information about its location, size, and shape, but how is it possible to judge its attributes until we know what "it" is? Which comes first, the attributes or the whole?

Experience with modern systems for processing information has taught us that such circles need not be vicious. Minsky and Papert (1972) remark in this connection that it is quite common in computer programs—and presumably in thought processes—for two different procedures to use each other as subprocedures. When the system is forming a percept, object-forming procedures can call on shape-recognizing procedures as subprocedures; when it pays attention to shape, shape-recognizing procedures can call on object-forming procedures as subprocedures. The assumption that one set of procedures must in every case precede the other imposes a rigid and unnecessary constraint on the complexity of our hypotheses about object perception.

If there is no need to assign priority either to the formation of an object percept or to the recognition of the object's attributes, why do we assume that $\text{Obj}(x, 3d)$ should be given priority? Our reason derives from our decision to characterize perception in terms of the attentional-judgmental predicates it must provide rather than in terms of mechanisms whereby percepts could be achieved. Deliberate judgments based on attention to particular attributes of an object normally occur only after the object percept is achieved. We say "normally" because in some situations the object-forming procedures may fail, in which case people become conscious of them and may be able to facilitate object formation by attending to particular features of the scene. But failures are the exception, not the rule. Since the success of linguistic communication about perceptual objects and their attributes presumes the successful operation of perceptual mechanisms for identifying those objects, we take the "normal" functioning as given, that is, we assume that the object percept is achieved prior to any conscious, attentional-judgmental abstractions of such particular attributes as size, place, or shape.

Place and size are purely spatial characteristics; we will postpone discussion of them until section 2.3. We will begin here with the extremely complex spatial attribute called the shape of a perceptual object. (A thorough and useful review of work on the visual perception of shape has been provided by

Zusne, 1970.) We will include under shape the perception of the parts of an object, including such parts as its surfaces, edges, and corners, and their perceptual properties—not only the visual properties of brightness, color, texture, contour, and so on, but also properties perceived by touch or kinesthesis. Thus, we are including under shape somewhat more than is customary in psychological discussions of shape perception.

2.2.2   Parts and Wholes

A thing may be a discrete entity, or it may be part of another thing. Any adequate theory of object perception will have to provide some way to deal with this relation between parts and wholes. The gestalt principle of common fate—all parts of a thing move through space together—is quite compelling for the perception that the parts form a whole, but the part-whole relation must depend on more than common fate; the edges and surfaces of an object are normally integrated even in the perception of stationary objects yet remain recognizable as parts. We can assume, therefore, that a perceptual theory must provide a predicate $Part(x, y)$ denoting that x is perceived as having a part y. Given this predicate, we can say that x and y are identical if each is a part of the other:

(2) $Ident(x, y) \equiv Part(x, y) \ \& \ Part(y, x).$

(Here, and subsequently, universal quantifiers are deleted when their scope includes the whole formula.) If x has a part y but x is not a part of y, then x has a proper part y:

(3) $Pprt(x, y) \equiv Part(x, y) \ \& \ notPart(y, x).$

Pprt will be one of the hardest-working predicates on our list. If no part of x is a part of y, then x and y are discrete things:

(4) $Disc(x, y) \equiv [Part(x, z) \supset notPart(y, z)].$

In other words, if the perceptual mechanism is able to determine that one percept is a part of another, then it will also be able to recognize when two percepts are discrete. Note that we need not assume here that Part must be a psychologically primitive predicate in terms of which Ident, Pprt, and Disc are defined; the same formal structure could be described by stating equivalences for Part, Pprt, and Ident in terms of Disc. Lacking an adequate perceptual theory, we have no way to determine which, if any, of these predicates should be considered primitive.

It should be understood that $Part(x, y)$ is not defined in terms of the connectedness or disconnectedness of x and y. That is, a pile of bricks consists of many proper parts that are not connected to one another. As we noted above, the arguments x and y need not be restricted to individual objects; the first argument can represent the total scene from which some particular object (or group of objects) has been isolated as a proper part. Connectedness, on the other hand, involves the existence of a continuous path, internal to the object, from every part to every other part. The parts of an object may or may not be connected. In order to discover whether some unfamiliar object is connected, it is at least necessary to explore it with the eyes, and manipulation is helpful if the object is of an appropriate size. Indeed, Hebb (1949) has claimed that motor responses in general, and eye movements in particular, are indispensable in learning to recognize any object, but even if this claim were true, active exploration would have to be supplemented by the symbolic construction of some representation of the object being explored. Whatever the mechanism, we will assume that $\text{Conn}(x)$ represents the judgment that x is connected. It will be convenient to use $\text{Conn}(x, y)$ when x and y are proper parts of some object percept z and $\text{Conn}(z)$.

If every part of an object percept x can be connected to every other part by a straight line containing no point external to the object, it is said to be convex, $\text{Cnvx}(x)$; otherwise it is concave, $\text{notCnvx}(x)$. Containers, $\text{Cont}(x)$, are a subclass of concave three-dimensional objects important for human use. These predicates can be used to describe either the perceived object itself or the shape of the perceived object. That is to say, we can write

(5) $\text{Shap}(x, y)$ & $\text{Cnvx}(x) \equiv \text{Cnvx}(y)$
          $\text{Shap}(x, y)$ & $\text{Cont}(x) \equiv \text{Cont}(y)$

and so forth. These predicates are intended to characterize the shape of a whole object. For shapes of particular parts or surfaces of an object, more detailed descriptions would be required in order to identify the part as well as to characterize its shape.

English has a variety of names for connected objects whose shapes are distinctive: cubes, blocks, cylinders, cones, pyramids, spheres, prisms, oblate spheroids, toroids. Although the three-dimensional shapes so named are characterized by perceptual symmetry and simplicity, each one designates a class of particular shapes that our culture has decided to group under a single label; the assignment of labels to classes of similar objects will be discussed in chapter 4. However, we can indicate here rather briefly the kind of perceptual mechanisms that might underlie such a classification.

We assume that a person familiar with this classification of shapes must have a general shape concept that is probably divided according to dimensionality. Under the three-dimensional shapes there will be a variety of more specific shape concepts. The perceptual system can gain access to some particular shape concept—the cube concept, for example—either via perception of the word "cube" or by identifying some perceptual object as an instance of the concept. Cubes can be conceptualized rather abstractly in terms of their six flat faces, all square; their twelve straight edges meeting at eight vertexes, each forming three right angles; each face being adjacent to four other faces and parallel to the fifth; their symmetries under rotations; and so forth. This cube concept must be distinguished from a cube percept. In addition to this conceptualization of cubes, therefore, there must be a set of perceptual tests that will enable us to determine whether some particular object percept is an instance of the cube concept. In dealing with real objects, of course, these tests must allow for some range of variation from the ideal concept, since the edges will not be infinitely sharp, some corners may deviate from exactly 90 degrees, opposite faces may not be perfectly parallel, and so on. The degree of tolerable variation must itself be an adjustable parameter, since the situational context does not always demand the same precision in the use of such words as "cube." How rules should be written in order to admit good as well as exact matches to a criterion is a question we will not try to answer, but some mechanism to account for our impressions of the relative goodness-of-fit is obviously necessary.

In order to specify how to identify an object percept as an instance of a cube, we could write out a routine (or set of routines) for testing the percept. For example, an identification routine might test whether anything in the object percept is inconsistent with the judgment that x has six congruent, square faces. This routine might identify x as a cube, Cube (x), but it would not, in and of itself, constitute the concept of cubes. The concept, as we saw above, is much richer and more abstract. An identification routine is merely a device to categorize x, to establish a connection between the particular percept and the abstract concept.

The perceptual isolation of individual objects in a scene and some identification of their shapes is only a beginning of the process of describing a whole scene. In addition, people are also able to appreciate various relations among those objects: they may be touching; one may be on top of, inside, or behind another; they may form a configuration having some common label, such as "pile," "wall," "stack," "line," "arch," "ring." Gestalt psychologists, always concerned about relations of parts to wholes, have used these configurational properties to argue that the whole is greater than the sum of its parts, that the configuration of the whole has properties of its own, over and above the properties of the individual objects that constitute it.

For example, imagine an arch formed, as in figure 2.2, by three blocks, two

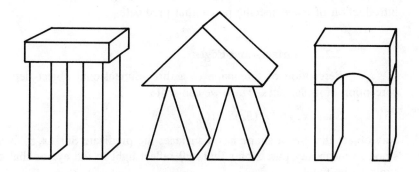

Figure 2.2   Sample arches. (After Winston, 1970.)

forming the base of the arch and the third resting on top of the other two. Not only must the perceptual system analyze this scene into the three blocks that compose it, but it must also characterize the relations among the blocks that lead to perceiving them as an arch. We might proceed as follows: let w point to the total perceptual configuration and x, y, and z point to the perceptions of the three blocks. Now we can list the following relations among these components: Obj(w, 3d), Obj(x, 3d), Obj(y, 3d), Obj(z, 3d); Pprt(w, x), Pprt(w, y), Pprt(w, z); Supports(x, z), Supports(y, z), notTouching(x, y). Minsky and Papert (1972), who have analyzed such arches in some detail, represent these relations the same way they represent relations among the various surfaces that go together to form a single connected object: each component is designated by a node in a directed graph, and the relations are indicated by labeled arrows between these nodes. Any configuration of blocks that satisfies this set of relations (that can be mapped into this graph) will be identified as an arch. The list of predicates can be regarded as a list of perceptual tests to be performed; the total configuration must satisfy all of these tests. This method of recognizing simple structures has been implemented by Winston (1970, 1973) in a computer program that can learn, through inspection of a sequence of instances and noninstances, to construct an appropriate list of tests.

When a computer (or, presumably, a person) learns to recognize arches in this manner, it is not easy to decide whether it is learning to perceive arches or acquiring a general concept of arches. We will argue that a concept of something must include more than just a routine for identifying instances of it, although learning to recognize instances must be part of learning the concept. So in a sense the learner is doing both—both learning to perceive and learning to conceive. We assume that the identification routine is part of the concept whose instances it identifies, but not the whole of it—just as perception is not the whole of conceptualization.

We will not pursue such examples further at this point, since they almost necessarily involve predicates (Supports and Touching in the case of arches) that have not yet been introduced or defined, and since this discussion has anticipated matters to be discussed more fully in chapter 4. This indication of the general line we are pursuing, however, should serve to motivate the further introduction of more specific perceptual predicates.

2.2.3   Surfaces and Edges

Perception of the shape of a three-dimensional object depends on perception of its surfaces. Thus, we can write

(6)   Shap(x, y) $\supset$ ($\exists z$)Surf(x, z).

Any object that has a shape has a surface; the predicate Surf(x, z) is understood to mean any part z of x that will reflect light to the eye or that can be explored by touch.

By Surf we mean the total surface of an object. Although the surface is a proper part of an object, we do not usually perceive a surface as a discrete object in itself, although streets, lawns, ceilings, and the like seem to be special exceptions. For concave objects in general, and containers in particular, it is useful to distinguish between internal and external surfaces, Intsurf and Exsurf.

A more difficult judgment to characterize is the distinction we make among faces, edges, and corners. All these are proper parts of surfaces, of course, and edges and corners are proper parts of faces, so there is a natural hierarchy. And corners are perceived differently from tips on or pits in the surface. We need a predicate $Exten(x, y)$ to indicate that y is perceived as an extension out from the body of object x and a predicate $Indent(x, y)$ to indicate that y is perceived as an indentation into the body of object x; we will not attempt to characterize the details.

What do we understand by a "face" of an object? If we are thinking of some idealized object like a cube, then the answer is reasonably obvious: it is one of the six planar squares bounding the object. Perceptually, a face of a cube is flat (although it may have a rough texture), is normally more or less evenly illuminated, and can be oriented at right angles to the viewer's line of regard. Exactly how rough the texture can be is a variable; under some conditions we would accept quite large variations from an ideal plane as an approximate face of a cube. A cylinder would seem to have only three faces: the circular top and bottom, plus the curved surface around the sides. Perceptually, there is a characteristic gradient of illumination and of texture indicating the curvature of the surface. In short, a face seems to be any extended, more or less continuously varying part of the surface that is bounded by relatively abrupt edges.

The perception of an edge of a three-dimensional object is generally taken as evidence that two faces intersect to form it. When three faces intersect, they form a corner; the projections of these corners can be classified, as noted on page 40, and used as evidence about both the integrity of the object as a whole and its particular shape. Thus, the perception of edges and corners probably plays a central role in shape perception.

Edges are usually perceived as abrupt gradients in color, particularly in brightness. The angle between the faces adjoining an edge can vary from small interior angles through color borders on flat surfaces to large angles of knifelike sharpness, with right angles (both interior and exterior) enjoying a special perceptual status. But the most important perceptual evidence for an edge is the qualitative difference in color (and/or texture) on either side of it. In order to characterize faces, therefore, we must first characterize edges; before we can deal with edges, we must first deal with color differences.

Every part of the surface of an object has some color. In order to refer to this property without having to specify a particular color, we can introduce a second-order predicate to say that z is a color, $Colr(z)$, and use it to define a heterogeneous relation between an object and its color: $Colr(y, z) = z(y)$ & $Colr(z)$. If we are given an object w having a surface x, and if y is any (sufficiently small) part of the surface, then y will have a unique surface color z:

(7) $\text{Surf}(w, x)$ & $\text{Pprt}(x, y) \supset (\exists z)\text{Colr}(y, z)$.

The normal perception of an edge, however, depends on a difference of color between adjacent areas y and y', so we must use the predicate Simlr (which we have already mentioned in section 1.2).

When we wish to say that two different percepts are similar, we usually specify the attributes with respect to which we judge them to be similar. Thus, a book and an apple can be similar in color, though different in all other attributes, so we might write

(8) $\text{Colr}(y, z)$ & $\text{Colr}(y', z')$ & $\text{Simlr}(z, z')$

to indicate that y and y' are similar in color. If y and y' are similar in every respect, then we can write simply $\text{Simlr}(y, y')$. Our ability to judge similarity is not limited to perceptual similarities, of course; judgments of conceptual similarities are also important. For the moment, however, we will assume that Simlr is a perceptual predicate, and we will leave open the possibility that perceptual acts can call on conceptual processes of this sort, just as conceptual processes can call on perceptual judgments. In any case, people are rather skilled at judging similarity, and many perceptual experiments exploit that skill. People are even able to estimate degrees of similarity; if we wish to include that ability in our notation, we can write, for example, $\text{Simlr}(y, y', d)$, where d is the degree of similarity, comparable to degrees of similarity estimated for other attribute pairs.

Armed with Colr and Simlr, we can introduce the notion of a visual edge between two adjacent areas y and y' by some such formulation as

(9) $\text{Colr}(y, z)$ & $\text{Colr}(y', z')$ & $\text{Adjcnt}(y, y')$ & $\text{notSimlr}(z, z')$
           $\supset (\exists v)[\text{Edge}(y, v)$ & $\text{Edge}(y', v)$ & $\text{Betw}(y, v, y')]$.

$\text{Betw}(y, v, y')$ denotes that the edge v is between areas y and y', and $\text{Adjcnt}(y, y')$ denotes that areas y and y' are spatially adjacent. (These two predicates will be discussed further in section 2.3.) The predicate notSimlr is understood to incorporate some arbitrary level or degree of similarity d that must not be exceeded. Boundaries, $\text{Bound}(y, v)$, are a special class of edges.

In (7) and (9) we assumed that area y was some part of the surface x of object w small enough to be relatively homogeneous in color and texture. Now if we expand area y to include as much of the surface x as we can without crossing any edge, then y will be a face of the object w, bounded by the edge v:

(10) $\text{Face}(w, y) \equiv (\exists x)[\text{Surf}(w, x)$ & $\text{Part}(x, y)]$ & $(\exists v)\text{Bound}(y, v)$.

That is to say, y is a face of the object w if and only if y is a part of the surface x of w and is bounded by the edge v. (10) is reasonably satisfactory except in the case of spherical objects having no edges; discussion with several speakers of English indicated that they were uncertain whether to say a sphere has one face or none at all. Given this uncertainty, and the tentative nature of this whole formulation, we are content to leave spheres in the faceless state indicated by (10).

The perceptual mechanisms required to "expand" the area y up to but not crossing any edge, or, conversely, to track a connected edge around the face y, must be reasonably complex and subject to error introduced by local variations in the surface or by such artifacts as highlights, shadows, or reflections. We will not attempt to describe mechanisms whereby the perceptual system could achieve such results, but we will point out that if there is doubt about instances of any importance, the visual mechanism for isolating faces can often be supplemented by tactual exploration and/or manipulation of the object. The object concept must be some kind of sensorimotor schema that includes more than a visual representation.

Not only can change in color signal an edge; color similarity can provide evidence for continuity. For example, when one object interrupts the view of another—as a ruler interrupts the view of a paper under it—the fact that the paper has the same color on both sides of the ruler provides evidence linking those disjoint surfaces perceptually. Similarity of texture and gradients of texture also provide clues for object perception (J. J. Gibson, 1950). These perceptual mechanisms make it possible to judge that one extended object intersects the perception of another, or $\text{Cross}(x, y)$.

The face of an object can be curved or round if the rate of curvature relative to the size of the object is insufficient to produce the impression of an edge. Flat faces and straight edges enjoy a special perceptual status, at least for people who live in carpentered environments. The perception of a face as flat, $\text{Flat}(y)$, or of an edge as straight, $\text{Straight}(v)$, is presumably facilitated by the fact that light travels in straight lines. A number of perceptual predicates are required to capture this aspect of object perception.

For example, the perceptual system must provide a basis for such predicates as

(11) $\text{Flface}(x, y) \equiv \text{Face}(x, y) \,\&\, \text{Flat}(y)$
             $\text{Stedge}(y, v) \equiv \text{Edge}(y, v) \,\&\, \text{Straight}(v)$

Although the notion that faces or edges are parallel is not easily defined without more geometrical terminology than we wish to introduce, the perceptual impression is sufficiently direct and immediate to justify a predicate Parallel (x, y), where x and y are flat faces or straight edges. Parallel judgments play an important role in judging relative orientations of objects.

Figures inscribed on flat faces can, of course, be considered as two-dimensional objects having connectedness, convexity, or various types of symmetry, just as three-dimensional objects can. In such inscriptions, of course, points and lines are perceptually salient, so we must introduce such predicates as $\text{Spot}(x)$ to denote that x is perceived to be a small mark suitable to represent a conceptual point, $\text{Line}(x)$ to indicate that x is a continuous path traced out by a moving spot, and $\text{Stline}(x)$ for straight lines. Moreover, simple patterns of spots on a flat surface can be perceived as if they were the corners of figures formed by connecting the spots with straight lines, so we also need such predicates as Inline(x, y, z) to indicate that a single straight line could be passed through the three spots x, y, and z; Intri(x, y, z) to indicate that connecting the spots x, y, and z by straight lines would form a triangle; and perhaps even Inquad(w, x, y, z) when lines connecting four spots are perceived as forming a quadrilateral. The strong association of spot patterns with simple geometric forms (up to patterns of four or five spots) may provide a basis for estimating the number of spots in a display from direct visual inspection and without deliberate counting.

2.2.4   Constancy

The stability of the perceptual world is generally believed to depend heavily on a phenomenon called perceptual constancy. The term refers to the fact that people usually see things as retaining relatively constant colors, shapes, and sizes even though the pattern of stimulus information they receive about color, shape, and size at the retinal surface may vary over wide ranges. This phenomenon has been studied in considerable detail by gestalt psychologists. We will describe it here briefly for color and shape and postpone size constancy to 2.3.3.

First, color constancy. The predicate Colr includes all three dimensions—hue, saturation, and brightness—discussed in sections 1.3 and 1.4 as characteristic of small homogeneous spots of light. (Perceptual theory must account for the other modes of appearance of color as well.) Moreover, we will simply assume that Colr(x, y) refers to the perceived color of x, not to its "true" color, whatever that might be. The problem of how to define true color has received extensive consideration, both from psychologists and from philosophers interested in perception.

A particular area, reflecting a given distribution of radiant energy, will not always be seen as constant in color. If it is spatially adjacent to a different color, the two colors will contrast, that is to say, the area to be judged will be seen as more different from the adjacent color than it would appear against a neutral (achromatic) background. Or, if a visual scene is illuminated by a particular color of light, it is possible under some circumstances to take account of the illuminant color and to perceive the spot as having a color more like what it would have if viewed in daylight. Contrast effects can usually be explained in terms of the opponent-process theory of color perception. The relative constancy of perceived color under variations in the color of the incident illumination—which, of course, can change radically the energy distribution of the light reflected from the object—is a more challenging problem.

In physical terms, the light reaching the eye (the luminance l of the object) depends on the energy distribution in the incident light e, multiplied by the reflectance r, which depends on the properties of the surface of the object: $l = er$. If perceived color depended only on the energy distribution in the light l reaching the eye, then it would change whenever the incident light e

changed. On the other hand, if perceived color depended only on the properties of the surface of the object that determine its reflectance r ($= l/e$), then it would remain constant when the incident light e changed. In fact, judgments of perceived color when e is varied seem to fall somewhere between l and r. Many experiments have explored conditions that contribute to constancy of perceived color (see the review by Hochberg in Kling and Riggs, 1971). Under normal viewing conditions it is possible to maintain good constancy— to judge the reflectance of the surface, rather than the light reaching the eye— over a wide range of variations in incident illumination, but constancy is not perfect. And when the cues required to judge the ratio l/e of luminant to incident light are removed—for example, by a reduction screen—constancy vanishes and only luminant color can be judged.

Is it possible to take account of the color of the incident light under normal viewing conditions? If a scene is illuminated by light of some particular color, that color will predominate in the scene. Perhaps the perceptual system reverses this implication: if some color predominates in the scene, then that is probably the color of the incident light. When some particular color dominates, therefore, the perceptual system might add a correction that would transform the dominant color into white. If, say, the dominant color is red, the visual system might add the opponent color, green, to a degree appropriate to cancel the red and produce white. It is known that color adaptation leads to afterimages in the complementary color; perhaps color constancy is one of the benefits of the elaborate organization into opponent processes that is superimposed on the trichromatic color receptors in the mammalian retina. A reduction screen, of course, deprives the visual system of its estimate of the predominant color in the scene and so would prevent the appropriate correction by such a system.

Mechanisms whereby color constancy is achieved provide a major topic for perceptual theory; theorists are not wholly agreed as to whether we take account of relations between the colors of adjacent areas or make "unconscious inferences" based on knowledge of the color of the incident light. We assume merely that some such mechanisms exist to support attentional-judgmental abstractions of the sort necessary for linguistic communication. The perceptual predicate $\mathrm{Colr}(x, y)$ makes no claim that y is determined by either l or r, which are presumably the two plausible definitions one might offer for the "true" color. However, the fact that observers can, and normally do, take an attitude of judging the object rather than the illuminant, so that y remains relatively constant in spite of variations in the illumination, obviously facilitates object recognition; words denoting the colors of objects would be of little use if this judgmental attitude were not easily taken.

When a common, three-dimensional object is seen in some familiar illumination—sunlight, for example—the intensity of the light reflected from different surfaces of the object varies according to the shape of the object and its orientation to the light. Indeed, this pattern is perceived not as a pattern of intensities but as the shape of the object. As Evans (1948) remarks, "this perception is usually so strong that it is almost impossible for the untrained observer to see the 'shading' on the objects at all. Yet it is just this shading which the artist must see . . . if he is to reproduce the perception of the shape in the mind of the person observing his reproduction" (p. 171). Color constancy and shape constancy are closely related in normal viewing.

A two-dimensional shape that would be clearly rectangular if viewed full on will not project a rectangular image to the eye if viewed from some oblique angle, yet the perceived shape normally remains approximately constant. Perceived shape depends on the perspective transformations produced by perceived motions, and shape constancy reflects the invariants under such transformations. The relative constancy of these judgments is critically important for the way people label shapes in linguistic communication.

One way to describe shape constancy is to say that the perception of an object is characterized not by some particular, momentary pattern of stimulation that it can produce on the retinas but by the whole set of patterns it can produce. If we ask how it would be possible for the visual system to appreciate whole sets of patterns as equivalent, an answer must be sought first in projective geometry, where the properties that remain invariant under projective transformations have been studied. If we assume that the visual system is somehow biased in favor of seeing rigid objects, then changes of the retinal pattern could be attributed to projective transformations rather than elastic deformations.

The tendency to attribute changes in the shape of the retinal image to projective transformations of a rigid, three-dimensional object rather than to deformations in the shape of the physical object has been demonstrated by experiments with two-dimensional patterns. Wallach and his colleagues (Wallach and O'Connel, 1953; Wallach, O'Connel, and Neisser, 1953; Wallach, Weisz, and Adams, 1956) used a variety of solid objects and forms constructed from wire to cast shadows on a screen. When these objects were rotated, the two-dimensional shadow patterns on the screen changed shape, but the changes preserved projective equivalences (J. J. Gibson, 1957; Hay, 1966). The shadow patterns were generally perceived as rigid objects in motion, not as elastic objects being deformed. Green (1961) and Johansson (1964) obtained similar results with figures generated on a cathode-ray tube, where nonperspective transformations can also be produced and are seen as deformations. Johansson concluded that simultaneous change in both the lateral and the vertical dimensions of the image was the effective stimulus for the perception of motion in the third dimension. In such experiments it is difficult to know whether the phenomenon being studied is shape constancy, depth perception, or the perception of motion. When we adopt a predicate like Shap to denote that people can treat as equivalent the entire set of projectively equivalent images created by an object, we are taking for granted an extremely complex visual mechanism.

With respect to shape, moreover, it is important to remember that information can be acquired tactually, so the perceptual mechanisms for the predicate

Shap must include more than the visual modality. And, of course, the viewer as well as the object viewed can move about, so transformations that the retinal image undergoes with movement must also be coherent with respect to proprioceptive information. Perceived shape is not an exclusively visual matter. Indeed, when people wish to explore some new and interesting shape in detail, they usually feel it as well as look at it, and either move it around or move around it, until a total conception of its shape is achieved, a conception that goes well beyond the information conveyed by any single modality.

Perceptual theory must also account for the fact that the perceived size of a familiar object remains constant over a wide range of variations in the size of the image it casts on the retina. Size, however, depends on spatial characteristics, which we must consider next.

2.3   SPACE, PLACE, AND SIZE

How do places in the visual field, which shift as the eyes shift, give rise to fixed places in a stationary, three-dimensional visual world? It is not enough for a thing recognizer to be invariant over translations of the eye; it must also have information about *where* the thing is. For example, a device that recognized letters anywhere in a sensory array would not thereby be able to read text; location in the array gives the order of the letters. As Minsky and Papert (1969) remark, a device that recognized only what letters were on a page, but not where they were, would have to solve anagrams to extract the message.

It may be an expository mistake to introduce space perception by pointing out that the visual image is constantly changing, although that fact has traditionally posed a central problem for theories of perception. As J. J. Gibson (1966) has stressed, ambient light has a significant three-dimensional structure that the eye explores. The structure of ambient light is normally quite stationary; it is the moving eye that creates most of the fluctuations at its own sensory surface. That a moving eye could gather information about a stationary world, much as a moving finger might gather information about a stationary object, is no great puzzle as long as we can imagine mechanisms to coordinate exteroceptive information on the retina with proprioceptive information about eye movements. The puzzle is somewhat deeper, however, when we ask how this coordination might be acquired. Do infants have to learn to stabilize the perceptual world by subtracting out the effects of their own movements, or is some mechanism for correlating the two sources of information a part of their innate endowment? In either case, must there not be some a priori concept of a stable, three-dimensional world to guide an infant's learning and/or correlating?

The history of man's efforts to abstract a formal concept of space from his experience of it has featured two rival theories, relative and absolute. Relative space is defined by spatial relations among things; absolute space is defined by a coordinate system independent of any things the space might contain. Relativistic theories dominated Western thought until Descartes and Newton and now have reappeared in modern relativity theory. Absolute space seems to be simple common sense to those educated under the influence of Newtonian thought. Cognitive theory should allow for both conceptions, of course, but the perceptual space to be characterized by a theory of perception must be relative in character. We will try, therefore, to avoid perceptual predicates that presuppose an understanding of metric distances in a euclidean space, in favor of predicates of a more relativistic—topological, perspective—character.

Perhaps the simplest spatial attribute of an object is its place. Early attempts to conceptualize space identified it with place. As defined by Aristotle in book 4 of the *Physics*: (a) place is what contains that of which it is the place; (b) place is not part of the thing; (c) the immediate place of a thing is neither less nor greater than the thing; (d) place can be left behind by the thing and is separable. Then Aristotle added that all place admits the distinction of up and down, and each of the bodies is naturally carried to its appropriate place and rests there, and this makes the place either up or down. After logical elimination of other alternatives, he concluded that the innermost motionless boundary of what contains is place. The universe, presumably, is the place that the universe occupies. In short, Aristotle stripped the place of one thing from any relation to the places of other things; place is merely a container coincident with the thing contained. Aristotle's definition of place does not determine how particular places are to be identified.

According to Jammer (1954), "The first major contribution to the clarification of the concept of absolute space was made by Philoponus, or John the Grammarian, as he is often called (*fl. c.* A.D. 575) . . . To Aristotle, place is the adjacent boundary of the containing body . . . Inconsistencies . . . proved to Philoponus that a new definition of 'place' or space was necessary. According to him, the nature of space is to be sought in the tridimensional incorporeal volume extended in length, width, and depth, different altogether from the material body that is immersed in it" (pp. 52–54). Modern scientific conceptions of space are not intuitive givens but have evolved from many centuries of thought and analysis.

Fillmore (1971d; see also H. Clark, 1973) has proposed a psychological characterization of "egocentric" perceptual space in terms of coordinates established by the vertical, unmistakably defined by gravity, and by reference to anatomical properties—front and back, bilateral symmetry—of the perceiver. Although the vertical enjoys special status for earthlings, the other coordinates are more difficult to establish as perceptual attributes. Defining spatial coordinates in terms of a point of origin at the perceiver is necessary but not sufficient, because his orientation is constantly changing, whereas the fact to be accounted for is that perceptual space is stable and stationary in spite of the observer's movements.

What remains stable as a person moves is the spatial relations between the fixed objects in his environment. A person's awareness of his own orientation in that space will, of course, rely heavily on his awareness of his own front and back, left and right, relative to those fixed objects. But first let us consider the perceived spatial configuration of objects relative to each other; then at least we will have a world in which an observer can orient himself and move about.

In order to take account of spatial relations, the perceptual process must not only register place, but relations between places, which entails perception of a spatial region containing the place of the thing. The region of a thing can be thought of as a rather indeterminate penumbra surrounding it. The advantage of region over place as a perceptual predicate is that regions can overlap even though things cannot. Thus, two things whose regions overlap can be seen in spatial relation to each other. We will say that object x is in the region of object y when x is spatially close enough to y to have the sort of interactions with it that normally occur between x's and y's. This definition of region is deliberately vague, because the perceptual attributes of a region are correspondingly vague.

The central concept involved probably develops from a distinction between those things a person is himself close enough to interact with and those things that he could interact with only if he (or they) moved. This personal and highly relative differentiation, between what is judged to be "here" (in my region) and what is not, presumably generalizes to spatial relations between other objects, and seems consonant with the plausible and widely held view that our conception of space depends on our motility in it.

There is some evidence that most people feel a personal space surrounding themselves (personal in the sense that they begin to feel uncomfortable if strangers invade it), and anthropologists have claimed that the limits of tolerable proximity vary from one culture to another. Evans and Howard (1973) have reviewed what is known about personal space—its dependence on sex, culture, and friendship—and have concluded that it is a conceptual construct, not a perceptual one. Moreover, when the notion of a characteristic region of interaction is generalized from people to inanimate objects, its extent and orientation must depend on experience with each particular kind of object. For example, the first time a child notices a chair he is unlikely to have any clear impression of its characteristic region of interaction; an adult, on the other hand, could probably judge the extent of its region and might say that the characteristic region is larger on the side that he recognizes as the front of the chair. The appreciation of an object's region must depend not only on the perceiver's ability to recognize what kind of object it is, but also on his familiarity with the functions such objects serve, on what they do or what can be done with them. For all these reasons, regions might better be discussed as concepts rather than percepts. But it is a difficult line to draw. Once an object has become familiar, its characteristic region of interaction seems to be appreciated with the same immediacy as many simpler perceptual attributes. So we will include it here and leave open the question of whether it is, say, a conceptual subroutine of some kind that can be called by the perceptual system.

A region is of interest for what it can contain, so two related predicates are needed: $\text{Reg}(x, y)$ denotes that y is the region within which characteristic interactions with x are possible; $\text{Incl}(y, z)$ denotes that y includes z (z is totally inside of y). If we let $\text{Reg}(x)$ mean that $(\exists y)[\text{Reg}(x, y)]$, we can combine these two predicates in such expressions as

(12) $\text{Incl}(y, \text{Reg}(x)) \equiv (\exists w)[\text{Reg}(x, w) \ \& \ \text{Incl}(y, w)]$

when y is judged to be included in the region of interaction with x, or

(12') $\text{Incl}(\text{Reg}(y), x) \equiv (\exists w)[\text{Reg}(y, w) \ \& \ \text{Incl}(w, x)]$

when the region of y is judged to be included in x. (12) represents a perception of y as near enough to x to interact with it; (12') represents the perception of the area of interaction with y as being contained in some other object (in a room, for example).

We have noted the need for some developmental account of Reg as a learned perceptual predicate. It is less obvious, but apparently equally true, that Incl also has a developmental history. T. G. R. Bower (1974), in commenting on Piaget's theory of the development of a concept of object identity in infants, argues that the young child follows a rule to the effect that "two objects cannot be in the same place simultaneously"; it is not until the child is fifteen to eighteen months old on the average that he learns to qualify this rule by adding "unless one is *inside* the other." The amalgamation of the relational concept "inside" with the general concept of "object" constitutes the last major step in the child's understanding that objects endure even when they have passed from view. Here again we discover how artificial the boundary between perception and conception must be. When we talk of things like "objects," or properties like "regions," or relations like "inside," are we talking of percepts, concepts, or both? One useful way to think of it is that perceptual judgments are the result of applying conceptual knowledge to sensory inputs.

Earlier, when we tried to suggest how the conceptual system could call on the perceptual system for judgments it needed in carrying out higher-order routines, we suggested that something corresponding to a "find" instruction is theoretically necessary, and we proposed that the arguments of this instruction should include whatever information (if any) was available about the domain of search and the characteristics of the target. The predicate Reg is a natural one to use in specifying the domain for a perceptual search: $\text{find}(\text{Reg}(x), F(y))$ would be an instruction to search the region of interaction with the percept indexed by x in order to find some target y described by the predicate F. Because we so often identify particular objects by their locations, this use of "find" plays an important role in understanding ordinary speech. For example, if we were asked to do something with the book on the table (and if we decided to comply), we would first have to locate that particular book by searching the region of the table. And that, of course, is precisely the kind of routine for which $\text{find}(\text{Reg}(x), F(y))$ is appropriate.

In order to identify one object relative to the location of another, however, English has a rich supply of prepositions and adverbs that can provide much more specific information about their spatial relation than mere regional proximity. Therefore, we must consider what kinds of perceptual predicates would be needed to support such linguistic constructions.

One of the most important relations in visual space is "between." Since light travels in straight lines, interposition is an informative cue for space perception, and therefore we will have to have some predicate expressing betweenness. If object x would block the view of part or all of object y for observer z, then x is judged to be between z and y. Of course, betweenness can be generalized to any three objects related rectilinearly; an observer need not be one of the three arguments of the relation;

(13) $\text{Betw}(x, y, z) \equiv \text{Betw}(z, y, x)$

expresses the relation of y located between x and z. (For some purposes $\text{Betw}(y, x \,\&\, z)$ might be a more perspicuous notation.) The negation

(14) $\text{not}(\exists y)\text{Betw}(x, y, z)$

says there is nothing between x and z, which might be true either if the space between them were empty or if they were touching.

Touching, however, is a more complex idea, since two things may touch at one point yet have something between them at other points, in which case (14) would be false even though x and z were touching. Therefore, we adopt a predicate $\text{Adjcnt}(x, y)$ to mean that there is no distance between two discrete objects x and y, and use it to introduce touching:

(15) $\text{Tch}(x, y) \equiv \text{Tch}(y, x) \equiv (\exists u)(\exists v)(\exists w)(\exists z)[\text{Surf}(x, u)$
            $\&\, \text{Pprt}(u, w) \,\&\, \text{Surf}(y, v) \,\&\, \text{Pprt}(v, z) \,\&\, \text{Adjcnt}(w, z)].$

Discrete objects x and y are said to be touching if there is at least one part of the surface of x at zero distance from some part of the surface of y. Since adjacency and touching are important relations, both between objects and between people, any formal description of the perceptual world will require some means of dealing with them.

Perhaps the most important use of Tch occurs when one of the arguments is the observer himself. The extent to which tactual exploration can support space perception is indicated by studies of the congenitally blind, who combine hearing and touching to create a remarkably satisfactory conception of space; their most difficult problems are in navigation, of course, but even there they are often able to dead reckon their course with remarkable skill (Nye, 1971). For small objects, the tips of the fingers can be used to explore the surface and construct an object concept having a shape, size, and location. In some respects it is easier to build an object percept by touch than by vision; unlike the eyes, the fingers send back reports about their own orientation. The principal point to remember, however, is that the understanding of space is not derived entirely from seeing it, and that touch, proprioception, and hearing make their own contributions, which must be integrated with the visual information into a spatial concept that transcends any single sense modality.

When two discrete things are not touching, they are separated:

(16) $\text{Sep}(x, y) \equiv \text{notTch}(x, y)$.

The perception of two discrete objects as separated by empty space can be described by saying that they are separated and that there is no other object between them:

(17) $\text{Space}(x, y) \equiv \text{Sep}(x, y) \ \& \ \text{not}(\exists z)\text{Betw}(x, z, y)$.

This space, of course, is relativistic—it is described relative to the objects x and y that bound it.

Shadows contribute to the appreciation of visual space; the perception that x casts a shadow on y can also be formulated in terms of betweenness:

(18) $\text{Shdw}(x, y) \equiv \text{Betw}(\text{light}, x, y) \ \& \ \text{Space}(\text{light}, x) \ \& \ \text{Space}(x, y)$.

Given a point source of light, such as the sun, the predicate Shdw provides a rich source of information about the relative locations of, and spaces between, visible objects; it is as if an alternative angle of regard was simultaneously available to the viewer.

Betweenness can also be used to define relations with respect to altitude above the earth; in most perceptual situations Above(x, y) would mean that y was between x and the earth. Moreover, since gravity determines a straight line of descent from any object, we can use Over(x, y) to denote that object x is vertically above object y. Thus,

(19) $\text{Over}(x, y) \supset \text{Betw}(x, y, \text{earth})$.

The perception of verticality, however, must be more complex than this notation suggests, since gravity is invisible. Physiologists have analyzed the system of postural reflexes that enable organisms to maintain a characteristic position with respect to gravity. An important component of this system is the otolith organs in the inner ears. The otoliths rest at the top of sensory fibers in such a way that when the head is tilted the fibers bend, providing information for estimating the position of the head and for correcting the visual perception of the vertical. According to von Holst (1957), "vertical constancy" depends on two sensory systems acting in opposition. When you tilt your head to one side, the visual image of your environment moves in the opposite direction across the retina; without correction you would perceive that the environment had moved. But the otolith organs are simultaneously activated and readjust your orienting system so that the visually induced error is roughly compensated. The hypothesis that observers judge visual verticality relative to their perception of their own head position contributed to the "sensory-tonic" theory of perception developed by Werner and Wapner (1952), a theory that emphasizes the importance of motor as well as visual data in space perception (see Witkin et al., 1954, for experimental tests of this theory). In any case, we can assume that perceptual theory will provide predicates for Vert and Horiz, in addition to Over.

It is interesting to note in this connection that the vertical is easier for young children to appreciate than the horizontal. In her summary of work on perceptual development, E. J. Gibson (1969) commented that "distinguishing what is up and what is down is a primitive accomplishment. The other axis in space, right and left on the horizontal plane, notoriously results in more confusion than does up and down" (p. 376). It seems that the vertical and horizontal axes both provide very obvious and stable spatial coordinates for the child, but it is far easier for him to differentiate vertical directions (by and large, up stays up and down stays down as he moves about) than horizontal directions (right becomes left and front becomes back every time he turns around).

A simple test of children's ability to deal with these relations is to present three lines, of which one has the same orientation as the center line and the other does not, and to ask the child to point to the line that is different. When all three are shown simultaneously the task is simple, even for young children, but when the lines are presented successively, four- and five-year-old children make many more mistakes on oblique lines than on horizontals or verticals. In a simultaneous presentation the child can judge which lines are parallel, but in successive presentation he must remember their orientation. Bryant (1974) argues that a young child can solve the successive problem for horizontals and verticals because he can note and remember that they are parallel with something in the environment; he has difficulty with obliques because he knows they are not parallel to anything, but he has no other way to represent their orientations and remember them until subsequent lines are shown. By seven or eight years, however, he will have developed internal categories for representing and remembering such orientations.

Bryant also considers the problems young children have in distinguishing between two figures like ⊏ ⊐. The pair ⊔ ⊓, on the other hand, poses no problem. The difficult pair differs in left-right orientation, whereas the easy pair differs in up-down orientation, so one might conclude that left-right judgments are more difficult than up-down judgments for young children. But Huttenlocher (1967) has shown that the left-right difference ⊔ is much easier than the up-down difference ⊓, so the answer is not that left-right judgments are difficult in such tasks. Huttenlocher's results might be explained if children have difficulty distinguishing figures that are mirror images of one another, but Bryant proposes a different account: what a child notices is whether the figures are "in line" or "out of line." It is easy for him to see that ⊓ ⊓ are the same because their horizontals are in line, and it is easy for him to see that ⊓ ⊔ are different because their horizontals are out of line. Both ⊏ ⊏ and ⊏ ⊐ have their horizontals in line, however; the in-line cue does not suffice to distinguish them, so it is necessary to note the less obvious difference between their vertical lines.

Thus, not all of the troubles young children are supposed to have with the left-right dimension can be attributed to mirror symmetry about the vertical axis. As long as young children can use a simple, relative judgment, like

Parallel or Inline, they can handle such tasks regardless of their orientation. It is when a task requires some internal frame of reference or some nonsalient perceptual judgment that performance is inferior.

If x and y are discrete objects and are touching, and if x is over y, then y will normally be perceived as supporting x:

(20) $Over(x, y)$ & $Tch(x, y) \supset Suprt(y, x)$.

The direction of implication cannot be reversed, because y can also support an x that is hanging from it. In order to include the case in which some part of x that is over y supports the rest of x, we can rewrite (20) as

(20′) $Part(x, v)$ & $Over(v, y)$ & $Tch(x, y) \equiv Suprt(y, x)$.

Given the ubiquity of the gravitational field, the predicate Suprt is critical for the stable organization of the objects in the perceptual world. The perceptual formulation given in (20′) is conceptually inadequate in at least one respect: if one object is placed on the edge of another in such a manner that its center of gravity is not over the supporting object, it will fall. The mechanics of this situation are not perceptually obvious to young children, and considerable experience in placing one object on top of another is required to establish it. Moreover, since $Suprt(x, y)$ requires $Tch(x, y)$, the formulation in (20′) does not admit transitivity: if $Suprt(x, y)$ & $Suprt(y, z)$, you usually (but not always) judge that $Suprt(x, z)$. We will allow (20′) to stand, however, as a representation of the perceptual predicate; when you perceive x to support y, you will also perceive that some part of y is over x and touches it. The additional constraints we might impose on this relation are largely conceptual, not perceptual. Falk (1972) should be consulted for a more detailed analysis of the information that is available visually for determining that one object is supported by another.

We are now ready to consider the perception of spatial distances, since Adjcnt defines zero distance and $Betw(x, y, z)$ would imply that x and y are closer than x and z, barring unusual configurations. The obvious solution to rule out "unusual configurations" would be to define distances between points on a straight line, rather than between objects, but the abstract refinements involved in the definition of a point seem more conceptual than perceptual. One "point" we can rely on, however, is the eye, so we can use Betw to represent the perceptual cue called interposition. If y masks the view of some part of z, then some part of y is closer to the eye than the masked part of z is (see fig. 2.3):

(21) $(Space(eye, y)$ & $Space(y, z)$ & $(\exists v)(\exists w)[Surf(z, v)$ & $Pprt(v, w)$ &
            $Betw(eye, y, w)]) \supset ((\exists v')(\exists w')[Surf(y, v')$ & $Pprt(v', w')$ &
            $Pprt(v', w')$ & $(Dist(eye, w') < Dist(eye, w))])$.

This much a perceptual theory would surely account for. Whether the extraction of the relation Dist from (21) and its application to distances from the observer to objects at different azimuths, or to distances between objects

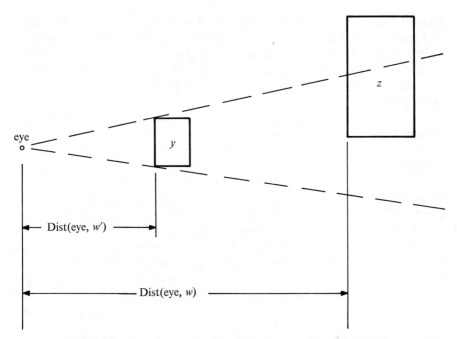

Figure 2.3   Depth cues resulting from interposition of *y* between observer and *z*, as represented in formula (21).

other than the observer, should properly be a part of perceptual or conceptual theory can be debated. Our own opinion is that because so many phenomena of perceptual grouping depend on an appreciation of unequal distances, an adequate perceptual theory would necessarily include at least an ordinal relation for perceived distance in general, and not just an ordering along a straight line starting from the eye of the observer. We will therefore assume that, for appropriate choices of pairs of objects (w, x) and (y, z), the expression

(22) $\text{Dist}(w, x) \leq \text{Dist}(y, z)$

represents a perceptual judgment that people (adults, at least) can make with some accuracy, and that this ability contributes part of the input available to the conceptual system. Note that (22) gives an appreciation of relative, not absolute, distances.

   An ability to make the judgments implied by (22) is related to an ability to deal with space in terms of a three-dimensional frame of reference. Shepard (1962) has demonstrated that from nothing more than a rank ordering of the observed distances between all pairs of *n* objects it is possible to construct the best-fitting hypothetical configuration of points in euclidean spaces of different dimensionality and, by observing the degree of departure of the ordering of the observed distances from the orderings of the hypothetical distances, to reach a decision as to the minimum number of orthogonal dimensions required to fit the observed data. The only perceptual configurations that could account for the perceived inequalities of all the distances among a set of ten or more objects scattered about in physical space must have at least three dimensions; a two-dimensional space would not account for all the inequalities among the perceived distances. In short, (22) is a very strong assumption.

We conclude, therefore, that the ability to make judgments of the kind indicated in (22) depends on prior development of an ability to perceive space three-dimensionally. That is to say, from what we know about the development of visual space perception in children, we are led to suppose that (22) does not represent a primitive visual ability but is a consequence of other, more basic perceptual processes for dealing with spatial relations. In order to provide some rationale for (22), therefore, we must consider how the visual appreciation of a three-dimensional space could develop from the proximal information that projective geometry tells us is available to the eyes. Since vertical and horizontal relations between objects are faithfully registered at the retinas, this problem has usually been construed to mean that we must give some account of the origins of the third dimension, depth.

2.3.1   Depth

Traditional accounts of depth perception rely on lists of "cues" that are supposed to provide information about the spatial relations of objects. Typical cues are the interposition of objects, binocular disparity, perspective, texture gradients, atmospheric effects, accommodation of the lenses and convergence of the eyes, motion parallax, size of familiar objects, and so on. All of these cues, singly or in combination, can be shown to contribute information on which judgments of depth can be based. From a theoretical point of view, however, such a list is unsatisfactory, for it includes no hint as to how all these various sources of information are integrated into coherent spatial perception.

Most research on depth perception has been concerned with static observers viewing "frozen" scenes. In part, this preoccupation with the static perception of depth was a consequence of difficulties in controlling dynamic displays experimentally, but the principal reason was probably the historical concern with building perceptions out of simpler, static elements of sensation. As early as 1875 Exner argued that motion is a sensory element in its own right, but the suggestion did not fit into the developing theory of sensory attributes and was not seriously pursued for the next thirty-five years.

The difficulties inherent in inferring depth from static visual displays are obvious from the projective relations involved. Any given pattern of proximal stimulation (the pattern of stimulation at the sense organ) can be the result of an infinite variety of distal situations (the physical situation about which information is desired) all of which are projectively equivalent. For example, a large object at a distance can project exactly the same proximal stimulus onto the retina as a smaller object nearer the eye. The indeterminancy of Dist(eye, x) in a static scene has been demonstrated in a variety of projective illusions (A. Ames, 1955).

If the same distal configuration is viewed from different angles, the resultant differences in the proximal patterns can provide information about the third dimension of space. A person with two eyes can use binocular disparities to perceive depth; indeed, Julesz (1960) has demonstrated that binocular disparity can lead to depth perception in the total absence of any contours or objects in the scene. But even a person with one eye can obtain different proximal patterns of stimulation by moving his head. Since motility and eyes have evolved together in the animal kingdom, it is not unreasonable to suppose that the visual system has evolved mechanisms to exploit the rich source of information about the depth that motion can provide.

The physical world of everyday experience is well characterized by euclidean geometry, that is, by a geometry in which parallel lines never meet. The proximal stimulus for vision, however, must be characterized by projective geometry, that is, by a geometry in which parallel lines converge toward some point at infinity. We must assume, therefore, that the visual system has evolved mechanisms sensitive to those projective properties that are invariant under the transformations produced by motion of the organism or the object viewed (J. J. Gibson, 1957; Johansson, 1972). For example, a straight line remains straight under all projective transformations, and a point on that line will remain on it; the ratios of the distances between points on a line will remain constant under all projective transformations; two things that are touching will remain touching; a region enclosed by an edge will remain enclosed; and so on. Perceptual judgments based on such projective invariances should thus have some priority in perceptual theory.

We will return to the perception of motion in section 2.5, but the point to be emphasized here is that perception of three-dimensional objects in three-dimensional space is based on an ability to appreciate projective equivalences under the transformations induced by movements in three-dimensional space. The kind of invariances involved in these projective transformations are nonmetric, in the sense that large metric differences in proximal stimulation may be projectively equivalent, yet they suffice to support the semimetric judgments of distance we have assumed are possible in (22).

There is evidence that a visual appreciation of depth develops reasonably early in life. It could hardly be present at birth, since the neonate seems unable to control his convergence or accommodation and so can make little use of binocular disparity. By the end of the first month of life, these basic reflexes begin to function, and by the time the human infant is able to crawl about, his depth perception is good enough to enable him to avoid dangerous cliffs (Walk and Gibson, 1961).

One might ask whether judgments of Dist(eye, x) are in any sense more primitive than judgments of Dist(x, y), that is to say, whether egocentric judgments are somehow prior to the judgment of distances between other objects. Such a speculation might arise from a consideration of the emphasis that Piaget has placed on "decentering" as a developmental accomplishment. Decentering is the transition from an initial egocentric state in which everything has the child's own body and actions as its origin to a more mature state in which the child's body and actions assume their objective relations to all other perceived objects and events. (The general concept of decentering plays an important role in Piaget's theory of sensorimotor, cognitive, social, and moral development.) With respect to space perception, a typical experiment is the "three-mountain problem" (Piaget and Inhelder, 1948), where it has been shown that children under five years are unable to indicate what a model of three mountains, differing in height and color, would look like to a person viewing them from a perspective different from their own. Before a child can solve such problems, his spatial world must be decentered; he must be able to appreciate another person's point of view. According to Piaget (1961), "It is by this decentration that the progressive construction of perceptual coordinates takes place: spatial directions, which were judged initially with reference to the position of one's own body, are decentered in order to be related to wider frames of reference" (p. 298).

This view might be interpreted to imply that self-centered judgments of Dist(eye, x) should be ontogenetically earlier, and that nonegocentric judgments of the type called for in (22) would not develop until age five—which seems implausible. Masangkay et al. (1974) showed that a two-year-old child can infer that another person sees an object not visible to himself; what he finds difficult is to infer how an object that both currently see appears to the other person. "See the same thing" is ambiguous between (a) "the same object" and (b) "the same perspective." For children, (a) is easy, but (b) develops later and involves processes going well beyond the simple perceptual judgments we are cataloging here. We assume, therefore, that very young children are capable of nonegocentric space perception when tasks are presented in appropriate forms. The development of space perception probably depends on the child's mobility in space and active engagement with objects whose relations define space, as Piaget contends. But the role of spatial decentering, whatever it may prove to be, should not be misunderstood as limiting this early perceptual development. (A reader interested in pursuing the topic of perceptual development further might begin with the chapters by Kessen and by Pick and Pick in Mussen, 1970.)

Whatever its ontogenesis, given (22) we can proceed to redefine the predicate Above in terms of distances from the earth:

(23)   Above$(x, y) \equiv (\text{Dist}(x, \text{earth}) > \text{Dist}(y, \text{earth}))$

indicates that x is above y. Below(x, y) can be defined by reversing the inequality. Given Above, it is possible to define Top as the uppermost part y of an object x:

(24)   Top$(x, y) \equiv \text{Pprt}(x, y)$ & not$(\exists z)[\text{Pprt}(x, z)$ & Above$(z, y)]$.

The unique role of verticality is indicated by the fact that Top can easily be defined in this manner, and Bottom analogously:

$$(24') \qquad \text{Bottom}(x, y) \equiv \text{Pprt}(x,y) \ \& \ \text{not}(\exists z)[\text{Pprt}(x, z) \ \& \ \text{Below}(z, y)],$$

whereas left and right cannot. Even a rock has a top and bottom that can be ascertained by looking at it, but how can we see which part of the rock is *its* right and which *its* left?

2.3.2   Stability

Why does the spatial world remain stationary? As J. J. Gibson (1954) has asked, when the eyes track a moving object, "Why do we perceive a motion of the *object* in the environment instead of a motion of the *environment*?" (p. 304).

One possible answer is that the observer has information about his own position and his direction of regard at any moment and somehow uses that information to discriminate between those changes in the retinal image that are produced by changes in his angle of regard and those that are produced by motion in his environment. The autokinetic effect, however, suggests that stability can be a fragile phenomenon. A person asked to watch a small point of light in an otherwise dark room will usually report that it moves, even though it does not (Sherif, 1935). This instability may be due to the fact that people do not have reliable proprioceptive information about their eye movements. Or it may be due to sudden changes in their judgment of their own position—the observer's own body is invisible in the dark room, and so provides an uncertain point of origin for judging relative positions.

Passive shifts in eye position are not perceived proprioceptively; intentional shifts and, of course, any consequent visual changes are all that people seem to know about (Brindley and Merton, 1960). Since there is no afferent feedback from the eye muscles, von Holst (1957) has argued that there must be an "efference copy" of the intention to move the eyes. If the eye is moved mechanically (unintentionally), the visual world is seen to move in the opposite direction; if the eye is held fixed mechanically while the person intends to move it, the visual world is seen to move in the direction he intended. When the two occur simultaneously, they cancel each other out and the result is that he sees the observed environment as immobile, despite the active movement of his eyes.

It has long been known that afterimages change in apparent size as a function of their apparent distance. If you stare fixedly at a bright window, for example, until a strong afterimage forms, you can then project the afterimage onto a piece of paper held in your hand and as you move the paper away from your face you will see the afterimage of the window increase in size. This change in apparent size cannot be attributed to any change in the size of the retinal image, since that is the aftereffect of your original viewing. It is attributable instead, according to von Holst, to the efference copy of your intention to move your eyes in such a way as to focus on the surface of the paper. As the intention changes, the perceived size changes, since there is no opposing change in the retinal image to cancel the intentional change.

Prisms that displace the apparent location of an object can be used to analyze the integration of visual information with information about the orientation of the eyes. Held (1961; Held and Hein, 1958) has argued that the normal correlation of the efference copy with its visual effects must be learned by active, intentional practice; when prisms disrupt the normal correlation, a person must actively reestablish it under the new conditions; passive viewing of the displaced scene is not sufficient.

The hands, which are the major tools people use for interacting with concrete objects, must be especially well integrated into the visual world; there must be some accurate representation of where the hands are, what they are holding, what they are doing with what they hold. It is essential for a person to see his hand appear in his visual field at the place he intended it to go; if prisms distort the usual relation, however, he will begin to learn the new relation with a speed that is quite surprising in view of the amount of prior practice he must have had on the normal relation between hand and eye. C. S. Harris (1965) has argued that what the person wearing prisms over his eyes is learning is an altered perception of the position of the parts of his body, and that felt position is more adaptable than seen position.

In any case, we can assume that when a person who is intentionally holding his hand and head stationary scans his eyes over a scene that includes his own hand and nose, he will not attribute the changing positions of the images of his hand and nose on his retinas to any objective motion of his hand or head. And if his body is perceived as stationary in spite of the changes in his visual field, then all other objects that retain their spatial configuration unchanged relative to his body will also be seen as stationary. The perceived location of other body parts must be consistent over modalities, too, but the hands and nose are probably the most important.

To explain the stability of the perceptual world in terms of one's perception of his own hand and nose may suggest that we are building a pyramid upside down; an elaborate perceptual system seems to rest quite insecurely on a small point of fact. However, White, Castle, and Held (1964) have observed that most children begin to hold their hands up in order to look at them at about two-and-a-half months. By three months they are spending long periods of their waking time staring fixedly at their hands, moving them toward and away from themselves, turning them, swiping at objects with them, moving them together and apart. By four months they can glance back and forth from one hand to the other as they bring them together. Piaget and Inhelder (1948), who believe that space perception depends on the prior development of appropriate sensorimotor schemata, have suggested that these hand observations are experiments the child is conducting in order to learn the geometry of perceptual space. If the point of evidence is small, it is at least firmly enough established to support some theoretical weight.

This brief review of some perceptual mechanisms is, of course, outside our present mandate. It would suffice for our present purposes to assume that perceptual theory must explain the stationary character of the visual world somehow, even though we are uncertain how such a property might be stated formally. Nevertheless, there are two reasons for discussing these mechanisms. First, they indicate that some account of intention is apparently necessary even at the level of perception. And, second, by emphasizing the spatial relations between body parts and those objects people intend their body parts to interact with, we hope to strengthen our assumption that the perception of regions of interaction is fundamental to spatial perception.

2.3.3 Size Constancy

Given relative distances in a stationary, three-dimensional world, we can return to the spatial properties of objects implied in (1): place, shape, and size. One way to characterize these attributes of objects is in terms of distances. We will introduce Dset to denote the set (or matrix) of distances from every member of one class of objects to every member of another class. Since (22) admits only an ordering of these distances, not an actual measurement, we will think of Dset as arranged in a ranking from the smallest distance in the set to the largest. We will say that two Dsets are equal if they arrange the distances between equivalent objects in exactly the same rank order.

If we define π as the class of all proper parts of object x,

$$(25) \qquad \pi = \hat{y}(\mathrm{Pprt}(x, y)),$$

and if σ is the set of stationary objects in the perceptual environment of x, then we can represent the location z of x as

$$(26) \qquad \mathrm{Place}(x, z) \equiv \mathrm{Dset}(\pi, \sigma).$$

Note that (26) is not equivalent to Aristotle's definition of place as the minimal container of x; since (22) provides only an ordering, not a precise measure, (26) will usually allow a somewhat larger volume of physical space with which x can vary without altering the order of $\mathrm{Dset}(\pi, \sigma)$. (This volume should not be confused with $\mathrm{Reg}(x)$.)

We can also represent the shape of x more abstractly than in (5) by

$$(27) \qquad \mathrm{Shap}(x, y) \equiv (y = \mathrm{Dset}(\pi, \pi)).$$

Here, the shape of object x is the set of distances between all the proper parts of x. Note that this characterization of shape enables us to say that two objects of different size can have the same shape; all that is assumed in (27) is that the rank ordering of distances is the same; the order will remain unaffected by changes of scale; it is also invariant under variations in brightness or location in the visual field. Shape constancy implies that our judgments of these interpart distances remain invariant even when we view the object from different directions.

We regard Dset as a sort of theoretical placeholder, representative of shape-descriptive schemes in general; the reader can substitute for it whatever equivalent notational devices for shape he prefers. Since Minsky's (1961) suggestions for a notation to characterize shapes, workers in automatic pattern recognition have developed a great variety of picture languages. If it were necessary to develop this aspect of perceptual theory in detail for our present purposes, we would probably favor some form of the system developed by Leeuwenberg (1968, 1971), which begins with angles between line segments and gives efficient methods for coding and structuring sequences of these elements into two- and three-dimensional patterns. Leeuwenberg's coding, like Dset, is invariant under rotations, translations, and expansions. Simon (1972) has discussed the relation of Leeuwenberg's method of coding to several other proposals for representing patterned sequences of elements; he finds considerable agreement in fundamental principles and concludes that all the superficially different notations are variations on a common theme.

Whereas shape depends only on the distance relations within an object, differences in size between two objects depend on comparisons of distance relations between objects. The judgment should be simplest when two objects of the same shape are seen simultaneously, since it is then necessary merely to compare the maximum internal dimension, maxDset, of the two objects:

(28) $(\mathrm{Shap}(x, y)\ \&\ \mathrm{Shap}(x', y')\ \&\ (y = y')\ \&\ \mathrm{Size}(x, z)\ \&\ \mathrm{Size}(x', z'))$
         $\supset (z < z' \equiv (\mathrm{maxDset}(\pi, \pi) < \mathrm{maxDset}(\pi', \pi')))$.

If the objects are seen successively, however, it is necessary to have some standard s that persists from the first to the second viewing and supports a transitive inference. For example, if d is the maximum internal dimension of one object and d' is the maximum internal dimension of the other, then $d < s$ and $s < d'$ imply $d < d'$. Bryant (1974) has shown that young children can make such perceptual inferences if s is provided by the external frame of reference, that is, if the two objects are seen against the same background. If the external frames of reference are different, an internal frame of reference is often needed—a memory of the expected size of objects of a given shape. Children begin to form such expectations quite early, presumably establishing what Helson (1947, 1948) has called an adaptation level. An adaptation level is an average value established by "pooling" all experience with objects of a given type, and serves as a reference against which new instances can be judged. The establishment of such internal standards for judgments of magnitude is a general perceptual process, not limited to judgments of size.

People can also compare the sizes of objects having very different shapes. Sometimes they can take advantage of their own bodies to provide an ever present yardstick, since they have considerable practice in estimating which things they can pick up, manipulate, shove around, or otherwise disturb. The importance of one's own body as a reference for size judgments is reinforced by man-made objects whose sizes depend on their users; most of them would be useless to a race of men half or twice as tall as most people are. Extensive experience thus contributes to such an adaptation level, so it is probable that when no other reference point is indicated people take their own proportions as the intended frame of reference.

An important fact about judgments of objective size is that they usually remain relatively constant as an object moves closer or farther away. A person approaching seems to stay the same size, even though the size of his image on the retinas may increase drastically. For nearby objects, where size constancy is best, the efference copy of the commands to accommodate the lenses and converge the eyes may be used to correct the change in the retinal image. But this cannot be the whole story. If objects were always seen as a constant size, how could one judge the distances as changing? Under normal conditions adult observers can rather reliably estimate either objective size (independent of distance) or angular size (related to the size of the retinal image), depending on the instructions they are given. It is this capacity to pay attention to either or both meanings of "size" that sets the theoretical problem.

The geometry involved is simple: if S is the distal size of an object and D is its distance from the eye of the observer, and if s is the proximal size of its retinal image and d is the distance from the optical node of the eye to the retina, then $S/D = s/d$. Since d is a constant, the size of the retinal image will be proportional to S/D; as D decreases, s will increase inversely. If perceived size remains constant when D changes, it would seem that people have some way to estimate sD, the product of the retinal size and the distance of the object from the eye. This would be possible if they had separate sources of information about s and D. One hypothesis holds that s is directly given on the retina and that $\text{Dist}(\text{eye}, x)$ can be estimated by the use of depth cues, and therefore all the necessary information is available for estimating sD. Moreover, when all cues needed to estimate D are eliminated, size constancy breaks down (Holway and Boring, 1941). This notion, that people estimate s and D separately and then take their product in order to estimate S, might be called the metric hypothesis of size constancy, since it depends on the appreciation of space in terms of a euclidean metric.

If we think about the problem in terms of projective rather than euclidean geometry, however, the phenomenon of size constancy appears in a different light. Presumably the representation of a three-dimensional world is created by a visual mechanism sensitive to projective equivalences under the continuous transformations induced by movement. Such a mechanism must be able to assign very different patterns of proximal stimulation—different in the metric sense—to equivalence classes when one pattern is a perspective transformation of the other. To say that the visual system extracts these projective equivalences is to describe the basic phenomenon of size constancy. According to this view, the problem of size constancy vanishes or, more precisely, is replaced by a far more general problem of describing mechanisms for recognizing projective equivalences and the way this mechanism relates proximal stimuli to subjective perceptions. The constancy of sD is merely one of many invariants under perspective transformations.

Some psychologists assume that this ability to see an object as retaining constant size, independent of the size of its retinal image, must be learned during infancy. The argument has been summarized by E. J. Gibson (1969):

> Because maintenance of object constancy implies appreciation of the spatial relationships over which the transformations occur, it has often been assumed that the child first learns the dimensions of space, like near, far, up, down; that he conceives some kind of metric for quantifying displacement of an object along the spatial axes; and then, when an object appears, plugs into an equation in his head the size of the retinal image projected by the object and some values for the spatial parameters, thereby correcting the retinal image and achieving constancy. (P. 369)

Gibson considers this "an outlandish hypothesis," because the dimensions of things are not abstracted, let alone quantified, until well after object constancy can be demonstrated in the child's perceptions. Her own view is that an object tends to be perceived in its true size very early in development, not because the child has learned to correct for distance but because he "sees the objects as such," and does *not* abstract from them their projected sizes or distances. It is the ability to abstract retinal size *s* and distance *D* that children must acquire through learning, not the ability to see objects as remaining constant in size.

What "sees the objects as such" might mean can presumably be explained projectively. In viewing a stationary scene the relative sizes of and distances between objects will remain invariant as their distance from a viewer changes. As long as these Dsets remain invariant, the perceived size of any object will remain invariant. Adults can be instructed to ignore the frame of reference and are able to do so—to judge *s*—with partial success. Whether children can ignore the frame of reference with equal success is dubious, but data are lacking because it is difficult to explain to a young child what you want him to do.

If the size of an object changes relative to other objects in the scene, the visual system must decide whether the perceived change is attributable to changes in *S* or in *D*. Since motion is common and expandable objects are relatively rare, experience would probably bias a viewer to favor changes in *D* under ordinary conditions and to see *S* as constant. In a psychological laboratory, though, the external frame of reference can be eliminated and objects can be presented for which the viewer has no valid size expectations. Under those conditions there are no grounds for attributing changes in *s* to either *S* or *D*, and size constancy breaks down.

2.3.4   Direction

We have now summarized some of the major judgments of perceptual space that any adequate theory of perception must account for, and have applied the results to some of the spatial properties of objects. Except for Betw, Over, Above, Horiz, and Vert, however, we have not yet dealt explicitly with the important spatial relation of direction. We assume that a direction can be assigned to a straight line, Stline(w), extending between (and sometimes beyond) any two objects in the perceptual world. Since the perception of direction in general probably has its genesis in the perception (both visual and auditory) of directions relative to the observer himself, and since the observer provides a natural point of reference for orienting the line from himself to the object (he cannot look simultaneously in both directions along it), directions are perceived as having an orientation from one of the objects toward the other. Thus, direction z is determined for an ordered couple of objects, Dir(x, y, z) by taking the first member of the couple to be the place of origin: the direction from x to y is z.

In the case of moving objects, the direction of motion can be determined either by a line originating at an earlier and going to a later location of the object, or by reference to the origin or destination of the motion. The space through which a moving object will pass on its way to its perceived destination is seen as being in front of it, and the space through which it has passed is behind it. We can introduce the predicate Before(y, x) in order to indicate that y is in front of the moving object x and define it in terms of Betw(x, y, z), where z is the perceived destination of movement. Similarly, Behind(y, x) can be defined in terms of Betw(y, x, z) in order to indicate that y is behind x as x moves toward the destination z. The English words "before" and "behind," of course, are culturally determined and should be distinguished from the perceptual predicates Before and Behind, which are defined here solely for the perception of moving objects. A characterization of "before," "front," "top," "right," and "left" is given later as a part of cognitive theory (sec. 6.1).

There is, of course, an auditory as well as a visual space. Auditory judgments of the distance of a sound source are not reliable, although for such familiar sounds as the human voice there are cues provided by loudness and by one's knowledge of timbre changes that accompany differences in distance and in level of effort (from whispering through normal speech to shouting). However, the ears are much more accurate in discriminating the direction of a sound source. For brief or intermittent sounds the directional cues are provided by differences in time of arrival of the sound impulse at the two ears. For steady sounds there are phase differences between the ears at low frequencies, and intensity differences (due to the shadow of the head) at higher frequencies. Auditory appreciation of directions must, of course, be integrated with visual judgments; when the two sources of information disagree, the visual localization seems to dominate the auditory. The visual field is limited, though, in a way that the auditory field is not, and the ears are most reliable in picking up the location of events occurring to the right or left of the person in the horizontal plane—events that will often be out of his field of view. Auditory judgments of Dir(person, y, z) thus extend significantly the extent of the perceptual world that people can monitor and to which they can respond.

Communication about particular objects is often accompanied by some kind of ostensive gesture indicating the direction of the object from the speaker. When the hand is used, the person perceiving the gesture is able to extrapolate the line established by the speaker's eyes and hand until he finds a potential target in that direction. Such perceptions could be described well enough in terms of the predicates Inline and Dir, but ostension is so important for linguistic communication that a special predicate, Osten(x, y), will be introduced to denote that an ostensive relation is perceived from a pointer x to a target y. The pointer may be provided by a speaker's gesture, or by a directional arrow, or even by a person's angle of regard (Gibson and Pick, 1963). Judging another person's angle of regard might seem to be a sophisticated skill, but babies under a year of age are able to follow their mother's eyes to discover what she is looking at (J. S. Bruner, personal communication).

Directions given in terms of some arbitrary coordinate system independent of the observer's perceptual world are assumed to be defined conceptually, not perceptually.*

2.4 TIME

Psychological investigations of the experience of time (see Woodrow, 1951; Frankenhaeuser, 1959; Fraisse, 1963; Ornstein, 1969) seem to fall into four main categories: the experience of short intervals of time such as the phenomenal present or the detection of rhythm; the estimation of duration; the perception of simultaneity; and the experience of temporal perspective, that is, the placing of events with respect to the past, present, and future. Considerable effort has been expended in the search for the psychological principles governing the "perception" of time. But, as Ornstein has argued, the metaphor of perception may be misleading. He offers an intriguing hypothesis that the experience of duration is a function of the amount of storage space required to represent an interval in memory. Thus, anything that leads to demands for a greater storage space—an increase in the number of events, or in their complexity, for example—will also lead to an experience of lengthened duration. The process of constructing an experience of duration from the storage size of an episode is clearly subject to the usual advantages and adversities of information processing, such as "chunking" (Miller, 1956). Some of the neural mechanisms that are required by this approach to time may have been isolated by the work of Pribram (1971) and his associates. The amygdaloid complex seems to be involved with the initial registration of events, and the intrinsic cortex (the "association" areas) seems to carry out subsequent information processing, as in the reduction of redundancy. But the main advantage of this approach to time is that it provides a natural basis for the child's development of an explicit concept of time. The growth of a child's grasp of temporal relations and concepts requires a number of years, as Piaget (1927a, 1937) has shown, and the final articulated system is likely to depend on the technology of the culture in which the child is raised (Nakamura, 1966).

*A reader who wishes to pursue spatial aspects of perception in more detail will find the summary by Howard and Templeton (1966) extremely helpful.

For most purposes of communication, however, one is less concerned about time as an object of perception than as an attribute of the perception of other things. Since things change and move about in space as a function of time, a perceptual theory must provide a temporal coordinate that can be used to indicate that x was in a particular state or region at some time or during some interval.

There are psychological studies to support the assumption that time is experienced in quantized moments (Stroud, 1956, 1967; C. T. White, 1963; Harter, 1967). We will therefore adopt the convention that subjective time is divided into discrete moments and that these moments can be numbered: t, $t + 1, t + 2, \ldots, t + i, \ldots$, where $t + 1$ is the psychological moment that follows immediately after moment t and $t - 1$ is the moment immediately preceding t.

How long does a psychological moment last? Various estimates have been proposed, all of them in terms of fractions of a second. Some theorists have argued that moments are determined by the alpha frequency of the brain waves, and some have tried to use the optimal time interval between flashes that is required for the perception of apparent motion in order to measure the duration of a moment. Some claim that the eye is intermittently blind, others that the eye reports continuously but is checked only intermittently. Kolers (1972) has argued against the notion that there is some kind of neural clock that drives the visual system: "Not clocks but encoding routines of finite and measurable duration may explain many of the perceptual processes now thought to reveal an intrinsic periodicity in the visual system" (p. 148). In adopting our present notation we do not intend to take sides in this discussion, for many of the issues are still to be sorted out. The use of integers to represent the order of events in time is simply too convenient to resist. We assume that if subsequent research were to show that subjective time must be mapped into the real continuum, it would not affect our discussion below in any significant way, because we will be concerned primarily with ordinal, not metric, properties of time. The advantages of a discrete notation for time do not emerge until one considers how people talk about it (see, for example, the meaning of "next" moment, discussed in 6.2.1).

An event can happen at a particular moment, whereas an action or a process may persist throughout some interval. This information could be represented by some such predicate as $\text{Time}_t(S)$, where S specifies some state of affairs and t is the integral value of time at the moment S obtains. Alternatively, we could append time indices to the relation or property to which they apply. For example, $\text{Incl}_{t,t+k}(y, \text{Reg}(x))$ would denote that y is included in the region of x from time t to time $t + k$. If only a momentary event was involved, we would append only a single time index. The logical interpretation of such time indices is that the predicate to which they are appended is realized at the times indicated. Thus, for example, the subscripts above would assert that $\text{Incl}(y, \text{Reg}(x))$ is true during the $k + 1$ moments from time t to time $t + k$, but no assertion is made concerning the truth of this relation at any other times. One can think of a "time vector" associated with such a relation as an ordered sequence of 0's and 1's extending from minus to plus infinity, where 1 means that the relation obtains during that moment of time and 0 means that it does not; the indices denote that the time vector is 1 for all moments from t to $t + k$, inclusive.

It will frequently happen that the conceptual system will use a "test" instruction in order to obtain certain information from the perceptual system. In ordinary discourse this information is of a transient character, so, as we have previously suggested, it is convenient procedurally to specify the time at which the status of the predicate is of interest, and to give this time as the first argument of "test." When a perceptual predicate appears as the second argument of "test," therefore, the time indices can be shifted from subscripts to arguments. For example, test(from t to $t + k$, Incl(y, Reg(x))) is an instruction to test whether y was in the region of interaction with x from time t to time $t + k$. We will not try to choose between the logical and the procedural notations but will use whichever is convenient in any given context.

These time indices can, of course, be considered as dates (or pseudodates) relative to some arbitrary origin $t = 0$. (If the origin is the one used by the conventional calendar, t is a true date; if the origin is arbitrary, t is a pseudo-date.) The indices could enable us to state directly the transitive relation "later than," where "t is later than t'" is equivalent to "$t > t'$." However, such a relation is not in general directly perceptible; one does not *perceive* that the time men first stepped on the moon is later than the time Napoleon was born. The phenomenal present extends over a measurable period of physical time, but the period is relatively short; the relation "later" can only be inferred, not perceived, between moments further apart than are experienced together. Perhaps we should claim no more than that one perceives—allowing for iconic memory—temporal relations between contiguous events. However, we will stipulate that the relation "later than" represents the more or less immediate succession of one moment by another within a specious present that includes k moments, where k is some integer between, say, 2 and 10:

(29)   Later$(t, t') \equiv t > t'$, where not$(t - t' > k - 1)$.

The logical properties of this concept will be discussed in 6.2.1. Here we note merely that no first or last moment is assumed.

Additional assumptions are required to include the experience of "now," since "now" is not a date, but something that dates pass through on their way from future to past. Once the predicate Later has been established between two moments it does not change as a function of time; the date of "now" does change. It is convenient to reserve a particular symbol for "now," and we will use n for this purpose. Thus, the future is indicated by $t > n$, the present moment by $t = n$, and the past by $t < n$. There are many pretty puzzles here for philosophers, who have developed "temporal logic" (Cocchiarella, 1966; Prior, 1967; Rescher and Urquhart, 1971) by adding time indices and tense operators to the ordinary first-order predicate calculus. The psychological requirement, however, is that the perceptual world being experienced now can be compared with the memory of perceptual worlds experienced earlier. Other things being equal, the comparison is more accurate with the immediately preceding moment than with moments more remote in time.

A theory of time perception must also provide some explanation for temporal groupings and rhythms, which are important in auditory and proprioceptive perception, and for the recognition of simultaneity of events in different sensory modalities. The accurate timing of the component parts of a skilled synergic act is critically important for sensorimotor mechanisms—eye-hand coordination, for example—that contribute to our impression of a stable perceptual world, and speech production and perception both require very accurate appreciation of the temporal relations between different speech sounds. Such temporal relations, however, are usually built into mechanisms so automatic that they are inaccessible to introspection and will not support the kinds of attentional-judgmental abstractions about time that the conceptual system can call for. Such temporal relations reflect the machinery, not the content, of perceptual experience.

2.5   CHANGES, MOTIONS, AND EVENTS   *why people perceive differently*

We will use "change" to denote the perception that the pattern of stimulation at some particular moment is different from the pattern of stimulation at a preceding moment. We will use "motion" to denote changes of a particular kind, namely, changes of spatial relations. And we will use "event" to denote changes of the kind people talk about. None of these definitions is precise; we will try to clarify them in the following discussion.

It is a well-established fact of physiological psychology that when a sensory receptor is exposed to a constant, unchanging pattern of stimulation, the receptor quickly begins to adapt. That is to say, the amplitude or frequency of its response decreases with continued exposure to unchanging conditions and may disappear entirely. Then, when stimulation is terminated, the adapted receptor may give a strong response to its termination. Even at this level of analysis, therefore, sensory systems demonstrate an acute sensitivity to change, as if change carried information of great biological significance. Sensitivity to change, and a conservative tendency to attribute changes to intelligible sources, is characteristic of the perceptual system at every level of its functioning.

Any attribute of a percept may change its value from one moment to the next. A spot on a television screen can change its color, a tone can change its pitch, a taste can change from sweet to bitter, a touch can change from rough to smooth, an object can change from heavy to light. The nature of the physical world being what it is, however, and the natures of mobile animals being what they are, it is change in the spatial attributes of things that plays the most important role in perception: change of location, change of orientation, change of angle of regard. We will review some of the facts about how we perceive

d attempt to suggest some reasonable perceptual predicates to expli-
ay we talk about perceived motions.

r to keep this review within reasonable scope, we will consider pri-
_, ... visual perception of motion, although it should be obvious that
visually perceived motion must be integrated with motion perceived through
other receptor organs. Indeed, as we have already noted, there must be a
proprioceptive component even to visual perception if we are to keep track of
those visual changes that result from our own movements, so it is impossible
to ignore other modalities completely. A complete sensorimotor schema of an
object may involve integrating information from several modalities.

Once we have considered the visual perception of motion, we will raise the
question of why some changes are regarded as events and others not, since
this distinction has considerable importance for the way we talk about change.

2.5.1   Visual Perception of Motion

It is traditional to divide discussions of the visual perception of
motion into two parts, one dealing with real motion and the other with apparent motion. Real motion, as the name indicates, is the normal kind of motion
people perceive when they move about or when objects around them move
about. Apparent (or "illusory") motion refers to all those cases, familiar in
societies accustomed to motion pictures and television, where there is an impression of movement although nothing really moves. Having drawn this
distinction, the stage is then set for a debate as to whether the perceptual
mechanisms involved are the same or different. Most experiments on the
visual perception of motion—experiments that try to uncover the principles
involved under highly controlled conditions of stimulation—are easier to conduct with apparent than with real motion. In order to justify the relevance of
his research to the perception of real motion, the investigator is usually motivated to argue for the identity of the two perceptual mechanisms. Reasons for
thinking that the generalization may not always be as simple and direct as has
usually been assumed have been summarized by Kolers (1972), who finds
that none of the current theories of apparent motion is satisfactory in the light
of available data. We will therefore avoid this traditional distinction and
approach the subject instead in terms of an analysis of the information available in the proximal stimulus—the image projected on the retina by a moving
object.

J. J. Gibson (1957), arguing on the basis of experiments on the perception
of depth in shadows projected by three-dimensional rotating objects, has
suggested that the visual system is able to invert the projective relations between the three-dimensional object displacements and the two-dimensional
optical motions projected on the screen, and so to recover the object displacements from the perceived motions of the shadows. A detailed analysis of the
projective transformations and of the nature of the information they preserve
about the rigid, three-dimensional object whose displacements generate them,

would be required in order to evaluate this suggestion. Hay (1966) has extended Gibson's analysis and has concluded that (if one ignores elastic changes in the size or shape of the object) there are eight relevant parameters of the projected motion, parameters that can specify the initial position of the displaced object as well as its displacement. These eight parameters can be classified into four types, each applying to both the vertical and the horizontal axes of the projected image: translation, stretching, shearing, and foreshortening.

"Translation" is motion of the unchanged image up or down, left or right, in the image plane; diagonal translation involves motion in both the vertical and horizontal axes. "Stretching" is a multiplication of the image by some constant factor, so it becomes wider or narrower, shorter or taller; equal stretching in both axes creates a magnification of the image. "Shearing" converts a rectangle into a parallelogram; horizontal shearing moves the top of the image horizontally to the right (left) the same amount the bottom of the image moves to the left (right); vertical shearing moves the right side of the image up (down) the same amount the left side moves down (up); rotation of the image results from equal horizontal and vertical shearing, supplemented by suitable stretchings. "Foreshortening" increases the size of one side of the image while decreasing the size of the opposite side; under foreshortening, parallel lines meet at a point at infinite depth.

Projective transformations are defined from one plane P onto another plane P^*. If P represents a flat surface of the object being displaced and P^* the retinal surface onto which P is projected, then all the optical rays originating from P will move together in the sense that they will remain coplanar; that is to say, on P^* straight lines will remain straight although their lengths and orientations may vary. A visual system that is able to respond selectively to optical motions that preserve straight lines will have the basic capacity needed to discriminate spatial displacements of flat surfaces.

If x' and y' are the horizontal and vertical coordinates of the points of an image on the retina *after* displacement of an object, and x and y are the horizontal and vertical coordinates of the corresponding points on the retina *before* displacement, then the relation between them is given by the equations

(30) $$x' = \frac{ax + by - c}{gx + hy - m}$$

$$y' = \frac{dx + ey - f}{gx + hy - m}$$

There are nine coefficients in these equations, but only eight independent parameters. The value of a is related to the horizontal stretching of the image; b is related to horizontal shearing; c to horizontal translation; g to horizontal foreshortening. Changes in $d, e, f,$ and h are similarly related to the vertical coordinate.

A visual system capable of detecting these four types of parameters, both laterally and vertically, could extract all of the information contained in the projective optical transformations of an object's image. When a flat object moves, there will usually be changes in several of these parameters of its projected image, and as the displacement continues it becomes possible to compare many successive estimates of the transformations, thus providing much redundant information about the object's surface and its motion. In the case of solid objects having several flat surfaces, each face will induce a separate projective transformation of its own image; since all of these transformations must be induced by the same object displacement, even further redundant information about the object and its motion is available. Objects with curved surfaces present special problems; the accuracy of judgments about the motions of curved objects is relatively low.

It is clear from a mathematical analysis, therefore, that projective transformations of the retinal image provide a rich source of information about displacements of objects in three-dimensional space. It should be emphasized, however, that there is not a one-to-one correspondence between the parameters of image transformation given in (30) and the parameters of object displacement; inverting the transformations of the image in order to extract information about object displacements is not a simple and direct operation. Although it is clear that a plentiful supply of information is available in the structure of the projective transformations on the retinal image, it is still an empirical question to determine which aspects of this information the visual system is sensitive to and how object displacements are inferred on the basis of this information.

It should be obvious that transformations of the retinal image can result either from leaving the eye stationary and displacing the object, or from leaving the object stationary and displacing the eye. Moreover, as Hay points out, when you observe a moving object it is sometimes possible to simplify the transformations of the projected image on the retina by moving your eyes. For example, reflex pursuit movements of the eye to track a target moving at a constant distance from the eye will hold foveal image points stationary on the retina, which is equivalent to reducing the translation parameters of the projected motion to zero. To put it another way, the visual system must be able to substitute information about intended changes in the angle of regard for information about translations of the retinal image. Or, again, if your eyes are turned in such a way that the line of sight lies along the translation axis—as when you walk forward with your eyes focused straight ahead—stretching and foreshortening will be the only image transformations (Gibson, Olum, and Rosenblatt, 1955). But even if we assume the closest possible coordination of the exteroceptive and proprioceptive components of vision, the problem of characterizing how the visual system extracts and evaluates the information from the proximal stimulus remains.

In order to infer object displacements from the translations, shearings, stretchings, and foreshortenings that they project onto the retina, it seems necessary to have some kind of three-dimensional frame of reference for visual perception—a perceptual space within which perceptual objects can be seen to move. That this perceptual space is not isomorphic with physical space is obvious from the perceptions of apparent motions through three dimensions which can result from physical motions through only two. Given a perceptual frame of reference relative to which motions can be perceived, it then seems necessary to have some kind of vectorial analysis of motion into the horizontal, vertical, and line-of-sight (distance) coordinates of that frame of reference.

The frame of reference might seem to be provided by processes like those discussed in section 2.3, where we considered the question of the stability and three-dimensionality of the perceptual world. That discussion was limited, however, to those cases in which the environment really is stable and there is little uncertainty about the appropriate frame of reference. But, as physicists have shown, it is possible to have other frames of reference. If we are traveling in a moving vehicle, for example, a falling object will have a parabolic track with respect to the stationary environment and a vertical track with respect to the moving vehicle. In such cases, a physicist is free to choose either coordinate system, but a viewer is not. Perceptually, the vehicle is the frame of reference; a viewer can see only the vertical, not the parabolic track. The visual system extracts the component of motion relative to the background against which it is seen; motions common to both the displaced object and its background are seen as quite distinct from displacements with respect to the background. The importance of the surround for judgments of relative motion was first made explicit by Duncker (1929).

Johansson (1950) has demonstrated the relativity of judgments of motion in a series of simple experiments with moving dots. For example, two dots, one always above the other, move horizontally across the face of an oscilloscope in triangular, sawtooth paths that are in opposite phase, that is, come together and go apart, return together and then go apart again, and so on. Perceptually, this pattern of motions is analyzed into two components: (a) vertical motion of each dot with respect to the other, and (b) horizontal motion of the pair with respect to the face of the oscilloscope. The vertical motion is seen with respect to one frame of reference, the horizontal with respect to another. The horizontal motion "carries" the vertical motion in much the way a moving vehicle carries the falling object. Johansson termed such a dissociation of a physically given motion into two or more perceptual components kinematical vector analysis.

In his subsequent research Johannson (1964) generated a rectangle that changed continuously in its vertical and horizontal dimensions at a rate of once every two seconds. Consider the case in which the vertical dimension changed more than the horizontal. This changing display was usually seen as a translation of a surface in distance, combined with a rotation around the horizontal axis. This perception resulted even though such motions of a flat physical object would *not* have generated the pattern that observers saw—rotation would normally produce foreshortening in the projection of a physical surface. The perceived translation in depth accounted for motion of all points on the surface toward a point at infinity. This translatory motion then carried (provided a frame of reference for) the difference in stretching of the vertical and horizontal dimensions, which was attributed to rotation. When the absence of foreshortening was pointed out to sophisticated observers, they reported that they could see it as a third motion resulting from an elastic deformation in the shape of the surface. Such results suggest to Johansson that there is a hierarchy among the kinds of change people see when several aspects of a pattern are varying simultaneously. Insofar as possible, people attribute the perceived changes to translatory motions of a rigid object; if translation does not account for all the changes, they perceive rotary motion relative to the translation; if further components remain, they see elastic changes in the shape of the object. This hypothesis is probably too simple to account for all the known facts, but it indicates the kind of rules governing motion perception that might serve as a basis for a theory of this important phenomenon.

In any case, the visual system does seem to analyze perceived motions into components relative to various frames of reference. On that basis, therefore, we are justified in introducing perceptual predicates for translation (change of location), for rotation (change of orientation), and for deformation (change of shape): Trans, Rot, and Deform, respectively. What the arguments of these predicates should be is a question that we will postpone for the moment. But it is clear that the visual system discriminates among these various kinds of spatial changes, and it is equally clear that we require such judgments to account for how people use such words as "shift," "spin," "roll," "bend," and so on, to describe them.

With this brief indication of the nature of the pertinent perceptual processes, we turn now to another problem involved in fashioning an account of the relation between the perception of and talk about motion. There is a useful distinction to be drawn between the perception of changes and the perception of events. We will try to make this distinction more precise.

2.5.2   When Is a Change an Event?

The perception of events has important implications for language. Indeed, one feels inclined to say that English (and other languages) deals with objects in terms of nouns, events in terms of verbs, and properties in terms of adjectives. Although there is much psychological sense in this division, it is linguistically unacceptable. Noun, verb, and adjective are syntactic categories, not semantic categories. There are many English nouns that denote events and many verbs that do not. The syntactic distinctions cannot rest on some psychological discrimination among objects, events, and their properties.

If we wished to postulate some deeper level of cognitive analysis at which "noun" and "verb" were defined as semantic categories, we would have to defend the position that, underlying the surface syntax, there is a deeper cognitive level at which we deal with objects as semantic nouns and events as semantic verbs. We might argue, for example, that the syntactic noun "act" is a surface reification of the underlying semantic verb "act"; that the syntactic noun "occurrence" derives from the semantic verb "occur"; that the syntactic noun "event" is understood in terms of a semantic verb "come out" (from the Latin "ex" + "venire"); and so on. Similarly, we would have to defend the existence of a level of semantic adjectives underlying all surface specifications of properties. In short, we would have to endorse the hypothesis that at the level of "root" morphemes root nouns denote objects, root verbs denote events, and root adjectives denote properties. But even this version of the hypothesis can easily be shown to be false.

If there were some simple relation between syntactic categories and our psychological notions, of course, it would provide a very convenient shortcut connecting perception and language; our theories of how language is learned, for example, could be considerably simplified. Unfortunately, such is not the case.

The introduction of semantic verbs, semantic nouns, and semantic adjectives extends these syntactic terms into realms they are poorly suited to describe. Moreover, the extension is unnecessary; we have perfectly serviceable terms to describe the semantic distinctions we really have in mind. The faulty intuition that verbs describe events and nouns describe objects is less important to us at this stage of our argument than the psychological fact that events and objects represent two basically different ways of categorizing experience.

The analysis of perception seems to require at least four primitive categories: objects and attributes, states and events. The cognitive category corresponding to "state" is basic to the object-event distinction. Events are perceived when changes occur; not all changes are perceived as events, of course, but all events involve changes of some kind. And the perception of change cannot occur in a psychological vacuum. The generic term used for the thing that changes is "state." For example, if you perceive an object change from a state of rest to a state of motion, you may mark that change of state as an event and use the word "start" (noun or verb) to refer to it.

We must, therefore, present some analysis of the perception of states and events comparable to the analysis of perceptual objects and attributes. In undertaking this analysis, however, we find peculiarly little in the psychological literature on vision to guide us. As far as we know, the optimal conditions giving rise to a change of state being seen as a temporally connected event have not been studied extensively. Studies of the perception of motion have usually been considered to be investigations of event perception (see, for example, Johansson, 1950); under laboratory conditions, of course, this equivalence is probably justified, because observers are instructed to regard all perceived motions as events to be reported to the experimenter. Since we wish to make a distinction between changes and events, we will not use "event perception" to mean what it usually means in psychological journals.

We began our discussion of object perception with a consideration of how an integrated object could be segregated from its surround. This figure-ground distinction is also necessary for event perception. We assume that there is constant change in the sensory input; by some kind of attentional-judgmental abstraction people are able to focus on a limited portion of that flux, and, given appropriate conditions, to organize it into a unitary whole, an event. This far, at least, the achievement of a perceived event parallels the achievement of a perceived object or configuration of objects.

Unlike objects, however, events are transient. They have a temporal as well as a spatial location. One can return to an object and examine it again for further information. One cannot return to a prior event unless photography has converted it into an object that can be revisited. It is possible, though, to control changing patterns of stimulation in the laboratory—either by photography or by generating the patterns with a machine—so that the temporal aspects of perception can be investigated experimentally.

Event perception must also include proprioception and audition. The motion of a limb or the sound of an utterance will not support the Obj predicate to which so much of the visual machinery is dedicated; motions and sounds are not concrete objects. There seems to be a strong tendency to attribute them to objects, however, perhaps because of the desirability of integrating information received from different modalities. When one talks of some motion as an attribute of the arm, or of some sound as an attribute of its source at a particular moment, these perceptual events have much the same status in perceptual theory as the attributes of shape, color, size, or place. The principal distinction we must draw between them is in their need for temporal indexing. Objects retain relatively constant perceptual shapes, colors, and sizes, but locations can change with time, and the perception of those changes is fundamental to the perception of motion; sounds come into being and fade away, and their time of occurrence frequently serves to mark the time of an event. Hearing makes a particularly important contribution to the event character of experience; events are frequently noisy and the sounds of collisions punctuate the visual flow. The importance of hearing for event perception is attested by the fact that traumatically deafened persons frequently become depressed and complain of the loss of the event character of experience, as if they were "living in a glass coffin" (Ramsdell, 1947).

These remarks should suggest the general line we will follow. We will treat perceptual changes as properties or attributes of experience and characterize them in terms of their temporal and spatial locations. In order to specify the perceptual content that is changing when the event is perceived, we require at least two state descriptions (see Carnap, 1956), one of the perceptual content before the change and one after. These two descriptions can be formed by conjunctions of predicates describing various objects in the perceptual world to which the perceiver happens to be attending, and when changes are occurring the state descriptions will differ with respect to at least one of their component predicates. Let us denote these conjunctive constructions by $S_t(x, y, \ldots)$, where $x, y, \ldots$ are the various arguments of the predicates constituting S at the moment t. Then we can write

(31) $\text{not}(S_{t-1}(x, y, \ldots) \equiv S_t(x, y, \ldots)) \equiv (\exists z)[\text{Chng}_t(S_t(z))],$

where $S_t(z)$ is understood to be any component predicate true at $t - 1$ and not true at t. We assume it is possible to abstract the changing attributes from all the other components of S; in chapter 1 we saw that the ability to perceive independent variation in something was one of the criteria for calling it an attribute.

For example, if all the predicates describing a perceptual content remain unchanged from $t - 1$ to t except Place, then we would presumably have as one component of S_{t-1} the predicate $\text{Place}_{t-1}(x, y)$, and as one component of S_t the predicate $\text{Place}_t(x, y')$, where y and y' indicate different locations. Then, by (31), we could write $\text{Chng}_t(\text{Place}(x, y'))$ to represent the attentional-judgmental abstraction of this particular attribute difference from the rest of the predicates in S. That is to say, the conceptual system can give an instruction of the form find(search domain, all F such that $\text{Chng}_t(F(\underline{\quad})))$.

This way of introducing Chng makes it explicit that Chng is a higher-order operator that can take attribute predicates (properties) as its argument; change is an attribute of an attribute. (The same could be said of Simlr; similarity is a relation between attributes.) An alternative way (compare (8) above) to describe a change in place would be

(32) $\text{Place}_{t-1}(x, y)$ & $\text{Place}_t(x, y')$ & $\text{Chng}_{t-1,t}(y, y')$.

In the present context, however, Chng(Place(x, y)) seems to catch the intuition that change is a more complex perception than location, inasmuch as it presupposes the perception of the attribute that is changing.

We must consider event perception in more detail, but first it is necessary to point out a shortcoming in the formulation just given for state descriptions. As defined above, S_t is a static description of the perceptual contents at moment t. It does not provide any obvious way to characterize dynamic states, such as states of motion. In order to cope with dynamic states, it is necessary to introduce temporally extended states that have momentary states as their components. Since the phenomenal present integrates several successive moments, there should be no psychological barrier to such an assumption. Let S'_t denote an extended state description consisting of the sequence of momentary states S_{t-k} to S_t, where k is the number of moments spanned by the phenomenal present. If some object x is moving, then from S'_t we can abstract a sequence of Chng operators between $t - k + 1$ and t which can form the components of a dynamic, higher-order state description Σ_t. If Σ does not change from t to $t + 1$, x is perceived as being in a constant state of motion. We have no desire to rediscover the integral calculus, but it is necessary to recognize that the perceptual system is able to abstract such dynamic states and that the mechanisms for accomplishing it must be correspondingly complex. We will therefore generalize our definition of S to include extended and higher-order as well as momentary states of the perceptual world.

We return now to the perception of events. We assume that events are usually complex patterns of change, just as objects are complex patterns of edges, corners, and surfaces. For example, an event might consist of a glass's being knocked from the table, falling to the floor, and shattering. This total event would consist of a sequence of momentary changes, first in Place and later in Sound and Shap, but these would be perceptually integrated over space and time into a perceptual whole. We assume, therefore, that we could introduce some such perceptual predicate as $Event_t(e)$, which would be interpreted to mean that e is an event occurring at moment t. Event would be a predicate that denotes dynamic objects in much the same way that Obj denotes concrete objects.

It is not obvious why some changes or patterns of change are seen as events and others are not. All that seems to hold successive changes together in an event is adjacency in space and time, and it is easy to see that this is not sufficient. For example, imagine that nothing is happening except that a small circle of light is going off and on in alternate moments. An observer would perceive changes in its illumination, and they would be coherent in space and time, but he would probably not perceive this flickering light as an event unless the flickering started and stopped within a relatively short period. In principle, he could regard each successive change of illumination as an event, but this would be impractical where nothing serves to distinguish any particular change from the sequence of similar changes in which it is embedded. Presumably, it is easier to perceive some (higher-order) state of flickering.

Alternatively, imagine a visual display of pictures that changed haphazardly at a rapid rate (as fast as or faster than, say, the eye normally moves from one fixation point to the next). The whole episode might be regarded as an event, but each individual, momentary change probably would not—less than half the pictures would even be recognized subsequently (Potter and Levy, 1969). Presumably, it is easier to regard such a display as in a (higher-order) state of flux, although it is by no means clear how such a state could be defined in terms of invariance from moment to moment. However, any particular momentary change can be regarded as an event—the appearance of an image of the Statue of Liberty, for example. An observer can be set to look for the appearance of some particular image in the flux (Potter, 1975), and when it occurs his recognition of it might constitute an event. It seems obvious that with events, even more than with concrete objects, a person's perception is strongly influenced by his set: by what he is doing, what he expects, what he is attending to.

Haphazard changes are the exception in normal viewing. An event is usually a distinctive local change set in a context of great redundancy from moment to moment. Barlow (1961) has summarized an argument, endorsed by many students of perception, to the effect that the perceptual system is designed to preserve information and discard redundancy. Things that change take priority over things that remain constant; constancy is expected, the perceptual system tries to minimize surprise; wherever possible, sensory changes are relegated to predictable states, so that the amount of unpredictable information that must be processed will not overload the conceptual system. Once the state of the world has been conceptually established, the perceptual system needs to report only the information required to update it, only the information about significant changes. Within this context of discussion, therefore, we might speculate that sensory changes are perceived as events when they contain information needed to update the conceptual representation of the world. Which changes will constitute an event will thus depend not only on the sensory input to the system but also on the nature of the conceptual representation of the world to which the sensory input is being assimilated. Since that conceptual representation will depend on what a person is doing at any moment, there is no sure way to predict, solely from a description of the sensory input, which changes or patterns of change will be regarded as events.

The view that the perceptual system is designed to protect the stability of some conceptual representation of the world also gives us a way to talk about the preservation of object identity. Not only must an event be abstracted from a redundant context; the local change itself must preserve many features of a changing object. An object may move, but it remains the same object; the illumination may change, but it remains the same scene; a person may speak, but he remains the same person. When does an observer decide, as a result of changes in x, that x is no longer the same entity but has become some new entity x'? According to Michotte (1962), if one attribute—color, size, or shape —of an object changes, observers will say it is the same object; if two aspects change simultaneously, they are likely to say that the original object has been replaced by another; if three aspects change simultaneously, everyone agrees that replacement has occurred. (Michotte's observations should interest philosophers who would like to state criteria for the identity of individuals from one "possible world" to another.)

Just as an object must have a place, size, and shape, so an event must have place and a duration. Paralleling (1), therefore, we can write

(33) $\text{Event}(e) \supset (\exists y)\text{Place}(e, y) \ \& \ (\exists t)\text{Time}(e, t).$

Concerning the Place predicate, little need be added to our earlier discussion; the location of an event is the location of the concrete objects that serve as arguments for the predicates whose changes are perceptually integrated into the perceived event.

The Time predicate in (33) is intended to capture our tendency to select some moment in the interval from t to $t + i$ as the particular moment at which the event occurred. For example, a sunrise is a slow, steady change in illumination, but it can be seen as an event marked in time by the first appearance of the edge of the solar disc over the horizon. Hearing can contribute to this selection of a particular moment; when the glass falls to the floor, the impact provides an auditory signal marking the particular moment in the episode at which the event is perceived to occur. And touch can provide a similar service; an event consisting of moving the hand to grasp an object can be temporally focused at the particular moment the hand makes contact with it.

When we wish to characterize the translatory movement of some object x, we can, as we have seen, use $\text{Chng}_t(\text{Place}(x, y))$. This is such a common occurrence, however, that it is useful to have a single predicate to represent it:

(34) $\text{Travel}_t(x) \equiv \text{Chng}_t(\text{Place}(x, y))$.

If Travel applies in every successive moment over an interval of time from t to $t + i$, we may write $\text{Travel}_{t,t+i}(x)$ to represent the entire sequence of momentary changes of location beginning in place y_0 at time t and continuing to place y_i at time $t + i$.

When a moving object traces a path through space, the whole set of places through which the object passes can be perceived at least as clearly as any of the individual places through which it passes. Moreover, this spatial configuration can be perceived more or less independently of the object whose motion it describes. If we define ρ to be the set of locations related as momentarily successive locations in $\text{Travel}_{t,t+1}(x)$, then ρ is the path of x. If we wish to indicate the perception of the path independent of the object that moved along it, we can write simply ρ; if we wish to associate that path with a particular object x, we will write $\text{Path}(x, \rho)$.

Now, if we wanted to say that an observer regards $\text{Travel}(x)$ as a significant event, in the sense discussed above, we might write $\text{Event}(\text{Travel}(x))$, or $\text{Event}(\text{Chng}(\text{Place}(x)))$, which makes it clear that Event is a higher-order operator. And when we wish to use procedural notation, the "assign" instruction can be used: $\text{Assign}(e, \text{Travel}(x))$. A variety of notational options are available; which we choose is of less importance to us at this point than a reasonably clear understanding of the kinds of judgments about changes and events the perceptual system can be expected to provide.

Just as concrete objects can be related in larger configurations, so events can be parts of larger events. Given a sufficiently long conceptual perspective on time, some extended episode can be regarded as an event; a trip, say, might be seen as an event beginning with a departure, incorporating various events in transit, and ending with an arrival. Extended events of this sort do not always seem to have a single focus; they are marked multiply in time by the times of their several component events. The integration of extended events is clearly conceptual, not perceptual.

Because the perception of a change or pattern of changes as an event is highly subjective, our talk about events is even more dependent on conceptualization than our talk about objects. That is to say, some pattern of change may be regarded as an event simply because that is how we talk about it, not because we perceive it that way. This is particularly true of social events— parties, conversations, meetings, games, trips—which extend over an interval of time far greater than the phenomenal present and for which it is difficult to assign some unique moment as the time of their occurrence.

2.5.3   The Role of Perceptual Memory

In 2.5.1 we referred to the fact that motion is perceived relative to a particular frame of reference, and in 2.5.2 it was implicit in our discussion of dynamic states that memory is available to sustain such temporally extended states long enough to permit the extraction of the transformations associated with object displacements. The relation between these two assumptions has been clarified in an experimental analysis by Kinchla and Allan (1969).

In 2.3.3 we defined the location of an object in terms of the Dset of distances from its various parts to the parts of surrounding objects. It follows from such a relativistic formulation that an object will be seen to change place whenever its Dset changes, and the Dset to change either if the object's absolute position changes while surrounding objects remain fixed, or if its absolute position remains fixed while the surrounding objects change position. The former case is the usual one, of course, but the latter is also possible; it is called induced movement (Duncker, 1929). If object y provides a spatial frame around object x, and x and y are seen in an otherwise homogeneous (for example, dark) surround, then physical movement of the frame y in one direction will be perceived as movement in the opposite direction by the object x. Consideration of such perceptual judgments led Kinchla and Allan to distinguish between relative movement perception, when an observer judges the movement of one object by reference to some other object, and absolute movement perception, when the moving object is so far from all other objects (more than about 10 degrees of visual angle) that their presence does not affect his judgment of its motion. Outside this 10-degree angle, x is no longer functionally included in $Reg(y)$.

Absolute movement perception is rare but not impossible, and its accuracy has been of considerable interest to many perceptual psychologists. Kinchla and Allan have accounted for the experimental data on absolute movement perception in terms of a mathematical formulation involving a single free parameter which characterizes the observer's accuracy in remembering an object's previous location. His ability to remember an earlier position and compare it with the present position declines during intervals as short as two seconds. The accuracy of his memory seems to be limited by random variability in his eye-positioning system, which is cumulative with time.

The fact that movement perception is facilitated when a stationary reference object is provided near the moving object indicates that when the distance involved is small an observer's memory for relative position is more accurate than for absolute position—presumably because variability in the eye-positioning system affects both the moving and the reference objects in the same way. As the distance to the reference object increases, however, the accuracy with which an observer can estimate it declines rather rapidly, so that eventually he can do better by simply ignoring the reference object and judging the absolute movement of the target object.

Both relative and absolute movement perception depend on memory, therefore, although when reference objects are provided and the time elapsed is quite short, spatial memory seems to be relatively accurate. When a much longer span of time elapses between the successive perceptions of an object, memory of the earlier position is usually fallible and untrustworthy. Small changes, of a kind that could easily be detected from one moment to the next, will seldom be noticed when long periods of time elapse. When, after an interval, a difference in place is noticed, however, people can (and do) infer that some kind of spatial change has occurred, even though they did not witness the event occurring.

This situation can be described by assuming that after a sufficient interval of time only large changes—which we can take as changes sufficient to remove x from the $\text{Reg}(x)$ it defined previously—are likely to be noticed. More precisely, the inference can be formulated

(35) $\text{not}(\text{Incl}_{t+i}(x, \text{Reg}_t(x))) \supset \text{Travel}(x)$.

It is clear that the direction of implication in (35) cannot be reversed, since, if i is large, it is perfectly possible that x might have traveled extensively during the interval yet return to $\text{Reg}_t(x)$ by $t + i$. On the other hand, if $i = 1$, (35) would still be valid, but if x had not traveled far enough in a single moment to escape $\text{Reg}_t(x)$, the reverse implication would be invalid. The contrapositive of (35)—if x has not been perceived to travel, then it has remained in the same region—will be true if observation of x has been continuous during the interval, and it will usually be assumed true even when observation has not been continuous.

Although $\text{Incl}(x, \text{Reg}(y))$ gives a general way to say that x and y are perceived together, some more precise measure—Dset or an equivalent representation—must be assumed for the description of spatial changes. If we define the location in terms of Dset, however, a variety of spatial changes can affect Dset, not all of which lead to the same perceptual results. For example, the Dset of an object x will change if x is changing in shape: $\text{Chng}_t(\text{Shap}(x, y)) \equiv \text{Deform}_t(x)$. By this formulation, though, a man moving his hand would be said to be changing his shape. Why people prefer to regard such an event as a change in the location of his hand is not obvious. Or again, Dset will change if x is changing size: $\text{Chng}_t(\text{Size}(x, y))$. How to tell whether a balloon is being inflated or is coming closer, for example, requires a rather subtle visual analysis. Again, Dset will change if x is rotating: $\text{Chng}_t(\text{Orient}(x, y)) \equiv \text{Rot}_t(x)$. Here the problems concern the axis of rotation and its relation to the direction of translatory motion (if any). The perceptual system can discriminate among these various kinds of spatial changes, however, so we assume that such perceptual predicates are available.

2.6   CAUSES AND INTENTIONS

In the preceding pages we have reviewed, however briefly, most of the psychological processes that have traditionally been regarded as sensory or perceptual. At this point we might well abandon the traditional approach and turn directly to an attempt to construct an account of conceptual organization. In a sense, that is what we will do. We will turn to a consideration of cause and intention, two topics that are essentially conceptual in nature. Conceptions of the causes of events and the intentions of people provide some of the major furniture of the mind.

We will, however, approach these topics first under the rubric of perception. We adopt this approach not out of sheer perversity or slavish adherence to an expository device. There is some precedent in the psychological literature for talking about the perception of causation and the perception of intentions. Many experiments have explored conditions under which observers *see* one event as the cause of another; how a person can *see* another person's intentions is one of the central questions that have been asked by students of "person perception" (Kelley, 1973). We may believe that this kind of seeing is more conceptual than perceptual, but that is a relative matter, a question of degree. All perceptions are to some extent conceptually shaped and controlled. In deciding to treat cause and intention first as perceptual objects, we are not arguing that they are more perceptual than conceptual. Such opinions would have little utility, even if we could agree on them. The appreciation of causes and intentions does seem to have some basis in perception, and it is that base we propose should be included in theories of perception. The relatively greater contribution of conceptual processes will, of course, aggravate the problem of formulating this perceptual base, but that is not a new problem; we have struggled with it continually in the preceding pages.

One of the possible arguments against treating causal and intentional judgments as perceptions exploits the improbability of finding any simple neurophysiological correlates for them. When we deal with simple sensory attributes, it is often possible to find convincing correlates of experience in patterns of neural activity. When we move up to perceptual phenomena, correlates are more difficult to find, but we are not completely at a loss for reasonable hypotheses. But the more abstract perceptual judgment becomes, the less likely it is that we will ever find correlates that correspond to natural generalizations about the structure and function of the brain. This is not to deny that correlates exist; we assume that causal and intentional judgments can be given a satisfactory characterization both in terms of some eventual psychological theory and in terms of some eventual theory of neurophysiology. What we doubt is that the events classified as similar for psychological purposes would also be classified as similar for neurophysiological purposes; events judged psychologically to be perceptions of causation or intent may correlate with patterns of neural activity that, in terms of the natural generalizations of neurophysiology, would be extremely diverse and of little interest to that science. If one insists that for every natural generalization about perception there must be a corresponding natural generalization about brain processes, and if one recognizes the extreme diversity of events that might be perceived as causal or intentional, then one is almost forced to exclude such judgments from perceptual theories. Alternatively, if one accepts such judgments as perceptual, one should be prepared to abandon the hope that the psychological theory of perception can ever be reduced to a branch of sensory neurophysiology.

Since we believe that the natural generalizations of a completed psychological theory of perception could (in principle) be instantiated by an enormous variety of electromechanical automatons that would have no neurophysiology at all, we would feel no great loss if the reductionist program had to be abandoned. In that frame of mind, we are willing to dismiss one of the possible arguments for excluding judgments of causation and intention from the domain of perceptual phenomena. There may be valid psychological reasons for excluding them—on the grounds that they do not constitute natural generalizations in our (eventual) theory of perception—but that is a question we are unable to answer decisively in terms of existing theories of perception.

We will therefore review the kinds of attentional-judgmental abstractions we assume perceptual theory will ultimately provide in order to account for perceptions of causation and intention.

2.6.1   Perceptual Dynamics

In physics it is customary to divide kinetics, the study of motion, into two branches: kinematics, which treats of motion without regard for the influences of mass and force, and dynamics, which concerns the relation between motion and the forces that produce it. This conceptual distinction has its perceptual analog. The studies of perceived motion described in 2.5.1 might be regarded as perceptual kinematics; the studies of perceived motion with which we are concerned here can be regarded as perceptual dynamics. Motion that is seen as the result of something done to an object is perceived in terms of the forces that produced it; how the perceptual system appreciates this relation is the heart of the problem that has been called the perception of causation.

In kinematic perception, people see motion simply as something an object "has" in its own right. In dynamic perception there seem to be two different ways of taking account of the relations between motions and their causes. Motion can be seen either as something that is "done" to an object or as something an object "does" to itself. Psychologically, this distinction between extrinsic and intrinsic causes of movement may be more fundamental than the distinction between kinematic and dynamic perception. Objects that cause their own motions fall into a very special class. The motions of all other objects must have some extrinsic cause; if those extrinsic causes are perceived, the motion will be perceived dynamically, otherwise kinematically.

It is only the perceptual phenomena that concern us here. In particular, these phenomena have little to do with anything we may know about "real" causes of motion. If, for example, we constructed a device that would move a spot of light over the surface of a wall according to whatever trajectory we requested, people would probably see the motion kinematically, even though they might know that it was under the precise control of our machine. Moreover, if we used two of these devices to project two spots of light in such a way that they maintained a constant spatial relation—one of them always 5 centimeters below the other, say—then, by the gestalt principle of common fate, observers would see the two spots as a single perceptual object, having a (kinematic) motion of its own. But if we projected two spots in such a way that the lower spot seemed to hang freely from the upper one, as if the upper one were a hinge for a rod extending to the lower one, then people would see the motion of the lower spot dynamically in the frame of reference of the motion of the upper spot; the upper spot would be seen as pulling the lower spot, even though the observer might know that the two spots were controlled by separate machines; the upper spot would have a kinematic motion of its own, but the lower would be seen dynamically as caused to move by the upper spot.

The appreciation of dynamic relations can exploit extremely subtle clues. It is possible to make moving pictures of five lights placed on a person's body in such a way that all that is seen is one light at the hips, two lights on the knees, and two lights on the ankles. As the person walks, the five lights move together as a unit; the basic frame of reference is provided by the top light representing the hips; the lights on each knee are seen as hinges for the motions of the corresponding lights on each ankle. Johansson (1971) has demonstrated that the perception of walking is quite compelling under these severely reduced conditions of viewing. Now, one can make a Fourier analysis of the pendular motions of the spots and use it to generate such patterns of five spots on the face of a cathode-ray tube; when only the fundamental components of the motions are used to generate the pattern, it looks as though a person's legs are dangling freely below him; as higher-frequency components are introduced, however, they produce the appearance of resistance from an invisible surface on which a person is walking. With this rather small difference between the two patterns, the perceptual dynamics are completely altered. Apparently the visual system can be exquisitely sensitive to components of motion that provide information about dynamic relations between moving objects. If the lights are placed between the walker's joints, however, their motion does not create a perception of a person walking.

It is even possible to program the motions of two spots in such a manner that one spot is seen as chasing another; in addition to each spot dynamically generating a motion of its own, people see one spot as intending to catch the other, and the other as intending to escape. Heider and Simmel (1944), for example, used animated motion pictures to explore the impressions of social interaction that could be evoked by the movements of triangles and circles. Objects that can cause their own motion are seen as peculiarly lifelike and are often regarded as alive by young children.

Although the matter is debatable, it seems unlikely that the human visual system has special-purpose, innate mechanisms for seeing biological and social movements comparable, say, to the mechanisms for seeing color. Perhaps the visual system has evolved general-purpose mechanisms for *learning* to see patterns of movement in special ways, for there is a large conceptual component in this particular kind of seeing. Regardless of their origins, however, these interpretations of moving objects are very compelling. Only a deliberate effort to dissociate the pattern will enable an adult to see these motions in any other way than as causal or intentional.

In order to describe such perceptual relations between moving objects, therefore, it is necessary to introduce two complicated and often controversial predicates: causation and intention. Much has been written about both of these relations, and our principal task here will be to limit our discussion to their perceptual, not their conceptual attributes. Whether such attentional-judgmental abstractions are the product of learning based on experience with moving objects, or whether they are the product of some innate mechanisms of perception that contributed to the survival of our ancestors, is a difficult question that will have to be fought out in the construction of a perceptual theory. For our present purposes, it is the fact that people can make such judgments, not their genesis, that is of central concern.

2.6.2   Perceived Causes

The two most common situations in which people perceive that the motion of one object causes the motion of another are when one object carries the second, or when one object collides with the second. In the former case the motion is sustained by some kind of holding relation between the two objects; in the latter case, the motion of one object is transferred to the other. We require perceptual predicates, therefore, to characterize these relations of holding and transfer.

Consider first the relation of holding. A great variety of spatial configurations might be perceived as relating two objects in such a way that the motion of one would cause the motion of the other. There seems to be no term in English that captures this relation in its most general sense; lacking a better term, we will introduce the perceptual predicate $\text{Hold}(x, y)$ to mean that x is perceived to be in charge of y in such a way that if x begins to move, y will move with it. This way of phrasing it assumes that people can perceive a relation between the (potential or actual) motion of x and the motion of y. We will use $\text{Cause}(\text{Travel}(x), \text{Travel}(y))$ to denote that relation:

(36) $\text{Cause}_{t,t+k}(\text{Travel}(x), \text{Travel}(y))$ & $\text{Suprt}_{t,t+k}(x, y)$
          $\supset \text{Hold}_{t,t+k}(x, y)$.

We assume that perceptual judgments of this type would be required by organisms that spend so much of their time moving things about.

The predicate Cause denotes a perceived dynamic relation between x and y, or, more precisely, between the motion of x and the motion of y. Since Travel is itself defined in terms of a higher-order operator, $\text{Chng}(\text{Place}(x, y))$, we begin to see a building up of successive layers of operators. In (36), Cause denotes a perceived relation between the perception of a change of location in one object x and the perception of a change of location in another object y that x is holding. This building up of successive layers seems characteristic of conceptual processes, and may indeed be a reflection of the way the human nervous system has evolved—by adding higher mechanisms to control and exploit existing mechanisms at lower levels. The layered complexity of Cause supports our feeling that even these apparently perceptual causes are more like concepts than percepts.

The consequence of this hierarchical organization for the conceptual system is that instructions involving Cause presuppose considerable advance preparation. If we wished to use the instruction test(now, Cause(e_1, e_2)), we would first have to assign values to e_1 and e_2. Thus we would need an instruction to assign(e_1, Travel(x)) and also an instruction to assign(e_2, Travel(y)). But these instructions, in turn, presuppose that we have located the x that is traveling, which means that we need a prior instruction to find(Reg(z), x), followed by an instruction to test(now, Travel(x)), as well as an instruction to find(Reg(x), y), followed by test(now, Travel(y)). Once all these pointers are assigned, we can then test perceptually whether x supports y and the motion of x causes the motion of y, which will, of course, imply the Hold relation between x and y. This routine rivals many conceptual routines in complexity.

The temporal subscripts in (36) are critical for distinguishing the causal relation involving holding from the causal relation involving transfer. Both x and y are traveling and x is supporting y throughout the interval from moment t to moment $t + k$. Compare this situation with the relation involved in collisions.

If an object has a motion of its own, that motion can be transferred to another object by a collision. Take the case in which the first object approaches the second until it contacts it and then stops, at which instant the second begins to move off in the direction initially set by the first. If the velocities and time relations are correctly adjusted, the intrinsic motion of the first will be seen as transferred to the second, a perceptual phenomenon that Michotte (1954) called ampliation. When ampliation occurs, observers judge that the first object caused the second to move.

By carefully controlling the rate at which one spot of color moved toward a second spot, the time the spots remained touching, and the rate at which the second spot took off in the direction set by the first spot, Michotte was able to determine the conditions necessary for a person to see the first spot cause the second to move. We will again use Cause(Travel(x), Travel(y)) to denote this relation of ampliation, but now Suprt and the subscripts must be changed from (36):

(37) $\text{Cause}_t(\text{Travel}_{t-j,t}(x), \text{Travel}_{t,t+k}(y)) \ \& \ \text{Tch}_t(x, y) \equiv \text{Ampl}_t(x, y).$

Thus, the predicate for ampliation is introduced in much the same way as the predicate for holding, but the temporal relations are different, as the temporal subscripts indicate.

Because collisions have a temporal location, the predicate $\text{Event}_t(e)$ applies; that is to say, we can talk about them as "events" that occur at specifiable times. What we have called holding relations, on the other hand, may extend over much longer periods than can be integrated into the phenomenal present, so they do not always satisfy (33); the predicate Event does not usually apply. When we can use Event, the conceptual system will have a time index pointing to the moment of occurrence, so the time that various tests are to apply can be stated relative to that moment. In (37), for example, an instruction to test Cause might presuppose the definition of three indices: e is the collision at time t; e_1 is the motion of x prior to t; and e_2 is the motion of y subsequent to t. The first arguments of the relevant test instructions, therefore, can be stated simply as t, earlier than t, and later than t, respectively. That is, in calling for a perceptual test of the Cause relation between e_1 and e_2, the conceptual system does not have to specify explicit values for the constants j and k in (37). Thus, the routine might include instructions something like this:

      (i) find$(\text{Reg}(z), \text{Tch}(x, y))$ and call it e
    (ii) assign$(t, \text{time of } e)$
  (iii) test$(\text{earlier than } t, \text{Travel}(x))$
  (iv) test$(\text{later than } t, \text{Travel}(y))$

When the instruction to test$(t, \text{Cause}(e_1, e_2))$ is executed, therefore, the presupposed relations among the temporal indices will already have been confirmed. Our purpose in making the procedural representation of these time indices explicit is that later, when temporal indices required by the tense and aspect of verbs are discussed, it will be recognized that this machinery is not introduced merely as a linguistic convenience but is an essential component of the perceptual predicates themselves.

Not all causes are perceived, of course, and not all perceived causes are real. Obviously we are not concerned here with causes as scientists know them, or even with the objections Hume raised against the attribution of cause and effect when only co-occurrences are observed. The perception of one event as the cause of another is a psychological fact, unaffected by any doubt one may have about its scientific status or inductive basis. Perceived causes must be accounted for regardless of any more precise analysis such naive or "magical" impressions may undergo conceptually. For our present purposes it is necessary to make three points about perceived causes: (a) the perceived effect cannot precede the perceived cause in time; (b) the perceived cause must be spatially contiguous with the perceived effect; and (c) both the perceived cause and the perceived effect must be changes or events, not objects.

Depending on one's philosophical position, one might wish to add: (d) recognition of the relation of cause to effect must be acquired through prior experience. The difficulties with a strong version of (d) are well known; it is not obvious how any amount of exposure to perceptual causes and effects could lead inductively to a general concept of causation if human beings were not prepared in advance to make such an induction. A weaker form seems more plausible: the capacity to organize experience into cause-effect relations would be wasted if people were not exposed to consistent patterns of events that could be so organized. Fortunately, however, conditions (a)–(c) are sufficient to characterize the perceptual judgments; questions of their genesis need not be settled for our present purposes.

Conceptually, the temporal relation (a) between cause and effect is honored, but the spatial relation (b) is not; scientists long ago recognized that action can occur at a distance. One might argue that spatial contiguity is not necessary even for perceived causes: a child might perceive the throwing of a switch as causing a distant light to come on. Within the motional contexts used to define Cause in (36) and (37), however, spatial contiguity seems essential perceptually.

Since few topics have received more careful attention from philosophers of science than the concept of causation, it is important to be clear about the status we ascribe to Cause. Cause should not be confused with, say, some truth-functional operator of the predicate calculus, whose value could be determined from the truth values of the predicates it relates; the value of Cause must be determined by the perceptual act of looking at the events it takes as arguments and determining whether the event indicated in one argument is perceived as causing the other. Nor should Cause be confused with an instruction from the conceptual system to make something happen.

The perceptual predicate Cause means only that when two events are perceived in a certain way, a causal relation is seen between them. The validity of that perception is not to be settled by arguments about "real" causes. Indeed, in Michotte's experiments, no "real" causes were ever involved. Perhaps the concept of causation is deeply ingrained in the language as a consequence of the availability of this perceptual test. But for the present, we wish to emphasize that it is the percept, not the concept, that is intended by the predicate Cause. The *concept* of cause seems to imply that the state of the world would have been different if the antecedent event had not occurred, but are worlds-that-might-have-been perceptual objects? It seems unlikely that there are any purely perceptual criteria for determining whether causes really exist or are mere artifacts growing out of experience of invariable co-occurrence. In order to keep the perceptual and conceptual predicates typographically distinct, we will use CAUSE, rather than Cause, when the concept is intended.

We assume that Cause is transitive:

(38) $\text{Cause}(e_1, e_2) \ \& \ \text{Cause}(e_2, e_3) \supset \text{Cause}(e_1, e_3).$

If e_1 is perceived as causing e_2, and e_2 in turn is perceived as causing e_3, then e_1 is perceived as causing e_3. (We assume, of course, that all three events are included in the phenomenal present.) Moreover, we will assume that if some state of affairs S_1 implies some motion, or if some motion implies some state of affairs S_2, then we can substitute the one for the other:

(39) $(S_1 \supset e_1 \ \& \ \text{Cause}(e_1, e_2)) \supset \text{Cause}(S_1, e_2)$

(40) $(e_2 \supset S_2 \ \& \ \text{Cause}(e_1, e_2)) \supset \text{Cause}(e_1, S_2)$

Thus, Cause can take as arguments either perceived changes (or sequences of perceived changes) or states of affairs that imply such changes.

The most ubiquitous cause of perceived physical motion, of course, is gravity, but gravity cannot be included as a perceptual cause of motion. Aristotle, who knew nothing of gravity, saw objects seeking their natural places, either up or down. A heavy object will move downward until it comes to be supported by some other object, and there it will remain until something removes the support. Perceptually, what causes an object to fall is not gravity, but the removal of support. We can, therefore, consider perceptual predicates for prevention and permission:

(41) $\text{Prevent}(e_1, e_2) \equiv \text{Cause}(e_1, \text{not-}e_2)$

(42) $\text{Permit}(e_1, e_2) \equiv \text{notPrevent}(e_1, e_2)$

Although there seem to be no definitive experiments to show that the relations of prevention or permission can be perceptual judgments, some of Michotte's experiments on "releasing," and experiments by his colleagues on the perception of braking and removal of support, might be used to advance such an argument. We will include them here as perceptual judgments because they seem so closely related to the perception of causation, although it will be necessary in section 6.3 to promote them to the status of concepts. In any case, the predicates Prevent and Permit should not be confused with the senses these terms have in authority relations between persons.

2.6.3   Perceived Intentions

A particularly interesting question is how a person appreciates the cause of a voluntary motion by one of his own body parts. The question is important because so much of spatial perception depends on sensorimotor skills; for example, we have previously suggested that knowledge of your intention to move or to remain stationary contributes to your perception of the visual world as stationary. How should the perceived causal relation be represented in this instance?

A simple approach would be to substitute the name of a person as the first term in a causal relation. If John moves his hand voluntarily, we might describe the motion of his hand as an event that John caused: Cause(John, Travel(John's hand)), since we would normally think of animate objects as causing their own movements. This notation, however, provides no simple way to describe motions of his hand that John might cause involuntarily, and it is inconsistent with our earlier assumption that the perceptual predicate Cause is not defined for objects but only for perceptual changes (or states of affairs that imply perceptual changes). That is to say, such a description would require a different definition of Cause from the one we proposed in 2.6.2.

An alternative approach would be to introduce intention as an explicit predicate describing some internal state of affairs that can entail certain events and so, by (39), could serve as the first term for the perceptual predicate Cause. We have already noted that some way of handling intention is needed in order to account for such dynamic perceptual phenomena as the impression that one spot of light is chasing another with the presumed intention of catching it; an intentional predicate might serve both purposes. In adopting this approach, however, we must repeat all the disclaimers we made above for the predicate Cause. That is, we will be concerned here only with the perception of intentionality; the corresponding concept requires much deeper analysis.

Most English verbs of motion do not imply intention, so for our purposes it might be tempting to ignore it entirely. In the sentence "John moved," for example, no claim is made that he did so intentionally, and in such sentences as "The wind moved the curtains" it would seem odd to ask whether it was intentional or not. There are motion verbs, however, that do imply intention— "chase" is a good example. It would be redundant to say "John chased the burglar intentionally." And, of course, there are all those adverbs—voluntarily, deliberately, inadvertently, accidentally, intentionally, for example—that demand some kind of psychological grounds for their semantic analysis. We will have to face the issue eventually in any case.

In favor of introducing an intentional predicate for describing our perception of voluntary movements is the fact that people not only perceive most of their own motions as intentional but normally perceive other people as intending to achieve various goals or to bring about various states of affairs, not merely as moving their body parts about. People attribute intentions to other people even when they are uncertain what their intentions were; they assume they had *some* intention, and try to infer from their behavior what it could have been. One reason they ascribe intentions to others is that they perceive their own movements that way—as actions rather than mere movements.

There is a clear difference between announcing one's own intentions and ascribing intentions to others. An intentional statement involving oneself as agent is usually a description of one's state of mind at the time of the statement; an intentional statement about another person's intentions has more of the character of an explanation for predictions of his future behavior. It would involve some kind of intellectual leap, therefore, to use the same intentional predicate in both cases. To say that one makes the leap from himself to others because that is the way he sees himself sounds very similar to the "argument from analogy" for the existence of other minds, a venerable argument that has been under strong attack in recent years (Malcolm, 1963, 1971), so a word of explanation is in order.

We are not arguing here for the existence of other minds but for the existence of other persons. Some innate awareness of the similarities between oneself and others does not seem to us, on evolutionary grounds, to be an extravagant claim. Every species (for obvious biological reasons) has some mechanism for recognizing other members of its own kind; the interest displayed by human infants in the appearance of the human face and the sound of the human voice indicates that human beings have not been neglected in this respect. So a primitive concept of what human beings are and do is probably given to every normal person very early in life; the person concept is, like the self concept, a cultural universal (Hallowell, 1958). It is not necessary to discover what a person is by observing ourselves and then reasoning by analogy from ourselves to the existence of other persons.

We assume that "person" is a psychologically primitive, unanalyzable concept, and that intentional predicates must take persons as their first argument —other persons as well as oneself. In this way we hope to avoid such claims as that intentions describe mental states controlling bodily movements, with all the attendant problems of how to justify ascribing anything to minds other than one's own, or how immaterial minds could control material bodies. Strawson (1958) has argued that there are predicates, and intention would be one of them, that people apply to others on the basis of behavioral criteria, and to themselves without the use of behavioral criteria. If people did not use and understand such predicates, there would be no body-mind problem for philosophers to debate, and there would be no need for the concept of persons to stand as the subject of such predicates. In short, we accept Strawson's position that "we should acknowledge the logical primitiveness of the concept of a person and, with this, the unique logical character of certain predicates" (p. 352). The use of such predicates is not the result of some intellectual decision made in the history of Western thought, or achieved by children reflecting on their experience with certain animate beings, but is inherent in the very nature of human perceptual processes.

Moreover, there is good reason to think that the perception of intentions is not a uniquely human achievement. Students of animal behavior refer to such ritualized actions as baring the fangs, crouching in anger, and so on, as "intention movements" that are interpreted as signals by other animals. Indeed, some theorists have speculated that such intention movements, once they can be performed outside their original behavioral contexts, constitute initial elements for the development of symbolic communication leading ultimately to human language. Of course, the lack of any satisfactory theory of linguistic evolution has always been an embarrassment for evolutionary theory, so these speculations may represent little more than attempts to make the descent of man seem more plausible. Even if we discount them as linguistic antecedents, however, intention movements do serve as signals to control the social behavior of animals, and thus we should not assume that perception of the intentions of others is a highly specialized skill that presupposes some uniquely human development of conceptual intelligence.

Probably humans can appreciate a wider variety of intentional signals, but in all cases the basic distinction seems to be between affiliative and agonistic, good intentions and bad intentions. That is to say, there is usually an affective context to one's perception of the intent of others. Affect may be associated with any percept, of course, but positive and negative expectations seem to provide basic categories for perceived intentions. Once the other person's intention has been generally assessed as helpful, neutral, or threatening, this assessment will color the perception of his intentions with respect to the various constituent acts in his larger pattern of behavior.

The perceptual evidence, of course, is largely provided by movements. Insofar as observers organize those movements into behavioral events, they perceive them as acts. They attribute intent to those acts in terms of the objectives they believe the actor hopes to achieve. If they regard his objective as agonistic to themselves, they usually attribute bad intentions to him; if they regard his objective as beneficial to themselves, they usually attribute good intentions to him. Thus, perceived intentions provide a classification system for acts and their imputed objectives.

What stimulus conditions underlie this classification? How a person holds himself, whether he stares directly at you, whether he approaches on a straight line or by a slightly indirect path, his facial expressions and tone of voice, his gestures and other expressive movements, how close he stands—all these and more signal his intentions. But precisely the same actions can be perceived as affiliative in one context and agonistic in another. If he gives you signals of friendship, he may be trying to catch you off guard. If he says "How are you?" he is interested in your health and may hope to learn you are dying of cancer. And so on. It is because they are so susceptible to multiple interpretations that perceptions of intent seem so different from perceptions of concrete objects and their attributes. It is not the validity of perceptions of intent, however, that is at issue here. Right or wrong, the perceived intention is an integral part of the perception of the other person and his actions.

Given this defense of our introduction of intentional predicates into perceptual theory, we still face the task of deciding how to formulate them in a predicate notation. Let us survey some of the possibilities, disregarding, for the moment, our preoccupation with perceptual grounds for such judgments. We might represent the perception, say, that John moved his hand intentionally as Intend(John, Travel(John's hand)). It is possible, however, that John intended to move his hand but then changed his mind and therefore the intended motion did not occur. One difficulty with ascriptions of intent, of course, is that we seem to have no way to validate them independently of their effects, but it is certainly possible that John might intend at time t to do something at time $t + i$, yet fail to do it when $t + i$ arrives.

A conjunctive representation, along the lines of Intend(John, Travel(hand)) & Cause(John, Travel(hand)) would avoid the implication that what was intended was done, since we could simply delete the causal predicate involving the motion when it did not occur. But this is clearly a step backward. Not only are we still misusing Cause, as noted above, but we have separated the intention and the event completely; the notation does not indicate that the motion of his hand that John intended was actually the motion of his hand that John caused.

These formulations also omit the purpose of the action. Suppose that the movement of John's hand involves the contraction of his biceps. Do we say that John intentionally contracted his biceps? The answer depends on the purpose of the movement. If John was displaying the size of his muscles, the contraction would be primary and the motion of his hand would be derivative;

if John was scratching his nose, the motion of his hand would be primary and the contraction of his biceps would be derivative. In short, there must be some context into which the intentional action fits before an observer can decide whether a particular instance is a purposive intention or a derived intention. It is just such distinctions that the ascription of intentions should clarify. We need some way to say what an intention is about, what its objective is—which may or may not be identical with what actually occurs.

Meiland (1970) lists a variety of objectives that intentions can have. The objective of an intention may be an action by the agent himself, as when John intends to scratch his nose. Or it may be an event, as when John intends to be elected to public office. Or it may be a state of affairs, as when John intends to keep a supply of ink in his desk drawer. Or it may even be an action by another person, as when John intends to persuade Jane to do something. Yet even though the objectives of an intention may include things other than the agent's own actions, the agent must intend to do something that he believes will play a role in achieving his objective.

It might seem, therefore, that we need at least three arguments for an intentional predicate: Intend(person, action, goal), perhaps with time subscripts to indicate when he intended, when he intended to act, and when he intended to achieve his objective. Intend would be interpreted to mean that the person intended to perform the action because he believed that the action would help to bring about his objective. For example, Intend(John, Travel(his hand), Scratch(his nose)) might mean that John intended to move his hand because he believed that moving his hand would help him scratch his nose. More difficulties lie in this direction, however, since it is perfectly possible to imagine that John intended to scratch his nose but did not intend to move his hand—he intended to ask Marilyn to scratch it for him, or to rub it against his knee. His intention to achieve his objective need not commit him to intending any particular action more than various others. The relation between intended objectives and actions instrumental in bringing those objectives about is enormously complex, as centuries of discussion about the relation between means and ends will testify.

Intention is notoriously difficult to explicate; any formulation we propose is sure to have defects of one kind or another. The problem has been discussed extensively by philosophers interested in the theory of action (Anscombe, 1957; Melden, 1961; Rescher, 1967; Mischel, 1969; Brand, 1970; and many others) and by psychologists interested in the difference between molecular and molar description of behavior (for example, Tolman, 1932; Miller, Galanter, and Pribram, 1960). We are concerned here, however, only with perceived intentions. People perceive themselves and others as doing some things intentionally, others accidentally; they perceive intentional actions in a context of attributed goals and subgoals, even when those attributions may be logically indefensible or actually false. Apparently the perceptual system makes judgments of causation and intention that the conceptual system, in its analytic mode, cannot accept as valid criteria for the attribution of causality or intentionality. Regardless of how such perceptual judgments may be rationalized conceptually, the fact that people make them can be ignored by psychologists only at great peril. They not only make them, they entrust the planning and direction of their personal lives to their highly questionable validity.

We propose the notation

(43)   *Intend*(person, goal)

to mean that the person identified in the first argument intends to bring about the objective described in the second. We assume that his intention implies that he must do something, so his intention to bring his main objective about implies his intention to take some action that he believes will advance his purpose. Carrying out this action establishes a subgoal that the person intends to bring about on his way to the main goal. The same argument repeated establishes subsubgoals that the person intends to achieve, and so on. The regress can, we assume, continue back into a biomolecular level that neither we nor the person involved understands. The underlying structure can be viewed as a hierarchically organized plan for bringing the objective about, and when the person carries out or executes his intention he sets in train a sequence of causally related events that he believes will help to achieve his goal. Since we have no way to characterize that sequence of causally related events in any detail, we will adopt the convention of representing it by the intention that created it. Thus, *Intend*(John, scratch his nose) is both an intention to achieve a particular objective and, implicitly, an intended sequence of events. Execution of the intention, therefore, causes various events to occur:

(44)   Cause(*Intend*(John, scratch his nose), Travel(his hand)).

Why John adopted this plan rather than some other for achieving his objective is, we believe, irrelevant to the perception that he acted as he did (whatever he did) in order to bring about the objective attributed to him as his intention.

The formulation in (44) involves all three terms: person, action, objective. *Intend* is a relation between person and objective that implies action; Cause is a relation between *Intend* and action that holds when the intention is carried out, and thus results in the perceived movements. And, we hope, this formulation is as applicable to oneself as to others, that is to say, it is the type of predicate that can be applied to persons in general. In this respect, *Intend* is similar to *Perceive*, and we have marked its special status by italics.

How could all this be represented in procedural terms? Consider first the case in which someone is "perceiving" his own actions. We assume that intentional movements are instigated by some higher-order routine. In order to represent this assumption, we must introduce an instruction "achieve," which, when given a description of a goal, will try to make that description true. How an instruction to achieve(goal) goes about its task is a vast topic; we assume that something like a General Problem Solver (Newell and Simon, 1972) or a store of recipes for action as Winograd (1971) utilizes in a PLANNER formulation is available to implement "achieve." Execution of an instruction to achieve some described goal will cause the system to devise a plan for doing it. If the goal is to scratch one's nose, then it is highly probable that a subgoal will be created by an instruction to achieve(Tch(nose, hand)), which will initiate movement of the hand to the nose.

We assume that control instructions can deploy various motor commands: move(x, y), where x is a body part and y a destination; grasp(y), which presumes a hand and gives y as a pointer to the target; applyforceto (x, y) where body part x applies force to some object indexed by y; ingest(y), where y points to something to be taken into the body; expel(y), where y points to something to be pushed out of the body; and perhaps others. These motoric components of the control instructions are necessary if the system is not to be forever lost in thought, and they may provide a psychological basis for concepts incorporated in such English verbs as "touch," "move," "grasp," "throw," "eat," "exhale," and so on (Schank, 1973a). We will not pursue these efferent instructions here, since they seem to have a different formal status from the perceptual predicates that are our central concern. But we assume that they must play a central role in any sensorimotor schemata that support perception.

Given that "achieve" can initiate movements of various kinds, let us focus on the hierarchical structure of the plan for achieving a goal. As a movement occurs, it will be perceived as a consequence of the next-higher goal instruction. That is, if someone were to ask, "Why did you move your hand?" you could reply, "In order to touch my nose." If he then asked, "Why did you touch your nose?" you would probably reply, "In order to scratch it." And if he persisted long enough to ask, "Why did you scratch your nose?" you could reply, "Because it itched," which would be understood to mean that you had perceived something undesirable about your nose and had initiated a routine to change that perception. The questions stop here.

In order to answer such questions, you must be able to execute some such instruction as find(plan, goal such that achieve(goal) led to e), where the search domain, "plan," is the general routine the system is executing, e is a pointer to the action whose occurrence is questioned, and "goal" is the description given in the immediately higher "achieve" instruction in the plan. In short, in order to determine a reason for e, search the plan you are pursuing to find the immediate goal that e was expected to achieve. Since the general plan must be somehow available if you are to follow it, such a "find" instruction should not be difficult to execute. It should be noted, however, that the domain of search for the "find" instruction is not some region of the perceptual world but is internal to the system itself. Thus it sounds odd to say, "I perceived my intention to move my hand"; the direct statement that "I intended to move my hand" reflects your nonperceptual access to the plan you are executing. "I perceived his intention to move his hand" is far less odd, however.

Although you do not need to "perceive" your own immediate intentions when making voluntary movements, *Intend* is the kind of predicate that can be applied to others on the basis of your perception of their behavior. When another person x does something e, therefore, your efforts to discover his reason will lead to the execution of some such instruction as find(model of x, value of goal such that achieve(goal) led to e). This is formally very similar to the "find" instruction we suggested for determining your own reasons, but with a different domain of search. The "model of x" is a poorly defined search domain, but we use this phrase to suggest that the search must take into account not only what the person is doing at the moment but any other information you may have about him. If he is an old friend, you may already have a highly complicated model of him including information about the kinds of goals he frequently attempts to achieve; this information will influence your speculations about his immediate goal in doing e. If he is a total stranger, you may have to construct your model of him on the spur of the moment, with no specific evidence about him other than the evidence his appearance and current behavior provide.

Whatever the source of the model, this "find" instruction will institute a search for a goal description having the characteristics that it is consonant with the model of the person and that achieve(goal) would, directly or indirectly, lead to the observed behavior. You can try first any goals that you believe to be important to the person. If that source produces nothing satisfactory, you can execute an instruction to generate(goal), which will—again by conceptual operations beyond the scope of this discussion—provide other goal descriptions that you can try. This "generate" instruction should be easy to execute, because it must be used constantly to formulate descriptions of the goals and subgoals that guide your own behavior. Given any goal description, remembered or generated, you then explore the consequences of giving that goal description to an "achieve" instruction. That is, you execute an achieve(goal) instruction but block all motor responses; you exit whenever a subgoal is found that, if executed, would lead to e. You may test several goals in this manner and try to estimate which goal that leads to e is most probable in the light of your model of x.

This process as described is, of course, highly conceptual. If diligently pursued, such a search could consume hours of careful thought. Surely this is not what is meant when you say you can perceive another's intentions. To suggest that all this consideration goes into the impression that one dot of light intends to escape another or that an animal must execute such routines in order to interpret another animal's intention movements seems absurd.

Suppose we look at the system we have been describing in terms of its input and output. Given a goal description as input, the system generates either a subgoal or an action as output. At the more molecular levels of behavior, where actions occur, there must be enormous familiarity with these goal-action relations; psychologists interested in motor skills have studied in detail how people learn to make their actions more appropriate to the goals they are given. When you want to scratch your nose, you seldom need to devise some elaborate plan to achieve it; years of experience make the appropriate action for achieving that goal automatic. It is appropriate to think of these frequently repeated goal-action sequences as preprogrammed units available to the skilled individual and to speak of them as habits (see theorems in PLANNER; Winograd, 1971).

As some psychologists have used the term, "habit" might suggest that the behavioral units can be thought of as an automatic association between stimulus and response. That is not at all what we wish to propose. The goal is not a stimulus, and the response needed to achieve a particular goal will differ given different initial conditions. Scratching your nose is not a fixed motor response to a nose-tickling stimulus; the response will differ depending on whether you start with your hands in your pockets or holding a book. Henry Head (see Bartlett, 1932, chap. 10) long ago recognized that the brain is not a storehouse of unrelated habitual movements; Head spoke of a constantly changing postural model of the body, which he called a schema, against which subsequent movements are measured before they occur. Moreover, it is not the tickle stimulus that "causes" the response, but your intention to alter your perception of your nose, to change the tickle. In speaking of these goal-action relations as habits, therefore, we assume something considerably more complicated than many psychologists have hoped would be necessary. We take it as a general rule that behavior can be explained only in terms of its goals.

This complexity is not incompatible with the assumption that many goal-subgoal and goal-action relations are highly practiced, until people learn to "see" the goal as part of the action itself. People build a general model of human behavior sufficiently explicit at the level of simple acts that they can execute instructions to find(in perception of behavior, value of goal such that achieve(goal) led to e). By taking a brief perceptual sample of what a person is doing—perhaps noting the context and two or three actions in sequence— you can usually identify his goal.

How are goals to be characterized? If behavior is always intended to maintain certain perceptual conditions invariant, then goals can be characterized in terms of perceptual predicates. For example, instead of saying that John's goal is to scratch his nose, we could say that his goal is to perceive his nose as not itching. In general, (43) could be written: Intend(person, Perceive(person, x)), where x is a description of his objective phrased in terms of perceptual predicates. However, since we have followed the notational tactic of omitting Perceive as redundant, this becomes simply Intend(person, x), where the objective x is characterized in terms of perception rather than action. Similarly, the goal argument of the achieve instruction can also be characterized by a perceptual specification.

Since objectives are usually related hierarchically, an observer may not immediately appreciate another person's full intentions on the basis of a perception of his initial moves in some behavioral episode. But the observer can appreciate subobjectives and ascribe intentions to the initial moves—often quite incorrectly, to be sure—even before he knows what those actions are ultimately leading to. Judgments of intent are often wrong, of course, because people do not have the same access to the intentions of others that they have to their own. The point at issue here, however, does not concern either the particular or the general validity of perceptual judgments of intent, but rather the psychological fact that the perception of the movements of other people constantly involves such teleological judgments.

Some theorists might find it attractive to explore an even closer connection between the perception of intent and the perception of cause. For example, if the perception of intent has its ontogenesis in the observed correlation between one's own intention to move and the resulting movement of one's body or body part, it is not unreasonable to suppose that this might also be the origin of one's conception of causation. Initially, causation might be simply the relation between an intention to achieve some perception and the resultant movement. Generalization to other persons would be automatic. Subsequently, however, this causative relation might also be generalized to admit other arguments when movements of inanimate objects were observed. If F denotes the early, undifferentiated relation between goal and event, $F(\text{goal}, e_2)$, subsequent observations would necessitate a differentiation of F into $\text{Cause}(e_1, e_2)$ when no agent was present and $\text{Cause}(Intend, e_2)$ when there was an agent.

2.7 PROCESSES UNDERLYING PERCEPTION

We have been concentrating on the contents of perceptual experience; the person doing the perceiving has been kept largely in the background. This emphasis is, in a sense, antipsychological; it is the behaving, experiencing organism that provides the proper subject matter for psychological investigations.

Our reason for concentrating on the content rather than the process of perception is that the content provides a referent for linguistic identification. It is obvious, however, that the uses of language are not confined solely to labeling objects and events. Although much of what people say to one another concerns things and events that are perceivable, or have perceivable aspects, they are not struck dumb when more complex relations and processes capture their attention. Even the sentence "I see the moon" demands some account of "I" and "see" as well as of the definite reference to a particular perceptual content. A consideration of perceptual processes, therefore, is not an empty gesture intended to put perceptual contents into better psychological perspective. The processes themselves can be objects of verbal reference, so the system must have some way of evaluating not only contents but also its own relation to those contents.

Thus far we have introduced only two predicates, *Perceive* and *Intend*, that take "person" as an argument. *Perceive*(person, x) was introduced on page 31, but our discussion focused primarily on aspects of x that could be attended to and judged, and only secondarily on the system that attends and judges. In section 2.6 *Intend*(person, x) was introduced, but again the discussion focused mainly on x. Since "person" is otherwise an undefined term, all we have said so far is that a person is the kind of thing that can perceive objects and events and can intend to achieve certain objectives.

The most obvious oversight in this list, of course, is a predicate to express the fact that a person can store information and retrieve it for later use. Let us add, therefore, *Remember*(person, x), where x can range over the contents of the person's memory (just as, in *Perceive*(person, x), x can range over the contents of the person's perceptual world). At various points in the preceding pages it became obvious that some kind of perceptual memory must integrate the phenomenal present and support the perception of change in general and motion in particular, but no special notice was taken of these facts; we tucked them into perception under the name of perceptual memory. That is to say, we assumed that the memory involved in perception was short-term and required little more than memory buffers in or near the receptors in order to store perceptual contents long enough for them to be processed by the higher centers of the brain. If we had said more about perceptual recognition, it would have become clear that much more memory is needed in order to store some record of previous perceptions in such a form as to make them comparable with present perceptions. And, the most glaring omission of all, we simply took for granted memory for all the different routines that we assume a person can acquire and execute.

In order to put *Remember* on a par with *Perceive* and *Intend*, we should indicate what control instructions the conceptual system has available for manipulating remembered contents. This account would be at least as extensive as that for *Perceive*, since much is known about the processes of human learning and forgetting. We will discuss *Remember* in chapter 3, but even there we will not go into details. For the moment we wish merely to add it to our list of psychological predicates that must support perception; we assume that all of the control instructions we have mentioned for manipulating the contents of our perceptions and intentions are also available for manipulating the contents of memory.

What further predicates of this type do we require? We claim that this list is almost complete. In order to talk about an information-processing system, we have to talk about its inputs, outputs, and memory. *Perceive, Intend,* and *Remember* correspond to these three subsystems. Everything else is just a description of routines for transforming information in these various subsystems.

If this claim seems too strong, consider some candidates for addition to the list. Since a person can pay attention selectively, what about some centering process like *Attend*? This predicate seems unnecessary if we are allowed an instruction "find" which the central processor can use to control the system. What about some decision-making predicate like *Judge*? Here we already have the instruction "test." What about a behavioral predicate to *Do* something, or an introspective predicate to *Imagine* something? For these we already have the control instructions "achieve" and "generate." What about a cognitive predicate *Think*? The entire system does that, so we cannot identify it with any particular instructions. It will be useful, however, to introduce a concept of knowledge, *Know*(person, *x*), since in ordinary language people frequently claim to "know" certain facts when they can provide no grounds for their knowledge. We assume that *Know* can find grounds in *Perceive, Intend,* and *Remember,* but it leaves open the possibility of as yet unknown sources of knowledge (see 7.4.5).

Why do we take *Perceive, Intend, Remember,* and the generic predicate *Know* as one category of predicates, and the control instructions "find," "test," "assign," "achieve," and "generate" as another category? Since this distinction will be respected in what follows, we will try to be explicit about it.

If we approach the person as an information-processing system, we will try to define as simple and basic a set of control instructions as possible in order to characterize the processing that the system does; the set just listed, plus a few more that we will introduce as needed, represents our choice of the basic order code in terms of which processing will be described. The control instructions represent commands that the central processor can attempt to execute, and so we assume they are under voluntary control. *Perceive, Intend,* and *Remember,* on the other hand, are not instructions that the central processor can execute; they denote relations of the system to the sources of information on which its central processor can operate. That is to say, we can sit a person down at a window and ask him to find a tree and test whether it has green leaves, but we cannot ask him to *Perceive* something that is not there —a battleship, say, or Napoleon. He perceives what he can and, whatever it is, it provides the information for processing, the values to which indices can be assigned. Similarly, the central processor cannot have an instruction to *Remember* Napoleon or a battleship, although it can have an instruction to find in memory any information that may be stored under those concepts and test it for this or that characteristic. He remembers what he can and, whatever it is, it provides values to which indices can be assigned. Again, *Intend* is something a person does, but it is not a control instruction; we can ask a person to achieve some goal and, if he is cooperative, he may try, but we do not instruct him to intend to achieve the goal. *Intend* provides a data structure to which the processor can assign pointers, but the decision to intend or not to intend at any given moment is not under processing control. In short, instructions can control *what* information is perceived or remembered, or *what* goals are intended, but they cannot control the fact that perceiving, remembering, and intending occur.

We said that this list was almost complete. The information-processing system that emerges from these remarks is fearfully cognitive and dispassionate. It can collect information, remember it, and work toward objectives, but it would have no emotional reaction to what it collected, remembered, or achieved. Since in this respect it is a poor model of a person, we should add at least one more predicate to the list of those that take "person" as their first argument. We will use *Feel*(person, *x*) to indicate that people have feelings as well as perceptions, memories, and intentions. It might be possible to subsume *Feel* under *Perceive* on the grounds that our feelings are a special class of perceptions of inner states. Or we might discuss feelings under *Remember;*

the recognition that some word or object is familiar is, after all, a matter of feeling a certain way about it. Or, since we have already recognized that there is a strong affective component to our intentions, we might link *Feel* to *Intend*. Moreover, much of our speech expresses or inspires emotions; a complete account of the psychological foundations of language would have to treat *Feel* in considerable detail. All of these considerations testify to the systematic importance of this psychological predicate.

Nevertheless, we will have little to say about *Feel* in the following pages. Our central interest is in the relation between perception and language and in the information processing they entail. Feelings do not respond to control instructions in the same way that perceptions, memories, or intentions do. It has been claimed that a major weakness of psychological theories deriving from the study of information-processing systems is that these systems do not provide any adequate way to represent the emotional forces that are such an important part of human life. Since we have not attempted to analyze this question in any detail, we must suspend judgment. It is obvious, however, that *Feel* is an indispensable predicate for any complete psychology and that it probably lies much closer than *Perceive, Remember*, and *Intend* to the basic sources of energy that keep the whole system running. If it were impossible to incorporate such a predicate into our theory, that fact would stand as an extremely serious criticism of the whole approach. In these pages, however, we have more than enough to employ us already, and therefore we leave the issue open.

We have now indicated the first step involved in taking seriously the idea that linguistic knowledge can be reduced to associations between words and percepts; we have developed an illustrative list of perceptual predicates that the system can evaluate. In order to give an empiricistic account the benefit of every doubt, we have included such abstract things as causes and intentions as perceptual predicates; we have provided mechanisms (via "find," "test," "achieve") to control the application of those predicates; and we have even allowed the system to reflect (via *Perceive, Intend, Remember, Know, Feel*) on its own operations. The next step is to consider how these predicates, or appropriate combinations of these predicates, might be associated with linguistic labels.

2.8   SUMMARY OF NOTATIONS

In the following chapters we will attempt to use the various perceptual predicates introduced in this chapter as a basis for object-recognition routines whose outputs can be taken as criteria for the applicability of linguistic labels. For convenience of reference, the various predicates and other notations that we have chosen are listed here in alphabetical order, along with an English paraphrase of their general sense and the number of the section in which they are discussed.

First, the predicates denoting attentional-judgmental abstractions that are possible for the perceptual system:

Above(x, y)	x is higher than y.	2.3, 2.3.1
Adjcnt(x, y)	The distance from x to y is zero.	2.3
Ampl(x, y)	Motion of x is transferred to y (ampliation).	2.6.2
Before(x, y)	x is in front of the moving object y.	2.3.4
Behind(x, y)	x is in back of the moving object y.	2.3.4
Below(x, y)	x is lower than y.	2.3.1
Betw(x, y, z)	y is between x and z.	2.3
Bottom(x, y)	x has the lowermost part y.	2.3.1
Bound(x, y)	x has boundary y.	2.2.3
Cause(e, e')	Event e causes event e'.	2.6.2
Chng(x)	x is changing.	2.5.2
Cnvx(x)	x is convex.	2.2.2
Colr(x)	x is a color.	2.2.3
Colr(x, y)	x has the color y.	2.2.3
Conn(x)	x is connected.	2.2.2
Conn(x, y)	x is connected to y.	2.2.2
Cont(x)	x is a container.	2.2.2
Cross(x, y)	x and y intersect.	2.2.3
Cube(x)	x is a cube.	2.2.2
Deform(x)	x is changing shape.	2.5.3
Dir(x, y, z)	The direction from x to y is z.	2.3.4
Disc(x, y)	x is discrete from y.	2.2.2
Edge(x, y)	x has the edge y.	2.2.3
Event(e)	e is an event.	2.5.2
Exsurf(x, y)	x has the exterior surface y.	2.2.3
Exten(x, y)	x has the extension y.	2.2.3
Face(x, y)	x has the face y.	2.2.3
Flat(x)	x is flat.	2.2.3
Flface(x, y)	x has the flat face y.	2.2.3
Greater(x, y)	x is greater than y.	1.2
Hold(x, y)	If x moves, y moves with it.	2.6.2
Horiz(x)	x is horizontal.	2.3
Ident(x, y)	x is the same thing as y.	2.2.2
Incl(x, y)	x is included spatially in y.	2.3
Indent(x, y)	x has the indentation y.	2.2.3
Inline(x, y, z)	x, y, and z lie in a straight line.	2.2.3
Inquad(w, x, y, z)	w, x, y, and z are corners of a quadrilateral.	2.2.3
Intri(x, y, z)	Lines connecting x, y, and z form a triangle.	2.2.3

Intsurf(x, y)	x has the interior surface y.	2.2.3
Later(t, t')	Moment t is later than moment t'.	2.4
Line(x)	x is a line.	2.2.3
Magn(x)	x is a magnitude.	2
Magn(x, y)	x has the subjective magnitude y.	1.2
Obj(x, 3d)	x is a three-dimensional object.	2.2.1
Orient(x)	x is an orientation.	2.5.3
Orient(x, y)	x has the orientation y.	2.5.3
Osten(x, y)	x is pointing toward y.	2.3.4
Over(x, y)	x is vertically above y.	2.3
Parallel(x, y)	x and y are parallel.	2.2.3
Part(x, y)	x has the part y.	2.2.2
Path(x, ρ)	x travels along the path ρ.	2.5.2
Permit(e, e')	Event e permits event e' to occur.	2.6.2
Place(x)	x is a location.	2.2.1
Place(x, y)	x has the location y.	2.2.1, 2.3.3
Pprt(x, y)	x has the proper part y.	2.2.2
Prevent(e, e')	Event e prevents event e' from occurring.	2.6.2
Qual(x)	x is a subjective quality.	2
Qual(x, y)	x has the subjective quality y.	1.2
Red(x)	x is red.	2
Reg(x, y)	y is the characteristic region of interaction with x.	2.3
Rot(x)	x is changing orientation (rotating).	2.5.3
$S_t(x)$	x is in the state S at the moment t.	2.5.2
Sep(x, y)	x is not touching y.	2.3
Shap(x)	x is a shape.	2.2.1
Shap(x, y)	x has the shape y.	2.2.1, 2.3.3
Shdw(x, y)	x casts a shadow on y.	2.3
Simlr(x, y)	x is perceptually similar to y.	1.2, 2.2.3
Size(x)	x is a size.	2.2.1
Size(x, y)	x has the size y.	2.2.1
Small(x)	x is small.	2
Space(x, y)	The space between x and y is unoccupied.	2.3
Spot(x)	x is a spot.	2.2.3
Stedge(x, y)	x has the straight edge y.	2.2.3
Stline(x)	x is a straight line.	2.2.3
Straight(x)	x is straight.	2.2.3
Suprt(x, y)	x supports y.	2.3
Surf(x, y)	x has the (total) surface y.	2.2.3

Tch(x, y)	x is touching y.	2.3
Time(e, t)	Event e occurs at the moment t.	2.5.2
Top(x, y)	x has the uppermost part y.	2.3.1
Travel(x)	x is changing location.	2.5.2
Vert(x)	x is vertical.	2.3

Although it is intuitively obvious from these paraphrases that not every percept can serve as an argument for every predicate, we have made only a preliminary and inadequate classification of arguments: e indexes events and t indexes moments, but $x, y, z, \ldots$, are used to index a variety of objects, attributes, motions, and so on. A more ambitious attempt to characterize perceptual theory would certainly introduce a more systematic classification of variables, but we will rely on context and the reader's intuition to enable us to keep our formal machinery to a bare minimum.

In addition to the predicates listed above, a number of symbols were introduced for particular concepts:

Dist(x, y)	distance from x to y	2.3
Dset(α, β)	matrix of distances from each member of the set α to each member of the set β	2.3.3
d	degree of similarity	2.2.3
e	index for an event	2.5.2
earth	horizontal base of reference	2.3.1
eye	the observer's viewing point	2.3
goal	objective to be achieved	2.6.3
light	a point source of light	2.3
n	index for the present moment (now)	2.4
person	a human being	2.6.3
Reg(x)	region of interaction with x	2.3
t	index for a discrete moment of time	2.4
$x, y, z, \ldots$	indices assigned to perceptual contents	2.2.1
π	set of all proper parts of an object	2.3.3
ρ	path of a moving object	2.5.2
σ	set of all stationary objects in the visual field	2.3.3

Finally, there are five psychological predicates underlying the perceptual processes:

Feel(person, x)	A person feels x.	2.7
Intend(person, x)	A person intends to achieve x.	2.6.3
Know(person, x)	A person knows x.	2.7
Perceive(person, x)	A person perceives x.	2
Remember(person, x)	A person remembers x.	2.7

Notations denoting various control instructions whereby the conceptual system can direct the operation of the perceptual system were also introduced. Those instructions are a central concern of chapter 3. We will postpone an inventory, therefore, until a fuller discussion has been provided.

3

Routines: A Fragment of Conceptual Theory

Saying that we always come to know the existence of individual objects through sense-perception is like saying that one comes to London from New York by bus when what one means is that one flies over and then takes a bus to London from the airport.
—*Jaakko Hintikka (1973)*

How are objects related to the words that name them? One's naive impression is that the relation is direct and immediate. There are aboriginal societies where a person keeps his true name a secret because it could be used to harm him. Young children may say a needle is called "needle" because it is sharp; "snake" is a long word because snakes are long; "rose" is as much a part of the flower as its scent. The sensorimotor pattern of uttering the name may seem to a child as much a part of that object as any other sensorimotor pattern contributing to his schema for the object. The idea that labels are arbitrary, that a rose by any other name would smell as sweet, requires sophistication about words and things. The more sophisticated one becomes, the more complicated the relation appears.

The absence of direct, tangible connections between physical objects and the acoustic patterns used as names for them is a foundation assumption for studies of linguistic meaning. The alternative is that words are magical. Any linguistic association between sound and substance must be mediated by a nervous system complex enough to learn the association.

The conceptual distance separating word and object can be reduced if we take a more proximal definition of the relation between them—replace the physical object by a perception of it, and replace the acoustic pattern by behavioral processes required to say it or by perceptual processes involved in hearing it. Those substitutions at least admit the nervous system as the mediating agency.

How much this maneuver reduces the conceptual distance from word to referent has inspired considerable disagreement. On one side are optimists who see the remaining distance as short indeed, hardly more than one might find between the stimulus and response of a conditioned reflex. At the other extreme are pessimists who see an intervening conceptual system of such complexity that they despair of finding any path of determinate length between perception and language. We ourselves are closer to the pessimists.

To revert to an earlier example, how does "lamp" come to be associated with lamps? Can we take seriously the claim that children are conditioned to utter "Lamp" by pairing lamps as the unconditioned discriminative stimulus with reinforcement for an appropriate vocalization? This approach might be used to explain why people say "Lamp" when they see a lamp, although people seldom do. It would not explain how "lamp" becomes incorporated into the communication system that we call language.

A corollary of the view that words are learned more or less automatically by virtue of repeated association between their vocalization and visually perceived things is the assumption that those things *are* the meanings of the vocalizations; that the meaning of "lamp" *is* the set of objects to which conditioned individuals will, under appropriate conditions, give the vocal response "lamp." To know this meaning is to be able to give the response. But how can such a theory account for words like "the" or "of" or "if"? No doubt people can be conditioned to make particular responses to particular stimuli. But a word is part of a linguistic system of great flexibility and complexity. One who holds that words are conditioned responses must explain how they differ from other responses a person can be conditioned to make. An associative account must be sufficiently complex to admit the use of those associations in linguistic communication. When this task is taken seriously, problems appear that are of a different order of difficulty from the phenomena that conditioning theory is intended to explain: How do children get the concept of labeling, or learn that labels are related in many ways and play various roles in sentences? How do they learn to interpret novel combinations of words, or understand predication, or appreciate truth and falsehood? How does the theory explain the variety of well-formed sentences? Faced with problems of this complexity, the notion that language is a process of associating vocal noises with perceptual stimuli seems too simple; even Pavlov recognized the need for a "second signaling system" to account for symbolic processes.

If, for some metapsychological reason, one were to hold to conditioned reflexes as the basic atoms of all behavior, the complexity of human linguistic communication would still require a correspondingly complex theory to account for the compounds into which such atoms might enter. The architecture of a great building cannot be adequately characterized by saying that it is constructed of bricks, even if that claim is true.

Conditioning theories are but one variety of associationistic theory. It is undeniable that, in some sense of the term "association," many words are associated with percepts. The question is how. Are word-percept associations direct "bonds" established inductively by repeated pairing? Are they mediated by elaborate networks of other associations? Or are there some even more intricate processes of information and control that mediate them? We believe that these associations are but a surface manifestation of an enormously complex cognitive system, a system that could only be characterized adequately by a correspondingly complex theory.

But where should psycholinguists turn for this more complex theory? Logicians and grammarians can be helpful as long as we remember that they are not psychologists, that they deal in idealized abstractions of particular aspects of the psychological processes of language. If one hopes to characterize the psychological processes themselves, the most promising source of ideas rich enough to capture the architecture of this system is the modern theory of information processing. Hypotheses formulated in terms of information processing may also prove inadequate or inappropriate to the task, but they are the best available in our present state of knowledge. We see no feasible alternative for psycholinguistic theory but to pursue these ideas as far as possible.

One cannot pursue linguistic meanings very far before discovering that words have the meanings they do as a consequence of the ways they are used in sentences. We can think of understanding a sentence as a form of information processing, as if the sentence were a program being fed into a computer. A listener, if he knows the language, has a variety of mental routines and subroutines that he can call and execute. Our problem is to specify in as much detail as possible what these routines might be, how they could be assembled into plans, how their assembly depends on the contexts in which they are used, what kind of representational system they entail, how they might relate to one another and to the perceptual world.

We can assume, at least tentatively, that a listener who understands a sentence that is used in a particular context *translates* it into the routine it represents. What use he makes of the routine is then up to him. If he decides to verify the sentence, he can try to *execute* the tests and operations it calls for. The tests may be performed on things and events in his environment, or may rely on stored information about them, or may even be performed on imaginary situations. Often, however, he simply assumes that the sentence is true without attempting to test it; he treats the assembled routines as a program for enriching or correcting his data base. Then he may use the information it contains by speaking or acting at some later time as if the tests and operations called for by the sentence could have been satisfied.

These remarks take us ahead of our story and might best be considered a preview of things to come. For the present, note that if some such approach is accepted, then one contribution of perception to language is to provide tests that can be performed as needed by the linguistic routines people know how to execute.

Because the relations between words and things are so complex, however, we cannot plunge immediately in. We cannot, for example, start writing identification routines for recognizing objects that share particular linguistic labels. We must first survey the problem we face and construct at least a fragment of conceptual theory to guide our efforts. In this chapter we will develop more fully our ideas about the role such routines might play in language. Without some notion of the functions they must serve, it would be impossible to choose wisely between alternative formulations of the word-percept connection. Our first task, therefore, is to define the problem we face, assess the theoretical resources at our disposal, and map our general strategy. Then we will be ready to make particular proposals about particular semantic questions. We will leave until later the application of our fragment of conceptual theory to specific conceptual domains.

In the preceding pages our survey of perceptual phenomena did not pretend to present new findings. Much is known about perception, both from intuition and from controlled observation. Our problem was to organize that knowledge in such a way that we could appreciate how it might be incorporated into some future theory of perception and how it could be exploited by some future theory of conceptual thought. Loose ends were left dangling and no doubt important relations were overlooked or incorrectly understood, but we attempted to suggest a general framework within which the major types of perceptual judgments could find a plausible niche.

We approach conceptual theory in a similar spirit. We will not report new empirical facts but will attempt to systematize facts already known. A major difference will be in coverage. We have attempted to mention all of the major categories of perceptual phenomena. A comparably ambitious survey of conceptual phenomena is out of the question, not merely because these phenomena have been studied less exhaustively but also because the variety of conceptual systems developed by men in different cultures, ages, and professions defies any but the most encyclopedic survey.

The part of conceptual theory that we wish to introduce in chapter 4 is a theory of lexical knowledge, of how people know the meanings of words in their language. But even lexical knowledge is a vast subject; we intend to focus on those parts of the lexicon where dependence on perceptual phenomena is reasonably apparent. Before we can undertake even this limited objective, however, it is necessary to have some kind of theoretical framework for our discussion.

3.1 MEANING, VERIFICATION, AND UNDERSTANDING

The impression that perception and language are closely related may stem from a feeling that people use language primarily to talk about what they perceive. Most linguistic communication does not serve that purpose, of course, but the impression persists nonetheless. Descriptive language seems simpler; its meaning seems to be given by what it describes; questions of truth can be resolved by the fit of the description to the perception.

This apparent simplicity of descriptive sentences recommends them as the starting point for attempts to construct a theory of linguistic meaning. Since their simplicity derives from the fact that they are often easy to verify, this starting point also suggests that we should take verification as a primitive semantic operation and try to define all other semantic concepts in terms of it. Reference, for example, might be defined as the relation that must hold between the world and the nominal constructions in the sentence in order for the sentence to be true. Synonymy might be defined as the relation that holds between two sentences when their truth values are the same in all possible situations. Understanding might be defined as knowing the conditions under which a sentence would be true or false. And so on. The goal would be to establish a correspondence between each sentence in the language and conditions for its verification.

This approach would make verification the fundamental source of evidence for determining linguistic meanings. In order to be able to regard the mechanical act of uttering some string of vocal noises like "That book is blue" as a meaningful speech act, it must be possible to relate it to whatever observations are required to determine whether or not the speaker holds it true at the time and place of utterance that the book in question is blue. This sort of correspondence would get a verificational theory of meaning started, because it could provide meanings for a large but finite set of simple predicates. But sentences expressing such simple predicates are only a fraction of the sentences people use. In order to extend the theory to all sentences, we would require some way to deal with more complicated sentences in terms of simpler ones.

To construct such a semantic theory, it is necessary to deal with the negation of predicates, with conjunctive, disjunctive, and implicative relations between predicates, with identification and quantification, with questions and commands, with indexicals and temporal relations, and so on. Many of these problems have been solved, in the sense that it is now possible to construct semantic theories that can interpret every well-formed sentence in certain artificial languages. The hope would be to extend this work until it became possible to construct a similar explicit theory of meaning, assuming only the possibility of verification, for any natural language.

One approach that is open to us at this point—since we have introduced a set of perceptual predicates that people can make judgments about—is to follow in this logical path: to try to show how a theory of meaning could be developed by decomposing every sentence into its component predications and determining its truth value in terms of the truth values of its components.

According to this program there are certain truth rules of the general form "a is an instance of P" is true if and only if a is an instance of P. Verification is a matter of testing whether some particular object a satisfies some particular predicate $P(x)$ when a is substituted for the variable x.* Psychologists would rely on philosophers to solve the more difficult semantic problems of language

---

*A verificationist would add the stipulation that if $P(a)$ cannot be computed, then "a is an instance of P" would, under the given substitutions for a and P, be a meaningless sentence. And if he were a radical verificationist, he would add the further stipulation that the sentence would be meaningful only if the computation of $P(a)$ could be re-

and could limit their psychological responsibility to an account of the perceptual and judgmental processes involved in verification.

For example, verifying the assertion "That book is blue" would involve testing a perceptual predicate like Blue(x). In order to assign a value to x, some perceptual predicate for recognizing books would be needed; such a predicate is not on the list developed in chapter 2, but we might construct a routine to identify books by using the available perceptual predicates in some appropriate combination. The demonstrative adjective "that" is presumably to be interpreted as instituting a search for some book that is ostensively identified by the speaker, that satisfies the perceptual predication Osten(speaker, book). Then the propositional function underlying the sentence "That book is blue" could be represented by some such logical expression as Osten(speaker, x) & Book(x) & Blue(x). Given the context in which the sentence is used, the listener should be able to substitute a particular, individual object for x and so convert the propositional function into a testable proposition. If an object could be found that satisfied the propositional function, the assertion would be considered to have been verified.

These remarks on the verifiability program are informal and indefinite. They could be improved in various ways, however, until, if we were lucky, we might be able to fashion an account of what people would do—what perceptual tests they would perform—if they were trying to verify such simple declaratives as "That book is blue." It is not the program we will follow, although we will begin as though we wanted to; from that beginning we will revise our theory to make it better suited to the needs of psychology.

Theoretical revisions should proceed one at a time. The present point is that a verifiability approach imposes an important qualification on our initial assumption that all language can be reduced to, or explained in terms of, word-percept associations. A word-percept association either exists or does not exist. Assertions about its existence might be subject to verification, but the association itself is not the kind of thing that is either true or false. Uttering the word "lamp" in the presence of a lamp could be an automatic response; as such, it would assert nothing. In order to think about verification, we must regard the utterance as asserting something that could be verified or falsified, for example, "That object is called lamp."

If a word-percept association is to be regarded as a working constituent in the process of verifying the propositions that utterances express, it must be supplemented by some kind of "test" framework within which it can be exploited. A theory of word-percept associations that did not enable us to stipulate the conditions under which tests should be performed would be an inadequate basis for a verifiability theory of language.

As we try to develop this modified version of the associative hypothesis we

---

duced, indirectly or directly, to computations on perceptual evidence. In his *Aufbau* (see sec. 1.1) Carnap undertook to carry out this reduction by formalizing a language of sense data that could serve as the canonical form to which all meaningful discourse could be reduced. He later abandoned this attempt. Wittgenstein (1953) is generally credited with having disproved any possibility of a private language of sense data.

will encounter difficulties that will call for still further modifications. These difficulties will have little or nothing to do with the value or validity of a verifiability approach to natural-language semantics. We assume it is defensible for a philosopher to try to confine natural language in a logical straitjacket—defensible in the sense that it is not obvious what arguments or observations could dissuade him—but there are several reasons to believe that such an approach cannot lead to a *psychological* theory of language use or linguistic competence.

First, a psychologist must recognize that verification is only one of several different conceptual operations a person might perform as a consequence of understanding a sentence. As Davies and Isard (1972) have pointed out, it is difficult to refuse to understand a sentence in a language you know well, but it is often easy to refuse to verify it. And for many kinds of sentences (most questions and commands, for example) the possibility of verification does not arise. An emphasis on verification distorts the nature of the descriptive task faced by psycholinguistics.

Second, a psychology of communication should characterize what people are doing when they use language. Insofar as verification might be something they do, it qualifies as one process that psychologists must consider. But to make it the cornerstone of a psychological theory of language places undue emphasis on the receptive side of linguistic communication. It may be possible to gain insight into the listener's role in a linguistic exchange by considering what he would have to know and do in order to verify any propositions expressed by the sentence he hears, but a complete account must also say something about where sentences come from and what they are used for. There is a reciprocity between understanding and meaning; a listener tries to understand what a speaker means. It was no accident that when Wittgenstein (1953) criticized the verificational approach he chose "language games" played by two or more people, where the speaker must be considered along with the hearer. To ignore the speaker leaves us contemplating a mute listener who verifies sentences that appear magically out of a social vacuum.

Declarative sentences are usually uttered or written by someone who wants his audience to believe that he believes whatever propositional meanings the sentences may express (Grice, 1968). To utter a sentence with the intention of contributing to the furtherance of some bona fide social interaction is to perform an act (Austin, 1962b). Acts may be wise or foolish, successful or unsuccessful, appropriate or inappropriate; they may be performed skillfully or clumsily, rapidly or slowly; but acts are not true or false. It is difficult to see how a psychological account of the speaker's contribution could be based wholly on verification. At the very least, a psychological theory would have to provide an elaborate superstructure to relate verification to speech production.

Third, the vagueness of ordinary language is a problem for the verificational approach. Many objects may not lead to a determinate truth value for a sentence such as "That object is a lamp." If people must rely on observation to determine whether certain terms in their language are applicable to certain objects, then their language *must* contain terms that are vague. If we equate the meaning of a statement with a representation of its truth conditions, it is not at all obvious how we will be able to provide such representations for many vague but meaningful sentences.

Vagueness is not the only problem one faces when one tries to go from sentences to truth values. For example, the sentence "That book is blue" will be true on some occasions and false on others, depending on what particular book the speaker happens to be indicating. It is not the sentence per se that is true or false; it is the sentence-in-a-given-context-of-use that must be verified. One way to accommodate this complication is to speak of sentences as expressing meanings, or propositions; it is the proposition that the speaker uses his sentence to express that can be true or false, not the sentence itself. In this view, a two-step analysis is involved in verifying a sentence. The first step is to recover the proposition that the speaker is expressing when he uses the sentence in a particular context; the second step is to verify that proposition by testing it against the facts as the listener knows them. Semantics can then be said to be the study of how propositions plus facts lead to truth values; the study of how sentences plus contexts lead to propositions can be called pragmatics (Stalnaker, 1972).

As valuable as this suggestion is for sorting out the kinds of problems we face, it is still not a psychological theory. If we were to misinterpret it as a theory to the effect that when people talk to each other they are always busily engaged in translating sentences into propositions and propositions into truth values, we would have a very strange and abstract idea of what conversation is all about. People talk to one another for a great variety of reasons. Even when their purpose is to exchange information, they are inclined to accept what the other person says as true, or to accept that he believes it to be true— or, at least, to accept that he wants them to think that he believes it to be true. If a listener were to interrupt a conversation every time he heard a sentence that expressed a proposition whose truth value he was unable to determine, he would seldom learn anything he did not already know. It is disruptive enough if a listener interrupts only when he hears something inconsistent with what he knows.

For various reasons, therefore, a semantics of propositions based exclusively on verification seems ill suited to the needs of psychological description. One alternative is a procedural semantics in which sentences are decomposed into a variety of procedures or operations that speakers and listeners can perform. That variety of operations provides a broader foundation for psychological theories of language than propositional verification does alone. In a procedural theory, word-percept associations play an even more peripheral role than they seem to play in a truth theory; word and percept are "associated" only in the sense that they can be alternative ways of gaining access to the same underlying procedures.

We will part company with many psychologists by placing word-percept associations in a verificational context, thus changing them from automatic connections to component parts of an information-processing system for evaluating particular attentional-judgmental predicates. As we develop our ideas about that system, we will discover that operations other than verification are required, and at that point we will part company with many philosophers.

Although we intend to follow this alternative path, the simple sentences that express perceptual predicates most directly still provide a convenient point of departure. We will begin by considering an example. A person holds an object where you can see it and says to you, "Is this a book?" What must you do in order to reply?

The first thing you have to do, of course, is understand the sentence. You must understand that it is a question. You must understand that it is a serious question, that the speaker expects a reply. You must understand that it is addressed to you, that the speaker expects you to provide the answer. You must understand that an answer involves performing certain operations: determining the reference of "this," applying tests associated with the class of objects conventionally labeled "book."

Once you understand the question, the second thing you have to do is decide in what way, if any, you are going to respond to it. This decision will depend on your knowledge of the speaker's intentions in asking the question on this occasion and on its possible relation to your own intentions as a participant in the interaction. The decision will include whether you should answer it truthfully or untruthfully.

If you understand the question and decide to answer it truthfully, the third thing you must do is perform the operations called for in your understanding of the question. That is to say, you must look at the object and try to recognize whether it is the kind of thing you have learned to label "book." If so, you utter "Yes"; if not, "No." If you answer "Yes," then the sentence "This is a book" is, according to your best judgment, true; otherwise, it is false or indeterminate. The semantic condition for "This is a book" to be true is that the object in question is indeed the kind of thing you call a book.

If these three steps can be taken as a rough outline of the processes we want to study, the next question might be: What kind of evidence is available from which we could infer the exact nature of those processes? This question directs our attention forcefully to the third step, where the processing finally surfaces into observable behavior. The first step, understanding, is directly accessible only to introspection, and the processes involved are so rapid and automatic for a competent speaker of English that they go on outside of conscious awareness. We may be able to infer what is happening, but we have no way to observe it directly. The second step, decision, is a more voluntary process, more accessible to introspection, but the conditions controlling the outcome— your motives and intentions on this particular occasion—are notoriously difficult to specify with satisfactory accuracy. We can infer the outcome from subsequent behavior and try to control it on different occasions by varying the consequences for the respondent, but, again, direct observation is difficult, if not impossible.

It is the third step, performance, where something observable occurs: your eyes move to the indicated object and you utter sounds. At this point a behavioral scientist finally has something to work with, and he can begin to fill in the details implied by "look at the object," "recognize," and "learn to label," since these phrases suggest processes that psychologists have studied intensively. Let us begin here, therefore, and consider whether these apparently innocuous phrases pose any hidden difficulties.

When a person says "That is a book," in order to verify his claim you must search the region around him until your eyes fall on the object he seems to be interacting with. If he is holding the object in his hand where you can clearly see it, or if he is conspicuously pointing toward it with his arm or his eyes, you can be reasonably confident that you have reached agreement with the speaker as to which object he is describing. But such gestures are themselves a form of communication, based on social conventions and subject to misunderstanding.

If verification depends on prior agreement in identifying the referent, what happens when a speaker says "That is a book" while clearly indicating nothing? Suppose it is perfectly evident that no object at all is present. You will surely be puzzled, because the existence of some object is usually a precondition for using this sentence in this way. That is to say, neither "That is a book" nor "That is not a book" can be verified if there is no object to which a label might be attached. You can understand the sentence, but how can you say whether it is true or false? Understanding a sentence is possible even when verification is not.

Although in this odd situation it is recognized that the sentence is not being used in a conventional way, one would not ordinarily say it was false. If the speaker holds up an apple and says "That is a book," you will recognize that the sentence is false, because "book" is not the conventional label for apples. But if he presents nothing at all, you will probably assume that he is using language in some special way: perhaps he wants you to imagine, for innocent reasons of his own, that he has a book when in fact he has nothing; perhaps the object is hidden in some inadvertent way; perhaps he is joking; and so on. Listeners usually try to put some construction on the situation compatible with their expectation that the speaker is behaving conventionally; they do not immediately assume that every unconventional use must be false.

Efforts to put some sensible construction on what another person is saying are usually aided by knowledge of the context in which he says it. The context provides a pool of shared information on which both parties to a conversation can draw. The information, both contextual and general, that a speaker believes his listener shares with him constitutes the cognitive background of his utterance. Information that he adds constitutes the focus of his utterance, and his sentence will usually be phrased in such a way as to make it clear that this new information should be the focus of the listener's attention. To speak as if the listener shared information that he clearly does not share—to suppose that there is a book when there is nothing, for example—is to violate a basic convention of conversational intercourse. To violate this convention deliberately is to invite failure of communication. It would be paradoxical for someone to fail deliberately; to succeed in failing is to fail in one thing in order to succeed in another, so people look behind the deliberate failure to find the real success. That is, listeners assume that there must be some interpretation that will clarify the speaker's real intention. In Grice's terminology, a speaker may "implicate" things very different from what he actually says.

Normally, of course, you can identify which object a speaker supposes you know about; in that case your next step might be to verify his assertion—to decide (in the present example) whether it is the kind of thing you have learned to label "book"—by applying a set of perceptual tests that you have learned to associate with "book." There are deep difficulties here, but the general idea is that (barring computational errors) if the object satisfies the tests, the assertion is true; if not, the assertion is false and you may protest; and if you cannot decide, the assertion is neither true nor false, but open for debate. The criteria for verification are set by your knowledge of conventional usage, as formulated in rules for recognizing and labeling. Note, however, that a meaning of the sentence must be clear before you undertake to verify it; if it were not, you would not know how to proceed with its verification. Understanding is antecedent to verification, not a consequence of verification. It may be necessary to acquire the conceptual knowledge needed to understand sentences in situations where immediate and decisive verification is possible, since if a learner does not perform appropriately, a teacher cannot assess his progress. But the requirements for use should not be confused with the requirements for teaching.

It has frequently been noted by critics of the simpler behavioristic theories of language learning that inducing a correct set of rules for the perceptual recognition of books from repeated pairings of books and "book" solely on the basis of the objective evidence ostensively provided would be impossible. The mapping of words onto things is many:many. That is to say, if a particular book is taken as the object, it can serve as the referent for many words: bible, big, book, brown, cover, object, page, paper, print, readable, square, thing, volume, and so on. How are the different meanings of all these shared labels to be sorted out? On the other hand, if a particular word "book" is taken as the label, there is an indefinite variety of hypotheses a learner could entertain as to what "book" should be paired with: with the particular books shown and only those; with some property of books, like color or weight; with the demonstrative gestures used; with some parts of books, like the cover or the pages; with what books do or with what can be done with them; with portable objects in general; with various locative coincidences in space or time; or with any complicated combinations of such conditions that would serve to characterize the specific evidence that has been received.

Defenders of the view that ostensive definition works because of some necessary inductive logic inherent in the laws of association have generally proposed more elaborate methods of teaching. For example, various instances of books are paired with "book" in many associations involving wide variations in all irrelevant aspects. Such variations probably help establish the degree of tolerable generalization, but the reason induction works is presumably that if it had not our ancestors would not have survived. The fact that children do get the idea so readily—that they do not seem to explore the full range of hypotheses theoretically available but settle rather quickly on the labeling relation that the teacher intends—should be taken to mean that they are prepared, both by heredity and by previous experience, to induce certain rules and not others. That is simply how the human mind works, a conclusion that is often denigrated as "psychologism" by those who aspire to more insightful accounts in other terms.

As psychologists, we are perhaps less fearful of psychologism than we should be. We have taken such speculative steps as postulating, in chapter 2, that the isolation of enduring objects from their perceptual surround is one of the givens of the mammalian visual system. That is simply how human vision works; if it did not, there would be nothing to label and hence little chance for a child to get the idea of labeling in the first place. We assume that a complete account of how a child learns to label objects and events would have to include considerably more than an inventory, however detailed, of the physical stimulations impinging on the child's receptor surfaces.

In order to determine that "That is a book" is true, therefore, some rather complicated and poorly understood procedures—searching, recognizing, labeling—must be brought into play. We will discuss each of them in the following pages. The important point is that people would not be able to apply these skills in an appropriate way if they did not first achieve some understanding of the utterance. The meaning of "That is a book" is not to be found in the operations of search, recognition, or labeling; as we will try to show, the meaning depends on the place that "That is a book" occupies in a conceptual structure determined by the linguistic conventions of the society and the particularities of the situation in which it is used. If this conceptual place is understood, then you can proceed with the verification of "That is a book"; if not, if the words cannot gain access to appropriate concepts, there is no way to determine what operations to perform.

So detailed a discussion of "That is a book" runs the risk of making an almost reflex act seem peculiarly complicated. The very simplicity of the example makes analysis verbose, but without it there is a danger of suggesting something more than, or something different from, what we have in mind. The meaning of "book" is not the particular book that was designated, or a perception of that book, or the class of objects that "book" can refer to, or a disposition to assent or dissent that some particular object is a book, or the speaker's intention (whatever it may have been), or the set of environmental conditions (whatever they may have been) that caused him to use this utterance, or a mental image (if any) of some book or other, or the set of other words associated with books, or a dictionary definition of "book," or the program of operations (whatever they are) that people have learned to perform in order to verify that some object is conventionally labeled a book. We will argue that the meaning of "book" depends on a general concept of books; to know the meaning is to be able to construct routines that involve the concept in an appropriate way, that is, routines that take advantage of the place "book" occupies in an organized system of concepts.

Conceptual theories of meaning have had many critics. One example of the arguments against them is the following (to the extent that we understand Quine, 1960, we might attribute it to him, but we wish to simplify in the interest of brevity): (a) it is impossible to account for people's habitual intuitions about the concepts expressed by a language in terms of the observable behavior of language users in the presence of observable stimulus events; (b) the only objective evidence a language learner has to go on is the stimuli he sees affecting native speakers of the language and their subsequent behavior, vocal or otherwise; and, therefore, (c) there is no objective way to determine whether our habitual semantic intuitions are right or wrong. According to this view, two people who both speak English and seem to understand each other may be doing so on the basis of entirely different concepts of the "meanings" of the words they are using, even though each person's intuitive theory is self-consistent and consistent with all the objective evidence available to them both. A stronger phrasing of (c) would be that there is no objective matter for our semantic intuitions to be right or wrong about.

Since we espouse a conceptual theory of meaning and propose to analyze habitual semantic intuitions about the meaning of words and phrases, we cannot accept conclusion (c). Where would we disagree? Certainly not with (a); the impossibility of inducing the subjective meanings of words and sentences solely from stimulus-response pairings has been convincingly argued by many critics of behavioristic psychology. It is with (b) that we would take exception. Why should we assume that a language learner has nothing to go on but the stimulus-response pairings he encounters among users of the language? An alternative to (b) is psychologism: to assume that people are prepared by nature and nurture to make certain inferences and not others, and that they can exploit this preparation in addition to the evidence of their senses. A first-language learner is prepared, as we have noted, to organize his visual field into segregated objects. He is prepared to believe in the existence of other persons. It is not implausible to suppose that he is also prepared to be interested in communication with others, and to pay special attention to vocal sounds as a means of communication. By the time he is a year old he seems also to be prepared to grasp the principle that all the visually segregated objects he sees have vocal labels. He is probably prepared by then to understand the usefulness of labels for identifying what he wants to communicate about; the principle that labels are most numerous and differentiated for those things of greatest communicative interest does not have to be learned, but merely accepted. He is prepared to pay special attention to the temporal order of speech elements. The sorts of syntactic relations that will seem most obvious to him must be those most basic to all languages of the world. By the time he is ten years old he will surely have mastered the important principle that it is self-defeating to believe in contradictions. In short, he will learn his first language from people whose minds work in much the same way as his own.

Proponents of (b) would argue that none of these psychologistic principles are "objective evidence" that a language learner can use. There is, of course, objective evidence supporting the validity of these principles, and hence there is an objective basis for believing that different language learners will arrive at very similar semantic intuitions about their language. Those who support (b) interpret "objective evidence" in a narrowly empiricistic sense. If the psychologistic principles are true, however, this restriction of "objective evidence" to the physical energies impinging on the learner's sense organs provides no compelling reason to believe that what a learner will make of this evidence is either unknowable or indeterminate, even though the particular evidence he receives will differ in detail from that received by other learners.

This defense of a conceptual approach to semantics is somewhat premature, since we have not yet developed any coherent version of a conceptual theory worth defending. Let us return, therefore, to the procedural approach.

We assume that understanding the meaning of a sentence depends on knowing how to translate it into the information-processing routines it calls for. This notion has been particularly attractive to workers in the field of artificial intelligence, where attempts to program computers to "understand" natural language have helped to clarify what meaning is and what a semantic theory must do. When you tell a computer to "add 13 and 58," for example, the meaning of the instruction "add" would seem to be the sequence of operations the machine is expected to execute. It is natural for anyone familiar with this way of thinking to generalize it from machines to people, but some care must be taken in its formulation. For example, Woods (1967) has said, in describing the kind of semantics he needed for an automatic question-answering system, "The meaning of the word 'dog' (for example) consists of an operational procedure for determining whether a given object is a dog—e.g., by looking at it, feeling it, noticing the number of legs, the hair, shape of body, tail, type of teeth, etc." (p. 5–8). Such operational procedures are obviously a necessary part of the meaning, since they are required in order to identify instances. But our procedure for identifying a dog is not, as we will see, the same as our concept of dogs.

Although perceptual identification procedures are not to be confused with conceptual meanings, they do provide a mechanism whereby perception can gain access and be of service to conceptual processes. As such, they play a central role in any discussion of the relation between language and perception, and we must consider how identification routines might best be characterized.

One advantage of a procedural over a propositional approach is that it enables us to make greater use of functions. We can think of a predicate as a kind of function, of course, but computing such a function yields truth values. If we believe there are psychological reasons for computing things other than truth values, then we need a more general kind of function. If we are concerned merely with identifying instances of lamp, book, dog, or whatever, the advantages of the broader notion of function are not obvious. For example, in the discussion of color perception we introduced the perceptual predicate $Colr(x, y)$, which is true if surface x has color y. (More precisely, the predicate is true if, when some particular surface is substituted for x and some particular values of red-green, yellow-blue, and black-white oppositions are substituted for y, the person who attends to his perception of that surface judges it to have that particular color.) Instead of this perceptual predicate, we could equally well have introduced a perceptual function $C(x)$, where C denotes the attentional-judgmental processes involved in calculating the color of x. As long as we are interested only in identifying the color, it makes little difference whether we think of a sentence like "This book is blue" as based on the speaker's judgment that $Colr(book, blue)$ is true or as based on his calculation that the value of $C(book)$ = blue.

Where the more general kind of function begins to make an appreciable difference is when we want to talk, as psychologists must, about decisions as to what action is to be taken. Then it is not sufficient merely to evaluate predicates identifying the action that was taken. What we want is some more general decision function that, given situations and goals as arguments, can calculate actions (not truth values) as its output values. Inasmuch as deciding what word to use in identifying something is a special case of the general decision problem, even here we can anticipate advantages of the procedural approach that may not be obvious at first consideration. In chapter 4 we will try to bring out those advantages in the context of a conceptual theory of linguistic meaning. For the present, we will focus on procedures that are obviously necessary, even in the context of a verifiability theory.

We have said that the routines involved in verifying "That is a book" include visual search, recognition, and labeling. These procedures have a firm base in perceptual reality. They entail some private data processing, but they are quite different from the private sense data that philosophers have debated and, by and large, have rejected. We believe that perception is a matter of confirming or disconfirming attentional-judgmental predicates, not a matter of identifying sense data. And we believe that the programming of these perceptual judgments must be under the control of instructions that enable us to perform computations far more diverse and powerful than the propositional approach would seem to require.

By starting with the procedures of search, recognition, and labeling and their contributions to the task of verification, we seem to be assigning special priority to perceptually verifiable expressions. That is not our intention. We see no need to insist that every meaningful use of language must be reducible to perceptual tests. For our current purposes it is enough to recognize that this is one way of using language meaningfully.

Obviously, we cannot limit our account to direct perceptual verification. In the sense that seeing is believing, perceptual verification is often decisive, but it is not the only recourse. Certain sentences can be verified by logic alone. Another alternative is verification by memory test—by interrogating stored information. Indeed, in studies of artificial intelligence these are often the only tests available, since computers come with great logical power and very large memories but with rudimentary sense organs. Although humans are much better than computers at perceptual tests, there are many common expressions that force people to rely on inference and memory. For example, "That is my uncle" cannot be tested entirely by perception of the designated object; you can test perceptually whether "that" indicates a man, but no perceptual observations will settle his avuncular status; the test must rely on information stored in some personal or archival memory. Similar inferential and memory tests are needed to verify "This is Monday," "This is a democracy," "That is impossible," "That is mine," and so on. Of course, these tests may use perception indirectly (by testing memory of previously perceived things or events), but in such cases as "An uncle is a relative," "January is a day of the week," and "Democracy is a form of government," you need consult only your memory of the language itself; someone who knows English can evaluate such sentences without perceiving the things or events that are named.

The psychological processes we have identified—search, recognition, and labeling—need some generalization to cope with a wider range of operations than those entailed by direct perceptual verification. We must consider search in general, memory search as well as perceptual search. And that, in turn, obliges us to say something about organizing memory to facilitate search. Moreover, our account of recognition and labeling will depend on our theory of memory: people must be able to remember that they have seen something before; they must be able to remember labels and their truth rules. In the most general terms, computations presume representations on which to compute, and those representations presume some medium—some memory—in which they can be held.

Chapter 2 gave preliminary glimpses of the control instructions we believe are necessary if the conceptual system is to call on the perceptual system for information. We must now rationalize those instructions psychologically and develop them far enough to discuss how a simple sentence might be translated into a routine that locates a sentence in a conceptual system and that may include instructions to conduct various perceptual or memorial searches and tests. We will begin by trying to clarify our ideas about search and the role that memory is expected to play in such processes.

3.2   SEARCH AND THE MANAGEMENT OF ATTENTION

We have had frequent occasion to refer to the role of attention, for an ability to pay attention to particular parts or attributes of the perceptual world is an indispensable prerequisite for the kinds of judgments we assume as primitives in conceptual theory. Obviously a person's ability to pay attention will depend on his level of arousal and general motivation (for a review of these matters see Kahneman, 1973), but our concern is with the ability of the conceptual machinery to control attention, to exploit perceptual processes in the service of thought. Since this capacity to manage attention is basic to everything else the conceptual processes do, we must try to characterize its contribution in some detail. Probably the simplest place to begin is with its contribution to the process we call searching.

In section 3.1 we said that one of the mental operations required to verify "That is a book" is to search the environment for an object of a particular kind. The ease with which this operation is usually performed might tempt us to take it for granted and to move on to more complicated operations. There are several reasons, however, for pausing first to consider the search process in more detail. One is that search is a component operation entailed by many expressions; if our assumptions about it are faulty, the trouble will spread. Another reason is that searching entails close control of the perceptual process by conceptual processes; if we are really interested in the interface between perception and conception, then search would seem an obvious place to study it. Moreover, there are several kinds of searches; distinguishing among them is an interesting exercise in its own right.

The ability to search makes perception a useful mode of acquiring information. It is search more than anything else that makes perception an active process, not a passive registration of energies impinging willy-nilly on the receptors. When a person is task-oriented, he searches for things needed in the task; when he is not task-oriented, he searches for things that interest him, that have personal value for him.

We take it as axiomatic that perception guides behavior. In the simplest examples, people move their bodies in order to gain a clearer perception of some object or event. The movements they make in order to readjust their perceptions become more complex when they incorporate the movement of objects other than their own bodies, but the guiding role of perception is the same; they have a current percept and they have a goal that describes a different percept, and they respond in such a way as to reduce the discrepancy between them (Powers, 1973). This characterization extends even to some appetitive behaviors, where people try to reduce a discrepancy between their current internal state and some state of satisfaction that they take as their goal. When behavior is seen in this context, everything people do is part of an active search for some goal percept. For the present discussion, we will focus on the simple instances where people are searching for some perception of the environment, and we will assume that comparable searches can be pursued in memory as well as in the external environment.

The importance of exploratory activity with the hands and the mind as well as the senses has been emphasized by Piaget (1961), who holds that perceptual development is a consequence of enrichment of perceptual structures deriving from the prior development of intelligent actions and operations beginning with sensorimotor organization; conceptual operations are not mere extensions of general laws already at work in perception—on the contrary, perceptual development must await the development of the structures of intelligence. If this thesis is correct, if the nature of perception is so strongly influenced by the conceptual uses to which it is put, perhaps our characterization of search should be included as an integral part of perceptual theory. Our reasons for preferring to treat search as an executive process in the conceptual system will become clear in the discussion that follows, but none of those reasons should be interpreted as dictating one or the other order of ontogenetic development. The importance of active search for perceptual development is not in question here; its importance in making perception useful, both for children and for adults, is the point we would emphasize.

People do not respond equally to all the stimuli impinging on their receptors; different parts of the sensory field are brought into the focus of attention at different times, and different parts of the same field may be scanned depending upon the task in hand (Yarbus, 1967). The perceptual mechanism is so constructed that surprising stimuli have the power to capture attention involuntarily; the survival value of this reflex is reasonably obvious. But the fact of interest here is that people do have some degree of voluntary control over attention; they can decide what parts of the perceptual world they wish to center on and in what order. Voluntary control makes search possible. How it is used is one aspect of the more general problem of the management of attention.

The paradigm case is visual search through objects in the environment. The retina of the eye has a small, central area, the fovea, where people usually center the image of any object they wish to see clearly. The periphery of the retina can provide information about the general location of an object, and this information can be used to guide the rotation of the eyeball until the object is in foveal vision. It is as if there were two focuses of perception, one given by the fovea and the other given by attention; the perceptual system tries to reduce any disparity between them, and consequently as attention shifts, the eyes try to follow. Thus, the simplest kind of visual search brings different objects successively into foveal vision until a desired object is recognized.

Two aspects of this process deserve comment. First, efficient scanning depends on some plan for conducting the search. Second, recognition of the object once its image is in foveal vision depends on matching its visual properties to the properties that define the kind of object one is looking for. Let us consider these in turn.

Plans for searching may be either algorithmic or heuristic. Given some internal representation of the space to be searched, an algorithmic plan first bounds the search area, then organizes it in some sequential order that, in principle, eliminates the likelihood of skipping parts or searching the same part more than once. Attention is then moved successively from place to place until either the object is found or the searcher decides it is not there. Algorithmic search has a high probability of providing a definite answer for the area searched (assuming that the recognition process is accurate), but it can be tiring and time-consuming; sustained control of attention requires a tedious exertion of the will in order to avoid momentary lapses. Algorithmic search is usually the court of last appeal.

Heuristic plans controlling the order of search draw on contextual information to increase the probability of finding the target without looking in every possible place. Such information is of various kinds: you may remember (that is, search your memory for) where you saw it last; you may follow gestures made by others trying to help; you may receive verbal information about the object's general location; you may rely on the organization of the environment (furniture usually sits on the floor, pictures hang on walls, books may be arranged alphabetically by author, and so on). Heuristic searching is usually relatively rapid but has the disadvantage that if the target is not discovered, you cannot be certain that it is not there.

Looking for a missing object is a common type of search, but there are others. For example, when you compare two objects to see whether they are alike, you search for a difference. If you do not know what kind of difference to expect, you cannot preset yourself with a description of the target. This kind of visual search is difficult; Vurpillot (1968) has shown (by an analysis of eye movements) that the ability to scan systematically back and forth and to sample a variety of features continues to improve until at least age nine.

The critical point is that searching is a complex skill under the control of higher mental processes. Representing the search area, deciding how much to include and organizing it sequentially, deciding when to stop—these are executive decisions that differ from the perceptual judgments discussed in chapter 2.

Efficient organization of search is learned; children do not spontaneously search for things in an efficient way. Still, one can understand what spatial search is without knowing how to do it efficiently. That is to say, one can understand that "What is this?" involves searching for the referent of "this" without knowing how to undertake that search efficiently. Most adults appreciate this fact intuitively; when they try to teach a child conventional labels for objects, they ease the search process by moving the object into the child's foveal vision and so, presumably, into the center of his attention. In order to start a child learning his vocabulary, the adult tries to remove any obstacles set by the child's inability to control his attention long enough to conduct a true spatial search. Recognition is the critical process; organizing the search is a skill that can be acquired later.

So we turn to the second aspect of searching: testing objects once they are in the focus of attention. Visual recognition of a target object in an array of other objects has been intensively studied experimentally by presenting the array to foveal vision, but limiting the exposure time to a period so short that no eye movements are possible. Most of this work has been done with arrays of letters and/or digits. Accuracy and speed of recognition under these conditions depend on the number and variety of the target objects, on the number and variety of nontarget objects, on the spatial separation and arrangement of the objects, on familiarity with the objects and amount of previous practice, on the size of the set of alternative objects from which the target object is drawn, on the size of the objects and their contrast level with the background, on the spatial orientation of the target, and probably on other factors. Various theories of this kind of visual processing have been proposed to explain the data (see, for example, Sperling, 1963; Rumelhart, 1970; Gardner, 1973).

During the second stage of searching, what the visual system does is usually so rapid and automatic that any control over it must be exercised in preparation for it, not during the time it occurs. We will concentrate on this preparatory process.

One notion of how an observer sets himself in advance to recognize a particular target is that he summons up in his mind's eye a memory image representing a class of objects; this image can then serve as a template to compare with the perceptual image of any particular object. (Not all template theories of recognition assume the use of imagery; we are concerned here with only one species of template theory.) If the image matches the percept, the object can be assigned to that class; if not, it is something else. This characterization may fit such simple cases as, say, recognizing the color red, but what kind of image could provide a template for recognizing such generic classes of objects as, say, animals or furniture? Potter (1975) reports that viewers of a rapid sequence of pictures can recognize a target picture as accurately and almost as rapidly when they know only its name ("boat," for example) as when they have seen the picture itself in advance.

There are a number of difficulties with image theories of recognition; we will not review them here (see Neisser, 1967; Paivio, 1971; Pylyshyn, 1973a). Our own preference is to think of a memory image not as a template for matching a perceptual image but as a substitute that can be invoked when a perceptual image is not available. For example, when you are searching for a book you may generate a visual memory image of a book (or an auditory memory image of "book") as an aid in maintaining control of attention. A visual memory image can serve as a reminder of the features such objects have and of the tests you wish to apply to each object as you examine it. Once the object itself is in view, however, its perceptual image may bear only a slight resemblance to the image you have used as a crutch for attention and memory.

Imagery has been studied extensively by psychologists. It has been found, for example, that some words evoke images much more readily than others. Paivio, Yuille, and Madigan (1968) had thirty university students rate 925 English nouns for the ease with which they produced images—rating 7 for the easiest and 1 for the hardest. A sample of their results, selected to suggest the range of differences, is shown in table 3.1. They found a correlation of 0.83 between these ratings of imageability and ratings of the same words for concreteness (reference to perceptible objects), but only 0.23 with relative frequencies of word usage; the nouns for which people have the clearest images are those that refer to objects with which they have had frequent perceptual experience. Although the effects of picturability on search strategies seem not

Table 3.1 Ratings of the ease with which nouns arouse mental imagery. 7 = maximum ease; 1 = maximum difficulty. (Selected from Paivio, Yuille, and Madigan, 1968.)

Noun	Rating	Noun	Rating	Noun	Rating
girl	6.87	elbow	6.30	nephew	4.30
cat	6.80	monarch	6.20	encore	4.00
blood	6.70	furniture	6.17	length	3.73
mother	6.67	animal	6.10	honor	3.50
green	6.60	soil	6.00	idiom	3.00
wife	6.53	love	5.60	amount	2.73
table	6.50	angle	5.50	magnitude	2.50
book	6.43	wench	5.30	fact	2.20
grandmother	6.43	death	5.00	instance	2.00
body	6.40	barnacle	4.50	inanity	1.83
square	6.37	form	4.30	surtax	1.63

to have been studied, Paivio (1971) has summarized an extensive body of experimentation showing that concrete imagery can facilitate perception, learning, and memory. Imagery obviously plays an important role in the cognitive economy, but we would attribute its importance to its making available the large information capacity of the perceptual system to support other mental processes, not to replace them. An image can provide a kind of vicarious perception on which conceptual processes can operate much as they operate on percepts.

The images people use in the absence of a perceptual referent have a platonic character. That is to say, they are usually idealized images based on all previous experience with objects of that class and viewed from stereotyped angles. After practice in identifying objects in a given class, people develop an imaginary typical instance, and any given perceptual instance can be judged for its similarity to that imaginary typical instance. Thus, most people judge a German shepherd to be a better dog than a dachshund—better in the sense that it is more similar to their typical instance, a "doggier" dog. When such an image is used as a memory crutch, recognition of a particular instance will usually be faster and more accurate if the percept is similar to the typical instance. But such facts do not necessitate the conclusion that recognition is accomplished by some neural correlation of the percept with a memory image of the typical instance.

Although there are other versions of the template theory that are more adequate to the facts and do not assume that explicit images are formed of the stored trace (see, for example, J. A. Anderson, 1970, 1972), we assume that at some stage in the recognition process there is a component that is functionally equivalent to the application of a set of perceptual tests. It is easier to describe how such a component might work than to specify precisely what the tests are, but we assume that the mechanisms underlying the perceptual judg-ments cataloged in chapter 2 must provide at least a partial answer. Prepara-tion for the moment of recognition consists of selecting in advance the particular set of tests to be applied (Bruner, 1957).

We will therefore consider a feature theory of recognition, where we take "feature" to mean any particular value of an attribute that a percept must have in order to satisfy a test based on the perceptual predicates. A feature enables us to partition a set of objects into those having it and those either lacking it or of indeterminate status with respect to it. A set of features, tested in series or in parallel, defines a set of categories. If tests are applied serially, they can be arranged hierarchically (the application of test $n + 1$ depends on the outcome of tests 1 through n in the hierarchy); successive tests limit the identification to successively narrower ranges of possibilities. Once the range is sufficiently narrow to permit association with a label, the recognition process can termi-nate. (Perhaps we could think of the tests as rapidly narrowing the range of templates against which to correlate the percept, in which case we would have a dual mechanism; such speculations are difficult to evaluate in ignorance of the processes involved.)

A hierarchy of perceptual tests can categorize a heterogeneous collection of objects exhaustively. Even unfamiliar objects will have a place, so it is unnec-essary to have seen everything and been told its category before being able to assign it a plausible place relative to other objects. Finer distinctions can be made by adding more features to the hierarchy.

The simplest version of a feature theory would not require that tests for different attributes be arranged hierarchically. If the use of any test did not require knowledge of the prior outcome of any other tests, all tests could be conducted in parallel. For example, a tactual test might be independent of a visual test; if neither dominated the other, both tests could be conducted si-multaneously, with a consequent saving of time. Many visual attributes seem to have this kind of independence, but not all do. For example, visual tests to determine whether a person is male or female would be applied after tests to determine whether the object was a person, because such tests are simply irrelevant for books, clouds, colors, and so on. Since some tests have limited domains of relevance, hierarchical organization is required for some parts of the system.

People have some voluntary control over the features they will attend to. They cannot voluntarily see what is not there, but they can control to some extent which features are most salient. For example, in searching for hidden figures (fig. 3.1 is an example from Gottschaldt, 1926), it is possible to give priority to those features that define the target and make it stand out against the ground in a way that it would not normally be seen. This process is ordi-narily called search, but it differs from a spatial search that has as its goal to bring the object into foveal vision; you can look right at the target and not recognize it through the camouflage. Here the search is almost purely a matter of controlling attention to particular features.

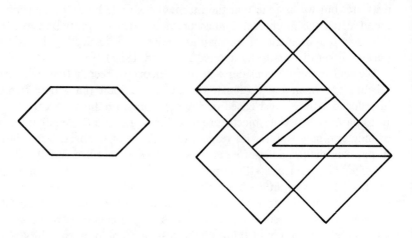

Figure 3.1   A hidden figure. (After Gottschaldt, 1926.)

As we saw in chapter 2, the perceptual mechanism provides a variety of tests for features of objects—color, shape, location, motion, and so on; a particular outcome of a set of such tests might define a familiar category of objects. And the nature of attention is such that people can abstract the outcomes of some tests and ignore others. For example, "red" is a vocal noise used when attending to the outcome of color tests, "rectangular" is a vocal noise used when attending to the outcome of shape tests, and so on. These noises are not associated with objects or classes of objects but are used to communicate the results of tests applied to particular objects in answer to such attention-directing questions as "What color is it?" or "What shape is it?" These questions may be asked either by another person or by the observer to himself.

As we have stressed, to speak of "properties" or "attributes" of an object or event presupposes an ability to pay attention to the outcomes of some perceptual tests and not to others. A property or attribute *is* an attentional domain, and the ability to apply different labels to different attributes can only be understood in terms of the ability to shift the domain of attention from one set of tests to another. Psychologists have various ways of discussing this fact: attention is selective; a person can be set to see one thing rather than another; his interests control what he is likely to notice; and so forth. But most of these locutions can be misunderstood to refer only to external search, to changes in the content of the perceptual field. It is critically important to recognize that attention varies over properties and attributes as well as over objects and events and that in this respect the control of memory search is very similar to the control of perceptual search.

A person's ability to attend to some properties and ignore others is not unlimited. His degree of success will depend critically on what the competing properties are. Size and hue, for example, are easily judged independently;

under most conditions it is difficult to combine them as a single perceptual property. On the other hand, it is difficult not to combine the saturation and brightness of a color. Factors relating to the "integrality" or "separability" of properties are discussed by Garner (1974). We do not wish to oversimplify complex psychological processes, but we believe that the separability of perceptual properties is the fact that should be emphasized in a psychological account of linguistic categorizing and labeling.

To summarize. We assume that it is possible for people to conduct spatial searches voluntarily with the goal of bringing objects successively into foveal vision, that they can prepare themselves to apply some perceptual tests rather than others, that tests can be rapidly performed on object percepts to assign them to categories, that it is possible to pay attention to the outcome of some tests while ignoring (or not performing) others, and that conventional labels can be used to communicate the outcomes.

In order to represent these abilities in our theory, we resort to the control instructions "find" and "test," mentioned in chapter 2. The instruction "find" sets up a search; it uses any information available about the domain to be searched—whether, for example, it is to be a search of the perceptual world or of information stored in memory—and some general characteristics of the target. Once an entity having those characteristics is found in the search domain, further instructions test whether it is the particular entity that is sought. Procedurally, of course, "find" is just a "test" embedded in a search routine, so in principle all of the information about the target could be allocated to the "find" instruction.

By dividing target information between "find" and "test," we hope to leave open options that language seems to exploit. For example, a person might search for a red rectangle by scanning the field for red things and then testing their shape, or by looking for rectangles and then testing their color. He might even be able to search for anything that was either red or rectangular and, on finding one, test it for the other feature. In short, people can adopt different search strategies in different situations.

What considerations might influence the choice in dividing target information between the "find" and "test" instructions? Lacking any definite reason to prefer some other division, language seems to suggest that certain strategies are to be preferred. In English, for example, it is more natural to speak of a "red rectangle" than a "rectangular redness," which we take to imply that the conventional procedure is to find a rectangle and test its color. If someone asked for a "red RECTANGLE," stressing the second word, it might be taken as a suggestion to reverse the usual division—to find something red and test its shape. In English, stress can indicate which attribute is to be the focus of attention; perhaps the focus should be taken as the argument of the "test" instruction. If this suggestion is correct, of course, then the information supplied to the "find" instruction should correspond to background information. Asking for a "RED rectangle" seems natural when there are many rectangles around and color is a distinguishing feature; asking for a "red RECTANGLE" seems natural when there are many red things around and shape is a distinguishing feature.

We assume a person is free to divide the information he has about the target quite flexibly between these two control instructions; the context will indicate what is background (and thus appropriate for the "find" instruction) and what is focus (and thus appropriate for the "test" instruction). By dividing the work between them in this way we hope to parallel procedurally an important distinction between the presupposition and the assertion of an utterance; by leaving as optional the division of information between them we hope to capture procedurally the fact that a normal or customary distinction can sometimes be neutralized or even reversed in actual usage.

We have taken visual exploration of the environment as our paradigm of search and of the management of attention that search involves. It should be noted, however, that when these procedures are viewed more abstractly, search provides a general model for many functions of intelligent systems. Whenever a system can be described abstractly as selecting, on the basis of a criterion given in advance, one or more out of an array of alternative states or actions, its operations can be described, at least metaphorically, as searching.

For example, a negative-feedback system can be thought of as searching for a state of equilibrium defined in advance by the parameters of the system. An information-retrieval system can be thought of as searching through a memory for entries meeting a given criterion (we have already adopted this generalization explicitly and must develop it in more detail). A decision maker can be thought of as searching through a set of permissible actions for those that optimize (or minimax, or satisfice) certain aspects of his situation. A problem solver can be thought of as searching through a set of decision sequences for a path leading from the problem situation to a solution situation. A language user can be thought of as searching through the set of possible sequences of linguistic elements for those that are grammatical sentences in a language, or as searching through the set of grammatical sentences for one that expresses a particular propositional or conceptual content. A game player can be thought of as searching through the set of permissible continuations of the game for a sequence of moves that will insure a win. A forecaster can be thought of as searching through a set of possible worlds for those that seem most probable, given reasonable constraints on the transformations that can occur. The search paradigm provides a general theoretical framework in terms of which a great variety of intelligent processes can be characterized abstractly; all of these varieties of metaphorical search have received extensive analysis and discussion.

In principle, therefore, if a system is complex enough to conduct a search, it is complex enough to perform a wide variety of intelligent functions. Hintikka's (1973) game-theoretic analysis of the quantifiers "some" and "all," which are essential to modern logic, suggests that existential statements can be regarded not as claims about existence but as claims about the outcome of a search through the appropriate domain: $(\exists x)Fx$ can be interpreted to mean that if you search through the x's, you will find one or more that satisfy F. To assume that an information-processing system can execute "find" and "test" instructions, therefore, is to assume that it is capable of performing some of the fundamental operations of logical thought.

It is apparent, however, that descriptions of intelligent systems in terms of search processes are usually quite abstract. Particular instances differ greatly, both in the nature of the domains searched and in the way the search can be conducted. An adequate psychological account of a particular instance of intelligent behavior by a human being should not characterize it merely as the outcome of some abstract or hypothetical search process; a serious account should characterize the representations searched and the procedures followed as explicitly as possible. In the present context, we will confine our discussion to searches of the environment or of memory, where the possibility of providing plausible psychological accounts of the domains and procedures of search seems most promising.

3.3   ORGANIZATION OF MEMORY

In order to use a language, a person must be able to remember many different kinds of information. Leont'ev (1973, p. 85) has provided a catalog that can serve to illustrate the diversity:

— "Situation memory" enables us to react unambiguously to the repetition of the same set of external factors determining a verbal utterance
— Retention of components of an utterance in memory while it is being processed
— Storage and retrieval of the plan or program of an utterance
— Storage and retrieval of the content of an utterance
— Storage and retrieval of the form of an utterance, as in rote memorization
— Storage and retrieval of grammatical structures
— Storage and retrieval of stereotyped verbal constructions
— Storage and retrieval of sound sequences

Leont'ev contrasts these memory requirements for language use with the kinds of experiments that constitute the bulk of psychological research on verbal memory, experiments that concentrate on the processes of storage, retention, and retrieval but that frequently ignore the nature of the information itself or the use a person might make of it.

This discrepancy between linguistic and psychological interest in memory poses a problem for anyone who wishes to apply psychological results to linguistic processes. We will select from the psychological studies of memory only those hypotheses we deem relevant to linguistic problems. As a consequence, the following discussion differs from the usual reviews of verbal memory and should not be taken as a substitute for them. We will provide only the minimum account necessary to support our discussion of relations between perception and language; we will not attempt to review or evaluate all the evidence for or against various assumptions we will make. Fortunately, there are many reviews where these matters can be pursued; a reader who begins with the collections of papers edited by Norman (1970) and by Tulving and Donaldson (1972), perhaps supplemented by Frijda (1972) and Anderson and Bower (1973), will quickly discover paths into the technical literature relevant to these assumptions.

A parsimonious approach would assume, at least initially, that people have a general innate ability to change as a consequence of their experience; to the extent that those changes persist, they can be regarded as constituting the contents of memory. Then "memory" is a broad term for the representational system, whatever it may be, in which these changes are preserved and from which they can be retrieved. As we proceed, however, we will find that this generic concept has to be differentiated functionally into memories of different types. Our problem is to try to make some match between the types of memory that might be defended on the basis of psychological theory and research and the types of memory that seem to be required in order to support linguistic performance.

We can begin by noting some parallels between memory and perception. The conceptual system must be able to search memory as well as the perceptual world. When we search perceptually, the appropriate domain of search is limited in space and time; it is less obvious how the appropriate domain for a memory search can be indicated in advance. William James (1890) believed that "the machinery of recall" is the same as "the machinery of association." "In short," he wrote, "we make search in our memory for a forgotten idea, just as we rummage our house for a lost object. In both cases we visit what seems to us the probable *neighborhood* of that which we miss" (I, 654). We turn over the ideas associated with the one we are seeking until at last it comes into active consciousness. By that view, the "neighborhood" in which to search for a forgotten idea is given by those remembered ideas with which it has come to be associated through prior contiguity or similarity in perception or thought. Other psychologists have felt that association is not a sufficient explanation— that further principles of organization are required in order to account for the way memory search is actually conducted.

Perception and memory are the two great sources of information available to the conceptual system. One is largely external and contemporaneous, the other largely internal and historical. We say "largely" external or internal because a person can perceive the internal state of his own body and because writing and other memory crutches enable him to externalize memory. But the point is that these two domains, perception and memory, must provide values to which pointers can be assigned in routines. Since we assume that a "find" instruction can be used to search memorial as well as perceptual representations, we must consider how the arguments of that instruction should be stated for memorial search. The first argument of "find" is a specification of the domain to be searched; at the very least, the first argument must say whether the domain is perceptual or memorial. But just to say find (in memory, x) is hardly enough; with only that much indication, an exhaustive search of memory would be required. What further limitations can be placed on the search domain must depend on how memory is organized. Since the organization of memory is currently a controversial topic (some psychologists hold that associative networks are sufficient without further organizing principles, and those who see a need for more explicit organization are far from agreement about its nature) we must emphasize that suggestions are all we can offer at this time.

The second argument of a "find" instruction must be a description based on what is known of the target. The simplest instances, given the theoretical machinery now at our disposal, are searches for information that has been perceptually encoded, since a description can then be given in terms of perceptual predicates we have already defined. Insofar as generic concepts refer to classes of concrete, perceptible objects, these can be described in the same way. But for impalpable and abstract concepts and relations, and for motor skills, we have introduced no notation; we will rely on informal expressions in English to describe any such psychological entities we wish to index in our routines.

Our task is thus to provide an account of memory sufficient to determine how these two arguments of "find" should be formulated. Before we undertake it, however, we must draw an important distinction in terms of the dynamics of memory systems.

3.3.1   Primary and Secondary Memory

Those familiar with modern information-processing systems draw distinctions between buffer memories, which generally have a limited capacity and hold information only until the central processor is ready for it; working memories, where information is processed according to instructions; and central memories, where large amounts of information can be stored for indefinite periods of time. When one begins to think of people as information-processing systems, it is natural to ask whether they also have these rather different forms of memory. Several psychologists have argued that they do, and that their buffer and working memories must be described rather differently from their central memory.

Although the time differs for different modalities, stimulus-induced activity in the receptor organs may persist for times having an order of magnitude of a tenth of a second. The phenomenal present seems to integrate times on the order of magnitude of one second. And there is a transient memory of perceptions that, if undisturbed, rapidly fades away with a duration having an order of magnitude of ten seconds. Because phenomena having short durations are easy to study, and because these short-term memories can often be investigated with procedures developed for perceptual experiments, short-term traces of the perceptual input have been extensively analyzed (Murdock,

1967; Norman, 1969). The shortest of these transient memories is usually called sensory or iconic memory, and the longest is frequently called short-term or primary memory. More permanent memory traces are usually said to be stored in long-term or secondary memory.

It is natural to identify primary memory as the memory that supports on-going processes at the center of attention. It holds whatever information is required for the particular instruction being executed at the moment. Conrad (1964) and Baddeley (1966) have provided evidence from studies with linguistic materials that information in primary memory is usually in phonemic form—a kind of covert vocal rehearsal, perhaps. Although the capacity of primary memory is clearly limited (Miller, 1956), when a person is listening to discourse in a familiar language the immediate sentence or the immediately preceding clause is retrievable verbatim (Jarvella, 1971). Once the current subroutine is executed, rapid loss of the exact form of the input is necessary in order to permit execution of the next subroutine. Of course, if the current sub-routine is a loop—as might be the case if a person were actively rehearsing—information can be maintained in primary memory for a longer period of time, but at the price of ignoring subsequent information. "Maintaining information in primary memory" and "maintaining information in the focus of attention" seem to be two ways of describing the same psychological process. Once attention shifts to something else, primary memory decays fairly rapidly, but it does not usually fall to an asymptote of zero recall. Even after a much longer period than would normally be considered within the span of primary memory, some items or features of the information can still be recalled. Waugh and Norman (1965) have suggested that there is some constant probability that any information in primary memory will be transferred into secondary memory, and that one effect of rehearsal is to keep information in primary memory longer and so to provide more opportunity for this transfer to occur. Craik and Lock-hart (1972), however, have argued that there are different kinds of rehearsal and that a memory trace will be strengthened only if the information that is being maintained at the center of attention is also being analyzed, enriched, or elaborated (not merely recycled); the greater the "depth of processing," the more durable the memory will be. Thus, they propose not different storage devices but different levels of processing of the perceptual input.

If, for example, a person is asked to cross out all occurrences of the letter *e* in a particular text, his processing of the information conveyed by the text will be superficial and little of it will be recalled later. If, on the other hand, he is asked to read the same text for comprehension and to prepare himself to answer questions about it, he will process the information at a much deeper level and the probability of its being strengthened (transferred to secondary memory) is much greater. This difference, of course, presumes the person's ability to process at deeper levels; if the text is in an unfamiliar language or contains many unfamiliar words or difficult constructions, he may not be able to perform the deeper processing, to extract the gist of what he is reading.

There is a hierarchy of skills involved in understanding a linguistic message, and the more superficial skills must be automatic before deeper processing can occur; if attention is filled with superficial details, there may be no room for analyzing, enriching, or elaborating the message and hence little secondary memory for its content. LaBerge and Samuels (1974) have proposed that the criterion for deciding when a subskill is automatic should be that it can be performed accurately while attention is directed elsewhere, that is, the processing can occur outside the focus of attention. Once a subskill has become automatic, of course, a person has little voluntary control over it—it is difficult for him to refuse to process the information if he has built up automatic skills for doing so; unnatural proofreading tasks are required to block their operation. Normally, however, these automatic skills free the focus of attention for deeper levels of information processing that seem necessary to establish more permanent memory traces.

In any case, the probability of transferring an item of information into secondary memory, like the probability of finding some target during the course of a search for it, can be influenced by control instructions available to the conceptual system. We will therefore introduce another instruction that the conceptual system can use to program its operations. The instruction store(in x, this information) will, when executed, result in the system's doing whatever it can, from simple looping to complex transformations in depth, to increase the probability that the information will be remembered. In a modern computer an instruction to store will result in almost instantaneous copying, at the indicated location, of the information in the accumulator; barring malfunction, that copy will be perfect and will persist until some subsequent instruction changes or erases it. The human analog is a much more probabilistic operation and probably a much more complex one. Moreover, a computer will not store unless instructed to, but a person may remember even when he has not voluntarily executed any routine to increase his likelihood of remembering (just as he may find something without deliberately looking for it). If the transfer from perception to memory depends on the kind and depth of the analysis that the person performs on the information, as Craik and Lockhart maintain, then the storage location(s) for the control instruction "store" may perhaps be thought of as one of the computational consequences of that analysis.

Intermediate storage in primary memory may not even be a necessary stage in establishing secondary memory for processed information. Shallice and Warrington (1970) studied a brain-damaged patient with a severely impaired primary memory as measured by such conventional indices as his digit span. Yet this patient (and others like him; Warrington, Logue, and Pratt, 1971) experienced little difficulty in understanding and remembering ordinary language, provided it was free of embedded or parenthetical constructions. These patients may have defects only in the management of attention that is required for active rehearsal of phonemic material. They may have nothing wrong with the automatic subskills required for the analysis involved in comprehension and in strengthening information for secondary memory. This interpretation has been suggested by Baddeley and Hitch (1974) as a result of their studies of "working memory" in normal (non-brain-damaged) people. It appears that only when people are asked to hold in memory a number of items approaching their digit span is there any impairment of their performance on verbal reasoning or comprehension tasks. Baddeley and Hitch conclude that the central executive component of working memory, governing comprehension and transfer of information, is distinct from the storage component governing phonemic retrieval.

Pending the outcome of further experimental studies, however, we will assume that "find" and "store" are complementary instructions. When "find" is executed, the system tries to produce in working memory a pointer to the target in secondary memory; when "store" is executed, the system attempts to produce in secondary memory a representation of information currently in working memory.

What sort of subroutines can the "store" instruction invoke when it is executed? Psychologists have explored a variety of likely candidates, which Meacham (1972) has grouped under the general headings: organizing, labeling, rehearsing, and visual and verbal elaboration. Although the execution of a "store" instruction is intended to correspond to a voluntary use of these activities, much evidence indicates that they are effective even when they are undertaken incidentally, with no expectation of future recall tests. Meacham suggests that the development of memory skills in children depends, at least in part, on their growing recognition that these activities are in fact appropriate when they encounter tasks requiring them to remember. Both "store" and "find" are acquired skills.

If the execution of a "store" instruction can initiate such activities, it must also be able to terminate them. In order to terminate them at an appropriate time, a learner must be able to estimate rather accurately how successful they have been; in order to decide that "store" has been successfully executed and that the activities so initiated can stop, he must know that he knows it (Hart, 1967). Moreover, the ability to monitor memory in this way also has a developmental history (Flavell, Friedrichs, and Hoyt, 1970).

Both "store" and "find" take as their first argument a memory location. We must return now to the question of how that location might be characterized theoretically.

3.3.2   Memory Locations and Fields

In order to account for people's capacity to understand the sentences they hear, it is helpful to suppose that routines (or schematized information on which routines can be based) corresponding to words (or morphemes) are stored in their memories. Since adult knowledge of most of those routines is permanent, we assume they are stored in what has been called secondary memory. And since there are obvious relations among them—"tree" and "bush" must be closer together in some sense than, say, "tree" and "square"— we assume some organization of the secondary storage system, so that similar concepts are stored in functionally related locations. By using "location" in this manner we do not wish to imply that we are thinking of some topographic location in the brain, for it is possible that the brain's operations are widely distributed and frequently parallel. What we have in mind is an analogy to locations in computer memories, but we need the analogy only to allow the introduction of indices that "point" to those "locations." The brain mechanisms, if any, that might correspond to such pointers are of no concern here.

One might suppose that memory for word routines is sufficiently different from memory for other things that we can differentiate it as a separate domain of search. Tulving (1972) has suggested that a sharp distinction should be drawn between semantic memory and episodic memory. What he calls episodic memory is a more or less faithful record, temporally organized, of a person's experiences. What he calls semantic memory includes all the timeless, organized knowledge a person has about words and other symbols and their relations, and about rules, formulas, and algorithms for manipulating them. Episodic memory holds "mere facts"; semantic memory holds abstract knowledge. Leont'ev (1973) draws a related distinction between "verbal memory" and "word memory." Verbal memory is mediated and voluntary; word memory is immediate and involuntary. Verbal memory is temporary; word memory is permanent.

If we accept this distinction, we can think of memory locations as partitioned into two rather distinct fields. Tulving points out that most experiments psychologists conduct on memory for linguistic materials relate to episodic memory—memory for events during an experimental episode. Episodic memory can exploit semantic memory, but it is organized differently. Miller (1972) tried to suggest the nature of the difference: "Suppose you were asked to remember a word, say, *boat*. What would you do? You have, in one sense, known and remembered the word *boat* ever since you were a child, and will probably continue to remember it until you die. The only sense you might make of such a request would be to associate *boat* with some special situation, cue, or contingency designated by the person who made the request" (p. 367). A request to remember "boat" is not a request to remember the abstract concept but to remember some new pattern of information, specific to the situation, from which a control instruction to utter(boat) can be derived under specified conditions. The request would normally institute some storage instruction, but the storage would add nothing to semantic memory. Tulving would say that such a request would lead to the storage of a specifically encoded memory involving "boat" in episodic memory and that attempts to retrieve it would have to begin with recall of the particular episode in which the request was made.

The difference between episodic and semantic memory is reflected in ordinary language. When describing a particular episode, a speaker will usually be able to supply an identification of the objects, events, or persons involved; when he speaks more generally, however, he may not be able to supply pointers to particulars, and only the listener's semantic knowledge will enable him to construct an interpretation. English provides linguistic devices to indicate whether a speaker is referring to some particular individual or to any member of a class whose attributes are given in semantic memory. The analysis of these linguistic devices has challenged both linguists and philosophers, for they are as complicated as they are important. Consider the following sentences:

      (a) Tom was introduced to Doris.
      (b) Tom was introduced to the wealthy woman.
      (c) Tom wanted to be introduced to the wealthy woman.
      (d) Tom wanted to be introduced to a wealthy woman.
      (e) Every man wants to be introduced to a wealthy woman.

A speaker who utters (a) is probably describing some episode that he has knowledge of; identifications of the participants are provided explicitly for the listener, who can assign pointers to his representations of those individuals and can enter the sentence into his episodic memory of the occasion the speaker is discussing. A speaker who utters (b) or (c) is also presumably describing some particular episode; use of the definite article "the" in "the wealthy woman" would normally be understood to mean that the referent had been previously identified or that the speaker could provide further identification of the particular person if he were asked to. Of course, if the listener knows that "the wealthy woman" was "Doris," he can store (b) in the same form he would store (a). It is possible, however, that a definite reference by the speaker will not enable the listener to identify the particular person referred to, in which case some kind of pointer to a generically characterized but otherwise unknown individual will be all the listener can supply in his interpretation.

The situation grows more uncertain for the listener if he hears (d). The use of the indefinite article "a" in the referentially opaque context created by "want" is ambiguous. It is not clear whether the speaker is describing some remembered episode in Tom's life in which a particular wealthy woman was involved or some episode when Tom wanted to be introduced to any wealthy woman. The ambiguity may be resolved by context: if the speaker adds "but I didn't know any," then the reference is to an indefinite wealthy woman.

If the speaker says (e), the problems are still more complex. Out of context, "Every man wants to be introduced to a wealthy woman" would probably be understood as an expression of the speaker's opinions. Neither the speaker nor the listener would be referring to particular persons, male or female. It would not be correct to say the sentence had no reference at all, however; the speaker is talking about somebody, even though his reference does not identify a particular somebody. Alternatively, (e) could be used to describe a particular episode in which the speaker and listener are participating; perhaps every man in the room with them wants to be introduced to a particular wealthy woman, in which case the speaker has definite pointers in mind that he could provide if the listener requested them.

How these alternatives are to be characterized poses serious problems for pragmatic and semantic theory. Our present interest in them derives from the fact that language distinguishes between particular referents and arbitrary referents, which we take to be related to the difference between episodic memory for particular events and semantic memory for linguistic knowledge. It would seem, therefore, that some sentences create pointers to particular episodic-memory traces and that other sentences create pointers to general semantic-memory traces. A listener who heard "Tom was introduced to Doris" might add it to his episodic memory, but the generic interpretation of "Every man wants to be introduced to a wealthy woman" would (in the unlikely event of its being believed) be added to his semantic memory along with such other general knowledge as "Every man has a liver."

The difference depends on the values that can be assigned to the arguments of the various functions. When no particular referent can be assigned, the listener is left with something more like a general formula than a specific fact. That is to say, a sentence without definite, particular reference is like a whole set of particular sentences at once. Given any particular instance that satisfies the subject description, the general formula can be used to infer that that instance also satisfies the predicate: if Tom is a man, then Tom wants to be introduced to a wealthy woman. Or, if Doris is a wealthy woman, then every man wants to be introduced to her. And so on. The economy of the general formula is obvious. English provides devices for achieving such economies, and any adequate cognitive theory of linguistic competence must include an account of how those devices function.

Speakers of a language, moreover, will exploit those devices whenever they can in order to lighten the burden on their memories. If a set of specific facts can be reduced to a single general rule, the rule is more easily remembered than the specific facts independently. Exploiting such generalizations, however, would lead to intimate cross-referencing between episodic and semantic memory. For example, a person may formulate a general rule for remembering the events in a particular episode; the general rule will be stored in semantic memory, and a pointer from episodic memory to the general rule will have to be assigned. The cooperation between these two memory domains is so intimate, in fact, that it seems misleading to think of two different *kinds* of memory. Two different *ways* of retrieving information from memory might be a better characterization.

Tulving's distinction between episodic and semantic memory (or ways of addressing memory) suggests one kind of restriction on the search domain for a "find" instruction. We could write find(episodic memory, x) for one type of information and find(semantic memory, x) for the other. For our purposes, however, this distinction does not go far enough.

For example, every person has a repertoire of motor skills along with a model of himself that must include the information that these particular skills are available. Knowing how to tie a certain kind of knot requires a sort of memory that we would not like to call either episodic or semantic. A third memory field is required, which we might call action memory.

Some kind of action memory must support the instruction "achieve," which uses whatever skills are at the disposal of the system in order to reduce the difference between the present state and the goal state. For example, a person may know that in a situation of some particular kind the action a will cause the situation to change in a specific way. An analysis of "knowing how" would surely require a great number of such action-change schemata. In order to construct conceptually a sequence of actions calculated to achieve a goal without unnecessary trial-and-error experimentation, there must be stored in memory a set of rules having the general form: action a is possible in context c and will cause event e, where a may be some complicated pattern of movements acquired through considerable practice.

Psychologists often talk as if memory for motor skills and memory for verbal symbols were basically different. Motor skills seem to require some kind of analog representation, verbal knowledge seems more digital. It is possible, though, to defend the hypothesis that here too there is only one kind of secondary memory, but different ways of addressing it. Speaking is a motor skill, after all, so the two memory fields cannot be totally unrelated.

Probably the strongest advocate of the view that verbal and motor skills are closely related was Bartlett (1932), who adopted Henry Head's concept of motor schemata* (the organized settings that provide the bodily contexts for any particular occurrences of a skilled movement) and extended it into a theory of verbal memory. A motor schema is a representation of the bodily state at the moment, and so can be viewed as a summary of the past changes that have led into that state. Bartlett generalized the schema into a description of the state of the organism against which any event—motor, perceptual, symbolic —is measured. When an event is stored, it is as a part of the schema for subsequent events. Consciousness, according to Bartlett, enables an organism "to turn around on its own schemata," that is, to reinstitute a schema that existed in the past and so to remember how the past episode developed. In his own experiments on remembering, Bartlett claimed to find that the first stage began with the reinstatement of a general attitude toward the episode to be remembered; as the person put himself back into that attitude, he began to remember more and more details of his earlier schematization.

As a theory of episodic memory, Bartlett's approach has the interesting implication that general attitudes, undifferentiated as to motor, perceptual, or symbolic content, are stored most faithfully in memory. If these attitudes can be revived, other information schematized along with them can often be recovered with remarkable accuracy and detail. What makes us feel that seman-

*Werner and Kaplan (1963, p. 91) note that this notion of "schema" has a long history, dating back to formulations by Kant in the eighteenth century.

tic and action memory are somehow different from episodic memory is not that words and movements are intrinsically different from episodes, although they may be. The difference in memory organization arises out of the frequent recurrence of these events in so many different episodes that episodic retrieval becomes impractical. For rare words or little-used skills, one may recall the episode in which they were acquired, but this is the exception. As words and skills acquire too many episodic settings to remember, they acquire a timeless character independent of the particular episodes in which they occurred. Which is to say that people develop more direct methods of retrieving information that they use frequently.

Once Tulving's dichotomy is breached, there seems to be no reason to stop with three memory fields. A good case can be made for a geographic memory, in which all of the information a person has about where particular things are and where particular behaviors are appropriate might be stored. We have argued that space and time are organizing principles for the perceptual world; it is reasonable to suppose that memory would be organized in such a way as to accept retrieval cues reflecting these important perceptual coordinates. Episodic memory is characterized by organization in the time dimension; geographic memory would be comparably organized in spatial dimensions.

Moreover, since so much time is spent interacting with and thinking about other people, it would not be unreasonable to propose a person memory. Each person is a nexus of individuating information of considerable personal and social importance; ready access to organized attitudes toward and information about other people is essential for the regulation of interactions with them. Moreover, the agentive role that people can play is reflected linguistically in many diverse ways; person memory would be an important source of support for a human language-processing system.

We could thus replace Tulving's dichotomy with a fivefold classification: semantic, episodic, action, geographic, and person memories. No doubt other distinctions could be made to sound plausible, but grounds for defending this sort of proposal are sufficiently vague that we hesitate to pursue the classification further at the present time. Our immediate need is for some rubric to identify the major fields of memorial search; this fivefold classification will at least serve to illustrate how that need might be met. More experience with such theories is required before they can be intelligently criticized and either improved or discarded.

It does not require experimental analysis, however, to recognize that any boundaries between these memory fields cannot be sharp or impermeable. Imagine an episode in which you are reading aloud to another person in the park. If each memory field were an independent mental organ, the content of what you read would be stored in semantic memory, the occurrence of the episode itself would be stored in episodic memory, your practice in reading aloud would be registered in action memory, the location of the park would be entered in geographic memory, the listener's presence would be stored in person memory. Having scattered all this information about in different places, some mechanism would then be required for its reintegration in recall. Lacking any evidence to the contrary, therefore, it seems simpler to think of a single, long-term, content-addressable memory to which you can gain access by a variety (five or more) of different kinds of contents.

We will assume that these various fields of memory enable people to search their memories in a variety of ways. They can enter memory with an episode and try to remember the details, or they can enter with a person and try to remember episodes in which he was present, or they can enter with a place and try to remember what it looks like, and so forth. In chapter 4, where the concept of semantic fields is introduced, we will attempt to carry the partitioning of semantic memory much further. In that context there will be little temptation to think of the concepts common to many words as defining separate memories. Both there and here our argument is not for a variety of memory organs but for a variety of ways of addressing a single memory organ. For a content-addressable memory, there are as many different modes of addressing as there are content fields to be stored.

One case of addressing memory temporally in search of a particular episode requires special comment. Much use of language is conversational, and a conversation is an episode. As a conversation proceeds the participants must construct some schema for the current episode, some representation of what information is shared at successive moments in the conversation, of what has been said and so is background and of what has not been said and so can be the focus of new contributions. We assume, therefore, that some special priority is assigned to remembering a current episode, in the sense that "find" instructions having the present episode as their search domain can operate with special efficiency and dispatch. One might argue that the schema for the current conversational episode is in some kind of memory intermediate between primary and secondary—a staging area, so to speak, for transfer of information from one to the other. We have no objection to such hypotheses, although it seems simpler to think of the current episode as just another episode like all the rest, distinguished only by recency and accessibility.

However conceptualized, one's representation of the communicative episode in which he is currently involved provides an indispensable basis for understanding what is going on, for analyzing the incoming messages and translating them into appropriate responses. It is possible to study how context affects understanding by comparing people who are given a context with people who are not. For example, two groups might be told to remember a particular textual passage, where one group is given antecedent context and the other sees only the passage itself, as if they had opened a book at random and started reading or walked in during a conversation. Any resulting differences in understanding or memory would be heavily dependent on the particular passage chosen, of course, but it is not difficult to construct passages that are almost incomprehensible without prior knowledge of context.

Bransford and Johnson (1972) read the following passage to high school students who were asked to try to comprehend and remember it:

> If the balloons popped, the sound wouldn't be able to carry since everything would be too far away from the correct floor. A closed window would also prevent the sound from carrying, since most buildings tend to be well insulated. Since the whole operation depends on a steady flow of electricity, a break in the middle of the wire would also cause problems. Of course, the fellow could shout, but the human voice is not loud enough to carry that far. An additional problem is that a string could break on the instrument. Then there could be no accompaniment to the message. It is clear that the best situation would involve less distance. Then there would be fewer potential problems. With face to face contact, the least number of things could go wrong.

After hearing this passage, the students tried to recall it in writing; of the 14 ideas Bransford and Johnson identified in the passage, the students recalled 3.6 on the average. Students who heard the passage twice recalled only 3.8 of the ideas. Some of them reported later that they had actively searched for a situation that the passage might be about; they were generally unable to find one suitable for the entire passage, although they could make sense of parts of it. In Bartlett's terminology, they had no appropriate schema against which the passage could be measured.

Bransford and Johnson also read this passage to students who had seen a picture in advance. They were allowed thirty seconds to inspect the picture before hearing the passage. The picture portrayed an implausible but appropriate situation in terms of which the various sentences could be interpreted and related. (It showed a guitar player serenading a woman who is in an open window at the top of a building. He is using an amplifier system; the loudspeakers hang just outside her window, suspended from balloons.) Students given this pictorial representation of the context in advance were able to remember 8.0 of the component ideas after hearing the passage only once. They also rated the passage as easily comprehensible, whereas students without the context had rated it as difficult to comprehend. If the picture was shown after hearing the passage, but before attempting to recall it, only 3.6 ideas were remembered; it was as if no context had been given. Context aided memory if it was available at the time of input, but not if the input processing had already occurred.

Obviously, this passage was designed to make a point; it is not representative of passages from most books or excerpts from most conversations. But it does make the point: it is not sufficient to know the meanings of all the words and to be able to parse and interpret all the sentences out of context. In order to participate in most communication situations, it is also necessary to be able to construct certain cognitive structures that represent and relate the meanings of the communications, that provide a schema in terms of which new information can be given a conceptual place.

3.3.3   Memory Search

What happens when the executive system tries to execute a control instruction to find something in memory? Let us consider one current account in order to illustrate the kind of answers psychologists are now pursuing. We will choose one that shares our own bias toward computational hypotheses about psychological processes.

One of the more comprehensive theories of memory search is that proposed by Atkinson and Shiffrin (1965, 1968; Shiffrin, 1970). We will not attempt to review the mathematical formulation of their theory or its various applications to a wide variety of psychological experiments. A brief overview of the processes they assume should serve to illustrate the theoretical issues. They propose as their model of memory search a recursive procedure that can be described as a routine:

(i) A request is received for information.

(ii) An executive decision maker decides whether to search, whether to search primary or secondary memory, what strategy to use, whether to respond, continue, or terminate the search, and what search set is to be defined, that is, what set of memory images is to be searched.

(iii) Given a search set by the executive decision maker, an image is randomly selected from that set.

(iv) This image is examined and any relevant information it contains is given to the executive decision maker; the procedure beginning at (ii) is then repeated, but with additional information now available from the recovered image.

The cycle repeats until the requested information is found and recognized, or until the executive decision maker calls a halt. On each cycle the search set may be further constrained and, consequently, the probability of recall increased. Considered as a model for the "find" instruction, the search set corresponds to the domain in memory to be searched and the request corresponds to the description of the target.

The selection of a search set lies at the heart of this retrieval system. The selection will depend not only on the person's general strategy but also on the nature of the request—the information it provides and the response it demands—and on any information recovered during the course of searching. When the system searches episodic memory the search set is frequently delimited in time; Tulving would say that it is delimited by the episode in which the image to be found was acquired. The request may not only delimit the time but also provide other characteristics of the target. For example, if asked what you had for breakfast last Thursday, you would first have to reconstruct the episodes stored for that day and examine them for information that would define a further search for the breakfast in question, which would then be examined for information about the foods eaten. By assigning probabilities to the outcomes of successive steps in such searches, Atkinson and Shiffrin were able to evaluate alternative strategies and to predict the probabilities of successful recall in a variety of experimental situations.

We will assume that this recursive routine, or something like it, is called when the instruction to find information in memory is executed. That is to say, in the example just described, the instruction find(M(Ep), Thursday breakfast) starts a recursive search of episodic memory for last Thursday, for breakfast, for the particular foods in that breakfast episode. Or, again, if asked to name cities in West Virginia, an instruction find(M(Geo), place names in West Virginia) would provide information necessary for the search to begin. As the search set is progressively limited, the probability (at step iii) of drawing an image that will be recognized as the one requested increases. It increases as long as successive cycles continue to provide a more precise characterization of the memory domain to be searched. The search set of Atkinson and Shiffrin is, of course, much more narrowly defined than the general fields of memory that we have tentatively enumerated. People do not usually have to search their whole personal history when they search episodic memory, nor do they usually search all of geographic memory to find some particular place name. The organization within each memory field is a complex subject that we can better discuss in the light of specific examples; we will return to it for the case of semantic memory in chapter 4.

Target specifications will usually have some predicate with a missing argument. That is to say, the predicates "I ate ⎯⎯ for breakfast last Thursday" or "⎯⎯ is a city in West Virginia" would be a natural way to describe the targets. Then the control instruction becomes: find the values of x such that "I ate x for breakfast last Thursday" ("x is a city in West Virginia") is stored in episodic (geographic) memory. This instruction sets up an index x which has no values assigned to it yet, so in order to distinguish indices for which values have not been assigned we will use the notation $?x?$. Then find(M(X), F(?x?, y)) is the schema for a control instruction that tries to evaluate x—that searches the indicated memory domain for something that bears the relation F to y. Similarly, $?F?$ would start a search for relations between x and y.

We do not assume that information is necessarily stored and retrieved in the form of images. Although they seem to be thinking of images, Atkinson and Shiffrin speak of "I-units" that are recovered. Some such neutral designation seems preferable. It is possible, we assume, to execute a control intruction generate(image of I-unit), and in difficult searches such images may provide an economical representation of the information for further processing. In many cases, however, the information will be found almost immediately, so the assumption of images seems gratuitous.

Some critics see the term "executive decision maker" as little more than modern jargon for the implausible claim that there is a homunculus in the head who searches for things. Those who have had experience with complex programming systems, however, understand that such components are merely routines that control the sequencing of other routines. The critical question to ask is whether any decisions are expected from the executive decision maker that could not be made automatically, given the initial conditions of the search. If there is a stage of its operation that demands some ill-defined operation, like "think up the answer," the putative routine is indeed little better than a homunculus. Although Atkinson and Shiffrin are careful to define precisely what their executive decision maker is expected to do, some critics have found certain points less well defined than they would like.

For example, an assumption of most retrieval models is that once the correct information has been located, it will indeed be recognized as correct; recognition would fail only if the trace in episodic memory had deteriorated or been lost. If this assumption were correct, recognition scores would always be higher than recall scores, since recall involves retrieval in addition to recognition. In a review of work relevant to this point, Tulving and Thompson (1973) point out that this consequence of the theory can be contradicted under certain circumstances. For example, if the information is stored with a retrieval cue that leads the person to think about it one particular way, he may fail to recognize it as the same information when it occurs under conditions that do not reinstate the same cue-word association. If "cold" is to be recalled from the cue "ground," and later the person responds "cold" to the stimulus "hot," he may not recognize it as the item to be remembered. Tulving and Thompson argue from such observations that the pairing of a target word with a retrieval cue at input creates a specific meaning for the target word and that this specific meaning, not some generic representation of the word, is what is stored in episodic memory. (Indeed, such arguments led to Tulving's distinction between episodic and semantic memory.) On the principle that "only that can be retrieved that has been stored," Tulving and Thompson argue for an "encoding specificity principle" in episodic memory. In order to retrieve the target, it must be characterized for the "find" instruction by the specific encoding used in that episode.

Reder, Anderson, and Bjork (1974) propose a semantic interpretation of Tulving and Thompson's principle of encoding specificity. They show that the principle does not hold for rare words, which have few senses (Zipf, 1945), and conclude that what must be encoded specifically is the sense of the word. That is to say, when a person in this situation wants to remember a word, he tries to retrieve the specific sense that the word expressed—the same phonological or orthographic shape may not be recognized as the same word unless it is thought of as expressing the same sense. The original cue is effective because it is likely to remind the person again of that specific sense; words having few different senses offer few opportunities for mistakes. For example, when "ground" is the cue, "cold" may make a person think of death; when "hot" subsequently leads him to utter "cold," he may be thinking of temperature; consequently, he may fail to recognize that these different senses are both expressed in English by the same phonological unit. But when the target is an infrequently used word, like "ludicrous" or "ecumenical," most people do not know enough different senses to get into trouble. The point, however, is that people are not aware simultaneously of all the senses a frequently used word can express, and so they can sometimes find a word they are searching for without realizing that they have found it.

During a conversation events may be mentioned that lead to memory searches. Having once found memories of these events, it should not be necessary to keep on finding them; pointers to them are in one's memory of the conversational episode itself, so it is necessary merely to establish that a current phrase is coreferential with an index already assigned.* Very specific encoding is needed to keep straight the difference between memory for the episode under discussion and memory for which subepisodes have already been mentioned in the conversational episode itself. To what extent specificity is achieved by differentiating between episodes or by accumulating more details in the target description (or both) is too difficult a question for idle speculation.

Episodes have a temporal organization. In order to recall an episode, it is necessary not only to remember specific events that occurred but also to have some idea about their order in time. Since most languages—Standard English rather compulsively—express these temporal relations by a variety of devices, we will conclude this discussion of memory search with a brief comment on psychological studies of temporal coding.

If a person is presented with a long series of items and then asked which of two items in the series occurred more recently, his accuracy will be a regular function of their separation and their distance in the past (Yntema and Trask, 1963). From a number of studies of this type it has become clear that people do indeed retain information about temporal order; the major source of disagreement has been about the mechanism of such judgments. One hypothesis is that when an item occurs it creates a memory trace that slowly fades as a function of time; when a person is asked to judge which of two items is more recent, he will select the one whose memory trace is stronger because it has decayed less and so has spent less time in memory. Tulving and Madigan (1970) call this strength hypothesis "a product of desperation" (p. 463) and suggest the following thought experiment. Include the person's own name in the series of items. All subjects will remember seeing their own name, so the trace strength of the name must be very high, yet they will not judge it to have been the last item presented. Such arguments do not imply that trace strength cannot be used as a basis for inferring trace age, but they do suggest that people can have other, more direct information on which to base such judgments.

We assume, therefore, that some part of the encoding of specific items in episodic memory is a "time tag" that helps people distinguish that item from

---

*Phrases associated with discourse referents sometimes change. For example, if in a motor race "the second car" passes "the first car," these phrases exchange their referents; other names, like car A and car B, can be substituted to avoid confusion. The discourse referents of anaphoric pronouns (or superordinate terms used anaphorically) pose special problems, some of which are mentioned in section 3.5.

other items in the same episode and that helps them distinguish one episode from others that resemble it. The incorporation of these time tags seems to be automatic in the sense that it occurs even when a person is instructed only to remember what the items were, and it does not reduce the amount of item information recalled. Tulving and Madigan speculate that temporal coding is related to a variety of interference effects that have been observed in experiments on rote memorization, and deplore the fact that it has received so little systematic study.

Fortunately it is the availability, not the mechanism of such time tags, that is important for our present needs. Not only does temporal organization underlie our assumption that a "find" instruction can search episodic memory, but our inclusion of a temporal argument for the "test" instruction assumes that such tags are available when memory of an event is used to verify some past-tense predicate.

3.4 ROUTINES

In order to understand what people do when they produce or understand language we need a catalog of things people can do. Our review of the perceptual tests people can make and the manner in which they can control their attention to perceived and remembered information might constitute the beginnings of such a catalog. Before we can bring these component operations to bear on linguistic skills, however, we must consider how they are to be combined in compound operations of sufficient complexity.

It should be emphasized that we are concerned here to find some way to talk about how language is *used*. The proposal that we should put the use of language foremost is not novel, of course. Wittgenstein (1953) is probably the most illustrious author of such views, and a whole school of ordinary-language philosophers have helped to light the way. But Wittgenstein's proposal of a model for the use of language was "ein Spiel," which, when translated as "a game," does not immediately suggest the kind of theory we need. Certainly it is true that learning the rules for using language is much like learning the rules of a game, and certainly there are many different uses of language, just as there are many different games. But the formal theory of games has had more relevance to economics than to linguistics or psychology. Nevertheless, linguistic philosophers have kept alive a form of analysis that encourages us to think that an emphasis on use is not an entirely fruitless undertaking if only we can find a better model on which to base a formal theory.

Theories of linguistic usage should be clearly distinguished from theories of language. The difference has been most clearly defined by Chomsky (1963, 1965, 1968), although it was implicit in Saussure's well-known distinction between "langue" and "parole." Chomsky speaks of theories of language as descriptions of an ideal language user's basic *competence* in his language, and of theories of linguistic usage as descriptions of actual *performance* by language users. The linguist's theoretical task is to characterize competence; this Chomsky proposes to do by means of transformational generative grammar. The psycholinguist's task is to characterize performance; no clear notion is offered as to how this should be done, but it is usually assumed that the rules of generative grammar must provide one component of any performance model. According to Chomsky (1965), "a reasonable model of language use will incorporate, as a basic component, the generative grammar that expresses the speaker-hearer's knowledge of the language" (p. 9).

As Pylyshyn (1973b) has pointed out, however, "component" must be interpreted very generally. Proponents of transformational generative grammar claim that it represents the most parsimonious account of a language user's intuitive knowledge of his language. A broader cognitive theory of the user's competence would attempt to account for other data in addition to linguistic intuitions. But a theory that is most parsimonious in describing X need not be part of, or even have the same form as, a theory that is most parsimonious in describing $X + Y$. It is not necessary to incorporate transformational generative grammar as formulated for X into the broader theory that we are attempting to construct for $X + Y$. What is necessary is that the broader theory should also account for the type of structure captured by transformational generative grammar. Because the phrase "incorporated as a component" is so easily misunderstood, we prefer to characterize the relation between these grammatical theories and the broader psychological theory of competence as one of abstraction. If the broader theory is to be adequate, it should be such as to allow all of the valid abstractions of transformational generative grammar. In our view, however, this broader psychological theory of linguistic competence must be formulated in procedural terms.

The competence we will try to characterize is that of a user of so-called Standard English. Thus, the judgments of acceptability that we will rely on may not apply to other kinds of English—child English, Pidgin and Creole English, or various other dialects—but we are limited by our own linguistic experience. When we say that a particular usage is odd or unacceptable, therefore, the judgment is relative to our understanding of Standard English and is *not* a prescriptive judgment about other varieties of English.

3.4.1   Linguistic Devices

What seems to be needed is a wedding of Wittgenstein and Chomsky, a theory as explicit as Chomsky has shown us how to construct about the phenomena that Wittgenstein has shown us are important. Harrison (1972), working within a frame of reference he attributes to Wittgenstein and Chomsky, has provided a version of linguistic philosophy that seems to point in the direction we should go. The part of Harrison's philosophy that we wish to discuss is his description of what he calls linguistic devices. Although he conflates translation and execution, his ideas merit consideration here.

Harrison (1972, chap. 7) illustrates what he means by a linguistic device by stating some explicit procedures that a child might learn to carry out in the course of learning to use the English verb "bring" (a choice presumably inspired by Wittgenstein's account of language games played between a builder and an assistant who brought him slabs to build with). A child learning English might begin to learn the word "bring" by learning the following procedure:

(A)   The learner is shown an object, for example, a ball, and is taught to bring it to the teacher on the command "Bring the ball."

Although the command "Bring the ball" is part of a linguistic system, (A) is a sterile and circumscribed ritual of the sort that could be taught to a dog. A learner who knew only (A), therefore, could not be said to know the meaning of "bring" or to have recognized the separate functions played by "bring," "the," and "ball."

Next the learner acquires labels for everyday medium-sized physical objects in his environment: "book," "doll," "dog," and so on. Harrison emphasizes that a learner of this primitive taxonomy is merely learning to "execute a performance" and is not learning names in the usual sense of "naming." He is simply learning to make certain vocal noises when certain sorts of objects are presented to him. The rules of this linguistic device would be

(B)   (i) When someone says "What's this?" and presents an object in the usual way, utter one but not more than one of the following responses: "book," "doll," "dog," "cat," and so on.

           (ii) To determine which response to utter on a given occasion, apply the following criteria: . . .

The missing criteria in (Bii) would then have the form of a taxonomic schema for identifying instances taking the same label. At this point, of course, the learner has no idea how to use these labels in discourse. He has merely learned another sterile and circumscribed ritual.

If (B) is to be of any use in communication, it must be incorporated into some other linguistic device of wider scope. This is in effect what happens in

(C)   To generate correct responses to utterances of the form "Bring———," in all cases in which the blank is filled by one of the labels whose applications has been learned in (B), apply the following set of rules:

           (i)   Examine all the objects visible in the vicinity and determine (by means of (Bii)) what the correct vocal response would be in each case if the teacher were to ask of that object, "What's this?"

           (ii) As you determine the correct vocal response for each object, utter it subvocally.

           (iii) Detach "bring" from the teacher's utterance and compare the remainder successively with each of your subvocalizations.

(iv) When this comparison produces a match (defined within certain phonological limits), perform on the object which generated the matching subvocal utterance the operation that you learned in (A) to perform on balls in response to the command "Bring the ball."

Harrison comments that the rules of (C), like those of any other linguistic device, are essentially instructions for executing a certain set of procedures. Learning (C) does not involve understanding the syntactic function of "bring" —that it is a transitive verb, or that sentences beginning with "bring" express commands. Children learn to use words in the conventional way long before they are able to understand grammatical rules in the form in which linguists state them.

The important feature of (C) is that it makes essential use of (A) and (B). A learner who has mastered (C) understands something of the meaning of "bring" even though he could not use it in conversation and has no resources for defining or paraphrasing it. His understanding consists of knowing how to perform certain sequences of operations in response to certain cues, and to continue or terminate them according to the outcomes of various tests. A psychologist might want to consider alternative formulations of (C) in order to reduce the amount of subvocal muttering involved, but that is a minor point. Some such device must be available when a child has learned to respond correctly to a command to bring something. If he has not acquired such a linguistic device, he will not know what "Bring the ———" means. If he has learned it, he still may not bring the object requested, but at least he will have some understanding of what he has been asked to do. When he does not bring the object you may be in some doubt as to whether he understands the command, but when he does comply, you can be reasonably sure that he did understand how it is used in this situation. Compliance, of course, is the best evidence a teacher can have that his pupil is learning; compliance is essential if a teacher is to give his pupil instructive feedback concerning his performance. But performance is an imperfect indicator of competence.

Whereas (A) and (B) alone are sterile rituals, (C) is fertile, because its rules refer to other linguistic devices. Harrison proposes that fertility in language is made possible only by the existence of hierarchical relations of presupposition between different linguistic devices—relations of the sort illustrated in (C). The fertility of this system (A)–(C) is quite limited, however, and needs to be enriched by further devices. For example, the child might next learn how to command.

(D)   To get someone to bring you an object that you wish to have hold of:
     (i) Utter the noise "Bring."
    (ii) Look at the object you wish your hearer to bring and by using the rules of (Bii) generate the noise you would utter if you were being shown the desired object in the context of (B).
   (iii) Utter this noise.

Whereas (A)–(C) have little utility for the learner, he can use (D), or something like it, to get people to bring him things. Harrison claims that this discovery exemplifies one of many small but important advances in the use of language that a learner will make as he adds more devices to his equipment. There is no great moment of insight when he can say to himself that now at last he knows what "bring" means. He simply continues to discover more ways to use "bring" in further devices.

The last linguistic device Harrison presents in this context is intended to suggest how a learner might be taught to deal with questions involving "bring":

(E)   The teacher says to a third party, "Bring x" (this being an utterance generated by the rules of (D)). A few moments later he asks the learner, "Is he bringing x?" The rules by which the learner generates an answer to this question are as follows:

(i) Answer either "Yes" or "No."

(ii) Determine which answer to give by reference to the following instructions:

(a) Determine whether the person A to whom the request "Bring x" was directed has moved his position. If he has not, answer "No"; if he has, proceed to (b).

(b) Determine whether A has any object visibly in his possession or attached to him. If he has not, answer "No"; if he has, proceed to (c).

(c) Generate the name of each object noted in (b) using the rules of (Bii).

(d) Detach the noise "bring" from the original request ("Bring x" in this example) and compare the remainder successively with the products of (c). If no match is discovered, answer "No"; if a match is discovered, proceed to (e).

(e) Observe whether A is moving toward the teacher. If so, answer "Yes"; otherwise, answer "No."

Here again one might wish to add details or modify the sequence of procedures in order to obtain a more plausible account, but these are details. Harrison's point is that some such linguistic device is necessary if a learner is to understand questions involving "bring."

Harrison comments that instructions in (E) do not require any detailed description of A's posture or movements—whether he is walking, riding, running, or whatever, or how he is carrying x—so any theory that would explain the meaning of "bring" as an association between certain perceived movements and that vocal noise would have difficulty in accounting for this degree of generalization. But even if the possibility of appropriate generalization were granted, such an associationistic account would leave out the social context in which A's movements were executed (that someone has in fact issued a request addressed to A to "Bring x") because that critically important information is no part of a description of *A*'s movements, however detailed that description might be.

The linguistic device described in (E) makes explicit what some semanticists would call the semantic components or markers of the verb "bring"—that it is a causative, directional, deictic, motion verb. These components of meaning will not be apparent to the learner, of course, since he will master them simply as integral parts of (E). It may be easier for him to learn step (d) in (E) if he has previously learned (C), but even this similarity may at first escape his attention. Eventually the fact that (A)–(E) share subroutines, plus the suggestive hint provided by the phonetic occurrence of "bring" in all of them, should insure that these devices will be integrated in memory as different aspects of a single concept. However, it will not be until steps like (a), (b), and (e) have appeared in many different linguistic devices and the learner has attained sufficient mastery to reflect on them that he may begin to recognize semantic similarities on the basis of shared subroutines. Any explicit appreciation of this basis for impressions of semantic similarity must await the development of a motion concept in terms of which verbs like "bring," "take," "move," "carry," "come," "go," "travel," and many others can be given their conventional places.

A learner who masters the devices (A)–(E) knows how to respond to, how to request, and how to recognize bringing, because he has routines for all of these things. But he will not have—because he does not need—any way to describe to other people how he does it. Still, someone who has mastered (A)–(E) could fairly be judged to know something of the meaning of "bring." That is to say, he would have learned to execute a variety of procedures related in these and other ways, and would presumably have begun to form a concept in terms of which the meaning of "bring" would find a natural place.

A number of difficulties and complications are passed over in this account in order to give a general picture of what might be happening when a child learns to use a word like "bring." The most obvious omission is in (B), where tests for particular object labels are missing; how this gap might be filled will be considered in chapter 4 when the control instruction "identify"—provide a distinguishing label for some percept—is discussed in detail. Less obvious, but equally important, is the fact that the verb "bring" is relatively simple. If we had taken another verb—"grow," for example—it would have been necessary to develop several devices for such different uses as "Fred grew," "Fred grew weary," and "Fred grew roses." It is sometimes assumed that each verb must have associated with it a list of the various verb-phrase constructions into which it can enter (Chomsky, 1965, has referred to this as "strict subcategorization"), but we could assume that each of these uses is simply another device: GROW1, GROW2, and so on, each of which a child would learn separately at first. The realization that these devices share many component tests, as well as their phonetic shapes, could be left to a later stage of linguistic and conceptual self-consciousness.

We might simply leave the matter here, with the conclusion that understanding the meaning of an utterance involves (among other things) knowing how to operate a set of linguistic devices. The whole exercise would be pointless, however, if other people did not execute the same procedures on similar occasions. It is essential for communication that (A)–(E) be functionally equivalent to the linguistic devices used by almost all others in the learner's social group. And since truthfulness is a basic maxim of linguistic communication, learning to use these routines in the conventional way is much the same as learning the conditions under which certain utterances are true. But we do not wish to reduce "knowing the meaning" of an utterance to "knowing the conditions under which it would be true," for reasons considered in section 3.1. If Harrison's analysis is accepted, the opinion that there is some relation between knowing the meaning and knowing what must be done in order to assign a truth value could be given a basis in how language is conventionally learned and used, although the relation would not be one of equivalence. Even children can understand some sentences (such as "There is a gorilla in your closet whenever no one is looking for him") that defy verification.

A person who has learned (A)–(E) will understand the meaning of "bring" even in situations where these procedures are not actually executed: where the command is not obeyed or the answer is not uttered. Analogously, a person can understand the meaning of some arithmetic problem, such as "Multiply 4085 by 799," without actually performing the operations entailed by the problem. The execution of the appropriate procedures demonstrates that he has mastered them, but failure to execute is no proof that he has not. It is not clear from Harrison's account, though, how a person who has mastered (A)–(E) could have any voluntary control over them. Perhaps very young children do not have such control, although this is a claim we would be reluctant to defend. For an adult speaker, however, some of the steps in Harrison's linguistic devices are performed quite automatically, whereas others are very much under voluntary control.

Since we believe that the distinction between translating a sentence into routines and deciding to execute those routines is fundamental, we cannot accept Harrison's theory of linguistic devices in the form presented. Although we share his general view of the proper approach to descriptions of linguistic competence and performance, we must disagree with important details of his attempt to implement that approach. We will therefore propose a different view of what the child must master and the adult can exploit.

3.4.2   Procedural Semantics

It is clear that Harrison is describing linguistic devices that correspond rather closely to routines used to program the operations of a computer.

In order to develop these suggestions further, let us consider how computers are used. The machines themselves operate on patterns of electrical pulses. Different instructions are represented by different patterns. Each make of machine comes equipped with its own list of instructions, most of which are closely tied to the detailed electronic operations that the machine can perform. Human programmers cannot think clearly about complicated problems when they must be translated into such detailed instructions, so higher-level languages have been invented to provide commands more closely related to the problem to be solved. In order for some particular machine to carry out those commands, of course, they must first be translated into the machine language of that particular computer. This translation is usually performed by the machine itself operating under a translating program known generically as a compiler. A compiler for FORTRAN, for example, takes instructions written in the FORTRAN language and translates them into instructions in the language of whatever machine is to make the computation. Once a program has been compiled, it can then be run on the machine. So there is a two-stage process involved, first compiling the program, then executing it.

Programming languages have both syntactic and semantic aspects. Their syntax—the rules for writing commands that the compiler will accept—is usually rigid. The methods used to specify the syntax of programming languages are much the same as those used to describe the syntax of any formalized language (such as formal logic); they are, in fact, the same methods that mathematical linguists have used to characterize transformational generative grammars for natural languages.

The semantics of higher-level programming languages, on the other hand—the rules for assigning performable operations to syntactically well-formed commands—differs from the semantics of logical languages, which assign truth values to well-formed formulas. Assigning "true" or "false" to a particular expression is merely one procedure that a programming semantics must include. Since Harrison's account provides specific procedures that the learner must carry out, it clearly falls within the realm of procedural semantics rather than propositional semantics. We wish to develop this suggestion further in terms of an analogy with the operation of compilers, but in order not to distort Harrison's ideas we will speak of the "routines" a language user has acquired, instead of his "linguistic devices."

In the case of linguistic communication between speakers and listeners, what might be analogous to a higher-level programming language? An obvious suggestion is that natural languages might be so regarded. For example, Woods (1967) writes that "in a question-answering system . . . each question which the user poses to the system is a command or instruction for the system to perform some action or actions. The output of the semantic interpreter is a formal representation of the action which the system is to take. Thus the parser and the semantic interpreter constitute in effect a natural language compiler which translates the input natural language questions into a formal query language" (p. 8–1). Davies and Isard (1972) have carried this analogy further; they suggest that all sentences can be regarded as bits of higher-level programming, and that understanding any sentence is analogous to compiling the program it encodes.

Once compiled, a program may or may not be run. One obvious advantage of the Davies-Isard suggestion is that it provides a natural way to disconnect the understanding of a sentence from any actions it might entail, thus dissolving a bond that has always bedeviled associationistic theories of language and that has led to the invention of such intervening variables as "dispositions to respond" or "representational mediation processes." Davies and Isard propose that the compilation and execution processes can be separated by the earliest possible "point of refusal." Neither man nor machine can refuse to obey a command until the command has been understood. Presumably, compilation occurs automatically without conscious control by the listener; he cannot refuse to understand it. Davies and Isard comment that loss of conscious control over one's compiler may correspond to knowing a language fluently.

We are led by such arguments to consider the nature of compilers and their suitability as analogs for the human process of interpreting grammatical sentences. Because it is only an analogy, and in order to avoid too close identification of understanding with compilation, we will speak of the process as translation rather than compilation; the goal of the translator is to produce sequences of instructions. The output of the translator will be available to another component of the system, which we call the executor. If the listener decides to run the routine, the executor will undertake to do so.

If we imagine that the listener-translator takes spoken words a few at a time and stores them in some working memory until they can be translated into a program of instructions to operate the neural computer, then there must be available in secondary memory an extensive set of subroutines for each word. If no translation can be produced, the input sentence is not understood. If more than one translation is possible, the input sentence is ambiguous.

According to this interpretation of Harrison's linguistic devices, knowing a word is defined as being able to construct well-formed programs when that word is part of the input sentence. This definition implies the existence of something like a lexicon, a set of subroutines that can be called when different words are used, but this procedural lexicon would be very different from the dictionaries of everyday use and the subroutines would not resemble a familiar dictionary entry. (Deciding on an appropriate formulation of such routines is the subject of chapter 4.) But the obvious implication is that knowledge of any word need not be compacted and deposited in any single place corresponding to *the* lexical (or conceptual) entry for that word. Procedures can be composed and related much more flexibly and freely than, say, lists of semantic components. The theoretical problem is how best to exploit that freedom.

The output of the translator would be a program in the sense made most explicit by Newell and Simon (1972), who have proposed an extensive theory of human problem solving based on the computer metaphor. In order to simplify their task, Newell and Simon deliberately ignored the perceptual inputs and behavioral outputs of their hypothetical information-processing system. The general nature of their enterprise, however, makes it clear that the perceptual processes involved in hearing and understanding a sentence must translate it into some kind of notation usable by the programs involved in problem solving. The Davies-Isard proposal, therefore, is compatible—in spirit if not in detail—with the Newell-Simon proposal, and might be regarded as filling a gap left in the more general theory. (For alternative views on how this gap might be filled, see Minsky, 1968; Rumelhart, Lindsay, and Norman, 1972; Simon and Siklossy, 1972; Anderson and Bower, 1973; Rustin, 1973; Schank and Colby, 1973; Norman and Rumelhart, 1975.)

One of the most impressive applications of this kind of thinking to the understanding of natural languages has been the work of Winograd (1971), who programmed a hypothetical robot to move blocks in response to commands given in English. Such applications do much to clarify what a semantic theory must be and do in order to describe such information processing. Winograd's program will not be described here, but everyone with a serious interest in psycholinguistics should study it carefully. Winograd's work is the clearest glimpse yet of how procedural semantics can be applied to natural language.

Consider some advantages of this approach (Miller, 1974a). In addition to separating translation from execution, a procedural approach does not suffer from the old referential embarrassment about the meanings of the little words, for these are critically important signals as to the order in which subroutines must be assembled. Nor is there any reluctance to deal with clauses or whole sentences rather than isolated words; the verb will be recognized as the basic operator in any clause, for it organizes the roles of the various noun phrases that can serve as its arguments. Rules of syntax will be seen as abstractions from, not components of, the user's competence; syntactic rules are not rules that children must discover and learn but generalizations about what children learn, generalizations against which a psycholinguist can test his more specific procedural hypotheses.

The output of the translator, therefore, must be something like the linguistic devices that Harrison describes. It is obvious that the translation will have to differ depending on whether we are dealing with a command, a question, or a declarative statement. Before we can know how to formulate routines for particular words, we must have at least a preliminary notion of the translations by which they will be called as subroutines.

3.5   TRANSLATION INTO ROUTINES

The theoretical problem we face is to characterize how a sentence might be articulated in some central language in terms of which cognitive operations can be carried out. As Fodor, Bever, and Garrett (1974) remark, "it seems clear that the speech event must at some point be assigned an analysis in such a central language, and that the object of the elaborate series of recodings which underlies speech perception is precisely to effect the assignment. Utterances can communicate thoughts only because hearers know how to translate them into the language in which thinking is done" (p. 508).

We have claimed that this process of translation can be profitably likened to the compilation of a routine that can be executed. We will now try to illustrate how this might be done for a few simple sentences, all involving "bring" in order to maintain a parallel with Harrison's discussion of linguistic devices for using this verb. Our choice of examples is not intended to reflect a possible order of acquisition; it is simply for expository purposes. As we saw in Harrison's examples, it is necessary for various reasons to embed each sentence we analyze in some context of social interaction; the contexts we will use differ from those envisaged by Harrison, again for expository convenience.

By embedding examples in a conversational context we hope to leave room in our theory for those aspects of linguistic communication that confer on mere utterances the status of being what some philosophers have called speech acts: questions, assertions, greetings, denials, promises, requests, commands, and so on. Philosophical interest in speech acts seems to stem from Austin's (1962b) discussion of such sentences as "I bet you sixpence it will rain tomorrow," which are declarative in form yet have no obvious truth value; they are not so much sentences that say something as they are sentences that do something—in this case, offer a wager. Such sentences perform what Austin called illocutionary acts. His analysis of these acts led him to conclude that statements are also acts with an illocutionary force, that every genuine speech act has both a propositional content and an illocutionary force.

Searle (1969) has elaborated on Austin's work, taking the speech act as the basic unit of linguistic communication and exploring connections among speech acts, what the speaker means, what the sentence uttered means, what the speaker intends, what the listener understands, and what the rules governing the linguistic elements are. When a person utters an appropriate sentence in an appropriate context, that speech act has not only a propositional content but also an illocutionary force that depends on what the person thought he was trying to do when he uttered it. The rules that govern the felicitous performance of speech acts go well beyond the rules of syntax and semantics; many of them might be considered pragmatic rules (J. J. Katz, 1972).

Although we will not consider speech acts in detail until section 7.4, it is obvious that a listener's impression of what speech act a talker is performing will have important implications for the way he will translate it into a routine. One of the most dramatic examples is irony. If a speaker detests some person, he may say "Isn't he a great guy" in order to communicate exactly the opposite opinion. He will be correctly understood only if the listener knows his true opinion in advance or if some exaggerated intonation signals that he does not mean what he is saying. The pragmatic rules for translating such sentences into the routines they express must rely on the listener's sophistication. In his William James Lectures at Harvard in 1967-68, Grice dubbed such usages conversational implicatures. The speaker apparently violates a conversational maxim to speak the truth; the listener recognizes the violation, but has no reason to think that the speaker is being deliberately uncooperative; moreover, the listener knows that the speaker knows that the listener will recognize the violation and that the speaker knows that the listener is clever enough to make out what the speaker really means; so the listener searches for a related statement that will express what the speaker really means—in this case, the opposite.

We will avoid such complex inferential processes in the examples that follow, but even in simpler situations it is necessary to keep in mind that the routines into which sentences are translated are subroutines in some higher-order program controlling the person's participation in the social interaction. The higher-order program may itself be a subroutine in some more general plan the person is trying to execute. Such higher-order routines not only determine whether the translated routine for a sentence is to be executed; they can also affect the choice of particular control instructions to use in the translation and often provide information about arguments on which control instructions operate. In short, we assume that a psycholinguistic account of a language user's competence should not be limited to the syntactic and semantic processing that provides the focus for narrowly linguistic accounts. Other considerations must be included in a procedural approach to semiotics.

An important source of mismatch between what a speaker actually says and the program he expects his listener to compile is conversational etiquette. In English, according to traditional grammatical dogma, statements are expressed in the indicative, assumptions are posed in the subjunctive, and commands are issued in the imperative mood of the verb; questions are signaled by interrogative pronouns or word order. If this were true, describing rules for translating sentences into executable routines would be much simpler than it is. But as language is actually used, such signals are very unreliable. The simplest counterexamples are provided by the various ways we have of requesting another person to do something.

One might say, for example, "Pass the salt." Between social equals, however, this way of phrasing a request for action would be rather brusque. At the very least the speaker would probably soften it by adding "please." But even the imperative mood of "Pass the salt, please" is often too formal, and etiquette generally dictates an interrogative version: "Would you pass the salt?" or "Can you pass the salt?" or "Could I bother you to pass the salt?" or "Can you reach the salt?" or whatever. The fact that "please" can be appended to these interrogatives suggests they are not mere questions—one would not ordinarily say, for example, "Is your father dead, please?" although "please" can sometimes be used to soften requests for an answer as well as requests for action. If these interrogative sentences are interpreted as true questions, rather than as requests for action, they can be answered yes or no, but such a response would be a form of verbal play for anyone old enough to understand this conversational convention, that is, anyone older than about three. Indeed, a declarative sentence can also express a request for action: "You have the salt" or "I need some salt" or "There's not enough salt on these beans" or "We ought to get another saltcellar" or the like will usually do the trick, although if the request is too covert—"I wish my arms were longer"—the hearer may not respond appropriately.

Sinclair et al. (1972), on the basis of an analysis of how teachers request actions of their students, formulated the following rules. (a) Any interrogative containing one of the modal auxiliaries "can," "could," "will," "would" (and sometimes "going to"), with the addressee as subject and the predicate describing an action that is feasible for the addressee to perform, is to be interpreted as a command. (b) Any declarative or interrogative referring to an action or activity that is forbidden or not supposed to be occurring at the particular time is to be interpreted as a command to stop. (c) Any declarative or interrogative referring to an action or activity that teacher and pupil know ought to have been performed or completed and has not been is to be interpreted as a command. For example, according to rule (a), "Can John bring me your paper?" would be a question because the subject of the sentence is not the addressee, and "Can you swim a length?" would be a question because teacher and student are in the classroom, but "Can you bring me your paper?" would be a command. "May I have your paper?" would also be a command, but presumably such sentences did not occur in the corpus analyzed by Sinclair et al.

In general, rules can be stated for etiquette, whereas unraveling a conversational implicature is a form of problem solving not easily characterized or automatically executed. Somewhere between the two are cases Grice calls conventional implicatures. For example, "Dinner lasted until ten" suggests that dinner ended at ten, but if it had continued until eleven, it would still be true to say that it lasted until ten. That its ending at ten is not entailed is demonstrated by the ease with which the implicature can be canceled: "Dinner lasted until ten or later." Conventional implicatures might be regarded as conversational implicatures that have become automatic and so might be formulated as rules of usage. But the boundaries here are not easily drawn. To what extent these ways of translating are frozen into social conventions and to what extent they are shared by different social groups are fascinating topics for descriptive sociolinguistics.

In order to illustrate as simply as possible how a listener might translate a sentence into an executable program, we will deliberately forgo these complications. Instead, we will try to suggest how the process might go for relatively simple, straightforward examples, and postpone the complications until we have something in hand to complicate.

3.5.1   Yes/No Questions

As a first example, assume that a person A has participated in an episode Ep that he now remembers; call his memory of the episode M(Ep). Person B did not witness Ep but knows that it occurred and is learning what happened by talking to A about it. That is to say, persons A and B can both identify the episode Ep by some nominal construction, for example, "the dinner party at the Smiths' house." At the time our first example occurs, this episode has been identified by both participants as the topic of their conversation. In order to learn more details, B might ask some such question as

(1)   Did Lucy bring the dessert?

A must translate this sentence into a routine for producing an answer of the form "Yes," "No," "Yes, she brought chocolate cake," "I don't remember," "I think so."

Questions should lead to routines for finding or inferring information needed to formulate answers. In yes/no questions the task is to search somewhere—in memory in this example, although a different example might require perceptual search—for information that would confirm or disconfirm the declarative form of the sentence. In short, is "Lucy brought the dessert" true or false? Note, however, that understanding this question does not require verification of the implicit declarative. To understand the question it is necessary to understand what the implicit declarative statement means and that verification of it has been requested.

Note also that the sentence "Did Lucy bring the dessert?" is lacking any spatial locatives. Hence, it might be paraphrased as "Did Lucy serve the dessert?" (bring it to the table) or as "Did Lucy provide the dessert?" (bring it to the party). A third person who arrived just in time to hear *B*'s question might interpret it either way. It is possible, of course, that *B* deliberately asked an ambiguous question—asked two questions at once—and hopes *A*'s answer will explicate the appropriate relation between Lucy and the dessert. In order to avoid this ambiguity, we will assume that the participants' general knowledge and the antecedent conversation resolve it: both *A* and *B* know that Lucy was a guest and not a member of the Smith household, and *A* has already informed *B* that different guests provided different courses for the dinner. In this context, *A* might search his memory for Lucy's arrival at the party and test whether she was carrying a dessert. The point is that in a slightly different conversational context exactly the same question might lead *A* to search his memory for the serving of the dessert in order to test whether Lucy participated. The particular routine that a listener constructs from a given sentence is not usually determined solely by the form of the sentence itself but depends also on the context in which it occurs.

Since the information processing that occurs depends on what is known in advance, we can begin the analysis by trying to distinguish between what *B* knows before he asks the question and what he knows after it is answered. If we assume that B is asking "Did Lucy bring the dessert to the party?" and that this is a sincere question directed to *A* (who is expected to do something that will add to *B*'s knowledge), then *B* must hold certain beliefs about the episode under discussion. That is to say, *B*'s information about the episode prior to asking the question must be sufficient to support such sentences as

    (a) There was a person named Lucy.
    (b) There was a dessert.
    (c) There was a time at which Lucy was not present.

B's knowledge of the episode may include more than this, of course, but we are concerned here merely with what he must know in order to ask (1) as a sincere question. If these facts correspond to what *A* knows about the episode, then it is possible for *A* to construct a routine that finds in his memory the information needed to answer the question. If *A* answers "Yes," he confirms (a)–(c). An affirmative answer also confirms certain other sentences, such as

(d) Lucy came.
(e) Lucy brought food.
(f) Someone brought the dessert.

After an affirmative answer, *B* can add such facts to his information about the episode—information on the basis of which the conversation can continue.

All of the sentences (a)–(f) are entailed by an affirmative answer to (1), in the formal sense that it would be contradictory if "Lucy brought the dessert" were true and any of (a)–(f) were false. However, there is a pragmatic difference between (a)–(c) and (d)–(f). If *B* were mistaken about (a)–(c), *A* could not reply sincerely with a simple "no"; he would probably reply in some manner that would correct the misconception of the episode that *B* took as the basis for the question. Both *A* and *B* have to know (a)–(c) in advance. On the other hand, it is not necessary that *B* know (d)–(f) in advance in order to ask (1) sincerely; if he were ignorant or mistaken about them, a simple "no" would be a perfectly plausible answer. We will say that sentences like (a)–(c) are (pragmatically) *presupposed* by "Lucy brought the dessert," whereas sentences like (d)–(f) are merely entailed by it.

Presuppositions have been discussed extensively by philosophers and linguists interested in semantics. According to Strawson (1952), statement *S* (semantically) presupposes statement *S′* if *S′* is a necessary condition for the truth or falsity of *S*. For example, "John has children" is a necessary condition for the truth or falsity of "All John's children are asleep." If John has no children, then, according to Strawson, the statement made by the sentence "All John's children are asleep" is neither true nor false; it has no truth value in a bivalent logic. According to this view, formal analyses of presupposition must be stated in three-valued logics, where statements can be true, false, or neither (van Fraassen, 1971).

Strawson views presupposition as a relation among statements, not sentences, because the same sentence can be used to make different statements on different occasions; the same sentence might have different presuppositions in different contexts. The presuppositions of a sentence are relative to the context in which it is used, but these contextual relations are not an integral part of the formal definition of semantic presuppositions.

There is another definition of presupposition, not as a formal condition for a statement to be true or false but as a pragmatic condition for the felicitous use of a sentence (Karttunen, 1973a). The pragmatic definition, which regards presuppositions as sincerity conditions that must be satisfied for the sincere use of the sentence, is relevant to the ways sentences are conventionally used. These two definitions have enough in common to be easily confused, but no satisfactory statement of the relation between them is presently available. Our problem is to characterize the routines involved in sentences not only in terms of syntactic and semantic relations among their constituent parts but also in terms of the semantic conditions for their verification and the pragmatic conditions for their sincere use in particular contexts.

All three aspects of the problem—pragmatic, semantic, and syntactic— impose conditions on the kind of information processing that will occur. Obviously *A* must know how to interpret (1) semantically. And the routine *A* must execute in order to answer (1) will reflect the fact that it is a yes/no question; other kinds of questions would be indicated by other grammatical forms, so it is also obvious that *A*'s routine must reflect syntactic relations as well as semantic relations and sincerity conditions.

If the question were "Who brought the dessert?" the task would be to find information relating some particular individual to the dessert by the operator associated with "bring" and to give an answer that would identify that individual. "Why did Lucy bring the dessert?" must set up a search for goals; it would be necessary to find the event in memory and then to determine what larger goal of Lucy's created this event as a subgoal; "why" presupposes an affirmative answer to (1) and, if the presupposition is satisfied, institutes a search for information about the related goal structure underlying the behavior. "How did Lucy bring the dessert?" sets up a search for details about the instrumentalities involved in the event. And so forth. We will postpone consideration of these questions with missing arguments until we have disposed of (1).

Questions of fact lead to searches for information, and various types of questions specify various types of searches. The routines into which such sentences are translated, therefore, must have "find" as their basic instruction. And "find," of course, requires not only a description of the object or event that is the target of the search but also an indication of the domain to be searched. The domain of search will usually be inherited from the context, although some of the most interesting questions provide little or no guidance on this point. For instance, "Is a man's life worth more than the Louvre?" or "Did God die?" could be answered yes or no, but the justification of the answer would be of more interest than the answer itself; where a person decides to search for information to justify his answer is the crux of such questions. We will limit our discussion here to questions about matters of fact, where the locus of relevant information is reasonably clear. The task we have set ourselves is to characterize the procedural semantics of (1), and for that we must translate it into a routine to search through memory.

We will assume that translation proceeds left to right, although primary auditory memory can support limited backup in cases of incorrect analysis. Since we are interested primarily in semantic processing, syntactic details will be suppressed, but we must assume that information about syntactic category is available in the lexicon and that the translator is guided by its knowledge of syntactic rules (see 3.5.4). For example, the translator will recognize that "did" in initial position signals a question about an event prior to the time of utterance, and in this situation institutes a find-in-episodic-memory routine. The translation of "did" thus becomes

(2)   find(M(Ep),———),

where the blank leaves a place for a description of what is to be found. M(Ep) is not a necessary interpretation of "did," of course; in other situations, other search domains would be appropriate.

"Lucy" is a proper name; let us assume that it suffices to enable A to identify a particular individual who participated in Ep, so a pointer is created to A's concept of that individual; let the pointer be x. (If we used "Lucy" as the pointer, we could confuse the word "Lucy," which may be shared by many different individuals, with the particular individual identified by A and B; if we assign x the value of A's concept-of-particular-Lucy, then x is unambiguous in this routine.) The verb "bring" provides the basic operator of the sentence; for the moment, let us assume that this operator is stored in lexical memory as BRING(agent, object, recipient). (Note that BRING is not the word "bring" but an operator that characterizes the meaning of the word.) A pointer —call it F—is created to this operator, and x, the pointer to Lucy, is taken as its first argument. So now, after translating "Did Lucy bring," we have

(3)   find(M(Ep), $F(x,$———, ———)),

where blanks are left for pointers to the object and recipient that remain to be supplied. The definite article "the" suggests that reference has already been justified by the context. Syntactically, however, "the" does little more here than signal segmentation; it is simply a left adjunct of a noun that will follow. The noun "dessert" supplies a pointer to A's concept of desserts; let this pointer be y. The sentence ends here with one argument missing. We assume that A knows implicitly—that is to say, that his translator has a rule—that the indirect object or recipient can be deleted in operators like BRING and that y can thus be taken as object and the second argument of F. (Alternatively, A could supply a value for $z = $ location of Ep, but we will take the simpler formulation here.) This completes the translation and leaves us with a routine that can be represented as

(4)   find(M(Ep), $F(x, y)$).

This representation, is, of course, incomplete. A "find" instruction must also indicate what to do next. For example, if the description is found in memory, go next to an instruction to utter "yes"; if it is found to be contradicted by information stored in memory, go next to an instruction to utter "no"; if nothing in memory is relevant to the description, go next to an instruction to utter "I don't know." Although these provisions for answering are an integral part of the routine that is compiled when a question is asked, they clutter a description of how a sentence is translated into a retrieval routine; we will suppress them here for expository convenience.

In place of the original sentence, we now have an instruction to find, followed by a string of pointers. The first argument is a pointer to the place we must search, the second argument is a description of the thing we are searching for. The description is a pointer to the BRING operator, followed by pointers to the individual and the class of things that are to be taken as its arguments, namely, Lucy and the dessert.

If *A* knows English well, and if he has heard and attended to the question, this translation is automatic and involuntary. At this point, however, he has an option. He can ignore the question or he can try to answer it. His decision will depend on a variety of considerations relating to the social context of the conversation. For example, his decision to answer will be influenced by his judgment that the question was addressed to him, the prestige or affective relations between *B* and himself, the importance of the answer relative to his larger goals, his impression that *B* is sincere or joking. Such considerations go far beyond the kind of information processing we are trying to analyze here. We will, therefore consider only the case in which he decides to answer. In that event, he must try to run routine (4). That is to say, if he decides to answer the question truthfully, he must search his memory of the episode for the information required to verify the description, and he must respond according to the outcome of that search.

We have assumed that *A* has correctly identified the episode in question and that his memory of it is not blank, because he has been talking to *B* about it. His task, therefore, is to apply the various tests that define BRING to any information about Lucy and the dessert in M(Ep).

Let us assume that the tests defining BRING are of the following form:

(5) (i) find(domain, COME(agent)) and call it *e*
  (ii) test(during *e*, Hold(agent, object))

The "find" instruction in (5i) is needed in order to identify the event to which tests are to be applied. Since the event for which the system must search is described as satisfying COME, which we must also define shortly, (5i) expresses the hypothesis that simple sentences with "bring" entail similar sentences with "come" in ordinary discourse. That is to say, if "Lucy came" were false, then "Lucy brought the dessert" would also be false. (Note that "Lucy brought the dessert" does not semantically presuppose "Lucy came," but merely entails it, since the truth value of "Lucy brought the dessert" is not indeterminate when "Lucy came" is false.)

Once the event corresponding to "Lucy came" is identified, (5ii) tests whether an appropriate relation between agent and object actually obtained during the event. Presumably, BRING would also include tests to determine that the object was delivered to the recipient, but since the recipient is omitted in (1), we can temporarily ignore this complication. What the operator BRING will try to do is search some indicated domain for an event that satisfies the description COME(agent) for someone coming and, if such an event is found, will call it *e*; then it will test whether during *e* that person had some object with him in such a way that his movements caused the object to move with him (which is the meaning of Hold, introduced as a perceptual predicate in 2.6.2).

As BRING is stated in (5), of course, it cannot be executed, because its arguments have not been given values. However, when BRING is called by routine (4), appropriate values can be transferred to it: the domain of search is $M(Ep)$, agent is x, and object is y. Thus, (4) enables us to formulate (5) as an executable routine:

(6)   (i) find($M(Ep)$, COME(x)) and call it e
          (ii) test(during e, Hold(x, y))

If either instruction fails, we assume that processing is interrupted and that control is turned over to the executive system, which will then try to find alternative ways to answer the question.

We say that (5) is not executable because values for its arguments have not been provided. In a more general sense, however, it is executable, because it is possible to provide those values in appropriate contexts. It would be more accurate to speak of (5) as being potentially executable and of (6) as being immediately executable. In order to convert a potentially executable routine into an immediately executable routine, it is necessary to provide pointers to the values on which it must operate. We will say that if the context is such that appropriate values can be provided to make the routine immediately executable, the context satisfies the routine.

This notion of a context satisfying the routines that a sentence involves is closely related to the pragmatic definition of presupposition. If a context does not satisfy the presuppositions of a sentence, the sentence cannot be uttered sincerely. If a context does not satisfy the routines of a sentence, the routines cannot be executed. If this analogy is accurate, it means that sentence routines should be characterized in such a way that their satisfaction corresponds to the satisfaction of the presuppositions of the sentence.

When a test routine is executed, it can terminate in "yes," "no," or "don't know." Let us say that the routine fails if the outcome of the tests is "no" or "don't know." Consider some of the ways routine (4) could fail:

—If A did not witness Lucy's arrival, his search of $M(Ep)$ would fail to find the event required in (6i). Consequently, the "find" instruction would not provide an appropriate argument for the "test" time in (6ii). Should this be regarded as a presuppositional failure on the grounds that the argument of a test could not be found? Clearly not. The fact that A did not see Lucy arrive does not imply that she did not arrive; A's perception of her arrival is not presupposed by the question. A routine is satisfied if values for its arguments can be found, but the fact that arguments have not been found does not mean that it could not be satisfied. In order to know that a routine could not be satisfied, the context must be known to violate the presuppositions of the sentence. If the context neither satisfies nor violates the routine, the routine should be written in such a way as to lead to the outcome "don't know."

—If A saw Lucy arrive but has forgotten it, a similar failure would occur and should lead to "don't know."

—If A remembers seeing Lucy arrive but has forgotten whether she had the dessert with her, test (6ii) would be executable with the result "don't know." This outcome might lead to the utterance "I don't remember."

—If A saw Lucy arrive and remembers that she did not have the dessert, test (6ii) would be executable with the result "no," in which case A could say, simply, "No."

As we have described A's efforts to answer the question so far, we seem to have assumed that the only way he could have learned whether Lucy brought the dessert was to see her carry it in. This simplifies our account of what A is doing, but at the cost of ignoring highly probable alternatives (Norman, 1973). Suppose, for example, that providing the dessert was indeed Lucy's project but that her escort did the actual carrying. We could still say that she "brought" it, even though she delegated the actual delivery. Presumably we have some way of allowing an instrumentality to intervene between an agent and the motions of objects for which the agent is responsible. When we say, for example, "Johnny Bench hit the ball over the fence," it is understood by people who know anything about baseball that Johnny Bench himself never touched the ball; it was his bat that caused the ball to travel over the fence. Similarly, it was Lucy's escort who caused the dessert to travel to the location of the episode under discussion. We must allow a penumbra around the test for $\text{Hold}(x, y)$ sufficient to permit the employment of some complex instrumentality.

If A remembers that the episode was a dinner party where each participant brought and served one of the courses, and if he also remembers that Lucy served the dessert, he might well infer that Lucy brought the dessert, even though he did not actually witness her bringing it. When A searches M(Ep) and finds no event corresponding to Lucy's bringing the dessert, he does not immediately utter "I don't know" or "I don't remember." He first transfers control to a problem-solving routine that would search for alternative ways to test "Lucy brought the dessert." Only when this more complex routine fails would the failure be communicated to B.

The most common alternative to witnessing an event, of course, is being told about it. Someone might have said to A, "Lucy brought the chocolate cake." A would have translated this sentence into a routine to store the information in memory and, lacking any information to the contrary, would have run it; if the storage was successful, A might find in M(Ep) some such fact as, say, $G(u, v, w)$, where G is a pointer to BRING, u to Lucy, v to chocolate cake, and w to the dinner party. Under these circumstances, routine (4) would succeed directly without further testing of memory.

The difference between remembering a fact and remembering a witnessed event can lead in English to different forms of expression. Thus, "I remember that Lucy brought the dessert" usually means the fact is remembered, whereas "I remember Lucy's bringing the dessert" usually means the event itself is remembered. We will pursue the linguistic analysis of sentential complements in 7.3.1, but it is worth noting here that R. M. W. Dixon (personal communication) has attempted to account for a variety of semantic distinctions among English complement constructions on the basis of this difference between remembered facts and remembered events. We assume that in one case the retrieval system finds a stored proposition that entails the target description and that in the other it finds a stored perception of an event that can be tested to verify the target description.

Although the many different ways in which (4) could fail, and the many different ways it could succeed other than by satisfying (6), must be borne in mind, they should not distract us from our present purpose. Having considered them, we now turn to the special case where an affirmative answer can be given from memory of the event in question.

Let us assume that Lucy did bring the dessert, that A witnessed this event, that he remembers it at the time of his conversation with B, and that he decides to answer the question. Then we can ask whether (4) really represents an executable routine and answer the question by tracing its execution.

Routine (4) tests M(Ep) for something satisfying the description $F(x, y)$. F calls BRING, and appropriate values are transferred to it, giving (6). The first instruction in (6) has the same format as (4), but a different operator. Assume that COME is an operator that involves the following tests:

(7)   (i) find(domain, Obj(3d)) and call it w
             (ii) find(domain, Travel(w)) and call it e
             (iii) test(start of e, notIncl(w, Reg(speaker or listener))) &
                   test(end of e, Incl(w, Reg(speaker or listener)))

In (7i) only the existence of the object is presupposed. The arguments in (7) can be given values transferred from (6); the domain of search is M(Ep); the object sought is Lucy, for whom we already have the pointer x; the listener is A, and the region of the listener is his location at the time of e, namely, the place where the episode occurred. Thus, (7) becomes

(8)   (i) find(M(Ep), x)
             (ii) test(during Ep, Travel(x)) and call it e
             (iii) test(start of e, notIncl(x, Reg(Ep))) &
                   test(end of e, Incl(x, Reg(Ep)))

Hence, M(Ep) is searched for memories of Lucy; each memory is tested until an event is found that satisfies the test of motion; then e is tested to determine whether Lucy was not in the region of the episode at the beginning but was there at the end. Subroutine (8) will deliver an affirmative signal to routine (6), along with the pointer e. Then (6ii) tests whether Lucy had y with her during e.

M(Ep), however, contains a memory of a particular chocolate cake, whereas y points to the more generic concept of desserts. It is necessary to determine whether the particular chocolate cake that is remembered belongs to the category of things labeled desserts. The fact that chocolate cakes are often served as desserts must be represented somewhere in memory; this is general information, not a fact about the episode. Precisely how this test should be represented will be discussed in chapter 4, but for the moment let us assume that some mechanism exists to categorize the remembered object as an instance of the concept pointed to by y, so the test for $Hold(x, y)$ gives an affirmative signal. Now routine (6) has been successfully executed, and the response "Yes" can occur.

The point of this account is that the linguistic competence of a user of English should be characterized in such a way as to account for such operations. The translation of "Did Lucy bring the dessert?" in the context we have assumed does indeed provide a routine that a hearer can execute. A host of difficult details are avoided by assumption and by the simplicity of the example; we will deal with some of them later. For the moment, we are concerned to indicate the general setting within which these details are to be considered.

3.5.2   Present Progressive

While this example is before us, we should note the role of tense and aspect. Question (1) is posed in the past tense, which signals a search of memory. How would B phrase his question if he wanted A to perform a perceptual search of the environment? Obviously he would remove the past marker from the verb, but that change alone would yield:

(9)   Does Lucy bring the dessert?

In this form, however, the question would not normally be interpreted as relating to the present situation. Although "Lucy brought the dessert" is clearly marked as past tense, "Lucy brings the dessert" is not marked as present; it is merely unmarked for past. Thus, (9) could be regarded as a question about Lucy's habitual behavior, and the routine would have to indicate that fact by designating person memory as the appropriate domain of search.

In order to indicate that A should search the environment, B would probably phrase his question in the progressive aspect:

(10)   Is Lucy bringing the dessert?

But now the question is ambiguous. It might mean "Is Lucy in the act of bringing the dessert right now?" It would probably be interpreted to mean "Is Lucy planning to bring the dessert at some future time?" The first interpretation could translate into a routine for searching the environment, the second into a routine for searching person memory for information about Lucy's plans. This ambiguity can usually be resolved in context, however; A and B have already identified the particular episode they are discussing, and thus they know whether it has already happened, is happening now, or is anticipated in the future. If the episode occurred in the past, then search would have to be conducted through memory of that episode; the form of (10) clearly excludes that alternative. If the episode is to occur in the future, then a search for knowledge of Lucy's intentions would be instituted, and some nontrivial inferences might be required. If the episode is occurring at the time of the conversation, then the event in question may be part of the immediate past, the actual present, or the immediate future, where past, present, and future are now understood to be within the temporal scope of the ongoing episode. For a current episode, therefore, the search may be in episodic memory, in perception, or in person memory, and (10) remains ambiguous. In the context of a current situation, however, *A* will usually be able to judge what information *B* is requesting—perceptual or intentional—from his knowledge of the information available to *B*; lacking any idea of *B*'s perceptual field or knowledge of Lucy, *A* can supply whatever information he has about Lucy and the dessert or ask for clarification. The point is that the routine into which (10) should be translated depends on far more than the actual form of the question.

The semantics of tense and aspect must cope with two sets of temporal relations simultaneously. There is, first, the time of the episode itself relative to the time of the conversation, and, second, the time of a particular event within the episode relative to other events in that episode. Some of these meanings can be signaled unambiguously. "Lucy had brought the dessert," for example, is past-in-the-past; "Lucy will have brought the dessert" is past-in-the-future; "Lucy has brought the dessert" is past-in-the-present; and so forth. But since English lacks any clear marking of the nonpast as present or future, it is not possible to use syntactic form as the sole criterion for present or future reference. When the domain of search is syntactically ambiguous, the appropriate value can frequently be transferred from some higher-order routine controlling the conversation. If such transfer is not possible, then the domain of search must be enlarged to include all possibilities. If (10) remained ambiguous in context, for example, it would be translated into a routine to search both the memory for Lucy's intentions and the current environment; indeed, both searches might be conducted more or less simultaneously.

Since both participants in a face-to-face conversation normally have the same perceptual opportunities, it is seldom necessary for one to ask the other questions requiring a perceptual search, so (10) would usually be interpreted as a request for information about Lucy's plans. If *B* is somehow preoccupied, he might use (10) to request a perceptual search by someone else. Since *B* is aware of the ambiguity of (10) and the improbability of the perceptual request, he would probably mark his meaning specifically with a perceptual verb: "Can you see whether Lucy is bringing the dessert?" But even this question could be interpreted as a request to inquire rather than as a request to look. "Look to see whether Lucy is bringing the dessert" is unambiguous; the fact that it is a command rather than a question indicates how closely related the imperative and interrogative really are. Alternatively, if *B* has conducted his own perceptual search and is uncertain of the outcome, he might ask *A* for confirmation: "Is that Lucy (I see) bringing the dessert?" This sentence would be translated into a routine for perceptual search of the environment (or a limited part of the environment indicated by *B*'s direction of regard) to determine whether, in fact, Lucy is now bringing the dessert.

The moral of this somewhat tedious consideration of alternatives is that only under rather special circumstances do English questions translate into routines for perceptual search. Questions beginning with "where is" can set up perceptual searches, but even these can often be answered more easily from memory. Since our purpose here is to consider the relation between perception and language, the particularity of questions requiring perceptual verification is a matter of some interest. At the very least, it helps put this extensively discussed relation into better perspective—we seem to theorize about it more than we exploit it in social interaction.

If conditions are such that (10) is interpreted as requiring a perceptual search—if the value for domain of search transferred from a higher-order routine points to the environment—then we could translate (10) into the routine

(11)   find(Env, $F(x, y)$),

which is identical to routine (4) except that Env, a pointer to the environment, has been substituted for M(Ep), the previous pointer to memory for a past episode. This value for domain of search would be transferred into the operators for BRING and COME, and all would proceed as before, except that the search process would be very different. However, no changes in the definitions of these operators would be required. Indeed, the perceptual tests called in the definitions of these operators would now be truly perceptual—that is to say, they would be applied to current rather than stored input. Thus, (11) is also a routine *A* can try to execute.

If *A* decides to run (11), however, he may find himself in trouble with test (8iii). Let us assume that he looks around and finds that Lucy is indeed holding the dessert as she moves toward *B*. She seems to be in the process of bringing the dessert, but she has not yet completed the act. Hence, test (8iii), which calls for information about the location of Lucy at the end of the event, will fail because the event has not yet ended. This failure might seem a mere detail—*A* must somehow extrapolate, and *B* understands that the event has not yet ended—but it is nonetheless a frequent problem and deserves comment.

Verbs like "bring" and "come," which require information about the end of the events they describe, are sometimes called performance or accomplishment verbs. For example, Kenny (1963) observes that if V is a performance verb, then "He is now V-ing" entails "He has not yet V-ed"; if Lucy is now bringing the dessert, she has not yet brought it. If V is an activity verb, however, then "He is now V-ing" does entail "He has V-ed"; if Lucy is now carrying the dessert, she has already carried it. And, of course, if V is a stative verb, the progressive "He is now V-ing" is odd; if Lucy loves desserts, we do not say "She is now loving desserts." (This classification is complicated by verbs like "read," which can be either an activity or a performance verb: "He is now reading the book" entails "He has read the book" in the sense of "read" as an activity verb, but also entails "He has not yet read the book" in another sense of "read" as a performance verb.) Attempts to categorize verbs in this manner have been discussed by philosophers and linguists; we will not review that discussion here. For our present purpose it is sufficient to point out that verbs whose meanings involve information about outcomes of events have posed a problem for linguistic analysis, a problem that is most clearly revealed by their use in the present progressive.

The question of how this difficulty should be handled is sufficiently general, therefore, to justify proposing a procedural answer for it. What is needed is some routine that will have the effect that whenever in the course of an environmental search a test is encountered that requires information about the outcome of an ongoing event, a goal description will be generated and the test will be replaced by a test of progress toward that goal, that is to say, by a test indicating that the difference between the perceived situation and the goal description is decreasing:

(12)   If find(Env, event) leads to test(end of event, description), where time(end of event) is later than now, then generate(goal) and test (diff$_t$(goal, percept) is greater than diff$_{t+i}$(goal, percept)).

In the present example, if routine (11) leads to condition (8iii) while Lucy is still traveling with cake in hand, routine (12) will substitute for (8iii) a test to determine whether her motion is reducing the distance between her and *B*.

It may be necessary to generalize (12) to cover all uses of the present progressive. The distinction between events in progress and events completed is usually called the imperfective/perfective distinction by grammarians. In some uses, however, a temporary/permanent distinction seems to be involved: "Lucy is being rude," like "Lucy is bringing the dessert," suggests a temporary or uncharacteristic state of affairs, whereas "Lucy is rude," like "Lucy brings the dessert," suggests a more permanent disposition. Routine (12) does not seem adequate for the temporary/permanent distinction, and there may be cases where it is inadequate for the imperfective/perfective distinction. For example, if the question had been "Is Oscar solving the problem (right now)?" then a perceptual test at two moments would probably not serve; the respondent would have to know a great deal more about the problem and about what Oscar was doing than could be given by just looking at him.

Even if (12) could be formulated appropriately, there would still be the question of where, in the general scheme of things that we have been describing, the routine belongs. It clearly does not belong as part of BRING or COME, because it is a general routine that would be invoked for any performance verb; (12) is not part of the meaning of those verbs. Nor does it belong in routine (11); if we wish to think of (11) as representing the procedural meaning of "Is Lucy (now) bringing the dessert?" we can surely understand that meaning (translate the sentence into routine (11)) without knowing whether the event in question has ended. However, we could assume that the translator is constructed in such a way that when it encounters any routine of the form find(Env, event), as it would whenever F was a pointer to a non-stative verb, it would add a pointer—call it prog for progressive—to routine (12) or some reasonable facsimile. Then, instead of (11), we would have

(11′)   find(Env, $F(x, y)$)(prog).

Now if A decides to execute routine (11′), the executor will find this pointer to (12), will search for tests involving an end of event, and will substitute the progressive test instead. When the edited routine is run, if the event has already ended, the routine will fail to find the event perceptually and an exit will be made prior to the progressive test; if the event is in progress, then the progressive test will determine whether the goal is being approached. Alternatively, we could retain (11) and assign (12) exclusively to the executor.

Although the solution in (11′) may seem more complicated than necessary, it does serve to illustrate how routines might be modified dynamically in the process of running them. If we allow ourselves this facility, we can use it in various situations where we would like to attach special markers to sentence routines. A lexical alternative—to claim, for example, that performance verbs have one meaning in the past or future and a different meaning in the present progressive—is even more complicated and counterintuitive. Whether or not (12) is an adequate formulation of this particular modification, some such capacity for dynamic modification seems necessary.

3.5.3   Missing Arguments

Let us return now to the original context of question (1) and consider in more detail the relation between its focus and its background. So far we have assumed only that the questioner believes that A and B both know that there was a dinner party to which Lucy came and that dessert was served. If this were really all that B knew about the episode, his suddenly asking, "Did Lucy bring the dessert?" would seem a wild leap in the dark. Without any apparent hint, B has guessed that Lucy brought something, that somebody brought dessert, and that Lucy had something to do with the dessert. In order to give a more plausible account of the conditions under which B might have asked this question, we should fill in more of the information he must have already acquired from A about the episode. That is to say, we must give a more realistic account of the context of his question.

There seem to be three possibilities: (a) B has gathered (presumably from the previous conversation) that somebody brought the dessert, and he wonders whether it was Lucy; (b) B has gathered that Lucy had something to do with the dessert, and he wonders whether she brought it; or (c) B has gathered that Lucy brought something, and he wonders whether it was the dessert. These different possibilities would normally be signaled by differences in intonation:

(13)   (a) Did LUCY bring the dessert?
          (b) Did Lucy BRING the dessert?
          (c) Did Lucy bring the DESSERT?

The different focus of each sentence is indicated by the stress given to the corresponding word (Chomsky, 1971; Jackendoff, 1972). Natural answers corresponding respectively to these three intonations would be:

(14)   (a) No, SONNY brought it.
          (b) No, she SERVED it.
          (c) No, she brought VEGETABLES.

If the pairing of question and answer is permuted—if, say, (13a) is answered by (14b) or (14c)—the answers are not directly responsive to B's question. At best, they serve to correct the contextual information on which his question is based.

When the focus of the question is indicated by stress, therefore, the person questioned knows more precisely which element of the description $F(x, y)$ the questioner is trying to discover. In situation (a) the pointers for "bring" and "dessert" have already been assigned during the preceding context—they are available—and a pointer to the agent is requested: $F(?x?, y)$. In situation (b) he is asking A to complete $?F?(x, y)$, and in situation (c) he is asking for $F(x, ?y?)$. As the questions in (13) are phrased, however, the questioned element is not really missing; B has offered a guess as to what it was. If he had been unable or unwilling to guess, he would have asked:

(15)   (a) Who brought the dessert?
          (b) What did Lucy do about the dessert?
          (c) What did Lucy bring?

In these questions the missing argument is explicitly indicated; it is represented by an interrogative pronoun.

Consider first the routine that A might construct for (15c). Using the same pointers as before, (15c) would translate into

(16)   find(M(Ep), $F(x, ?y?)$),

where $F(x, ?y?)$ stands for "the value of y such that $F(x, y)$." The first part of this routine is essentially what we had from (1) after we had translated "Did Lucy bring" to obtain (3). Since (15c) does not supply the object argument for "bring," however, the translation cannot be completed as in (4). The question marks around the missing argument signal that the executor should try to assign a value to it. Thus, (16) tries first to find $F(x, ?y?)$ in memory. Since the description is less adequate in (16) than in (4), the likelihood of failure is greater, but we assume that the executor will try to run routines even when some of their arguments are missing.

Command (16) will call BRING, which will inherit values for its arguments as before:

(17)   (i) find(M(Ep), COME(x)) and call it e
          (ii) test(during e, Hold(x, *?y?*))

The COME subroutine will, as before, return with e having the value of A's memory of Lucy's coming, and (17ii) will test that memory to determine what she had with her. The value of y will then be discovered to be the chocolate cake, so an event described by $F(x, y)$ is found. Since the description in (16) calls for the value of y, not for verification of $F(x,$ y$)$, this value will be passed to the executor, which may then identify y—may produce a pointer to some such label as "dessert," "cake," "chocolate cake"—and stop with a routine: utter (z), where z is a pointer to the label that identifies what Lucy brought. Then A may or may not decide to execute the instruction.

   If, instead of (15c), B had asked (15a), "Who brought the dessert?" then the translator should produce the routine

(18)   find(M(Ep), $F(?x?, y)$).

This routine is exactly parallel to (16), except that the other argument of BRING is requested. When A runs (18), BRING will have the following arguments to work with:

(19)   (i) find(M(Ep), COME(y)) and call it e
          (ii) find(M(e), Hold($?x?, y$))

If (19i) succeeds in retrieving a memory of the dessert's arrival, then (19ii) will search that memory for the person who was holding the dessert on arrival. In this way (19) will find that Lucy was the agent who brought the dessert and will return to (18) with the result $x =$ Lucy. Then A may identify x by some such label as "Lucy," "Ms. Lindsay," or "Lucy Lindsay" and stop with a routine ready to utter that label.

   It has often been noted that questions with missing arguments are similar to relative clauses. For example, in the sentence "The dessert that Lucy brought was delicious," the restrictive relative clause "that Lucy brought" resembles (15c) in that both omit the object of brought. In this case, of course, the missing argument can be transferred from the main sentence, where the dessert has been explicitly identified, so the domain of search must be the sentence, not M(Ep). In the sentence "What Lucy brought was delicious," however, the "what" translates into a routine to find in memory the value of y such that $F(x, y)$, just as in (16). Since "what Lucy brought" is an identifier, not a question, the value of y will simply be taken as the argument for the stative predicate "was delicious."

   In the sentence "Lucy, who brought the dessert, served it," the nonrestrictive relative clause "who brought the dessert" is word for word identical to (15a). In this case, if x is the pointer to Lucy, it can be directly transferred from the main sentence to $F(x, y)$ if (18) searches the sentence rather than M(Ep). In "The person who brought the dessert served it," however, the restrictive relative clause "who brought the dessert" will inherit "person" as agent; let the pointer to "person" be z. If A's memory of the episode is adequate, he may then decide to execute (18) to find the particular person "who brought the dessert"; if this routine is successful, he can then substitute x, a pointer to Lucy, for z as the first argument of "served."

3.5.4   The Role of Syntax in Translation

The preceding discussion reveals something of how syntactic information guides the translator—determining whether the sentence is interrogative, finding a relative clause, separating the subordinate clause from the main sentence, and so forth. We have avoided grammatical complexities by selecting simple examples and by assuming that syntactic operations are possible without saying how they might be performed. We will not try to treat syntax comprehensively, but a few comments on the kind of processor we have in mind should help to reduce the aura of magic. (A good introduction to the sort of syntactic theory presupposed here can be found in Akmajian and Heny, 1975.)

As the contribution of syntax to the procedures of sentence interpretation has been discussed by some linguists, the translator first parses the sentence; it assigns each word to a constituent and each constituent to a syntactic category. Once the surface string has been parsed, a search is instituted for one or more deep structures that can be transformed into that surface structure. Finally, the deep structures are interpreted semantically. These procedures have been proposed as the most direct actualization of the theory (Katz and Postal, 1964; Chomsky, 1965) that sound and meaning are related transformationally. According to that theory, the surface structure of a sentence is realized phonologically and the deep structure is interpreted semantically; relations between those two structures are stated in the form of transformational rules.

Whatever the advantages of that approach as an abstract linguistic characterization, the difficulties in using it as a description of a translator's actual operations are well known. Davies and Isard (1972) suggest that the linguist's parsing tree for the surface structure of a sentence might correspond to the historical record (or "trace") of a translator's operations in formulating a routine. If this is correct, the parsing tree would provide valuable guidance to a theorist in his attempts to characterize the translator, but it would not necessarily represent an intermediate state in translation. The output of the translation process should be a routine ready to run, not a phrase-structural description of the sentence.

The most explicit accounts of how a translator might operate can be found in the literature of artificial intelligence, where mechanical question-answering systems have been designed to accept interrogative sentences and recast them as routines for retrieving relevant information from some stored data base. A powerful technique called augmented transition networks (ATN) has been developed to express syntactic rules in the form of a natural-language compiler

(Woods, 1970). ATN notation evolved from experience with several language-processing systems (Thorne, Bratley, and Dewar, 1968; Bobrow and Fraser, 1969; Woods, 1970, 1973) and has been used to formulate psycholinguistic hypotheses about the processes of sentence comprehension (Kaplan, 1972, 1974, 1975; Wanner and Maratsos, 1975). The ATN approach appears to be the best way presently available to characterize what a translator must do.

We will try to illustrate how a translator might work by going through an example in some detail, using ATN-inspired notation for the syntactic aspects. By limiting our attention to simple sentences we will greatly reduce our problems—an expository strategy for which there is considerable precedent in theoretical linguistics. The fragment of a system that we will present, however, should in no case be mistaken for a complete grammar.

The grammatical rules we require are represented graphically in ATN notation in figure 3.2, which is taken from an illustration used by Woods (1970), with minor complications to accommodate relative clauses (Wanner and Maratsos, 1975). The syntactic categories whose names are abbreviated in the networks are indicated in the key to figure 3.2. Circles represent states, and arrows (or arcs) represent possible transitions between states; initial states of each network are placed to the left, and terminal states are indicated by a slash after the state name: $q_4/$ is a terminal state. The system is given a string of words to process, starting in state S; if it can go from S to a terminal state ($q_4/$ or $q_5/$), it accepts that string of words as a grammatical sentence. The network whose initial state is S represents the syntactic rule that a sentence must have a noun phrase, NP, and a verb phrase, either Aux V or Aux V NP. In order to go from state S to state q_1 the initial words of the string must form a noun phrase; in order to determine whether that is the case, control is transferred to state NP and the system attempts to reach a terminal state ($q_8/$, $q_9/$, or $q_{11}/$) in that network. The network whose initial state is NP represents the syntactic rules defining noun phrases; if the system can go from NP to one of its terminal states, it accepts that string of words as a grammatical noun phrase. If a noun phrase is found, transition from S to q_1 is possible, so control passes to state q_1; if the initial words fail to satisfy the conditions for a noun phrase, control is returned to state S, which called NP, and the system next asks whether the first word is an auxiliary verb.

For example, "Did Lucy bring the dessert?" begins with the auxiliary verb "do" with a past-tense marker; this signals that the sentence is a yes/no question and transfers control to q_2. A noun phrase is needed next, so control goes to NP, where "Lucy" is found to be a proper noun and control goes to $q_8/$, which is a terminal state; the noun phrase has been found and control can now be returned to state q_3. In q_3 the next word is found to be the untensed verb "bring" and control is transferred to $q_4/$. (Note that since $q_4/$ is a terminal state this system would accept "did Lucy bring" as a sentence, like "did Lucy come"; distinguishing between transitive and intransitive verbs is feasible, but it would complicate our illustrative discussion.) In state $q_4/$ the

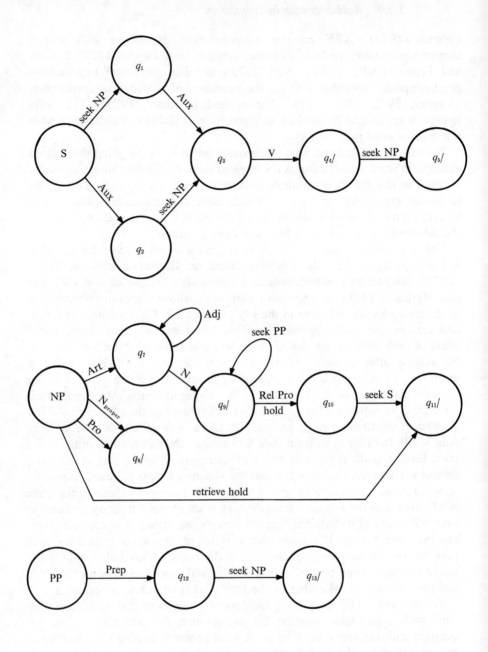

Figure 3.2 An augmented transition network. Adj = adjective; Art = article; Aux = auxiliary verb; N = common noun; NP = noun phrase; N_{proper} = proper noun; PP = prepositional phrase; Prep = preposition; Pro = pronoun; Rel Pro = relative pronoun; S = sentence; V = main verb. (After Woods, 1970, and Wanner and Maratsos, 1975.)

Table 3.2 Steps in constructing a routine for sentence (20).

Step	Input	State	Action	Syntactic trace	Translation	Execution
S01		S	seek S	S	test(——, ——): **push**	
S02		S	seek NP	NP: SUBJECT		
S03	the	NP	Art	Art: THE	mood = declarative: modality	
S04		q_7	Adj			
S05	person	q_7	N	N: PERSON		
S06		q_9	assemble NP		find(——, PERSON(?x?)): **push**	
S07	who	q_9	Rel Pro	Rel Pro: WHO		
S08		q_9	hold NP			
S09		q_{10}	seek S	S		
S10		S	seek NP	NP: Subject		
S11		NP	Art			
S12		NP	N proper			
S13		NP	Pro			
S14		NP	retrieve hold			
S15		q_{11}	assemble NP	(NP: THE PERSON)	$t < n$; search domain = M: modality	
S16	brought	q_1	Aux	VP: Past tense	pop: find(M, BRING(PERSON(?x?), ——)): *push*	
S17		q_3	V	V: BRING		
S18		q_4	seek NP	NP: OBJECT		
S19	the	NP	Art	Art: THE		
S20		q_7	Adj			
S21	dessert	q_7	N	N: DESSERT		
S22		q_9	assemble NP		find(M, DESSERT(?y?)): exec	DESSERT = CAKE = y
S23		q_9	Rel Pro			
S24		q_9	seek PP			
S25		PP	Prep			
S26		q_5	assemble S		pop: find(M, BRING(PERSON(?x?), y)): exec	PERSON = LUCY = x
S27		q_{11}	assemble NP		$t < n$; search domain = M: modality	
S28	served	q_1	Aux	VP: Past tense	pop: test($t < n$, SERVE(x, ——)): push	
S29		q_3	V	V: SERVE		
S30		q_4	seek NP	NP: OBJECT		
S31		NP	Art			
S32		NP	N proper			
S33	it	NP	Pro	Pro: IT	find(context, IT(??)): exec	
S34		q_8	assemble NP		test($t < n$, SERVE(x, y)): exec	IT = DESSERT = y
S35		q_5	assemble S			TRUE

system seeks a noun phrase and, since English noun phrases (except for some pronouns) have the same characteristics whether they are the subject or the object of the verb, network NP is again usable; this time "the" and "dessert" satisfy Art and N, so terminal state q_9 is reached; since neither a preposition nor a relative pronoun follows, control passes to state $q_5/$, which terminates successfully.

As the system proceeds, it performs a number of operations in addition to testing the well-formedness of the sentence. The sentence is identified as a question, each word is assigned to a syntactic category, words are grouped into noun phrases, the first noun phrase can be identified as the subject and the second as the object, and so on. A record, or trace, of these operations would reveal the phrase structure of the sentence.

This example indicates how an ATN system might parse a sentence, but we have claimed that the translator is only incidentally concerned with parsing— syntactic analysis is merely one aspect of compiling a routine for the executor. In order to suggest how these syntactic decisions could contribute to the routine, we will take the sentence

(20)   The person who brought the dessert served it.

We will try to describe the translator's operation step by step.

Concurrent with the operations we wish to consider here, there is a representation of the sentence available in short-term, working memory and some kind of perceptual processing is being performed on it. As part of this perceptual processing, the signal is segmented into words. This segmentation and matching process initiates dictionary look-up and the syntactic *and* semantic features of each word become available to the translator as an immediate consequence of recognizing that it is a word (Marslen-Wilson, 1975). Our present concern is not with this perceptual processing but with the sequential organization of strings of words and their translation into routines for the executor.

Table 3.2 presents a list of steps that the translator might perform in processing (20) according to the syntactic rules represented in the augmented transition network of figure 3.2. In addition to the syntactic analysis, table 3.2 indicates how a routine would be constructed to verify the sentence relative to one's memory of a particular episode. That is to say, we will augment the network with more operations than would be required to construct a syntactic description of the sentence.

S01. The first step activates the network to seek a sentence. Speech is automatically distinguished from other kinds of acoustic signals; recognition that a speech signal is being heard should suffice to start the process. We will suppose that the executor, for reasons of its own, has decided to verify what is being said, and therefore a control instruction to test it must be compiled. We will think of this instruction from the executor as occupying the top location in a pushdown store where the routine will be compiled. Initially, of course, there are no arguments for the "test" instruction; it is not well formed and could not be executed. In order to preserve the instruction until subsequent processing can provide appropriate arguments, it is "pushed down" in the store, leaving the top of the store free to accept any new control instructions that may emerge from subsequent analysis. Later, when it is needed, this "test" instruction will be popped back to the top.

S02. As a consequence of S01, control is passed to state S, where, in order to recognize a sentence, the system will seek a noun phrase, or, failing that, will try to categorize the first word as an auxiliary verb. A more complete set of rules would recognize many other ways of beginning a sentence; Woods and Kaplan (1971) distinguish eight different initial possibilities, which enables them to determine whether the sentence is declarative, imperative, yes/no question, "wh" question. Any noun phrase that enables the system to move from S to q_1 will be taken to be the subject of the sentence. (As developed thus far, ATN systems deal only with full or "initial" sentences; one-word answers to questions, for example, would require special processing.)

S03. As a consequence of S02, control is passed to state NP, which tells the system to look first for an article. By this time the perceptual processor will have recognized the first word as "the," which makes available any stored information about this word, such as that "the" is an article and so satisfies one of the questions posed by state NP. If intonation is ignored, the system can assign declarative status to any sentence beginning with an article, and this assignment is retained in a special memory buffer called (for lack of a better term) modality.

S04. Recognition that the first word is an article results in control passing to state q_7, which inquires whether the next word is an adjective. Since "person" is not an adjective, this query fails.

S05. The system remains in q_7 and tries the second alternative: Is the next word a noun? This time the answer is affirmative.

Since "person" is recognized as a word, syntactic information about it should be immediately available, in which case one might think of S04 and S05 as a single step: the system is in q_7 and has recognized "person," so it might simply look to see if this word matched any of the transitions available in state q_7. This would seem to obviate the apparently meaningless step S04 of asking whether "person" is an adjective. If, instead of "person," however, the second word had been "red," both of the transitions available would have been satisfied; the system would either have to follow both paths or would have to choose which path to follow first. The convention adopted in figure 3.2 is that the adjectival possibility should be explored first.

S06. Since $q_9/$ is a terminal state reached by Art $+$ Adj^i $+$ N (where $i = 0, 1, 2, \ldots$ is the number of adjectives in the phrase), it can assemble the noun phrase just completed and try to assign a value to it: find(———, PERSON($?x?$)). This control instruction is put at the top of the pushdown store. Lacking any information as to where to search for an x such that PERSON(x), the instruction is not yet well formed, so it must be pushed—

preserved in the pushdown store on top of the already pushed instruction to "test" the sentence—leaving the top free for subsequent instructions.

S07. Before the system can leave $q_9/$ and return to q_1 with its NP mission accomplished, it must look to see whether there is a relative pronoun or a prepositional phrase. Thus it discovers that the next word is "who," which is a relative pronoun; the analysis of the noun phrase must continue.

S08. When a relative pronoun is discovered in state $q_9/$, the important "hold" operation must be executed. This operation stores the noun phrase that has just been processed and holds it until it is called for. The strategy in dealing with relative clauses is to treat them like sentences with a missing argument: the system is going to look for a sentence and, when a missing argument is encountered, retrieve the noun phrase it is holding in order to fill the gap. The "hold" facility enables ATN systems to deal conveniently with a variety of constructions that are described by preposing transformations in transformational generative grammars, and so to go directly from a surface sentence to its deep structure without first parsing the surface sentence and then trying to find inverse transformations to recover the deep structure. Wanner and Maratsos (1975) argue that the transient memory load created by this holding process is the major source of difficulty in understanding nested relative clauses.

S09. The system, pursuing the strategy for relative clauses just described, has now moved to state q_{10}, where it must seek a new sentence embedded in the main sentence that the system is analyzing.

S10. As a consequence of S09, control is now transferred back to S. Note that S first called NP as a subroutine; then NP called S as a subroutine. In S10, S again calls NP as a subroutine.

S11–S13. In state NP the system tries to find an article, a proper noun, or a pronoun; all three fail.

S14. The attempt to find a new sentence has now encountered a missing argument, so NP retrieves the noun phrase "the person" that it has been holding since S08.

S15. As a consequence of S14, control is transferred to the terminal state $q_{11}/$ of NP, so the noun phrase just retrieved is adopted as the subject noun phrase of the embedded sentence.

S16–S17. Since the attempt to find a noun phrase has now succeeded, control is passed to q_1 and then to q_3, in which the word "brought" is analyzed as the past-tense marker on the transitive verb BRING. The past tense indicates that the search domain should be memory for the episode in question, and this assignment is stored in "modality." When the verb is found, the pushdown store is popped, which retrieves the "find" instruction that was pushed in S06, and this instruction is reformulated to include all the information currently available: find(M, BRING(PERSON(?x?), ——)). Since this instruction is still not well formed, it is pushed down in the stack again.

S18. As a result of S17, control is transferred to $q_4/$, which seeks the object noun phrase of the embedded sentence.

S19. In state NP again, the system looks for an article and finds it in the next word, "the."

S20–S21. In q_7 the next word, "dessert," is not an adjective, but it is a noun.

S22. Having reached $q_9/$ by completing a noun phrase, the system assembles it and tries to assign a value to it. Unlike the situation in S06, the search domain is now established as memory, so the instruction is find$(M, \text{DESSERT}(?y?))$. The operation "exec" tells the system to transfer this instruction to the executor's memory and so clears the top of the pushdown store.

At this point the executor might decide to postpone execution, but we will assume that finding the value for y is a simple operation and is executed as soon as the instruction is formulated. Given the context discussed in 3.5.1, execution will result in finding the memory of a chocolate cake that was served as dessert, and that memory will provide the value for y.

S23–S25. Before the system can leave $q_9/$ it must look for a relative clause or a prepositional phrase. Both attempts fail, so NP terminates.

S26. As a consequence of terminating the NP analysis, control passes next to state $q_5/$, which assembles the embedded sentence and tries to evaluate it. In order to do this, it first pops the instruction that was pushed in S17 and, drawing on the executor's memory for y, completes it: find$(M, \text{BRING}(\text{PERSON}(?x?), y))$. The instruction is now well formed and so, by "exec," is transferred to the executor's memory. We will assume that the instruction is executed immediately, with the result that the person to be remembered is Lucy, so LUCY is assigned to x.

S27. The embedded sentence that was sought in S09 is complete, so control can pass now to $q_{11}/$, which is a terminal state for the analysis of the subject noun phrase of the main sentence.

S28–S29. As a consequence of successfully finding the subject noun phrase, control now passes to state q_1 and then to q_3, in which the word "served" is analyzed as a past-tense marker on the transitive verb SERVE. Past tense indicates that the search domain is memory, and this information is stored in "modality." When the verb is found, the pushdown store is popped, which retrieves the "test" instruction that was preserved in S01, and this instruction for the main sentence is now reformulated to include all the information currently available: test$(t < n, \text{SERVE}(x, \text{---}))$. Since this instruction is still not well formed, it is pushed down in the stack again.

S30–S33. Control is now in $q_4/$, which seeks a noun phrase. In NP the next word, "it," is not an article or proper noun, but it is a pronoun.

S34. As a consequence of S33, control passes to $q_8/$, which assembles the noun phrase and attempts to assign a value to it. This attempt leads to the instruction find$(\text{Context}, \text{IT}(??))$, where Context includes both the linguistic context and the conversational situation, and IT is a special-purpose routine for searching the context that we will discuss below. Since this instruction is well formed, it can be transferred, by "exec," to the executor's memory. We will assume that the instruction is executed immediately, with the result that "it" is found to be coreferential with "dessert," which has already been remembered as chocolate cake and assigned as the value of *y*.

S35. Since the object noun phrase has been found, control passes to $q_5/$, which is the terminal state for the analysis of the main sentence. The sentence is assembled and an attempt is made to evaluate it: the pushdown store is popped, retrieving the instruction preserved at S29, which can now be completed, test(t $<$ *n*, SERVE(x, *y*)), and transferred to the executor. If the instruction is again executed immediately, it will, given the conditions we have imagined, lead to the result "TRUE," which verifies the sentence.

This completes our step-by-step account of how the translator might go from perceptual input to a set of instructions corresponding to a routine for verifying the sentence. Note that if we had not assumed that the instructions were executed immediately, the translator's operation would have led to the following instructions stored in the executor's memory:

find(M, DESSERT(*?y?*))
find(M, BRING(PERSON(*?x?*), *y*))
find(Context, IT(*??*))
test($t < n$, SERVE(x, IT))

In order to indicate the general type of system that we think is feasible we have made a number of arbitrary decisions in the interest of being definite. For example, we have given the task of finding the reference of "it" to the executor; we could just as well have given this task to the translator, in which case the third instruction above would not appear in the routine and the fourth would have *y* as the second argument of SERVE. Many other details could probably be similarly revised; perhaps some better notation than ATN could replace the whole account. Our purpose is not to defend this particular formulation but to illustrate that such formulations are not inconceivable and that they can provide a context in terms of which our subsequent discussion of lexical concepts should eventually find its place.

It is instructive to compare the account just given with an account of relative clauses that has been given in transformational generative grammars. In both cases, sentences like (20) are assumed to have two sentences at the level of deep structure: the main sentence is "the person served the dessert" and, embedded inside it, the subsidiary sentence is "the person brought the dessert," yielding: (the person (the person brought the dessert) served the dessert). A transformational account starts from this deep structure and applies syntactic transformations to delete the second "person," to introduce "who," and to pronominalize the second "dessert." If these transformations were regarded procedurally, they would seem to be procedures for producing the sentence, not for interpreting it, which would make comparison difficult. In fact, however, transformational generative grammarians are explicit that their account is an abstraction having nothing to do with the actual performance of operations; the sense of "generative" they have in mind is that used in mathematics to describe any system able to select all well-formed strings and reject all ill-formed strings, not the sense corresponding to "production." Consequently, the transformational account can be viewed as relevant to interpretation and so comparable in some sense to the procedural account just given.

In a transformational account, the deep structure of (20) is separated from the surface structure by something Chomsky (1965) has called an erasure transformation. In this example, the erasure transformation uses the first occurrence of "the person" in the deep structure to delete the second occurrence of "the person." Various types of erasure transformations have received extensive analysis since they are required in forming relative clauses, in pronominalization (with especially complex constraints for reflexive pronouns), in sentential complement constructions ("Mary wanted Mary to bring the dessert" becomes "Mary wanted to bring the dessert" if the two occurrences of "Mary" are coreferential), in preposing predicate adjectives ("The red ball bounced" is related to a deep structure (the ball (the ball is red) bounced) via (the ball that is red bounced)), and elsewhere. In many of these applications of erasure transformations it is necessary to establish that the second noun phrase is not just formally identical with the first but is also coreferential. Reference is not a matter for syntax, of course, so the convention was adopted of using subscripts as referential indices: if two noun phrases have the same subscript, an erasure transformation can be applied to delete the second (Bach, 1968). This solution seems to make the applicability of the transformation depend on a semantic contingency. In order to avoid this consequence, Jackendoff (1972) has suggested that the erasure transformation be dropped from the grammar by simply using, in place of the second noun phrase, a dummy symbol Δ that is marked as coreferential with the first but has no semantic realization in the surface sentence. There is no need to evaluate these complex arguments here, but we wish to point out that transformational accounts are often so abstract that special constraints must be introduced to limit the applicability of transformations—in this case, a semantic constraint.

The need for purely syntactic constraints can be illustrated by the following use of relative-clause transformations. Suppose the deep structure includes three sentoids, related so: (this is the box (Lucy brought the dessert (the dessert was in the box))). The relative-clause transformations applied to the second two would delete the second "the dessert" and convert it into: (this is the box (Lucy brought the dessert that was in the box)). A second relativization will now delete the second occurrence of "the box" and so give the surface structure: (this is the box that Lucy brought the dessert that was in). Since this result is ungrammatical, a special constraint is needed to prevent relativization of a noun phrase that is already inside a relativized clause (Ross, 1967, chap. 3).

One might hope that a procedural account would eventually explain the need for these ad hoc constraints on what otherwise seem to be extremely general abstractions about English grammar. The semantic constraint should be explicable somehow in terms of cooperation between translator and executor; in (Mary wants (Mary brings dessert)) the system should work in such a way that referential indices to one or two Marys would be clear to the executor. Similarly, the syntactic constraint on relativization to prevent sentences like "This is the box that Lucy brought the dessert that was in" should follow naturally from a correct formulation of the "hold" facility of the ATN grammar of figure 3.2. For example, when the system works its way to the end of the string, the "hold" register should be empty, so the analysis could not be completed in a terminal state and the string of words would not be accepted as a sentence. Although the theoretical possibilities remain to be explored, if some of the problems discovered by transformational analysis could find more natural explanations in procedural terms, it would be an important theoretical advance.

A particularly thorny set of problems arises from pronominalization; a useful review of transformational studies can be found in Stockwell, Schachter, and Partee (1973). It seems natural to assume, for example, that "Lucy brought the dessert and served it" is the surface form of a deep structure corresponding to "Lucy brought the dessert and Lucy served the dessert," where "the dessert" and "it" are coreferential. The person who utters the sentence may be quite clear about the coreferentiality of "the dessert" and "it." A person who hears "Lucy brought the dessert and served it," however, will not know whether "it" has replaced a second occurrence of "the dessert" that is coreferential with the first; a hearer should be prepared for "it" to refer, say, to some other dish. If the speaker utters the sentence with contrastive stress on "it" while making a gesture toward the meat, the natural syntactic analysis of the sentence must be overridden. There are sentences, like "The dessert, if she ever serves it, will be delicious," where "it" and "the dessert" must be coreferential, so the question can sometimes be answered on purely syntactic grounds. But in most cases "it" is a free variable, and special procedures must be instituted to evaluate it.

How should the semantics of "it" be represented? Since "it" can be used to mean almost anything, it is natural to think of it as a variable that may be syntactically bound but is often a free pointer whose value is to be determined. When it is a free variable, the routine for determining its value in any context would have to be complex. Winograd (1971) treats "it" not as a free variable but as an operator, IT( ), which tries to find the referent and provide a pointer to it. The peculiarity of this operator is that it has no arguments, but in other respects it resembles other semantic operators. That is to say, IT is a heuristic routine that looks into the text and context for possible referents: Could "it" refer to some preceding object or event? Has a word referring to "it" already appeared in the same sentence? In the immediately preceding sentence? And so forth. The search would, of course, be subject to a consistency condition (Jackendoff, 1972) to the effect that two noun phrases cannot be coreferential unless both can describe the same referent. And if two or more possible referents are found, as in "The dessert was on the table the first time I saw it," the routine might have to estimate probabilities. If the referent cannot be determined, IT should interrupt and call the executor, where the importance of finding a value can be estimated and, perhaps, explicit questions might be phrased. In any case, it is obvious that IT must be a very complex routine, dependent on inferential procedures (see Charniak, 1973b).

These comments on the role of syntax in the process of translation are not intended as an alternative to linguistic theories of grammar or as an attempt to reduce syntax to a branch of semantics or pragmatics. Any satisfactory psychological theory of linguistic information processing must be compatible with—must provide a basis from which can be abstracted—the valid generalizations of theoretical linguistics. But a grammar does not specify how this processing is done.

Fodor, Bever, and Garrett (1974) survey a large body of linguistic and psycholinguistic research that lies beyond the limits we have set for this book. They conclude that sentence perception cannot exploit grammatical information as it is represented in the grammars that have been proposed by linguists. In particular, they find no evidence for the psychological validity of syntactic transformations—for perceptual processes that correspond to unraveling the transformational history of a sentence. Instead, they suggest heuristic strategies a listener might use to decode sentences, for example, "Take the verb which immediately follows the initial noun of a sentence as the main verb unless there is a surface-structure mark of an embedding" (p. 356). How this strategy might work is illustrated, of course, by the ATN system in figure 3.2. Fodor, Bever, and Garrett assume, however, that "the decoding processes compute the same structural description that a grammar does" (p. 369), as if parsing were an end in itself, rather than an abstraction from (or trace of) the computations required to translate a sentence into an executable routine.

Systematic exploration of heuristic strategies for the translator is not our concern. Our intention is merely to indicate how we believe the present work might be extended in that direction.

3.5.5 Commands

In ordinary usage, assertions and questions can have the illocutionary force of commands or requests: "I need salt" or "Can/will/would you pass the salt?" will, in appropriate contexts, elicit the same response as the imperative "Pass the salt." Indirect requests can be conveyed by asserting what you want or by questioning your addressee's ability, intention, or willingness to do what you want them to (Gordon and Lakoff, 1971; Labov, 1972b, chap. 8). These complications can be analyzed, but the analysis would lead us far afield.

Instead, let us take a simple case that is clearly a command in the imperative mood. Since Lucy and her dessert have become a bit tiresome, we will begin again with a new context. Suppose that a child has a broken toy that he wants his mother to fix. Suppose that in the course of their conversation about the toy the mother says

(21)   Bring it here.

And suppose that the child's mastery of English is more than adequate to enable him to translate this sentence into a routine.

The semantics we will propose for such sentences—and for nonimperatives that are interpreted as commands—is that they are translated into routines for doing something that will bring about the described state of affairs. Whereas we treated yes/no questions as if they meant "Is it true that S?" we will treat requests as if they meant "Make it true that S." For example, (21) would become "Make it true that you brought it here." Since "Make it true that" is just another imperative, this approach has no value as a syntactic or semantic analysis; it is intended rather as a gloss of the routine that a listener will construct on hearing an imperative.

Let us assume that untensed "bring" in initial position signals the imperative mood, that is to say, it sets up an instruction to achieve(description), and—since the agent in imperatives is an implicit "you"—it sets up a pointer x to A himself, which will serve as the first argument of the verb. If we again assign F the value BRING, from the first word alone the translator can produce: achieve($F(x, \underline{\hspace{1cm}}, \underline{\hspace{1cm}})$).

Note, incidentally, that it is necessary to know to whom the request is addressed. If a third person overheard (21), he would realize that the command was not addressed to him and so would not obey it (unless, perhaps, the child was unable to comply). Hence, some other routine is also created by hearing (21), a routine like find(Environment, person addressed by speaker) and call him x, then test(now, x = ego). This routine would not be specific to imperatives; it is needed in any conversational interaction and the results provide information that a listener needs in order to decide whether to execute the routines his translator produces (see sec. 7.4). Since the operation of the translator is automatic and involuntary for a person who knows the language well, someone who overheard (21) would also translate it into an "achieve" instruction, but presumably the first argument of BRING would not be a pointer to himself.

The second word of (21) is "it," which calls the IT operator; IT institutes a search of the context (verbal and nonverbal) and returns with a pointer y to the toy. "Here," like "bring," is a deictic word; HERE is a routine that tries to find the region of the speaker, Reg(speaker), and sets up a pointer z with that location as its value. The translated routine, therefore, is

(22)   achieve($F(x, y, z)$),

where F calls BRING, x is A, y is the toy, and z is B's location.

Having translated the sentence, A now has the option of executing it. If he decides to run it, his executor will turn to a complicated bag of tricks involving motor skills, perception of the problem environment, and planning how to achieve the described goal. When the problem is sufficiently difficult, the "achieve" instruction may call on linguistic routines for various purposes, but it is the nature of "achieve" that it will try to do whatever it can to make the description it is given true. That is, it will generate(goal) and test(Diff(goal, percept)) and try to reduce that difference. How this might be accomplished is discussed at length by Newell and Simon (1972), and we will not attempt to improve here on their theory of problem solving. We will simply assume that "achieve" calls other routines and will not try to specify what they are. The plan, when executed, will have to incorporate such motor control instructions as "grasp," "transport," and "release"—instructions that we believe are as important for lexical concepts as the perceptual predicates we have tried to catalog are—but we will not offer a detailed characterization of these basic actions.

Since voluntary motor acts are executed under perceptual guidance, our concentration on perceptual predicates is not as limiting as it might at first seem. What is involved is a control loop, with both efferent and afferent branches. A complete description of these loops would have to include both branches, but our present purposes seldom require us to consider more than the perception that the goal has been attained. Where the efferent branch seems important in its own right, we will discuss it informally. (However, cf. Werner and Kaplan, 1963.)

3.5.6 Declaratives

Declarative sentences pose a question for procedural semantics. It is usually clear what a listener should do about requests for attention, confirmation, information, or action; what he should do about assertions is not. If declaratives were rarely used, we might try deriving them from underlying imperatives. But they are not rare, and many of them, such as "He is old," have no obvious imperative counterparts. Both linguistic and logical intuition would derive imperatives from declaratives. If the translator must compile all sentences as sequences of control instructions for the executor, what kind of instructions should it turn assertions into?

Sometimes a listener wants to remember what a speaker says; an instruction to "store" the information in memory could serve a role similar to "find" and "achieve" in the translation of questions and commands. Although situations in which everything a speaker says is to be stored are unusual, any serious participant in a conversation must remember enough of the gist to ensure that his own contribution will be relevant. So it is worthwhile to consider how the system might apply the "store" instruction to declarative sentences.

Presumably, a declarative sentence can be translated into a series of pointers to appropriate referents—into descriptions or routines for future use—in much the same way we have proposed for questions and commands. When a "store" instruction is executed, however, many problems can arise. What happens, for example, if there is already information in memory that is inconsistent with the new information? A partial answer is provided by assuming that listeners store not merely the content of the utterance but certain aspects of its context: who said it, to whom it was addressed, whether the speaker appeared sincere, and so forth. The fact that John said *p* and Jane said not-*p* need not lead directly to a contradiction, as it would if the unadorned contents of their utterances, *p* and not-*p*, were to be stored.

This convention for contextualizing what is stored will nevertheless have to be supplemented by conventions for the straightforward updating of memory. One must repeatedly update one's memory of the location of one's movable possessions; when the new location is to be stored, the old location must somehow be discarded. Davies (1974) has devised a computer program that incorporates procedures that might be used in this process. In updating its data base, Davies's program searches for any previously stored assertions inconsistent with the incoming assertion, and deletes them. It is not enough, though, merely to look for direct inconsistencies; often an assertion will be incompatible with what can be inferred from the data base, or the data base will be incompatible with what can be inferred from the assertion. For example, if the information that Arthur has no son is stored in memory, then "Arthur has a son" will be in direct contradiction, "Arthur is a father" will contradict an inference that can be drawn from the information stored in memory, and "Arthur's son is asleep" will entail a presupposition that contradicts the stored information. Inference also plays an important role in answering questions and in determining the best way to comply with a command.

Consequently, we will introduce a control instruction, infer(x, y), where x and y range over routines and descriptions, which will call procedures to try to infer x from y. When one of the arguments is not given, we will use infer($x, ?y?$) to mean that the system will try to find some basis for deducing x, and infer($?x?, y$) to mean that the system will try to draw some conclusion from y. The nature of the inferential procedures need not concern us here; our understanding of them is fragmentary, to say the least (Wason and Johnson-Laird, 1972). However, it appears that we may usefully distinguish among lexical inferences, based on the meanings of simple lexical items; propositional inferences, based on the meanings of connectives between clauses and sentences; and quantified inferences, based on the meanings of quantifiers and related terms (Johnson-Laird, 1975). We assume that "infer" can both call and be called by other control instructions.

Listeners do, indeed, often remember what is said to them, but to insist that a "remember this" command is automatically instituted for all declarative sentences would close options that might better be left open. There must be many speech acts involving declarative sentences where the speaker cares nothing for what the listener does with the information and where he certainly has no intention of instructing him.

We assume, therefore, that declaratives are free to take whatever control instruction a listener wishes to apply to them. His decision will depend on other considerations extraneous to the sentence. For example, in a conversation he may pick up anything the speaker mentions, search his memory for related information that has not already been discussed, and make that information the focus of his next remark. In an argument he may take the sentence and test it, hoping to find some basis for refuting it. In a task-oriented situation he may translate it into a routine to achieve some subgoal that the sentence suggests to him. In an instructional situation he may set up an instruction to store the information in secondary memory. In listening to a story he may use an instruction to generate an image of successive events. How he will use a sentence will depend on what he is trying to do at the time and on what speech act he thinks the talker is trying to perform. It is no small component of the beauty of declaratives that they leave these options open.

If we did decide to select one control instruction for all routines produced for declaratives, a plausible choice might be "generate." The capacity of primary memory is too small to hold much more than the information being processed by the translator. If a listener wants to keep some memory of the gist of what has been said, he needs a larger store; imagery can provide such a store, at least temporarily. His normal mode of operation, therefore, might be deliberately to generate an image of what he is hearing. This operation would be interrupted by questions and commands, which are specially marked to signal a changed mode of operation. The model that the listener is building would not contain the words that had been spoken, but their referents would be represented (and related) by imagery and could be searched quickly for information presupposed in new sentences. Since imagery is known to facilitate transfer of information from primary to secondary memory—most mnemonic tricks exploit that fact—a "generate" instruction would insure the construction of an organized memory trace that could become part of episodic memory. Thus, a "generate" instruction would accomplish much the same result as a "store" instruction, at least for picturable sentences, but in a more indirect way.

Alternatively, the "assign" instruction, which sets up pointers to the percepts, memories, or concepts associated with words, could be the instruction used by default. That is to say, we could think of some string of pointers, like $F(x, y)$, as representing a mental construct (not necessarily an image) that would have an asymptotic probability of being transferred from primary to secondary memory even without an explicit instruction to store or generate an image.

There is a difficulty with this idea that the listener is generating mental representations and storing them in episodic memory. We must leave open the possibility that a listener can seize on any phrase or sentence that seems particularly relevant to some higher-order routine he is trying to execute and make it an argument of whatever instruction that higher-order routine might dictate. It is hard to understand in procedural terms how he might do this in advance of hearing the sentence. Do we assume that he normally begins translating the sentence into "generate" or "assign" instructions, then notices its relevance to the higher-order routine, and replaces the initial instruction by a more appropriate one? It would not be impossible to devise an executive procedure whereby high-order routines of preemptive importance could monitor all incoming information and interrupt the normal processing when relevant information occurred. The problem has to do with the fact that "generate" and "assign" do not automatically preserve all the information that might be required by the arguments of any other instruction the system might decide to substitute.

A possible solution would be to assume that the main control instruction is usually not chosen until the sentence has been heard and most of the processing has taken place automatically. But this suggestion appears to contradict our assumption that understanding a sentence requires an ability to translate it into a routine that the system can execute. Are we now saying that you must be able to understand the sentence *before* it is translated into a routine in order to know what kind of routine you want to translate it into? Since the exact moment at which you understand a sentence you are hearing is impossible to determine, this objection is more formal than substantive. We can, therefore, consider a formal way to dispose of it, one that will turn out to have certain other advantages in relating our procedural account to the descriptions of sentence structure that some linguists have given.

3.5.7   The Suspension of Instructions

One knows intuitively that there are many situations in which a listener just listens. Speech flows over him much as music would. People often listen to radio programs in this frame of mind. The translator is working, but the executor is not running higher-order routines that would use the translator's output. If something preemptive is heard—one's own name, for example—the system may be stirred to action, so the translator must be doing something. But the person is just listening idly. This state of volitional idling is a possibility for which our theory should allow.

In order to characterize idle listening, we should be able to distinguish it both from no translation at all and from active listening. Active listening is characterized by the kinds of information processing by the executor that we have described; zero translation occurs if the speech is inaudible or in a foreign language, or (presumably) if the person is deeply asleep. But what is idle listening?

In order to sharpen the question, consider a situation in which a person is so engrossed in his thoughts that he pays no attention to the speech—he is awake, he knows the language, he hears the speech, but he is not listening to it. Should this situation be classed as zero translation or as idle listening? Introspection cannot answer the question; in a familiar language translation is so automatic that it normally occurs outside conscious awareness. Mere inattention does not suffice to prevent translation (Solomons and Stein, 1896; LaBerge and Samuels, 1974). In the words of Deutsch and Deutsch (1963), "a message will reach the same perceptual and discriminatory mechanisms whether attention is paid to it or not; and such information is then grouped or segregated by these mechanisms" (p. 83). They based this conclusion on a review of studies in which an unattended message had disrupted perception of an attended message.

Such experiments can be performed by presenting different messages to the

two ears; unattended words in one ear may interfere with the processing of
attended words in the other. For example, synonyms in the unattended ear
cause more interference with shadowing (repeating aloud words heard in the
attended ear) than unrelated words do (J. L. Lewis, 1970); unrelated words
cause more interference with the recall of attended words than nonsense syllables do (Davis and Smith, 1972). Since the meaning of the unattended signal
is related to the magnitude of these interference effects, some degree of semantic
processing must occur even though the listener is not aware of what words he
is hearing.

Lackner and Garrett (1972) have provided evidence that sentences are
processed even when a person is not attending to them and cannot report their
content. They asked people to attend to and to paraphrase a sentence heard
in one ear while another sentence, fainter and slightly delayed, was presented
to the other ear. Some of the sentences to the attended ear were ambiguous
("The spy put out the torch as our signal to attack") and were accompanied
by related but unambiguous sentences in the unattended ear ("The spy ex-
tinguished the torch in the window"). Although listeners reported not hearing
the unattended sentence, its presence significantly biased their paraphrase of
the ambiguous sentence toward the sense of the unattended sentence. Lackner
and Garrett take their results to indicate that "there is structural analysis of
the material in the unattended channel" (p. 359). MacKay (1973) has obtained similar results, although there may be some disagreement as to the depth
of processing that an unattended message can affect. In any case, there is
positive support for the claim that translation does not depend on conscious
awareness—that idle listening cannot be equated with zero processing.

We will assume, therefore, that idle listening corresponds to the operation
of the translator without executive involvement. That is to say, the translator
will probably be forming "find" instructions for questions and "achieve" instructions for commands, since these instructions are rather consistently
associated with interrogative pronouns and initial verbs. But when declarative
sentences are heard, a control instruction may not be assigned at all; the
translator goes involuntarily about its business of looking the words up, grouping them into constituents, assigning pointers, and formulating descriptions
that could be used as arguments for some control instruction, but, since the
executor has no use for them in the idle-listening mode, selection of an appropriate instruction is irrelevant.

A simple way to represent this nondirected operation of the translator is to
introduce a dummy instruction that we will call "instruct." If the executor
receives a routine starting with an "instruct" instruction, it has no operations
it can execute until this dummy instruction has been replaced by some specific
instruction for controlling information processing. If the arguments of "instruct" are related to an activity of sufficient interest to the listener, his executor
can select an appropriate control instruction—"generate," if nothing else—and
substitute it for "instruct"; then the routine can be executed. But this insertion
of a specific instruction will be the exceptional case when the translator is in

its idle-listening mode. Ordinarily, if nothing is done with it, an "instruct" instruction will quickly be forgotten.

What are the arguments of "instruct"? Since the translator in this mode of operation has no way to anticipate which instruction may be imposed on its arguments, it must be able to formulate arguments with enough information that any instruction the executor decides to impose will find what it needs for its own operations. Let us consider what this requirement entails. First, all of the specific instructions we have introduced require something we have called a description of the perceptual, memorial, or conceptual content that the system is expected to find, test, infer, store, generate, achieve, identify. The description will be a string of pointers, like $F(x, y)$ for "Lucy brings dessert." So the least we must demand from the translator is some such functional structure to serve as one argument of "instruct." The instructions "find" and "store," however, have two arguments. In addition to a description, they require a specification of the domain to be searched or the domain in which the information should be stored. And the instruction "test" requires information about the time at which the description is supposed to be applicable. So "instruct" must also contain information about domains and times; this information will provide another argument for the "instruct" instruction, an argument we will call modality.

The general format of this dummy instruction will be instruct(modality, description), where "modality" refers to all the information that may be required in order for any specific instruction to be subsequently substituted for "instruct."* We choose to call the first argument modality because we believe that the information it must contain is similar, if not identical, to the information that some linguists have assigned to a "modality constituent." Fillmore (1968) writes, "In the basic structure of sentences, then, we find what might be called the 'proposition', a tenseless set of relationships involving verbs and nouns (and embedded sentences, if there are any), separated from what might be called the 'modality' constituent. This latter will include such modalities on the sentence-as-a-whole as negation, tense, mood, and aspect" (p. 23).

Let us compare Fillmore's modality constituent with the modality argument we would require. It is clear that the argument of "instruct" that we are calling

---

*If we wished to preserve the distinction that some philosophers have recommended between the context of use of a sentence and the possible world in which the proposition that the sentence expresses is to be verified, we could impose a further constraint on the modality argument. The information that a "find" instruction will need concerns the context in which to search; this is particularly clear for sentences having deictic reference. The "test" instruction requires a time at which it is to be applied; the variable t could be considered an index to the possible world in which the test is to be executed. Distinctions between contexts of use and states of affairs are difficult to maintain, however, even when one is working within an abstract logical system of semantics and pragmatics. When one begins to consider the performance of language users in ordinary conversations, the distinction that is so helpful at an abstract level becomes even more difficult to define. We will therefore forgo any systematic attempt to partition the modality argument into that information required to translate the sentence into an executable program and that information required to execute it in some possible world.

modality will include information about time that is critical for tense and aspect. The moods in English are generally taken to be indicative, to express factual statements; subjunctive, to express dubious or hypothetical statements; and imperative, to express commands and requests. (Fillmore includes the interrogative form along with these traditional moods.) The natural control instructions for the three moods would be "test," "generate," and "achieve," respectively. If the translator immediately adopts one or more of these instructions, it will not use "instruct," so the modality argument will be displaced by the specific information needed by the chosen instruction. Insofar as the translator does not select specific instructions in advance (even, possibly, for questions and commands), this kind of information must be preserved by the modality argument of "instruct."

Fillmore also includes negation in his modality constituent, at least when it applies to the sentence as a whole. We have so far avoided the syntactic and logical complexities of negation, but it should be clear that there is little place for negation in the kind of descriptions we have proposed. The description is a string of pointers to perceptual, memorial, and conceptual entities; in our formulation, we have no way of assigning a pointer to such nonexistent entities as not-percepts, not-memories, or not-concepts. Negation, in procedural terms, means that the outcome of a "test" instruction should be negative. In order to allow for negation, a "test" instruction could have three arguments: one for the description to be tested, one for the time at which the test is applicable, and one to specify whether a positive or a negative outcome is to be judged confirmatory. In computer programming, however, it has been found more convenient to write such instructions as test $F(x)$; if true, go to next instruction; if false, go to instruction n. Whichever way one decides to represent the consequences of negative test outcomes, if "instruct" is to preserve all of the information that might subsequently be required for "test," the modality argument will have to include information about the consequences of negative outcomes. (Similar comments would hold for the unsuccessful execution of a "find" instruction.)

We believe, therefore, that "modality" is an appropriate term to use for this argument of "instruct" and does little or no violence to the linguistic concept from which we have borrowed it. A noteworthy difference between our procedural modality and the linguistic version is that the linguist assumes that there is a modality constituent in every sentence, whereas we have introduced it merely to characterize how the system would operate until (if ever) it had some particular use for the sentence it was translating.

As we view the whole system, the translator is normally under the executive control of some higher-order routine, from which it can inherit appropriate instructions to process incoming sentences. A theoretical linguist, however, is not often concerned with the goal-oriented behavior that provides a context for linguistic communication. Instead, he usually takes a sentence in isolation from any context, verbal or social, and attempts to characterize precisely what is contained in or presupposed by the sentence itself. Judging from the success of this context-free approach, one would be foolhardy to criticize it as inferior or inadequate for achieving the linguist's descriptive goals. As an approach to the problems of psycholinguistics, though, it is less satisfactory. A context-free analysis of a sentence (or group of formally related sentences) deliberately ignores what use a person might make of such utterances, which means that the linguist places himself deliberately in that mode of operation we have called idle listening. We maintain that it is just in this state of suspended instructions that the translator must accumulate all the heterogeneous modality information that might be relevant to any subsequent choice of a control instruction. So it is no accident that the two approaches should converge on "modality" in this way.

Once it is recognized as a special situation, the analytic convenience of suspending the choice of instructions cannot be denied. Instead of specifying all possible instructions that might be chosen for a sentence in different contexts, we can use "instruct" to hold a place for them while we proceed, as a linguist would, to formulate the modality and description arguments in such a way as to prepare for all eventualities.

Inasmuch as no particular procedure or subprogram is invariably associated with "instruct," it represents a step backward from a strictly procedural semantic theory, toward a mixture of procedural and propositional elements; "instruct" enables us to introduce propositions as arguments for a null function. In chapter 4 we will find further reasons to mix commands and assertions in an effort to take advantage of both approaches at the same time.

One might ask whether there is any similarity between this representation of modality and the illocutionary force of a speech act. We have considered three reasons for wanting to split up the meaning of a sentence into two parts:

(23)   (a) Procedural: modality versus description
         (b) Linguistic: modality versus proposition
         (c) Speech act: illocutionary force versus proposition

We have argued that (a) and (b) are roughly equivalent. Can we generalize further and equate modality with illocutionary force? The similarity of (b) and (c) has been noted by Ingram (1971) and Dore (1973) in the context of child language, but whether modality could be generalized to include everything that a speech-act theorist would require to characterize adult speech acts is dubious. We prefer to view modality as the part of the information about the illocutionary force of a speech act that can be represented in the utterance itself.

As J. J. Katz (1972) has pointed out, Searle includes both semantic and pragmatic conditions in his theory of speech acts. Katz argues for distinguishing between them. He assigns responsibility for determining the literal illocutionary force of an utterance to the semantic component of his theory and responsibility for determining the intended illocutionary force in the actual context of use to the pragmatic component. According to Katz (forthcoming), a pragmatic theory is a function, PRAG, whose arguments are a grammatical description of some sentence type $D(S_i)$ and a specification of all the relevant information about a context in which some token of S_i occurs, $I(C)$. The output of the function is a grammatical description of some sentence type $D(S_j)$, where $D(S_j)$ may differ from $D(S_i)$. In short:

(24) $PRAG(D(S_i), I(C)) = D(S_j)$.

For example, let S_i be "Lucy didn't bring a pencil" and let $I(C)$ be information about a schoolroom context in which all students are required to have pencils and in which S_i is addressed to the teacher by a friend of Lucy's. And suppose that the teacher responds to S_i by giving Lucy a pencil. Then PRAG would be a function translating "Lucy didn't bring a pencil" in that context into S_j, "Give Lucy a pencil." After evaluating PRAG, the teacher responds to S_i as if S_j had been uttered instead.

If we were to adopt Katz's proposal directly into our present account, the first argument of PRAG would be a routine, not a grammatical description. In the example, the teacher might first translate "Lucy didn't bring a pencil" into a routine for verification: test(t, BRING(Lucy, pencil)). Then this routine, plus the contextual information $I(C)$, would be transformed by PRAG into another routine to supply the pencil: achieve(HASA(Lucy, pencil)). The trouble, as we have noted, is that "test" and "achieve" require different information. Since the purpose of "instruct" is to retain all information in S_i that might be needed for any outcome of PRAG, we must adapt Katz's proposal as follows:

(25)   PRAG(instruct(modality, description), $I(C)$) = achieve(goal).

The outcome of PRAG would not always be an "achieve" instruction. In order to determine what the output routine would be for any sentence uttered in any context requires a detailed pragmatic theory that would encompass higher-order routines dealing with far more than linguistic information.

Even in the absence of a satisfactory formulation of the necessary pragmatic rules, there is much to be done before we understand the illocutionary force of sentences interpreted literally. In order to get on with the development of his semantic theory of illocution, Katz assumes the existence of a class of "zero contexts" such that PRAG becomes an identity function:

(26) $PRAG(D(S_i), 0) = D(S_i)$.

As an example of a zero context, Katz and Fodor (1963) imagined someone finding an anonymous letter containing one sentence in his language, with no clue as to the motive or circumstance of its transmission. We do not believe that this situation is truly contextless, since it is a written sentence and its location would surely give some clue to its origins, but such objections are beside the point; zero context is to Katz's theory what a perfect vacuum is to a physical theory—an idealized situation in which certain other relations can be more clearly and simply analyzed.

If we were to adopt zero contexts in our present account, it is clear from

(25) that an identity function would simply leave the dummy instruction "instruct" unmodified and still unexecutable. The general purpose of zero contexts is to set aside pragmatic rules in order to concentrate on semantic rules; we can accomplish this purpose within our procedural formulation by assuming the existence of some minimal level of automatic processing of sentences that falls short of PRAG—a level of idle listening that goes as far as the "instruct" instruction and no farther. This assumption is consistent with various psychological hypotheses relating comprehension and memory to the depth of processing the receiver performs.

Is it possible to point to situations in which this procedural vacuum might be approximated? One place we would *not* expect to find it would be in conversations. A person actively engaged in conversation would have various higher-order routines actively analyzing, enriching, or elaborating what his conversational partner was saying—suspension of instructions for deeper processing would violate the implicit mutual agreement to cooperate on which normal conversation is based. A conversation has a structure (Sinclair et al., 1972; Sudnow, 1972; Schegloff and Sacks, 1973; Duncan, 1974; Sacks, Schegloff, and Jefferson, 1974) that must influence a person's way of going about the translation and deciding what routines to execute. In a conversational context many speech acts have a purpose that can only be understood from extensive context. There are speech acts that open or close a topic of conversation, that let a speaker enter or withdraw from the discussion, that are interpolations or asides, that repair misunderstandings, that express solidarity or encourage continuation or tie the conversation together—these acts involve pragmatic and rhetorical and social rules that go far beyond anything a linguist would find necessary to include in the modality constituent. It would be impossible to participate normally in a conversation without extensive information processing of the sort PRAG is intended to represent.

The idle-listening mode is most likely to occur when a person is not expected to respond—when he is listening to others converse, or listening to a monologue, or reading a text. We have couched most of our discussion of how sentences might be translated into routines in terms of dialogue. The listener's role in a monologue is different.

Take a reader's processing of written text. The structure of written texts has received attention from both linguists and psychologists. Psychologists— Dawes (1966), Frase (1969, 1972), Fredericksen (1972), and Crothers (1972), for example—have generally attempted to analyze text structures in logical or set-theoretical terms. Frase considers passages containing such sentences as "The big thing was green. The green thing was a box. The box was empty." Symbolically, big → green → box → empty. A young reader is asked questions about those sentences and about inferences based on them: "Was the big thing empty?" The reader who thinks about what he reads—who actively processes the text in depth (and so is most likely to remember it later)— should translate these three sentences into a representation of a big, green, empty box, a representation from which answers to questions requiring inferences could be readily retrieved. Frase's results indicate that few readers take this active attitude; most come away from a text with some memory of statements made explicitly in the text, but not enough to support a later reconstruction adequate to answer questions requiring inferences from those statements. These results may not be representative of readers who are personally interested in understanding well-written texts, but they probably are representative of performance on most standardized tests of reading comprehension. Apparently the usual level of processing such texts runs deep enough to translate sentences, but seldom deep enough to integrate those translations into larger programs. This level of performance is a visual counterpart to idle listening; the active and voluntary use of those automatic translations is presumably suspended by many readers under the conditions in which the texts are presented.

Texts involving logical structures appropriate for such studies are rare and usually have to be constructed by the experimenter for his own purposes. Linguists who have considered suprasentential structures have normally worked with less artificial texts and have tried to extend the general methods used for analyzing sentence structure into the structural analysis of these larger units. For example, Grimes (1968) has attempted to catalog various "rhetorical predicates" that an author can use to signal the structure of his text. Paratactic rhetorical predicates have two or more arguments of equal weight; hypotactic rhetorical predicates indicate that one argument is of greater weight than the others. For example, the syntactic transformation that is said to underlie relative-clause constructions appears at the rhetorical level of analysis to be a hypotactic predicate for indicating subordination. The syntactic machinery can combine the structures underlying "The boy lived next door" and "The boy broke the window" into "The boy who lived next door broke the window" or "The boy who broke the window lived next door." The rhetorical effect of the first combination is to give greater weight to his breaking the window and to make his living next door subordinate information; the second combination reverses the emphasis. This example is at the sentence level, but rhetorical predicates are not limited to that level—long passages can be organized in a similar manner.

Paratactic and hypotactic rhetorical predicates enable a writer to impose an outline structure on the content of his text, to indicate which are the more important ideas and which are subordinate and to indicate which are equally important. The result of analyzing a well-written text in this manner is essentially an outline with major headings, subheadings, subsubheadings, and so on. By continuing the analysis into the lexical predicates of individual sentences, the text can be analyzed as deeply as required. B. J. F. Meyer (1974) used Grimes's method to analyze several texts; then she asked people to read them and to write out all that they could recall. By placing the same information high in the hierarchical structure of one passage and low in another, she was able to demonstrate that recall was significantly better for information high in the content structure of the text. Although Meyer did not investigate individual differences in reading ability, she speculates that poor readers are probably those who do not discover the structure of the texts they read and who report low-level information with little or no integration of the various ideas they remember.

Although investigators of these difficult problems have understandably avoided the additional complications posed by ambiguous sentences, their methods must be related to the well-known fact that most ambiguous sentences in ordinary usage are disambiguated by context. For example, "The monkey makes an ideal pet" is ambiguous out of context; it can mean either that any monkey would make an ideal pet or that some particular monkey is an ideal pet. Consider this sentence in two different contexts:

(27)   (a) The monkey makes an ideal pet. I know a man who owns a female rhesus. She is housebroken and almost no trouble to care for.

(b) I know a man who owns a female rhesus. The monkey makes an ideal pet. She is housebroken and almost no trouble to care for.

Texts (a) and (b) differ merely in the order of the first two sentences. In (a) the sense of "the monkey" is generic. In (b) it refers to a specific monkey, the one mentioned in the preceding sentence. At a semantic level of analysis, one might say that "the" is interpreted generically if there is no antecedent discourse referent, but if such a referent has been provided, "the" is interpreted specifically. At a rhetorical level, on the other hand, one would say that (a) establishes "The monkey makes an ideal pet" as the superordinate idea and the rest of the text gives supporting evidence for that thesis, whereas (b) makes "I know a man" the superordinate idea and subordinates his various interesting attributes to that central topic. How a reader or listener will translate an ambiguous sentence will depend, in part at least, on its position in the discourse.

How these various syntactic, semantic, pragmatic, and rhetorical devices are to be integrated in an eventual procedural theory of semiotics remains unclear, but we trust we have said enough about them to indicate the general theoretical context into which our analysis of lexical relations in the following pages must fit.

3.6 SUMMARY OF CONTROL INSTRUCTIONS

The conceptual system has two parts, a translator (corresponding roughly to a compiler), which converts grammatical sentences into routines containing control instructions, and an executor (corresponding roughly to the computer that runs the compiled program), which accepts the output of the translator, decides whether to execute it, and, if so, proceeds with its execution. The executor must be able to obey the following instructions:

$find(x, y)$ Search the domain indicated by x for the entity (percept, memory, or concept) described by y; if

	found, proceed to the next instruction; if not, go elsewhere.
assign(x, y)	Give the pointer (index, variable) x the value of the entity y.
test(x, y)	Determine whether the description given by y is true at time x; if so, proceed to the next instruction; if not, go elsewhere.
store(x, y)	Try to add the information given by y to the memory field indicated by x.
generate(x)	Form or modify an image that includes the information indicated by x.
achieve(x)	Act in such a way as to make the description x true.
identify(x, y)	Provide symbols (vocal or gestural) to distinguish the entity indexed by y from other entities in domain x.
infer(x, y)	Try to deduce the description or routine x from the information indexed by y.
utter(x)	Output the symbols x.
instruct(x, y)	Dummy instruction: must be replaced by another instruction before execution is possible; x denotes modality information and y denotes propositional information.

Except for "assign" and "instruct," all of these instructions are intended to correspond to some voluntary cognitive operation that the conceptual system can perform. No attempt has been made to design a computer language (for use, say, in simulating cognitive processes) based on this list of instructions; any order code intended for use on a digital computer would require many more, and more specific, instructions. Out of respect for the reader's memory load and for our own ignorance of the psychological processes represented by these instructions, we have deliberately kept the list as short as possible, given our purpose of developing a framework within which to discuss procedural semiotics.

In order for the system to respond with movements of the body (other than "utter"), the list must be supplemented by efferent control instructions. For example, "find" must be able to move the receptors through an environmental search domain; "achieve" must be able to order movements of body parts, grasping, applying force, ingesting, expelling objects; "identify" must be able to command pointing gestures as well as to provide distinguishing descriptions. A catalog of motor acts comparable to the catalog of perceptual predicates has not been attempted.

4

Labels, Words, and Concepts

To grasp the meaning of a thing, an event, or a situation is to see it in its relations to other things: to note how it operates or functions, what consequences follow from it, what causes it, what uses it can be put to. In contrast, what we have called the brute thing, the thing without meaning to us, is something whose relations are not grasped.
—John Dewey (1910)

We have introduced predicates to characterize perception and have sketched the kind of information processing required to use language. We are ready now to consider how these systems work together—how perception and language are related. The relation between perceived objects and their names is probably the easiest place to begin.

Labeling cannot be a simple process. Object recognition and object permanence are so complex that no satisfactory account is yet available; using labels is part of the very complex process of using language; the intricate connection between the labels people use and their conceptions of the things labeled is poorly understood; little is known about the acquisition of labeling skills—about what is learned, or how a child gets the idea of labeling in the first place, or what motivates him to extend his mastery. Given this morass of complexity and ignorance, any account must be speculative and incomplete.

Harrison (1972) speaks of labeling as a sterile and circumscribed ritual; labels qualify as names only after people learn to use them in discourse. But learning to use them in discourse involves more than learning to incorporate them into routines for understanding and producing grammatical utterances. The way labels are used also depends on the conceptual distinctions and relations they represent. To leave conceptualization out of account would ignore the part of the story of greatest interest to cognitive psychologists.

Although it is common sense that labels are related conceptually as well as linguistically, this is a peculiarly difficult idea to explicate. One reason is that "concept" is a vague term. Frontal attacks that begin with "Concepts are ———," followed by some putative definition, never seem to clarify the subject. A flank attack may be more successful.

We will not impose some initial definition of concepts or conceptual relations from which consequences can be derived. Instead, we will begin with labels as if they were a collection of arbitrary, conceptually unrelated rituals linking words and objects. For all we know, that may be how they seem to young children. As we try to work with this concept-free hypothesis we will discover that some kind of structure has to be hypothesized. That structure, whatever it may be, and the information it organizes are what we take lexical concepts to be. In order to explore different kinds of lexical concepts, we will consider structures needed in various parts of the lexicon. By this inductive approach we hope to discover some lexical concepts of English—by characterizing the roles they play in relating English words. If we understood that, of course, we would have little need for a more formal definition of concepts.

Even before we become entangled in such abstract notions as concepts we face serious theoretical difficulties in understanding how unrelated percept-label associations might be characterized. It may seem a sterile and circumscribed ritual to Harrison, but it is a baffling problem to students of perception. So it is by no means obvious how to phrase an initial simple hypothesis—one that we might complicate later by conceptual relations.

The immediate task is to characterize what a person knows when he knows that an object x is labeled W. We reject the view that W is a vocal noise he has been conditioned to utter (or is predisposed to utter) whenever he perceives an appropriate object. We believe that a person who knows which x are labeled W knows something of the meaning of W, even though he may not be able to use W in sentences or to explain to someone else what he knows. We want to say that he knows something like "W" *means* M, even though he could not himself say " 'W' means M." More precisely, we want to say that the person, A, has learned a rule of the form x is a W if and only if $F(x)$. According to this formulation, the problem is to specify $F(x)$ in terms of whatever procedures we believe A follows when he examines x to see whether it is labeled W. In the present context we can limit $F(x)$ to A's perceptual judgments. At least initially, $F(x)$ will involve something like *Perceive* (A, x) and test$(t,$ $G(x))$, where G gives the perceptual description that x must satisfy before A will label it W.

So the problem is to specify G. At this point the perceptual predicates introduced in chapters 1 and 2 become relevant. We will concentrate on how those perceptual predicates could be used to provide descriptions of the kind required for object labeling. This concentration on G should be seen in terms of the role G plays in the more general theoretical scheme.

In formulating perceptual descriptions suitable for a discussion of labeling, we will draw heavily on ideas developed in the field of artificial intelligence, where object recognition by machines is an important focus of research. These mechanical systems have been limited in the main to recognizing line drawings of stylized objects, but some of their limitations are probably attributable to difficulties involved in providing a computer with the full range of perceptual tests available to human observers. As a starting point, we can assume that artificial intelligence models are correct in principle and could be made to work if all the various perceptual judgments people can make, and the ways in which the judgments are integrated, could be automated for the machine.

Object recognition depends heavily on shape perception. Variations in size, brightness, color, or location are not unimportant, but the major factor is shape. In chapter 2 we assumed that the perceptual system is able to attend to and make judgments of shape; indeed, we assumed that it is able to perceive the shape of a rigid three-dimensional object as invariant under variations in angle of regard, so we have simplified the problem to that extent. But even given that the perceived shapes of rigid objects stay constant, we face difficult questions.

It would not suffice to design a system that could do no more than recognize two shapes as the same, even under perspective transformations. The kind of object recognition needed for labeling must make it possible to assign the same label to objects of different shapes. It is not the set of all shape distinctions a person can make that we are interested in, but rather how he acquires just those distinctions his elders have found significant and comes to see as similar just those things they have judged to be similar.

Moreover, not all objects are rigid; the same object may have different shapes at different times. Consider how many shapes a person can have as he moves about. Any object with movable parts—books, animals, clouds, folding chairs, clothing, bags—can take a variety of shapes without changing labels. And some things—like a rhombus or a 6—can change their labels without changing their shapes.

A device able to answer correctly the question "Have you ever seen this object before?" could do little more than assign proper names to individual objects. But labels can be assigned correctly to objects never seen before. Psychologists invoke generalization to explain correct responses to novel instances; some such mechanism is required, but we should not underestimate its complexity.

We assume that a general description is associated with each label. General descriptions for categories of equivalent objects we will call perceptual paradigms. Recognition thus involves assigning a label to each percept on the basis of whatever perceptual paradigm matches it best. A perceptual paradigm presumably emerges inductively from experience with many exemplars whose labels were told to us, or, after a certain level of linguistic competence is attained, from a more direct verbal specification of the paradigm. If no single perceptual paradigm is adequate for all the various objects that take the label —if, as seems likely, there is no real perceptual essence of bookness or house-hood—then we might imagine a disjunction of several paradigms. If any one of the alternative paradigms provides the best match to a perceived object, the label can be applied.

The difficulties of this approach should not be minimized. To list some: we do not know how perceptual paradigms develop from the perception of a finite number of exemplars. Conditions affecting the rate and accuracy of inductive learning have been studied in psychological experiments, but the process itself remains a mystery. Winston (1970) demonstrated that a mechanistic account of such learning is not impossible in principle (he programmed a computer to do it in certain simple cases), but the fact that the discrete feature tests he used could be made to work in his artificial universe cannot be used to argue against alternative theories. We do not even know, for example, whether a paradigm might be conceived as a sort of template, as J. A. Anderson (1970, 1972) has proposed, or whether it might be more abstract—a program, say, for generating a template appropriate to the occasion. Nor do we understand the relation, if there is one, between paradigms used for recognition and the memory images people can generate for familiar objects.

The problem becomes very complex when there is no paradigm that matches the percept exactly. Finding the paradigm that gives the best match to a percept is far more difficult than finding an exact match. As Minsky and Papert (1969) point out, finding the best match implies some measure of discrepancy in terms of which alternative matches can be compared. They speculate that there is no way to find the best match without conducting a large search through many paradigms stored in memory. To make this difficulty concrete, imagine that an object percept is specified by n pieces of information, each of which must be compared with specifications laid down in memory in the form of stored paradigms for various labels. If no exact match is found, the system could try to maximize the similarity to some paradigm by modifying the input; each of the n pieces of input information could be altered individually, which leads to n more attempts to find an exact match to a stored paradigm. If no exact match was found, all possible pairs of the n features could be modified, which leads to $(n^2-n)/2$ more attempts to find an exact match. As long as no exact match is found, the search continues to expand factorially. Thus, even when all feature discrepancies are weighted equally, the search for a best match is discouragingly complex. The problem does not appear to be one that will yield more easily to parallel than to serial search through memory. And all this computation is required for a process that seems rapid and spontaneous in normal perception.

Faced with the difficulty of finding the stored paradigm that best matches a percept, one is motivated to search for constraints that could be placed on the memory search in order to rescue the valuable hypothesis of perceptual paradigms from computational disaster. For example, if finding the best match is impractical, we might settle for a satisfactory match (see Simon, 1957, on "satisficing"), one closer than some predetermined threshold. And we should know when to quit. If after two steps, say, no satisfactory match is found, terminate the search and say, "I don't know what it is." If there is no reasonably near neighbor, give up.

Another heuristic device would reduce the number of features with respect to which a match is sought. Let n be the number of features given in the percept and m the number of features specified by the perceptual paradigm. There is nothing that can reduce n, perhaps, but certainly m can be kept to a minimum, with the understanding that if a match is obtained for these m features, the other $n-m$ features are irrelevant. Thus positive weights can be assigned to shape features for the purpose of labeling objects, and zero weights to positional, chromatic, or size features. The shorter paradigm accepts a larger class of percepts as equivalent, which is one of the phenomena of labeling we would like to understand.

As m is reduced, a paradigm comes to accept a larger volume in the n-dimensional percept space and there is nothing to stop the boundaries of two paradigms from overlapping. The price of shortening paradigm specifications is that a given percept may match more than one paradigm. But, again, this is a price we should be glad to pay. Not only would the reduction of m speed the search process, but it promises to explain—in part, at least—how the same percept can have many different labels.

We must consider, therefore, the effects of overlapping. First, paradigms can accept overlapping sets of percepts if they specify values for disjoint sets of attributes. For example, if "rectangle" specifies acceptable values of m_i shape attributes and "red" specifies acceptable values of m_j color attributes, then both paradigms will accept red rectangles.

Second, if two paradigms specify values for some of the same attributes—if their feature sets intersect—they will label overlapping sets of percepts if they specify the same value for all shared attributes. For example, the paradigm for "man" might specify values for male and person and "driver" for activity and person, where person features are common to both paradigms, yet each paradigm specifies additional features. In such cases there can be percepts that would admit both labels. If two paradigms specify different values for the same attribute, however, they will not accept overlapping classes of percepts. In the most extreme cases exactly the same attribute is specified for each label, but each paradigm specifies a different value for that attribute.

Finally, a common source of overlap could be accounted for by inclusion of one paradigm as a component of another, which might happen in two ways. The more specific paradigm may include the less specific as one of its parts; a paradigm for "table" would include a paradigm for "leg." Or the more specific paradigm may include the less specific as a more general class; a paradigm for "table" would include a paradigm for "thing."

These various stratagems might help to avoid difficulties in finding the best match between a percept and a store of perceptual paradigms. And they would seem to increase the speed of search while having other consequences that are characteristic of lexical organization. As an initial hypothesis, therefore, we will propose that a perceptual paradigm can be described by a set of abstract perceptual predicates like those introduced in chapter 2. Precisely how the search for the best paradigm is implemented is a question yet to be answered, but some mechanism must exist so that a percept can be tested, more or less in parallel, against all stored paradigms, and many paradigms may be satisfied simultaneously. And by an act of attention a person can select one matching paradigm from all others.

These remarks are little more than a review of arguments implicit in our decision in chapter 2 to treat the output of the perceptual system in terms of predicates that describe attentional-judgmental abstractions.

4.1 LABELING OBJECTS

Our initial hypothesis is that phonological strings can label object percepts when a perceptual paradigm included in the labeling routine describes that percept. The perceptual paradigm, in turn, is some expression constructed from perceptual predicates like those introduced in chapter 2. The first problem, therefore, is to formulate labeling routines in such a way as to characterize these relations.

In order to increase the flexibility of the system, we distinguish between the procedures for labeling and the information utilized in the process. Assume that there is some perceptual paradigm F that is stored in conjunction with a label W; this information may be called by the procedure for labeling objects. The procedure will test whether the paradigm applies to percept x at a given time t. Thus, its general format would be

(1)   Label(x): $test(t, F(x))$; if so, utter(W); if not, exit,

where F and W range over perceptual paradigms and their labels. An equivalent format:*

(2)   Label(x):   In order to determine whether some x can be labeled "W" at time t, execute the following routine:
         (i) test$(t, F(x))$

The simplest way to understand what this formulation implies is to consider a specific instance, and one of the simplest examples is labeling a percept a "thing."

4.1.1 Labeling Routines

The existence in English of such a general word as "thing" (in the sense applicable to any percept judged to be a three-dimensional object) means

---

*Strictly speaking, quotation marks around the variable W are not required, although Quine's (1951) quasi quotes might serve as a reminder that the variable ranges over labels.

that there is *some* label you can apply to every concrete object, even when you are uncertain about the applicability of a more specific label. For this very general case, the paradigm can be captured by a single perceptual predicate, Obj. It sounds odd to refer to an extremely large object—the world, say, or even a mountain—as a "thing." The limitation is probably perceptual: if you are unable to get it all into view at once, the perceptual predicate Obj$(x, 3d)$ is not applicable and "thing" does not seem appropriate. This simple paradigm could be stored in the format

THING(x):   Obj$(x, 3d)$.

Thus, a routine for labeling a percept as a thing would be formulated as follows:

(3)   THING(x):   In order to determine whether some x can be labeled "thing" at time t, execute the following routine:
(i) test$(t$, Obj$(x, 3d))$

We will consider more extended paradigms, but before rushing into complexities there are several points to note about routine (3). First, the perceptual predicate Obj$(x, 3d)$ is taken as an argument for the instruction "test." A perceptual test seems to pose a yes/no question; if the answer is yes, x satisfies the test and the system moves on to the next test (if any) in the paradigm. If all tests are satisfied, the label ("thing" in this case) can be applied to the percept indexed by x. If the answer is not yes, however, the situation becomes more complicated. If x is a percept that has values outside the range of values specified for some attribute by the paradigm, it can be judged unequivocally to have failed the test, and the answer is a clear no. But sometimes the results may be indeterminate, neither clearly yes nor clearly no. For example, the percept may be near the boundary of the category; under some conditions the label might apply and under other conditions it would not. Or the test may call a recursive routine that leads to a long, repetitive computation that never ends. Since the halting problem is undecidable, some arbitrary rule to halt long computations is probably invoked and the resulting output is neither yes nor no; indeterminate computations will produce the output "indeterminate" and will not continue for indefinitely long times to give no output at all.

Since people can reply to questions about the applicability of a particular label by saying "Yes," "No," or "I don't know," the system seems to operate with a three-valued logic. This requirement poses certain formal problems; to deal with them at length would interrupt our discussion of labeling, but we cannot ignore them entirely. For the present, we will assume that routine (3) must lead to a clearly affirmative answer; if the answer is not affirmative the system exits to some unspecified routines where other instructions for dealing with the situation can be found. It is worth noting, however, that at category boundaries people say things like "It is either red or orange, but I can't decide which." If this judgment entails "It is either red or not red," the law of the excluded middle is preserved even though the observer is unable to decide which disjunct is true. In this case, what must be given up is the program of assigning truth to composite propositions on the basis of an evaluation of their component propositions.

Second, although the paradigm incorporated in routine (3) contains only one perceptual test, the Obj predicate represents a perceptual routine that is here called as a subroutine. In more general cases, a perceptual paradigm will include several perceptual predicates. When more than one perceptual predicate is required, the paradigm will be regarded as their conjunction, that is, the paradigm will match and the label will apply only if all components are satisfied. In order to distinguish between negative and indeterminate outcomes, we will make a distinction between parallel and serial conjunctions. Let F and G denote perceptual predicates. Then in a trivalent logic the instruction to test$(t, F \& G)$ will mean to test F and G in parallel, and the instruction to test(t, F) & test(t, G) will mean to test F first and, only if the result is affirmative, to test G second. In a bivalent logic, this distinction would be meaningless. It makes a difference, though, just in case testing F leads to an indeterminate outcome and testing G leads to a negative outcome. Under those conditions, test$(t, F \& G)$ would lead to a negative output, whereas test(t, F) & test(t, G) would halt after the first test with an indeterminate output.

Third, routine (3) incorporates only one paradigm, but we wish to leave open the possibility that a labeling routine might incorporate two or more alternative paradigms. Multiple paradigms will be regarded as disjunctively related, that is to say, the label will be applicable to the percept if any one of the paradigms matches it. Here again, it is necessary to distinguish parallel and serial disjunction in order to retain information as to whether the outcome was negative or indeterminate. In a trivalent logic the instruction to test$(t, F$ or $G)$ will mean to test F and G in parallel, and the instruction to test(t, F) or test(t, G) will mean to test F first and, only if the result is affirmative, to test G second. The outcomes will be different just in case testing F leads to an indeterminate outcome and testing G leads to an affirmative outcome. Under those conditions, test$(t, F$ or $G)$ would lead to an affirmative output, whereas test(t, F) or test(t, G) would halt after the first test with an indeterminate output.

Fourth, the perceptual apparatus does not wait for a routine to be executed before carrying out the information processing necessary to construct the percept. The index x points to the particular percept that is to be tested. Execution of a routine simply directs attention to particular aspects of the percept and ignores others.

Fifth, the label is associated with a perceptual paradigm, not with an object or pattern of stimulation or class of entities. It will sometimes be convenient to treat the label as though it were the name of the paradigm rather than a label for objects that satisfy the paradigm. The paradigm is expressed in terms of perceptual judgments introduced in chapter 2. Incorporating the paradigm in a "test" instruction indicates that a person can consciously attend to the outcome of tests included in this paradigm and can signal a successful paradigm match. Since predicates included in a paradigm themselves represent routines and may require extensive sensorimotor activity to modify the percept in such a way as to facilitate the test, the actual processing that is performed to determine whether the label is applicable can vary considerably from one occasion to the next; execution of the routine should not be thought of as a relatively passive matter of attending to whatever static percept chance provides. It is also convenient to talk sometimes as though perceptual paradigms and their associated labels were labeling routines, rather than information called by the labeling routine. In a discussion of labeling it makes little difference whether we regard $F(x)$ as a routine or as a recipe for the ingredients of a routine. Later, however, the reader will encounter more complex functions where the same paradigm-label formula can be used in different ways (with different control instructions) in different situations, and then it will be necessary to bear in mind the distinction between the control routine and the subroutines it calls. For example, in chapter 3 we considered cases in which a routine is used to replace a label by a pointer to some suitable percept or memory. The word "thing" (in the intended sense) might have occurred in a sentence and the listener wants to replace it by a perception of its referent. In that case he might try to execute the instruction find(Env, $F(?x?)$). This instruction calls the perceptual paradigm and searches the environment for a percept that satisfies it; if the procedure succeeds, it assigns the pointer x to that percept and so makes the pointer available to the routine that called for it. All that it is necessary to assume is that the spoken label "thing" is attached to the routine THING so that the appropriate perceptual paradigm can be used to evaluate percepts.

Sixth, because this paradigm is so short, it will be satisfied by an enormous variety of percepts. Although this particular paradigm does little to partition the perceptual world, it does serve to define a domain to be partitioned. Test (i) will be incorporated in many paradigms used in different labeling routines. The formation of a hierarchical system of labels is implicit, as is the notion that every object has at least one label.

Seventh, a person who has this routine stored in memory and who knows that when a percept matches its paradigm he can utter "thing" knows something of the meaning of the word. He is not able to say "A thing is a three-dimensional object," because that would involve both conceptual knowledge about dimensions, numbers, and objects and how to use the word "thing" in a sentence. Routine (3) indicates how to apply the label, but not what it means or how to use it in discourse.

Eighth, routine (3) might also hold for the labels "object," "article," and "entity" in addition to "thing." A careful lexicographer would find consistent and useful distinctions among these labels when used as words in normal discourse. Whatever those distinctions might be, they are unlikely to involve alternative perceptual paradigms. Routine (3) is therefore not a complete definition of the word "thing." The most we can say is that it provides information relevant to the definitions of a set of closely related words—it can be an incomplete definition.

Ninth, the paradigm is not a visual (or sensorimotor) image. People can voluntarily form imagination images which may or may not resemble any paradigms for which they have common labels. Given this ability, it is not implausible to suppose that a paradigm might provide specifications for image formation, although the image could contain many more features than the paradigm. Any image that a person might form according to the paradigm for "thing" would necessarily be an image of some specific thing, as Bishop Berkeley noted long ago, but it would still be an image of a thing in the sense that if tested against the store of paradigms, the "thing" paradigm would give a confirmatory result. That is to say, imagination images can be tested just as perceptual images are, and can be modified in various features until they fit a paradigm. But we do not require the paradigm to *be* an image, and we believe there are persuasive reasons for keeping images and paradigms distinct.

If a constructed image can function in much the same way as a perceptual image, it can provide input not only to the routine for which it was generated but to other routines as well. Imagery can thus provide a communication channel between labels; it is possible to enter the system with a label, generate an image, and retrieve other labels as output.

Finally, when a label is sought for an object, a "find" instruction is needed in order to search through semantic memory (through the store of perceptual paradigms) to find a paradigm that fits the percept. In this case the appropriate control instruction is find(M(Sem), ?Label?(x)). This instruction will initiate a comparison of x with all stored paradigms. If THING(x) is satisfied, then the system can utter "thing."

This account of labeling objects is still inadequate in at least one respect. Execution of the instruction find(M(Sem), ?Label?(x)) will usually provide more than one paradigm that fits x. Why should THING be selected instead of any other? Various heuristic strategies for selecting a particular label could be imagined: the first one found, the most specific one, the one used most often in the past, a random choice. If we think about situations in which labels designate particular objects, we recognize that they frequently serve a selective function for a listener. The speaker is composing a program that he wants the listener to be able to translate back into a routine that can be executed, and that fact puts certain constraints on his choice of words. The word "thing," for example, will not often be used alone to identify an object because it provides no criteria for distinguishing the intended object from all the other objects that normally clutter the environment. If a label is to play a role in successful communication, it must be informative enough to select an intended object from a set of alternative objects (see 4.2.3).

Selecting a label adequate to distinguish a particular object from all others in the domain of search poses a problem to be solved by the system. We will use the instruction identify(search domain, x), where x is a pointer to the percept; when executed, this instruction causes the system to select a label (or string of labels) adequate to identify that percept in that search domain. Like most of the control instructions we have introduced, "identify" represents a complex cognitive skill that must be acquired. It presupposes an ability to recognize a listener's difficulties in understanding labels that are overly general; this insight is something children have been said to lack until they are old enough to decenter—to see the world from another's point of view. For adults, the labeling task will usually call on a control instruction to identify, rather than merely find. That is to say, the instruction identify(search domain, x) will call the instruction find(M(Sem), ?Label?(x)) as a subroutine. This "find" instruction will not stop with the first labeling routine that x satisfies but will continue to provide suggestions until the "identify" instruction has found a distinguishing label.

It is clear that the identification process is an important component of the way adults label objects (Olson, 1970, 1972; Osgood, 1971). The implication is that even simple labeling is complicated by the requirements of communication. If one thinks of labeling as a private activity, it may not matter which label is selected. But as soon as labels are used for communication, other considerations intrude.

If the difference between words and labels is that some words are labels that people know how to use in ordinary discourse, and if identifying an object by a label is one way to use labels in ordinary discourse, then our discussion has already passed from the realm of labels into the realm of words. The transition is accomplished not by complicating the labeling routine in some way but by using the routine differently, by using it for communication. If one thinks of a label as a response to the question "What's this called?" accompanied by an appropriate pointing gesture, the response is more than a label—it is an answer. To provide answers is to engage in discourse. As an answer, even a one-word response is a word, not merely a label.

If a labeling routine is to function in the manner suggested in section 3.5, various kinds of syntactic information must be attached to it somehow. How this attachment should be represented theoretically—whether by pointers to relevant information stored elsewhere or by explicit statement as part of THING —is a question we will not try to answer here. For the moment we need merely note that words and labels differ in that words must have such linguistic information attached to them, whereas labels need not.

These comments on labeling should suffice to explicate the hypothesis with which we wish to begin. Our next step in developing this hypothesis will be to apply it to some more interesting word, to note the problems we encounter, and then to propose remedial complications. Since there is no compelling reason to suppose some objects more important than others, we will arbitrarily plunge into the middle of things.

Consider the noun "table." How should a labeling routine be written for this perceptually complex concept? We will try to answer this question by recasting a conventional definition of "table" into a labeling routine.

According to the dictionary,* a table is "an article of furniture supported by one or more vertical legs and having a flat horizontal surface on which objects can be placed." How can we convert this definition into a series of perceptual tests that could be incorporated as a perceptual paradigm in a labeling routine for tables?

The dictionary gives two proper parts of a table, leg and top, and says that the legs are vertical and the top is flat and horizontal; this description suggests perceptual tests, if it is possible to recognize legs and tops. The dictionary also gives another fact: it should be possible to place objects on a table—presumably objects smaller than the table itself—but this information has less to do with form than with function. And it gives a genus, furniture, of which table is a particular species.

We turn next to see how "furniture" is defined. Furniture is "the movable articles in a room or establishment that render it fit for living or working." The perceptual information provided here is that furniture—and so, presumably, a table—is movable, and that you can expect to find it inside rooms or establishments. If you are looking for a table, of course, the best search domains are indoors, but if you were to encounter one outside you would still be able to recognize it. (It is interesting to note, incidentally, that "table" is a count noun and "furniture" a mass noun, which would seem to eliminate any simple perceptual test for distinguishing between those two categories of nouns.)

Pursuing the same course one step further in the dictionary, an article is "an individual thing in a class; an item." There is no perceptual information here except that a table is a thing.

Next we must seek perceptual information about legs and tops. For "leg" the dictionary provides several senses to consider, the two most relevant being that a leg is "a limb or appendage of an animal, used for locomotion or support" (which can be ruled out because tables are not animals) and that a leg is "any supporting part resembling a leg in shape or function" (which refers to animal legs via a dead metaphor). This definition suggests that first you must learn to recognize animal legs; once you have done that, you can look around at things indoors and see if any of them have parts that, were they on animals, would be legs. For top we are told that it is "the uppermost part, point, surface, or end of anything," so we know to look for the flat horizontal surface as the part of the table farthest from the floor.

The information from the dictionary about the meaning of "table" falls into two parts, one having to do with the conventional function of tables, the other with their perceptual appearance. The perceptual information, in turn, falls into three parts, namely, that a table is a movable object, that it has a flat, horizontal top, and that the top is supported by vertical legs. We are ready now to formulate this information as a perceptual paradigm associated with the phonological string "table." We will divide the perceptual paradigm into four serially conjunctive parts:

---

* Here and elsewhere references to "the dictionary" should be understood to mean the *American Heritage Dictionary of the English Language* unless otherwise indicated.

(4)   TABLE(x):

    (i) x is an object: Obj(x, 3d).

    (ii) x is connected and rigid: Conn(x) & Rigid(x).

    (iii) x's top is flat, horizontal: Top(x, y) & Flface(y) & Horiz(y).

    (iv) Vertical legs support the top: Exten(y, z) & Vert(z).

It will be noted that the information in a perceptual paradigm is apparently stored in the form of assertions. We say "apparently" because one of the functions of the labeling routine is to take these apparent assertions and to convert them into perceptual tests. On the other hand, if a person is asked to say what a table looks like, he will simply try to convert (4) into words.

The ambivalence of much of the information in semantic memory—sometimes functioning as an assertion, sometimes functioning as a procedure—will be a persistent theme of these pages; it will be useful on occasion to mark the distinction notationally. We will continue to use our ordinary notation for tests and procedures; where they are frozen into nonoperative assertions we will represent them within brackets. [Obj(x, 3d)] represents the assertion (strictly, the predicate) that x is a three-dimensional object, and the only difference between it and [THING(x)] is that "thing" is introduced as a label for x. The brackets may be regarded as insulating procedures from actual execution. Unless it is crucial to our argument, we will for convenience ignore the distinction, simply writing THING(x) for both the test and the predicate. This distinction is another step away from a strictly procedural representation —the first step was the introduction of the null instruction "instruct" in 3.5.7—toward a mixture of procedural and propositional representations.

Turning to the actual content of (4), a number of points require comment. Paradigm (4) is a combination of several perceptual predicates and might be viewed as another perceptual predicate little different from those discussed in chapter 2 except that it is longer and is organized into subparts. Line (i) is equivalent to calling THING as an initial subroutine of TABLE. That is to say, we have included THING(x) as an entailment of TABLE; if x satisfies paradigm (4), it necessarily satisfies paradigm (3). Line (ii) imposes further tests on the properties of the object. Line (iii) is intended as a paradigm for the WORKTOP of a table and line (iv) for the LEG; if these routines had been written previously, they could be called explicitly.

These remarks, which are intended to illustrate how a definition of "table" might be phrased as a labeling routine, could be developed in more detail, but before investing too much notational refinement in their formalization we should consider some consequences of this general approach. Since the reader knows what a table is, he could easily overlook the shortcomings of the dictionary definition and the perceptual paradigm based on it.

4.1.2 Objections to Labeling Routines

The first and probably the most apparent criticism of the line we have been illustrating is that a variety of unusual objects would pass as tables according to the dictionary and paradigm (4). Some examples borrowed from Carelman (1969) are reproduced in figure 4.1. The "table à pieds groupés" (*A*) is physically improbable; the "table tête-à-tête" (*B*) is merely unusual. If these were included along with some other pictures of tables and if people were asked to judge how closely each picture resembled their conception of what a table should look like, the two pictures in figure 4.1 would probably rank close to the bottom. Obviously, not all instances that satisfy the definition are equivalent. Rosch (1973) uses people's ability to judge (and to agree on) the distances of various instances from the most typical instance of a natural category as evidence that there are prototypes for each category. What the most typical "thing" would be is difficult to imagine, but people clearly have much more specific "table" expectations than are captured by paradigm (4).

G. Lakoff (1972b) has noted various hedges that speakers use to signal degrees of category membership. For example, "technically" is a hedge in "A whale is technically a mammal"—it means that whales satisfy the defining criteria but do not have other properties characteristic of most mammals. "Loosely speaking, a whale is a fish" illustrates a different hedge—"loosely speaking" means that whales satisfy characteristic though incidental properties of fish. In "Harry is a regular fish," "regular" means that Harry shares a property characteristic of fish—swimming, drinking—but is not a member of the class. Lakoff lists more than sixty such hedges. In order to account for these expressions, it is necessary to recognize, at the very least, a distinction between features that are defining and features that are merely characteristic. A typical instance would satisfy both types of criteria.

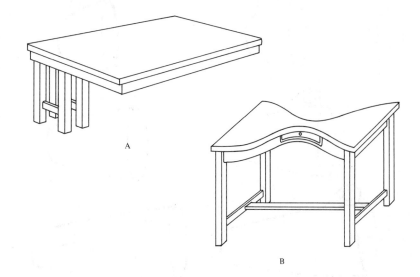

Figure 4.1 Improbable tables. (After Carelman, 1969.)

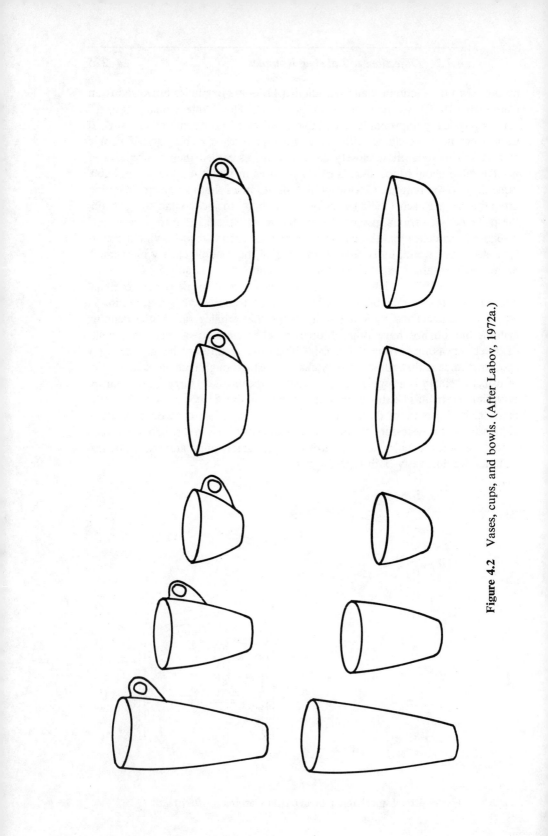

Figure 4.2 Vases, cups, and bowls. (After Labov, 1972a.)

A drawing of a packing case might look more like a typical table than either of the drawings in figure 4.1. Nevertheless, Carelman's drawings satisfy the defining criteria for tables—they are "technically" tables, to use an appropriate hedge—and a drawing of a packing case does not. If the judged distance from a prototype were the only mechanism available for categorization, it would be impossible to explain such violations. Lack of equivalence of instances is not a sufficient reason, therefore, to abandon lists of discrete tests. But it is a shortcoming of paradigm (4) that it ignores nonequivalence of instances.

Not all boundary disputes can be settled. There are some objects that fall so close to a boundary that either or both labels could apply. It would not be difficult to design a series of objects graded between a table and a bench; somewhere in the series we would find speakers of English just as willing to use "bench" as "table," and no amount of learned lexicology would suffice to select either label as more correct. Labov (1972a) has demonstrated the problem in a study of containers. Figure 4.2 reproduces some of the drawings he asked people to label. When the ratio of width to height is about 1:1, people use "cup"; when the width is much greater than the height, they use "bowl"; when the height is much greater than the width, they use "vase." The proportions of judgments in each category varied as a function of the height:width ratio, with "cup" and "bowl" being about equally probable when the ratio was 1:2, and "cup" and "vase" being about equally probable when the ratio was 2.5:1. The "best" cups in the series were around 1:1 to 1.2:1, which are presumably closest to the prototypical cup. But paradigm (4) makes no provision for the vagueness of labels.

There are some properties that are not essential (in the Aristotelian sense) for assigning a label to an object but that contribute when they are present to increasing the probability that the label will be used. For example, when Labov used the same drawings without handles, the probability of "cup" dropped sharply for the wider containers. Cups usually have handles, although they do not always; bowls usually do not have handles, although they may have. There is an interaction between the height:width ratio and the presence of a handle; a wider range of height:width ratios will be labeled "cup" when a handle is present than when a handle is absent. But the best instances are still labeled "cup" even without a handle. It is a shortcoming of paradigm (4) that it assigns no weights to reflect the relative importance of various features.

Another shortcoming is that (4) will not recognize tables on end or upside down. Although rotational invariance is not one of the perceptual constancies (Rock, 1974)—familiar faces, for example, are not familiar upside down—that does not mean that people are unable to recognize tables in any but their characteristic orientation. Nor can we argue that there is something about the shape of tables that dictates what their characteristic orientation should be, something that would make the flat, horizontal surface be seen as the top even if it were not physically above everything else, because all of the relevant psychological experiments on preferred orientations for unfamiliar shapes indicate that people tend to judge that the concentration of mass and the horizontal faces of unfamiliar objects should be their bottoms (Howard and Templeton, 1966). The only way a person can know which part of a table should be uppermost when it is in its characteristic orientation is by experience with tables.

We might consider inserting another test into paradigm (4), a test that would ask, "Is x in its characteristic orientation?" We could then define the intrinsic top of x as the part that was uppermost (that satisfied Top) when x was in its characteristic orientation. But a test for the characteristic orientation of x cannot be part of a paradigm for recognizing x, since that creates a very small circle: you cannot know what it is unless it is in its characteristic orientation, but you cannot know whether it has a characteristic orientation until you know what it is.

There are other alternatives, however. We could imagine some perceptual mechanism that on failure to recognize an object tried rotating it various ways in imagination. Certainly this mental feat is not impossible, and undoubtedly people use it on some occasions (Shepard and Metzler, 1971), but it is probably not their method of choice. Another possibility might be based on previous experience with tables in arbitrary orientations; perhaps the TABLE routine has a whole battery of perceptual paradigms for various orientations. People who see some mono-oriented object in a new orientation for the first time are slow to recognize it, but recognition is faster with increasing practice; perhaps practice has the effect of making more paradigms available to the labeling routine.

Orientation is related to a general process that we took for granted in the discussion of perception, namely, the process of integrating a variety of specific views of an object into a general percept independent of angle of regard. If people can have a perception of a table that is independent of the spatial relation between themselves and it, it is not implausible that they could also have a perceptual paradigm for tables that would be independent of the spatial relation between it and other objects. We might rephrase the paradigm as follows:

(5)   TABLE(x):
        (i) x is an object.
        (ii) x is movable, connected, and rigid.
        (iii) x has a flat surface.
        (iv) There are parts of x that extend out from the side opposite
              to the flat surface.

Here, all the predicates in paradigm (4) that involve horizontal or vertical orientation are simply eliminated. We might imagine that when paradigm (5) is satisfied in a labeling routine, the percept is then rotated (in imagination) until its flat surface is uppermost and then paradigm (4) is tried.

It may seem that we are making too much of orientation, but characteristic orientation is not a minor idiosyncrasy limited to tables. Many objects, including people, have intrinsic tops—parts that remain the top regardless of orientation. We will return to this problem in more detail later.

All of these criticisms—equivalence of instances, lack of vagueness, omission of ancillary features, reliance on characteristic orientation—may be related to a further shortcoming of paradigm (4). Unlike the dictionary, (4) says nothing about the function that tables serve. This oversight is unfortunate, since the uses people can make of a firm horizontal surface are the real reason for having tables in the first place. Function is a critical aspect of most human artifacts.

A functional definition might go something like this: "A table is used for working or eating or playing games; the top is used to support various smaller objects required in the course of those activities." From this functional definition it is possible to infer what tables should look like. A table should have a WORKTOP, a surface that is horizontal so that objects will not roll or slide off and flat so that objects can stand on it. Moreover, the surface would be useless if it were not firm and at a convenient height from the floor (not horizontal upside down), so rigid legs are required to support it. Since normal function determines such matters as the nature of the top and the characteristic orientation of tables, a functional definition is needed in order to escape the shortcomings of the simple perceptual predicates of paradigm (5). Function—at least for artifacts—is more basic to the definition than form.

Consider the many varieties of tables: tea tables, billiard tables, end tables, drafting tables, typing tables, operating tables, bridge tables, conference tables. How can these be distinguished perceptually? In some cases it would be possible to add perceptual tests in order to differentiate among them, but often the difference is purely a matter of function, not form. Exactly the same physical object may, at different times of day, function as a breakfast table, kitchen table, worktable, lunch table, conference table, coffee table, dinner table, poker table. In order to know which label to use, one needs to know what function the table is serving. If we tried to specify such distinctions perceptually, we would require tests for the time of day and the location of the table, the objects on it, the activities of any people in the region of the table, and so on; some of these tests would be awkward to formulate in terms of the perceptual predicates of chapter 2. It is more economical to define such differences functionally.

In his study of containers, Labov (1972a) asked his judges to imagine that the same pictures (fig. 4.2) they had labeled in a neutral context were now used in various ways. For example, they were to imagine they saw someone holding the object, stirring in sugar with a spoon, and drinking coffee from it. Or they might be asked to imagine that it was on the dinner table filled with mashed potatoes, or sitting on a shelf with cut flowers in it. Labov reports that imaginary contexts (in addition to the presence or absence of a handle) had strong effects on category boundaries. Imagining that the container was functioning as a vase significantly increased the probability that it would be labeled "vase." What an object is being used for has measurable effects on what people are likely to call it.

The well-known utilitarian character of children's definitions may be relevant here (Krauss, 1952). Children frequently offer such definitions as "a hole is to dig," "a tree is to climb," "a book is to read," "a table is to sit at." The child does not seem to learn the labels first and later learn to use them in sentences. As Harrison (1972) claims, referents and uses are learned together. A child learns to use "table" in sentences: "That table is where we eat dinner," "Dinner is on the table," "Sit down at the table," "Daddy works at his table." They learn which verbs—"eat," "sit," "work"—"table" is used with, and such information is dependent on functions that the object serves.

Blank (1973) argues that children's predisposition to define concepts spontaneously through function should be exploited by good teachers. For example, if "corner" is to be taught, instead of presenting multiple instances accompanied by "This is a corner" or "This is not a corner," the teacher can show the child where two walls meet and point out that you cannot keep going straight: "A corner is where you have to turn." Blank notes that some such functional approach is most important for abstract words, where it is unlikely that a child will be able to induce from multiple instances just what combination of attributes is intended.

Function is also related to problems posed by the nonequivalence of instances. Consider what is meant by "That is a good table." Theories of the good are too complex to review here; we assume that to say a thing is a good table means that it has in greater than average degree those attributes that it is rational to want in a table, given what tables are expected to look like, or be used for, or do (Rawls, 1971). The ways in which things can be good are various and depend on what people think it is rational to expect of them; obviously, all those expectations cannot be part of the definition of "good." Semantically, it is as if the meaning of "good" were given by some component of the head noun that it modifies; all "good" does is assign that component a positive evaluation (J. J. Katz, 1964a).

Most people will sense some ambiguity about "a good table." On the one hand, it might mean that it is near the prototypical idea of what tables should look like—the sense of "good" understood in "a good red." On the other hand, "a good table" might mean that it performs its normal function well—the sense of "good" understood in "a good knife." As we have seen, the perceptual form of a table is closely related to what tables are used for, so these two senses of "good," a typical instance or a useful instrument, become almost indistinguishable in "a good table." The point at issue here is that nonequivalence of instances can result from functional as well as perceptual expectations, which implies that functional as well as perceptual information must be part of the meaning of "table."

There are some categories where all instances do seem equivalent; Katz gives as examples liquid, electricity, planet, molecule, scribble, truth, speck, mote, noun, amoeba, integer, and grain of sand. When an instance of one of these categories is said to be good, you generally need some context, either implicit in the discourse or expressed by an explicit phrase, to decide what the speaker thinks is good about that instance. For nouns that can be used to label instances regarded as nonequivalent, Katz has proposed that a theoretical representation of their meaning must include information about the expected use for their referent, with the understanding that unless otherwise indicated by context any evaluative adjective will be interpreted as relevant to the performance of that function. The representation of "knife," for example, would include the information that knives are used to cut; "chair" would include the information that chairs are used to sit in. When the adjective "good" (or "bad") is applied to these nouns without any explicit indication of a basis for the evaluation, it is understood implicitly that they are good (or bad) for cutting, sitting in, and so forth. Since some nouns, such as color names, are evaluated implicitly in terms of how typical they look, Katz's proposal should probably be broadened to include the possibility that an evaluative term could also denote judged perceptual distance from a prototypical instance. But, there are many cases where nonequivalence of instances arises from functional nonequivalence, so a functional definition, properly phrased, might avoid some problems arising from nonequivalence of the instances accepted by paradigm (5).

There are several reasons for including functional information along with the perceptual tests of paradigm (5). But it is at this point that "table" would start to lose its labellike quality and begin to take on more of the characteristics of a word. As we conceived it originally, a label is tied to a percept simply by virtue of the satisfaction of a specified set of perceptual predicates. It is feasible, as paradigm (5) demonstrates, to set up a perceptual paradigm for tables. Yet this approach has an air of artificiality about it. It is psychologically implausible to suppose, for example, that people identify worktops purely in terms of the predicates introduced in chapter 2. It is much more plausible to suppose that they rely on predicates motivated by the function of worktops. So a theoretical revision is indicated: the association of simple perceptual judgments into compound perceptual paradigms is not, by itself, adequate to account for the ways we identify objects.

Suppose we wished to specify a paradigm for WORKTOP that incorporated functional information. Such a paradigm might be

WORKTOP(x):
  (i) x has a flat surface.
  (ii) x is large enough, and rigid enough, so that, if it is supported horizontally at an appropriate height, it will support objects for a person to manipulate with his hands.

It does not seem implausible that people are able to judge whether a percept satisfies such conditions. In order to make this judgment it is necessary to go beyond the predicates of chapter 2—it is necessary to have developed a schema of a worktop, which incorporates such predicates (Flface(x), for example) along with sensorimotor predicates (manipulate(x, y)). And these predicates are integrated by knowledge of the function of the object. We must distinguish between an ability to perceive what an object *is* being used for (what it is currently functioning as) and an ability to perceive what it *could* be used for. It is this latter notion, the ability to perceive potential functions, that is required here; hence the occurrence of the conditional clause in line (ii) of WORKTOP. Such an ability may involve construction of a *possible* state of affairs—imagining, for instance, that the object is supported by brackets from a wall. We will say more about a procedural analysis of possibility in 6.3.5; here, the essential point is that a person can imagine what an object could be used for without straining its functional potential. Presumably, both visual imagery, based on a perceptual paradigm, and sensorimotor imagery, based on functional information, can be exploited. On the other hand, it is often unnecessary to engage in this process, as when identifying a table that is being used in a conventional way.

It might be tempting to suppose that a perceptual paradigm can always be derived from knowledge of the function of an object, and hence that paradigms should be discarded and replaced by functional definitions. But that approach would go too far in the opposite direction. There are natural objects that have no intrinsic functions—clouds, trees, pebbles. More important, the schemata of many artifacts weld together form and function, as we have tried to illustrate in WORKTOP. It would be a mistake to rely wholly on one or the other.

The amalgamation of form and function can also be illustrated by the formulation of a more satisfactory paradigm for "leg":

LEG(x):
   (i) x has a maximal dimension.
   (ii) x is rigid enough that if one of its ends is connected to a proper part y of an object z which is oriented so that x is between y and the earth and the other end of x touches the earth and prevents y from falling, then x supports part of z.

Line (i) lays down the simple criterion that legs are longer in one dimension than in the other two—a criterion that reduces to a combination of chapter 2 predicates. Line (ii) represents an interrelation between such predicates and an overriding functional requirement. Note, again, the conditional form of this requirement, and its consequent claim, not that a leg necessarily supports an object, but that it supports part of an object. If line (i) is omitted, the remaining analysis is appropriate for a SUPPORT, which includes LEG as a special case.

With these analyses it should be possible to offer a more functional description of TABLE. But knowing what tables are used for does not exhaust one's knowledge of tables. Knowledge of their function is useful for understanding metaphorical extensions of the term to such objects as crates, but calling a crate a table does not make it one. Function may determine many aspects of form, but centuries of debate over the relation of form to function should convince us that we cannot ignore either in favor of the other. The crux of the matter is that in specifying function it is often necessary to refer to form. On the other hand, if we limited ourselves to perceptual information about things, it would indeed be difficult to explain why the variety of differently shaped tables merit a common label. What they share, of course, is a common function. Perhaps the most plausible organization for the concept of TABLE is a single schema, largely functional in nature, that integrates a disjunctive set of perceptual paradigms. Where an individual has never seen a particular sort of table, he will lack its perceptual paradigm and be unable to provide a specific lable for it. He may nevertheless recognize it as a table by relating its perceptual characteristics to his schema of tables.

Because of the uncertainty of the boundary between purely perceptual information and perceptual information incorporating conceptual knowledge, it would be foolish to insist that there is no conceptual basis for the predicates introduced in chapter 2. It would be a simple matter to introduce paradigms that raised them from one level to the next in the manner in which we defined THING(x) in terms of Obj(x, 3d). We will accordingly assume that we have written such paradigms, and mark this assumption by referring from now on to all predicates as though they had a conceptual basis. We will write, for example, FLFACE(x, y) rather than Flface(x, y) in subsequent analyses. (We postpone discussion of this assumption to 4.1.3.)

The desired schema for tables may now be written as follows:

> TABLE(x):
>   (i)   THING(x)
>   (ii) MOVABLE(x) & CONN(x) & RIGID(x)
>   (iii) PPRT(x, WORKTOP(y))
>   (iv) PPRT(x, SUPPORT(z)) & SUPPORT(z, y)

Our claim is that any object that would normally be labeled "table" should satisfy this schema. The labeling routine, however, may call on much more specific perceptual paradigms, formulable in terms of the simple perceptual predicates of chapter 2, that have been acquired by experience with different sorts (and shapes) of table.

It is the schema that provides the beginnings of the concept of a table, since a label does not acquire meaning simply through association with some class of percepts. A perception of an object is not necessarily, in and of itself, a meaningful experience. Bransford and McCarrell (1974) illustrate this important point in terms of relatively unknown tools designed to perform very special functions. One could imagine learning to recognize such a tool, even learning to call it by some label—a "glump," say—without having any notion what it is used for, by whom, in what circumstances. Alternatively, one could imagine learning to use it under appropriate circumstances in a skillful manner without having learned any particular word to distinguish it from other tools. Neither the perception of a glump, nor the label "glump," nor an association of the label with the percept suffices to endow the object or the label with meaning. In order for them to be meaningful, there must be, underlying both the percept and the label, a concept that has its place relative to other concepts. The development and differentiation of this concept and its relation to the rest of the conceptual system is a long learning process that may continue into highly advanced stages of expertise. What any word or percept means to a person will depend on how much he already knows about it; his knowledge of his world will be considerably richer than his knowledge of the perceptual characteristics of isolated objects. In short, learning to utter some conventional label whenever objects of a certain type reappear does not make the label meaningful unless such objects have already become meaningful in terms of their relations to other knowledge.

It is easier to learn the conventional label for a meaningful object than for a meaningless one, and many psychologists have speculated that conceptual development must precede lexical development. It is difficult to know, however, what concepts prelinguistic children have mastered. There is some evidence (Ricciuti, 1965) that infants engage in sorting and grouping objects in a consistent way before they have acquired labels for the categories they are forming. Nelson (1973a; see also Werner and Kaplan, 1963) has suggested that these prelinguistic categories are predominantly functional in nature—acquired, perhaps, as part of the period of sensorimotor learning. It is frequently assumed that infants learn conceptual categories by noting the perceptual features shared between objects that are instances of the category and not shared with noninstances. Although attention to between-object variations may be important, Nelson suggests that a more important basis for conceptual learning is the within-object variations that a child notices in the course of using, eating, or manipulating objects. It is noteworthy that the first names of things children learn are for movable, manipulable objects (Nelson, 1973b); they are not names of things that—however obvious or important—just sit there: sofas, tables, walls, windows, trees, grass. Once a schema for an object has been formed through its actions and reactions, new members (or candidates for membership) may be recognized in terms of their perceptual similarity to typical instances. According to Nelson (1973a), "young children generate rules on the basis of function and generalize on the basis of form" (p. 23).

This hypothesis, that children form concepts on the basis of function, resembles the view (Werner, 1912; Piaget, 1948) that early concepts are interiorized actions. As Blank (1973), Nelson (1974), and others have pointed out, more than mere action must be involved. If actions are to enable a child to identify instances of a concept, they must incorporate some function characteristic of the instances; action and function must be integrated into a schema.

Even at early stages of language acquisition, however, there begins to emerge a conceptual basis more extensive than functional or perceptual similarities. The schemata for individual objects become related to one another. The meanings of "ball" or "table" depend in part on their schemata and in part on their place relative to other schemata. When such relations are grasped, one may speak of *concepts* of balls and tables. In section 4.2 we will explore these larger conceptual systems by considering hierarchical relations that can hold labels together in organized semantic structures.

We conclude, therefore, that much more than perceptual paradigms must be acquired before a label can be used as a word. But the theory of reference that we are considering is not merely incomplete. Even when perceptual paradigms are supplemented with functional information and the resulting schemata are embedded in larger semantic structures, the theory of reference with which we began is still false. It is not always sufficient, in order to determine what a word really refers to, to know the concept that the word expresses.

Probably in all societies, but certainly in technologically advanced ones, individual differences in the mastery of certain identification procedures are so extreme that an average person's schemata are only superficially related to an expert's. Not everyone to whom the identification of gold, edible mushrooms, or cancer is important is able to make the identification correctly. As Putnam (1975) points out, a division of linguistic labor is required to identify elm trees, aluminum, or H_2O that is not required (for adults) to identify balls, tables, or chairs. The average English-speaking adult associates appropriate concepts with such technical terms and uses them correctly in many contexts—by most standards he understands their meanings—although he is himself unable to determine their true range of application.

Note what this means for the theory we are considering. It is not necessary to have acquired a schema that will identify correctly any instance of a concept in order to understand and use the word that expresses that concept. For technical terms, verification is the responsibility of experts. This does not mean that the average person has no basis for identifying instances of technical terms; it does mean that he can be easily deceived because his identification procedures are superficial and stereotypical.

Since our psychological interest is in the average person's use of words, we want to characterize *his* range of applications, not the true range; it is *his* superficial stereotypes, not the expert's latest theory, that we must determine. This distinction will make no difference for most of the common expressions we will analyze; even for technical terms it would mean little more than allowing that a person may realize that his schemata are superficial, that an expert should be consulted. But it is important to recognize that the schemata we will propose are intended as descriptive psychological hypotheses about an average person who speaks English. No claim is being made that some more general theory of reference could be constructed along these lines, or that the success of some such general theory is a precondition for psychological studies of word meanings.

4.1.3   The Relation between Perceptual Predicates and Concepts

Before turning to hierarchical relations between words, we owe the reader some further discussion of the move, taken on page 233, promoting all perceptual predicates to conceptual schemata after the general manner of routine (3) for THING. In one view, little more than a typographical convention is altered. In another view, however, a basic assumption seems to be involved about the relation between perceptual judgments and conceptual categories. Since the relation of perception to conceptualization is one of the traditional battlegrounds of cognitive psychology, further comment is required.

The effect of formulations like (3) is to connect three theoretical entities: a perceptual predicate, a label (usually), and a concept. This connection is not necessary in any absolute sense; one can easily imagine nonverbal organisms, or even mechanical devices, capable of evaluating a perceptual predicate without linking it in any way to a label or relating it to any conceptual organization. Our concern, however, is to understand how people relate perception and language. It is simply an empirical fact that people speak languages, that those languages provide labels for the outcomes of most perceptual judgments, and that those labels are related in elaborate conceptual systems. What formulations like (3) are intended to do is to recognize this empirical fact. English does have words to label the outcomes of perceptual judgments, and so these processes do lead a double life, both perceptual and conceptual.

The principal danger in taking (3) as our model for representing this double role is that it might lead us to think we have reduced these concepts to "nothing but" perceptual predicates. It may be true in some cases that the concept includes "little more" than a perceptual judgment, but such a simple relation is certainly not universal. For an obvious counterexample, consider the perceptual predicate Cause(e, e'), introduced in 2.6.2. It would be absurd to propose that CAUSE should link "cause" and Cause after the manner of routine (3). The concept of causation goes far beyond anything that might be captured in a perceptual predicate and is incorporated as a semantic component of many more words than "cause." Unfortunately, at this stage in our argument we are not yet ready to discuss the nature of those conceptual supplements—the concept CAUSE will be discussed at length in section 6.3, where some of the missing conceptual structure will be supplied. And CAUSE is but one of several similar examples. Indeed, most of the rest of this book can be regarded as an attempt to discover what the underlying conceptual structures of various domains are and how they should be characterized.

We can anticipate the outcome of that exploration with the comment that the complexity of the relation between perceptual predicates and their related concepts varies enormously from one example to the next. Relatively simple examples are perceptual predicates like Yellow(x) or Obj$(x, 3d)$, although even here we will find that their conceptual counterparts, YELLOW(x) or THING(x), give the system access to information about colors and things that goes well beyond perceptual judgments. At this level the conceptual components are so intimately incorporated into a language user's perceptual judgments that it is difficult to separate them theoretically. Probably much of the psychological controversy over relations between percepts and concepts has arisen in just these cases.

At the other extreme, where there is little danger of confusing perceptual and conceptual components, are relatively complicated examples like Reg(x, y), S$_t(x)$, Chng(x), Event(e), Time(e, t), Cause(e, e'), and *Intend* (person, x), which we can relate to the conceptual level only after careful consideration of elaborate conceptual organizations. Clearly, the promotional move made on page 233 does not apply even approximately in these instances. To anticipate still further, it will generally turn out that these are the most complicated and ubiquitous concepts of all—concepts that become elaborated into important semantic operators incorporated into highly diverse lexical items. In what follows we will have much to say about these concepts that is not suggested in our promotional move.

Finally, one consequence of this move, even when it works more or less smoothly, is the disappearance of explicit perceptual predicates from the following pages. This sudden switch in notation may give the false impression that in chapters 1 and 2 we introduced a lot of theoretical machinery we do not need. It is indeed true that we will tend to take the simpler perceptual predicates for granted, since introducing them repeatedly to remind the reader of their perceptual basis leads to unnecessarily clumsy exposition. But it is just as essential to a balanced view of our subject to recognize that many concepts originate in the nature of the perceptual processes as it is to recognize that many more do not.

With these warnings clearly posted, we are ready now to consider what we can learn about conceptual organization from analyses of concepts frozen in the English lexicon.

4.2   HIERARCHICAL FIELD PROPERTIES

In approaching the question, how are words related to one another, we must take care not to drown in the diversity of answers. We can protect ourselves in part by recognizing at the outset that we are interested primarily in semantic relations between words. There are also relations based on similarities of sound, relations derived from syntactic function, and relations idiosyncratic to each person's experience, but these can be ignored for the moment. Our concern here is with relations that hold between words by virtue of what the words mean.

The intuitive impression that some words are more closely related in meaning than others is compelling. In order to characterize that impression theoretically, some linguists argue that words are organized into "semantic fields." This approach at least gives the phenomenon a name. It enables us to rephrase our question: how are words related in semantic fields? As we will discover, however, this restriction of the question does little more than set aside the kinds of relations between words that are easiest to explain. Relations of meaning are by all odds the least well understood and most difficult to explicate. The task we face is enormously complex. It is also enormously important if we hope to make a serious contribution to the theoretical foundations of psycholinguistics.

What is a semantic field? Different linguists have used the term in different senses (see Ullmann, 1962; Nida, 1975). There seems to be a consensus that the term means something, but precisely what is open to question.

The term "Bedeutungsfeld" (semantic field) was introduced by Ipsen (1924) to mean a group of words that form some kind of semantic unity. Ipsen gave as an example the Indo-European words used to discuss sheep and sheep raising. These words are not all related etymologically, nor should they be thought of as strung together on an associational thread. They fit together like pieces of a mosaic in such a way that together they cover all aspects of this particular field of activity.

Trier (1934) offered a more detailed interpretation of fields that integrates them into the Humboldtian notion that each language has its own "inner form" which determines the world perspective of those who speak it. Trier's theory begins with the assumption that every word's meaning depends on the meanings of others words in the language, and that different languages divide up reality among their words in different ways. According to R. L. Miller (1968), "Next to and above every word (to return to the image of the mosaic) stand other words which are closely or remotely related to it conceptually. These 'conceptual relatives' taken together constitute a lexical field (*Wortfeld*) and must be distinguished from the conceptual field (*Begriffsfeld*) of which it is the outward manifestation" (p. 66). The conceptual field covers the same area as the lexical field, and all parts of it are represented in the lexical field. In order to study the conceptual field, however, it is necessary to infer it from relations observable in the lexical field. Smaller lexical and conceptual fields combine to form larger ones until the entire vocabulary is an integrated, articulated whole. How this articulation is achieved constitutes the world picture presupposed by those who speak that language.

For Trier, the meaning of each word depends on its position in a conceptual field relative to other words in that field. Where the meaning of one word leaves off, the meaning of another must begin; the boundaries of the one, therefore, can be understood only in terms of the boundaries of the other. To understand the meaning of any word, the total field must be known to users of the language. Trier's notion of the dependence of the meaning of one word on the meanings of related words defines the central feature of what is meant by a "field property."

There are alternative interpretations of field theory in linguistics. Porzig (1934), for example, criticized Trier for assuming the existence of conceptual fields without providing any linguistic justification for their existence. Porzig preferred to begin with a more linguistic approach that revealed essential semantic relations between verbs and nouns. Verbs like "walk," "drive," "ride," "grasp," "see," "hear," "lick," "kiss," presuppose a human on foot, in a car, on a horse, hand, eye, ear, tongue, lips. The semantic relations go out from the verb unidirectionally; "grasp" implies hands, but hands have many other functions than grasping. Adjectives, like verbs, serve as predicates, and have similar close semantic relations with the nouns they qualify: "blond" is predicated of "hair." These data are linguistically given, Porzig claimed, and provide the elementary semantic fields from which more abstract fields can be derived.

Many of the examples Porzig cited involve selectional restrictions: dogs bark, horses neigh, flowers bloom, organisms grow, people fell trees. These selectional restrictions are usually on semantic categories of nouns: on all dogs, all horses, all flowers. The verb denotes a situation and restricts the range of subjects and objects that can appear in that situation. Thus, Porzig advocated selectional restriction as the preferred linguistic route into the analysis of semantic fields.

In spite of Porzig's criticisms, Trier's field theory has been very influential in German linguistics, and particularly in the work of Weisgerber (1962). Weisgerber places primary emphasis on "the law of the field": "blue" can only be defined in terms of its position in the total color field. There is a structural principle that delimits the domain of shades of blue from all other color shades and causes one to conceive of these variations as the same color; this structural principle is a reflection of the operation of a linguistic field.

Weisgerber has proposed a variety of different field structures for different parts of the vocabulary. Trier illustrated this notion of the field by arguing that a word like "poor" would have a different meaning in a rating scale that had seven designations of proficiency from the meaning it would have in a scale that had only three designations; to know what "poor" means you must know what the alternatives are. For Weisgerber, such one-dimensional "serial structures" are only part of the story. Kinship terminology, he claims, provides a two-dimensional "surface structure"; terms are ordered by generation and lineality. Color terminology provides a three-dimensional "solid structure" reflecting the three dimensions of the color solid. German verbs for dying illustrate a "multilayered field": there is an inner layer for human dying ("sterben"), a second layer for animal dying ("verenden"), and a third for plant dying ("eingehen").

In order to illustrate the complete development of a semantic field, Weisgerber analyzes German terms used to describe misdemeanors. He postulates two semantic coordinates: (a) the offender's degree of responsibility, which may be inadvertent, with possible knowledge, with knowledge required, with inklings of knowledge, acting almost deliberately, acting deliberately with intent, acting out of natural disposition; and (b) the social norms that are violated by the act, which include norms of appropriateness, acceptability, reasonable conduct, propriety, statutory law, what is right, what is ethical. For example, an inadvertent offense against norms of appropriateness is "Versehen" (oversight); a deliberate, intentional offense against statutory law is "Vergehen" (misdemeanor); an offense against ethics by a person who knows better is "Schandtat" (infamy). Every combination of the two coordinates is represented by a particular term.

Hörmann (1971) has criticized Weisgerber's work as unduly subjective, amounting to little more than an expression of Weisgerber's personal opinion. For example, Weisgerber's distinction between "Irrtum" (error), which he defined as an inadvertent offense against reasonable conduct, and "Fehlgriff" (blunder), which he defined as an offense against reasonable conduct by a person who might have possible knowledge "certainly does not reflect accepted usage to such an extent that everyone would unquestioningly agree with it" (p. 172). As a more objective approach, Hörmann advocates word-association tests and cites as an example Deese's (1965) application of factor analysis to word-association data in order to define his concept of associative meaning.

The Humboldt-Trier-Weisgerber conception of semantic fields has been criticized repeatedly on the grounds of vagueness and subjectivity, yet even critics seem willing to grant that there is something of semantic and psychological importance underlying the general conception. The theoretical task, therefore, is to try to formulate these ideas more clearly in the hope of dispelling some of the uncertainties and misunderstandings that surround them.

As a starting point we will take the observation that some labels have a wider scope of application than others. The referential scope of the word "thing," for example, is wider than the scope of "furniture," which in turn has wider scope than "table." Words with wide scope are generic; those with narrow scope are particular, or specific. Generic words may or may not be abstract. As Ullmann (1962) remarks, "The generic nature of our words has often been described as an element of *'abstractness'* in language. There is some danger of ambiguity here since the usual opposition between abstract and concrete does not correspond to that between generic and particular" (p. 119). When used to denote a concrete object, "thing" is no more abstract than "table," but it is far more generic.

These scope relations are often characterized hierarchically; words higher in the hierarchy have wider scope than those they dominate. Words related in this way can be said to form a semantic field, and one of the field properties can be called the hierarchical property.

4.2.1   Relations That Generate Hierarchies

In order for a set of elements to be hierarchically related, there must be some asymmetrical and transitive relation between them. We will consider three such relations that hold between the meanings of words: locative inclusion, part-whole, and class inclusion. If v and w are two elements related by locative inclusion, we will use [IN(v, w)] to mean that v is in w; for the part-whole relation we will use [PPRT(v, w)] to mean that v has the proper part w; and for class inclusion we will use [ISA(v, w)] to mean that v is a w.

The simplest of the three is locative inclusion, illustrated by such sentences as "The woman is in the room," "The room is in the house," "The house is in the town," which represent spatial inclusion. Events are located in time as well, and locative inclusion can also be temporal: "The dinner is in the evening," "The evening is in September," "September is in the fall." That the relation is asymmetrical can be seen by noting that when the arguments are reversed, the resulting sentences are false. That the relation is transitive can be seen by evaluating the inference of IN(x, z) from IN(x, y) & IN(y, z): "The woman is in the town" and "The dinner is in the fall" follow from the illustrations just given.

The part-whole hierarchy is illustrated by such sentences as "The body has a head," "The head has a face," "The face has a mouth." When the arguments are reversed the resulting sentences are false, so the relation is asymmetrical;

transitivity, however, seems a bit strained: "The body has a mouth." The part-whole relation can also be used temporally: "The year has fifty-two weeks," "The week has seven days," "The day has twenty-four hours." In this use, transitivity must be supplemented by arithmetic, and asymmetry is clouded by poetic license; "Fifty-two weeks has the year" might be acceptable in some contexts, although "The week has fifty-two years" would be satisfactorily false. Locative inclusion and part-whole relations are sometimes difficult to distinguish: "There are five burroughs in New York" and "New York has five burroughs" are effectively synonymous.

The class-inclusion relation differs from the other two; one is not sure whether it really is more complicated or only seems so because it has received so much more attention from students of logic and language. The most familiar examples are taxonomic: "A pine is a (kind of) tree," "A tree is a (kind of) plant," "A plant is a (kind of) living thing." As before, asymmetry can be demonstrated by reversing the arguments and transitivity by deleting connecting terms: "A pine is a (kind of) living thing." It is necessary to understand these sentences in their generic sense, however. "A tree is a (kind of) pine," when interpreted generically, is false, but "That tree is a (kind of) pine," when interpreted specifically, is a perfectly acceptable way to tell someone what kind of tree it is. But in this case it is class membership rather than class inclusion that is expressed.

It might be interesting to explore the hypothesis that locative inclusion is psychologically the primitive hierarchical system, with part-whole and class inclusion being adaptations of the locative hierarchy for special purposes. This seems to have been what Piaget (1927a) had in mind when he wrote that space and time are the logic of things: "the process of fitting its parts into a meaningful whole (colligation) is analogous to the colligations and series that class and relations introduce among concepts, and its metric system is that of numbers and numerical operations" (p. 1).

The structural similarities among these hierarchies become obvious when we consider their graphical representations; drawing a picture maps the relation into spatial inclusion. Drawings of the parts of an object will be parts of the drawing of the object, that is, they will be located inside it; to the extent that part-whole relations can be represented graphically, the part-whole hierarchy must be isomorphic with a locative-inclusion hierarchy. And since Euler circles are a convenient way to translate class inclusion into locative inclusion for the benefit of beginning students of set theory, the structural similarities between these two types of hierarchies are also well known. Thus, it is no accident that spatial imagery can provide valuable support for attempts to reason logically about hierarchical systems of relations.

The relation of class inclusion between labels is so common in all languages that semanticists have invented a name for it: "hyponymy," by analogy with "synonymy" and "antonymy" (Lyons, 1968, p. 453). A hyponym is a subname; since the referents of the word "table" are included among the referents of the word "furniture," "table" is a hyponym of "furniture." Hyponymy can be defined in terms of entailment: if the sentence "It is a W" (in the appropriate sense of "is") entails the sentence "It is a V," then W is a hyponym of V. Lyons suggests that if the sentences are equivalent (mutual entailment), then W and V are synonyms, which would make synonymy a special, symmetrical case of hyponymy. The opposite of a hyponym should be called a hypernym, but the two words sound so much alike that the entailed term is usually referred to as superordinate with respect to its hyponyms.

The part-whole relation is equally common, but it has received less attention from theorists and so has not been specially designated. We suggest the term "partonymy." Partonymy might also be defined by entailment: if the sentence "It is a W" entails the sentence "It has a V" (in the appropriate sense of "has"), then V is a partonym of W.

We have now identified the kind of word relations we intend to consider. The next question is how people know whether these relations hold between any two labels. For example, how would people be able to determine whether W is in V? The answer depends on what they know about W and V; it is necessary to distinguish two situations. First, how do they know that Hiroshima is in Japan and that Japan is not in Hiroshima? Hiroshima and Japan are place names corresponding to various representations stored in geographical memory; the information is something people have to learn. We cannot even suppose that the question could be settled by going to look; one would not know whether to go to Japan and look for Hiroshima or vice versa, and when one got there it would not be clear what to look at. It might seem that this information imposes a heavy burden on people's memories, but since the referents are not movable the information has a permanence that makes the learning worthwhile.

Most things people talk about are movable, however. Their locations are so variable that you can never be entirely sure of them, although the ability to update information about the locations of personal friends and possessions is remarkable. One can verify that the car is in the garage either by remembering where it was left or by looking inside the garage. In this case there is little trouble with reversal of arguments: to say that the garage is in the car could only be understood to mean it was a toy garage, not a real garage. This information is available because, along with everything else people know about cars and garages, they have stored information about expected sizes. (The relative way such adjectives as "large" and "small" are used can only mean that expected size is available as a basis for comparison.) Given this information, one needs only the simple rule that a smaller object cannot contain a larger one in order to invalidate many incorrect statements that W is in V. For example, if you are told that the baby is in the pen, you will understand that he is in a playpen, not a fountain pen. We conclude that even though size information may be less important than shape information in labeling objects, expected size is nonetheless retained as part of the perceptual paradigm and exploited in understanding sentences.

With respect to partonymy, how would people determine whether W has

V (as a part)? If the referent of W is some familiar object, they simply remember the fact that V is part of W. It is absurd to think of someone examining pianos in order to determine whether they have keyboards; anyone who understands what these words label knows that "keyboard" is a partonym of "piano." Here again, however, part-whole relations are often variable; one might have to check to see whether the cup has a handle or the book has an index. Yet one knows that indexes are parts of books and not the other way round, that a cup does not have an index, and so on. We must assume that a great deal of partonymic information is stored in memory.

With respect to hyponymy, how do people determine whether W is a (kind of) V? Again we must distinguish two situations. A person knows that a monkey is an animal if he knows what the labels "monkey" and "animal" denote; the matter can be settled by consulting his memory for these labels. But if he is told that a monkey is a pet, he must have other evidence than the meaning of the labels in order to validate the claim. His memory for these labels must be so organized that he can know that "monkey" is a hyponym of "animal" and that it is not a hyponym of "pet."

In all three cases we find that sometimes people know from the meanings of the words whether the relation holds and that sometimes they must collect (or remember) empirical evidence if they wish to verify it. The evaluation of statements involving IN, PPRT, and ISA seems to require two parts. A reasonable hypothesis is that people first try to settle the question from their knowledge of the meanings of the words; failing that, they try next to perceive or remember relevant evidence. For expository purposes it is simpler to consider first the routines that could be written for empirical verification.

Consider how one would verify empirically that the coat is in the closet. This would be translated into the routine test(now, $F(x, y)$), where F is a pointer to the routine IN, x a pointer to the coat, and y a pointer to the closet. If this routine were executed, it would call IN, which might look like this:

(6)   IN(x, y):   In order to determine whether x is "in" y:
         (i) find(y, x).

(A more detailed analysis of "in" will be given in 6.1.1; (6) will serve our present purposes.) Routine (6) presupposes that the translator, in order to assign values to x and y, has already identified the particular coat and closet, so (6) will determine whether closet y has coat x in it by trying to find x in the search domain y.

At least two important details are neglected in (6). For one thing, no stop rule is indicated. What stop rule will be appropriate in which circumstance is, of course, no part of the meaning of "in," but somehow the translator must determine how to complete the "find" instruction in (6i): what to do next if x is found in y, and what to do next if x is not found in y. If there is a particular, individual coat involved, the stop rule is obvious: as soon as you find x, stop testing. In other cases, however, the stop rule might be much more complicated ("Some of Jane's coats are in a closet at her mother's house") or even ambiguous ("Everyone's coats aren't in the closet"). We will not try to fill this gap, because the semantics of quantificational expressions are complex in ways that would only distract us from our present concern with lexical relations, but we would not wish to mislead anyone into believing that translation involves only identification of the appropriate search domain and test criterion.

A second thing missing in (6) is any recognition of the transitive character of the relation: if the coat is in the closet and the closet is in the house, then the coat is in the house. In order to add this feature we could write (6) in such a way that, in addition to testing $IN(x, y)$, the system would search for any z such that $IN(x, z)$ and $IN(z, y)$. (This addition is unnecessary for the predicate Incl, which expresses a perceptual relation. The routine for IN, however, is not limited to directly perceived relations; it is available for conceptual relations that are not directly visible.) The question is whether transitivity should be expressed as part of the routine IN or should be allocated to the executor. That is to say, the IN routine might be recognized by the executor as one of a set of inclusion relations, all of which share the abstract feature of transitivity; then the executor would decide whether to institute a search for some intervening z.

A more attractive hypothesis is that transitivity is a part of IN, not as an explicit principle but as a direct consequence of the representation of $IN(x, y)$. The drawback with the idea of having a separately stated principle of transitivity to which the executor may refer is that the set of such principles needed to accommodate spatial inferences would be extremely large. Consider the principles needed to justify the following inference (from Johnson-Laird, 1975):

> The black ball is directly beyond the cue ball.
> The green ball is on the right of the cue ball, and there is a red ball between them.
> Therefore, if I move so that the red ball is between me and the black ball, then the cue ball is on my left.

The obvious way to make such an inference is to utilize the routine for "beyond," "right of," and so on, to generate a representation of the scene rather than to try to rely on separately stated rules of inference. Logical properties such as transitivity and asymmetry then become abstractions that may be observed by reflection on the behavior of verbal relations when they are used in this constructive manner. This solution seems psychologically reasonable and also enables us to keep lexical routines relatively simple.

Next, consider how one would verify empirically that a table has a drawer (as a part). This, too, would translate into a routine: test(now, $F(x, y)$), but where F is a pointer to PPRT, x is a pointer to the table, and y is a pointer to the drawer. The routine for PPRT, which is based on the corresponding perceptual predicate, might look like this:

(7)   PPRT(x, y):   In order to determine whether x "has a" y as a proper
           part:
           (i) test(time, Pprt(x, y))

(The "has a" relation will be analyzed in greater detail in 7.2, especially the
"has" of possession.) The comments about the stopping and transitivity rules
of IN also apply to PPRT, with appropriate substitutions.

Finally, consider the verification of such claims as that a particular monkey
is a pet. If we proceed as before, the translator would again require an instruction: test(now, $F(x, y)$), but with F being ISA, x monkey, and y pet. As we
try to parallel (6) and (7), however, we discover a difficulty. For IN and
PPRT there are two percepts, x and y, whose relations we wish to test; here
there is only one percept, x, and we wish to determine whether two labels can
refer to it. The translator must compile such operations as

> find(search domain, MONKEY$(?x?)$)
> test(now, PET(x))

The executor locates the monkey in question and provides a pointer to it.
This pointer then serves as the argument of PET(x). No special routine for ISA
need be written. That is to say, the "is a" that appears in English sentences of
this type has no deeper semantic significance; it is introduced syntactically
whenever a sentence expresses the applicability of two labels to a single object.
Many languages (including child and Black English) dispense with a copulative verb in this role, and even in Standard English we drop it when "the monkey is a pet" is nominalized as "the pet monkey."

This analysis slides over a point that logicians have learned is important,
namely, the differences between class membership and class inclusion. In
English, both relations can be expressed by "is a." Class membership is expressed by such sentences as "Eric is a Christian"; class inclusion by such
sentences as "Baptists are Christians." Whenever the test has to be applied to
an individual object or person, the relation is one of class membership. For
sentences expressing class inclusion, however, there is often no percept to which
a pointer can be assigned, and hence nothing to be tested in the usual way. The
idea is not merely that the two labels can both be applied to some particular
x but that they can both be applied to any x that satisfies the hyponymic label.
The usual way to state this relation of entailment can be captured by

(8)   ISA(w, v):   A w "is a" v if and only if it is not possible for there
           to be an x such that w (x) and notv (x).

In this form the relation applies both to generic inclusion ("A monkey is an
animal") and to specific inclusion ("Those boys are Canadians"). It also
applies to abstract properties as well as to concrete objects ("Honesty is a
virtue").

Our concern has been how these three relations can be subjected to perceptual tests. As we have pointed out, perceptual tests are often unnecessary,

however, because the relation can be verified from what is already known about the meanings of the words themselves. In such cases it is necessary to search one's general knowledge of those words rather than to search for their perceptual referents. In order to verify that Hiroshima is in Japan, or that a table has a top, or that a monkey is an animal, examine what you know about Hiroshima, tables, monkeys; do not go to Hiroshima and look around for Japan, or visually inspect every table for its top, or test every monkey to determine whether it really is an animal.

How do people go about verifying a sentence of the form "A monkey is an animal"? We will argue that there are three distinct procedures that may be used. First, a person can simply examine the contents of his semantic memory in order to determine whether an assertion of the form [ISA(MONKEY, ANIMAL)] is stored there. Such an assertion may be stored as part of his concept of monkey, as part of his concept of animal, or both. It may even be simply stored as a link between the two concepts in the manner of a semantic network. Second, if there is no direct representation of the sentence or of its negation ("A whale is not a fish"), it may be possible to infer it from assertions that are represented. Thus, one of the procedures that may be called by infer(x, y) allows such inferences as

[ISA(POODLE, DOG)]
[ISA(DOG, ANIMAL)]

[ISA(POODLE, ANIMAL)]

Equivalent assumptions have been made by Collins and Quillian (1969), among others. Third, if there is no inferential evaluation forthcoming, a person may have recourse to a still more sophisticated strategy. To anticipate an argument from 4.2.2, a person presented with a sentence like "A poodle is a mammal" may lack both a representation of this fact and representations that allow it to be directly inferred. In such a case, he may retrieve conceptual information about mammals, perhaps a sufficient condition such as [PPRT(MAMMAL, HAIR)], and use this information to set up test(t, PPRT(x, HAIR)). This test can then be applied to his concept of poodle, either directly or by way of an inference to DOG, and its result will determine the evaluation of the sentence. There is no restriction of such tests to perceptual predicates. In particular, pointers can be assigned to concepts, just as they can to percepts and routines, and a concept can be searched for specific information and tests applied to what is found. The translator automatically uses the words to call the concepts, and (for adult speakers of the language) these concepts are searched for the necessary information. Only if the information is not directly available conceptually, or available from a simple inference, will the more complex test procedures be called. Children, who may not have the conceptual information or who may not have learned to search concepts prior to empirical testing, would be expected to treat these relations differently from adults, even though their routines for "is in," "has a," and "is a" might be similar to adult versions when perceptual testing is required.

If these arguments are correct, we have placed further constraints on the way adult semantic memory is structured. We began by assuming that it contained paradigm-label pairs that could be used in routines for labeling objects, finding them in the world, and so on. It became clear that purely perceptual predicates could not cope satisfactorily with items like tables, so it was necessary to allow not only disjunctive perceptual paradigms but also the introduction of functional information in the form of unifying schemata. It has now become evident that explicit predicates must be introduced in order to interrelate schemata in semantic memory. All of this information is required in order to capture the underlying *concept* represented by a word. We will continue, for convenience, to use small capitals to denote concepts, which contain specifications of any appropriate perceptual paradigms. Thus, the TABLE concept must contain the information [PPRT(TABLE, WORKTOP)] and [ISA(TABLE, ARTICLE OF FURNITURE)]. These assertions locate TABLE in different conceptual hierarchies and so enable the system to move rapidly between different concepts.

The effect of cross connections between concepts is to organize conceptual fields. The words attached to the concepts often form a hierarchical lexical field that speakers can use to express conceptual relations and that psychologists can exploit to investigate conceptual hierarchies. Taken together, the conceptual and lexical fields form a semantic field. We have considered three kinds of hierarchical relations and suggested how they might be characterized in a procedural theory of semantics. We turn next to a brief review of some methods for studying these relations experimentally.

4.2.2   Methods of Eliciting and Exploring Hierarchical Relations

The relations that we have been discussing have marked effects on the way people respond to words, remember words, and classify words. Psychological research into these effects has a long history, and we will interrupt our theoretical development to indicate something of the variety of studies that have been conducted.

Probably the oldest psychological experiment for probing into the organization of lexical memory is the word-association test. Indeed, some psychologists still consider this procedure ("Give me the first word you think of when I say ———") the method of choice for investigating the subjective lexicon. Certainly its convenience and apparent objectivity have contributed to its considerable popularity. The relative frequency with which a particular word is given in response to a particular stimulus is regarded as a measure (or at least an index) of the strength of association between those words, and reasonable predictions of the rates of learning verbal materials have been based on the hypothesis that frequency of spontaneous association can be used to estimate the degree of transfer from previous experience to a present learning task. Consequently, extensive tables of word associations have been compiled and published in order to calibrate the verbal materials used in memorization

Table 4.1   Words associated with "table" by 500 fourth graders and 1,000 college students (not including responses by only one person). (From Palermo and Jenkins, 1964.)

Associated word	Fourth graders	College students	Associated word	Fourth graders	College students
able	2	0	furniture	5	0
big	7	1	hard	2	0
brown	5	4	kitchen	2	6
cards	0	2	lamp	1	8
chair	216	691	leg	2	11
chairs	3	2	legs	5	7
cloth	19	29	maple	0	2
dark	1	2	plate	4	3
desk	10	33	round	1	2
dinner	4	4	salt	0	4
dish	2	8	set	1	3
dishes	3	4	silverware	2	1
eat	70	23	sit	6	1
eating	9	2	spoon	3	5
flat	7	3	tablecloth	1	3
floor	1	2	tennis	0	2
food	45	59	top	1	30
fork	0	5	wood	10	7

experiments (Kent and Rosanoff, 1910; Postman and Keppel, 1970; and many more in between). As an illustration of data obtained by this method, the responses to the word "table" that were obtained from fourth graders and college students by Palermo and Jenkins (1964) are reproduced in table 4.1.

A word-association task elicits a great variety of responses, reflecting the variety of ways words can be related. A person who responds "able" to "table" has one relation in mind, a person who replies "chair" has another, and a person who responds "eat" differs from both. Because it is frequently unclear which relation a person had in mind when he gave his answer, attempts to classify responses have never been wholly satisfactory. Moreover, since many association theorists hope to simplify their basic assumptions by deriving all these apparently diverse responses from a single principle of learning, usually association by contiguity, differences among them have often been deliberately underemphasized in psychological reports.

One result from word-association tests is the discovery that association can be asymmetric. For example, "white" is the response to "black" more often than "black" is the response to "white." One explanation is based on the claim that "black and white" is more frequent in everyday speech than "white and black." According to this explanation, word associations draw strength from two different sources, which have been dubbed paradigmatic and syntagmatic.

Two words are considered to be paradigmatically related to the extent that they can be substituted in identical contexts, syntagmatically related to the extent that they can follow one another. "Cat" and "dog" are paradigmatically related, since they have similar privileges of occurrence in discourse; they can serve as arguments of the same verbs and can be qualified by many of the same adjectives. There is little reason to expect that "cat" would evoke "dog" more often than "dog" evokes "cat"—unless "cat and dog" is more frequent in everyday usage than "dog and cat." It is the syntagmatic component, presumably, that contributes a directional difference. For example, the probe "doodle" almost never elicits the reply "Yankee," but "Yankee" frequently elicits "doodle," for syntagmatic reasons. Young children give relatively more syntagmatic associations than adults; the so-called syntagmatic-paradigmatic shift at around six years of age has been studied extensively (Brown and Berko, 1960; Ervin, 1961; Entwisle, 1966).

If we consider the hierarchical relations expressed by "has a" and "is a," we see that these order the words they can take as arguments in a syntagmatic relation. If people have stored in memory "A dog is an animal," we might expect that "dog" would elicit "animal" more often than "animal" would elicit "dog." We would expect more responses to be superordinate than hyponymic, which is indeed the case (Woodrow and Lowell, 1916; Russell and Jenkins, 1954; Jenkins and Russell, 1960; Palermo and Jenkins, 1964; and others). This direction from narrower to wider scope is reversed by the partonymic hierarchy, however. If people have stored "A table has a top" in their memories, "table" should elicit "top" more often than "top" elicits "table." This prediction is confirmed—many more whole-part associations are given than part-whole associations where the direction is from wider to narrower scope. Miller (1969a) has argued that these asymmetries indicate the syntagmatic effects of "is a" and "has a" on the direction of word associations.

Such influences can only be statistical, for the processes whereby a person makes his response are complicated and poorly understood. Indeed, an adult subject seems able to set himself in advance to give certain types of associations in order to simplify the task (Moran, 1966). Moreover, it is clear from an inspection of responses given only once that many associative relations are arbitrary and idiosyncratic. Disentangling the effects of linguistic and non-linguistic associations is a persistent headache in psycholinguistic experimentation; it would be absurd to suggest that arbitrary responses are of no importance or that linguistic analysis can somehow explain them away.

Some psychologists interested in verbal memorization processes seem to have accepted, perhaps implicitly, the following line of reasoning: since nonlinguistic associations are necessary anyhow, it is more parsimonious to explain all word-association results in those terms rather than introduce linguistic hypotheses of dubious relevance. This argument rests on the premise that the only reason for considering linguistic relations is to explain word-association results. As soon as we take a broader view of our theoretical task, the absurdity of this premise becomes apparent. For example, any general theory of linguistic performance must have some way to account for the fact that "A table is a chair" is false and "A table is an object" is true, even though the table-chair association is far more frequent (far stronger) than the table-object association.

It might be worthwhile to consider the converse argument: since linguistic hypotheses are necessary anyhow, it is more parsimonious to explain all word-association results in those terms rather than introduce idiosyncratic associations of unknown origin. We will not advance this argument, because both linguistic and nonlinguistic mechanisms are required, but we regard it as the more interesting of the two.

People first learn to produce and understand sentences; that ability must explain, insofar as possible, why they give the word associations they do. The stimulus-response bonds between words that seem to be demonstrated in word-association tests are not the psychological atoms out of which speech is built. Rather, they are a consequence of making people use their linguistic competence in an unusual, not to say aberrant, test situation. If we could first characterize how a person uses sentences, we might be able (if anyone still cared) to explain why he behaves as he does on tests of word association. Efforts to move in the opposite direction have had little success.

Other methods that psychologists have used have yielded data of greater relevance to hierarchical semantic relations than word-association tests. For example, it is now well known that when educated people are asked to recall a list of words they have heard only once, they usually organize their recall in such a way that words that are conceptually related are recalled adjacently (Bousfield and Cohen, 1956; Tulving, 1962; Mandler, 1967). The words are organized in memory into conceptually related categories, and words in the same category are recalled together. When the list contains hierarchically related words, people usually recall superordinate words first, then hyponyms of that category. That is, they use the hierarchic principle as a retrieval plan for cuing recall, with candidates so generated being monitored for their membership on the list before they are overtly recalled. If the words are presented to the learner in the form of a diagram depicting the hierarchic relations among them, he is relieved of the task of discovering these relations for himself and recall is vastly improved (Bower, Clark, Lesgold, and Winzenz, 1969). Although these experiments have not been used systematically to explore hierarchical relations between words—those have been taken for granted in designing the word lists to be recalled—this technique could be adapted to testing hypotheses about lexical organization.

The effects of semantic organization can also be studied by measuring the extent to which it interferes with color naming. In the Stroop test (Stroop, 1938) an observer is asked to name the color of the ink in which color names are printed. If the word "red" is printed in blue ink, the observer is supposed to say "blue." For people who are literate, this task activates two conflicting response systems. The tendency to read the color name interferes with the tendency to name the color; it takes longer to name the color when the letters spell an antagonistic color name than when the letters are simply a row of X's.

The interference is strongest when the words are antagonistic color names, but there are measurable effects even for other words. As the string of letters is changed from X's to nonsense words to infrequent words to common words to color names, the degree of interference increases (Klein, 1964). Warren (1972) has shown that if a person is given a list of three hyponyms to remember, it will interfere with his ability to name the color in which the superordinate word is printed. For example, if the person is asked to name the color in which "fuel" is printed, it will take him longer if he is simultaneously remembering "oil-coal-gas" than if he is simultaneously remembering "doctor-lawyer-nurse." The activation of the fuel concept by "oil-coal-gas" activates a competing response system to read "fuel," which interferes with the color-naming system.

Response times can also be used to test the recognition of letter strings as words. Strings of letters can be presented visually to a literate adult who is asked to press one key if the letters form an English word and another key if they do not. Response times are much faster for words than for nonsense syllables, presumably because an exhaustive search is required before you can conclude that it is nonsense (Rubenstein, Garfield, and Millikan, 1970). Words that occur frequently are recognized faster than infrequent words, which probably reflects something about the way people read words, and homographs (two words with the same spelling) are recognized more rapidly than nonhomographs, probably because the likelihood of finding the word quickly is increased if there are more entries for it in the subjective lexicon. But when frequency of occurrence is equated concrete words (words used to label perceptible things) are not recognized faster than abstract words.

There is a sequential effect in such experiments that can also be used to investigate relations between words (Meyer, Schvaneveldt, and Ruddy, 1972). If successive tests are rapid—if the next stimulus pattern is presented 250 milliseconds after the judge's response to the preceding pattern—the time required to say that the pattern spells a word will be shorter if the preceding pattern was a related word. For example, the time required to recognize that "butter" is a word is shorter if the preceding stimulus pattern was "bread" than if it was "nurse." Indeed, the effect persists over two preceding words; the recognition of "butter" when it occurs in the sequence "bread-star-butter" will not be as fast as in the sequence "star-bread-butter," but it will be faster than in the sequence "nurse-star-butter." The facilitating effect of semantic relations on the lexical decision task can also be demonstrated when the strings of letters to be judged are presented simultaneously, two or three strings at a time (Meyer and Schvaneveldt, 1971; Schvaneveldt and Meyer, 1973).

It is also possible to record response times in judging the acceptability of sentences that violate selectional restrictions. Some linguists have argued that strings of words like "Rocks eat grass" violate syntactic rules, but if such constructions are prohibited by syntactic rules, it becomes impossible to account for such perfectly grammatical sentences as "It makes no sense to say that rocks eat grass." We conclude, therefore, that selectional restrictions are semantic, not syntactic, rules. That is to say, "Rocks eat grass" is a grammatical sentence to which the system is able to assign an appropriate semantic interpretation; it is not ungrammatical, it is simply false. Response times in judging such sentences true or false can be taken as relevant to the organization of lexical memory. Just as it takes longer to decide that a string of letters does not spell an English word, so it takes longer to decide that a string of words does not form a true sentence (Wason, 1961; Collins and Quillian, 1969; Kintsch, 1972; Jorgensen and Kintsch, 1973; Smith, Shoben, and Rips, 1974).

Differences in response times to acceptable sentences may provide an indication of the complexity of the semantic search that is required to verify them. Collins and Quillian (1969) found that it took their judges longer to respond to "A canary is an animal" than to "A canary is a bird." This suggests that some iterative search process is required to verify "A canary is an animal"; first it is determined that a canary is a bird, then that a bird is an animal, and so a canary is an animal. Moreover, they found that it takes longer to verify "A canary can fly" than "A canary can sing," which they interpret to mean that the latter is stored in your memory for canaries, but the former must be retrieved by a two-step process: a canary is a bird and birds can fly. (Note, incidentally, the banal similes "sing like a canary" and "fly like a bird.")

D. Meyer's (1970) results cast some doubt on the hypothesis advanced by Collins and Quillian. Meyer found it necessary to propose a two-stage hypothesis about the retrieval mechanisms required to verify such sentences as "All legs are limbs." The first stage is to decide whether the two words so related have any intersection—whether there can be anything such that both labels apply to it—and the second stage is to decide whether the first word labels a subset of the second. Meyer found the fewest errors and fastest response times in judging such sentences as "All legs are trees," which can be rejected at stage one. The most mistakes and longest reaction times were obtained in judging such sentences as "All limbs are legs," which requires both stages.

Meyer's results provide evidence specific enough to support discussion of the formulation we gave for the ISA routine in 4.2.1. Meyer's sentences were generic; their truth or falsity could be determined from the meanings of the words themselves. In our terms, therefore, routines for testing percepts or memories of particular objects need not be executed at all. Instead, we assume that the translator, given the sentence "All limbs are legs," will first retrieve the concept LIMB and then search that concept for the information [ISA(LIMB, LEG)]; we might assume that this search takes a relatively long time because the target is not there. If Meyer's hypothesis is correct, however, we should divide this conceptual search into two steps: first, LIMB is searched for any occurrence of LEG; second, if LEG is found, it is tested further to determine whether it is the second argument of [ISA(LIMB, LEG)]. Since the similar [ISA(LEG, LIMB)] will be present in the LIMB concept, this test must be precise. (It would be interesting to repeat Meyer's study with the "has a" hierarchy to see whether a two-stage mechanism is also necessary there.)

Although on many occasions it may be unnecessary to do anything more than search concepts in order to verify hierarchical statements, our hypothesis about the representation of conceptual relations does allow that actual testing may occur. As we argued earlier, an individual presented with the sentence "A poodle is a mammal" may have no direct information about the relation between these two concepts. In that case, he is likely to retrieve whatever conceptual information he has about mammals, such as [PPRT(MAMMAL, HAIR)], and use this information to set up a test to be applied to his concept of POODLE. A response to this sort of sentence is accordingly likely to demand a greater latency, and to yield a more uncertain answer, than a response to a statement calling on directly represented conceptual information. Such responses do, indeed, occur, as Rips, Shoben, and Smith (1973) have demonstrated. They found that the evaluation of class-inclusion statements about mammals took reliably longer than those about animals, even though the set of all mammals is included in (is smaller than) the set of all animals. Such findings present difficulties for theories that allow only for a direct representation of hierarchical information.

Jorgensen and Kintsch (1973) have obtained evidence consistent with our view that conceptual information is sometimes represented directly and sometimes, in effect, procedurally. They found that three-word sentences expressing partonymic relations ("Truck has oil," "Book has cover") are responded to more rapidly than three-word sentences having some arbitrary verb ("Ear produces wax," "Knife cuts steak"). Although they do not comment on the reason for this difference, it is difficult to resist the view that many "has" relations are represented directly in lexical memory, whereas the recovery of arbitrary relations demands the execution of test procedures. Test procedures may also be called in the evaluation of false partonymic relations such as "Rock has hair." The false sentences took longer to evaluate than the true ones; hence it would seem that the two-stage retrieval process was not operating here. However, the experimenters did not reverse the partonymic relation ("Cover has book") and their results cannot be compared with Meyer's in detail.

The major effect observed by Jorgensen and Kintsch was that response times are shorter for sentences that describe easily imageable relations: "Book has cover" was faster than "Truck has oil," and "Knife cuts steak" was faster than "Ear produces wax." This evidence that imagery facilitates verification suggests that it may be easier for people to form an image and then apply a test to it than to search through a concept for a particular item of information. Jorgensen and Kintsch suggest that the results of Collins and Quillian might also be explained in these terms: it is easier to form an image of "A canary is a bird" than of the more abstract "A canary is an animal." But *why* some images are easier to form than others remains unanswered. And, indeed, how does an image of a canary represent that it is a bird, unless one is prepared to countenance the testing of images? It may therefore be a mistake to attempt to conflate the Collins and Quillian results with those of Jorgensen and Kintsch. An alternative hypothesis is that the findings are explicable in terms of the difference between the direct representation of information and its procedural retrieval, since the direct representation of information may involve an image. The representation of an assertion in the form of an image should be relatively easy when it involves only a simple perceptual predicate; but it should be relatively difficult when it involves a considerable number of perceptual (or conceptual) predicates. Thus, an image of a book is likely to represent the fact that it has a cover, but an image of a truck is unlikely to represent the fact that it has oil. The same principle probably underlies the construction of images; it may explain why "Knife cuts steak" was evaluated faster than "Ear produces wax."

Another technique that can be used to study word relations is to ask people to rate words on the basis of their similarity of meaning. For example, Rubenstein and Goodenough (1965) asked people to rate pairs of nouns for their similarity of meaning on a five-point scale, where zero indicated the lowest degree of synonymy and four the highest. Their averaged results for sixty-five pairs of nouns included those reproduced in table 4.2. Although Rubenstein and Goodenough did not obtain a complete comparison of every noun with every other, their results do show that people are able to make estimates of this somewhat ill-defined relation between words.

A variation of the rating method is the sorting method, which is relatively direct and has the advantage of convenience of administration and minimal effort for the judges. In the method of sorting (Miller, 1969b), a list of words—preferably a list whose relations are of some theoretical interest—is selected and each word is printed on a separate card. The pack of cards is given to a judge who is asked to sort them into piles on the basis of similarity of meaning. If n words are used, a matrix containing $n(n-1)/2$ entries (one for each of the pairs of words) is constructed, and the number of times each pair is put into the same pile is counted. After many judges have performed the sorting, the entries in the matrix give the number of judges who thought each pair similar enough to put them in the same pile; those entries can be regarded as measures of semantic proximity between all pairs of words on the list and can be analyzed by any of several alternative procedures to discover the underlying structure. Fillenbaum and Rapoport (1971) have

Table 4.2 Ratings of the similarity of meaning of noun pairs. 5 = maximum similarity; 0 = maximum difference. (Selected from Rubenstein and Goodenough, 1965.)

Noun pair		Rating	Noun pair		Rating
midday	noon	3.94	hill	woodland	1.48
serf	slave	3.46	forest	graveyard	1.00
asylum	madhouse	3.04	cushion	jewel	0.45
sage	wizard	2.46	cord	smile	0.02
magician	oracle	1.82			

compared the sorting method with graph-theoretic methods that rely on judgments of "most similar" pairs of words in nine semantic domains; their results strongly indicate that no single structural principle obtains throughout the lexicon.

If as few as ten words are to be studied, the method of triads can be used. There are 120 triads that can be formed from a set of ten items. Each triad can be presented separately to a judge who marks which of the three words is most different in meaning from the other two. A convenient statistic to use is the number of times each pair of words is judged similar; if there are ten words in the list, every pair is judged with respect to the eight others, so the statistic can range from zero to eight. When results from many judges are added together, the result is a matrix of proximity measures for every pair, and the matrix can be analyzed in various ways to determine the underlying structure (see, for example, Wexler and Romney, 1972).

One of the few studies of locative inclusion used a version of the triad method (Preusser and Handel, 1970). Judges were given triads of place names, like "Kansas-Topeka-Omaha," and told to group them in any way that seemed to make sense. If they grouped "Topeka" and "Omaha" separate from "Kansas," they were presumably judging on the basis of categorical information: Topeka and Omaha are both cities. If they grouped "Topeka" and "Kansas" separate from "Omaha," they were presumably judging on the basis of hierarchical inclusion: Topeka is in Kansas. If they did anything else, their response was judged "miscellaneous." For this example, 70 percent of the judges put "Topeka" and "Kansas" together (locative hierarchy), 25 percent put "Topeka" and "Omaha" together (hyponymic hierarchy), and the remaining 5 percent gave the miscellaneous response. The difference could be exaggerated by using "Michigan-Detroit-Toronto," where Toronto is in Canada and Michigan and Detroit in the United States; in this case 80 percent put "Michigan" and "Detroit" together (locative hierarchy). Apparently, the "is in" relation has a strong effect on performance under these conditions.

Many variations on these experimental strategies are possible; our intent is not to review all that has been done but to indicate some avenues that are presently open to psychologists for testing the kinds of hypotheses we have proposed. Another dimension is added to this research when children are used as judges; there is considerable evidence that the organization of children's knowledge of semantic relations continues to grow long after they are able to use language as a means of communication.

Eliciting judgments about relations between words is also a task that ethnologists face when they try to understand how people in other cultures think about their world. Since linguists and anthropologists are generally less committed to experimental methods of gathering data than psychologists are, they take the direct route: they ask questions. The procedures differ from one practitioner to another, but they share the general goal of exploring hierarchical relations: "What kind of tree is that?" should elicit a hyponym of "tree."

Some ethnologists have tried to formalize the elicitation procedure in order to increase the replicability of the data. For example, Black and Metzger (1965) take as the basic unit for their analysis a stable question-and-response pair produced spontaneously by a native informant. The initial (and most difficult) task is to discover how to ask questions in the native language, questions that are grammatical, unambiguous, and natural to an informant. Once found, the questions consist of two parts, a general frame, like "Does *A* notify the authorities when a man dies?" and a specific term for *A* that directs attention to some content area, like "his father," or "his wife." Once the frames and terms are standardized, a number of informants can be questioned. The frame, term, informant, and response can be coded for machine process-ing, so that the ethnographer can receive printouts of what questions he has asked what informants in what order. The computer enables him to search for all occurrences of some word or distinction, concordances can be assembled for each frame or each specific question, and co-occurrences of different types of frames, terms, or responses can be compiled. Since the corpus quickly grows too large for the investigator to keep an accurate record of, the computer enables him to fill any gaps while he is still working with informants and to make various inferences that can then be tested further.

These methods need not be confined to fieldwork in exotic cultures. Black and Metzger used them to study terminological categorizations of lawyers by an American law student. Analysis of his answers revealed hierarchical rela-tions between terms; for example, anyone who is called a defense attorney can also be called a trial lawyer, but not all trial lawyers are defense attorneys. Although psychologists have made little use of this method, it makes possible the rapid accumulation of an extensive data base and, by checking for reliable question-response units across different informants, can provide information as dependable as that collected by experimental techniques. Since psychologists pioneered in the development of questionnaire and interviewing techniques, it is odd that their application to the investigation of semantic memory has so far been left largely to linguists and ethnologists.

4.2.3   Identification

How people identify objects so that another person can recognize them in a given search field has been studied by psychologists in a situation that is sometimes called the communication experiment. In one simple version of this experiment (Cole and Scribner, 1974), two people, seated at opposite ends of a table but visually separated by a screen, are given identical sets of objects; one person is designated as the speaker, *S*, and the other as the addressee, *A*; the experimenter places one object from *S*'s set on the left side of his end of the table and *S* describes it to *A*, who, on the basis of the descrip-tion given, attempts to select the corresponding object from his set and places it on the right side of his end of the table; the experimenter then selects an-other object from *S*'s set and places it beside the first, and the procedure is repeated; when all objects have been ordered, the screen is removed and the two rows of objects are compared. The objects to be matched are usually selected in such a way as to be difficult to describe—no simple, single-label responses serve to identify them—and the lengths of the descriptions as well as the accuracy of identification are scored.

Different forms of this experiment have been conducted under a variety of conditions with different kinds of people serving as the communicating dyad. Krauss and Weinheimer (1964, 1966) found that descriptions would be abbreviated with repeated use when the two people could talk to each other about the objects; Glucksberg, Krauss, and Weisberg (1966) found that four- and five-year-old S's who performed well with familiar objects did not give descriptions of novel objects adequate for others to identify the referents, although they could themselves identify later the novel objects from their own descriptions; Krauss and Glucksberg (1969) found that with children as participants the success of the dyad depended more on S's than on A's communication skills. These studies have been reviewed by Glucksberg, Krauss, and Higgins (1974).

Olson (1970) describes a communication experiment conducted by William Ford in which a gold star is placed under a small wooden block. An observer is then asked to tell a listener, who did not see the placement, where the star is. Suppose the star was always placed under the same small, round, white wooden block. If there was one alternative block present which was small, round, *black*, and wooden, S would usually say "It's under the WHITE one." If the alternative block was small, *square*, white, and wooden, S would usually say "It's under the ROUND one." If there were three alternative blocks—a round black one, a square black one, and a square white one—S would usually say "It's under the ROUND, WHITE one."

In every case, of course, the description "It's under the small, round, white wooden block," would have been unambiguous, but since much of that information was redundant for the task at hand, the description differed depending on the set of objects from which S wished to distinguish the target. The information S provided was no more specific than required for identification.

We have proposed that one of the control instructions available to the conceptual system is "identify," which tries to determine what information is required to designate a particular target in a given search domain and provides the system with labels expressing just that information and no more. Perhaps "identify" starts with the most general designation, tests whether it differentiates the target object, and then adds whatever further information is required to obtain a designation that could denote no other object in the search domain; once an identifier is found, "identify" stops and gives the label to the routine that called it. In other words, semantic memory may be so organized that "identify" can proceed more or less systematically from labels of greater scope toward labels of narrower scope.

Suppose the experiment was done with a dachshund instead of a small, round, white wooden block. If the alternative was a block, the identification might be "under the animal." If the alternative was a cat, the identification might be "under the dog." If the alternative was a collie, the identification might be "under the dachshund." If the alternative was another dachshund, the identification might require the use of specific features of the target dog— place, size, sex, color. In this context a more precise identifier than is actually required might often occur—the label "dog" is so short and readily available that it might be used instead of "animal" even to distinguish a dachshund from a block. Thus, we cannot assume that "identify" necessarily enters a hierarchy at its most general level and works down from there. The rule seems to be one of minimizing the effort expended. If a less general term suggests itself first, people may give more information than is required by the task. But they will not usually exert themselves in a search for finer distinctions than necessary.

Since agreement between speaker and listener in the identification of refer- ents is so important for successful communication, we can suppose that for adults the operation of "identify" is rapid and automatic. We have imagined a sequential search of semantic memory from broader to narrower labels, but other hypotheses are possible. The system might begin with the narrowest pos- sible identification and then omit features that were redundant, thus moving from narrower to broader scope. Or it might consider all possible labels in parallel, discarding those that did not apply or did not differentiate and, on the assumption that more detailed identifications would take longer to process, accepting the first differentiating label that the parallel search produced. We hold no strong brief for any of these hypotheses. The interesting point is that, whatever hypothesis we espouse, efficient execution of "identify" requires a special organization of semantic memory. Broad-to-narrower and narrow-to- broader searches imply a hierarchical organization of the relevant labels; a hierarchical organization is implicit for parallel search on the assumption that more precise labels should take longer to test—they require all the tests in- volved in less precise labels plus a residuum of additional tests, some of which may take a longer time to perform.

It seems reasonable that experience would provide extensive practice in finding distinctive identifiers, and that this practice would eventually strengthen a hierarchical organization of semantic memory for the terms being searched. If so, the hierarchical field property would not be a consequence of a self-conscious effort to be tidy or logical but would grow organically from psychological requirements for successful linguistic communication. A corol- lary would be that if a person has not been frequently required to use the terms in some semantic field distinctively for the purpose of identification, hierarchi- cal relations among them in his semantic memory might be relatively weak— not absent, but less salient and accessible, so that inferential processes would be required more often.

Developmentally, the selection of an appropriate identifying expression to guide a listener's perceptual search is probably the central task of "identify." When the problem is viewed more broadly, however, it is obvious that a lis- tener's need to identify the speaker's referent is not limited to situations in- volving perceptual search of objects in the environment. In the course of a conversation several objects or events may be referred to; a listener must be able to identify which of those discourse referents the speaker intends. In this case, the search domain is the memory of the conversational episode, but the speaker must still select appropriate identifying expressions to guide the listener's search.

The general principle of identification is aptly formulated by Davey (1974): treat your hearer like the tax man, give him no more than you have to. Davey has written a computer program that gives a commentary on games of tick-tacktoe (naughts-and-crosses). A typical sample of its output runs as follows: "The game began with my taking a corner, you took an adjacent one, and I took the middle of the same edge." It also makes hypothetical remarks like "You could have forked me but you took the square opposite the one you had just taken." The program builds up such comments from a representation of the game. It selects the most significant and general verb ("forked" in the previous example). It generally constructs economical referring expressions; it does not bother to say "square" where the term would be redundant. It makes extensive use of context, both explicitly and implicitly; thus, it will use the expression "the same edge" even if it has not mentioned an edge before (see the first example above). Many of its referential problems are solved by virtue of the simple universe of discourse with which it operates.

The signals that guide textual search are subtle and complex. Since the search set in a discourse is seldom given perceptually, it can grow and change as the discourse progresses. Not only must the speaker provide sufficient information to identify which discourse referent he intends, but if he wishes to introduce a new referent he must indicate somehow that it has not been previously established. In English, the articles "a" and "the" help keep these matters straight. As they are frequently used, a noun phrase preceded by "a" indicates that the listener does not need to search his memory for an already established referent; "the" usually means that a referent has been introduced. For example, "I saw a tall man. The man had a gun" involves one man, whereas "I saw a tall man. A man had a gun" involves two men. These important little words are used in other ways, of course, but this is one frequent function they serve.

In either case, perceptual or textual, identification requires a speaker to use an expression that will be true for a unique element (or set of elements) in the search domain and false for all others. In the perceptual case, the speaker will usually be able to locate and recognize the elements his expression identifies; in the textual case, he may not. A speaker can introduce hypothetical elements to serve as discourse referents and then identify them anaphorically later, even if he knows nothing about them beyond what he must know in order to distinguish them from other discourse referents. In this sense it is possible to identify something without knowing what you have identified; anaphora must depend more on co-identification than on coreference. Some of the complexities of discourse that follow from this textual definition of identification have been explored by Stenning (1975).

4.3 CONTRASTIVE FIELD PROPERTIES

The hierarchical field property is manifested in a series of levels of terms of different scope. Within a given level the terms have different meanings, meanings that often contrast with one another. The most striking examples of contrast are between antonyms. "Alive" and "dead" provide a typical example where one or the other term may be applicable in a certain situation, but never both. The meaning of one excludes the meaning of the other. But "table" and "rug" are also mutually exclusive, even though they do not show the same degree of opposition as "alive" and "dead." J. J. Katz (1964b) has suggested that we could treat all these sets of terms similarly if we assumed that there are many special antonymy relations. For example, sex antonymy would pair "man" and "woman," "cow" and "bull," "bride" and "groom"; species antonymy would relate "child," "cub," "puppy"; age antonymy would relate "infant," "child," "adolescent," and "adult," or "cub" and "lion." The color adjectives, "blue," "yellow," "green," "red," would form an antonymous n-tuple based on "distinguisher antonymy." Katz treats these sets of words in terms of semantic markers: two terms so related have all of their semantic markers in common except for the one marker—sex, species, age, distinguisher—that distinguishes among them.

To refer to such sets of words as antonymous n-tuples seems to overgeneralize the usual meaning of antonymy. Most people believe, with the dictionary's sanction, that antonymy is the relation that holds between two words that have opposite meanings. Katz does tie together negation and disjunctive concepts with the observation that a negation of one term in a disjunction entails an affirmation of the disjunction of the remaining terms, so his terminology is logical. In the traditional sense, however, the denial of one pole of an antonymous pair does not entail the assertion of its opposite; "big" and "little" are antonyms, yet you do not always interpret the denial of one as the assertion of the other. Conversely, if the context indicates that you are dealing with an age disjunction of "puppy" or "dog," the denial of one may entail the assertion of the other, even though most people would regard "puppy" as a hyponym of "dog." Antonymy and synonymy are best left to play their more narrowly defined (and often controversial) role in semantic theory. There is an opposition between antonyms (usually adjectives) that does not seem to characterize all sets of coordinate terms.

The disjunctions that we are interested in here are held together by some kind of field property; they consist of coordinate terms; the terms exclude one another; only one of them can be applied at a time. Lyons (1963) uses the term "incompatibility" to capture the property of mutual exclusivity and makes antonymy a special case of incompatibility. We will borrow from the ethnologists (Conklin, 1962; Frake, 1962) and speak of these lists of incompatible terms as contrastive sets. To say that two words contrast is to say more than that they are incompatible or mutually exclusive; it says that they are in the same semantic field. "Table" and "ambition" are incompatible, in the sense that anything labeled by one cannot be labeled by the other, but they are not in contrast, because they are not in the same semantic field.

What is meant by a contrastive set is clarified by considering how ethnologists elicit such sets. Frake (1961) gives the following example from English to illustrate the method. Suppose we confront an English-speaking person with a dog—a poodle, say—and collect from him all the terms he might use to refer to it. We would eventually have a list including "quadruped," "vertebrate," "mammal," "canine," "animal," "poodle," "dog." All of these words can designate the same object, so they cannot belong to the same contrastive set. They are not synonyms, either, since they are defined at different levels in the taxonomic hierarchy. The problem is to get them sorted into their appropriate levels.

Frake suggests that, still pointing to the poodle, we ask our informant the following questions:

      (a) Is that a plant?
      (b) Is that a cat?
      (c) Is that a collie?

The responses will be, respectively:

      (a) No, it's an animal.
      (b) No, it's a dog.
      (c) No, it's a poodle.

From these answers we know that "animal" contrasts with "plant," "dog" with "cat," "poodle" with "collie." In this way it is possible to elicit the contrastive sets that constitute various levels in the hierarchy. Once these are known, it is relatively simple to arrange them vertically according to degree of generality. Frake illustrates the procedure in terms of his analysis of the Subanun terminology for skin diseases.

This method of constructing lists of terms belonging to the same contrastive set relies on the conventional use of negation in ordinary discourse. The convention of negation within contrastive sets can be demonstrated by playing a simple guessing game. You announce, "I am thinking of something and I want you to quess what it is. I will give you a hint: it is NOT a dog." Asked to think of something that is not a dog, the average adult will think of cats, or some other domesticated animal comparable to dogs. To use "is a" in the hint would elicit hyponyms; to use "is not a" elicits contrasting terms. Why "is not a" has this effect is puzzling, because to say that something is not a dog logically eliminates only such terms as "dog," "collie," and "poodle," but says nothing more about what it is. In the context of the guessing game, "is not a" logically eliminates hyponyms, yet most people interpret it as calling for contrasting terms. That the logic of the situation is clear is indicated by those few people who guess "the Volga" or "a basketball team" instead of the banal "cat."

Undoubtedly the strength of this tendency can be attributed in part to people's preconceptions: about what a hint is; about the difficulty of any task you might set in the time available for performing it; about your intentions in asking the question in the first place. It is not uncommon to get a partonymous response, and there is always the clever person who jumps as far from the contrastive set as his imagination permits. But even granted that a contrastive response is not universal, the phenomenon is remarkably robust.

There is a simple explanation for this illogical behavior. People frequently use negation in common speech to indicate that some customary or expected state of affairs is not the case. (See Wason and Johnson-Laird, 1972, for a review of experiments on the use and interpretation of negation.) That is to say, people do not ordinarily go about uttering such denials as "George Washington is not a table" or "Sealing wax is not a dog," even though they are perfectly true. It is difficult to imagine a situation that would call for such speech acts; there is no reason to suppose that anybody who knows English would need to be disabused of a belief that George Washington is a table or that sealing wax is a dog. These denials seldom occur because their corresponding affirmations seldom occur. In short, the way negation is conventionally used in ordinary discourse limits attention to contrastive sets of terms, and extensive experience with this convention leads to an organization of semantic memory into such contrastive sets. (This organization appears even in word-association tests, where contrasting terms constitute the most frequent type of response; Woodworth, 1938, p. 352.)

The definition of a contrastive set would be simple if we could add to the incompatibility requirement a requirement that all terms in the set be direct hyponyms of some single superordinate term. But what if the language contains no such superordinate term? Linguists tell us of languages that have several contrasting labels for kinds of snow but no generic term translatable as "snow"; many contrasting labels for trees, but no generic "tree"; several contrasting labels for colors, but no generic "color." Such languages are often said (misleadingly) to be more concrete than Indo-European languages, but there is reason to believe that people who speak these so-called concrete languages are capable of conceiving of contrastive sets and capable of abstractions that their language does not happen to express directly. The existence of an explicit superordinate term for every contrastive set cannot be a necessary condition. This fact places a responsibility on the investigator, who should not multiply nameless concepts without limit; he must at least determine that there is an acceptable nominal phrase that informants can agree on to serve in place of a single superordinate term. For our theoretical purposes, the implication is that there must be a nameable, if not explicitly named, superordinate concept for the contrastive field.

We will say that two words are in contrast, therefore, only if both are included in a minimal contrastive set. By "minimal" we mean that every word in the set has exactly the same superordinate terms and/or concepts as every other; by "contrastive" we mean, as before, that they are incompatible, so one and only one word in the set can apply to any given particular. Ethnologists carry the definitions another step and distinguish between direct and indirect contrast (Kay, 1971). Two terms are in direct contrast ("poodle" and "collie") if they are both members of the same minimal contrastive set; two terms are in indirect contrast ("poodle" and "cat") if one or both are hyponyms of words in direct contrast.

We have taken some pains to define what we mean by a minimal contrastive set because it is a basic building block of lexical and conceptual memory. As we have defined it, it may seem a special and complicated relation, yet it is of primary psychological importance and can be appreciated intuitively by anyone with linguistic self-consciousness. The notion is so obvious that we must analyze it in detail in order to become aware of its not inconsiderable structure. Minimal contrastive sets occur not only among perceptual paradigms but generally throughout the lexicon. Indeed, much of what people must do when they choose their words is to select among such sets of contrasting alternatives.

In sum, contrast is a linguistically important psychological fact. Strawson (1974) argues that the very nature of predication—the basic combination of subject and predicate in language and logic—"must reflect some fundamental features of our thought about the world" (p. 20). He claims that the duality of subject and predicate reflects the duality of spatiotemporal particulars and general concepts. He points to the asymmetry between concepts and particulars. Concepts contrast: there are sets of concepts so related that, for every particular, if one concept is exemplified by that particular, other concepts in the set are not. But particulars do not contrast: there are no sets of particulars so related that, for every concept, if one particular exemplifies that concept, other particulars in the set do not. According to Strawson, subjects are like particulars, predicates like concepts. On the basis of this analogy he undertakes to explain all of the formal and grammatical differences between subjects and predicates.

A psychologist in search of reasons for this asymmetry between particulars and concepts might look to the fundamental processes of attention and discrimination. A word like "cube," for example, not only activates the contrastive set of shape concepts, it also directs attention to the perceptual attribute of shape, and it may lead to ignoring other attributes. The incompatibility of the concepts and the words that express them arises from the incompatibility of the perceptual experiences; restriction to a minimal set corresponds to the ability to attend to one aspect at a time.

Sutherland and Mackintosh (1971) provide an extensive summary of the experimental evidence that discrimination learning involves two stages. If a hungry animal is given the problem of learning which visual patterns are associated with food, its first task is to discover which attributes of the patterns are relevant and must be attended to—is it their shape, size, color, location, orientation, or what? Once the animal has discovered the significant attributes, its next task is to associate an approach response with the correct value of that attribute. If shape is the attribute, should it approach circles, triangles, or squares in order to obtain food?

Since a visual pattern may be simultaneously square, large, red, and on the right, these attributes are not mutually exclusive. The first stage, according to this theory of discriminative learning, is a matter of discovering which contrastive set to attend to; the second stage involves discovery of that one among all the mutually exclusive values within the contrastive set that signals food. Thus, the contrastive organization of experience may not be peculiarly linguistic, or even limited to human beings. It may derive from a basic design feature of discriminative learning, which would be a prime example of the influence of perception on language.

We should not overestimate the similarities, however. Unlike animals, a person partitions these attentional domains and assigns labels to them. There is reason to think that the contrastive field property among labels is much stronger than among percepts. For example, on word-association tests, if the stimulus is a color term, adults tend to give another color term or "color" as their response. But Dorcus (1932) found that if they are actually shown the color and asked to give the first word they think of (other than the name of the color), people will usually give names of objects having that color, not names of other colors. The name of a color draws our attention to the attribute of color more forcefully than the perception of that color does.

A color term is not a vocal noise that can be substituted for the color it denotes; the word has its meaning by virtue of its place in the partitioning of a particular attentional domain, and the occurrence of a color term retrieves the conceptual field in which the name is defined. Given that this concept is activated, other color terms are immediately available. On the other hand, when a color is seen (with explicit instructions to withhold its name), it is not necessary to retrieve the color concept in order to interpret the stimulus or think of a response. A color term makes no sense except as an element in a contrastive semantic field that partitions the color domain; the color itself does not require a definitional context. Color terms are in conceptual contrast with each other; color percepts are not.

Words related by membership in a contrastive set lend themselves to definition in terms of genus and species. It is possible to state first the general class to which they belong and then the respect in which they are contrasted with other terms belonging to that class. A table, for example, is an article of furniture (generic class) that has one or more supports for its top (species characterization). A cook is a person (generic class) who prepares food by using heat (species characterization). Red is a color (generic class) that is characteristic of fresh blood (species characterization). These definitions consist of a head noun that names the genus followed by a relative clause that differentiates the species.

We have seen that the cognitive effect of negation—*x* is not a table, *y* is not a cook, *z* is not red—is to leave most people still thinking in terms of the same genus, but searching for another species. If *x* is not a table, perhaps it is a chair; if *y* is not a cook, perhaps he is a waiter; if *z* is not red, perhaps it is green. In short, this kind of negation is conventionally interpreted as applying to the species, not the genus; the genus is taken to be the same for "is a table" and "is not a table." For this reason, Miller (1969a) suggested that in copulative predicate phrases we might say that the genus is (cognitively) presupposed and the species characterization is asserted, since presuppositions, unlike assertions, are unaffected by negation. To speak of presupposition in this context, however, creates terminological confusion; if "table" presupposes "furniture," "x is a table" should have an indeterminate truth value when x is not an article of furniture, whereas in fact it will be clearly false. Logically, the species does not presuppose the genus, it merely entails it. It is a psychological fact that people usually take the genus for granted and search for a different species.

It is perhaps obvious, but sufficiently important to emphasize again, that minimal contrastive sets are the basic building blocks from which semantic hierarchies are constructed. This follows from the fact that the superordinate term of a contrastive set may itself be a member of another contrastive set. This relation was evident in the discussion above of the relations among "poodle," "dog," and "animal," each of which can denote the same object but at different levels of contrast.

Not all hierarchies are as compelling as the poodle-dog-animal example, however. Consider the following example:

(9)   knight: a *man* who has been raised to honorary military rank
         man: a *person* who is male and adult
         person: a *being* that is human (a human *being*)

"Knight" is coordinate with "commoner" and both entail "man"; "man" is coordinate with "woman" and both entail "person"; "person" is coordinate with "animal" and both entail "being."

It is important to remember, however, that such schematizations have a tidiness that is more apparent than real—a tidiness which people aspire to for convenience in cognitive processing but which they never completely succeed in imposing on an instrument that must adapt itself to the changing purposes of human communication. Note how many exceptions one can find to the hierarchical implications of (9): "commoner" entails "man" only when it is contrasted with "knight," for commoners can be women; "man" is contrasted with "woman" in one usage, with "child" in another; "man" has a double role as both a specific and a generic term, so it can also contrast with "animal" or "machine"; and "person" is in many ways a unique concept, taking intentional predicates and contrasting only metaphorically with other "things." There does seem to be a hierarchical plan somewhere in the background, but it is never implemented fully.

Once we get away from labels for simple perceptual properties we lose the kind of neatness that comes from having all the members of a contrastive set distinguishable in terms of a single attribute. The definition of a minimal contrastive set does not assume dimensional purity; it is merely simpler to illustrate and understand for pure cases. In more complex instances there may be considerable structure within a contrastive field; a set of words that are all of equal generality, are mutually exclusive, and are directly dominated by a single superordinate term or cognitive presupposition may still differ with respect to several perceptual or conceptual attributes. Indeed, some words in the set may not necessarily contrast with one another. Think, for example, how articles of furniture differ, and whether "chair," "couch," and "bench" can never be applied to the same object.

The internal structure of a contrastive set does not admit hierarchical organization. The simplest kind of internal structure is probably ordinal: names of the months, letters of the alphabet, ages of man. But more complex contrasts are possible. Only hierarchical relations within a minimal contrastive set are excluded by definition.

We can think of hierarchical relations as characterizing the *external* structure of a contrastive set—how one set of contrastive terms is related to other sets—and of the dimensions of contrast within the set as characterizing its *internal* structure. The hierarchical field property, based on external relations between contrastive sets, reflects the way labels include one another; the contrastive field property, based on internal relations among members of a contrastive set, reflects the way labels exclude one another. Both field properties must be representable in whatever hypothesis we adopt for characterizing general concepts.

These comments should suffice to indicate why hierarchical and contrastive field properties play such an important role in language and in conceptual thinking. As Lyons (1963) remarks, the relation of synonymy, which has received so much attention from writers on semantics, is far less important. One can conceive of a language that would make no use of synonymy; it is hard to imagine how a language in which contrastive and hierarchical field properties played no part could function at all. Viewed psychologically, these field properties are closely related to processes of attention and discrimination. Viewed formally, they provide a cognitive basis for logical operators and perhaps for predication itself. Viewed grammatically, they are closely related to what are usually called restrictions of co-occurrence or selectional restrictions —restrictions on the words that can serve as arguments of a predicate. Viewed semantically, they provide the basic pattern of entailment relations between words in the same field. However they are characterized, it is clear that any adequate theoretical formulation must somehow deal with these field properties and their implications.

Characterizing the internal structure of contrastive sets turns out to be considerably more difficult than demonstrating the importance of conceptual contrast in general. There are several reasons. Contrastive fields serve as components in a great variety of hierarchies—not merely as contrastive sets of nouns used for labeling objects, but throughout every corner of the lexicon. They vary enormously in size: from pairs like "male" and "female" to infinitudes like the integers. They may be as generic as "solid," "liquid," and "gas" or as specific as the most precise nomenclature in chemistry or taxonomic biology. They vary heterogeneously in dimensionality: from the single dimension of age names through the three or four dimensions of color names and the half-dozen or more dimensions of kin terms to the unknown dimensionality of shape designations. Some of them have attributes that are clearly graded, like "hot" and "cold"; some are discrete, like "married" and "single"; and the gradability of some is debatable, like "true" and "false." Some contrasting terms have precisely defined boundaries, like the names of the days of the week; some have very fuzzy boundaries, like color terms. Sometimes the terms in a contrastive set are absolutely anchored, like the names for units of measurement; sometimes they are deictically anchored, like personal pronouns; sometimes they are not anchored at all, like "fast" and "slow." Sometimes they are expressed by affixes, like singular and plural, or by words and affixes, like English tenses, or by words alone. Sometimes membership in the contrastive set is precisely known, as it is for the names of the points of the compass, and sometimes it is vaguely open-ended, as for names of articles of furniture. They may be ordered or unordered. Even their incompatibility may be fuzzy, as it is for the names of emotions. It is impossible to select any one example that fairly represents all the kinds of problems posed for semantic analysis.

4.4   CONCEPTUAL INTEGRATION

What we have called a label is essentially a rule involving a description of objects or events that can be used to determine whether an object or event is a member of the class of objects or events to which the label applies. Given such a rule, a logical conclusion to draw would be that a perceptual paradigm *is* the concept one has of that label, and the class of objects or events *is* the meaning of that label. This conclusion is certainly part of what we are saying, but not the whole of it.

If we were to take as our definition of concepts the unadorned statement that concepts are routines that can be used in labeling, we would still have to face a central issue in psychology, how concepts are related. In order to explore relations between concepts, it is necessary to examine particular concepts—to analyze them explicitly and to try to discover what it is about them that leads to the organizational properties underlying their use in ordinary discourse. This is, more or less, the line we have been following. But we have encountered complications.

Our first discovery was that descriptions of objects or events solely in terms of their perceptible attributes are insufficient. In order to recognize the denotation of a label, one must also know what objects and events bearing that label can be used for or what they are expected to do. With this schematic information, the complexity of possible relations between concepts is greatly increased.

Moreover, although it might be possible to define a concept in terms of a rule for labeling its instances, we must remember that labeling is, in Harrison's words, "a narrow and circumscribed ritual"; before labels can become words used in ordinary discourse they must be incorporated into routines for pro-

ducing and interpreting meaningful sentences. A word must be correspondingly more complex than the same sound used as a label. When information
about the use of a label as a word is added to the schema, the complexity of
possible relations between concepts is again increased.

At the very least, a psychological hypothesis about the concept someone
has of a given word must include much information that is not essential for
the perceptual recognition of instances labeled by that word. Labeling routines
must be included in many concepts, but they cannot be the whole of any
linguistically encoded concept.

When we considered the kinds of relations between words that have led to
the claim that lexical knowledge is organized into semantic fields, we first noted
the phenomenon of shared labels. Many shared labels differ in generality,
which led us to consider hierarchical relations between them. The hierarchical
field property can be explained in part by relations between the perceptual
paradigms incorporated into the labeling routines. That is to say, if the paradigm for label W is a part of the paradigm for label V, then any object or event
that is recognized as an instance of V will also be recognized as an instance of
W; w will be the more general concept, and v a more specific subconcept.
Since this relation between W and V can be recognized by adults in the absence
of perceptual tests applied to specific objects or events, we must assume that
the conceptual system is sufficiently complex to be able to represent not only
the labeling routines themselves but also relations between labeling routines.
As a very preliminary hypothesis, therefore, we suggested that this information
might sometimes be represented memorially by including the specific assertion
[ISA(v, w)] as part of both concept w and concept v.

Next, we noted the phenomenon of contrasting labels. Once again, the
contrastive field property can be explained in part by relations between the
perceptual paradigms incorporated into labeling routines. If the paradigm for
label W excludes by its very nature the paradigm for label V—if no single
object or event can satisfy both labeling routines—then the labels are mutually
exclusive, or incompatible. But since it is possible for adults to distinguish
direct from indirect contrast, it is necessary to define a minimal contrastive set
of labels that share all their superordinate labels. Since a language may not
have an explicit label shared by all members of a minimal contrastive set, we
must assume that the conceptual system is sufficiently complex to be able to
represent, in addition to the concept of a label, concepts for which no label has
been adopted in the language. Not only is a labeling routine merely a part of
its concept, it is not even a necessary part.

Such arguments have led us to a conception of lexical concepts far more
abstract than our conception of labels. At this point it seems appropriate,
therefore, to offer some general comments on conceptual theories of meaning.

By separating that part of a lexical concept required to identify instances
from all other information associated with it, we have arrived at a theoretical
position similar in many respects to that which philosophers of language generally attribute to Frege (1892). According to Church's (1951) modification

of the Fregean approach, "A name is said to *denote* its denotation and to *express* its sense, and the sense is said to be *a concept of* the denotation" (p. 102). The schema that we suppose must identify instances of a lexical concept determines the denotation of the word; additional information about the location of the lexical concept in a field of related concepts and about those things that the word denotes extends its sense, or meaning. Church provided a tentative list of principles that such a theory assumes, which we can take as a guide for the following comments.

—Every concept is a concept of at most one thing. It may be a concept of an individual, a function, a class, a proposition. But it is not a concept of two or more things, for then it would be two or more concepts. The variety of concepts is unlimited.

—Every word has either a unique concept as its meaning or, if its meaning can vary, it has a nonempty class of concepts over which its meaning can range. It is not assumed that every concept or class of concepts is expressed by a unique word; it may be expressed by two or more words, or none at all.

—The denotation of a word is whatever its meaning is a concept of. We must not combine a schema for identifying the sun with a concept of the moon. The range of a variable word is the class of things that the members of its range of meanings are concepts of. We must not combine a schema for lamps with a class concept of apples. It is not assumed, however, that two words having the same denotation must express the same concept. In natural languages it may be possible to have words that have a meaning, that express a concept, yet denote nothing ("unicorn," "the present king of France"). In such cases we could propose a schema for recognizing instances even though no instance would ever be encountered.

—These comments are not limited to the meaning and denotation of lexical concepts. In a Fregean system declarative sentences are taken to be a kind of name. The meaning of a sentence is the proposition it expresses and its denotation is its truth value. Hence, the above assumptions about the meaning and denotation of words are assumed to hold equally for sentences. If a sentence contains a word whose meaning is variable, however, the meaning of the sentence will depend on the meaning assigned to that word.

—If a particular meaning in the appropriate range is assigned to each of the words in a well-formed sentence, that sentence will have a unique concept as its meaning. Given the notorious ambiguities of sentences in natural languages, this is a strong assumption; it may be necessary to weaken "a unique concept" to "at least one concept." In any case, it is not assumed that a particular concept can be expressed in only one way.

—If a sentence S contains a variable word W, and if P is the meaning of S when concept A is taken as the meaning of W, then the value of S for that concept A is that which P is a concept of. Suppose the sentence is "That is a lamp," where "that" is a variable word. And suppose that when the concept A of some individual object is taken as the meaning of "that," the meaning of "That is a lamp" is LAMP(A). Then the value of the sentence "That is a lamp" for "that" = A is whatever LAMP (A) is a concept of. For Frege, the proposition expressed by "That is a lamp" is a concept of its denotation, and its denotation is its truth value, so the value of "That is a lamp" for "that" = A is truth or falsehood. We generalize this propositional formulation, claiming that a sentence expresses a program of operations and (to keep terminology as close as possible) denotes the consequences of executing the program, and its program is a concept of its denotation. In the special case where the program happens to be test(t, LAMP(A)), its value can be truth or falsehood, but in other contexts the same sentence might express a different meaning that was a program of operations conceptualizing different procedural consequences, having a different value.

—If an expression is changed by substituting for one word another word with the same sense, the new expression will have the same sense. If it is changed by substituting another word with the same denotation, the new expression will have the same denotation.

Church distinguishes a logistic system, for which it is sufficient to give a vocabulary, rules of formation, rules of inference, and certain axioms, from a formalized language, which is a logistic system together with an assignment of meanings to its expressions. For a conceptual theory of meaning of the sort contemplated here, this assignment falls into two parts. The extensional part of the semantics will include rules of denotation for constants, rules of range for variables, and rules of value to determine the value of expressions. The intensional part will include rules of sense to determine the meaning of constants, rules of sense range to determine the range of meanings of variables, and rules of sense value to determine the propositional meanings of well-formed expressions. If English is thought of in these terms, there are such rules of denotation as: "round" denotes the class of round things; "the world" denotes the world; "the world is round" denotes the truth value thereof that the world is round. And there are rules of sense such as: "round" expresses the property of roundness; "the world" expresses the individual concept of the world; "the world is round" expresses the proposition that the world is round.

The intensional part of our procedural analog to this theory would include procedures for forming routines incorporating schemata for identifying instances of constant and variable terms and procedures for executing programs including such routines. At this point in the development of our ideas the intensional part of our procedural analog would differ little from Frege's, except for our claim that the meaning of a sentence is the program, not the proposition, that it expresses.

There is a sense in which a logistic system together with only extensional semantic rules can be thought of as a formalized language. Either the metalinguistic phrase used in stating the rule of denotation can be taken as indicating the corresponding rule of sense, or the need for any intensional part can simply be denied. Intensional rules seem to introduce an infinitude of abstract entities that in formal logic or mathematics might better be omitted entirely. To those who object to abstract entities on ontological grounds, Church's reply is that there are more important criteria by which a theory should be judged. A theory of human language that prohibited any discussion of concepts that the language expresses could not be an adequate psychological theory, and on those grounds we are prepared to accept an ontological commitment to the existence of such abstract entities.

We were led into this commitment by considerations relating to the conceptual organization of words, by the realization that the intensional part of the theory must provide the structure underlying the extensional part. Frege and Church provide little guidance for psychologists who ask how concepts in general, and lexical concepts in particular, are related to one another. For that part of the theory we must rely on psychological arguments, and a good place to begin would seem to be with the concepts that social convention has fixed in the lexicon.

When we survey the variety of conceptual structures that the English language expresses we see that they are far too heterogeneous to submit to any simple formula. No single blueprint can adequately characterize the internal structure of every semantic field; the architecture of the lexicon is at least as diverse as the architecture of houses, skyscrapers, bridges, gardens. If we wish to discover generalizations about semantic structures, the best place to look would seem to be in the ways lexical concepts can be put together rather than in the shapes of the finished products.

4.4.1   Associative Networks

One implication of lexical field properties is that memory for the meanings of words does not have the property known to computer scientists as random access. The accessibility of any particular item of information is not independent of the current state of the system. This conclusion can be supported by a variety of experimental techniques that demonstrate the facilitation of recognition produced by prior exposure to semantically related information. Meyer and Schvaneveldt (1971) have considered the possibility that such facilitation could be explained in terms of the time it takes to move from one memory location to another. In computer systems, for example, information stored on a magnetic tape or disc takes longer to retrieve if the reading head happens to be located far from the target item. If it were assumed that semantically related items are close together in memory, then when a prior item was semantically related to the target item the metaphorical reading head would already be nearby and retrieval time would be reduced.

The usual assumption made by psychologists is not merely that semantically related items are in some sense close together in memory but that they are actually connected to one another in some way. These connections between memory items are called associations. An association is a two-term relation. There has been much disagreement as to whether the associative relation is symmetric or transitive, and even about what the related terms represent, but there has been no disagreement that associations relate two of something.

When more than two elements are to be associated, therefore, the pairs must form an associative network. It is generally assumed that when some item is activated by recall, the activation spreads over these connections to all related words, which are thereby more readily accessible for subsequent recall.

We have suggested that one way to integrate concepts into larger structures would be to include specific statements of each relation in the information available about each concept, as in the two-term relation [ISA(Y, X)]. This cross-referencing scheme can be thought of as an associative network. In figure 4.3 a fragment of such a network is represented diagrammatically, where the nodes represent the concepts and the arrows are cross-references labeled according to the relation between the concepts. Associative networks can be constructed in almost any shape with almost any kinds of relations needed to match the diversity of conceptual structures. The hypothesis is that the conceptual system can search through an associative network for a concept having certain specified characteristics.

Since 1969, when Collins and Quillian proposed associative networks as models of semantic memory, this hypothesis has been examined in detail by psychologists interested in verbal learning. Some psychologists prefer a theory of associative networks built up entirely through contiguity in prior experience —the arrows between nodes would not reflect hyponymic or partonymic relations, as in figure 4.3, but would simply be labeled with measures of strength of association (strengths that might be inferred, for example, from frequencies of occurrence on word-association tests). Others prefer something closer to the network we have shown here, where the arrows represent semantic relations, not strengths of association. In both cases, however, it is assumed that the difficulty of memorizing arbitrary lists of words should be predictable—in part, at least—on the basis of transfer to a new learning task of previously learned associations, and that the long-term consequences of previous learning can be represented by some kind of associative network.

One way to test this hypothesis is by computer simulation. An associative

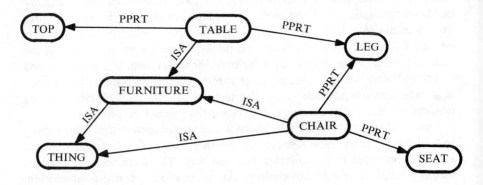

Figure 4.3   Fragment of an associative network.

network can be created in a computer's memory, a procedure can be defined for indexing the nodes and arrows so as to simulate what a person might be doing while he studies the list, and another procedure can be defined for searching for indexed nodes so as to simulate what a person might be doing when he recalls the list. Building the computer model is difficult, and many arbitrary and heuristic decisions are required along the way to get the system to run at all. But it has been done, and the results obtained when the computer learns a list are sufficiently like the results obtained when people learn the same list to justify the assumption that it has been done well.

J. R. Anderson (1972; see also Anderson and Bower, 1972, and G. Bower, 1972) calls his model FRAN, for Free Recall in an Associative Net. It has a vocabulary of 262 noun concepts, each with from three to nineteen associations (determined from *Webster's Dictionary*) to other concepts. Unlike figure 4.3, the connections between concepts are unlabeled, that is, they are all of the same type; although Anderson made provisions for including labeled connections, he did not exploit it. The network is multiply connected; it is possible to trace a path from any node to any other node in the network through varying distances. When a list is presented to FRAN, it indexes each node that occurs on the list and searches each node for paths that would connect it with other indexed nodes; when such a path is found, it too is indexed. After several repetitions of the list FRAN will eventually succeed in finding and indexing the shortest paths between all the nodes representing words on the list. During recall, the system takes a word that has been selected as a "starter" and follows indexed paths from there to find other indexed nodes.

In order to simulate human experiments, the list of words to be learned is presented once to FRAN, which then tries to recall it; the list is presented a second time and FRAN again tries to recall it; this presentation-and-test cycle is repeated until the list is mastered, just as it would be for a human learner. The rate of learning, the order in which items are recalled, the effects of rate of presentation, the effects of interference from interpolated learning, and many other features of FRAN's behavior are directly comparable to human data.

FRAN's deficiencies are more instructive than its virtues, however. One deficiency is that it is not equipped to keep track of a common relation. Unlike the associative network shown in figure 4.3, FRAN's memory is connected by unlabeled arrows; when two nodes are connected, FRAN has no way to know whether the connection is, say, hyponymic or partonymic. Without that information, the system has no way of noting that several items on the list might all be hyponyms of the same superordinate item, so it would not be able to take that superordinate term as a useful starter for retrieving the indexed hyponyms. Consequently, FRAN shows significantly less clustering on recall of conceptually related items than human learners. This deficiency might be corrected by adding labels to the arrows representing different kinds of semantic relations and providing FRAN with some way to use those labels to reduce search time.

Another deficiency is that FRAN recognizes nothing special about a list of words that happens to form a grammatical sentence. People, of course, recognize the linguistic structure and remember a sentence much better than a haphazard list of words. FRAN was not designed to support sentence comprehension but rather to explain data obtained from experiments with free recall of lists of independent words. In order to correct this deficiency, Anderson and Bower (1973) developed HAM, Human Associative Memory, which attempts to simulate the learning and retrieval of propositions rather than lists of isolated words.

HAM parses input sentences (top-down and left-right) into two parts in working memory. One part represents the fact that the sentence expresses and the other part represents its context (location and time the fact is said to be true). The output of the parser is a phrase-structure tree whose terminal elements point to preexisting concepts. The relations in this tree are transformed into long-term memory associations and matched against structures already in long-term memory. Unlike FRAN, HAM does not assume direct connections between words; words become interconnected only as they occur in particular propositions. In HAM, therefore, two words are linked by way of the relations expressed between them, not by direct connections; the distinction between episodic and semantic memory is not respected. HAM can deal with many sentences that FRAN could not, but HAM does not ameliorate FRAN's reluctance to cluster conceptually related ideas.

Memory for a proposition is represented in HAM as a network of labeled associations between the words constituting the sentence (Rumelhart, Lindsay, and Norman, 1972, also analyze sentences into associative nets). Anderson and Bower say that these associations are functionally independent of one another and that any node is accessible from some other node if and only if there is a sequence of associations leading to it from the other node; they present evidence to support their claim that sentence memory does not depend on configurations of nodes. The evidence is not general, however: Foss and Harwood (1975) report results that cannot be explained by any purely associative theory like HAM—results they take as evidence that a more complex, configural theory of sentence memory is required.

FRAN and HAM provide lower bounds for the complexity of the system we are trying to characterize. It is instructive that an associative system can be shown to require more than just the information that two concepts are connected, either in secondary memory or in a list of propositions.

Smith, Shoben, and Rips (1974) observe that associative networks provide no way to account for nonequivalence of instances. Although connective links can establish, say, that a robin is a bird and a chicken is a bird, considerable complication would be required to represent the fact that a robin is a more typical bird than a chicken is, or to give any principled account of why people agree on this difference. Such an account would have to incorporate schematic similarities over and above the satisfaction of definitional criteria —birds characteristically fly, robins characteristically fly, but chickens do not characteristically fly. Clearly, a more complicated representation of the links between concepts is required; the simple two-term relation of association is insufficient.

Moreover, to record in the associative network no more than that "robin" and "chicken" are both hyponyms of "bird" provides no basis for distinguishing robins from chickens. One would like to list further distinguishing information along with the fact that a robin is a bird: it is a songbird, has a red breast, has gray and black upper plumage, lays pale blue eggs; whereas a chicken is large, domesticated, flightless, lays white or brown eggs, is used for food. How such information might be included in a network has been explored by Moore and Newell (1974) as part of an artificial-intelligence system called MERLIN.

MERLIN's basic data structure is called a β-structure. Its general form is α:[β α1 α2 . . .], which can be read as "α is a β further specified by α1, α2, . . ." For example, the memory might contain such β-structures as

> ROBIN: [SONGBIRD [BREAST RED] [WINGS GRAY-BLACK] . . .]
> SONGBIRD: [BIRD [SONG MELODIOUS] . . .]

β-structures play the same role in MERLIN that nodes play in a semantic associative network; Moore and Newell refer to the set of all β-structures as a knowledge net. A node may have a number of β-structures, or "alternate views," simultaneously. For example, one view of CHICKEN might record that it is a bird with certain distinguishing features, another view might record that it is food with distinguishing features appropriate to that category. Given some problem to solve, MERLIN can try alternative views in search of one that will succeed.

The basic operation on these nodes is to ask whether one node X can be viewed as another Y, which is represented as X/Y. If it were asked, given the β-structures listed above, whether a robin can be viewed as a songbird, the attempt would obviously succeed, since ROBIN is there expressed as a hyponym of SONGBIRD. If it were asked whether a robin can be viewed as a bird, the attempt would again succeed, yielding a new β-structure:

> ROBIN: [BIRD [SONG MELODIOUS] . . . [BREAST RED] [WINGS GRAY-
> BLACK]. . .].

This operation is quite powerful. It can be used, for example, to ask whether a problem can be viewed as a solution, that is, whether the β-structure that describes a goal G can be mapped into the β-structure that describes an existing situation s. The result of such a request may be nothing, if the problem cannot be solved, or it may be something like s:[G s1/G1 s2/G2 . . .] which says the present situation is the solution, providing the submappings si/Gi . . . are acceptable.

In such a knowledge network there is no restriction on the kinds of information that can be included in a node. Although the superordinate term is given special recognition, partonyms can be included and characteristic as well as defining criteria can be stated. Moreover, the basic operation exploits the transitivity of the network: if x/y and y/z, then x/z. Although MERLIN can solve simple problems in an apparently intelligent manner, no attempt has been made to replicate results of experimental studies of verbal learning. It should be obvious, however, that networks adequate to represent the general knowledge of a human being cannot—and need not—consist merely of undifferentiated nodes connected by unlabeled associations.

4.4.2   Associative Redundancy

An obvious defect of the method of cross-referencing concepts is that it would be enormously redundant. We have considered the possibility that if every W is a V, then a statement to that effect can be stored both in concept w and concept v. Under TABLE, for example, we could store the fact that a table is furniture and that a table is a thing. Under FURNITURE we could store the fact that a table is furniture and that furniture is a thing. And under THING we could store the fact that a table is a thing and that furniture is a thing. The absurdity of this solution becomes apparent as soon as we think of all the specific information that would be stored under THING. James Mill once wrote, while extolling the virtues of associationistic psychology, that his ideas of brick, mortar, position, and quantity were all associated in his idea of a wall, and that his idea of a wall was one of many ideas associated in his idea of a house. "How many complex ideas," he asked, "are all united in the idea of furniture? How many more in the idea of merchandize? How many more in the idea called Every Thing?" (Mill, 1829, quoted in Herrnstein and Boring, 1965, p. 377). We must avoid repeating that mistake. At the very least, cross-references should allow for transitivity.

Suppose we think of cross-references or associative links under the name some semanticists have given them, semantic markers. Semantic markers can be likened to references upward; each concept would include a list of all its superordinate concepts. This strategy eliminates any need to list specific instances under general items, to list, for example, all labels for things as part of the concept THING. Of course, the price for discarding this much of the redundancy of cross-referencing is the requirement to devise some special cognitive organ for discovering specific instances, given a general term. But if we had such a device, it might be possible to reduce the redundancy even further.

Consider the kind of redundancy we wish to avoid in terms of the following example: What is odd about saying that Jane is a female woman? The adjective "female" does not add anything that the noun "woman" does not already say. If we imagine that we have a concept WOMAN and another concept FEMALE—linked perhaps by cross-references of the form [ISA(WOMAN, FEMALE)]—we have not exploited the fact that the information needed to identify instances of FEMALE is also included in the information required to identify instances of WOMAN. It would seem more efficient to store it in only one place and to refer to it from the other.

The nature of the problem can be well stated in terms of the theory of semantic markers, a theory most fully developed in the work of J. J. Katz (Katz and Fodor, 1963; Katz, 1966, 1972; for a sympathetic evaluation of the relation of Katz's work to cognitive psychology, see Savin, 1973). The semantic "reading" of each word can be thought of as including a list of abstract semantic markers that serve to distinguish the meaning of that word from the meanings of all other words. When words are strung together grammatically to form sentences, a person who knows the language will know rules to combine these markers to construct a compound reading for the whole sentence. Although it is a mnemonic convenience to assign familiar names to these markers, they are not themselves words, but abstract concepts or properties; they may or may not be represented in English by single words.

In the simplest version of what a marker could be, we might have abstract features like "proper" and "count." (These are probably better classified as syntactic markers, but we will use them for illustration as if they were semantic). English nouns are generally divided into proper and common; this division can be characterized by a marker that can have one of two values: — Proper, or unmarked, would indicate common nouns, and + Proper, or marked, would indicate proper nouns. Thus, each noun would have a + or — marking for Proper. Common nouns might then be further classified as count or mass nouns: mass nouns ("virtue," "sugar," "furniture") would take — Count, and count nouns ("dog," "foot," "table") would take + Count. In this way various markers are defined and used to categorize meanings of words. For example, "female" might have the markers — Proper, + Count, + Living, + Female. "Woman" would have all the markers that "female" has, plus the markers +Animal and +Human. "Wife" would have all the markers that "woman" has, along with +Married. Since "female" does not add any semantic markers that are not already present in "woman" and "wife," saying "female woman" or "female wife" is redundant. (This description of the hierarchical relations between words suggests the psychological hypothesis that responses on word-association tests tend to be words that have many of the same semantic markers as the stimulus word; Marshall, 1969; Johnson, 1970; H. Clark, 1970.)

If we think of semantic markers as a more concise notation for what we have called cross-references between concepts, the problem of redundancy is simply this: all of the markers required to interpret "female" must also be included in the markers required to interpret "woman." Katz and Fodor suggest that this situation could be handled theoretically by assuming that there are certain "redundancy rules" that are not part of any particular concept but that are general rules the system can use to interpret a particular word. For example, if it is always true that +Human entails +Animal, this fact can be stated as a general redundancy rule, so that any words marked +Human need not be further marked as +Animal; if +Married entails +Human, then any word marked as +Married need not be further marked as either +Human or +Animal.

Redundancy rules summarize the most general hierarchical relations between concepts; their function is similar to that of Carnap's (1956) "meaning postulates." Is anything more than a system of redundancy rules required to account for the relations between words that we have called a semantic field? Katz (1972) has argued that shared markers capture all that is meant by this phrase. It should be noted, though, that semantic markers deal only with the hierarchy described by the "is a" relation. When we turn to the partonymic "has a" relation, the notion of semantic markers does not seem to have the same degree of generality; parts of objects may be specific to those objects and have little relevance in other lexical domains. Moreover, some different scheme of marking seems to be necessary in order to distinguish hyponymic from partonymic markers; otherwise a marking on "carburetor" of +Gasoline Engine might be taken to mean that a carburetor is a kind of, not a part of, a gasoline engine. The more explicit notation that we have used for cross-references between concepts does not encounter this difficulty, but the problem of redundancy remains.

Bever and Rosenbaum (1970) have argued on the basis of the "has a" relation (and other observations) that hierarchical structure plays such an important role in determining how words can be used together in sentences that it is necessary to have general rules that apply to whole hierarchies, not to particular words in a hierarchy. For example, it is acceptable to say that a rifle is more dangerous than a pistol, but there is something silly about saying that a rifle is more dangerous than a gun or that a gun is more dangerous than a rifle. A general rule is needed to prevent comparative constructions from combining superordinates and hyponyms, and it would be easier to state such a rule for all hierarchies than to repeat it explicitly in each one. Or, again, some rule is needed that will say: if a word cannot be used in a particular position in a particular sentence, no word dominated by it in the "is a" hierarchy can be used. It is more efficient to state such rules for hierarchies as a whole than to leave them implicit in the redundancy rules of a marker system for individual concepts. But that implies the existence of cognitive entities of a hierarchical nature to which such rules can refer.

One of the psychological arguments for the intimate integration of hierarchically related concepts is the speed with which you can move back and forth between "is a" and "has a" relations. For example, you have no difficulty in understanding that if every mammal has a face, and if a kangaroo is a mammal, then a kangaroo has a face; if a face has a nose, then a kangaroo has a nose. Yet you can avoid such mistakes as claiming that an arm has a knee on the grounds that an arm is a limb, a limb has a joint, and a knee is a joint. This kind of logic flows easily, in sharp contrast to other kinds of logical inferences. We assume that such *lexical* inferences are made by executing an infer(x, y) instruction. The key to the smoothness of their operation is the structural organization of lexical information.

Bever and Rosenbaum point to the difference between "the boy's knee aches" and "The statue's knee aches." The verb "aches" requires an animate noun as subject. Since "knee" is acceptable as the subject of "aches" in one case and unacceptable in the other, we assume that "knee" cannot be marked as +Animate but inherits that marker from "boy" in the acceptable case and does not inherit it from "statue" in the unacceptable case. The oddity of "The statue's knee aches" arises from information that is not contained in the labeling routine for "knee" but is inherited from "statue" via the partonymic hierarchy or imposed on "knee" by "aches," so that in this context "knee" becomes incompatible with "aches." In either case, it is as if the entire hierarchy were immediately available to provide the required information.

The problem, to state it once again, is that although the hyponymic and partonymic hierarchies can be defined in terms of "is a" or "has a" relations between pairs of concepts, the hierarchical structure seems to be appreciated as a whole. What we need is some way to activate a hierarchy of concepts simultaneously. When a language user masters his vocabulary he organizes it into memory structures in such a way that whenever a particular concept in that structure is activated, the whole structure becomes activated and available to attention. It is as if every word in the structure were a part of the meaning of every other word—and that is what has generally been meant by a semantic field.

What we have to account for is how memory is organized in order to avoid associative redundancy. The system is somehow capable of recognizing such redundancies and organizing itself to take advantage of them. The results of this organization manifest themselves as semantic fields—groups of lexical concepts integrated by their relative positions in a more abstract concept. We will speak of the conceptual core of a semantic field as this more abstract idea that integrates the various lexical concepts designating different aspects of it.

Our technical terminology is growing; let us attempt to recapitulate it. Figure 4.4 illustrates the relations between the main terms. A lexical concept

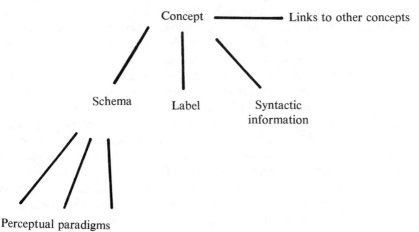

Figure 4.4 Relations between some technical terms.

consists of a label ("table"), a schema, and rules for the syntactic behavior of the label. (Indeed, in this case one may speak of a word rather than a label.) The schema consists of functional and perceptual information, and integrates whatever perceptual paradigms there are for the object. It is entirely possible that the schema will include memorial information that has no direct perceptual consequences. Indeed, in the case of certain schemata, there may be no perceptual paradigms whatsoever ("truth," "justice," "value"). Concepts are not isolated entities; they are related to one another to form semantic fields (their corresponding labels form a lexical field). Although such relations between concepts could, hypothetically, be haphazard or arbitrary, in fact they are not. Relations between lexical concepts in the same field appear to be a consequence of a deeper, more abstract conceptualization of the world, a conceptualization that for a given semantic field may be termed the conceptual core. The core is more abstract than an associative network of relatively independent concepts linked in pairs, or even a superordinate system of redundancy rules for eliminating transitive relations from the network.

Given the diversity of abstract ideas underlying semantic fields, it is impossible to be more specific about the nature of a conceptual core without considering examples. We will begin with the example of furniture, since we have already discussed the analysis of "table." All we learn from the dictionary is that furniture is "the movable articles in a room or establishment that render it fit for living or working." There is no perceptual essence of furniture that can be captured in a single perceptual paradigm. The question is whether there is a single simple schema for furniture.

James Hampton (personal communication) asked English-speaking people a series of questions about how they conceive of furniture. The first question was: "What generally important characteristics do you feel may be relevant to deciding if something is a piece of furniture or not?" Of the thirty-two people who answered this question, twenty-eight mentioned that furniture is used by people for a specific function or purpose, twenty-two that it is found in buildings, eleven that it is for sitting on, ten that it is for putting things on, eight that it is used for personal comfort, convenience, or satisfaction, seven that it is wooden, four that it is decorative, three that it is man-made, and one that it has legs. (These response classes are not mutually exclusive, of course.) From a series of such questions Hampton constructed a list of features that he applied to thirty object labels, ranging from objects that are clearly articles of furniture (sofa, table, stool, bed, lamp, dresser, crib) to articles about which people might disagree (television, shelf, carpet, mirror, hammock, clock, wastepaper basket, curtains, vase, picture, refrigerator, lights, radio) to articles that would probably not be thought of as furniture (ashtray, trunk, sewing machine, door, desk blotter, hutch, ladder, secretary, van). Then he measured the reaction times of people who were asked to respond from one (definitely yes) to seven (definitely no) as to whether each of these words labeled an article of furniture. For example, all thirty people tested gave "one" as their response to "table" with a latency of 1.39 seconds; twelve gave "one" in response to "shelf" with a latency of 1.73 seconds; nine gave "one" to "clock" with a latency of 2.69 seconds; and no one gave "one" to "van." According to Hampton's feature evaluation, a table possesses ten of the eleven features people think of as characteristic of furniture, a shelf has eight, a clock has seven, a van has three.

No single feature that Hampton elicited is sufficient to distinguish all articles of furniture from everything else. Perhaps people judge that an object is furniture if the number of features exceeds some threshold, or if the sum of the weights associated with the features exceeds some threshold (see Smith, Shoben, and Rips, 1974). Alternatively, people may define "furniture" in terms of a disjunctive list, and the features they give in response to questions like Hampton's may be abstracted from subsets of different sizes, that is, may be characteristic of many but not all items on the list.

This hypothesis suggests that we analyze FURNITURE as a disjunctive list— that we list explicitly the schemata for particular articles of furniture:

(10)   FURNITURE(x): TABLE(x), or SEAT(x), or CUPBOARD(x), or
         BED(x), . . .

This schema would be of little use, of course, if a person had not already mastered the schemata TABLE, SEAT, CUPBOARD, BED, . . . However, it is possible to know that a label belongs on the list—that it labels an article of furniture—without having a schema for it. For example, a person may know that "commode" labels an article of furniture without knowing what it looks like or is used for; the list may include labels that lack schemata. A more crucial difficulty with (10) is that a person may recognize a novel item as an article of furniture without having a specific label for it or any certain knowledge of its particular function.

There are many general terms in English that have this quasi-disjunctive character: foods, animals, flowers, toys, tools, clothing. Wittgenstein (1953) used games as an example; he apparently believed there was an important philosophical lesson to be learned from the fact that nothing is common to all games. If one thinks of such concepts as having extended disjunctive schemata, there must be something that indicates which schemata can be included in such an enumeration and which cannot. Wittgenstein spoke of "family resemblances" (p. 32). It is surely no accident that English does not have a word "bittler," say, defined by an arbitrary disjunction: table or heel or glove or carburetor or hammer. Whatever it is that constrains the disjunctive list enables a person to identify novel instances; we refer to it as the conceptual core.

4.4.3 Taxonomies, Keys, and Decision Tables

Students of classification—see, for example, Simpson (1961) on animal taxonomy, Conklin (1964) on ethnographic classification, or Dunnell (1971) on archaeological classification—draw an important distinction between what they call a key, which is used for identification, and the system of taxonomic concepts on which a key is based. Once a conceptual analysis is accepted, a key can be constructed as a mechanical aid in assigning particular samples to various categories defined by that analysis. A key cannot replace a conceptual classification.

For example, the theory of evolution provides a conceptual scheme in terms of which fossils can be classified. The conceptual scheme derives from observations of living species, from geological information, from studies of genetics and mechanisms of inheritance and mutation, from hypotheses about fertility and environmental pressures, and much more. When a new fossil is to be identified—when its position in the evolutionary scheme relative to other fossils is to be determined—most of this information on the basis of which the theory was constructed becomes irrelevant. What is needed then is a key, which will usually be arranged as a program of questions about the characteristics of the fossil that the scientist should ask in a certain order. Each question will usually tell him which branch to take through the key, which questions to ask next. When he has proceeded through all of the questions, the key will provide him with the label that identifies that particular fossil. If it is a fossil of some kind that has never been seen before, the key will usually be unable to deal with it—at some point the key may start posing unanswerable questions —but a scientist who knows the theory will be able to make an educated guess as to the correct place to assign a novel fossil, and he may write a scholarly article describing his discovery and its implications (if any) for the general theory.

Since good keys are important in the daily work of many scientists, much effort has been invested in designing and developing them. Some keys are better for some purposes than others; it is rare to find a single key that will serve every classificatory need. A key for identifying insects in North America would not be useful for African insects, even though they would both be based on the same underlying biological concepts. There is considerable latitude available to a key builder in selecting features to ask questions about, in ordering the questions, and in arranging the labels, so there is no hope of finding the unique key most suitable to any particular theory—there are always many keys possible for the same purpose, and certainly there are alternative keys for different purposes. In this respect, keys are very unlike the theories on which they are based; given alternative (and nonequivalent) theories, we are inclined to believe that one must be nearer to the truth than another. It is one of the great practical advantages of a key that all the conceptual baggage essential to the theory but irrelevant for identification can be stripped away.

This general distinction between a taxonomy and a key may be adapted to our discussion of how labels are assigned to objects in more familiar situations. The taxonomy that derives from a general theory corresponds to what we have called the conceptual core; the key that is used to identify instances corresponds to an integrated set of schemata. If we are willing to assume that speakers of English have an intuitive understanding of the underlying theory, we can proceed to devise keys that would be hypotheses about how the native speaker of English assigns labels to objects and events.

The important difference between our enterprise and that of a conventional taxonomist is that we would like to know the "true" key, the key that people really use. Ethnologists, who have been exploiting this analogy for several years, have discovered that it is not always easy to decide whether some identification procedure is "god's truth" or "hocus-pocus" (Burling, 1964). For example, it cannot be settled on the basis of an intuitive understanding of the conceptual basis for the classification, since the same conceptual core can be respected by a variety of different identification procedures. It can be settled, presumably, by empirical methods—by collecting intuitive impressions from many speakers and analyzing them, by measuring reaction times or noting confusions between labels in use or in memory—if one is willing to spend the time and effort required. Before one can test the psychological validity of an identification scheme, however, the scheme must be stated explicitly. Some have been, and we hope to provide more.

In order to understand what we are doing, it is essential to bear in mind the distinction between the conceptual core and the integrated schemata that we will provide. This task is all the more difficult because we have yet to describe either in detail. The conceptual core of FURNITURE can be considered to be a master plan for integrating schemata, but it should not be confused with the actual resulting set of integrated schemata. The problem that we now address is how schemata may be integrated so as to make for the efficient identification of objects. In 4.4.4 we will take up the question of how the conceptual core might be formulated.

It is possible to suggest a compact representation for the information required for integrating schemata—not a description of any structure we might imagine to exist in the brain, but an abstract characterization of the kind of information that we believe must be represented, however it may be realized.

In order to illustrate some relations among alternative ways of stating the same key a simple example may be helpful. Suppose that there is an imaginary world in which there are only three kinds of things, called chairs, tables, and beds, and that only two perceptual judgments (which can be either satisfied or not) are required to distinguish among them: if a thing has a SEAT, it is called a chair, but if it does not have a SEAT, it is called a table if it has a WORKTOP and a bed if it does not have a WORKTOP. This classification can be represented in the usual manner of writing keys:

KEY:
  (i) Does it have a SEAT? If so, call it a chair; if not, go to (ii).
  (ii) Does it have a WORKTOP? If so, call it a table; if not, call it a bed.

The same procedure can be represented in a flowchart of the kind used to summarize the logic involved in writing computer programs. In figure 4.5 the flowchart corresponding to this key has been drawn in order to illustrate that it is merely an alternative representation of exactly the same identification process. People familiar with flowcharts usually feel that the graphic display enables them to discover more quickly what is going on, but such charts require some skill and patience in drafting, particularly when the system gets large and complex or involves recursions. A computer programmer often

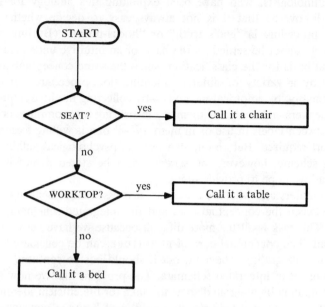

Figure 4.5   Flowchart for an identification procedure.

begins his work by laying out the logic in a flowchart that he can use to guide him in writing a program of instructions for the computer; the program will then bear much the same relation to the flowchart as the key given above bears to figure 4.5.

A decision table (Pollock, 1971) is usually viewed as an alternative to a flowchart when one is organizing the logic of a process to be programmed. It is more or less the engineering cousin of the logician's truth table. For example, a logician might write the tautology A or $(\text{not}A \ \& \ B)$ or $(\text{not}A \ \& \ \text{not}B)$, where A denotes "it has a SEAT" and B denotes "it has a WORKTOP." If A is true, call it a chair; if $(\text{not}A \ \& \ B)$ is true, call it a table; if $(\text{not}A \ \& \ \text{not}B)$ is true, call it a bed. This logic can be represented in a decision table:

Decision table

	1	2	3
Conditions			
(i) It has a SEAT?	Y	N	N
(ii) It has a WORKTOP?		Y	N
Actions			
"chair"	x		
"table"		x	
"bed"			x

The three numbered columns of the decision table can be thought of as three different rules, where each rule corresponds to a different possible path through the flowchart. In rule 1, for example, if condition (i) is satisfied—which is indicated by "Y" (yes) in the table—then the action marked "x" in that column can be taken—the object can be called a chair. The blank space in the table opposite condition (ii) in rule 1 means that the action to be taken is indifferent to the outcome; a yes or a no answer will lead to the same action. In a sense, rule 1 is really two rules. The truth tables of the propositional calculus can be represented in this form by taking the propositions p and q as the conditions and the various compound propositions—$p \& q$, p or q, $p \supset q$ —as the actions.

The narrative description, the key, the flowchart, the truth table, and the decision table all say the same thing; we can translate freely from one to the other. For our present purposes, however, the decision table has a distinct advantage in that it does not constrain the sequential order in which the process must be realized. In both the key and the flowchart, order is fixed: first test SEAT, then test WORKTOP. The opposite order of testing would give a different key and a different flowchart, although they would be functionally equivalent to the ones presented above. In a decision table, on the other hand, conditions can be listed in any order; all that is required is that the action taken must depend on the pattern of yes and no given by its rule. Thus, a decision table provides a more abstract representation of the decision process than a key or flowchart does.

The advantages of this abstractness are obvious. If a psychologist uses a flowchart to represent his hypothesis concerning a cognitive activity that he believes must occur when people perform certain kinds of information processing, he is forced to make definite (and often arbitrary) decisions about the order in which successive operations are performed. Since there is some reason to suspect that parallel operation is possible in the brain, these requirements of sequencing may be unrealistic. A decision table, by corresponding equally well to all equivalent flowcharts of the same process, enables a theorist to characterize his system without committing himself as to whether the information processing is done serially or in parallel, or, if serially, in which order.

The disadvantage of decision tables is that they tend to grow exponentially with the number of conditions included. With two conditions, each having one of two outcomes, there are four possible rules; with ten binary conditions, there are 1,024 possible rules. Ten conditions each having three possible outcomes would yield 59,049 rules to be considered. As we saw in the example above, a decision may be indifferent to some combinations of conditions, which can reduce the number of rules, so these numbers are upper limits. Yet the exponential specter is always lurking in the background, and careless use of blanks to indicate indifference can easily lead to contradictions or ambiguities. There is good reason, therefore, to make the number of conditions as small as possible—but this restriction limits the number of actions that can be related in a single table.

Fortunately, there is a compromise between decision tables and flowcharts that enables us to factor a problem into subparts. The device we need is called table linkage. To take a trivial example, let us factor the decision table given above into two tables:

Decision table (i)

	1	2
Condition		
It has a SEAT?	Y	N
Actions		
"chair"	x	
call decision table (ii)		x

Decision table (ii)

	1	2
Condition		
It has a WORKTOP?	Y	N
Actions		
"table"	x	
"bed"		x

The second decision table is linked to the first by the action "call decision table (ii)" in the first table. Note that we now have a tabular version of the flowchart in figure 4.5; by splitting the larger table into two smaller ones, we have imposed an order on the performance of tests for SEAT and WORKTOP. Note also that if we had imposed the reverse order, we would have needed three decision tables (just as the corresponding flowchart would require three conditional diamonds), because the outcome of condition (ii) alone is insufficient to determine a decision.

If we were faced with ten binary conditions, we could handle five of them (thirty-two possible rules) in one table and use "call table two," "call table three," . . . , up to, at worst, "call table thirty-three." Under the worst condition, there would be no savings in this division, but if it is possible to analyze the total process into relatively independent subprocesses, then decision table (i) can often be used as a traffic officer to decide which other table is to be consulted. The result can be thought of as a flowchart having decision tables at each branch point. When the subdivision is carried to the limit—to one condition per table—the result is simply a flowchart of the familiar kind. The usual solution is a compromise that imposes a little sequential constraint in order to reduce the number of rules that must be dealt with in any given decision table.

The effect of a "call" action is to transfer control to the decision table that is referred to; control will not be returned to the first table. Recursion is possible if a table calls itself. It is also possible to have a "do" action that returns control to the first table when the work of the second is done, so the first table continues with the next action in that column. Obviously, care must be taken in ordering such actions, but borrowing these tricks from the programmer greatly increases the flexibility of decision tables.

Some of these ideas can be used in order to construct an integrated set of perceptual paradigms for a more realistic analysis of FURNITURE. Obviously, a person will not attempt to identify something as FURNITURE unless it satisfies the predicate THING. Thus, it seems likely that the initial decision table will simply determine, granted that the THING predicate is satisfied, which of a number of fairly broad domains should be consulted for further analysis— furniture, vehicles, utensils, tools, clothes, and so on. The list is so enormous that it is difficult to know where to begin. We will simply assume that a percept is referred to the initial decision table for FURNITURE in order to undergo further analysis. Such a table is likely to have the general format (though we have simplified many details) of table 4.3.

At the next level there are clearly a number of separate decision tables, and we have illustrated only one, the decision table for SEAT (table 4.4). The four conditions in this table are virtually self-explanatory, but we should explain that FORONE(x) denotes that a seat has a width for one person only.

A number of points should be made about table 4.4. First, it by no means exhausts the schemata for seats. Many of the entries (such as, CHAIR) would, in fact, call additional decision tables for a more refined analysis. Second, the conditions and actions of a decision table are essentially assertions. The conditions become perceptual tests only by virtue of the use of a decision table in an identifying routine, or a routine that is searching for a particular sort of percept. In trying to find a particular kind of seat such as a chair the system would enter the table at the entry CHAIR(x) and then retrieve its required set of perceptual tests: find(Env, G$(?x?)$), where G in this case would involve

Table 4.3   A decision table for FURNITURE(x).

	1	2	3	4
Conditions				
c1. PPRT$(x,$ SEAT$)$	Y	N	N	N
c2. PPRT$(x,$ WORKTOP$)$		Y		N
c3. INTSURF(x, y) & EXTSURF(x, z)		N	Y	N
Actions				
a1. call table for SEAT(x)	x			
a2. call table for TABLE(x)		x		
a3. call table for CUPBOARD(x)			x	
a4. call table for BED(x) or ORNAMENT(x) or ...				x

Table 4.4   A decision table for SEAT(x).

	1	2	3	4	5	6	7	8	9	10	11	12
Conditions												
c1. FORONE(x)	N	N	N	N	N	Y	Y	Y	Y	Y	Y	Y
c2. PPRT(x, BACKREST)	Y	Y	Y	N	N	Y	Y	Y	N	N	N	N
c3. UPHOLSTERED(x)	Y	N	N			Y	N	N	Y	Y	N	N
c4. PPRT(x, LEG)	Y	N	Y	N		Y	N	Y	N	Y	N	N
Actions												
a1. SOFA(x)	x											
a2. PARKBENCH(x)		x										
a3. PEW(x)			x									
a4. BENCH(x)				x	x							
a5. PIANOBENCH(x)				x								
a6. CHAIR(x)						x	x	x				
a7. KITCHENCHAIR(x)							x					
a8. STOOL(x)									x		x	
a9. FOOTSTOOL(x)									x	x		
a10. OTTOMAN(x)										x		
a11. exit												x

PPRT(x, BACKREST) and FORONE(x) and, by reverting to the FURNITURE decision table, PPRT(x, SEAT). It is for such reasons that table linkage must provide a link in both directions between decision tables; hence, we assume that an entry such as "do decision table x" sets up a simple class-inclusion link that can be traversed in either direction.

Careful examination of all possible situations characterized by a given set of conditions and the words appropriate in each can discipline a semanticist's imagination. But that service in itself would not provide sufficient reason to publish the tabulations. The broader import of the decision table for SEAT(x) is that it is a concise summary of the results of a semantic analysis. Not only does a decision table display in compact form the hypothesized relations among several words in a semantic subfield, but the use of a decision table—the execution of the conditions it contains—can be thought of as a hypothesis about the way semantically related words are activated simultaneously by the occurrence of any one of them. A speaker can enter this information structure by testing its conditions and find a word or words corresponding to the pattern of outcomes. A listener can enter it with a word and gain access to conditions that relate it to others in the same semantic subfield. In addition to the particular semantic analysis that it contains, the decision table illustrates how we believe a complex cognitive organ might be described: it is a specific realization of how schemata can be integrated.

What the decision table for SEAT establishes is that the integration of furniture schemata is not as tight as might occur in an idealized language. The set of terms "sofa," "park bench," "pew," and so on, do not form a precise contrastive set; as the table shows, an article of furniture may be correctly labeled "footstool" or "ottoman." This state of affairs—a structure part contrastive, part hierarchical—is probably more typical of the lexicon than a neat regimentation of minimal contrastive sets into a hierarchy. One way to look at it is to consider that although language allows a speaker to label anything there are often lexical gaps. There is no contrastive pair of terms in English, for instance, that distinguish between benches that have legs and benches that have end supports. There is no term for items that have yet to be constructed. Among the possible objects that the conditions of the table for SEAT permit are: an object that consists of legs and a backrest but no seat; an object that consists solely of an upholstered worktop. English has no terms for these objects— though some might label the latter item a "bed"—because they do not exist.

A further consequence of a partial contrastive set is that a speaker will often find that he has a choice of words, represented by multiple occurrences of "x" in the same column of the table. As decision tables are ordinarily used, all actions that are marked must be taken, usually in the order they are listed. That is, the actions (as well as the conditions) are thought of conjunctively. In this respect, our practice will differ from the custom: the conditions are thought of conjunctively, but the actions (insofar as they are lexical elements) are thought of disjunctively. This convention leaves the speaker with a further decision to make: Which word or combination of words that the conditions allow should he use? The control instruction "identify" presumably contains subroutines that, given the discourse context, look for the shortest phrasing adequate to distinguish the particular object from all the others in the search domain.

A hearer seems to face a similar variety of alternatives. He may hear that something is a chair and not know which of the rules in the decision table was the basis for the speaker's choice. His dilemma is more apparent than real, however. He does not need to know precisely what led the speaker to use the word. If he wishes to find the chair that the speaker is talking about, he can search the domain (perceptual or memorial) with the four conditions active in order to determine whether any pattern satisfying CHAIR is realized; the word "chair" serves merely to indicate the semantic subfield whose decision table is appropriate.

We have said that decision tables can be translated into programs. Indeed, one of their principal uses is in computer programming, and there are "preprocessors" available that take a decision table written in a prescribed format and translate it into a program of instructions that can be run on a machine. This possibility can be used to redeem our earlier claim (sec. 3.4) that learning to use words is a matter of learning to execute routines that include them— but now the claim can be put in a more complex form than we could defend initially. The kind of routines that result from these decision tables are executed more or less automatically; the voluntary control instructions that are operating at an executive level do not become involved directly in these retrieval operations. It is at this lower level of relatively fixed routines that the system collects all of the relevant information required by the higher-level "instruct" instruction (3.5.7). What use the system makes of the results of these lower-level procedures depends on pragmatic considerations—on the general situation and the goals of the system at the time.

Decision tables provide a useful way to conceive interrelations between schemata. They can be linked so as to accommodate conceptual relations in a semantic field, and in this way they provide a parsimonious solution to the problem of associative redundancy. What is yet to be explained is the process by which knowledge comes to be structured in a way that can be captured by a decision table.

Consider, for example, that "chicken" has a place in the lexical fields for both birds and foods, and that "piano" has a place in the lexical fields for both musical instruments and articles of furniture. What changes when we think of such words in one sense or the other is not their denotation but the conceptual context in which they are located.

4.4.4 Conceptual Core

Conceptual theories of semantics posit both extensional and intensional rules for assigning meanings to expressions. We have discussed how extensional rules might be formulated in terms of shared perceptual and functional conditions for the identification of instances. Our next task is to consider how intensional rules might be organized and how their organization relates to the organization of extensional rules.

When we introduced keys to illustrate identification devices, we contrasted them with the scientific theories on which keys are based. We will try to use this contrast to suggest how the intensional component of the system should be characterized. That is to say, we will take scientific theories as our model for the conceptual core of a semantic field.

In adopting this model, we do not wish to imply that it is impossible to use words correctly unless one knows all the scientific theories about their referents. We would argue only that the layman has some kind of theory—"prototheory" might be a better term—that plays a role in his ordinary use of language that is in some sense analogous to the role theories play in scientific discourse. Since the view of man as a problem solver, doing daily at a simpler level what scientists try to do with sophistication, has been important in the history of cognitive psychology, the line we are taking does not break with tradition. The view we hold is probably more familiar in cognitive anthropology, however, where lay theories of animal and plant taxonomies have been studied for many years.

The layman's theories frozen in his vocabulary probably express general points of view that provide starting positions for the development of scientific theories. As science advances, the meanings of words can change as a consequence of increasing knowledge—Feyerabend (1962) notes the shift from a unidirectional meaning of "up" to an earth-centered meaning when the flat-earth hypothesis was abandoned. Or science may introduce new words;

"mammal" was inserted between "dog" and "animal" when animals were systematically cataloged. Such changes do not alter the denotation of words already familiar, but they do reflect profound changes in meaning—in the conceptual core underlying those words.

Characterizing a conceptual core as a prototheory says almost nothing about its structure or organization. What little it does say is that conceptual cores must come in all shapes and sizes, just as scientific theories do, and, perhaps, that they are subject to disproof. One would not say that a language can be disproved; language can be used to express true or false concepts, but the language itself is not true or false. When one looks at the concepts that a language can express, though, the picture changes, for then it is of considerable practical importance to determine whether one's conceptions are correct. So to speak of core concepts as verifiable, in the sense that scientific theories are verifiable, does not seem inappropriate. But in order to gain a deeper appreciation of the structure of core concepts expressed in the lexicon, we must examine particular concepts. Chapters 5, 6, and 7 will do precisely that, and we will return to these questions after analyzing some core concepts of English. For the present, however, we are forced to speak in generalities.

We assume that a semantic field consists of a lexical field and a conceptual core. A lexical field is organized both by shared conditions determining the denotations of its words and by a conceptual core, by the meanings of what the words denote. A conceptual core is an organized representation of general knowledge and beliefs about whatever objects or events the words denote— about what they are and do, what can be done with them, how they are related, what they relate to. This lexical-conceptual relation is complex. To say that a lexical field covers a conceptual core like a mosaic is suggestive, but it greatly oversimplifies.

The mosaic metaphor captures much that is important: it is only in terms of the core that the choice of particular conditions to identify instances can be rationalized; it is only in terms of the core that a particular lexical concept can be assigned a location relative to other lexical concepts in that field. But that is not all we need to say about the lexical-conceptual relation. It is also necessary to realize that a conceptual core is an inchoate theory about something and that the same lexical field can cover very different theories. In particular, we must keep in mind that it is only in terms of the core that lexical concepts can be generalized and extended, or nonliteral uses of words interpreted. The mosaic can be stretched in some directions and not others; which stretchings can be interpreted depends not on the mosaic but on the conceptualization it covers. Theories of linguistic relativity to the contrary, thought is not forever bound by the words in which it must be expressed.

Discussions of the nonliteral use of language, both in literature and science, are too extensive and controversial for review here. But even a limited exposure to these discussions suffices to establish that figurative language is not the special province of creative writers. Indeed, some linguists have argued that metaphorical extensions are a basic means whereby languages change and grow; the observation is not limited to languages with recorded bodies of literature. The lexical mosaic is constantly being stretched to cover more than it should; these stretchings are important, and to understand them we need some account of their conceptual bases. In order to explain why some extensions are seen as apt and others merely confusing, for example, we would need to formulate rules for construing them. At present, we know almost nothing about such rules, because we know almost nothing about the conceptual structures in terms of which the rules would have to be formulated.

Grammar characterizes the major dimension of creativity in language; explaining the limitless variety of grammatical sentences in any natural language poses a central question—if not *the* central question—for linguistic and psycholinguistic theories. But grammar does not exhaust the creative potential of language; the enormous variety of metaphorical extensions in any natural language poses a similar question at a different level of description. Whereas grammatical productivity is the result of combinatorial possibilities inherent in phrases and sentences, conceptual productivity is the result of combinatorial possibilities inherent in lexical and sentential concepts. Although grammatical and conceptual productivity usually work hand in hand, it is not always so. Syntax admits combinations that are conceptually vacuous and thought admits combinations that are grammatically inadmissible. How the bounds of admissibility are extended is critical for any psychologist interested in thought and cognition.

Although metaphorical extensions provide the most spectacular evidence that a conceptual core is not an idle foundation for a lexical field, there are more mundane consequences of the lexical-conceptual relation that should not be overlooked. We have spoken in almost platonic terms of conceptual cores, as if they existed in an ideal form independent of actual people. Indeed, we have argued that people who speak the same language must share core concepts implicit in the lexicon of that language. But we would not go so far as to argue that shared concepts have any significant existence independent of the people who share them. And insofar as a concept is a personal thing, we must be prepared for individual differences. If we are to understand many of the failures of communication between people, we must insist on individual differences. But conceptual differences are usually peripheral ones, not core. For example, using "doggie" to label a cat indicates a difference in conceptual refinement, not in the core concept; using "doggie" to ask for a drink of water violates the core concept.

As long as people respect the conceptual core, as long as they agree what the core is a theory of, there is room for considerable difference concerning the details and explicitness of their prototheories. It is even possible that in many situations these differences will offer no impediment to successful communication—one would have to devise special circumstances to discover that a conversational partner was using "up" unidirectionally rather than relative to the center of the earth. Probably the most important source of individual differences in conceptualization is differences in age and education.

If adults could not extend their literal interpretations of utterances, they would have great difficulty understanding young children. (And, as Mac-namara, 1972, has noted, the child must be able to return the favor.) Take a typical example: a child touches a briefcase and says "Daddy." A literal interpretation would be that the child is naming the object, in which case the child has made a fundamental error about the core concept underlying "daddy." The parent must judge the likelihood of such an error. If it is highly unlikely that a core confusion has occurred, the next interpretation would be that the child is offering an assertion to the effect that this object and the individual referred to as "daddy" have frequently occurred contiguously in the past. If the parent has recently observed similar assertions from the child, it may even be justifiable to conclude that the child is attempting to assert a possessive relation but has not yet mastered the linguistic signals used to express that concept. (A psychologist might want controlled observations before drawing conclusions about the child's concept of ownership, but successful communication between parent and child can proceed on a more inconclusive basis.) As the child develops, his conception of possessive relations between people and things will undergo many enrichments and refinements, but lack of the adult concept does not block conversation with adults.

Students of child language and cognitive development face the problem of finding ways to determine what a child's concepts—his "protoprototheories" —really are at any stage. If lexical-conceptual relations were always simple, a child's concepts might be inferred directly from what he says. But because a child uses much the same lexicon to cover conceptual cores that are rather different from those most adults hold, the psychologist has to contrive situations in which conceptual differences behind linguistic similarities can become apparent.

Children begin learning their first language by acquiring a heterogeneous variety of relatively specific routines for applying labels and for using simple utterances. At first, therefore, their lexical information may well be in a relatively unorganized state that might be represented by independent lexical entries. As this information accumulates, it begins to organize around simple conceptual cores. Probably the psychological integration of the lexicon must await developments in the conceptual realm that are only indirectly reflected in language (Slobin, 1971). But how the learning proceeds—how core concepts are acquired to relate lexical items and how lexical items are acquired to be related—is still poorly understood. The two kinds of learning, lexical and conceptual, must reinforce each other, but the details differ from word to word, from concept to concept, and from child to child.

Consider the lexical field of animal terms, which has a relatively simple hierarchical organization. Lexical evidence indicates that people do not usually talk of people as animals—evolutionary continuity is an insight not yet integrated into lay theory. The lay theory might be characterized as having a superordinate concept of "living things" partitioned into many hyponymic domains: people, animals, birds, fish, snakes, bugs, plants, where "animal" is understood as covering the range of living things more accurately denoted by the technical term "mammal." A child must first learn this lay theory; with further education he may learn the scientific theory.

The child begins with a relatively clear notion of "person." Other varieties of living things must be differentiated from people, but "person" seems to provide a focal concept. According to S. Carey (personal communication), a young child's uncertainty in answering various questions about animals increases as the morphological differences between the animals and people increase, but at first there is no recognition of defining conditions. That is, the child's uncertainty about the answers to "Does this bug have bones?" and "Does this bug eat?" are roughly equivalent; he does not seem to know that all animals must eat but that only some have bones. His answers can be understood as involving a judgment of the creature's similarity to people; if he judges the similarity great enough, he believes the creature has whatever properties people have.

If this characterization of the initial state is correct, then a child's task is to learn the scope of various conditions that differentiate living things into the classes recognized in the English lexicon. We are unable to describe this learning in detail, but comparison with the adult concept indicates that "animal" must expand to include mammals, birds, fish, and bugs, and eventually even people, but not plants, with a concomitant sharpening of definitional criteria for various kinds of animals. As these conceptual changes occur, more and more animal terms are added to the lexicon, each being given its location according to the prevailing conceptual core.

According to this description, the core concept is "living thing," which undergoes progressive change as a function of learning. But is this all there is to the core concept? What about the concept of class inclusion? The child is learning that collies are dogs and that dogs are animals. Does not such learning imply that the child is also learning another core concept, the ISA concept? Is not ISA what really integrates animal terms into a semantic field?

The account of semantic memory that we have given requires us to take the position that ISA is not a core concept. ISA is *not* what the child is learning but is a consequence of what he is learning. The child is developing a prototheory about living things and is using it as a basis to determine appropriate conditions governing the assertibility of various animal terms. Class inclusion has nothing to do with animals. Once the semantic field is mastered, reflection on what has been learned can support the development of an ISA concept, but that is a derivative concept, not part of the core concept ANIMAL. Whatever knowledge a child gains of ISA in the course of learning animal terms is implicit. As in the case of grammatical rules, logical rules of class inclusion and transitivity become explicit only with formal education, and even their implicit use seems to depend on prior learning from which they can be abstracted.

If this view is correct, ISA should develop relatively late, and there is considerable evidence that it does. The following well-known passage from Piaget (1947) illustrates the kind of observations that have been made:

To study the formation of classes, we place about twenty beads in a box, the subject acknowledging that they are "all made of wood", so that they constitute a whole, B. Most of these beads are brown and constitute part A, and some are white, forming the complementary part A'. In order to determine whether the child is capable of understanding the operation A + A' = B, i.e., the uniting of parts in a whole, we may put the following simple question: In this box (all the beads still being visible) which are there more of—wooden beads or brown beads, i.e., is A < B?

Now, up to about the age of 7 years, the child almost always replies that there are more brown beads "because there are only two or three white ones." We then question further: "Are all the brown ones made of wood?"—"Yes"—"If I take away all the wooden beads and put them here (a second box) will there be any beads left in the (first) box?"—"No, because they are all made of wood." —"If I take away the brown ones, will there be any beads left?"— "Yes, the white ones." Then the original question is repeated and the subject continues to state that there are more brown beads than wooden ones in the box because there are only two white ones, etc." (P. 133)

Apparently it is possible for children to understand each of the independent referents without relating them appropriately, that is, without appreciating class inclusion. Piaget comments that when a child centers his attention on part A he destroys the whole, B; he is able to attend to B alone, or to A + A' alone, but not to both at the same time. The relation of class inclusion is not inherent in the individual definitions of any of the terms it relates but is an implicit consequence of their being embedded in a conceptual field. When this abstract relation is appreciated, complex inferences can be based on it; when it is not, even a simple one-step inference may fail. But appreciating it is not a necessary condition for learning hyponymically related words.

It is unlikely that the abstract idea of class inclusion could emerge from extensive overlearning of the particular lexical concepts involved. According to this line of argument, not only must a child have labeling routines for wooden, white, and brown beads, but he must be able to stand back from those specific concepts and see a more general relation between them; it is not a view he would acquire by virtue of more training on individual labeling routines.

Such observations of young children are often used by those who would conclude that children are unable to understand relations. ISA develops late, they say, not because it is derivative but because it is relational. This is a bold conclusion in view of the fact that children are heavily dependent on relations, not absolute values, within perceptual frames of reference. Indeed, Bryant (1974) has proposed a different conclusion, that many of the difficulties young children have are attributable to their almost exclusive reliance on relational information.

The limitations of purely relative judgments have been widely overlooked. Much psychological theory has been cast in terms of connecting particular responses to particular stimuli; in that theoretical context the appreciation and use of general relations between stimuli has seemed a more complicated skill, presumably slower to develop. And so it seems natural to conclude that the young child cannot appreciate a relation—in Piaget's example, the relation of class inclusion. But, as Bryant points out, perceptual relations are almost all that a child has to go on, and a relativistic approach is adequate only for direct perceptual comparisons between objects presented simultaneously. In order to get around this weakness it is necessary to develop absolute values internally that can serve to anchor the relational system to something more permanent.

We might adapt Bryant's argument to the problem involving different kinds of beads as follows. An adult has an absolute system available—he can count the number in order to settle such questions definitively. A young child relies on perceptual relations, but the most salient perceptual relation may not provide a correct answer to an experimenter's questions. In Piaget's example, brown and white can be compared simultaneously; in order to compare brown and wooden perceptually it is necessary to see a bead first as brown and then see it again as wooden, a successive judgment that is more difficult for the young relativist.

The possibility that abstract relations like ISA are difficult for children to appreciate and express verbally because children are unable to understand relations is therefore an oversimplification. A more likely account might feature processes whereby a child could organize particular kinds of relations into internalized frames of reference anchored to certain absolute values established through experience. But the relatively late mastery of ISA must be explained on some grounds other than its relational character. We suggest that it is late because it presumes conceptual developments from which it can be abstracted.

A child may use the same words an adult uses, but with different, more perceptual bases for them. Probably the first words a child learns are overgeneralized. "Papa" may be used to name any man, "doggie" any small furry animal. This is sometimes taken to mean that children begin with general distinctions and learn later to differentiate them into the particular subclasses labeled by the language. But this view, too, is an oversimplification. Any undergeneralizations—failures to apply a label to a referent that adults would include in the category—will go unnoticed because they do not lead to amusing mistakes. It is possible that a child's initial concepts sometimes need further broadening as well as further sharpening. Moreover, it is possible that many initial overgeneralizations are metaphorical extensions necessitated by the small size of his vocabulary rather than misunderstandings of the words themselves. Considerable attention has been devoted to this question, but the answer for the youngest children is still unclear.

Welch (1940) has pointed out that vocabulary growth for generic terms occurs later than for specific terms. He tried to teach young children both generic and specific labels by pairing them ostensively with appropriate objects. Between their twentieth and twenty-sixth month children were given several thousand repetitions of specific and generic labels. "By the end of the six months they knew no more concerning genus and species than they did in the beginning. If this training had any effect on them it was to retard them, since it destroyed their motivation to associate words with these materials" (p. 370). Welch's study can be interpreted as a demonstration of the inadequacy of ostensive definition as a method of teaching young children new labels; he concluded that the ability to deal with more general terms develops later than the ability to learn specific labels. Both interpretations are probably correct. Children who learn shared names for objects are learning names; they are not learning the genus-species distinction, and even the most intensive drill devoted to this distinction will fail to impart it to them.

By the time children approach school age it is possible to obtain relatively clear evidence that they understand superordinate terms less well than their hyponyms—as if their first attempts at conceptual integration, their first prototheories, are often specific and limited in scope. Anglin (1970) had school-children sort written words into piles on the basis of similarity of meaning and found that younger children (third and fourth graders) did not include the superordinate terms along with their hyponyms. Another example is provided by Schaeffer, Lewis, and Van Decar (1971), who used semantic oddity problems. Pictures of objects, or words naming the objects, were presented three at a time, and children were asked to pick the picture or word that did not belong with the other two. If a cow, a tree, and a boat were presented, a child who selected the boat as different from the other two would give evidence of understanding the animate-inanimate distinction. First graders understood little about this distinction; they used the categories plant, animal, vehicle, and utensil somewhat better, but not as well as fifth or ninth graders.

Evidence that children's concepts can be fragmented has been advanced by Saltz (1971; Saltz and Sigel, 1967), who concludes that younger children depend more on perceptual than conceptual attributes for categorizing objects. Saltz, Soller, and Sigel (1972) asked children to pick which of seventy pictures of common objects were instances of furniture. Kindergarten children showed a narrow and confused sense of furniture and were likely to consider objects to be instances because they looked alike or were commonly seen around the house. In a replication, however, Niemark (1974) included adult judges and found little difference between them and second graders.

As we have noted, furniture is a highly disjunctive concept. It is not obvious what conceptual integration could develop. If the youngest children have difficulty, it may not be a conceptual difficulty—perhaps they have not yet learned the full disjunctive list of instances. If we are correct that this concept is little more than a list, it would appear to be a poor field on which to fight this particular battle. (The other concepts that Saltz, Soller, and Sigel used—food, animals, transportation, clothes, toys—are almost equally disjunctive.)

Such disjunctive concepts have a bare minimum of conceptual integration. It is no accident, for example, that 1,000 college students whose word associations were tested by Palermo and Jenkins (1964) gave 691 responses of "chair" to the stimulus "table," but no responses of "furniture" (table 4.1); they gave "table" 421 times in response to "chair," but "furniture" only 10 times; "rug" in response to "carpet" outnumbered "furniture" 311 to 1; "lamp" elicited "light" 706 times and "furniture" not at all—and this in spite of an overall tendency to give more superordinate than hyponymic responses on word-association tests. Responses to words related by such disjunctive concepts are far more often contrastive than superordinate. For concepts such as these, it might seem that one requires little more conceptual organization than is implicit in an associative network.

The reader will recall that the functional notion of a table comes from the schemata of WORKTOP and SUPPORT (or LEG). Similarly, the functional notion of a chair derives from the schemata of SEAT and BACKREST. What they have in common is the *function* of allowing people to sit and work. For furniture in general there is a core of indoor human activities—eating, sleeping, working, playing. In addition, furniture is movable: it is not usually part of the building (hence one talks of "built-in" wardrobes). Furniture is not the object of the activities, it is not the immediate instrument that is used for them; in other words, it is not the food, utensils, tools, and so on. Furniture exists to accommodate people's bodies and the objects and instruments they use as they engage in those activities. That is the conceptual core that permits (but is not directly represented in) the integrated schemata of the FURNITURE decision table. Of course this conceptual core is vague, and its vagueness is reflected in the language. (Is a telephone an article of furniture? Is a washing machine? An alarm clock?) But its vagueness should not be construed as insubstantiality. A conceptual core is needed for the child to be able to construct an integrated set of schemata and for the adult to recognize novel items. Sometimes it even becomes a matter for verbal debate, as in a discussion about whether a certain exotic tribe has any furniture.

In order to have something to contrast with the vagueness of this situation, consider the concept of the human body. This concept is so central that it seems reasonable to suppose it must develop very early in children, and it provides a conceptual core for a large number of other concepts. The lexical field built around the body concept includes all the names of body parts in an elaborate partonymic hierarchy: the whole body; the head, trunk, arms, and legs; hair, face, ears; chin, forehead, eyes, nose, mouth; teeth, lips, tongue; hip, thigh, knee, ankle, foot; heel, arch, sole, toes; and so on. The internal parts provide another partonymic hierarchy. There are also hyponymic relations: ankles, hips, knees, shoulders, elbows, wrists, and knuckles are joints; arms and legs are limbs; stomach, lungs, liver, heart, and brain are organs.

In learning the names of his body parts a child presumably begins with a good grasp of the conceptual core. He has a problem, however, that is usually overlooked by adults because the answer is so plain to them, namely, what is the scope of the label? When a parent touches the child's foot and utters "Foot," the child, even if he already understands the concept of naming, has no way of knowing whether the sound is to be associated with just that part of his anatomy that is touched or with more of it; if more of it, how much more? He cannot know in advance whether he is learning English, where the applicability of "foot" leaves off at the ankle, or one of the Papuan languages of New Guinea, where "nesok" includes the leg as well (Bromley, 1967). In order to learn the scope of "foot," he must also learn "ankle" and "leg." Languages carve the body up for labeling in different ways, but always exhaustively— every part has some label—so the denotation of one label depends on its place relative to other labels. Once a child has grasped the fundamental concept of labeling he must still discover the boundaries between the labeled parts. But a boundary is a relation; it cannot be understood for only one of its terms. It is inherent in the meaning of "finger" that it does not apply to the palm, but where one leaves off and the other begins is part of the learning of both labels. One boundary relation implies another, until the whole body and its parts form an integrated system of labels. This system would be poorly represented in an associative network of pairwise relations between labels, but once a child has recognized the conceptual core of this semantic field, he will recognize a need for the labels that designate its parts and will have a ready-made conceptual system for integrating them into a single schema.

It is also a part of the body concept that bodies have a front and a back, a top and a bottom, a left and a right side. This aspect of the concept generates a whole system of spatial designations: facing, in back of, in front of, ahead, behind, to the right or left of, underfoot, overhead, beside, and so on. It would be possible to store in an associative network the fact that the head is at the top of the body, or that the face is on the front of the head, but it would be a clumsy and redundant business, better replaced by a more general schema of the body in which all these facts are directly represented. Since the body is a spatially extended object, it should probably be represented conceptually the way space is. We might think of it in terms of landmarks bearing a topographic relation to one another; the lexical field includes labels for the landmarks and the language enables us to identify any particular location by expressing its spatial relation to the nearest landmark. The denotation of any label for a body part is given by its place in this spatially related system of landmarks.

It is always possible, however, to assign some landmark a kind of priority in description of a spatial manifold by making it the point of origin; then other landmarks can be located relative to this origin. In the body schema some such role seems to be assigned to the head, which defines the intrinsic top, and particularly to the face, which contains major sense receptors and defines the intrinsic front of the body. If the point of origin had to be located even more precisely, most people would probably choose the eyes—perhaps that Cyclopean eye in the middle of the head where "I" seems to be.

Not only does the body schema provide a spatial reference system, it also is a rich source of figurative extensions. For example,

> "body": of water, of an airplane, of people, of knowledge
> "head": of a page, of a committee, of cabbage, of a pin
> "arm": of a coat, of the sea, of a chair, of government
> "leg": of a race, of a table, of a pair of trousers
> "foot": of a mountain, of a bed, of a stocking, 12 inches

Sometimes these extensions are confusing (a golf club has a head and a face, but it also has a heel, toe, and sole) but usually there is an obvious analogy between the body and the concept to which the label is extended. Names of body parts can also serve as verbs (head him off, arm the natives, hand him the cup, foot the bill, finger the cloth, stomach an insult, toe the mark, nose around, face the foe, sole the shoe).

The human body provides one of the most obvious and well-developed schemata. With respect to degree of integration, it must stand at the opposite extreme from such concepts as furniture; if people were as vague about their body parts as they are about articles of furniture, the human race would not have survived as long as it has. The integration of the body schema would seem to be a simple consequence of the fact that bodies are integrated entities. A child's perception and direct experience of the behavior of bodies naturally reflect their integrated nature and give rise to a conceptual core, perhaps a sensorimotor image, that readily integrates the semantic field.

To recapitulate what we have learned about the function of core concepts: they are essentially commonsense theories about the way the world works. People rely on them in much the way scientists rely on their theories—to interpret the world, to make sense of phenomena, to predict the behavior of entities. They lie behind the use of language, integrating semantic schemata and accommodating them to novel instances. Novelty, or an unexpected event, may lead to a revision in the lexical field—new terminology may need to be invented to deal with it—and, exceptionally, to a revision in the conceptual core itself. Once again there is a sensible analogy with what happens when a scientist encounters, say, a novel fossil: if it cannot be accommodated within the key, it may be necessary to modify the key or, exceptionally, the theory that the key is based on.

How should we attempt to characterize in formal terms the conceptual core of a semantic field? Unfortunately, the most plausible answer seems to vary from one field to another. An image for the human body. A procedure for a social notion such as possession. A list for furniture. At the present time the most powerful general form of representation for the various kinds of concepts we must consider is that provided by the language of information processing, so we will assume that conceptual cores can be characterized in procedural terms. It is seldom the case that we can offer more than the barest sketch of the contents of a conceptual core, let alone any explicit procedural proposals. It will turn out, however, that a broad and general statement of what the conceptual core is a theory *about* will serve most purposes of lexical analysis.

The expository problem is further aggravated by the fact that not every core concept forms the basis for a lexical field. The core concept PERSON, for example, is certainly important, but it does not seem to have a single, homogeneous lexical representation. We will consider how persons are labeled in the next section, where we hope to show something of what lexical fields are not, as well as something of what they can be.

4.5   LABELING PERSONS

The resources in English for labeling persons are extremely rich, as befits a topic of personal and social importance. A division of these terms into individual and generic labels would seem to provide an obvious and convenient first step in any analysis. Among the individual labels would be proper names (Martha Washington, Martin Luther King, Xavier Cugat, Millard Fillmore) and for the generic labels we would have common nouns (person, man, woman, child, boy, girl, wife, father, citizen, lawyer, client, owner, friend). Then we could proceed to analyze the hierarchical and contrastive field properties of the generic terms.

Although a distinction between terms that label definite individuals and terms that label classes of individuals is extremely important, several difficulties arise if we take this distinction as the foundation of our analysis. Proper names may be the lowest level in the hierarchy of person labels, in which case to set them aside as a special category would violate their natural incorporation into this lexical domain. More serious difficulties would arise from the fact that many labels for persons can be used in either sense, as individual or generic, definite or indefinite. The personal pronoun "you," for example, can refer to a specific individual on some occasions and to a generalized anybody on others; the personal pronoun "I" refers to a specific individual, but to a different one whenever a different person utters it. It is not obvious where such deictic labels fit in an individual-generic dichotomy. And what would we do with definite descriptions, with phrases like "the person who invented the wheel," or "the man who was king of France in 1650," or "that person" accompanied by some appropriate gesture—phrases compounded of generic labels but intended to designate specific individuals? Kin terms also have both an individual and a generic use: "mother" can denote the particular woman who happens to be the speaker's mother or the whole class of women who bear this relation to other people. Indeed, in their generic sense the kin terms are probably better thought of as denoting a relation between pairs of individuals rather than as labels for single individuals—as "mother of," not simply "mother."

Faced with this degree of diversity, the best course would seem to be to reserve judgment as to whether all the different ways of referring to persons make up a single semantic domain. That is to say, we should probably consider a variety of person-labeling strategies as if they were separate semantic domains, postponing any decisions as to whether some or all are subdomains of the more general concept PERSON.

How should the lay concept of persons be characterized? In Western society the core concept seems to involve a live body that possesses such abstract characteristics as mind, soul, personality, and will. Other cultures have different ideas, and even in our own culture there is room for disagreement about how much further one can go in characterizing "person" than to say "a living human being." A considerable measure of socialization is built into one's expectations of how a person should behave, individually and socially. Perhaps the conservative approach is to assume that the common sense on which English rests embraces some kind of body-mind dualism, and to concentrate instead on how this abstract and ill-defined general concept is particularized into individual persons. We will begin, therefore, with an attempt to characterize how people organize information about particular individuals.

4.5.1 Proper Names

Consider the proper names that people answer to. At first glance, this would seem to be the simplest case of all; the internal structure can be little more than a disjunctive list, perhaps partitioned by sex. At a very early age each person is christened by some adult who occupies the appropriate social position to perform this act, and thereafter that person is referred to by all who know him with the label so assigned. What more is there to say about proper names?

He is fortunate who can leave the matter so simply formulated. If one goes on to ask what proper names mean, or how they are used, or why we bother to confer them, one quickly becomes entangled in deep and perplexing problems.

What does "John Brown" mean? The label "John Brown" can refer to a particular individual, and when it is so used its meaning is apparently given by what it refers to. "The man" can also refer to a particular individual, but it means something more than its momentary referent—it assigns this particular referent to a class of similar referents. Does "John Brown" assign its referent to the class of individuals who share that name? Well, yes, but people do not use it that way. We might try to argue that they do not use it that way because the individuals so named share nothing but their name—that they learn nothing about a person by virtue of knowing his membership in that class. But that argument is false. "John Brown" suggests that its referent is a male human being, so it must mean almost as much as "the man" means. It may even suggest something, whether right or wrong, about his ethnic origins. A name like "Never Say Die"—if it were a name—would be recognized immediately as one not for a human being but for a racehorse or sailboat (see Levi-Strauss, 1966). All such information, however, is irrelevant to the referential function of a proper name.

Frege tried to untangle some of these questions by sometimes drawing a distinction between what a word refers to (or denotes) and what it means (or expresses, or connotes). In a sentence like "The man is John Brown," one understands that "the man" and "John Brown" both refer to the same individual. But they do not have the same meaning (or sense). Two labels that have the same meaning can be substituted for one another without changing the meaning of the sentence in which they appear, but if in this example we substitute "John Brown" for "the man," we get the new sentence "John Brown is John Brown," which obviously has a different meaning because its truth can be determined by inspection, in total ignorance of John Brown. So even on an occasion when "the man" and "John Brown" refer to the same thing, they are not synonymous—they do not mean the same thing. Alternatively, we might say that "John Brown" refers to the same individual in every possible state of affairs in which it refers to anything, but that "the man" may refer to John Brown in some possible states of affairs but not in others. (In this way we could please semanticists who dislike the notion of meaning.)

J. S. Mill (1843) concluded that proper names like "John Brown" do not mean anything—they are meaningless sounds used to designate particular individuals. According to this view, a proper name is simply a logical constant —it is a singular term, without internal semantic structure, that designates a unique object.

Frege and Russell, independently, rejected Mill's argument and proposed instead that the meaning of "John Brown" is given by a definite description of the individual it names. For example, one meaning of "John Brown" might be "the American abolitionist hanged at Charlestown." The view that proper names are constants has trouble with the fact that there may be more than one object with the same name. If someone had asked Mill which John Brown he was referring to, it is not clear how he could have answered, since for Mill a name had no descriptive content; it is not even clear that Mill could have understood such questions as "Did John Brown actually exist?" Given a definite description of John Brown, however, such questions can be answered by determining which individual, if any, answers to the description. According to this view, a proper name has the logical status of a predicate—it assigns certain properties to its argument, just as a common noun does.

Russell's (1905) notion that proper names have definite descriptions as their meanings is not above challenge. For most people, the meaning of "Jonah" would be given by the description "the man who lived in the belly of a whale," even though there is evidence that this description is false. Scholars who are supposed to know about such matters say that a man named Jonah did exist but that none of the popular beliefs about him are true. How can the meaning of the name of a real person be given by a definite description of a person who never existed? The trouble is that proper names do *not* describe anything. Consider the fact that "John Brown" can be associated with one description for Tom and a totally different description for Mary, yet both descriptions can fit the same individual and no barrier to communication between Tom and Mary need arise from the fact that (if the meaning of a name is synonymous with the definite description that could replace it) "John Brown" means something different for each of them.

If two people can have entirely different information about a referent and yet experience no communicative difficulties in identifying that referent through the use of his name, perhaps the same situation could exist with respect to common nouns like "table" or "cup." If so, exploration of people's intuitions about meanings of common nouns might uncover nothing but idiosyncratic information based on their individual experiences with those nouns. This possibility would undermine any attempts to construct a conceptual theory of meaning of the sort we have been developing, and so must be rejected—our reasons for rejecting it were discussed in section 3.1 and need not be repeated here. But it must be recognized that our present project commits us to the view that meanings of proper nouns differ somehow from meanings of common nouns. We cannot accept the apparent simplification in the theory of reference that follows from treating proper and common nouns in the same way—as predicates that can be applied only to objects having certain properties.

The difference between proper names and common nouns results from the fact that a proper name applies to (is true of) an object if and only if the object bears a certain *pragmatic* relation to that name, that is, if and only if the object has been given that name in an appropriate manner. An object can be a man —can have all the properties of a man—even if the common noun "man" is never used, but it cannot be a John Brown unless somebody uses "John Brown" to name it.

As Burge (1973) points out, a proper name plays much the same role as a phrase consisting of a demonstrative pronoun or adjective followed by a predicate. For example, both of the sentences "John Brown is six feet tall" and "That man is six feet tall" can only be assigned a truth value in particular contexts of use. Out of context, it is impossible to know which John Brown or which man is intended, so neither sentence can be completely interpreted. This is not to say that "John Brown" and "that man" have the same meaning but only that both are deictic terms. If exaggeration can help make the point, a proper name can be thought of as a pronoun with an arbitrarily limited range of reference. If proper names, like demonstrative and personal pronouns, can only be fully interpreted in their context of use, they are clearly more a topic for pragmatic than for semantic theories of language.

Let us consider a pragmatic question: How do people teach proper names to children? Suppose you want a child to learn that "Millard Fillmore" is the name of a particular individual. An obvious strategy would be to present Millard Fillmore and, having gained the child's attention, to utter a naming expression like "This is Millard Fillmore." Proper names and associative learning seem to have been made for each other; the task is practically a paradigm of "paired-associates" learning. The student has merely to acquire an individuating perceptual paradigm for the object and the vocal skills to produce the sound—association will do the rest. When we objected to this view as a characterization of how a child might learn to use a common noun like "book" (sec. 3.1) we noted the problems of abstracting just those properties common to the class of objects called books and of placing books in some larger conceptual structure. In the case of proper names, however, rote memorization of a connection would seem to be all that is involved. Proper names are labels par excellence.

The simplicity is vitiated by the fact that a child must somehow learn which sounds label individuals and which label classes of individuals. The linguistic signal is that proper names are seldom preceded by articles, whereas common nouns usually are. Katz, Baker, and Macnamara (1974) exposed small children (seventeen to twenty-four months) to nonsense names for dolls and blocks, with and without an article preceding the nonsense syllable. When the syllable was used as a proper name (without an article) for a doll, children learned it, whereas when it was used as a proper name for a block, they did not. They conclude that young children do individuate people, but not objects; by bearing in mind this semantic distinction, the child is in a position to detect the syntactic signal, the presence or absence of "a" or "the," and to discover that people can be referred to by both kinds of nouns, common as well as proper. Girls noticed these regularities by the age of seventeen months.

In order to relate a spoken sound to a particular object, it is essential that the speaker somehow draw the learner's attention to the pertinent entity. The speaker must be able to single out a specific person from everything else. At its simplest, this may involve pointing or the use of such deictic words as "this" or "that"; at a more sophisticated level, it may involve such linguistic forms as definite descriptions. But in all cases we find at the root a simple act of picking out a single individual.

Of course, it would be absurd to announce "This is Millard Fillmore" if no one were there. And it would be equally absurd to persist in identifying Millard Fillmore as "Millard Fillmore" prior to each remark about him. Once a learner is able to move easily from the name to the individual and from the individual to the name, a speaker can usually say whatever he has to say directly: "Millard Fillmore hopes to be president some day" need not be accompanied by gestures indicating the individual involved. Just "Millard" or "Fillmore" will on occasion suffice, depending on whether there are other Millards or Fillmores with whom the listener might confuse him, and sometimes a mere pronoun will pick him out. If by chance there should be a room full of Millard Fillmores, then "Millard Fillmore" can no longer function as a proper name should because it will fail to pick out a unique individual. The essential point, though, is that once the name has been learned it is not necessary to continue to identify the individual it labels—the name itself can be used to refer to the person.

Pragmatically, therefore, what might be taken as the meaning of a proper name is the set of perceptual and conceptual tests that an individual must pass in order for the name to be correctly bestowed upon him. So a word about these tests is in order. They are not the same sort of tests that we have been considering to label objects like books or tables. Some, perhaps many, of the facts associated with named entities must be idiosyncratic to the particular entity in question. Consider the sorts of information a person might associate with the name "Anthony Eden":

(11)   Anthony Eden
    (i)   Name may be prefaced by "Sir"
    (ii) Visual image of male face (mustache, bushy eyebrows, wear-
          ing homburg hat)
    (iii) Political career
        (a) Foreign secretary in Tory government
        (b) Churchill's righthand man
        (c) Prime minister
        (d) Suez fiasco in 1956; Bevan in public meeting exclaims
           "Eden must go!"
        (e) Retires owing to ill health
    (iv) Becomes Lord Avon
    (v)   Makes an appearance in a documentary film on occupied France

This information (or misinformation) might reasonably characterize what a particular individual knows about Anthony Eden; it might be taken as a person's concept of Eden. It is obvious from its ad hoc and factual nature, however, that (11) cannot be considered to represent the meaning of "Anthony Eden." And, although a definite description might be based on such information, we would certainly not wish to claim that a proper name is equivalent to such a set of facts. Both Donnellan (1972) and Kripke (1972) have pointed out difficulties to which such claims lead. Yet such putative facts as those in (11) are likely to be available in person memory, if only to facilitate recognition of individuals from their photographs and to aid in the coherent recall of historical episodes. But there need be no general, universally shared set of facts (or definite descriptions based on them) that would constitute a unique and valid criterion for identifying the referent of a proper name.

As (11) is formulated, it seems to give some special status to "Anthony Eden" as the name of the information we have about Anthony Eden. But that way of characterizing it would be misleading, for "Anthony Eden" is the name of a person, not the name of what we know about him. A better way to think of (11), therefore, is that the conceptual core is a particular individual who serves as a focus for (or a mental peg on which to hang) a variety of putative facts, one of which is that this person answers to the name "Anthony Eden." It is possible to remember a great deal about a person without being able to remember his name, and some person concepts may even contain such idiosyncratic information as "that man in Essex whose name I can never remember" or "the girl I met in Rochester who wouldn't tell me her name." It is possible to gain access to a person concept by a variety of retrieval cues: by "Anthony Eden," by a perception of Anthony Eden, by "the prime minister in 1956," by "the Suez fiasco." It is characteristic of associative memory that a whole entry can be recovered from any part of it—no single part is an indispensable "address" for retrieval—and it is just this property of memory that enables people to substitute descriptions for proper names.

Free associations to proper names might reveal something of the organization of person memory. One observes informally a variety of responses, such as the occupation of the person named ("Picasso"—"painter"), his common personal associates ("Eden"—"Churchill"), some outstanding event ("Lenin"—"revolution"), or evaluation ("Hitler"—"evil"). The "tip of the tongue" phenomenon is another potential source of information. William James (1890) wrote: "That nascent cerebral excitations can effect consciousness with a sort of sense of the imminence of that which stronger excitations would make us definitely feel, is obvious from what happens when we seek to remember a name. It tingles, it trembles on the verge, but does not come" (I, 673–674). Brown and McNeill (1966) introduced a method to study the phenomenon, with striking results, but proper nouns seem not to have been investigated.

Johnson-Laird is susceptible to forgetting the names of famous people, so some years ago he resorted to free association out loud whenever a name trembled on the verge. This procedure invariably led to successful recall, and often produced demonstrations of how person memory was being searched. It usually proceeded in terms of the person's occupation and the phonemic shape of his name (its initial sound, number of syllables, and so on). For example, in searching for the name of the painter of *Nude Descending a Staircase* and other Dada works, the following sequence occurred:

	/d/
	Daumier
	Derain
Jacques	Villon
	Vlaminck
Max	
Max	Ernst
Marcel	Duchamp!

Every surname is the name of a painter, and they are mainly drawn from the appropriate period with suitably French names. And there are phonemic relations between the target and its precursors; the initial /d/ was present from the start.

The facts a person knows about another person at any given time will necessarily be criterial for him at that time, although they may still fail to identify a unique individual. Since different people may know different facts about the individual, there is always a possibility of confusion, but, in general, communication about him can proceed in spite of these knowledge differences. As

Searle (1969) has written, the "convenience of proper names in our language lies precisely in the fact that they enable us to refer publicly to objects without being forced to raise issues and come to an agreement as to which descriptive characteristics exactly constitute the identity of the object" (p. 172).

If a person has no information associated with "Anthony Eden," as far as he is concerned its referential use in a sentence is problematic. "Anthony Eden has long since retired" may or may not express a verifiable statement for the listener—indeed, as far as he knows there may not be such a person. He may inquire "Who is Anthony Eden?" Suppose, however, that what the speaker said, in full, was: "A man called Anthony Eden was the English prime minister during the Suez crisis. Anthony Eden has long since retired." In his second sentence the speaker has used "Anthony Eden" to refer, and it does so on condition that "a man called Anthony Eden" identifies an actual person. Thus, in order to establish that a proper name X refers, it is necessary only to establish the truth of a statement of the form "There is a y called X."

It may help to put these ideas in procedural terms. Suppose that a person decides to verify "Anthony Eden was prime minister." In the course of translating this sentence into a routine he may execute these instructions:

(12)   (i) find(person memory, Anthony Eden) and call it x
          (ii) find(semantic memory, prime minister) and call it Y

Since he decides to try to verify the sentence, the control instruction for the resulting routine will be "test":

(13)   test(in past, $Y(x)$); if so, the sentence is true; otherwise, false or indeterminate.

The result of (12i) will be to create a pointer x to the listener's concept of Anthony Eden, which we can imagine to be something like (11); similarly, (12ii) creates a pointer to the listener's concept of prime minister. When he attempts to execute (13), therefore, the "test" routine can search x, where it will find, in (11iiic), the necessary information. The information can then be added to the schema the listener is forming for this conversational episode, at which point it becomes part of the context in terms of which subsequent sentences can be processed, that is, it modifies the state of the translator by adding new entries to its list of variables for which values have been assigned and by adding new relations among those entries.

Suppose that "Anthony Eden" cannot be found in person memory. Even a person who had never heard of Anthony Eden would, if he knew English, be able to recognize that "Anthony Eden" is the name of a person, probably a man, so the first argument of "find" in (12i) could be correctly assigned. But if "Anthony Eden" could not be found in this memory field, one of the prerequisites for executing (13) would have failed. If the truth of the sentence were of sufficient importance to the listener, however, he might exit to a different routine that would assign(z, "Anthony Eden") and assign(w, person), then try to test (in past, there is a w such that NAME (z, w)). Attempts to execute this "test" instruction might lead him to ask "Who was Anthony Eden?" and to use the answer in order to create a new person concept as the core of whatever information he received in reply; if he did not trust the speaker, he might address the question to someone else; if he did not trust anyone, he might search for Eden himself. But he cannot verify the sentence from his own personal knowledge unless that knowledge includes the facts that are asserted.

Alternatively, suppose that the person has heard of Anthony Eden but has somehow forgotten or never learned that Eden was once prime minister. Then (12i) will find the person concept and create a pointer x to it, but (13) will not be able to verify that Eden was prime minister. In that case, (13) would give an indeterminate (not a negative) outcome; falsehood would normally be assigned only if (13) turned up a positive memory that Anthony Eden had never been prime minister. If the outcome of (13) is indeterminate, therefore, the "otherwise" should send the person to some routine that will try to find more information about Anthony Eden; if that search is successful, the listener's concept of Anthony Eden can be enriched sufficiently to allow a successful execution of the test in (13). Since finding independent evidence requires an expenditure of time and energy that only a highly motivated skeptic would be willing to afford, most people would abandon the attempt at verification and probably would execute a "store" instruction to add this information to the facts they already have about Anthony Eden.

It is remarkable how seldom people attempt to verify statements. This observation appears to apply equally well to statements that identify individuals. People are usually content to assume that someone exists simply because someone else has presupposed or asserted his existence—a special case of trust in the pragmatic convention of truthfulness governing the use of language.

Several philosophers, including Strawson (1950), have argued that it is a mistake to think of proper names as referring expressions. More properly, they argue, a speaker may be said to refer; an expression by itself does not refer. To refer is to perform a particular kind of communicative act. A speaker may refer to an individual when he uses that individual's name in a sentence uttered to make an assertion, ask a question, or whatever, but it is the speaker, not the name, that does the referring. This distinction makes psychological sense, but it turns out that discussions of reference quickly become tangled and clumsy when we try to phrase them always in terms of acts rather than expressions. "Referring expression" is a convenient abbreviation and, as long as one keeps in mind what it is an abbreviation for, need not lead to confusion or misinterpretation. Speakers do exploit the regularities of their language and the conventions that govern its use when they perform referential acts, so it is not altogether wrong to think of expressions as referring to things in the world. We will feel free to use this way of talking about the matter in trying to characterize those linguistic regularities and conventions.

By no means every occurrence of a proper name actually refers. Existential assertions or denials, such as "Millard Fillmore does not exist," plainly do not involve a referential use of names, for that would beg the question. It is an interesting exercise to consider what the meaning of such a denial might be. It seems to assert that there is no individual to whom one can refer by using the name "Millard Fillmore." The claim that "there was no such person as Shakespeare" means either that no individual (or no one individual) ever existed who would satisfy the tests conventionally associated with the label "Shakespeare" or that the label itself is a pseudonym for some individual who satisfies these tests and more—Francis Bacon, perhaps.

A failure of names to refer may also arise in certain opaque contexts. For example, "John is looking for Millard Fillmore," or "John believes that Millard Fillmore is a brute." Such assertions could be true even if there was no such person as Millard Fillmore (see, for example, Geach, 1967). In other contexts, a name may be mentioned without being used to refer; for example, " 'Millard Fillmore' sounds like the name of an American president."

For our purposes, the most important aspect of reference is that it is an act carried out by the speaker to which a listener must be sensitive. On the one hand, a speaker may use an entirely appropriate referring expression yet fail to communicate whom he is talking about simply because of some unforeseen gaps in the listener's knowledge. On the other hand, a speaker may use a totally inappropriate name or expression yet succeed in communicating whom he is talking about, perhaps because the listener shares the same misinformation or because he exercises skill or intuition to correct the misleading label. And there are other interactive possibilities. Different individuals may associate different tests with a given name, or they may have different names for the same person, that is, different names associated with the tests he satisfies.

A philosopher sensitive to the delicacies of referring might wish to distinguish: (a) the correct performance of the act of referring, (b) its correct interpretation by the listener, and (c) the successful communication of the reference—the "full consummation" of the act, as Searle terms it. From a psychological point of view, however, it seems sensible to concentrate on the communication of a reference, which may succeed in spite of mistakes by the speaker or the listener. Success will depend on the speaker's and listener's general knowledge of their world and of the particular context of their discourse (including the intended referent), and their knowledge of each other's knowledge.

Since the semantics of proper names is so different from the semantics of common nouns, combining them into a single semantic domain seems inappropriate. The kind of information people associate with various persons they know, like the kind of information they associate with various episodes they have lived through, differs from the kind of perceptual and functional information they associate with common nouns in semantic memory. To the extent that this difference implies a difference in how they address their memories for such information, we may be justified in thinking of person memory, episodic memory, and semantic memory as differentiable. That is to say, a proper name for a person can give access to information retrievable from person memory, whereas a generic term gives access to information retrievable from semantic memory.

Although we may believe there is an abstract conceptual core underlying all the different instances of "person" that we know, our discussion of how persons can be distinguished and identified by name for purposes of reference or address reveals nothing about this general concept. "Person" is still a primitive term in our theory.

4.5.2   Personal Pronouns

The individuals identified and referred to by hundreds of thousands of proper names are also referred to in English by a mere handful of personal pronouns. In order to map so many individuals into so few terms, of course, it is necessary to group people in various ways; the bases for this grouping are obligatory knowledge for speakers of English—in order to use the personal pronouns, to substitute them for proper names or noun phrases, a speaker must have information about the referents that enables him to select the appropriate pronoun. The information required for pronoun selection has to be stored in memory with each of the nominal entries in the subjective lexicon.

One might expect, therefore, to extract valuable clues about semantic organization from an inspection of pronouns. These expectations are disappointed, however, when one discovers what the bases for pronoun substitution really are. Except for number and gender (which is preserved in English only for "he," "she," and "it") all of the semantic criteria are deictic, that is, they are determined by the situation in which one is speaking.

Before considering semantic attributes of the personal pronouns, we should first be sure we agree on what they are. A pronoun is usually defined to be a word that can be used instead of a noun or noun phrase, and sometimes instead of a clause or sentence. A personal pronoun should be any pronoun that can be used in place of a noun phrase that denotes a person, but this definition is more permissive than the one we find in most grammar books, which generally list the personal pronouns exhaustively and discuss all the others that can replace person names under other subheadings. This strategy makes it possible to avoid mixing them up with such pronouns as "one," "myself," "somebody," "each other," "anyone," "this person," "who," "whomever," "others," and even such quantifiers as "some," "all," "more," "five" (as in "Some/all/more/five were released")—all of which are words that can be used instead of proper names or noun phrases to denote people. Since we have no desire to cause unnecessary trouble for ourselves, we will follow the grammarians' lead.

The personal pronouns (plus "it") can be listed in the following form:

(14)   *Singular*   *Plural*

   Nominative case
     First person   I   we
     Second person   you   you
     Third person   he, she, it   they

   Accusative case
     First person   me   us
     Second person   you   you
     Third person   him, her, it   them

   Genitive case
     First person   mine   ours
     Second person   yours   yours
     Third person   his, hers, its   theirs

By arraying the pronouns in this way, which we have borrowed from traditional grammarians, we have already displayed some of the attributes that can be used to classify them. Three attributes are apparent in (14): case, number, and person. A fourth attribute, gender, is concealed in the "he, she, it" grouping. (We can include "it" as a personal pronoun because it is sometimes used to refer to babies.) A fifth attribute, the relative status of the participants, was once expressed by a thou-you distinction but is now obsolete; most speakers of English would not know how to add "thou," "ye," "thee," and "thine" to (14) without consulting a dictionary.

This way of arranging the personal pronouns is so familiar that we can easily overlook its implications. Not only does (14) represent the internal structure of a set of contrastive terms, but the grouping represents components of the meaning of those terms. At some point in the history of attempts to describe language somebody had to decide that these were the correct semantic components for English (and other Indo-European) pronouns. It might have been otherwise, for there is no logical necessity that pronouns should oblige anyone to express person and number; it is simply an empirical fact that speakers of English are so obliged. In many Philippine languages, for example, the semantic components of personal pronouns are different. Thus, the Hanunóo (Conklin, 1962) observe different obligatory semantic relations: minimal or nonminimal membership (close to, but different from number), inclusion or exclusion of the person sending the message (not quite the same as first person versus other), and inclusion or exclusion of the person receiving the message (different from second person versus other). If we attempt to impose semantic dimensions of English on their set of pronouns, the result will not represent the distinctions they use to indicate various individuals or collections of individuals pronominally.

The traditional analysis of personal pronouns in English into five components suggests that any labeling routine for these words should involve a subset of five components as tests. For example, the routine for "I" might include

   (i) find(search domain, x such that PERSON(x))
  (ii) test(t, x is source of message)
 (iii) test(t, no other x is source of message)
 (iv) test(t, x is the subject of message)

Since these tests involve "message," they are in some sense metalinguistic; we have used informal English phrases to state the criteria that must be met. Test (ii) is intended to determine person, (iii) to determine number, and (iv) to determine case.

Given appropriate tests, we could write labeling routines for each personal pronoun separately. Such routines, however, would encounter all the difficulties mentioned in 3.5.4, where the problem of locating the most probable referent for "it" was discussed. These difficulties are usually minimal for "I," since the nature of the speech-communication situation makes the source of a message obvious, but all other personal pronouns are potential sources of ambiguity. Adult speakers usually anticipate a listener's problems and provide antecedent context adequate to disambiguate pronominal references—the listener can expect to find the referent somewhere in his list of previously assigned pointers—but children are notoriously careless: "He came and he hit him and he fell down" can involve two, three, or four persons with a variety of coreferential possibilities that only another witness of the episode could unravel.

Although the major work of determining reference must be carried out by heuristic routines processing contextual information, there are still important semantic leads provided by the pronoun used. In the child's utterance just quoted, for example, a listener knows to search for animate, male referents other than the speaker and addressee. The information that a user of English can extract from the choice of pronouns is our central concern here.

Even if we ignore the additional information processing that personal pronouns require, routines like the one suggested above for "I" do not reveal the structure of this semantic domain. A list of routines would be redundant, and redundancy would conceal the relations that serve to integrate them. We can, however, cast (14) in a format resembling a decision table.

In table 4.5 the five tests that we need—for case, number, person, status, and gender—are given across the top and the pronouns that these tests define are listed on the left. The table cells give the outcome of the tests associated with the definitions of the pronouns. (Complications introduced by the possibility of indeterminate outcomes are ignored.) The first row of the table says that "I" is the appropriate pronoun when the outcome of the case test is nominative, when the outcome of the number test is singular, and when the outcome of the person test is first person; since the outcomes of tests for status and gender are irrelevant (any outcome is acceptable), these cells are left blank. Note that no two rows of the table are identical; moreover, every possible combination of test outcomes is associated with some pronoun. Since this method of representation is economical, we have included the archaic pronouns "thou," "thee," "thine," and "ye" along with the rest, but if they are eliminated

Table 4.5   English personal pronouns.

Pronoun	Case (N = nominative; A = accusative; G = genitive)	Number (S = singular; P = plural)	Person (1 = first; 2 = second; 3 = third)	Status (T = intimate; V = formal)	Gender (M = masculine; F = feminine; N = neuter)
I	N	S	1		
me	A	S	1		
mine	G	S	1		
we	N	P	1		
us	A	P	1		
ours	G	P	1		
thou	N	S	2	T	
thee	A	S	2	T	
thine	G	S	2	T	
ye	N	P	2	T	
you	N, A		2	V	
yours	G		2	V	
he	N	S	3		M
him	A	S	3		M
his	G	S	3		M
she	N	S	3		F
her	A	S	3		F
hers	G	S	3		F
it	N, A	S	3		N
its	G	S	3		N
they	N	P	3		
them	A	P	3		
theirs	G	P	3		

(along with the test for status), it is still true that every possible combination of outcomes is associated with some pronoun.

Each row in table 4.5 corresponds to a separate labeling routine. We can think of the five tests as performed more or less in parallel, and of the table as an identification device for selecting the pronoun appropriate to their possible outcomes. Thus, table 4.5 makes explicit the kind of integration that must underlie this lexical domain: each pronoun is related to the others in terms of the five tests that define them all.

Other words that can be substituted for person nominals could be represented in the same format. For example, when used as a pronoun, "one" is third-person singular, nominative or accusative; it provides a genderless alternative to "he," "him," "she," and "her." Thus, if "one" were included in table 4.5, the table would no longer provide a unique resolution for pronoun selection; some additional criterion would be required to decide whether "one" or some other third-person singular form was appropriate. Since "one" may be used when a speaker is uncertain of the gender of the referent person, it is semantically less definite than the pronouns in table 4.5. For example, in "Bill visited a lawyer and Alex visited him, too," we would ordinarily understand "him" to refer to a definite person, namely, the lawyer Bill visited, whereas in "Bill visited a lawyer and Alex visited one, too," we would ordinarily understand "one" to refer indefinitely to some other lawyer. A case can be made that the pronoun "one" is related to the indefinite article "a" in much the same way the pronoun "mine" is related to the adjective "my"; indeed, all of the personal pronouns in table 4.5 may be related to the definite article "the" in the same way. The syntactic arguments supporting these relations are presented by Stockwell, Schacter, and Partee (1972) and need not be reviewed here. We are concerned only with the suggestion that the additional criterion required to decide between "one" and "he/him/she/her" has something to do with definite versus indefinite reference, which is a topic that would lead us far outside the domain of person labels. In order to confine our discussion within manageable limits, therefore, we will not explore relations between personal pronouns and various determiners (particularly quantifiers) that can be used as pronouns when their head nouns can be deleted.

Each of the five tests included in table 4.5 is different from the others, and all raise important issues concerning the way words refer to persons. Since case seems more purely syntactic than the other four criteria, we will consider it first. Until recently (probably until Fillmore's presentation of "The Case for Case" in 1968), linguists who talked about case had in mind the inflections on nouns, pronouns, and adjectives that serve to indicate the syntactic functions these words can serve. Case inflections play an important role in many languages, but in English their importance is negligible. The contrast between nominative and accusative in contemporary English is retained only for the pronouns listed in (14) and table 4.5 and for "who" and "whom." The genitive case is also preserved in the personal pronouns and in the apostrophe + "s" ending for nouns.

Case has to do with the different functions that nouns can serve in sentences. The nominative case is generally said to be used for the subject of a sentence, accusative for the direct object of the verb, dative for the indirect object, genitive for a possessive relation, locative for location in space or time, and so on. There are many exceptions to these designations, exceptions that are the despair of struggling students, particularly when the language in question is highly inflected. Considerable research into the history of case inflections in different languages has failed to systematize the semantic relations that case inflections are generally supposed to express. All in all, the grammar of case would not seem a profitable place to look for insight into the deeper psychological aspects of language.

One difficulty faced by students of case has been the superficial nature of the inflections expressing it. Case inflections seem to depend on a variety of different rules in different parts of the grammar; it has been difficult to discover any convincing regularities, either syntactic or semantic, in their behavior. Comparisons of different languages have led to equally confusing results. Some languages maintain elaborate systems of case inflections, whereas others have dispensed with them almost completely. The inflectional system in English is superficial. Pronouns illustrate the point: "He saw her" uses the nominative "he" to denote the agent and the accusative "her" to denote the patient, but in the passive, "She was seen by him," not only is the order of agent and patient inverted, but the agent is now denoted by the accusative "him" and the patient is denoted by the nominative "she." Apparently we use case inflections to indicate the superficial syntactic relation of subject and direct object of the verb, not to indicate the deeper semantic relation of agent and patient.

What we have called case in (14) and table 4.5 does not serve the same purpose as what Fillmore (1968, 1971a) calls case in his discussion of the semantic relations of verbs in their nominal arguments. What we, following traditional grammar, have called case is the superficial syntactic relation of the subject of the sentence and the object of the verb, whereas Fillmore is concerned with the deeper relation of the agent of the verb and the patient of the verb. In order to avoid confusion one could adopt Langendoen's (1970) suggestion to use the term "role" to distinguish Fillmore's approach from the traditional one. In Langendoen's words, "The semantic relationships are most easily and directly described in terms of *roles*—as if each sentence were a miniature drama, whose plot is given by the main predicate and whose actors (in their various roles) are the nominal expressions that occur with them" (p. 62). In our view, such roles are defined by the underlying schema of the verb; the actor role requires an argument that *does* something that *causes* something else to *happen* (see 6.3.2).

The genitive case seems to have a simple semantic interpretation in English, but the differences between nominative and accusative are syntactic details of the sort we have not attempted to analyze. As far as we are concerned, "I" and "me" are simply variant spellings of the same concept; they contrast syntactically rather than semantically; which is to be preferred depends on its place in the sentence structure.

This leaves number, person, status, and gender as semantic dimensions of the personal pronouns.

A semantic analysis of personal pronouns should exploit the fact that they are deictic words. Since their meaning is situationally determined, the analysis should reflect the situation of communication. Communication requires a source and a receiver. For a given speech signal the role of source S can be played by only one person, but the role of receiver can be played by one or more persons, some of whom may be intended receivers (addressee, A) and some not. Anyone who is not the source S or addressee A can be designated as other, O. Hence, there are three roles that persons can play in a speech-communication situation at any time: S, A, or O, and these roles are mutually exclusive.

If the personal pronouns are to refer to the roles that persons are playing, they should be able to denote not merely S, A, or O but all possible combinations of these roles. Given three roles, any one of which may or may not be referred to, there are seven possible combinations: SAO, SA, SO, S, AO, A, and O. The way these combinations are denoted in English can be illustrated as follows:

(15)   *Singular*   *Plural*

 First person
  SAO   —   You, Ed, and I deserved what *we* got.
  SA   —   Only you and I know *we* are here.
  SO   —   *We* didn't invite you.
  S   *I* am hungry.   —

 Second person
  AO   —   You and Ed said *you* knew each other.
  A   *You* are one.   *You* are all listening to me now.

 Third person
  O   *He* is alone.   *They* are together.

The correspondence of S, A, and O with first, second, and third persons, respectively, holds only for singular pronouns. In plural pronouns there is considerable ambiguity, the best known being the difference between the so-called inclusive (SAO or SA) and exclusive (SO) "we." As Postal (1966) points out, "we" is certainly not the plural of "I" in the same sense in which "boys" is the plural of "boy" (except in the case of writing, where it may refer to plural authors—a case that we are ignoring).

If the analysis in (15) is correct, the test for person in table 4.5 should be replaced by three tests: one each for reference or nonreference to source, addressee, or other. The advantage of representing person in this manner is not only that it characterizes some of the ambiguities of these pronouns but also that it enables us to phrase the analysis in terms of plausible universals of language. The social structure of source, addressee, and other provides the conceptual core underlying this semantic field. Note that it is a social concept, however, involving little more of the person concept than the fact that people talk to each other.

On the basis of this conceptual core we can construct an identification device in the form of a decision table, as in table 4.6. Conditions $c1$-$c3$ indicate whether the source, addressee, or other is referred to. These three tests can do some of the work of determining number as well, but not all of it, since they do not distinguish singular from plural "you," or "he/she/it" from "they." Consequently, condition $c4$ must also be included, but entries under $c4$ are given in parentheses where they are redundant—where number is not required in addi-

Table 4.6   A decision table for deictic reference to persons.

	1	2	3	4	5	6	7	8	9	10
Conditions										
c1. *S*?	Y	Y	Y	Y	N	N	N	N	N	N
c2. *A*?	Y	Y	N	N	Y	Y	Y	N	N	N
c3. *O*?	Y	N	Y	N	Y	N	N	Y	Y	N
c4. Singular?	(N)	(N)	(N)	(Y)	(N)	Y	N	Y	N	
English Actions										
a1. WE	x	x	x							
a2. I				x						
a3. YOU					x	x	x			
a4. HE								x		
a5. THEY									x	
Hanunóo actions										
a6. TAM	x									
a7. TAH		x								
a8. MIH			x							
a9. KUH				x						
a10. YUH					x		x			
a11. MUH						x				
a12. YAH								x		
a13. DAH									x	
a14. exit										x

tion to the first three conditions in order to determine the English pronoun. In addition to the English pronouns, as a minor test of the generality of this method of analysis, the Hanunóo pronouns are also given (according to our understanding of Conklin, 1962).

Person and number are the major semantic features of personal pronouns in English. Status and gender also are important in other Indo-European languages. In English, gender depends on sex, although, as Weinreich (1966) points out, "any physical object can in English be referred to by *she* with a special semantic effect" (p. 405). In French, every noun must be marked as either masculine or feminine, but this categorization is only loosely related to sex even for animate referents. In German, nouns are masculine, feminine, or neuter, but again linguistic gender is only vaguely related to sex. According to Bloomfield (1933), Algonquian languages have animate and inanimate genders, although some inanimate objects belong to the animate gender, and some Bantu languages have as many as twenty such classes with gender and number distinctions combined. Mastery of these categories of nouns imposes a heavy load on a learner's memory (Tucker, Lambert, and Rigault, 1973).

Status relations between speaker and listener provide a richer source of psychological observations, with respect to both the language itself and the society that speaks it. It is generally assumed that some democratic impulse in the history of English-speaking nations led people to abandon "thou" and "thee," which, in Shakespeare's time, were used to express affection toward friends, superiority to servants, and dislike for strangers, in favor of impersonal "you," and that in its consequent deficit of such status indicators English contrasts sharply with such languages as Japanese, where honorifics are consistently used to debase the speaker and honor the addressee—"Will the honorable guest please enter my humble home," to give a typical translation. There is some reason to think this contrast has been exaggerated, however. Brown and Ford (1961) analyzed the use of titles or first names—"Mr. Steiger" or "William"—and such greetings as "Good morning" or "Hi" by American speakers of English. They were able to distinguish five levels of intimacy: (a) titles alone between complete strangers; (b) title plus last name between newly introduced adults; (c) last name alone between some enlisted men or slightly antagonistic acquaintances; (d) first name between friendly acquaintances; and (e) multiple names, including nicknames, between intimate friends. R. Lakoff (1972) has pointed to various ways in which modal verbs, intonation, subjunctives, and tag questions are used in English to convey subtle shades of politeness according to the status and attitude of the speaker, and she argues that in order to characterize these forms correctly it is essential to take extralinguistic context into account. Among the extralinguistic factors she lists respective status of speaker and addressee, the type of social situation in which they find themselves, the real-world knowledge or beliefs the speaker brings to a discourse, his lack of desire to commit himself on a position.

Although their dependence on nonlinguistic context makes such forms difficult to analyze syntactically, this very dependence makes them of particular interest to students of social relations; nonreciprocal use of a given form of address can indicate social distinctions among members of any social group. If one member of a social dyad consistently addresses the other as "Mr. Noble" and is addressed in return as "Charlie," it reveals something of psychological importance about how they view their relationship. Brown and Gilman (1960), on the basis of questionnaires answered by speakers of Indo-European languages that have preserved the thou-you distinction (tu-Lei in Italian, tú-usted in Spanish, tu-vous in French, du-Sie in German, or generically *T-V*) distinguish two dimensions of social organization underlying the choice of which second-person pronoun should be used: status differences can motivate nonreciprocal address; social solidarity can motivate reciprocal address. The two motivations sometimes conflict; an employer, for example, may want to use the *V* of status to his employee at the same time he would like to express the *T* of solidarity. According to Brown and Gilman, solidarity has largely won out over status, and reciprocal *T* seems to be gaining over reciprocal *V*.

Both status and solidarity are relations between people, not properties of individuals. In order to determine whether some individual should be addressed as "tu" or "vous," a Frenchman must consider not only person and number but also the social relation between himself and his addressee. Since a relation involves at least two terms, any schema for the choice of the second-person form will require two arguments rather than one, and thus will be more complex than the schemata we have considered so far. That is to say, we cannot define some class X of individuals such that "X is addressed as 'tu' " because every individual can be addressed as "tu" or "vous" by different speakers. How routines should be written for words that label relations rather than individual persons, objects, or events is a topic for chapter 5. This consideration of status relations has taken us ahead of our story.

Since kin terms label relations as well as individuals, we will postpone discussion of them, even though they are obviously a domain of person labels, until we have considered in more detail how relational routines should be represented procedurally.

4.5.3   Generic Person Labels

A great variety of English words are available to designate different kinds of persons. Those with some reliable perceptual foundations include: person, adult, man, woman, child, youngster, kid, boy, girl, baby, infant. Occupational designations are far more numerous but require memorial rather than perceptual recognition: doctor, lawyer, miner, farmer, sailor, politician. Occupants of certain social roles may be denoted by distinctive terms as long as they hold that role: president, director, chairman, colonel, congressman. In sports, team members are designated by the positions they play: fullback, shortstop, center, server. There are many relational designations in addition to kin terms: employer, employee, assailant, victim, seller, buyer, friend, enemy. Some labels, once applied, can haunt a man for years: convict, addict, thief, deserter, traitor, coward. And we have labels for race (Caucasian, Oriental, Bushman), religion (Jew, Christian, Catholic, Protestant), place of origin (Swede, Italian, Israeli) political party (Tory, Liberal, Communist, royalist) temperament (optimist, crank, curmudgeon, saint), ability (fool, genius, expert, novice)—and so the varieties go on and on.

The heterogeneity of such person labels defies any attempt to analyze their underlying semantics. More accurately, any analysis of these labels would necessarily cut across many semantic domains. The heterogeneity becomes most obvious when we recall that almost any verb in English can be used to label a person who could serve as its subject: be/being, run/runner, own/owner, fly/flier, range/ranger, shave/shaver, listen/listener. Given the productive use of the "-er" morpheme in English, the variety of person labels is as great as the variety of agentive verbs.

We should consider what implications this heterogeneity might hold for the organization of lexical memory. There is nothing sufficiently coherent here to be called a semantic field. But it is clear that people have a well-developed and highly differentiated concept of person. Apparently there are some concepts so general and so important that they can enter into a great variety of semantic fields. In chapter 6 we will discover others in the same class: object, event, place, time, state, cause, intention, quantity. When we try to track down the linguistic resources available for expressing these general concepts we find ourselves moving back and forth across lexical and grammatical categories of the most diverse sorts. When some concept leads us on a merry chase, the only sensible conclusion to draw is that it does not provide a conceptual core for any single, well-defined semantic field.

If this argument is correct, a complete catalog of the semantic domains of English would not be a complete catalog of the general concepts that serve to organize semantic memory. In addition to concepts that are sufficiently specific to serve as the conceptual core for a lexical domain we would expect to find others of a more general nature that enter into and help to differentiate the more specific concepts. Such a characterization is unfortunately vague; the only way we know to sharpen it is to explore several semantic domains in sufficient detail to enable us to look for these recurrent general concepts in a variety of different contexts.

5

Properties and Relations

*A rough road into the empirical semantic wilderness is preferable to
a well paved one timidly skirting the borders.*
—Edward H. Bendix (1966)

A language must make it possible for people to identify and refer
to entities by describing their properties and characterizing various relations
among them; a psychology of language must recognize that people are biologically equipped to attend to and discriminate among those properties and
relations. We have attempted to catalog the properties of and relations among
objects and events that can be abstracted and judged perceptually. We have
also suggested how the conceptual system might exploit such judgments in
order to provide labels. We will now consider, by way of examples drawn from
English, how these labels are organized in semantic fields and systems of
relational thought.

Before entering into details of particular fields or systems we will raise three
general issues by way of introduction. The first concerns the difficulty of deciding whether a word expresses a property or a relation. The second concerns
the psychological status of definitions phrased in terms of semantic components. And the third concerns the difficulty of deciding whether some proposed
definition of a word is complete.

Certain words in any language have as their major purpose to denote properties that seem natural to the users of that language. In English the predicate
adjectives (adjectives that can be used in such constructions as "The sky was
blue," "The soup is hot," "Lions are dangerous," or any other that fits the
general formula NP + *be* + Adj) obviously specify values of such properties.
But many nouns are also best thought of in this way: to call something a

table is to say that it has all the properties, whatever they may be, of tables. The critical point is whether, as a predicate, the term takes a single argument. Adjectival and nominal properties can be combined in the schemata of some entities. For example, all tables have some color and some tables have a gray color; one can denote by "gray table" all objects that have the properties of tables and whose color is gray. If gray tables became of some importance, a new word, "grable," might be introduced to denote objects exhibiting all those properties—in which case it would be redundant to speak of a "gray grable." It is even possible to express properties of properties: an object that is moving has the property of motion; the adverb "rapidly" specifies a property of the property of motion.

If a predicate takes two or more arguments, it is a relation. But a relation can also be thought of as specifying a property. For example, if Mike is Ike's father, then "father of Ike" is a property applying to Mike, and "father of" is a property applying to the ordered pair, Mike and Ike. (They must be an ordered pair, since reversing the order of the arguments changes the relation from "father of" to its converse, "son of.")

What it is that makes a relation seem natural is even more slippery to define than the naturalness of a property, but it has something to do with the ability of people to recognize relations intuitively, and that ability must be characterized in terms of the nature of human intelligence, not in terms of the infinite variety of combinatorial possibilities. Or, to turn the argument around, an algorithm that would select from the abstract class of all possible relations (and properties) just those that seem natural to a human intelligence would tell us a great deal about human intelligence. We cannot offer such an algorithm, so we must rely on intuition to suggest the restricted notions of "property" and "relation" that we require.

We will continue to use [F(x)] to indicate properties, which can usually be rendered linguistically by a sentence of the form "x is F." [GREEN(x)], for example, corresponds to "x is green," and [TABLE(x)] corresponds to "x is a table." The reader will recall that a schema is essentially an assertion, and that brackets indicate this fact. In general, we will forgo this notational device for the sake of simplicity, but it is important to bear in mind that a schema excludes any specification of particular control instructions. This exclusion allows a schema to be used by a variety of control instructions.

We will use F(x, y) to indicate two-term relations; it can often be rendered linguistically by sentences of the form "x is the F of y." FATHER(x, y), where x points to Mike and y points to Ike, corresponds to "Mike is the father of Ike." And similarly for n-term relations, although natural relations between more than three arguments are rather rare. In the case of two-term relations, F(x, y), we will order x and y in such a way that the first member of the pair is the "referent" and the second is the "relatum" (see Reichenbach, 1947, pp. 112ff).

This notation is convenient for some purposes, but it tends to obscure differences that are linguistically important. For example, the three sentences

(1)   (a) Mike is a policeman.
         (b) Mike is tall.
         (c) Mike is groaning.

could all be represented abstractly by $F(x)$, where x is evaluated as "Mike" and F is variously "a policeman," "tall," and "groaning." Whether a property is to be expressed by a noun phrase, a predicate adjective, or an intransitive verb has implications for grammar. Moreover, we can word the sentences differently:

(2)   (a) Mike is a member of the police force.
         (b) Mike is taller than the average man.
         (c) Mike is uttering groans.

Although the sentences in (2) are virtually synonymous with their corresponding versions in (1), we would probably want to represent them abstractly as relations, $F(x, y)$: membership is a relation between Mike and the police force, "taller than" is a relation between Mike and the average man, "uttering" is a relation between Mike and the groans. On the other hand,

(3)   (a) Mike is that policeman.
         (b) Mike is unique.
         (c) Mike is dying.

cannot be reworded in the same ways; (3a) identifies Mike not as a member of a class but as a particular member of a class; (3b) does not permit a comparative construction; (3c) does not have an obvious transitive paraphrase. Exactly when a sentence is expressing a property and should be construed as an instance of $F(x)$ or when it is expressing a relation and should be construed as an instance of $F(x, y)$ cannot be settled by a simple rule of thumb.

Many adjectives seem at first glance to express simple properties but on further analysis are better characterized as relations, after the manner of (2b). "Tall" denotes one height for a building, another for a tree, and still another for a man. "Tall" must be interpreted relative to some standard expectation for objects of the same general type as those identified by the noun it is used to modify (Sapir, 1944). That is to say, in order to verify that some x is tall, one must test whether the height of x is greater than some value y that characterizes the expected height of things like x.* In order to perform such a test, therefore, one must remember or compute the norm y against which the height of x should be tested. Although "tall" would seem to specify a property of an individual object, on closer inspection it looks relational.

In the relation $F(x, y)$ there are two free variables, x and y. Actually, these

---

*The phrase "things like x" conceals important questions. Stanley Peters (personal communication) points out that "tall" does not have the same expected value in "The kindergarten built a tall snowman" as in "The football team built a tall snowman," although $x =$ snowman in both sentences. It is not obvious how propositional semantics would represent the difference in truth conditions for the propositions expressed by these two sentences; we assume that procedural semantics could call on operations to determine the domain of x before estimating an expected value of the relevant property.

variables are not completely free; one would not say "Jonas's weight is taller than Maggie's wealth." If F is the relation "taller than," it is presupposed that x and y denote objects having vertical extents; it is the heights of x and y that F relates. So we need a way to represent height. Let HEIGHT(x) denote a function, the height of x, whose values can be expressed in some conventional units. Thus, "Mike is 6 feet tall" can be represented by HEIGHT(Mike) = 6 FEET. And "x is taller than y" can then be represented by

$$(4) \qquad \text{GREATER}(\text{HEIGHT}(x), \text{HEIGHT}(y)),$$

where GREATER is a conceptual version of the perceptual predicate introduced in chapter 1.

Let us return to (1b), "Mike is tall." If we interpret (1b) to mean "Mike is taller than the average man," as in (2b), and use (4) to expand it again into "Mike's height is greater than the height of the average man," we can see that (1b) must have the structure MAN(x) & GREATER(HEIGHT(Mike), NORM(HEIGHT(x))), where NORM(HEIGHT(x)) is a function yielding the elusive norm by considering the heights of the set of individuals assigned to x. The point to note about this formula is that it has, in effect, only one free variable, the variable whose value here is "Mike." Once a substitution has been made for this variable, the predicate denoting the superordinate term should be defined automatically.

It may help to put the matter in a different context. Suppose we let DIVISIBLE(x, y) represent the relation "x is divisible by y without remainder," where x and y are natural integers. Now we could represent the formula "x is an even number" either as a property of x, EVEN(x), or as a relation of x to a constant, DIVISIBLE$(x, 2)$. That is, if we replace one of the free variables by a constant, we get something that acts very much like a property. We can talk about "even" as if it expressed a property, a relational property, but when we wish to test whether any value of x has that property, we must treat it in terms of the relation DIVISIBLE. "Tall" is like "even"—it expresses a relational property.

How do children learn words like "tall" and "taller"? One problem they have is to differentiate them as special forms of "big" having to do with vertical extent. Another problem is to internalize expected values for the heights of different classes of objects—to develop internal frames of reference for judging heights. If one accepts what Piaget has said about egocentricity, one standard they might easily internalize is their own height. But children begin learning the expected sizes of things quite early and so are probably ready to understand "tall" as a relational property as soon as they differentiate the dimension to which it applies.

But why is "taller" more difficult for children than "tall"? If they really learn "tall" as "taller than average," the order of acquisition should be the other way round. One reason may be that the comparative construction is syntactically more difficult. Another reason may be that "taller" can be used to describe differences between different sorts of objects, whereas "tall" involves differences within one sort of object. Since children are frequently more attentive to within-object variability than to between-object variability (Nelson, 1973a), they might be more attentive to within-class variability than to between-class variability. Still another reason might be that "taller" usually places heavier demands on absolute memory. Children who understand "tall" have little difficulty with "taller than" as applied to two objects seen side by side, but they have trouble when two objects having no expected values—wooden rods, for example—are to be compared successively (Bryant, 1974).

The order of development seems to go from attending to vertical height, which is a property $F(x)$, to noticing deviations from expected values, which is a relational property $F(x, k)$, to expressing general relations between heights, which is a relation $F(x, y)$. The reasons for this order are complex and involve both the nature of the language and the demands of the tasks used to test children's competence. The order is not to be explained in terms of some basic inability to deal with relations but rather in terms of anchoring those relations they can appreciate to certain memorable landmarks.

We began by noting that adjectives like "tall" are usually thought to express properties, then argued that "tall" expresses a relation, and concluded that it involves a function, "height." Once we start decomposing properties in this way we must know where to stop. For example, it does seem to be a part of the meaning of "height" that it denotes a distance, since "It reached a height of 40 kilograms" is semantically anomalous. Moreover, it must be a distance in the vertical direction, since "From Atlanta to Boston is a height of 937 miles" is also odd. In short, "height" can be analyzed in terms of another more basic function, DISTANCE. If the height of an object is 6 feet, then VERT (DISTANCE(earth, z)) = 6 feet, where z is the top of the object.

According to this argument, an apparently simple assertion like "Mike is tall" decomposes into something monstrous,

$$\text{MAN}(x) \ \& \ \text{GREATER}(\text{VERT}(\text{DISTANCE}(\text{earth, TOP}(\text{Mike})))),$$
$$\text{NORM}(\text{VERT}(\text{DISTANCE}(\text{earth, TOP}(x)))))),$$

and there is no guarantee that this decomposition is complete.

What are the psychological implications of such a decomposition into semantic components? On the one hand, we want to say that a person who knows the meaning of the adjective "tall" knows something like this. On the other hand, it is absurd to say that every time a person who knows English hears the word "tall" in a sentence he must think about—work through, construct, be aware of, compile, or compute—such a decomposition. Kintsch (1974) points out in this connection what people *can* do and what they *will* do are often different. Some tasks require a person to make comparisons or draw inferences that exploit such decompositions; in those cases the time required to perform the task may bear some relation to the compositional complexity of the terms it contains. But Kintsch also conducted studies in which the tasks did not require people to analyze lexically complex words into their components; his results argue against automatic decomposition. A decomposition is a description of the language user's lexical competence; his performance on any particular occasion may not fully exploit that competence.

One advantage of having a procedural dimension to our theory is that differences in depth of processing seem to represent a natural aspect of the information processing that must be performed on different occasions. In order to exploit our computational metaphor, let us consider an arithmetic analogy. Probably the strongest decompositional claim a lexicologist could make would parallel the fundamental theorem of arithmetic: any lexical item can be expressed as a unique (Cartesian?) product of prime lexical items. Now, many arithmetic computations involving 30 can be carried through successfully without factoring it into $2 \times 3 \times 5$, but some computations (finding a least common denominator, for example) would require such a decomposition. If the lexical situation were analogous to the arithmetical, very strong claims about lexical decomposability would have no general relation to, say, reaction times for tasks involving complex lexical items.

Probably the weakest claim one would care to make about decomposability is that each lexical item is a unique prime in its own right. Just as one human being cannot be decomposed into a combination of other human beings, so no lexical item can be decomposed into others. Even in this case, however, various relations might be found to hold between many pairs of lexical items, although such properties and relations would not be regarded as conceptual atoms from which lexical items are built or into which they can be reduced. Here again no correlation would be expected between complexity and reaction times, since all lexical items would presumably be equally complex gestalts.

Although experimental evidence on processing times or errors does not seem relevant to deciding between these two theoretical extremes, there are various indirect arguments that would seem to discredit them both. Strong decomposition is implausible in view of the difficulty that lexicographers have in providing complete definitions; some residuum of meaning, often but not necessarily affective, usually vitiates the synonymy of the lexical item and its definition. On the other hand, complete individuality is inadequate to explain the rich and relatively consistent patterns of properties and relations found in the lexicon. Perhaps the reasonable approach would be to regard these two views as upper and lower bounds between which one might search for a plausible theory.

Suppose there were many lexical items having the characteristic that whenever they occurred in a simple declarative sentence, verification of the proposition they expressed would require execution of a particular cognitive (perceptual or memorial) test. That test would partition the lexicon into those items that need it and those that do not, but the lower bound—the individuality hypothesis—would not be violated. One might go further and argue that the need to perform this test (and its acceptable outcome) must be indicated explicitly in the information associated with those lexical items, and so, in a real sense, the test can be said to be "incorporated" into their meanings (Gruber, 1965). Then the goal of analysis would be to determine which lexical items incorporate the test—in short, to decompose such items into that test plus anything else they require. This program falls short of strong decomposition in that (a) it is a decomposition of words into cognitive entities, concepts or tests, rather than into other words; (b) the method of incorporation is left unspecified but would surely be more complex than a Cartesian product; and (c) there is no guarantee that decomposition would be complete without introducing more cognitive entities than there are lexical items to be defined, so the problem of the residuum is unresolved. But a sort of limited decomposition would be possible.

We might imagine, therefore, that every lexical item incorporates several primitive lexical concepts and that no primitive lexical concept is expressed directly in a single lexical item. Certain patterns of primitive concepts might recur frequently, and so give an impression of underlying concepts into which surface words could be decomposed, but individuality and the appearance of residual meanings would result from the existence of unique lexical primitives not expressed directly by any single word and not entering into recurrent patterns. Although underlying concepts (patterns of primitives) would reflect the considerable order that has been repeatedly found in the lexicon and in selectional restrictions for word combinations, it would not be obvious that there could be any unique solution to the decomposition problem (alternative formulations might seem equally plausible) and theoretical economy would be highly unlikely (there would not be fewer lexical primitives than there are lexical items).

These speculations are intended primarily to alert the reader to theoretical alternatives he might keep in mind while exploring various lexical domains in the following pages. Our attempts to use decomposition in order to discover some of the primitive lexical concepts of English should not be taken as a claim that decomposition is automatically performed as a necessary part of understanding the use or meaning of every lexical item we hear.

The limits of the semantic analyses that a listener must perform may be related to the limits of the semantic analyses that a lexicologist can perform. It is usually easy to identify one or more components of the meaning of a word. But it is not clear that any workable criterion could be proposed for deciding when a semantic analysis had exhausted every possible semantic distinction that could be drawn by a skilled speaker of the language.

What is a semantic analysis an analysis of? Is it an analysis of a word or an analysis of the meaning of a word? It cannot be an analysis of a word. To analyze a word would be to give an account of the syllables it contains and of the phonemes in each syllable. So it must be an analysis of the word's meaning, of the concept that the word expresses. But this alternative leads straight into "the paradox of analysis" (Langford, 1942), which is the source of many puzzles in this area. The paradox goes as follows. If a word and a semantic analysis of that word both express the same concept, we have a trivial statement of identity, like A = A. Yet if they do not express the same concept, the semantic analysis must be wrong. We seem to face an uncomfortable choice between error and triviality.

How can we avoid this paradox? How do we establish that a statement of synonymy is far from trivial, or that a statement of some relation other than synonymy is not necessarily wrong? Consider an example. Suppose the word to be analyzed is "brother," the semantic analysis is "male sibling," and the claim is that these express the same concept, that $\text{BROTHER}(A, B) = \text{MALE}(A)$ & $\text{SIBLING}(A, B)$. What is the significance of putting an equal sign between these two conceptual formulas? In what sense does that equation say anything more than the truly trivial $\text{BROTHER}(A, B) = \text{BROTHER}(A, B)$? Our answer is that the significance of the analytic claim lies in the conceptual connection it creates between different words. The question whether a semantic analysis is an analysis of words or of meanings is misleading; it is not concerned solely with words or solely with meanings but with the connections between words that meanings create. Discovering those connections and stating them precisely is far from a trivial task.

Finding two or more words or phrases that express exactly the same concepts is so far from trivial that some would reject it as impossible. If that is true, we are on the other horn of the dilemma: error. But must every incomplete analysis be wrong? In order to answer that question we must consider what it would mean for a semantic analysis to be complete.

To ask for a complete semantic analysis of a word is like asking for a perfect definition. This translation of the question moves it into the realm of lexicography, where considerable practical knowledge exists. According to Weinreich (1967), "we need not restrict lexicography by requiring that a definition be a *perfect* rendition of a meaning, or that the definiendum be recognizable from the definiens by mere inspection. Much less can we claim for natural-language lexicography that the definiens should be literally substitutable for the definiendum in normal discourse" (pp. 29-30). In practice, definitions are incomplete.

The practical question, therefore, is whether incomplete definitions are of any value to us. Is Lakoff (1971a, p. 272) correct in his claim that only an inclusion relation is required—that the meaning of the incomplete definition must be included in the meaning of the term defined—in order to justify the kind of semantic analysis we wish to undertake? If our goal is to identify semantic components that serve to differentiate and relate words in different semantic fields, is a complete analysis necessary?

In 4.2.1 we discussed hyponymy and defined it as the semantic relation that holds between two words W and V when, by virtue of the meanings of W and V, "It is a W" (in the appropriate sense of "is") entails "It is a V." For example, "It is a typewriter" entails "It is a machine," so "typewriter" is a hyponym of "machine." Note that although hyponymy is a relation between words it is defined here in terms of an entailment relation between sentences. "Typewriter" cannot entail "machine" except in an appropriate sentential context, for entailment is not a relation that can take single words as its arguments.

A superordinate word will generally occur in definitions of its hyponyms. Our dictionary defines "typewriter" as "a keyboard machine that prints characters and numerals by means of a set of metal hammers bearing raised, inked type that strike the paper when actuated by manually pressed keys." Because this definition is overly descriptive, technology has passed it by, but the part that has stood the test of time is the superordinate term, "machine." For our analytic purposes we could make good use of an incomplete definition like "a keyboard machine for printing," for this would suffice to connect "typewriter" conceptually with other words in the same semantic field. The word to be defined entails its incomplete definition even though the incomplete definition does not entail the word to be defined. For other purposes the definition might be woefully inadequate.

Our interest in such unsatisfactory definitions arises from the fact that people tend to judge that words and their hyponyms are similar in meaning. The word "typewriter," for example, expresses a meaning that is much more similar to the meaning expressed by "machine" than either of those is to the meaning expressed by "tree." If pressed to explain this intuition of semantic similarity, people would probably say that the meaning of the hyponym includes the meaning of the superordinate, plus some additional semantic components to distinguish it from hyponyms of the same superordinate. The more semantic components two words share, the more similar people judge their meanings to be.

Considerations of this sort provide psychological justification for factoring the meanings of many words into component parts: meaning of hyponym = meaning of superordinate + residuum. In terms of schemata, these relations imply that the schema for the superordinate is (or could be) part of the schema for the hyponym. Since we are interested in discovering the widely shared schemata that account for the structure of semantic fields, we are necessarily interested in incomplete definitions. That is not to say that we are uninterested in complete definitions but rather that it is sufficient for most purposes of semantic analysis to establish incomplete definitions. That we may not be able in every case to provide definitions of a word that will differentiate it from all the other words in the language does not imply that we are unable to begin a semantic analysis.

All of this no doubt seems obvious. The difficulties associated with incomplete definitions do not really arise until we consider questions of substitutability. Words acquire whatever meanings they have by virtue of the routines in which people have learned to use them to perform and understand conventional speech acts. That is, words have their meanings by virtue of their contributions to sentences used for communication. To consider their meanings without considering the sentences into which they can be substituted is at best an uncertain, if not impossible, task. And to compare the meanings of two words requires—implicitly, at least—sentence contexts within which the comparison can be made. We must take substitutability into account.

Linguists have long used interchangeability in context as a test for membership of two or more linguistic elements in the same category, and some have even suggested that two elements having exactly the same privileges of occurrence would have the same meaning. One might ask whether incomplete definitions are paraphrases that can be substituted wherever the words that they define occur. But this question is not well phrased. Anything *can* be substituted. The real question is what effects the substitution will have. For the purposes of linguistic analysis, the method of substitution requires criteria specifying what must remain invariant under substitution. In phonetics, two phones are regarded as allophones of the same phoneme if the substitution of one for the other does not change a native speaker's identification of any spoken word. In syntax, two words are regarded as belonging to the same syntactic category if the substitution of one for the other does not make any grammatical sentence ungrammatical. In semantics, two words are regarded as synonyms if substitution of one for the other does not change the meaning of any sentence. These substitution tests are used by linguists as part of their "distributional methods"; their convenient, semimechanical nature has earned them more admirers than their analytic value merits.

When we ask about the substitutability of an incomplete definition for the word it defines, we must specify what should remain invariant. The obvious criterion, since definitions are supposed to provide meanings, is that the meaning must remain invariant. Consequently, there is a school of thought that considers definitions to be synonymous with the words they define, and synonyms to be interchangeable in most contexts. Those who hold this opinion would regard an incomplete definition as a contradiction in terms, or, if they wished to be generous, a bad or incorrect definition. There is little we can say to them, for we do not accept their basic premise that definitions must be synonymous with the words they define.

Consider some examples of the difficulties involved in giving complete, fully substitutable definitions. Gleitman and Gleitman (1970) give "garbage man" as a case in point. Most people would accept "a man who collects garbage" as synonymous with "garbage man," and a linguist might even provide a transformational rule to derive one from the other, just as he might derive "a tall man" from "a man who is tall." Although a garbage man collects garbage, a man who collects garbage need not be a garbage man, however; "a man who collects garbage" is an incomplete paraphrase because it lacks the occupational meaning of "garbage man." Again, "cause to change location" is an incomplete definition of the transitive use of "move," because you can cause someone to change location (by being sufficiently obnoxious, for example) without your actually moving them, although you cannot actually move them without causing them to change location.

If a definition is incomplete, substituting it for the word it defines will change the meaning of the sentence. After substitution, the sentence will usually have a more general meaning. If we take "warm-blooded animal" as an incomplete definition of "elephant," the sentence "Harold likes all elephants" will, after substitution, become "Harold likes all warm-blooded animals," which certainly has a different meaning. Indeed, one sentence may be true and the other false, depending on the generality of Harold's attitudes about animals. The most obvious price we must pay for accepting incomplete definitions, therefore, is to abandon the premise that substitution is useful in semantic analysis only if meaning is always preserved unchanged.

In complex sentences, replacing a verb by a verb phrase can lead to odd results even when the two are fully synonymous. Fodor (1970) has pointed out that a phrase having two verbs can exhibit degrees of freedom unavailable to a single verb. Suppose there was a verb "moofs" that was fully synonymous with "causes to change location." In the sentence "He moofed the chair by falling" it is reasonably clear that he fell against the chair and caused it to change location. When we substitute the synonymous phrase we obtain "He caused the chair to change location by falling," where it is no longer clear whether he fell or the chair fell. Since the adverbial phrase "by falling" can now attach to either of the verbs, the substitution has introduced ambiguity. The meaning has changed, even though we made "moof" and "causes to change location" fully synonymous by fiat.

Difficulties can also arise when, conversely, we substitute a verb for its synonymous definition. For example, the sentence "I caused the chair to change its location and its color" contains the definition of "moof," but when we substitute the verb we obtain the questionable result "I moofed the chair and its color." Substitution into the surface structure of the sentence inadvertently removed an implicit second occurrence of "change" in the underlying structure of the sentence. Even when we create perfect synonymy by decree, substitution can change the meaning of a sentence—which we take to mean that the scope for synonymy is far more restricted than some theorists have admitted.

This last example suggests that if we want to work with substitutions we should not think of them as being made in the surface structure. This point has been clear to linguistic theorists, although there has been disagreement about how deep the substitution must be—whether, for example, all substitutions should be made before any syntactic transformations are applied, or whether substitution itself should be regarded as a kind of transformation, equal in dignity to any other. Our preference is to avoid thinking of lexical substitutions as if they were grammatical transformations. We assume that the semantic similarity one feels between, say, "zebra" and "horse with stripes" should not be explained in terms of the substitution of a so-called surface noun "zebra" as a transformational derivative from an underlying phrase corresponding to "horse with stripes," but rather in terms of subroutines shared by these two expressions.

We will use substitution because it is difficult to judge the meanings of words when no context is given, but we will use it only for the purpose of comparing meanings, not equating them. Our claim is merely that incomplete definitions can help us gain an overview of a semantic field, and that for this purpose it is not necessary (even if it were possible) to have complete definitions substitutable without change of meaning in all conceivable contexts.

What, then, does remain unchanged when we use substitution in semantic analysis? Invariance of meaning under substitution in every context is the strongest demand we could make. It is not difficult to weaken it. We will take the definition of hyponymy as our model. We can demand a relation of entailment (not equivalence) in appropriate contexts (not all contexts). That is, when an incomplete definition is compared with the word it incompletely defines in an appropriate context, the sentence containing the word defined should entail the sentence containing the incomplete definition.

As for what contexts are "appropriate," the best answer we can give is that they should be no more complex than required to test the entailment. For example, "Dumbo is an elephant" entails "Dumbo is an animal" so simple, affirmative, copular sentences provide an appropriate context in which to test noun hyponymy. Negative or quantificational contexts, however, can be too complex. "Dumbo is not a horse" does not entail "Dumbo is not an animal," and "All elephants have trunks" does not entail "All animals have trunks." The appropriate contexts in which to test verb hyponymy are less well understood, but entailment still seems to be the appropriate test (see discussion of the "but" test in 6.3.1).

When phrased in terms of entailment in appropriate contexts, our requirements are weaker, but more realistic. The claim is that nothing stronger is needed in order to undertake preliminary explorations of semantic structure.

The method of incomplete definitions is most useful when dealing with many words together. With rare exceptions, it will not be the method of choice when one is examining some small set of closely related words in great depth and detail. The virtue of the method is that it enables us to converge gradually toward complete definitions while leaving open the possibility that complete definitions are unachievable within the scope of the schemata with which we hope to identify major semantic components. The guiding criterion is that the semantic components we identify should leave us with groups of words that seem intuitively similar in meaning. As long as this criterion is met, incomplete definitions enable us to direct our attention to the larger dimensions of the problem without becoming hopelessly entangled in the numerous and often baffling details idiosyncratic to particular words.

The factorization of meaning begins when sentences are taken out of their situational contexts of use. It continues when words are taken out of their sentential contexts. Our goal now is to take semantic components out of the words in which people have learned to package them. But we could just as well think of the analysis as taking semantic components out of situations— that way of describing it would at least remind us of the context that gives the enterprise its purpose. And it would explain the otherwise puzzling frequency with which it is necessary to use sentences and even situations in order to indicate the particular semantic distinctions among the properties and relations that we will analyze.

5.1   COLOR

Color terms have served for centuries as a favorite example for empiricist philosophers concerned with language. Psychologists have found color perception and color blindness a challenging field of study and their interest has frequently spilled over into color naming. Anthropologists have been interested in the ways different cultures can partition the continuous gradations of the spectrum and so, often working within the tradition of the linguistic relativity hypothesis of Humboldt, Sapir, Whorf, Hoijer, and others, have provided much comparative data. Painters sometimes consider their art in verbal terms. And recent developments in color photography and television have created a whole new color technology. The facts needed to test almost any conceivable hypothesis about color terms can probably be found somewhere in the vast literature that has accumulated around the topic. We will not attempt to review all the previous work; the literature is enormous and highly technical, far beyond the needs of our present argument.

According to Hering (1920), as early as 1865 Hermann Aubert said that "the words black, white, red, yellow, green, and blue suffice as main designations" of color sensations, and Ernst Mach also selected red, yellow, green, and blue as fundamental color sensations "since these are the only ones in which one perceives no other colors in direct observation." Then, in a footnote, Hering comments, "If one were to designate the nomenclature used by Aubert as a four-color theory, then not only Aubert but *language* itself would be its author, for language has long since singled out red, yellow, green, and blue as the principal colors of the multiplicity of chromatic colors" (p. 48). Although the Young-Helmholtz three-color theory could account for the process of excitation, the process of sensation was said by Hering to require four colors for its description, and these four colors, which correspond to the color terms "red," "green," "yellow," and "blue," are generally referred to as the psychological primary colors.

In terms of the hierarchical structures discussed in chapter 4, we interpret Hering's comment that language has singled out "red," "yellow," "green," and "blue" to mean that these color terms, along with "black" and "white," form a contrastive set having "color" as its superordinate term, and that each of these primary color terms can have its own hyponyms; secondary color terms for "red" would include "scarlet," "pink," "vermilion," "crimson," "magenta." There is room for considerable disagreement as to which color terms are superordinates and which are hyponyms—the scheme just given could be criticized on several grounds—so the crux of our discussion must concern how we could determine a minimal contrastive set of primary color terms. That is to say, our principal interest will be in the internal structure of this contrastive set of terms.

The internal structure of a contrastive set can be as simple as an unordered list, or it can be a complex system of cross classification with terms related by any number of perceptual or conceptual attributes. In the case of color terms, more than one attribute is involved and the quality to be named varies continuously through the spectrum and the ranges of possible lightnesses. The relations among the three basic dimensions of color—hue, lightness, and saturation—are generally conceptualized in the manner indicated in figure 5.1 as providing coordinates for a three-dimensional space. The whole set of pos-

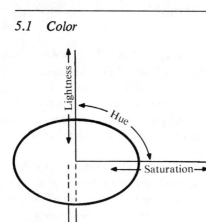

Figure 5.1   Coordinates of the color solid.

sible color sensations is usually represented by a so-called color solid, a sphere with a vertical axis from white at the top through gray in the middle to black at the bottom; around the equator are the spectral colors from red to blue, with nonspectral violets completing the color circle; from the equator inward toward the axis the colors become progressively less chromatic. Any possible color will have a place somewhere in this configuration. We will assume that the color solid is one way of representing the basic schema of the semantic field of English color terms. The problem is to find some way to characterize how a minimal contrastive set of primary color terms can represent this three-dimensional configuration.

Since we already have a three-dimensional representation of the color sensations, it is not difficult to arrange English color terms in a similar three-dimensional array isomorphic with the sensations they label, where every term labels some volume in the total configuration. In this case, thanks to more than a century of investigation of color and color perception, the relations between the sensations, the terms used to label sensations, and the conceptual core underlying this semantic field are relatively clear. What is not so clear is the relations between the color terms themselves.

—Why do we have so many labels for colors? In their *Dictionary of Color* Maerz and Paul (1930) list over 3,000 English color terms.

—Why are some color labels so much more useful than others? Some color sensations have several possible names, whereas others seem ambiguous or even nameless.

—Do the useful color terms label sensations that are perceptually salient in some way? There are psychophysiological reasons for thinking red-green, yellow-blue, and black-white should be coordinates of the color solid.

—Is English color terminology purely arbitrary and conventional? Other languages, especially those outside the Indo-European family of languages, carve up the color solid differently.

One might ask why anybody would care about these words, since physics provides a precise system for specifying colors. A physicist talks about light as radiant energy characterized in terms of wavelengths and areal densities. Surely this is a better way to describe it than laymen have been able to devise. Why not simply adopt the language of physics and abandon all these vague and imprecise terms that were introduced before scientists discovered how to do the job properly?

The trouble with physical specifications of the stimulus as a language for talking about color is that it does not describe what people *see* when they are exposed to those stimuli. The perceived color of a patch of light is not uniquely determined by the wavelength of the radiant energy that produces it. A psychologist must be interested in the experience and behavior of organisms exposed to such stimuli, and that depends on far more than the physical characteristics of the stimulus. Lay terminology for color reflects the perception of it; the physical specification does not.

As indicated in 1.3.1, a basic distinction must be drawn between the color people see when they view an object normally and the color they see when they view a small, homogeneously illuminated part of its surface through a reduction screen. When they see an object in relation to other objects illuminated by a known source of light, they are able to use the information inherent in the ratios between them in order to perceive a relatively constant "true" color for each object; changes in illumination do not affect the ratios of reflected light as drastically as they affect the absolute values. When a reduction screen deprives viewers of these relations, however, they can judge only the absolute value reflected from the surface; obviously, changes in illumination do affect the absolute values of the reflected light.

Some theorists have tried to explain why objects viewed normally maintain a constant color in spite of variations in ambient illumination by appealing to memory of the "real" color of familiar objects. Thus Hering (1920) spoke of familiar objects as being seen "through the spectacles of memory color" (p. 8). But gestalt psychologists have convincingly demonstrated that familiarity is not necessary for color constancy (Koffka, 1935). The maintenance of constant ratios throughout the visual field provides a more adequate explanation.

With respect to color memory, a useful distinction can be drawn between intrinsic colors, landmark colors, and accidental colors. By "intrinsic color" we mean a remembered color that is part of the conception of an object. Just as a table has an intrinsic top, so snow is intrinsically white, soot intrinsically black, blood intrinsically red, grass green, lemons yellow, the sky blue, ashes gray. That particular instances of these objects may depart considerably from their intrinsic color (just as the intrinsic top of a table may not always be uppermost) is irrelevant to one's memory of their intrinsic color.

By "landmark color" we mean memory of the primary hues that provide points of reference for applying the color terminology to perceived colors. Such landmarks are remembered for at least black, white, red, green, yellow, blue, and perhaps gray. It is possible that landmark colors are retained in memory by association with the intrinsic colors of certain objects (or vice versa), but we think a neurophysiological basis is more plausible. We will return to the role of landmark colors in more detail below.

By "accidental color" we mean a remembered color for some object a person is familiar with but that is not intrinsic to all objects in that class. A person may, for example, try to remember the color of a sofa in order to purchase pillows that match it. Since sofas can be upholstered in a variety of colors, the color of any particular sofa is accidental, not intrinsic to it. Memory for accidental colors (other than those falling close to landmark colors) is notoriously inaccurate (Brown and Lenneberg, 1954; Lantz and Stefflre, 1964; Lenneberg, 1967; Miller and McNeill, 1969).

In order to apply the correct label to a perceived color you have to perform some kind of comparison. The most accurate method is to compare the unknown sample side by side with samples whose color names you know and to continue until you find the known sample that most closely matches it. Few people have access to standardized and labeled color samples, however, so most talk about colors is based on a comparison of the perceived color with some kind of remembered color. Part of our task is to explain how this comparison is made. But first we must survey the resources of the English language for labeling colors.

5.1.1   English Color Terms

The noun "red" is defined by our dictionary as a color "whose hue resembles that of blood," the adjective as "having a color resembling that of blood." For "green" the definitions are similar, but emeralds are substituted for blood. "Blue" mentions the clear sky. "Yellow" mentions ripe lemons. These four are the "psychological primaries." "Violet" and "purple" are defined as falling between red and blue; "orange" as between red and yellow; "brown" as a dark orange of low saturation; "pink" as light red. "Black" is defined as the darkest achromatic visual value; "white" as the lightest; and "gray" as any intermediate achromatic value.

The generic term "color" is said to mean "that aspect of things that is caused by differing qualities of the light reflected or emitted by them." Then our dictionary devotes half a page to an "Explanation of the Color Definitions" based on the recommendations of the Inter-Society Color Council as developed by the National Bureau of Standards. The discussion based on the ISCC-NBS recommendations makes no mention of the intrinsic colors of blood, emeralds, clear skies, or ripe lemons, but it explains the terms "hue," "lightness," and "saturation," gives the recommended contrasting terms under each, describes the color solid, and indicates that there is a standard way of partitioning the color solid into 267 blocks, each of which defines a color name constructed by combining terms for hue, lightness, and saturation: "vivid purple," "deep purple," "light purplish gray." The ISCC-NBS recommendations provide a standardized lexicon and grammar for talking about color that can serve the purposes of science, art, industry, and, it is hoped, the general public.

The ISCC-NBS lexicon includes the following words. For the attribute of hue:

(5)
red	purple
reddish orange	reddish purple
orange	purplish red
orange yellow	purplish pink
yellow	pink
greenish yellow	yellowish pink
yellow green	brownish pink
yellowish green	brownish orange
green	reddish brown
bluish green	brown
greenish blue	yellowish brown
blue	olive brown
purplish blue	olive
violet	olive green

The attribute of lightness varies from black through gray to white. The contrasting terms recommended for applying the lightness scale to hues are

(6)   very dark, dark, medium, light, very light.

The contrasting terms recommended for degrees of the saturation attribute are

(7)   grayish, moderate, strong, vivid.

Certain combinations of lightness and saturation have special names:

(8)   brilliant (light and strong)
pale (light and grayish)
deep (dark and strong)

Perhaps the most notable feature of this nomenclature is that most of the color words in English are not included: amaranth, amber, aquamarine, ash, auburn, bay, beige, blond, bronze, chartreuse, chestnut, cinnamon, coral, cream, crimson, cyan, emerald, flaxen, fuchsia, gamboge, geranium, gold, indigo, lavender, magenta, maroon, mauve, ocher, platinum, puce, roan, rose, russet, rust, saffron, salmon, scarlet, silver, tan, tangerine, taupe, ultramarine, umber, vermilion, viridian, wine, to list only a few. If one pursues these missing terms in the *American Heritage Dictionary,* one finds they are defined in terms of the ISCC-NBS nomenclature. For example, amber is a fossil resin; when it lends its name to a color, it designates "medium to dark or deep orange yellow." The name of the gemstone aquamarine designates "pale blue to light greenish blue."

It is apparent that we are dealing here with at least two levels of terminology. The basic color terms of this system are those used for the standard nomenclature in (5): red, orange, yellow, green, blue, violet, purple, pink, brown, and olive for chromatic colors; black, gray, and white for achromatic colors. These thirteen terms, plus some adjectives and a rule involving the use of "-ish," comprise the basic terminology of this system. Secondary color terms are defined in terms of these.

The array of terms recommended by ISCC-NBS is intended to provide a contrastive set; in this system, something cannot be both red and orange at the same time, or, to take a more uncertain pair, violet and purple at the same time. The secondary terms do not contrast directly with the primary terms; something can be amber and yellow, or aquamarine and blue, at the same time. Many of the secondary terms are not well known or frequently used; many are variable in focus and lack saliency; many are names of objects or loanwords from other languages.

The ISCC-NBS nomenclature is contrived rather than natural—the result of an intelligent effort to impose some organization on a sprawling suburb of the lexicon. By taking it as the object of our analysis, rather than collecting direct evidence of usage from native speakers of English, we run some risk of misrepresentation. It is possible, however, to regard the people who developed this nomenclature as highly sophisticated informants and to treat their usage as we would treat data from any other native speakers of English. But the possibility that they may not be representative of other native speakers should be kept in mind.

Primary and secondary terms are distinguished in this system. Is there any reason to think there might be terms superordinate to the primary terms but hyponymic to "color"? In English we speak of light and dark colors, warm and cool colors, chromatic and achromatic colors (or real colors and shades of gray). Should such terms be included in the hierarchy?

Rather than include these adjectives as superordinates of the primary color terms, it is more accurate to regard them as separate semantic fields whose meanings can be combined with color terms to yield more precise specification. It is a common and useful practice in all languages to partition one semantic field by combining it with another—to take their Cartesian product. For example, you can partition names for articles of furniture by combining "furniture" with names for rooms in order to obtain "dining-room furniture," "kitchen furniture," "bedroom furniture." These possibilities lead us into the combinatorial aspects of semantics, where we must consider the selectional restrictions on various combinations: why "warm red" seems redundant, "light black" contradictory, and "kitchen bed" anomalous. Unlike "red," "green," "yellow," and "blue," which are primary color terms, "light," "warm," and "bright" are adjectives that qualify but do not name colors. In "bright black" the adjective "bright" is understood to refer to a mode of appearance different from what we mean here by color. We conclude that only the word "color" is directly superordinate to the thirteen contrasting color terms designated in the ISCC-NBS standards.

The ISCC-NBS terminology implicitly incorporates a simple grammar. First, note the adjectives listed in (6) for lightness, in (7) for saturation, and in (8) for lightness and saturation combined. These terms must be used according to rules for prenominal adjectives in English, which, in this case, amounts to using terms from (6) first, (7) second, and (5) third—lightness, saturation, and hue, in that order.

The grammar of "-ish" is more revealing. To see how it works when fully exploited, consider the following sequence extracted from (5):

(9)   yellow, greenish yellow, yellow green, yellowish green, green.

"Yellow" and "green" anchor the sequence; the other three terms refer to colors that are intermediate between yellow and green. "Yellow green" refers to a color halfway between, one that is just as yellow as it is green. (We might ask why it is not "green yellow," but this seems merely a matter of conventional usage.) "Greenish yellow" refers to a color intermediate between yellow and yellow green (a quarter of the way from yellow to green); "yellowish green" is a color intermediate between yellow green and green (more green than yellow). Thus, we see from (9) that the suffix "-ish" means "just a hint of." Note, incidentally, that "-ish" can be repeated: a "greenish, yellowish, grayish color."

Now consider the selectional restrictions implicit in the hue terms of (5). In order for two hue terms to combine, there must not be a named color between them. Thus, we find reddish orange in (5), but not reddish yellow or reddish green; purplish red, but not purplish olive. Indow and Ohsumi (1971) report that observers are unable to estimate the degree of similarity between colors that are very different; a saturated red and a saturated green are simply "extremely different," and observers are unable to scale the degree of difference between them. The neutral "gray" is the only term that can combine with every hue term. If one writes down all the terms in (5) that are used in isolation and connects pairs of them with lines whenever those terms can be combined to label an intermediate color, one discovers that the only way to simplify the diagram (to make the lines as short as possible and minimize crossing lines) is to array the color names in the familiar circular pattern. The way the color terms can be combined in (5) reflects directly the arrangement of the colors themselves that has resulted from experiments on color mixing.

If we wished to characterize the grammar of "-ish" as it is used in constructing compound color names (taking the ISCC-NBS nomenclature as our sample of educated usage), we could do little more than either accept all combinations as grammatical or list all the acceptable combinations, as in (5). These selectional restrictions are not linguistic in origin. Underlying this array of terms is a concept of color that reflects judgments of perceptual similarity; the field property of the terms related by the concept is specific to this attentional domain. The internal structure of this contrastive set of terms does not reflect some general linguistic strategy for carving up and labeling domains in general; it reflects the nature of color perception.

The use of "-ish" implies something about the way people recognize colors. How, for example, do people decide whether a sample is reddish purple or purplish red? If this decision can be made without resorting to direct inspection of the sample side by side with standard samples of reddish purple and purplish red, we must assume (a) that a person who speaks English carries about in his memory some typical red and some typical purple, and (b) that he can recognize whether the sample is nearer the former or the latter. Thus, "-ish" assumes that people can estimate degrees of similarity.

The ability to make absolute identifications of color is not unlimited, however; Halsey and Chapanis (1954) studied confusions in naming colors of equal luminance and concluded that there are about eleven to fifteen identifiable colors. The number of color terms in the ISCC-NBS recommendations falls (not accidentally) well within the bounds of human competence. But the twenty-eight terms listed in (5) go considerably beyond the average person's ability to identify colors absolutely without confusion. In short, the limited size of the basic array of hue terms is no accident; it reflects human limitations in identifying color.

The color terms selected for the ISCC-NBS standards reflect rather well the most frequent color terms used in the nonspecialized vocabulary of the English-speaking community as a whole. Battig and Montague (1969) gave 442 college students thirty seconds to write down as many color names as they could think of, then tabulated the results to determine which names were most frequently included. The first color name written by 319 people was "red." The twelve color names most frequently given were, in order of decreasing frequency, blue, red, green, yellow, orange, black, purple, white, pink, brown, violet, and gray. This order has the names of the primary colors first and includes all of the basic ISCC-NBS terms except olive.

Psychological constraints on the language of color can be seen more clearly in experiments that apply multidimensional scaling to color names (this work is reviewed in Fillenbaum and Rapoport, 1971, chap. 3). A scaling technique was first applied to judgments of the perceptual similarity of the colors themselves and was found to reproduce with satisfactory accuracy the color space inferred from color mixing (Indow and Kanazawa, 1960; Indow and Uchizono, 1960). When applied to color names—to the words, with nothing more colorful in view than black print on white paper—the color wheel is recovered just as if the colors themselves had been used. Judgments of the similarity of color terms give the same spatial arrangement that we find to represent perceptual judgments and the same arrangement that emerges from an analysis of the combinations permitted in (5).

Given that a hierarchy can be determined and that the primary color terms do seem to be combined on the basis of perception rather than grammar, the next question must concern the particular set of terms that are taken as contrastive in the ISCC-NBS terminology. At this point it seems necessary to disagree with our expert informants. Consider "olive" as a primary color term. Many people do not think of olive when they are asked to list color names;

olive is a fruit first, a color second. For most people, "olive" will not take the "-ish" suffix, a limitation characteristic of most secondary color terms. Similar objections can be raised against "violet" as a primary color term: a violet is a familiar flower, and it does not combine easily with "-ish" for most people. When we examine the place of violet on the list given in (5), we see that it could easily be replaced by "bluish purple."

If we discard olive and violet, we are left with eleven terms: black, white, red, yellow, green, blue, brown, pink, orange, purple, and gray. These are the eleven terms that Berlin and Kay (1969) selected as the "basic color terms" of English. If we wished to reduce this list still further, we could argue that brown is any warm color of low saturation, pink is light red, orange is a fruit, and purple (in addition to being nonspectral) is really the purpura dye. It is not clear how much weight should be given to such arguments. If we limit ourselves solely to linguistic criteria, brown, pink, orange, and purple probably qualify as primary color terms. But perception is a better guide than linguistic rules for understanding color usage. If we take as our criterion for a minimal contrastive set that it should be the smallest set that exhausts the domain denoted by their superordinate term, then brown, pink, orange, purple, and gray can all be dispensed with. That is to say, we can use black and white; red, yellow, green, and blue for the primary chromatic hues; combinations and "-ish" for intermediate hues; and the adjectives in (6)–(8) to indicate variations in brightness and saturation. That such a perceptually minimal contrastive set requires only these terms has been conclusively demonstrated by psychological experiments in color naming.

5.1.2   Color Naming

Since the same wavelength of light can produce different color sensations under different conditions of viewing, it is not possible to tell from the wavelength what color a person will see in any particular situation. The only way to tell is to ask him to name the color. This obvious solution to the problem was not exploited systematically until Thomson (1954) asked observers to name the colors of monochromatic lights. Since there was a danger that different observers would use entirely different terms and so would give data that could not be combined, Thomson limited his observers to five color terms: red, orange, yellow, green, blue. Beare (1963) also used these five terms, but allowed her viewers to give two-word responses: the hue term plus anything else, such as "dark" or "pale."

Since the method seemed to give reliable results, Boynton and his colleagues (Boynton, Shafer, and Neun, 1964; Boynton and Gordon, 1965; Kintz, Parker, and Boynton, 1969) developed and used it to study a variety of phenomena in color vision. For example, an observer would be allowed only four terms, "red," "yellow," "green," and "blue," but he could use them in pairs for intermediate hues, giving the name of the most intense hue first. The proper response to a greenish blue would be "blue, green," in that order. Each judgment was allotted three points. If only one term was used, the stimulus would receive all three points for that term; if two terms were used, the stimulus would receive two points for the first and one point for the second term. This method provides the observer with sixteen responses, four being single terms and twelve being pairs of the four terms in different orders. Since red and green were never paired, and yellow and blue were never paired, only twelve of the sixteen possible responses were actually used. This method was found to be sufficiently sensitive to permit accurate measurement of even second-order effects like the Bezold-Brücke hue shift (change of color as a function of intensity of light). Jacobs and Gaylord (1967) have used the method to study the effects of chromatic adaptation.

The method of scoring points invented by Boynton is plausible but arbitrary; most recent studies have used a variant of the method developed by Jameson and Hurvich (1959). Their observers gave percentage responses based on their judgments of the perceived ratios of red, yellow, green, or blue in the total hue sensation, where the percentages had to total 100. Wooten (1970) has used this method to study simultaneous and successive color contrast.

What interests us about these studies is that observers were never at a loss for a response. They did not insist that some stimulus must be called chartreuse or scarlet or whatever; the response alternatives that were provided were sufficient to label every spectral hue. Of course, since such experiments are usually confined to the visible spectrum, purple is not included; since no wavelength corresponds to purple, it is clearly a compound, not a basic hue. Moreover, since brightness is held uniform, pink and brown are unnecessary; and since only chromatic colors are used, black, white, and gray do not appear. We must therefore focus our attention on orange, which the earlier studies did allow as a possible response but later studies were able to eliminate with no inconvenience to the judges.

Sternheim and Boynton (1966) examined whether orange is a basic hue or a compound in an experiment using the continuous judgmental method of percentage estimation. Since they wanted to introduce orange as a possible response, however, they did not insist that the percentages add up to 100; if orange is not a basic hue, including it should mean that the percentages could sum to more than 100. They compared four conditions. The colors ranged through the orange region, from red to green, and observers were allowed different response alternatives in different experiments: (a) red, yellow, green; (b) red, green; (c) red, orange, green; and (d) red, orange, yellow, green. Sternheim and Boynton found that "orange" was used the least reliably. Moreover, at wavelengths where "red" was assigned its highest percentages, no percentage of "yellow" was given, and at wavelengths where "yellow" was assigned its highest percentages, no percentage of "red" was given; the highest percentage was assigned to "orange" in regions where percentages of both "red" and "yellow" were also assigned. Since the percentages did not have to total 100, it was possible in condition (b) to calculate the missing "yellow" percentage, but they were unable to calculate a missing "orange" curve when that response was prohibited. Thus the data were consistent with the conclusion that orange is not a basic hue but might just as well be called yellow red.

The results of the color-naming experiments are in fairly good agreement with the results of electrophysiological studies reviewed briefly in chapter 1. At the level of the lateral geniculate nucleus and above, the visual nervous system of monkeys works on the basis of red–green and yellow–blue oppositions. Intermediate colors are represented by the relative intensities of the activities of these two systems. Thus, there is evidence that the four hues— red, yellow, green, and blue—are psychologically primary and that the color terms corresponding to these primary sensations are a minimal contrastive set. To these we must add a black–white opposition in order to characterize the whole color solid.

We conclude that these six primary color sensations represent landmark colors. Anyone with normal color vision will be able to recognize these landmarks and to estimate how much each of them contributes to any particular sample whose color he is asked to identify. Since he is able to make relatively precise judgments about the proportion of each landmark, he should be able in theory to label a great variety of colors. In practice, however, many sources of variability limit his ability to make and to remember fine discriminations.

We might suppose that a person is able to make a rough discrimination with respect to each opposition. To take the coarsest scale possible, say he can make only three judgments with respect to each opposition. For example, he can judge that there is more red than green, that there is more green than red, or that they are about equal. Three such judgments on each of three scales would divide the color space into twenty-seven subspaces. In this manner we can devise a schema that associates every possible outcome of these three tests with a color term. Since no one opposition dominates any other, we can assume that all three tests are performed simultaneously.

A schema has been constructed for the twenty-seven possibilities in table 5.1; appropriate labels have been suggested for each possibility. Each row of the table corresponds to a perceptual paradigm that, once the labels are learned, is incorporated into a test as part of a labeling routine. If we wished to accommodate the "-ish" construction, we would have to allow finer degrees of judgment about the relative amounts of each opposition. For example, if violet is purple with a hint of blue, the decision rule would have to be white — black = 0; red — green = +; and yellow — blue = — —; where the scale runs through five steps, + +, +, 0, —, and — —, and allows for $5^3 = 125$ spaces in the color solid. A five-point scale would also enable us to label degrees of saturation, but a seven-point scale would be required to distinguish all the levels of saturation and lightness allowed for in (6) and (7).

If we were to treat only the chromatic colors—to ignore lightness and saturation—we would use only the first eight rows in table 5.1. We would call both pink and dark red simply red, both light orange and dark brown simply orange, and so on; black, gray, and white would not, in this use of the system, be regarded as colors at all. Since this sense of the word "color"—which excludes achromatic colors—is fairly common, we should probably think of the top third of table 5.1 as the basic schema of the color concept and of the

Table 5.1 An identification procedure for color terms based on judgments of the six landmark colors. (The symbols +, 0, and − indicate the result of subtracting the second color from the first.)

Label	White − Black	Red − Green	Yellow − Blue
red	0	+	0
orange	0	+	+
yellow	0	0	+
yellow green	0	−	+
green	0	−	0
blue green	0	−	−
blue	0	0	−
purple	0	+	−
gray	0	0	0
pink	+	+	0
light orange	+	+	+
light yellow	+	0	+
light yellow green	+	−	+
light green	+	−	0
light blue green	+	−	−
light blue	+	0	−
light purple	+	+	−
white	+	0	0
dark red	−	+	0
dark brown	−	+	+
dark brown	−	0	+
olive	−	−	+
dark green	−	−	0
dark blue green	−	−	−
dark blue	−	0	−
dark purple	−	+	−
black	−	0	0

bottom two-thirds as the product of color terms and lightness terms. It is simply an accident of history that light red is called pink, that dark yellow and orange are called brown, and that dark yellow green is called olive. When only the top third of table 5.1 is included, the white–black opposition is irrelevant and only the red–green and yellow–blue oppositions are required to define the familiar color circle with gray at the center.

   The basis of the system is the six landmark colors and their labels: red, green, yellow, blue, black, white. One might wonder why, if these landmarks are truly given by the nature of the visual nervous system, children take so long to get them straight. If they were simply learning to associate labels with sensations, the acquisition of color terms should progress at least as rapidly as it does for the names of concrete objects and people. (We will return to this question in 5.1.4.)

It should be noted in passing that table 5.1 represents the color terms as denoting not simple properties but relational properties. They are related to one another. Knowing what is to be called red involves knowing what is not to be called red or, as Lyons (1968) puts it, "the incompatibility of *red, green,* etc., is not a secondary consequence of the sense which each of them has (independently as it were) but is necessarily involved in learning and knowing the sense of each of the terms in the set" (p. 458). Just as the adjective "tall" contains a hidden constant depending on the average height of the objects denoted by the noun it modifies, so the adjective "red" contains a hidden constant depending on the landmark red given by the response of the visual system. Actually, "red" involves several hidden constants and so may be psychologically more complex than adjectives like "tall." To say that x is red means that x is closer to red than it is to any other focal color—to green, yellow, blue, black, or white. At the linguistic level of analysis, "red" may seem to be a simple property of surfaces, but when we analyze the operations required to use or verify it, we see that we are dealing with a complex system of perceptual relations.

We have now given one concrete example of what we mean by the difference between a conceptual core and an identification procedure based on that core. As an example of what is required for semantic analysis, and of the effects perception can have on the relations between labels, the discussion should be reasonably clear. Less satisfactory is the match between the primary color terms selected on the basis of psychophysiological considerations and the basic color terms that ethnologists have suggested for English. In particular, why do orange, purple, brown, pink, gray, and perhaps olive and violet have basic labels when other intermediates do not? Until better criteria for recognizing basic color terms from linguistic usage are proposed, we are forced to assume that ethnologists are simply wrong. We take the set of primary color terms that are in direct contrast to be the common names for the landmark colors: white, black, red, green, yellow, and blue. All other color terms are identified in terms of their intermediate location relative to these landmarks.

5.1.3   Color Terms in Other Languages

If the landmark colors are truly distinctive on neurophysiological grounds, not merely an arbitrary expression of linguistic convention, we would expect to be able to translate these terms into any other language. But such a translation is not possible. One reason is that some languages do not have as many basic color terms as the Indo-European languages. Some have only two basic color terms (for what we might call light and dark); all finer distinctions of color are made with secondary color terms; the word for fresh leaves may denote green, the word for blood may denote red, the word for ashes may denote gray. Nomenclatures comparable in elaboration to English exist only in the industrialized countries.

If English has six primary color terms and another language has two, we cannot translate the English terms directly into that language. It might still be the case, however, that the two or three basic color terms in the other language would correspond to particular primary terms in English, so that their terms could be translated faithfully into English even though the direction could not be reversed. Berlin and Kay (1969) surveyed basic color terms for nearly a hundred languages, as described in the ethnological literature, and tested informants speaking twenty of them. They concluded that there are certain focal colors—the best examples of the basic color terms—that are the same for all the languages they studied. Since this conclusion contradicts the usual interpretation of the linguistic relativity hypothesis, there has been considerable discussion (Heider, 1972) and some criticism of their work (Hickerson, 1971; N. McNeill, 1972). With respect to their experimental methodology, however, the work of Berlin and Kay follows standard practices developed by psychologists interested in color vision.

Berlin and Kay also revived and extended an observation by Woodworth (1910) concerning the sequence in which basic color terms appear in a language. According to Woodworth, color nomenclature begins almost always with red and spreads to the other colors in spectral order, skipping such transitional colors as orange, blue green, and violet. That rule would imply the order red, yellow, green, and then blue, with other terms emerging later. Berlin and Kay argue for the order black and white, red, yellow or green, blue, brown, and pink or orange or gray or purple.

Woodworth supposed that the order is attributable to the development of needs for fixed color terms in the culture. In many cases the development of these terminological needs is linked to the development of technology. The introduction of a new pigment or dye frequently results in a new color term, often the name of the substance or its source. As people's daily work becomes more technical, their need for precise terminology, including color terminology, increases correspondingly.

In many societies these natural evolutionary forces have been disrupted by technological developments in the industrialized nations—by the invention of chemical dyes in the nineteenth century and their worldwide distribution in the twentieth. It is possible to argue, therefore, that the agreement about focal colors found by Berlin and Kay for color terms in unrelated languages would not have existed prior to the universal availability and use of these dyes. For what it is worth, however, the comparative evidence available today indicates that every language has at least two basic color terms, which always include the colors that we call black and white. When there are only two basic terms, they are extended far beyond our rather limited notions of black and white; they are used to refer to chromatic as well as achromatic colors. Bromley (1967) translates the two basic terms of some Papuan languages of New Guinea as "brilliant" (which labels most of our reds, yellow, and white) and "dull" (most greens, blue, and black). Heider and Olivier (1972) tested forty New Guinea Dani, who have two basic color terms, and found by multidimensional scaling techniques that the same three dimensions are required to describe the Dani color space as are required for English color terms. And on tests of memory for colors the Dani gave data that were even more similar to American data than those obtained from both cultures on the color-naming test. It would seem that the same conceptual core can underlie languages with very different terminologies.

If a language has three basic color terms, it has a term for red. In many three-term languages the word for red and the word for blood are the same, but this is not necessarily true; some American Indians use the same word for red that they use for the red ocher that produces it for them. Why red should be the color everyone would choose to name if he were naming only one has been a matter for speculation for many years. People who speak these three-term languages are often surrounded by green foliage, blue skies and water; against such a background red is a striking visual quality. Moreover, red is associated with both blood and fire, which have emotional and sometimes ritual connotations; red affects the autonomic nervous system (Wilson, 1966). The term for red is used to designate a broad range of colors in the red, orange, yellow, and brown range, so red–other is roughly correlated with such distinctions as hot–cold, dry–wet, animal–plant. There are even traces of this red saliency in the languages of industrialized countries: Spanish "colorado," for example, or the fact that black, white, and red are the only color terms in English that can form verbs by adding "-en" (Dixon, 1970). The remarkable discovery by Berlin and Kay, however, was that if people who speak one of these three-term languages are asked to pick the best example of red from a large display of colors, they will pick a color that is very close to what we would regard as a landmark red. The boundaries between terms may vary enormously, but the landmark color—what Berlin and Kay called the focal color—is apparently universal.

According to Berlin and Kay, languages with four basic color terms have a term either for the green-blue region, which complements the red-yellow term, or for yellow, which divides the warm colors into two regions. Languages with five basic terms have terms for both yellow and green. Languages with six basic color terms have a term for blue. In all the cases Berlin and Kay tested, the focal colors representing these terms were close to focal colors for their English equivalents. Hence, there is evidence that all of the landmark colors, at least insofar as they are given by common focuses, are universal.

Berlin and Kay argue that since this pattern of inclusions characterizes existing languages today, it probably characterized languages throughout man's history. The order of terms they observed, black and white, red, yellow/green, blue, represents a universal pattern of linguistic development. Berlin and Kay feel that they have some evidence to continue the sequence, with brown as the seventh color term and pink, gray, orange, and purple added in any order. We will not comment on their hypothesis beyond the first six terms.

Why the order of introduction of terms should be what it is has stimulated considerable speculation. The primacy of the terms for black and white is perhaps understandable. When chromatic terms are introduced, however, one might expect the four primaries—red, yellow, green, and blue—to come in together. Given the special importance of blood, it is not too surprising to find that this term is more general than the other three. Then it would seem that yellow, green, and blue should be equally noteworthy; but blue lags behind, and the reason for the absence of a term for blue in many languages has long puzzled ethnologists. One clue is the greater variability observed in applying the terms "green" and "blue" in color-naming experiments. Some have wondered whether darker skin pigmentation, which reduces the sensitivity of the eye slightly in the short wavelengths, might be responsible (Bornstein, 1973). Whatever the reason, the case of the missing term for blue is well documented. With the term for red advanced and the term for blue delayed, the result is the pattern of basic terms in different languages that Berlin and Kay describe—at least through the first six colors.

Although some aspects of Berlin and Kay's thesis are hotly debated by ethnologists, there is reason to believe that the three fundamental oppositions of the visual system—black–white, red–green, and yellow–blue—are reflected in the color terminology of many, if not all, of the world's languages. Moreover, no known language seems to have a basic color term for brown, pink, gray, purple, or orange without also having all of the six landmark terms.

A major qualification to this generalization is that in some cultures the attentional domain of color may not be as completely abstracted from objects as it has been in ours. Our technological capacity to manipulate color independently of other aspects of objects makes more obvious to us what people in less developed societies might have little reason to suspect—at least until our merchandise began to invade them. Conklin (1955) reports that the Hanunóo in the Philippines use their words for red and green to signify dessicated and succulent: "A shiny, wet, brown-colored section of newly cut bamboo is *malatuy*" (p. 343), the basic color term we would usually translate as green. Such confounding makes the work of the ethnologist more difficult and requires us to qualify our generalization: to the extent that color is abstracted from all other illumination or surface properties, the color name will be assigned in terms of a judgment as to the nearest landmark color.

The different possible modes of appearance of color may be related to the absence of a term for blue in many languages. Speakers of English have learned to see a blue surface, a blue light, a blue shadow, or a blue three-dimensional volume as all having the same color, although these modes of appearance are very different. A nontrivial abstraction is required to see them as the same. If almost the only blue a people saw was in the sky or in the water, which are not only highly variable, but where the blue color is not attached to a surface the way it is for red meat, green leaves, and yellow fruit, it might easily be the case that they would not include blue in their abstraction based on experiences with surface colors.

Because colors are continuously graded with no obvious boundaries suggested by the physical properties of the stimulus, it had been widely assumed prior to the work of Berlin and Kay that different cultures could partition and label color in any way local customs required. Color-naming practices were believed to be an ideal arena in which to demonstrate how an arbitrary linguistic convention could shape the way people perceive the world. Insofar as the color attribute is not completely abstracted from other aspects of visual experience and insofar as the boundaries between color terms must vary as the number of basic color terms in the language varies, there is some basis for this assumption of linguistic relativity. But the fact that focal colors are much the same everywhere, regardless of language, and that these colors are more codable and more memorable than nonfocal colors, regardless of language, puts strong limits on the generality of this assumption. Heider (1972) concludes that these special attributes of focal colors are all "derived from the same underlying factors, most likely having to do with the physiology of primate color vision. In short, far from being a domain well suited to study the effects of language on thought, the color space would seem to be a prime example of the influence of underlying perceptual-cognitive factors on the formation and reference of linguistic categories" (p. 20).

5.1.4   Color Terms in Child Language

Philosophers interested in word-percept relations often take color terms as their examples and sometimes venture so far as to take the learning of color terms as their example of how simple referential associations are formed. An instance, noteworthy both for its recency and the eminence of its author (Quine, 1973), can be cited:

> Thus consider the learning of the word 'red.' Suppose the child happens to utter the word in the course of the random babbling that is standard procedure in small children, and suppose a red ball happens to be conspicuously present at the time. The parent rewards the child, perhaps only by somehow manifesting approval. Thus in a certain brief minute in the history of overall impingements on the child's sensory surfaces there were these features among others: there were light rays in the red frequencies, there were sound waves in the air and in the child's headbones caused by the child's own utterance of the word 'red', there were the impacts on the proprioceptors of the child's tongue and larynx occasioned by that utterance, and there were the impacts, whatever they were, that made the episode pleasant . . . As a history of variously similar episodes accumulates, the traces compete and determine the net resultant drive as by the adding of vectors, or composition of forces. (P. 29)

It is true that certain psychological theories might lead one to believe that this is how the learning should occur, but anyone who has carefully followed a child through his mastering of the color terms must deplore such armchair accounts of the roots of reference. There is still much to be learned about the process, but it is reasonably certain that no such simplistic picture will suffice.

Color terms are taken as examples of how children learn words because they are considered to be relatively simple and because we know a great deal about the physics, physiology, psychology, and cultural variation of color perception and color naming. Whereas adjectives like "tall" or "fast" are incorrigibly relative, color terms are often assumed to be absolute in their denotations. By beginning with color terms, the theorist hopes to avoid what seem to be irrelevant details that complicate the learning of other words. If learning color terms were really so simple, these words would be among the first that a child would master, but they are not. And if color terms had an absolute range of applicability, they would not vary depending on the head nouns they modify—yet consider the different senses of "red" in "red hair," "red bricks," "redskins," "red cheeks," "red paint," and "red sunset." The simplicity of learning color words is more in the eye of the theorist than in the eye of the child.

The correct use of color terms by children generally develops rather late, certainly long after emergence from the babbling stage. Infants as young as fifteen days have been shown able to discriminate between colors (Chase, 1937), but discriminating and naming are very different skills. In the 1911 version of Binet and Simon's Metrical Scale of Intelligence about half of the seven-year-old French children they tested were able to name four primary colors. Today the average American child is able to do this by his fourth birthday—a difference attributable not to any superiority in native intelligence but to the introduction of wax crayons at school and in the home. Given more opportunities for learning, children learn earlier. In view of a four-year-old's mastery of other seemingly more complex linguistic skills, however, this still seems a late date for mastering terms that refer to so salient a perceptual property. If color naming required merely the conditioning of vocal responses in the presence of appropriate discriminative stimuli, children should be ready to learn it at any age.

That color terms appear so late in the language of the average child presumably reflects the fact that there is more to learn than one would expect. In order to discuss this learning process, it is convenient to divide it into two aspects, conceptual and linguistic. On the conceptual side there seem to be three basic aspects that a child must appreciate: (a) he must make the appropriate abstraction of color from other attributes of visual experience; (b) he must establish certain landmark colors; and (c) he must learn to locate all colors with respect to those landmarks. On the linguistic side there seem to be three kinds of conventions that the child must learn: (a) he must learn specific uses of color terms in particular contexts; (b) he must isolate the color terms from other words as a contrastive set; and (c) he must learn the referential values of each term.

The outcome of conceptual development should be a frame of reference onto which the color terms can be mapped, after the manner of table 5.1. A child may have difficulty discovering this structure for many reasons. His parents or peers may not use color terms frequently; he sees all kinds of intermediate colors for which he hears no names; colors of objects are generally irrelevant to the goal-action relations that a young child must master; textures, surfaces, spaces, lights, pigments, and shadows have diverse ways of confusing the appearance of colors; the color solid is never encountered (it is an abstract concept, not a real solid), nor can its principles be easily explained to a young child. Quite a lot of color information must get sorted out, and sorting it out is far from being the most pressing task a child faces.

Abstracting the appropriate attribute is complicated by the ubiquity of color. At a gross level, color must be distinguished from size, shape, texture, temperature, and weight. Since an exemplar of an English color term will usually be an object having all of these attributes, a nontrivial induction is required to determine what remains constant while other attributes vary from one exemplar to the next. At a finer level, even after a child has hit on the general attribute that "color" refers to, he must still learn to disregard striking differences in the mode of appearance of colors. Fortunately, other aspects of this conceptual and linguistic learning process need not await the fine tuning of these abstractions and generalizations; a child might master his color terms for surface colors before he generalized them to luminous colors, or vice versa.

Identifying landmark colors is facilitated by the nature of the visual system. Bornstein (1975) tested infants between four and five months of age and determined that when given a choice they will spend more time looking at primary colors than at colors near the boundaries between them. Istomina (1963) found that Russian children (aged twenty-four to thirty-six months) were more accurate both in matching a sample and in grouping similar colors when papers or objects were red, green, yellow, or blue than when they were nonprimary colors. Heider (1971) gave American children (aged thirty-six to fifty-five months) an array of color chips and said to them: "Show me a color"; their choice of focal colors was much more frequent than would be predicted by chance. Heider also found the children were more accurate in matching a test sample when it was one of the focal colors. Such results are compatible with the hypothesis that primary colors are more salient perceptually long before color terms are known for them.

Some of the child's difficulties initially may arise from what Bryant (1974) calls the limitations of relative codes. A child can appreciate relations between colors seen simultaneously; his difficulties are in making absolute judgments of colors presented in isolation. In order to overcome them, he must internalize an absolute code. That is, he must select certain colors from the heterogeneous variety of possibilities and remember them so that they can serve to anchor relational judgments over an interval of time. The obvious candidates for these internal anchors are the primary colors; the child has merely to accept the colors his perceptual system makes salient and learn to use them as transfer standards for comparing colors seen at different times.

Once these landmark colors are recognized, the child must learn to use them as a stable frame of reference in terms of which any intermediate colors can be located. At this point, for example, a child told that puce is a color from deep red to darkish purple should have a fair notion of this color—he should be able to locate it in his frame of reference—even without seeing an instance of it. Of course, this assumes that his color vocabulary has kept pace with his color concept, so let us turn to the linguistic side of his development.

Linguistically, an average three-year-old seems to have all the tools necessary to learn the color terms. He is a fluent speaker, able to pronounce the terms and already familiar with them in some uses. He can discriminate all the color differences that adults can see and he can sort colored papers into piles correctly on the basis of either shape or color. Yet he is often totally confused about the color-naming game. He may respond "I don't know any" when asked to name the colors but list half a dozen color terms when asked what color crayons he owns. "Color" is not yet an adequate retrieval cue for color terms. He may even know that grass is green and use a green crayon to color the lawn in a picture yet not put these facts together to infer that the crayon is called green.

Some of the earliest uses of color terms are associated with particular objects or contexts. A child may know a story about Snowwhite or Little Red Ridinghood, he may know that Santa wears a red suit or that Mary had a lamb whose fleece was white as snow, he may sing a song about blue skies or demand a glass of orange juice. Although color words are included in such expressions, it is not clear that they have any particular color reference for the young child. Indeed, there is reason to think that the child has not initially sorted out the color terms from all other words. He may say "Round" when asked the color of a yellow bucket or "A plate" when asked the color of a white plate. He has learned something about "orange" and something about "round" and something about "plate," but these facts are often used as if they were unrelated, like independent entries in a dictionary. He has not yet overlearned that color words belong together in a single semantic domain.

And he has certainly not learned that they are contrasting hyponyms of "color." Children are relatively slow to notice the contrasts between such antonymous pairs as "long" and "short," "alive" and "dead." If it takes a while to relate two antonyms, it is not surprising that relating six contrasting terms to each other is even more difficult. To say that something is not long suggests that it is short, but to say that something is not red gives little information about what color it is. The difficulty of getting these relations clear surely provides part of the explanation as to why color terms are mastered relatively late.

Even after a child has distinguished color terms from the other words he knows, he still has much to learn. In particular, he has to learn what color each term refers to. A child who knows what the color words are will always give some color term when naming the color of something, but often the wrong one. A common strategy for learning referential values is to pick a favorite color word and use it to answer all questions about color; Istomina (1963) found that 32 percent of Russian two-year-olds did so. One might conclude that such a child has not discovered that different colors have different names, but this would ignore the possibility that it is a deliberate strategy for discovering what color terms mean—for exploring both the range of attributes that color terms denote and the range of applicability of that particular term within the appropriate attribute. It is certainly a more powerful strategy than, say, waiting passively until somebody remembers to condition you.

The actual connecting of color terms with colors—the part of the process that has received the lion's share of discussion—does not come until considerable preliminary learning has prepared the child for it. Terms come in one at a time and sometimes a term previously known seems to be forgotten. One child followed for several months by Elsa Bartlett (personal communication) took three or four months to master them. When first tested (at age three years and three months) he named black, orange, and purple objects correctly; two weeks later he named black, orange, blue, red, and yellow, but missed purple; five weeks after that he named black, orange, blue, red, green, and white, but missed both purple and yellow; two months later he had mastered the whole list of eleven terms that Berlin and Kay consider basic. This repeated testing drew the child's attention to colors, which may have accelerated his learning, but even so, the complete system was not mastered overnight.

The evolutionary order proposed by Berlin and Kay might lead one to wonder whether ontogeny recapitulates phylogeny—whether the same order could be found in the mastery of the terms by children. Although there seems to be considerable variation within individual children, one might hope to find that on the average those words were learned first that evolved first. There are some data relevant to this hypothesis.

The use of color naming as an item on intelligence tests inspired Bateman (1915) to test American children just entering the first grade. He found that they were more accurate in using some terms than others, with the progression from best to worst being *white, black, red, blue, yellow,* orange, *green,* purple. Hopmann (1972) replicated this work, testing both recognition and production of color terms with children aged thirty-nine to fifty-one months. When the errors for both tasks are pooled, the progression from best to worst is *white* = *red* = *green, black,* brown = pink, *yellow* = orange, *blue,* purple, gray.

If landmark colors are in some sense given by the nature of the visual system, we might expect the names of these six (italicized above) to be learned first and used most accurately. There is some support for this expectation, but the orderings may not be reliable and the particular colors used in the tests may not have represented the landmarks accurately. In the tests by Heider (1971) mentioned previously, focal colors were included. The number of children who could correctly identify one of the chips that adult judges would accept as instances of each color term differed, with the order from best to worst being *red,* orange, *yellow* = *green, blue,* pink, brown, purple. Except for orange, this ordering also puts the psychological primaries earlier than the intermediate color terms. In this study, Heider could identify which of her chips corresponded to the focal colors determined by Berlin and Kay. The number of children who pointed to a focal chip as an instance of the color term ordered the terms from best to worst: *yellow,* orange, *green = blue, red* = brown, purple, pink. Yellow and orange seemed to be salient.

Given the variety of influences at home and at school that must affect the order in which children master color terms, the existence of any preference at all for the primary terms indicates that the hypothesis of a physiological basis for this learning cannot be dismissed. The alternative hypothesis is that children master color terms in an order determined by the frequency with which they hear them used. We can get a rough estimate of relative frequencies of adult use from Kučera and Francis's (1967) counts for written materials, where the eleven terms used by Berlin and Kay are ordered from most to least frequent: *white, black, red,* brown, *blue, green,* gray, *yellow,* pink, orange, purple. Although this order seems to predict the children's order of acquisition as well as anything—that is to say, not well—it is not truly an alternative hypothesis. These relative frequencies of use must also be determined by the same complex of social, psychological, and physiological factors that determine children's learning.

An adequate account of how children learn to use color terms would have to relate the conceptual and linguistic developments that we have merely listed here. Although such an account is not presently available, it is clear that something much more complicated is required than attaching vocalizations to stimuli with the glue of pleasure.

5.1.5   Use of Color Terms

English color terms can be used as nouns or as adjectives. As nouns, they simply denote the position of a particular perceptual property relative to the color concept. As predicate adjectives, color terms specify (assign a value to) a particular perceptual property of the denotation of the head noun— usually of the illumination or of the surface of a concrete object denoted by the head noun. If the noun denotes something more abstract, unrelated to illumination or lacking a surface, the color adjective must be interpreted metaphorically.

A general feature of predicate adjectives, not limited to color adjectives, is that their interpretation depends on the head noun they modify. This dependence can be illustrated by comparing three adjective-noun combinations: (a) "red ball" is an unexceptional combination with minimal interaction between the adjective and the noun; (b) "red hair" requires that the values of "red" be limited to a range appropriate to hair; and (c) "red music" is semantically anomalous and, if it is to be interpreted at all, must be interpreted metaphorically—politically, for example. One way to deal with this would be to propose alternative meanings for "red": (a) a standard chromatic meaning of the sort we have been discussing; (b) a special chromatic meaning related to hair color; and (c) a special nonchromatic meaning related to politics. Which meaning to assign to any given occurrence of "red" would be indicated by including with each separate meaning some semantic indication of the class of nouns to which that meaning applies. Once we start down this path, however, it is hard to know where to stop. If "red" has a special meaning for hair, it should have special meanings for skin, leather, clay, brick, and so on; if it has a special meaning for politics, it should also have special meanings for economics, emotions, traffic control, violence—for synesthesia generally. Lexicographers provide a valuable service by collating all these possible uses, but the heterogeneity of the information admitted to the lexicon in this fashion defies the usual methods of linguistic analysis.

It would seem that this situation provides a particularly appropriate place to exploit the computational power of procedural semantics. The adjective and the noun provide access to particular lexical concepts; the computational problem is to provide an interpretation for their combination. In simple cases like (a), the computation should be relatively straightforward; in special cases like (b) and (c), the simple computation should fail and the system should fall back on alternative procedures. The theoretical task is to characterize these computations, bearing in mind that the particular concepts involved can provide most of the information required for the computation. That is to say, rather than store a separate rule for each special use of the adjective, it should be possible to compute its value according to some general rules for combining the information given by the adjective in its context of use.

We will survey some of the problems a procedural approach should be able to handle, but first we must note that, in comparison to most predicate adjectives, color adjectives are relatively independent of the meanings of their head nouns. Color adjectives are sometimes categorized as "absolute" by comparison with "relative" adjectives like "tall," which always depends for its value on its head noun, or "good," which seems to take a different sense for every noun it modifies (4.1.2). The difference can be put procedurally. If you are asked to find a red rectangle, you have an option (sec. 3.2). You can look first for something red and then test whether it is a rectangle, or you can look first for something rectangular and then test whether it is red. Color and shape are sufficiently independent that either search procedure can be adopted, depending on the search environment. On the other hand, if you were asked to look for a good table, it would not be a sensible strategy to look first for good things and then to test whether they were tables. The evaluation is so dependent on the nature and function of the head noun that it cannot be computed first.

To classify all adjectives as either absolute or relative, however, dichotomizes what is essentially a continuum. Color and shape adjectives are near one end, evaluative adjectives are near the other end, and the majority of predicate adjectives are somewhere in between. The differences are of degree, not of kind. For example, "black chair" allows a direct interpretation of "black," unaffected by the meaning of the head noun; "good chair" places strong restrictions on "good," since what is good about a chair is unrelated to what is good about, say, a knife; and "tall chair" is intermediate, since it depends on one's conception of chairs and their expected heights, but in all cases it is the vertical extent of the referent that is specified by "tall." Since we want to exploit a procedural approach for the evaluation of adjective-noun phrases, we would argue against classifying adjectives as absolute or relative and in favor of drawing a graded distinction in terms of the complexity of the procedures they entail.

Let us try, then, to characterize a general system that would interpret predicate adjectives procedurally. In the course of this attempt we will gain a better appreciation of the problems we face.

Given the concept of the head noun, a set of formal and functional properties is available to the system. These properties can be roughly grouped into three types: definitional properties, whose values are fixed; characteristic properties, whose values for most instances can be assumed although variation is possible; and peripheral properties, whose values can be regarded as free variables. We think of these as graded distinctions, not as a true trichotomy, but in order to survey the semantic problems that can arise, it is sufficient to sample three instances along the continuum.

Given the concept of the adjective, it should be possible to compute the value of one or more properties of the particular referent of the head noun. The simplest cases would seem to be those in which the adjective specifies a value for some otherwise indeterminate property. A child's ball, for example, must be some color, but the value for this peripheral property can vary freely from one instance to the next; color is a free variable that appropriate adjectives can specify.

In the especially simple case of a relatively independent adjective and a peripheral property of the head noun, one can speak of the interpretation of the phrase as the Cartesian product of the interpretations of the adjective and the noun. "Red ball" might be the logical product of red things and spherical things that bounce and roll: all things that are both red *and* balls. Procedurally, this amounts to little more than conjoining the color schema with the ball schema; instances satisfying both schemata independently will satisfy the compound description. It seems reasonable to take this situation as prototypical of adjectival modification. In view of all the possible complications we have anticipated, however, it does not seem reasonable to take the logical product as the universal procedure for interpreting adjective-noun combinations. But we can take it as a starting point; possible deviations from it represent the real problems for theoretical analysis.

Consider first the case of modifying characteristic properties. We can take size as representative of a characteristic property for most familiar, concrete objects. A child's ball can come in a range of sizes, but size is not a completely free variable. Adjectives like "big" or "small" must be evaluated relative to this characteristic range. "Red hair" presents a similar example: hair comes naturally in a range of colors—information about that range must be part of the hair concept—but color is not a completely free variable. When an adjective specifies the value of a characteristic property, therefore, its evaluation is normally constrained by the concept it modifies. That is, the value assigned must be compatible with both the adjectival and the nominal information about that property. The implication for a procedural account, of course, is that these two sources of information cannot be simply conjoined. The nominal information must be given priority; the adjectival information is then evaluated within the range allowed by the nominal information.

The procedure must not be so inflexible, however, as to block the assignment of noncharacteristic values. Given modern technology, green hair is not inconceivable, although it is certainly uncharacteristic. To take less outrageous examples, we must be able to deal with such uncharacteristic entities as flightless birds, portable bridges, inedible foods, dry lakes, and so on. Apparently we need a three-stage procedure: first the system looks to see whether the noun has a property that the adjective could specify, and if it is found to be a peripheral property the two schemata are simply conjoined; if the property is found to be characteristic, the second step is for the system to interpret the adjective within the characteristic range of that property for that noun; if that attempt fails—if the adjective cannot specify a value within the characteristic range—the third step is simply to replace the characteristic value by the adjectival value of that property. In either case, if the adjective specifies a characteristic property the computed concept is not simply a product of its component concepts; the nominal concept is modified, either by limiting or replacing the usual information about a characteristic property.

One would expect adjectival specification of a defining property to lead either to redundancy (if the adjective specifies a value already specified by definition) or to nonsense (if the adjective specifies some other value). The redundancies are plain enough ("red crimson," "unmarried bachelor," "canine dog") and can serve to provide information about the semantic components of the head noun. Such expressions may even occur in ordinary usage when redundancy is judged to be a necessary antidote to misunderstanding. The nonsense, though, is more complicated. What happens when an adjective specifies a value incompatible with the value for that property fixed by the meaning of the head noun? For example, what interpretations do people give to such contradictory phrases as "colorless green," "married bachelor," "noisy silence," "dry water"? These phrases are semantically anomalous, but what does that imply? It does *not* imply that they are ungrammatical, and it certainly does not imply that such combinations will not occur in poetic, exaggerated, or humorous uses of language. It *does* imply that their translation poses special problems.

When people are introduced to the notion of semantic anomaly by way of such examples, a common reaction is to resist on the grounds that one can invent situations in which it might be plausible to use the anomalous expression. Such inventions involve higher-order processing much more complex than the usual automatic translation of nonanomalous combinations. In general, much more context than usual must be included in the computation of a plausible value, and there will usually be several alternatives to choose among, so social consensus is low, but the point is that such computations are not precluded by any syntactic or semantic rules.

A similar situation arises when an adjective specifies a value for some property that is not included in the concept of the head noun. For example, what interpretations do people give to such vacuous phrases as "green idea," "waterproof integer," "angry wheelchair," "intelligent rock"? Vacuous combinations are also semantically anomalous and, like contradictory combinations, require higher-order interventions in the normal processes of translation. In both cases we assume that the system attempts to compute a value for the adjective as if it specified some characteristic or peripheral property of the nominal concept, fails to complete the computation, and interrupts, calling on higher-order routines for assistance.

These remarks sketch an initial approach to a procedural account of one type of semantic dependency that is often called a selectional restriction. In 5.1.1 we noted the selectional restrictions governing the use of color terms to label intermediate colors and commented that they derive not from arbitrary linguistic conventions but from the nature of color perception, from the meanings of the terms that are being combined. In this section we have sought to extend this approach: to explain why different senses of the same adjective are selected when different head nouns are involved and, again, to base the explanation on the meanings of the words that are being combined.

The argument makes essential use of the conceptual component of word meaning; adjective-noun interpretations are not based solely on those properties, specified in their schemata, that are necessary in order to identify instances of the concept. In order to formulate the theory in a workable form, therefore, it would be necessary to provide a sufficiently rich conceptual theory to account for such facts as that "red ball" is interpretable because "ball" denotes a concrete object, concrete objects must have surfaces, surfaces must be colored, and "red" denotes a color. This conceptual information, simple as it is, goes well beyond the defining properties of "ball," "sphere," or "object"; it involves in addition a prototheory of the nature of physical objects, a conceptualization that provides room for characteristic and peripheral properties as well as defining properties.

In order to develop this sketch into an explicit procedural theory of adjectival modification, it would also be necessary to consider a number of complications that do not arise with color adjectives: evaluative adjectives like "good" that assess properties of an instance relative to expectations; nonpredicate adjectives like "utter" or "former" that follow different syntactic rules; hedging adjectives like "regular" or "artificial" that suspend whole classes of characteristic or defining adjectives; and so on. Most important, a complete theory of adjective-noun interpretation would also explicate the executive processes to which appeal must be made when conventional processing fails. Some generalizations are much easier to interpret than others, and such differences raise very difficult questions about the role and nature of metaphor. Even lacking a general theory of metaphor, however, it might be possible to say something about the generalization of sensory adjectives (Williams, 1975). Why, for example, are touch adjectives so easily generalized (to tastes that are coarse/cold/dry/harsh/sharp/smooth; to sounds that are dull/heavy/rough/ soft; to colors that are light/soft/warm), or why are sounds so easily described by nonauditory adjectives (as heavy/rough/soft like touch; as bright/brilliant/ clear/dark/dim/faint/light/vivid like colors; as big/deep/even/flat/high/hol- low/low/thin like objects), whereas other directions of generalization (green/ shallow/heavy taste; blue/loud/sweet touch; yellow/quiet/rough smell) are unusual and difficult to interpret?

Perhaps it is a mistake to think that the concept expressed by a word like "sharp," which can describe touch, taste, sound, intelligence, terrain, strict- ness, eagerness, and objects, is legitimately applicable only to touch and must be generalized for other applications; SHARP may be a concept of more than just a sensory quality. Perhaps, as Asch (1958) argues, such adjectives express general concepts of "functional properties or modes of interaction" (p. 93). A sharp mind may be as good an instance of SHARP as a sharp pain; a warm person may be as good an instance of WARM as a warm tactual sensation.

These are some of the problems a procedural theory of adjectival modifica- tion would have to solve. With such a theory well in hand, we might then see how to extend it to other types of selectional restrictions. But much remains to be done.

5.2 KINSHIP

According to Goodenough (1956), the problem of determining what a linguistic form means is well illustrated by kinship terms: "In essence it is this: what do I have to know about A and B in order to say that A is B's cousin? Clearly, people have certain criteria in mind by which they make the judgment that A is or is not B's cousin. What the expression *his cousin* signifies is the particular set of criteria by which this judgment is made" (p. 195).

Although Goodenough does not bother to point it out, the criteria involved have little to do with perception. There is no way you can tell from perceptual evidence alone whether A is B's cousin; kin terms have about as little percep- tual basis as any semantic field in the lexicon. Kinship terminology is not a topic one would ordinarily expect to cast light on the relations between perception and language.

There are two reasons to include kinship here. The first is to provide a con- trast with color terminology. Whereas colors grade continuously into one another, kinfolk are discrete entities. Whereas color terms refer to properties, kin terms refer to relations. Whereas color information is given perceptually, kinship information is given memorially. Whereas disagreements between people about the appropriate color term may never be satisfactorily resolved, the appropriate kin term can almost always be determined. Whereas color terms always refer to the same properties, a particular kin term can refer to different people depending on who utters it. Precisely because these two semantic fields are so different, any generalizations that apply to both should have special significance for our understanding of conceptual schemata.

Both color and kinship illustrate minimal contrastive sets having relatively complex internal structures, involving more than one attribute as a basis for classification. In both cases it is possible to describe relations among the contrasting terms in such a way that every term has a value for nearly every attribute. Such structures occur in phonology, where they are called matrices of distinctive features; they occur in ethnology, where they are called paradigms and subjected to componential analysis; they occur in psychometrics, where they are called multidimensional spaces; no doubt they occur in other fields under still other names. Since color and kinship terminologies share this paradigmatic structure, a search for generalizations that will apply to both will not be fruitless, but it will require a considerable degree of abstraction.

A second reason for discussing kinship terminology is that a great deal is known about it and how to analyze it. The remarkable concentration of research on the semantics of color and kin terms is probably at least partially attributable to the opinion that the value of any new fact is a function of the number of old facts to which it can be related. Social anthropologists have found kinship an invaluable guide to understanding social organization; it is often related to marriage practices, property rights and inheritance, family life and residence arrangements, population control, social roles and obligations, political preferences, and many other features of social organization. Consequently, data on kinship have been collected systematically for every culture that has been seriously studied. Formal methods for analyzing these data have been developed and basic types of kinship systems have been proposed. Moreover, methods of psychological scaling have recently been applied to kin terms, both by anthropologists and psychologists. As a consequence of all this work, a great deal more is known about kinship and kinship terminology than an uninterested party might feel necessary. The rigor with which kinship terminology can be analyzed may make it somewhat unrepresentative of the rest of the lexicon, but that very rigor also makes it particularly attractive as a test of semantic theories.

All societies take some account of the biological facts involved in mating and birth relations between individuals, but how they do so and what cultural or behavioral significance they attach to these relations vary greatly from one culture to another. Some systems of kinship terminology are more highly differentiated than others; English—or, more appropriately, Anglo-American —terminology, which will be our principal interest here, is relatively undifferentiated. The kind of analysis we will give is applicable to any kinship system, however, as the extensive and technical literature on kinship will attest.

The terms with which we are concerned include: father, sister, father's sister, aunt, child, parent, ancestor, mother's brother's son, cousin, mother-in-law. The problem is to arrange these terms—which are not all contrastive—in some way that will represent their relations in a revealing and intuitively satisfying manner. This task is complicated by the fact that people use these terms in several different ways. When they say "This is the child," the kin term "child" is part of an expression used to refer to a particular individual and serves the same identifying role as any concrete noun. When they say "Come here, son," the kin term "son" is used as a term of address and serves the same purpose as a proper name. When they say "This is my foster child," the kin term "child" is used to express what is essentially an analogy. When they say "He is like a father to me," the kin term "father" describes a social role. And when they say "Hans is the child of Frieda and Gottlob," the kin term "child" —or, better, "child of"—denotes a relation between people. The kinds of contrast that we can observe between kin terms varies according to contexts and ways in which they are used.

All cultures seem to make multiple uses of these words, but the effects of context on the interpretation of kinship terminology varies from one culture to another. It is not even clear that the semantic field of kinship is the same for every culture; ritual relationships (other than adoption and marriage), age, death, and so on, often supplement the categories recognized as resulting from birth and mating. (Greenberg, 1949, has discussed how a logical analysis of kinship can be extended to include relations not recognized in Anglo-American terminology.)

Consider first the set of terms required to characterize members of the nuclear family: father, mother, son, daughter, husband, wife, brother, sister. These terms can be used to specify any individual's genealogy with respect to all his known relatives by forming higher-order combinations: father's father, father's mother, father's mother's sister's son, and so on. Since genealogy can be described independently of culture, these primary terms and their higher-order combinations provide a convenient way for a field worker to indicate the possible relations between kinsmen in the culture he is studying. These genealogical designations are related to kin terms in much the same way a physical description of a light stimulus is related to color terms. Any given community will group these genealogical designations into a smaller number of kinship classes for which they have labels. English groups together the father's brother's children, the father's sister's children, the mother's brother's children, and the mother's sister's children and calls them all cousins. Other cultures have other groupings. In general, kinsmen who are given the same label have the same duties and privileges with respect to the individual who so labels them.

Our interest here is not in the social, political, or economic implications of kinship for a social group, but merely in the linguistic and logical analysis of the terminology that is used. Our initial task is to try to find contrastive sets of terms and to arrange them in an appropriate hierarchy.

At first glance one might think that kin terms are not contrastive at all. Our criterion is that two contrasting terms should not refer to the same thing. But a single individual can be simultaneously a mother, daughter, aunt, sister, cousin. Many English kin terms designate the sex of the referent, so we do find a contrast on that basis: the same person cannot be referred to both as mother and as father. Thus it is apparent that sex must be one dimension of this semantic field. Indeed, there are both sexed and sexless terms for every nuclear relation:

parent	father	mother
child	son	daughter
spouse	husband	wife
sibling	brother	sister

This arrangement of kin terms can be continued outside the nuclear family:

grandparent	grandfather	grandmother
grandchild	grandson	granddaughter
—	uncle	aunt
(nibling)	nephew	niece
cousin	—	—

The table is less complete for the more remote relatives. Ethnogenealogists report that many languages have a sexless term for child of sibling—they have coined the word "nibling" for it, which we have included above—but that a sexless term for sibling of parent is rare.

This much of the semantic structure is clear. There are pairs of contrasting sexed terms (father-mother, son-daughter, ...) that are hyponyms of the sexless superordinate terms (parent, child, ...). Since "relative" is the direct superordinate for the sexless terms, we can see three levels of the hierarchy.

We can simplify the problem if we factor sex out as a semantic component and deal only with sexless kin terms. In order to complete the set of sexless terms for the purposes of this discussion, we will adopt "nibling" and introduce "auntuncle" for sibling of parent.

But now we must return to the question of contrast. Since the same individual may be simultaneously a parent, child, spouse, sibling, grandparent, grandchild, auntuncle, nibling, and cousin, in what sense can we say that these form a contrastive set? The obvious answer is that they are contrastive with respect to any given origin. For example, if we take Leslie Grigsby as the origin of the system, then the same person cannot be both Leslie's parent and Leslie's child, Leslie's parent and Leslie's spouse, and so on. Kin terms are labels for relations between pairs of people, so in order to see the contrasts among them it is necessary to anchor one term of the relation.

This anchored interpretation is the usual way people think about their kinfolk. Each individual is the center of a circle of relatives, his kindred. He uses kin terms to refer to specific members of his kindred. No two individuals have the same circle; full siblings have almost identical circles except for themselves, but second cousins may have few kin in common. The individual at the center of this circle has certain duties to his kindred and can turn to them for help in some situations. Two individuals who wonder whether they are related search through each other's kindred for common members. Let us refer to this circle of relatives as the personal core of the kinship concept for each individual. Given this conceptual core, the problem is to place each kin term with respect to it.

Let us use "ego" to designate the basic landmark of the system. Then our set of contrastive terms becomes: parent of ego, child of ego, spouse of ego, sibling of ego, and so on. It is a relatively simple matter to arrange ego's kindred around him according to their genealogical distance. In table 5.2 this is done in such a way as to display three dimensions of this semantic field. The middle column gives the terms used for those who are in ego's direct line of descent, ordered by their generation. Thus, generation is a dimension of this semantic field. To the left are the terms used to designate relatives by marriage (affinal), and to the right are the terms used to designate blood relatives (consanguineal). Thus, consanguinity is another dimension. The consanguineal terms have been classified in the manner proposed by Wallace and Atkins (1960), with lineality as another dimension; they define lineals as the direct ancestors of descendants of ego, colineals as nonlineals all of whose ancestors include or are included in all the ancestors of ego, and ablineals as blood relatives who are neither lineal nor colineal.

The semantic components of English kin terms, therefore, are sex, generation, consanguinity, and lineality. These provide the basic dimensions (or oppositions) in terms of which the schema of egocentric kinship can be organized. Wallace and Atkins say their analysis is adequate to define the set of terms chosen; they leave open the possibility that it may not be the best representation. The reason for their caution in this respect is that there are other features of English kin terms that are not clearly revealed by this particular analysis.

In English the kinship system is bilateral (or cognatic). Descent is reckoned through both the father's and the mother's side of the family. This feature is important because it serves to distinguish this type of kinship system from those of other cultures. The symmetry is reflected in the fact that the same term is used for the mother's relatives and the father's relatives: both maternal and paternal grandparents are simply called grandparents. Similarly for maternal

Table 5.2   Kin terms in relation to ego.

| | Consanguineal | | |
Affinal	Lineal	Colineal	Ablineal
	grandparent		
parent-in-law	parent	auntuncle	
sibling-in-law, spouse	(ego)	sibling	cousin
child-in-law	child	nibling	
	grandchild		

and paternal auntuncles, niblings, cousins. In order to recognize this symmetry, it is necessary to dig beneath the componential analysis of table 5.2.

There is another kind of symmetry that is obscured by the analysis shown in table 5.2. If person A is related to ego, then not only will there be a kin term expressing that relation but there will also be a converse term expressing the relation of ego to A. If A is ego's grandparent, then ego is A's grandchild. Since the terms grandparent and grandchild have this reciprocal function in the dyadic interactions of A and ego, one might expect them to be closely related terms in some psychological sense. In table 5.2, however, grandparent and grandchild are five generations apart. Romney and D'Andrade (1964) have shown by psychological tests, and their results have been confirmed by Fillenbaum and Rapoport (1971), that most adults consider "grandparent" and "grandchild" similar in meaning. If the semantic analysis is to reflect the cognitive organization of the people who use these terms, anchoring to ego does not seem the correct way to analyze this semantic field.

So far we have discussed kin terms as if they were terms that ego could use contrastively to identify his various kindred. Suppose, however, that we look at them more abstractly as labels for relations rather than as labels for relatives (Bierwisch, 1970). Consider the relation "A is the F of B" as if it were a logical predicate of the form $\text{F}(A, B)$, where B is no longer anchored to ego, but both A and B are variables. What kind of logical analysis of these relations is possible? We will follow the general line developed by Greenberg (1949), although with a different notation and order of development.

The conceptual core of the kinship concept is derived from one fundamental biological relation, which it is convenient to express in two converse relations: $[\text{P}(A, B)]$ will mean that A is a parent of B, and $[\text{c}(B, A)]$ will mean that B is a child of A. The task of specifying what is involved procedurally in these basic relations would be more laborious than revealing. Let us merely note three logical properties of their routines. First, they would be irreflexive—the old song notwithstanding, a man cannot be his own grandpa, precisely because he cannot be his own parent. The values of A and B must be different. Second, the routines would be nontransitive: if A is a parent of B and B is a parent of C it does not follow that A is a parent of C. Indeed, if the fundamental relations were transitive, the lexical field could be considerably simplified; kinship terms would consist of "ancestor of" and "descendant of," modulated by gender. On the other hand, the fundamental relations are not intransitive, either. If A is a parent of B and B is a parent of C, it is biologically possible for A to be a parent of C provided A and B are of different sexes. Third, the routine for $\text{P}(A, B)$ will be the logical converse of the routine for $\text{c}(B, A)$.

We have already adopted the terminology of traditional logic, where the first argument of a relation is the referent and the second is the relatum. In "Maude is a parent of Claude," Maude is the referent and Claude is the relatum. In "Maude is a parent," the relatum is omitted and only the referential function remains. The relation is not one-to-one, of course, for Claude has another parent and Maude may have other children. Note that when the dimension of sex is added, only the sex of the referent is important; Maude is called a mother regardless of whether her children are male or female. For that reason it is possible to place a sexless ego at the center of table 5.2; it does not matter for English kin terminology whether the relatum is male or female.

Just as we thought of ego as the landmark in terms of which table 5.2 is anchored contrastively, so we can think of the relatum as the landmark in terms of which the logical relations are anchored. In "Maude is a parent of Claude," Claude is the landmark relative to which Maude's kin status is defined. Lacking contextual indications to the contrary, this sentence would usually be understood to mean that knowledge of Claude is presumed and that an assertion is being made about Maude's relation to him; the new information communicated would be about Maude. Logically, of course, "Maude is a parent of Claude" and "Claude is a child of Maude" are equivalent—both are true or false under the same conditions—but they have a different focus. In procedural terms, "Maude is a parent of Claude" would usually imply that the sentence should be verified by first finding the Claude concept and then testing it to see whether Maude was related as a parent; "Claude is a child of Maude" would reverse the arguments of "find" and "test." Because the two predicates are converses, however, it is easy to proceed in either order— and so it is also easy to overlook the different roles played by the two arguments, referent and relatum.

The sexless terms "parent" and "child" are specified in terms of the primitive relations P and C. To define "grandparent" and "grandchild" in terms of these relations, we observe that a grandparent is the parent of a parent and a grandchild is a child of a child; their meanings must reduce to some kind of product of P and C with themselves. What is needed is a procedural equivalent to what is known in logic as a relational product (or resultant), which is defined as follows (Reichenbach, 1947, p. 123):

$$(10) \qquad f(x, z) = (\exists y)g(x, y) \ \& \ h(y, z).$$

By definition, f is the relational product of g and h: $f = gh$. The term "grandparent" is the relational product of parent with itself, that is, g and h are the same relation. Hence, a schema for grandparent can be specified as follows:

(11)   PP(A, C):   Referent A is a "grandparent of" a relatum C if and only if there is a B such that:
          (i) [P(A, B) & P(B, C)].

The same procedure can be used to define grandchild:

(12)   CC(C, A):   C(C, B) & C(B, A).

"C is the grandchild of A" is defined to mean that there is some person B such that C is the child of B and B is the child of A.

But now recall that P and C are converse relations. Therefore, in (12) we can substitute P(B, C) for C(C, B), and P(A, B) for C(B, A). The substitution makes the right side of (12) equivalent to condition (i) of (11), so

PP(A, C) = CC(C, A). That is, PP and CC are also converse relations. This logical representation has converse relations playing an important role that was not represented in table 5.2: although your grandparent and your grandchild are very different people, "grandparent" and "grandchild" are simply converse labels for the same relation.

The remaining consanguineal relations can also be defined in terms of P and C; we will run through them quickly in order to complete the logical structure. "Sibling" can be defined as the resultant of C and P:

(13)   CP(A, C):   C(A, B) & P(B, C)
                    $\equiv$ P(B, A) & C(C, B)
                    $\equiv$ CP(C, A).

"A is a sibling of C" is defined to mean that there is a B such that A is the child of B and B is the parent of C. (Since these arguments cannot be coreferential, $A \neq C$, a person is not his own sibling.) Note that CP is a symmetric relation —CP is its own converse. This use of CP (rather than PC) may be slightly confusing to someone who would be more likely to speak of Claude's siblings as "Claude's parents' other children" than as "the other children of the parents of Claude." We will retain this order of the letters designating the relational product because CP corresponds more closely to the conventions of logical notation.

We need two more functional products for auntuncle and nibling. Auntuncles are siblings of parent; sibling is CP and parent is P, so sibling of parent should be CP of P, or CPP:

(14)   CPP(A, C):   CP(A, B) & P(B, C).

Similarly, niblings are children of siblings, which should be C of CP, or CCP:

(15)   CCP(C, A):   C(C, B) & CP(B, A)
                    $\equiv$ P(B, C) & CP(A, B)
                    $\equiv$ CPP(A, C).

Thus, CPP and CCP are converse relations; if A is an auntuncle of C, then C is a nibling of A.

Although we have introduced CPP as if it were (CP)P, and CCP as if it were C(CP), these groupings can be disregarded, because relational products are associative. In order to prove this for CPP, for example, we can expand CP in (14) by using (13) and then regroup the terms by (11):

(16)   (CP)P(A, C):   CP(A, B) & P(B, C)
                    $\equiv$ C(A, D) & P(D, B) & P(B, C)
                    $\equiv$ C(A, D) & PP(D, C)
                    $\equiv$ C(PP) (A, C).

In short, auntuncles are described either as siblings of parents or as children of grandparents. The former is less confusing, however, because the restriction against coreference need not be stated; to speak of auntuncles of C as children of grandparents of C requires an explicit addendum to the effect that they are not also parents of C, that is, $A \neq B$. When the same argument is applied to (15), it shows that child of sibling is logically equivalent to grandchild of parent, but again the latter formulation requires an explicit addendum to the effect that they are not children of A, that is, $A \neq B$.

The final consanguineal term is "cousin," for which there are various degrees in English. If we limit ourselves to first cousins, they are the children of auntuncles, C of CPP, or niblings of parents, CCP of P:

(17)   CCPP(A, C):   C(A, B) & CPP(B, C)
                          $\equiv$ P(B, A) & CCP(C, B)
                          $\equiv$ CCPP(C, A).

So CCPP is also symmetric; if A is a cousin of C, then C is also a cousin of A. (Second counsins are related by CCCPPP.)

Let us collect all these relations and arrange them by generation differences, with the older referent on the left and the converse younger referent on the right:

(18)   *Generation*   *Older*   *Younger*
         difference   *relation*   *converse*
            2   PP   CC
            1   P, CPP   C, CCP
            0   CP, CCPP

According to this analysis, three semantic components—generation difference, direction of generation difference, and collaterality—are required instead of just generation and lineality as in table 5.2. (The dimensions of sex and consanguinity are ignored in this comparison.) Which analysis is correct? The one in (18) is essentially that developed and tested by Romney and D'Andrade (1964), who found it reflected rather accurately the results of judgments of similarity of meaning. If we take such psychological evidence as relevant for deciding which analysis is to be preferred, then no better solution than (18) for this set of terms is known at the present time.

However, the possibility should be considered that there are two ways to use the kinship concept. In one way, you put yourself at the center of your circle of relatives and think of the different people who take the different kin terms; in this attitude you are exploiting what we have called the personal core of kinship terminology. In the other way, you think more abstractly of the converse relations between relatives, since these determine not only how you should behave toward them but also how you expect them to behave toward you; for lack of a better term, let us call this the logical core of kinship terminology. These are simply two ways of thinking about the same set of contrastive terms, so it is difficult to say that either is more correct than the other. The difference between them is that in the former case you take a single landmark, ego, to anchor all the relations simultaneously, whereas in the latter case you can take a different landmark for each term. Since these two ways of using the conceptual structure are incompatible, some of the difficulties in tracing complex paths between relatives may be attributable to the difficulty of keeping clearly in mind which way you are trying to exploit the concept at any given time. In 4.4.3 we pointed out that more than one identification device, or key, could be based on the same general theory; neither key is more correct than the other, though one may be more useful than the other in certain situations. Presumably, the personal and logical analyses represent a cognitive illustration of this possibility.

In table 5.2 we included affinal as well as consanguineal relatives. In order to represent affinal terms in the logical notation we have developed, we introduce a third basic relation, M, for "spouse." If M were interpreted as "mated" rather than "married," it might be defined as PC: if A is the parent of B and B is also the child of C (where $A \neq C$), then PC$(A, C) \equiv$ M(A, C). Greenberg (1949), for example, used $+$ for our P, $-$ for our C, and $+-$ for our M. Since none of the relational products in (18) use P to the left of C, the use of PC to represent mates would nicely round out the set of letter sequences available for designating kinship relations. However, since A and C can be married without having a child B, the relational product would not always go through; spouse, in-law, and step relations depend on marriage, not mating, so we prefer to introduce a separate term.

We note first that M is symmetric: M$(A, B) \equiv$ M(B, A). If M(A, B), then A can have a set of in-laws consisting of B's father, mother, brother, and sister, and conversely for B. Also, at the time of marriage A's parents acquire B as a new child, whom they can call son-in-law or daughter-in-law, and conversely for B's parents. Moreover, A's children by any previous marriage acquire a stepmother or stepfather, and perhaps stepbrothers and stepsisters, whereas B acquires a stepson or stepdaughter. Step relations provide new persons to play the customary roles of blood relatives to A, but in-law relations provide A with a whole new set of kinfolk.

These affinal relations can be defined by relational products. For example,

(19)   MC(A, C):   M(A, B) & C(B, C)

is a relation such that it defines "child-in-law" as either "son-in-law" or "daughter-in-law." In this manner we can define

(20)
M	spouse	symmetric
MC	child-in-law	converse of PM
PM	parent-in-law	converse of MC
MCP $=$ CPM	sibling-in-law	symmetric
CM & notC	stepchild	converse of MP & notP
MP & notP	stepparent	converse of CM & notC
CMP & notCP	stepsibling	symmetric

The step relations are structurally equivalent (Goodenough, 1965) to normal consanguineal relations and thus require an additional negated relation to deny that the normal blood tie exists between the referent and the relatum. This list omits auntuncular relations created by marriage. For example, if A is the wife of C, then she is the (affinal) aunt of C's (consanguineal) niblings, and so might be called their aunt-in-law. However, she is structurally equivalent to a consanguineal aunt and so might be called their stepaunt. Since neither designation is more defensible than the other, the issue is generally resolved by using neither qualification; MCPP is simply "aunt" or "uncle," and CCPM is simply "niece" or "nephew."

All together, therefore, there are seven or eight semantic dimensions to kinship terminology. It would be a simple matter to set up a formal identification procedure (a key or a decision table) based on these dimensions and to incorporate each outcome in a separate labeling routine.

The logical character of kinship systems has always fascinated people who like conundrums. For example, "What people are not the descendants of those who are not my ancestors?" (Answer: the descendants of my ancestors.) Even such a simple question as "If I am the son of the daughter of the mother of the father of Edna, what relation is she to me?" can require considerable thought. (Answer: CCPP defines first cousins.) What relation is my uncle to my cousin? (Answer: it depends.) People are no more facile in using the kinship concept for answering such questions than they are at solving syllogisms—in marked contrast to their ability to exploit the hierarchical trees generated by "is a" and "has a."

Kin terms are ordinarily used to communicate information about particular genealogies—your own or another's. Thus it will happen that you are in receipt of certain fragments of information about someone's genealogy but with large gaps in your knowledge. You may know something about A's relatives and something about B's relatives without knowing that A and B are siblings, so when you hear "A is B's sister" you must understand from your kinship concept what bond is to be added to their genealogies in your person memory.

The effect of adding such a relation is to convert two genealogies into one, which implies that additional work should be done. In this example, A's known offspring can be recognized as niblings of B, and vice versa; the unknown C and D who are A's parents can be identified with the unknown E and F who are B's parents; and so on. Considerable restructuring of memory is entailed, and the logic behind it consists of tracing out inferentially the various P–C–M bonds that might exist between the different individuals.

Lindsay (1963) has described a computer simulation of this process and compared it with the inferences produced by high school students provided with the same genealogical information. Given the sentence "Joey was playing with his brother Bobby in their Aunt Jane's yard when their mother called them home," what can you conclude about Joey's genealogy? Some conclusions can be definite, but others involve alternative possibilities; are Aunt Jane and Joey's mother sisters or sisters-in-law? As more information accumulates, more uncertainties may arise. The memory required to store all the alternative genealogies compatible with the available evidence may be quite large. People simplify the problem by ignoring many of the contingent implications when the set of such possibilities is too large. In a culture that regulated much of its social behavior according to kinship, such uncertainties could be embarrassing, which might create pressures in the society either to change their conventions or to develop more informative terminology—to make it obligatory to distinguish between paternal and maternal aunts, or affinal and consanguineal aunts, for example. Genealogies are relatively unimportant in Anglo-American life; they are seldom known more than three or four generations back.

Because the conceptual core of kinship is complex, it takes children several years to master it. A child learns kin terms first as terms labeling individuals —equivalent to proper names—and only later develops an integrated conception of kinship adequate to understand the relational properties involved. Piaget (1924) reports the following conversation with Raoul, aged four: "Raoul, have you any brothers?—*Gerald.*—And has Gerald a brother? —*No, only me has a brother.*—Oh, come! Hasn't Gerald got a brother? —*Raoul? . . . No, he hasn't got one*" (p. 84). For Raoul, the label "brother" is clearly not understood in terms of a system of kinship relations. Piaget's study of the stages in the child's conception of "frère" and "soeur" was replicated for "brother" and "sister" by Elkind (1962) and Swartz and Hall (1972) and extended to other kin relations by Danziger (1957) and Haviland and Clark (1974).

Danziger asked children questions about brother, sister, daughter, uncle, and cousin. Five-year-olds typically gave what he called a categorical response, such as "A brother is a boy." The first relational responses indicated understanding that the terms denote a relation between individuals, but it was not integrated into a system of relationships: "A brother is a little boy that you live with." Older children understand a more abstract relation: "A brother is a boy who's got a sister or a brother." While the relation remains isolated, it depends for its meaning on specific people the child happens to know as examples. Once it is seen as part of a system, the system introduces what Danziger calls objective necessity into the child's thinking—a necessity that is "irrespective of the intent or other irrelevant characteristics of the individuals whose relationship to each other constitutes the system" (p. 229). By eight most children had given up categorical definitions, but even then they did not handle all kin terms at the same level of conceptualization. Terms they had had most experience with were integrated first into their developing concept.

Haviland and Clark considered the possibility that the order of development of different terms might be explained in terms of the complexity of the relation, where "complexity" is defined, in our present notation, by the number of P and C relations required to define it: they suggest that single P or C is simplest, then CP, then PP or CC, and CPP or CCP is most complex. This hypothesis accounted for about half the variance they observed in order of acquisition by children between the ages of three years and eight years ten months.

For any particular term, development might be characterized as going from properties, $F(A)$, to relational properties, $F(A, k)$, where k is fixed on ego, to relations, $F(A, B)$, with two free variables. The child first learns that A is

called father, then realizes that A is called my father, and finally, after sufficient familiarity or maturation allows it, he recognizes "father" as a true
relational term. The egocentric use of these words as relational properties provides an intermediate step toward mastery of the more complex system of
relations with two free variables. When it becomes possible for him to free the
terms from their anchor to ego, the logical possibilities of the system of relations become available for exploration. Kin terms involving ego as the relatum
continue to be used after the general system is understood, of course, but then
they can be seen not as properties but as special instances having their place
in the more general system.

A great deal more could be said about kinship and its effects on the behavior of peoples who talk about it in different ways. There is much more
information stored in the kinship concept than the semantic components we
have been discussing. It is clearly one important ramification of the core concept
of person. We will not pursue the topic further, however. Our purpose was
to contrast kinship with color, so we should consider now whether there are
any similarities that we might abstract from these two very different semantic
fields.

We can draw some generalizations. Both semantic fields involve contrastive
sets of terms organized paradigmatically with respect to a limited number of
dimensions of opposition. Both involve a limited hierarchy of terms. And in
both one is able to recognize dimensions of contrast whose psychological validity can be tested experimentally. Kinship is cognitively more complex than
color; seven or eight semantic dimensions are required for the analysis of kin
terms and only three for the analysis of color terms. Moreover, there seem to
be two ways to exploit the kinship concept—an egocentric (or deictic) way
and a decentered way—but only one for color. Yet in both cases it is possible
to formulate paradigms that will permit the translation of the underlying conceptual core into a labeling routine. These similarities are remarkable evidence
of the power of the human mind to impose its classificatory strategies on the
most diverse kinds of subject matter.

The ubiquity of contrastive sets nested in hierarchical relations suggests
that such an organization represents a formal, universal semantic characteristic of language. More than that, like all linguistic universals, it is not a part of
language per se but a part of the psychological and biological foundations on
which language rests, a capacity that all human languages can take as given by
the nature of the language-using organism. As such, this type of organization
must play a central role in any account we try to give of man's attempts to
discover structure and meaning in his world and his experience of it.

The general characterization of these concepts that appears to emerge from
our two examples is that they consist of at least a conceptual core and a lexical
field. The conceptual core shares many aspects with a scientific theory; it is, if
you like, a lay theory about the nature of a particular part of the world. The
lexical field, on the other hand, enables people to map this logical core into
language, and the mapping can usually be represented in the form of a key or

a decision table based on perceptual or memory tests that are selected for their relevance to the conceptual core and that reveal the place of each lexical item relative to all the others in that field. The field properties that hold among words are in part a lexical reflection of the conceptual core and in part a result of the hierarchical and contrastive structures that make possible the different levels of generality at which people are able to talk about aspects of the concept.

Semantic analysis is generally most successful when we have a reasonably clear understanding of the underlying conceptual domain. The semanticist's favoritism for color and kin terms, for example, and his success in characterizing their relations are not accidentally related to the availability of independent analyses of the perceptual and biological relations that these terms denote. Other favorites, only slightly less well analyzed, are number terms and terms for plants and animals, where there are independent conceptual analyses from mathematics and biological taxonomy. Where semantic analysis becomes difficult and semanticists are likely to lose their way is in domains for which there is no independent conceptual base or where conceptual analyses do not seem isomorphic with the lexical resources of natural languages.

Many students of child language are now convinced that mastery of basic concepts must precede a child's mastery of language that expresses those concepts. A semanticist's situation may be similar to a child's. If adequate conceptual analysis must precede adequate lexical analysis, the semanticist's task may be even more difficult than he has realized.

A further similarity between our analyses of color and kinship terminology is the importance of relations for determining the place of each lexical item in the general concept—both relations between terms in the domain and relations that the terms express. In both cases the system of relations has to be anchored to certain fixed landmarks. In the case of color terms, the landmarks are provided by the basic oppositions of primate color vision. In the case of kin terms, the whole system may be anchored to a single landmark, or each separate term may express a relation between its referent and an arbitrary landmark (the relatum). Semantic relativity has long been recognized as a valuable resource of human language, but we would enlarge its role and supplement it by the introduction of landmark terms that serve to anchor a whole system of relations to certain fixed points that are perceptually or conceptually salient.

6

Some Fundamental Concepts

The purpose of psychology is to give us a completely different idea of the things we know best. —*Paul Valéry (1943)*

Color and kinship have received more attention from semantic theorists than they deserve, but they do have the virtue of illustrating clearly what is meant by a semantic field. The clarity dissipates, however, when one tries to duplicate these analyses elsewhere in the lexicon. Many critics have complained that, outside a few special topics, the notion of semantic fields is too vague for serious investigation.

The notion could be made considerably less vague if it were possible to decide, for any two words (or two senses of words), whether they are in the same semantic field. Or, since the question will probably not admit a yes/no answer, if we could decide how large is the smallest field containing them both. Two approaches have been proposed, one analytic, the other intuitive. The analytic approach assumes that any two words that can be analyzed into common conceptual components are to that extent in the same semantic field; the more conceptual components two words have in common, the smaller is the smallest semantic field that contains them both. The intuitive approach asks people to make intuitive judgments of the similarity of meaning between any two words; the greater the judged similarity of meaning, the smaller is the smallest field that contains them both. This whole enterprise could be considerably strengthened, moreover, if both of these approaches gave the same results, in which case one might hope to find that an analytic hypothesis would explain the observations of judged similarity. In the introduction to chapter 5 we phrased this hope as a criterion to be met: "the semantic components we identify should leave us with groups of words that seem intuitively similar in meaning" (p. 333).

Unfortunately, the two approaches do not always support each other. All is well in the fields of color and kinship, where the conceptual components required for analysis do seem to provide plausible explanations for people's intuitive judgments of similarity of meaning. Trouble appears when we look at concepts like PERSON. In chapter 4 we found that this important concept did not have an intuitively coherent lexical field associated with it. The language of personal identifications and personal relations is enormously complicated and cuts across many semantic fields—even across color, where a red is a communist, a blue is a graduate of Yale, a white is a Caucasian, and a black is variously colored, beautiful, or cool. In short, there is no set of intuitively similar terms that covers this conceptual field; it is not a semantic field.

If we assign primary importance to a native speaker's intuitions about similarities of meaning—and we believe that is the only defensible approach for a psychologist to take—we are forced to recognize at least two different kinds of concepts that are incorporated into lexical entries. On the one hand are concepts like color and kinship that are central to semantic fields. On the other hand are concepts like person, whose lexical role is still unclear.

In this chapter we take up three more concepts that, like person, are important and ubiquitous, yet are not mapped onto intuitively coherent lexical fields. With more examples in front of us, the correct generalizations about them may become more obvious.

6.1   SPATIAL RELATIONS

The primacy of spatial organization for human cognition has frequently been noted; it gives this topic an importance that extends far beyond any literal interpretation of spatial locations and directions. Urban (1939) writes that "our intellect is primarily fitted to deal with space and moves most easily in this medium. Thus language itself becomes spatialized, and in so far as reality is represented by language, reality tends to be spatialized" (p. 186). Other authors could be cited in the same vein. The variety of uses people make of spatial words in nonspatial contexts is but one example of the extent to which spatial metaphors and analogies dominate speech and thought. We have already commented (4.2.1) that the system of locative inclusion seems psychologically basic to part-whole and class-inclusion hierarchies.

Although linguistic consequences of the biological and psychological importance of space are plain enough even in Indo-European languages, in many other languages the specification of spatial attributes of objects is obligatory, just as temporal specification is obligatory in the English tense system. Friedrich (1970) has concluded that "the overt, obligatory morphology of perhaps the majority of the world's languages functions partly to express categories of shape" (p. 403). According to Friedrich, no language illustrates this better than Tarascan, an American Indian language spoken in southwestern Mexico. Tarascan grammar requires a speaker to add to his use of numerals a "classifier" that indicates whether the objects are sticklike, tortillalike, or ball-like—one, two, or three dimensional. Moreover, a considerable number of verbal roots in Tarascan are marked for spatial features of the nouns that can serve as their subjects or objects. The language uses a distinct set of suffixes of locative space, suffixes indicating features of a location such as its dimensions and shape; some of these suffixes refer to body parts, some refer to certain noncorporal kinds of location, often of a typical shape, some combine body and nonbody referents. Friedrich comments, "These suffixes of space are largely obligatory when discussing any one of their wide range of referents; one is forced to code the location of the action in terms of spatial features, many of which are shape-differentiated" (p. 391). In Tarascan, grammar compels a language user to conceptualize in terms of "a stream of abutting shapes and adjoining surfaces and lines that is reminiscent of Cézanne's dismemberment of objects into their geometrical components" (p. 399).

According to Hoijer (1945), the Navaho language also has classificatory verbs that depend on shape categories, and Casagrande (Carroll and Casagrande, 1958) found that Navaho-speaking children would solve a non-linguistic, object-sorting task on the basis of the shapes of the objects at distinctly younger ages than English-speaking children on the Navaho reservation would. English-speaking children in Boston, however, performed much as the Navaho-speaking children did, so this evidence that obligatory grammatical categories affect perceptual and cognitive development is not compelling. No doubt the perception of shape depends on certain universal neurophysiological characteristics of the perceptual system, just as color perception does; talking about it by option or obligation may have only minor psychological consequences (Rosch, 1973). However, the possibility of discovering very different ways of relating perceptual and linguistic space in different cultures will probably continue to interest anthropological linguists.

In any event, the languages of the world differ widely in their treatment of space. Although English, like other Indo-European languages, may be among a minority in not having obligatory spatial morphemes—in not treating spatial features on a par with tense, gender, person, and number—its lexical resources for optional reference to shape, space, and spatial relations are rich and complex. One part of the spatial lexicon of English is the elaborate system of coordinates available for metric descriptions. A careful analysis of these labels would have to distinguish a great variety of metric subfields. For example, we could analyze the terms used for points of the compass (north, south, east, west, and their permissible combinations); latitude, longitude, altitude, and their appropriate measure phrases; units of length, area, and volume and labels for such properties as height, length, width, breadth, depth, and thickness. In principle, there is nothing to stop people from partitioning space as finely as they wish and assigning labels to it; coordinate systems and measures of length enable a speaker to be very precise about space and spatial relations. Since nothing can be in two places at the same time, the conditions for creating contrastive sets of place identifiers seem ideal. Outside of scientific or technological discourse, however, coordinate positions specified by measure phrases are rare.

Another part of the spatial lexicon is an elaborate system of place names for geographic and political areas: Alaska, the Caspian Sea, Kanawha County, Indochina, the Vatican. These labels form a hierarchical lexical structure based on the semantic relation of locative inclusion and complicated by historical and political information of the most diverse kinds. We assume that this lexical field maps onto a conceptual core that organizes adults' geographic knowledge of the world. Since this concept can contain an indefinitely large amount of information and goes well beyond any perceptual space that people are likely to experience, it is not surprising that the construction of this intellectual space is a relatively slow process in children (Flickinger and Rehage, 1949).

For dealing with the space in which people live and work, there are still other resources. Take the extensive system of labels in English for various kinds of containers, pathways, and boundaries.

—Containers: archives, attics, bags, baskets, bins, boats, bottles, bowls, boxes, buildings, canisters, cans, cars, caves, cellars, chambers, chests, cities, closets, continents, countries, crates, cribs, cups, drawers, envelopes, glasses, holes, houses, jars, lakes, libraries, lockers, luggage, mouths, mugs, museums, oceans, packages, pails, pans, parlors, pens, phonebooths, pits, pockets, pools, pots, prisons, purses, receptacles, rooms, sacks, satchels, sinks, states, tanks, trunks, tubs, vases, vessels, wallets, wardrobes, yards, zones

—Pathways: airways, aisles, alleys, arteries, avenues, boulevards, bridges, canals, channels, courses, detours, drives, driveways, footpaths, freeways, halls, hallways, highways, lanes, overpasses, passages, passageways, paths, pipes, rivers, roads, routes, shortcuts, sidewalks, stairways, steps, streets, subways, throughways, tracks, trails, tubes, tunnels, turnpikes, underpasses, walks, waterways, ways

—Boundaries: backs, banks, barriers, beaches, blockades, borders, bottoms, bounds, brinks, ceilings, cliffs, coasts, confines, contours, covers, curbs, edges, ends, extremes, fences, floors, fringes, frontiers, fronts, hindrances, limits, lines, linings, lips, margins, perimeters, rims, shores, sides, sills, surfaces, thresholds, tops, walls

Architects have probably collected more data about the ways people talk about space than psychologists or linguists have. In an essay recounting his attempts to discover how people conceptualize the spaces in which they live, Lynch (1960) developed a list of spatial elements and graphical representations that he used to summarize what people told him about cities they knew well. Lynch found he needed to distinguish among districts, nodes, landmarks, paths, and edges. This set of spatial elements for cognitive maps may have some generality for entities other than cities.

Districts, according to Lynch, are the medium-to-large sections of a city, conceived of as having two-dimensional extent, which a person mentally enters "inside of": downtown, the Irish district, the West Side. Nodes are the strategic places in a city into which a person can enter, and which are the focuses of a district to and from which he travels; they can be junctions, transportation stops, public squares, street-corner hangouts. Landmarks, for Lynch, are point references external to the person. In a city, landmarks may be distant buildings or geographical features that can be seen from many angles and distances, or they may be primarily local: buildings, signs, trees, storefronts, doorknobs, or other urban details. Paths are the channels along which people move—streets, walkways, transit lines, canals, rivers, railroads; they are generally conceived of as linear, one-dimensional entities. Edges are linear elements not used or considered as paths, the boundaries or seams along which two regions are related and joined together. In a city they include shores, railroad cuts, edges of development, walls, barriers in general.

How such elements come to be organized in a person's memory relative to one another as a cognitive map of his world poses a fascinating problem for developmental psychology. Siegel and White (1974), who have reviewed speculation and research on the development of spatial representations of large-scale environments, suggest that the developmental sequence begins when a child starts to notice and remember fixed landmarks in his environment; then the landmarks slowly become connected as he notices and remembers familiar routes between them; and, when a route representation is sufficiently rich and elaborated, it may be possible (although not necessary) to construct a survey representation incorporating configurations of landmarks. The available evidence, however, indicates that even adults do not have literal maps to represent their information about the geography of their environments and that when they try to draw maps based on what they know, the maps are usually fragmentary and distorted. Perhaps a final stage is possible when the person studies a topographically accurate map and tries to use that formal representation to organize spatial information he has acquired informally. The sophistication of survey representations can vary considerably with the individual's experience. In any case, Siegel and White's discussion suggests that the cognitive elements available for linguistic denotation of spatial relations can be classified as landmarks, routes, and configurations.

Not only do people remember a great deal of organized information about these spatial elements, but such environmental features have strong affective connotations as well. Lowenthal and Riel (1972) obtained ratings on a variety of subjective scales from people who were actually walking through particular urban neighborhoods and compared the pattern of intercorrelations with those obtained from another group of people who were asked only to judge the semantic relations between the terms that had been used in the rating scales. Although there was considerable agreement between the patterns obtained when people were looking at actual environments and those obtained when people were only thinking about them, there were interesting differences as well. For example, both sets of data showed that beautiful/ugly was strongly correlated with fresh/smelly, interesting/boring, vivid/drab, pleasant/unpleasant, clean/dirty, like/dislike, and light/dark; but people who were judging actual urban environments showed strong correlations also between beautiful/ugly and ordered/chaotic, smooth/rough, rich/poor; and people who were only thinking about urban environments gave strong correlations of beautiful/ugly with natural/artificial, open/bounded, quiet/noisy. Wealth, texture, and order made a more consistent impression on observers of environments than on those who were merely thinking about environmental concepts. And although people thought they liked openness, they did not always like it when they saw it.

A thorough exploration of cognitive and affective language for space would be a much more ambitious project than we wish to undertake here. We will, instead, select a part of the larger problem. We will try to analyze those prepositions that can be used to express spatial relations: in, on, at, by, on the right of, to, toward.

These words are sometimes called locatives (or spatial locatives, to distinguish them from temporal locatives) because their grammar is too complicated to justify calling them simply prepositions. For example, "in" is a preposition in "in the harbor" and "in the harbor" is a prepositional phrase. But a prepositional phrase can occur either as the complement of a verb ("It sank in the harbor"), in which case it plays an adverbial role, or as the complement of a noun ("the channel in the harbor"; see Chomsky, 1970), in which case it plays an adjectival role. In these examples, "in" is used transitively ("the harbor" is the object of the preposition "in"); it can also be used intransitively. As a verb-complement intransitive "in" is an adverb ("It sank in") and as a noun complement it is an adjective ("the channel in" or "the in channel"). Thus, to call "in" simply a preposition underestimates its grammatical potentialities.

On the other hand, to assign "in" always to its correct syntactic category suggests diversity where there is considerable semantic uniformity. Since our interests are semantic, we will adopt a single grammatical frame in which to work: NP + (Prep + NP), as in "a boat in the harbor," "faces at the window," "life on a farm." In these adjectival constructions the preposition can be seen as a relation taking an ordered pair of arguments: $R(x, y)$, where the referent x is a target identified by the head noun phrase, the relatum y is a landmark identified by the object noun phrase, and R is a spatial relation indicated by the preposition. Psychologically, these constructions presuppose the existence of some landmark whose location is known, or easily discoverable, by both participants in the communication—something that can help to narrow the domain of search for the target. Moreover, when a spatial (or temporal) locative establishes a locale, it usually creates a context that governs subsequent discourse until it is explicitly changed.

Nothing of semantic importance is neglected by ignoring adverbial uses. Spatial locatives in adverbial constructions also narrow the search domain, but the target is identified by the subject of the verb. In "The plumber worked in the kitchen," for example, the adverbial "in the kitchen" seems to locate where the work occurred, but since it is impossible for the plumber to work anywhere other than where he is located, locating the work has the same effect as locating the worker. Thus, "The plumber worked in the kitchen," "The plumber was in the kitchen," and "the plumber in the kitchen" all express the same spatial relation between the plumber and the kitchen. (Geis, 1975, notes that these generalizations are not true of temporal locatives, since "The plumber worked in the morning" is not paralleled by "The plumber was in the morning" or "the plumber in the morning." Temporal locatives locate events or activities; spatial locatives locate things.)

Semantic analysis of spatial locatives is complicated by strong interdependencies between the preposition and the relatum. It is appropriate, for example, to speak of a referent as "in France" or "at the corner of Sixty-sixth and York," but one would not ordinarily say it was "at France" or "in the corner of Sixty-sixth and York." These selectional restrictions in English are complex and often seem arbitrary, but it is not possible to analyze spatial locatives without taking account of the kinds of landmarks that can serve as their relata.

6.1.1 Location

The Newtonian conception of space as an infinite, continuous, stationary, three-dimensional box enables a speaker to label locations by their coordinate values as precisely as he might wish (given a point of origin). Needless to say, this way of labeling space is not the usual practice in everyday affairs. Ordinary languages are designed to deal with relativistic space; with space relative to objects that occupy it. Relativistic space provides three orthogonal coordinates, just as Newtonian space does, but no fixed units of angle or distance are involved, nor is there any need for coordinates to extend without limit in any direction. Children acquire their initial familiarity with relativistic space in infancy as they learn to move about and to construct a stable, three-dimensional, perceptual world. When they first learn to talk about space, they learn to describe and interpret spatial relations between two or three things that are perceptually relatable. As in the case of color and kin terms, the spatial words children learn first have their meanings by virtue of their place in the whole field of words and phrases used to represent the conceptual core of relativistic space.

The logic of space is complex, as students of geometry can attest, yet people deal with it reflexly most of the time and have little trouble understanding it at the level of concrete operations. There is a Hungarian story about two mountain climbers lost in the Alps who consult their map until one suddenly points to a distant peak and announces, "We are on that mountain over there." The story is absurd because this is not the kind of confusion about space people are liable to. People sometimes get lost, but they never think that they are anywhere other than where they are—they just do not know where where-they-are is. "Where I am" is always "here." Except in the dead of night a person can look around him and see where he is. He is in trouble only if he does not know the spatial relation between his own "here" and any place he might prefer to be. That is to say, he can usually deal with space locally, but he sometimes loses track of it in the large. Instances in which two people converse from different locations—by telephone, for example—can lead to difficulties that language evolution may not have allowed for and that may require novel conventions (see Schegloff, 1972), but such instances are special. The spatial concept is basically relativistic, and sometimes people lack one or more of the basic relations. But as long as people deal with local spaces, their intuitions are remarkably accurate.

Because the relativistic conception of space is more natural and primitive, it is tempting to dismiss the absolute conception as a special scientific derivative of no linguistic interest. Whatever the merits of this opinion, it should not lead us to overlook the fact that people do often talk about locations in terms of coordinate systems that remain, if not absolute, at least reasonably permanent. Consider William James's (1907) famous problem:

> The *corpus* of the dispute was a squirrel—a live squirrel supposed to be clinging to one side of a tree-trunk; while over against the tree's opposite side a human being was imagined to stand. This human witness tries to get sight of the squirrel by moving rapidly round the tree, but no matter how fast he goes, the squirrel moves as fast in the opposite direction, and always keeps the tree between himself and the man, so that never a glimpse of him is caught. The resultant metaphysical problem now is this: *Does the man go round the squirrel or not?* He goes round the tree, sure enough, and the squirrel is on the tree; but does he go round the squirrel? (P. 41)

James solved the problem by distinguishing two different coordinate systems:

> If you mean passing from the north of him to the east, then to the south, then to the west, and then to the north of him again, obviously the man does go round him, for he occupies these successive positions. But if on the contrary you mean being first in front of him, then on the right of him, then behind him, then on his left, and finally in front again, it is quite as obvious that the man fails to go round him, for by the compensating movements the squirrel makes, he keeps his belly turned towards the man all the time, and his back turned away. (P. 42)

The coordinate system based on north, east, south, and west is permanent for earthbound humans and so must be treated linguistically in much the same way one would treat locations in Newtonian space. The coordinate system based on front, right, behind, and left is always relative to the organism that provides its point of origin and so requires a different linguistic treatment.

Consider the most comprehensive system for designating permanent locations that is generally familiar, the system of latitude, longitude, and altitude.

The locative preposition that seems to go most naturally with such place designations is "at":

(1)   Greenwich, town at 0 degrees longitude
            the plane at 13,000 feet
            the main office at 123 East Forty-fifth Street

The third example shows that street addresses can be treated as a two-dimensional system of the same type. The easy adoption of "at" into absolute systems of spatial designation suggests that it naturally adapts to the fiction of "point" locations.

Relative locations, on the other hand, can be talked about in a variety of ways. There seems to be a basic split between relative designations in terms of bounded areas or volumes and relative designations in terms of "point" locations. When people wish to indicate an area or volume containing some location, the preposition of choice is usually "in":

(2)   a town in England
            the plane high in the sky
            the office in Chicago
            the dish in the cupboard

There are at least three distinguishable systems for designating locations relative to landmarks, paths, and boundaries. When the reference object supports the object whose location is to be indicated, people generally use "on":

(3)   a building on Long Island
            the plane on the runway
            the office on the third floor
            the dish on the table

When people wish to indicate the direction in which an object lies with respect to a reference object, a variety of possibilities are available for different directions and distances:

(4)   a town near London
            the plane over the field
            the office by/beside/behind/over/at the bank
            the dish with/beneath/against/under the cup

The system of spatial designations that is probably most primitive psychologically is the deictic system, in which the current location of the speaker or listener is taken as a landmark:

(5)   a town 15 miles from here
            the plane right over us
            the office to the left of you
            the dish in front of me

This summary suggests the basic plan. In actual usage there are many variations on this plan, variations that are the frustration of all learners, adults and children alike. The difference between "Ross is at the hospital" and "Ross is in the hospital" is not explained in terms of the differences between (1) and (2). The difference between "the house on the street" and "the car on the street" would never be clear from (3). And many ambiguities result from other uses than designating locations: "The painting was by Picasso," "The book is beneath me," "He was behind the class," "Her hat was over her shoes."

We will concentrate on the principal senses of these words when they are used to denote relative locations and will select "in," "on," and "at" as in some way simpler and probably more generic than the others. Although T. Bower (1974) makes an interesting case that the relation "inside" is not understood by infants younger than fifteen to eighteen months, Brown (1973) lists "in" and "on" as among the earliest morphemes that children produce when they begin to combine words into longer utterances. "In" was the easiest of the twenty-three locative prepositions tested on children by Aaronson and Schaefer (1968), and "on" was the tenth most difficult ("at" was not included; "between" was the most difficult). E. Clark (1972; 1974b) has reported studies of the comprehension of "in," "on," and "under" by children as young as twenty-one months that also indicate that they may understand "in" before they understand "on." She notes, however, that there is a strong response bias. Young children act out commands to place a referent relative to a relatum on the basis of the physical properties of the relatum. That is to say, if it is possible to place the referent in the relatum, the children will do so regardless of the preposition used in the instruction; if the relatum cannot serve as a container, the children will place the referent on it even when asked to put it under the relatum. The request to "put" the referent somewhere is respected, but the child shows little understanding of the spatial relation denoted by the accompanying preposition and simply exhibits his own preference for putting one thing inside another. By thirty-three months the children Clark studied responded appropriately to all three commands, but the nature of their response preference makes it difficult to say from their performance whether they "really" understand "in" before "on."

We have found no comparable data suggesting that "at," or the closely related preposition "with," is among the first to appear in child language. As we will see, "at" is dependent on a more abstract notion of a region, a more complex notion than perhaps occurs with "in" and "on," which can be used in the absence of any general spatial frame of reference for the relatum.

In considering the semantics of spatial reference we are fortunate to have a number of excellent studies of English prepositions; we have benefited from the work of White (1964), Bennett (1968, 1972, 1975), Cooper (1968), Becker and Arms (1969), and Leech (1969). Their studies have in the main concentrated on the componential relations in the language and have often achieved enviable comprehensiveness. We can begin, therefore, by considering what some of these authors say about "in," "on," and "at."

Bennett (1972), although primarily concerned with other issues, offers the following sketch of the relations among these three locative prepositions:

(6)   in y: locative(interior(y))
         on y: locative(surface(y))
         at y: locative(y)

A more elaborate functional analysis, in a notation sharing several features with our own, is provided by Cooper (1968):

(7) x in y: x is located internal to y, with the constraint that x is smaller than y.

         x on y: A surface of x is contiguous with a surface of y, with the constraint that y supports x.

         x at y: x is near or in y, with the constraint that x is portable relative to y and y is not a geopolitical area.

         x near y: x and y are separate and x is located internal to the space z which is contiguous with y.

Leech (1969) has carried out the most exhaustive study of English spatial terms, analyzed in a semantic notation of his own. The following paraphrases of his interpretations are based on those that Leech himself provides:

(8) x in y: x is "enclosed" or "contained" either in a two-dimensional or in a three-dimensional place y.

         x on y: x is contiguous with the place of y, where y is conceived of either as one-dimensional (a line) or as two-dimensional (a surface).

         x at y: x is contiguous or juxtaposed to the place of y, where the dimensionality of y is not significant.

There are both resemblances and conflicts among these accounts, and one could even demonstrate some inadequacies.

One purpose of locative descriptions is to narrow the domain of search for a referent. They are particularly useful for making object identifications distinctive—for providing definite descriptions—because they can be used to narrow the search domain to the point where only one object of the type described is contained in it. In thinking about such routines, it is helpful to distinguish two search domains. The first domain is the one in which to search for the relatum y; the second is a subdomain of the first in which to search for the referent x. The first search domain is given by the context in which the communication occurs; the subdomain depends on both the relation expressed by the preposition and the characteristics of the particular relatum. It is necessary, therefore, to specify the subdomain as a function of the preposition and the relatum.

We can make these remarks less abstract if we consider the general format of a schema for "in." A brief glance at any dictionary will confirm that "in" has a great variety of uses. We can set aside several senses: "the woman in the club" indicates class membership; "the hydrogen in the water" is some kind of constituent relation; "the switch in the circuit" indicates a part-whole relation. The locative uses we will analyze are

(9)   (a) a city in Sweden
         (b) the coffee in the cup
         (c) the spoon in the cup
         (d) the scratch in the surface
         (e) the bone in the leg

Underlying all these uses of "in" is a concept that Bennett (1972) refers to as "interior," Cooper (1968) as "internal location," and Leech (1969) as "enclosure" or "containment." This concept can be represented by making the subdomain of search the relatum itself, which implies that the relatum must be the kind of thing that has an interior to serve as a search subdomain.

The sense of "in" in (9a) is locative inclusion, discussed briefly in 4.2.1. The senses in (b) and (c) involve containers, with the complication that something sticking out of a container can still be said to be in it; (c) implies that a container need not always be larger than the object it has "in" it, as in "the club in his hand." The senses in (d) and (e) involve partonymic relations with a contrast between two- and three-dimensional objects; it should be noted that although "in" and "on" usually contrast, when the subdomain is a two-dimensional area the difference seems to be a matter of judgment as to how far the referent goes into the relatum. The following schema would appear to fit all these senses.

(10)   IN(x, y):   A referent x is "in" a relatum y if:
         (i) [PART(x, z) & INCL(z, y)]

The question here is whether part (some or all) of the referent is included in the relatum. The schema leaves uncertain how much of the referent must be inside the relatum before one is willing to say it is "in" it, but such uncertainty is not inappropriate.

Since a schema is an assertion—as indicated by the brackets—and excludes control instructions, it can be used in a variety of ways. What is presupposed and what is asserted in any particular use of a relation will be left open as far as semantic memory is concerned, and only the components to be tested will be stored in semantic memory. The flexibility of this approach can be illustrated by considering first the case in which the system tries to execute a command to find(search domain, x such that IN(x, y)), where the search domain is given by the context of the discourse. The "find" instruction will use (10) to determine that part of x is included in y, and so will try to find(search domain, y) and, if successful, will then substitute y for the general search domain, thus changing the control instruction to find(y, x such that IN(x, y)), and this will cause the executor to search y until either part of x is found within it or the subdomain of search is exhausted. If the "find" instruction incorporates such subroutines for narrowing the search domain, it will be able to use the information given in (10) even though (10) itself contains no control instructions.

Consider next the case in which the system tries to execute a command to identify(search domain, x), where again the search domain is given by the context of the discourse, and x is a pointer to the perception of some particular object. If the most precise label for x that is available to the system does not distinguish it from other objects in that search domain, "identify" may try to narrow the search domain until only one object bearing that label is included in it. Then "identify" may execute an instruction to find(search domain, y such that $\text{IN}(x, y)$) and, if successful, will use (10) to construct $\text{IN}(x, y)$, which can then be used in an identifying phrase of the form "the x in the y." If the "identify" instruction incorporates such subroutines for narrowing the search domain, there will be no need to include such instructions in (10).

Consider next the preposition "on." Here again, some of the many senses of "on" can be set aside: "the man on the committee" indicates class membership; "the dog on the chain" indicates connectedness and differs from "the chain on the dog" only with respect to focus; "the nose on your face" expresses a part-whole relation; "the man on the move" indicates movements. In the phrases

(11)   (a) the house on the river
         (b) the scratch on the surface
         (c) the label on the box
         (d) the picture on the wall
         (e) the rug on the floor
         (f) the table on the rug (on the floor)
         (g) the lamp on the table (on the rug on the floor)

the relata for "on," except in (11a), seem to be surfaces, which suggests that the subdomain for search should be the region of the surface of the relatum. Since surfaces are parts of objects, this subdomain is not defined for abstract relata; one can be "with" a group "at" a party "in" Westport, but one cannot be "on" any of these surfaceless things.

"The house on the river" is not usually understood in the same way as "the canoe on the river," although a large boat could be moving the house to a new site. Ordinarily, "the house on the river" is understood to mean "the house by the river." The ambiguity arises from the nature of paths, which can be thought of either as surfaces along which traffic can pass or as edges marking the boundary of something. As long as you use "on" for surfaces and "by" for edges there is no problem of interpretation. When you use "on" for edges, however, ambiguity is possible if the edges have surfaces. We need some way to represent these two uses of "on."

(12) $\text{ON}(x, y)$:   A referent x is "on" a relatum y if:
         (i) $(\text{INCL}(x, \text{REGION}(\text{SURF}(y))))$ & $\text{SUPRT}(y, x))$; otherwise go to (ii)
         (ii) $\text{PATH}(y)$ & $\text{BY}(x, y)$

Here we assume that whatever control instruction is used will first try to interpret "on" as a surface relation; if that fails, it will try to interpret the relatum
as a path and will call BY to determine whether an edge relation is involved.

This solution supposes that either "on" or "by" is acceptable when the
relatum is a path, which is not literally true. Some path relata are preferred
with "on," others with "by": "apartment on Seventieth Street" or "entrance on
the hall," versus "room by the stairway" or "buildings by the bridge." Here
again a better analysis of locative relata would be required to untangle these
relations. Lacking that, we must adopt the always unsatisfactory assumption
that these are idiomatic exceptions to the general rule.

"The scratch on the surface" will satisfy (12), just as "the scratch in the
surface" satisfies (10), and with the same judgmental distinction required
between them. The surface need not be horizontal, as (c) and (d) illustrate;
(c) assumes that the referent is supported by some kind of attachment to the
relatum, whereas (d) assumes that there is some part of the referent that is
over a part of the relatum (over a hook, for example) and that this part supports the rest of the referent.

Probably the sense of "on" that comes first to mind is that in (e). The
supported referent is "on top of" the supporting relatum. This sense is also
expressed in (f) and (g). Note that one might say "the table on the floor,"
given the situation in (f), even though there was a rug between them. We
might attribute the dispensability of "on the rug" to the transitivity of the
support relation. If we try to interpret "on" as a transitive relation, however,
we discover a peculiar limitation on the extent of its transitivity. A lamp may
be on a table that is on a rug on the floor, as in (g), but we do not describe
that situation by saying the lamp is on the floor. Similarly, a roof may be on a
house that is on a foundation, but we do not say the roof is on the foundation.
The subdomain of search for "on" must be the *region* of interaction with the
surface of the relatum rather than merely the surface. We can say the table is
on the floor even though it is not touching it because when we search in the
region of the floor we will encounter the table legs. We cannot say the lamp
(on the table on the rug on the floor) is on the floor because when we search
in the region of the floor we will not encounter it. Hence the limited transitivity
of "on" as used to describe a pile of objects.

Schema (12) has committed us to an analysis of "by," but before we
analyze that complicated preposition we should consider "at" in order to
establish something of the semantics of REGION, to which we have also resorted
in (12).

A central problem in characterizing relative designations of location is that
you can speak of them simply, without qualification. A point in space is rarely
specified precisely by a speaker; locative expressions are relatively indeterminate with respect to their truth conditions. This freedom is particularly
salient in the case of "at." For example, there is no clear demarcation between
what would and what would not satisfy the following: "the man at the desk,"
"the man at the office," and "the man at the university." Leech (1969) tries

to capture this characteristic indeterminacy by using the words "contiguous" or "juxtaposed." Yet, if we take these formulations literally, they seem too precise, like H. Clark's (1973) notion of punctual location. It is not really necessary to be contiguous or juxtaposed to something in order to be at it. The concept of REGION is needed here. To say "x at y" is to say that x is included in the region of y, that is, x is where it can interact with y socially, physically, or in whatever way x's conventionally interact with y's: "at the party," "at the cleaners," "at work." It is just this indeterminate region of potential interaction that we tried to capture in perceptual terms by Reg(w, y): w is the region of possible interaction with y.

The perceptual predicate Reg(w, y) needs to be generalized slightly in order to accommodate the absolute usage of "at," since it is not clear what the conventional region of interaction with a coordinate position might mean. When you say that Greenwich is at 0 degrees longitude, you are making a very precise statement, since Greenwich is the point of origin for this system of spatial designations, but when you say that a plane is at 13,000 feet, you may mean merely that it is closer to 13,000 than to 12,000 or 14,000. The absolute "at" need not be absolutely precise but may (by metaphorical extension) designate a region around the value given. A more important point is that the relatum y is not an object; the abstract character of the relatum distinguishes absolute from relative designations. One knows that "A plane is at 13,000 feet" means 13,000 feet above sea level, so the ultimate point of reference is sea level, but the sentence should not be interpreted to mean that the plane is in the region of sea level. (The difficulties of specifying exactly what point of origin and what system of measurement are required to locate the relatum y when it is a coordinate position in some abstract space are, of course, no part of the meaning of "at.")

When we introduced Reg as a perceptual predicate, we really had in mind one of those schemata like SEAT that combined perceptual and functional information. A person can make a perceptual judgment involving the region of an object, but in order to do so he must utilize conceptual information about the use or function of the object. This aspect of the predicate is naturally highlighted by considering its conceptual version, REGION(w, y). Indeed, if some class of human artifacts is totally unfamiliar to a person, if they stir in him no meaningful expectations of what they do or what is to be done with them, he will hardly have any clear perception of a characteristic region of interaction with them. Common sense would decree that the judgment could only be made on the basis of a firm conception of what kind of thing y is. Given such a concept of y, the way one characteristically interacts with it (if such a way exists) would surely be a part of that concept, and those conceptual routines would have to be called as subroutines by the perceptual system. An appropriate schema for "at" would therefore seem to be

(13)   AT(x, y):   A referent x is "at" a relatum y if:
          (i) INCL(x, REGION(y))

So much seems necessary, but is it really sufficient? On the positive side we can note that the unacceptability of such constructions as "a city at California" or "the table at the living room" follows from the nature of regions. Geopolitical entities like California and containers like living rooms do not *have* regions, they *are* regions. All the other types of relata, however, can serve as arguments of REGION and so can serve as relata for "at." Moreover, this formulation of "at" clearly admits a variety of truth conditions: "the woman at the piano," for example, could be playing the piano, leaning against it, or even attacking it with an ax. The relation is neither transitive nor intransitive; "He is at the window" does not follow from "He is at the table" and "The table is at the window." And, finally, it is implicit in (13) that the referent must not be too large to be included in the region of the relatum; an expression such as "the plane at the door" suggests either a toy plane or a hangar door.

It seems to be a general rule that relata for "at" should be less mobile and larger or more salient than the referents they locate. This implies that people must store as relevant information about objects not only some impression of their expected sizes but also some impression of their expected mobilities and, perhaps, of their expected salience. It also seems to be true that the notion of "interaction" includes considerably more information than at first may meet the eye. One is much more likely to say "The chair is at the table" if it is upright and facing the table than if it is lying on its side facing away from the table. But chairs do not strictly interact with tables—people sit on chairs in order to use tables. We will not try to write routines to take these facts into account but will simply note once more that perceptual and conceptual routines can each function as subroutines of the other. A judgment that x is at y may depend on what x is doing with y; a judgment of what x is doing with y, if anything, may depend on where x is in relation to y. The one plain fact is that x must be small enough to be included in the region of y if x is to be at y.

A careful analysis of the characteristics of preferred relata would be an interesting psychological study. Large, immobile objects make good landmarks because a person is unlikely to overlook them when making a quick survey of the search domain. But smaller objects can serve if they are perceptually salient, and some locative prepositions seem to presuppose nothing about the relative sizes of the referent and the relatum. Perceptual salience would be one important variable to consider. For example, if there is one red spot in a search domain of gray spots, the red spot might make a natural relatum. A flashing light might provide a useful landmark for similar reasons, and people seem to have special privileges to serve as locative relata. Mobility would be another obvious variable to investigate; motion serves to make an object perceptually salient, although moving objects are uncertain landmarks.

The importance of immobility can be inferred from the work of Huttenlocher and Strauss (1968), who studied children's comprehension of such statements as "The red block is on top of the green block" or "The green block is under the red block." The child was asked to build a pile at the experimenter's instruction; this was done by placing one block relative to a second, where the second was fixed in position on the middle rung of a ladder. If the instruction called for x under y the task was much easier if the relatum y was the immobile block and the referent x was the movable block. When the relatum y was movable, the instruction x under y had to be mentally translated into the converse relation, y over x, before the child understood what to do; this translation took extra time even for older children, and caused five-year-olds to make many mistakes. Even though y over x is logically equivalent to x under y, they are not psychologically equivalent; the first term in the relation should designate the thing whose location is to be determined; the second, the immobile landmark that can be used to determine it.

INCL in (13) places certain restrictions on the characteristics of the relatum for "at." A special problem arises, however, when the referent and the relatum are commensurate in size and mobility. This symmetrical state of affairs is expressed in English by the preposition "with." One says "the boy with Buddy," not "the boy at Buddy"; "the pen with the pencils," not "the pen at the pencils." This locative sense of "with" is symmetric; if Buddy is with the boy, then the boy is with Buddy. The symmetry suggests that this sense of "with" can be treated as a symmetric form of "at":

(14)   WITH(x, y):   A referent x is "with" a relatum y if:
          (i) INCL$(x,$ REGION$(y))$ & INCL$(y,$ REGION$(x))$

This shows what the trouble with (13) is—it needs a condition that will explicitly exclude "with," which might be phrased:

(15)   AT(x, y):   A referent x is "at" a relatum y if:
          (i) INCL$(x,$ REGION$(y))$
          (ii) not(INCL$(y,$ REGION$(x))$)

According to this analysis, "at" and "with" are contrasting terms; either INCL is symmetric, in which case you use "with," or it is not symmetric, in which case you use "at." Hence, like articles of furniture, but unlike color and kin terms, locative prepositions do not fall into a simple hierarchy of minimal contrasting sets. The differences between locatives are characterized primarily, though not exclusively, in terms of limited subdomains of search. When those subdomains happen to be mutually exclusive, the prepositions contrast, but mutually exclusive subdomains of search are not the rule. In the case of "at" and "with," the contrast derives from a more complex constraint.

Since "in" requires search inside of y whereas "at" does not, it might seem that these prepositions should contrast, too. Usually they do, but we should not overlook noncontrasting pairs like "the man at the store" and "the man in the store," or "the furniture at the office" and "the furniture in the office," or "a student at the university" and "a student in the university." These pairs stand in sharp opposition to pairs like "the man at the hospital" and "the man in the hospital," or "the furniture at the swimming pool" and "the furniture in the swimming pool," or "a student at his desk" and "a student in his desk." We assume that violations of contrast are acceptable for some relata—pre-

Table 6.1   A decision table for LOCATION(x).

	1	2	3	4	5	6	7	8	9	10	11	12	13	14	15
Conditions															
c1. PART(x, z) & INCL(z, y)	Y	Y	Y	Y	Y			N	N	N	N	N	N	N	N
c2. INCL$(x, \text{REGION}(\text{SURF}(y)))$ & SUPRT(y, x)	N	N	N	Y	Y	Y	Y	Y	Y	Y	N	N	N	N	N
c3. PATH(y) & BY(x, y)	N	Y	Y	N	N	N	N	Y	N	N	N	Y	Y	Y	N
c4. INCL$(x, \text{REGION}(y))$		Y	N	Y	Y	N		Y	Y	Y	Y	N	Y	Y	N
c5. INCL$(y, \text{REGION}(x))$				Y	N			Y	N	Y	N		Y	N	
Actions															
a1. IN(x, y)	x	x		x	x										
a2. ON(x, y)								x	x						
a3. AT(x, y)											x		x		
a4. WITH(x, y)												x		x	
a5. error						x	x								
a6. exit			x							x					x

sumably those with fuzzy boundaries, those for which the difference between the domains inside and outside are unclear or unimportant, or those where the characteristic region of interaction with the relatum is inside it.

The schemata of "in," "on," "at," and "with" are related in table 6.1. Its details are complicated and the analysis may be open to doubt in some respects, but some such representation is required for this set of terms. It can be tested by confronting native speakers of English with various arrangements of objects, selecting one as the referent, and asking them to identify it by its location. If necessary, their choice of locative prepositions can be limited to a set of alternatives—the four in table 6.1, for example. Then their choices can be compared with the choices that would be predicted from the semantic analysis. We have not collected such data from others, but we have tried to perform the test as a thought experiment. More systematic and critical methods of investigation would surely lead to improvements.

6.1.2   Location and Distance

A referent may be located by stating something about its distance from a relatum or its direction from a relatum. We will take up the question of direction in 6.1.4; here we will consider relations between location and distance. These relations have already been touched on in discussing "in," "on," and "at." Indeed, it might be thought that these locatives are subordinates of "near" if it were not in contrast with "in." "Near" would also contrast with "on" if it were not for examples like (11a): a house on the river can be said to be near the river. And "near" contrasts with "at" in just those cases where "in" does not contrast with "at": a man at or in his office would not be said to be near his office, although a man at his typewriter could be said to be near (but not in) the typewriter. These complex contrastive relations naturally suggest that it would be wise to begin by considering distance by itself.

"Near" can be used as a verb, adverb, or adjective, as well as a preposition. It can take comparative and superlative forms, which can also be used as prepositions: "the chair near the door," "the chair nearer the door," "the chair nearest the door." And there is a marked resemblance between "near" and an adjective like "tall." The resemblance that particularly interests us is in their underlying semantics. The reader will recall that "tall" denotes not a simple property but an underlying relation to an implicit norm. The same sort of analysis applies to "near." The actual distance between referent and relatum that is needed to satisfy "near" depends considerably on the nature of referent and relatum. Compare "The car is near the gate," "The house is near Oxford," "Oxford is near London." Rather than attempt a direct assault on the semantics of "near," however, let us resort as before to the analysis of the comparative.

The meaning of "x is nearer to y than z is" can be simply paraphrased as "the distance from z to y is greater than the distance from x to y":

(16)   GREATER(DISTANCE(z, y), DISTANCE(x, y)).

The parallel with our analysis of "taller than" (p. 325) should be obvious. That x is nearer to y than z is does not entail that x is near y (any more than that x is taller than y entails that x is tall). Obviously, there is more to the semantics of "near." First, if a referent is near a relatum, it cannot be touching the relatum—in that case one would use "on" or "against"—and it cannot be in the relatum or have the relatum in it. Second, although it may be within the region of the relatum, it need not be. People are likely to describe any referent within the region of a relatum (but not touching it) as near the relatum, but they are also likely to describe more distant referents as near the relatum. The actual distances here are fuzzy rather than precise. They are determined, as the examples above indicate, by the nature of the referent and relatum. But just what aspects of these entities are relevant, or how they determine the critical distance, remains to be investigated. People seem to have sets of norms for geographical distances, for distances with respect to buildings, persons, vehicles, domestic interiors, tabletops, and so on. The existence of some such hierarchy of spatial domains is perhaps supported by the oddity of sentences that take a referent from one domain and a relatum from a domain distant in the hierarchy, as in "The table is near Oxford" and "The ashtray is near the town hall." Perhaps the following conditions would serve to characterize "near":

(17)   NEAR(x, y):   A referent x is "near" a relatum y if:
       (i) GREATER(NORM(DISTANCE(y)), DISTANCE(x, y))
       (ii) SEPARATE(x, y)
       (iii) not(IN(x, y) or IN(y, x))

where NORM(DISTANCE (y)) yields a norm, which in any case is a distance that includes the region of the relatum. This formulation assumes that the system must have a schema for IN in order to use "near" correctly; there is some evidence from child language (see, for example, Aaronson and Schaefer, 1968; Brown, 1973) that this may reflect the usual order of cognitive development.

With these comments on "near" and "nearer" in mind, let us turn next to "by." One meaning of "by" given in our dictionary is "next to or close to." We discover that "next" has two meanings: (a) "nearest in space" and (b) "coming directly after in time or sequence." The etymological origin of "next" is Old English "neahst" (the superlative of "neah"), or "nearest." We assume the temporal use derives from the spatial, given that the objects one is concerned with are lined up in a spatial series or sequence. In the more general use of "next to," however, things are not necessarily lined up in sequence, so we will concentrate on meaning (a), "nearest in space." The dictionary also informs us that the appropriate sense of "near" is "to, at, or within a short distance or interval in space or time." So we can summarize what our dictionary has to say about the spatial meaning of "by" as

(18)   by = next to
              = nearest in space to
              = at the shortest distance in space from.

If the dictionary is correct, to say that John is by the car would mean that there was no one closer to the car than John. Something is wrong here.

As it stands in (18), the wording "at the shortest distance in space from" is clearly inadequate. The shortest possible distance between two objects is zero, when they are touching, but "by" does not imply contact. In this respect, "by" resembles "near," but there is a difference, since "by" implies there is nothing else between the referent and the relatum. (In this respect "by" resembles "nearest.")

Cooper (1968) analyzes "by" as BY(x, y): x is located internal to the space z which is contiguous to a vertical side of y. We assume that what Cooper means by "the space z" is not just any conceivable space contiguous to a vertical side of y but the space we have called the region of conventional interaction with y. If we use REGION(SIDE(y)) as a subroutine of BY, this criterion will apply. Then we must add another condition to determine that there is no other object between x and y.

Cooper's analysis points to a further difference between "by" and "near." Whereas we can use "near" in relation to any border, "by" seems to demand a side: "a state by Kansas" sounds awkward because Kansas, although it has borders, does not have sides; "a state near Kansas" or "a state next to Kansas" is more acceptable. Cooper's restriction to vertical sides seems too strong, however, so we suggest substituting for it the condition that the referent and relatum are both in the horizontal plane:

(19)   BY(x, y):   A referent x is "by" a relatum y if:
              (i) INCL(x, REGION(SIDE(y))) & not(BETWEEN(x, z, SIDE(y)))
              (ii) not(ABOVE(x, y) or (ABOVE(y, x))

This formulation involves the concept SIDE, which is an important component of our conceptualization of spatial relations, to which we will return shortly. When a control instruction incorporates (19) it will try to find a side of the relatum and will look for the referent within its region in the horizontal plane. If the referent is not found, it will find another side of the relatum and look again in that region. When all the sides of the relatum have been searched without finding the referent, it will reject the assertion that the referent is "by" the relatum.

A word must be said about the effects of negation on these relations, since negation defines a related set of prepositions. Following Gruber (1965), we will take these negations to be

(20) x is not at $y \equiv x$ is away from y.
         x is not on $y \equiv x$ is off of y.
         x is not in $y \equiv x$ is out of y.

In (20) we consider only the sense of "on" appropriate for surfaces; when "on" is used to express a relation to an edge or path, it can take a different negative, usually "away from."

The prepositional constructions "away from," "off of," and "out of" indicate locations only by elimination—they are relations of nonlocation. They do little or nothing to narrow the subdomain of search and can be interpreted as meaning that if routines based on "at," "on," or "in" were executed, no object matching the referent would be found in that subdomain.

We could continue this investigation with other locative prepositions, but the examples we have given should be more than enough to illustrate a procedural approach to these terms. It will not have escaped an attentive reader that these locative prepositions are a heterogeneous collection of special-purpose devices exhibiting little of the contrastive or hierarchical simplicity of color names or kin terms. No doubt we have missed some of their subtleties and misunderstood others, but we consider it highly unlikely that a simple pattern of semantic relations could be found in this lexical domain. Each term differs from the others in different ways, so that a person acquiring the language has little alternative but to learn each locative preposition individually. A better classification of the spatial entities we take as their relata would certainly help to account for the complex selectional restrictions we have noted, but that important task has not been undertaken here.

6.1.3   Deictic and Intrinsic Systems of Spatial Reference

The conceptual core of space probably originates, as Cassirer (1923) and others have maintained, with the body concept—with what is at, in, or on our own bodies. The first spatial relatum we learn to use is ego. The primitive meaning of "here" is "where I am"; "from" is probably first understood as "from me"; "to" as "to me"; and so on. Piaget and Inhelder (1948) claim that escape from this egocentric space requires considerable cognitive development, and Laurendeau and Pinard (1970) have traced the successive steps toward intellectual decentration of spatial relations. The ability to decenter does not displace the egocentric conception of space, but it supplements it; egocentric space comes to be seen as merely one among all the other possible perspectives.

Although egocentric space is just one of many ways an adult can exploit the space concept, it retains an immediacy and personal value that set it apart from the other perspectives that are intellectually possible. Semantic analysis shows that adults have two ways of talking about space. In the case of kinship we noted that the concept could be used to describe the circle of relatives around any given individual (with special priority given to the circle around ego) or to describe more abstractly the relation between any two kinsmen. It is probably no accident that the same is true of space. One can use the space concept to describe the relative locations of objects around any given individual (with special priority given to the locations relative to ego) or to describe more abstractly the relation between any two objects. There are usually many possibilities for confusion as to which way a speaker is using the space concept; a complex set of conventions is needed to keep things straight.

Egocentric use of the space concept places ego at the center of the universe. From this point of origin ego can lay out a three-dimensional coordinate system that depends on his own orientation. With respect to this landmark other objects can be directionally located as above or below (ego), in front or in back (of ego), to the left or to the right (of ego). "Here" is the region x of interaction with ego. Both his location (the point of origin) and his orientation (the directions of the coordinate axes) are essential for the interpretation of most words expressing his spatial relations to other objects. Since two people cannot be in the same place at the same time, the location of ego defines a unique spatial manifold. In order to understand what a person means when he talks about space egocentrically, therefore, you have to know where he is and in which direction he is facing.

When it is necessary to know the conditions under which a word occurs in order to interpret it, linguists, following Bühler (1934), speak of the word as deictic. (Some philosophers, following Peirce, 1932, call it an indexical term.) "Deixis"—which is the Greek word for pointing or locating—refers to those aspects of a communication whose interpretation depends on knowledge of the context in which the communication occurs. There is a strong argument that interpretation is always dependent on context, but for some words dependence is unavoidable. Personal pronouns, discussed in 4.5.2, are the most obvious examples; in order to know whom "I" refers to, you need to know who is speaking. But there are also words with time deixis; the reference of "now" depends on the time it is used. And our present concern is with space deixis: "here" refers to different places depending on the location of the speaker. Deictic words "introduce particulars of the speaker's and hearer's shared cognitive field into the message" (Rommetveit, 1968, p. 197).

Deictic terms for space in English include "here" and "there," "this" and "that." These words are learned early, presumably in terms of the distinction between INCL(x, REGION(ego)) and not INCL(x, REGION(ego)) and also the distinction between locations and objects. Probably this system originates with some prelinguistic ostensive gesture that directs attention to an object or a location (Lyons, 1973), and the distinctions among these words are initially understood as vocal alternatives to gestural ostension (Werner and Kaplan, 1963). Since the semantic and syntactic distinctions between these words in adult speech are complex, we will limit our discussion of deixis to locative prepositional phrases.

We will call the linguistic system for talking about space relative to a speaker's egocentric origin and coordinate axes the deictic system. We will contrast the deictic system with the intrinsic system, where spatial terms are interpreted relative to coordinate axes derived from intrinsic parts of the referent itself. Another way to phrase this distinction is to say that in the deictic system spatial terms are interpreted relative to intrinsic parts of ego, whereas in the intrinsic system they are interpreted relative to intrinsic parts of something else.

Consider the imperatives

(21)   (a) Put it in front of the chair.
           (b) Put it in front of the rock.

A chair, like a person, has an intrinsic front, so (21a) is ordinarily understood to mean that "it" should be put in a location determined by the orientation of the chair. A rock, on the other hand, does not have an intrinsic front, so (21b) is potentially ambiguous. The rock establishes a landmark, but it does not serve to orient a unique three-dimensional coordinate system around it. In that case, the coordinate system must be borrowed from one of the participants in the conversation—usually from the person who says it, but possibly from the person who hears it. Deictically, the front of the rock is usually the side of the rock that ego is facing, the side that is momentarily in front of ego, but if ego is thinking of himself as in a row of objects behind the rock, "in front of the rock" can mean on the far side from ego. It is possible to interpret (21a) deictically, too, which leads to further opportunities for confusion. The remarkable fact, however, is not that confusions are possible but that adults have so little trouble avoiding them.

The difference between these two ways of talking about space can be illustrated in terms of the difficulties people have with "left" and "right." Imagine yourself facing two people, Tom and Dick, who are also facing you. Suppose that from your point of view Tom is on the left and Dick is on the right, so you can say "Dick is to the right of Tom." But note that in this spatial arrangement Dick is by Tom's left side, so you can also say "Dick is to the left of Tom." There is something wrong with a language that permits you to describe the same situation in two directly contradictory ways: "Dick is to the right of Tom" and "Dick is to the left of Tom." One description should be correct, the other incorrect. Yet both are correct. The only escape is to recognize that "right" and "left" can be used in two ways: deictically, when Tom and Dick are described from the speaker's point of view; intrinsically, when Dick is described in relation to Tom's body parts.

Consider the problem in terms of mirrors. A common misconception is that mirrors reverse left and right. Many people when asked why mirrors reverse left and right but not up and down are genuinely puzzled. (For a discussion of four alternative interpretations of this question, see Block, 1974.) They will hold a page of writing so they can see it in the mirror and observe that left and right are backward, but top and bottom are not, then conclude that there must be something special about the vertical dimension of space. In order to explain what has happened it is necessary to make them start this exercise by looking directly at the page, then note that in order to see it in the mirror they must turn it around (which rotation they will almost inevitably make in the horizontal plane); it is not the mirror that turns the page around, but they themselves. It is also possible to rotate the page in the vertical plane until it faces the mirror, in which case it will be upside down, but, once again, it is the viewer who reverses the page, not the mirror. At this point some people will be even more puzzled, and may ask, "But if a mirror doesn't reverse left and right, why do I have so much trouble shaving or combing my hair when I use a mirror?" What makes the world so strange through the looking glass is that near and far are reversed; as your hand moves away from you toward the mirror, its reflection moves toward you in the mirror.

These are relatively simple observations. One wonders why mirrors are so maligned about left and right when the real trouble is with near and far. Do people expect to have left/right troubles and simply assume that mirrors provide another instance of a recurrent difficulty? The truth is more complicated. Simply because mirrors do *not* reverse left and right, the view you have of yourself in a mirror is not the view you would have of your twin facing you. Your twin facing you *would* reverse left and right; your twin's right hand would be opposite your left hand. So people must accommodate their left/right terminology to two situations that are perceptually very similar.

Space has one vertical coordinate, two horizontal; the horizontal coordinates are easily confused, both when you are learning the appropriate terms and when you use them in communication. It has been claimed that children master "up" and "down" first, then "front" and "back"; "right and "left" are so difficult that many adults have trouble with them (Ames and Learned, 1948). It is probably gravity that makes the vertical dimension unique. Since people are all in the same gravitational field, "over" and "under," "up" and "down," "above" and "below," are physically anchored in the same way for everyone. "Near" and "far," "in front of" and "in back of," "before" and "behind," are more difficult because an anchor must be specifically indicated; what is near the speaker may be far from the hearer, what is in front of the relatum from the speaker's point of view may not be in front of it from the hearer's point of view. "Left" and "right" are the most difficult because nothing external to the person can anchor them; they can be defined for him only in terms of his own body. A child must begin his mastery of left and right by learning which is his right hand and which is his left. According to Piaget (1924), children can identify their own right and left hands by the age of five but are not able to use the terms correctly with respect to a person facing them until seven or eight. And it is not until age eleven that they can, when presented with a row of three objects, say whether the middle object is to the right or left of the end objects. These observations have been replicated by Elkind (1961) and Swartz and Hall (1972).

The terminology for these spatial relations is complicated by the fact that people use these words not only to indicate perceived relations between objects but also to label parts of the objects themselves. We encountered this complication in 4.1.2, where we noted that a table has an intrinsic top—a part that remains the top regardless of whether it happens to be uppermost at the moment. There are also objects, like cars, chairs, desks, that have intrinsic fronts. And if an object has both an intrinsic top and an intrinsic front, it will have intrinsic right and left sides. Thus there are two systems for indicating spatial relations, involving much the same terminology but requiring different interpretations. The meaning of "x is to the right of y," may be either (a) that x is closer than y to the right hand of some person viewing them face on from a given location, or (b) that, if y is an object that has an intrinsic right side, x is closer to the right side of y than to its left. The deictic system is based on (a); the intrinsic system on (b).

The addition of the intrinsic system introduces complexity and potential misunderstanding, but it has the advantage of freeing spatial indications from the immediate context of a shared situation. The instruction "Put the lamp to the right of the chair," for example, can be understood to mean that the lamp should be placed near the intrinsic right side of the chair, regardless of the speaker's or hearer's locations or orientations. If the speaker is present and viewing the chair from some arbitrary angle—from the side, say—he may have intended this order to be interpreted deictically, in which case the intrinsic interpretation would not lead to the desired result. But intrinsic interpretations usually dominate deictic ones; if a deictic interpretation is intended when an intrinsic interpretation is possible, the speaker will usually add explicitly "from my point of view" or "as I am looking at it." If the relatum does not have an intrinsic right and left, only a deictic interpretation is possible: "Put the chair to the right of the tree" must be understood deictically to mean that the chair should be placed so as to be seen to the right of the tree from where the speaker is standing, since trees have no intrinsic right or left sides.

In order for this example to be strictly correct, one must think of the tree as located in a forest or large field, away from anything that has an intrinsic front that could be used to define the front of the tree. A tree is not normally conceived of as having an intrinsic front, but it may acquire an accidental front by virtue of its location, say, in a yard in front of a house; then the front of the tree will usually be understood to mean the side of the tree facing the street, and back, right, and left sides can be understood relative to this accidental front. Similarly, a rectangular table does not normally have an intrinsic front, but if you shove one long side of it against a wall, the table will acquire an accidental front. The situation with respect to deictic and intrinsic fronts is sufficiently complex without this additional complication, however, so we will not add to the difficulties by discussing accidental fronts.

Leech (1969) has proposed that there are three basic senses for the phrase "at the side of" (which he claims is synonymous with "beside"). He gives the examples

(22) (a) Star x is at the side of star y.
     (b) I placed my hat at the side of his.
     (c) His car was at the side of mine.

He suggests that they involve the following progression of concepts:

(23) (a) spatial proximity
     (b) spatial proximity on a horizontal plane
     (c) spatial proximity on the secondary horizontal axis

These distinctions arise from the nature of stars, hats, and cars. Leech's examples do not represent three different senses of "at the side of" but merely demonstrate that the intrinsic system of labeling parts of objects must be taken into account in the locative interpretation of such phrases.

In interpreting spatial indications, people first determine whether the landmark has intrinsic parts. If it does, they try to interpret the spatial relation intrinsically unless they are explicitly informed to the contrary. If the landmark does not have intrinsic parts relevant to the spatial indication, they must rely on context to provide a deictic interpretation. If both strategies fail, they may ask for more explicit information.

The deictic system is relatively straightforward. In chapter 2 we introduced the predicate Over(x, y) to denote the perceptual judgment that y is between x and the ground, and this perceptual test is sufficient to define the deictic interpretation of "over," which we can represent as OVER$_d$(x, y). (There is, of course, another sense of "over" meaning "covering.") FRONT$_d$(x, y) is the routine involved in the deictic interpretation of "x is in front of y" and can be defined in terms of the perceptual predicate Betw(ego, x, y). RIGHT$_d$(x, y) can be defined in terms of the relative distances of x from the observer's hands (assuming he stands in a normal orientation with y in front of him):

(24) RIGHT$_d$(x, y): A referent x is "to the right of" the relatum y deictically if FRONT$_d$(y, ego) and:
     (i) GREATER(DISTANCE(x, ego's left hand), DISTANCE(x, ego's right hand))

An argument could be made that (24) should be phrased in terms of relative rotations of the observer's eyes rather than distances from his hands, thus avoiding the restriction that he must stand in a normal orientation facing the referent. In either case the principle involved in the definition of deictic "right" and "left" would be the same, however.

The deictic system can be characterized rather simply in perceptual terms because it is based on one's direct perception of the objects that are related and because it maintains the mirror relation between left and right. The intrinsic system, on the other hand, necessitates reference to memory, to our conception of the relatum and any intrinsic parts it may have. Thus, the intrinsic system requires a more careful analysis.

The question whether an object is considered to have an intrinsic top is relatively straightforward; it depends on whether it has a characteristic orientation to the vertical. The same question with respect to fronts is more difficult. Teller (1969), in trying to provide a general definition of "front," makes a useful beginning. According to Teller, "front" can be defined in terms of something that is functionally prominent, that is "outstanding or attention catching by virtue of the function of the object" (p. 210). Unfortunately, as he himself admits, this is too catholic a definition. One does not think of spoons or pencils as having fronts. Alternatively, he suggests that "front" might follow from three more restricted notions: (a) positive sense of the axis in the direction of motion (cars, bullets); (b) the "side" oriented toward an observer (mirrors); and (c) positive sense of the axis along which motion or vision proceeds through the object (telescopes).

But even these criteria are not entirely satisfactory. Part of the trouble seems to be that Teller is trying to define fronts in general rather than just intrinsic fronts. Moreover, he has omitted an important criterion, one that Fillmore (1971d) has stated: "For animate beings having a certain degree of complexity, the front is that portion of it which contains its main organs of perception." Children frequently identify the front of their bodies as the part they can see, the back as the part they cannot see (Harris and Strommen, 1972). Fillmore notes that for animals the location of the main organs of perception outweighs the direction-of-motion criterion, since people speak of crabs as moving sideways, not as having heads on the sides of their bodies. And he speculates that if we were to find a race of people who moved around the way people move in reverse motion pictures, we would say that they walked backward, not that they had faces on the back of their heads.

How many sides does an object have? The problem that is posed for perceptual identification can be illustrated by an example of Fillmore's. A cube in the abstract has six sides. If it is used as a table, two of the six sides are called the top and bottom. If it is used as a desk, two more sides become the front and back. How many sides it has depends on what concept is assigned to it, not on its perceptual properties. The problem is to formulate criteria for deciding when a side becomes a particular kind of intrinsic side, top or bottom, front or back, left or right. We have seen that the uppermost side is called the intrinsic top when the object has some normal function that it serves in a characteristic vertical orientation. The intrinsic front of an object requires a more complex specification:

(25)   Intrinsic front:
(a) The side containing the main perceptual apparatus (either literally or figuratively, as with toys or cameras)
(b) The side characteristically lying in the direction of motion
(c) The side (inside or outside) characteristically oriented to the
observer

Criterion (a) is Fillmore's; (b) is Teller's; (c) was introduced by Bierwisch
(1967). Fillmore prefers a more complex formulation of (c) to account for
the fact that what is taken to be the front of a church depends on whether
the observer is inside or outside. We will accept the simpler formulation of
Bierwisch and Teller and assume that the term is ambiguous when applied
to halls, churches, and so forth.

This brings us back again to left and right. People tend to treat objects as
six-sided. If an object has both an intrinsic top and bottom, and an intrinsic
front and back, the remaining two sides are intrinsically left and right—although further distinctions are needed here. We have supposed that a child
must memorize which hand is his right and which his left. In the deictic system, this memorized distinction is generalized to inanimate objects by the relation exploited in (24). For example, a street has no intrinsic right side; which
side is the right side depends on which is nearer your right hand as you travel
along it. The intrinsic system seems to try to observe this same rule, with one
major exception: animate beings with a perceptual apparatus that defines their
fronts will be assigned intrinsic left and right sides by analogy with human beings, so that when one faces another the mirror relation does not hold; one
person's right hand is opposite the other person's left, and vice versa. With
this exception, the deictic rule of mirroring seems to carry over into the intrinsic system, but it is complicated by the fact that we must introduce the notion
of characteristic orientation. The rule then is: if an inanimate object has an
intrinsic top and front, the parts that are characteristically adjacent to your
right hand are said to be its intrinsic right side, and those characteristically
adjacent to your left hand are its intrinsic left side.

This is simple enough, except that there are two kinds of characteristic
orientation: inside and outside. If people assume a characteristic orientation
inside an object (car, chair, clothing), the part of it adjacent to their right hand
will turn out to be labeled the intrinsic right side in a manner analogous to the
body itself. But if people assume a characteristic orientation outside an object, facing the front of it (desk, cupboard, stove), the part of it adjacent to
their right hand will turn out to be labeled the intrinsic right side according
to the mirror relation of (24), just as in the deictic system. For example, the
right drawer of a desk is the one nearest your right hand as you face the front
of the desk, but the right arm of a chair is the one nearest your right hand as
you sit in (face away from the front of) the chair.

"Front" and "back" are easier. De Villiers and De Villiers (1974) found
that four-year-olds could correctly answer questions like "Is it in front of the

wall or behind the wall?" either from their own or the questioner's point of view, but two-and-a-half-year-olds could not. Harris and Strommen (1972) have demonstrated that middle-class American children in kindergarten and first grade are in good command of both intrinsic and deictic uses of "front," "back," and "beside." The children they tested made no errors in placing objects in front of, in back of, or beside themselves; they made virtually no errors (only one child in eighty was egocentric in the Piagetian sense) in placing objects relative to a relatum with an intrinsic front (doll, bug, car, chair); and only 7 percent of their responses to a relatum having no intrinsic front (glass, block) could be regarded as errors. In the deictic situation, 67 percent of the responses to "Put it in front of the glass" (or "block") were placements of the referent object between the child and the relatum, and 26 percent were placements on the far side of the relatum; either interpretation of the request can be defended, of course. Even when errors occurred, however, "front" and "back" were on opposite sides of the relatum.

In view of the complexity of (25), it is surprising how early children recognize intrinsic fronts of familiar objects. Susan Carey (personal communication) has found that two-year-olds can arrange toy objects (either characteristically stationary or movable) in a "parade" with their intrinsic fronts correctly oriented if the experimenter first establishes the direction of the parade by correctly orienting three objects in a row. One might expect children to master the apparently simpler deictic system before the intrinsic system, but evidence for "front" and "back" does not support that expectation. Of course, it is not clear what should be counted as "simpler" here; the deictic system may be simpler for a talker and the intrinsic system simpler for a hearer.

Since for the intrinsic system "left" and "right" presuppose a knowledge of "front" and "back," and since for most objects with intrinsic parts "front" and "back" presuppose a knowledge of "top" and "bottom," the order of mastery of these terms during childhood would seem to be predictable. Tracing out the actual course of this development in detail, however, would be an extensive and difficult undertaking, and the results might lead one to consider the possibility that cognitive development explains the relations between the intrinsic parts rather than the other way around.

A child who has not mastered the linguistic conventions for expressing this system of relations usually shows a variety of heterogeneous confusions when asked to identify intrinsic sides of common objects. He may place a toy bureau upside down and misidentify the top and bottom yet identify the front correctly by pointing to the drawers; he may point to the back of the headboard of a toy bed when asked where the top of the bed is; when asked to point to the top of a jacket that a doll is wearing he may point to the doll's head; and so on. He may correctly identify the top of containers that have lids but be confused about the top of a glass that is upside down. He may call the parts of an object that he can handle or do things with the front, which leads to success in the case of a bureau with its handles and drawers but to failure when the burners on a toy stove are thought to identify its front. The general impression is that young children (aged three or four) have learned a number of specific labeling routines that will often lead to successful identifications, but the conceptual structure that underlies the adult linguistic system is still unknown to them. Whether or not intrinsic tops are really mastered before intrinsic fronts must vary according to the objects that are used to test a child's knowledge.

The system that we have used to characterize intrinsic parts (which is based largely on the work of Fillmore) can be summarized as a key. The key will not represent anything that a speaker of English must know but it helps to crystallize our hypothesis about the kinds of information that must be stored in every concept if we are to assign the correct labels to intrinsic parts of objects. The following key is intended purely for the convenience of the theorist and does not represent an identification device based on some explicit concept that English speakers "have."

(26)   Hypothesis: Objects can be categorized with respect to the kinds of information about their intrinsic parts that must be stored in memory according to the following rules:

   (A) Is there a side characteristically uppermost? If so, store information that that side is the intrinsic top and the opposite side is the intrinsic bottom. If not, go to (B).

   (i) Is there a side containing perceptual apparatus? If so, store intrinsic front, back, left, and right by analogy with the human body (person, animal, doll, camera). If not, go to (Aii).

   (ii) Do people take a characteristic orientation with respect to the object? If so, go to (Aiia). If not, go to (Aiii).

   (a) Inside the object? If so, store intrinsic front, back, left, and right by analogy with the human body (car, chair, clothing). If not, go to (Aiib).

   (b) Facing toward a side of the object? If so, store intrinsic front, back, left, and right according to deictic labeling system (desk, radio, mirror).

   (iii) Store information that the object has a maximum of four sides (table, vase, tree).

   (B) Is there a side lying in the characteristic direction of motion? If so, store information that that side is the intrinsic front and opposite side is the intrinsic back (arrow, bullet, torpedo). If not, go to (C).

   (C) Store information that object has a maximum of six sides (block, cube, ball, star).

There is a sense in which people who speak English must know these rules, because they seem to conform to them. But their conformity is incidental to the task of learning the intrinsic parts of each object as they become familiar with it and its normal functions. Certainly (26) should not be taken as a hypothesis about the lexical development of children, who probably master (Ai) before they master (A).

Where a theorist who knows English is uncertain about the outcomes of tests in (26) he should find some corresponding public uncertainty among other English speakers about the assignment of labels to intrinsic parts. For example, if you think of a telescope as an extension of the perceptual apparatus, the eyepiece will be in back, but if you think of it as an object toward which people assume a characteristic orientation, the eyepiece will be in front. Or, again, if you think of the characteristic orientation as being inside a church, you will assign a different part to be the front than if you think of being outside it. In short, hypothesis (26) should predict ambiguities where ambiguities exist; otherwise it would explain too much.

In (Aiii), (B), and (C) the hypothesis indicates the maximum number of sides. There may be fewer. A curvilinear object will be deficient in this respect; as a general rule, a curved surface or line is regarded as bounding a single side (Bierwisch, 1967). Certain geometric figures, such as an octagon, may be regarded as having more than six sides, but "octagon" is a term from technical discourse; the vast majority of three-dimensional objects are treated in common language as having no more than six sides.

To round out this discussion we should mention one other deictic test that is related to sides. If a horizontal dimension of an object happens to be its maximal dimension, the deictic system labels that dimension the "length" of the object; the secondary horizontal dimension is its "width." As Teller (1969) remarks, one sense of "side" is merely those extremities that bound the width of an object, that is to say, its sides as opposed to its ends. This deictic usage generalizes without difficulty to the intrinsic system as long as the maximal dimension of the object runs from the intrinsic front to the intrinsic back— cars, for example. When the intrinsic front-to-back dimension is the secondary one—most desks, for example—deictic usage conflicts with the intrinsic system and, as usual, intrinsic terminology dominates.

Since "top," "bottom," "front," "back," "right," and "left" form a contrastive set of terms, with "side" as the superordinate term, there must be a SIDE concept somewhere behind this lexical repertoire. There is little reason to think that this concept is separately defined for intrinsic parts, however; the same contrastive set of terms can be characterized in the deictic system for labeling parts. Recognizing the intrinsic nature of the parts of some objects seems to be something that users of English manage to do without self-consciously conceptualizing it; they know how to refer to intrinsic parts, but they have never organized the rules underlying this ability into a distinct concept. We conclude that there is no independent concept of intrinsic parts, that the necessary information about characteristic orientation with respect to the vertical, the viewer, or the direction of motion must be stored redundantly as part of the conceptual information about each class of objects. The clothing concept, for example, must include the information that every article has intrinsic parts labeled by analogy to the human body; the schema for tables as part of the furniture concept includes functional information that determines its characteristic vertical orientation by way of its intrinsic worktop.

We now have a reasonably complete picture of the information required to interpret such statements as "*x* is in front of *y*" and "*x* is to the left of *y*." A hypothesis about the information processing required might be formulated along the following lines. People determine whether the kind of relatum that is used has an intrinsic top, front, or side, and, if so, they assume the referent is located adjacent to that part. If the relatum does not have the relevant intrinsic parts, they determine the deictic relation between *x* and *y* as seen from the speaker's position. So much for the six contrasting locative prepositions "over," "under," "in front of," "in back of," "to the left of," and "to the right of."

The complexities we have discovered in these prepositional indicators of spatial relations arise less from the prepositions themselves than from the distinction between deictic and intrinsic usage. Deictic usage is context-specific, it requires anchoring to observables in the communication situation, it is the language of "here" and "now." Intrinsic parts complicate the perceptually based deictic system and require conceptual knowledge of the normal functions and characteristic orientations of the things one is talking about. But the role played by the locative prepositions, once these deictic-intrinsic matters are straightened out, is relatively simple. Although they are often considered abstract by comparison with, say, concrete nouns, their use and interpretation is based directly on perceptual tests and relations, and their meaning is given by their place in the lexical field used to express the logical core of the space concept.

In summary, the core of the concept of space is a relativistic, three-dimensional universe of locations. In order to talk about that concept, however, it is necessary to define a point of origin and to orient coordinate axes from that landmark. English allows two strategies for doing that. Ego's location and orientation can define the space deictically, or some other object can provide the point of origin, in which case its intrinsic parts orient the coordinates. In either case, the role of locative prepositions is to define a subdomain of search relative to the landmark that defines the point of origin.

6.1.4   Paths and Directions

The locative expressions we have considered so far enable people to identify static locations, but English also has devices that let people talk about dynamic locations. A moving object passes through many locations successively; any one of those locations might be included in a description of its path, and English has resources that allow a speaker to make the path description as detailed as he desires (Bennett, 1972). The origin and terminus of the path have a distinctive status, and "from" and "to" (or various alternatives similar to them) are used to indicate these end points. We will take "along" as representative of the prepositions used to indicate intermediate points.

Although "along" retains its path-descriptive implications in most usages, "from" and "to" are used in many constructions that have nothing to do with paths or motions along them. "The house was a gift to him from his mother" does not imply that either the gift or the house traveled through space; the traveling is a purely symbolic transfer of ownership. Similarly, "The meeting lasted from Wednesday to Saturday" implies no change in spatial location, and "Politicians' incomes vary from low to high" implies no change in altitude. The general sense of "from" is that a relation hitherto the case no longer holds, and the general sense of "to" is that a relation hitherto not the case now holds. It is spatial relations expressed by "to" and "from" that we wish to consider here; other relations will be discussed later.

The conceptual core of the system for indicating movement is the path, which usually has a distinctive beginning and end. As an object traverses a path it passes each successive location at a later moment in time, so time indices can be associated with each location. What the linguistic expressions must describe, therefore, is the logical equivalent of a sequence of AT relations:

$$(27) \qquad \text{AT}(x, y_0), \text{AT}(x, y_1), \ldots, \text{AT}(x, y_i), \ldots, \text{AT}(x, y_n),$$

where the successive relata y_i constitute the path (sec. 2.5), and associated with each location y_i is a time index $t + i$. The first relatum in the path is where the referent moves from, the last is where the referent moves to, and the intermediate terms denote where the referent moves along.

Nothing in this characterization prevents y_0 from being the same as y_n. People may wish to describe motion along a closed path that has no distinctive beginning or end, and in such situations "from" and "to" are inappropriate. The sentence "He moved from the chair to the chair" means to most people who know English that two different chairs were involved. However, it may be a mistake to characterize "from" and "to" with the constraint that when both are used with the same referent the locations that they indicate must be different. Such a characterization might lead to difficulty with the semantics of a sentence like "He led from start to finish" when a race is run on an oval racetrack.

Gruber (1965) suggests that "from" is the negation of "to"; to move from y is to move to not-y, that is, to the area denoted by the logical complement of y. This plausible observation indicates that we must consider both AT and notAT as components of "from" and "to." Sentences of the form "x moved from y" presuppose that x was at y for some interval of time and assert that x was then not at y. Sentences of the form "x moved to y" presuppose that x was not at y for some interval of time and assert that x was then at y. In section 6.2 we will consider how to deal with intervals of time; meanwhile these analyses of prepositions can be represented more formally as

(28)   FROM(x, y):   A referent x is "from" a relatum y if, for an interval ending at time $t - 1$, AT(x, y) and:
     (i) notAT(x, y) at time t

(29)   TO(x, y):   A referent x is "to" a relatum y if, for an interval ending at time $t - 1$, notAT(x, y) and :
     (i) AT(x, y) at time t

"From" negates "to," but in a dual and more complex fashion than Gruber proposed.

As for the intermediate points, we can utilize the concept of a PATH, which is clearly related to a perceptual predicate, to provide a schema for "along":

(30)   ALONG(x, y):   A referent x moves "along" a relatum y if, for an interval of time, x moves and:
   (i) PATH(y)
   (ii) If AT(x, z) during the interval, then PPRT(y, z)

Taken together, (28)–(30) indicate the schemata that underlie such expressions as "along a path from y to z."

A speaker may wish to specify the locations at the beginning or end of the path in more detail than "from" and "to" convey. He can do this by using the format of "from" and "to," but with "in" or "on" instead of "at," to obtain "out of" and "into," or "off of" and "onto." For example:

(31)   OUTOF(x, y):   A referent x is "out of" a relatum y if, for an interval ending at time $t - 1$, IN(x, y) and:
   (i) notIN(x, y) at time t

(32)   INTO(x, y):   A referent x is "into" a relatum y if, for an interval ending at time $t - 1$, notIN(x, y) and:
   (i) IN(x, y) at time t

A similar substitution of ON will serve to characterize "off of" and "onto."

Combinations of "in" and "on" with "along" are expressed by "through" and "across." If the path that the referent is moving along is in the relatum, it moves through it; if the path that the referent moves along is on the relatum, it moves across it. Hence, THROUGH(x, z) involves ALONG(x, y) & IN(y, z). In paraphrase: "x traveled through z" corresponds to "x traveled along a path in z." Similarly for "across."

The strategy for indicating the location of moving objects is built on the strategy for locating stationary objects, except that when an object is moving you must indicate the location of its path. Locating the path involves locating its origin, intermediate points, and terminus, but English uses the same "at," "in," and "on" distinctions to locate the path that it uses to locate stationary objects. Given this strategy, the full range of locative prepositions becomes available for locating moving objects. The prepositions "over," "under," "in front of," "in back of," "to the right of," "to the left of," "next to," "beside," "by," can all be used to locate paths, as can "above," "below," "beneath," "beyond," "among," "around," "between," "toward." Specific locations along the path can be designated by such prepositions as "by way of," "past," "via."

That English uses the same locative prepositions for paths that it uses for objects and events creates many opportunities for ambiguity. "He ran in front of the house" can mean either that there was an event, his running, that occurred in front of the house, or that the path along which he ran passed in front of the house. Even where distinctions are available, they are often ignored in colloquial speech: people may use "at" when they mean "toward," "in" when they mean "into," "on" when they mean "onto."

English offers another way to describe movement that does not locate the path but merely indicates its direction. Such directional indications are given by adverbs, but many of these adverbs are exactly the same words that serve as prepositions when location is to be indicated.

In order to talk about directions a coordinate system is necessary; the basic coordinate system is supplied by the human body. "Up" and "down," "front" and "back," "left" and "right," are the major directional adverbs of English (with "north," "east," "south," and "west" as a similar but less important set), and each can be supplemented with the suffix "-ward" to make its directional use unambiguous. There is also a way of indicating directions that is analogous to that of locating paths, but with "toward" instead of "to" and "away" instead of "from," or with "inward" instead of "into" and "outward" instead of "out of"; in this system the origin or terminus of the imaginary path is taken as the relatum. ("Toward" is the exceptional case, since it is the only one of the directional words that cannot be used as an adverb: "He walked toward her," but not "He walked toward.") The morpheme "-ward" is productive. It can combine with directions, as in "eastward"; with landmarks, as in "homeward"; or with movements, as in "windward"; it can even be used to form such nonce words as "treeward" or "chairward." The general idea of "-ward" is that successive positions are further in that direction or closer to that landmark. (Perhaps we think of "-ward" words as derivative from "toward" —"toward the sea" becomes "seaward," and "toward up" becomes "upward" —in which case we might explain why "toward" is exceptional: it cannot be used to define itself.)

There is an element of futurity in "-ward" words, since the path of motion must be extrapolated to the landmark. Osgood (1971) found that most observers describe a ball rolling in the direction of a tube by using "toward," but some use the future, "will hit." He offers this observation as an example of a paraphrase relation that demands perceptual rather than syntactic explanation.

Vertical and horizontal provide a conceptual frame of reference for path and directional descriptions. Indeed, one might think of them as internalized landmarks anchoring judgments of direction and orientation in much the same way primary colors anchor judgments of hue. Rosch (1975) has used linguistic hedges to illustrate the special status assigned to vertical and horizontal directions, exploiting an observation by Wertheimer (1938) that a line of 85 degrees is almost vertical, but a vertical line is not almost 85 degrees. She presented people with the sentence frame "A —— is almost a ——" and drawings of lines in various orientations and asked them to fill the blanks with the drawings. Other hedges used were "essentially," "basically," "roughly," "sort of," and "loosely speaking." The two drawings that people were given always showed lines that differed by 10 degrees in orientation. In half the tests, one of the two lines was at 0, 45, 90, or 135 degrees—directions that people have internalized, if the hypothesis is correct—and in the other half neither line was a landmark direction. When landmark directions were not included, the use of either drawing as the relatum in the sentence frame was random, but when one of the drawings depicted a horizontal, vertical, or oblique direction, that drawing was used as the relatum far more often than chance would allow—the only exceptions being in the case of the oblique lines at 45 and 135 degrees.

Given an internalized reference for vertical and horizontal directions, other directions can be remembered in relation to them. Obliques are halfway between, and other intermediate directions can be coded with hedges: "almost vertical," "almost horizontal but tipped up to the left." The situation is closely analogous to what we observed for color terms with "-ish": "greenish yellow," "yellow green," "yellowish green." Rosch also tested color terms in hedged sentence frames and found a similar use of focal colors as the relata.

Bryant (1974) has reviewed studies of how children judge and remember directions of lines. He argues that young children can judge orientation correctly for successively presented lines only if the frame of reference in which they are presented can be used as a transfer standard—under normal testing conditions, this means only vertical and horizontal, which are given by the cards on which the lines are usually drawn. That is to say, young children have not yet internalized these directional landmarks, and so must rely on external features to help them remember the orientation of a line. For example, Witkin (1959) has found that when young children are asked to adjust a luminous rod to the true vertical, they are strongly influenced by the frame of reference in which the rod is seen. The magnitude of the frame-induced error decreases as children grow older, indicating greater reliance on internal cues. Bryant concludes that "between the ages of four and eight years there is a transition from external to internal categories in orientation perception" (p. 75).

It would seem, therefore, that children learn to use expressions describing paths and directions on the basis of relativistic perceptual information; the relatum is given by external features of the environment. This dependence on external context can be overcome by internalizing vertical and horizontal reference directions and learning to rely on them when external cues are missing or in conflict with internal cues.

In discussions of case grammar it is commonly said that the prepositional phrases we have been discussing are instances of the locative case. For example, one can treat the intransitive verb "travel" as if it had three arguments: TRAVEL (Agent, from Source, to Destination). One trouble with this analysis is that a path description can vary so much in detail. It can be omitted entirely, as in "He traveled rapidly," or it can be elaborated into such sentences as "The smoke traveled upward from the hearth around the mantle through the heavy air to the ceiling," where there is an adverb and four prepositional phrases. With just a little ingenuity, path descriptions can be made as detailed as patience permits. This situation exemplifies what is sometimes called the problem of variable polyadicity: How do we decide how many arguments to provide for path descriptions in the case frame for the verb "travel"? Someone who favored a case approach to locatives could argue that only one path is ever described for any motion verb, so a single "path case" is all that is needed; it can be freely expanded, but it is a single case. The whole question is avoided, however, by treating locatives as adverbials rather than as cases.

Finally, a word about deixis. Our introduction of deictic spatial relations extends our treatment into a realm that is usually called pragmatics. In order to translate deictic spatial terms into routines that the system can execute, it is necessary to know the context in which the words are spoken; that requirement makes the enterprise pragmatic. When one associates a lexical concept with a word like "lamp," much the same concept is expressed whenever the word is used. For deictic uses of "front" or "top," on the other hand, the concept expressed seems to vary from one use to the next. What varies, however, is not the concept but the reference; even though the results may be different from one context to the next, the procedures involved in determining reference are always the same. Thus, a procedural representation of lexical concepts is as appropriate for deictic as for nondeictic words.

Spatial language is used primarily to indicate where things are; indicating where things are is frequently an important aspect of identifying or referring to them; identification and reference are critical aspects of linguistic communication. We see no way to deal with all the procedures whereby specific objects in particular locations are identified or referred to without including deictic relations, so the virtues of including them as procedural schemata, similar to other schemata proposed for nondeictic words, seem to us to outweigh any problems that may result from our failure to draw sharper distinctions between our semantic and pragmatic hypotheses.

6.2   TEMPORAL RELATIONS

The core of the time concept is relatively simple, perhaps even universal, and grows more or less directly out of the experience of successive moments. In section 2.4 we described a notation for time perception based on the assumption that time is a unidimensional variable with a past-to-future orientation that can be divided into discrete moments, and that the order of those moments can be designated by numbering them. In order to experience successive moments as successive, however, it is necessary to be able to conceive of the present moment and past moments together. As William James (1890) said, "A succession of feelings, in and of itself, is not a feeling of succession" (I, 628). It is the *relation* between the present moment and past moments that creates the feeling of succession, and the feeling of succession leads to a conceptualization of time as a line extending from past to future.

As in the case of space, there is both a relative and an absolute version of the time concept. The relative version concerns merely the ordinal relations between moments or intervals of time; the absolute version assumes units of measure. The influence of spatial concepts on the concept of time has frequently been noted; many expressions of temporal relations borrow directly from spatial language (at midnight, in September, as long as, before Tuesday, the next day). The intimate relation of space and time concepts is most apparent in motion, which involves both spatial and temporal changes. It is likely that the perception of motion is ontogenetically prior to both the time and space concepts, which take their adult form only after a child is able to differentiate these two aspects of voluntary and perceived movements. As in our discussion of space, we assume the structure of the time concept is reasonably apparent, although some of its logical implications may not be.

Whereas the expression of spatial shapes and relations is optional in English, the expression of temporal relations is obligatory. Quine (1960) has written, "Our ordinary language shows a tiresome bias in its treatment of time. Relations of date are exalted grammatically as relations of position, weight, and color are not. This bias is of itself an inelegance, or breach of theoretical simplicity. Moreover, the form that it takes—that of requiring that every verb form show a tense—is peculiarly productive of needless complications, since it demands lip service to time even when time is farthest from our thoughts" (p. 170). Quine exaggerates a little; not every verb has to carry a tense marker, but every sentence does. Such requirements can be dropped in artificial languages. For many purposes of logical analysis, the complex and obligatory indications of temporal relations in ordinary English are simply dropped; the present tense is used not to indicate the present time but as the closest approximation to a temporally neutral, timeless, untensed form of expression. In this way it is possible to dodge many of the problems posed by natural languages. Our present concern, however, is not to substitute some timeless and well-behaved canonical notations that might enable us to ignore the problem but to explore the psychological bases for the diverse and apparently "needless complications" of temporal expressions in ordinary language.

It might seem that the simplest approach to the question of how people express temporal relations would be to analyze linguistic expressions and to infer from them what the conceptual core might be. We have chosen the opposite approach. The reason becomes apparent when we consider some of the obstacles that lie in the path of a purely linguistic approach.

Interpreting the temporal significance of sentences is one of the most complex problems in linguistics. Part of the difficulty is that temporal relations can be expressed in many ways. It is not merely that every verb form must show a tense. The lexical resources for expressing temporal information are also very rich. Consider the following examples:

> Verbs: end, postpone, precede, recur
> Nouns: day, month, precedent, tomorrow
> Adjectives: former, later, present, successive
> Adverbs: eventually, often, shortly, subsequently
> Prepositions: at, during, in, on
> Conjunctions: as soon as, before, until, when

Temporal information is provided by words in all the major syntactic categories. The categories are a poor guide, however. For example, in "It happened before," "before" is an adverb; in "It happened before noon," "before" is a preposition and "before noon" is a prepositional phrase that functions adverbially; in "It happened before he left," "before" is a conjunction that connects two sentences and "before he left" is a subordinate clause. The same semantic relation can assume a variety of grammatical disguises.

Tense is the major grammatical mechanism for expressing temporal relations. Temporal information given lexically must coordinate with temporal information given by tense markers. In order to assign correct temporal indices and quantifiers for the formal specification of the temporal meanings of English sentences, we must take account of auxiliary verbs, of the type of main verb, of time adverbials, and sometimes even the subject or object of the sentence. In English, auxiliary verbs carry information about tense, aspect, and phase; we must consider not only the tense markers on the main verb but the full verb group—the main verb plus any auxiliaries. The role of the other elements— the type of verb, the adverbials, the noun phrases—is less obvious and perhaps worth exemplifying.

The role of the main verb can be illustrated by comparing verbs that denote states (love, know, contain) with verbs that denote events (kiss, hit, speak). The distinction between stative and nonstative predications has profound consequences for the temporal interpretation of sentences. For example,

(33)   (a) Gilbert loves Mary.
         (b) Gilbert kisses Mary.
         (c) Gilbert kisses Mary today.

The first two differ solely with respect to the stativity of the verb. "Gilbert loves Mary" suggests an enduring state; "Gilbert kisses Mary" can be taken either as a statement of a habitual phenomenon or as a running commentary on a specific event. As a commentary, (b) may be a report of what happened (the historic present), a report of what is currently happening (the instantaneous present), or a statement of what is yet to happen (the future). In (c) the ambiguity is resolved by the use of an adverb. In "Gilbert kisses Mary today," "today" establishes that the sentence is about what is yet to happen.

The effect of the noun phrase can be brought out by a comparison suggested by Leech (1969):

(34)   (a) He climbed a mountain.
         (b) He climbed several mountains.
         (c) He climbed mountains.

Here the nature of the object of the verb determines whether the sentence is construed as (a) a single event that occurred at a definite though unspecified time; (b) a series of events taking place in a definite though unspecified interval of time; or (c) a habitual series of events—"He was a mountain climber." Hurtig (1974) has illustrated the importance of the noun phrase in terms of the difference between

(35)   (a) Mary lived with the dead man.
         (b) Mary lived with a dead man.

In (a) the time of being together is more naturally taken as preceding the time of death, whereas the salient interpretation of (b) is that the time of death preceded the time of being together.

These examples should illustrate some of the difficulties of working from a grammatical analysis of temporal language toward an account of its conceptual basis. English provides an amazing variety of ways to express temporal relations and they interact in complicated patterns. It is little wonder that despite the sophisticated efforts of many linguists there is still no comprehensive account of the English grammar of time. Given the diversity of temporal meanings that any form may carry, it is difficult to discern any systematic principles.

When such situations have arisen in other domains, we have generally tried to provide a procedural account that would explain what was going on psychologically and why it is so difficult to abstract from those psychological processes any simple, general, syntactic rules. What is going on psychologically in the case of time is the construction of serial representations of events, processes, and episodes ordered and/or anchored along the real time line or along expected time lines in the future or along imaginary alternatives to the real time line. In order to talk about these constructions we need ways to identify which time line is involved and then to locate a moment, interval, or event as a landmark in terms of which earlier, simultaneous, or later real or hypothetical states of affairs can be discussed. Most of the cognitive work involves creating or re-creating the particular contents of these serial representations; the details of the processing that must occur will vary considerably depending on the particular history, whether it is or was real or imaginary, the discussants' shared knowledge of it, the discourse context, and what is said about it. It is difficult to think of any aspect of cognitive psychology that might not be involved. Whereas in our discussion of spatial relations we could presume the existence of a physical space to support the symbolic processes, in the present discussion the symbolic processes must denote largely nonexistent (past, future, or imaginary) states of affairs whose representations are complex psychological constructions.

In short, a procedural account of temporal relations would be exceedingly complicated and those complications largely a consequence of the abstract nature of time. What such an account might look like can be suggested by extrapolating from Isard's (1975) procedural semantics of "when" used in questions about games of ticktacktoe. Isard describes a computer program that plays the game and answers such questions about it as "Had you taken x when I took y?" or "Could you have taken x when I took y?" or "If I had taken x when I took y, what would you have done?" The program uses the "when" clause and associated tense markers to locate the particular situation that the questioner describes (checking its record of the game to make certain that such a situation actually arose), then computes an answer appropriate to that situation. Isard's procedural account of "when" is sufficiently complex, even for the reduced universe he considers, that the prospect of expanding it to include all temporal locatives, all tenses, all grammatical constructions in which they can occur, and, especially, all alternative situations that people can take as temporal landmarks in ordinary discourse should suffice to indicate why we will not undertake a full procedural account.

Instead, we will abstract one aspect of the larger problem for discussion here. In the control instruction test(t, S) the description S is to be verified relative to time t. In order to produce such instructions in executable form, however, the translator must have (a) some explicit characterization of what is meant by the phrase "relative to time t" and (b) some way to determine what state of affairs obtained at that time. Most of the really difficult problems for any procedural account are associated with (b). How the first argument of "test" should be formulated is not a simple question, but (a) is certainly far less formidable than (b). We will therefore focus our attention on (a).

As a consequence of this decision, the following discussion of temporal relations will be considerably more abstract than we would like, or than we have attempted for other domains. We will begin by noting some of the implications of the core concept of time—a strategy adopted by Bull (1960) and defended in principle by Chafe (1970). Moreover, since the aspects we wish to abstract from the procedural account we cannot give are far more conceptual than procedural, we will allow ourselves the luxury of describing them in propositional rather than procedural notations. Although this lapse from our general program slants the following discussion rather differently from the rest of the book, the expository convenience of quantificational and temporal logic in this context is too great to resist. We only hope that the notation we use here will remind the reader of the important aspects of temporal thought and language that we must regretfully neglect.

6.2.1   Representations of the Time Concept

The simplest way to visualize time is as a line without beginning or end. Conceptually, the time line and the number line are very similar; they may develop together in children. The number line can provide an ordering of magnitudes; the time line can provide an ordering of events. We will say that events are mapped onto the time line by linguistic expressions. In figure 6.1 two symbols, A and B, are ordered in this way by mapping them onto points on the time line.

A more precise term would be "time vector." The time line has an orientation as well as an extent. In figure 6.1 the time line runs from left to right, but the direction is arbitrary. Familiarity with Cartesian coordinate systems in which time is conventionally represented as running from left to right makes this a preferred orientation for most educated adults. Young children are just

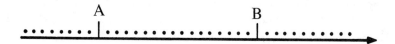

Figure 6.1   A time line.

as happy with a right-left orientation for ordering events in a story and may even adopt a vertical orientation, as if they were moving upward or forward into the future. Since it is not a question of which orientation is correct, but only of being consistent, we will adopt the left-right convention to represent the conceptual core of the time concept.

Although we will use the time line as the basis for discussing temporal relations, it should be noted that the time concept may be represented as circular. The clock face provides a familiar example, and "clockwise" sets the dominant orientation for ordering events. The circle provides a better representation for cyclical time terms like the names of the days of the week, and one might propose a spiral representation to reflect the fact that not all Tuesdays map onto the same interval of time. For historical and autobiographical memory, however, the rectilinear representation seems to be what most people think of.

We assume that time is a continuum and should be represented by a continuous line. For psychological and linguistic purposes, however, it is convenient to think of time as a sequence of moments. In figure 6.1 the dots above the line are intended to suggest this discrete interpretation. Since the concept is used primarily to represent ordinal relations between events, it makes little difference whether we use a continuous or a discrete representation, or even whether equal extents along the line represent objectively equal intervals of time, however that might be defined. The discrete representation is more convenient for understanding such expressions as "the next moment," but most of the uses we will make of the time line will hold under either a continuous or a discrete interpretation of the concept.

Given this linear conceptual core, we must introduce some metalinguistic symbols to discuss it and to enable us to formulate definitions of English time terms. First we need a variable t that can take integral values for successive moments. Since temporal language must describe relations between two or more moments in time, symbols are required to indicate different moments. In order to *refer* to a particular moment, we need constants like t_a or t_b or $t_a + 1$. In order to *identify* a moment, we need to introduce quantifiers: "There exists a t such that t is a moment of time, and at t . . ." We will continue to use $(\exists t)$ for the existential quantifier and (t) for the universal quantifier.

In section 2.4 the perceptual predicate Later(t, t') was introduced to accommodate the fairly immediate succession of one event at time t' by another at time t, with Earlier(t', t) as the obvious converse relation. There we assumed that the succession of moments is perceived within the specious present. Given a perceptual grasp of this succession, there presumably comes a stage during a child's development when the relation Later is generalized to

longer intervals of time. Once this has occurred, the core of the time concept has
been grasped and we can denote this conceptual relation by LATER. The logic
of time can accordingly be made explicit by making explicit this unrestricted
relation LATER:

(36)   Asymmetric: $(t) (t')[\text{LATER}(t, t') \supset \text{notLATER}(t', t)]$
           Transitive: $(t) (t') (t'')[\text{LATER}(t, t')$ & $\text{LATER}(t', t'')$
                            $\supset \text{LATER}(t, t'')]$
           Connected: $(t) (t')[\text{LATER}(t, t')$ or $\text{LATER}(t', t)]$

where $t \neq t' \neq t''$. These properties define a series and, granted moments of
time exist, moments are serially ordered by the relation LATER. Graphically, the
moment labeled B in figure 6.1 is later in time than the moment labeled A, so
if we refer to those moments as t_A and t_B we can write $\text{LATER}(t_B, t_A)$ or
$\text{EARLIER}(t_A, t_B)$. Since the order of moments is paralleled by the order of
integers, it will often be convenient to represent LATER and EARLIER more
briefly as $>$ and $<$, respectively; thus, figure 6.1 could be described by either
$t_B > t_A$ or $t_A < t_B$.

The serial nature of time could be defined on a relation NEXT, in the sense
of the immediate succession of one moment by another (see, for example, the
"T-calculus" of von Wright, 1963). Then LATER could be defined in terms of
NEXT. Such a definition would introduce the idea that between any two moments that are not NEXT to each other there are always other moments such
that you can get from the earlier to the later by going "and NEXT and NEXT and
NEXT and . . . " for a finite number of times. If the concept of a finite number
is assumed, or if mathematical induction is assumed, there is no problem.
Since these are large assumptions, it seems more plausible psychologically to
begin with the relation LATER and to define NEXT in terms of it. In this case we
must assume that moments of time are discrete; insofar as people are prepared
to talk about "the next moment," they are prepared to think of time as a succession of discrete moments. Let us add a discreteness condition to the logic
of LATER:

(37)   Discrete: $(t') (\exists t)(t'') [\text{LATER}(t, t')$ & $\text{LATER}(t'', t') \supset$
                        $(\text{LATER}(t'', t)$ or $t'' = t)]$.

To paraphrase the discreteness condition: For every moment t' there is a
moment t such that t is later than t' and, for any moment t'', if t'' is also
later than t', then either t'' is later than t or t'' equals t. In short, there is
no moment between t' and t. The definition of $\text{NEXT}(t, t')$—t is the next moment after t'—follows at once:

(38) $\text{NEXT}(t, t') =_{\text{df}} t > t'$ & $(t'') [t'' > t' \supset (t'' > t$ or $t'' = t)]$.

Since the discreteness condition says that for every moment t' there is a next
moment t, there is, at least conceptually, no last moment. In order to insure
that there is an immediately preceding moment for every moment in time, and
hence that there is no first moment, we could restate the discreteness condition
with EARLIER in place of LATER.

With this much notation in hand we are able to characterize the sequential order of temporal moments. People have two ways of thinking about this order, however. Following the lead of the logician Prior (1967), we can pose the problem by quoting McTaggart (1927). McTaggart is perhaps best remembered as an Idealist philosopher who sought to prove that Time is Unreal. This enterprise forced him to scrutinize the conventional notion of time with considerable care. We can borrow some of his ideas without endorsing his ultimate conclusion.

"Positions in time," McTaggart wrote, "as time appears to us *prima facie* are distinguished in two ways." In the first place, "each position is Earlier than some and Later than some of the others"; and "in the second place, each position is either Past, Present, or Future. The distinctions of the former class are permanent, those of the latter are not. If M is ever earlier than N, it is always earlier. But an event, which is now present, was future, and will be past" (quoted by Prior, 1967, pp. 1-2). It follows that we can distinguish two different series of time positions, which McTaggart called the A-series and the B-series. The A-series is the series of positions in time that runs from the past through the present to the future. The B-series is the series of positions in time that runs from earlier to later. Any relations expressed in terms of the B-series can also be expressed in terms of the A-series: event e is earlier than event e' if it is ever in the past while e' is in the present, or in the present while e' is in the future. The converse is not true; there is no way to define past, present, and future in terms of the B-series.

We have described the order of moments in time as a B-series. In order to describe the A-series, we must introduce "now." Given "now," the A-series can be defined in terms of the B-series:

(39)   past = earlier than now
          present = not earlier and not later than now
          future = later than now

where the A-series is on the left and the B-series plus "now" is on the right.

It would seem that the A-series and the B-series are not different conceptions of time but merely different ways of talking about the same concept. But the core concept must include, in addition to the time line, a privileged moment "now." The A-series takes the present moment as its point of origin and the B-series does not, but if "now" is added to the B-series, either way of thinking about time can be translated directly into the other.

As Rescher and Urquhart (1971) point out, "now" is neither a constant nor a variable. It is not a constant because it does not refer to the same moment on each occasion that it is used; it is not a variable because it cannot be quantified. It refers to a unique moment in any given context, though not the same moment in every context. In short, "now" is a deictic term whose interpretation depends on the context of use. The A-series is deictic; the B-series is not. In order to complete our characterization of the conceptual core of the time domain, therefore, we must add the deictic moment "now," which we will symbolize n, and define past and future in terms of it:

(40) $(\exists t)\,[t = n]$

PAST$(t) \equiv$ LATER(n, t)

FUTURE$(t) \equiv$ LATER(t, n)

Although we can now describe the sequential order of temporal moments with respect to the present, we are still in need of some way to map events onto the time line. People usually take the order of moments for granted; what they talk about is the order of events. Consider how "later" is used. In the sentence "I'll do it later" we understand that there is a moment t, later than the time of utterance t_s, for which the event is promised. We can write LATER(t, t_s), and the time of utterance can be associated with the moment t_s as a standard convention. But what is our notation for indicating that the promised event is associated with moment t? We need some way to say "There exists a t such that I'll do it at t."

Although any two moments can be related by LATER, the same cannot be said about events. Two events can occur at the same time. Indeed, states or processes can persist over indefinite intervals, during which many other things may be happening. So, whatever notation is adopted for mapping onto the time line, it must be able to map persisting states or processes in addition to momentary events.

Let S represent a sentence describing or identifying an event or process whose temporal location on the time line is to be identified or referred to. For example, if S is "I do it" and t_s denotes the time S is uttered, we want to write something like $(\exists t)\,[$LATER(t, t_s) & S is true at $t]$. What "S is true at t" means is that if the control instruction "test" is given t as its first argument and S as its second, the result should be confirmatory. "S is true at t" corresponds to the statement-forming operator R used by Rescher and Urquhart (1971) in their system of temporal logic. If S is some temporally indefinite statement, the operator R can form another statement from S by specifying the time at which S is asserted to hold: $R_t(S)$ is interpreted to mean that S is realized at moment t. If S is AT(x, y), for example, $R_t($AT$(x, y))$ means that x is at y at time t. $R_t(S)$ makes a claim only about moment t; it says nothing about $t - 1$ or $t + 1$ or any other moment.

We will not develop the system of temporal logic that can be based on R (details can be found in Rescher and Urquhart, 1971) but will list some of the axioms required to follow derivations in our subsequent discussion:

(41)   (a)   not$R_t(S) \equiv R_t($not$S)$

(b) $R_t(S \,\&\, S') \equiv (R_t(S) \,\&\, R_t(S'))$

(c) $R_n(S) \equiv S$

(d) $R_{t'}((t)S) \equiv (t)R_{t'}(S)$

(e) $R_{t'}(R_t(S)) \equiv R_t(S)$

(f) $R_t(n = t') \equiv (t = t')$ and $R_t(t' = t'') \equiv (t' = t'')$

(g) $R_t(n < t') \equiv (t < t')$ and $R_t(t' < t'') \equiv (t' < t'')$

These axioms make it possible to incorporate R into the ordinary predicate calculus. For example, $\text{not}R_t(S)$ means that S is not realized at t, which is equivalent, according to (a), to saying that $\text{not}S$ *is* realized at t. $R_t(S \ \& \ S')$ means that both S and S′ are realized at t, which is equivalent, according to (b), to saying that S is realized at t and S′ is realized at t. Given negation and conjunction, of course, all of the propositional calculus is available in the temporal logic. $R_n(S)$ means that S is realized right now; according to (c), to say S is true right now is the same as to say S. Quantification is introduced in (d), which allows R to move in or out of the scope of quantifiers. According to (e), if S is a temporally definite statement, then $R_t(S)$ is taken as the equivalent of S. The exception to this rule involves "now" in any of its various disguises. When S is a temporally definite statement involving "now," Rescher and Urquhart take $R_t(R_n(S))$ to be equivalent to $R_t(S)$, not to $R_n(S)$. On this interpretation, which is formulated in (f) and (g), yesterday's today is not today, but yesterday. Readers familiar with the first-order predicate calculus should have no trouble in following the arguments to be presented below, although occasional reference to (41) may be necessary.

R_t enables us to map an event onto the moment t on the time line, and we can map persisting states or processes onto intervals by the use of quantifiers. For example, if the temporally indefinite state S is realized throughout an interval from t_i to t_{i+k}, we can write

(42) $(t) [t_{i-1} < t < t_{i+k+1} \supset R_t(S)]$.

For all t, if t runs from t_i to t_{i+k}, S is realized at t. In order to see what this means in terms of the time line, let $R_t(S) = 1$ denote that S is realized at t, and let $R_t(S) = 0$ denote that S is not realized at time t. Then we can think of $R_t(S)$ as a function of t that has the value one for every moment between the two stated bounds, as shown in figure 6.2. Since the expression tells us

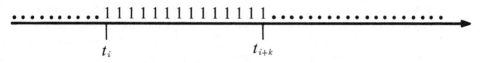

Figure 6.2 $R_t(S) = 1$ for all moments from t_i to t_{i+k} inclusive.

nothing about the realization of S outside of those bounds, we cannot put "0" before t_i or after t_{i+k}; the dots indicate that the moments still exist, but we have no information about the truth value of S outside the indicated interval.

Thus, for any temporally indefinite statement S, $R_t(S)$ enables us to define a characteristic function over all t with values of either one or zero for each successive moment on the time line. The characteristic function tells us, for any moment, whether or not S was realized at that moment. The expression in (42) describes a finite part of the characteristic function for that statement. The expression $(t)R_t(S)$ would denote that the characteristic function of S was one for every moment of time. The axioms in (41) should be understood as holding for any t in the characteristic function—for any point along the time line—not merely for one particular moment t.

We could thus use R and quantifiers over t to identify or refer to any interval we like during which some statement can be said to be realized. To do so, however, would necessitate a cumbersome imposition of quantifiers and temporal inequalities. It is a natural step, therefore, to use R to define four other statement-forming operators that will enable us to denote intervals, rather than discrete moments, during which a statement is realized:

(43) $F_{t_a}(S) =_{df} (\exists t) [t_a < t \quad \& \quad R_t(S)]$

$G_{t_a}(S) =_{df} (t) [t_a < t \supset R_t (S)]$.

$P_{t_a}(S) =_{df} (\exists t) [t < t_a \quad \& \quad R_t(S)]$

$Q_{t_a}(S) =_{df} (t) [t < t_a \supset R_t(S)]$.

The F operator denotes that S is realized at *some* moment or moments in the future with respect to t_a; P denotes that S is realized at *some* moment or moments in the past with respect to t_a. If $t_a = n$, F is the simple future and P the simple past. The operator G is also a future indicator, but it differs from F in that S is realized at *all* moments subsequent to t_a. And Q is a past indicator, differing from P in that S is realized at *all* moments prior to t_a.

Suppose that we wanted to describe something that was realized for the first time at t_a and continued to be realized for all subsequent time. We need merely write

(44) $Q_{t_a}(notS) \& R_{t_a}(S) \& G_{t_a}(S)$

to represent the sequence of values

(45) $\dots 00000000001111111111111111 \dots$

along the time line. In both (44) and (45), notS is realized for all t earlier than t_a, S is realized at t_a, and S is realized for all t later than t_a. We will make extensive use of the operators F, G, P, and Q in the subsequent discussion, so some important relations between them are worth noting:

(46) $F_{t_a}(notS) \equiv notG_{t_a}(S)$.

(47) $P_{t_a}(notS) \equiv notQ_{t_a}(S)$.

In paraphrase, if notS is realized at some future (or past) time, then S is not realized at all future (or past) times.

To summarize: we take the oriented time line containing a privileged moment "now" to represent the conceptual core of the time domain. We think of events, processes, or states as being mapped onto the time line in the order of their occurrence. This mapping can be represented graphically by drawing the time line and indicating by appropriate symbols the location of events, processes, or states; something resembling such a drawing may be what people construct when they try to imagine some past or future sequence of happenings. In order to discuss such mappings without having to draw pictures, some formal notation is required, and we have adopted for that purpose the temporal logic as presented by Rescher and Urquhart (1971). Our task now is to explore how English time expressions can be defined—or at least clarified and interrelated—by such logical concepts.

6.2.2   Names for Times

Names for particular spaces leave off somewhere around spaces the size of rooms; finer designations of spatial locations are made relative to fixed landmarks. An absolute system for spatial locations is available, but no one would use longitude, latitude, and altitude to indicate the location of a book on a shelf. Most people have no clear notion of these coordinate values for the town they live in. With respect to time, however, the coordinate system given in terms of the cyclical names and numbers of the Gregorian calendar is known and used by almost everyone, even though it burdens memory and requires frequent recourse to clocks and calendars to establish the correct coordinate value. In terms of this system, every moment and interval can be given an identifying designation as precise as the situation demands and patience allows. In industrialized societies, coordinate representation of time is much more important than coordinate representation of space, a fact that links time concepts and number concepts in a most intimate relation. The whole system is based on the assumption that those who use it will have mastered at least the elementary numerical concepts.

Linguists have sometimes puzzled as to which unit of time should be taken as primitive. Whichever one they take, the other units can be defined easily by reference to it. A little reflection indicates that there is no determinate way in which the objective units of Western time technology can be identified with the subjective temporal order that we have postulated. One might assume that the perceptual moment has an objective duration of, say, one-tenth of a second (see Stroud, 1967), but this seems altogether too arbitrary, too unlikely. We need make only the rather weak assumption that a number of subjective moments are included in each objective second in order to obtain a viable system. This assumption ensures that moments will be brief enough that such deictic terms as "today" can be satisfactorily defined in terms of "the day that contains the moment 'now.' " And other deictic time expressions can be similarly defined: "this morning" is "the morning of the day that contains 'now' "; "this week" is "the week that contains the day that contains 'now' " (although there is some uncertainty here, because people cannot agree whether the week starts on Sunday or Monday).

At any level of time measurement—that is to say, for any particular unit—there is a set of contrastive terms that, like the color terms, is exhaustive. The internal structures of these sets are serial orders:

(48)   Season: spring, summer, autumn, winter
         Month: January, February, . . . , December
         Day: Monday, Tuesday, . . . , Sunday
         Hour: one, two, . . . , twelve
         Minute (or second): one, two, . . . , fifty-nine

Taken together with the A.M./P.M. contrast, we can name a time rather precisely as, say, "1:36:25 P.M., Sunday, April 14, 1974." The terms in (48) are cyclical; in order to complete the specification of a particular date, it is necessary to go to a noncyclical contrastive set of chronologically stable terms: A.D./B.C.; millennium; century; decade; year—A.D. 1974, for example.

Rescher and Urquhart (1971) distinguish between "dates," which are stable, and "pseudodates," which are deictic and specify different dates on different occasions of use. "Now" is an obvious pseudodate, and since "now" is involved in the definition of "today," it too is a pseudodate. Even "January" or "Monday," which do not seem to involve "now" in their definitions, are often used as pseudodates: "Next Monday" selects one Monday out of the repeating cycle of weeks by reference indirectly to "now"—"the next Monday from now." The serial and exhaustive nature of the cycles at each level of contrast enables us to exploit the notion of an element that is "immediately before" some unit of time or "immediately after" it, and so to define the temporal terms "previous" and "next." Leech (1969) has noted the confusion that these terms can lead to; "the previous January" may be construed to mean either the most recent January or the January of the preceding year. Such confusions are most likely to arise when "previous" or "next" are combined with the cyclical terms on the right-hand side of (48); combinations with the superordinate terms on the left—"the previous day" or "next month"—are more clear-cut. Indeed, we can define "yesterday" as "the day previous to the day that contains 'now' " and "tomorrow" as "the next day after the day that contains 'now.' "

The terms in (48) form contrastive classes with the left-hand terms as superordinates: "Spring is a season," "January is a month." The relations between the lines in (48), however, is partonymic: a year is a part of a century, a month is a part of a year, a week is a part of a month. The whole, of course, is the time line, which is partitioned into successive intervals or units of different lengths. When some happening is to be mapped onto the time line, various locatives—on, in, at, between, from . . . to—are borrowed from the spatial lexicon and used as temporal locatives.

The deictic terms for time, on the other hand, do not require these relational prepositions. People say "It happened yesterday"; it sounds odd to say "It happened on yesterday." Sentences like "It happened Tuesday" seem to be an exception, since a partonym is used without a locative, but even here one can argue that "Tuesday" is being used deictically; the context should establish that the reference is to the most recent Tuesday. The omission of the locative seems to be the signal that "now" is the time with respect to which the reference is to be interpreted. If this observation is correct, then "the present time" would seem to be the B-series translation of "now." Although "It is happening now" does not require a locative preposition, "It is happening the present time" is distinctly odd. "The present time" is obviously deictic, yet it is used as if it is not.

The vagueness of "the present time" has often been noted, since this expression plays an important role in defining what is usually called the present tense. To take an example of the vagueness, "He is working at the present time" can mean "He is working at the present moment" or "He is working this week" or even "He is working this year." "The present time" can denote any interval of time that includes the present moment. Since "this month" includes the present moment, the present tense can be used in "He is working this month"; on the other hand, "last month" does not include the present moment and it is odd to say "He is working last month." The complexities of the temporal relations that are usually discussed under the rubric of "tense" will be explored in more detail in 6.2.4.

6.2.3   Time Adverbials and Connectives

English offers a variety of temporal locatives—in, on, at, when, while, before, since. Syntactically, these words are sometimes prepositions, sometimes adverbs, sometimes conjunctions, but their semantic role is to locate events on the time line—by relating them to a specific time or to other events. We will try to take care of the semantic relations and hope the syntactic relations will take care of themselves.

The use of "in," "on," and "at" as temporal locatives is by analogy with the spatial use of these terms. ("Between" and "from . . . to" are also loans from the spatial lexicon and have much the same meaning for time lines as for spatial lines.) "At" is used for punctate identifications: "at 9:05," "at dawn." "In" is the most generally useful: "in the morning," "in January," "in 1900." Why "on" is preferred to "in" when the relatum is the name of a day is not clear, but neither "in Tuesday" nor "in the tenth of May" is used. "In" and "on" can also be used to relate two times: "in five minutes" refers to a time five minutes later than some time to be inferred from context. "In time," "on time," "ahead of time," "behind time" are even vaguer, but seem to mean "earlier than," "at," or "later than" some time established contextually.

"Later than" and "earlier than" can be used to relate a statement S to a definite date t_a ("It happened later than six") or to some contextually established date ("It happened later than usual"). This use of "later than" is an extension of the formulation for LATER given in 6.2.1, where it was used formally to relate two moments t and t'. The sense of "later" defined there is expressed in such sentences as "400 B.C. is later than 800 B.C." In order to relate an event statement to a date, we need something like

(49)   LATERTHAN(S, t_a):   An event, state, or process described by S is "later than" some particular time t_a if:

      (i) $[F_{t_a}(S)]$

That is to say, S is later than t_a if there is some time t such that S is realized at t and LATER(t, t_a). The relation expressed by "sooner than," or "earlier than," can be given similarly in terms of $P_{t_a}(S)$. Sentences like "Sooner or later it happened" combine F and P and so reduce to $(\exists t) R_t(S)$ or, since this sentence is past tense, $P_n(S)$.

"Sooner than t_a" and "later than t_a" are adverbial prepositional phrases. They are not used freely as sentence connectives—"It happened sooner than he ate" and "He left later than it happened" are awkward. When a second statement S' is used as the relatum, the preferred terms seem to be "before" and "after." "Before" and "after" can also take t_a as the relatum, a use important for telling time, so we must formulate them to accept either S' or t_a as the relatum.

There has been considerable discussion of the semantics of "before" and "after"; for a useful review see Heinämäki (1974). We will assume that sentences of the form "S before S'" are interpreted to mean that there is some moment t such that S has been realized at t but S' has not yet been realized—that there is an interval between the first realization of S and the first realization of S'. Kroch (1972) has analyzed "before" in essentially this manner and has considered the potential counterexamples provided by such sentences as "Before the arrival of the rebel army, the government forces controlled the town." The problem here is that such sentences would normally be construed to mean that the government forces controlled the town for *all* moments prior to the arrival of the rebel army, and not merely that there was *some* moment prior to their arrival at which the government forces controlled the town. Kroch suggests that where the context permits it, the existential "some" is extended to the universal "all," but Heinämäki argues persuasively that such interpretations are better regarded as implicatures than as general rules. We will accept Kroch's formulation and express it in terms of the operators given in (43):

(50)   BEFORE(S, S'): $(\exists t)[P_t(S) \ \& \ \text{not} P_t(S')]$.

For example, in the sentence "He jogs before he eats breakfast," let S denote "he jogs" and S' denote "he eats breakfast"; then (50) says that there is some moment t such that "he jogs" is realized before t and "he eats breakfast" is not yet realized (cf. Geis, 1970).

Heinämäki (1974) proposes a somewhat more complex statement of the truth rules for "before." She notes that in sentences like "Mark built a sailboat before he knew how to sail" it is understood that Mark completed building the sailboat before he started learning to sail; hence, "before" relates the terminal moment (not the first moment) of the building to the first moment of the learning. In order to take account of the fact that "before" can sometimes relate the terminal moment of the antecedent to the initial moment of the subsequent referent, Heinämäki defines a "reference time" for an interval that is the final point if the referent describes an accomplishment, like building, but is otherwise the initial point of the interval. We prefer the formulation given in

(50), however, on the grounds that the antecedent accomplishment is not realized—R_t(Mark built a sailboat) $= 0$—until the outcome is accomplished. Thus, the first moment at which (50) is satisfied turns out to be the last moment of the interval spent accomplishing the outcome. To take another example, in "He jogs before he eats breakfast" the relation is between the first moment of jogging and the first moment of eating breakfast, but in "He jogs a mile before he eats breakfast," the antecedent is not true until a mile of jogging has been accomplished. We prefer to account for such facts in terms of aspectual relations (6.2.5) rather than by complicating the logical formulation of "before."

"Before" and "after" can also be used, like "sooner than" and "later than," to relate a statement S to a particular time t_a: "He jogs before 8:00 A.M." As a short tutorial in the use of temporal logic, consider how BEFORE(S, S') reduces to EARLIERTHAN(S, t_a) when S' is a statement about time. For this purpose, let S denote "he jogs" and S' "it is now 8:00 A.M." or "$n = 8$." Then we can write (50) as

$$(\exists t)[P_t(S) \ \& \ \text{not}P_t(n = 8)]$$
$$(\exists t)\,[P_t(S) \ \& \ \text{not}(\exists t'')\,[t'' < t \ \ \& \ \ R_{t''}(n = 8)]]$$
$$(\exists t)\,[P_t(S) \ \& \ \text{not}(\exists t'')\,[t'' < t \ \ \& \ \ t'' = 8]]$$
$$(\exists t)\,[(\exists t')\,[t' < t \ \ \& \ \ R_{t'}(S)] \ \ \& \ \ t \leq 8]$$
$$(\exists t)\,(\exists t')\,[t' < t \leq 8 \ \ \& \ \ R_{t'}(S)]$$
$$(\exists t')\,[t' < 8 \ \ \& \ \ R_{t'}(S)]$$
$$P_8(S) \equiv \text{EARLIERTHAN}(S, 8)$$

A similar argument for the sentence "It is 8:00 A.M. before he eats breakfast" would show that BEFORE$(n = 8, S)$ implies $P_8(\text{not}S)$.

AFTER can be analyzed in the same manner as BEFORE, but we should be careful about calling these relations converses. "He jogs before he eats" is for all intents and purposes synonymous with "He eats after he jogs," but such conversions are possible only when the events are incompatible, like eating and jogging, or momentary. If S and S' describe states or processes that can be realized at the same time, then S' can be realized both before and after S. For example, "It was raining after he was working" is not equivalent to "He was working before it was raining." Whereas "before" relates the two beginnings, "after" relates the beginning of the relatum to the termination of the referent. The formulation for "after" is

(51)   AFTER(S', S): $(\exists t)[P_t(S) \ \& \ F_t(S')]$.

Hence, "before" and "after" are not converse relations in the same sense that "sooner than" and "later than" are converse relations between moments, "longer than" and "shorter than" are converse relations between lengths, or "parent of" and "child of" are converse relations between kinfolk. Of course, if S' denotes a momentary event, then, assuming that it occurs, if it has not happened in the past, $\text{not}P_t(S')$, then it will happen in the future, $F_t(S')$, so the formulations given in (50) and (51) for BEFORE(S, S') and

AFTER(S′, S) will indeed be equivalent; but that fact should not be taken to mean they are converses in the more general sense.

A further difference between "before" and "after" concerns their presuppositions. In both cases, the subordinate clause expresses the presupposition. "He finished before he left" and "He didn't finish before he left" both entail that he left, so "he left" is a presupposition of "He finished before he left." But both "He left after he finished" and "He didn't leave after he finished" entail that he finished, so "he finished" is a presupposition of "He left after he finished." Hence, "He finished before he left" and "He left after he finished" make different assertions and have different presuppositions. The difference is most apparent in imperatives and interrogatives. Compare "Finish before you leave" with "Leave after you finish," or "Did you finish before you left?" with "Did you leave after you finished?" If people's understanding of "before" and "after" were tested by using them in commands or questions, these presuppositional differences might well affect the outcome.

G. Lakoff (1971b) points out that the presuppositions of "before" are not as simple as this account would imply. "He rested before he saw the ambassador" presupposes "he saw the ambassador," but "He died before he saw the ambassador" does not. Lakoff concludes that there must be two meanings of "before." It is sometimes difficult to decide which sense of "before" is intended. "He dodged before it hit him" is ambiguous and only one of its interpretations is equivalent to "It hit him after he dodged." Heinämäki (1972, 1974), however, argues that the difference between factual and nonfactual (or counterfactual) "before" is not to be explained by introducing two definitions of this connective—the temporal relations expressed are the same in both uses—but rather by taking account of the contexts in which it is used. If the sentences are expanded as restrictive relative clauses ("He rested before the time at which he saw the ambassador" and "He died before the time at which he saw the ambassador") the nonfactual version is odd on the grounds that we have a basic belief that seeing is impossible after death; in order to rescue it, a notion of expectation must be introduced ("He died before the time at which he would have seen the ambassador"). In the nonfactual use of "before," a temporal relation is still expressed, but it is a relation between two events, the second of which would have occurred if the first had not prevented it. Therefore, we prefer, with Heinämäki, to account for such facts in terms of contextual information that, together with the main clause, enables the listener to infer a preventive relation (6.3.6) in addition to the temporal relation, rather than by complicating the logical formulation of "before." When a parent says "Eat your spinach before I spank you," he has in mind the same temporal relation as when he says "Eat your spinach before you eat your ice cream," but he does assume that the child is capable of using the context to infer that the second event will occur if the first does not prevent it.

In order to explore some presuppositions of expressions of temporal relations, consider a simpler case: "at." As a temporal locative, "at" requires a temporally definite, momentary relatum. Let AT_t represent the temporal sense of "at," where the subscript is not a variable but serves simply to distinguish it from "at" used as a spatial locative. Then we can define

(52) $AT_t(S, t_a):$ $(t)[t = t_a \supset R_t(S)].$

Since $\supset$ is material implication, (52) will be true for all moments $t \neq t_a$; it will be false only when $t = t_a$ and S is not realized at t.

Given this simple formula, consider the effect of negating (52). Four cases must be compared:

(53)   (a) $AT_t(S, t_a):$ $(t)\,[t = t_a \supset R_t(S)]$
          (b) $AT_t(notS, t_a):$ $(t)\,[t = t_a \supset R_t(notS)]$
          (c) $notAT_t(notS, t_a):$ $(\exists t)\,[t = t_a \ \& \ R_t(S)]$
          (d) $notAT_t(S, t_a):$ $(\exists t)\,[t = t_a \ \& \ R_t(notS)]$

In terms of our example, these correspond to the sentences

          (a) He always jogs at 7:00.
          (b) He never jogs at 7:00.
          (c) Sometimes he jogs at 7:00.
          (d) Sometimes he doesn't jog at 7:00.

In traditional logic, (b) is called the contrary of (a), (c) the subaltern, and (d) the contradictory. The sentence "He doesn't jog at 7:00" is usually regarded as ambiguous between the contrary and the contradictory of "He jogs at 7:00."

The traditional doctrine of the "square of opposition" has been discussed extensively by authors of introductory texts on logic, and the problems involved in translating it into quantificational notation are well known. In particular, if the antecedent referent does not exist, the antecedent will be false; a false antecedent assures a true (material) implication. For example, "On February 29, 1973, Tullio was in Milano" identifies a nonexistent date; hence, $t = t_a$ will be false for all t, so both (53a) and (53b) will be true, and both (53c) and (53d) will be false—hardly a satisfactory set of evaluations. It was his analysis of just such problems that led Strawson (1952) to propose that formulations like those in (53) logically presuppose the existence of members of the antecedent class. If there is no t such that $t = t_a$, then (52) and (53) are neither true nor false; the conditions for evaluating them are not fulfilled. In the present instance, $AT_t(S, t)$ presupposes $(\exists t)\,[t = t_a]$.

Caution is required in translating (52) into procedural terms. In general, we have assumed that presuppositions can be translated into control instructions to "find" the presupposed entities before testing whatever is asserted about them. If the "find" instruction fails, the tests are neither passed nor failed; they are simply inoperative. Moreover, in this case the presupposition contains an existential quantifier, and Hintikka (1973) has argued that an existential quantifier can be viewed as an occasion for search. It would seem, therefore, that this situation calls for the system to institute a search for a time t satisfying the condition that $t = t_a$.

How is this call to be answered? It is not difficult to imagine how you could search for a place, but how can you search for a time? Only "now" is available to direct experience; if t ($= t_a$) is not "now," what do you do? If t is in the future, there is nothing to do but wait. If t is past, you can search episodic memory. If t is some time that recurs, like "noon every day," you can supplement memory with induction. But the whole business looks odd. The only way it makes any sense to search for a date is in episodic memory, but—with obvious exceptions for birthdays, holidays, certain dates of personal significance—one feels intuitively that dates are not good probes with which to enter episodic memory. Although episodic memory is probably organized sequentially, only a few specific dates are available as landmarks. Most questions about what you were doing on such-and-such a date require considerable reconstruction—a process that does not seem to occur in understanding simple sentences like "He jogs at 7:00 A.M."

Such considerations make it implausible that temporal presuppositions of the form $(\exists t)F(t)$ should be taken as providing targets for a "find" instruction. Rather, they specify a time at which some "test" instruction is supposed to apply. Procedurally, $R_t(S)$ amounts to test(t, S) = yes, where "yes" is an informal way of indicating how the part of the test that specifies "if so, go to . . . ; otherwise, go to . . . ," is to be completed; "yes" means "choose the 'if so,' not the 'otherwise.' " A "test" instruction is not well formed unless a temporal argument is provided; "test" presupposes $(\exists t)F(t)$ in the sense that the test cannot be performed without it. That is to say, test(t, S) not only presupposes that whatever S points to can be found; it also presupposes that t exists. If t is a future time, the test must be conducted very differently from the way it is conducted if t is a past or present time.

In introducing quantificational formulas to characterize the times at which tests are to be applied we do not intend them to represent procedural instructions; they are simply a convenient notation in which to represent the information that the executive system must have in order to formulate the appropriate "test" procedures. In a sense, $R_t(S)$ is a way to introduce the control instruction "test" into the conditions that our lexical formulations impose. By using R rather than "test," we maintain the rule that our definitions simply provide the information from which routines can be constructed, not the routines themselves. In practice, R constrains the translator considerably and we could obtain much the same results by stating (53) as

(53')   (a) test$((t)[t = t_a], S)$ = yes
         (b) test$((t)[t = t_a], \text{notS})$ = yes
         (c) test$((t)[t = t_a], \text{notS})$ = no
         (d) test$((t)[t = t_a], S)$ = no

If there is no moment t such that $t = t_a$, the test cannot be performed, and the system must return for further instructions.

English has several cotemporal terms. "At" seems to be related to "when," "while," and "as long as" in much the same way as "earlier than" is related to "before" and "later than" to "after." ("During" resembles "while" except that the relatum must be a noun phrase rather than a clause.) These terms can map a clause onto a moment or interval on the time line and once that time of reference has been established it usually persists until a different reference time is explicitly indicated. Consequently, these terms often relate an extended series of clauses or sentences to a reference time established in one clause—Isard (1975) gives a detailed analysis of this phenomenon for the conjunction "when." The logic of these terms, however, is unaffected by the length of the description of processes or events that the terms serve to locate in time. How they relate two clauses will show as much about their truth conditions as will how they relate twenty.

Let "when" relate two clauses. The clauses can denote momentary events or enduring states or processes. If "explode" and "arrive" are momentary events (having what is sometimes called punctual aspect) and "sleep" and "rain" are enduring states or processes (having what is sometimes called durative aspect), then we can consider the four possible combinations with "when":

> (a) It exploded when he was sleeping.
> (b) It exploded when he arrived.
> (c) It rained when he was sleeping.
> (d) It rained when he arrived.

These sentences are all acceptable; the important condition seems to be that both clauses are realized at some moment:

(54) $\text{WHEN}_t(S, S')$: $(\exists t)[\text{AT}_t(S, t) \ \& \ \text{AT}_t(S', t)] \equiv (\exists t)R_t(S \ \& \ S')$.

There is another sense of "when" that resembles "if"; the subscript in (54) is intended to distinguish the temporal from the conditional use of "when."

As Heinämäki (1974; see also Isard, 1975) notes, there are uses of "when" that can be interpreted as denoting succession rather than simultaneity. These uses seem most natural when both clauses describe momentary events. For example, (b) above could be understood to mean that first he arrived and then it exploded. Accomplishments, which behave like momentary events, also admit a sequential interpretation: "When John wrecked the car, Bill fixed it" or "I want to be a fireman when I grow up." The meanings of these sentences would be little changed by substituting "after" for "when." Moreover, there are sentences like "It had just exploded when he arrived" where "before" could be substituted for "when." Such sentences would seem to be exceptions to the conditions stated in (54).

These exceptions suggest a relatively short interval between the two events, whereas "after" and "before" suggest nothing about the length of the intervening interval. "As soon as" or "as soon after as possible" suggests the sense of immediate succession that seems to be involved in these exceptions. We could assume that there is another sense of "when" that incorporates NEXT, or we could try to show that (54), properly interpreted, also accounts for the apparent exceptions. The latter argument might go as follows: it requires only a slight rewording of the exceptional cases to make them conform to (54). "It exploded when he had arrived," "When the car had been wrecked (by John), Bill fixed it," "I want to be a fireman when I am grown up." This suggests that the correct interpretation of these sentences is that once the *state* described in the "when" clause is realized, then the main clause is realized— which conforms to (54). In the case of "It had just exploded when he arrived," the state of being exploded (although not the explosion itself) and the arrival do overlap in time.

The importance of the difference between durative and punctual aspect is more apparent in the case of "while." Consider the following event-process combinations:

(a) It exploded while he was sleeping.
(b) It exploded while he arrived.
(c) It rained while he was sleeping.
(d) It rained while he arrived.

Although (a) and (c) are acceptable, (b) and (d) suggest that the arrival, which is usually a momentary event, is extended in time. That is to say, the relatum of "while" is an ongoing process or state; if a clause denoting an event occurs as the relatum, that event is thought of as enduring for an interval.

Let P represent some temporally indefinite statement about an ongoing process or state. We can write

(55)   WHILE$_t$(S, P): $(\exists t)R_t(S \,\&\, P)$.

The only difference between (54) and (55) is that the relatum for "while" cannot be momentary. (The subscript is to distinguish the temporal sense of "while" from the senses that can be paraphrased "whereas" or "although.")

Finally, "as long as" requires that both the referent and the relatum be ongoing processes or states. Consider

(a) It exploded as long as he was sleeping.
(b) It exploded as long as he arrived.
(c) It rained as long as he was sleeping.
(d) It rained as long as he arrived.

All of these event-process combinations except (c) sound odd; (c) combines two clauses with durative aspect. So we can write

(56)   ASLONGAS$_t$(P, P'): $(t)[R_t(P') \supset R_t(P)]$.

As (56) is formulated, the "as long as" clause can denote a shorter interval than the main clause; if the subordinate clause is realized, the main clause must also be realized, but if the subordinate clause is not realized, the main clause may or may not be realized. There is usually an implicature that both processes begin and end at the same time, but, as Heinämäki points out, this implicature can be canceled without contradiction: "He was depressed as long as he was ill, and maybe even longer."

Given the aspectual distinction between momentary events and ongoing processes, it is natural to introduce the temporal senses of "until" and "since" for ongoing processes or states as

(57)   (a) UNTIL(P, t_a): $Q_{t_a}(P)$
            (b) SINCE(P, t_a): $G_{t_a}(P)$

Heinämäki (1974) gives a more complicated analysis of these temporal connectives; in particular, she points out that "since" (but not "until") can take main clauses denoting momentary events. That is, "It has exploded since Wednesday" is acceptable on the interpretation that the explosion occurred at some time between Wednesday and the moment of speech. Moreover, "since" clauses can only be in the past, either in the simple past or perfect (if we ignore idomatic uses like "Since when did he go?"). A more precise formulation of "since," therefore, would be

(57′)   SINCE(S, t_a): $F_{t_a}(P_n(S))$.

"Until" and "since" are thus not converses of one another. (57′) should be compared with (49), LATERTHAN.

Note that "until t_a" does not entail that P terminates at t_a, although that would normally be understood. For example, "He slept until noon" suggests that he awoke at noon, but this implicature is not an entailment because it can easily be canceled: "He slept at least until noon" or "He slept until noon or later." Similarly, "since t_a" does not entail that S began at t_a, although it would frequently be understood that way.

When negation is introduced into sentences containing "until" or "since" clauses, the picture becomes more complicated. Three complications deserve comment. First, if the statement denotes a state or ongoing process, the negative is ambiguous: "He didn't sleep until noon" can mean either that he stayed awake until after noon or that he awoke before noon; "It hasn't rained since Wednesday" can mean either that there was no rain at all or that the rain was not continuous during that interval. Second, momentary events become acceptable in negatives: "He didn't arrive until noon" and "It hasn't exploded since Wednesday" are both acceptable, although the affirmative with "until" is unacceptable. Third, sentences involving negation of momentary events are not ambiguous: "He didn't arrive until noon" can mean only that he stayed away until noon (or later), not that he arrived before noon; "It hasn't exploded since Wednesday" can mean only that there was no explosion at all, not that the exploding was not continuous during that interval.

These apparent anomalies can be explained as consequences of the formulations proposed in (57a) and (57′). First, the ambiguity of negating "P until t_a" arises from the possibility of construing the negation either as the contrary or as the contradictory. The contrary, UNTIL$($not$P, t_a)$, means that not$P$ was realized at all moments prior to t_a ("He stayed awake before noon"); the contradictory, not UNTIL(P, t_a), means that P was not realized at all moments prior to t_a but that there was some moment before t_a at which P was not realized ("He awakened before noon"). The ambiguity of negating "S since t_a" can be similarly explained. The contrary, SINCE (notS, t_a), means that notS was realized at all moments between t_a and the time of speech ("There was no rain at all between Wednesday and now"); the contradictory, notSINCE (S, t_a), means that S was not realized at every moment between t_a and the time of speech but that there was some moment between t_a and n at which S was not realized ("The rain has not been continuous since Wednesday").

Second, a durative statement entails that there is an interval during every moment of which the statement is realized. Let E represent a temporally indefinite statement about a momentary event. If a momentary event does *not* occur, we might say there is an interval during every moment of which notE is realized. According to this view, a nonevent resembles a state or process with respect to its temporal shape. Consequently, UNTIL(notE, t_a) is an acceptable formula, although UNTIL(E, t_a) is not.

Third, notUNTIL(E, t_a) is not acceptable because UNTIL(E, t_a) is not acceptable. Consequently, "notE until t_a" can only be understood as the contrary, not the contradictory of "E until t_a," so the negation of "until" sentences involving momentary events does not lead to ambiguity: "He didn't arrive until noon" can only be understood to mean the contrary—that his arrival did not occur before noon—and not the contradictory—that his arriving did not continue throughout all moments before noon. For the case of the negation of "since" sentences involving momentary events, the contradictory, notSINCE (E, t_a), which is equivalent to $G_{t_a}(\text{not}P_n(E))$, provides the only acceptable combination with a momentary event.

The formulations in (57) deal with some of the problems discovered in characterizing "until" and "since." There are others, however. Sentences like "It didn't last until noon" are not ambiguous, even though "last" is nonmomentary. We have only the contradictory interpretation, "It ended before noon," and not the contrary, "It began lasting after noon." This apparent exception to the rule is attributable to the aspectual verb "last," which has a special meaning as "not end" (see (65) below). Consequently, the contrary, UNTIL(notLAST(P), t_a), becomes UNTIL(END(P), t_a), or "It ended until noon," which is unacceptable. So only the contradictory of "It lasted until noon" is available as an interpretation of "It didn't last until noon." Durative verbs that entail not ending are an exception to the general rule that the negation of statements denoting a process "until t_a" are ambiguous, but the exception does not require revision or supplementation of (57).

This general rule also applies when the relatum is an event rather than a definite time (see (58) below): "Don't drink until Dino arrives" is ambiguous. However, "Don't drink until you are drunk" is only humorously ambiguous—the contrary, "Don't drink before you are drunk," is not practicably actionable, leaving only the contradictory, "Stop drinking before you are drunk." Here again the apparent exception to the general rule arises from the meanings of the related clauses, not from alternative senses of "until."

Another problem arises from the fact that "He didn't sleep until noon" is not two-ways ambiguous, but three-ways. The two interpretations considered above were "He was awake until noon" (the contrary) and "He awoke before noon" (the contradictory). Since it is acceptable to say "He didn't sleep until noon, he slept until one," there must be a third interpretation, "He awoke after noon." The problem here is not restricted to temporal expressions. "There are not ten people in this room" can be interpreted to mean that there are either more than ten or less than ten. "He didn't sleep until noon" can mean that he awoke either before or after noon. Still, people interpret it to mean that he awoke before noon more naturally than they interpret it to mean that he awoke after noon. The reason is that the affirmative, "He slept until noon," entails only "He slept at least until noon." The contradictory of "He slept at least until noon" would be "He awoke at least before noon," which greatly reduces the salience of the third possible interpretation of "He didn't sleep until noon," namely, that he slept until after noon. The problem here does not seem to be that (57) is incorrect; it has something to do with the law of trichotomy for numbers. To define "until" in such a way as to eliminate this problem would be to explain too much.

The most questionable part of the analysis given above is the assumption that notE can be treated as if it were P. If this is taken to mean that "He didn't awaken" is synonymous with "He slept," there are difficulties immediately: "He slept soundly" is not equivalent to "He didn't awaken soundly"; "He slept in the hotel" is not equivalent to "He didn't awaken in the hotel"; "He slept before he left" is not equivalent to "He didn't awaken before he left." Even if the claim is taken to mean that "He didn't awaken" is synonymous with "He remained asleep," the problems persist: "He remained asleep to enjoy his dreams" is not equivalent to "He didn't awaken to enjoy his dreams." It must be emphasized that it is only with respect to temporal matters that notE can be taken to resemble P.

Next, consider the use of "until" and "since" to relate P temporally to an activity described by some statement S rather than to a definite time t_a: in "He slept until it rained" or "He arrived since it rained," "until" and "since" are used as connectives, not as prepositions. We take these sentences to mean "He slept until the time at which it started raining" and "He arrived since the time at which it stopped raining." "Start" and "stop" are aspectual verbs that we will not analyze until 6.2.5, but we can anticipate that analysis in order to round out the discussion of temporal connectives:

(58)   UNTIL(P, S): $(\exists t)[R_t(S) \ \& \ Q_t(\text{not}S) \ \& \ Q_t(P)]$

      SINCE(S′, S): $(\exists t)[R_t(S) \ \& \ G_t(\text{not}S) \ \& \ F_t(P_n(S'))]$

These formulas differ from those given for "until" in (57a) and for "since" in (57′) only insofar as the beginning and ending of the clause S that serves as the relatum is substituted for the definite time t_a. Note that SINCE(P, S) is vague as to whether P lasted throughout the entire interval from t to n; "He has slept since it rained" can mean either that he slept and awakened during the interval or that he slept continuously throughout the interval. "Ever since" is often used to remove that vagueness, if continuous P is intended:

    EVERSINCE(P, S): $(\exists t)[R_t(S) \ \& \ G_t(\text{not}S) \ \& \ G_t(P)]$.

When speakers want to indicate that a process continued throughout a bounded interval, they can also use a from–until construction that is similar in many respects to the from–to construction used as a spatial locative. On this analogy, the simplest way to construe "P from t_a until t_b" would be as

UNTIL(EVERSINCE$(P, t_a), t_b)$, or $Q_{t_b}(G_{t_a}(P))$.

When expanded, this becomes

$$(t)[t < t_b \supset R_t(t_a < t \supset R_t(P))] \equiv (t)[t_a < t < t_b \supset R_t(P)].$$

This formulation is also appropriate for sentences of the form "P from t_a until n," where n would replace t_b. Sentences of the form "P since t_a" have an implicit "now" bounding them to the time of utterance, so that they are often understood as meaning "P from t_a until n" but this relation does not always hold: "He has been dead since yesterday" would not be understood as equivalent to "He has been dead from yesterday until now."

6.2.4   Tense Operators

"Tense" means the system of adding inflections to verbs in order to indicate the time—in terms of the A-series "past," "present," "future"—of the action or state. This definition slides over a host of difficult questions, some of which we will discuss below, but let us begin by noting that the A-series is defined in terms of the privileged moment "now." In order to indicate whether a verb denotes an action in the past, present, or future, a speaker must utter a sentence that expresses the indication. The sentence must be uttered "now" and must express past, present, or future with respect to the time it is uttered. If a sentence is recorded or written down and preserved to some later time, events that were future when it was uttered will have become past, so a sentence that expressed a true proposition at the time it was uttered may well have been falsified during the interim. A speaker who says "The phone is ringing" truthfully at time t will not lightly accept the charge that he is not telling the truth ten minutes later when the phone is no longer ringing. A sentence is to be evaluated at the time and in the context in which it is used. So the "now" that is the basis of the tense system is not the time at which the sentence is processed by the receiver but the time at which it is uttered by the speaker. In particular, the tense markers that are built into the sentence must be understood relative to the time that the sentence itself is uttered.

Confusions about the time relative to which a sentence is to be interpreted are largely the result of technological advances—writing, printing, audio recording, and the like—that enable us to preserve sentences beyond their occasion of use. If we hold firmly to ordinary conversation as the situation in which sentences are used, "now" is the most accessible moment of time to take as a point of origin for temporal relations. In spoken discourse, "now" is the time of utterance; "now" is the same for speaker and listener; "now" is the time of encoding and decoding the message. For all these reasons the time of utterance plays a central role in anchoring the tense system.

To speak of the time of utterance as a particular moment is to adopt a convenient fiction. It may take several moments to execute an utterance. "It is going to explode . . . , didn't it?" illustrates the idealization involved in identifying the time of utterance with the particular moment "now." Thus it is very difficult to state the precise time in a sentence; by the end of the sentence the time will have changed by a few seconds. Still, we will speak of the time of utterance as "now."

A similar idealization is frequently adopted when one speaks of events as occurring at some moment t, since even brief events usually require an interval of time for their occurrence. This idealization reflects a psychological aspect of the concept of time. As we noted in discussing the difference between "when" and "while," one can think of an event either as occupying an interval or as being a durationless occurrence. Many languages, like English, reflect this distinction in their systems of tense—"the present time" sometimes refers to a single moment and sometimes to a more extended period including that moment.

A second time that is important to the tense system is the time of the event that is being identified or referred to. If t_s is the time of utterance, then the time of an event, t_e, can be either past, present, or future with respect to t_s. Imagine a very simple tense system in which one inflection is given to the verb if $t_e < t_s$, another inflection if $t_e = t_s$, and a third inflection if $t_e > t_s$. In such a system, the relative order of t_e and t_s on the time line could be represented simply by the tense operators (let $t_s = n$):

(59)   Past: $P_n(S) \equiv \text{BEFORE}(S, n)$
        Present: $R_n(S) \equiv \text{AT}_t(S, n)$
        Future: $F_n(S) \equiv \text{AFTER}(S, n)$

where S denotes a description of the event at t_e. This system would correspond to the tense operators used by Rescher and Urquhart (1971, chap. 5).

The threefold distinction of (59) is conceptual. It does not correspond to the tense system of English, which has inflections only for the twofold distinction, past versus nonpast. We must keep clearly in mind the differences between them.

Most discussions of the grammar of tense in English include much more than the simple distinction between past and nonpast.

(60)

		Nonprogressive	*Progressive*
Nonperfect			
	Past	He worked	He was working
	Nonpast	He works	He is working
	Modal	He will work	He will be working

	Nonprogressive	*Progressive*
Perfect		
Past	He had worked	He had been working
Nonpast	He has worked	He has been working
Modal	He will have worked	He will have been working

In some languages these distinctions that English expresses by auxiliary verbs are expressed by suffixes on the main verb. The various headings—"progressive," "perfect," "past"—are more or less traditional and seem to have been chosen with some thought of the conceptual relations these surface tenses are generally used to express. As we have seen, the variety and complexity of the exceptions are great. Grammatically, it is probably safer to think of progressive as "be" + "-ing," perfect as "have" + "-ed," past as "-ed," and modal (or future) as "will," with present being the absence of any of these special markers.

Since the tense operators in (59) give us only three alternatives and the array in (60) distinguishes twelve, it is obvious that, as they stand, the operators are insufficient to account for the variety of forms that are usually called tenses in English. A simple way to enrich the operators would be to use them in combination. For example, $P_n(P_n(S))$ applies the past operator twice and so might be expected to give us the past-in-the-past. The result of this double operation is $(\exists t, t')[t' < t < n \ \& \ R_t(R_{t'}(S))]$, which orders the times and says (S was realized at t') was realized at t. Rescher and Urquhart seem to feel that this result is an intuitively acceptable translation of the past perfect, and for many purposes they may be right. It appears to us, however, to lack the completive sense that is usually associated with these linguistic forms. But even if $P_n P_n$ is taken as an acceptable correlate of the perfect, it is not clear how this device should be used to account for the progressive, nor how a grammar would account for the complex relations between such formulas for conceptual tense and the multiple surface forms that can express them in English.

A grammar might also explain how tenses and time adverbials are matched —why "He is arriving yesterday," "He arrived tomorrow," and many other possible combinations are not acceptable. One school of thought (Chomsky, 1965) holds that tense is first assigned to the verb, then the choice of permissible time adverbials is determined by the tense; another school (McCawley, 1971) holds that a time adverbial is first selected, then tense markers are assigned to the verb by copying them from the adverb. Since we have approached the problem from a conceptual rather than a linguistic point of view, it seems to us that the conceptual information underlying both tense and time adverbials is very similar, and that the problem is not which imposes selectional restrictions on the other but how to ensure that the two mechanisms can identify or refer to the same time.

We assume time indices are applied to a conceptual representation of some real or imagined episode. We have finessed the difficult problem of characterizing how that representation is constructed, but any representation must have a serial structure in which the date or ordinal position of a particular event can be identified or referred to. If two devices—an adverb and a tense, say— are used in a syntactic construction that makes them both apply to the same event, then it must be conceptually possible for them both to apply to the same event. In the absence of explicit rules for what is conceptually possible, this comment does little to unravel the enormous complexities of temporal identification and reference in English, but it does suggest that considerably more than syntax is involved.

In (59) we defined tense operators in terms of adverbials. This formulation might suggest that we believe that the adverbial is chosen first and that it then imposes selectional restrictions on the tense markers. The particular formulation of (59), however, is an accident resulting from the fact that we happened to discuss adverbials before we discussed tense. We assume that what come first conceptually are the statement-forming operators P, R, and F. That we use these operators to define both time adverbials and tense operators means that we believe the two mechanisms can be coordinated conceptually; it does not mean that we believe they must be introduced in a particular order.

For the purpose of exploring the problem in more detail, let us develop one version of the suggestion in (59) far enough to discover its limitations. Suppose that S is "He arrive," where the verb is given without a tense marker to make it seem tenseless. Then (59) might suggest that adverbial operators are first applied to S, yielding something like "He arrive before now," "He arrive at now," and "He arrive after now." We assume that the information ($t < n$, $t = n$, and $t > n$) introduced by the adverbials can then be used to put tense markers on the verb. The simple tense markers would yield "He arrived before now," "He arrives at now," and "He will arrive after now." These tense markers are obligatory in English and have the effect of making the adverbial phrase redundant. So we can further assume that these redundant and awkward adverbials are erased transformationally, leaving us with the usual "He arrived," "He arrives," and "He will arrive."

Whatever the virtues of this account, it suffers the fatal defect of explaining the wrong thing. The basic distinction in the English tense system is twofold, not threefold. It can distinguish past from nonpast; it cannot distinguish the nonpast present from the nonpast future. The trouble begins to appear when we stop to realize that the simple present, as in "He arrives," is more often than not understood as habitual or future, not as "He arrives right now." Of course, there are situations in which the so-called present tense is used to mean "right now"—by a witness describing an ongoing episode, in narratives, in stage directions—but it usually occurs more naturally with such adverbs as "regularly" or "today" rather than with "right now." When people want to communicate the "right now" sense, they generally use the present progressive, "He is arriving."

But to substitute "He is arriving" for "He arrives" to express the conceptual present tense compounds the syntactic difficulties without resolving the basic problem. "He is arriving" is not past: "He is arriving yesterday" is unacceptable. But it can be either present or future: "He is arriving right now" and "He is arriving tomorrow" are both acceptable. What we have is a division between past, "was arriving," and nonpast, "is arriving." "English *grammar*," writes Joos (1964), "has *no device whatever* for cutting future time away from the time of speaking." How does a listener decide between the present and future interpretation? According to Joos, "if the hearer has sufficient reason to believe that the sentence would be false if taken to apply to the time of listening, he subtracts that . . . now he has left—and he *always will* have left as a solid residue—reference to future time" (pp. 135-136). If the speaker says "I am speaking German," the listener has sufficient reason to believe the sentence would be false if taken to apply to the time of speaking, so he should assume that the speaker intends future reference—"I am speaking German when I read my paper at the conference in Bonn next week."

Palmer (1965) points out that in addition to present and future reference the present progressive can also have a habitual interpretation: "He's working right now," "He's working tomorrow," and "He's always working." The difference between the habitual present, "He always works," and the habitual present progressive, "He's always working," seems to have something to do with duration of the activity. "He always works when the boss appears" suggests a more limited duration of working than "He's always working when the boss appears." But whatever the difference is, it is not appropriate to contrast the present tense as habitual with the present progressive as the actual present tense.

Without going further into the subtleties or complexities of these verb phrases it should be clear that the threefold distinction between past, present, and future in (59) is not simply reflected in English grammar, which must constantly be rescued by adverbials in order to make important conceptual distinctions between present, future, and habitual activities. There is still another lesson to learn from (59), namely, that two reference moments, t_s and t_e, are not enough to express all the temporal relations of (60).

Sentences in the past perfect, like "It had spoiled," introduce a third reference time between t_e and t_s, between the time of spoiling and the time of utterance. If we represent this intermediate time as t_r, the time point of reference, then the past perfect orders the three points: $t_e < t_r < t_s$. As we noted above, we can obtain this ordering by applying the past operator, P_n, twice. Reichenbach (1947) has argued, however, that three points do not constitute some idiosyncrasy of the past perfect but are involved in all the tenses. For example, "He works right now" would be represented as $t_e = t_r = t_s$. "He worked yesterday" would be $t_e = t_r < t_s$. And so on. (As J. J. Katz, 1972, points out, the past (or future) operator moves t_r to the left (right) on the time line, and the perfect operator moves t_e to the left of t_r.) Time lines of the sort Reichenbach used to illustrate his analysis are shown in figure 6.3. The corresponding progressives—I am agreeing, I have been agreeing, I was agreeing, I had been agreeing, I will be agreeing, I will have been agreeing—are given the

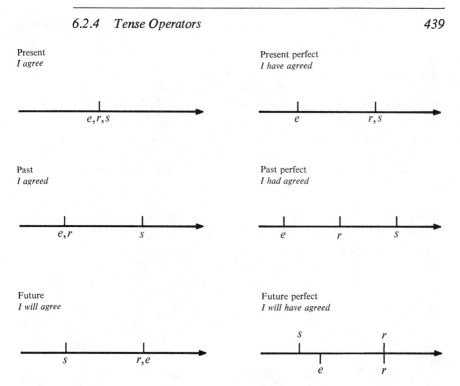

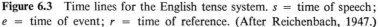

Figure 6.3   Time lines for the English tense system. s = time of speech; e = time of event; r = time of reference. (After Reichenbach, 1947.)

same temporal orderings, but the time of the event, t_e, is extended to indicate an interval.

The difference between the simple past and the present perfect is, according to this analysis, a difference in the time of reference, t_r; the relation between t_e and t_s is the same for both. This difference is subtle. To borrow an example from Chafe (1973), "Steve just fell in the swimming pool" and "Steve has just fallen in the swimming pool" are almost interchangeable. Clark and Stafford (1969) found that college students tend to simplify the verb group in their memory of sentences, omitting perfective and progressive markers that had been present in the sentences they were asked to remember. Such omissions could be accounted for in terms of forgetting either syntactic or semantic features of the original sentences. However, there was a strong tendency to confuse the simple past with the present perfect ("I agreed" with "I have agreed") and the past progressive with the present perfect progressive ("I was agreeing" with "I have been agreeing"). These confusions seem to require a semantic explanation.

As Palmer (1965) argues, the fact that an event occurring in the past can be reported in either the simple past or the present perfect shows that they indicate overlapping periods of time. What determines the choice between them? According to Palmer, the present perfect is chosen when the event reported has special relevance to the present situation. For example, a child who says "I've finished my homework" may be asking to be allowed to go out and play; "I finished my homework," on the other hand, is merely a report of a past event. Or, to return to Chafe's example, if you saw someone running toward the pool and asked "Why are you running?" he would more naturally reply "Steve's fallen in (and needs help)" than "Steve fell in." This sense of current relevance that the present perfect conveys is indicated in figure 6.3 by placing the point of reference, t_r, together with the point of speech, t_s. That is, if you like, why it is called the present perfect form.

The simple past takes definite time reference more naturally than the present perfect. "I finished my homework at five o'clock" is acceptable, whereas "I have finished my homework at five o'clock" suggests that the task was not merely to finish the work but to finish it precisely at the appointed time of five o'clock. Adding "at five o'clock" to the simple past requires no special contextual assumptions, so reference to a definite moment t_a seems implicit: $t_a < n$ & $R_{t_a}(S)$. Adding "at five o'clock" to the present perfect, however, introduces a need for contextual support, so there seems to be no implicit reference to a definite time: $(\exists t)\ [t < n$ & $R_t(S)]$. This would justify placing the point of reference, t_r, at the time of the event, t_e, for the simple past in figure 6.3.

The past perfect combines these two operators. The result can be ambiguous. For example, does "I had finished at five o'clock" mean that the finish occurred at five o'clock or before five o'clock? It is not clear whether "at five o'clock" is intended to denote the event time ($5 = t_e < t_r < t_s$) or the reference time ($t_e < 5 = t_r < t_s$). These interpretations correspond to different orders of application of the operators. If we apply the perfect to the past, we obtain

$$(\exists t)\ [t < n\ \&\ R_t(t_a < n\ \&\ R_{t_a}(S))] \equiv (\exists t)[t_a < t < n\ \&\ R_t(R_{t_a}(S))],$$

which corresponds to interpreting t_e as "at five o'clock." On the other hand, if we apply the past to the perfect, we obtain

$$t_a < n\ \&\ R_{t_a}((\exists t)[t < n\ \&\ R_t(S)]) \equiv (\exists t)[t < t_a < n\ \&\ R_{t_a}(R_t(S))],$$

which corresponds to interpreting t_r as "at five o'clock."

If two or more sentoids are combined in a sentence, their tenses must be adjusted to secure agreement. Rules governing this agreement are called sequence-of-tense rules and are sometimes stated: make a verb in a subordinate clause agree logically with the verb in the main clause. Although there are many exceptions to the rules in English, the general idea is that if the main verb is marked as past, the subordinate verb should also be marked as past, and if the main verb is not marked as past, the subordinate verb should not be either. For example, "He smiled as she entered" is correct, but "He smiled as she enters" is poor; "He will smile when he sees her" is correct, but "He will smile when he saw her" is poor.

Reichenbach (1947) suggests that "we can interpret these rules as the

principle that, although the events referred to in the clauses may occupy different time points, the reference point should be the same for all clauses" (p. 293),
a principle that demands the "permanence of the reference point." To take one
of Reichenbach's examples, "I had mailed the letter when John came" combines
a past perfect with a simple past. "I had mailed the letter when John has come,"
on the other hand, is poor; it combines a past perfect with a present perfect.
Using the representations given in figure 6.3, the three time points for the correct sentence can be lined up as

(61)   I had mailed the letter: $t_e \ldots \ldots .t_r \ldots \ldots .t_s$
         John came: $t_e = t_r \ldots . .t_s$

The corresponding arrangement for the incorrect sentence is

(61′)   I had mailed the letter: $t_e \ldots \ldots .t_r \ldots \ldots .t_s$
         John has come: $t_e \ldots . .t_r = t_s$

The times of reference are the same for both clauses in the correct sentence;
they are different for the incorrect sentence.

As Reichenbach, admits, English does not always respect the permanence of
the reference point. "He was happier yesterday than he will be tomorrow" combines $t_e = t_r < t_s$ with $t_s < t_r = t_e$, and, since there is no alternative to lining
up t_s for all clauses, there is no way the times of reference for these two clauses
can coincide. In such cases, Reichenbach says, the rule of the permanence of
the reference point is replaced by the more general rule of the "positional use of
the reference point." That is, when the three time points for each clause are
lined up, the ordinal positions of the reference points determine the tenses that
can be used. Permanence of t_r is thus a special case of positional use of t_r, where
both events have the same t_r.

According to this positional-use rule, "before" and "after" should relate reference times, not event times. But consider such sentences as "He will discover
everything before he has finished." The main clause has the temporal indices
$t_s < t_r = t_e$ (or $t_s = t_r < t_e$; Reichenbach accepts both for the future forms),
and the second has $t_e < t_r = t_s$. When these are aligned on t_s the reference point
for "he will discover everything" is either after or the same as the reference
point for "he has finished," not before it. The positional-use rule would block
"before" in this context, yet the sentence is acceptable. Perhaps t_s for the subordinate clause could be omitted from the analysis, freeing "he has finished" to
move wherever it likes—in this case, to the future of "he will discover everything." But then it would not be clear why "He will discover everything before
he had finished" is incorrect. Huddleston (1969) claims that two events related
by "before" or "after" must both occur in the past, or both in the present, or
both in the future. Although "he has finished" would normally denote a past
event (or a present state), the main clause denotes a future event, so the subordinate clause must also refer to the future.

The reference point is valuable to indicate that some event is further in the
past than (or not as far in the future as) another event. To borrow an example

from Gallagher (1970), "The man who was on the porch was in the garden" is acceptable English to most people, although it seems to say the man was in two places at the same time. Any ambiguity can be settled by the perfect: "The man who was on the porch had been in the garden." Or it could be settled by an adverb: "The man who was on the porch was in the garden before that."

Perhaps one should, with J. J. Katz (1972), use the point of reference only with perfectives, where it can be thought of as the time of some "undescribed event" occurring later than the event described. "He had earned the money," for example, invites a further event description—"before he spent it," perhaps—where t_r can be taken as the time of this later, undescribed event. With "He earned the money," on the other hand, one does not feel that some other event has been left undescribed, so there is no comparable argument for introducing t_r.

This sketch of English tense is obviously incomplete. We have made no attempt to indicate syntactic transformations that would be required to relate formulations of conceptual tense to the surface structures of sentences with tense markers. We have not provided any mechanisms to get the correct adverbials and tenses together. Our central concern is with the temporal structure that a language user builds for the events described in a sentence; tense provides one mechanism for relating that structure to "now," to the time of utterance. We will leave it at that and turn next to other temporal structures and relations that the language can express.

6.2.5   Aspect

Linguists usually distinguish between tense and aspect when describing the grammar of temporal relations. In principle the distinction is clear enough. Tense has to do with grammatical devices whereby the time of occurrence of a referent event is related to the time of utterance. Aspect has to do with the time course of the referent event itself, independent of its time of occurrence. Thus, tense is deictic, aspect is not. For example, "depart" has the sense that something was at a given place up until some time at which it moved away from that place. Such is the temporal shape of a departure, or, in Vendler's (1967) phrase, the "time schema" of the verb "depart." The temporal shape of departure is independent of the time at which it occurs, whether before, during, or after the time at which it is referred to.

When this distinction is imposed on natural languages, the hypothetical independence of tense and aspect is less apparent. In actual usage the two systems merge (Lyons, 1968, p. 316), leaving a grammarian with such questions as whether the English perfect ("John has walked to school") is better classified as a relative tense or an aspect. We have little to contribute to the resolution of such complex questions. We prefer to start from an analysis of the temporal relations to be expressed. What we should learn from the grammarian's difficulties is that the temporal shape of an event is not determined solely by the verb that is used but can be supplemented and modulated by other devices.

The progressive is usually interpreted as denoting an extension of the reference time to include an interval, which modulates the aspect of the verb. But the effect of the progressive differs depending on the temporal shape of the event or process that the verb denotes. Consider sentences where present reference is intended. "Arrive" is an event verb; "He is arriving (right now)" seems to expand a momentary event into a process filling an interval. "Hit" is also an event verb, but "He is hitting it (right now)" suggests repeated occurrences of the event. "Work" is a process verb; since working is understood to fill an interval, "He is working (right now)" seems more natural than "He works (right now)," although there is no aspectual difference between them. The effect of the progressive, therefore, depends on the time schema of the verb it is applied to.

So it is necesary to characterize the temporal shapes of verbs. Compare "travel" and "reach." People say "Shadlow traveled until noon" or "Harriet reached Cambridge in three hours," but not "Shadlow traveled in three hours" or "Harriet reached Cambridge until noon." Reaching is an event; traveling is a process. One of the basic facts about aspect is that events and processes have different temporal shapes.

In order to deal with this difference we might introduce a semantic marker, Momentary, to distinguish verbs like "reach," which can be combined with momentary time indicators, from verbs like "travel," which cannot. For example, if "travel" were marked as —Momentary, it might enable us to account for the oddity of "Shadlow traveled in three hours"; the phrase "in three hours" identifies a particular moment by relating it to some earlier moment, and —Momentary "travel" would not combine with momentary temporal locatives. This solution is clearly too simple, since it leaves us with the question of why "Shadlow traveled to Cambridge in three hours" or "Shadlow will travel in three hours" are acceptable even though they combine nonmomentary "travel" with momentary "in three hours." We would not want to define "travel" one way and "travel to destination" and "will travel" another. We might try to formulate rules for combining certain categories of verbs with certain expressions of time or duration in such a way that aspectual information is associated not with the verb but with the predicate phrase or the whole sentence (Verkuyl, 1972).

We recognize two types of action verbs, those that describe processes ("travel") and those that describe events ("reach"), and we will continue to represent simple statements about momentary events by E and simple statements about nonmomentary (durative) states or processes by P. (For convenience, statements about transient states—"in the house," "is ill," "is a candidate" —can be included in the class of statements denoted by P. The time course of permanent states—"is an animal," "is mortal"—is obvious and will not be discussed.) In simple sentences, event verbs indicate E statements with momentary time adverbials and process verbs indicate P statements with durational adverbials. But if an event verb occurs with a durational adverbial, it can be interpreted iteratively ("He hit the punching bag until noon" indicates repeated hitting) and if a process verb occurs with a momentary adverbial, it can be interpreted as initial aspect ("He traveled in three hours" can indicate when he began traveling).

It would be natural to define a verb like "reach" in terms of a verb like "travel" (see sec. 7.1), in which case we would need to add certain conditions to "travel" in order to characterize the kind of traveling that is called reaching. For one thing, "reach" should include a provision for the place to which the traveling occurs, since it is a transitive verb. But if we define "reach" simply in terms of "travel to," we will have ignored the aspectual differences between reaching and traveling. Contrast "Harriet finished reaching Cambridge in three hours," which sounds odd, with "Harriet finished traveling to Cambridge in three hours," which is clumsy but not unacceptable English. Another test, also borrowed from Dowty (1972b), is that "Harriet almost traveled to Cambridge" is ambiguous to most people, since it could mean either "Harriet didn't travel" or "Harriet stopped traveling before she got to Cambridge." "Harriet almost reached Combridge," on the other hand, is not ambiguous, since "reach" entails "Harriet traveled."

What we must add to "travel to" in order to capture the meaning of "reach" is that "reach" asserts the existence of some moment t such that "Harriet is in Cambridge" is false at $t - 1$ and true at t. That is, we must impose a temporal shape on "travel to" in order to define "reach"; we must change it from a process verb to an event verb.

What we have said so far would define "arrive" as well as "reach." Certainly these two verbs are similar in many respects, yet there are some puzzling differences. For example, "arrive" differs from "reach" in that the destination can be omitted if it is understood from context; "arrive" is intransitive. A more important difference for semantic analysis is that "x arrived at y" is understood to mean that y is the destination of x, whereas x can reach an intermediate point y on the way to a destination z. Thus, for most people "Harriet arrived in Cambridge for three hours" sounds better than "Harriet reached Cambridge for three hours." When you arrive somewhere, you stay for a while; when you reach somewhere, you may or may not stay. So here is another difference in the temporal shapes of verbs.

These examples stir up enough problems to suggest the complexity of aspectual relations. In order to decompose the temporal components of such verbs, we require expressions like "at," "before," "after," "until," and "since" and verbs like "happen," "begin," "continue," and "end." Taken together, these enable us to say that something "began before" something else, "continued until" something else, and so on. Given a semantic analysis of these expressions, we could use them to make explicit the temporal shapes of English verbs.

We introduced these adverbs in 6.2.3; "happen" will be discussed in 6.3.3. Our major lack at this point is an analysis of "begin" and "end," which we must try to provide. Before we formulate the abstract concepts BEGIN and END, however, we should pause to consider the grammar of the English verbs "begin" and "end" and their equivalents, not only to guide our semantic analysis but also to evaluate our assumption that the concepts underlying these verbs are sufficiently important to earn them special status in the language.

"Begin" has stimulated discussion within the context of transformational theories of grammar because of its unusual privileges of occurrence in combination with other verbs. Chomsky (1965) once proposed—in order to account for differences between such verbs as "persuade" and "expect"—that the base component of English grammar must contain a rule that permits a predicate phrase to consist of a verb and a sentence, in addition to rules that permit a predicate phrase to consist of a verb and a noun phrase and that permit the noun phrase to consist of a noun and a sentence. For example, "I expect John will be examined by a specialist" would be analyzed as having a predicate phrase consisting of the verb "expect" plus the sentence "John will be examined by a specialist." The sentence can take various forms, like "I expect John to be examined by a specialist" or "I expected John's being examined by a specialist," where the sentential constituent is not literally a sentence in the surface structure; it is usually called a sentential complement. The verb-plus-sentence rule in the base component of the grammar provides for "verb-phrase complementation." Although noun-phrase complementation is obviously necessary in any adequate grammar of English, considerable doubt has been expressed as to whether verb-phrase complementation is also necessary. A review of this question has been provided by Stockwell, Schachter, and Partee (1973, chap. 8), who conclude that the distinction between noun-phrase and verb-phrase complementation "is not fully viable" (p. 513).

The verb "begin" became involved in this discussion because Chomsky (1962) and Rosenbaum (1967) included it as one of a small class of English verbs that allow what Rosenbaum called intransitive verb-phrase complementation. For example, in "Kenneth began to make trouble" we have the predicate phrase "began to make trouble," which might be analyzed in the deep structure as the verb "begin" plus the sentence "Kenneth made trouble." Transformational rules would delete the redundant "Kenneth" and change the sentence into an infinite or participial construction: "to make trouble" or "making trouble." The bulk of the verbs that Rosenbaum included in this class have a common aspectual theme (begin, cease, commence, complete, continue, finish, recommence, start), although several others do not (condescend, dare, decline, endeavor, hasten, manage, proceed, refuse).

The group of aspectual verbs is discussed in more detail by García (1967), who refers to them as "aspectual semi-auxiliaries" because they "share properties of both the true lexical verbs and the true auxiliaries" (p. 858). Considered as lexical verbs, they have the unusual property that the subject of the complement sentence must always be the same as the subject of the aspectual verb and must always be deleted: "Kenneth began for Kenneth to make trouble" or "Kenneth began for Morton to make trouble" are clearly unacceptable. Moreover, these aspectual verbs impose very weak constraints on the sentences they can take as complements: "The well began to be deep" is odd, so verbs that denote persisting states should probably be excluded on semantic grounds, but García argues that there is nothing syntactically objectionable about "He began to be dead" and similar sentences. The aspectuals can also have odd effects when used with verbs describing momentary events ("The car began to hit the tree" suggests temporal expansion by high-speed photography), but again the objections are semantic or pragmatic, not syntactic.

Since "begin" seems to impose no syntactic restrictions—it can be inserted into any sentence—García is led to compare it to the tense auxiliary verbs "have" and "be" and to the modal auxiliary verbs "will," "shall," "can," "may," "ought," "must," and perhaps "dare" and "need." She points out that "begin" behaves like auxiliaries under passivization, whereas the nonaspectual verbs in Rosenbaum's list do not: "Many people began to read his books" goes into "His books began to be read by many people," just as "Many people have read his books" goes into "His books have been read by many people," whereas if "Many people condescended to read his books" is transformed in the same way, it goes into the very different sentence "His books condescended to be read by many people." Unlike auxiliary verbs, however, aspectuals require suppletive "do" in questions and negatives: "Did she begin to fight?" and "She didn't begin to fight," versus "Has she fought?" and "She hasn't fought." "Begin she to fight?" and "She begann't to fight" are not available in normal English, and "She didn't begin to fight" says something very different from "She began not to fight." Moreover, unlike "have" and "be," aspectuals can be combined in any order: "He began to finish washing the dishes" or "He finished beginning to wash the dishes" or even "He stopped finishing to begin washing the dishes." These differences are sufficient to cast doubt on the classification of aspectuals as true auxiliaries.

García concludes that there is not a dichotomy between the major verbs and auxiliary verbs but rather a continuum from tense markers to tense auxiliaries to modal auxiliaries to aspectuals to lexical verbs. It is clear that tense markers should be accounted for in the grammar of the language and that the lexical verbs are to be chosen freely from the lexicon, but intermediate levels might be allocated to the grammar or the lexicon or both. Many of the problems that aspectuals pose for syntactic analysis stem from their intermediate position on this linguistic continuum. García suggests a simple way to account for the behavior of aspectuals under passivization, their lack of selectional restrictions, their need for "do" suppletion, and their iterativity: "All that is needed is to regard *begin* and its group as verbs taking sentences not as their objects, but as their subjects. In other words, they can be thrown into the class of *happen*, *seem*, and *appear*" (p. 867).

We will comment in 6.3.3 on the fact that "happen" can take a sentence as its deep structure subject and on its lack of selectional restrictions. "Happen" also resembles the aspectuals with respect to passivization, "do" suppletion, and iterativity ("John appeared to happen to seem to be clever"). A deep structure like "(Kenneth makes trouble)s happen," where the sentential complement is represented as the subject of "happen," is transformed into the surface structure "Kenneth happened to make trouble" by inserting "happen" into its own subordinate clause and changing the subordinate verb to an infinitive. Since this syntactic machinery is available for subject noun-phrase complementation in the case of "happen," it is simple enough to use it also for the aspectuals: a deep structure like "(Kenneth makes trouble)$_s$ begin" would be transformed in the same way to the surface structure "Kenneth began to make trouble" by inserting "begin" into its own subordinate clause and changing the subordinate verb to an infinitive.

Although the "happen" solution for aspectuals gives a formally correct representation, García cautions that the subject-predicate relation in "Kenneth began to make trouble" is intuitively different from the subject-predicate relation in "Kenneth happened to make trouble." On the other hand, this difference seems to vanish between sentences like "It began to rain" and "It happened to rain," or "There began to be a commotion" and "There happened to be a commotion," where the dummy subjects "it" and "there" clearly come from "It rained" and "There was a commotion"—which makes implausible the alternative analysis: "It began (it rained)$_s$" or "There began (there was a commotion)$_s$," where the sentential complement is represented as the object of "begin."

Perlmutter (1970) argues that two verbs "begin" should be recognized: an intransitive "begin" that resembles "happen" in taking sentential subjects in deep structure and a transitive "begin" that resembles "try" in taking complements as objects, with the constraint that the subject of transitive "begin" (or "try") and the subject of the sentential complement must be identical. According to Perlmutter's analysis, "It began to rain" would have a deep structure "(It rained)$_s$ begin" with a sentence as the subject of intransitive "begin," whereas "Kenneth began to make trouble" would have a deep structure "Kenneth begin (Kenneth makes trouble)$_{NP}$" with the complement as the object of transitive "begin." The transitive "begin" takes only animate subjects and its object is not a sentence but a noun phrase (which can, of course, have a sentential constituent).

The fact that "begin" can be used either as a transitive or as an intransitive verb is not a novel insight. We have intransitive uses like "Life begins at forty" and transitive uses like "Carl began the discussion." Since we have much the same relation between "Carl began the discussion" and "The discussion began" that we find between such sentences as "Freeman grew the flowers" and "The flowers grew," or "Tom moved the boulder" and "The boulder moved," we assume that some general convention is required for representing these verbs that permits deletion of their agents (see secs. 6.3 and 7.1). That is, the difference between the two kinds of "begin" is not unique to "begin" but is required for a variety of other verbs. (To anticipate, we assume that the conditions are divided into two parts: the first condition, that something happens for the first time, is essential; the second, that something was done that caused the happening, is optional in the sense that if the agentive argument is not provided the condition is not applied.)

The grammatical problems posed by "begin" arise from the fact that unlike "grow" or "move" or other verbs that can take the object as the subject, "begin" can take a sentential complement as one of its arguments. The formula must be something like BEGIN$((x),$ S$)$, where the parentheses around the pointer to the animate beginner x indicate that it is optional, and S denotes a sentential constituent describing whatever began. When the object is a simple noun phrase—"the discussion," for example—S can be replaced by a pointer to the referent; when the object is a sentence complement, it will refer to a process that has a beginning (not to a momentary event that merely happens), so S can be replaced by P, a description of a process or state. When the actor is not indicated, therefore, we will have BEGIN$($P$)$.

"Begin" is a representative member of a class of aspectual verbs in English; others with a similar meaning are "commence," "recommence," "set about," "start." These verbs are interchangeable with "begin" in such sentences as

(62)   Harriet $\left\{\begin{array}{l}\text{began}\\\text{commenced}\\\text{recommenced}\\\text{set about}\\\text{started}\end{array}\right\}$ $\left\{\begin{array}{l}\text{traveling.}\\\text{to travel.}\\\text{her traveling.}\end{array}\right\}$

They are not mutually interchangeable in all contexts, since you can say "Harriet's traveling began" but not "Harriet's traveling set about," and you can say "Harriet started the engine" but not "Harriet began the engine," and you can say "Harriet began to be lonely," but "Harriet commenced to be lonely" is a bit odd. We take "begin" and "start" to be the important members of this group; the principal difference between them seems to be that "start" does not impose the like-subject constraint; "Harriet started Chuck working" is acceptable, but "Harriet began Chuck working" is awkward.

At the terminal end of an ongoing process, English offers a larger variety of lexical options: cease, complete, conclude, desist, discontinue, end, finish, halt, leave off, quit, stop, terminate, wind up. Ross (1972a) argues that, like "begin," some of these verbs have both a transitive and an intransitive use—"stop," for example—but that "finish" has only the transitive use and "cease" has only the intransitive use. That is to say, "It stopped/ceased being muggy" is acceptable, but not "It finished being muggy"; and "I suggested that they not talk anymore, so they stopped/finished" is acceptable, but not "I suggested that they not talk anymore, so they ceased." Our own intuitions about these sentences are less clear than Ross's, but if such differences exist, we assume they must reflect idiosyncrasies of usage—like the fact that "cease" is the only verb in this terminal group that admits the infinitive of the complement verb. There is, however, an important semantic difference between "finish" and "stop," so that sentences like "The wind finished blowing" or "The ball finished rolling" are not ordinarily used; some agentive condition seems obligatory for "finish," whereas it is optional for "stop" and "quit." The real syntactic sport among these terminal aspectuals is "end," which (unlike "stop") does not substitute for "begin" in such sentences as "Zeke began working" or "It began raining" or "Kenneth began making trouble," yet does take animate subjects in transitive uses, like "Carl ended the discussion," and also takes inanimate subjects in intransitive uses, like "Zeke's working ended" or "The rain ended."

It is apparent that these aspectual verbs have syntactic features that have not been fully understood. In undertaking a semantic analysis of beginning and ending aspects of action, therefore, we cannot hope also to provide a definitive account of the English verbs "begin" and "end." The formal conditions we will suggest for BEGIN and END do bear some general relation to the meanings of "begin," "end," and their close relatives, but our purpose is to define some plausible semantic operators that can be incorporated into verbs of action. The difficult task of unraveling the subtle differences among alternative aspectuals will not be attempted here. The important points to note in these syntactic analyses are that aspectuals as a class play a unique role in English grammar, and that their acceptance of sentential complements as subjects and objects justifies our use of statements, S, P, or E, as arguments of BEGIN and END.

The abstract notions that aspectuals express are probably well anchored to perceptual and behavioral phenomena starting early in life. Most children hear "Stop that" rather often, and comparable imperatives with "start" are probably not infrequent, beginning at an early age. Bloom (1970) reports the use of "more" and "no more" by children under two years to describe or command the recurrence or nonexistence of processes as well as things; it may be the case that "start" and "stop" develop out of the same conceptual matrix as affirmation and denial. We speculate that a child first notices the difference between persisting states and momentary changes; the happenings are then differentiated into events or processes according to their temporal shapes. Such distinctions would be achieved well before a child demonstrated any mastery of tense, auxiliary verbs, or time adverbials in his spontaneous speech; how these early, primitive concepts of processes and transient states coming to be and passing away accommodate to a child's expanding conception of time and temporal order is too difficult a question for idle speculation. Before any serious attempts are made to answer it, we need better formulations of the adult conceptual system that should result from the developmental process.

When an object begins or stops moving the transition is generally perceived as a momentary event. In dealing with events that can be conceived of as occurring at a single moment, we can use R_t to assert the existence of a particular moment at which they occur. Thus BEGIN and END must entail R_t, but they must say something more. A beginning has some sense that the event has not occurred before; an ending, that it does not occur thereafter. The operator R_t does not capture this difference; it is confined to a particular moment. R_t says merely that the state or process could be observed at some moment. In order to see what is required, consider how a state transition should be characterized abstractly.

Suppose we are concerned with a situation that is initially in some state Σ and, after remaining in Σ for a time, changes to Σ'. This state transition is

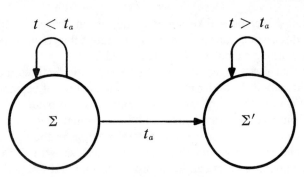

$$t < t_a \qquad\qquad\qquad t > t_a$$

$$\Sigma \qquad\qquad\qquad \Sigma'$$

$$t_a$$

Figure 6.4   State transition at time t_a.

illustrated in figure 6.4. If S is the temporally indefinite statement "situation in state Σ" and S' is the corresponding temporally indefinite statement "situation in state Σ'," we can think of the characteristic functions as

$$R_t(S): \quad \ldots 1111111111110000000000 \ldots$$
$$R_t(S'): \quad \ldots 0000000000011111111111 \ldots$$

where t_a is the first moment that the situation is in the new state. $R_t(S) = 1$ until the transition occurs; thereafter $R_t(S) = 0$ and $R_t(S') = 1$. As the situation has been described, S' is equivalent to notS, so we might describe the transition, as we did earlier, by

(63) $Q_{t_a}(S)\ \&\ R_{t_a}(\text{notS})\ \&\ G_{t_a}(\text{notS})$.

The moment t_a at which the situation shifts from Σ to Σ' is the moment at which its being in Σ ends. So we can consider (63) a candidate for the definition of END(S). A similar expression could be formed for BEGIN(S'); see (44) above.

Troubles with (63) begin to appear when we consider its contradictory, notEND(S). Since (63) calls for an unbroken string of ones to the left and an unbroken string of zeros to the right of t_a, a single exception to this pattern would suffice to establish the truth of notEND(S). That is clearly not what one would ordinarily mean by "S hasn't ended." That sentence would ordinarily mean there was an unbroken string of ones right up to the time of utterance. This proves that although (63) is a correct description of the situation depicted in figure 6.4 it is not a correct formulation for END(S).

When a person says that S ends, he is saying that there will be an unbroken string of zeros to the right of the moment t that was the last occurrence of S; he will not normally feel committed to any claims about how long S persisted before it ended, although he does presume that at *some* time S was the case. So we will introduce "end" as follows:

(64)   END(P): $(\exists t)[R_t(P)\ \&\ G_t(\text{notP})]$.

According to (64), "P ends" can be paraphrased roughly as "there was a time when P, but notP since then." If we consider the contradictory, we obtain

(65)   notEND(P): $(t)[R_t(P) \supset notG_t(notP)]$
$(t)[R_t(P) \supset F_t(P)] \equiv \text{LAST}(P)$

We might propose (65) as a definition of CONTINUE(P), since to say that P continued is much the same as to say that P did not end. This formulation would not be completely precise, however. Compare "Elsa didn't continue to work after dinner, but her working had not ended" with "Elsa's working had ended, but she continued to work after dinner," which is odd. "End" implies "not continue," but "not continue" does not imply "end." For "continue," therefore, we propose

(66)   CONTINUE(P): $(t)[R_t(P) \supset R_{t+1}(P)]$.

By induction on (66), of course, it becomes equivalent to (65), which accords with the intuition that if something does not end, it continues. But if we consider the contradictory of (66), we obtain

(67)   notCONTINUE(P): $(\exists t)[R_t(P) \,\&\, R_{t+1}(notP)]$.

Comparison of (67) with (64) reveals that although END implies notCONTINUE, notCONTINUE does not imply END, which accords with the intuition that something not continued at the moment may not have ended once and for all.

The universal quantifiers in (65) and (66) need not be assumed to range over all time. They will range over some finite interval T whose boundaries will be given, often imprecisely, by the context or by some accompanying adverbial phrase. How those boundaries are determined is an important problem, but we will avoid it for the present discussion.

Next, we must define "begin" in a manner analogous to "end." When one says that S begins, he is saying that there is an unbroken string of zeros to the left of the moment t that is the first occurrence of P; the speaker will not normally feel committed to any claims about how long P will persist after it begins, although he does presume that at *some* time notP was the case. Therefore,

(68)   BEGIN(P): $(\exists t)[Q_t(notP) \,\&\, R_t(P)]$.

Since BEGIN(P) presupposes that the antecedent state was notP, the correct formulation of the contradictory is

(69)   notBEGIN(P): $(t)[Q_t(notP) \supset R_t(notP)]$.

BEGIN(P) is not equivalent to END(notP), since the former says that P has not occurred before some time t, whereas the latter says that notP will not occur after t. BEGIN is based on knowledge of the past, END on the future.

At this point it may be useful to summarize and relate various formulas for temporal relations in terms of a decision table (table 6.2). In order to keep the table to a reasonable size, we have adopted three simplifying conventions: (a) we assume that the temporally indefinite statements have been checked for well-formedness (S) and their process (P) or event (E) character prior to entering this table; (b) we do not attempt to distinguish between conditions that are presupposed and conditions that are asserted—such distinctions are possi-

Table 6.2 A decision table for temporal relations.

	1	2	3	4	5	6	7	8	9	10	11	12	13	14	15	16	17	18	19	20
Conditions																				
c1. $R_{t\rightarrow}(S)$	A	A	A	A	A	A	I	I	I	I	I	I	E	E	E	E	E	E	A	E
c2. $R_{\leftarrow t}(S)$	A	A	I	I	E	E	A	A	I	I	E	E	A	A	I	I	E	E	A	
c3. $R_t(S)$	Y	N	Y	N	Y	N	Y	N	N	N	N	N	Y	N	Y	N	Y	N	N	Y
c4. $R_{t+1}(S)$	Y	Y	Y	Y	Y	Y	Y	N	Y	N	Y	N	Y	N	Y	N	Y	N	N	Y
Actions																				
a1. LATERTHAN(S, t)	x	x	x	x	x	x	x	x	x	x	x	x	x	x	x	x	x			
a2. EARLIERTHAN(S, t)	x	x	x	x			x	x	x	x			x	x	x	x				
a3. AT$_t$(S, t)	x	x	x		x		x	x	x		x		x		x		x			
a4. UNTIL(P, t)	x	x		x				x					x	x						
a5. END(P)													x		x					
a6. BEGIN(P)					x						x									
a7. CONTINUE(P)	x																			
a8. exit																		x		
a9. error																			x	x

ble within the decision-table format (by "initialization" conventions), but to introduce them would complicate the summary at no apparent gain in understanding; and (c) we use $R_{t\rightarrow}(S)$ to represent both $F_t(S)$ and $G_t(S)$, and $R_{\leftarrow t}(S)$ to represent both $P_t(S)$ and $Q_t(S)$. In order to distinguish the quantifiers associated with all moments, some moments, and no moments in both the future and the past, we enter in the table A, I, and E, respectively, instead of the binary yes and no.

The four conditions required after these simplifications are future, past, present, and present-plus-one moment. R plays its usual role in forming statements that S is realized for some, all, or none of the future or past moments, or for the present or present-plus-one moments. The major dependency between conditions occurs in the case of $R_{t+1}(S)$, which must be yes when $R_{t\rightarrow}(S)$ is A and no when it is E; these combinations lead to an "error" output. Of the $3 \times 3 \times 2 \times 2 = 36$ possible rules, the 20 shown in the table remained after consolidation.

Little comment on table 6.2 is required; to consider each rule in turn would recapitulate the discussion already presented. We assume that since time markers are obligatory in English, this table and the information it contains would have to be consulted for every clause.

An interesting feature of "begin" is that, like the auxiliary verbs, it absorbs the tense markers of its complement verb. Semantically the situation can be described by saying that BEGIN requires a temporally indefinite argument P, that is, the complement cannot have a tense marker (one does not say "Harriet begins traveled" or "Harriet begins will travel") because P must have nonfinite or indefinite temporal reference. To indicate the tenseless character of the complement, English uses three devices: gerundive, infinitive, and nominal. All three are available for the complement of "begin," as (62) illustrates. Since P must be temporally indefinite, any tense markers the speaker introduces into the sentence containing "begin" must be associated with "begin," not with the complement verb. The effect of the "past" operator on BEGIN(P) is to anchor the beginning of P to n, thus anchoring the time of P indirectly:

(70) $P_n(\text{BEGIN}(P))$: $(\exists t)[t < n$ & $Q_t(\text{notP})$ & $R_t(P)]$.

The opposite order, BEGIN($P_n(P)$), has the effect of removing the deictic anchor n, so this order is not correct.

UNTIL(P, S) and SINCE(S', S) were introduced in 6.2.3 with the comment that "until S" means "until S begins" and "since S" means "since S ended." The formulations given in (58) for these two uses of "until" and "since" conform to those for "begin" and "end" in (68) and (64). When nonmomentary processes are the relata for temporal locatives, it is generally understood that it is their momentary beginnings or endings that anchor the temporal relation. If S has no beginning or ending, it cannot provide a temporal relatum—"She has been working since two plus two are four" or "She is working until all men are mortal" are not acceptable.

In this context it is interesting to consider "still" as a temporal adverb. In sentences like "She is still traveling" there is no obvious temporal relatum, as there is in the case of "before" or "until"; in this respect the grammar of "still" resembles that of "now," as in "She is now traveling." In order to provide an explicit temporal relatum for "still" you must add a temporal adverbial ("She is still traveling at the present time") or infer it from the tense of the verb ("She was still traveling" or "She will still be traveling"). "Still," like "now" and "then," must be deictic in making reference (implicitly) to the present moment. Then, by applying a tense or adverbial operator to it, the implicit reference to "now" can be shifted in the appropriate temporal direction (the "present" operator will, of course, leave it unchanged).

If "She is still traveling" can be paraphrased roughly as "Her traveling hasn't ended before the present time," we can formulate "still" as follows:

(71)   STILL(P) = notEARLIERTHAN(END(P), n):
          $\mathrm{not}(\exists t) \, [t < n \; \& \; R_t(R_t(P) \; \& \; G_t(\mathrm{not}P))]$
          $\equiv (t)[t < n \supset (R_t(P) \supset F_t(P))].$

According to (71), STILL incorporates EARLIERTHAN(S, n), which is the operator given in 6.2.4 for the past tense. This formulation gains some intuitive support from comparisons of sentences like "She is still traveling," in the present tense, with "She has not stopped traveling," in the present perfect. That "still" incorporates something more than the past-tense operator is indicated by the difference between "The door is still open" and "The door has been open," where the present perfect leaves vague the current state of the door—we can say either "The door has been open, and it still is" or "The door has been open, but it isn't anymore" (Morrissey, 1973). For sentences like "His trial is still to come," which could be paraphrased as "His trial hasn't begun before the present time," we assume the correct interpretation is that the state described by "His trial is to come" has not ended before the present time.

The oppositions based on (71) are

(72)   (a) STILL(P): $(t)[t < n \supset (R_t(P) \supset F_t(P))]$
          (b) STILL(notS): $(t)[t < n \supset (R_t(\mathrm{not}S) \supset F_t(\mathrm{not}S))]$
          (c) notSTILL(notS): $(\exists t)[t < n \; \& \; R_t(\mathrm{not}S) \; \& \; G_t(S)]$
          (d) notSTILL(P): $(\exists t)[t < n \; \& \; R_t(P) \; \& \; G_t(\mathrm{not}P)]$

There is a striking difference between the contrary (b) and the contradictory (d): "She is still not traveling" versus "She is not still traveling." The construction "not still" feels awkward, however, and most people would prefer to express (d) by "not anymore." Similarly, "not still not" is impossibly clumsy, so (c) is usually represented lexically by "already." And "still not" is often replaced by "not yet." (One difference between "still" and "yet" is their behavior in interrogatives and imperatives—"Is he here still?" versus "Is he here yet?" and "Don't leave yet" versus the questionable "Still don't leave." We will not attempt to resolve the complexities of "yet.")

Other temporal adverbs that include a deictic component are "just" and "recently," which are oriented back from the moment to which they are deictically anchored, and "soon" and "shortly," which are oriented ahead of the moment to which they are anchored.

Although these adverbials extend the list analyzed in 6.2.3, our major interest here is in aspect, and our analysis has focused on an appropriate definition for "begin." Since we will use "begin" to discuss the aspectual properties of verbs in chapter 7—particularly of motion verbs in section 7.1—it will be useful to provide an explicit formulation of BEGIN for reference later.

It is usually assumed to be a presupposition of "begin" that the process or state that is beginning has not occurred before in the period under discussion. So we can rewrite (68) as

(73)   BEGIN$((x), P_x)$:   An animate x "begins" a nonmomentary process described by the statement P_x at time t if $Q_t(\text{not}P_x)$ and:
   (i) $R_t(P_x)$
   (ii) DO(x, S)
   (iii) CAUSE$(S, (i))$

The subscript in P_x reminds us that the subject of the complement verb (if one is provided) must be the same as the subject of "begin." If the subject of "begin" is not provided, P_x becomes the subject and only condition (i) need be satisfied. If an animate x is provided, it becomes the subject of "begin" and conditions (ii) and (iii) must also be satisfied; these conditions will be discussed in 6.3.1 and 6.3.7; for the moment it is sufficient to understand them as "x does something that causes P_x to be realized at t."

We have treated $Q_t(\text{not}P)$ as a presupposition of BEGIN and have included it in the introductory sentence as a condition that must be satisfied before the subsequent conditions apply. If it is not satisfied, sentences using "begin" cannot be evaluated. Although the assumption that "begin P" presupposes "notP in the past" has support from other students of aspectual verbs (see Givón, 1972), Karttunen (1973b) points out that sentences involving "begin" can be used in a natural way that violates this assumption. "Harriet may have begun taking drugs" can be offered by the speaker as a speculative explanation of Harriet's strange behavior; such a speculation can be offered in total ignorance of whether Harriet did or did not take drugs in the past. If Harriet has been taking drugs for years, the speaker's speculative use of "Harriet may have begun taking drugs" is not impossible to evaluate; in the use imagined it is simply false, she has not "begun." Indeed, the question "When did Harriet begin taking drugs?" can completely reverse presupposition and assertion; it can presuppose "Harriet is taking drugs now" and inquire about her behavior in the past.

Nevertheless, one can assume that the *sentence* "Harriet may have begun taking drugs" does presuppose that Harriet was not using drugs in the recent past, even though the *speaker* who uses the sentence in the situation described may not presuppose that Harriet was not using drugs in the recent past. The listener has to compile the sentence that the speaker provides and may well be ignorant of the speaker's presuppositions in using that particular sentence on that particular occasion. What he has to go on is what the speaker says and his own understanding of "begin." If he knows that Harriet is a longtime user, a presupposition of the sentence is violated and he can say so—in which case the speaker will have achieved his purpose in using the sentence.

There are other subtle problems in aspectual presuppositions, however. Both "John began to study" and "John didn't begin to study" seem to entail "There was a time before which John was not studying," so the presupposition seems to hold. Yet "John began to study at noon" entails "There was a time (noon) before which John was not studying," but "John didn't begin to study at noon" does not, since it is not incompatible with the further clause "he began before noon," so the presupposition does not hold (cf. R. J. Harris, 1974). Similarly, "John can begin to study" entails "John is not studying now," but "John can't begin to study" does not—perhaps the reason he cannot begin is that he is already studying.

A strong case can be made that BEGIN(P) does not presuppose $Q_t(\text{notP})$ but asserts it, in which case the impression that in many contexts notBEGIN(P) negates $R_t(P)$ rather than $Q_t(\text{notP})$ would presumably be explained as a conventional implicature rather than as a presupposition. Although it would be a simple matter to move $Q_t(\text{notP}_x)$ out of the introductory sentence of (73) into the list of conditions to be tested, most of the published work on aspectuals treats them as having this presupposition. So, having issued this caveat, we will adopt the conventional treatment given in (73). Pragmatic constraints affecting the use of sentences in particular contexts and the effects of conventional implicatures pose important questions for psycholinguistic theory, but they would lead us far from the questions of lexical analysis that are our central concern here.

A more complete discussion of aspectual relations would include a discussion of verbs whose action must be completed: "He came" is not true until he arrives, whereas "He left" is true as soon as he starts. And the concepts BEGIN, END, and CONTINUE would be used as incorporated components of other verbs having various aspectual properties. But these matters are better left for chapter 7.

6.2.6   Some Psychological Implications

In our review of some of the conceptual and linguistic complexities of temporal relations in English, we have concentrated on analyzing truth rules for the various expressions considered and relating them to the conceptual time line. This approach poses more psychological problems than it answers. For example, although the language of time borrows heavily from the language of space, the psychology of time is very different from the psychology of space. Such differences are not explicated by formal semantic analysis.

One matter that presses for consideration concerns the use of quantification over temporal variables. In particular, why have we exploited the quantifiers of the predicate calculus far more heavily for temporal than for spatial relations?

We could have dealt with spatial semantics by introducing a statement-forming operator comparable to R; for example, we could let $L_s(S)$ mean that statement S is realized at location s, where S is some description innocent of geography. Then a spatial L-logic, or topological logic, could be based on this operator, just as temporal and tense logic is based on R (Rescher and Urquhart, 1971, chap. 2). In such a system, the spatial location s would presumably be a position in a three-dimensional system of Cartesian coordinates, and the formal concepts of geometry would be applicable. In section 6.1 we rejected this approach in favor of a system based on REGION(w, x); even though the notion of a characteristic region of interaction with x is less well defined than a position in a coordinate system, we believe it provides a better representation of the perceptual and cognitive bases of our descriptions of spatial relations. More consistent authors would probably have followed the same course in dealing with temporal relations. We could have introduced some temporal analog of REGION, calling it EPIS(T, e) to mean that T is the rather uncertain interval of time during which the episode that includes event e is conceived to extend. Just as the region of x defines a spatial domain in which to search for presupposed landmarks, so the episode T would define a temporal domain in which to search for presupposed events.

We have chosen to be inconsistent for several reasons. From a psychological point of view, the most important reason is that searching for an event is very different from searching for an object—moving around in time is impossible. Memory search is a complex and poorly understood exercise of the imagination. Hence, some of the obvious advantages of REGION would be missing in EPIS. Since people can imagine states of affairs at times other than the present moment, some kind of temporal indexing for these alternative states of affairs is required to distinguish and relate them; in our present ignorance of how people accomplish this feat, we have chosen temporal logic as a formal notation for describing what the unknown psychological mechanism must accomplish.

Second, because English does exhibit "a tiresome bias in its treatment of time," some fairly rigorous way to specify the times at which "test" instructions are to apply seems advisable. The obligatory preoccupation of English speakers with tense markers on verbs also calls for greater precision of notation than is required for spatial locations, and the deliberate vagueness of REGION is inappropriate.

Third, in the culture most familiar to us an elaborate system of names is available for absolute temporal locations that is not available for absolute spatial locations. The lexical resources of English for designating objective moments in time were noted in 6.2.2; they are obviously rich. A theoretical notation involving discrete moments t thus seems less objectionable than a theoretical notation involving discrete positions in spatial coordinates. Not only does ordinary talk about time involve numbers in a way that ordinary talk about space seldom does, but the core concept of the time line is intimately related to the concept of the number line.

For these and related reasons we have taken a more formal approach to time than to space. We must emphasize that we regard temporal logic not as a theory of the psychological processes that people must execute as they speak and understand English sentences but as an abstraction from such a psychological theory. When we understand the psychoneural engine that keeps these temporal relations straight, we will probably find that it bears little resemblance to any logic machine. But however it realizes its functions it will have to deal with the kind of information that we have here represented abstractly in terms of R, t, and quantificational formulas. We are merely proposing rather abstract boundary conditions on the kind of psychoneural engine that we can expect to find.

By resorting to quantificational logic we have embraced an idealization that is obviously incorrect—for everything there is a price. When a serious logician writes an expression like $(t)F(t)$, he means that F is to hold for all t. In ordinary language, statements are rarely made about indefinitely long periods of time, although they can be. For example, when you say that Igor died at t, most people will understand that "Igor is dead" will be realized for all moments thereafter. When you say "This is the first cigarette Flora ever smoked" most people will understand that "Flora is not smoking a cigarette" has been realized for all moments prior to the moment she started smoking it. Usually, however, time spans are more limited. You say things like "Flora didn't smoke before noon today" and are usually understood to mean that "Flora is not smoking a cigarette" has been realized for a finite span of time since yesterday. "Osa got here at noon" is understood to mean that for some finite period prior to noon Osa was not here; it is not taken to mean that Osa had never been here before. We have not attempted to build into our notation an indication of the limits of the time span that speakers and hearers assume when they use the cyclical, and hence potentially ambiguous, time units of English. It would be possible to incorporate such discourse limits, effectively introducing a temporal REGION into the theory, but it would greatly complicate the notation. We have already made a reasonably obvious matter look difficult; to add precise outer limits would make something difficult look impossible.

Nevertheless, distinctions between the present episode, the near past or future, and the distant past or future are psychologically important, and if Chafe (1973) is right these distinctions receive linguistic expression by speakers of English. It is at this point that a regional notion like EPIS(T, e) would be a convenience. We might prefix our temporally limited formulas with some such warning expression as $(\exists T)$EPIS(T, e), followed by an indication that the temporal index t is limited to values before, during, or after the period T of the current interactive episode. Although considerable psychological justification for such a move could be found, we will not develop it here. For both spatial and temporal variables, agreement between parties to a discussion as to the limits beyond which variables are not expected to range depends on complex pragmatic factors that lie well outside the limits we have set for the present discussion.

Violations of the strict sense of "all" go even further than a failure to provide explicit outer limits. Even when the interval over which the quantified variable ranges is clear, English does not insist that "all" have no exceptions. "André worked until noon" does not mean literally that he was working every single moment—André may have answered the telephone, gone to the bathroom, insulted a visitor, or looked out the window during the course of the morning and still reply truthfully to a question about his activities "I worked all morning." The liberties taken with words like "all" should lead to logical perplexities, but somehow people avoid them.

We have used the symbol S to denote some kind of timeless and untensed statement or proposition; t, t', t_a, and n have represented the temporal information required in order to formulate S as a tensed sentence in ordinary English. This device for factoring the surface sentence into a propositional and a temporal component enables us to treat temporal information in much the same way we treat spatial information—by such paraphrases as "after now" or "before then," comparable to "west of here" or "over there" (Quine, 1960). The advantage is that it provides temporal information explicitly and the temporal argument of the control instruction: test(t, S) is available for execution once a sentence has been translated.

This factorization amounts to a psychological assumption that temporal information is represented conceptually in an abstract form. The logical formulas do not explain the formation of grammatical English sentences; they are intended to capture how events are to be mapped onto a conceptual time line. Moreover, this mapping is not limited to individual sentences. Much discourse describes sequences of events; indices assigned in one sentence must be related to indices assigned in other sentences. We must assume that temporal mapping can be suprasentential, that the temporal organization of a narrative can grow as the narrative unfolds over many sentences. Thus, part of the context in which a sentence is translated is provided by the temporal organization inferred from preceding sentences. How the temporal organization of a discourse should be represented has been considered by linguists, but little is known of the cognitive processes that must be involved in such memory. Litteral (1972) assumes that each event described has associated with it a double index (t_a, t_b) for the interval it fills—momentary events are (t_a, t_a)—and that these indices can be accumulated in correct order as the discourse proceeds. Some of the indices, of course, can be dates.

Psychological research on the expression and understanding of temporal relations has focused primarily on "before" and "after," which seem simpler than the nonlexical formatives of the tense system. Let us review some of the ways these words are used in sentences. We will limit ourselves here to the use of "before" and "after" as conjunctions relating two nonstative predications:

(74)   (a) He ate before he napped.
        (b) He napped after he ate.
        (c) Before he napped, he ate.
        (d) After he ate, he napped.

Since eating and napping are incompatible processes, (a) and (b) are understood as if "before" and "after" were converse relations: "He finished eating before he began napping" is very close in meaning to "He began napping after he finished eating." Moreover, the only difference between (a) and (c) is that the subordinate clause has been preposed in (c), so they can be understood as equivalent in meaning, and a similar relation holds between (b) and (d). In short, given the statements we have chosen to conjoin, (74) lists four different ways to express the same temporal relation.

Experiments show that even though these four sentences can be regarded as alternative phrasing of the same temporal relation between two activities, they are not psychologically equivalent. When Clark and Clark (1968) asked adults to remember such sentences verbatim, they found that recall was more accurate for the forms (a) and (d), where the order of the clauses in the sentence is the same as the temporal order of events. When Smith and McMahon (1970) presented such sentences and asked people to say which event came first or which came second, responses were faster and more accurate when the correct answer was the main clause. But when a person was allowed to view the sentence until he felt he was ready to answer a question about it, he spent significantly less time studying sentences with "before" in them—sentences (a) and (c). K. H. Smith (unpublished) found that when the events were irreversible ("He made the coffee before he drank it" versus "He drank the coffee before he made it" in all four forms), judgments of acceptability were fastest and most accurate when the "critical event" ("He made the coffee") occurred in the subordinate clause with the conjunction "before" or "after," and that no effect was attributable either to the order of the clauses or to a favoritism for "before." (It might be instructive to repeat some of these experiments with a perfect tense—"The man who was napping had eaten" versus "The man who had eaten was napping.")

The difficulty of interpreting these various sentence forms depends critically on the task a person is trying to perform. Any psychological account that reconciles these diverse results will necessarily be complex. We can indicate some of the factors a theorist might consider in formulating his explanation.

First, in the relation BEFORE(S, S'), S is the referent and S' is the relatum. We have seen that the relatum generally has the psychological properties of a landmark with respect to which a referent can be located. If the experimental task involves first establishing the temporal landmark and then positioning the referent event before or after it—which might well be the critical task when irreversible events are involved—we might expect the nature of the subordinate clause to be the important consideration.

Second, in sentences based on BEFORE(S, S'), S is the assertion and S' is normally the presupposition. Bever (1970) notes that "Did he eat before he napped?" does not have a yes-or-no answer if he did not nap, but it does if he did not eat; hence, his napping is presupposed and his eating is to be asserted or denied. (Note, incidentally, that this difference implies that even in (74) the sentences (a) and (b) are not strictly synonymous, since they assert different things.) Bever suggests that comprehension of the assertion in the main clause may be the basis for understanding these sentences and that comprehension of the presupposition in the subordinate clause may be psychologically subsidiary. If there is a tendency to judge that the event identified in the main clause occurred first, then (a) and (c) should be the easiest forms to understand, since they present the first event in the main clause.

Third, preposing the subordinate clause leads to a more complicated syntactic construction that might cause difficulty in comprehension. If the experimental task involves not only understanding the sentence but also remembering its syntactic form, as might be the case in verbatim recall, more must be remembered about the syntax of (c) and (d).

Fourth, as Clark and Clark (1968) note, (a) and (d) preserve the temporal order of events in the order of the clauses. If the experimental task involves remembering the order of the events, and if the sentence is processed by starting with the first event mentioned and then organizing events mentioned later as subsequent to the first, (a) and (d) should be easier.

Fifth, some semanticists (such as Leech, 1969, p. 110; E. V. Clark, 1971) feel that "before" is the semantically positive member of the before-after pair and that "after" is the negative term with respect to "before." Clark analyzes "before" as bearing the semantic markers +Time, —Simultaneous, +Prior and "after" as +Time, —Simultaneous, —Prior. There are grounds for questioning this analysis (see the discussion following (51) above), but if one accepts it, understanding sentences with "after" might require an additional semantic step, and (a) and (c) should be easier; if one rejects it, one might argue that "before" sentences are easier when the task requires subvocal rephrasing of (c) and (d) as (a) and (b), respectively, where (a) is easier than (b) because the order of its clauses is congruent with the order of events.

Sixth, an interaction might occur between the temporal connective and the aspect of the verb in the predicates it connects. If both predicates are nondurative, "before" and "after" behave like converse relations; with durative predicates the situation is more complex. Suppose it rained for several hours and while it was raining someone arrived. This situation can be described correctly by "It was raining before he arrived" and by its apparent converse, "He arrived after it was raining." And it can also be described correctly by "It was raining after he arrived," although the apparent converse of that, "He arrived before it was raining," is false. This asymmetry arises from the following facts. "S before S'" requires a comparison of the beginning of S with the beginning of S', whereas "S after S'" requires a comparison of the end of S with the beginning of S'. "Before" requires consideration of two initial moments, "after" requires consideration of the initial moments of S or S' relative to the terminal moments of S' or S. If S and S' are both in durative aspect, "after" requires selection of the appropriate initial-terminal comparison, whereas "before" does not require a similar selection because only one initial-initial comparison is possible. If this factor caused slower processing of "after," (b) and (d) would be more difficult than (a) and (c).

Seventh, there might be combinations of the preceding factors. Jarvella and

Lubinsky (1975) point out that "S after S'" is the only one of the four sentence forms that cannot be correctly interpreted either on the grounds that the main clause describes the antecedent event or on the basis of clause order. If both of these factors contribute to performance, there should be fewest mistakes on (a) and most on (b), with (c) and (d) intermediate.

It would seem that the theoretical possibilities are at least as diverse as the experimental findings and that the variety of cognitive strategies a person might adopt in dealing with temporal relations of the B-series stands in sharp contrast with the apparent simplicity of the logical core of this concept. Perhaps it is the very simplicity of the time concept that enables speakers of English to afford such a rich diversity of linguistic expressions for this important aspect of their lives.

When we turn to the psychological problems posed by the deictic A-series, the salient fact to be remembered is that the cognitive processes involved in evaluating statements referring to past events are different from those involved in evaluating present events, and both differ from those involved in evaluating future events. Somehow memory, perception, and expectation are integrated linguistically in the service of talking about before now, right now, and after now in a conceptually coherent manner. Much of the speculative literature about the psychology of time centers around this conversion of expectations into memories by passage through the present moment of experience. The achievement of this integration in terms of the time line must constitute one of the major cognitive developments of childhood.

We have talked about the time line from past to future as a static concept, to which "now" adds the dynamic element. Language users are inescapably anchored to "now," but "now" is somehow conceived of as moving along the time line. We believe this is how most adults think of time, but the mysteries that are concealed therein should not be overlooked. Taken literally, this conception begs the question, since to speak of motion presupposes what is to be explained, namely, time. It is reasonable to ask how many miles per hour an object is moving, but what could it mean to ask how many hours per hour "now" is moving? Clearly, the conceptual core of the time domain is a representational convenience, not an explanation of the nature of time. That the static time line appears to demand a further notion of time has led some thinkers to conclude that time does not exist and others that there is an infinite series of times. It would be unfair to demand of the lay conception of time that it resolve a mystery so baffling to philosophers. We ask only that it serve to support linguistic communication about time and temporal relations.

As Fillmore (1971d) has emphasized, conceptualization of time in terms of movement seems to be a central feature of the Western concept of time. Indeed, when a person is in motion through space, there is a reciprocity between temporal and spatial designations. He can refer to distances by using temporal expressions ("The house is about five minutes away"), and he can refer to time by using spatial expressions ("He started to feel ill about 5 miles ago"; this usage is appropriate only when he is in motion).

When a person moves from one place to another, he can conceive of his journey in two ways: either he travels through a landscape that is stationary relative to his movement, or else (since the invention of self-propelled vehicles, at least) he remains conceptually stationary while the landscape travels past him. (The importance of this mode of conceptualizing motion in a native Polynesian system of navigation has been stressed by Gladwin, 1970.) These two distinctive modes of conceiving spatial movement also apply to time when it is thought of as movement. According to McTaggart (1927), "the movement of time consists in the fact that later and later terms pass into the present, or—which is the same fact expressed in another way—that presentness passes to later and later terms. If we take it the first way, we are taking the B series as sliding along a fixed A series. If we take it the second way, we are taking the A series as sliding along a fixed B series" (quoted by Prior, 1967, p. 2). There are seeds here of an important distinction drawn by Fillmore (1971d). Like a man in a vehicle (a time machine), one can think of the world as moving along the static dimension of time or one can think of time itself as moving past a static world. This ambivalent metaphor is reflected in the distinction between such descriptions as "He has yet to reach his best period" or "His best period is yet to come." It is also reflected in the way certain spatial terms can be applied to temporal matters. For example, the leading part of an object in motion can be called its front. Hence, something in advance of a moving object can be described as "in front" of or "ahead" of it. If one thinks of the world as moving along the stationary time axis, then events in the future are "ahead" of it. If one thinks of events laid out on the time axis, which passes by the world, then each event has a "front," and one can refer to the moments of time lying "ahead" of it. The distinction is subtle, reflected in the contrast between the meaning of "ahead" in "His trial lay ahead of him" and "His trial lay ahead of his imprisonment."

We should add to this analysis, which we borrow from Fillmore (1971d), the fact that the two conceptualizations are clearly interrelated; if his trial is (now) ahead of his imprisonment, then his trial is (now) ahead of him. In other instances the distinction is not subtle at all: when someone writes that he has "advanced the date of the meeting by two days," do you decide to attend two days earlier or two days later? If you think of time as static and of yourself as advancing into the future, you will believe the meeting was postponed; if you think of yourself as static and time advancing toward you, you will believe the meeting was moved two days earlier.

We have seen that the complexity of the time concept lies more in its lexical (and linguistic) field than in its conceptual core. Although the time concept may seem easy to an adult who has mastered it, there is evidence that its simplicity is not obvious to young children. A variety of experiences, both situational and linguistic, involve this ubiquitous abstraction in one way or another, but apparently they are not perceived by the child as being related in any simple way. It is not until he reaches what Piaget calls the stage of concrete operations that he seems to have the conceptual basis needed to integrate his diverse temporal experiences in the adult manner. The ability to decenter may be the critical skill (Cromer, 1971), since someone unable to escape "now" would certainly have difficulty understanding temporal relations. But that is a relatively late development. We should begin by considering the earlier stages.

An infant lives in the present, reacting to stimuli in a reflex or learned fashion, and has no consciousness of time. Only when he can grasp the contrast between the present "now" and the nonpresent "then" can an awareness of time emerge. An early sign of such maturation is the infant's appreciation of the permanence of objects. Piaget (1937) has claimed that a young infant treats an object hidden under a cloth as though it has ceased to exist. By the age of nine months or so he engages in an active search for the vanished object, grasping the cloth and trying to remove it; by the end of his first year he is capable of taking into account the sequence of events leading to the disappearance of the object. By this age, presumably, the succession of feelings has been supplemented by the feeling of succession.

A considerable period elapses from the development of this primitive conceptualization of time until a child is able to talk. His early utterances tend to center on current activities or needs: single-word utterances are integrated into the child's ongoing physical activity. He utters words as though to direct his attention, or that of his listeners, to pertinent aspects of the temporally immediate environment.

The child's problems in going from a concept of brute persistence to something more like an adult's concept of time are attributable in large measure to the abstract character of time. Three-year-old children who can easily distinguish between one and two concrete objects have difficulty distinguishing between one and two flashes of light (Blank and Bridger, 1964). In order to succeed, they must use some kind of verbal coding scheme. Blank (1973) comments that "the concept of two is defined not by the light itself, but by the idea that 'something went before.' This requires that the previously perceived but now absent stimulus (i.e., the first light) be retained and combined with the second light so as to form a meaningful distinctive entity. In the vast percentage of cases, this achievement seems to demand of the child that he resort to a coding system" (p. 45). In this sphere, accurate perception seems to depend critically on language.

The ability to combine an earlier with a later event is presumably generalized somehow to span longer periods as a child grows up. But memory of earlier events can be only part of the story. The adult concept of time extends in two directions from "now." How does a child come to anticipate the future?

Since thinking about future events is a matter of setting up and manipulating expectations, it must be based on a memory of past sequences of events. But it is possible to have memories without expectations. The nature of memory and anticipation would seem to support the commonsense intuition that the past is a simpler concept than the future. On the other hand, the future is probably more important, more worthy of comment than the past—especially for a young child.

Investigators have generally been reluctant to classify children's initial references to the nonpresent, claiming it is unclear whether they are referring to the past or to the future (Lewis, 1937). But some have claimed that children refer to the future before they refer to the past (L. B. Ames, 1946), or that they refer to the past before they refer to the future (Court, 1920). Although children may differ, it seems more likely that such contrary claims stem from differing linguistic and conceptual criteria used by the investigators. A child may use a word without really understanding what it means; an experimenter may take as his criterion any appropriate reference to the future, or an appropriate use of the future tense. Since the future tense in English involves an auxiliary verb, whereas the past merely involves a suffix, the appearance of the future tense may be delayed because of its more complex surface structure.

Some such difference in surface-structure complexity may also account for subsequent difficulties with the future tense. Cromer (1971) gave children a task in which they had to indicate what would be an appropriate utterance to use at one time about an event at another time. He found that when children become able to decenter in this way—usually between their fifth and sixth years—they can do so equally well for all tenses except the future (Cromer, table 4, p. 361).

To return to the younger child, it seems that his first temporal expressions are locative in function and deictic in form ("now," "today"). Only later does he begin to express temporal relations, durations, and frequencies, and at first with one term of the relation anchored to the present moment. Although there is no definitive information on the emergence of these different sorts of expression, it seems plausible that children's grasp of the language of time develops out of their grasp of the language of space. This relation has been suggested by a number of investigators (including Piaget, 1927a; H. Clark, 1973), and is consistent with the many parallels between these two linguistic systems (at least in English).

Piaget has shown how children up until the age of seven or so readily confound differences in distance with differences in time. The following dialogue demonstrates an extreme confabulation of this sort. The experimenter has just run with the child, starting and stopping simultaneously but leaving the child some distance behind him. "Did we start together? *Yes.* Did we stop together? *Oh no.* Which one stopped first? *I did.* Did one stop before the other? *I did.* When you stopped was I still running? *No.* And when I stopped were you still running? *No.* So we did stop at the same time? *No.* Did we run for the same length of time? *No.* Who went on longer? *You did*" (Piaget, 1927a, p. 99). There is a real confusion about simultaneity here, yet this child, and others like him around five years of age, showed considerable sophistication in his use of temporal expressions. Piaget puts his predicament in a nutshell: "If 'before' and 'after' in time are confused with spatial succession, and if duration is identified with distance, it goes without saying that simultaneity at a distance, or with different velocities, can have no meaning for the child: he cannot possibly grasp that bodies moving in different places with different velocities can be fitted into a unique and homogeneous time scale" (pp. 101–102).

This confusion between time and place has been reported elsewhere. According to Ervin-Tripp (1970), children start to ask "where" questions before they ask "when" questions, and E. V. Clark (1971) found that young children sometimes confuse "when" questions with "where" questions. It seems to be true that the acquisition of spatial terms is generally slightly ahead of the acquisition of temporal terms. This disparity is evident in many of the early descriptive accounts of the development of vocabulary (see Nice, 1915, and numerous other studies of this period reported in *Pedagogical Seminary*). It is also borne out by more recent studies. Cromer (1968) found that such words as "before" and "after" are used to relate two objects in space before they are used to relate two events in time. Ames (1946) and Ames and Learned (1948) recorded the spontaneous utterances of twenty children in a nursery-school setting at six-month intervals beginning when the children were around eighteen months old and continuing until they were around four years old. They also put specific questions to the children about time and space. Both procedures revealed that the period of greatest growth in spatial vocabulary is from two to two-and-a-half years, whereas the spurt in temporal vocabulary occurs about six months later.

There is some reason to believe that children master McTaggart's B-series before the A-series, although the difference may be attributable more to linguistic complexity than to conceptual mastery. Children seem to understand such B-series relations as "before" and "after" a little earlier than they are able to master the kind of temporal decentering from "now" that is required by the tense system. But even for B-series relations the child's comprehension seems to pass through a series of stages, with BEFORE(S, n) perhaps mastered before BEFORE(S, S').

Evidence on the acquisition of "before" and "after" comes from experiments in which children are asked to act out with toys the events described by sentences like "The boy kicked the rock before he patted the dog." This task requires a child to remember the sentence long enough to find the appropriate toy objects and perform with them the indicated actions in the correct order. All four of the sentence forms listed in (74) are generally tested. According to results reported by E. V. Clark (1971), a three-year-old child will respond to such requests as if "before" and "after" were little more than nonsense syllables, or alternative pronunciations of "and." About 85 percent of the time he acts out the events in the order that the sentence describes them, which means he is right 85 percent of the time with the forms "S before S' " and "after S, S' " but wrong 85 percent of the time with "S' after S" and "before S', S." Bever (1970) obtained a similar result, but with slightly less favoritism for the spoken order, and so did Hatch (1971).

Since sentences in which the order of the clauses preserves the order of events do not show any developmental trend, we must focus on the results for the sentence forms "S' after S" and "before S', S," where events are referred to in the reverse order. Although the research seems to have been well designed and executed, the results have not been consistent enough to support any simple interpretation.

If we consider only the data of E. V. Clark (1971), who tested children aged three to five, and of Weil (1970), who worked with somewhat older children (aged four to eight), correct responses to "before S', S" are consistently more frequent than correct responses to "S' after S." Clark takes this result as evidence that "before" is somehow simpler (positive, unmarked), and that "after" must be learned as the converse of "before." However, since there is no other justification for this semantic analysis—the pair do not appear to be exemplars of the marked-unmarked contrast that is found between such adjectives as "small" and "large" (Bierwisch, 1967)—and since both words occur equally frequently in adult speech, one is led to search for an alternative explanation. Weil suggests that "before S', S" tells a child in its first word that the order of events will have to be reversed, so he is prepared to think of event S as preceding before he even hears what it is; in "S' after S," on the other hand, it is not until the middle of the sentence that the child discovers he must reverse the order, and this reversal may require some recoding of S. According to Weil's hypothesis, by age five an average child understands the meanings of "before" and "after" equally well, but the two tasks he is set are not equally difficult. E. V. Clark (1970; but see Cromer, 1968) reports that "before," both as a preposition and as a conjunction, appears to precede "after" in the spontaneous speech of young children—which may or may not be relevant to the greater difficulty that Weil observed with "S' after S" in children as old as eight.

The situation seems more confused if we also consider the data of Barrie-Blackley (1973). Using essentially the same method to test first graders, she found sentences with "after" to be more accurately understood than sentences with "before"—and both were significantly easier than sentences with "until." Amidon and Carey (1972) found no significant difference between "before" and "after" in five- and six-year-old children they tested—but both "before" and "after" were much harder than sentences with "first" and "last." Something more than the children's understanding of "before" and "after" must affect the results of such experiments.

One observation that is constant in all accounts of the conceptual development of time is that as a child grows older his temporal horizons widen. He looks further into the future and further back into the past (Lewis, 1937; Gesell and Ilg, 1943). Similarly, he is progressively better able to orient himself to the calendar—starting from the unit of the day and working up to the year and the day of the month—and to the clock (Oackden and Sturt, 1922; Bradley, 1947; Farrell, 1953).

Accompanying this growth of time perspective is the growth of episodic memory. If we think of episodic memory not as an isolated memory system but as one way we have of organizing our general memory in order to facilitate search for particular information, the development of the time concept and its use in organizing memory must be a critical component of normal cognitive development. Presumably, the various linguistic devices that are available contribute in some way to this organization (the kinds of relations between memory and language that Chafe, 1973, has suggested deserve careful study), but it seems more likely that episodic organization and the ability to judge fairly accurately the relative age of an episodic-memory trace are general-purpose cognitive mechanisms, independent of language. As episodic memory grows, and as it enables the child not only to retrieve the past but to extrapolate more imaginatively into the future, the need for more flexible and precise ways of referring to time and temporal relations also grows. But before we can decide whether temporal language is the cause or the consequence of episodic organization, we will need much more study and analysis of how a growing child masters the intricate system of temporal concepts that our semantic analysis has claimed to find in the language of normal adults.

6.3   CAUSAL RELATIONS

The lay conception of causal relations that is implicit in the English language outruns considerably our analysis of the perceptual predicate Cause in 2.6.2. In modern English causality is incorporated lexically as a semantic component of many verbs, there are morphological devices for adding affixes to nouns and adjectives in order to form causative verbs, and there are periphrastic constructions that express causal relations explicitly. But no special status is assigned to the distinction between perceived and inferred causal relations.

The lexical expression of causality can be appreciated most directly by contrasting particular verbs. The difference between "die" and "kill" is frequently taken as an example: "Sid died" says nothing about causes, whereas "Bruce killed Sid" means that Bruce in some way caused Sid to die. Moreover, the causal entailments of verbs like "kill" can be further complicated by intentional entailments: "Bruce killed Sid" does not say that Bruce brought about Sid's death intentionally, whereas "Bruce murdered Sid" means that the killing was deliberate. We will focus on the causative distinction, but the intentional distinction is so closely related psychologically that we cannot ignore it.

Although the argument for the incorporation of a causative semantic component in a particular verb is especially persuasive when the language has another verb that differs from it primarily in that the causative component is lacking, the identification of such pairs has given rise to considerable disagreement among linguists. Some pairs, like "die" and "kill," are reasonably clear. "Persuade" is "cause to believe," "bring" is "cause to come"—but even here one can argue that something more than a causative component distinguishes the paired meanings. Other pairs stimulate other objections: Is "give" the causative of "have"? If so, is "take" also the causative of "have"? Is the causative of "see" to be taken as "show," "look," both, or neither? Is "teach" the causative of "learn" when so much teaching produces so little learning? If "sell" means "cause to buy," is some special initiative assigned to the vendor? One can imagine situations in which "buy" meant "cause to sell," in which case "buy" and "sell" would be causatives of each other. Is "frighten" the causative of the verb "fear," or is it better thought of as a morphological causative based on the noun "fright"? In defense of those who have made such proposals, it should be said that they have not claimed the pairs are semantically equivalent in every respect except for the presence or absence of a causative semantic component. One can defend the plausibility of causative semantic components even when the elimination of that component does not suggest a particular noncausative verb already established in the language.

The status of the causative semantic component is further complicated by verbs that are causative when used transitively but noncausative when used intransitively. "He turned the wheel" will accept the causative periphrastic equivalent "He made the wheel turn," whereas "The wheel turned" says nothing about cause; one may believe that if the wheel turned, something must have caused it, but that belief is not entailed by "The wheel turned." As representative examples of such double-purpose verbs Baron (1972) lists: bake, bend, boil, break, burn, change, close, cook, cool, dissolve, drown, dry, fill, flood, fly, freeze, grow, hang, hide, melt, move, open, pass, pour, run, sink, slip, stop, tear, turn, wake up, walk (in 6.2.5 we noted that "begin" and "end" have this character). Bowerman (1974) observes that her daughter began to impose this double-purpose pattern inappropriately—saying "She came it over here," for example—at the same age she began to use periphrastic causatives with "make" and "get."

Noncausative-causative pairs of verbs are morphologically related in many languages, and in some the relation is productive; by changing a vowel or adding a suffix, any noncausative verb can become a causative, much as in English a present-tense verb can become a past-tense. According to Baron, the derivation of causative from noncausative verbs was never productive in English, although Old English did contain a number of instances where the distinction was marked by a vowel difference. For example, Old English contained the verb "cwelan" (which was replaced by borrowing the Old Norse "deyja" from which "die" derives) and the related causative "cwellan" (from which come modern "quell" and "kill"). In modern English there are now only four frozen relics of this kind of morphological pairing: fall-fell, lie-lay, rise-rear, sit-set. (The rise-rear pair is etymologically defensible, although today most English speakers would think of "raise," which derives from the Old Norse "reisa," as the causative version of "rise.") Since even these vestiges of a morphological system for expressing causal relations are rapidly weakening in popular speech, it is appropriate to classify these verbs as lexical rather than as morphological causatives.

Morphological causatives in English derive from adjectives or nouns by the addition of appropriate affixes: -ify, -ize, -en, en-, or dis-. Among the examples cited by Baron as deriving from adjectives: falsify, modernize, deepen, enrich, disable. Deriving from nouns: beautify, capitalize, lengthen, encode, discourage. The system is not productive, that is, the affixes are not freely interchangeable; even though they are not uninterpretable, English does not contain: falsize, deepify, coden, encapital. It is an interesting question whether people know these verbs as lexical entries independent of their corresponding adjectives or nouns or whether they interpret them by rules for combining the meaning of the root with the meaning of the causative affix. If such verbs were rare, a separate-lexical-entry hypothesis would be attractive; if the system were productive, a general-rule hypothesis would be attractive; since the system is intermediate, it poses a problem for psycholinguistic research.

The English verbs that express causal relations with the least contamination from other semantic features include: allow, cause, force, get, have, let, make. The use of these verbs as causatives is illustrated in

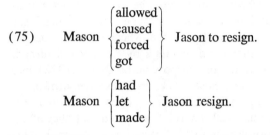

(75)   Mason $\begin{Bmatrix} \text{allowed} \\ \text{caused} \\ \text{forced} \\ \text{got} \end{Bmatrix}$ Jason to resign.

Mason $\begin{Bmatrix} \text{had} \\ \text{let} \\ \text{made} \end{Bmatrix}$ Jason resign.

Baron (1972), who calls these periphrastic causative verbs because they can be used as the initial part of constructions expressing causation, has provided a detailed account of three of them—have, make, get. Apart from any differences in meaning, these verbs differ syntactically in the kinds of complements they can take. For example, "get" can take a variety of complement constructions:

Mason got Jason $\begin{cases} \text{to resign.} & \text{(infinitive)} \\ \text{excited.} & \text{(past participle)} \\ \text{active.} & \text{(adjective)} \\ \text{out of the room.} & \text{(space adverbial)} \end{cases}$

whereas "cause" takes only the infinitive. The syntactic features of these verbs are complex.

Semantically, it sounds odd to combine periphrastic causative verbs with complements that describe something impossible. "Mason is causing Jason to have resigned" seems to say that Jason's resignation antedates whatever Mason is now doing to cause it; causes should precede effects. "Mason allowed a stone to die" is unacceptable because "die" demands an animate subject. Similarly, it sounds odd to use periphrastic causatives with complements that are necessarily true: "Mason forced two to be a number" is just as bad as "Mason forced two not to be a number."

Since intentionality is so often involved when causality is considered, we should note three periphrastic intentive verbs that are frequently used in combination with causatives, "intend," "try," and "plan." Sentences like "Bruce intended to kill Sid," "Bruce tried to kill Sid," or "Bruce planned to kill Sid" do not entail that Bruce caused Sid to die; indeed, there is an implicature that

Bruce did not fulfill his intention or succeed in his attempt—both "Bruce tried to kill Sid, and he succeeded" and "Bruce tried to kill Sid, but he failed" are acceptable. Periphrastic intentives can be combined with periphrastic causatives: "Mason intended to allow Jason to resign," "Mason tried to get Jason out of the room."

Semantically, intentive verbs are notoriously opaque. The truth or falsity of statements expressed by sentences containing such verbs does not depend on the truth or falsity of the statements expressed by the complements of the verbs. "Mason intended that Jason resign" does not depend for its truth value on the truth of "Jason resigned." People can truly and seriously intend, try, or endeavor to cause all manner of peculiar things. What is odd about "Mason planned to get a stone to die" or "Mason tried to allow two to be a number" is not so much their truth or falsity, or even their status as grammatical sentences, as Mason's state of mind. A listener is left with an uneasy feeling that he does not understand what Mason could do in order to accomplish what he is said to have intended or tried. There is nothing odd about "Mason intends to prove the Axiom of Choice from the postulates of set theory," even though mathematicians have proved that the task is impossible. The constraints on what people may intend to do certainly do not exclude the impossible or the nonsensical; Mason might intend to make colorless green ideas sleep furiously, and for all we know there may be people whose beliefs could lead them to try to get a stone to die. What seems odd or reasonable for someone to intend or try to do depends on a complex system of beliefs, not on linguistic rules. If the task indicated in the complement really is impossible, of course, it is an open question how long a person will persist in trying it—to say he is trying means that he has not yet given up. Probably that is what "try" means —that the execution of a plan of action has not yet been completed or abandoned—so that opacity is a consequence: as long as the outcome is uncertain, its value cannot affect the truth of the sentence as a whole.

Some theorists, like Schank (1972), have argued that cause is a conceptual relation between events and should be understood linguistically as expressed by relations between statements or sentences denoting those events. Although the relation may be expressed in a single verb, as in "Bruce killed Sid," two conceptual statements are involved, "Bruce did something" and "Sid died," along with a causal relation between them. The difficulty of identifying the source of a causal relation by a semantic analysis of particular lexical items is illustrated by such sentences as "Arnie hit the ball into the cup"; the two causally related events here are expressed by "Arnie hit the ball" and "The ball went into the cup," but "hit" cannot be paraphrased as "caused to go"— "Arnie hit the floor" does not mean that Arnie caused the floor to go somewhere. "Arnie hit the ball and it went into the cup" could be interpreted to mean that the hitting occurred at one time and entering the cup occurred at some other, unrelated time; the causal relation is implicit, but the conceptual machinery for supplying it is obviously well oiled. In order to account for the natural interpretation of "Arnie hit the ball and it went in the cup" by some lexical device, one would have to include a sense of "and" as expressing causal relations; this alternative seems less plausible to us than the assumption that the conceptual system is constantly alert to discover causes, in described as well as witnessed events, and that the various lexical, morphological, and periphrastic devices English provides to denote causal relations explicitly are merely surface indicators of the conceptual core underlying our understanding of causal relations.

We would like to start with a conceptual analysis of the causal relations that have to be expressed and move from that to the linguistic means that English provides. As we have seen, the linguistic resources are largely verbs. Because we have not previously considered the kinds of semantic relations that can hold between verbs, we must preface our discussion with enough information about verbs to provide a context for causative verbs. This indirection will delay our consideration of the expression of causal relations in English, but the result will be a better foundation for discussing the semantic domains of verbs to be introduced in chapter 7.

6.3.1   Semantic Classification of English Verbs

Werner and Kaplan (1963) write that "in Indo-European languages, the model used for connoting states of affairs and articulating them linguistically is the *human action model*. A total event is basically articulated into agent, action, and object . . . In Indo-European languages, one is even constrained to formulate attributive propositions and propositions about conceptual relations in terms of that *action model*" (p. 57).

Given the importance of this human action model, it is understandable that some traditional grammarians tried to use it to define syntactic categories. Verbs, for example, were the words that express the action. This notional definition is generally rejected today because there are so many exceptions to it. For example, "know" is a verb but not an action, and "action" is a noun. Still, there seems to be some sense to it, if one is not inclined to be too critical. In such simple sentences as "Marvin ran," the noun labels the actor and the verb labels his action. But even here we must be careful. "Run" is not a label for running in the same way that "Marvin" is a label for Marvin. Marvin remains Marvin whether or not he is running, whereas running without somebody to do it is like addition without numbers. The verb corresponds to a function; the noun provides its argument. In this respect, English sentences reflect the structure of the perceptual world they can be used to describe. It might be more accurate to say that Indo-European languages use a function-argument model and then to note that the function is frequently an action and the argument is frequently an actor.

"Be" is a prime example of a verb that is used to label states, not actions. In "The sky is very blue today," the verb "is" does not express action. What is its role? It seems that if no other verb is available to turn a formula into a sentence, in English and languages like it there is a copulative verb that can serve by default. This same verb serves to produce the surface structures corresponding to "Marvin is at the door" or "The car is between Marvin and Simon." In Standard English, therefore, some form of "be" serves to mark the property or relation as a predication: it marks the fact that an utterance is a sentence. Given the nature of this linguistic device, it is obvious that "be"— the hardest-working verb in English—does not express action and so stands as the most glaring exception to any definition of "verb" in terms of notions about actions or events.

It is worth mentioning some of the uses of "to be." (a) It can express co-reference in such "equative" sentences as "That woman is Donna" or "The president is the commander-in-chief." (b) It can express class membership and inclusion, as in "Charles is a fool" and "A monkey is a primate." (c) It can assert existence, as in "There is a hole in my pocket" or "There is a Santa Claus." (d) It can assert adjectival properties, as in "The sky is blue" or "The woman I love is beautiful." (e) It can assert locative relations in space or time, as in "The chair is by the door" or "The funeral is tomorrow." (f) It can assert possessive relations, as in "The car is Simon's" or "It's his." (g) It can be used as an auxiliary verb, either with a participle, as in the progressive "Carl is reading," or in the passive "The book was written by Hemingway."

The heterogeneity of these examples suggests the syntactic and semantic complexity of this verb; but none of these uses justifies the notional claim that verbs denote actions. For this reason "be" is usually considered a "stative" verb, a verb used to express something about the state rather than the action of the referent: (a) equality, (b) membership and inclusion, (c) existence, (d) attribution, (e) location, (f) possession, and even, perhaps, (g) participial or passive "states."

Given the need for a class of stative verbs, it is natural to look for other instances. Predicate adjectives are possible candidates. This suggestion is motivated by the similarity of such sentences as "John died" and "John is dead" and by the existence of languages in which no copula is necessary and adjectives are a subtype of verbs. The idea would be that English verbs are divided into two classes, adjectival and nonadjectival (Lakoff, 1970); in order to form a sentence with an adjectival verb, it is necessary to introduce some form of "be" into the surface structure of the sentence, if only to carry tense markers ("I like her" corresponds to "I am fond of her" in the present; "I liked her" to "I was fond of her" in the simple past, and so on). Not all predicate adjectives can be classified as stative verbs, however. Although "dead" is clearly stative, adjectives like "noisy" are more transient; "Alice had been noisy" is an occasional description, unlike "John had been dead."

We could try to identify a variety of predicate adjectives that denote relatively unchanging states or processes and cite them as examples of stative verbs. The advantages of calling adjectives verbs are not obvious, however, and if this departure from traditional syntactic categories is pursued systematically, it should include predicate nominals as well (compare "He cooks" and

"He is a cook"), which might lead to the extravagant conclusion that nouns are also verbs.

English has other stative verbs apart from "be." The most obvious examples are verbs that describe enduring psychological states: believe, know, like, love, need. The usual linguistic test for a stative verb is that it does not freely take the progressive form (Kenny, 1963; Ota, 1963). One says "He believes in Santa Claus," but not "He is believing in Santa Claus"; "Ludwig knows English," not "Ludwig is knowing English"; "Linus loves classical music," not "Linus is loving classical music"; "Animals need oxygen," not "Animals are needing oxygen." The participial form denotes a temporal extension of the reference time, which can mark the verb as descriptive of a state; if the verb already describes a state, it is redundant to add "be" and "-ing" to it. Since relations of class inclusion, existence, and possession are treated linguistically as states, such verbs as "include," "contain," "exist," "live," "own," and "have" do not freely take the progressive form and so are probably best classified as stative verbs. One says "The book has a preface," not "The book is having a preface."

The stative verbs of English are not freely used in imperatives. People seldom issue such orders as "Be 7 feet tall," "Know the answer," "Need money," "Exist for ten years." Although both of these criteria—limited use in the progressive form and in the imperative mood—are usually considered syntactic, even young children respect them. According to Brown (1973), both the progressive "-ing" and the imperative occur in the earliest sentences children utter, but never with stative verbs. Brown comments, "This is surprising because all the other inflections, the past and present indicative on the verb, the plural and possessive on the noun, were overgeneralized to unsuitable stems" (p. 140). Apparently the conceptual difference between states and events is primitive. Yet its representation in language by means of stative and nonstative verbs may not be universal, as Brown is careful to point out (p. 328).

Another way to diagnose whether a verb is stative—a way that is probably more relevant for semantic analysis—is to consider whether it would answer the question "What happened?" Events happen, states do not. Answers to questions about what happened ordinarily use nonstative verbs. The conversational exchange

> "What happened?"
> "He believed in Santa Claus."

strikes most people as a non sequitur; there would have to be considerable contextual support for such an exchange. In contrast, as an answer to "What happened?" such sentences as "It rained" or "He died" or "He ate an apple" or "He killed a hawk" are acceptable—so "rain," "die," "eat," and "kill," like most other verbs, can be nonstative. Strictly speaking, as Mark Steedman (personal communication) has pointed out, it is the predicate as a whole that is stative or nonstative—although "He ate an apple every day of his life" uses the verb "eat," in this predicate phrase it does not describe an event but a sort of habitual state, a disposition to eat apples. However, it is tedious to keep such subtleties always in mind and we will frequently adopt the convenient fiction of talking of nonstative verbs rather than nonstative predicate phrases.

Nonstative verbs can be further classified by another question: "What did he do?" The answers "He rained," "He died," "He received the letter," or "He happened" seem odd without a supporting scenario. "Rain" and "snow" do not take animate subjects. "Die" entails "cease to live," and "live" is stative; inasmuch as "die" entails a change of state, it is nonstative and can be used to answer "What happened," but since the change of state is not a voluntary act, it cannot convey a sense of agency. Moreover, since imperatives generally command the audience to do something, verbs that cannot convey a sense of agency are not freely used in imperatives.

Agency is a difficult notion to explicate, both in linguistics (Lyons, 1968) and in philosophy (Davidson, 1967), but it is generally thought to involve not only the idea that what happened was something the actor did but that it makes sense to ask whether his action was intentional. In "He killed the chicken," the killing might have been accidental, so it makes sense to ask whether it was intentional. In "He died" it does not make sense to ask whether he died intentionally; if he died intentionally, the appropriate expression is "committed suicide." The "he" in "He killed the chicken" can be an agent, but the "he" in "He died" is not. In "He chased the chicken," however, it sounds odd to ask whether he chased it intentionally, since "chase" denotes a voluntary act; intentionality is incorporated into the meaning of the verb "chase."

Nonstative verbs like "rain," "happen," "occur," "die," and "lose" might, therefore, be further classified as nonagentive (Lee, 1969). Agentive nonstative verbs could then be further classified as causative or noncausative. Causative verbs are those that express a relation between two events, the first of which is something that an agent does, the second an event that his action causes. In "He killed the chicken," he did something; what he did caused the chicken to die. On the other hand, in "He saw the star" he did something perhaps, but what he did caused nothing to happen. So "kill" is a causative verb and "see" is not. A test that will usually distinguish between causative and noncausative verbs involves asking a question of the form "What properties of y are changed by x's action?" Killing changes the chicken's state of life; being seen changes nothing about the star.

We can use this diagnostic question to uncover some of the complexities of the linguistic expression of causal relations. If we take a case where there are two related verbs, like "raise" and "rise," the analysis is initially simple enough. For example, "He raised the car" implies that x's action changed the location of y, so "raise" is a causative verb. "The car rose" can be used to describe the same event, but "rise" is an intransitive verb and the diagnostic question simply cannot be asked, so "rise" is noncausative in this usage. Complications began to appear when we ask about "The man rose." Now when we ask "What properties of y are changed by x's action?" we must decide whether x and y are to be taken as coreferential. If so, the man's location was changed by his own action, so "rise" is causative in this usage. But if one takes x not to be coreferential with y, then once again the question about x's action simply cannot be asked, so "rise" is noncausative, as it is in "The car rose." It would seem that "rise" is both causative and noncausative; the man may have risen by his own efforts or he may have risen because, say, he happened to be standing in an elevator.

There is a similar difference in meaning between "He turned the wheel" and "The wheel turned." Are there accordingly two different senses of "turn," one causative and the other noncausative? This conclusion, both for "rise" and "turn," offends one's intuition that the motions are precisely the same in both uses. Perhaps the causative component appears only when there is an agent and vanishes when he is not mentioned? If he must be explicitly mentioned in the sentence, the answer is presumably negative, because the diminished passive, "The wheel was turned," is causative whereas the intransitive, "The wheel turned," is noncausative, yet neither mentions an agent explicitly. In the underlying structure, however, the answer is presumably affirmative, because an agent is implicitly present (although syntactically deleted) in a causative-diminished passive, whereas it is explicitly and implicitly absent in the noncausative, intransitive use. So the question becomes how the underlying concept TURN can be formulated so as to change its meaning from noncausative to causative when an agent is present, either implicitly or explicitly.

Suppose the information underlying transitive "turn" requires two arguments, TURN(x, y), related something like this:

(76)   (i) y moves around an axis.
           (ii) x does something.
           (iii) (ii) causes (i).

In order to account for the vanishing causative, we merely add that intransitive TURN(y) must satisfy condition (i) but, since there is no underlying agentive argument x, conditions (ii) and (iii) are dropped. Since condition (i) alone suffices to define intransitive "turn," the intransitive schema is incorporated in the transitive schema (Bierwisch, 1970). An obvious way to indicate this inclusion is to write TURN$((x), y)$, where the added parentheses indicate that x is optional (Fillmore, 1970; Langendoen, 1970).

Some syntactic rule is also needed, since y, which serves as the grammatical object of transitive "turn," must be promoted to the grammatical subject of intransitive "turn." Fortunately, the same rule serves for all of these double-purpose causatives in English. It is probably a special application of some more general rule about the order of assignment of arguments to syntactic roles—subject, direct object, indirect object—which has the consequence that whenever there is only one argument, it must serve as the subject, and when there are two, the actor is the subject and the second argument is the direct object of the verb. When properly formulated, this rule should allow a sequence of possibilities: "The window broke," "Melvin broke the window," "A hammer broke the window," "Melvin broke the window with a hammer."

If the argument *y* that moves is inanimate in (76), it cannot be an agent, but if *y* is animate and *x* is omitted, there can be uncertainty. The apparent ambiguity of "The man turned" derives from the possibility of either TURN(y, y), with the causative sense that he did something to cause himself to turn, or intransitive TURN(y), with the noncausative sense that he happened to turn—presumably owing to some unspecified cause. Note, however, that a speaker who says "The man turned" may be just as uncertain as the hearer; he may have chosen that sentence precisely because he did not know whether the man's turning was self-initiated or not.

We began this discussion of verbs by trying to partition them into large classes: stative or nonstative, agentive or nonagentive, causative or noncausative. The methods available for this analysis are syntactic (does it take the progressive freely? is it used in imperatives?), semantic (does it answer "What happened?" or "What did he do?" or "Was it intentional?"), and mixed (does the action by the subject of the verb change something about the object of the verb?). These are tests that linguists and philosophers use in order to discipline their linguistic intuitions, and many similar tests can be invented; we have only scratched the surface here. We could ask "Was he successful?" in order to distinguish verbs like "aim" and "hit"—the question makes sense following "He aimed at it" but seems odd after "He hit it" (Ryle, 1949). Or we might ask "At what moment did he do it?" in order to distinguish verbs like "climb" and "reach"—the question makes sense after "He reached the top" but seems odd after "He climbed the mountain" (Vendler, 1967). Or we might classify verbs according to the kinds of complement constructions they can take—"He looked for something" and "He saw that something was there" are acceptable, but not "He looked that something was there" or "He saw for something" (Rosenbaum, 1967; Kiparsky and Kiparsky, 1970; we will consider the semantics of complements in 7.3.1.) Tests of this sort are standard tools of semantic analysis, and they can be adapted to whatever hypothesis the analyst is currently exploring.

It must be noted that most of the tests that have been widely used do not converge on intuitively satisfying semantic fields. They partition the verbs in such a way that verbs of very different meaning may be in the same class and, much worse, verbs that seem close in meaning may be in different classes. If one has some independent criterion for what a semantic field is and can construct a list of verbs that, in one or more of their senses, belong to it, then one can use tests of this sort to explore differences among the verbs in that field. But the same contrasts one finds within one semantic field may also exist within a very different semantic field. Such tests are most useful to explore the internal structure of a semantic field; they are much less useful for identifying that field as a distinct conceptual system.

Tests for semantic fields are more difficult to construct, but they are not impossible to find. Bendix (1966) used the "but" test to discover whether two verbs have semantic components in common. If two verbs have nothing in common, they can be freely combined with "but." For example, both "He brought it, but he lived" and "He brought it, but he died" are acceptable. We can take this fact as suggestive that "bring" is semantically unrelated to "live" and "die." If the verbs are related, however, the result can be anomalous. Both "He brought it, but he came" and "He brought it, but he didn't come" sound odd on most interpretations, so we can argue that "bring" and "come" are semantically related. Since "He came, but he didn't bring it" is acceptable, whereas "He came, but he brought it" is odd, we can argue further that "come" is a component of "bring" and not vice versa—"bring" sentences entail "come" sentences.

Although the "but" test can be useful in exploring close semantic relations, it is less helpful for more distant relations. For example, "He came, but he walked" and "He came, but he didn't walk" are both acceptable, as are "He walked, but he came" and "He walked, but he didn't come." So "come" and "walk" would, by this test, seem unrelated. Yet both are verbs that describe motion and have in common some notion of change of location, as we can show by applying the "but" test to "come" and "change location" and to "walk" and "change location." So the "but" test must be used with caution; anomalous results indicate semantic relations, but nonanomalous results do not necessarily indicate the absence of semantic relations.

If we wish to study semantic fields of English verbs, we need tests that will help us identify membership in those fields. Most of the tests that have been used to partition verbs into classes are really more appropriate for analyzing the internal structure of a semantic field. Within each field there are usually statives and nonstatives, agentives and nonagentives, causatives and noncausatives. In discussing color terms, we could plausibly claim that we were exploring a relatively well defined semantic field. In the case of kin terms, we were forced to admit that the general concept of person does not have a coherent lexical representation, although personal pronouns and kin terms can be isolated and treated in a manner consistent with our initial picture of contrastive sets arranged hierarchically. Similar subfields of place names and dates can be identified for the expression of spatial and temporal relations, but contrastive sets among the locative prepositions are not easily characterized and temporal relations can be expressed by nonlexical devices that bear little resemblance to the field properties with which we began.

Now, in considering causal relations we find that the notion of a hierarchical lexical field covering a conceptual domain like a mosaic is totally inadequate. Presumably, people have some concept of cause, and a few words—cause, force, make, get—seem to express it directly. But causation and intention are expressed ubiquitously in different semantic fields. So we cannot pretend here to be isolating any simple lexical field and looking for its conceptual foundations. We must work from the concept toward its linguistic expression, as we did in the case of temporal relations, but here realizing that the linguistic expression is usually implicit, a component of the meanings of verbs in many semantic fields.

6.3.2   Actors and Actions

A majority of the causal relations people talk about involve effects that are brought about intentionally by other people. Since people recognize that some effects are caused accidentally, the language must provide ways to draw that distinction; since people recognize inanimate as well as animate causes, that distinction must also be honored; since people recognize that some things simply are the case, without being attributable to any particular cause, that distinction, too, must be expressible. But the linguistic machinery of central concern and major use relates an animate, purposive actor to the actions he initiates, so what he intends to do and what he causes to happen are inextricably confounded.

In sentences like "Bruce murdered Sid" the purposive character of Bruce's action is clearly entailed. What is not intuitively clear is whether that purpose is communicated by (a) a semantic component of the verb, (b) a semantic component of the subject of the verb, or (c) the combination of certain subjects with certain verbs. Is the oddity of "A knife murdered Sid" to be explained by the fact that "murder" is intentional, or that "knife" is inanimate, or that this combination of "knife" and "murder" violates some semantic principle?

Consider a case where the purposive character of an action is ambiguous. Then we can try to identify which of these three alternatives might account for the ambiguity. In "The man moved," whether the movement was self-generated or not is ambiguous, and where the movement is self-generated there may be a further ambiguity between whether it was intentional or not. It would be difficult to keep track of both sorts of ambiguity. Therefore, take the sentence "The man traveled." Since "travel" is intransitive, the causative sense of "The man traveled himself," paralleling "The man moved himself," is not available. With the causative component set to one side, we can consider whether "The man traveled" is ambiguous with respect to intention—between whether he deliberately and actively caused himself to travel or whether he traveled in a passive and unintentional manner, perhaps because he inadvertently sat in a ski lift—because of some ambiguity of "travel," or some ambiguity of "the man," or some ambiguity attributable to their combination.

If we take purpose to be a property expressed by the verb, we should have two senses of a verb like "travel," one indicating that the grammatical subject is the intentional cause of the traveling, the other compatible with the idea that something else caused the subject of the verb to travel. The first sense of "travel" would be marked in the lexicon as agentive and the second as non-agentive. The major trouble with this approach is that most people do not feel that there are two meanings of the English verb "travel" that differ in this way.

If we reject this solution, the apparent ambiguity must arise either from some semantic property of the noun phrase that is the subject of the verb or from an interaction of the noun and predicate phrases. If we take the ambiguity to arise from the noun phrase, we should have in the lexicon two senses for every animate noun like "man," one indicating that the subject is the intentional cause of the action and the other that he is not. (In ergative languages, different suffixes might be attached to the subject noun, as if in English we said "He traveled" when the subject caused his own traveling and "Him traveled" when he did not.) The trouble with this approach is the same as the first. People do not feel that there are two meanings of "the man" that differ in this way.

We are left with the possibility that purpose arises from the combination of certain noun phrases with certain verbs. What kind of rule for combinations could express the fact that "The man traveled" can denote either purposive or nonpurposive traveling? The components, "the man" and "travel," are the same in both interpretations and their combination results in exactly the same surface structure.

There are various possible answers, all of which assume two different structures underlying the sentence. One underlying structure contains some feature that corresponds to a purposive interpretation and the other does not. Whatever that feature is, it does not receive explicit expression in the surface sentence.

Fillmore (1968) has argued that there is a special case, called the Agent case, that can provide one of the arguments of the verb. When there is a noun phrase in the Agent case in the underlying structure, it develops into the surface subject of the verb (if a passive transformation is not applied); the result is the purposive version. There is also a case called the Object case (or Patient case) that would normally develop into the direct object of the verb in the surface sentence, but if a noun phrase in the Agent case is not provided, the noun phrase in the Object case sometimes serves as the surface subject; the result is the nonpurposive version. If this argument is applied to intransitive verbs like "travel," which do not ordinarily have an Object (or Patient) case, it seems less persuasive than in the examples Fillmore has analyzed; it says little more than that sometimes the surface subject derives from an underlying Agent and sometimes it does not.

Lee (1969) has suggested that sentences express purpose if and only if they have "deep structure subjects." Sentences that express purpose have agents marked as such in the underlying structure because they are the subject of the verb; sentences that do not express purpose do not have subjects of the verb in the underlying structure—the noun phrase that appears as the subject in the surface sentence bears some other relation to the verb. This suggestion would make it unnecessary to introduce linguistic entities like Agent and Patient cases in addition to the usual syntactic categories like noun, noun phrase, and verb, or syntactic relations like subject of and object of. It is not clear, however, what other relation than grammatical subject "the man" could have to "travel" in the structure underlying the nonpurposive sense of "The man traveled," and the complications for syntactic analysis that would result from Lee's proposal would be forbidding.

In answer to the question "What did he do?" the nonpurposive sense of "He traveled" is not appropriate—if the man was not an agent, an appropriate reply would be something like "He didn't *do* anything, he just traveled along." This relation between agency or purpose and constructions involving "do" has often been noted. In the nonpurposive sense of "The man traveled," the man does not *do* anything; in the purposive sense, the traveling is what he does. One might suppose—with Ross (1972b)—that somewhere underlying the purposive version is another verb, *do*(he, event), where the event is his traveling; this verb can be made explicit in such surface sentences as "What the man did was travel." We do not agree, however, that "What the man did was travel" is closer to the syntactic structure underlying the purposive sense of "The man traveled" than is "The man traveled" itself. Ross's *do* may be present conceptually, but that does not mean it must be incorporated into the underlying phrase structure of the purposive interpretation.

To recapitulate: since sentences like "The man swam" seem to have only a purposive sense in which "the man" plays the role of an agent who intentionally does the swimming, the purposive sense must be inherent either in the verb, in the noun phrase that serves as the subject, or in the way the two are combined. But when we consider sentences like "The man traveled," which can describe either purposive or nonpurposive motion, none of these three possibilities gives a coherent explanation of the putative ambiguity; the verb in both interpretations is the same verb, the noun phrase in both interpretations is the same noun phrase, their combination into a sentence is accomplished in the same way in both interpretations. So we must consider a fourth alternative, namely, that sentences like "The man traveled" are not ambiguous at all.

It may be the case that the speaker saw a man change location but was unable to determine whether the man did so on purpose or not. A virtue of verbs like "travel" is that they permit a speaker to say what he saw even when he is unable or unwilling to decide whether it was intentional. If we adopt some hypothesis that builds agency or purpose inextricably into the linguistic machinery at a speaker's disposal, the hypothesis would imply that the speaker must decide, for he would have only two options: either he intends the purposive version or he intends the nonpurposive version, that is, either the linguistic structure underlying his sentence contains Ross's *do* (or Fillmore's Agent case, or Lee's deep structure subject, or whatever) or it does not. In order to say "The man traveled" he must first adopt one or the other of these underlying structures before the "ambiguous" surface sentence can be derived from it.

Although a speaker may have the information necessary to decide whether a motion was purposive, that information is no part of the sentence "The man traveled." Consider a parallel situation. Suppose the speaker also has the information necessary to decide whether the man's motion was northward. Directional information is certainly no part of the sentence "The man traveled"; you do not feel this sentence is ambiguous because the motion may or may not have been toward the north. Why should anyone feel it is ambiguous because the motion may or may not have been intentional?

On the one hand a few verbs are clearly nonagentive: happen, rain, snow, die. On the other hand many verbs are clearly agentive: murder, eat, swim, chase. When someone says "The man ate," anyone who knows what eating is will know that it is something you do, not something that can just happen to you. But there are also many verbs that are neither one nor the other: raise, turn, break, travel, move. When someone says "Melissa moved the bed" it is not a part of this sentence that she was a deliberate agent; she may have moved it accidentally—it is not odd to ask whether she moved it intentionally. But if you say "Peter chased Melissa," it is distinctly odd to be asked whether he did so intentionally.

In sentences like "Melissa moved the bed" we will not assume that the verb "move" has an Agent case associated with it, or that "Melissa" is in the Agent case when she moves the bed intentionally. We will assume only that Melissa did something, and whatever she did caused the bed to move. We can think of Melissa as a causal factor who may also have been an intentional agent, but we will not incorporate such distinctions into the lexical information associated with "move." We will retain the notion of agent but will not use it to define an Agent case in the grammar.

Some of the semantic issues here can be sorted out if we assume there are four basic semantic operators available for incorporation into complex verbs. We will use HAPPEN, CAUSE, INTEND, and DO for this purpose. After introducing them as simply as possible in order to get the structure clear, we will consider the necessary qualifications. These operators are characterized by the fact that they can take statements, S, as their arguments.

We will use HAPPEN to conceptualize the Event predicate of 2.5.2.:

(77)   HAPPEN(S):   An event x characterized by the statement S "happens"
         at some time t if:
         (i) Event$_t(x)$

We will use DO to conceptualize the relation between an object and the event in which it participates:

(78)   DO(x, S):   An object x "does" something characterized by the state-
         ment S if:
         (i) Chng(x) $\equiv$ HAPPEN(S)

We will use CAUSE to conceptualize the Cause predicate of 2.6.2:

(79)   CAUSE(S, S'):   Something characterized by the statement S "causes"
         something characterized by the statement S' if:
         (i) HAPPEN(S)
         (ii) HAPPEN(S')
         (iii) Cause((i), (ii))

We will use INTEND to conceptualize the *Intend* predicate of 2.6.3:

(80)   INTEND(x, S):   An animate x "intends" to achieve a goal g charac-
        terized by the statement S if:
        (i) *Intend(x, g)*

The general idea is that "Melissa moved the bed" corresponds to DO(Melissa, S) & CAUSE(S, TRAVEL(bed)), or "Melissa did something that caused
the bed to travel." This representation does not assume that what Melissa did
was intentional, but, whatever she did, it had the effect of moving the bed.
The sentence "Melissa intends to move the bed" would correspond to INTEND
(Melissa, MOVE(Melissa, bed)), where the second argument of INTEND is
taken as a goal description. In order to represent "Melissa moved the bed
intentionally," we need something like INTENTIONALLY(MOVE(Melissa, bed)),
where the adverb would be

(81)   INTENTIONALLY(S_x):   An animate x does something characterized by
        the statement S "intentionally" if x has a goal g and a plan p to achieve
        that goal such that p entails S and:
        (i) CAUSE(INTEND(x, g), DO(x, S))

The complete analysis of "Melissa moved the bed intentionally" would be
CAUSE(INTEND(Melissa, g), MOVE(Melissa, bed)), where g—Melissa's ultimate
goal—may have been either to move the bed or to achieve some state of
affairs of which this was only a part or a precursor. Since many verbs incorporate the meaning that the action is done intentionally, it will be convenient to
have at least one further operator of this type:

(82)   ACT(x, S):   INTENTIONALLY(S_x).

This is the general plan we will follow in analyzing these components of verbs,
but first we should note some of the more obvious shortcomings of these preliminary formulations.

All of these operators are abstract, yet we have introduced them in terms
of perceptual predicates; the bridge from perceptual to conceptual status must
be discussed. It should also be noted that they are introduced to account for
certain distinctions between English verbs; it would be desirable to know
whether the same operators would be needed for languages outside the Indo-
European family, but we are not competent to make comparative analyses.
We believe that the concepts involved are sufficiently basic to qualify as psychological universals, but whether these concepts are expressed by verbs in
all the languages of the world—whether they are linguistic universals as well—
is dubious, though not impossible. But even as operators for English semantics we must ask what their relation is to the particular English verbs that
we have borrowed as mnemonic aids in designating the operators: What is
the relation of HAPPEN to "happen," of DO to "do," of CAUSE to "cause," or
of INTEND to "intend"? We will take them up in turn and will comment on
their conceptual status and their relation to particular senses of the English

verbs that seem to express them most directly, but we will have little to say about their universality.

6.3.3   HAPPEN

The definition of HAPPEN in (77) suggests that the only events that can happen are those identified perceptually as occurring at some location during some brief span of time—those satisfying the perceptual predicate Event. People think and talk of many events that are not perceptual, although they do involve some change of state. HAPPEN is so basic to human conceptual life that it is difficult to analyze it further; psychologically we can do little more than point to a need for developmental study. We assume that (77) characterizes the perceptual origins of the concept but that as a child acquires increasing familiarity with perceptual objects, states, changes of state, and their linguistic representations, he generalizes his conception of events to a wider variety of state changes, extended in space and time, abstract in character.

The major use we will make of HAPPEN will be to introduce locatives—particularly temporal locatives—that will specify where and when the happening occurred. The stative verbs do not easily take such locatives: "Ivan knows English in New York on Wednesdays" is odd, although "Ivan walks to work in New York on Wednesdays" is acceptable. Joos (1964) notes that with nonstative verbs we can say things like "Don't worry: he leaves next week," whereas "Don't worry: the baby resembles his father next year" is not good English. Stative verbs require an explicit timeshifter such as "will" or "be going to." Joos remarks, "This turns out to be a fairly economical criterion for sorting out the status verbs when we need to" (p. 118). Since happenings can be located in space and time, we assume that absence of a temporal locative introduced by the HAPPEN operator characterizes the semantics of stative verbs (and predicate adjectives denoting permanent states).

It must follow that HAPPEN is somehow incorporated in such nonstative verbs as "rain." It is not clear whether "rain" passes Joos's test or not. Is "Don't worry: it rains next week" acceptable? If not, perhaps its oddity is due to the general unpredictability of the weather. We believe that "rain" is a nonstative verb and that Joos's test must be used with caution.

The question, then, is how HAPPEN could be incorporated into "rain." Presumably "rain" relies on "fall," and "fall" means to change location in a downward direction. Since a change of location is a change, and a change can be an event, the formula for HAPPEN might apply. However, the formula given in (77) uses the predicate Event, which denotes the perception of a momentary change of state, whereas raining is not a momentary event but a process—a sequence of related momentary events that can persist for an indefinite time.

We will distinguish two subforms of HAPPEN: HAPPEN$_t$ to denote a momentary event, and HAPPEN$_i$ for a process extending over an interval. Then we can say that the semantic operator incorporated in "rain" is the durative HAP-PEN$_i$, not the punctual HAPPEN$_t$.

We now require three operators: HAPPEN, HAPPEN$_i$, and HAPPEN$_t$. Since the distinctions between them are temporal, we can use the temporal logic, introduced in 6.2.1:

(77′)   (a) HAPPEN(S):   An event or process characterized by the statement S "happens" if:

(i) $(\exists t) R_t(S)$

(b) HAPPEN$_i$(S):   A process characterized by the statement S "happens" if there are moments t' and $t'' > t' + 1$ and:

(i) $(t)[t' < t < t'' \supset R_t(S)]$ & $(\exists t''') R_{t'''}(\text{not}S)$

(c) HAPPEN$_t$(S):   An event characterized by the statement S "happens" if $(\exists t')[R_{t'}(\text{not}S)]$ and:

(i) $(\exists t)[R_{t-1}(\text{not}S)$ & $R_t(S)]$

As before, S represents some temporally indeterminate statement and $R_t(S)$ means that S is realized at the moment t. Note that HAPPEN$_i$ and HAPPEN$_t$ both imply HAPPEN, but not conversely. Note also that notHAPPEN(S) $\equiv$ HAP-PEN(notS), but that notHAPPEN$_i$(S) is not equivalent to HAPPEN$_i$(notS), and notHAPPEN$_t$(S) is not equivalent to HAPPEN$_t$(notS). HAPPEN$_t$(S) is equivalent to notCONTINUE(notS), given in (67).

HAPPEN$_t$ is closest to the sense of the Event predicate introduced in (77). The formulation of HAPPEN given in (77′a) is much more general than that given in (77); it amounts to little more than the assertion of S. One might think that so general an operator would be of little use, yet there is a sense of "happen" that seems to correspond closely to HAPPEN. "Happen" is one of a small class of intransitive verbs that can take sentences as their deep structure subjects (Rosenbaum, 1967). "Hassler has come from New York" can be taken as the subject of "happens," and grammatical transformations turn the combination into such surface sentences as "Hassler happens to have come from New York" or "It happens that Hassler has come from New York." When "happens" is used in this way, it has the force of "it happens to be the case that," which we take as close to (77′a). Moreover, the fact that "happen" can take a sentence as its subject seems to justify our use of the statement S as the argument of HAPPEN. As García (1967) has observed, for any English sentence there is a counterpart that contains "happen," either with "it happens that" or with "happens" taken to be the superficial main verb. This is equally true for sentences like "Kurt happens to know English," even though the stative verb "know" does not incorporate HAPPEN, so the sentence cannot be understood either as an event or as a process.

When "happen" does not take a sentence as its subject it is generally used together with a temporal locative for an event. "An explosion happened" is unsatisfying, like "He put the book"; a locative is wanted. "Homer saw the accident happen" says little that "Homer saw the accident" does not; "happen" in such contexts invites an identifying locative and serves little purpose when it is not provided. Therefore, when "happen" does not take a sentence as its subject, it is HAPPEN$_i$ or HAPPEN$_t$ that is involved. In that case, the subject must be an event nominal: "The apple happened at noon" is not conventional English.

Our present concern, however, is more with the incorporation of these operators into other verbs than with their adequacy in accounting for all the uses of "happen." Among the motion verbs it is obvious that HAPPEN$_i$ is incorporated into some, like "travel," and HAPPEN$_t$ is incorporated into others, like "reach" or "arrive." We encountered this distinction in 6.2.5, where we distinguished two types of temporally indeterminate statements: P statements characterizing ongoing processes, and E statements characterizing momentary events. In that discussion we noted that temporal locatives for P statements are somewhat more complex than for E statements. It will turn out that HAPPEN$_t$ is generally more useful to us; it permits the introduction of a specific moment prior to which S was false and at which S is true. We will therefore omit the operator HAPPEN$_i$ as redundant in such process verbs as "travel," but we will not suppress HAPPEN$_t$ when it permits us to introduce t as an argument of event verbs.

Among the most important happenings are beginnings and endings. The formulation for END(P) given in (64) implies HAPPEN$_t$(notP), and the formulation for BEGIN(P) in (68) implies HAPPEN$_t$(P). P can characterize locations, properties, or even the identity of an object. If something "changed into a pumpkin," the statement P could be represented as ISA(x, pumpkin); then BEGIN(P) would correspond to "x began being a pumpkin" and HAPPEN$_t$(P) would correspond to "x being a pumpkin happened." The natural way to say such things, however, is "x changed into a y" or "x turned into a y." We can introduce a formulation for such expressions:

(83)   CHINTO(x, y):   An entity x "changes into" being an entity y if there
is a time t such that Q_t(notISA(x, y)), and:
(i) R_t(ISA(x, y))

Since (83) is modeled after BEGIN(P), it too will imply HAPPEN$_t$(P), where P is ISA(x, y). In order to indicate what x was before it changed, there is a parallel formulation of "change from":

(84)   CHFROM (x, y):   An entity x "changes from" being an entity y if there
is a time t such that Q_t(ISA(x, y)), and:
(i) R_t(notISA(x, y))

Since (84) is modeled after END(P), it too will imply HAPPEN$_t$(notP), where P is ISA(x, y).

These routines are appropriate for abrupt changes of status, but sometimes the change to be described is more gradual. It may be difficult to recognize exactly what moment an entity ceases to be a weapon, say, and becomes a plowshare. At some time, however, the new status of the entity will be recognizable, so CHINTO is at least part of what is happening. But it must be supplemented by the notion that the change was going on for some appreciable interval prior to the final state. So we can propose a routine for "becoming":

(85)   BECOME(x, y):   An entity x "becomes" an entity y if:
   (i) HAPPEN$_i$(CHNG(x))
   (ii) CHINTO(x, y)
   (iii) UNTIL((i), (ii))

Condition (i) requires some interval of changing prior to accomplishing the final state.

If an entity does not change from being y, it "remains" or "doesn't stop being" y. A routine for REMAIN(x, y) can be modeled on (65) for notEND(P):

(86)   REMAIN(x, y):   notEND(ISA(x, y)).

REMAIN(x, y) is equivalent to notCHFROM(x, y).

Sentences like "He made a plowshare" incorporate an additional argument, the agent, into BECOME. This sense of "make" can be formulated:

(87)   MAKE(x, y):   An x "makes" an entity y if there is an entity z and:
   (i) BECOME(z, y)
   (ii) DO(x, S)
   (iii) CAUSE(S, (i))

Arguments specifying the something z from which y is made may be added to MAKE by combining it with CHFROM(y, z). This sense of "make," which resembles "build" or "manufacture," is but one of the senses of this useful verb. It can also be used as a general causative verb, as in "He made Cora angry" or "He made the saucer spin." This more general sense of "make" should be formulated as MAKE(x, S'), where HAPPEN$_t(S')$ or HAPPEN$_i(S')$ would replace BECOME in the first condition of (87), but conditions (ii) and (iii) would remain unaltered: "x does S and S causes S'."

As defined in (77'c), HAPPEN assures the existence of some moment $t - 1$ at which S is false and a next moment t at which S is true; the moment need not be identified, but its existence is asserted. When we say "Tom reached Chicago" we mean there was some moment t at which "Tom is in Chicago" was false and a next moment $t + 1$ at which "Tom is in Chicago" was true. If we wish to identify that moment, we can add a temporal locative, as in "Tom reached Chicago at 11:23 A.M. yesterday." If we say "Tom didn't reach Chicago" we deny there was a moment t at which "Tom is in Chicago" was true, but we do not deny there was some moment at which "Tom is in Chicago" was false; the falsity of "Tom is in Chicago" at some moment of time is a presupposition of "Tom reached Chicago."

This presupposition is stated explicitly in (77'c), where $(\exists t')R_{t'}(\text{not}S)$ is given as a precondition for the application of test (i). The reason for this stipulation becomes clear when we consider the contradictory of HAPPEN$_t(S)$:

notHAPPEN$_t(S)$:   not$(\exists t)[R_{t-1}(\text{not}S)$ & $R_t(S)]$
$\equiv (t)\text{not}[R_{t-1}(\text{not}S)$ & $R_t(S)]$
$\equiv (t)[R_{t-1}(\text{not}S) \supset R_t(\text{not}S)] \equiv (t)[R_t(S) \supset R_{t-1}(S)]$.

Something can "not happen" only if no change occurs; no change will occur if either $R_t(S)$ or $R_t(\text{notS})$ is always true. The contrapositive equivalence in the last line above admits either possibility. Since we generally mean that $R_t(\text{notS})$ is true when we say that S has not happened, we must presuppose that at some moment t', S was not true. Then we can conjoin the presupposition with the negative (but not the affirmative) assertion

$$(\exists t')R_{t'}(\text{notS}) \;\&\; (t)[R_{t\text{-}1}(\text{notS}) \supset R_t(\text{notS})].$$

Although the presupposition stated in (77'c) seems unnecessary at first glance, it must be included to ensure a correct interpretation of the contradictory. It will be noted that the nonoccurrence of an event is temporally equivalent to a state.

6.3.4   DO

HAPPEN and DO are closely related (see (78)). We use DO to introduce an argument representing the object that participates in a happening, and to introduce it in a nonpurposive way. Of course, events and processes exist only insofar as they happen to objects; it might seem that any nonstative verb would involve some object. We have noted the verbs "rain" and "snow," however, which are nonstative yet do not involve objects to "do" them; they are functions without arguments, which satisfy HAPPEN, but not DO. Hence the two operators cannot be combined into one. Since HAPPEN will not suffice for the vast majority of nonstative verbs—because it provides no way to indicate what the participating object is—we need $\text{DO}(x, S)$ to say not only that S happened but that x was the object that did it.

Although this operator represents a simple addition to our semantic analysis, its very simplicity can lead to misunderstanding by those who would expect more from it. In particular, we must consider its relation to the very complex English verb "do," and we must consider whether it expresses intentionality.

We are not concerned here with the suppletive and essentially meaningless "do" that can be introduced transformationally for insistence or negation or interrogation, as in "Do try it" or "I don't know" or "Did you go?" The sense of "do" we have in mind is incorporated in more complex verbs; it surfaces only in sentences like "He left and so did I" or "What the engine does is drive the propeller."

Such constructions convey a sense of action, and verbs that incorporate DO are called action verbs. When an action involves an actor, $\text{DO}(x, S)$ should suffice to define x as the actor. In many cases x may be an intentional agent as well as an actor. Although the distinction between actors and agents will do no theoretical work here (we regard the basic distinction as between DO and ACT) we will generally use "actor" in the nonpurposive sense of (78) and reserve "agent" for animate, intentional actors.

Other theorists adopt other conventions. Ross (1972b) argues on linguistic grounds that "every verb of action is embedded in the object complement of a two-place predicate whose subject is identical to the subject of the action verb, and whose phonological realization in English is *do*" (p. 70). In a very general sense, that much of Ross's analysis is roughly compatible with ours. But then Ross suggests, and Dowty (1972b) endorses the suggestion, that the notion of agent should be identified with the first argument of this two-place predicate. We have indicated our objections to this analysis in our discussion of "The man traveled" (6.3.2), where we wanted to leave open the possibility that his change of location might or might not have been an intentional act on his part. We prefer to distinguish actors and agents, and to regard "intentionally" as a special manner of doing, characteristic of actors who are also agents. We will return to this matter in the discussion of INTEND and ACT.

The notion of "action" is important for any semantic analysis of verbs, as the history of grammatical theories has shown, but precisely how a semantic category of "action" and a syntactic category of "verb" should be related has never been satisfactorily explained. Insofar as $DO(x, S)$ represents this relation —insofar as DO is a semantic operator dependent on the grammatical relation of a subject x to a sentence whose predicate phrase is an event description (whose predicate entails HAPPEN)—we must recognize that it is undefined.

For the purposes of the present work, DO will be used principally as a placeholder. That is, $DO(x, S)$ will be restricted to contexts where S can be a dummy variable, as in "x does something." If S cannot be a dummy variable— if what x does is important to the meaning that is being analyzed—then DO will be replaced by a verb schema that makes x's action explicit. However, the aspectual distinction between momentary events and continuing processes can be represented by $DO(x, E)$ or $DO(x, P)$.

6.3.5   CAUSE

In 6.3.2 we suggested the following analysis of "cause":

(79)   CAUSE(S, S'):   Something characterized by statement S "causes" something characterized by statement S' if:
    (i) HAPPEN(S)
    (ii) HAPPEN(S')
    (iii) Cause((i), (ii))

Here again we have used a perceptual predicate to introduce an extremely complex concept. As anything more than a hypothesis about the ontogenetic origins of the adult concept of causation, (79iii) is woefully inadequate; it may not even be a plausible ontogenetic hypothesis. One could propose that the perceptual mechanism for Cause is innate and that visual causation provides the point of origin for later conceptual refinements; in his discussion of visual causality Piaget (1961) reports that he never found any great differences between age groups. He argues, though, that the child's concept of causality originates in action. The sensorimotor organization achieved during the first two years "prefigures" visual causality and is also the origin of more abstract notions of causation that develop between the ages of two or three and eleven or twelve years. In 2.6.3 we speculated that the perceptual predicate Cause may itself be a product of considerable cognitive development, which may originate with intentional movements and generalize through some kind of decentering to other persons and inanimate objects.

The simplest formulation of the conceptual core of CAUSE for sophisticated adults living in a contemporary industrial society would probably be that all events have causes. On that basic hypothesis a person then seeks valid and socially acceptable criteria for asserting that events of particular types are the effects of such-and-such types of causes. This hypothesis, that all events are caused by something or other, has not always been accepted, even by educated people. It is not a hypothesis that young children would be expected to formulate independently, nor does English (or any other language we have heard of) obligate a speaker to incorporate causes in every event description. The ontogenetic development of this conceptual core of causation is plainly something of a mystery. It cannot develop by means of inductive learning (Goodman, 1955); since the concept has varied so much in different cultures at different times, it is difficult to accept any psychologistic hypothesis that this is simply how the human mind works. If there is some innate psychological basis, it probably derives from the innate ability to profit from experience, to learn brute facts about which subsequent events frequently follow which antecedent events. It is the nonindependence of events that makes past experience useful for prediction and planning, and self-conscious awareness of dependencies between events presumably leads to some attempt to categorize those dependencies—to distinguish cases where the dependency arises from the action of human or superhuman agents from cases where it arises from natural sources, or to distinguish cases where the antecedent event is merely an indicator of the subsequent event from cases where the antecedent event necessarily (in some physical sense of necessity) leads to the subsequent event, and so on. Children may begin with an innate ability to register correlations between events, but what they are able to make of those correlations conceptually must depend on their experience, on their education, and the culture in which they live.

Laurendeau and Pinard (1962) have summarized extensive psychological research on the development of causal thinking in children. After considering a variety of objections to Piaget's (1926, 1927b) description of the process, they concluded that their own experiments substantially corroborated Piaget's theories. The youngest children do not seem to comprehend questions about "Why..." or "How is it that..." Many answers indicate that the average child between four and six has not clearly distinguished between subjective and objective, and the external world shares such characteristics of the self as purposiveness, awareness, and so on. At that age men are seen as responsible for everything that happens, or, when that will not suffice, some omnipotent magician created in the image and likeness of man is held to be responsible. Parallel with explanations in terms of human agency, but lasting somewhat longer (until about age ten) is a failure to distinguish clearly between animate and inanimate things and a tendency to endow inanimate objects with strength and energy similar to man's. Answers in terms of objective causality do not predominate until a child is ten or eleven years old, but even adults sometimes react to novel problems in ways that resemble the precausal thinking of children.

Of particular interest is the child's concept of life. According to Laurendeau and Pinard, very young children do not comprehend questions about "alive." The earliest justifications for judgments that something is alive are appeals to its motions, activities, or usefulness. Then a distinction is made between things that can move independently (the sun and wind) and those that do not (bicycles). Finally, only plants and animals are said to be alive, but even here the importance of motion can be detected in some children's restriction of the category to animals and people. A willingness to attribute life to inanimate objects is not completely missing in the responses of many adults.

Apparently it takes at least ten years for an average child to get his ideas about causation and animacy sorted out. Before this is accomplished, he is already a very competent (and often prolific) speaker of his native language. Since language is something that children can learn and use even before they have mastered adult concepts of causation and animacy, we must be careful not to impose too much of our sophisticated adult understanding on the linguistic forms. That is to say, CAUSE should be formulated in such a way that a variety of conceptual grounds for understanding the relation between two events will be compatible with it. For example, a child might begin with the idea that spatially and temporally contiguous events are crucial to the relation; then, by generalizing his own powers for causing events, he might impose a restriction that the relation must be intended by somebody or some manlike thing; only later does he replace the purposive relation with some more abstract relation involving the notion of possibility. This hypothetical progression might reflect a progressive unfreezing from CAUSE(ego, event) to CAUSE (person, event) to CAUSE(event, event). Throughout this progression the child must be able to use "cause," and verbs incorporating CAUSE, in his speech and in understanding the speech of others, which might lead to the kinds of answers that Piaget and others have observed. Let us leave this question of the ontogenesis of CAUSE and consider what is involved in its adult conception.

Schank (1973a, b) has argued that, conceptually, causation is a relation between two events; that aspect of the perceptual formulation proposed in (79) seems to be accepted at the conceptual level. The statements S and S' that describe the two events assumed in (79) may not appear explicitly in the linguistic expression of causality—typically, the description S of the causal event is omitted and must be filled in conceptually as "x does something" in order to provide both terms of the relation—but we assume that when people are thinking about causal relations they are thinking about relations between ordered pairs of events. The problem that requires discussion concerns the criteria that people will respect when they decide that some ordered pair of events, or some general class of ordered pairs of events, is related causally rather than in some other way. Phrased in more philosophical terms, what is the semantic basis for propositions about causal relations? Given a semantic analysis at the conceptual level, we could then address the problem of how those conceptual relations are expressed in English.

Dowty (1972a) suggests that von Wright's (1963, 1968) deontic logic could provide a semantic basis for the analysis of cause in English sentences. According to this view, in order to assert that an object's actions caused some event to happen, a speaker must believe that the event happened and that it would not have happened on that particular occasion if the object had not acted and all else had been the same. This interpretation of causation relates to a logical analysis of conditionals proposed by Stalnaker (1968), and Dowty argues that it is the most adequate interpretation available for causative verbs in ordinary language. It is complex in that it involves a comparison of the actual situation with the situation that would have prevailed (the "possible world") if the person had not acted and all else had been the same. (We encountered such a situation earlier in the discussion of nonfactual "before" in 6.2.3.)

In order to understand the relations between counterfactual conditionals and such concepts as causality, it is worth exploring this notion of "possible worlds" in more detail. The ideas underlying possible-world semantics go back at least to Leibniz, but they probably became respectable in logical circles only with the successful development of semantical models for modal logic (as in Kripke, 1963a, b). Semantical models provide a formal method to specify the truth conditions of sentences (usually in a formalized language) in terms of more elementary sentences, and ultimately in terms of the extensions of the constituents of the elementary sentences. The models provide an elegant way to characterize the semantics of many logical systems whose axioms may have nonobvious consequences.

Following Leibniz, one may say that if a certain state of affairs is to be found in at least one possible world, that state of affairs is "possible." If it is "impossible," it is not to be found in any possible world. If it is "necessary," it is found in any possible world. These notions, which are closely related, are called modal notions. They are represented formally in terms of statement-forming operators that take statements as their arguments and transform them into new statements. For example, if p is a statement and M is the modal operator for possibility, Mp is a new statement corresponding to "It is possible that p" or "p is possible." Impossibility is defined by negation: $notMp$; necessity is defined by $notMnotp$. The truth value of "It is necessary that p" cannot be determined from the truth of p, and elaborate systems of modal logic for determining which modal formulas should be taken as valid have been explored. Hughes and Cresswell (1968) provide a valuable introduction to this kind of logic and to the methods used to prove the consistency and validity of various alternative systems.

We have seen one variety of modal logic in 6.2.1, where the statement-forming operator R_t was introduced to formalize temporal relations. The temporal index t can be thought of as indicating possible worlds—different states of affairs at different moments. Possibility might be thought of as the existence of some moment t at which a statement is realized; if there is no moment at which the statement is not realized, the statement may be thought of as necessary.

A key role in the semantics of modal logics is played by the relation of accessibility. In order to talk about the truth of statements in worlds other than the one you happen to be in, you must have some kind of access to those worlds. One way to think of this relation is that there are only certain possible worlds that people can conceive. A necessary action, for example, might be defined as an action that occurs in all the possible worlds that you can conceive. An individual in one possible world may be able to conceive of another possible world, but it may not be the case that an individual in the second possible world could conceive of the first world; for example, we can conceive of a world without war, but inhabitants of such a world might not be able to imagine our world. In such a case, the relation of accessibility is not symmetrical. One's conceptions of possibility and necessity will depend on what worlds one can conceive of, and the variety of modal logics reflects the variety of ways that conceivable alternative worlds can be defined.

It might help to introduce a concrete example. Consider the game of tick-tacktoe. At the outset of any play of the game there are 9! ($= 362,880$) conceivable sequences of moves the two players can choose (if they fill every square). Each successive choice of a move changes the current state of the game into a new state; at any given point in the game, only certain choices—only certain state transitions—are available to a player. If we think of the state of the game at any particular point as a possible world, then a player must be able to conceive of possible worlds other than the one that actually exists at the moment.

Isard and others (Isard and Longuet-Higgins, 1971; Davies and Isard, 1972; Isard, 1975) have used ticktacktoe, played between a person and a machine, to explore the semantics of such English modal verbs as "can," "might," and "will." The machine was programmed to play the game and to answer questions like "What would you have done if I had taken square x on move three?" or "What can you do if I take square x on the next move?" The machine had to remember the course of events and to compute its moves for a variety of possible situations other than the actual situation at the moment. Although this example may seem trivial, it provides a simple setting in which many of the complexities surrounding the linguistic description of alternative states of affairs can be explored in terms of procedural semantics.

The machine that plays modal ticktacktoe can compile and respond to such nonfactual conditional questions as "If I had done this, what would you have done?" because the set of possible worlds is well defined by the rules of the game. In normal conversation, however, there is much more uncertainty about the possible worlds that are to be considered as alternatives to the actual world. Stalnaker (1968) proposes a way of analyzing nonfactual conditionals, like "If the Russians invade Germany, the United States will use nuclear weapons," in terms of model theory. What he suggests, in essence, is that such a conditional is true if its consequent is true in the possible world that is most similar to the actual world except for what is required by the conditional's antecedent clause. This approach has been extended by Dowty (1972a, b) to incorporate the apparent counterfactual nature of conditionals expressing causal relations. He has explored the apparent equivalence between the following sorts of sentences:

(88)   John's doing it caused Mary to leave.
         If John had not done it, Mary would not have left.

Dowty argues that "S caused S′ " is true if (a) "S and S′ " is true and (b) "notS′ " is true in the possible world that is most similar to the actual world except that the event described by S does not occur in it.

A number of philosophers are persuaded that this sort of approach offers the best analysis of causal language in ordinary life. In our view, any decision on this issue at the present time is likely to be premature. One of the disadvantages of a semantical model for the purposes of psychological theory is, indeed, its very precision. The general idea is obviously of great psychological importance; people *can* envisage states of affairs alternative to what actually happens, and this ability probably plays an important part in the semantics of causal and moral concepts. When this idea is formalized in terms of sets of possible worlds, accessibility relations, and extensionalist ways of thought, however, the results are normative, not descriptive. For example, many of the philosophical debates over the interpretation of possible-world logics have centered around the determination of the identities of individuals in different possible worlds. In unreal worlds some existing individuals may be absent and nonexisting individuals may appear. Is Hitler still Hitler, for instance, in a possible world where he became a successful but minor artist in Vienna? Or would Hitler disappear in that world? What would consitute evidence that could be used to settle the matter? The answer to such questions is easily tainted with essentialism—what are the essential attributes of Hitler?—which offends the metaphysical sensibilities of some philosophers. The argument is whether this way of thinking can be justified on logical grounds and what assumptions are required for the justification. Although it may not be logically justifiable, the man in the street has little difficulty in doing it—in thinking of what might have happened to an individual under different circumstances, or in thinking of the same individual with attributes other than those he actually possesses. The layman can even imagine worlds in which there are two instances of the same individual (entities that can be in two places at the same time) who may or may not have the same attributes.

Insofar as modal logics help keep our psychological theories straight, they are valuable aids. As theories about the mental operations of ordinary language users, however, we prefer to reserve judgment. We favor a more flexible procedural semantics to characterize the ways in which people can set up cognitive representations of various states of affairs.

The conceptual core—the layman's notion that some if not all events have causes—implies that events are not always independent of one another; the occurrence of one event may affect the possibility of another event. Indeed, an ability to foresee outcomes of one's own behavior is an essential component of intelligent adaptation to the environment and entails an ability to foresee the consequences of other events as well. It is this predictive ability, we believe, that ultimately underlies the linguistic expression of causal relations. In order to make predictions, one must envisage possible states of affairs other than the present state. So we will assume the availability of the operator POSSIBLE, which can apply to a description S of some state of affairs. The mechanism for testing POSSIBLE(S) presumably involves the execution of some sort of control instruction to "generate" a representation of the state of affairs specified by S, and the execution of that instruction will exploit any relevant experience or knowledge about such states of affairs that happen to be available to the system.

As in modal logic, we assume that notPOSSIBLE(S) defines IMPOSSIBLE(S), and that notPOSSIBLE(notS) defines NECESSARY(S). What we do not assume is that these are *logical* operators. They may be or they may not, depending on the domain of discourse. Logical necessity, for example, concerns statements that could not fail to be true under any circumstances; "There are no round triangles" may be necessarily true in this logical sense. A nonlogician recognizes also what might be called physical necessity: "No object travels faster than the speed of light" is thought to be necessarily true in this physical sense. This distinction raises many philosophical difficulties that we will simply ignore. If one listens to how people ordinarily talk about possibilities and necessities, it is clear that the states of affairs they are capable or incapable of conceiving vary enormously as a function of the domain of discourse and their experience with it; logical necessity characterizes one domain of discourse, but it is not a domain of preeminent concern to the average person. Sometimes it is difficult to know which domain one is in; if someone asks whether it is possible for time to flow backward, he may be asking whether it is logically possible (whether the notion is self-contradictory) or whether it is physically possible (whether there could be some place where it actually happens). Deciding such questions of classification is of considerable philosophical importance, but it does not seem to lead to psychologically interesting constraints on the kinds of states of affairs for which people are able to generate cognitive representations.

One domain of discourse to which these operators can be applied is the domain of causal relations. It is important to distinguish between generic and specific assertions about causation. Generic causal assertions are universally quantified and often lawlike: "If an object is heated, it expands." Specific causal assertions are existentially quantified: "This object expanded because it was heated." It is sometimes claimed that generic causal assertions are nothing but universally quantified implications; this thesis, in effect, was advanced by Hume. It is sometimes claimed that specific causal assertions contain an implicit resort to established laws (generic causal assertions); this thesis, in effect, was advanced by Carnap. But these ideas were explored in the context of a philosophy of science; they could prove false when applied to the semantics of ordinary English.

We will try to apply POSSIBLE to the analysis of generic causal relations and associated concepts in order to provide a theoretical basis for introducing the semantic component CAUSE(S, S') as a relation between two statements S and S'. Since we must allow that the product of our analysis of the generic concept may differ from the concept that is incorporated into causative English verbs, we will observe a minor notational distinction. For the purposes of conceptual analysis we will use CAUSES(e_1, e_2) to represent a generic causal relation between conceptual representations of the temporally ordered pair of event types e_1 and e_2, where (to avoid self-causing events) $e_1 \neq e_2$. Given an analysis of generic CAUSES in terms of POSSIBLE, we will then take it as the model for defining the linguistic concept CAUSE.

Although the linguistic concept of causal relation that is incorporated into English causative verbs relates pairs of statements, the generic concept of causation must accommodate long strings of causally related events. Making explicit the causal chains underlying phenomena that may be treated in ordinary language as pairs of causally related statements is often a problem requiring intensive scientific research. Since an analysis of causal chains would involve us in scientific details extraneous to our present interest, and since the basic building blocks of causal chains are pairs of events, and since our linguistic needs do not exceed pairs of statements, we will limit our analysis of the generic concept CAUSES to pairs of events. This limitation may reduce the value of the analysis as a basis for constructing a philosophy of science, but our purpose here is merely to construct a plausible psychological account.

Accordingly, as a first approximation, a simple conceptualization in terms of POSSIBLE might posit the following analysis of generic causal relations: CAUSES(e_1, e_2) is accepted whenever a person is willing to accept both POSSIBLE(e_1 & e_2) and IMPOSSIBLE(e_1 & not-e_2). If a person accepts that it is possible to heat an object and for the object to expand, and that it is impossible to heat an object and for the object not to expand, then he should accept that heating an object causes it to expand. Given this formulation, CAUSE(e_1, not-e_2) $\equiv$ POSSIBLE(e_1 & not-e_2) & IMPOSSIBLE(e_1 & e_2) can be taken as defining PREVENTS(e_1, e_2). And, if not to cause or prevent something is to allow it, then ALLOWS(e_1, e_2) might be defined as POSSIBLE(e_1 & e_2) & POSSIBLE(e_1 & not-e_2). (Note that the conditions for ALLOWS(e_1, e_2) also satisfy the conditions for ALLOWS(e_1, not-e_2).) If neither (e_1 & e_2) nor (e_1 & not-e_2) is possible, generic causal relations between e_1 and e_2 do not apply.

One obvious deficiency of this approach is that it takes no account of what happens when e_1 does not occur. One term of the relation, e_1, is fixed, and only the other term is allowed to vary. This formulation might correspond to some intermediate stage in a child's development of a concept of causality (e_1 might be fixed at first on personally initiated events), but a full causal analysis must also consider not-e_1. Indeed, the state of affairs that would result from not-e_1 is the critical element in the counterfactual interpretation of causal relations; see (88) above.

We must consider the possibility or impossibility of all four combinations: (e_1 & e_2), (e_1 & not-e_2), (not-e_1 & e_2), and (not-e_1 & not-e_2). Since the combinatorial complexity is formidable, the consequences of this expanded set of conditions for generic causal relations are spelled out in table 6.3, where it is again assumed that e_1 occurs before e_2. As before, PREVENTS(e_1, e_2) is taken as equivalent to CAUSES(e_1, not-e_2); PREVENTS(not-e_1, e_2) is similarly taken as equivalent to CAUSES(not-e_1, not-e_2). ALLOWS(e_1, e_2) is taken to mean that not-e_1 would prevent e_2, but if e_1 occurs, e_2 might or might not occur; the other ALLOWS arise from appropriate substitutions for e_1 or e_2. Rules specifying that the action should be to exit from the decision table are taken to mean that e_1 and e_2 are not causally related. Rules indicating that an error has occurred serve to reject inconsistent combinations of conditions.

Table 6.3 contains two situations in which the generic CAUSES is satisfied. This fact has important consequences for the analysis of specific causal relations. A person may, for example, accept that Bruce's stabbing causes Sid's death whenever he accepts that the stabbing and the dying are possible and that the stabbing and not dying are impossible, that is, when condition c1 is is affirmative and condition c2 is negative. Given that these conditions are

Table 6.3 A decision table for generic causal relations.

	1	2	3	4	5	6	7	8	9	10	11	12
Conditions												
c1. POSSIBLE(e_1 & e_2)	Y	N	Y	Y	Y	N	Y	N	Y	N	Y	N
c2. POSSIBLE(e_1 & not-e_2)	N	Y	Y	Y	N	Y	N	Y	Y	N		Y
c3. POSSIBLE(not-e_1 & e_2)	Y	Y	Y	N	N	Y	Y	N	Y		N	N
c4. POSSIBLE(not-e_1 & not-e_2)	Y	Y	N	Y	Y	N	N	Y	Y		N	N
Actions												
a1. CAUSES(e_1, e_2)	x				x							
a2. PREVENTS(e_1, e_2)		x				x						
a3. CAUSES(not-e_1, e_2)			x			x						
a4. PREVENTS(not-e_1, e_2)				x	x							
a5. ALLOWS(e_1, e_2)					x							
a6. ALLOWS(e_1, not-e_2)				x								
a7. ALLOWS(not-e_1, e_2)		x										
a8. ALLOWS(not-e_1, not-e_2)	x											
a9. exit								x	x	x		
a10. error										x	x	x

satisfied, however, there are still two possibilities involving not stabbing to be considered. The speaker may consider either (a) that Sid might or might not have died if Bruce had not stabbed him (rule 1), or (b) that Sid would not have died if Bruce had not stabbed him (rule 5). The distinction is between (a) a sufficient cause and (b) a necessary and sufficient cause:

(89)   Sufficient cause:
                IMPOSSIBLE(e_1 & not-e_2)
         Necessary and sufficient cause:
                IMPOSSIBLE(not-e_1 & e_2) & IMPOSSIBLE(e_1 & not-e_2)

The meaning of POSSIBLE does not correspond to any simple logical notion. A formulation like IMPOSSIBLE(e_1 & not-e_2) looks at first sight like a "strict implication," as defined by C. I. Lewis (1918). A strict implication consists of a material implication that is a necessary truth, and Burks (1951) has proposed a notion of causal implication relying on such an analysis. But there are reasons to suppose that IMPOSSIBLE(e_1 & not-e_2), and its equivalent NECESSARY(if e_1 then e_2), do not behave as strict implications. Stalnaker (1968) has shown that counterfactual conditionals fail to behave like strict implications for three reasons. First, transitive inferences with counterfactuals are not always valid:

> If Edgar had been born in Russia, he would be a communist today.
> If Edgar were a communist today, he would be a traitor.
> Therefore, if Edgar had been born in Russia, he would be a traitor.

Second, contrapositive inferences (as Goodman, 1965, also pointed out) are not always valid with counterfactuals:

> If the match had been struck, it would have lighted.
> Therefore, if the match had not lit, it would not have been struck.

Third, it is a fallacy to suppose that where a counterfactual of the form "if p then q" is true, a counterfactual of the form "if p & r then q" is true. One cannot generally strengthen the antecedents of counterfactuals by conjoining additional propositions:

> If Mike had stayed at the party, Mary would have stayed.
> Therefore, if Mike and his wife had stayed at the party, Mary would have stayed.

All three of these patterns of inference are valid for strict implications but invalid for counterfactuals.

This difference makes for considerable complication in the construction of a possible-world semantics for counterfactuals (see D. Lewis, 1973). More important, however, if there is an intimate connection between generic causal assertions and specific causal assertions (expressible by counterfactuals), it is likely that the three patterns of inference will also be fallacious for relations of the form IMPOSSIBLE(e_1 & not-e_2). This suspicion is confirmed. The following examples are all invalid. First, transitivity:

> Richard's rudeness causes Patricia's crying.
> Patricia's crying causes Jane's headaches.
> Therefore, Richard's rudeness causes Jane's headaches.

Second, contrapositive:

> Not having fresh fruit causes one to have scurvy.
> Therefore, not having scurvy causes one to have fresh fruit.

Third, strengthening the antecedent:

> Striking a match causes it to light.
> Therefore, soaking a match in water and striking it causes it to light.

The failure of POSSIBLE to conform to a simple logical interpretation also eliminates any attempt, such as Karttunen's (1972), to construe the word "possible" in terms of conventional modal logic. Admittedly, Karttunen takes Hintikka's (1962) epistemic modal logic as his model, but, as both he and Hintikka seem to have overlooked, this epistemic logic is essentially C. I. Lewis's system of strict implication in an epistemic guise (see Chisholm, 1963). There is still no adequate *logical* account of the ordinary language concept of possibility.

Recognizing the distinction between a sufficient and a necessary and sufficient cause makes it possible to suggest solutions to a number of riddles. For example, Dowty's (1972a,b) analysis in terms of counterfactual conditions yields the following sort of paraphrase of Bruce's stabbing causing Sid's death:

(90)   Sid would not have died on that particular occasion if Bruce had not stabbed him and all else had been the same.

But suppose that Mark had also stabbed Sid mortally at the same time Bruce made his assault. Then one could properly say of either assailant that he had killed Sid. This alternative, however, does not tally with the semantics of (90). Dowty considers this anomaly and takes refuge in the fact that cases of simultaneous causation are rare in the real world. (Actually, simultaneous causes are not so rare, as attested by law cases that have hinged on them; see Hart and Honoré, 1959, chap. 8.) But simultaneity may be irrelevant here. Cause is a relation between events and has itself no time index. Sid may die hours later; the precise moment of his death is not critical for asserting a causal relation between it and the stabbing(s). Hence, if Bruce and Mark inflict mortal wounds one after another, a speaker might still wish to say either that Bruce killed Sid or that Mark killed Sid. It seems slightly odd to say that the analysis in (90) is saved because one can now talk of two separate occasions. In our view, a more satisfactory solution to the problem raised by such joint causes is simply to recognize the distinction between a sufficient cause (e_1 = Bruce stabbing Sid, or e_1 = Mark stabbing Sid) and a necessary and sufficient cause (e_1 = Bruce and Mark stabbing Sid).

Although this conceptual distinction is important, English does not make it obvious which concept a speaker intends; the semantic component incorporated in causative English verbs expresses merely sufficient cause, and when a speaker wishes to make it clear that he has something stronger in mind he must say so explicitly.

Since there are also two separate situations in table 6.3 in which PREVENTS may be used, the corresponding riddle about "prevent" can also be solved. If either e_0 or e_1 is sufficient to prevent e_2, then, contrary to a counterfactual formulation, e_2 does not occur even if e_1 fails to prevent it, provided that e_0 does so. Once again, a conceptual distinction must be drawn between a sufficient sense and a necessary and sufficient sense of "prevent":

(91)   Sufficient prevent:
            IMPOSSIBLE(e_1 & e_2)
        Necessary and sufficient prevent:
            IMPOSSIBLE(not-e_1 & not-e_2) & IMPOSSIBLE(e_1 & e_2)

It is sometimes suggested (G. Lakoff, 1972a, for example) that there is a direct connection between "cause" and "allow." Not to cause something is to allow it not to happen; not to allow something not to happen is to cause it to happen. Yet it is simple to think of counterexamples: a sentence such as "Dropping a teacup does not cause a door to open" would not ordinarily be paraphrased by "Dropping a teacup allows a door not to open." Indeed, as table 6.3 indicates, there is no direct connection between generic relations of a causal and a permissive form. The reason is that there are no simple negations of CAUSES and ALLOWS: if e_1 does not cause e_2, it may allow it, or it may prevent it, or the two events may be causally independent of one another.

We have been focusing primarily on generic causal relations; let us turn now to specific causal relations. A specific causal relation must be taken as falling within a conceptual framework established by some generic state of affairs. That is, one must have in mind a generic state of affairs when considering specific causes for what actually happens (or fails to happen). A generic causal relation—as specified by one of the first six rules of table 6.3— always eliminates as impossible at least one combination of events, and in the case of a necessary and sufficient relation (rules 5 and 6) it eliminates two combinations of events as impossible. Thus, one way to analyze specific causal relations is to consider how the remaining outcomes would be described in the light of the generic state of affairs characterized by the rule.

Consider the generic state of affairs characterized by rule 1 in table 6.3. This rule says that the state of affairs specified by the outcomes (Y, N, Y, Y) for the four conditions can be described generically by "e_1 causes e_2, and not-e_1 allows not-e_2." In any specific instance where this generic situation is thought to prevail, any one of three potential observations can be expected: (c1) e_1 followed by e_2; (c3) not-e_1 followed by e_2; or (c4) not-e_1 followed by not-e_2.

If the fourth possibility occurred—(c2) e_1 followed by not-e_2—the person would have to revise his assumption about the prevailing generic state of affairs. Suppose that on some occasion the person does observe one of the three sequences of events or nonevents compatible with his generic assumption, and consider in turn how each of these observations could be described.

First, if a person who views the generic situation as that characterized by rule 1 were to observe e_1 followed by e_2, he would be justified in asserting either:

(92)   (e_1 & e_2): e_1 caused e_2.
                      If e_1 hadn't happened, e_2 might not have happened.

Both assertions are appropriate and both indicate that e_1 and e_2 actually occurred. As long as one takes as given the generic state of affairs that the observer has in mind, the counterfactual modal assertion might be regarded as equivalent to the causal assertion. If he had had in mind the generic situation characterized by rule 5, however, the appropriate counterfactual equivalent would have been "If e_1 hadn't happened, e_2 wouldn't (couldn't) have happened." It would be pointless to argue which counterfactual is the correct equivalent of the causal assertion, since either can be correct under the appropriate generic assumptions. We maintain, however, that even when the generic situation characterized by rule 1 is taken for granted, it is too strong a claim to say that the causal assertion and the counterfactual assertion are "equivalent." The counterfactual assertion is based on the generic assumption that not-e_1 allows not-e_2, whereas the causal assertion is based on the generic assumption that e_1 causes e_2; both assertions are required for a complete specification of how the person views the specific causal relation involved in the observed event.

This pairing of causal and counterfactual assertions appears in all of the specific situations that might occur. Consider next the case where a person who views the generic situation as that characterized by rule 1 observes not-e_1 followed by e_2:

(93)   (not-e_1 & e_2):   Not-e_1 didn't prevent e_2.
                     If e_1 had happened, e_2 *must* have happened.

In order to provide intuitive support, consider the case where e_1 is "You touched the soap bubble" and e_2 is "The soap bubble burst," and assume that this is a pair of events for which rule 1 is appropriate. The specific observation is that you did not touch the bubble and it burst. The assertions proposed in (93) would be "Your not touching the bubble didn't prevent it from bursting" and "If you had touched the bubble, it *must* have burst" (or "Even if you had touched the bubble it would still have burst"). Perhaps the second of these last two assertions is more satisfactory, since the first would be equally suitable on the occasion that you did not touch the bubble and it did not burst—it leaves open to doubt whether e_2 occurred.

It is tempting to suppose that, in general, not to prevent an event is equivalent to allowing it to happen. Following this supposition, we might replace "Not-e_1 didn't prevent e_2" by "Not-e_1 allowed e_2" in (93); "allow" might seem more consonant also with table 6.3. There is a subtle difference, however, between "Your not touching the bubble didn't prevent it from bursting" and "Your not touching the bubble allowed it to burst." The assertion with "allow" suggests that the bubble would not have burst if you had touched it—that touching it would *not* have allowed it to burst. Given the generic assumption governing this specific situation, "Your not touching the bubble allowed it to burst" would be misleading. Hence, "not to prevent an event" is not invariably equivalent to "to allow an event."

Consider next the case where a person views the generic situation as that governed by rule 1 and observes not-e_1 followed by not-e_2. The following assertions seem justified:

(94)   (not-e_1 & not-e_2):   Not-e_1 allowed not-e_2.
                                     If e_1 had happened, e_2 would have happened.

In this case the assertion with "allow" is appropriate, since "Your not touching the bubble allowed it not to burst" suggests (correctly, this time) that the bubble would have burst if you had touched it. "Your not touching the bubble didn't prevent it from not bursting" contains at least three negatives and is unintelligible without pencil and paper; when deciphered, it suggests that touching the bubble would have prevented it from bursting, which may be true, but it is certainly an odd way to talk.

To take a different generic state of affairs, let e_1 be "An insomniac is given a tranquilizer" and e_2 "The insomniac falls asleep," and assume that this is a pair of events for which rule 4 is appropriate—without a tranquilizer the insomniac cannot sleep, with it he may sleep. According to table 6.3, this generic state of affairs can be described by "Not-e_1 prevents e_2, and e_1 allows e_2."

If the insomniac is given a tranquilizer and falls asleep (e_1 & e_2), a speaker who believed generic rule 4 applied might say "The tranquilizer allowed the insomniac to sleep" or "If he hadn't been given a tranquilizer he still wouldn't have fallen asleep." If the insomniac is given the tranquilizer but does not fall asleep (e_1 & not-e_2), a speaker might say "The tranquilizer didn't allow the insomniac to sleep" or "If he hadn't been given the tranquilizer, he still couldn't have slept." If the insomniac is not given a tranquilizer and does not sleep (not-e_1 & not-e_2), a speaker might say "Not giving the insomniac a tranquilizer prevented him from sleeping" or "If he had been given a tranquilizer, he might have slept." If it should happen that the insomniac falls asleep without the benefit of a tranquilizer (not-e_1 & e_2), the speaker would have to revise his generic assumption.

Beyond its value as an illustration of the complexities involved in describing causal relations, this example bears on a theoretical question raised by the counterfactual analysis of causative assertions. Dowty (1972a) considers the case where an election is won by a single vote. Under those circumstances it is appropriate to say that if Jones had not voted for Wilson, Wilson would not have won, and if Smith had not voted for Wilson, Wilson would not have won, and so on, naming each person who voted for Wilson in a separate counterfactual. On Dowty's claim for the equivalence of these counterfactuals with causal assertions, it should be equally appropriate to say that Jones caused Wilson to win, and Smith caused Wilson to win, and so on. Yet the causal usage would be rather odd. In table 6.3 it is rule 4 that appears to apply, where e_1 is "Jones voted for Wilson" and e_2 is "Wilson won the election." We would not say "Jones's voting for Wilson caused Wilson to win the election," because it would have been possible for Wilson to lose in spite of Jones's vote. The only condition that is eliminated in this situation is c3: it would not have been possible for Wilson to win without Jones's vote. So in this case the counterfactual corresponds not to a causal assertion but to an assertion of the form "Jones's voting for Wilson allowed Wilson to win" or "Jones's not voting for Wilson would have prevented Wilson from winning." This characterization in terms of "allow" rather than "cause" seems appropriate for each person who voted for Wilson.

We have probably said more than enough to illustrate the complexities of causal relations and, perhaps, less than enough to suggest how the present approach might meet them. Endless puzzles are still to be solved, but rather than continue in the same way to deal with each potential outcome for the four remaining generic situations, we simply summarize our analysis of the complete set of six generic situations and their specific outcomes in table 6.4. It should be noted that no description involving "cause" or "prevent" (or their associated counterfactuals) is unique to a single combination of generic situation and specfic outcome.

So much for simple generic causal relations. Ordinary language admits of a more complex form of causal relation. Consider the relation between two classes of events: e_1 is "A teacup drops" and e_2 is "The teacup breaks." It is common knowledge that sometimes when a teacup is dropped it breaks and that sometimes when it is dropped it does not break. It is also common knowledge that sometimes a teacup breaks when it is not dropped and sometimes— perhaps most times—a teacup does not break when it is not dropped. The generic situation appears to be one in which all four conditions to table 6.3 are satisfied: rule 9 applies. But rule 9 corresponds to there being no causal relation between e_1 and e_2. Yet sometimes there *is* a causal relation between dropping a cup and its breaking. How are we to resolve the apparent paradox?

Suppose you drop a cup and it breaks. You are likely to claim: "Dropping the cup caused it to break." You may be arguing *post hoc ergo propter hoc*— that cause can be inferred from temporal sequence—but you could substantiate your claim if you could show that any cup of the same sort dropped from the same height onto a floor of the same hardness will break. Your "experiment" would establish the generic causal relation CAUSES(e_1, e_2). There is no problem with such a relation or even with an experimental outcome in which the cup never breaks. But an experiment might show that a particular sort of cup dropped onto a particular sort of floor will sometimes break and sometimes not break. This situation is one that, according to table 6.3, fails to establish a causal relation between e_1 and e_2. And this conclusion is perfectly correct

Table 6.4 Summary of the observed outcomes of events e_1 and e_2 and the pairs of sentences that can express them, for each of the six generic rules in table 6.3.

Observed outcomes	Assumed generic states of affairs
	Rule 1: CAUSES(e_1, e_2) & ALLOWS(not-e_1, not-e_2)
e_1 & e_2	e_1 caused e_2. If e_1 hadn't happened, e_2 might not have happened.
not-e_1 & e_2	Not-e_1 did not prevent e_2. If e_1 had happened, e_2 must have happened.
not-e_1 & not-e_2	Not-e_1 allowed not-e_2. If e_1 had happened, e_2 would have happened.
	Rule 2: PREVENTS(e_1, e_2) & ALLOWS(not-e_1, e_2)
e_1 & not-e_2	e_1 prevented e_2. If e_1 had not happened, e_2 might have happened.
not-e_1 & e_2	Not-e_1 allowed e_2. If e_1 had happened, e_2 would not have happened.
not-e_1 & not-e_2	Not-e_1 did not allow e_2. If e_1 had happened, e_2 could not have happened.
	Rule 3: CAUSES(not-e_1, e_2) & ALLOWS(e_1, not-e_2)
e_1 & e_2	e_1 did not prevent e_2. If e_1 had not happened, e_2 must have happened.
e_1 & not-e_2	e_1 allowed not-e_2. If e_1 had not happened, e_2 would have happened.
not-e_1 & e_2	Not-e_1 caused e_2. If e_1 had happened, e_2 might not have happened.
	Rule 4: PREVENTS(not-e_1, e_2) & ALLOWS(e_1, e_2)
e_1 & e_2	e_1 allowed e_2. If e_1 had not happened, e_2 would not have happened.
e_1 & not-e_2	e_1 did not allow e_2. If e_1 had not happened, e_2 could not have happened.
not-e_1 & not-e_2	Not-e_1 prevented e_2. If e_1 had happened, e_2 might have happened.
	Rule 5: CAUSES(e_1, e_2) & PREVENTS(not-e_1, e_2)
e_1 & e_2	e_1 caused e_2. If e_1 had not happened, e_2 would not (and could not) have happened.
not-e_1 & not-e_2	Not-e_1 prevented e_2. If e_1 had happened, e_2 would (and must) have happened.
	Rule 6: PREVENTS(e_1, e_2) & CAUSES(not-e_1, e_2)
e_1 & not-e_2	e_1 prevented e_2. If e_1 had not happened, e_2 would (and must) have happened.
not-e_1 & e_2	Not-e_1 caused e_2. If e_1 had happened, e_2 would not (and could not) have happened.

as far as it goes. What *has* been established, however, are two separate relations between e_1 and e_2—a higher-level description that we will call a metacausal relation. The relevant metacausal relation in the present example is

> POSSIBLE(IMPOSSIBLE(e_1 & not-e_2)) & POSSIBLE(POSSIBLE(e_1 & not-e_2)).

If this nesting of modal operators is too perplexing, the first conjunct can be expressed as POSSIBLE(CAUSES(e_1, e_2)), and, since POSSIBLE(e_1 & not-e_2) is the contradictory of IMPOSSIBLE(e_1 & not-e_2), the natural way to express the second conjunct is POSSIBLE(notCAUSES(e_1, e_2)), in short, the metacausal relation is POSSIBLE(CAUSES(e_1, e_2)) & POSSIBLE(notCAUSES(e_1, e_2)), which we can construe in terms of our example as "Dropping the cup may or may not cause it to break."

The existence of metacausal relations shows that in everyday life speakers are prepared to consider *possible* causal relations. In logical terms, the present metacausal relation might be construed as saying that there is at least one possible world w (alternative to the actual world) where e_2 holds in each of the alternative possible worlds to w in which e_1 holds; and that there is at least one other possible world w' (alternative to the actual world) which possesses alternative possible worlds where e_1 holds but e_2 does not.

The description of specific events in the light of this metacausal relation is relatively straightforward. An observation of the teacup being dropped and breaking (e_1 & e_2) can be described according to rule 1 (or rule 5), since the speaker is likely to assume a causal relation between the two events. It can therefore be described by "Dropping the teacup caused it to break." A more skeptical speaker alert to the other component of the metacausal relation might admit: "Even though the teacup was dropped it might not have broken." An observation of the teacup being dropped and not breaking (e_1 & not-e_2) will lead the speaker to assume notCAUSES(e_1, e_2) as his generic frame. This relation does not correspond to any of the rules in table 6.3, but its natural description is simply "Dropping the teacup did not cause it to break." The skeptical speaker might also add: ". . . but it might have broken." The description of these two events by counterfactual conditionals will depend on how the speaker views the consequences of not-e_1, not dropping the cup. He may very well conceive of a metacausal relation in this case, too. Perhaps it will be easier to understand the argument if we revert to the bubble example.

Sometimes if you touch a bubble it bursts, and sometimes it does not burst; but even if you do not touch it, sometimes it bursts and sometimes it does not. Depending on what you observe, you are likely to consider the relevant constituent of the appropriate metacausal relation. If you try to use a counterfactual conditional in order to describe the case where you touch the bubble and it bursts you have to examine the metacausal relation—whichever one you think appropriate—governing the consequences of not touching it. If you think the bubble would not otherwise have burst, you might say: "If I hadn't touched the bubble it wouldn't have burst." Your choice of constituents from the two metacausals thus coincides with rule 5. If you think the bubble would have burst anyway, your choices really do converge on rule 9 and you are not entitled to make any causal claim either directly or by way of a counterfactual— you might say "Even though I touched it, it would have burst anyway." If you think the bubble might have burst without your touching it, your choices converge on rule 1, and you might say "If I hadn't touched the bubble it might not have burst." What makes such descriptions a complicated business is that different metacausals are possible, and you can choose either of their constituents. The combination of a metacausal for e_1 and a straightforward generic causal relation for not-e_1, or vice versa, fortunately presents us with no new problems.

We can now attempt to pull together our thoughts on CAUSE and to propose a schema for it. Since sufficient cause is ubiquitous throughout the lexicon, we will propose a routine for it. Routines for the other notions may easily be constructed with the aid of table 6.3.

The presuppositions of CAUSE pose a special problem. It is difficult to decide precisely what is being denied when a causal statement undergoes sentential negation. If someone asserts "John didn't kill Mary," are you to understand that John did something and Mary died but that there was no causal relation between the two events? Or are you to understand that John did something (to Mary), but (fortunately) Mary did not die? Or what? Out of context the answer is difficult to discern, and therefore we will not attempt to separate any presuppositions of CAUSE from its assertions:

(79')   CAUSE(S, S'):   An event, process, or state characterized by the statement S "causes" an event, process, or state characterized by the statement S' if:
          (i) HAPPEN(S)
          (ii) HAPPEN(S')
          (iii) BEFORE((i), (ii))
          (iv) notPOSSIBLE(S & notS')

Condition (iii) is added to respect the metaphysical assumption that causes must precede effects.

The sense of CAUSE that is probably incorporated into most causative verbs involves a relation between events or processes, yet by using S we have allowed relations between states in (79'). Fillmore (1971a) suggests that the verb "cause" must have at least two senses: an active sense for sentences like "Susan's screaming caused Fred to drop the tray" and a stative sense for sentences like "Susan's living nearby causes me to prefer this neighborhood." It is certainly true that there are oddities about the verb. Vendler (1967) argues that its antecedent clauses specify "facts" whereas its consequent clauses do not, since there is a clear contrast in the acceptability of such sentences as

(95)   The fact that Susan screamed caused Fred to drop the tray.
         Susan's screaming caused the fact that Fred dropped the tray.

(We will resist this view in considering the interpretation of sentential complements in 7.3.1.) Whatever may be the case for the verb "cause," there is no reason that our analysis of CAUSE should not allow for relations between states; in many respects the nonoccurrence of an event is the persistence of a state. Therefore we have used the general formulation, HAPPEN(S), in (79′). Likewise, although theorists often distinguish physical cause from so-called personal cause ("John made Mary angry"), we assume that the distinction is one of domain rather than one requiring a different analysis of CAUSE.

Executing the tests required to evaluate an assertion about a specific causal relation is very difficult. How can one be sure that a particular combination of events (or nonevents) is not possible? Perhaps one's only hope is to rely on generic knowledge stored in memory about the characteristic behavior of objects, or else to seek to establish such knowledge by a series of empirical observations. In this way, too, specific and generic causal assertions must be related.

6.3.6 Acts, Intentions, and Deontic Judgments

In (80) we defined INTEND in terms of the predicate *Intend*, which is not a truly perceptual predicate. We can add little to the discussion in 2.6.3, but we assume that *Intend* (ego, goal) describes a result of early sensorimotor learning, that ego can be replaced by person as a consequence of decentering, and that our ability to perceive the intentions of others from their behavior is later rationalized into our adult notions of intention. On this account, the ontogenesis of INTEND and CAUSE are closely related.

If we consider (80) as an analysis of the verb "intend," its major defect is that it fails to make explicit the complex tense restrictions that "intend" imposes. Sentences like "Marshall intended (for) Felix to be happy" are formed by taking the sentence as the complement of the verb—in this case, taking the infinitival "Felix to be happy" as the complement of "intended." In "Marshall intended to be happy," "intended" takes "Marshall to be happy" as its complement and the redundant "Marshall" is omitted. Thus, the arguments of "intend" must be an animate subject (capable of having intentions) and a sentence that describes a goal that the subject intends to achieve. Since (80) provides places for these two arguments, it is to that extent satisfactory. But (80) does not make clear that sentences like "Marshall intends (for) Felix to be happy yesterday" are odd. Intended activities are limited to some time subsequent to the time of intending. We should use BEFORE(S, S′) to make this restriction explicit:

(80′) INTEND(x, S): An animate x "intends" to achieve a goal g characterized by the statement S if:
   (i) *Intend*(x, g)
   (ii) BEFORE((i), HAPPEN(S))

We assume that the opacity of "intend" arises from the fact that as long as x continues to *Intend*(x, g), execution of his plan to achieve g has not yet terminated, so that the truth or falsity of any assertions about its outcome cannot be evaluated.

The adverb "intentionally" denotes a particular manner of doing something, a manner restricted to actors capable of having intentions. Since this manner arises from a causal relation between INTEND and DO, and since (79′) imposes a temporal order on cause and effect by virtue of condition (79′iii), we need not introduce a similar modification of (81) to ensure the appropriate temporal relations. The selectional restrictions on "intentionally" seem to follow naturally from the analysis already given: "Kurt knows English intentionally" is inadmissible because "know" does not incorporate DO and so cannot serve as the second argument in (81i); "The apple fell intentionally" is inadmissible (or must be interpreted metaphorically) because apples cannot INTEND and so cannot serve as the first argument in (81ii); "Felix chases Pamela intentionally" is redundant because "chase" incorporates the idea that the intention to catch Pamela caused Felix to travel after her, so "intentionally" adds nothing that is not already implicit in "chase"; "Deane discovered the missing money intentionally" is contradictory, though it may have a metaphorical use, because discoveries are fortuitously, not causally, related to the actor's intentions.

The use in (81) of CAUSE as the relation between INTEND and DO implies that voluntary acts are caused. Since this comes dangerously close to perplexing philosophical questions of freedom of will, some comment seems necessary. Our immediate concern is not with the truth, falsity, or intelligibility of claims about the freedom or determination of apparently voluntary acts but merely with the way people use English to talk about their reasons for taking various actions, so it should not be necessary for us to defend any particular position in this ancient debate. The philosophical question concerns a person's freedom to intend. Once an intention is adopted—once a decision is made to institute a particular plan of action—the behavior that follows can legitimately be said to be caused by that intention. That is the general sense of CAUSE we have in mind in (81): if the agent had intended otherwise than he did, the behavior observed would not have happened.

In a larger context, of course, any serious psychologist must also be concerned with the philosophical question. Our general position on that larger issue is that the question should be rephrased from "Are people free to intend?" to "Why do people believe they are free to intend?" We suspect the answer will have something to do with people's inability to foresee the outcome of physical causes and effects transpiring in their own bodies, but this opinion is independent of any defense we would offer for the incorporation of CAUSE in our formulation of INTENTIONALLY.

There are a number of subtle contrasts within the domain of intention; as Rescher (1967, pp. 215–219) has pointed out, one should consider all the fine shades of meaning that reside within the following pairs of adverbs:

(96)   intentionally/unintentionally
         voluntarily/involuntarily
         deliberately/inadvertently (or accidentally)

consciously/automatically
knowingly/unwittingly
willingly/unwillingly

"I am willing to write a novel" does not entail "I intend to write a novel," though the converse inference does seem to follow. It appears that willingness presupposes that some obligation has been created, perhaps by a request or an order, whereas no such presupposition is involved in an intention. For our present purposes, however, we will accept INTEND as adequate; finer distinctions among the words in (96) are unnecessary for our analyses of English verbs.

The concept of ACT formulated in (82) involves no new ideas; it is intended merely to provide a specialization of DO when the doing is intentional in manner. We will refer to x in ACT(x, S) as an "agent," without implying that it is in the Agent case grammatically.

We see little connection between ACT and the verb "act," which is most frequently used in ordinary discourse to refer to some kind of pretense, whether theatrical or otherwise. There is a sense of "act" that is often used in philosophical discourse, however, that is related to our present argument, namely, that acts are voluntarily and intentionally undertaken, that a person is responsible for his own acts, and so on. Since we have chosen to call the subject of DO the actor and the subject of ACT the agent, we forsee potential misunderstandings resulting from any effort to redefine ACT in such a way as to reflect more adequately the usual meanings of "act." Perhaps something like DOI for "do intentionally" would be more felicitous, but we will trust the reader to remember the interpretation we intend. Needless to say, ACT will be used only as a semantic component of verbs other than "act."

It often happens that an action is performed intentionally for the benefit of someone other than the actor himself, and this relation is frequently signaled by a "for" phrase: "He wrote it for Clara," "He did it for his mother." The argument introduced in this way is sometimes said to be in the Benefactive case. The beneficiary seems to be introduced by way of the goal that the agent intends to achieve. If we assume some relation BENEFIT(z) as a way of specifying that the goal is to benefit z, then "x acted for z" could be written as CAUSE(INTEND $(x,$ BENEFIT(z)), DO(x, S)). In such verbs as "build," "cook," "make," "buy," "find," "get," and "dance," this schema underlies the role of the indirect object of the verb, and many of these verbs admit constructions in which the "for" is deleted: "He built a coffee table for Kay" versus "He built Kay a coffee table." The truth value of such statements does not hinge on whether S actually did benefit z, only on whether x's intention to benefit z caused him to do S. There is sometimes an ambiguity about the interpretation of "for" (Stephen Isard, personal communication): "He did it for her" may mean either that he did something for her benefit or that he did it so she would not have to.

A final word about moral causes. There appears to be an overlap between notions of permission and obligation and notions associated with causality, since one can talk of one person allowing another to do something in either a causal or a deontic sense.

At the conceptual core of such deontic matters is the concept of permissibility, which plays a role analogous to the role played by possibility in the causal domain. We talked earlier of the way in which judgments of POSSIBLE(S) could be restricted to particular domains; we assume that when they are restricted to the moral domain they yield an analysis of what is morally possible: POSSIBLE(S) becomes PERMISSIBLE(S). Although we can define what it means for an action to be morally permissible, we cannot (and need not) define the conditions that determine whether any particular act is permissible. To judge particular acts would require taking into account the whole fabric of the social life of a culture, since most people recognize, besides the letter of the law, deeper, ineffable, and sometimes contradictory principles governing their moral judgments. In other words, what we are dealing with are the "constitutive" conventions of permissibility rather than the "regulative" conventions that obtain in any given society (Searle, 1969, chap. 2). What we are dealing with is the meaning of "permissibility," granted the existence of some arbitrary set of regulative conventions.

Permissibility is a special sort of possibility; the parallel has been exploited by many theorists, including those who have sought an analysis of deontic logic in terms of semantical models. There are, however, two important distinctions between them. First, an act that is physically impossible cannot occur, but an act that is morally impermissible can. It follows that the language used to describe particular events in the light of generic deontic assertions is often straightforward ("He prohibited her from leaving the house, but she left anyway"), since speakers seldom have recourse to counterfactuals unless they wish to imply that a deontic state of mind *caused* a particular outcome ("If it weren't for my honesty, I wouldn't have been obliged to stay in office"). Second, since permissibility characterizes human acts, it is appropriate to specify the person who is permitted to perform them. So we will use PERMISSIBLE(x, S_x) to indicate that x is the appropriate individual and S_x is some event in which x is a participant.

It is a simple matter to use PERMISSIBLE(x, S_x) to construct a decision table analogous to table 6.3 in which such notions as PERMITS(a_1, a_2) and PROHIBITS (a_1, a_2) are analyzed. But, although one does speak of customs, laws, rules, regulations, and so forth "prohibiting" or "permitting" certain acts, it is more interesting to examine the semantics of such sentences as "The boss allowed us to smoke" or "Victoria prohibited the telling of dubious jokes in her presence." There is a whole class of deontic statements created by the fact that people, by virtue of authority or of the particular circumstances they are in, may create certain obligations in others.

The vast majority of deontic states are probably created by speech acts; there is a close connection between the language of such speech acts and the language used to describe the resulting deontic state. As Moravcsik (1972) points out, an assertion such as "You may smoke" can be a speech act granting permission or a simple description of a deontic state of affairs. The verbs "prohibit" and "permit" can also be used in this ambivalent manner. Of course, not everyone has the authority to grant permission. If you say to a friend, "I permit you to take things from Woolworth's without paying for them," the manager of Woolworth's, not to mention the police, is likely to question your authority. What has gone wrong is your speech act—its meaning is clear, but it is hardly felicitous. On the other hand, virtually everyone has the power to create obligations on his own part; an appropriate speech act, a promise, say, will usually succeed (see Austin, 1962b).

One situation in which an obligation can be created is where one person has authority over another. This social relationship may be the result of custom or tradition, or it may arise from a mutual convention—perhaps supported by an associated set of rewards and punishments; in consequence of it, when *A* tells *B* to do something, *B* is placed under an obligation to carry out the order. The nature of the obligation depends on the nature of the "regulative" convention. With a purely mutual convention, in each of *B*'s morally permissible future states, *B* carries out *A*'s order. Where there is no such convention and where, say, obedience is reinforced solely by inescapable punishment for disobedience, obviously there is no obligation. However, *B* may appreciate that failure to carry out the order will result in punishment. There is, accordingly, an implicit threat of the form "Do that, or else . . . " hanging over the order. We can formulate this state as

$$\text{CAUSE}(\text{ACT}(A, \text{S}), \text{KNOW}(B, \text{CAUSE}(\text{notACT}(B, \text{S}'), \text{PUNISHED}(B)))),$$

where S' specifies the state of affairs *B* is ordered to bring about. This underlying meaning is asserted in at least one sense of the verbs "force," "compel," "coerce"—they presuppose that *B* carried out the act leading to S'. And some such formulation must underlie uses of the nonfactual "before" discussed in 6.2.3 ("Give me your money before I shoot you").

We will return to the topic of speech acts and commands in section 7.4; our present concern is the description of deontic states regardless of how they are created. We will define "prohibit" and "permit" more formally:

(97)   PROHIBIT(x, y, z):   Someone x "prohibits" someone y doing z if:
      (i) ACT(x, S)
      (ii) notPERMISSIBLE(y, DO(y, z))
      (iii) CAUSE(S, (ii))

(98)   PERMIT(x, y, z):   Someone x "permits" someone y to do z if:
      (i) ACT(x, S)
      (ii) PERMISSIBLE(y, DO(y, z))
      (iii) CAUSE(S, (ii))

There does not seem to be any common English verb with the appropriate sense of "act so as to make it obligatory for someone to do something"; verbs like "compel" go beyond a purely deontic framework. But the verb "obligate" does have an appropriate meaning, admittedly with legalistic overtones, so we will use it to stand in for this important concept:

(99)   OBLIGATE(*x*, *y*, *z*):   Someone *x* "obligates" someone *y* to do *z* if:
           (i) ACT(*x*, S)
           (ii) notPERMISSIBLE(*y*, notDO(*y*, *z*))
           (iii) CAUSE(S, (ii))

By separating the sense of these verbs from the notion of a speech act, we have
avoided the question of specifying all the conditions that must be felicitously
fulfilled in order to succeed in making a prohibition, such as having the necessary authority, speaking sincerely, and so on. The analyses formalize the conditions that must be satisfied if a sentence such as "He permitted them to leave"
is to be true, not as the report of a speech act but as a description of a deontic
state of affairs.

It might be thought necessary to introduce into PROHIBIT, PERMIT, and OBLI-
GATE a component specifying that *y* knows the consequences of *x*'s act—just
as such a component is necessary in the discussion of "force," "compel,"
"coerce." Since there is nothing wrong with sentences like "The queen permitted them to eat cake, but they never learned of her gracious permission,"
we have forsworn the cognitive component.

6.3.7   Causative Verbs and Instrumental Adverbials

Causative verbs are grammatically transitive. They express a relation
between two or more arguments, one of which is usually the cause and another
the effect. Frequently there is an associated verb with a similar meaning, except
that the causative relation is not present. In order to illustrate how CAUSE would
be used to formulate routines for causative verbs, we will give a few representative examples; in order to focus on the causative component, we will assume
that the associated noncausative verb has already been formulated and can provide a subroutine.

Suppose we have DIE(*y*) for the concept expressed by the intransitive verb
in such sentences as "John died." Then the hypothesis that "kill" is the causative associate of "die"—that "kill" can be incompletely defined as "cause to
die"—can be expressed as follows:

(100)   KILL(*x*, *y*):   Something *x* "kills" some animate *y* if:
           (i) DO(*x*, S)
           (ii) CAUSE(S, DIE(*y*))

The causative component of the verb "kill" is given in condition (ii).

No condition is included in (100) to ensure that what *x* does and *y*'s death
must occur within a limited time—the next moment, for example. CAUSE is a
relation without a temporal index. "Kill" is mapped onto the time line indirectly
by the times S happened and *y* died; it is useless to argue whether the killing occurred at the moment of S (which need not be momentary) or at the moment of
death or throughout the interval between them. The oddness of "Bruce killed
Sid until noon" indicates that "kill" is nondurative; it is an accomplishment
verb, in the sense that "Bruce killed Sid" is not true until Sid is dead. This fact

is not to be accounted for by dating the causal relation but by including BECOME in the routine for noncausative DIE.

The use of $DO(x, S)$ in condition (100i) means that intentionality is not incorporated; S may or may not have been intentional. A schema for "murder" would be very similar to (100), except it would presuppose that y was a person and the intentional $ACT(x, S)$ would be substituted for $DO(x, S)$ in condition (100i).

Adverbs and adverbial phrases can modify either "kill" or the semantic components of "kill." For example, "Bruce almost killed Sid" is ambiguous between almost DO, almost CAUSE, and almost DIE (Morgan, 1969). In "Bruce probably killed Sid skillfully and painlessly," "probably" is a sentence modifier, "skillfully" modifies what Bruce did, and "painlessly" modifies what happened to Sid. Using the notation we have at the moment, these adverbs could be introduced into (100) as PROBABLY(SKILLFULLY($DO(x, S)$) & CAUSE(S, PAINLESSLY ($DIE(y)$))). Since "skillfully" is not a manner of doing something accidental, its modification of DO suggests intentionality; if Sid is a human being, "Bruce killed Sid skillfully" is understood to mean that Bruce murdered Sid. Instrumental phrases—"Bruce killed Sid with a car"—can be thought of as manner adverbials; like "skillfully," they modify what the agent does, so (100i) might become $WITH_i(DO(x, S), z)$.

Case grammarians would give instrumental phrases a special status by adding an Instrument case as a third argument of "kill," with some indication that the Instrument z is optional: if a value for z is not provided, $WITH_i$ need not be evaluated. In support of this special treatment of instrumental phrases they might point to the difference between "Bruce killed Sid with a car" and "Bruce killed Sid with skill," where "with skill" is a manner adverbial quite different from "with a car." Although instrumental phrases are not limited to causative verbs—"He saw the scratches with a microscope" contains an instrumental phrase, although "see" is not a causative verb—they are especially common with causatives. We should pause to consider some of the problems they pose.

First, let us review the possible ways to characterize instrumental phrases. One strategy is to include an Instrumental case as an argument of the verb in some such formula as

(101) $KILL(x, y, WITH_i(z))$,

where there would be a general rule that Instrument could be omitted, or, if Agent were omitted, Instrument could serve as substitute Agent. This way of introducing instrumental phrases, however, limits our freedom in accounting for the great variability of instrumental phrases. One symptom of the difficulties in settling on the cases that verbs can take as their arguments is the variation between one case grammarian and another (Fillmore, 1968, 1971a; Chafe, 1970; Langendoen, 1970; J. M. Anderson, 1971; and others; see Nilsen, 1973), and even within the same case grammarian on different occasions. These difficulties suggest that deletable cases may not be the best way to think of all the combinations into which English verbs can enter.

A second alternative, one that preserves our freedom to combine phrases, is to introduce WITHᵢ conjunctively: "*x* killed *y and* it (the killing) was with *z*," which would lead to something like

(102)   KILL(x, y) & WITHᵢ(e, z),

where *e* is understood to be the name of the event in the preceding conjunct. This approach would treat the instrumental phrase not as a case but as an adverb. "Bruce killed Sid with a knife" would be treated the same way as "Bruce killed Sid quickly," that is, "*x* killed *y and* it (the killing) was quick." The logical simplicity of (102) appeals to some philosophers, but, as Parsons (1972) points out, the trouble with it becomes apparent when we compare such sentences as (a) "Bruce deliberately killed Sid quickly" and (b) "Bruce killed Sid deliberately and quickly," which are not synonymous. A conjunctive notation would reduce them both to something like "Bruce killed Sid *and* it was deliberate *and* it was quick," which is appropriate only for (b).

This difficulty can be avoided by the notation we have used previously. This approach would make WITHᵢ an operator that can take concepts like KILL as its argument:

(103)   WITHᵢ(KILL(x, y), z).

When KILL is expanded according to (100), the natural place to attach an instrumental phrase is to what the actor does:

(104)   WITHᵢ(DO(x, S), z) & CAUSE(S, DIE(y)).

If adverbs were all introduced in this manner, the difference between the two sentences given above could be simply expressed as (a) deliberately(quickly (kill(Bruce, Sid))) and (b) deliberately(kill(Bruce, Sid)) & quickly(kill(Bruce, Sid)).

This notation is also useful with adjectives like "former." The adjective "blue" can occur in "*x* is blue," so it would be possible to represent "*x* is a blue book" either as book(x) & blue(x), after the manner of (102), or as blue (book(x)), after the manner of (103). But the representation of "*x* is a former mayor" must be former(mayor(x)); the conjunctive form would be mayor(x) & former(x), but former(x) is ill formed—"*x* is former" is not acceptable.

If we were to continue to follow this general line, sentences like "Bruce deliberately killed Sid quickly and painlessly in the kitchen yesterday with a knife" would introduce all of the adverbs in the same way, yielding something like

YESTERDAY(DELIBERATELY(IN(WITHᵢ(QUICK(PAINLESS(KILL(x, y))), z), w))).

One supposes that the various schemata of these modifiers would have constraints built into them that would help to determine their appropriate order, but even so there are reasons to believe that this solution is too simple.

Thomason and Stalnaker (1973) argue that the theory of adverbials must allow for two kinds in English, some modifying sentences, others modifying predicates. One of four criteria they propose for recognizing sentence modifiers is "Only if *Q-ly* occurs as a sentence modifier can one paraphrase the sentence by deleting the adverb and prefacing the resulting sentence by *It is Q-ly true that* " (p. 205). For example, "probably" would be a sentence modifier in "Bruce probably killed Sid" because that sentence can be paraphrased by "It is probably true that Bruce killed Sid." "Quickly" would not be a sentence modifier in "Bruce quickly killed Sid" because that sentence cannot be paraphrased by "It is quickly true that Bruce killed Sid."

Spatial locatives seem to be borderline cases. "In some restaurants" is a sentence modifier in "Women are not admitted in some restaurants" because that sentence can be paraphrased as "It is true in some restaurants that women are not admitted." But "It was true in the kitchen that Bruce killed Sid" is a little odd, and a directional phrase, like "It was true at Sid that Bruce threw the knife" sounds sufficiently strange to suggest that "at Sid" is not a sentence modifier.

On other grounds, however, Thomason and Stalnaker conclude that both place and time locatives can serve as sentence modifiers. Another of their criteria can be stated: "If a conditional sentence begins with an adverb, and if one cannot paraphrase the sentence by putting the adverb in the consequent, then . . . the initial adverb modifies the sentence" (p. 204). For example, "Yesterday, if John was told to buy stock, he bought IBM" would become "If John was told to buy stock, he bought IBM yesterday," which means something different and so is not a paraphrase; hence "yesterday" acts like a sentence modifier in this example. Similarly, "In the kitchen, if Bruce was told to kill Sid, he killed him quickly" is not paraphrased by "If Bruce was told to kill Sid, he killed him quickly in the kitchen," so "in the kitchen" is a sentence modifier. The result of preposing a predicate adverb in a conditional sentence is generally unacceptable. We will assume that locatives are usually (but not necessarily) sentence modifiers and that directional adverbials are predicate modifiers.

By both criteria, instrumental phrases fail to qualify as sentence modifiers. "Bruce killed Sid with a knife" is not paraphrased by "It is true with a knife that Bruce killed Sid," and "With a knife, if Bruce was told to kill Sid, he killed him" is awkward, but if it means anything at all, it is equivalent to "If Bruce was told to kill Sid, he killed him with a knife."

We have been largely concerned with space and time adverbials, many of which we can now recognize as sentence modifiers. Now we wish to consider instrumental adverbials, which are predicate modifiers. How should this distinction be recognized in our notation?

A sentence modifier can take a sentence as its argument and the result is another sentence. A predicate modifier can take a predicate as its argument and the result is another predicate. If this characterization is correct, then we might recognize the distinction as follows:

(105)   (a) He killed frequently: frequently(kill(he))
         (b) He killed quickly: (quickly(kill))(he)

"Frequently" is a sentence modifier taking kill(he) as its argument to form a new sentence; "quickly" is a predicate modifier taking "kill" as its argument to form a new predicate (quickly(kill)) that, in turn, takes "he" as its argument to form a sentence. This formulation would conform to one's intuitions about the correct phrase structure of these sentences. And it would explain why "He frequently killed quickly" is acceptable, but "He quickly killed frequently" sounds bad—"quickly" requires a predicate as its argument, not a sentence: frequently((quickly(kill))(he)) is acceptable according to (105); (quickly (frequently(kill(he))))( ) is not, because the argument is missing from ( ).

Thomason and Stalnaker point out that the distinction between these two kinds of adverbs influences logical relations between sentences that contain them, so the correct formulation is a matter of some importance. The correct formulation of just those sentences that occur in English, however, is not a simple matter. The scheme used in (105b), for example, is not adequate for adverbs modifying complex predicates. The sentence "He drives slowly to Sag Harbor and Montauk" has one interpretation that is equivalent to "He drives slowly to Sag Harbor *and* he drives slowly to Montauk," which can be represented as (slowly(to(drive)))(he, SH) & (slowly(to(drive)))(he, M). But it also has another interpretation that he drives slowly only when he is going to both destinations; he might not drive slowly to either one alone. This second interpretation would require something like (slowly((to(drive))(SH) & (to (drive))(M)))(he), where "he" is the argument of a very complex predicate. Thomason and Stalnaker propose a logical analysis adequate for such complex predicates and suggests that it might cast light on the complexities of English adverbs.

The space and time adverbials that we have been considering include both sentence and predicate modifiers. The distinction between (105a) and (105b), although inadequate for many problems posed by adverbials, is still more perspicuous than treating every adverbial as if it took a sentential argument. The instrumental adverbials that concern us now, however, require an extension of the notation of (105b). We will represent them by $(\text{WITH}_i(\text{DO}))$ (x, S, z), rather than as in (104). Thus, to summarize our notational practice, we must consider two dichotomies: sentential modifier versus predicate modifier, and adverb versus adverbial phrase. These four conditions are represented as follows:

	Sentential modifier	*Predicate modifier*
Adverb	FREQUENTLY(DO(x, S))	(RAPIDLY(DO))(x, S)
Adverbial phrase	IN(DO(x, S), z)	(WITH$_i$(DO))(x, S, z)

We must consider other causative verbs, but while these distinctions and caveats are in mind, we should ask what operational difference there is between predicate and sentence modifiers.

The most obvious difference is that $G(F(x))$ corresponds to the instruction to compute first the value of $F(x)$ and then to take that value as the argument of G, whereas $(G(F))(x)$ corresponds to the instruction to compute first a new function $(G(F))$ and then to apply it to x. In order to make this difference less abstract, let us consider the sentence "Bruce killed Sid intentionally." The adverb is a predicate modifier, so our representation would take the form

(106)   (INTENTIONALLY(DO))$(x,$ S) & CAUSE(S, DIE$(y))$.

The predicate in the first conjunct is the predicate ACT$(x,$ S), so the system has an option. "Kill intentionally" and "murder" are both appropriate expressions of (106). For "kill intentionally," the system presumably computes the new compound predicate; for "murder" it looks up an already stored predicate. (In order to attend to the fact that the result is the same in either case, the system would have to do both and compare the results.) A person who knows the meaning of "murder" retrieves the combination automatically—it is already entered in some decision table, if that manner of speaking is accepted—whereas a higher level of information processing is required for "kill intentionally." It is this automaticity of the retrieval that we have in mind when we say that an adverb—"intentionally" in the case of "murder"—is incorporated into the verb.

In any case, the system must have a capability to compute—not merely look up—many compound predicates from the values stored for their individual predicates. Even if "kill intentionally" were prepackaged in memory, there are so many other acceptable combinations—"kill quickly," "kill blindly," "kill accidentally," "kill obediently"—that to assume they must all be stored in memory in advance would greatly underestimate the productivity of adverb-verb combinations. To propose a specific form for this capability, however, would be to propose a mechanism capable of building the great variety of compound predicates in English, and only those. We will not formulate any detailed proposals, but will simply leave it that the system does have this capability—that the system can, for example, distinguish HAPPILY(DO$(x,$ S)) from (HAPPILY(DO)) $(x,$ S) by different computations based on its schemata for HAPPY and DO, and will arrive at two different interpretations corresponding to "fortunately" for the sentence modifier and "gladly" for the predicate modifier.

For apparently accidental historical reasons the bulk of the discussion of English causatives has concentrated on "kill." There are many other causative verbs in English, and not all of the problems they raise can be illustrated in terms of "kill." Consider another example. The verb "feed" is sometimes said to be the causative form of "eat." Assuming that we had a schema for EAT, this hypothesis could be captured by substituting EAT(x, y) for DIE(y) in (100ii). It is inaccurate, however, to paraphrase "feed" as "cause to eat." You can lead a horse to water, but you can't make him drink; the same probably holds for eating. A more conventional definition of this sense of "feed" would be "give food to," without the stipulation that what was given must be eaten. And since you can feed someone poison, it may be too strong to claim that what he is fed must be food. Let us explore a schema based on the paraphrase "allow to eat":

(107)   FEED(w, x, y):   Something w "feeds" something y to an animate x if:
         (i) DO$(w,$ S)
         (ii) ALLOW(S, EAT(x, y))

The argument y is syntactically optional—"He fed the dog" omits it—and if a value for w is not provided, either a passive, "The dog was fed meat," or a change of verb, "The dog ate meat," is possible. The point is that "feed" can be interpreted as a permissive rather than a causative verb.

"Eat," on the other hand, really is a causative verb. It might be paraphrased as "do something intentionally that causes something to enter the body through the mouth." In order to distinguish eating from drinking it would be necessary to characterize the "something" that is done with the ingested substance in more detail, presumably by making explicit the personal or impersonal instruments employed in each. We will neglect these instrumental niceties in order to concentrate on the causative component in the following crude approximation:

(108)   EAT(x, y):   An animate x "eats" something y if there is a z such that
             z is the mouth of x and:
             (i) ACT(x, S)
             (ii) CAUSE(S, (INTO(THROUGH(TRAVEL))))(y, z, x)

Here again the argument y is syntactically optional—"He ate in the restaurant" omits it. When a value is not provided for y, condition (108ii) cannot simply be dropped; it must be understood that a dummy variable "something" is substituted for the value of y. That is to say, although y is syntactically optional, it is not semantically optional.

If this analysis is correct, eat-feed is not an example of a noncausative-causative pair but rather an example of a causative-permissive pair. The full paraphrase for "feed" would be "do something that allows x to do something that causes y to travel through the mouth into x." There is a causative component to "feed," but only as a result of its incorporation of the causative "eat."

The question of when an argument that can be omitted syntactically can also be omitted semantically is a delicate one. In order to see the distinction clearly, consider a causative verb whose subject can be omitted. "He broke the knife" and "The knife broke" are both acceptable. If we assume that we have some schema for characterizing the broken state utilizing the concept of USE (which will be analyzed shortly), then, following (76), we can write

(109)   BREAK((x), y):   Something x "breaks" something y which an animate
             w uses to do S_w if:
             (i) BECOME(notPOSSIBLE(USE(w, y, S_w)))
             (ii) DO(x, S)
             (iii) CAUSE(S, (i))

If "break" is used intransitively, conditions (ii) and (iii) cannot be tested; only condition (i) remains. By assuming that x can be semantically omitted—that the system can execute BREAK((), y), where no value is given for x—we are assuming that there are two uses for (109): one for the full causative sense, the other for the intransitive, noncausative sense. Yet there is no need for two different schemata; (109) serves both purposes. We need merely assume that when a value for x is provided, all three conditions, including the causative condition, must be evaluated; if a value for x is not provided, only condition (i) is tested. Thus, when x is omitted the causative component can vanish, leaving "break" as a verb whose noncausative and causative versions are phonologically identical. For such verbs, omitting the argument x has a clear semantic consequence—it turns a causative into a noncausative—whereas omitting the argument y for verbs like "eat" does not have comparable semantic effects. This is the difference we have tried to express by distinguishing between syntactic and semantic omissions of an argument and by indicating permissible semantic omissions by placing the argument index in parentheses. The simplest example of a syntactic omission is the diminished passive: "The knife was broken," where the missing actor is understood and "broken" is an adjective.

The appearance of an animate subject in a sentence is not adequate to determine whether such double-purpose verbs are being used transitively or intransitively. In "He avoids breaking windows," "he" is the actor in "avoid," but "he" may or may not be the actor in "break." The sentence can be interpreted either as the causative "He avoids breaking any windows" or as the noncausative "He avoids any breaking windows." If we ignore aspectual complications, the former can be represented as WINDOW(y) & AVOID(x, BREAK(x, y)), with transitive "break," whereas the latter can be represented as WINDOW(y) & BREAK(y) & AVOID(x, y), with intransitive "break." (A complete account would also distinguish two senses of "avoid"—"refrain from" and "stay out of the region of interaction with.") The same semantic distinction underlies the ambiguity of "Breaking windows can be dangerous," which allows two interpretations, "Breaking any windows can be dangerous" and "Any breaking windows can be dangerous." The former is causative, even though all explicit reference to a causative actor x has been syntactically omitted in the nominalization that relates "x breaks y" and "breaking y." The resolution of such ambiguities in actual discourse depends on the presence or absence of a value for x in the surrounding text or context.

Let us return now to the matter of instrumental phrases. Some case grammarians have claimed that "with" is a reliable marker of the Instrumental case, although "by" is also common. Nilsen (1973), however, has demonstrated both that "with" and "by" have many other uses and that "the Instrumental case can be preceded by probably any preposition in the English language" (p. 85). Nilsen makes this point as part of an argument that the Instrumental case must be identified on semantic, not syntactic grounds, but since we have no theoretical investment here in case grammar we can accomplish a similar result by simply limiting our discussion to tools and body parts, that is, to hyponyms of the generic noun "instrument" (which is what linguists usually have in mind anyhow). In the present context, tools and body parts are noteworthy for their easy incorporation into verbs—"He hammered the nails," "He handed me the book," "He kicked the dog" (incorporates "foot"). In order to represent the relation (incorporated or explicit) of tools and body parts to the actions in which they are instrumental, we will use the notation WITH$_i$. The subscript is a reminder that this is an instrumental relation, and only a rough resemblance to the surface prepositions "with" or "by" is intended. The goal is to formulate a plausible schema for this instrumental relation.

G. Lakoff (1968) has proposed that instrumental "with" is a verb at some deeper level of analysis and should be derived transformationally from the same underlying base as "use." Although it is true that the objects of the preposition "with" and the objects of the verb "use" are constrained by very similar selectional restrictions, they are not identical (Chomsky, 1971). We will therefore deal first with instrumental "with" and then consider how "use" might differ from it semantically.

If one can say "Bruce killed Sid with the car," one can also say "The car killed Sid," but even if one can say "He ate the soup with a spoon," one cannot say "The spoon ate the soup." The difference seems to be that an inanimate instrument can provide a substitute actor only with verbs that accept inanimate subjects. KILL(x, y) includes DO(x, S) as a condition and DO accepts inanimate subjects; EAT(x, y) includes ACT(x, S) as a condition and ACT does not accept inanimate subjects.

A schema for one important use of instrumental "with" when the verb contains a DO condition can be formulated as follows:

(110)   (WITH$_i$(DO))(x, S, z):   Something x does S "with" something z if:
         (i) DO(x, S')
         (ii) CAUSE$(S', DO(z, S))$

In other words, WITH$_i$ simply inserts another causal link for a causative verb: "He broke the window with his elbow" is, roughly, "He did something that caused his elbow to do something that caused the window to break." When the main verb contains an ACT condition, however, the insertion of another causal link according to (110) adds DO(z, S), which can lead to complications.

For example, "x kills y with z" would be

(WITH$_i$(DO))(x, S, z) & CAUSE$(S, DIE(y))$.

Expanding WITH$_i$ according to (110) gives

DO(x, S') & CAUSE$(S', DO(z, S))$ & CAUSE$(S, DIE(y))$.

If all terms involving x are deleted when x does not occur, we obtain

DO(z, S) & CAUSE$(S, DIE(y))$.

This result satisfies (100) and so justifies "z killed y." On the other hand, "x murdered y with z" would be

(WITH$_i$(ACT))(x, S, z) & CAUSE$(S, DIE(y))$.

Expanding ACT and reassigning WITH$_i$ in the plausible way gives

CAUSE$(INTEND(x, g),(WITH_i(DO))(x, S, z))$ & CAUSE$(S, DIE(y))$.

Expanding WITH$_i$ according to (110) gives

CAUSE$(INTEND(x, g), (DO(x, S')$ & CAUSE$(S', DO(z, S))))$ & CAUSE $(S, DIE(y))$.

Deleting all terms involving x gives, again,

DO(z, S) & CAUSE$(\text{S}, \text{DIE}(y))$.

But this result satisfies KILL, not MURDER. So, if one can say "Bruce murdered Sid with a knife," one can also say "A knife killed Sid" but not "A knife murdered Sid."

Closely related to instrumental "with" is the causative verb "use" in one of its senses. "He ate the soup with a spoon" and "He used a spoon to eat the soup" are, for all practical purposes, synonymous. The difference between "with" and "use" becomes apparent when we consider nonintentional verbs: "He broke the window with his elbow" is not synonymous with "He used his elbow to break the window." "Use" carries an intentional entailment that is lacking in "with."

In sentences like "Peter used the knife to make a spear," "use" takes sentential complements with infinitive or participial forms: "Peter used the knife (Peter made a spear)$_s$." becomes "Peter used the knife to make/for making/in making a spear"; the like-subject constraint applies and the redundant subject is deleted in the surface sentence. This analysis suggests that the correct semantic formulation might be something like USE(x, z, S_x), where x is the agent, z the instrument, and S_x a sentential complement having x as its subject. If we base a formulation of "use" on paraphrases like "Peter did something intentionally that caused the knife to do something that allowed Peter to make a spear," we obtain

(111)   USE(x, z, S_x):   An animate x "uses" something z to do S_x if:
    (i) ACT(x, S)
    (ii) CAUSE$(\text{S}, \text{DO}(z, \text{S}'))$
    (iii) ALLOW(S', S_x)

When S' and S_x are identical ("He used his elbow to break the window," for example, where what he did and what his elbow did are the same) S' can be replaced by S_x so that (111iii) becomes redundant and we have a shortened version of "use" similar to the version of "with" given in (110), but with ACT providing the sense of intentionality that characterizes "use."

Many complex and interesting problems are posed by the causative verbs, and the present discussion falls far short of exhausting them. As an example of the perplexities calling for study, we can mention the "do so" construction, as in "He broke the knife and I was surprised that he should do so." It seems plausible to attribute the "do" to the DO(x, S) of condition (109ii) in the formulation of BREAK. Many speakers of English also find "He broke the knife and I was surprised that it should do so" an acceptable sentence. If this sentence is accepted, and if "do so" again signals DO, one presumably accepts the notion that breaking is something the knife *does* and condition (109i) should more clearly entail DO(y, S'). For "kill," however, DO(y, S') is clearly not indicated, since "He killed the hawk and it surprised me that it would do so" is very odd; death is something that happens to the hawk, not something it does. On the other hand, "He caused the knife to break and it surprised me that it would do so" is perfectly good, and even "He caused the hawk to die and it surprised me that it would do so" is considerably better than the corresponding version with "kill" instead of "cause to die." Fodor (1970) and Fodor, Bever, and Garrett (1974) use such observations to cast doubt on the analysis of "kill" as the causative form of "die," or transitive "break" as the causative form of intransitive "break." Given the present theoretical uncertainty about the status of "it" and "do so" in such constructions, however, we find it difficult to draw conclusions from such arguments.

It would be convenient to have some test that would indicate whether a verb incorporated DO(y, S'), but there are many difficulties in the way of using "do so" constructions for that purpose. For example, one might argue from the acceptability of "He moved the bookcase, although it surprised me that it would do so" to the conclusion that DO(bookcase, S') is involved, that moving is something the bookcase does. On the other hand, "He ate the apple, although it surprised me that it would do so" is odd in spite of the fact that the apple's traveling into him—condition (108ii)—would normally be considered something the apple does. In one case, travel is something that y does, and in the other case, travel is something that happens to y, but the basis for this distinction is far from obvious.

The lesson to be learned from "do so" constructions seems to be that whatever the similarity of the semantic conditions for pairs like "kill" and "cause to die," they behave differently under syntactic rules. The extent to which syntactic rules can be reduced to semantic rules has been hotly debated by theoretical linguists, and causative verbs have played an important role in the controversy. Before any analysis of these verbs can be carried much further, several difficult theoretical issues will have to be resolved.

So we must leave the analysis of causal relations in this rather unsatisfactory state, where major philosophic, semantic, and syntactic questions are still unanswered. One point that should be clear, however, is that the English verbs that express causal relations do not form an intuitively coherent semantic field. A list of causative verbs would be semantically heterogeneous in all other respects, just as "kill," "eat," "break," and "use" are semantically heterogeneous. Apparently the common occurrence of a particular semantic component, CAUSE, is not in itself sufficient to define a semantic field.

These observations recall a question raised in the introduction to this chapter. As long as our analytic methods lead to groups of words that are intuitively similar in meaning, we can speak of conceptual and lexical fields that are integrated in semantic fields. That is the situation we find for personal pronouns, color terms, kin terms. But what do we do when our analytic methods lead to groups of words that are not intuitively similar in meaning? That is the situation we find for person, space, time, cause. What is the lexical role of these important and ubiquitous concepts which do not provide conceptual cores to organize intuitively similar words?

The answer to our question becomes obvious when we phrase our observations as follows. To try to find a semantic field built around PERSON, SPACE, TIME, or CAUSE is as fruitless as to try to find a semantic field built around ISA or PPRT. When we applied the class-inclusion relation to nouns and nominal expressions, we did not search for a lexical field of ISA words. We did not claim, for example, that "dog," "red," and "uncle" are in the same semantic field just because a dog is an animal, red is a color, and an uncle is a relative. Yet class inclusion and part-whole are concepts, just as person, action, space, time, cause, and intent are concepts. They are simply too important to be confined to any single semantic field. They are organizers. They impose patterns of meaning on other concepts and determine the internal structure of semantic fields, but they do not provide nuclei around which semantic fields can be organized.

How the concepts explored in this chapter can serve to organize semantic fields of verbs is a topic we have not yet discussed. Verbal semantic fields exhibit meaning patterns more complex than the relatively simple hierarchical structures we found in nominal semantic fields. We should reserve comment on this difficult subject until we have examined several examples in detail.

7

Some Meaning Patterns of English

It is enough to take up some single leading grammatical relation. I select for this purpose the verb as the most important part of speech, with which most of the others come into relation, and which completes the formation of the sentence, the grammatical purpose of all language. —*Wilhelm von Humboldt (1885)*

The claim that lexical knowledge is organized into semantic fields has been supported by semantic investigations in several languages. We have accepted this claim as a basis for formulating our hypotheses about structures within fields; it is therefore a general part of every specific hypothesis. Since it partitions the lexicon into manageable fields and subfields, this general claim greatly simplifies lexical research. But in our enthusiasm for its convenience in dealing with lexical diversity we should not overlook the difficulties it poses.

One difficulty with an approach to the lexicon via the hypothesis of semantic fields is that words can be related in many ways. And the more similar the words one is comparing, the subtler the relations among them are. Another difficulty arises from the vagueness of the boundaries of semantic fields and the problems of deciding whether any particular meaning of a word should be classified in this field or that field or both. Disregarding a few difficult words or word senses may simplify an analysis considerably, but at the risk of missing important semantic or pragmatic distinctions within the field, or between fields. There are obvious difficulties in getting the analysis right and consistent throughout a whole field, in analyzing one's intuitions about meanings correctly, in keeping track of the implications of the distinctions that have been drawn, keeping the whole field clearly enough in mind not to lose the forest in the trees, in checking one's analysis against the intuitions of others. There are many places in a semantic analysis where a theorist can lose his way; the problems encountered constantly remind one of the hypothetical character of the enterprise. In spite of all this the assumption that semantic fields represent a pattern of shared conceptual components is the most promising approach available at the present time.

In this chapter we will examine some semantic fields of English verbs. By basing the analysis on sets of verbs that seem to be sufficiently similar in meaning to qualify as semantic fields we can work with many verbs together —but not too many. We are mindful of the enormous effort required to construct dictionaries and thesauruses, and of our limited resources when viewed in comparison with decades of labor by small armies of lexicographers. Our goal is certainly not to compile a new type of wordbook written in semantic procedures. Instead, we hope to test our general claim on a reasonable sample of related words in order to discover what kinds of difficulties we encounter and, perhaps, to solve enough of the methodological and notational problems that other workers can criticize, revise, or extend the work in the spirit in which we have undertaken it. Our goal is to contribute to a theory of psycholexicology, not to apply our ideas to the practical problems of lexicography.

There is no guarantee that we will find the meaning patterns we are looking for, that every word meaning will have a place in some identifiable semantic field. Although natural languages did not evolve for the convenience of research in semiotics, we are confident that some efficient principles of organization exist in the lexicon in order to facilitate learning it and using it at the rapid rates of conversational communication. If there are not semantic fields, other principles of semantic patterning may emerge. But we will not discover them unless we search.

In conducting this search the reliance we must place on our own intuitions as speakers of Standard English deserves some comment, not to say defense. We maintain that speakers of a common language share their semantic intuitions—that there *is* a social uniformity to be explored. Yet we are aware of the social and cultural differences even among native speakers of English that limit the generality of our analyses to people who spend large portions of their time producing, receiving, or studying linguistic messages. And we are aware that other languages may slice the semantic cake very differently.

We would prefer to have objective methods to analyze the meaning patterns of other people. Such methods are not inconceivable; some steps toward the pooling of semantic intuitions have already been taken (see 4.2.2). Our experience in using these methods, however, has persuaded us that their utility lies primarily in testing hypotheses already formulated on other, usually intuitive grounds. It is those hypotheses that we are seeking here. Once formulated, they can be subjected to empirical study and revision. If our efforts are successful for the brand of academic English we ourselves speak and write, they may provide a model for how to study the meaning patterns of other dialects and even of other languages. Until such additional studies have been completed, the generality of our observations can be questioned; any discussion of semantic universals must be speculative. But we are not willing to abandon our most powerful tool for charting the semantic patterns we know best simply because the results cannot answer all the questions about meaning that we would like to ask.

We have elected to explore verbs of motion, possession, vision, and communication. Verbs of motion have an obvious perceptual basis that we should be prepared to deal with in terms of perceptual predicates. Verbs of possession differ from verbs of motion, yet resemble them in many ways. And in a book about relations between perception and language it is only proper to examine verbs of seeing and saying. The "subjects" in our studies were about 2,000 English verbs. Although they were not selected randomly, we believe, and will try to demonstrate, that they constitute a representative sample of the population we are interested in.

The following discussion is organized in terms of semantic fields of verbs. The organization should not be taken to mean, however, that we think we have proved the general claim we are trying to test. It is no logical consequence of a theory of linguistic competence phrased in terms of operational procedures that the lexical component of the system must be patterned in lexical fields. In our opinion, the most useful theory of linguistic procedures would be one that would make it obvious that a natural language does not have well-defined, mutually exclusive semantic fields and also why people who speak the language and know its meaning patterns would feel intuitively that it might have. For our present purposes, a semantic field is not a theoretical entity whose psychological validity must be established and defended but rather is a useful intuitive device for gaining access to the kinds of semantic patterns we wish to study.

7.1   VERBS OF MOTION

Modern linguists of the structural school have been critical of notional definitions of parts of speech. They have found it all too easy to enumerate exceptions to proposals that a noun is the name of a person, place, or thing, that an adjective expresses a quality of a thing, that a verb describes the action that is performed. An extreme reaction to the traditional approach led some structuralists to an almost cryptographic analysis of linguistic forms; they boasted that their results were obtained without recourse to the meanings of the symbols whose patterns they analyzed. Systematic efforts to provide purely formal definitions of syntactic categories, however, have convinced many linguists that although reliance on notional formulations can be reduced considerably, it cannot be eliminated entirely. A middle ground is obviously preferable; the willingness of some linguists in recent years to discuss the relation of syntax to semantics is a clear advance over a situation in which students of language were forced to choose between bad semantics and no semantics at all.

In the more relaxed atmosphere that currently prevails it is even possible to see some virtue in what traditional grammarians were saying. Perhaps they did not really mean that everything labeled by a noun is a concrete object; perhaps they meant that when you use a noun to label something, you tend to conceptualize it as if it were a concrete object. Perhaps they did not mean that every verb denotes a perceptible action; they may have meant that when you use a verb to denote something, you tend to conceptualize it as if it were an action. Their definitions did not facilitate formal distributional analysis, but they may have expressed an observation of how people think of nouns, verbs, adjectives, and other syntactic categories.

Notional definitions of the parts of speech can be seen as evidence for one way that language can distort people's view of reality. If you call something electricity, the noun tempts you to reify it. If you say a cage contains a wild lion, the verb tempts you to think the cage is doing something. Versions of this idea have been explored by proponents of linguistic relativity. We will not review that theory here; it is enough to recognize a tendency to think of nouns as things and verbs as actions—pointing out counterexamples does not seem to have diminished it.

One could search for a statistical explanation. Many nouns name concrete objects, many verbs denote actions, and such nouns and verbs are among the most frequently used in everyday speech. To a psychologist it is especially interesting that concrete nouns and verbs of animate movement are even more predominant in the speech of children; Brown (1957, 1958) documented this favoritism in samples of children's speech and demonstrated experimentally that young English-speaking children will take the part-of-speech membership of a new word as a clue to its meaning. It seems that the nouns that name concrete objects and the verbs that describe movement are first learned, most frequently used, and conceptually dominant.

If one wished to identify the most characteristically verbal of all the verbs, therefore, one would turn to the verbs of motion, the verbs that describe how people and things change their places and their orientations in space. If evidence from children can be interpreted in the obvious way, these are the verbs that establish the pattern, and even adults as mature and judicious as traditional grammarians are not able to escape the action semantics associated with this syntactic category. In turning first to an analysis of the semantics of motion verbs, we believe we are launching our study of verbs with their purest and most prototypical forms. The semantic components that we can identify for the verbs of motion appear repeatedly in our analyses of less dynamic verb families.

Not only are verbs of motion ontogenetically primary, but their meanings have a strongly perceptual basis—a correlation that can hardly be coincidental. When someone cogitates or acquiesces or experiences it is not clear just what perceptible signals of those "activities" he will transmit, but when he runs or jumps or climbs there is little question. This feature also motivates our study of motion verbs, for it means both that motion verbs are an important link between perception and language and that they should fall within the scope of the perceptual predicates we have introduced. Here, if anywhere, we should have available some of the formal machinery necessary to construct plausible linguistic routines.

We define verbs of motion as verbs that describe how an object changes from a place p at time t to another place p' at a later time $t + i$. Miller (1972) has proposed that "travel," in one of its senses, captures this idea of change of location at least as well as any other single verb in English. We might take "travel" as the generic concept and use it in the "but" test to explore other verbs (6.3.1). For example, "He walked, but he traveled" and "He walked, but he didn't travel" both sound odd, so "walk" is semantically related to "travel." Any verb that produces anomalous sentences when substituted in this frame should be included in the semantic field of motion verbs.

The "but" test should not be applied too rigidly, however. We feel intuitively that "raise" involves a change of location, yet "He raised it, but he traveled" and "He raised it, but he didn't travel" are both possible. The problem is that in "He raised it," it is not "he" whose motion is at issue, but "it." We must test "He raised it, but it changed location" and "He raised it, but it didn't change location." Then the semantic relation becomes apparent. We have thus discovered a basis for classifying motion verbs into those in which the subject of the verb moves and those in which the object of the verb moves.

The ideal strategy for identifying all the motion verbs would be to proceed through the dictionary entry by entry, testing each verb against "but . . . travel." Although the spirit may be willing, the flesh generally proves too weak for algorithmic search. The heuristic strategy we have followed is to begin by jotting down verbs that come immediately to mind as involving motion: travel, move, come, go, rise, raise, lift, fall, walk, run. This process can go on for weeks, during which one is acutely sensitized to these verbs. After about the first hour, however, it is helpful to start looking up in dictionaries and thesauruses the words one has listed and to study the verbs given there for further candidates. Since semantic domains seem to be organized into many subfields, the danger in this approach is that one will compulsively exhaust many of them but accidentally overlook entire subfields. The best protection against such lacunae we have found is to study the analyses already proposed by other workers, when these are available, and to resort to algorithmic search through a few pages of the dictionary as a test. There is always a possibility that some obvious subfield has been completely ignored, but that is the risk one takes with heuristic searches.

During this preliminary verb hunt it is wise to accept everything that is even vaguely related to the semantic domain. (An uncertain penumbra surrounds every semantic field, and sharp boundaries should not be based on hasty preconceptions.) The verbs so collected may then be written on file cards and sorted into categories that seem roughly similar in meaning (Miller, 1969b). If, as is often the case, a verb has two senses that both seem relevant to the domain, separate cards should be made for each sense, since it is the

senses, not the phonological shapes or strings of letters, that we are interested
in. This can be done by copying each sense from the dictionary onto a card,
but usually it is more convenient simply to note on a card the number of
the sense given in the dictionary, and to refresh one's memory when necessary.
This anchors the work to a particular dictionary, which has advantages and
disadvantages.

As the sorting proceeds one discovers the gray areas. They pose the really
difficult decisions, and the best way to characterize what is involved is to give
some examples from the domain of motion verbs.

"Start" and "stop" are so frequently used with motion verbs that they seem
to be motion verbs themselves. Street signs use "stop" and "go" as antonyms,
and certainly "go" is a motion verb. We can use "start" in such sentences as
"She started to New York from her home," where "started to go" is apparently taken for granted. The "but" test is not very helpful: "He stopped, but
didn't change location" seems anomalous if we think of "stopped" as meaning
"stopped moving," but nonanomalous if we think of it as stopping something
else, as in "stopped singing," which leaves us right where we were. The nuclear
meanings of "start" and "stop" have nothing to do with motion; they can
refer to any change of state (6.2.5). Yet they have acquired a secondary
meaning as motion verbs. Since it is sense we are interested in, and since
"start" and "stop" have senses that are motional, we must include them in
the domain. Moreover, since we will probably have to deal with obvious motion verbs like "arrive" and "depart" in any case, including the motional
senses of "start" and "stop" should not complicate the analysis unduly.

Another borderline case is provided by verbs that describe bodily movements: breathe, cough, flex, gesture, shrug, smile, sneeze, swallow. If we take
"change location" as the generic concept defining this domain, the "but" test
would exclude these verbs: "He shrugged, but he changed location" and "He
shrugged, but he didn't change location" are both acceptable. On the other
hand, "He shrugged his shoulders, but they didn't change location" is odd,
so motion is involved here somewhere, even though we cannot make a parallel
argument for intransitives like "sneeze." These verbs remind us that not all
motion is locomotion. If we include them, we should include verbs for rotary
changes in orientation, since these motions can also occur without change
in location: oscillate, pivot, revolve, rotate, spin, spiral, turn, twirl, whirl.
We should also include verbs for changes in shape or size: absorb, broaden,
deepen, diffuse, empty, expand, extend, fill, grow, lengthen, narrow, shorten,
shrink, spread, widen. (These usually involve movement of boundaries, but
not change of location.) The dichotomy here between verbs of motion-in-
place and verbs of locomotion probably should be viewed in a broader
context: the verbs of motion are a subfield of the positional verbs (Gruber,
1965; Jackendoff, 1972), a larger semantic field of verbs used to describe
not only motion but location ("contain," "hold") and immobility ("remain," "stay") as well. We will arbitrarily confine our analysis to verbs of
locomotion and assume that body motions are an area of overlap with the

body concept, that changes in size are an area of overlap with the size concept, that rotary motions are a special case of motion verbs that can be analyzed as "travel round," much as "ascend" can be analyzed as "travel up," and that nonmotional verbs of location can be ignored without distorting our analysis of the verbs of locomotion.

Another example of semantic overlap is seen in the contact verbs: bang, bash, bat, batter, bounce, bump, butt, collide, contact, crash, deflect, dent, hammer, hit, jab, kick, knock, meet, pat, pound, pummel, ram, rap, rebound, ricochet, scrape, scratch, slap, smash, smite, strike, tap, touch, whack. These verbs presuppose that at least one of two objects is in motion, and some suggest that motion is imparted to the object contacted. For example, since "The car hit the tree, but the car changed location" and "The car hit the tree, but the car didn't change location" both sound odd, "hit" behaves like a motion verb. We will, again arbitrarily, omit contact verbs on the grounds that change of location is incidental to their meanings. Our first task is to unravel relations between the simpler verbs of locomotion; once these concepts are analyzed it should be easier to combine the concepts of moving and touching.

Our attempt to define verbs of motion as verbs that imply change of location is not completely satisfactory, since it leaves us with complicated decisions about various groups of closely related verbs. A list containing all and only verbs of motion seems to be an impossible ideal. There is a central group of verbs that clearly and unambiguously describe changes in location, and that group should be fully represented. Various peripheral verbs require us to sharpen our ideas; we must make arbitrary decisions as to whether to include them. The important point is not what decision we make—if we exclude them now we can always return to them later—but that such decisions are necessary. Given that they are necessary, the claim that there are semantic domains worthy of analysis must rest on one's subjective impression that the boundaries around them are not figments of a theorist's imagination. At what point do these decisions become too numerous or too arbitrary to justify the working hypothesis of a semantic field?

We have no compelling answer to this question, but our impression, after considerable trial and error, is that verbs of motion are relatively well behaved. It is possible to assemble a list of more than two hundred verbs that describe different ways to change location (Miller, 1972). Those verbs whose membership might be questioned themselves form intuitively related domains, so one decision can serve to include or exclude them. Many have other senses that belong in other patterns (you can move someone to tears, send a message, come across a discovery, take a bet, hand over ownership), but these are usually metaphorical extensions of the senses that entitle them to membership in the field of motion verbs. For all these reasons we feel that designating motion verbs as a semantic field of English is defensible, at least as a working hypothesis.

The real test is whether the meaning pattern of motion verbs can be analyzed in an intuitively satisfying manner that explains people's feelings of relation between them. A perusal of the motion verbs leaves one with a clear impression that they make up a complex, interrelated pattern of concepts. We find contrasting pairs like "open" and "shut"; pairs that describe motions in opposite directions, like "come" and "go," "raise" and "lower," "advance" and "retreat"; pairs like "start" and "stop" that contrast the initiation and the termination of motion; "walk" and "ride," which differ in the instrumentality employed; "walk," "swim," and "fly," which describe motion through different mediums. The challenge is to identify these common components and to represent them in a system of interrelated linguistic concepts.

7.1.1   Simple Verbs of Traveling

In chapter 2 we assumed that the perceptual system can support judgments of motion. We introduced the predicate Travel(x) to mean that something x is perceived by someone as changing location, as traveling through space. It would be convenient to start our analysis with a motion verb that captures Travel in a relatively pure form. It would be even more convenient, since we are discussing verbs of motion, if that verb could be "move." But "move" is a causative verb; its meaning involves more than change of location.

The most common and earliest acquired verbs of motion are "come" and "go," but they are also too complex to serve as generic verbs for our analysis. "Come" entails a change of location, but it also entails a destination—someone who is coming will not have come until he has reached the destination (although someone who is going will have gone before he gets there). Moreover, the destination of "come" must coincide with the speaker's or listener's location either at the time of utterance or at the time referred to (Fillmore, 1966, 1971d). Deixis of place and person are therefore involved in "come." "Go" is similarly complicated. These complications disqualify "come" and "go" as pure expressions of a Travel percept.

A motion verb that expresses change of location as simply as possible is intransitive "travel." "He travels" means simply that he goes from one place to another. It leaves open whether he causes or merely allows his location to change, and says nothing about where or how far he goes, how long it takes, or what else happens. The trouble is that "travel" has another sense that is probably more common—to visit distant places, as in "He traveled widely in Africa." Consequently, "travel" often leads to stilted test sentences: "He moved the chair, but it didn't travel." In such cases we can relieve some of the strain on our linguistic intuitions if we use "change location" instead: "He moved the chair, but it didn't change location." We must be careful with "change location," however, because "change," like "move," is a causative verb.

We might assume that a person who knows English knows something like

[TRAVEL(x)]:   Something x "travels" if Travel(x)

(where once again we use brackets to remind the reader of the assertive force of schemata). Such a paradigm would require a person who wished to evaluate sentences using "travel" to witness the change of location. The concept TRAVEL should not be limited to perceived motions. A modest degree of familiarity with moving objects should suffice to support inferences that traveling has occurred if something has either appeared in a place where it has not been before or disappeared from a place where it has been before. A weaker formula for the concept than for the percept might be appropriate. We could use AT to characterize the change of location (omitting brackets to simplify the notation):

> TRAVEL(x):   Something x "travels" if there is a time t and a place y such that:
> (i) Either: $R_{t-i}(\text{notAT}(x, y))$ & $R_t(\text{AT}(x, y))$
>   Or: $R_{t-i}(\text{AT}(x, y))$ & $R_t(\text{notAT}(x, y))$

where $i > 0$. The statement-forming operator from temporal logic is used here to denote that a statement is realized at a given time (see 6.2.1); this formulation implies that at some (one or more) t', where $(t - i) < t' < t$, HAPPEN$_t$(AT(x, y)) or HAPPEN$_t$(notAT(x, y)). Note that if x does not change location between $t - i$ and t, both disjuncts are false.

One advantage of this formulation of TRAVEL is its obvious relation to TO and FROM (6.1.4). The major differences are that TRAVEL does not have y as an argument and does not share the presuppositions of TO and FROM. A weakness of this formulation is its behavior under negation. In "x didn't travel," both of the disjuncts would have to be false:

> notTRAVEL(x):
> Either: $R_{t-i}(\text{AT}(x, y))$ & $R_t(\text{AT}(x, y))$
> Or: $R_{t-i}(\text{notAT}(x, y))$ & $R_t(\text{notAT}(x, y))$

The first disjunct is what would ordinarily be meant by "not travel"; the second disjunct is vacuously true, since the universe will be full of places where x was not, both at $t - i$ and at t.

Negation should not permit the second disjunct, so we will make it a presupposition of "travel" that the object in question has *some* location at $t - i$. That is to say, if x exists, both "x travels" and "x doesn't travel" entail that x is somewhere in space, that there is some location y such that x is at y. This suggests the formulation

> (1)   TRAVEL(x):   Something x "travels" if there is a time t and a place y such that $R_{t-i}(\text{AT}(x, y))$ and:
>   (i) $R_t(\text{notAT}(x, y))$

where the presupposition is stated in the introductory phrase. By including the prior location at $t - i$ as a presupposition for any test of the location at t, we insulate it against negation—if x does not travel, it stays where it was.

This version of "travel" is similar to that given for "from" in 6.1.4 except that the location y is not an explicit argument of TRAVEL. If TRAVEL is combined with FROM(x, v), v provides one specific value of y for which TRAVEL could be tested. In general, however, we should not assume that $y = v$; there is only one v, but there should be a sequence of locations y as long as the traveling continues. Both FROM and TO provide new information about definite locations of x, not about the indefinite place y that is presupposed in (1).

One trouble is that the sequence of locations y is not expressed in (1). There is more to motion than momentary appearances or disappearances. As (1) is formulated, "travel" would seem to be an event verb, which is clearly incorrect. In order to be explicit that traveling is a process that can continue throughout an interval (compare HAPPEN$_i$ in 6.3.3) we require something like

(1′) TRAVEL(x): Something x "travels" from time t_0 to time t_m if, for each t_i such that $t_0 \leqq t_i \leqq t_m$, there is a place y_i such that $R_{t_i}(AT(x, y_i))$ and:
(i) $R_{t_{i+1}}(\text{notAT}(x, y_i))$

Since (1′) is essentially a sequence of momentary instantiations of (1), (1′) entails (1). Although (1) does not entail (1′), if something that was known to be present at moment $t - i$ is noted to be absent at moment t, people will normally infer (1′) from that fact, although it is sufficient merely for (1). Since "travel" has durative aspect, however, we assume that (1′) is the preferred formulation. Note that when TRAVEL is defined as in (1′), there is little temptation to confuse the locations y_i with the locations specified by FROM(S, v) or TO(S, w).

In adopting (1′) as the nucleus of the semantic domain of motion verbs, we attempt to capture the basic intuition that motion involves a durative change of location—from somewhere y_i to somewhere else not-y_i—and we assume that "travel," "to," and "from" enable us to express different aspects of that concept on particular occasions. Various arguments can be supplied: "He travels" omits both spatial locatives; "He's from Liberia" omits traveling and one locative, as does "It's a long way to Leeds"; "The train travels from London to Glasgow" provides all three arguments of the full construction.

This threesome is such a coherent unit that we must consider in more detail how "travel," "to," and "from" work together. Since the prepositional phrases appear to be predicate modifiers by our usual tests (see 6.3.7), "x traveled from v to w" can be written:*

(2) (TO(FROM(TRAVEL)))(x, v, w) $\equiv$ (FROM(TO(TRAVEL)))(x, w, v).

---

*This method of representing the arguments of a compound predicate can induce some confusion about which argument plays which role. Such uncertainties could be avoided: "x travels to w" could be considered as attributing the property "travels to w" to the term "x," or ((TO(TRAVEL))(w))(x), and "x travels to w from v" could attribute the property "travels to w from v" to "x," or ((FROM((TO(TRAVEL))(w)))(v))(x), and so on. Since the rapidly accumulating parentheses can also induce confusion, we have adopted the notation illustrated in (2) and will rely on the reader's knowledge of English to keep the arguments straight in any substantive application. Formally this amounts to an assumption that the role of every argument could be given separately as part of the selectional and strict subcategorization features (Chomsky, 1965).

"Travel" can be used in combination with a great variety of other adverbials, especially predicate modifiers: "travel through the air," "travel on water," where medium is indicated; "travel by conveyance," where instrumentality is indicated; "travel rapidly," where manner is indicated. These particular combinations are so common that we have verbs with special senses for traveling in these ways:

(3)   soar   travel through the air   (THROUGH(TRAVEL))(x, AIR)
          drift   travel on water   (ON(TRAVEL))(x, WATER)
          ride   travel in a conveyance   (IN(TRAVEL))(x, CONVEYANCE)
          hurry   travel rapidly   (RAPIDLY(TRAVEL))(x)

The descriptions "through air," "on water," and the like, are here assumed to be locative adverbials that modulate TRAVEL to form a more complex concept. TRAVEL can serve as an argument for such instrumental and manner phrases as long as the argument of TRAVEL is provided for the more complex operator that results. We will refer to the relation between the complex concept and its components as semantic incorporation; we will say, for example, that HURRY incorporates RAPIDLY and TRAVEL. Procedurally, the incorporation of F in G means that G cannot be verified without performing all of the computations that would be required to verify F. Note that this formulation does not say that the incorporated concept must be verified. Someone who has determined that HURRY(x) truly represents a given situation will not necessarily have determined that (RAPIDLY(TRAVEL))(x) also truly represents it, even though he will have performed all of the computations that such a determination would require.

If G incorporates F, G entails F, and we will say that the word expressing G can be analyzed into a formula or schema containing F. For example, the concept HURRY entails the concept TRAVEL and the verb "hurry" has a sense that can be analyzed as (RAPIDLY(TRAVEL)). The data on which this analysis rests are the judgments by speakers of English that sentences like "He was hurrying down the street and he was not traveling rapidly down the street" are contradictory. Our claim is that such judgments are possible because "hurry" is understood as HURRY, "travel rapidly" is understood as (RAPIDLY(TRAVEL)), and people can determine that HURRY calls for all the computations that would be required for (RAPIDLY(TRAVEL)).

The semantic field of motion verbs includes all those that entail traveling and can be analyzed into formulas containing TRAVEL. It is important to our argument, therefore, that sentences with motion verbs like "soar," "drift," or "hurry" entail corresponding sentences with "travel." This point deserves attention, because it is known that some adverbs block the normal entailments of constructions in which they occur. "John walks rapidly" entails "John walks," but this entailment seems to rest on the meanings of "walk" and "rapid," not on the general form of the sentence. Counterexamples to a formal generalization are provided by sentences like "John allegedly walks" or "John walks in his dreams," which do not entail "John walks." Most of the exceptions that have been discussed are sentence modifiers. Few predicate modifiers have been found that have the effect of blocking normal entailments, although Thomason and Stalnaker (1973) say that predicate adverbs like "halfway" may pose difficulties. For example, "John traveled halfway here" does not entail "John traveled here." This counterexample is tricky, since "John traveled halfway" does entail "John traveled." One might argue that "halfway here" is a place adverbial that must be treated as a whole, in which case it does not block the normal entailment relation.

Our present interest is in incorporated adverbials, and although predicate adverbials seem to be the main candidates for semantic incorporation, we must be alert to the possibility that a verb incorporating TRAVEL may not entail traveling. That is to say, our claim that an entailment relation holds between all verbs of motion and "travel" is subject to disproof. It is an open question whether sentential adverbs like "allegedly," "partially," or "halfway" are incorporated into English verbs and, if so, what their effects would be on the entailments we have assumed. We will proceed as though entailment relations always hold between those compound concepts for which English has special verbs and the simpler concepts they incorporate, and wait until counterexamples arise to worry about it.

The distinction between predicate and sentence adverbials is important, however, because the choice can lead to different interpretations. Consider the ambiguous sentence "It traveled in the car." The most salient interpretation is probably "It rode in the car," which corresponds to (IN(TRAVEL))$(x$, CONVEYANCE), as indicated in (3). Another interpretation is "It changed location within the car"; the car itself may not have moved. This second interpretation cannot be paraphrased in terms of "ride"; it corresponds to IN(TRAVEL$(x), y)$, where y is a pointer to "the car" and "in the car" is a sentence adverbial.

The problem posed is simply this: How should a schema or decision table be formulated in order to indicate that "ride" is appropriate for the former case and not for the latter? The second interpretation is simpler, so consider it first. The decision table for IN would presumably accept IN(S, y) if y is a container and if S is a description of a state or event that is realized in y. Since TRAVEL(x) qualifies as substitutable for S, the result is IN(TRAVEL(x), y). To complete the translation it would be necessary to determine that ISA$(y$, CAR) & ISA(CAR, CONTAINER). From information in these various schemata, the system could then construct a program to find x and y and apply appropriate tests.

The first interpretation requires that the translator have available in some decision table conditions for (IN(TRAVEL))(x, y) and ISA(y, CONVEYANCE); when these are both confirmed, RIDE(x) is an admissible action. How does the system compute (IN(TRAVEL))? One possibility is that some decision table for motion verbs combines such conditions as TRAVEL(y), IN(x, y), and HOLD(y, x) to define this concept. That is, the operator (IN(TRAVEL)) would not really be computed but would be looked up in a table where the defining information had already been stored. Then we could assume that (IN(TRAVEL))(x, y) underlies sentences corresponding to "x traveled in y" (in the appropriate sense) and that when *y* is a conveyance (not a pocket, suitcase, briefcase, or whatever else) it contributes to sentences of the form "*x* rode in *y*" or, more simply, "*x* rode."

To assume that predicates like (IN(TRAVEL))(*x*, *y*) are prepackaged and available in lexical memory would accord with the fact that interpretations of English verbs and the prepositional phrases they can take often seem arbitrary. For example, one can ride in *y* or ride on *y* or ride by *y*, in the appropriate sense, but if one rides under *y* or rides after *y* or rides in various other (preposition + *y*) ways, the adverbial phrase may be understood as a sentence modifier. It is not implausible that many incorporations of predicate adverbials are simply learned and stored in semantic memory by speakers of the language.

Whatever plausibility a prepackaging assumption may have, it is not sufficient to account for all predicate adverbials. To suppose that "travel slowly" and "travel widely" and "travel briefly" and "travel blindly" and travel in all the other acceptable ("travel" + predicate adverb) ways must be prepackaged in semantic memory would seriously limit the combinatorial productivity of the system. In 6.3.7 we claimed that the system must have a capability to compute compound predicates. We can illustrate this process by considering some other verbs of traveling.

In (3) we suggested how path descriptions of the medium traveled through, instrumentalities, and manner adverbials might be incorporated into incomplete definitions. The formulations given in (3) are incomplete both in that "soar," "drift," "ride," and "hurry" have other senses than those given and in that the senses considered are not completely specified. We will not attempt to complete these definitions, although the fact that additional specifications are needed is obvious from the existence of other words that satisfy these incomplete definitions yet are not synonymous. For example, "travel through air" would paraphrase not only "soar" but also various senses of "drift," "fly," "float," "sail," "spiral," "swoop," "wing," "zoom," where at least "wing" seems to include an instrumental component as well. Similarly, "travel through water" would paraphrase senses of "drift," "float," "row," "sail," "wade." Even "travels in boat on water"—(ON(IN(TRAVEL)))(*x*, BOAT, WATER)—which combines medium and instrument, would not be sufficient to distinguish between "row" and "sail." And "travel rapidly" paraphrases senses of "hurry," "race," "scurry," "speed," "sprint." The psychological point of formulations like those in (3) is that sets of verbs they incompletely define are semantically homogeneous—not contrastive sets, but similarity sets with overlapping privileges of occurrence.

Many motion verbs contain adverbial components that describe the direction of motion (Gruber, 1965). "The smoke rose" and "The smoke traveled upward" are, for all practical purposes, equivalent. "Rise" can therefore be paraphrased as "travel upward," where "upward" is a directional adverb that modifies "travel." Let us use this analysis to illustrate how a compound predicate might be computed. The essentials are that before any tests are carried out it is necessary to apply the procedure UPWARD to the procedure TRAVEL to

yield a new procedure representing "travel upward" or "rise." According to
(1′), TRAVEL involves a sequence of momentary realizations; the basic pair
(ignoring the distinction between what is asserted and what is presupposed) is

$$R_{t_i}(\text{AT}(x, y_i))$$
$$R_{t_{i+1}}(\text{notAT}(x, y_i))$$

In general, however, it will be more convenient to represent this information
in the format

$$R_{t_i}(\text{AT}(x, y))$$
$$R_{t_{i+1}}(\text{AT}(x, z))$$
$$\text{F}(y, z)$$

where, in the case of simple "travel," F is a relation of inequality. We may then
assume that the complex procedure UPWARD operates in the following way. A
subprocedure, which can be thought of as the -WARD component, locates in
the procedure to be modified the two locative arguments defining the process
—in the present case the arguments y and z. (If there is no such pair of arguments, the computation fails: the procedure to be modified violates the selectional restrictions on -WARD.) A further subprocedure, which can be thought
of as the UP- component, then inserts into the procedure to be modified a new
component specifying that the later location is OVER the earlier one. The result
in the present case is a new procedure:

$$R_{t_i}(\text{AT}(x, y))$$
$$R_{t_{i+1}}(\text{AT}(x, z))$$
$$\text{OVER}(z, y)$$

The new procedure is ready to be utilized in verifying that x is rising, or in any
other computation. A similar process would be involved in the computation
of any compound predicate, as in the following intransitive verbs of traveling
with directional-adverb components:

(4) | ascend, rise | (UPWARD(TRAVEL))(x)
     | pivot, revolve, rotate | (AROUND(TRAVEL))(x)
     | descend, fall, sink, drop | (DOWNWARD(TRAVEL))(x)
     | proceed | (ONWARD(TRAVEL))(x)
     | depart, flee, leave | (AWAY(TRAVEL))(x)
     | advance, progress | (FORWARD(TRAVEL))(x)
     | enter | (INWARD(TRAVEL))(x)
     | exit, emerge | (OUTWARD(TRAVEL))(x)

The fact that several verbs are listed on the left as having the same directional-
adverb component is another reminder that these are incomplete paraphrases
at best. For example, "sink" could be (THROUGH(FALL))$(x, $ LIQUID$)$; "flee"
requires an intentional component; "exit" has a suggestion of x's moving out
of view whereas "emerge" suggests moving into view.

   Some of these directional motion verbs also have transitive uses. "Rotate" can be a causative motion verb, ROTATE$((x), y)$, where x causes y to travel around; "advance" can express ADVANCE$((x), y)$, where x causes y to travel forward. We will return to problems raised by such verbs in 7.1.3.

"Travel away" is a satisfactory paraphrase of the intransitive use of "leave," and "from" and "to" phrases can be added as freely as they can be added to "travel." There are transitive uses of "leave," however, that can omit the preposition "from": "leave town," "leave the office." When the origin of travel is an argument of LEAVE, it is as if "away from" were incorporated: $(\text{FROM}(\text{LEAVE}))(x, v)$. (There is also a transitive use in phrases like "leave a gift" or "leave the book," where the second argument is not an origin.) "Ascend" and "descend" have similar transitive uses that indicate locations without a preposition ("ascend the mountain," "descend the stairs") and could be similarly represented as $(\text{UP}(\text{ASCEND}))(x, y)$ or $(\text{DOWN}(\text{DESCEND}))(x, y)$.

A variety of motion verbs incorporate locative prepositional phrases as adverbials modifying predicates based on TRAVEL. Some verbs with such senses are

(5)	leave, depart	$(\text{FROM}(\text{LEAVE}))(x, v)$
	accompany	$(\text{WITH}(\text{TRAVEL}))(x, y)$
	ascend, climb	$(\text{UP}(\text{ASCEND}))(x, y)$
	cross, traverse	$(\text{ACROSS}(\text{TRAVEL}))(x, y)$
	descend	$(\text{DOWN}(\text{DESCEND}))(x, y)$
	follow, chase	$(\text{AFTER}(\text{TRAVEL}))(x, y)$
	jump, leap	$(\text{OVER}(\text{TRAVEL}))(x, y)$
	pass	$(\text{BY}(\text{TRAVEL}))(x, y)$
	penetrate	$(\text{THROUGH}(\text{TRAVEL}))(x, y)$
	reach, visit	$(\text{TO}(\text{TRAVEL}))(x, w)$
	enter, invade	$(\text{INTO}(\text{TRAVEL}))(x, w)$
	approach, near	$(\text{NEAR}_a(\text{TRAVEL}))(x, w)$

(NEAR$_a$ is the adverb.)

The incompleteness of these definitions is obvious. Several of these verbs will be taken up again as we discuss other semantic incorporations in this domain. The point of (4) and (5) is that many English verbs of motion incorporate adverbials of direction and location.

The directional and locative components of the verbs of motion are most explicit in Latinate verbs. For example, English has several motion verbs based on the Latin "pellere," to drive: dispel ("dis," apart), expel ("ex," from, out of), impel ("in," in, into), propel ("pro," before, forward), repel ("re," back, again). Other Latinate verbs that wear directional signals on their sleeves are: progress, regress, transgress; eject, inject, traject; proceed, recede, precede; deport, export, import, transport; exit, transit; dismiss, emit, transmit. In such cases there is etymological support for semantic analysis into a directional and a motion component of meaning. In (4) and (5) we have generalized this analysis to English verbs that are not explicitly marked for adverbial incorporations, on the assumption that the underlying conceptual processes are the same. The incorporation of path-descriptive components in the verb is a major device for generating the large variety of motion verbs available in English.

Ways of characterizing the path of motion are relatively well elaborated in English, no doubt because the path is one of the most obvious aspects of motion. We have exemplified verbs incorporating origin and destination, intermediate locations, medium, and direction. There may be other ways to characterize the path, but these are surely the most important.

7.1.2   Deictic Verbs of Motion

The deictic verbs of motion in English are a small set—bring, come, go, send, take—but they are among the most frequently used verbs in common speech. Like most common words, they have a variety of senses that challenge lexicographers. Our present interest is in their use as motion verbs. We will concentrate on "come" and "go," since "bring" can be paraphrased as "cause to come," and "send" and "take" can be roughly paraphrased as "cause to go." (E. Clark, 1974a, suggests that "send" be paraphrased as "cause to begin to go" and "take" as "cause to go with.") The semantic feature of major interest here is deixis, and the complexities involved can be well illustrated by the intransitive use of "come" and "go" as simple verbs of traveling.

The uses of "come" and "go" on which we wish to focus are those that presuppose something about the place to which the traveling occurs. Motion that one speaker might refer to by saying "It came here" another speaker in a different place might refer to by saying "It went there." The choice of verb depends on who is speaking and where he is located relative to the destination of the motion; deixis of both person and place is involved.

Characterizing deictic conditions is not a simple task. Perhaps the best analysis is Fillmore's (1971d, 1973). It seems to make little difference where the traveling was *from*, but where it was *to* is critical. According to Fillmore, "come" indicates motion toward the location of either the speaker or the addressee at either the time of reference or the time of utterance, or toward the home base of either the speaker or the addressee at the time of reference; "go" indicates motion toward a location that is distinct from the speaker's location at the time of utterance. To these general conditions Fillmore adds two special uses of "come": (a) "come" also indicates motion at the time of reference in the company of either speaker or addressee, and (b) "come" also indicates, in discourse in which neither the speaker nor the addressee figures as a participant, motion toward a place taken as subject of the narrative, toward the location of the central character at the time of reference, or toward the central character's home base at the time of reference. The fact that "bring" shares all these special conditions on the use of "come" (Binnick, 1971) is strong evidence for interpreting "bring" as "cause to come."

Fillmore's analysis of "come" is more complete than his analysis of "go," which he considers only in the sense that contrasts with "come." "Go" enters into other motional contrasts, however, that endow it with meanings that easily confuse one's intuitions about its deictic conditions. For example, when "go" contrasts with "stay," it is closely similar in meaning to "travel"; the contrast is between changing location and not changing location. (Indeed, the contrast is sometimes between changing and not changing, as in "go sour" versus "stay fresh," where motion is not entailed.) When "go" contrasts with "stop," it is closely similar in meaning to "start"; the contrast is between commencing to change location and ceasing to change location. (Again, the motion component is sometimes ignored, as in "He went pale" versus "He stopped blanching.") When "go" is used to mean "travel" or "start," the locations of the speaker or his addressee are not important; "travel" and "start" are not deictic verbs.

Deictic uses of "go" may or may not indicate travel away from the speaker. "Go away!" is a command to travel away from the speaker; "He went to Biloxi in 1974" entails nothing about his or the speaker's prior location. In both cases it is understood that the travel is to a location other than the location of the speaker at the time of utterance, so Fillmore's analysis covers both uses.

There are differences, however, between "He has gone" and "He has gone to Biloxi." The latter sentence seems to presuppose that the speaker is not in Biloxi at the time of utterance; both "He has gone to Biloxi" and "He hasn't gone to Biloxi" entail that the speaker is not in Biloxi at the time he is speaking. On the other hand, "He has gone" does not presuppose that the speaker is not wherever "he" is at the time of utterance, but merely entails it, that is, "He hasn't gone" does not entail that the speaker is not wherever "he" is at the time of utterance. "He hasn't gone" means simply "He stayed"; without some indication of a destination, "go" is not a deictic verb. Still, when "to" is added to "go" there must be constraints on the location "to" assigns, constraints that depend on the speaker's location at the time he is speaking. The simple solution would be to distinguish two senses of this verb, a nondeictic sense of "go" roughly equivalent to "travel" and a deictic sense of "go to" that incorporates restrictions against going to the speaker's location at the time of utterance. Since this solution offends one's intuitions that there are not really two concepts of going that differ in this subtle way, we are motivated to combine them in a single paradigm.

We will complicate (1'), therefore, by including a deictic condition to define "go" in such a way that when it is used with "to" it will have a presupposition that it does not have when it is used without "to." This can be done in the following way:

(6)   GO(x):   Something x "goes" at time t_0 if for each t_i such that $t_0 < t_i < t_m$ there is a place y_i such that $R_{t_i}(\text{AT}(x, y_i))$; there is an utterance time n and a place z such that $R_n(\text{AT}(\text{speaker}, z))$; if a destination w is indicated, then $w \neq z$; and:

   (i) $R_{t_{i+1}}(\text{notAT}(x, y_i))$

   (ii) $R_{t_m}(\text{notAT}(x, z))$

As before, conditions described in the lead sentence are presupposed; they must be satisfied before the conditions listed in the paradigm can be tested. In this case, the presuppositions amount to little more than the presuppositions of TRAVEL plus the assumption that the speaker must have been somewhere z at the time he was speaking. The deictic constraint, $w \neq z$, is vacuous as long as w is not given. Note that it is possible for y_0 and z to index the same location, that is, for x to have been where the speaker is now at the time of utterance—at z—and to have traveled by t_m to some other, any other, location. This case is particularly simple, since, if $y_0 = z$, conditions (i) and (ii) are identical. Since $y_0 \neq z$ is also possible, however, x can "go" from other places than the speaker's location.

Consider the effect of negation. "He hasn't gone" will be true if (i) or (ii) or both fail. If (i) fails, x is still at place y_0 at time t_m; x has stayed wherever it was and has not traveled at all. If (ii) fails, x has traveled to the speaker's location z at time t_m; x has not *gone* to z, x has *come* to z. If both (i) and (ii) fail, x has been at $y_0 = z$ all the time; x has stayed at z. These three failures correspond to

$$\text{He hasn't gone.} \quad \begin{cases} \text{He's stayed where he was.} \\ \text{He's come (here).} \\ \text{He's stayed here.} \end{cases}$$

Note that as long as w is unspecified "He hasn't gone" does not entail that he is not at z at the time of utterance; it is not a presupposition of "go" that the speaker's location at the time of utterance must differ from x's location at time t_m.

Now consider the effect of adding a "to" phrase. Recall that TO(S, w) presupposes $R_{t-i}(\text{notAT}(S, w))$ and asserts $R_t(\text{AT}(S, w))$. If we assume that the presuppositions of GO and TO are simply added in "go to," and if we let $t - i = t_0$ and $t = t_m$, we have at t_0 both AT(x, y_0) and notAT(x, w), from which it follows that $y_0 \neq w$; it is presupposed that the somewhere y_0 that x had been was not the destination w to which x traveled. Moreover, the conditional presupposition in (6) now comes into play, since w is given, and we have $w \neq z$; the destination w is not the speaker's location z. If we also combine the assertions of GO and of TO, we have at time t_m: notAT(x, y_{m-1}) and notAT(x, z) and AT(x, w). From the second and third we infer that these conditions are consistent with the presupposition that $z \neq w$—that the destination w must be different from the speaker's location z at the time of utterance. In the special case that $y_0 = z$, the sense will be that x went to w from "here."

Finally, consider the effect of negation on "go to." Sentences of the form "x hasn't gone to w" will be true whenever it is true at t_m that AT(x, y_0) or AT(x, z) or notAT(x, w). If AT(x, y_0) is true at t_m, then "x hasn't gone to w" will be true because x has not moved (in which case, since it is presupposed that $y_0 \neq w$, notAT(x, w) must also hold). If AT(x, z) is true at t_m and if, as presupposed, $w \neq z$, "x hasn't gone to w" will be true because x has come to z instead. And if notAT(x, w) is true at t_m, "x hasn't gone to w" will be true because x is not at w; x has gone somewhere else. In the special case that

$y_0 = z$, all three of these conditions will hold, so "x hasn't gone to w" will be true because x stayed "here," at the speaker's location. These various bases for negation correspond to

$$\text{He hasn't gone to Biloxi.} \begin{cases} \text{He's stayed where he was.} \\ \text{He's come (here).} \\ \text{He's gone somewhere else.} \\ \text{He's stayed here.} \end{cases}$$

If we wished to add "He was in Biloxi all the time," we would have to weaken the presupposition of TO and include $R_{t-1}(\text{notAT}(S, w))$ among its assertions instead. Nothing essential in the analysis just given hinges on the status of this condition.

The important point to note is that "x hasn't gone to w" does entail that the speaker was not at w at the time of utterance, because the condition $w \neq z$ is incorporated as a presupposition in (6) and so is immune to negation. By phrasing this presupposition as conditional on a value for w, the presupposition is empty for "x hasn't gone."

There seem to be no additional problems posed by "go from" or "not go from" that require analysis, since "from" does not indicate a destination and "go from" is presumably comparable to "go." The awkwardness of sentences like "He went from Biloxi," without an accompanying "to" phrase, is presumably attributable to the availability of "leave" (see (5) above).

Having found all these complexities in the relatively simple verb "go," we may perhaps be forgiven if the analysis of "come" is less detailed. We will ignore Fillmore's addenda about "home," about traveling together, and about third-person narratives and concentrate instead on the deictic restriction that the destination of "come" must be the location of either the speaker or the addressee at either the time of reference or the time of utterance. "It'll come to the office tomorrow" is acceptable if the speaker expects to be at the office tomorrow or if the speaker expects the addressee to be at the office tomorrow or if the speaker is at the office at the time he says it or if the addressee is at the office at the time it is said or if any combination of these conditions holds. This is clearly a more complicated deictic condition than is required for "go"; "It'll go to the office tomorrow" is acceptable if the speaker is not at the office at the time he says it. As these conditions are listed, it is easy to see that under many circumstances either "come" or "go" is acceptable.

How can speakers of English remember such a complicated deictic condition? Is there some simpler concept behind it which, once grasped, has all these specific conditions as consequences? Perhaps it is related to the notion that in any serious conversation a context of information is shared by the participants. This line of thought suggests that the acceptable destinations of "come" might be characterized as the locations that have been established for the participants by their antecedent discourse. If the condition stated above is to be applied correctly, they must have established where they were, are, or would be at the time of the events under discussion. If these locations are not clearly established in the conversational context, a speaker should be forgiven for violating the deictic restrictions of "come"; if they are established, violations can lead to misunderstanding.

We can simplify our formulations if we introduce λ to represent this shared information about the participants' locations; λ will denote the locations of the speaker and the addressee at the times of reference and the times of utterance, insofar as they are known to the speaker. The deictic presupposition can then be stated simply as requiring the destination to be a member of λ, which we can state using ISA since the destination will be a single entity:

(7)   COME(x):   Something x "comes" at time t_m if for each t_i such that $t_0 \leq t_i \leq t_m$ there is a place y_i such that $R_{t_i}(\text{AT}(x, y_i))$; if a destination w is indicated, then ISA(w, λ); and:

     (i) $R_{t_{i+1}}(\text{notAT}(x, y_i))$

     (ii) ISA(y_m, λ)

Analysis of notCOME(x), $(\text{TO}(\text{COME}))(x, w)$, and $(\text{notTO}(\text{COME}))(x, w)$ would proceed in a manner parallel to that illustrated above for GO.

Comparison of (6) and (7) with (1′) will show that GO and COME entail TRAVEL; (6) and (7) state the presupposition of TRAVEL explicitly, and condition (i) is identical in all three. In order to make the incorporation of TRAVEL into GO and COME explicit, we can rewrite (6) and (7) as follows:

(6′)   GO(x):   Something x "goes" at time t_0 if there is an utterance time n and place z such that $R_n(\text{AT}(\text{speaker}, z))$; if a destination w is indicated, then $w \neq z$; and:

     (i) TRAVEL(x)

     (ii) $R_{t_m}(\text{notAT}(x, z))$

(7′)   COME(x):   Something x "comes" at time t_m if, when a destination w is indicated, ISA(w, λ), and:

     (i) TRAVEL(x)

     (ii) $R_{t_m}(\text{AT}(x, \lambda))$

If a predicate-modifying adverb like "rapidly" is used in combination with "go" and "come," as in "He came/went slowly into the room," the adverb, as (6′) and (7′) indicate, must modify TRAVEL(x) in condition (i); x cannot be rapidly "at" some location. The system must be able to modify these schemata by substituting such operators as $(\text{RAPIDLY}(\text{TRAVEL}))(x)$ in condition (i).

"Go" and "come" enter into many idiomatic combinations with adverbials. "Go about" can mean undertake; "go after," pursue; "go at," attack; "come across" can mean find; "come by," acquire; "come through," survive or provide. One might assume that each of these idioms is learned as if it were a separate verb, unrelated to "go" or "come" in the senses analyzed above. On the basis of such contrasts as "The plane came down in Texas" and "The plane went down in Texas," however, E. Clark (1974a) suggests that the "deictic center" toward which events can come and away from which they can go is some normative, positively evaluated state of affairs—how the addressee might hope or expect things would be—and that the deictic conditions described by Fillmore for "go" and "come" are a special extension of this more basic contrast. This hypothesis, which reverses the customary direction of explanation, is attractive psychologically, but it remains to be seen how wide a variety of "go" and "come" idioms can be characterized in this way.

7.1.3   Causes of Motion

We have noted that "move" is a causative verb. In analyzing sentences like "Melissa moved the bed" in section 6.3 we assumed a causal relation between two associated events: "Melissa did something" and "The bed moved." When "move" is used intransitively, however, the causative component can vanish: "Melissa moved," like "Melissa traveled," can be interpreted to mean either that Melissa did something that caused herself to move or that her change of location was attributable to motive forces other than her own. The latter interpretation does not require a causative component. We take this duality of interpretation to mean that intransitive "move" is vague, not ambiguous, about causation.

In order to accommodate these various possibilities in a single conceptual schema, we proposed in 6.3.7 to formulate such verbs as follows:

(8)   MOVE$((x), y)$:   Something x "moves" something y if:
     (i) TRAVEL(y)
     (ii) DO(x, S)
     (iii) CAUSE$(S, (i))$

S indexes the same statement in (iii) as in (ii), even though no interpretation of S—of what x did—is provided. The parentheses in (x) mean that this argument of MOVE is semantically optional; if no value for x is given, conditions (ii) and (iii) are simply omitted and MOVE$(( ), y)$ reduces to TRAVEL(y) by condition (i). There is no restriction against $x = y$, which would be explicit in such sentences as "Melissa moved herself," but it is syntactically acceptable to omit the pronoun, leaving some uncertainty about the speaker's intended message. The uncertainty—between MOVE$((y), y)$ and MOVE$(( ), y)$—is precisely the uncertainty one feels about TRAVEL(y). When x is not supplied, uncertainty about causation is therefore appropriate, particularly if y is animate.

Many English verbs of motion share with "move" this option of being either transitive causatives or intransitive noncausatives. For example, "advance":

(9)   ADVANCE$((x), y)$:   Something x "advances" something y if:
     (i) (FORWARD(TRAVEL))(y)
     (ii) DO(x, S)
     (iii) CAUSE$(S, (i))$

It will be seen that (9) differs from (8) only in condition (i), where the formulation suggested in (5) for intransitive "advance" has been substituted for the simple "travel" condition. The causative motion verbs of English that we have identified as having senses that take this general form are: advance, assemble, bend, bounce, close, empty, expand, fill, flap, flex, fly, gallop, halt, move, nod, open, pass, pour, race, return, roll, rotate, run, sail, scatter, separate, shake, shift, shrink, shut, sink, slide, slip, spin, spread, start, stop, swing, tilt, trip, turn, twist, walk, wave, whirl, wiggle. For all of these verbs the definitional problem is to characterize their intransitive sense of motion; the causative component can be added as in (8) and (9) whenever an actor x is provided as an argument.

There are also causative motion verbs from which the actor cannot be omitted. Although they can contain directional or locative constraints on the traveling involved, they are transitive verbs that do not have an intransitive, noncausative use. In general, they follow a schema that can be illustrated for "raise" (or "lift"):

(10)   RAISE(x, y):   Something x "raises" something y if:
      (i) DO(x, S)
      (ii) CAUSE(S, RISE(y))

The causative motion verbs that we have identified as having senses that take this general form are: attract, bear, bring, carry, depress, drag, drive, eject, elevate, emit, fling, flip, hand, hurl, inject, insert, interpose, jerk, launch, lay, lift, lower, place, project, propel, pull, push, put, raise, remove, replace, send, set, shove, substitute, take, throw, thrust, toss, tow, transport.

For verbs following the pattern of (9), when a value for x is not provided, y can become the grammatical subject; that possibility is not available for verbs following the pattern of (10). For both types of verbs, however, x can be omitted if an instrumental phrase is available instead. (We will ignore here the nonappearance of x in incomplete passives—"y was raised"—since this syntactic transformation does not affect the semantic recoverability of an actor; "by something" is understood to have been deleted.)

In 6.3.7 we pointed out that causative verbs containing DO(x, S) can take an instrument as their subject. Both "Tom moved the boulder with a crowbar" and "A crowbar moved the boulder" are acceptable. To review our account of how this substitute actor develops from an instrument, let us begin with "x moves y with z." If we assume that "with z" modifies what x did, not the way y traveled, this type of sentence would be represented:

(WITH$_i$(DO))(x, S, z) & CAUSE(S, TRAVEL(y)).

If we expand the first conjunct according to (110) in 6.3.7, we obtain

DO(x, S') & CAUSE(S', DO(z, S)) & CAUSE(S, TRAVEL(y)).

If we suppose that the actor x is omitted and that the consequence is the deletion of all terms in which x is involved, we are left with

DO(z, S) & CAUSE(S, TRAVEL(y)).

This result satisfies the formulation of MOVE given in (8), but with the actor x replaced by the instrument z. Hence "z moves y." The instrumental phrase inserts another causal link in the chain from actor to effect; if either is omitted, the other can serve as grammatical subject. The collapse of such causal chains in our linguistic descriptions of them often requires considerable conceptual reconstruction by the addressee (Schank, 1973b).

Most of the causative verbs listed above have further semantic components. For example, a deictic component can be added by basing a causative on "come" or "go":

(11)   BRING(x, y):   DO(x, S) & CAUSE$(S, (\text{WITH}(\text{COME}))(y, x))$
          TAKE(x, y):   DO(x, S) & CAUSE$(S, (\text{WITH}(\text{GO}))(y, x))$
          SEND(x, y):   DO(x, S) & CAUSE$(S, \text{BEGIN}(\text{GO}(y)))$

For these verbs the first argument is not optional and intransitive use is incorrect, although an instrument can serve as the grammatical subject by the substitutions described above.

The verbs "open," "close," and "shut" have received some attention as a consequence of their similarity to the adjectives "open," "closed," and "shut." G. Lakoff (1970) notes the similarity between "John opened the door," "John brought it about that the door opened," "The door opened," and "The door became open"; "become" he took as the basis for an inchoative transformation and "brought it about that" as the basis for a causative transformation applied to inchoatives. These observations can be represented in our notation if "John opened the door" is paraphrased as "John did something that caused the door to become open," where (85) in 6.3.3 is taken as the formulation of BECOME. As we noted in the introduction to section 6.3, English has a large number of morphological causatives derived from adjectives and nouns, all of which seem to require analysis in terms of CAUSE and BECOME. In the case of "open," "close," and "shut," the motional component is introduced by BECOME, which requires a change; since the adjectival forms denote a location, changing them will entail a change of location, that is, motion.

Some of the verbs listed above require a destination. The best example is "put," although "lay," "place," and "set" have similar senses. "He put the book" means that he caused the book to travel somewhere, but the sentence is incomplete without a locative adverb ("away," "down") or some such phrase as "on the shelf," "in his case," "against the lamp," "beside the typewriter." Many locative prepositions are possible, so the destination seems to be introduced by an adverbial prepositional phrase, but since the locative phrase is obligatory, the destination must be included as an argument of the verb. If we formulate "put" as

(12) $(\text{AT}(\text{PUT}))(x, y, w)$:   Something x "puts" something y at a place
          w at time t if:
          (i) $Q_t(\text{notAT}(y, w))$
          (ii) DO(x, S)
          (iii) CAUSE$(S, R_t(\text{AT}(y, w)))$

then the absence of any entry for PUT without the modifying AT would serve to indicate that a locative phrase—any phrase that entails AT—is obligatory.

Binnick (1968) considers "put" the "locative causative" of "be." "The sheriff put Robin Hood in jail" would thus be paraphrased as "The sheriff caused Robin Hood to be in jail." We regard "be" as a surface verb without semantic content (see 6.3.1). In our system, "y is at w" is simply AT(y, w). But if we were to formulate "put" more simply as DO(x, S) & CAUSE$(S, AT(y, w))$, traveling would not be entailed. It is necessary to include condition (i) asserting that y was not at w until x put it there at time t, and to rely on conditions (i) and (iii) together to entail TRAVEL. (Note that condition (i) is not a presupposition, because "x didn't put y at w" does not entail that y was not at w prior to some moment t.) We believe (12) is an appropriate way to capture Binnick's insight without losing the motional component of "put."

Most of the problems associated with the definitions of these verbs have to do with manner, direction, or location, not with the introduction of a causative component. We will therefore close this discussion, but not before mentioning the permissive motion verbs: admit, drop, release. These follow the same pattern as the causatives, but with ALLOW replacing CAUSE:

(13)   ADMIT(x, y):   DO(x, S) & ALLOW$(S, ENTER(y))$
         DROP(x, y):   DO(x, S) & ALLOW$(S, FALL(y))$
         RELEASE(x, y):   DO(x, S) & ALLOW$(S, TRAVEL(y))$

An instrument can also serve as the grammatical subject of these verbs: "He dropped a beam with the crane" or "The crane dropped a beam"; "They released the water by blowing up the dam" or "Blowing up the dam released the water." Here again a substitute actor can enter by virtue of the schema proposed for instrumental WITH, as described on page 520.

7.1.4 Agents of Motion

The verbs of motion we have been discussing do not have to take a human agent as their grammatical subject. It is possible to speak of either animate or inanimate things traveling, coming, going, moving, ascending, leaving, raising, taking, setting, admitting. Even when these verbs take an animate noun as their subject, the noun may not denote an agent. "He rode to Boston," for example, could mean either that he was a passive passenger in a conveyance operated by someone else or that he rode a horse to Boston, in which case it would be understood from general knowledge of horseback riding that he was a very active agent indeed. There are other intransitive motion verbs, however, that demand an agent as the subject: "He walked to Boston" or "He drove to Boston." You do not normally walk or drive without some intention to do so. We must consider how this semantic component is incorporated in such verbs.

In 6.3.2 we drew a distinction between DO(x, S), which relates x to the event or process S in which x participates actively, and ACT(x, S) where x is an animate thing that does S intentionally. In 6.3.7 we noted that verbs incorporating DO could be distinguished from those incorporating ACT by their behavior with instrumental phrases. In 7.1.3 we considered those causative verbs of motion that must incorporate DO because the instrument can serve as a substitute actor ("He lifted his hat with his cane," "His cane lifted his hat"). We will now consider verbs of motion that must incorporate ACT because an inanimate instrument cannot serve as a substitute agent ("He walked with his cane," but not "His cane walked").

Intransitive agentive verbs of motion like "walk," "swim," and "run" incorporate, in addition to an ACT and a TRAVEL component, components describing the path and instrumentality. That is to say, we understand these verbs to mean that the agent uses an instrument to allow him to travel along a path through the air or on land or water. The instrumentality is usually some part of the agent's body that is moved in such a way as to achieve the desired result, and cannot ordinarily become a substitute agent—"Upstairs, feet walked back and forth until I fell asleep" is an example of synecdoche.

There are many sorts of walking; we will use their variety as an excuse for a brief detour into verbs that describe bodily movements. The variety of gaits is possible because walking involves a system of reflexes that can be utilized in different ways depending on such immediate demands as the nature of the terrain. There is a normal mode of walking for crossing relatively smooth terrain, there is a tentative "seeking" mode for crossing an irregular terrain in the dark, and there are many other modes from a professional walker's heel-and-toe to a sailor's rolling swagger. The basic reflex, found in babies, is the stepping reflex, which ensures that when your center of gravity is in front of your feet, you step forward. A detailed account of the neuromuscular coordination involved in walking can be found in Bernstein (1967).

The important point is that although walking, like other motor skills, involves a complicated set of coordinated muscle movements taking into account intentions and visual, kinesthetic, and vestibular information, it may be a relatively simple activity at the highest level of neural computation. As Arbib (1972) remarks, "High level control seems to be kept free for settling broad questions of strategy, or fine details of manipulation, while intervening systems ensure that our motor activities issue in smooth, well-connected movements" (p. 147). A high-level decision to walk does not specify details of muscle movements. We assume that a control instruction, walk, is translated by an efferent interpreter into the language governing muscle movements. The translation is guided by other information concerning such matters as the positions of the limbs. Psychological evidence (see Miller, Galanter, and Pribram, 1960, chap. 6; Powers, 1973) suggests that there are hierarchies of motor control in which, at each stage, a relatively gross command is translated into instructions for action at the next lower stage. The translation would take into account, as Arbib argues, both feedback from lower levels and other parallel commands from above. By allowing "tuning" from lower levels, a gross command does not have to be finely specified; the control instruction to walk need not specify what will happen to the center of gravity when a leg is moved. Extraneous factors, such as gravity or the mechanical properties of skeletal linkages, also circumvent the need for detailed specification. Presumably, therefore, the way people think and talk about bodily movements has largely to do with their highest level of control, with control instructions of the sort described in chapter 3.

We imagine that children understand what it means to walk long before they have any communicable concepts of motion, causation, or intention. A child who knows how to walk can have a clear concept of what "walk" denotes without understanding fully the conceptual location of "walk" in the field of motion verbs. He has acquired the necessary computational machinery to compile and to execute the control instruction, and he learns first a simple label for it. It is only later that the semantic components incorporated in "walk" become clear, as an increasing understanding of the conceptual relations between movements relates the lexical concept WALK to all the other lexical resources available for describing motion—to speak loosely, as "walk" changes from a label to a word. That development continues throughout childhood, perhaps throughout life.

The conceptual core for bodily movements is, of course, the body. The various body parts are capable of characteristic movements, and some of them provide a model for the movements of other objects. Since the body is also a physical object, terms that speakers use to describe motions of objects can often be used to describe its motions. For example, limbs and their extremities can be lifted, waved, turned, twisted, and shaken. Eyes and mouth can be opened and closed. Skin surfaces can be wrinkled and stretched. Joints and vertebrae can be bent, flexed, arched, and straightened. Few of these movements are locomotory and we have not analyzed them here, but none of them would introduce insuperable analytical problems.

The lexicon contains a number of verbs that seem primarily restricted to bodily movements. Although they are probably learned initially as labels for specific efferent control instructions, they can be broken down into separate motional components. What is particularly interesting is the breakdown of global body movements involving an intentional component into simpler body movements that do not necessarily involve intention. We can illustrate this relation, which is perhaps a reflection of the hierarchical control mechanism, by considering some pertinent examples. The global activity of eating involves such components as biting, chewing, and swallowing. The global movement of picking something up by hand involves grasping or gripping it, and lifting it by lifting the appropriate arm. Dropping an object intentionally involves releasing one's grip, which thereby allows the object to fall. Catching an object intentionally presupposes that it is traveling and involves cupping the hand(s) around it, grasping it, maintaining one's grasp (that is, holding it), which thereby stops it from traveling and prevents it from falling. An especially interesting set of global movements are those that bring about a particular body posture: stand, sit, crouch, lie. These verbs denote either a posture or an act that brings it about, and, since there may be no gross movement in common between, say, standing from a sitting posture and standing from a crouching posture, it seems that the action component is relatively unspecified; the resulting posture is the main global concept.

The main global locomotory motions include walking, running, crawling, climbing, and swimming. We will consider in more detail the intransitive agentive verbs "walk" and "run." We might say simply that these verbs label control instructions for global movements. But just as there is a hierarchy in motor control so there is a hierarchy in descriptions of motor actions. At the next level down, a specification of "walk" might include: one leg steps forward, then the other leg steps forward, and so on. A still more detailed specification of lower-level bodily movements might include the following: $foot_i$ is lifted from the ground and moved by leg_i forward past leg_j and under the body (its center of gravity), $foot_i$ treads on the ground, leg_j pushes $foot_j$ against the ground causing the body to move forward so that it (its weight) is supported by leg_i and $foot_i$; the cycle is repeated with the roles of leg_i (and $foot_i$) and leg_j (and $foot_j$) interchanged. Like the stepping reflex, none of these components by itself requires an intention for its execution, and each of them could be submitted to a further conceptual analysis. Such an analysis, however, would take us from the conceptual framework of everyday life into the realm of neurophysiology.

A useful working analysis of "x walks" would be something like "x uses his feet to travel on land" or "x moves on his feet." There is an instrumentality here: a walker walks with his feet. The combination of intentionality and instrumentality yields

(14) $(\text{WITH}_i(\text{ACT}))(x, \text{S}, \text{FEET})$ & $\text{CAUSE}(\text{S}, \text{TRAVEL}(x))$.

When WITH_i is expanded according to (110) in 6.3.7, (14) becomes

(14') $\text{ACT}(x, \text{S}')$ & $\text{CAUSE}(\text{S}', \text{DO}(\text{FEET}, \text{S}))$ & $\text{CAUSE}(\text{S}, \text{TRAVEL}(x))$.

There are two obvious consequences. First, if we substitute x's feet for x and drop the intentional component, we are left with $\text{DO}(\text{FEET}, \text{S})$ & $\text{CAUSE}(\text{S}, \text{TRAVEL}(\text{FEET}))$, which presumably underlies such synecdochal uses as "feet walked back and forth." Second, since the verb is intentional, (14') entails

(14") $\text{ACT}(x, \text{S}')$ & $\text{CAUSE}(\text{S}', \text{DO}(\text{FEET}, \text{S}))$ & $\text{ALLOW}(\text{S}, \text{TRAVEL}(x))$,

and hence we can also paraphrase "x walks" by "x uses his feet to travel" according to the specification of USE in (111) in 6.3.7.

Although (14') may seem excessive, it is still incomplete. As it stands, it represents only "x travels by foot." We may easily add a path component: $(\text{ON}(\text{TRAVEL}))(x, \text{LAND})$. But even with this addition we have a paraphrase of many verbs of motion. Pedestrian pursuits are so important that English has a rich crop of verbs for talking about them. These verbs enable speakers to differentiate among a great variety of ways of traveling by foot, although there is no superordinate verb that means simply "travel by foot." Indeed, there is no superordinate verb that means simply "travel by foot on land," although "wade" may serve the purpose for "travel by foot through water."

The major categories of "traveling by foot on land" appear to be "walk" and its various subsets of hyponyms: march, strut, stride, pace; lumber, plod, trudge, tramp; saunter, stroll, promenade, amble; mince, slink; toddle, waddle; hobble, limp; stagger, stumble, totter; "run" and its hyponyms: sprint, jog, trot, scamper; and a few more specialized modes: dance, skate, hop, skip, tiptoe.

One's intuitive impression on scanning this list of verbs is that velocity must be one of the psychological dimensions along which they are differentiated. Young and Cliff (1971) obtained judgments of semantic similarity from college students for many of these verbs and analyzed the results as distances in a hypothetical mental space. They concluded that "the structure contains one dominant dimension, speed of movement" (p. 31). Verbs like "plod," "saunter," "amble," and "trudge" were at one end of the dimension and verbs like "run," "scamper," and "trot" were at the other. We might try to incorporate this distinction by introducing predicate adverbs: (RAPIDLY(TRAVEL)) or (SLOWLY(TRAVEL)). Since such operators will be needed to account for verbs like "hurry," "dash," and "inch," they should be available for the travel-on-land-by-foot verbs. Wierzbicka (1972, p. 107) cites K. Baumgärtner and G. Wotjak as advocates of this proposal to incorporate velocity in the meanings of these verbs.

If RAPIDLY is incorporated in the meaning of a verb, it would be contradictory to modify it with "slowly." It sounds odd to say "He sprinted slowly to the door" or "He sauntered rapidly down the street," from which we can argue that RAPIDLY must be incorporated in "sprint" and SLOWLY must be incorporated in "saunter." We can use this test to discipline our intuitions about the presence or absence of a velocity component in the analysis of traveling verbs.

The basic distinction among the travel-on-land-by-foot verbs is between walking and running. Since there appears to be a velocity difference between them, it might be proposed that "walk" incorporates SLOWLY and "run" incorporates RAPIDLY. Both Wierzbicka (1972) and Miller (1972) reject this proposal; the test just formulated indicates why. It is not odd to speak of walking rapidly or walking slowly, or to speak of running rapidly or running slowly. Such sentences as "He walked rapidly and I was forced to run slowly to keep up with him" do not seem semantically anomalous to most judges. Moreover, we would probably want to formulate "sprint" as "run rapidly," "jog" or "trot" as "run slowly," "stride" as "walk rapidly," and "amble" as "walk slowly." We conclude that the walk/run distinction must be based on something other than velocity of motion.

The usual distinction between "walk" and "run" is rather clumsy. When we run, both feet come off the ground at some point during the stride, whereas in walking one foot or the other is always on the ground. This difference is necessarily at a lower level of bodily movements—we can imagine adding a distinguishing clause for running to our earlier analysis of walking, namely, when leg_i pushes foot_i against the ground it causes it to cease touching the ground and the whole body to travel forward through the air. For convenience, however, we can denote the "walking" specification by the operator ATG for "always touching ground" and use it to define "walk" as ATG(FEET) and "run" as notATG(FEET). It is important to realize that these manner differentiations probably have no applicability elsewhere in the lexicon. We are really dealing with labels for efferent control instructions that are distinguished at a lower level when they are compiled; the same may be said for many other manners of walking: march, totter, strut, slink, stumble, pace. However, we will adopt ATG to illustrate how manner of traveling can be incorporated, and will assume that it denotes the appropriate pattern of muscular coordination stored in action memory.

Our semantic analysis of "walk" then becomes

(14''')   (WITH$_i$(ATG(ACT)))(x, S, FEET) & CAUSE(S, (ON(TRAVEL))(x, LAND)),

or "x acts with his feet in a walking manner to travel on land." (The restriction to land could perhaps be omitted from the semantic analysis. We have no trouble understanding "walking on air" or "walking on water," so the conventional restriction to land might be considered part of our general knowledge rather than our linguistic knowledge.) A verb like "totter" might be defined as (UNSTEADILY(WALK))(x), where further manner operators are incorporated.

We noted in 7.1.1 that simple verbs of traveling may incorporate a directional adverbial to characterize the path of motion. Agentive verbs of traveling can also have a directional component. For example, "visit" is agentive—visiting is something you do intentionally—and has a clear sense of "traveling to." Some directional agentive verbs of motion are

(15)   visit   ACT(x, (TO(TRAVEL))(x, y))
         invade   ACT(x, (INTO(TRAVEL))(x, y))
         lead   ACT(x, (BEFORE(TRAVEL))(x, y))
         chase   ACT(x, (AFTER(TRAVEL))(x, y))
         climb   ACT(x, (UP(TRAVEL))(x, y))
         jump   ACT(x, (OVER(TRAVEL))(x, y))
         withdraw   ACT(x, (FROM(TRAVEL))(x, y))

Both "enter" and "invade" have the sense of "traveling into," but you can enter something unintentionally, as in "He slipped and entered the water with a splash," whereas it sounds odd to say "The police invaded the apartment unintentionally." "Chase" (as contrasted with "chase away") usually has the sense of "intending to catch," so perhaps ACT should be expanded to include this component: CAUSE(INTEND(x, CATCH(x, y)), (AFTER(TRAVEL))(x, y)), or "x's intention to catch y caused x to travel after y."

The last three verbs in (15) have a special feature. "Climb" is ordinarily understood to imply upward motion and seems to differ from "rise" only by virtue of the intentional component. "Climb" is used with a greater variety of directional modifiers, though. You can "climb over" or "climb across" or even "climb down"; you can "rise over" or "rise across," but to "rise down" is contradictory. Similarly, "jump" is understood to mean "jump over" if no other direction is indicated, although you can "jump up" or "jump across" or even "jump under." And you can "withdraw into" as well as "withdraw from." Apparently there are some verbs whose incorporated directions can be over-ruled by explicit expressions to the contrary and other verbs for which any additional specification of direction must be consistent with the incorporated direction. Which verbs are which is something you have to learn when you learn English. Verbs whose normal direction can be overruled can be freely used without their second argument; they can be written with deletable arguments, like CLIMB$(x, (y))$. Since "x climbs" omits y, the condition UP(S, y) can-not be evaluated; because intransitive "climb" does not have UP in it, expressions like "climb down" can be understood as (DOWN(CLIMB))(x, z). When a value for y is given, as in "He climbed the stairs," the incorporated UP makes the pro-noun "up" unnecessary. Thus "x climbed y" would be CLIMB(x, y), whereas "x climbed up y" would be (UP(CLIMB))(x, y).

An even more complicated agentive verb of motion is "hand," which incor-porates the instrument that the agent uses. Sentences of the form "x hands w y" ("He handed me the book") entail that x uses his hand to cause y to travel to w. Moreover, the act of handing is not successfully performed unless the recipient accepts what is handed to him. The verb "hand" might be formu-lated as

(16)   HAND$_v(x, w, y)$:   Someone x "hands" someone w something y if:
      (i)   USE$(x,$ HAND$_n,$ S$)$
      (ii)   CAUSE(S, (TO(TRAVEL))(y, w))
      (iii)   ACCEPT(w, y)

Condition (iii) might be even stronger—USE(w, HAND$_n$, ACCEPT(w, y))—if one feels that the object must also be accepted by hand.

Since "He handed me the book" is so near in meaning to "He passed me the book by hand," the corresponding formulation for "pass" might be

(17)   PASS(x, w, y):   Someone x "passes" someone w something y if:
      (i)   ACT$(x,$ S$)$
      (ii)   CAUSE(S, (TO(TRAVEL))(y, w))
      (iii)   ACCEPT(w, y)

This formulation suggests that HAND$_v(x, w, y)$ might be (WITH$_i$(PASS))$(x, w, y,$ HAND$_n$) if it were not for the difference in their temporal shapes: "pass" will cover throwing whereas "hand" will not. (Such aspectual differences will be discussed in 7.1.5.) Moreover, in the case of "pass," the person w to whom something y is passed (the indirect object) can be omitted. In that case, TO(S, w) in condition (ii) and condition (iii) cannot be evaluated: "He passed the book" says nothing about the destination or whether anyone received it. (This sense of "pass to" should be distinguished from the sense of "pass by" considered in (5) in 7.1.1.)

The complexity of verbs like "pass" and "hand" arises in part from the fact that they can take three arguments—they are often called double-object verbs.

Some other motion verbs of this type are: bring, carry, convey, deliver, drag, fling, haul, lift, lower, pitch, pull, push, raise, restore, return, send, shove, take, throw, toss. Many of them permit either order of the direct and indirect objects, as in "He passed the salt to me" or "He passed me the salt" (some exceptions: convey, deliver, lift, restore, return), and many of them allow two passive forms, as in "The salt was passed to me" or "I was passed the salt" (some exceptions: carry, haul, pitch, pull, push, take). The relations among these sentences are generally considered to be syntactic: a dative-movement transformation changes the structure underlying "He handed the salt to me" into the structure underlying "He handed me the salt" by inverting the order of the direct and indirect objects and deleting the preposition, after which a passive transformation can be applied. There are so many exceptions and special cases (Green, 1974), however, that one begins to suspect that the apparently simple transformational solution may be incorrect. An obvious alternative is to put the appropriate information into the lexical entries for each double-object verb—to include it along with other brute facts that an English speaker must learn by rote—but the details of how that should be done have inspired considerable disagreement among theoretical linguists. A rough semantic pattern can be discerned that fits most double-object verbs: usually the grammatical subject is an agent that does something intentionally that causes the indirect object to have the direct object (in some sense of the multiply ambiguous verb "have"). Since various meanings of "have" will not be discussed until section 7.2, we will not pursue the problem here.

7.1.5   Aspects of Motion

Motion occurs in both space and time, but so far we have paid more attention to its spatial than to its temporal properties. We should redress this imbalance by considering aspectual properties of motion verbs, properties that express the time course of action.

In order to see the full range of aspectual possibilities we would have to consider all the positional verbs, not just the verbs of motion. Motion can continue, begin, or end, but it can also fail to occur. Verbs that express a "remain at rest" sense include: hover, lie, linger, lodge, loiter, remain, rest, sit, stand, stay, tarry, wait. Moreover, many verbs of motion have nonmotional uses: cross ("A bridge crossed the river"), fall ("The land fell away to the east"), leave ("He left his umbrella"), reach ("The roof reached the trees"), rise ("This river rises in Colorado"), run ("This road runs all the way to Chicago"), soar ("The steeples soared toward heaven"). Verbs that express continued rest or continued motion, however, pose fewer aspectual difficulties than verbs that express changes from rest to motion or motion to rest; we will focus here on verbs that incorporate the operators BEGIN or END.

Let us return to the contrast between "travel" and "reach" that we introduced first in 6.2.5. The formulation for durative "travel" given in (1') makes it explicit that traveling continues throughout an interval. In (5) we suggested that "reach" might be defined as "travel to." Since "travel" is durative, this suggestion makes "reach" a durative verb, which is clearly incorrect. What we must add to "travel" in order to capture the temporal shape of "reach" is that reaching is momentary, that it is realized at some moment t. The existence of such a moment is precisely what HAPPEN$_t$ can add. According to (77′) in 6.3.3, HAPPEN$_t$(S) presupposes that there is a moment t' at which notS is realized and asserts that there is a moment t such that notS is realized at $t - 1$ and S is realized at t. If we assume that "x reaches w" means that x is at w for the first time at t, then S can be AT(x, w) and "reach" could be formulated as

(18)   REACH(x, w):   HAPPEN$_t$(AT(x, w)).

HAPPEN$_t$ asserts that x was in a different location at $t - 1$ from its location at t, which is sufficient to entail that x traveled.

The defects of (18) become apparent when we consider the consequences of negation. What is denied in such sentences as "Harriet didn't reach Cambridge"? If we define "reach" as in (18), its negation would say that there was not any moment t such that "Harriet is in Cambridge" changed from false to true. How could such a moment fail to occur? A change of truth value would not occur if, say, Harriet had been in Cambridge the whole time, but that would violate the presupposition of HAPPEN$_t$. We conclude that "Harriet didn't reach Cambridge" must mean that "Harriet is in Cambridge" remained false during the entire interval of time under discussion.

The presuppositions of "reach" go beyond the presuppositions of HAPPEN$_t$, however. If Harriet had not been traveling at all, or if she had been traveling away from Cambridge, it would also be inappropriate to discuss her reaching Cambridge. That is to say, both "Harriet reached Cambridge" and "Harriet didn't reach Cambridge" seem to entail that Harriet was traveling toward Cambridge, so "travel toward" would be a presupposition of "reach." Moreover, if Harriet was traveling toward Cambridge prior to t, then "Harriet is in Cambridge" must be false prior to t, so the presupposition of "reach" entails the presupposition of HAPPEN$_t$.

In order to make these entailments explicit, we must include them in the presupposition of "reach":

(18′)   REACH(x, w):   Something x "reaches" some place w if there is a moment t such that $Q_t((\text{TOWARD}(\text{TRAVEL}))(x, w))$ and:
          (i) $R_t(\text{AT}(x, w))$

Since (18′) entails (18), and since HAPPEN$_t$ characterizes momentary events, this formulation ensures that "reach" is nondurative.

The analysis just given for "reach" can be paralleled for other nondurative motion verbs, although the correct phrasing of the presupposition must be determined for each instance. To take an intransitive example, "depart" would be

(19)   DEPART(x):   Something x "departs" if there is a moment t such that $Q_t(\text{notTRAVEL}(x))$ and:
          (i) $R_t(\text{TRAVEL}(x))$

Comparison of (19) with (73) in 6.2.5 shows that DEPART is modeled after BE-GIN(P_x), where P_x is TRAVEL(x); "x departs" can be paraphrased as "x begins to travel."

To take a causative example, "launch" would be

(20)   LAUNCH(x, y):   Something x "launches" something y if there is a moment t such that Q_t(notTRAVEL(y)) and:
    (i) R_t(TRAVEL(y))
    (ii) DO(x, S)
    (iii) CAUSE(S, (i))

Since x can launch itself, it is possible for x and y to be coreferential. Comparison of (20) with (73) in 6.2.5 shows that LAUNCH is modeled after BE-GIN(x, P_y), where P_y is TRAVEL(y). The paraphrase of "launch" is "cause to begin to travel."

There is a sense of "throw" that can be paraphrased as "launch by hand through the air." The instrumental and path complications can be introduced as follows:

(21)   THROW(x, y):   Someone x "throws" something y if there is a moment t such that Q_t(not((THROUGH(TRAVEL))(y, AIR))) and:
    (i) R_t((THROUGH(TRAVEL))(y, AIR))
    (ii) (WITH$_i$(ACT))(x, S, HAND)
    (iii) CAUSE(S, (i))

"Fling," "flip," "hurl," and "toss" would share this incomplete definition of "throw." Although BEGIN does not appear explicitly in these schemata, it is clear that they all imply BEGIN(TRAVEL(y)).

Miller (1972) comments that "jump" provides a good review of most of the semantic components one can uncover in the motion verbs. In our present system it would be formulated thus:

(22)   JUMP($x, (y)$):   An animate x "jumps" something y if there is a moment t such that Q_t((notTHROUGH(TRAVEL))(x, AIR)) and:
    (i) R_t((THROUGH(TRAVEL))(x, AIR))
    (ii) (WITH$_i$(ACT))(x, S, LEGS)
    (iii) CAUSE(S, (i))
    (iv) OVER((i), y)

Note that motion, intention, causation, path direction and medium, and instrumentality are all included. Despite the apparent complexity of this analysis, children under five have little trouble recognizing jumping or applying the word correctly (Long, 1975). Presumably the concept of jumping is learned as an action pattern even before these semantic components can be appreciated individually—it is not acquired by first mastering the individual components and then combining them in the appropriate way.

As (22) is formulated, if a value for y is not provided, condition (iv) does not apply. Expressions like "jump under" are to be interpreted as the intransitive "jump," which omits "over *y*," with the predicate-modifying adverb "under." Inanimate objects can also jump—trains jump the tracks, needles jump out of their grooves—so there is probably a less elaborate formulation of "jump" that would omit intentionality and instrumentality, but (22) is probably the sense that children learn first, even though they themselves would not be able to appreciate this decomposition.

With these examples of nondurative verbs before us, consider the aspectual problems posed by our introductory comparison of "reach" and "arrive." In 6.2.5 we suggested that the difference was that you can reach one place on your way to some other place, whereas the place that you arrive at is your destination. We proposed a schema for "reach" in (18′) above. It says merely that the traveler *x* is located at *w* at a particular moment; it entails nothing about his staying there. A formulation for the intransitive verb "arrive" can be modeled after that for "depart" given in (19):

(23)   ARRIVE(*x*):   Something *x* "arrives" if there is a moment *t* such that $Q_t(\text{TRAVEL}(x))$ and:
     (i) $R_t(\text{notTRAVEL}(x))$

"Arrive," like "depart" and "reach," has no sense of agency; something can arrive intentionally or accidentally. This formulation of "arrive" implies that wherever *x* is at *t* is the destination of *x*, at least briefly, since that is where it stops traveling, or, more precisely, that is where its not-traveling begins. Note that "arrive," unlike "reach," does not presuppose that *x* must be approaching its destination; its presupposition is that *x* must be traveling. We could include in the presupposition of "arrive" an explicit stipulation notAT(*x*, *w*) until *t*, where *w* is appropriately defined, but since the destination must be provided explicitly by a spatial locative ("at *w*" in "*x* arrived at *w*," for example) we assume *w* is not part of the meaning of "arrive."

Formulations (18′) and (23) seem to account for the differences we have noted between these two verbs, yet one may be left with a vague sense of unease that a destination should be any place where not-traveling begins. A person who sets out on a journey with a specific destination in mind does not arrive until he is at the place he planned to be. This purposive penumbra of "arrive" is missing from (23), which says that anywhere a traveler happens to be when he stops traveling is the place where he has arrived at that moment. These misgivings about (23) can only be dispelled if one is willing to assume that not all the places at which one arrives are one's destination: "An hour after he arrived he discovered that this was not the party he had been invited to." We propose (23) in the belief that things often arrive where they were not intended to go, but we recognize how simple it would be to add further conditions to (23) in which an ACT operator would contain an explicit description of *x*'s intended goal as AT(*x*, *w*).

In 6.2.5 we proposed that the aspect of English verbs could be satisfactorily represented in terms of the relatively simple operators BEGIN(P), CONTINUE(P), and END(P), along with the temporal logic used to define them. The most obvious omission in this treatment is an operator for iterative aspect, for verbs like "hop" or "bounce" that can describe either a single nondurative event or a durative sequence of such events; we see nothing difficult in principle about the definition of an operator REPEAT(E), although the details might become complicated. However, we take (18') to (23) as examples showing how to formulate natural and relatively simple accounts of intuitive differences and similarities in the temporal shapes of many English verbs of motion.

There are still many puzzles worthy of analysis in this semantic field, but we will not pursue them further. Our results are already sufficiently rich to underwrite similar explorations of other fields.

7.2   VERBS OF POSSESSION

The concept of possession, like the concept of location, is fundamental to the English lexicon; indeed, transfer of possession in many ways resembles movement from one location to another (Gruber, 1965; Jackendoff, 1972). Unlike spatial location, however, possession goes beyond what is perceptible; as Snare (1972) remarks, a stolen apple does not look different from any other apple. Possession is primarily a conceptual matter.

If someone asks about one of your acquaintances, "Does he have any possessions?" you are likely to ask yourself: What does he own? What has he bought? What has he been given? What has he inherited? But if someone asks about an exotic tribe, "Do they have possessions?" such reflections may be inappropriate. The point of the question may be to establish whether the tribe has a concept of possession, whether possessions play any part in their social intercourse. Thus, at one level of discourse there are a number of notions, such as having, buying, giving, and inheriting, that can be partially interdefined because they revolve around possession. At a deeper level of discourse is the conceptual core, which stands in need of explication if one is going to be able to decide whether property exists in a given society.

The ordinary business of life can be conducted without explicit recourse to the conceptual core of possession; people need only grasp the interrelations between having, buying, giving, and so forth. Indeed, many people have only the vaguest notion of the conceptual core. There may be whole societies that do not grasp the core explicitly; it may be embodied in their conventions and forms of social behavior rather than in their mental lexicons. We will have to lay bare these conventions before attempting to analyze the verbs of possession.

7.2.1   The Concept of Inherent Possession

The inherent possession of property is an unequivocally social concept. Ask a layman what is meant by "property" and he is likely to reply that it is in the last resort a legal notion, a matter for the courts to decide. In fact, however, it is a good deal more fundamental than that, and a good deal more relevant to psychology. Our society revolves around property, its ownership, its exchange, its inheritance; one of the profound political questions of the age is the determination of what ought to be within the category of private property. The concept is so widely embracing of and embraced by linguistic usage and habitual ways of thinking that it is difficult to see it in perspective.

For a traditional Western philosopher like Locke, property is the foundation of all moral rights, as a famous chapter in the *Second Treatise on Government* bears witness. But for a modern philosopher, equipped with greater logical and linguistic sophistication, it is a social institution governed by a complicated set of conventional rights and duties, an institution much like that of promising. A recent analysis by Snare (1972) emphasizes the analogy with speech acts. Just as there are constitutive conventions that define what it is for a speech act to be a promise, and regulative conventions that concern the smooth running of the institution (see Searle, 1969, chap. 2), so there are constitutive conventions that define the conceptual core of property and regulative conventions that define its particular institutions within a society.

Regulative conventions presuppose that property exists. They govern such matters as who can own property, how ownership is to be decided, and what sorts of things can be property; they differ manifestly from one society to another. We might say, following Snare, that some such conventions are necessary for the institution, but no particular ones are necessary for it. On the other hand, constitutive conventions define the institution. They are universal, but perhaps only in a tautological sense—one would say of an apparent exception not that it shows that the conventions are erroneous but merely that it is not an instance of property.

Snare offers three main constitutive conventions for the concept of inherent possession expressed by "A has x":

(24)   (a)   It is not wrong for A to use x, but wrong for others to interfere with A's using x.

       (b)   If and only if A consents, it is not wrong for others to use x.

       (c) A may permanently transfer the rights in rules (a) and (b) to specific other persons by consent.

Further conventions (or laws) may govern the punishment of transgressors, the liabilities of property owners, and damages for the destruction of property. But it is these three conventions, often embodied in common law, that are crucial.

Do these three constitutive conventions tolerate exceptions? In *The Republic* Socrates questions whether you should return weapons belonging to a madman; even Locke admits that it may be necessary to destroy a man's property without his consent in order to prevent the spread of fire. According to Snare, such apparent exceptions show only that the conventions are to be considered to hold prima facie. It could not be wrong for an individual to use weapons just because they belong to him; rather our caution reflects an anticipated misuse of them. Property rights are not absolute; most cultures recognize an authority with an overriding option (see Hallowell, 1943).

Let us try to reformulate Snare's rules in terms of the conceptual apparatus we have been developing. His first rule introduces both a moral notion—an echo of Locke—and a notion of use—it is permissible for an owner to use his property and impermissible for other people to interfere with this use. Section 6.3 established appropriate concepts to accommodate both components. The general sense in which an owner can "use" his property includes a variety of operations: he can literally use it as an instrument (USE), he can make something from it (MAKE), and so on. The root of this general sense of "use" appears to be that he does something with or to his possession or experiences (perceives) it in some way. For simplicity, we will represent this disjunctive concept as USE(x, y, S_x), though of course it is broader than the notion defined in 6.3.7. Snare's first rule can be formulated as

(25)   PERMISSIBLE(x, USE(x, y, S_x)) & notPERMISSIBLE(z, PREVENT(z, USE (x, y, S_x))).

The second rule stipulates that another person may use property only with its owner's permission. But we need a further convention, not specified by Snare, in order to establish that it is indeed permissible for an owner to grant such permission. This right is important because in its absence the lending of property might be considered impermissible. These two rules can be formulated as

(26)   PERMISSIBLE(z, USE(z, y)) $\equiv$ PERMIT(x, z, USE(z, y, S_z))

and

(27)   PERMISSIBLE(x, PERMIT(x, z, USE(z, y, S_z))).

Where these three rules obtain, we can say that x possesses y inherently: POSSESS$_{inh}$(x, y).

Snare's third rule, perhaps surprisingly, is not a simple component of the definition of inherent possession, because not only may an owner transfer the exclusive right of use to someone else, but he may also transfer the right of transfer itself. If someone gives you a book, he also gives you the right to dispose of it how you will—you can throw it away, give it away, sell it, or whatever. Although such actions might be ungracious, they are hardly impermissible. In other words, Snare's rule should be reformulated so as to refer to itself. It is striking that a recursive definition should be necessary to specify an everyday concept:

(28)   POSSESS$_{inh}$(x, y) $\equiv$ PERMISSIBLE(x, ACT(x, S) & CAUSE(S, POSSESS$_{inh}$(z, y))).

The act of conveying possession, and the way it is achieved, will be discussed later.

We can review these four constitutive conventions by considering some of the consequences of omitting them from our analysis. It is clear that any notion of possession must involve the right of the owner to use his own property; rule (25) cannot be omitted. But if there were nothing more to possession, there might be no way to distinguish between owning something and merely borrowing it. This distinction is evident in the exclusivity implicit in rule (26), but without the right (27) to grant permission for others to use the object, property would always be exclusive to its owner. Suppose we sacrifice exclusivity but retain the power to grant use; then property could be used with or without the permission of its owner—the granting of permission would be a vacuous exercise. Full property ownership therefore requires all three conventions. But it is still impossible for an owner to dispose of his property to anyone else— a situation that can occur with certain sorts of possession, as when a person is a tenant for life or acts as a trustee. The regulative convention (28) is required in order to ensure transferability.

It may well be that property is governed by regulative rules that are essential in our society. An interesting case arises with property that is a source of production. It seems to be generally true that if an individual owns some raw materials and a machine that processes them, he owns the product too. We have deliberately avoided questions of what sorts of people may own property and what sorts of objects are considered to be property. These matters vary from one culture to another. In Western societies both individuals and organizations may own property. However, an individual may be legally debarred from exercising his property rights should he be judged mentally incompetent —a matter that was discussed by Socrates and remains controversial (compare Szasz and Alexander, 1972, with Stone, 1972).

Just what property can be conveyed, its mode of conveyance, and its inheritance on the death of its owner are legislated by the regulative rules of society. Anthropologists are naturally interested in these practices; something of their cultural variety may be learned from such authorities as Thurnwald (1932, chap. 10) and Herskovits (1952, chap. 14). But, diverse as the institution of property undoubtedly is, it seems to be ubiquitous. There appears to be no group of people to whom it is wholly alien. As with language itself, this universality has led theorists to look for antecedents in the behavior of other species; some psychologists, notably William James (1890), have speculated that people may have a "proprietary instinct" (II, 422). The territorial claims exercised by insects, birds, and primates may be precursors of human notions of real property; the hoarding behaviors of lower species may be precursors of human notions of personal property. Although such behaviors have been widely investigated and much is known about their innate and learned components (see, for example, Thorpe, 1963), it is not clear what would constitute decisive evidence for or against the continuity hypothesis. The issues clearly resemble those associated with the origins of language. Since property is a social notion, and presumably dependent on conventions made possible by the existence of language, the two problems may indeed be related.

7.2.2   Other Concepts of Possession

Is it merely coincidence that the language of kinship and proper parts and the language of location are related to the language of possession? It is tempting to see here the familiar anthropological contrast between "inalienable" and "alienable" possession. Partonymic and kin relations are inalienable; locative relations are alienable. In his brief but excellent discussion of the literature Fillmore (1968) argues convincingly that where the contrast is realized morphologically in a language it is a grammatical phenomenon operating essentially at the level of surface structure. In Fijian "uluqu" means "my head" in the sense of the inalienable object attached to my neck, whereas suffixing the possessive morpheme, "kequ ulu," means "my head" in the sense of the alienable object that, say, I own and am about to eat. The ambiguity of the English possessive in these examples is worth remarking (see Day, 1966), since it has sometimes been taken as an index of inalienable or inherent possession. If there is an underlying concept of inalienable possession, it must be in large part culturally determined. Fillmore cites such cases as a language where the term for left hand is treated as inalienable whereas the term for hand is treated as alienable, and the language of the Arapaho in which lice are treated as inalienable.

Relations between possession, position, proper parts, and kinship in English are apparent in their common use of the genitive case: his hat, his location, his face, his father. Some grammarians have assumed that the deep syntactic structure of such genitive phrases includes the verb "have"—that the genitive case ending in "Tom's hat" is derived transformationally from the structure underlying "Tom has a hat." Lyons (1968) argues both from the adjectival function of the genitive and from the late development of such "have" sentences in most languages that the structure underlying the copulative sentence "The hat is Tom's" is a more likely candidate. That is to say, the grammatical relation between "Tom's hat" and "The hat is Tom's" is the same as the relation between "black hat" and "The hat is black." Lyons concludes that "The hat is Tom's" is more similar in surface structure to what we may take as the deep structure of "Tom has a hat" than is "Tom has a hat" itself.

Semantically the situation is more complex. "Tom's hat" identifies a particular hat that Tom owns, whereas "Tom has a hat" leaves ownership vague—he might be accidentally in possession of an indefinite hat owned by someone else: "Tom has Bill's hat." "Tom's place," on the other hand, is vague with respect to ownership—it may refer to a definite location to which Tom has proprietary rights or it may refer to whatever accidental location he happens to occupy at the moment. "Tom's face" is uniquely Tom's; "Tom has Bill's face" can only be understood to assert similarity. "Tom's father" identifies a definite person to whom Tom stands in a particular kin relation; "Tom has Bill's father" would not be used to mean that Tom and Bill are brothers. Moreover, Tom's face's expression is Tom's expression and Tom's location's location is Tom's location, but Tom's hat's color is not Tom's color and Tom's father's father is not Tom's father. Although the genitive case provides a uniform syntactic marker for all these relations, their interpretation depends on conceptual knowledge about the domain of the head noun in the genitive phrase.

Perhaps a more revealing way to illuminate relations between possession, position, proper parts, and kinship is to focus on the highly versatile verb "have." Bendix (1966) distinguishes between the general meanings and the inherent meanings of "have." The general meanings in the main need not concern us, since they are largely transformational in origin (see C. S. Smith, 1964; Bach, 1967; Fillmore, 1969), but they do include the simple locative sense exemplified by "The table has a vase on it." The inherent senses of "*A* has *B*," Bendix claimed, can be paraphrased by "*C* is *A*'s *B*" where *C* = *B*. As a direct semantic specification he says only that

> a speaker, when he uses a form whose meaning we define as expressing an inherent relation between 'A' and 'B,' is making the assertion that there is a relation between 'A' and 'B' and that this relation is characterized as being subjectively identified as in some sense exclusive and special. In other words, a relation is inherent only when someone says it is or when it cannot be objectively observed as exclusive unless one is told by what objective criteria it is defined as exclusive by a speaker in the given context or by the speakers in the broader context of the culture. (P. 52)

In fact, as Bendix (1971) seems to acknowledge, it is often possible to observe more objective criteria. Any relation stable enough to be represented by a relational noun in the lexicon—kinfolk, proper parts—together with inherent possession can be expressed using "have." The verb "possess" is almost as flexible —"He possesses two nephews and a niece" or "The suitcase possesses a false bottom" is awkward but not unacceptable—whereas "own" can express only inherent possession. The factor common to possession, kinship, and proper parts appears to be that they are all durative relations, and perhaps after all this factor underlies the concept of inalienability. The exclusiveness of possession is also echoed in the exclusiveness of proper parts and of kinship conceived deictically (see sec. 5.2).

The relation between location and possession appears to be reflected in the history of the term "property." As Beaglehole (1968) describes it,

> The history of the English word *property* indicates something of the way Western man has thought about scarce objects. Both the Middle English term *propete* and the Old French term *propriete* are derived from the Latin word *proprietas*, itself the noun form of the Latin *proprius*, meaning one's own, which is akin to the French noun *propre*, meaning what is close or near. Thus, historically, property carries the implication that one has exclusive rights to objects because they are so close or near that they have became part of oneself through familiarity or common usage. (P. 590)

There is, however, a much more important yet subtle relation between location and possession. Consider in what sense you may be said to "possess" an object that you have borrowed from somebody. How are you to construe a sentence like "You still have my umbrella"? It is tempting to try to interpret the sentence in a direct locative fashion. There is a locative relation between you and the umbrella; you have it with you. Or there is a locative relation between a part of you and the umbrella; you have it in your hand. Or there is a locative relation between something that you own and the umbrella; it is in your car. This initial temptation must be resisted, because it oversimplifies the situation. It leaves out of account the sort of case illustrated by the dialogue

> "Do you still have my umbrella?"
> "Yes, but I left it at Carl's."

The reply might equally well have been "No, I left it at Carl's." Whether or not the borrower considers that he is still in possession of the umbrella depends less on its location than on how he thinks of it. There are a number of delicate issues here: Is Carl's house near or distant? Is the umbrella easy to retrieve from Carl's house? And so on. But we need not attempt to pin the conditions down in detail.

The crucial point is that a person ceases to have "accidental" possession of an object when it becomes impossible for him to use it. A borrower's assessment of his plight will thus hinge on his conception of the possibility of using (or retrieving) the umbrella in the immediate future. If there is a strong possibility, he may respond "I still have it"; if the chances are remote, he may respond "I don't have it anymore." The notion of accidental possession plainly falls short of inherent possession. It also goes beyond a locative or physical relation. If a person has accidental possession of an object, it is possible for him to use it and it may not be possible for anyone else to use it. It follows that where there is a close locative relation between the person and the object —a regional relation—he has accidental possession of it; but the converse does not follow.

Our temptation to pursue a locative analysis of possession reflects the subtle relation between position and possession that arises in the following way. The essential condition governing inherent possession is *permissibility* of exclusive use; the essential condition governing accidental possession is *possibility* of exclusive use.* In chapter 2 we introduced the idea of the perceptual region of an object, and in section 6.1 it proved to be an important basis for the expression of locative relations. Although we took the region of an object as a primitive, we did suggest that it was essentially that region within which interactions with the object were possible. But it is precisely this notion of interaction (use or experience of the object) that we have tried to capture in defining inherent possession. Thus, the concepts of region, use, and possession form a closely interrelated nexus of ideas. Use of an object implies your being within its region, or its being within yours. Accidental possession of an object entails the

---

*Deontic logicians sometimes suggest that whatever is permissible is possible. This is folly as far as everyday concepts are concerned. It may be permissible for you to do many things that, alas, are impossible for you to do. Likewise, inherent possession does not imply accidental possession.

possibility of using it. Inherent possession of an object entails the permissibility of using it. We will not try to relate these notions formally, because devising a minimal set of concepts is less important, from a psychological point of view, than establishing connections between them. For example, there is no reason to suppose that a child's conceptual growth proceeds according to any logical prescription for developing formal calculi; a child may learn initially separate concepts that only later become interdefinable.

Yet the relation between position and possession may be apparent in the early speech of a child. It has long been observed that a young child, still at the stage of one-word utterances, learns to point at objects and apparently name their owner. A child may point at a book and say "Daddy" when the book does in fact belong to Daddy. Greenfield, Smith, and Laufer (1976) have observed that at this stage a child also begins to point at locations and name the objects that customarily belong there. Sometimes it is difficult to distinguish between habitual physical location and possession, as when a child points at an empty bed and names its customary occupant. Greenfield and her colleagues argue that a genuine relation is being expressed by such one-word utterances because, in a space of about a month, a child may pass from never using people's names for their possessions to using all the names in his vocabulary in such a way—a development whose rapidity defies plausible explanation in terms of referential generalization. In our terms, it seems that a child's first step is to grasp an undifferentiated concept of possessing that embraces the inherent, accidental, and physical notions of an adult.

For an adult, inherent, accidental, and physical possession can be contrasted in the sentence "He owns an umbrella but she's borrowed it, though she doesn't have it with her." We define a verb of possession as any verb that incorporates one or more of these three separate notions of possession.

7.2.3   Simple Verbs of Possession

Many verbs of possession can convey the three senses of possession —inherent, accidental, and physical. We will use the unsubscripted symbol POSSESS to range over all of them. Some verbs, notably "have," convey a still broader range of meaning. The dictionary lists thirty-one main senses for "have," although many of them do not concern possession. Of the simple verbs of possession, "possess" is nearly as wide-ranging in meaning as "have," whereas "belong to" and "own" are considerably more restricted. "Belong to" expresses the converse of possession and can be used for proper-part relations and inherent possession. "Belong" can also take a prepositional object, as in "That cup belongs on the shelf," in which case it has a modal function. "Own" is restricted to inherent possession, although the adjective "own" has a wider usage, as an example that we owe to Harold Conklin illustrates: "The eye I own is not my own." These variations in range of meaning appear arbitrary; we suspect their explanation is etymological.

The simplest verbs of possession, like "possess" and "own," are statives; they merely specify that a possessive relation holds between their grammati-

cal subject and object over some period. Other verbs contain a presuppositional component concerning the prior relation between subject and object.
Since there may or may not be a presupposed possessive relation, and since
there may or may not be an asserted possessive relation, these relations in
combination yield four aspectual domains, exemplified by "keep," "find,"
"lose," and "elude," where possession continues, begins, ends, or fails to occur.
(Parallel aspectual distinctions among positional verbs were noted in 7.1.5;
Gruber, 1965, emphasizes the similarity.) The two domains that do not involve a change are relatively straightforward, so we will begin with them.

"Keep" presupposes that the subject was previously in possession of the
object and asserts that this state of affairs has continued. Both "He kept the
book" and "He didn't keep the book" entail that at one time he possessed
the book. "Keep" has this sense for any contingent state or relation ("He kept
silent," "He kept his car clean," "He kept hitting the ball"); it is scarcely surprising, therefore, that "keep" ranges over all types of the POSSESS relation but
usually not over inalienable relations such as kinship. Where a relation term
does occur with "keep," the verb usually takes on a special sense, as in "He
kept a wife and a mistress." "Keep" also has a specialized possessive sense
when it refers to a habitual activity: "He kept pigs" involves more than owning them. However, a general schema for "keep" in its simple possessive senses
may be written as

(29)   KEEP(x, y):   Someone x "keeps" something y if there is a time t
          such that Q_t(POSSESS(x, y)) and:
          (i) R_t(POSSESS(x, y))

It follows that KEEP(x, y) is equivalent to notCHFROM$(x,$ POSSESS(x, y)) and
in its most general sense is equivalent to notCHFROM$(x,$ G(x)), where G(x) denotes some property of x or some relation into which x enters.

Keeping something may simply involve refraining from getting rid of it
or it may involve an active effort to maintain possession of it. Thus if x holds
on to y or x saves y, x is plainly acting as an intentional agent:

HOLDONTO(x, y), SAVE(x, y):   (INTENTIONALLY(KEEP))(x, y).

Another sense of "hold on to" means simply "keep hold of," where
HOLD(x, y) is analyzed as DO$(x,$ S$)$ & CAUSE$($S, IN(y, z)) and z is a proper part
of x, such as his hand. We see here the overlap between position and possessing. This overlap is also evident in "store":

STORE(x, y):   (INTENTIONALLY(AT(PUT)))(x, y, w) &
KEEP$(x,$ AT(y, w)).

The most complex verb of keeping that we will consider is "reserve," which
has a sense that may be paraphrased as "put somewhere with the intention of
giving to someone." The appropriate sense of giving will be dealt with shortly;
in the meantime "reserve" can be analyzed as

RESERVE(x, y):   CAUSE(INTEND$(x,$ (TO(GIVE))(x, y, z)), STORE(x, y)).

The other domain in which there is no change in possessive status is represented by senses of "refuse," "decline," and "reject." Each appears to demand an intentional action and usually presupposes not only that x did not possess w but also that someone offered w to x. If we analyze $(\text{TO}(\text{OFFER}))(y, w, x)$ as $(\text{TO}(\text{SHOW}))(y, \text{PERMISSIBLE}(x, \text{POSSESS}(x, w)), x)$, relying on an analysis of "show" that will be described in section 7.3, a schema for "refuse" can be formulated as

(30)   REFUSE(x, w):   Someone x "refuses" something w if there is a time t such that $Q_t(\text{notPOSSESS}(x, w))$ and $R_t(\text{TO}(\text{OFFER}))(y, w, x)$ and:
    (i) ACT(x, S)
    (ii) CAUSE$(S, \text{notPOSSESS}(x, w))$

There seems to be no English verb that conveys the notion that a lack of possession simply continues, although the converse relation is sometimes expressed by "y eluded x." In this case it is not necessary that y act in any way; "The Van Gogh eluded him" might be said about a disappointed art collector. Hence

(31)   ELUDE(w, x):   Something w "eludes" someone x if there is a time t such that $Q_t(\text{notPOSSESS}(x, w))$ and:
    (i) $R_t(\text{INTEND}(x, \text{POSSESS}(x, w)))$
    (ii) $R_t(\text{notPOSSESS}(x, w))$

If we wished to stipulate that x tried to gain possession of w but failed, we could add the further conditions

    (iii) ACT(x, S)
    (iv) CAUSE$((i), (iii))$
    (v) notCAUSE$(S, \text{POSSESS}(x, w))$

The two domains that concern changes in status of a possessive relation consist of those verbs incorporating FIND or LOSE. Although the two concepts are obviously related, the manner of their relation is subtle. A sentence such as "He found it" can be paraphrased as "He came to see where it was." But the verb can also be used possessively in a sense that arises from an obvious implication: "He came to perceive where it was, and therefore was able to get it." This sense of "find," involving the idea that seeing the object created an intention to possess it, can be analyzed as follows:

(32)   FIND(x, w):   Someone x "finds" something w if there is a time t such that $Q_t(\text{notPOSSESS}_{\text{acc}}(x, w))$ and:
    (i) HAPPEN$_t(\text{SEE}(x, w))$
    (ii) ACT(x, S)
    (iii) CAUSE$(S, \text{POSSESS}(x, w))$
    (iv) CAUSE$((i), (ii))$

The antithesis of finding something is losing it. It too has a perceptual sense, exemplified in "He lost the mountain in the fog," which can be construed as HAPPEN$_t(\text{notSEE}(x, y))$. But its possessive sense is perhaps more common. The possessive sense of "lose" is noteworthy in that it cannot take an intentional component: one can only lose an object unintentionally, although there are colloquial senses extending the verb into the intentional domain ("Get lost"; "Lose this for me, will you?"). It would be a mistake to render the literal meaning with an analysis that merely lacked an intentional component since nothing would prevent a subsequent addition of one; we must incorporate the notion of UNINTENTIONALLY, which is equivalent to notINTENTIONALLY:

(33)   LOSE(x, w):   Someone x "loses" something w if there is a time t such that Q_t(POSSESS(x, w)) and:
     (i) R_t(notINTEND(x, notPOSSESS(x, w)))
     (ii) HAPPEN$_t$(notPOSSESS(x, w))

People can lose an object without doing anything—they may have it taken from them—but a lack of action is no bar to the UNINTENTIONALLY component, unlike its positive correlate, INTENTIONALLY. An action of some sort is necessary, though, in the case of "misplace," which involves the loss of accidental possession; if you do not know where something is, you cannot use it. The act may have been intentional, but the intention cannot have been to lose possession of the object.

So much for the four basic relations between an individual and an object: KEEP, FIND, LOSE, and ELUDE. Although a third argument, or "benefactive," can be introduced in many of these predicate phrases by the preposition "for" —"I found (kept, saved) a book for Gilbert," for example—and although they may behave like double-object verbs (dative movement, two passive forms) we will not explore these complications here. We will turn instead to the transfer of possession from one person to another.

7.2.4   The Transfer of Possession

There are many ways an individual can come to have an object and many ways he can lose it. Their apparent variety is increased by the fact that English contains converse pairs of verbs allowing the same event to be specified from the point of view of either participant:

(34)   "give to" versus "receive from"
     "lose to" versus "take from"
     "lend to" versus "borrow from"

The first distinction is between verbs concerning the acquisition of possession and verbs concerning its loss. Another distinction concerns which of the two protagonists, if either, acts as causal agent. Still another concerns whether the agent acts intentionally.

Descriptions of acquisition and loss usually exploit the prepositions "to" and "from": "He gave it to her," "She received it from him." This use of "to" and "from" is closely related to the locative use analyzed in 6.1.4, except that AT is replaced by POSSESS. In fact, we can introduce a useful generalization.

FROM(x, y) presupposes that a given relation G held between x and y and asserts that it no longer holds; the nature of G depends on the verb and other contextual aspects of the sentence, as in "He came from America," "He got it from John," "He hid it from the police." TO(x, y) presupposes that a given relation G did not hold between x and y and asserts that it has come to hold between them, as in "He went to America," "He gave it to Mary," "He showed it to the police." This function of "to" and "from" over a variety of semantic domains was remarked by Gruber (1965) and played an important role in the development of Fillmore's (1968, 1971a) version of case grammar. We can express the semantics of "from" and "to" as HAPPEN$_t$(notG(x, y)) and HAPPEN$_t$(G(x, y)), respectively, or, more formally:

(35)   FROM(S_x, y):   A referent x identified by the statement S_x is "from" a relatum y if there is a relation G and a time t such that $Q_t(\text{G}(x, y))$ and:
   (i) $R_t(\text{notG}(x, y))$

(36)   TO(S_x, y):   A referent x identified by the statement S_x is "to" a relatum y if there is a relation G and a time t such that $Q_t(\text{notG}(x, y))$ and:
   (i) $R_t(\text{G}(x, y))$

It should be noted that the presuppositional component of FROM is not invariably present.

When G is taken to be POSSESS, this analysis allows the following schema for "give to":

(37) $(\text{TO}(\text{GIVE}))(x, w, y)$:   Someone x "gives" something w "to" y if there is a time t such that $Q_t(\text{POSSESS}(x, w)\ \&\ \text{notPOSSESS}(y, w))$ and:
   (i) $R_t(\text{POSSESS}(y, w)\ \&\ \text{notPOSSESS}(x, w))$
   (ii) DO(x, S)
   (iii) CAUSE(S, (ii))

Exactly the same schema can be assigned to $(\text{FROM}(\text{RECEIVE}))(y, w, x)$. Schema (37) is appropriate, however, only when w is a concrete object that cannot be in two places at once. "Give" can be used in other contexts, where the giver loses nothing by virtue of his gift: "I gave her my cold," "They will give you all the information," "He gave me a look at it." A slightly more general schema would concentrate on what the recipient acquires rather than on what the giver loses:

(37′) $(\text{TO}(\text{GIVE}))(x, w, y)$:   Someone x "gives" something w "to" y if there is a time t such that $Q_t(\text{notPOSSESS}(y, w))$ and:
   (i) $R_t(\text{POSSESS}(y, w))$
   (ii) DO(x, S)
   (iii) CAUSE(S, (ii))

But (37′) does not seem appropriate for "receive from," which would normally presuppose $Q_t(\text{POSSESS}(x, w))$.

"Give" is a double-object verb; it permits the dative-movement transformation ("He gave the book to her," "He gave her the book") and both passives are acceptable ("The book was given to her," "She was given the book"). Its general semantic pattern is that the grammatical subject causes the indirect object to "have" the direct object. "Receive" follows the opposite semantic pattern ("She received the book from him" means that the indirect object ends up not having the direct object) and does not permit a transformation similar to dative movement ("He received her the book" is unacceptable English).

"He gave her the book" and "He found her the book" look much alike syntactically, but the former comes from "He gave the book to her" by virtue of dative movement and "to" deletion, whereas the latter comes from "He found the book for her" by virtue of dative movement and "for" deletion. It is not clear what kind of syntactic rules will keep these relations straight and also admit such apparent exceptions as "He gave her a party," although the semantic generalization—indirect has direct object—seems to cover all the double-object verbs of possession.

Too much weight should not be put on the possessive relation between the indirect and direct objects of double-object verbs. The association in English of the dative case with the semantic notion of possession ("father to the bride," "aide to the president," "index to the book") is old and a bit archaic. The dative use of "to" with double-object verbs, however, does not inevitably represent a possessive relation. There are double-object verbs of motion, possession, perception, and communication: bring, give, show, tell. The relation G in (36), which we have used to represent the relation between the indirect and direct objects, is different in these different semantic fields—$G(x, y)$ is variously $AT(x, y)$, $POSSESS(x, y)$, $PERCEIVE(x, y)$, $KNOW(x, y)$, and consequently very different senses of "have" are involved: having y nearby, having possession of y, having a view of y, having knowledge of y. Even the more limited sense of "having possession" covers a variety of relations between x and y that must be kept distinct.

The sentence "He gave her the book" may concern a gift, a loan, or merely the handing over of a book. His giving her the book, in other words, may involve inherent, accidental, or physical possession. It presupposes that he possessed the book in one sense, and it asserts that he did something that caused her to possess it. But in what senses may she be said to possess the book? Clearly, if he owned it, he could have transferred its ownership to her. If he had borrowed it, he could have transferred its accidental possession to her, but such a transfer could not ordinarily be effected without the book's coming into her physical possession—it would usually be handed over or picked up at some later time—and it would not be until it entered her physical possession that English speakers would regard her borrowing as having commenced. Finally, if he merely had the book in his hand and no title to its inherent or accidental possession, the most that he could genuinely have transferred was its physical possession. The sort of possession involved in the transaction has an important consequence for the semantics of "give." When inherent or ac-

cidental possession is transferred, (37) should be amended to incorporate an
INTENTIONAL component; this component is also necessary for "present,"
which appears to require a definite, not to say manifest, transfer of physical
possession. Other intentional verbs, such as "donate," refer to the transfer of
inherent possession; still others, such as "grant," "contribute," and "render,"
refer to varying combinations of the basic senses.

One of the striking features of the English lexicon is how systematic ambiguities can be passed on from one word to another. In 7.1.2 we noted such a
relation between "come" and "bring." Another example arises in the case of
"have" and "give." A simple paraphrase of "He gave it to her" is "He did
something that caused her to have it," where "have" ranges over many of its
customary meanings. In this respect, "give" is similar to "get," and, as Fillmore (1969) suggests in his review of Bendix's study, we might equally well
paraphrase "He gave it to her" as "He did something that caused her to get
it." Hence "give" and "get" possess a very general causal meaning. You can
give somebody a punch in the eye, a good time, an original idea, or German
measles, as well as a book, a car, or some real estate; and you may get all of
these things, too. The general meaning goes back to the range of meanings
conveyed by "have." It is certainly possible to "have" physical objects, attributes, states, ideas, titles, diseases, and even the services or assistance of
someone. But when a transaction involves an intangible object, there is not a
literal transfer of possession. It is absurd to suppose that when *A* gives *B* a
punch in the eye, first *A* possesses the punch in the eye and then *B* possesses
it. It is also absurd to suppose that hitherto *B* did not possess a punch in the
eye. One is dealing with an event, an act that can be given, received, taken,
suffered, but cannot enter a stative relation. Of course, to give someone a
punch is equivalent to punching him. Wherever a causal verb has a corresponding noun, a construction involving "give" is feasible. We may regard such a
construction as a periphrastic variation on the underlying sense. When we are
dealing with a state or an attribute a giver simply causes a recipient to be in the
appropriate relation to the state or attribute.

Transfer of mental objects or diseases resembles that of physical objects except that the giver does not thereby lose possession. Abstract entities like titles,
degrees, and honors are more mysterious. They fall outside the category of
inherent possessions since, once awarded, bestowed, or conferred, they are invariably nontransferable. Besides, what are they used for? How could one
grant permission for someone else to use them? The closest analogy would
seem to be with a proper part of their possessor—the appendix, perhaps. But
unlike that useless organ, abstract titles do bring with them certain rights, privileges, and responsibilities. They may even affect the manner of addressing
their recipients. Let us settle for a primitive category, TITLE, recognizing that
it involves a social concept of inalienable possession, as much a proper part
as (but no more than) a proper name.

Another problem that we could resolve by introducing unanalyzed primitives arises from the legal notion of property and its disposal. A society that

has civil laws governing property is likely to have a number of important legal notions governing its sale and inheritance. Several English verbs denote such transactions: bequeath, devise, convey. It would be out of place here to try to give a conceptual account of what is involved, but we could introduce primitive concepts expressed by manner adverbials that would describe how such transactions are supposed to take place.

Dixon (1973) would distinguish two senses of "give," one that involves giving in return for some service or object and the other that involves spontaneous giving. The spontaneous sense is involved in such hyponyms as "donate," "award," and "present"; the contractual sense is involved in such hyponyms as "pay," "lend," "sell," and "rent." "He gave money to the Red Cross" could mean either that he donated money or that he paid money to the Red Cross. We take such examples to indicate not that "give" has two senses but that "give" is vague with respect to the giver's motives. We will not try to impose Dixon's distinction on GIVE, therefore, but will try to develop in some detail the semantic components that must be added to GIVE in order to distinguish among its hyponyms.

First we should note that in addition to giving there is at least one other way in which a person may actively part company with an object. He may dispose of it, either to another party or to some unspecified destination. Although one speaks of accidentally disposing of, or getting rid of, something, in such usages there is a strong presumption that the act was intentional but involved the wrong object. This suggests the following analysis:

(38)   DISPOSEOF(x, y):   Someone x "disposes of" something y if there is a time t such that $Q_t(\text{POSSESS}(x, y))$ and:
          (i) ACT(x, S)
          (ii) CAUSE(S, notPOSSESS(x, y))

How does disposing of an object differ from giving it away intentionally? The answer appears to be that giving involves a recipient, a transfer of possession from one individual to another, whereas disposing does not necessarily involve another party—it may bring to an end a chain of transactions, as when an owner throws away one of his possessions. The focus is on the termination of possession, and a number of verbs, like "throw away," "toss out," and "dump," involve a fairly specific motion to bring this about. These verbs have a natural extension to the termination of inherent possession.

Let us turn from the case where the person parting with possession is a causal agent to the case where the person gaining possession is the causal agent —the case that involves the notion of obtaining or taking something from someone. A neutral way to express the notion of coming into possession of something is "x gets w from y," which leaves open the possibility that x was the agent, y was the agent, both x and y were agents, or neither x nor y was an agent (a possibility that can also be expressed by "w passed from x to y"):

(39)   GET(x, w):   Someone x "gets" something w if there is a time t such that:
          (i) HAPPEN$_t$(POSSESS(x, w))

Note that there is another use of "get," in such sentences as "He got a present for Joe," which permits a transformation to "He got Joe a present" but which is not synonymous with "Joe got a present from him." If "x gets w for z" is understood to mean that x is in possession of w, presumably with the intention of giving it to z, the full schema for "get for" would be

(39′)   (FOR(GET))($x, w, (z)$):   Someone x "gets" something w "for" z if there is a time t such that:
   (i) HAPPEN$_t$(POSSESS(x, w))
   (ii) (FOR(ACT))(x, S, z)
   (iii) CAUSE(S, (i))

Schema (39) represents the consequence of omitting the beneficiary z, and in that case conditions (ii) and (iii) in (39′) cannot be evaluated. The suggestion that w is eventually transferred to z is apparently a conversational implicature, not an entailment, since it can easily be canceled: "I got this for Harry, but it was so nice I couldn't give it to him." If $x = z$, as in "He got a cup of coffee for himself," the agentive, causative sense of "get" is clearly entailed, but if z is omitted, the possibility that $x = z$ leaves some uncertainty as to whether x was an agent. The argument z for the indirect object is in parentheses in (39′) to indicate that this is a case of semantic deletion: omitting z changes the verb from agentive and causative to nonagentive and noncausative. Combining "for" and "from" ("He got the tickets for Felicia from Max") gives an awkward but meaningful construction: (FROM(FOR(GET))) ($x, w, (z), y$), where y is syntactically deletable and z is semantically deletable.

There are also verbs, like "obtain" and "acquire," that introduce a causative component without either the intentional or the benefactive. If x does something that causes him to gain possession of w from y, then x obtains w from y:

(FROM(OBTAIN))(x, w, y):   DO(x, S) & CAUSE(S, (FROM(GET)) (x, w, y)).

A further intentional component can be added when required:

APPROPRIATE(x, w), PROCURE(x, w):   (INTENTIONALLY(OBTAIN)) (x, w).

The intentional verbs "win" and "gain" are more complex because they imply that the person parting with the object was striving to maintain possession of it:

(40)   (FROM(WIN))(x, w, y):   Someone x "wins" something w "from" someone y if:
   (i) (FROM(APPROPRIATE))(x, w, y)
   (ii) INTEND(y, KEEP(y, w))
   (iii) ACT(y, S)
   (iv) notCAUSE(S, KEEP(y, w))

There is a competitive sense of "lose" that can also be formulated as in (40): (TO(LOSE))(y, w, x). (Note, incidentally, that this "lose" is a double-object verb, but if "Max lost me five dollars" is grammatical, it is certainly not synonymous with "Max lost five dollars to me.")

The verb "take," which has been encountered among the verbs of motion (7.1.3), seems to have acquired a possessive sense by an obvious implication. The motional sense of TAKE(x, y) was construed as DO(x, S) & CAUSE(S, (WITH(GO))(y, x)), that is, x causes y to go with him; this entails that x has physical possession of y: WITH(x, y). A natural extension of this sense is to other sorts of possession: DO(x, S) & CAUSE(S, GET(x, y)), but there is a constraint on the sorts of entities that can be taken. In general, the verb may be used in its motional sense only when the object is portable or movable, and it may be used in its possessive sense in these cases, too. When the object is large and immovable, it may be used in a possessive sense provided that its accidental or inherent possession is recognized by regulative convention. Hence there are obvious, though more specialized senses, for such sentences as "He took the city" and "He took the apartment."

An important subclass of verbs incorporating TAKE includes "seize," "snatch," and "grab." These verbs seem to apply primarily to physical possession brought about by taking hold of an object in a sudden or forceful manner:

| seize, grab | (FORCEFULLY(TAKE))(x, y) & HOLD(x, y) |
| snatch | (RAPIDLY(TAKE))(x, y) & HOLD(x, y) |

These verbs are extended to cases of accidental possession. They lead us naturally to consider another subcategory, verbs of stealing.

Stealing involves deliberately taking something from its owner without his permission and with no intention of returning it to him. It follows that a thief's possession of a stolen object is at most accidental:

(41)   (FROM(STEAL))(x, w, y):   Someone x "steals" something w "from" someone y if:
   (i) notPERMIT(y, POSSESS(x, w))
   (ii) (INTENTIONALLY(FROM(TAKE)))(x, w, y)
   (iii) notINTEND(x, (TO(GIVE))(x, w, y))

There are special verbs for different sorts of stealing, depending on whether the object is taken from a person ("rob") or a place ("burgle"); whether the object is valuable ("steal") or of little worth ("filch"); the general manner or circumstances in which the theft occurs ("loot," "plunder"). There are also differences in the arguments they may take. It is grammatically acceptable to assert "Genet stole a book" but not "Genet robbed a book." On the other hand, if Genet burgled Sartre's house, it follows that he stole something from it, but it is odd to say "Genet burgled a television set from Sartre's house." The syntax of "burgle" contains no slot for the stolen object represented in its underlying routine.

Terms denoting the converse of an agentive relation are less common. We have represented the converse of the various GIVE and DISPOSEOF verbs by RECEIVE; only a small number of verbs denote the converse of the many OB-

TAIN and TAKE verbs. When a person plays a passive role, one speaks of his losing the object; when he plays a more active role, one speaks of his parting with it or surrendering it. "Surrender" suggests that although x may have parted with possession reluctantly, he did so intentionally:

(42)   (TO(SURRENDER))(x, w, y):   Someone x "surrenders" something w "to" y if:
     (i) ACT(y, S) & ACT(x, S')
     (ii) CAUSE(S & S', (GET(y, w) & LOSE(x, w)))

The concepts of getting and keeping are bound together in the representations of such verbs as "gather," "collect," and "hoard." What is involved here is a process in which over a period of time an individual gets a series of objects, which he keeps, enjoys the use of, and perhaps ultimately disposes of. The process may involve simply gathering the objects in some place; it may involve a rate of acquisition that is more rapid than the rate of disposal, as in "accumulate" and "amass"; it may involve aesthetic or miserly intentions. Its essential component, however, is simply

COLLECT(x, w):   HAPPEN$_i$(PROCURE(x, w) & SAVE(x, w)).

One final transaction, lending and borrowing, remains to be considered before we turn to the mutual exchange of possessions. Dixon (1973) notes that "lend" is a hyponym of "give," but its converse, "borrow," is not (we regard "borrow" as a hyponym of "obtain"). In Dixon's view, sentences of the form "A lent b to C" presuppose that A was willing to part with b and assert that C was willing to accept b, whereas sentences of the form "C borrowed b from A" reverse these entailments—they presuppose that C was willing to accept b and assert that A was willing to part with it. We question this analysis on the grounds that "A didn't lend b to C" does not seem to entail that A was willing to part with b, and "C didn't borrow b from A" does not seem to entail that C was willing to accept b. Consequently, we will not try to incorporate these presuppositions into our analyses of LEND and BORROW.

When an individual borrows property, he has at most an accidental possession of it. A borrowed object need not remain within the accidental possession of the borrower, however. Consider the following dialogue:

> "Do you have my copy of the *Kamasutra*?"
> "No."
> "Well, you borrowed it from me."
> "Yes, but I'm afraid I've lent it to my mother-in-law."

There seems to be a convention that, within reason, a borrower may lend a borrowed object. What he does not normally lend is the ultimate obligation to return it to its original owner; that obligation stays with him unless it is explicitly discharged by the owner. Other reasons that a borrower may no longer possess a borrowed object include his having lost it or sold it or given it away. To sell or give a borrowed object to a third party is plainly to violate the conventions governing the institution of borrowing. Such things happen, but they are incompatible with the concept of borrowing—to sell a borrowed object is tantamount to theft; indeed, a society might have laws allowing for the sale to be overruled and for the original owner to recover his property. When one gets permission to use someone else's property, one is often tacitly granted permission to give others permission to use it. But this feature is not part of the meaning of "borrow"; we cannot argue that since x borrowed y it follows that x may lend y. The convention that one may not sell or give away borrowed property follows directly from the fact that there is no transfer of inherent possession.

These considerations establish that the concept BORROW incorporates the following components: the borrower gets accidental possession of the object with permission to use it, and it is mutually understood that he is obliged to return it to its owner at some future time. This understanding, perhaps realized in a speech act such as a promise, creates the crucial component, the borrower's obligation to return the borrowed object.

(43)   (FROM(BORROW))(x, w, y):   Someone x "borrows" something w "from" someone y if:
  (i) (INTENTIONALLY(FROM(OBTAIN$_{acc}$)))(x, w, y)
  (ii) PERMITS$(y,$ USE$(x, w))$
  (iii) OBLIGATE$(x, x,$ (TO(GIVE))$(x, w, y))$

That the creation of the obligation is the critical feature is borne out by the fact that such sentences as "He borrowed the book but forgot to take it" are acceptable. But there is a looser sense of the verb in which one borrows something without its owner's permission, a sense in which an intention to return the object, rather than an obligation, is created.

"Lend" is not quite the converse of "borrow." Sometimes either verb is appropriate, but on other occasions—when only one of the parties has acted agentively—only one of the verbs is appropriate. Thus, LEND requires (INTENTIONALLY(TO(GIVE$_{acc}$)))(y, w, x). We may also note that "loan" and "entrust," which incorporate LEND, entail the transfer of possession. With certain objects and commodities, such as money, the borrower gets inherent possession but is obliged to return at some future time an equivalent amount of the commodity, or more. Such obligations, which may be created in other ways—by a simple promise, for example—create debts; the verb "owe" conveys simply the sense of obligation. If A borrows five dollars from B, it follows that A owes five dollars to B until the debt is discharged.

We have now examined the four basic possessive relations that may hold between a person and an object, KEEP, FIND, LOSE, and ELUDE, and the major ways of conceptualizing a transfer of possession, GIVE/RECEIVE, TAKE/LOSE, and BORROW/LEND. The psychological validity of this organization is supported by the noteworthy overlap between these concepts and the domains uncovered in multidimensional scaling studies of possessive verbs carried out by Fillenbaum and Rapoport (1971). Our next task is to explore the extension of such transactions to the mutual exchange of possessions.

7.2.5   Exchange and the Concept of Money

Transactions involving mutual exchange of possessions can be described in various ways. An episode that could be described as "He exchanged a picture for a sculpture with her" might also be described as "He gave her a picture and she gave him a sculpture." To paraphrase "exchange" as mutual giving is not precise, however; it would be sensible to say "He exchanged a picture for a sculpture with her, but she never gave him the sculpture," whereas the same addendum to the sentence about mutual giving would be contradictory. The "for" of exchange marks an obligation to give in return, but the obligation may not be honored.

The "for" of exchange must be distinguished from benefactive "for." "He exchanged the camera for Mary" is ambiguous in several ways; one of the least salient interpretations is the "for" of exchange, where Mary and a camera change hands. The benefactive sense is salient when the head noun in the "for" phrase denotes a human being; otherwise the exchange sense is salient. Both senses of "for" can occur in "He exchanged the camera for a radio for Mary."

A schema for "exchange" based on giving and obligation to give in return is

(44)   (WITH(FOR(EXCHANGE)))(x, w, z, y):   Someone x "exchanges" something w "for" something z "with" someone y if:

   (i) (TO(GIVE))(x, w, y)
   (ii) OBLIGATE$(y, y,$ (TO(GIVE))$(y, z, x))$

A small domain of verbs shares some of the semantic components of "exchange." "Interchange" usually applies to the exchange of accidental possessions, "barter" and "trade" to the exchange of goods or services; "swap," like "exchange," seems to cover both meanings. Verbs that admit two causal agents often have a property exemplified by "exchange"—they allow for joint action. A sentence like "Larry and Jim exchanged their hats" is ambiguous; it could mean that they exchanged hats with one another or that both exchanged their hats with unmentioned parties. In a joint action the schema for EXCHANGE is symmetrical and condition (44ii) can be omitted, since each party's action fulfills the obligation created by the other's action; with condition (44ii) omitted, the joint action is indeed one of mutual giving and the "for" is unnecessary. "Barter" can also be interpreted as a joint-action verb; it presupposes that neither of the exchanged objects is a sum of money. But certainly the most important verbs of exchange are those that denote financial transactions, particularly "buy" and "sell."

Before we can deal with buying and selling we must come to terms with the concept of money. Psychologists have not ignored this concept. Money is used as a reinforcement, its utility has been scaled, and the craving for it has been related to other personality traits. Yet the conceptual structure of money seems to have been neglected by psychologists. Money is the province of economists. Economists—economic anthropologists in particular—have contributed many informal definitions of the concept and informal conditions that must be met by a commodity if it is to be considered money. We will try to crystallize the essential components, as we see them, from a variety of authorities (Thurnwald, 1932; Herskovits, 1952; Sahlins, 1972). The reader should bear in mind that defining the meaning of money, like defining the meaning of possession, involves us deeply in cultural analysis.

A distinction is generally drawn between money and currency. For example, a debt of ten dollars may be discharged by the appropriate amount of cash, by a check for that amount drawn on a solvent account, or by the appropriate use of a credit card. In each case a transaction involving money occurs, but only in the first case is currency involved. Currency is a form that money takes as an actual medium of exchange, circulated from hand to hand. In some societies, including our own in historical times, a commodity with intrinsic value—gold, silver, feathers, salt, gunpowder, shells, the jawbones of pigs— is used as currency. Paper currency owes its origin to the writing of debt notes; to this day one may read on an English pound note the words "I promise to pay the bearer on demand the sum of one pound." The note was the medium and gold was the standard—the gold served to create confidence in the note. Since the gold is no longer exchanged, we are brought back directly to the question of what money is. That is, what is money as opposed to currency?

The article on money in the *Encyclopedia Britannica* cites Hawtrey (1928): "Money is one of those concepts which, like a teaspoon or an umbrella, but unlike an earthquake or a buttercup, are definable primarily by the use or purpose that they serve." The only use or purpose money can serve is in the exchange of goods and services. Money presupposes that the exchange of goods and services is permissible—it presupposes the institution of property. The basic psychological condition on money is that it is acceptable in exchange for other commodities because people know that they will be able to pass it on to others in the same way. The acceptability is a social convention, in the same sense that driving on the right is a social convention; the choice is arbitrary, but everyone benefits as long as everyone accepts it (D. K. Lewis, 1969).

If someone intends to exchange a possession for money, there is some amount of money that he will accept for it; if someone intends to exchange money for a possession, there is some amount of money that he will give for it. These requirements are part of the underlying cultural concept of money:

(45)   (a) For any person x who possesses inherently something w there
             is some amount of money u such that:
             INTEND$(x, ($FOR$($EXCHANGE$))(x, w, z))$ entails $(z = u)$
         (b) For any person x who intends to possess inherently something

z there is some amount of money u such that:

INTEND$(x,$ (FOR(EXCHANGE))$)(x, w, z))$ entails $(w = u)$

In a society where all exchangeable entities were equally valuable there would be little need for money. There is a presumption in the use of money that things have a value and that different things may have different values. If a commodity is to serve as money, therefore, it must be divisible into amounts that are equally valuable. It is these amounts, or cardinal numbers of them, that provide a sort of economic language in which, as Herskovits (1952, p. 245) puts it, people can determine the least common denominator of value for any exchangeable object. Such conditions appear to lie behind the use of cigarettes as a standard of value, and medium of exchange, in the economy of prisons and prisoner-of-war camps (see Radford, 1945).

These considerations can be formulated as two further conditions on money:

(45)   (c) If an amount of money u is equal to another amount of money v, then for any persons x and y:
           POSSIBLE (WITH (FOR (EXCHANGE)))(x, u, v, y)

           (d) For any amount of money u there is a name z such that:
           NAME(z, u).

The four conditions together appear to be essential for the concept of money. Other conditions seem more peripheral—that debts and deferred payments are standardized by reference to monetary value, or that money provides a way to store wealth.

Money is property, but clearly it is no ordinary sort of property. In practical terms, the institution of property does not undergo the same sorts of crises as the institution of money. In periods of anarchy effective ownership might cease to exist and the concept of permissibility might lose its meaning: there would be insufficient conventions for it to range over. Money crises, however, are of a different order. Money begins to lose its value and people become unwilling to exchange goods or services for it. A device that changes this climate of opinion may restore the exchangeability of money. In the financial crisis in Germany after World War I the authorities introduced the Rentenmark, asserting that it took its value from the value of land. How this magical valuation worked was never explained, but people believed it and the social convention was reestablished.

7.2.6   Verbs of Payment

The fundamental transaction involving money is its payment. If you pay someone for something, it follows that you have parted with your money, but it does not follow that you have received the goods—all that has been established is an obligation, not an actuality. The obligation seems to be represented superficially by the presence of "for"; its underlying representation can be handled by the semantics of exchange:

(46)   (FOR(TO(PAY)))(x, m, y, w):   Someone x "pays" an amount of
         money m "to" someone y "for" something w if:
         (i) (WITH(FOR(EXCHANGE)))(x, m, w, y)

A similar schema is required for a verb like "disburse." But "spend," as in
"He spent ten dollars on a meal," does seem to imply that the complete transaction was consummated. If money is spent on something, it is paid to someone, but the verb has no syntactic slot for an explicit statement of the recipient.
If money is paid, however, the syntax of "pay" allows for any combination of
arguments: he paid (Paolo) (a million lire) (for the picture). It is even possible
to assert "His million lire paid for the picture." A sentence of this form is close
to expressing the converse of "The picture cost him a million lire."

The basic sense of the verb "cost" is unusual in that it often behaves like a
stative in the present tense but like a nonstative in the past tense. A sentence
like "The picture costs a million lire" refers to an intention on the part of its
owner—he intends to sell at a certain price—whereas "The picture cost a million lire" may refer either to a specific transaction or a past intention—the
owner intended to sell at a certain price. A schema for the stative sense can
be formulated as follows:

(47)   COSTS(w, m):   Something w that someone y possesses "costs" an
         amount of money m for anyone x if:
         (i) INTEND(y, (WITH(FOR(EXCHANGE)))(x, w, m, y))

In other words, if something costs a dollar, its owner intends to create for
himself an obligation to give it to you if and when you give him a dollar.

The example, "The picture cost him a million lire," implies that he paid a
million lire for the picture, but it is not clear that he actually received it. In
fact, we assume that the receipt is merely implicated, not asserted:

(48)   (TO(COST))(w, m, x):   Something w that someone y possesses "cost"
         someone x an amount of money m if:
         (i) (WITH(FOR(EXCHANGE)))(x, m, w, y)

"Buy" and "sell," more complex verbs of payment, have been the object of
considerable attention from linguists. It might seem that such pairs of sentences as

(49)   He bought the flowers from her.

(50)   She sold the flowers to him.

are synonymous, in which case "buy" and "sell" must be so formulated that
(49) and (50) both express the same proposition. Indeed, Staal (1967) argues
that the relation between the two sentences is a syntactic one analogous to the
relation between active and passive voice. Gruber (1965) pointed out in anticipation of this argument that it is difficult to determine which sentence should
be the source and which the derived item. There is, moreover, a subtle suggestion in (49) that the man is the agent—the person who, as Gruber says, "willed

the action"—whereas (50) suggests that the woman is the agent. The interpretation of manner adverbials thus depends on which verb is used: "Stupidly, he bought the flowers from her" says that the stupidity was his, but "Stupidly, she sold the flowers to him" says that it was hers.

In our view transactions of buying and selling may involve both parties in an agentive role; the real distinction between them is more subtle. Consider a scenario for a sale. Suppose that Box wants a cigarette and knows that Cox has some. Box asks Cox "Will you sell me a cigarette for a nickel?" Cox replies "Yes." The deal has been made, and Box and Cox exchange nickel and cigarette. The final transaction is reciprocal, with both parties playing an agentive role. But there is a difference in initial intention. It was Box's intention to have a cigarette that inspired the whole transaction. In these circumstances you are likely to say "Box bought a cigarette from Cox." On the other hand, suppose that Cox's intention to come by a nickel led him to approach Box and to ask "Will you buy a cigarette from me for a nickel?" In these circumstances you are likely to say "Cox sold a cigarette to Box." Of course, both Box and Cox might have had intentions, and in that case either sentence would be appropriate. A violation of these constraints would hardly count as a solecism. But if one of the parties to a transaction is incapable of intentions, solecisms can occur; it would be odd to say "The vending machine sold him a bar of chocolate" instead of "He bought a bar of chocolate from the vending machine."

The intentions of vendor and emptor do not lead directly to the exchange of goods and money, but to intermediary acts that constitute striking a bargain. And in certain circumstances an individual may be said to have bought (or sold) something when the intermediate acts have been carried out. It is for this reason that Katz's (1972) examples "John sold the book to Mary but she never paid him for it" and "Mary bought the book from John but she never received it" are in no way anomalous. Indeed, there is nothing anomalous about "John sold the book to Mary but she neither paid for it nor received it." Such sentences demonstrate that financial transactions involve social conventions analogous to speech acts. When a bargain is struck, in whatever way, there is a sense of the verbs in which we may truly say "The object is sold" or "The object is bought."

How are we to represent the striking of a bargain? The felicitous performance of such an act involves more than an agreement between vendor and emptor (just as a promise involves more than saying that something will be done). The crucial convention is that by acting in certain ways a mutual obligation is created—the vendor is obliged to hand over the goods, the emptor is obliged to hand over the money. A component specifying a similar obligation is involved in such verbs as "rent," "hire," and "lease," with the last involving the adverbial LEGALLY.

Whether the complete senses of "buy" and "sell" require an actual transfer of possession is not obvious. Sentences like those just considered suggest that transfer does not need to take place, but others suggest that it must: "He owns it because he bought it." It seems that we need to distinguish between the preparatory act, which creates the obligation, and its ultimate consummation, which discharges it by the mutual exchange of goods and money. The preparatory act is what is involved in such verbs as "auction" and in such sentences as "By waving to his friend, Malcolm had bought a Victorian commode without realizing it."

If the consummation of a sale involves the transfer of possession, the question naturally arises as to what sort of possession is involved. Katz (1972) argues, in effect, that inherent possession is not necessary, because it makes good sense to assert "John sold some hot merchandise to Mary, who only after the sale found out that John did not own it." But we must also consider examples like "It is impossible that he sold it, because it wasn't his to sell." This sentence has a clear conceptual force. We must therefore try to distinguish between the meaning of the verb "sell" and the regulative conventions governing selling as a social institution.

The root of the problem is the ambiguity of "sell." It may denote either a preparatory act or both the act and its consummation. When the verb occurs in a sentence like "He sold me the Brooklyn Bridge, but it wasn't his to sell and I paid him with forged money," what is true (if the sentence is true) is that the preparatory act of striking a bargain was successfully completed. The bargain, however, was never properly consummated. Just as an unfulfilled promise is still a promise, so an improperly consummated sale is still a sale. In short, it is because "buy" and "sell" can be used to describe merely the act of striking a bargain that they can also be used when an actual inappropriate exchange of goods has taken place. Normally, though, exchanges are appropriate, and in order to satisfy the full routines of "buy" and "sell," or at least the usual conversational implications, an exchange of inherent possessions must take place.

Let us summarize what we have learned in the form of a complete schema for "buy":

(51)   (FROM(FOR(BUY)))(x, w, m, y): Someone x "buys" something w "for" an amount of money m "from" someone y if:
    (i) ACT(x, S)
    (ii) OBLIGATE$((x \& y), (x \& y), (FOR(TO(PAY)))(x, m, y, w))$
    (iii) CAUSE$(S, (ii))$

A schema for (TO(FOR(SELL)))(y, w, m, x) would be identical except that (i) would read ACT(y, S). When "buy" and "sell" refer to completed transactions, their schemata no longer incorporate the OBLIGATE part of (ii), only its third argument.

Analyses of "buy" and "sell" can easily be modified to apply to related verbs, such as "purchase," "market," "auction." With the introduction of the idea that ACT can also be a commodity—that it can serve as the referent of w in (51)—we can handle "earn," "gain," and "tip." Such verbs as "hire," "rent," "let," and "lease" are their own converse terms: "He rented a car to me" and "He rented a car from me." Their basic analysis is obtained by introducing "lend to," or "borrow from," into the notion of exchange.

Special terms cover the repayment of debts, the making good of losses, and so forth. They presuppose an obligation of the sort we are familiar with from (TO(LEND)) and (FROM(BORROW)), and their assertion discharges the obligation unless otherwise qualified. "Repay," and perhaps "reimburse," suggests that the obligation was created by a financial debt, whereas "recompense" and "compensate" suggest that it may have been damage or loss of property. The boundaries are vague, however, and we will not attempt to draw them.

Relatively little is known about children's mastery of this suburb of the lexicon. Gentner (1975) has studied the order in which children between the ages of four and eight learned eight verbs of possession. In a play situation the child was asked to act out various sentences involving different ways of transferring possessions between two dolls (or a doll and himself). The order was: give (which the four-year-olds knew), take, pay, trade (nondirectional), trade (directional), buy, spend money, and sell (which 73 percent of the eight-year-olds knew). Gentner argues that this order of acquisition reflects the semantic complexity of the verbs tested.

We undertook to review the verbs of possession in order to apply our theoretical apparatus to an essentially social domain. It turns out that we can leave unanalyzed most of the details of social convention. It is necessary only to introduce such modal concepts as PERMISSIBLE and to allow them to range over the set of regulative conventions of society. Once the underlying concept of possession is defined in this way, the bones of the semantic field can be fleshed out with largely familiar notions.

7.3   VERBS OF VISION

Having examined verbs whose meanings derive from an obvious perceptual property (motion) and verbs whose meanings derive from an obvious social convention (possession), we will now complicate the analysis by considering verbs that describe perception and verbs that describe a social process, the process of communication itself. Once again, native speakers of English are likely to agree that such verbs form semantic fields; we want to explore this intuition. We begin with perception and, in particular, with verbs of vision.

Austin (1962a) remarked "that our ordinary words are much subtler in their uses, and mark many more distinctions, than philosophers have realized; and that the facts of perception, as discovered by, for instance, psychologists but also as noted by common mortals, are much more diverse and complicated than has been allowed for" (p. 3). Our task is to uncover some of the complexities of perceptual language that are revealed in ordinary words; a suitable starting point is the familiar but mysterious verb "see."

"See" is one of the more complex verbs in English. Its complexity arises

partly from the complicated logic of perception and partly from the variety
of meanings that "see" conveys—our dictionary lists twenty senses for its
transitive use. This variety is illustrated in the following sentences:

> Isaak saw a fish.
> I see what you mean.
> They don't see him as president.
> Sinclair saw service in the Guards.
> We are seeing Pringle today.
> Did you see *Psycho?*
> Ambler was seen to the frontier.
> See that the drains are unblocked.

It should come as no surprise that a term expressing such a central perceptual experience has a multitude of meanings. But are these meanings really
different? Or is there something common to them all? One generalization that
seems to apply throughout the lexicon might be called the principle of implication. As Fillmore (1971c) notes, "Where one kind of activity is a possible
way of carrying out another kind of activity, the verb which identifies the
former activity has superimposed onto it certain syntactic and semantic properties of the verb which identifies the second or completing activity" (p. 385).
He gives the verb "tie" in "He tied his shoes" as an example. "Tie," which is
an action normally performed with stringlike objects, is here extended to mean
"fasten" or "secure," because if you fasten your shoes, in the ordinary course
of events you tie the laces. In "He tied his shoes," "tie" continues to identify
the original activity, but its meaning has been extended to take in the result of
such activity. It should not be necessary to include two lexical entries for these
two senses of "tie," since, given the original sense, a general "construal rule"
will account for the extended sense.

Abstractly, the principle of implication might be formulated thus: when a
simple implication of the form "if S_i, then S_j" is true in the ordinary course of
events, then the verb in S_j is likely to possess a meaning equivalent to the verb
in S_i. (The principle is presumably a generalization of the relation of hyponymy; if the verb in S_i is a hyponym of the verb in S_j, the superordinate can
usually be substituted in S_i.) For example, "If we met Pringle, then we saw
Pringle" will be true in the ordinary course of events when "see" is understood
to mean simply "perceive with the eyes," and "see" does indeed have the extended sense of "meet."

A weakness in this effort to formulate the principle of implication abstractly
is the vagueness of the phrase "in the ordinary course of events," which covers
an indefinitely large amount of information about how natural and social episodes normally develop. People obviously have such information. Knowledge
of what can ordinarily be expected to follow simple motor acts (what Bartlett,
1932, calls action schemata) must be acquired by children early in life. Knowledge of what can ordinarily be expected to happen when members of a society
undertake conventional activities in appropriate environmental surroundings

(what Barker, 1968, calls behavior settings) is critically important to successful participation in the life of that society; acquiring such knowledge is part of a child's socialization. Abelson (1973) has this kind of knowledge in mind when he speaks of "generic themes" integrated into "scripts" that combine to form human belief systems. The claim that people must have such information is neither new nor implausible. What is unclear is the relevance of such non-linguistic information for the subjective organization of lexical information.

How general knowledge supports language learning and use is an enormously complicated question. We will assume simply that people learn many scenarios for typical episodes; these scenarios are a storehouse of information about what can be expected to happen in the ordinary course of events. If a verb can be used to describe some aspect of a typical episode, its scenario is available as part of the schema for that verb (just as in section 4.1 functional information about objects was assumed to supplement perceptual criteria for the applicability of nominal labels). Thus verbs are associated by shared scenarios as well as by shared semantic components. When association by scenario is sufficiently regular—as "meet" and "see" are regularly associated in the scenario of typical personal encounters—the meaning of one of them may be extended according to the principle of implication.

In the case of "see" the principle is exemplified by the following scenarios: if you meet a person, in the ordinary course of events you see him; if you consult someone, in the ordinary course of events you see him; if you attend a performance of a play, you see the play; if you escort someone to the frontier, you see him get to the frontier; if you make sure the drains are unblocked, you see that they are unblocked. Each of these implications is true treating "see" as "perceive with the eyes."

If the various uses of "see" that conform to this principle are ignored, three main senses remain:

(52)   (a) to perceive with the eye
           (b) to have a mental image of; visualize
           (c) to understand; comprehend

Only the first of these senses is truly perceptual; we will concentrate on it here.

It will be helpful to begin by returning to the analogy of a person as an information-processing device. In chapter 2 we suggested a large number of predicates denoting the sorts of perceptual judgments people can make; in chapter 3 we described the sorts of control instructions that the central processor can attempt to execute. We pointed out in section 2.7 that *Perceive*(x, y) cannot be such a control instruction. It is a predicate that denotes the process involved when an internal representation of the external world is constructed out of information from the receptors. What we mainly have in mind is the construction of object percepts that can be submitted to various tests (via control instructions) to determine whether they satisfy perceptual predicates. Simply attaching "perceive" to the psychological predicate *Perceive*(x, y) would provide a vastly impoverished semantics for the verb.

Isaak may report "I see a fish" when *Perceive*(Isaak, x) and the following test is satisfied: test(t_a, FISH(x)). In this example *Perceive*(Isaak, x) denotes an internal process and FISH(x) denotes the outcome of a complex perceptual test. In responding to a question like "Is the boy holding a fish?" the system would have to examine its perceptual output for entities that satisfy appropriate tests for HOLD(BOY, FISH). But suppose the question is "Does the boy see a fish?" In order to answer this question we need a specification of the concept SEE. In other words, what conditions must be fulfilled if a statement such as "The boy sees a fish" is to be true?

A behaviorist might begin to list objective truth conditions: (a) the boy must be able to see—if this condition does not beg the question; (b) the boy must look at a fish, or toward it, or possibly at a reflected image of it, and there must be no opaque entity between the boy and the fish or its reflection; and (c) either the fish must be illuminated or else it must emit light; and so on. Such conditions may be necessary for the boy to have a veridical perception of a fish, but they are not sufficient. The most they can establish is that it is possible that the boy sees a fish. What is missing is the crucial mental event, seeing a fish. When the boy sees a fish, he is experiencing something rather than doing something. Phenomenologically, this event is an immediate and direct datum: it does not involve an intentional act of will, even though such an act may be part of the process leading up to it. Such a datum is something that only the individual himself is privy to.

The concept SEE is accordingly a special sort of generalization of the predicate *Perceive*(x, y). Seeing, of course, is a sort of perceiving. The meaning of PERCEIVE(x, G(y)) can be construed as *Perceive*(x, y) & [G(y)], where the brackets indicate the assertive nature of the satisfaction of perceptual tests. It follows that the concept contains neither a causal nor an intentional component: it is a primitive. The meaning of SEE(x, G(y)), however, can be analyzed as (WITH$_i$(PERCEIVE))(x, G(y), z), where it is presupposed that z denotes x's eyes.*

A number of important lessons can be drawn from the analysis so far. To revert to our earlier example, it is clear that there is no guarantee when Isaak truthfully reports "I see a fish" that he really is seeing a fish. It may be true that the output of his perceptual process is something that satisfies tests for fishiness even though it is, in fact, an old shoe—perceptual processes are not foolproof. He may make such a report when he is not perceiving, or even misperceiving, any object in the external world—when he is hallucinating. Even discounting human propensities for lying, the logic of "He sees a fish" is thus both referentially and intensionally opaque (Quine, 1960). This logic is made explicit in [SEE(he, ($\exists x$)FISH(x))], a formulation that is compatible with hallucinations or with misperceptions such as ($\exists y$)SHOE(y) & [SEE(he,FISH(y))]. A genuine

---

*Aravind K. Joshi suggests the analysis BY SIGHT(PERCEIVE(. . .)). We have greatly benefited from his alternative approach to this field, proposed in an unpublished paper, "Factorization of Verbs: An Analysis of Verbs of Seeing," and from many fruitful discussions of the topic.

and true perceptual report is not necessarily veridical, though perceptual verbs usually record an observational success (Ryle, 1949). However, a person cannot establish whether his percept is veridical simply by examining the output of his perceptual system. He cannot establish the truth of a statement of the form $(\exists x)\text{FISH}(x)$ & $[\text{SEE}(\text{ego}, \text{FISH}(x))]$ purely on visual grounds. Of course he can make such a claim ("There's a fish, I see it"), and he may be correct; but the claim goes beyond what is perceptually given.

When we speak of what others are perceiving, the situation is still worse. Barring spectacular advances in neurophysiology, we have no way to verify conclusively the assertion "The boy sees the fish." We can ascertain that it is overwhelmingly probable that the boy sees the fish, but it is always possible that we are wrong. We have no way to verify $(\exists x)\text{FISH}(x)$ & $[\text{SEE}(\text{BOY}, \text{FISH}(x))]$.

We are led ineluctably to the central paradox of perception. No claim about veridical visual perception can be visually verified. The individual himself is the only person to know what it is that he perceives; other persons cannot verify this component of a veridical claim. But the individual himself can have no perceptual grounds for moving from an opaque and potentially nonveridical report to a transparent and veridical report. It seems that SEE is a concept that has truth conditions that are easy to state but impossible to execute. Yet it is possible to determine that a veridical claim is *false*. The individual himself knows when he fails to tell the truth about what he perceives, and others can determine that a veridical perception of an object was impossible—the perceiver was not looking at it, he is blind, or whatever. Perceptual statements have an empirical content, but, like scientific conjectures, they may only be falsified. The output of the perceptual system is a hypothesis about the world; there are no facts except in the light of hypotheses.

There has been considerable argument among philosophers about such issues. Proponents of sense-data theories of perception, such as Berkeley, Hume, Russell, Ayer, and Price, have often argued that "see" and "perceive" have at least two distinct meanings. Ayer (1940) distinguishes a transparent meaning of "perceive" that entails that the perceptual object exists and an opaque meaning that does not entail that it exists—the incorrigible meaning in which one reports a sensory datum. Austin, a celebrated critic of sense data, simply denies the existence of these different meanings and claims instead that there are different ways of perceiving (Austin, 1962a, chap. 9). Although the dictionary distinguishes different meanings of "see," it is not the meaning of the verb that changes but the underlying logic of statements. We have to allow that "see," unlike "catch," can create opaque contexts. Generally speaking, "see" is used in a totally transparent manner. The logic of a sentence like "He has seen a volcano" seems to be $(\exists x)\text{VOLCANO}(x)$ & $[\text{SEE}(\text{he}, \text{VOLCANO}(x))]$; the logic of a sentence like "He has seen a lord," where the object has no obvious perceptual characteristics, seems to be $(\exists x)\text{LORD}(x)$ & $[\text{SEE}(\text{he}, x)$ & $\text{KNOW}(\text{he}, \text{ISA}(x, \text{LORD}))]$. In both cases the existence of the perceived object is being asserted by the speaker. It is even asserted in such utterances as "He saw a lord without realizing it." There are other cases where no such assertion is made, as in "He saw pink elephants dancing on the ceiling." Competent speakers of the language are capable of determining which interpretation is intended. The fact that it is difficult to verify perceptual statements of whatever variety in no way seems to impede their use or interpretation.

The logic of "see" evidently resembles that of other mental experiences like "think" and "believe" (Anscombe, 1965). This logic emerges naturally from the analysis of "see" as a generalization of an internal operation *Perceive*(. . .); it is implicit in the concept. An alternative conception of semantics, based on a possible-worlds approach, seeks to render the logic completely explicit in the form of a semantical model (Hintikka, 1969, pp. 151–183).

One of the traditional reasons for distinguishing between the meaning (or intension) of an expression and its reference (or extension) was to allow for the fact that it sometimes matters how a reference is made. Thus two expressions with the same reference are not always freely intersubstitutable. To take a much-used example, there is a difference between "Gottlob believes that the Evening Star is Venus" and "Gottlob believes that the Morning Star is Venus," even granted that "the Evening Star" and "the Morning Star" refer to the same entity. If Gottlob believes that the two expressions refer to the same entity, these two sentences have the same truth values. But if Gottlob believes that "the Morning Star" and "the Evening Star" refer to different entities—if he believes in a world that is possible but different from the actual world we live in—one of these sentences may be true while the other is false; that is, Gottlob may believe "The Evening Star" is Venus and "the Morning Star" is not, or vice versa. Whether two expressions that refer to the same entity are freely intersubstitutable in the opaque context created by "believe" depends on what the person in question happens to believe. The person's beliefs can be thought of as dividing all possible worlds into two sets: one set compatible with the two expressions having the same reference, the other set compatible with the two expressions having different reference. In the set of possible worlds corresponding to one belief, the two expressions are freely interchangeable in the context created by "believe"; in the other set, the expressions cannot be intersubstituted without changing the truth value of statements about the person's beliefs.

Similarly, one can argue from the truth of "Gottlob believes that Venus is a planet" to a claim about an *actual* entity only if one can establish that "Venus" refers to one and the same entity in all of the possible worlds compatible with Gottlob's beliefs. It is necessary to establish $(\exists x)[\text{Gottlob believes}$ that (Venus $= x)]$ in order to argue from "Gottlob believes that Venus is a planet" to the conclusion "There is something that Gottlob believes to be a planet." This style of analysis deals only in terms of extensions (in possible worlds); it is not necessary to talk of meanings or intensions.

What does all this have to do with perception? Hintikka makes the bold suggestion that sense data are analogous to meanings or intensions. One of the traditional reasons for postulating sense data was to allow for the fact that perception can be illusory. If a person has an illusory perception, there must be something that he misperceives. Suppose, however, that what someone perceives is also treated as a set of possible worlds, that what someone sees is a description of all the alternative possible situations that are compatible with his percept. One may then argue from the truth of "Gottlob sees that Venus has risen" to a claim about an actual entity only if one can establish that "Venus" refers to one and the same entity in all the alternative possible states of affairs compatible with what Gottlob sees. It is necessary to establish $(\exists x)[$Gottlob sees that (Venus $= x)]$ in order to deduce the conclusion "There is something that Gottlob sees to be a planet." This problem is similar to the problem of reidentifying individuals from one occasion to another (see Strawson, 1959). It may even be, as Hintikka supposes, that people can operate with logically distinct criteria. Thus, an individual may be cross-identified simply from a visual impression of him or, alternatively, from definite criteria about who he is—a contrast that corresponds to Russell's (1912, chap. 5) distinction between knowledge by acquaintance and knowledge by description.

From a psychological point of view, Hintikka's radical extensionalist approach to the verbs of perception has the clarity of a logical dream. It has something of the same order of relevance as an axiomatization of arithmetic does to a theory of how people add numbers. It lays bare a logic that may have to be adhered to but offers no insight into actual mechanisms. We have argued that a satisfactory psychological theory of semantics need not fight shy of intensions or meanings, and we have certainly embraced them in the form of procedures or programs. Since the essential logical requirements emerge from the concept SEE, we may regard Hintikka's proposals as a template against which to test the theory rather than as a rival theory. It would be folly to suppose that we need an explicit model of how individuals are cross-identified from one possible world to another in order to handle the distinction between such sentences as "He saw the thief without realizing it" and "He saw (and recognized) the thief."

The other main pillar of the visual verbs has a different, and simpler, underlying logic. The concept of LOOK that is expressed in "He looked at the author of *The Deer Park*" might almost delight a behaviorist. Its truth conditions, unlike those for SEE, involve a number of objective criteria, such as that the observer's eyes must be open and directed at the perceptual object. As befits a behavioristic notion, "look" is referentially transparent. If an individual looks at the author of *The Deer Park*, it follows that he looks at someone; since that author is Norman Mailer, it follows that he looks at Norman Mailer. Of course, the individual may not be aware that the author of the *The Deer Park* is Norman Mailer; indeed, he may not even be aware that the person at whom he is looking *is* the author of *The Deer Park*. Could he be unaware that he is looking at a person? Perhaps. Such hackneyed remarks as "He looked right at it and didn't see it" suggest that "looking at" is sometimes no more than directing the gaze toward a particular object. This important distinction between "see" and "look at" is not peculiar to English. Scovel (1971) finds this distinction in the Spanish "ver" and "mirar," the French "voir" and "regarder," the Thai "hĕn" and "duu," and the Chinese "kànjyàn" and "kàn." We speculate that this basic division of the English verbs of vision reflects some universal feature of human attempts to communicate about visual experience.

We can distinguish within the English verbs that describe vision a domain of LOOK verbs, a domain of SEE verbs, and a domain where the two concepts come together. Before exploring these domains, however, we need to consider the semantic function of English complement constructions.

7.3.1   Complement Constructions and English Verbs

A wide range of cognitive predicates can apply both to objects, events, or processes in the world and to certain mental objects, notably propositions. To express their application requires that one sentence be grafted onto or into another; this operation is complicated and requires considerable syntactic machinery.

The possibility of combining two or more sentoids into a single sentence provides the basic source of recursive productivity in a language. There are three major ways to accomplish it in English: (a) by connecting two sentences with a grammatical conjunction, as in "She left and he followed her"; (b) by subordinating one sentence to another in a relative clause, as in "She is the one whom he followed" or "He is the one who followed her"; and (c) by incorporating a sentence as an argument of the verb in another sentence, giving a complement construction, as in "She thought he followed her." (Sentential complements were discussed briefly in sections 6.2 and 6.3 in connection with the introduction of sentential arguments of the verbs "begin," "happen," and "cause.")

Many verbs of vision accept such sentential arguments. Their complexity can be illustrated by considering some typical sentential complements of the verb "to see": "He saw (that) the man had been injured," "He saw who ate the cake," "He saw Uri bending the spoons," "He saw Mary's dancing." The richness of this system forces us to consider English complement construction as a whole before we discuss its application to verbs of vision.

There has been considerable argument about the syntactic derivation of sentential complements. A view explored in detail by transformational linguists is that all the principal forms have the same underlying structure and that their respective complementizers (such as "that," "for ... to") are inserted transformationally; syntactic differences between complements are the result of different transformational histories (see Rosenbaum, 1967). Such an account, however, rides roughshod over obvious semantic differences, and its associated assumption that verbs have features specifying their acceptable sentential complements also runs into difficulties. An alternative view is that complementizers have a semantic function and are perhaps better conceived of as elements of underlying structure (Bresnan, 1970). We cannot hope to work back from the variety of surface forms of complement to a clear statement of their underlying meaning—a goal that has so far eluded linguists—but since we believe that the complements taken by a verb are largely determined by its meaning, we will attempt to specify the sorts of underlying meanings conveyed by complements and to illustrate how they might be realized in surface structure.

Sentences can be used to make statements, ask questions, or convey commands; since these uses are roughly correlated with the syntactic forms of declarative, interrogative, and imperative, it is hardly surprising that different complementizers are used to graft them onto other sentences:

(53)   He said that she had left.   ("that" complement)
       He asked whether she had left. ("wh" complement)
       He ordered her to leave.   (accusative + infinitival
                                        complement)

There are clear semantic distinctions within these basic sentence forms. We will begin by considering the ways in which declaratives can be formed into complements.

Two reasons for using a declarative complement construction should be distinguished. A speaker may wish to refer to what is, in turn, referred to by that sentence. Declaratives, depending on their temporal schemata, can describe events, actions, states, and processes; a speaker may want to relate such referents to other matters or to comment on them. On the other hand, a speaker may wish to refer not to what an utterance refers to but to its meaning (to the proposition it expresses); such metalinguistic expressions are exemplified in (53).

It is extremely useful to be able to convert a sentence into a noun phrase referring to the proposition expressed by that sentence. This procedure makes it possible, for example, to attribute a truth value to an indicative statement ("It is false that Mary is leaving"). Moreover, the process of forming "that" clauses is recursive: "He said that it is doubtful that it is true that . . . Mary is leaving." A speaker can thus express a variety of "propositional attitudes" about a statement. He can believe, disbelieve, know, or doubt it; he can learn or come to know it, he can remember or call it to mind, he can forget or cease to know it, he can prove or disprove it. An important distinction can be made here between those complement-taking verbs that concern objective aspects of a statement, principally the likelihood of its being true or false ("believe"), and those that take its truth for granted (and the fact that their subjects grasp it) and that express a subjective attitude toward the proposition ("regret"). There is even a group of bisentential verbs (prove, indicate, suggest, imply) that can relate one clause whose truth is taken for granted to another clause whose truth is not taken for granted: "That the theorem is valid proves that you are right."

Kiparsky and Kiparsky (1970) argue that when the truth of a statement is presupposed, the underlying structure of the complement is "the fact that S," and that "it" may stand in for "the fact" ("I regret it that Mary left"). There may also be counterfactive verbs that presuppose the falsity of the complement and semifactive verbs that lose their factivity in modal concepts ("He may discover that his car has been stolen"; Karttunen, 1970, 1971). It must be emphasized that not all subjective verbs presuppose the truth of the complement assertion, and that some objective verbs take its truth for granted. The subjective verb "know" appears to be factive and to allow a speaker to convey by presupposition his own objective attitude to a proposition while describing someone else's. Likewise, verbs that express a wish, preference, intention, expectation, or the like, can hardly presuppose the truth of their complements. Indeed, many of their complements are likely to be expressed in the subjunctive ("She preferred that he do it," "He wishes that she were there") or in a similarly nonindicative form ("She preferred that he should do it," "He wishes that she may be there").

To recapitulate, in referring to the meaning of a declarative, a speaker may use a "that" complement. He may apply an objective or a subjective predicate to it; he may assert or presuppose its truth, and when he can do neither he is likely to use a nonindicative mood.

English allows an alternative form of complementation for nonindicative clauses; such complements can be expressed in an infinitival form (see Vendler, 1968): "She preferred him to do it," "He wishes her to be there." It follows that there is a difference in meaning between "It is surprising that a bat is blind" and "It is surprising for a bat to be blind." The former presupposes the truth of its complement and tends to take a generic interpretation; the latter is close in meaning to "It is surprising that a bat should be blind," and is not factive and less easily takes a generic interpretation (see Bresnan, 1970; Spears, 1973).

A syntactic point raised in 6.2.5 is worth considering in more detail at this juncture. Rosenbaum (1967) distinguishes between complements of noun phrases (NP complements) and complements of verb phrases (VP complements). His distinction is drawn on the basis of whether a complement behaves like a noun phrase and, for example, permits a pseudocleft construction ("What worried John was for the doctor to have examined Bill"). It appears that such tests are not altogether reliable (Bowers, 1968; Wagner, 1968); even Rosenbaum expresses doubts about the category of verb-phrase complements. Nevertheless, there is a clear distinction between this pair of sentences, which are synonymous:

(54)   I believe the doctor to have examined Bill.
         I believe Bill to have been examined by the doctor.

and the following pair of sentences, which are not synonymous:

(55)   I persuaded the doctor to examine Bill.
         I persuaded Bill to be examined by the doctor.

Whatever the syntactic specification of these sentences, there is an underlying semantic difference between them having its origin in the representation of the verbs. "Believe" takes a simple complement referring to a proposition, and hence there is a close relation of the sentences in (54) to:

(56)   I believe that the doctor should have examined Bill.
         I believe that Bill should have been examined by the doctor.

("Should" is not to be construed here in its moral sense, "ought to.") "Persuade" has a more complex structure; we might paraphrase the sentences in (55) by the following pair:

(57)   I persuaded the doctor that he should examine Bill.
         I persuaded Bill that the doctor should examine him.

("Should" may be construed here in its moral sense.) These paraphrases suggest a semantic representation of the form

(58)   PERSUADE(x, y, S_y):   ACT(x, S') & CAUSE$(S', $INTEND$(y, S_y))$.

The advantage of this approach is that it provides a unified account (compare Kiparsky and Kiparsky, 1970) for the presence of accusative + infinitive complements in both (54) and (55). The complements arise from a reference to an underlying nonindicative complement, as is evident in the paraphrases (56) and (57). The need for this mood arises from the uncertain nature of beliefs and from the intentional aspect of persuasion. Since factive predicates cannot take anything other than indicative complements, it follows that, as Kiparsky and Kiparsky rightly observe, they cannot take accusative + infinitive complements.

Certain verbs can have a dual function. Consider the difference between (a) "He remembered that he locked the door" and (b) "He remembered to lock the door." In (a) "remember" functions as a factive verb; the sentence presupposes that he locked the door. But in (b) "remember" is not factive; it might be argued that it is an implicative verb (Karttunen, 1971). If he remembered to lock the door, he locked the door; if he didn't remember to lock the door, he didn't lock the door. But, as Karttunen admits, these are weak implications. One would hardly argue that if he locked the door he remembered to lock the door; he might have done it without thinking about it. We prefer to take the view that (b) derives once again from a nonindicative form and is therefore closely related to "He remembered that he should lock the door" and that the weak implications arise by way of a conversational implicature. (A similar point of view about presuppositions in general has been taken by D. Wilson, 1972, 1975.) If you remember to do something, the chances are that you do it; if you do not remember to do something, the chances are that you do not do it. The underlying distinction in (a) and (b) is between a memory for a fact and a memory for an intention.

We have established in a variety of cases that nonindicative sentences may be referred to by accusative + infinitive complements. This analysis even applies in the case where a speaker makes reference to an order or request (see (53)), since there is a close relation between an assertion such as "He told her to leave" and "He told her that she should leave." What we have not established is the converse inference: that all infinitivals are derived from, or relate to, underlying subjunctives. We will shortly encounter a clear counterexample to this inference, but let us turn first to the representation of reference to events and actions.

There is a gerundive construction that allows a complement to refer to the event or action denoted by its corresponding assertion. Thus, the gerundive in "Caruso's singing of the aria was coming to an end" refers to the action denoted by its related assertion: Caruso was singing the aria. It is a controversial question whether such "active" gerunds, and particularly nominal derivatives like "the explosion of the bomb," are derived syntactically from their related assertions in underlying structure (see Chomsky, 1970). But there is a striking difference between them and "factive" gerunds like "He resented Caruso's singing the aria." As a number of authors have pointed out (Lees, 1960; Vendler, 1968; Fraser, 1970; Chomsky, 1970), the contrast is both syntactic and semantic. Unfortunately, many gerundives are ambiguous, and their interpretation often depends on the matrix:

> He heard her screaming.   (active gerundive)
> He reported her screaming.   (factive gerundive)

In some cases even the matrix is ambiguous; "Caruso's singing of the aria was recorded" may mean that the fact that he sang it was noted (factive) or that his singing of it was tape-recorded (active). Similarly, a sentence like "Caruso's singing of the aria surprised us" may mean we were surprised that he sang it (factive) or were surprised at the way he sang it (active). It is a mistake to place too much emphasis on superficial form. It is even doubtful that only active gerundives can be subjectless. Certainly a sentence like "Eating cabbage is good for you" refers to an action, either a generic one or one concerning *your* purely private welfare (see Wasow and Roeper, 1972; Thompson, 1973), but "He mentioned eating cabbage" is entirely acceptable.

We find the same subtleties in distinguishing complements that refer to states and those that refer to propositions denoting states. Borkin (1973) has suggested that the difference between the sentences

(59)   (a) I find this chair to be comfortable.
          (b) I find this chair comfortable.

is that (59a) concerns an objective state of affairs whereas (59b) concerns a personal experience. She argues that the deletion of "to be" is only permissible when such personal experiences are concerned. In our view, however, (59a) contains a complement that can be construed as referring to a proposition: "I find that it is the case that this chair is comfortable," whereas (59b) contains a complement that can be construed as referring to a state. (Both complements may, of course, be considered ambiguous—our claim concerns their more salient interpretations.) This distinction between factive and stative complements is also evident in Vendler's (1968) examples

He felt John to be trembling.   (factive)
He felt John trembling.   (stative)

and in Chomsky's (1970) examples

John felt that he was angry.   (factive)
John felt angry.   (stative)

It might therefore be more appropriate to think of two seperate underlying structures rather than a transformational deleting of "to be" (see Matthews, 1967).

An important set of verbs, first isolated and analyzed by Karttunen (1970, 1971), take complements referring to events and actions but can express these complements infinitivally. (The reader was warned that infinitival structures do not always express a nonindicative clause.) Consider first the set of aspectual verbs, also discussed by Vendler (1968), that occur in the following sentences:

(60)   He happened to leave the house.
        He began to write letters.
        He ceased to breathe.

These sentences concern various events, as we can bring out by paraphrasing them in the following way:

(61)   His leaving the house happened.
        He began his writing of letters.
        He ceased breathing.

Vendler suggests that perhaps the infinitival form is used because, for example, merely beginning to write letters does not indicate that any letters were actually written; but this argument plainly fails with "happen." Moreover, Karttunen claims that the verbs are "implicative," that is, that the sentences in (60) imply that at appropriate times

(62)   He left the house.
        He wrote letters.
        He did not breathe.

He also claims that the negations of (60) imply the negations of (62). Following Yamanashi's (1972) lead, we can account for these inferences by considering the logical consequences of some underlying concepts. The following equivalences can be derived (see 6.2.5 and 6.3.3):

(63)   HAPPEN(S) $\equiv$ S   (positive two-way implicative verb)
        CEASE(S) $\equiv$ notS   (negative two-way implicative verb)

Karttunen also considers some implicative verbs that allow only a one-way inference. The most important is "cause." "Your touching the soap bubble caused it to burst" implies that the bubble burst, but its negation is ambiguous, as we were at pains to establish in 6.3.5, and it has no clear implications about whether or not the bubble burst. In short, a sentence of the form "*x* caused S" implies S, and "cause" is accordingly in Karttunen's nomenclature a positive "if" implicative predicate. Likewise, since "*x* prevented S" implies notS, "prevent" is a negative "if" implicative predicate. And since "S is impossible" implies notS, "possible" is a positive "only if" predicate. However, we can easily establish the following entailments (see (79') in 6.3.5):

(64)   CAUSE(S, S') entails HAPPEN(S').

         PREVENT(S, S') entails notHAPPEN(S').

         HAPPEN(S) entails POSSIBLE(S).

Hence CAUSE is a positive "if" implicative, PREVENT a negative "if" implicative, and POSSIBLE a positive "only if" implicative. It is now possible to account for the logical properties of a large number of verbs by simply considering the inferential consequences of their constituents. For example, granted analyses along the following lines,

(65)   FAIL(*x*, S):   notSUCCEED(*x*, S)

         ANGER(S, *x*):   CAUSE(S, ANGRY(*x*))

         (TO(VISIBLE))(*x*, *y*):   POSSIBLE(SEE(*y*, *x*))

         (FROM(RESTRAIN))(*x*, *y*, S):   ACT(*x*, S') & PREVENT(S', S)

it follows that "succeed" is a positive two-way implicative and "fail" a negative one, "anger" a positive "if" implicative, "visible" a positive "only if" implicative, and "restrain" a negative "if" implicative. It should be noted that verbs incorporating a negative component (restrain, prohibit, prevent, abstain, refrain) tend to take "from" + "-ing" rather than the infinitival construction (Vendler, 1968).

There are obviously other underlying components with important logical consequences; it remains to be seen whether all implicative verbs can be accounted for in the manner of (65). How, for example, are we to explain the possibility that "hesitate" is a *negative* "only if" implicative?

A further problem with the complements of causatives is that the verb "cause" can take either a simple subject or a sentence as subject. When it takes a sentence, a strange situation arises—the sentence appears to be a factive. This oddity led Vendler (1967) to claim that cause is a relation between a fact and an event. We have argued that it is a relation between events or states. How is the question to be resolved? Let us consider some of the typical sorts of subject complement that can occur with the verb:

> Ogden's playing of the sonata caused the piano to disintegrate.
> That Ogden played the sonata caused us considerable surprise.
> The fact that Ogden played the sonata caused Mary to be angry.
> Ogden's playing the sonata caused a sensation.
> The beautiful playing of John Ogden caused the critics to weep.

As far as its subject is concerned, "cause" seems to be, in Vendler's phrase, a "loose container"; it allows complements expressing either facts or events. Specific causal assertions appear to presuppose either that the proposition referred to by the subject complement is true (the factive complement) or that the event referred to by the subject complement took place (the active complement). The latter is a simple consequence of any sort of reference: reference presupposes the existence of what is referred to. Nevertheless, it is important to distinguish between referring to an event, which presupposes its occurrence, and presupposing the truth of a proposition describing an event. There does not appear to be complete freedom for the subject complement of "cause." The following sentence is somewhat odd: "That Ogden played the sonata caused the piano to disintegrate." One tends to interpret it to mean that Ogden played in such a way that the piano disintegrated and that anyone else might have had a less dramatic effect. One tries to force the complement into an active interpretation. It is tempting to suppose that where the consequence of a cause is a physical event or state of affairs, the antecedent complement must also refer to a physical event or state of affairs (or else listeners automatically attempt to complete the causal chain with an intermediary human action; see Schank, 1973b); but that where the consequence is a mental event or a human action, the antecedent complement may refer to a truth or to a physical event. Thus both "Ogden's playing caused Mary to be angry" and "The fact that Ogden played caused Mary to be angry" are acceptable. In the first Mary was angered by an unspecified aspect of Ogden's playing; in the second she was angered by the fact that he played. If this speculative analysis is correct, it should be inherited by those verbs that contain an underlying causative component, unless other factors overrule a direct incorporation of the causal schema.

We have now dealt with complements expressing declarative sentences, and we have mentioned in passing the infinitival complements expressing imperative sentences. The remaining category of sentences, interrogatives, as we mentioned earlier, can be accommodated by a "wh" complement. It is natural to wonder whether they too are open to the distinction between metalinguistic and ordinary reference. The complements in "He asked them whether it was raining" and "He inquired who was at the wedding" evidently refer in metalinguistic fashion to the meanings of certain questions; the following complements seem to refer to their answers: "He told them whether it was raining," "He said who was at the wedding." Such metalinguistic uses must be distinguished from a referential function mirroring that of relative clauses. Vendler (1968) has illustrated the distinction with a pair of contrasting examples: "We know what he lost" versus "We found what he lost." In the first we can be said to know what it is that he lost, but in the second we can hardly be said to have found what it is that he lost. In the first case we know something equivalent to an answer to a question, that he lost x, where x has a specific value. In the second case we simply found an object—the complement refers to the object referred to, in turn, by "that x which he lost." Thus the basic distinction between metalinguistic and ordinary reference can also apply to "wh" complements.

So much for English complementation in general, though we will return to the semantics of metalinguistic reference in dealing with verbs of communication in section 7.4. We note, finally, that prepositional phrases can introduce complements of nearly every variety, and now return at last to complements of the verbs of vision.

On page 584 we suggested something of the range of complements taken by perceptual verbs. Obviously they can take a variety of complements other than simple perceptual objects. The interpretation of these complements depends to some extent, however, on the temporal schemata of the verbs in question. We can illustrate this dependency by considering three verbs of vision: see, glimpse, watch. The temporal shape of "see" is essentially stative:* "He saw the picture" means that a particular relation held for an indefinite period of time in the past. It may have been for only a moment, HAPPEN$_t$(SEE(he, PICTURE)), or for an indefinite duration, SEE(he, PICTURE). The momentary aspect of "see," in which it resembles "arrive," makes its collocation with "until" somewhat awkward, as in "He saw the picture until noon." The temporal shape of "glimpse" is purely momentary:

(66)   GLIMPSE(x, y):   HAPPEN$_t$(SEE(x, y)).

To say "He glimpsed it between time t_a and time t_b" suggests either a single definite moment at which he saw it or else a number of such discrete moments. The temporal shape of "watch," which is an activity, involves a process persisting over an indefinite period of time—a schema that we represent by HAPPEN$_i$; but it is a simple matter to demarcate the interval by definite references, as in "He watched until noon."

How do these three verbs fare in taking complements? "See" is the most flexible (and has the most flexible semantics), since it can take many sorts of complement. It can take, for instance, the three major sorts of complement that make metalinguistic reference to propositions: "He saw that the bridge had been destroyed," "He saw who destroyed it," and "He saw John to be kind." As an activity, "watch" can take none of these complements; as a momentary verb of seeing, "glimpse" can take the first two sorts of complement, but it cannot take the last sort, which refers to a stative proposition. Turning to complements that refer to actual events and states, once again "see" is the most flexible, "glimpse" suggests a momentary perception of an object while it is engaged in an activity, and "watch" suggests a process of perceiving an activity. It follows that "see" and "watch" can take complements directly referring to events: "He saw/watched the man leave the bank," but such complements are barely acceptable for "glimpse." When the event is itself momentary, "watch" is also inappropriate: "He saw the cup shatter instantaneously," but the same sentence with "watch" does not seem instantaneous. And

---

*Ryle (1949) argued that seeing is neither an activity nor a state but an achievement brought about by looking. The argument is fallacious and, as Sibley (1955) has shown, rests on confusion between such verbs as "look for" and "look at." Nevertheless, the momentary sense of "see" does share a similar temporal schema with an achievement, such as reaching the summit of a mountain (Vendler, 1968).

"glimpse" fares little better in this case since it suggests a glimpse of an ongoing event or action: "He glimpsed the demolition of the building." All three verbs, therefore, are compatible with a process complement: "He saw/watched/glimpsed us crossing the bridge." The versions with "see" and "glimpse" can be paraphrased as "He saw/glimpsed us when we were crossing the bridge." The versions with "see" and "watch" can be paraphrased as "He saw/watched us as we crossed the bridge" or as "He saw/watched us cross the bridge."

Whatever the directly referential complement of a perceptual verb, it must clearly contain a perceptible referent—a referent that involves perceptual tests. It would be bizarre, for example, to assert "He saw the man dislike his father." Certain states or events cannot be observed. A speaker can report not the state itself but the fact of it: "He saw that the man disliked his father." Hence there is nothing paradoxical in the remark "I see that it is invisible." This possibility for "see" to accept metalinguistic complements is of crucial importance. Speakers often say such things as "I saw that he was very angry" or "I see from the dial that the battery is flat." But you cannot literally see either a man's anger or the flatness of a battery. It is possible, however, to see through a man's demeanor, and through the pointers and numerals on a dial, to facts that lie behind them. Of course, a behaviorist might argue that it is the demeanor and the pointers and numerals that are the facts. But such a metaphysics is not embodied in ordinary language; it is necessary to allow that the interpretative aspect of "see" extends to grasping the truth of propositions.

We established earlier that "see" is referentially opaque. It seems to be similarly opaque when it takes a complement. Admittedly, the verb can have a superficial factivity when it takes a metalinguistic complement. A sentence like "He saw that the auditorium was empty" and its negation, "He didn't see that the auditorium was empty," can be taken to entail that the auditorium was empty. However, this factivity can easily be destroyed by a glaring failure of reference within the complement, as in "He saw that the present king of France is bald." Such a sentence is likely to be construed as referring to a fictional or historical context, or else to a palpably nonveridical perception. Even when referential presuppositions are fulfilled, however, there is no guarantee that a true sentence reports a veridical percept. We find exactly the same conditions at work when the verb takes an event complement. For example, both "He saw the auditorium empty" and its negation suggest that the auditorium did empty. The convention is that most reports are veridical, but once an appropriate context has been established—the perceiver is prone to hallucinate, he has been drinking, he is in a situation where error is likely—the verb can be used to report nonveridical percepts. Of course, when speakers report dreams or tell stories the logic of that discourse is no longer to be taken literally: they are referring to fictional entities. But this referential shift applies to all expressions, including the simplest verbs. What is different about a verb such as "see" is that even when discoursing about the real world a speaker may wish to use it to report truthfully a nonveridical experience, as in "He saw an extraordinary rock formation and took great pains to avoid it; later he found out that it was an effect created by trees in the mist."

One final point about the complements of perceptual verbs. Caplan (1973) emphasizes that "see," "hear," and "feel" have abstract senses:

> He saw at last that the empire was doomed.
> He heard that the president had resigned.
> He felt that inflation was an insoluble problem.

but that "taste" and "smell" have no such abstract senses capable of accepting complements. Caplan suggests that an abstract interpretation demands that the subordinate verb be tensed and that a concrete interpretation demands that it be either in the progressive and the same tense as the matrix verb or else tenseless. But these rules will not do; such sentences as "He will hear that Mary is singing" and "He has heard that Mary shouts" can take a concrete interpretation despite their violation of these rules. Indeed, Caplan's distribution between concrete and abstract interpretation does not quite tally with the facts. The real situation is perhaps more accurately captured by distinguishing between complements referring to events and complements referring to propositions. When the verb takes a complement referring to an event, as in "He heard Mary singing," the verb must be interpreted in its literal perceptual sense. When the verb takes a complement referring to a proposition, as in "He heard that Mary was singing," its factive nature can sometimes be established by perceptual experience: "He heard Mary singing; therefore he heard that Mary was singing," but it can always have been established by someone telling him that she was singing. The fact that "hear" can function like the converse of "tell" has an obvious psychological explanation—it is again a case of the principle of implication, and it allows the verb to take factive complements referring to propositions that cannot literally be perceived, as in "He heard that inflation had increased." Caplan's constraints on tense are really an attempt to isolate those propositional complements whose truth could be established on perceptual grounds.

"Hear" can be used as a converse of "tell." "See" can be used as a near synonym of "read" ("I see that the Geneva Convention is over") or of "understand" ("After the riot the pope saw the need for reform"). "Feel" can be used to specify an emotional state ("He felt happy") or an intuitive belief ("He felt that the project was unrealistic"). But neither "taste" nor "smell" can take abstract interpretations, though both can take propositional complements provided their factive nature can be established by direct perceptual experience ("He tasted that the drink had been sweetened," "He smelled that the gas had been left on"). Why, then, can they not allow a more remote agency to establish the truth of such complements and thus a full abstract interpretation? Caplan offers some interesting speculations, but in our view it is doubtful whether any explanation can be submitted to a stringent test. Our own hypothesis is that the verbs lack an abstract representation because of the conceptual impoverishment of the world of tastes and smells. If, for example, messages could be coded in a succession of perfumes, the language might very well be extended to include such utterances as "He smelled that the Dow Jones index had fallen."

7.3.2   Intermodal Verbs

Like "perceive" itself, there are a number of verbs that can be used to refer to any sensory modality of perception. These perceptually neutral verbs are perhaps best distinguished by their temporal schemata and by the complements they can take. The crucial distinction between "perceive" and "witness" appears to be largely a matter of complements. "Perceive" is as flexible as "see," but "witness" has a narrower purview. One can witness events but not facts. Nor, indeed, can one witness simple perceptual objects. It is unacceptable to say "We witnessed a box" or, in a perceptual sense, "We witnessed that the car was damaged." The function of "remark" as a perceptual verb seems to be very similar to "witness," though our intuitions are less certain because this use is largely confined to literary quarters: "Remark the cat which flattens itself in the gutter,/Slips out its tongue/And devours a morsel of rancid butter."

Just as "glimpse" is a momentary variant of "see," so "notice" is a momentary variant of "perceive." "Notice" and "spot" seem to differ in terms of their suitability as arguments of an intention: it makes more sense to say "You have to spot where it's hidden" than "You have to notice where it's hidden." A definition of "spot" should involve an active component capable of bearing an intentional component. It is not obvious at first what this active component should be; because the verb is neutral with respect to modality, it may have to correspond to looking, listening, and so forth. Perhaps the best candidate is "attend," in the sense of "pay attention to." A definition of "spot" might run "momentarily perceive as a result of attending to . . . "

Of all the verbs that are neutral with respect to perceptual modality, perhaps the most interesting and important are "recognize" and "identify." These two stand halfway between perception and cognition. There is even a sense of "identify," arising from the principle of implication, in which it means not only a mental act of categorizing a perceived object but also a public announcement of its outcome. The perceptual sense of "identify" presupposes that an object is perceived, and it asserts that a judgment is made about the category to which it belongs. Thus it really has three underlying arguments: (a) the identifier, (b) the object perceived, and (c) the category to which it is assigned. These arguments are not always expressed, so the same fact may be conveyed by very different sentences: "He identified the animal as a baboon," "He identified the animal," "He identified a baboon." It is the more general term that features in the presupposition—to have identified the animal as a baboon he must have perceived an animal. To presuppose that he perceived a baboon would clearly presuppose too much: it would leave nothing to be asserted. On the other hand, to assert merely that the individual perceived a baboon would leave out of account the search for an appropriate categorization. This search is a cognitive operation. Its agentive nature is brought out by the compatibility of "identify" with manner adverbs, as in "He hastily identified the animal." Its intentional nature is brought out by the incompatibility of "identify" with such adverbs as "accidentally." We do not propose to analyze such a cognitive concept in detail here; we will simply represent the key notion as JUDGE—a concept that would derive from the control instruction test(x, y) (sec. 2.7). This predicate involves an intentional mental act; hence an observer may try to identify, or identify with difficulty, but it would be superfluous to say that he intentionally identified something. "Identify" may accordingly be analyzed as

(67)   IDENTIFY(x, y, z):   Someone x who perceives something y at time t
         "identifies" y as z if:
         (i) HAPPEN$_t$(JUDGE(x, ISA(y, z)))

A concept, IDENTIFY(y), based on the control instruction, identify(y), could be added as a further component in order to capture the implied sense of "identify" as the statement of an identification.

The dictionary tells us that "recognize" has two main perceptual meanings: (a) to know or be aware that something perceived has been perceived before; and (b) to know or identify from past experience or knowledge. The second meaning, like "identify," takes three main arguments: "He recognized the animal as a baboon." Such a statement presupposes that he perceived the animal, but it goes further than "identify," since it also presupposes that the animal actually is a baboon. In other words, "identify" allows that the perceiver may make a mistake, but "recognize" does not—it is contradictory to say "He recognized the animal erroneously as a baboon."

The first meaning of "recognize" involves only two arguments ("He recognized the man") since the perceiver merely judges that he has perceived the perceptual object before. In other words, this first meaning is simply a special case of the second meaning in which the categorizing term is replaced by a routine asserting that the object has been perceived before. The two senses of "recognize" accordingly involve the following procedures:

(68)   (a) RECOGNIZE(x, y):   Someone x "recognizes" something y if:
             (i) IDENTIFY(x, y, BEFORE(PERCEIVE(x, y), t))
         (b) RECOGNIZE(x, y, z):   Someone x "recognizes" something y as z,
             where y is a z, if:
             (i) IDENTIFY(x, y, z)

A further category of intermodal verbs concerns the perception of differences: discern, discriminate, differentiate. Once again, these verbs often have a meaning arising from the principle of implication, which concerns statements about differences rather than the mere perception of them. The perceptual meaning exemplified in "He distinguished the claret from the burgundy" presupposes that the objects were perceived and asserts that they were correctly identified and were different. "Differentiate," however, seems to convey a slightly weaker sense, simply that a difference between the two entities is detected. But the distinction is a fine one and we will ignore it here.

(69)   DISTINGUISH(x, y, z):   Someone x "distinguishes" two things y and
          z, where y is a w, z is a w', and $w \neq w'$, if:
          (i) IDENTIFY(x, y, w)
          (ii) IDENTIFY(x, z, w')

There is a definite relation between "distinguish" and the sense of "discern"
reflected in such statements as "He discerned a dirigible in the clouds." This
sense has a distinct connotation of difficulty, a connotation represented in the
dictionary's gloss: "perceive (something obscure or concealed)." The notion
of difficulty can be indirectly specified by using "manage"; what also seems
to be required is the notion of distinguishing an object from its surroundings
or background. Hence "discern" can be incompletely defined as "manage to
distinguish x from x's background."

Although we have concentrated on visual interpretations of the intermodal
verbs, applications of these verbs to other perceptual modalities do not appear
to raise any difficulties of principle.

7.3.3   Simple Verbs of Vision

There are two main pillars to the verbs of vision. There is the stative-
like "see," which has a flexible temporal schema capable of denoting momentary events or durative processes. Since it denotes a mental experience of its
subject argument "see" is capable of taking metalinguistic complements and
complements that are logically opaque. "Look" is more active, and we have
established only that it is logically transparent. We must open our discussion
of the simple verbs of vision with a more detailed consideration of this verb.

There is a similarity between looking at something and pointing at something: looking is directing an eye, pointing is directing a finger. Both actions
involve movement with a directional component; where they differ is in the
nature of this component. The direction of a finger is easily specified by using
its base and tip as arguments for a directional concept, INLINE. Although the
eye has no obvious equivalents to the finger's tip and base, the direction of an individual's gaze can be judged with considerable accuracy. Gibson and Pick
(1963) concluded from an experimental study that the factors taken into account in judging whether one is being looked at include the position of the other
person's iris in the visible portion of the sclera and the position of his eyes in
his head. These results have been replicated by a number of other experiments,
including one that involved merely line drawings of heads and eyes (Nachshon
and Wapner, 1967). The greater directional component in "look at" than
in "see" is confirmed by Legrenzi's (1972) finding that the field in which someone considers he can be looked at is much smaller than that in which he considers he can be seen.

If judgments of the direction of a look depend on perceiving the position of
the pupils and irises with respect to the face, the eyes must be perceived as
though they were two directionally oriented "fingers" that point toward a given
object. Such a principle calls for a schema that we might represent as

(70) $(\text{AT}(\text{LOOK}))(x, y)$:   Someone x "looks at" something y if u is the back of x's eyes, v is the pupil of x's eyes, w is a part of y, and:
  (i) $\text{INLINE}(u, v, w)$
  (ii) $\text{DO}(x, S)$
  (iii) $\text{CAUSE}(S, (\text{i}))$

A part of y is the third argument of INLINE so that if y is a large object the relation will hold over an interval of time in which the eyes are directed at different proper parts of y.

Does (70) capture an essential sense of "look"? Certainly it explains why "look" and its associated preposition cannot take complicated complements. Yet it might be argued that looking implies seeing. This implication may hold for some statements, like "I am looking at the frame rather than the picture" or "They spent the morning looking at the Picassos." But it is not invariably true. You can look at something without seeing it. It might also be argued that there should be an intentional component to looking: you look in order to see. Although there is often an intention to see, there often is no such intention. Rather, as a result of looking, you come to perceive whatever you happened to look at. Statements of the form "He accidentally looked at it" are not self-contradictory. These considerations suggest that a basic sense of the verb *is* adequately reflected by an entirely objective set of truth conditions.

Do we need to add anything to (70)? Presumably an observer's eyes must be open and there must be no opaque entity between them and y. Perhaps we need to specify that y must either be illuminated or emit light. A simple way to accommodate these constraints is to replace the INLINE component with a specification that at least part of y is visible to x: $\text{POSSIBLE}(\text{SEE}(x, \text{PART}(w, y)))$. It is also tempting to replace the rather vague causal antecedent, $\text{DO}(x, S)$, with a more specific action, such as $\text{MOVE}(x, x\text{'s eyes})$. But this would be wrong for two reasons. First, an individual may look at something by moving it into line with his eyes rather than by moving his eyes into line with it. Second, and more important, once the eyes have been aligned with an object, the motion may cease, and yet the individual may persist in looking at the object. If the more specific antecedent were adopted, certain temporal information would apply only to the INLINE relation instead of to the routine as a whole. These complications can be avoided by simply using the generic antecedent, $\text{DO}(x, S)$, and we may suppose that in continuing to look at an object an individual continues to do something. $\text{DO}(x, S)$ is sufficient, as Gruber (1967) emphasizes, to establish that "look" denotes a sort of action and can accordingly take manner adverbials and phrases expressing intentions.

We can now write the complete routine for "look at":

(70′) $(\text{AT}(\text{LOOK}))(x, y)$:   Someone x "looks at" something y if u is the back of x's eyes, v is the pupil of x's eyes, w is a part of y, and:
  (i) $\text{INLINE}(u, v, w)$ & $\text{POSSIBLE}(\text{SEE}(x, w))$
  (ii) $\text{DO}(x, S)$
  (iii) $\text{CAUSE}(S, (\text{i}))$

When the verb implies actual seeing, POSSIBLE is omitted from test (i).

The directional component of looking (Gruber, 1967) may take alternative prepositions, as in "He looked toward the house," "He looked up the chimney," "He looked along the corridor." The important distinction is between phrases that specify, as it were, the target of the look ("at the house," "toward the house") and those that simply specify its direction ("up the chimney," "round the corner").

In our view, the conceptual core of vision rests on LOOK and SEE, the first behavioral, the other experiential. There is, however, at least one other verb that might be taken as a third item underlying the field. This is the sense of "look" illustrated in "You look tired to me," "It looks difficult," "He looks keen to fight," "She looks as though she had a good time," "That mountain looks like the Jungfrau." The three verbs can be contrasted in "He was looking at TV when he saw someone who looked familiar." This use of "look" is sometimes called copular because it takes predicate adjectives: "He looked hot" and "He is hot," but not "He looked hotly" or "He is hotly." In this sense "look" is similar to "appear" and "seem," although there are some syntactic differences between them, and, as Austin (1962a, chap. 4) emphasizes, some differences in their usage. Linguists have proposed a variety of derivations of this sense of "look" (see Postal, 1971; Rogers, 1971, 1972), and we will accept that the concept is a derived one, resembling to some extent the converse of SEE. There is, however, an instructive contrast between "The man looked tired to her" and "She saw that the man was tired." The sentence with "look" presupposes the existence of its subject but does not imply that its complement is true—the man may be as fresh as a daisy. The sentence with "see," on the other hand, is referentially opaque; it may fail to refer to an actual man. But if it does refer, it presupposes the truth of its complement. Thus, from negation of the sentence "She didn't see that the man was tired," one is normally entitled to infer that the man was tired.

There is a further constraint on "look" in this context: it can occur only with a complement referring to a stative proposition. It is acceptable to say "The bomb looked to be about to explode" but not "The bomb looked to explode." "Appear" and "seem" can take nonstative propositional complements: "The bomb appeared to explode." This constraint, together with the existential requirement, is presupposed in the routine

(71)   (TO(LOOK))(G(y), x):   Something y "looks" to be G "to" someone x
        if there is something y such that:
        (i) SEE(x, [G(y)])

The function of the brackets is to yield the metalinguistic interpretation of the complement; G(y) is asserted. (This notational convention will be explained in sec. 7.4.)

Rogers (1972) proposes an interesting alternative analysis of this sense of "look," which can be paraphrased in our terms as CAUSE(SEE(x, y), THINK(x, [G(y)])). This has the advantage of accounting for the obvious relation between such sentences as "Harry looked drunk to me" and "My seeing Harry caused me to think that he was drunk." It has the disadvantage of failing to account for the referential transparency of the subject of the verb "look." It is difficult to assess what semantic function is served by THINK in Rogers's analysis, since he does not offer an explicit account of its meaning. However, it would seem that a sentence like "Harry looks drunk to me, but I don't think he's really drunk—he's only acting" receives an inconsistent interpretation on Rogers's analysis: "My seeing Harry causes me to think he's drunk but I don't think he's drunk. . ." The obvious route around this problem is to modify the thinking clause so that it can be paraphrased ". . . think that he appears to be drunk," but this strategem quickly leads to a circular definition " . . . think that he looks drunk." We prefer to avoid a causative approach—indeed, "look" does not incorporate the sorts of adverbial that CAUSE generally allows—and to exploit the fact that SEE can take metalinguistic complements directly. What is generally agreed is that "look" and the other "Psych-movement" verbs— "sound," "smell" (see Postal, 1971)—can be satisfactorily derived from the main perceptual verbs "see," "hear," "smell"; there is no need to postulate a third category of underlying forms.

Only a few verbs fall strictly into the domain of SEE. The majority of these verbs are adequately paraphrased by "catch sight of"—"glimpse," "sight," "spy"—which implies that they involve only a momentary perception: $\text{HAPPEN}_t(\text{SEE}(x, y))$.

One apparent consequence of the stative nature of "see," which it shares with other verbs denoting cognitive states, concerns its collocation with the modal auxiliaries "can" and "could." Consider two examples:

(a) He could have seen the mountain through the mist.
(b) He could see the mountain through the mist.

The sense of the modal in (a) is either "It is possible that he saw the mountain through the mist" or "He would have been able to see the mountain through the mist." This second interpretation, which assumes ability, is clearly counterfactual—it indicates that he did not see the mountain, presumably because he was not there. Sentence (b) is different. Although it too expresses a sense involving ability, the sense involving mere possibility has disappeared and in its place is a meaning expressing observational success: "He saw the mountain through the mist." This paraphrase is not quite accurate, however. The modal auxiliary functions more like a progressive. It is as though its stative quality is borrowed in order to express duration. It is inappropriate to say "He was seeing the mountain," but the sense of this statement is expressed by "He could see the mountain."

Momentary verbs behave in an analogous fashion. Consider the difference between the following sentences:

(a) He could have glimpsed the mountain through the mist.
(b) He could glimpse the mountain through the mist.

The sense of (a) is either "It is possible that he glimpsed the mountain" or "He would have been able to glimpse the mountain." Sentence (b), while expressing the second, admittedly slightly implausible, meaning, loses the first meaning. In its place is an interpretation equivalent to that of the progressive for momentary verbs: "He was catching glimpses of the mountain through the mist."

The verb "sight," as in "He sighted a ship on the horizon," is curiously difficult to analyze. It can usually be paraphrased by "see" together with a locative expression—"He saw a ship on the horizon." As with seeing, sighting need not be veridical: the object of the verb occurs within an opaque context. Thus it is acceptable to say "He sighted a ship on the horizon but it was actually a whale." What does seem to be veridical is the locational information in the prepositional phrase. The observer may be wrong about what he sights, but not about where it is. Sighting thus involves looking at a particular location—usually at some distance—and, since this verb is referentially transparent, the location at least must be veridical. One difficulty of analyzing "*x* sights *y*" is that although the locational information is veridical, it need not be stated. This aspect of the meaning of the verb is perhaps best handled in a presupposition:

(72)   SIGHT(x, y): Someone x who looks at location z "sights" something y at time t if:
         (i) HAPPEN$_t$(SEE(x, y))

Turning to the verbs of looking, we find that some are momentary, like "glance," and others durative, like "stare." This aspectual distinction is reflected in the interpretation of the progressive. "He was glancing at me" suggests a succession of momentary acts, but "He was staring at me" simply denotes a state. Indeed, "stare" seems to be satisfied by an appropriate INLINE relation and does not require any causal act on the part of the observer; it is acceptable to say "His eyes were staring at the door," but it would be odd to say "His eyes were looking at the door."

A number of subsidiary manner components are involved in the verbs of looking. For example, a look can be wide-eyed or narrow-eyed. "Gape" seems to demand that the eyelids be open wide, "peer" that they be narrowed. Another subsidiary component crops up with "peep" and "peek." They suggest that the perceiver is only partly visible from the point of view of the perceived object. Indeed, when an inanimate subject occurs as the subject of these verbs, as in "His tie peeped out from the bottom of his jacket," it is solely this sense of being partially visible that is conveyed.

Certain verbs of looking can be approached from both an objective and a subjective standpoint. This ambivalence is evident in the dictionary, where "gape" is defined as "to stare wonderingly, as with the mouth open." "Gape" evidently reflects a correlation between an emotion and a facial expression, a correlation often observed in the laboratory (Ekman, Friesen, and Ellsworth, 1972). The question of whether to include a mentalistic component in an analysis—whether, for instance, to include a component of wonder in dealing with "gape"—is probably best decided on the criterion of whether its omission would invariably yield erroneous truth conditions. An individual may be said to gape even if one is not privileged to know his state of mind; we opt in this case for an objective analysis. But some facial expressions, such as glaring, are difficult to characterize without recourse to the relevant emotion. A fine distinction might also be drawn between verbs that merely require the appearance of a certain emotion and those that require it, in addition, to be genuinely present. Someone can be said to glare even though he is not really angry, but can he be said to gloat even though he is not really pleased? If there is a reliable distinction here, verbs like "gloat" require a component specifying the agent's actual feelings. Unfortunately, a semantic theory of emotional terms is outside the scope of the present work; however, we will subsequently analyze the appropriate concept of SHOW incorporated in such expressions as "showing anger."

Some of the looking-at verbs are

(73)   glance at $\text{HAPPEN}_t((\text{AT}(\text{LOOK})))(x, y))$
       gaze at $\text{HAPPEN}_i((\text{AT}(\text{LOOK})))(x, y))$
       peep at $(\text{AT}(\text{LOOK}))(x, y) \ \& \ \text{PART}(w, x) \ \& \ \text{LOC}(y, v) \ \&$
                    $\text{FROM}(\text{not}(\text{TO}(\text{VISIBLE})))(w, y), v)$
       gape at $(\text{WITH}_i(\text{DO}))(x, (\text{AT}(\text{LOOK}))(x, y),$
                    $(\text{WIDELY}(\text{OPEN}))(\text{eyes}))$
       peer at $(\text{WITH}_i(\text{DO}))(x, (\text{AT}(\text{LOOK}))(x, y),$
                    $(\text{NARROWLY}(\text{OPEN}))(\text{eyes}))$
       glare at $(\text{AT}(\text{GAZE}))(x, y) \ \& \ \text{ON}((\text{TO}(\text{SHOW}))$
                    $(x, \text{ANGER}, y), x\text{'s face})$

The pattern exemplified by "glare" might also be used with an appropriate substitution of emotional concepts for such verbs as "gloat" and "ogle."

There are occasions, as we have mentioned, where LOOK entails SEE. This option appears to be open for all the verbs in the domain. There are certain verbs, however, that invariably incorporate both LOOK and SEE. The most important are the visual-process verbs, to which we will turn momentarily, but others include "regard" and "behold." The verbs "admire" and "contemplate" demand, in addition, that certain mental states be brought about as a result of the perception, and, once again, their perceptual senses seem to have arisen by the principle of implication from deeper, more conceptual, meanings.

7.3.4   Visual-Process Verbs

Certain verbs involve the concept of a visual process, a sequence of perceptual acts under the control of an observer. "Looking over" a perceptual object is such a process: it requires the eyes to be moved over the object in a more or less continuous fashion so that its major portion is ultimately examined. More precisely, for most of the relevant interval the observer is looking at some part of the object, and most of the object is looked at during this interval. Since both of these conditions raise problems, we will examine them in turn.

The first requirement involves an intentional process of looking at the object; the analysis of "look at" in (70′) allows that a different part of the object may be examined from moment to moment. Strictly speaking, (70′) needs only to be satisfied at most times during the interval; in looking over something you do not have to keep your eyes glued to it. Such an intermittent process raises no problems of principle.

The second requirement relates to an aspectual distinction that can be drawn between "activity" terms, such as "run" and "draw," and "accomplishment" terms, such as "running a mile" and "drawing a circle" (Ryle, 1949; Vendler, 1967). It makes sense to ask "How long did it take you to run a mile?" but it is odd to ask "How long did you run a mile?" (Verkuyl, 1972). But looking over an object (like reading a book) appears to be both an activity and an achievement: it makes sense to ask "How long did it take you to look over the object?" as well as "How long did you look over the object?" It takes a certain time for you to look over an object, but at any moment during this interval it is also true that you are in the process of looking it over. Both conditions demand that the perceptual object have proper parts. The first condition requires that all, or nearly all, be examined at some time or other during the inspection interval; the second requires that at all, or nearly all, moments in the interval, a proper part be in the process of being examined. Since the same time interval is involved in both conditions, we can resort to a simple notational convention to specify both.

What sorts of things can be looked over? The answer seems to be areas, surfaces, and objects. The fact that the examination may involve an exploration carried out on foot or by vehicle, or extensive manipulation of an object, is easily accommodated, since the LOOK schema contains the generic test $DO(x, S)$. The routine for this sense of "look over" is, accordingly,

(74) $(OVER(LOOK))(x, y)$:   Someone x "looks over" a surface or area or
        object y with proper parts $y_1, y_2, \ldots, y_n$ if:
        (i) $HAPPEN_i((INTENTIONALLY(AT(LOOK))))(x, y_i))$

where the subscripted y_i represents the fact that the proper parts $y_1, y_2, \ldots, y_n$ of y are looked at during the process. When the entity that is looked over is an object, "examine" can be used; when it is a surface, "peruse" can be used; and when it is an area, "view" can be used.

An analysis similar to (74) is also required for the process of looking through a set of objects or surfaces:

(75) $(THROUGH(LOOK))(x, y_i)$:   Someone x "looks through" the objects
        or surfaces $y_1, y_2, \ldots, y_n$ if:
        (i) $HAPPEN_i((OVER(LOOK))(x, y_i))$

The analyses of other verbs in the process domain follow in a self-evident manner:

(76)   glance over $\text{HAPPEN}_i((\text{AT}(\text{GLANCE})))(x, y_i))$
          glance through $\text{HAPPEN}_i((\text{OVER}(\text{GLANCE})))(x, y_i))$
          skim $(\text{RAPIDLY}(\text{THROUGH}(\text{GLANCE})))(x, y))$

These process verbs leave open the question of what actual seeing occurred, if any; they also leave open whether the observer had any higher-order intention apart from looking over or looking through the perceptual object. These questions are taken up in the set of verbs to which we now turn.

7.3.5   Intention and Vision

Seeing is not strictly an intentional activity, and consequently the role of intention in the verbs of vision is not simple. It is implicated in at least three ways. First, visual monitoring may be impossible unless you intentionally guide your perceptual system: you act in order to continue looking at a perceptual object ("look at"). Second, you may deliberately prolong an observation in order to see what happens to the perceptual object ("watch for"). Third, you may initiate a series of observations in order to come to be able to see a particular entity ("look for").

The sentence "She watched the man as he crossed the street" conveys the fact that she monitored his progress. This sense is lacking in "She looked at the man as he crossed the street." The way a perceptual system holds a moving object in its field of view is a highly sophisticated matter, but the underlying concept merely involves a process in which the perceiver intentionally looks at and sees the object. The connection between these two processes is not fortuitous; it is the perceiver's intention to see or continue to see the object that guides his actions. Since it is also possible to watch stationary objects, motion of the target is not essential and we may analyze the concept thus:

(77) $\text{WATCH}(x, y)$:   Someone x "watches" something y if:
          (i) $\text{INTEND}(x, \text{HAPPEN}_i(\text{SEE}(x, y)))$
          (ii) $(\text{AT}(\text{LOOK}))(x, y)$
          (iii) $\text{HAPPEN}_i(\text{SEE}(x, y))$
          (iv) $\text{CAUSE}((\text{i}), (\text{ii}))$ & $\text{CAUSE}((\text{ii}), (\text{iii}))$

This schema corresponds to the paraphrase "intentionally look at in order to see." But "watch" often suggests that the observer has an intention over and above the continuance of observation. With animate perceptual objects, this higher-order intention may be to learn what they do; with inanimate perceptual objects, it may be to learn what happens to them. Although an observer may be able to watch a moving object with no particular intention in mind, an intentional component seems to be necessary when the object is stationary. "He watched the house" implies that he watched it for a particular reason, perhaps to see who entered it. This implicit notion is rendered explicit in "He watched for her to leave," where "for" introduces the intended event, which, since it must be referred to nonindicatively, is expressed by an infinitival complement. It is also acceptable to say "He watched for Mary," but that would seem to imply that he was watching for a specific event, maybe for Mary to arrive. A slightly different sort of intention is conveyed by "He watched that Mary reached the other side of the river safely"; we might paraphrase the sentence as "He watched Mary in order to see that she reached the other side of the river safely." In this case the intention was not to see an event but to see that a proposition became true. In short, "watch" inherits the dual function of "see":

(78)   (a) (FOR(WATCH))(x, y, E):   Someone x "watches" something y "for" an event E if:
              (i) INTEND$(x,$ HAPPEN$_t($SEE$(x, E)))$
              (ii) WATCH(x, y)
              (iii) CAUSE$((i), (ii))$
         (b) (THAT(WATCH))(x, S_y):   Someone x "watches that" S_y is the case if:
              (i) INTEND$(x,$ HAPPEN$_t($SEE$(x, [(S_y)])))$
              (ii) WHILE$_t($WATCH$(x, y), S'_y)$
              (iii) CAUSE$((i), (ii))$

What y is doing while it is being watched (described by S'_y) need not be the same as the anticipated observation (described by S_y). You may watch Mary swimming in order to see that she reaches the shore. The sort of analysis in (a) is also appropriate for "spy on": you can spy on a person to see what he does or on an inanimate entity such as a house to see what happens. Higher-order intentions seem to be involved in the verbs "survey," "inspect," and "scrutinize" as well (see Sibley, 1955). Hence

(79)   spy on   (FOR(WATCH))(x, y, E)
         survey   (FOR(VIEW))(x, y, S)
         inspect   (FOR(EXAMINE))(x, y, S)
         scrutinize   (CAREFULLY(INSPECT))(x, y)

There are some instructive points of similarity and contrast between watching for something and searching for something. Both activities are perceptual and are motivated by a higher-order intention to learn something. When you are watching, the target is usually an event or an action, but when you are searching, it is usually an object. Watching is a relatively passive occupation: it involves maintaining the relation of looking at an object or a location; where you look is determined by the movements, if any, of the target. Searching, on the other hand, is a relatively active process: it involves looking over a surface, an area, or a set of objects, and the pattern of search is determined by the observer.

If you search for something you intend in some sense to find it. (Of course, you can find things without looking for them—Picasso remarked in another context, "I do not search, I find.") We encountered a sense of "find" in the verbs of possession (7.2.3) that we derived by implication from its perceptual sense. To find something in this case is to come to see where it is located, that is, to sight it. The perceptual sense of "find" is thus directly related to the control instruction find(x, y).

You can search for something that does not exist. The truth of the statement "Von Schliemann sought the site of Troy," to take Alonzo Church's example, in no way depends on whether there actually was a Troy. The referential opacity of verbs like "seek" and "search for" is a direct consequence of the fact that they permit a speaker to specify an intention—you can intend to do something that is impossible. Certain verbs allow the object of search to remain implicit, as in "He scoured the island," whereas others allow the search domain to remain implicit: "He looked for/sought the treasure." "Search" allows either option: "He searched the island," "He searched for the treasure." Apart from such syntactic differences, there appears to be little difference between these verbs. The schema for "search" captures their essential semantics:

(80) $(\text{FOR}(\text{SEARCH}))(x, z, y)$:   Someone x "searches" something z "for" something y if:
    (i) $\text{INTEND}(x, \text{SIGHT}(x, y))$
    (ii) $(\text{OVER}(\text{LOOK}))(x, z)$
    (iii) $\text{CAUSE}((\text{i}), (\text{ii}))$

This completes our survey of the ways in which intention can be incorporated into verbs of vision, and it completes our analysis of verbs that directly involve vision. We must now consider some domains that emphasize the perceptual object rather than the perceiver.

7.3.6   Objects of Vision

An object is visible if it is possible to see it. Four groups of verbs depend on the concept of visibility. An object can become visible (APPEAR) or can cease to be visible (DISAPPEAR); an agent can act to cause an object to become visible (SHOW) or to cause an object to cease to be visible (HIDE). These paraphrases mask some intricacies that we will attempt to unravel, but our aim is not to offer an exhaustive analysis; rather, we will try to outline the organization of each group with some examples.

Although "appear" has a sense shared with "seem likely," we are concerned here with visual appearances. In that sense, something may appear in two main ways: it may move into your field of vision or it may materialize before your very eyes like Aladdin's genie. In order to make explicit which sense of moving into the field of view is intended it is necessary to specify the appropriate movement. A need for motional specification also occurs in "show up," "emerge," and "surface." A motional sense of "emerge" was paraphrased in 7.1.1 as "travel outward," but we could have paraphrased it as "come out from," where the deictic verb "come" indicates that the speaker-observer is located outside some enclosure within which the object was formerly located.

"Surface," in turn, may be paraphrased as "emerge on the surface of." Our analysis of these verbs in their perceptual senses thus relies on their motional senses as causal antecedents.

A complication arises from the relativity of motion. The perceived object itself may move, or an interposed object may move aside to reveal the object, or the observer may move to a position where an interposed object no longer obstructs his view. For example, "The bus emerged from the fog" may mean that the bus came out of the fog or that the fog moved away to reveal the bus or that the observer moved to a point where the fog no longer obscured the bus. In short, any of the three arguments—observer, perceptual target, or interposed object—may feature in the motional component of the verb.

Since "appear" can also be used in a nonemergent sense, as in "A picture appeared on the screen," we must allow for a more general causal antecedent event, HAPPEN(E). It might be argued that including any sort of causal relation in the verb's schema is a mistake—the verb simply denotes the event of something's becoming visible. Nevertheless, we will include a causal antecedent because the various conditions that it contains seem to us to be well motivated:

(81)   (TO(APPEAR))(x, y):   Something x "appears to" someone y if:
        Either there is something z such that:
        (i) TRAVEL(x) or TRAVEL(y) or TRAVEL(z)
        (ii) notBETWEEN(x, z, y)
        (iii) BEGIN((TO(VISIBLE))(x, y))
        (iv) CAUSE((i), (ii)) & CAUSE((ii), (iii))
        Or there is an event E such that:
        (i) HAPPEN(E)
        (ii) BEGIN((TO(VISIBLE))(x, y))
        (iii) CAUSE(E, (ii))

The verbs "flash," "shine," "gleam," "glimmer," and "glint" are obvious candidates for conveying a specific causal antecedent, HAPPEN(E); if a light flashes, for example, it is possible to see it.

To cause something to be visible is to "show" it. The flexibility as to what can occur as the subject of "show" might lead one to suspect that it has separate meanings where, in fact, the same basic meaning is involved:

(82)   (a) He showed a picture to us on the screen with the projector.
        (b) He showed a picture on the screen with the projector.
        (c) The projector showed a picture on the screen.
        (d) The screen showed a picture.
        (e) A picture showed on the screen.
        (f) A picture showed.

When a perceiver is explicitly mentioned, as in (a), the verb usually requires a human agent to be explicitly mentioned as well. The agent makes it possible for the perceiver to see the perceptual object; other arguments specifying an instrumentality, as in (a)–(d), or a location, as in (a)–(c) and (e), can be added to "show" optionally. Although it is usual for the agent to act intentionally in such circumstances, it is not necessary. We simply assume that he does something:

(83)   (TO(SHOW))((x), w, y):   Someone x "shows" something w "to" someone y if:

   (i) (TO(APPEAR))(w, y)

   (ii) DO(x, S)

   (iii) CAUSE(S, (i))

The causal component (iii) ensures that "show" asserts that the perceptual object was not previously visible. When (iii) is omitted in the absence of an agent and instrumentality, as in (e) and (f), the verb takes on a stative quality more accurately paraphrased as "was apparent on" than as "appeared on"— the assertion is no longer made that the perceptual object was not previously visible. The assertion is a presupposition of the verbs "reveal" and "expose," however. Hence it is only to be expected that "reveal" defines a number of verbs, such as "uncover" and "unveil," that refer to the undoing of specific modes of hiding. In the sentence "The dress revealed her scar" all that is left of (83) is (TO(APPEAR))(scar, y); but going back to (81), the schema for "appear," we can reconstruct

   (i) TRAVEL(dress)

   (ii) notBETWEEN(scar, dress, y)

   (iii) BEGIN((TO(VISIBLE))(scar, y))

   (iv) CAUSE((i), (ii)) & CAUSE((ii), (iii))

or, alternatively, a simple relation between states:

   (ii) notBETWEEN(scar, dress, y)

   (iii) (TO(VISIBLE))(scar, y)

   (iv) CAUSE((ii), (iii))

We can work back from SHOW to SEE by way of two simple relations: to show something is to cause it to be visible, and if something is visible it is possible to see it. "Show" inherits a crucial property of its ancestor: it can take sentential complements, and these complements can refer either to states, processes, and events or to propositions: "He showed her the engine running," "He showed her that the engine was running." The fact that "show" can take such complements makes it appropriate for sentences that concern the visibility of attributes, symptoms, states, indices, processes, events, actions, as well as for the more mundane presentation of pictures on screens, posters on walls, and so forth.

Turning to more specific verbs, we find that some are particularly suitable for the more abstract sorts of presentation since they accommodate sentential complements: reveal, indicate, register, evince, evidence. Others demand a physical arrangement of objects and in consequence cannot accept sentential complements so readily. They are accordingly more suitable for the presentation of tangible objects: expose, exhibit, display. A specialized vocabulary is associated with the projection of pictures; some of these items are borrowed from the motion domain (project, throw), some from other domains (present, screen).

"Disappear" and "vanish" seem to be the only verbs that convey the sense of "cease to be visible"; they can be analyzed as follows:

(84)   (FROM(DISAPPEAR))(x, y):   Something x that is visible to someone y "disappears from" y's view if:
Either there is something z such that:
   (i) TRAVEL(x) or TRAVEL(y) or TRAVEL(z)
   (ii) BETWEEN(x, z, y)
   (iii) END((TO(VISIBLE))(x, y))
   (iv) CAUSE((i), (ii)) & CAUSE((ii), (iii))
Or there is an event E such that:
   (i) HAPPEN(E)
   (ii) END((TO(VISIBLE))(x, y))
   (iii) CAUSE(E, (ii))

One point of contrast between (81) and (84): "disappear" presupposes that the object was previously visible, whereas "appear" merely asserts that the object was previously not visible. This difference may explain why it is customary to talk of an object's disappearing from someone's view but not of an object's appearing to someone's view. Nevertheless, the modes in which an object may disappear are simple opposites of the modes in which it may appear: an object may disappear because it, the observer, or something else moves or because it "dematerializes" within the field of view. Not many English verbs convey such senses; "submerge," for instance, is an unusual way to indicate that an object has disappeared.

The extent to which "hide" parallels "show" is brought out by comparing the sentences in (82) with

(85)   (a) He hid the thimble from us with a handkerchief.
        (b) He hid the thimble with a handkerchief.
        (c) A handkerchief hid the thimble from us.
        (d) A handkerchief hid the thimble.

It is often true that if someone hides something he does so intentionally, but a sentence like "He accidentally hid the picture" is acceptable. It could mean that he acted unwittingly as a screen or that he was unaware that it was a picture that he was hiding; it could also mean that in putting the picture somewhere he was unaware that he was hiding it. The most prudent course, as with "show," is not to include an intentional component:

(86)   (FROM(HIDE))((x), w, y): Someone x "hides" something w "from" someone y if:
   (i) (FROM(DISAPPEAR))(w, y)
   (ii) DO(x, S)
   (iii) CAUSE(S, (i))

If there is no explicit agent, as in (85c), all that remains is (i) (FROM(DIS-
APPEAR))(thimble, y), but by retracing our steps to the schema for "disappear"
we can reconstruct

    (i) TRAVEL(handkerchief)
   (ii) BETWEEN(thimble, handkerchief, y)
  (iii) END((TO(VISIBLE))(thimble, y))
  (iv) CAUSE((i), (ii)) & CAUSE((ii), (iii))

or, alternatively, a causal relation between states:

  (ii) BETWEEN(thimble, handkerchief, y)
 (iii) not(TO(VISIBLE))(thimble, y)
 (iv) CAUSE((ii), (iii))

It should be noted that "hide" can take conventional locatives, as in "He hid
the jewels in his house." Indeed, "He hid the thimble behind the mirror" may
be construed as "His hiding of the thimble took place behind the mirror," as
well as in the more obvious sense of "His putting the thimble behind the
mirror hid it."

The most general senses of hiding are conveyed by "hide" and "conceal."
A number of agentive verbs, like "secrete" and "cache," require an intentional
act of putting the object somewhere: (INTENTIONALLY(AT(PUT)))(x, w, z). Another hierarchy of verbs singles out the idea of moving something between an
object and its potential perceiver (screen) and the idea that the screen touches
the object (cover) and the idea of still more specific constraints (cloak, shroud,
mask, veil, bury).

With some grammatical subjects of "hide" a separate sense emerges, as in
"Darkness hid the ghastly scene." Here there is a causal meaning but no animate agent; what is involved is a lack of visibility due to a lack of light. Certain
verbs refer explicitly to a lack of illumination (obfuscate, darken, dim, bedim,
shade, shadow, eclipse), but they may also be used by implication in a perceptual sense. "A cloud darkened the mountain" means literally that a cloud
came between the mountain and a source of light, causing the light to be cut
off. It takes on a perceptual meaning from the implication that this event in
turn caused it to be difficult to see the mountain distinctly: the cloud hid the
light from the mountain and thereby hid the mountain from the perceiver.
"The cloud obscured the mountain" can be analyzed in terms of "partially
hid"; "hide" and "obscure" are alike in that they both convey a sense involving lack of illumination as well as the more general sense. They differ, however, in that "obscure" is only partial hiding. This concept occurs in a number
of more specific verbs (befog, becloud, haze over, blur, fog, cloud, mist).

Verbs such as "disguise" and "camouflage" seem initially to resemble "hide."
The meaning of "He disguised the diamonds," for example, means essentially
that he carried out some action on the diamonds, changing them in some way,
with the intention that they should thereby be no longer recognizable as diamonds. We represent this meaning thus:

(87)   DISGUISE(x, y):   Someone x "disguises" something y if:
  (i)   INTEND$(x,$ notRECOGNIZE(anyone, $y, y))$
  (ii)   DO(x, S)
  (iii)   CHNG(y)
  (iv)   CAUSE((i), (ii)) & CAUSE(S, (iii))

The main reason for distinguishing "disguise" from "hide" is that it does not contain within its meaning a successful outcome. If something is disguised, it may nevertheless be immediately recognized for what it is; if something is hidden, by definition it cannot be seen until it is uncovered or removed from its hiding place.

7.3.7   Verbs of Other Perceptual Modalities

Only a handful of perceptual verbs concern audition. On first consideration the distinction between "listen" and "hear" seems to be parallel to the distinction between "look" and "see": "listen" denotes an action and behaves like action verb, taking manner adverbials; "hear" is a stative predicate denoting a psychological relation and does not take manner adverbials. Other languages also respect this distinction in the auditory domain: "oir" and "escuchar" in Spanish; "entendre" and "écouter" in French; "dâyyin" and "faŋ" in Thai; "tīngjyàn" and "tīng" in Chinese (Scovel, 1971).

On closer consideration, however, the parallel between modalities does not run entirely true (Rogers, 1971; Miller, 1974b). If you look at something you do not necessarily see it, but if you listen to something you hear it. We can construe listening as doing something that causes you to hear. Looking is a directional activity and presumes a space in which entities are located, whereas listening is only indirectly spatial. For example, in looking for something you are apt to scan the scene, to move around in search of the desired object, but in listening for something you are apt to wait quietly with your attention concentrated on what you hear. Rogers (1971) suggests that the differences between "look" and "listen" relate to physiology: if people had highly directional ears and an ability to close them with earlids, hearing would entail listening, and if people had omnidirectional vision and no eyelids, looking would entail seeing. We will reserve judgment, since Rogers does not take account of the nonveridical aspect of perceptual verbs. A more critical distinction between visual and auditory verbs (at least in English) is in the interpretation of simple direct objects. The statement "He heard an airplane" can be closely paraphrased as "He heard the sound of an airplane." As many philosophers have observed (Bouwsma, 1942, for example), no comparable paraphrase of "He saw an airplane" exists. Warnock (1967) comments on this point:

> There is . . . no common noun associated with the verb 'see' in the way in which the common nouns 'sound,' 'taste,' 'smell,' are familiarly associated with the verbs 'hear,' 'taste,' 'smell.' And this suggests the question: why not? Is this just a fact about the world—the

fact that, when I look for something that, in seeing my hand, functions as the sound does when I hear a car, there is, straightforwardly, no such thing? Or is it perhaps a fact about my senses—the fact that the sense differs in just this way, in human beings, from the sense of hearing? Or again, is it perhaps a mere accident of vocabulary that, in the vocabulary of vision, this billet has been left unoccupied? Or might it not rather be a conceptual truth that, our concept of an object being what it is, there is no room, as it were, between the seer and the seen, for visual "intermediaries" on the analogy of sounds and smells? (P. 6)

As a matter of fact, there are two nouns that fill Warnock's billet: "What he saw had the look of a weather balloon," "He had seen the sight of a Mirandian sunrise." The crucial point is that speakers do not ordinarily utilize this way of talking about their perceptions. The logic of a sentence of the form "He heard the sound of an airplane" is referentially transparent; but a claim is made about the sound, not about its source. Such claims are likely in the domain of sounds, tastes, and smells because these modalities are so impoverished linguistically that a perceiver would be hard pressed to establish a thoroughgoing model of the world from any one of them alone. Verbs of seeing presuppose a spatial manifold, and therefore locative prepositions denoting spatial relations are appropriate to them. Hence there is a contrast in the acceptability of "He could see into the cup" and "He could hear into the cup," or of "He looked about the room" and "He listened about the room." Evidently hearing and listening are only derivatively spatial. Strawson (1959) argues that audition, unaided by other modalities, would be insufficient to establish the existence of particular individuals, distinguishable one from another, located within a spatiotemporal framework. In other words, your model of the external world, insofar as it is perceptually based, derives primarily from what you see; what you hear, feel, and smell is compatible with such a world. But any attempt to base a model solely on the nonvisual modalities would be likely to fail to establish a spatial framework. It would have been most incongruous, for instance, if G. E. Moore (1959) had sought to demonstrate the reality of the external world by listening to the sound of his voice as opposed to looking at his hands. Ultimately it is the nature of sights and sounds that influences both physiology and the semantics of perceptual verbs.

The distinction between action and perception, realized in "look," "see," and "listen," "hear," is even less important in the remaining perceptual modalities. "Taste," "feel," and "smell" can be interpreted in either way. Everyday language recognizes two other senses, pain and bodily orientation. The perceptual verbs for pain are "ache," "hurt," and "pain," and there are verbs both for causing pain ("sting," "burn") and for alleviating it ("soothe," "anesthetize"). Bodily orientation, however, seems to be considered only when absent—when someone is (perceptually) "dizzy," "giddy," or "unbalanced." Proprioception seems to have no lexical representation suitable for ordinary discourse.

7.4   THE LANGUAGE OF COMMUNICATION

A large subdivision of the English lexicon supports talk about talking. The number of verbs it includes runs into the hundreds, and many others can be pressed into metaphorical service: "He really gave it to them," "The lawyer built a strong case," "She doubted that you were there." In order to hold our exploration of the semantics of linguistic communication to a manageable size, we will concentrate on speech as the primary medium. We will consider less than a dozen important domains and offer only sketches of some subdomains. These economies are forced not merely by the size of this lexical field but also by the fact that it is virtually a microcosm of the language as a whole.

As we have noted, there are a few underlying semantic components, like CAUSE and INTENTION, that cross-classify with such core concepts as TRAVEL, POSSESS, and SEE to yield semantic fields. Verbs of communication are organized in a similar way: a number of underlying components related to a language cross-classify with one another. The conceptual core seems to be a group of concepts that relate various aspects of communicating: uttering, expressing, meaning, addressing, understanding, knowing, and so on. A variety of aspects of linguistic communication can be incorporated in the meaning of a single verb: the physical character of an utterance, its meaning, its general topic, its expressive function, the sort of discourse in which it occurs. For example, "say," which seems intuitively to represent the whole field, may also be construed as contrasting with at least three entirely different sets of lexical items represented by "sing," "ask," and "deny." Since a typical lexical item is likely to cut across a number of aspects, we will often have to postpone for later analysis one or another component of a verb's meaning.

Our strategy will be to concentrate on the central component of each domain as we come to it. We will begin with verbs that denote the physical process of uttering sounds. Apart from specifying the speaker and what he says, verbs of speaking can take a number of additional arguments. In 7.4.2 we will treat two arguments of special importance: the audience and the location of an utterance within its context. An utterance can be reported in either direct or indirect quotation and, as 7.4.3 will make clear, both forms raise tricky linguistic problems. Only after we have offered some tentative solutions to them can we consider illocutionary force and the fundamental distinctions between statements, questions, and commands. Then we will consider verbs that characterize conversations and will close with a brief analysis of explicitly metalinguistic terms.

The field of communication verbs is much more complex than the three fields we have discussed so far. Workers who have seriously puzzled over the complex (and largely unresolved) linguistic, semantic, and logical questions posed by various verbs of communication will almost certainly find our treatment cavalier or wrongheaded at critical points. Our purpose, however, is to put forward a general description of this field that will illustrate the possibili-

ties offered by a procedural theory and provide a basis for further psycholinguistic studies. If we are successful, later work should rectify our mistakes,
both of commission and of omission.

7.4.1   Verbs of Uttering

One of the control instructions introduced in chapter 3 was utter(w),
which was said to be analogous to a computer instruction to print out the
contents of memory location w. This control operation is related to the notion
conveyed by the verb "utter," but we must be careful in specifying it; the schema
representing the verb should not be allowed to cause an utterance. What is
required is a transition from the control instruction utter(w) to the lexical
concept UTTER(x, W). Presumably the decisive psychological difference involves an appreciation that other individuals experience the world and act on
it in the same way as oneself—a difference represented in UTTER by the addition of the argument x, which can point to other persons. Thus utter(w) requires that the sounds indexed by w be uttered by the system executing the
instruction, whereas UTTER(x, W) represents the concept of an arbitrary individual, indexed by x, uttering the sounds W. In short, UTTER(x, W) is true if
and only if individual x executes the control instruction utter(w) and the content of w is W. The evidence that x has executed this instruction is that sounds
emerge from his mouth. Since UTTER depends on a control instruction, it has
the status of an activity—so too do all its dependents. The following paraphrase makes explicit the active, causative nature of the concept:

(88)   UTTER(x, W):   DO(x, S) & CAUSE(S, ((FROM(EMERGE))(W, x))).

Both human beings and animals can utter sounds that are not linguistic.
Some of the verbs that describe these vocal activities ("weep," "giggle") are
sometimes used metaphorically to refer to linguistic acts, but they are at best
on the periphery of the communicative lexical field. More interesting is the
set of intransitive "barnyard" verbs that characterize animal communication:
baa, bray, cuckoo, gaggle, mew, miaou, moo, quack, whinny, yelp. Their origin is usually onomatopoeic (within the constraints of English phonology);
such words have received much attention in speculations about the origins of
language. Their schemata can be represented by a couple of examples:

MOO(x):   UTTER(x, low-pitched(resonant(/mu/))),

where x denotes a cow, or

BAA(x):   UTTER(x, high-pitched(nasal(intermittent/ba/))),

where x denotes a sheep.

We assume in these schemata that listeners are equipped with perceptual
tests to distinguish a number of auditory contrasts: high-pitched or low-
pitched, continuous or intermittent, loud or soft. Such tests have not been
characterized, but there is no reason to suppose that they could not be accommodated by the sorts of predicates given in chapter 2.

Barnyard verbs occasionally take human subjects, in which case they suggest that a human being is imitating or behaving in a fashion similar to the normal subject. That they do not usually have a human subject is borne out by the fact that they do not allow reference to propositional content. For instance, "The queen mooed to the reporters" does not mean that she conveyed any sensible message; "The queen mooed something to the reporters" is almost as bizarre as "The queen mooed that the cost of living had outpaced her income."

In addition to mere noises, human beings utter words; phoneticians, psychologists, and kindred workers have convincingly established the peculiar sensitivity of the human perceptual system to speech sounds (Liberman et al., 1967). There is evidence for differential perception of speech as opposed to nonspeech sounds (Crowder, 1972), including hemispheric differences in the perception of the two sorts of sounds (Shankweiler and Studdert-Kennedy, 1967).

Not every sequence of sounds that conforms to the rules of English phonology and morphology is an English word. An individual can determine that an arbitrary sequence *could* be a word in English, but he can only identify it if there is an entry (or partial entry) in his semantic memory. Ignoring any difficulties in retrieval, or the fact that complex words may be derived from root morphemes, we can define a word informally thus: a string of sound segments with a suprasegmental patterning, $/ \ldots /$, is a word if and only if there is a positive outcome to an operation of the form find (M(Sem), $/ \ldots /$). We will not attempt to go beyond this informal working definition, plainly restricted to a given speaker.

With the exception of barnyard terms, utterance verbs characteristically take human subjects and their objects produce an instance of a word or sound ("He uttered 'shibboleth' ") or else refer to what was uttered ("He uttered the password"). Since this referential distinction is important, we will use W as a variable that ranges over actual sounds (or marks on paper) in a reported utterance and w as a variable that ranges over symbols referring to the reported utterance.

We will say that in producing an instance of a word or sound in such contexts a speaker names it. Thus, in naming a sound a speaker simply reproduces it. If we let w be the pointer assigned to W:

(88′)   UTTER(x, W):   Someone x "utters" W if it is true of x:
         (i) assign(w, W) & HAPPEN$_t$(utter(w))

In referring to a sound a speaker has all the referential resources of the language at his disposal, which we may represent by the concept REFER (to which we will return in 7.4.8). If we let w stand for a term referring to a sound W:

(89)   UTTER(x, w):   Someone x "utters" w if:
         (i) (TO(REFER))(w, W) & UTTER(x, W)

Both (88′) and (89) can be taken to include the case where a series of sounds or words are uttered.

UTTER can be incorporated in verbs that specify particular aspects of what is actually uttered. A major distinction is between verbs (like "shout to," "whisper to") that entail that words are uttered and those (like "bark," "roar," and, perhaps, "shout at") that do not. It is odd to say "He roared to the plumber," but the sentence is rectified (Zwicky, 1971a) by introducing a direct object that refers explicitly to a verbal message: "He roared his orders to the plumber." On the other hand, there is nothing odd about "He shouted to the plumber"; an explicit reference to a message is unnecessary because it is implicit in the meaning of "shout to."

The issue is complicated by verbs like "gibber," "jabber," and "babble." Onomatopoeic in origin, they convey a notion of rapid, unintelligible speech— speech that is perhaps foreign and appears too rapid to be intelligible. There is accordingly something odd about "The general gibbered that the Russians were coming"; if his utterance was gibberish, how was it understood? Once again it makes better sense to introduce a direct object: "The general gibbered something to the effect that the Russians were coming." It should be noted that when someone uses "gibber" to mean that the speech was incomprehensible to him, it was not necessarily incomprehensible to others. The acceptability of such sentences as "They gibber French at him all day, but he understands it, of course" demonstrates the point.

Another major distinction between verbs of uttering concerns the acoustic or phonetic characteristics of the utterance. It may be voiced, as in "speak," or unvoiced, as in "whisper"; if it is voiced, it may be musical, as in "sing"; and so on. We could capture this set of verbs in a decision table, but for the sake of readability we will merely sketch their schemata.

"Speak" entails that words are uttered; we assume that such utterances are intentional. "Speak" does not allow the spoken words to be directly named; they must be referred to. Thus "He spoke 'April is the cruellest month' " is unacceptable, but the problem is rectified in "He spoke the words 'April is the cruellest month' " or "He spoke the first line of a poem." Since it is possible to speak in a whisper or to speak with a shout, the only other constraint is that in speaking, the sounds are not musical:

(90)   SPEAK(x, w): Someone x "speaks" w if w refers to some words W and:
    (i) (INTENTIONALLY(UTTER))(x, w)
    (ii) notMUSIC(W)

The same pattern of reference is found in the contrasting verb "sing":

(91)   SING(x, w): Someone x "sings" w if w refers to some words W and:
    (i) (INTENTIONALLY(UTTER))(x, w)
    (ii) VOICED(W)
    (iii) MUSIC(W)

Direct quotation is possible, however, in the case of "whisper" and "shout":

(92)   WHISPER(x, w) or WHISPER(x, W): Someone x "whispers" w or some words W, where w refers to W, if:
     (i) SPEAK(x, w)
     (ii) notVOICED(W)

(93)   SHOUT(x, w) or SHOUT(x, W): Someone x "shouts" w or some words W, where w refers to W, if:
     (i) SPEAK(x, w)
     (ii) LOUD(W)

Other verbs of utterance evolve from these schemata: bawl, call, chant, croon, holler, mumble, murmur, mutter, yell.

Many of these verbs have emotional overtones. Their flexibility is indicated by the variety of syntactic constructions into which they can enter. (We hope to support the conjecture of Zwicky, 1971a, that many of these constructions are predictable from their semantic characteristics.) A typical set of constructions is

> He roared.
> He roared with laughter.
> He roared my name.
> He roared "It's late."
> He roared to us that it was forbidden.
> He roared for them to go.
> He roared at the man to get out of the way.

Evidently, "roar" incorporates UTTER; the utterance is loud and resembles the noises made by wild animals. But it can also suggest that the utterance expresses anger. Just what emotion each of these verbs expresses is often difficult to determine: they implicate emotions rather than convey them definitely. Nevertheless, there is something odd about such sentences as "He growled with happiness," "He hissed for joy," "He cackled with boredom." We make no definitive claims about the emotions associated with these verbs but will try to illustrate how they might be analyzed. For example, the intransitive verb "roar" calls for a specification of the physical aspects of the sound:

(94)   ROAR(x): Someone x "roars" if:
     (i) UTTER(x, W)
     (ii) VOICED(W) & LOUD(W) & (LOW(PITCHED))(W) &
         VOCALIC(W) & CONSONANTAL(W)
     (iii) SIMILAR(W, /r/ of wild animal)

Each of these tests has a function. A roar is loud, low-pitched, and both vocalic and consonantal. It is, or resembles, the cry of a wild animal. Transitive "roar" takes complements referring to the content of utterances; the resemblance to an animal sound is construed more metaphorically and the verb indicates that x was probably expressing anger:

     (iv) EXPRESS(x, ANGRY(x)).

The concept of expression is related to the perceptual notion "show": to express one's feelings, like showing them, is to do something that makes it possible for someone else to perceive them. It is also possible to express thoughts, beliefs, suspicions. If someone expresses his thoughts to an audience he does something that makes it possible for the audience not merely to perceive them but to know them. Hence the concept of expression involves knowledge. A complete analysis would take us well beyond the confines of language. However, since such verbs as "verbalize," "vocalize," "voice," and "air" seem to refer to putting thoughts or feelings into words, we can simply divide up the sorts of entities that are expressible into propositional attitudes and emotional states. A propositional attitude is typically reported with a sentential "that" complement; thoughts, beliefs, and judgments can be described in an indirect quotation. Emotions, on the other hand, have no propositional content. An individual may be angry with something or because of something, but his anger itself is devoid of propositional content. It is simply a state of the organism that, like any other emotion, can be described with a nominal construction:

(95) $(\text{TO}(\text{EXPRESS}))(x, y, z)$: Someone x "expresses" something y that x feels "to" someone z if:
    (i) $\text{DO}(x, \text{S})$
    (ii) $\text{CAUSE}(\text{S}, \text{POSSIBLE}(\text{KNOW}(z, \text{FEEL}(x, y))))$

The general pattern of the analysis of ROAR in (94) appears to be common to other onomatopoeic verbs that allow the transition from animal to human utterance. They are summarized in table 7.1, with the emotions characteristically conveyed by each verb.

Other manner-of-speaking verbs take their meaning from fundamental biological states: "squeal" usually expresses pain, "pant" expresses breathlessness, and so on. These verbs incorporate a physical characterization of the utterance and can be used to express an associated emotion after the fashion of onomatopoeic verbs:

(96) $\text{SQUEAL}(x)$: Something x "squeals" if:
    (i) $\text{UTTER}(x, W)$
    (ii) $\text{VOICED}(W)$ & $\text{LOUD}(W)$ & $(\text{HIGH}(\text{PITCHED}))(W)$ & $\text{VOCALIC}(W)$

A causal component may be included:

    (iii) $\text{CAUSE}(\text{FEEL}(x, \text{PAIN}), (\text{i}))$

But since "The children squealed with joy" is not anomalous to most people, condition (iii) need not include PAIN. Indeed, since a person can squeal without being in any sort of emotional state, it may be a mistake to build a causal component directly into the schema of the verb. Like the components of the onomatopoeic verbs that characterize resemblance to animal cries, this component is even less pertinent when a verb is used transitively—it tends to be replaced by

Table 7.1 Onomatopoeic manner-of-speaking verbs.

Verb	Sound characteristics					Animal with similar sound	Emotion expressed
	Loud	High-pitched	Momentary	Vocalic	Consonantal		
roar, growl, snarl, bellow	+	−		+	+	Wild animal	Anger
bark, snap	++	−	+	+	+	Dog	Anger
howl	+			+	−	Dog	Anger, sadness
grunt, snort		−	+	+	+	Hog	Disapproval
purr	−	−	−	+	+	Cat	Satisfaction
bleat, bray			−	+	−	Sheep	Nervousness
twitter	−	+	+	−	+	Bird	Nervousness
chirp	−	+	−	−	+	Bird	Amusement
coo	−	+		+	−	Bird	Satisfaction
cackle, chuckle, chortle			−	+	+	Bird	Amusement
squawk, croak			+	+	+	Bird	Dissatisfaction
hiss				−	+	Snake	Disapproval

an explicit component specifying a characteristic emotion. The biological verbs are summarized in table 7.2.

7.4.2 Arguments of Speaking

We know from our discussion of verbs of motion (sec. 7.1) that the relation of a traveling object to its goal is conventionally represented in a phrase of the form "to" + NP. Since speaking is both physically and metaphorically (Gruber, 1965) a transmission of a message *from* a source *to* a goal, a speaker's audience is likely to be specified in a phrase of the form "to" + NP.

But who is a speaker's audience? The question arises because, as we saw in the discussion of personal pronouns in 4.5.2, a speaker may have a dual audience: (a) his addressee, to whom he directs the utterance, and (b) others who hear it but to whom he is not speaking directly. This division of the total audience is important when imperatives or interrogatives are involved—there must be some way to indicate who should obey or reply. Consequently, there is an elaborate social code for identifying the addressee, involving direction of regard, loudness of utterance, explicit terms of address, identifying descriptions of the addressee that may or may not be known to the others, shared interest in the topic, communication of information known to the others but not to the addressee, and so on. Rules for addressing are part of the complex conventions governing order of speaking in conversational groups. Requests, questions, greetings, and offers are initial members of utterance pairs; when accompanied by an addressing expression or implicature they select the addressed person as having the next conversational turn. If some other listener responds inappropriately, the speaker may say "I wasn't speaking to you," which suggests that "speak to" selects the addressee, not the total audience.

We will therefore introduce the concept ADDRESS(x, y). Its schema will not be explicated, but it would include the various rules of address conventional in the speaker's social group. We do not assume that the y addressed must be a human being; a speaker can follow the rules in addressing infrahuman or even inanimate objects. And we assume something can be addressed without being spoken to; it can be addressed in writing, in song, in gesture. Given ADDRESS, the schema for "speak to" follows simply:

(97)   (TO(SPEAK))(x, y):   Someone x "speaks to" someone y if:
      (i) SPEAK(x, w)
      (ii) CAUSE((i), POSSIBLE(HEAR(y, W)))
      (iii) ADDRESS(x, y)

A speaker may address his utterances "to" an audience and, on occasion, he may address them "at" or "in the direction of" an audience. It is sometimes argued (Gruber, 1965; Zwicky, 1971a) that this contrast between indirect object and directional adverbial is related to the presence or absence of propositional content. For example, "She shouted at the boy" seems to be neutral be-

Table 7.2 Biologically based manner-of-speaking verbs.

Verb	Sound characteristics				Biological cause	Emotion expressed
	Loud	High-pitched	Voiced	Momentary		
cry, wail	+	+	+		Pain	Sadness, anger
scream, shriek, screech	++	++	++		Pain	Anger, fear
squeal	++	++	++		Pain	Dissatisfaction
whine		++	+	−	Pain	Dissatisfaction
groan, moan		−	+		Pain	Sadness, dissatisfaction
whimper, sob	−	−	−		Pain	Sadness
sigh			−		Fatigue	Sadness, relief
gasp			−	+	Breathlessness	Surprise
pant			−	−	Breathlessness	Excitement
titter, giggle		+	+	−	Nervousness	Amusement

tween shouting inarticulate sounds and shouting a definite insult, order, or whatever, whereas "She shouted to the boy" means that she attempted to communicate a message of some sort. According to Zwicky, there is a similar contrast between "The neighbors moaned 'Futz' " and "The neighbors moaned 'Futz' to me." Unfortunately, the semantic distinction does not correlate perfectly with the syntactic distinction. An indirect-object construction does not always indicate communication of content: "They hummed a wordless dirge to me," "The monkeys jabber to me all day long." And an "at" phrase is sometimes associated with the communication of content: "They shouted at him that he was trespassing," "He bellowed at me to get out of the room." The distinction seems to be related to the contrast between "He came to me with an umbrella" and "He came at me with an umbrella." Both expressions entail motion, but the choice of "at" indicates a violation of an individual's personal space, of his personal region. A similar sort of aggression on the part of the shouter is evinced in the contrast between "He shouted to me to get out of the way" and "He shouted at me to get out of the way." This supposition is supported by an increase in the acceptability of, say, "He spoke the words at me" when a suitable adverbial is introduced: "He spoke the words aggressively at me." Such views are speculative, however, and we will not attempt to specify a schema for "speak at."

Another specialized argument of "speak" is a kind of locative phrase. Locatives indicating where a speech act occurred ("He spoke in the courtroom") introduce nothing novel, but the total speech act itself provides another relatum for locative relations: "He spoke a few words of welcome in his opening speech." These locatives, such as "during z" or "at the end of z," locate events in time and must be construed temporally: DURING(SPEAK(x, w), z).

In summary, two kinds of arguments can be appended to verbs of speaking: one specifies the addressee, the other the location of the utterance. Describing the utterance, however, may be more important than either of these matters. We have noted in passing the difference between the direct naming of sounds (or words) and indirect reference to them; we turn now to an analogous distinction in referring to the meaning of an utterance.

7.4.3   Direct and Indirect Quotation

The metalinguistic nature of the language of communication is perhaps best illustrated by verbs that allow speech to be reported. A report may take the form of either direct or indirect quotation, and many verbs permit both forms. For example:

> The wizard said "My spell is working."   (direct)
> The wizard said that his spell was working.   (indirect)

In general, any verb that allows direct quotation also allows indirect quotation, but the converse is not true; verbs like "state" are not used to make direct quotations. However, if the direct quotation precedes the verb, the range of acceptable verbs is much wider. Indeed, the range extends to the ridiculous, as bad novelists demonstrate in their quest for elegant variation: " 'Haven't we met before?' he smiled. 'Yes!' she swooned."

It is sometimes claimed that *spoken* English has no simple and explicit way to indicate direct quotation (Partee, 1973). A speaker may use such clumsy locutions as "quote . . . unquote" or a parenthetical "and I quote" or state explicitly that his report is verbatim. These conventions suggest that direct quotation is a sophisticated device, probably literary in origin. Yet intonation can give strong indications of direct quotation in colloquial speech, and there is at least one simple semantic indication that exploits the deictic nature of personal pronouns. Sometimes a whole dialogue is reconstructed: "I said to him you can't do that and he said who are you to tell me I can't? and I said who do I have to be? and he said . . . " The contrast between "I said to him" and the following "you" immediately suggests that the speaker is using direct quotation; the impression is confirmed by subsequent contrasts of the same sort and by the use of questions following immediately after "said." (In certain dialects the use of the present tense—"He says to me"—signals direct quotation; presumably it enhances the immediacy of the "dialogue.") It is not that speech has no devices for indicating direct quotation but merely that it has no impersonal (nondeictic) devices. Perhaps direct quotation is not so sophisticated after all.

Direct quotation presents a problem because it is not obvious how to specify the structure of a sentence such as "He said 'I'm leaving.' " It might be argued that just as barnyard verbs are analyzed as strings of sounds, so the underlying representation of this sentence should contain a phonemic transcription of "I'm leaving." But, as Partee (1973) points out, this phonological solution does not handle connections between the quoted and unquoted parts: "He said 'I'm leaving,' but he didn't."

The problem is also apparent in quotations of foreign phrases. In a sentence like "The Italian said 'Sto male,' but I didn't understand it," the phonological solution seems apt. But in a sentence like "The Italian said 'Sto male,' but I knew he was really quite well," some semantic connection must be established between the Italian quotation and the English comment.

The structure of quoted sentences cannot be specified in the usual transformational way, since that solution does not tie down their actual surface form: "He said 'I rang the girl up' " and "He said 'I rang up the girl' " cannot both be true. Partee suggests that one solution to the problem is to borrow from Davidson's (1969) analysis of demonstratives and to treat a quotation as a separate sentence on the lines of

He said this.   I am leaving.

The relations between quotation and comment would then be comparable to those between two contiguous utterances in a discourse; such an approach might satisfy a logician or linguist when carried through in detail. For a psycholinguist, however, there is an alternative possibility.

Suppose Alice says to her husband, "I said to my boss you can't do that." If this is an instance of direct quotation, "you" refers to Alice's boss; if it is indirect quotation, "you" refers to Alice's husband. A listener will usually be able to determine from intonation, context, or both which reference is intended. If the utterance occurs in an account of an argument between Alice and her boss, it is probably direct; if it occurs as part of an argument between Alice and her husband, it is probably indirect. Suppose the context makes clear that it is a direct quotation: "I said to my boss, 'You can't do that.'" If the husband is a competent speaker of English, able himself to use either direct or indirect quotation, he will be able to reinterpret deictic elements in a direct quotation in a manner appropriate to the circumstances surrounding its original utterance. That is to say, he will first translate Alice's report into a form that might be paraphrased as "*A* said *W* to *B*," where *W* is the quotation "You can't do that"; then he will translate *W* into something like notPERMISSIBLE (DO(*B*, S)), where, given the circumstances, *B* is a pointer to Alice's boss and S is what *B* shouldn't do. The combined result will be something like "*A* said notPERMISSIBLE (DO(*B*, S)) to *B*," which is equivalent to an indirect quotation: "Alice said to her boss that he shouldn't S."

According to this account, a speaker who uses direct quotation leaves more of the interpretive work to his listener. He may do so because that creates a more vivid impression of what it was like to have participated in the original discourse or because it is important that the discourse be repeated verbatim— it may be a vehicle by which a message that one person finds incomprehensible reaches another who can understand it. The only limitations on direct quotation are set by the memory and the imitative (or phonetic) skills of the reporter; it is not essential that he understand what he is repeating. If he does understand it, he can introduce semantic relations between the quotation and his comment on it.

Since direct quotation crops up throughout the field, we will suggest a routine for it as part of a more general schema for SAY. It will be a simple variation on SPEAK, complicated only by the fact that we want to accommodate such cases as "The poster says '...'" or "The rule says '...'" That is, we want to allow "say" to take inanimate grammatical subjects when it is used to report writing. The grammatical subject may refer either to a concrete thing ("The signpost says 'Ten miles to London'") or to an abstract entity ("The poem says 'We must love one another or die'").

This difference between concrete and abstract grammatical subjects seems to be related to the difference between direct and indirect quotation; it hinges on whether a speaker is making a literal report or a propositional report. Indirect quotation can be used only to make propositional statements, but direct quotation can be used to make either literal or propositional statements. Reported speech may be ambiguous between the two interpretations of direct quotation: if a person's speech is being reported, a propositional interpretation is more likely, but if a parakeet's speech is being reported, a literal interpretation is more likely. In reported writing, if the grammatical subject is an abstract entity, it will be a propositional statement and if the subject is an inanimate, concrete object, it will be a literal statement. (A few nouns, like "newspaper," serve a double function, denoting either abstract or concrete entities.)

Literal reports are simply repetitions of an actual set of words, which may have been spoken or written. They require direct quotation and may concern any sort of utterance, departing in the wildest ways imaginable from English. Propositional reports, even when made in direct quotations, go beyond a mere statement of words. In our view, when someone makes a propositional report he attributes to the original source a particular semantic competence: the source knew the meaning of what he was saying. If someone is in a coma, or has been totally misled about the meaning of expressions in a foreign language, we should be reluctant to make a propositional report of his utterances. Sometimes, of course, a person does not understand what he has said until he has said it, so the correct constraint is that the original speaker comprehended his own words at the time he said them.

Acording to the theory we have been developing, comprehension is essentially a process of compiling a program written in a natural language into a mental language. We have tried to capture it generically by the control instruction instruct(x, y), introduced in 3.5.7, which is a dummy instruction representing the translation of an utterance into a "modality" component x and a "description" component y. The modality component consists of information about appropriate search domains, the time at which the description is supposed to apply, and so on, and it includes a specification of illocutionary force. The description component is the translation of the proposition itself. The executor can act on an utterance only if the "instruct" instruction is replaced by some specific instruction controlling information processing. Thus instruct (x, y) represents the passive comprehension of an utterance, but a comprehension sufficiently detailed to support subsequent action if necessary. We will accordingly introduce a general concept of comprehension, COMP(x, W), based on "instruct" in the following way:

(98)   COMP(x, W):   Someone x "comprehends" some words W if it is true of x at time t:
    (i) R_t(PERCEIVE(x, W))
    (ii) instruct(y, z)
    (iii) CAUSE((i), (ii))

Such terms as "comprehend," "understand," and "mean" are interrelated: if x comprehends W then x understands what W means. The resulting value of the function COMP(x, W) is the pair of arguments y and z of "instruct," but we can also represent it as $u = $ COMP(x, W). That is to say, u is x's concept of the consequences of executing a program compiled for W.

If the concept WRITE(x, W) is defined in a way comparable to SPEAK(x, w), the literal sense of SAY(x, W) can be formulated as

(99)   SAY(x, W):   Someone or something x "says" W if:
    (i) UTTER(x, W) or (ON(WRITE))(z, W, x)

The first disjunct, involving UTTER, is appropriate for such sentences as "The parrot said 'Who's a cheeky chap?' " The second, involving WRITE, is appropriate for such sentences as "The signpost said 'Ten miles to London.' " A propositional sense of SAY(x, W) is obtained by adding to (99) the condition

(ii) COMP(x, W).

With one exception we have established all the apparatus needed for an analysis of indirect quotation. But the exception poses perhaps the hardest problem of all. In order to determine the truth value of a sentence of the form "*A* said to *B* that S," it is necessary to test whether *A* said some words to *B* and whether *A* understood what he was saying. It is also vital to test whether the meaning of *A*'s words is adequately conveyed by the indirect quotation in the sentential complement S.

The essence of the problem is that the relation between the meaning of the words in an original utterance and the meaning of the words in an indirect description of them is many:many (Zwicky, 1971b). The speaker is faced with the problem of deriving any one of a number of acceptable indirect reports of an original utterance. A listener who hears an indirect quotation may have had the problem of comprehension eased for him, but should he wish to verify the description he is faced with the problem of working back to a set of acceptable original utterances. Let us concentrate on the listener's problem. We will divide it into four parts: the problem of reference, the problem of deixis, the problem of predication, and the problem of illocutionary force.

We will take as an initial text the following indirect report of an utterance: "He said that the sole remaining member of the Mirandian royal family has hemophilia." The problem of reference arises from the fact that a referring expression, such as "the sole remaining member of the Mirandian royal family," need not have occurred in the original utterance. However, a verb like "say" usually generates a referentially opaque context, and hence no information can be added to a reference unless it is clear that this is what the original speaker had in mind. The sentence is an erroneous report if the original utterance was simply "Some guy has hemophilia." But if the speaker used a definite description, such as "that gentleman," "the prince," "he," or "Frederick," the indirect report is justified provided that the original speaker was referring to the same individual and would have known at the time that the new referring expression also denotes that individual. Such conditions derive from a standard requirement for inference from opaque contexts, which is clearly violated if the original speaker was referring to the little old man who sells apples in the market and had no idea that he was the sole remaining member of the Mirandian royal family. Although information may not be added, it is sometimes necessary to drop information or to shift from a definite to an indefinite description. One may have to use an indirect quotation such as "He said that a foreign gentleman has hemophilia" to report an original utterance like "The foreign gentleman has hemophilia." This situation can also arise when the person making the indirect report is unable to determine the reference of the original speaker's definite description or when he considers that his audience will be unfamiliar with this reference.

We can formulate these referential requirements by ensuring that the following conjunction holds:

(100)   (*W* used by *x* refers to *r*) & (*V* used by Speaker refers to *r*),

where *x* is the original speaker and "Speaker" is the person making the indirect report. That is to say, if the original speaker *x* makes any reference, then the words *V* in the present speaker's complement refer to the same entity. (Strictly speaking, *V* has only to refer to a set of which *r* is a member in order to allow for the use of indefinite reference in place of definite reference.) If the original speaker referred to himself (herself) with the pronoun "I," the speaker making the report will, in order to fulfill condition (100), have to use "he" ("she"). In other words, condition (100) captures the deictic shift from direct to indirect speech. Such shifts involve not only a choice of pronouns but also spatial and temporal locatives that depend on the fact that the time and place of an original utterance become reference points for an indirect report of it. An illustrative set of deictic shifts is given in table 7.3.

A further condition is required in order to meet the opacity conditions of the verb "say": a novel referring expression can be used only if it refers to the same individual and does so according to the original speaker's knowledge:

(101)   KNOW(*x*, [(TO(REFER))(*W*, *r*) & (TO(REFER))(*V*, *r*)])

If, for instance, Warren said "All of John's children are asleep," his remarks may be truthfully reported by "Warren said that Ann, Bill, and Charles are asleep" provided that "Ann, Bill, and Charles" refers to all of John's children and Warren knows that fact.

But what if John has no children? In that case, no reference is actually made and the relation between the original utterance and a true report of it hinges on the relation between the *meanings* of the two sentences. An interesting phenomenon, noted by Karttunen (1973a), is that the referential opacity of verbs of saying disappears when they are used performatively—with first person, present tense. Thus, although "Warren said that all of John's children are

Table 7.3   Changes in deictic terms in indirect quotations.

Indirect quotation	*Acceptable original utterance*
He said that he was watching me at that moment.	I was watching you then. I am watching you now.
He said he would watch me there.	I will watch you there. I will watch you here.
He said he had watched me.	I watched you. I have watched you. I had watched you.

asleep" may be true even though John has no children, "I say that all of John's children are asleep" is vacuous in such a case. One way to provide for this feature of verbs of saying will be suggested in analyzing commands and orders in 7.4.4.

Turning to the pattern of relations between predicates in the original utterance and predicates in the indirect report, we find that, generally speaking, information can be omitted, but it can be added only when it corresponds to the implicit meaning of the original utterance. The opacity of indirect reports is further emphasized by the fact that they may well be true even if they contain self-contradictory or semantically anomalous predictions. The truth of "He said that the day was both frabjous and not frabjous" depends solely on the nature of the original speaker's utterance. The constraint is accordingly

(102) u entails u',

where $u = \text{COMP}(x, W)$; $u' = \text{COMP}(\text{Speaker}, V)$; and Speaker again denotes the person making the indirect report V. This constraint also captures the earlier referential constraint provided that it is stipulated that the original speaker *knows* that u entails u'. Likewise, the actual words spoken by the original speaker need not constitute a sentence in order to satisfy (102), since COMP takes into account the context of an utterance. For example, "He said that his name was John Doe," is true if the original speaker merely said "John Doe" in reply to the question "What is your name?"

The choice of an appropriate main verb for an indirect report—say, ask, request, deny—depends in general on the nature of the original utterance and in particular on its illocutionary force (Austin, 1962b). Until we have considered this topic, we must postpone a complete analysis of sentences of the form "*A* says to *B* that S."

We cannot leave the topic of quotation without mentioning semi-indirect quotation. An utterance can be reported directly, as in "He asked 'Could I have some more?' " or indirectly, as in "He asked whether he could have some more." But consider "He asked could he have some more." Fronting the auxiliary verb suggests direct quotation, but shifting the pronoun suggests indirect quotation (Gragg, 1972; Banfield, 1973). To revert to our earlier characterization of reported speech, semi-indirect discourse arises when a speaker does part—but only part—of the work of converting direct quotation into an indirect format more suitable for semantic representation.

7.4.4   The Nature of Illocutionary Acts

An assertion can be made without using a declarative sentence, a question can be asked without using an interrogative sentence, and an order can be given without using an imperative sentence. There is no reliable way to determine the intended illocutionary force of an utterance solely in terms of its syntax. As table 7.4 shows, each mode can be used on occasion to make an assertion, ask a question, and give an order.

Table 7.4   Relations between sentence type and illocutionary force in indirect quotations.

Indirect quotation	Acceptable original utterance
He said that he really liked lobster.	I really like lobster. Do *I* like lobster? Give me lobster any day.
He asked me whether it was time to leave.	I wonder if it is time to leave. Is it time to leave? Tell me if it is time to leave.
He ordered me to get a taxi.	You will get me a taxi. Will you get me a taxi? Get me a taxi.

This phenomenon is hardly surprising. Syntax is specified with respect to sentence types, whereas it is a particular use of a sentence—a sentence token —that determines its illocutionary force. A listener distinguishes between statements, questions, and commands by using his knowledge of the social conventions governing conversation. The essential idea, elaborated in several investigations (Gordon and Lakoff, 1971; R. Lakoff, 1972), is that there are pragmatic and rhetorical rules governing conversation that speakers and hearers exploit. The rules stipulate that an utterance should be no more and no less informative than the situation requires for clarity; they call for a speaker to tell the truth, to be relevant, to express himself clearly and unambiguously. The rules may be countermanded by the dictates of courtesy (R. Lakoff, 1973) or deliberately flouted for an expressive purpose; many derogatory remarks, as Larkin and O'Malley (1973) observe, tend not to be informative: "Your field is medicine, professor, not economics." Such examples are not incompatible with the notion of conversational conventions; they can be accommodated within a pragmatic theory granted that a speaker can choose to ignore a convention for a deliberate purpose when he believes his audience will understand that purpose.

In 3.5.7 we noted the need to distinguish between grammatical (syntactic and semantic) determinants and pragmatic determinants of illocutionary force. If a sentence is interpreted literally, it will have a literal force, that is, the illocutionary force it would have if the speaker intended it to be taken literally. Sometimes this literal force corresponds to the illocutionary force the speaker intended his utterance to have, but often it does not. Pragmatic rules are needed when a mismatch occurs, when the force of a literal interpretation is inappropriate to the context; they are rules a listener can use to infer the illocutionary force that the speaker intended. It would be impossible to detect such a mismatch, however, if the literal interpretation did not have some force associated with it. And this literal force of a sentence cannot be explained by pragmatic rules, which, according to this view, serve a very different purpose. We assume that the force of a literal interpretation must be explained by syntactic and semantic rules.

The rules that Searle (1969) offers for determining the illocutionary force of assertions, requests, and questions are summarized in table 7.5. According to Searle, the conditions listed in the table must be satisfied if the speech act is to be performed felicitously. Looking at the conditions for assertions, we can appreciate J. J. Katz's (1972) observation that both semantic and pragmatic conditions are included: (4) gives information that one might expect to find in a definition of "assert," whereas (1)–(3) seem to be general principles governing social interactions—have evidence for what you say, be informative, speak the truth—which are not limited to particular speech acts. Searle calls (4) in each case the essential rule. We would argue that (4) is the semantic rule in each case and that if one knows the meaning of each verb the remaining conditions can be inferred according to one's knowledge of general pragmatic rules governing conversation.

In short, given a set of conversational maxims, a literal interpretation of the utterance, and a specification of its context of use, it is in principle possible to infer its illocutionary force. Such inferences may go astray:

> Do you know how they do it?
> No, how do they?
> I don't know! I was asking if you did.

In this example of Hutchinson's (1971) the listener initially misconstrued the opening remark as a simple yes/no question, whereas it was intended as a request for information. Inferences in other situations may be easier. As Hutchinson points out, a listener will probably appreciate that the interrogative "Did you realize that Nixon is a Quaker?" is intended to inform rather than question, since "realize" is a factive verb that presupposes the truth of its complement.

The view of illocutionary force that we are advocating runs counter to the assumptions of several theorists (Ross, 1970; Sadock, 1971; Travis, 1971; Jackendoff, 1972). Ross suggests that all assertions have an underlying representation in which they are embedded in a clause roughly of the form "I declare to you . . . " He recognizes that there is a feasible pragmatic alternative but confesses uncertainty about the psychological consequences of deciding one way or the other. We agree with Ross that there is some assertive force inherent in the syntax and meaning of a declarative sentence under its literal interpretation, but we claim that the illocutionary force that the speaker intended in using the sentence on a particular occasion can only be inferred.

In our view, there are three substantial advantages in treating illocutionary force pragmatically rather than as a sentence constituent. First, it avoids the embarrassing linguistic question of the form to be specified for an utterance whose illocutionary force is unclear. If the force of an utterance is clear, it

Table 7.5 Conditions for felicitous speech acts. (After Searle, 1969, p. 66.)

Assertion	Request	Question
1. Speaker has evidence or reasons for the truth of S.	1. Addressee is able to S, and speaker believes addressee is able to S.	1. Speaker does not know whether S is true, or does not have the information needed to complete S truly.
2. It is not obvious to both speaker and addressee that addressee knows S.	2. It is not obvious to both speaker and addressee that addressee will S of his own accord in the normal course of events.	2. It is not obvious to both speaker and addressee that addressee will provide this information without being asked.
3. Speaker believes S.	3. Speaker wants addressee to S.	3. Speaker wants this information.
4. Speech act counts as an undertaking to the effect that S represents true state of affairs.	4. Speech act counts as an attempt to get addressee to S.	4. Speech act counts as an attempt to elicit this information from addressee.

is unnecessary, from a psychological point of view, to assert what is obvious to both speaker and listener; if the force of an utterance is not clear, it can hardly be clarified by postulating an underlying but unrealized semantic component. Second, it obviates any problem of specifying the intended audience of an illocution. It avoids, in other words, the problem of identifying to whom "you" refers in Ross's underlying clause. Identifying the audience is often a problematical matter; Ross's assumption leads to difficulties when another listener overhears remarks plainly directed to a particular addressee. Third, it avoids introducing information into the underlying form of a sentence which almost invariably has to be deleted in deriving the surface form of that sentence.

To argue that illocutionary force need not be represented explicitly in the underlying structure of a sentence is compatible with the notion that it is so represented in the case of sentences that do make their illocutionary force explicit, such as "I say to you that it is raining" or "May I ask you whether he is a friend of yours?" or "I order you to shut up." Conversation might be logically simpler—though unnecessarily cluttered—if speakers always declared the force of their utterances. The logical simplicity of explicit declaration is attested by the fact that a successful exercise in programming one robot to talk to another utilized such a device. Power (1974) arranged for control to pass from one robot to the other (actually, both robots were represented by separate but similar computer programs) by specifying various games in which the structure of interchanges was laid down explicitly: question followed by answer; assertion followed by its acceptance, rejection, or an indication that the fact was already known; and so forth. In order for each game to be recognized, the first move always established its identity:

> *Robot X*:   May I ask you something?
> *Robot Y*:   Go ahead.
> *Robot X*:   Can you move?
> *Robot Y*:   Yes.

In this way, Power finessed the problem of inferring illocutionary force from context.

How many sorts of illocution are there? Austin (1962b) said they could be identified by listing the "performative" verbs that make illocutionary force explicit; he claimed that there are over a thousand such verbs. However, Vendler (1970, 1972) has cogently argued that Austin's criteria were not stringent enough, since they also admitted many verbs of thinking (know, envisage, overlook). Yet even on Vendler's criteria there are still several hundred such verbs. We cannot attempt to analyze them all here, but we can at least consider whether they could be classified in some way.

There are several distinct sorts of performative utterances. As we have seen, one sort simply makes the illocutionary force explicit. The utterance "I state that he did not do it" is, as Austin (1962b, p. 134) noted, equivalent to the assertion "He did not do it." If one denies the former, he is taken to be denying the latter, not merely to be denying that the speaker is making an assertion.

Another sort of performative is exemplified by "I hereby declare Mabel Miss Weston-Super-Mare" or "I proclaim these games opened." These utterances are equivalent to "Mabel is Miss Weston-Super-Mare" and "These games are open" provided that various pragmatic prerequisites are felicitously fulfilled: the speaker has the necessary authority and means what he says. But the essential feature of these utterances is that the act of making them brings about a state of affairs. A telltale sign of such performatives is found in their sentential complements. The assertion "I declare that Herb is the winner" may be an explicit statement identifying who has won or the very words that, in part, make him the winner. The latter interpretation is obligatory in the case of "I declare Herb the winner." This sort of complement, lacking the copulative verb "be," characteristically refers to a state or event (see 7.1.1), and the speaker's words seem to create that state or event. The same pattern occurs in nonperformative reports of such utterances: "He declared Herb the winner." Only certain verbs of saying can take this sort of complement; one cannot say, for example, "I assert Herb the winner." They appear to fall into that class of performatives that Austin dubbed "exercitives": appoint, name, proclaim, christen.

By considering the complements that a verb permits, Vendler (1970, 1972) has established a classification of illocutionary verbs. We will not follow precisely in his footsteps, because our concern is less with complements than with underlying semantic components. It is these semantic components which, according to a view we have urged before, largely determine collocations with various sorts of complement. Moreover, what seems basic to us is not the categories recognized by Austin or Vendler but the triad of illocutions: asserting, requesting, questioning, if only because of their obvious correlation with declarative, imperative, and interrogative sentences.

The most obvious condition to impose on all these illocutions is that the speaker *means* what he says, just as a propositional account requires that he *understands* what he says. The notion that the speaker means what he says is essentially an intentional one, as a number of philosophers have argued (including Grice, 1957; Searle, 1969; Vendler, 1972). The line we will take in giving an account of "mean" closely follows their arguments.

In the case of assertions, we claim that for a speaker to make an assertion and to mean it the following conditions must hold. It is a prerequisite that the speaker x says something W to someone y: $(\text{TO}(\text{SAY}))(x, W, y)$. The first condition is that the speaker understands his words as specifying a certain concept. In section 4.4 we considered a Fregean theory of meaning in procedural guise: the meaning of W to a person x, $\text{COMP}(x, W)$, is a program of operations to be executed, and his program is his concept of the consequences of executing it. We can state the condition thus:

(i) $\text{COMP}(x, W) = u$.

The second condition is that the speaker intends his words to inform the listener of this concept u:

(ii) CAUSE(INTEND(x, KNOW(y, u)), (TO(SAY))(x, W, y)).

The third rests on a peculiarity of language noted by Grice: when a listener understands a speaker's intention in speaking he understands his meaning:

(iii) INTEND(x, KNOW(y, (ii))).

Finally, the speaker creates a recognition of his intention by exploiting the listener's ability to understand the language:

(iv) CAUSE(COMP(y, W), KNOW(y, (ii))).

In short, to paraphrase Vendler (1972, p. 62), if your intention in saying "I'll be there" is to cause your audience to believe, by means of its recognition of your intention from these words, that you will be there, you have made a statement.

Let us gather these conditions in a schema representing one sense of that highly ambiguous word "mean," as in "He means that it's raining." This verb allows indirect quotation of an original speaker's remarks; in addition to the intentional components, the appropriate relation between the complement and the original remark must be established along lines laid down in 7.4.3: the meaning of the complement (as understood by the present speaker) must be implied by the meaning of the original speaker's remarks, and the original speaker x must have sufficient knowledge to appreciate this relation:

(103)   MEAN$_a$(x, v):   Someone x who says some words W to someone y "means" v, where v = COMP(Speaker, W), if:
   (i) COMP(x, W) = u
   (ii) CAUSE(INTEND(x, KNOW(y, u)), (TO(SAY))(x, W, y))
   (iii) INTEND(x, KNOW(y, (ii)))
   (iv) CAUSE(COMP(y, W), KNOW(y, (ii)))
   (v) u entails v
   (vi) KNOW(x, (u entails v))

This formulation ensures that a speaker cannot *mean* something simply by intending his words to mean it. On the supposition that the speaker using the form "x means v" is a competent speaker of the language, the entailment in condition (v) ensures that the original remarks, when considered in their context, are capable of bearing a conventional indirect report of them.

If a person x issues an order, his intention is not merely that the addressee should be aware of that fact but also that the addressee should carry out the order. The same line of argument for, say, "He meant her to close the door," where x issued the order and Speaker reports it indirectly, gives

(104)   MEAN$_r$(x, y, z):   Someone x who says some words W to someone y "means" for y to do z, where v = COMP(Speaker, W), if:
   (i) COMP(x, W) = u

  (ii) CAUSE(INTEND$(x$, ACHIEVE(y, z)), (TO(SAY))(x, W, y))
 (iii) INTEND$(x$, KNOW$(y$, (ii)))
 (iv) CAUSE(COMP(y, W), KNOW$(y$, (ii)))
  (v) u entails v
 (vi) KNOW$(x$, (u entails v))

We have made extensive use of a concept KNOW; a few words about it are in order. "Know" has a seldom recognized aspect that has created many philosophical problems. Thinkers from Plato to Ayer have suggested that knowledge is simply *justified true belief* and that one cannot be said to know something that is false. If this suggestion were correct, however, it would be wrong to say "People in the Middle Ages knew the world was flat" (Griffiths, 1967, pp. 1–15). But in a sense they did know that it was flat.

In spite of the heavy weight of precedent, we believe the appropriate conclusion for psychology is that knowing is deictic. There is an instructive contrast between one speaker's asserting "Stuart knows that it's raining" and another speaker's asserting "Stuart believes that it's raining." This contrast need have nothing to do with Stuart's behavior or state of mind, although the two sentences could be used to refer to such a difference. The contrast we wish to illustrate arises when these sentences are used by different speakers to refer to the same situation; the contrast has to do with what the sentences commit the speakers to believing. The first sentence, with "know," presupposes that the speaker also believes that it is raining; the second sentence, with "believe," does not. If a speaker were to cease to believe that it was raining, then, regardless of Stuart's state of mind, he would be forced to abandon the first sentence. It is perhaps this presuppositional difference between "know" and "believe" that led Vendler (1972) to argue for an objective domain of facts, causes, and outcomes that can be known and a subjective domain of assumptions, predictions, and statements that can only be believed.

A complication arises from the use of these verbs in the first person singular: "I know that it's raining" versus "I believe that it's raining." There is no deictic contrast here, yet there is a difference in meaning. No matter how vehemently a speaker utters "I believe" it conveys an element of doubt incompatible with "I know." Since an assertion of the form "he believes that S" does not commit a speaker to the truth of its complement, it tends to be used whenever the speaker is in doubt about it. It follows that an assertion like "I believe that it's raining, but I may be wrong" is unexceptionable. (What would be odd would be for a person standing in a heavy downpour to say to his companion, "I believe it's raining," although such a remark could be interpreted humorously, whereas "I know it's raining" under those circumstances might seem querulous.) This first-person use has a direct consequence for the other use of "believe." The sentence "Stuart believes that it's raining" can be used when Stuart himself is in doubt but the speaker, perhaps, has no doubts at all; it can be used when Stuart is uncertain or the speaker is uncertain or both. Some of the philosophical problems about knowledge appear to have arisen because, although a distinction between ordinary usage and the epistemological concept has been recognized, an idealized use of "know" has sometimes been considered without regard to its deictic function.

A more pertinent observation for our purposes is that there is no satisfactory lexical candidate in English for expressing the relation between an individual and his knowledge: "know" is deictic, "believe" contains an element of dubiety. We will settle for a nondeictic concept KNOW that does not commit a speaker to the ultimate truth of its complement, a sense of "*x* knows that S" which means simply that S is part of the body of assertions that can be established from *x*'s memory, perception, intentions, or in some as yet unknown and ineffable way. KNOW(x, S) is evidently a conceptual generalization of *Know*(x, y), mentioned in section 2.7.

Since no obvious program is to be executed in the case of assertions, we suggested in 3.5.7 that it is useful to introduce a holding operation, the dummy instruction instruct(x, y), until an executive decision has been made about what to do with the asserted proposition. So much is straightforward, but how is the assertive nature of a statement to be represented within the arguments of the "instruct" instruction? Syntactically, the essence of an assertion is the specification of an n-place predicate together with values for its n arguments —some of them may not be given explicitly in the surface sentence, but at least the existence of values for them must be inferable. Semantically, the essence of an assertion is the notion that the tests involved in the predicate will be satisfied by applying them to the n-ary set of entities referred to by the arguments. This notion is captured in our notational convention of using brackets when dealing with schemata in an assertive setting; we can represent the underlying meaning of an assertion like "She possesses it" as [POSSESS(she, it)]. We assume that a listener initially represents this assertion in the format

instruct(modality, [POSSESS(she, it)]).

In 3.5.7 we said that the modality argument included any information about the illocutionary force of a speech act that can be represented in the utterance itself. Thus, strictly speaking, the assertive force of the brackets is also represented as part of the modality component along with information about tense, aspect, negation, and so on. Whether a listener will be able to determine a truth value for the assertion will depend on his being able to "find" the entities referred to in it. If the entities can be found, the assertion is either true or false depending on the outcome of a "test" instruction; otherwise it is empty, and many philosophers would argue that in the general case no proper "statement" has been made. Special operations are required in the case of a quantified assertion, but, following Hintikka (1973), we believe they can also be reduced to processes of finding and testing.

What about the modality component? Suppose that all utterances are initially (and involuntarily) represented in working memory thus: (TO(SAY)) (x, w, y), where x points to the speaker, w points to the utterance, and y points to the addressee. We take this representation as an initial formulation of the modality component.

We must distinguish between a listener's grounds for inferring that an utterance has the illocutionary force of an assertion and the way in which he will represent its meaning as an assertion. The initial representation of an assertion might be

$$\text{instruct}((\text{TO}(\text{SAY}))(x, [w], y), \text{POSSESS}(\text{she}, \text{it})),$$

where [w] is now a pointer to the description component, to the second argument of "instruct," and the brackets convey the assertive force of the proposition. Subsequently, higher-order routines may call on the executive to substitute "test" for "instruct," a translation that should ultimately yield test (POSSESS(she, it)). The result of such a test may be stored in episodic memory either with or without information about the individual who originally made the assertion or the person to whom it was addressed.

The procedural semantics of an order (see 3.5.5) suggests an initial representation in which the modality component includes ACHIEVE. For example, the order "Get it" would have the initial representation

$$\text{instruct}((\text{TO}(\text{SAY}))(x, \text{ACHIEVE}(y, w), y), \text{GET}(y, \text{it})),$$

where w is again a pointer to the description component. What this representative encodes is that someone x says to someone y to achieve a state of affairs described by the outcome of GET(y, it). If the system determines that y is a pointer to itself, the presence of ACHIEVE triggers a translation into an actual control instruction: achieve(GET(ego, it)), and the executor has to decide whether to execute this instruction. If a third party is the addressee, however, y will not point to the system itself and the operation replacing "instruct" with "achieve" will not yield a directly executable routine.

A question is a special case of an order or request in which the speaker wants a listener to give him information. We sketched the following sort of routine for a "wh" question in 3.5.3: find (M(Ep), the value of y such that G(x, y)). We can generalize the analysis to any sort of "wh" question and to any sort of search domain. We can even accommodate double-barreled questions: "What did Martha hit *whom* with?" The initial representation of a "wh" question like "Who possesses it?" might be

$$\text{instruct}((\text{TO}(\text{SAY}))(x, \text{ACHIEVE}(y, (\text{TO}(\text{TELL}))(y, w, x), y)),$$
$$\text{POSSESS}(?r?, \text{it})),$$

where w is a pointer to the description component. What this representation encodes is that someone x says to someone y that y is to achieve a state of affairs in which y tells x the value of r such that POSSESS(r, it). When the executor encounters the routine it looks as usual to see whether y points to ego. If so, the first step in translation is to a control instruction:

(i)   achieve((TO(TELL))(y, w, x)).

The next step should specify an appropriate search domain, such as

(ii) find(M(Ep), r).

The final step, contingent on TELL, is

(iii) utter(identify(r)).

Once again, the executor utilizes higher-order routines to determine whether these instructions should be executed.

One advantage of setting up an initial representation of an illocution the way we have imagined here is that it offers a simple explanation of what happens when a listener overhears a remark addressed to someone else. In such a case, where y is not a pointer to ego, a routine corresponding to a request or a question will not be executed.

This procedure might be generalized. When the executor encounters an initial representation of any sentence it looks first to see whether y points to ego. If it does, the executor must consider whether to execute the routine; if it does not, the routine need not be executed. If it is not to be executed, it does not matter whether its presuppositions are satisfied. Such a device might therefore block presuppositions of the complement sentence from appearing as presuppositions of the main sentence: "Max says that all John's children are asleep" does not presuppose "John has children" because (TO(SAY))(Max, [all John's children are asleep], y) contains no pointer to ego. Karttunen (1973a) points out, however, that such presuppositions are not blocked for verbs of saying in a performative use when the subject of the main sentence is the speaker himself: "I say (to you) that all John's children are asleep" does presuppose "John has children" because (TO(SAY))(Speaker, [all John's children are asleep], ego) contains a pointer to ego. This exception is provided by our initial representation of utterances if we assume that a performative use of "say" maps directly into that representation, thus providing a pointer to ego.

This proposal to use (TO(SAY)) in order to preserve the identities of the speaker and addressee is tentative. An alternative, given the general framework we are imagining, would be to represent the modality component of any utterance initially as (TO(SAY))(x, w, y) and to modify the modality component of orders and questions to ORDER(x, y, z) and ASK(x, y, z) as soon as the appropriate representation could be inferred from the sentence and its context of use. We have not yet considered ORDER and ASK, however. This analysis is best undertaken as part of a more general discussion of the verbs that mark the basic triad of illocutions.

7.4.5   Verbs of Asserting

In the verbs of assertion we encounter one of the more troublesome properties of this field: verbs appear to change their meaning as a function of the objects or complements with which they occur. For example, "say," "state," and "assert" are virtually synonymous when used to make indirect quotations; there are no obvious differences between the meanings of

> He said that the room was bugged.
> He stated that the room was bugged.
> He asserted that the room was bugged.

With other constructions, however, this virtual synonymy disappears.

Sentences of the form "*x* says that S" can be characterized according to the arguments of 7.4.4 by specifying that *x* says some words and means by them something that can be correctly reported in a sentential complement S with assertive force:

(105) $\text{SAY}_c(x, S)$:   Someone *x* "says that" S, where *W* expresses S and *v* = COMP(Speaker, *W*), if:

   (i) $(\text{SAY})(x, W)$
   (ii) $\text{MEAN}_a(x, v)$

What distinguishes (105) from the propositional sense of (99) that is used in (i) is its acceptance of a sentential argument S, which gives it the force of "says that."

A useful wedge for driving verbs of assertion apart is to consider their meaning with a direct object: "He said his name" versus "He stated his name." The divergence in meaning is readily explicable within the present theoretical framework. The expression "his name" refers to a sequence of words that is an individual's name. Hence, by (99), "he said his name" simply requires him to have uttered the appropriate words. But the verb "state" can only be used to describe an illocutionary act—in this case, the act of stating what his name is. "He stated his name" is thus equivalent to "He said what his name is," and this "wh" complement is essentially a nominalization of a clause, "His name is *w*." It follows that "He stated his name" has an underlying form corresponding to "He said that his name is *w*," where *w* is a pointer to his name, which is part of his original utterance. Indeed, there may be no difference in what a person actually does between uttering his name and stating it: context, such as a prior question, may make the utterance into a statement. Since "say" has both interpretations (99) and (105), it follows that from "He said his name" the only aspect of his utterance we can be sure of is that it contained his name. "State," on the other hand, has only a sense comparable to (105):

(106) $\text{STATE}(x, w)$:   Someone *x* "states" *w*, where *w* refers to some words *W*, if:
   (i) $\text{SAY}_c(x, w)$

When "state" takes an explicit "that" complement S, its content is substituted in condition (i) in place of *w*; in other words, the schema becomes identical to (105) for "say that."

Consider next the contrast between "state" and "assert": "He stated Kepler's first law" versus "He asserted Kepler's first law." Stating may merely involve saying what the law is, but asserting involves a commitment to it. If Kepler's first law is that each planet moves round the sun in an ellipse, the first sentence can be paraphrased as "He said (that Kepler's first law is) that each planet moves round the sun in an ellipse." The portion of the sentence in parentheses may be omitted since the original speaker may have stated Kepler's first law without realizing it. In this case, he may have stated it as some other law, misattributed it, or, indeed, he may actually have stated it with an assertive force. Hence two paraphrases for "He asserted Kepler's first law" are possible: "He said that each planet moves round the sun in an ellipse (which is Kepler's first law)" and "He said that Kepler's first law is true." We need to make this distinction since reports of speech are referentially opaque. If the original speaker said "Each planet moves round the sun in an ellipse," then, according to our analysis of indirect quotation, this utterance may be truthfully reported by "He asserted Kepler's first law," provided the original speaker was aware that what he asserted was Kepler's law. He may have explicitly attributed it with a clause such as the one in parentheses. Alternatively, the original speaker may have said "Kepler's first law is true," even perhaps while being under the delusion that the law was "All bodies fall toward the center of the earth." We propose the following schema for "asserts":

(107)   ASSERT(x, w):   Someone x "asserts" w if:
         (i) SAY$_c$(x, S)
         (ii) (TO(REFER))(w, S) or (S = TRUE(w))

When w refers to S, the schema underlies an original utterance like "Each planet moves round the sun in an ellipse"; when S = TRUE(w), the schema underlies an original utterance like "Kepler's first law is true." Schemata for REFER and TRUE will be given in 7.4.8.

One further assertive illocution should be considered before we discuss some variants. Consider the contrast between "He stated his name to them" and "He told them his name." A speaker may state something to an audience that fails to hear or to understand him, but, as Gruber (1965) points out, if he *tells* his audience something, it must grasp what he says. Thus there is an air of paradox about a sentence like "He couldn't understand what I told him"; "understand" here must mean something along the lines of "grasp the implication of." In the terminology of some philosophers, "tell" has a success grammar, whereas "say" does not. Indeed, you may say something to a brick wall or talk to trees, but you cannot tell them anything. One sign of success, according to Gruber, is the incorporation of "to": whenever a communicative act is consummated, it is possible (though not obligatory) to use such locutions as "John told Mary that he was tired," but if the issue is in doubt it is necessary to use such locutions as "John said to Mary that he was tired." However, there are verbs that imply success yet do not incorporate "to," such as "communicate," "convey," "report." "He informed the police of the accident" and "He reported the accident to the police" appear to be virtually synonymous.

A further complication with "tell" is illustrated in "She knows that it is snowing because we told her" and "She knows that it is snowing because we said that it was." If the truth of an assertion is presupposed, "tell" is the verb with which to make an indirect report of that assertion. One tends to construe the second example as a somewhat arrogant statement—its implicature is that we always tell the truth and are never misinformed. When truth is not presupposed, "say" is normal: "She believes that it is snowing because we said that it was." It is important to emphasize that the truth of a "that" complement is not always presupposed when it occurs with "tell": the verb is not factive (but see Vendler, 1972, p. 108). People do tell lies; it can be appropriate to say "He told me that he had resigned, but he hadn't."

"Tell" takes a variety of object complements and can be used to characterize assertions, requests, and questions. We specify here a schema for telling someone something ("He told the truth to Mary"); we assume that the speaker is satisfying all his intentions in saying something and meaning it:

(108)   (TO(TELL))(x, w, y):   Someone x "tells" w "to" someone y if w refers to W and:
  (i) STATE(x, w)
  (ii) PERCEIVE(y, W)
  (iii) COMP(y, W)
  (iv) KNOW(y, u)
  (v) ALLOW((i), (ii)) & CAUSE((ii), (iii)) & CAUSE((iii), (iv))

This schema is largely self-explanatory; however, u in test (iv) refers to the meaning that the original listener, y, places on x's words (see (102), p. 634). When "tell" takes a "that" complement, the appropriate modification is made in (i), as indicated in the case of schema (106) for STATE. However, the syntax of "tell that" differs from the syntax of "state that" because the listener should be designated: "x tells y that S" versus "x states that S."

A large number of verbs appear to be special cases of "say," "state," "assert," and "tell." We can relate them on the basis of their interpretations with direct objects. Among the cognates of "say" in (105) we find the technical terms "testify," "attest," and "swear," because none of the verbs takes a simple object but only "that" complements and constructions of the form "He testified/attested/swore to the defendant's innocence."

One other verb, "lie," is also reluctant to take direct objects; to lie is to say something that one knows to be false but that one intends to be believed:

(109)   LIE(x):   Someone x "lies" if:
  (i) SAY$_c(x, S)$
  (ii) COMP$(x, S) = u$
  (iii) KNOW$(x, \text{not}(u))$

"Announce," "declare," and "proclaim" behave in many ways like "state." If the eternal footman announces you as you enter the salon, he not only states your name but does so to everyone within earshot. Publicly displayed notices can also be said to announce their contents:

ANNOUNCE(x, w):   (PUBLICLY(STATE))(x, w).

"Declare" and "proclaim" differ from "state," however, in that they can be used performatively, and even "The clerk declared/proclaimed the proceedings open" reports performatives that were a necessary part of bringing about the specified state of affairs. The general form of these verbs appears to be

DECLARE(x, w), PROCLAIM(x, w):   CAUSE(ANNOUNCE(x, w), y),

where the result y of the utterance depends on its context and content. "Disclose" and "reveal" have senses that are variants of "state": they presuppose that the information stated had hitherto been kept from the listener (see the perceptual senses of these verbs in 7.3.7).

A presupposition distinguishes "maintain" from "assert": one maintains an assertion in the light of doubt about it. The other major assertive verb has an obvious derivation:

DENY(x, w):   ASSERT$(x, \text{not-}w)$.

The richest set of variants revolve around "tell," perhaps owing to the greater variety of complements it permits. Apart from its assertive sense analyzed in (108) the verb has a narrative sense exemplified in "He told a story." Here no assertions need be involved; this sense of the verb is not really within the illocutionary domain:

(110)   TELL(x, w): Someone x "tells" w, where w refers to some words W if:
    (i) (TO(SAY))(x, W, y)
    (ii) KNOW(y, w)
    (iii) CAUSE((i), (ii))

This schema, or something similar, underlies such verbs as "relate," "narrate," "retell," and "recite," which allow reference to be made to the nature of the discourse. "Communicate" and "convey" might also be included, except that these verbs are much broader in meaning—they are not strictly verbs of utterance.

Other verbs of telling introduce the notion of a topic of discourse. We can examine this notion in a simpler context by considering first "He commented/remarked on its behavior." Such sentences can be adequately paraphrased as "He said something about its behavior." The problem of defining the concept of a "topic" is analogous to the problem of working back from an indirect quotation to the original utterance that it describes. But, in the case of "comment on" or "remark on," nearly all the information in the original utterance has been lost. The original speaker's remarks may have been merely "Mmm, nice—very nice!" in which case it is not even true that the original utterance specified its topic explicitly. The critical feature is really not the utterance but the speech act as a whole, including its understood referents, presuppositions, and so forth. Aspects of the previous discourse may be important, as in defining a statement, for otherwise there would be no way to determine whether a remark such as "Well, John likes Jane" is a comment on John or on Jane (or both). If we argued that each referent in a statement should be treated as a topic of that statement, it would surely do violence to our intuitions about discourse. In the following dialogue *B*'s remark seems to be a comment on Jane:

> *A* :   Jane isn't very popular with the boys.
> *B* :   Well, John likes Jane.

But in

> *A* :   John doesn't care much for girls.
> *B* :   Well, John likes Jane.

B's remark seems to be a comment on John. The different topic (or focus) of his two remarks would probably be indicated by differences in intonation (see 3.5.3).

Linguists working with speech acts have attempted to pin down such concepts as "topic" and "comment" (Hockett, 1958; Pike, 1960; Firbas, 1964; Halliday, 1967). It should be clear that the notion of a topic concerns the organization and cohesiveness of discourse—it is a paradigm of a pragmatic factor in language. We merely stipulate the necessary condition that if x comments on y, then the meaning of what he says must be taken to refer, in part, to y:

(111)   (ABOUT(SAY))(x, W, y):   Someone x "says" some words W "about" something y if:
   (i) SAY(x, W)
   (ii) (TO(REFER))(PART(W), y)

Thus we establish

   (ON(COMMENT))(x, y):   (ABOUT(SAY))(x, W, y).

"Remark on" seems to have the same schema as "comment on."

The notion of a topic also enters into the analysis of a number of verbs of telling:

   (OF(INFORM))(x, y, z):   (ABOUT(TELL))(x, w, y, z).

This schema applies to "advise of" as well as to "inform of." "Report" also shares this schema, but when it takes a human object, as in "They reported him to the authorities," it requires

   (TO(REPORT))(x, z, y):   DO(z, S) & (ABOUT(TELL))(x, w, y, S).

There is another set of verbs, explored by Fillmore (1971b), in which the moral and expressive neutrality of "say" is abandoned in favor of value judgments: criticize, praise, blame. The main problem here is the representation of social and ethical values. For example, one can accuse someone of murder, but it seems odd to criticize him for so serious an offense. Syntactically, these verbs do not ordinarily admit "that" complements; they are used to report not an utterance but a relation between an utterance, a person, and an event or state. Because events or states are referred to gerundively (see 7.3.1), reports may take the form

> He accused James of stealing the jewels.
> He criticized Sarah for being clumsy.
> He blamed Bill for the accident.
> He praised you for being honest.
> He apologized for his absence.

If z is some bad event, state, property, class, or whatever, a speaker x can accuse another individual y of causing that event, being in that state, having that property, being a member of that class. For convenience we will represent these alternatives by $F(y, z)$. We can illustrate Fillmore's analysis of these verbs with two examples:

(112) $(\text{OF}(\text{ACCUSE}))(x, y, z)$:   Someone x "accuses" someone y "of" some bad thing z if:
        (i) $\text{SAY}_c(x, F(y, z))$

(113) $(\text{FOR}(\text{CRITICIZE}))(x, y, z)$:   Someone x "criticizes" someone y "for" $F(y, z)$ if:
        (i) $\text{SAY}_c(x, \text{BAD}(z))$ or $\text{SAY}_c(x, \text{BAD}(F(y, z)))$

As Fillmore observes, what is presupposed by one verb, the other very nearly asserts. This general pattern of analysis can be applied to a number of verbs: apologize, blame, censure, congratulate, praise, scold, thank. (Jackendoff, 1974, proposes that "blame" should be paraphrased as "cause responsibility for z to go to y." We disagree; you need not be responsible for everything you are blamed for.)

It is possible to report the content of an utterance that itself expresses a value judgment of some sort: "He assured her that the car was safe," "He protested that it was after midnight." Certain verbs allow both options, taking either a gerundive complement or a "that" complement, as in "He admitted/confessed to doing it," where the original speaker y is involved in some reprehensible act or situation z, $F(y, z)$, and says so, or "He admitted/confessed that his father was a politician," where the truth of the complement is presupposed and the original speaker asserts it, and either it is also presupposed that what it characterizes is reprehensible (a judgment of the current speaker) or the original speaker also asserts that what it characterizes is reprehensible.

"Tell" provides a bridge from verbs of asserting to verbs of requesting. It takes infinitival complements, characteristic of nonindicative clauses, and accordingly can satisfy a prerequisite for specifying desired states of affairs: "He told them to go." It is not obvious which aspect of the semantics of "tell" permits this sort of complement, but whatever it is it is shared by "warn" and "advise." To warn somebody that something is the case, or about something, is to tell him that it is dangerous. To warn somebody to do something is to tell him to do it in order to minimize or avoid a dangerous situation. The problems raised for semantic analysis by these verbs are best considered in the general context of verbs of requesting.

7.4.6 Verbs of Requesting and Questioning

Apart from its informative aspect, characterized by assertive verbs, language is perhaps most useful as an instrument for getting other people to do things. You can tell, order, instruct, request, or beg listeners to carry out actions for you, and English is rich in its variety of ways of making and reporting such requests. The way an order or request is given depends on a variety of social conventions. Among equals it is customary to request, not to command. There are many polite forms of speech that enable a speaker to make a request; indeed, it is usual to say "please" except when there is a distinct asymmetry in status (Haas, 1971). Requests among equals may be reported by using "request" or "invite" followed by an appropriate indirect quotation. The usual form of the indirect quotation, however, is not a "that" complement but an infinitival: "He requested her to leave." Such a complement is, as suggested in 7.3.1, a reflection of an underlying nonindicative clause.

Politeness may shade into obeisance. It is difficult to determine when, for instance, a request is more accurately described by "he begged" than by "he requested." Several verbs imply a distinct asymmetry in social status, or at least a distinct expression of it on the part of the original speaker. When someone beseeches, implores, or entreats a favor from his audience, he casts himself in an inferior role and his audience in an authority role.

There appears to be no neutral general English term for the domain of orders and requests—which tends to support the thesis that people who have much commerce with a class of entities often develop specialized vocabularies without generic terms. English is probably not unique in having a lexicon that reflects a high degree of specialization for what Skinner (1957), lacking any better term, calls "mands."

Although English has no generic verb for requesting and ordering, such speech acts can be described in a neutral way: "He told her to keep calm," "He asked her to keep calm." Nothing about the verb in these examples indicates whether he made a polite request or a peremptory demand. The choice of "ask," however, suggests (faintly) that the request or demand was couched in the form of an interrogative. The underlying sense of "*A* tells *B* to S" can be represented in a fashion parallel to the assertive schema (105) for "say that," since when a speaker tells someone to do something, the verb no longer has a success grammar:

(114) TELL$_c$($x, y,$ S):   Someone x "tells" someone y to S, where COMP
(Speaker, S) = ACHIEVE(y, z), if:
   (i) (TO(SAY))(x, W, y)
   (ii) MEAN$_r$(x, y, z)

If a speaker said, for example, "I order you to leave the room," an indirect report of the form "He ordered her to leave the room" would be justified. But orders can be given in other ways: indeed, they can be conveyed most politely. A general may communicate an order to an inferior in words more suitable to a tea party than a battlefield. "Order" really denotes a subtle speech act, resting on the notion that one individual has authority over another. This relationship can arise by a mutual convention, perhaps supported (or even entirely replaced) by associated rewards and punishments; in consequence of it, when x tells y to do something, y is placed under an obligation to carry out the order. The nature of the obligation depends on the nature of the convention. With a purely mutual convention, in each possible future state of the world compatible with the convention (in each of y's morally permissible future states), y carries out x's order. In the absence of mutuality, and when obedience is enforced solely by inescapable punishment, say, an order creates no obligation, although y may appreciate that failure to carry it out may result in punishment. An implicit threat, "Do it or else," hangs over all orders in these circumstances. Since it is not clear how this sort of quasi obligation should be represented, we ignore it in the following schema. What is clear is that "order" has a success grammar that is parallel to "tell to" (108):

(115) ORDER(x, y, S):   Someone x "orders" someone y to S if:
  (i) TELL$_c$(x, y, S)
  (ii) PERCEIVE(y, W)
  (iii) COMP(y, W) $= z$
  (iv) KNOW(y, notPERMISSIBLE(y, notACHIEVE(y, z)))
  (v) ALLOW((i), (ii)) & CAUSE((ii), (iii)) & CAUSE((iii), (iv))

In short, as a result of an order the addressee knows that he is obliged to achieve some state of affairs.

In the case of implorations, the original speaker will incur an obligation if the addressee achieves the requested state of affairs: the obligation devolves on the underdog whether he makes the request or receives the order.

(116) REQUEST(x, y, S):   Someone x "requests" someone y to S if:
  (i) TELL$_c$(x, y, S)
  (ii) PERCEIVE(y, W)
  (iii) COMP(y, W) $= z$
  (iv) KNOW(y, OBLIGATE(ACHIEVE(y, z), x, z'))
  (v) ALLOW((i), (ii)) & CAUSE((ii), (iii)) & CAUSE((iii), (iv))

Condition (iv) specifies that the addressee y knows that his achieving z obligates x to do something z' in return.

A variety of manner adverbials may modify these verbs. For example:

(117)   invite   (POLITELY(TELL))(x, y, S)
        command   (AUTHORATIVELY(ORDER))(x, y, S)
        implore, entreat, beseech, beg   (SUBMISSIVELY(REQUEST))(x, y, S)

Some of these verbs differ in terms of the direct objects they can take: "He invited Richard," "He ordered a meal," "He requested a hearing." There appear to be three basic meanings with these direct-object constructions: (a) *x* tells *y* to come; (b) *x* tells *y* to bring something; and (c) *x* tells *y* to achieve something. Only "invite" seems to allow (a); it would be odd to say "He ordered John" without adding "to come." Certain verbs convey the sense of ordering someone not to do something: forbid, enjoin from, prohibit. The underlying schema corresponds to "*x* orders *y* not to do *z*."

The last of our triad of major illocutions is questioning. This act is similar to requesting or ordering, but it also involves a stipulation that the original listener's task is to reply with information. It follows that the verbs of requesting and ordering can be used to make an indirect report of a question. For example, "He asked me her name" can be expressed as "He told/asked/commanded/ordered/requested/invited/begged/implored me to tell him her name." With such a wide range of possibilities available, it is scarcely surprising that only two verbs in the present domain allow the content of a question to be indirectly reported: "He inquired/asked what time it was." The remaining verbs are mainly concerned with the topic of a question or set of questions: "She quizzed/interrogated/examined/consulted the aide about his source of funds." "Interrogate" has a connotation of authority that occurs in some verbs of ordering, "examine" has a formal and "quiz" has an informal connotation of questions asked in a classroom, and "consult" suggests that the original speaker was seeking advice and acted with politeness and propriety.

More specialized meanings are exemplified in "He queried the source of the party's funds" or "He queried whether the party's funds were all reported." The first suggests that he asked for the value of a referential variable ("the source"), the second that he asked about the truth value of a statement ("The party's funds have all been reported"). There is clearly a relation between these statements and "He asked who the source of the party's funds was" and "He asked whether the party's funds were all reported." However, sentences with "query" presuppose that some statement about these matters had already been made and assert that the original speaker raised a question about that statement. This sense of "query" can also be expressed by the verb "question."

Since a question is a request to provide an answer, we can formulate its schema as

(118)   ASK(x, Q, y):   Someone *x* "asks" a question Q of someone *y* if:
           (i) TELL$_c(x, y,$ ANSWER$(y, Q, x))$

Answering, according to our general approach, involves compiling a program for finding the necessary information, executing it, and telling the answer to the questioner:

(119)   ANSWER(y, Q, x):   Someone *y* "answers" a question Q for someone *x* if ASK(x, Q, y) and:
           (i) COMP$(y, Q) = u$
           (ii) HAPPEN(execute$(u) = $ S)
           (iii) $($TO$($SAY$_c))(y,$ S, $x)$

Thus "answer" and "reply" presuppose a previous question and assert that an utterance is made in response to it. The content of this response may be specified in a "that" complement. In their linguistic senses, "respond" and "retort" have a similar presupposition, except that they allow a wider variety of illocutions both in the initiating remark and in the response they report.

ANSWER presumes a particular kind of relation between Q and S, between the question asked and what the respondent says. This relation has been discussed by J. J. Katz (1968, 1972), who argues that questions, like assertions, exhibit logical properties and relations even though questions cannot be evaluated as true or false. According to Katz, just as the logical features of assertions depend on their truth conditions, so the logical features of questions depend on their "answerhood" conditions. He defines what he means by a "possible answer," both to yes/no and to "wh" questions.

We have not discussed these relations between Q and S but have assumed they would be satisfied as a consequence of COMP. In (118) we did not specify how an utterance by x is to be recognized as an answerable question and in (119) we did not specify the type of utterance by y that would be recognized as an answer to the question rather than an evasion or rejection. The obstacles to providing such account, however, do not seem insuperable. The devices in English for forming questions enable speakers to request confirmation or to request values for various deleted arguments. It should be possible to characterize a relation $A(Q, S)$ in terms of those devices that would hold just in case interrogative Q was syntactically and semantically related to declarative S, in which case S would qualify as an answer to Q. The details would require us to go into the syntax of interrogatives far more deeply than in section 3.5, and the account would be complicated by the need for pragmatic rules to recognize indirect questions (not in the interrogative form) and by the acceptability of various paraphrases of Q and S. Since these pragmatic analyses would necessitate a detailed discussion that would add little or nothing to our lexical analysis of the verbs "ask" and "answer," we have not attempted to carry them through. (Nor have we attempted a similar analysis of the "compliance" conditions underlying the relation of commands to responses.)

This is as far as we will carry our survey of illocutionary verbs. Although we have discussed most of the verbs of requesting and questioning, even a casual glance at Austin (1962b), Vendler (1972), or Fraser (1975) will reveal a multitude of assertive verbs that we have not mentioned (affirm, claim, conclude, contend, postulate, predict, suggest).

7.4.7   Conversational Verbs

We have been examining speaking as if a speaker said things to a passive audience. Most speech, of course, occurs in some form of interactive dialogue; a key to the verbs that describe this two-sided process is provided by "talk."

Sentences with "talk" suggest success; a listener is believed to understand what is being said. To many people sentences like "He talked to me for five minutes, but I couldn't understand a word" are at least odd, if not contradictory. Moreover, if x talks to y about some matter, it is not strictly necessary for y to say a word; transition to conversation occurs when x talks *with* y. (Reciprocity is the key to the locative sense of "with"; 6.1.1.)

Consider four ways of characterizing a conversation between two participants:

> (a) x talked with y.
> (b) y talked with x.
> (c) x and y talked (with each other).
> (d) y and x talked (with each other).

Something more than a syntactic transformation must relate (a) to (c) and (b) to (d), since the meanings of (a) and (b) differ in a way that the meanings of (c) and (d) do not (see Lakoff and Peters, 1969). The difference between (c) and (d) is stylistic, although it may involve a rhetorical or stylistic choice. But the difference between (a) and (b) transcends style: the person denoted by the grammatical subject of the sentence is presumed to have initiated the conversation. This impression is strongest when someone reports a conversation in which he himself participated; compare "I talked with him about it" to "He talked with me about it." On the other hand, if x only asked questions and y only answered them, one would be more likely to say that x asked y about it than that they talked with one another; talking involves telling. The upshot is

> x talked to y (about it): x told y something (about it).
>
> x and y talked (about it): x told y something (about it) *and* y told x something (about it).
>
> x talked with y (about it): x told y something (about it) *and then* x and y talked (about it).

Talk is always addressed to someone: if no one is in the region of the speaker (and he is not on the telephone, recording his voice, or the like) he becomes the addressee of his own remarks—he is talking to himself. Even though it is not necessary to mention the listener explicitly, this facet of "talk" is implicit in the decision to analyze it in terms of "tell." "Talk," like "tell," can cover writing ("The author talks in his work of . . . ," "This book talks of. . . "). But when there is an explicit indirect object ("talks to y") or a collective subject ("x and y talked"), barring coauthorship, the verb concerns speech. Presumably this implication reflects purely practical considerations—it is difficult for correspondents to capture the to-and-fro of conversation by writing to one another.

Before proceeding to other conversational verbs, let us introduce three schemata for "talk":

(120) $(\text{TO}(\text{TALK}))(x, y)$:   Someone x "talks to" someone y if:
        (i) $(\text{TO}(\text{TELL}))(x, w, y)$

Given (120), the reciprocal sense of "x and y talk" is simply "x talks to y and y talks to x":

(121)   TALK(x & y):   Someone x and someone y "talk" to each other if:
        (i) (TO(TALK))(x, y) & (TO(TALK))(y, x)

Since "talk" cannot be used to make indirect quotations and can introduce only the topic of a conversation, not its propositional content, the topic phrase may be couched either in the form of "about" + NP or in the form of "of" + NP. There is no difference in the interpretation of such phrases, though they do differ when they occur with verbs describing propositional content (such as "tell"). Hence a schema for "x and y talk about w" can be framed as

(122)   (ABOUT(TALK))((x & y), w):   Someone x and someone y "talk about" something w if:
        (i) TALK(x & y)
        (ii) (TO(REFER))(x, W, w) & (TO(REFER))(y, V, w)

"Discuss" is similar but incorporates the preposition and demands that the topic be explicitly specified: "We discussed inflation." Other verbs of conversing have similarly straightforward analyses:

(123)   discuss   (ABOUT(TALK))((x & y), w)
        converse   TALK(x & y)
        discourse   (FORMALLY(CONVERSE))(x & y)
        chat, gossip   (INFORMALLY(CONVERSE))(x & y)

Some conversations have a particular character: negotiations, arguments, disputes. A speaker describing them may wish to bring out this aspect of the discourse as well as its topic. Terms for such overall features of discourse appear to derive from the dialectical possibilities of the minimal unit of dialogue: A tells B something, and B tells A something. Such pairs of statements may be compatible or incompatible. If they are compatible, the speakers may be agreeing with one another or their remarks may be relatively independent of each other. (They may be totally independent of one another, but in such a case we would say that the second speaker has changed the subject or that the dialogue is not cohesive. In either case, we are not really dealing with dialogue in a dialectical sense of the word.) If the speakers' remarks are incompatible with one another, they are probably disagreeing.

Logicians sometimes divide the universe of incompatible propositions into (a) pairs that are contrary to one another: both members of the pair cannot be true, but both could be false ("It's red"—"No, it's green"); and (b) pairs that are contradictory: both members of the pair cannot be true and both members of the pair cannot be false ("It's odd"—"No, it's even"). This distinction is prescriptive rather than normative; in ordinary conversation "contradict" is not used in accordance with these dictates. The philosopher Bernard Williams used to illustrate the difference between the ordinary and the logical use of this term by an anecdote about a builder who claimed that two cost estimates for a job were contradictory and was taken aback when confronted by a logician's retort that one of them must therefore be correct.

It is just as well that ordinary discourse seldom hinges on such details. A logician's map of incompatible statements may give rise to misgivings, but we will not try to modify it, since it already admits refinements to which ordinary language is insensitive. A more primitive notion of inconsistency—both statements cannot be true—suffices for psychological purposes. We could represent this notion in terms of a simple negation: not(u & v).

Some wags claim that disagreement is more fun than agreement because if everyone agreed, there would be nothing left to talk about. The English lexicon reflects this sentiment, for although a variety of verbs describe disagreements —argue, debate, dispute, haggle—there is no single word to describe a conversation consisting of agreements. Even "agree" is not unequivocally a verb of saying, for it can describe a state of mind: "He agreed with her, but said not a word to indicate it."

"Agree" and "disagree" can describe either statements or states of mind. Many other verbs share this ambivalence (see Vendler, 1970, 1972). We suppose that when a verb describes a state of mind, a person may use it to report his own thoughts: "I agree . . . ," "I doubt . . . ," "I suspect . . . " Since the verb is frequently followed by a complement conveying a propositional content, it is natural for others to report such a statement by using the same construction, "He agreed . . . ," "He doubted . . . ," "He suspected . . . ," rather than "He said that he agreed . . . " For example, "Jack agreed with Jill" can convey a variety of meanings. (Set aside the noncommunicative reading that might be paraphrased "Jack made Jill happy.") Jack and Jill may not have said a word to each other; the reporter may be comparing what he believes they have said independently. Another interpretation is that Jack and Jill talked to each other about something and that what they said about it was at least not inconsistent. That they talked to each other, however, is merely an implicature of "agree," not an entailment.

We can approach these verbs by beginning with a concept of "verify":

(124)   VERIFY(x, S):   Someone x "verifies" that S if:
         (i) COMP(x, S) $= u$
         (ii) HAPPEN(execute(u) $=$ TRUE)

This schema derives from the procedural semantics developed in preceding pages. We can incorporate (124) into a schema for "assent to," which can be used either to endorse the truth of some statement or to express a willingness to perform some act. We must bear in mind that a person may, for reasons of his own, assent to some statement he believes to be false or assent to some act insincerely. "Assent" means only that the speaker wants the addressee to believe that the speaker believes that what he assents to is true or intended. Since these indirections have already been detailed in (103), we can write

(125)   (TO(ASSENT))(x, z):   Someone x "assents" to z if z refers to S and:
         (i) SAY(x, W)
         (ii) MEAN$_a$(x, VERIFY(x, S)) or MEAN$_a$(x, INTEND(x, DO(x, S)))

According to this formulation, to assent to a proposal z entails nothing about the source of the S that z refers to. Indeed, it does not entail that x verified S or even understood S correctly. We will take "agree to" as semantically equivalent to "assent to": $(\text{TO}(\text{ASSENT}))(x, z) \equiv (\text{TO}(\text{AGREE}))(x, z)$.

We can formulate "agree" with a sentential complement in terms of "assent to":

(126)   AGREE(x, S):   Someone x "agrees" that S if z refers to S and:
         (i) $(\text{TO}(\text{ASSENT}))(x, z)$

The interpersonal notion of "agree with" would be

(127) $(\text{WITH}(\text{AGREE}))(x, y)$:   Someone x "agrees with" someone y if
         SAY(y, S) and:
         (i) AGREE(x, S)

What y said (or wrote) need not have been addressed to x, but it is presupposed that y said something: "Jack said nothing and Jill agreed with him" is a wry form of humor. Reciprocal interpersonal agreement, as in "Jack and Jill agreed," is presumably an elided version of a longer sentence telling what they agree on. We can include the object of their agreement by extending (126):

(128)   AGREE$((x \ \& \ y), S)$:   Someone x and someone y "agree" that S if:
         (i) AGREE(x, S) & AGREE(y, S)

This formulation leaves it open whether x and y agreed with each other or with a third party. If only the topic of their agreement is mentioned, it is usually introduced with "on" or "about":

(129) $(\text{ABOUT}(\text{AGREE}))((x \ \& \ y), z)$:   Someone x and someone y "agree about" some topic z if S is any sentence about z and:
         (i) AGREE$((x \ \& \ y), S)$ or AGREE$((x \ \& \ y), \text{not}S)$

In these variations on the schema for "agree" it is not necessary that the participants know they agree or even know each other. If, however, x and y agree to do something, $(\text{TO}(\text{AGREE}))((x \ \& \ y), z)$, where it is clear from context that the second disjunct of (125ii) is the correct value of z, the presumption is strong that they talked it over together and that both know of the other's intentions. But it is still merely a presumption.

This lexical gap on the affirmative side is well filled on the negative side. A verbal disagreement, of course, is an argument. But there is more to argument than mere disagreement; there is an active exchange and an intention on the part of each participant to persuade the other. Before we can formulate ARGUE we must pause to consider PERSUADE.

"Persuade" exemplifies what Austin (1962b) calls a perlocutionary act. It does not have a success grammar—one cannot say "I hereby persuade you that snow is green" or the like, although one can say "I hereby tell you that snow is green." The causal antecedent of "persuade" is not restricted to linguistic acts; the intended consequence is not restricted to mental states. We can treat "x persuades y that S" as meaning roughly that x does something that causes y to agree that S. What x does may be verbal or nonverbal; what y agrees to may be the truth of S or the truth of a statement about his intention to do something. Our schema for "persuade" is

(130)   PERSUADE(x, y, S):   Someone x "persuades" someone y that S if:
    (i) ACT(x, S')
    (ii) AGREE(y, S)
    (iii) CAUSE$(S', $ (ii)$)$

A similar schema would be appropriate for "persuade to," but with (TO(AGREE))(y, z) in condition (ii).

With (130) in hand, we can return to "argue." For sentences like "x argued that S," where S can be something like "The moon is made of cheese" or "John should feed the cat," the paraphrase would be "x says something by which he intends to persuade someone that S." There is a strong presumption that x believes the S he is arguing for, but the presumption can be canceled, as in "Max argued that four is a prime number, although he didn't really believe it." The schema is

(131)   ARGUE(x, S):   Someone x "argues" that S if:
    (i) SAY(x, W)
    (ii) CAUSE(INTEND$(x, $ AGREE(Addressee, S)), (i)$)$

One can, of course, "argue against" something z, where z denotes some statement: "He argued against the proposal," for example. (AGAINST(ARGUE))(x, z) is simply ARGUE$(x, $ notS$)$, where z refers to S. And the interpersonal sense of "Jack argued with Jill" is

(132)   (WITH(ARGUE))(x, y):   Someone x "argues with" someone y if SAY(y, S) and z refers to S and:
    (i) (AGAINST(ARGUE))(x, z)

To say that x argues with y does not entail that y argued back. The reciprocal interpersonal sense of "argue about," however, does seem to involve face-to-face interaction:

(133)   (ABOUT(ARGUE))$((x$ & $y), z)$:   Someone x and someone y "argue about" some topic z if:
    (i) DISCUSS$((x$ & $y), z)$
    (ii) (ABOUT(notAGREE))$((x$ & $y), z)$
    (iii) (WITH(ARGUE))(x, y) & (WITH(ARGUE))(y, x)

The remaining verbs of argument incorporate adverbials denoting the manner in which the argument was conducted:

(134)   debate   (FORMALLY(ABOUT(ARGUE)))$((x$ & $y), z)$
              haggle   (INFORMALLY(ABOUT(ARGUE)))$((x$ & $y), z)$
              quarrel, squabble   (ANGRILY(ABOUT(ARGUE)))$((x$ & $y), z)$

A final small domain of verbs of argument is concerned with arguments undertaken for the purpose of reaching an agreement: dicker, haggle, negotiate, parley. How an intention to reach agreement can be incorporated into the schema is illustrated by a schema for "negotiate":

(135)   NEGOTIATE$((x \& y), z)$:   Someone x and someone y "negotiate" z if:
      (i) INTEND$((x \& y), (\text{ABOUT}(\text{AGREE}))((x \& y), z))$
      (ii) $(\text{ABOUT}(\text{ARGUE}))((x \& y), z)$
      (iii) $(\text{ABOUT}(\text{AGREE}))((x \& y), z)$
      (iv) CAUSE$((i), (ii))$ & CAUSE$((ii), (iii))$

One might think that condition (ii) should be DISCUSS$((x \& y), z)$, but if x and y do not disagree, there is nothing to negotiate between them; the possibility that they disagree is what (133) adds to the concept of discussion.

7.4.8   Metalinguistic Verbs and the Concept of Truth

Most natural languages permit the topic of discourse to be language itself. English contains a variety of explicitly metalinguistic terms that can be roughly classified into reference terms, meaning terms, and truth terms. In order to do justice to this aspect of vocabulary, a well-articulated theory of the logic of language would be required. We have not developed such a theory, and the following remarks are therefore tentative.

Reference is an act. In chapter 3 we took ostensive pointing as a paradigm of the sort of convention that underlies, or is presupposed by, all linguistic acts of reference. When there is a relation between a proper name W and something x, a speaker may say "x is named W" or "x is called W." If x is an inanimate object, he may say "x is called W" or "x is labeled W." If x is an abstract object, such as a song or a play, he may say "x is entitled W." But the root of such reports is an original act of naming.

Naming can be a formal matter with an associated ritual or it can literally be done in a word. To name something is simply to make an appropriate performative utterance—appropriate, that is, to a culture's conventions governing the act. In English an object may come to be named by a variety of formulations: "I name this x W," "I christen this x W," "Let's call it W," or "We will call this x W." The same set of verbs can also be used to describe an act of naming: "We named him Bonzo," "He was christened Art." At least one verb, "nickname," seems to be used only to describe, rather than execute, acts of naming.

Apart from proper names, less permanent and more generic labels can be introduced by a speaker; several verbs conform to the pattern: "He refers to his wife as 'the Missus' " or " 'The Missus' refers to his wife." This pattern also occurs in more technical domains: denote, symbolize, signify, designate, represent. A verb that conforms to only one half of the paradigm, obligatorily taking a name as its subject, is "stand for." (Of course, many of these verbs can be used in a metaphorical sense to convey a property or attribute of an entity, "Fudpucker symbolizes/represents/stands for free trade," but this usage is not strictly metalinguistic.)

Although there are ways to introduce a transient name, label, or description that temporarily refers to a particular individual for a limited population of speakers, when the relevant expression refers to an individual relatively permanently and universally it becomes a proper name (or a definite description with many of the features of a proper name). A language denuded of proper names would be most inconvenient, and hence a specialized vocabulary is reserved for the purpose of introducing them. Alternatively, when an expression comes to function as a proper noun, it can become a frozen form: "The White House," "The Sun King," "Never Say Die."

Given an analysis of temporary acts of reference, it is evident that more permanent forms differ mainly in their universality—a notion that is easy enough to capture. But what is the core of a temporary reference? In our view, the semantics underlying a verb such as "refers to" is simply a decentered control instruction: identify(x). With the introduction of an additional argument specifying the individual making the reference, we have an appropriate routine for such sentences as "He referred to his wife." The schema can be completed by adding an argument to specify the expression used to make the reference:

(136)   (WITH(TO(REFER)))(x, W, y):   Someone x "refers" to something y with some words W if it is true of x:
   (i) HAPPEN$_t$(identify(y) = W)

When x is unspecified, the schema corresponds to "W refers to y"; the essence of naming something is performing an act—usually a speech act—that allows the entity in question to be referred to thereafter by the words uttered as its name.

(137)   NAME(x, y, W):   Someone x "names" something y W if:
   (i) ACT(x, SAY(x, W))
   (ii) (TO(REFER))(W, y)
   (iii) ALLOW((i), (ii))

If two expressions name the same entity, one might suppose that they mean the same thing, but this supposition must be rejected for natural-language expressions. We have discussed an intentional sense of "mean" in (103); here we must consider the definitional sense paraphrased by "means the same as." For example, " 'Kill' means 'cause to die' " was discussed in section 6.3, where we claimed that the relation is one of entailment: it would be contradictory to assert "x killed y and x did not cause y to die." We assume this relation expresses the fact that any sentence S_1 containing "kill" should translate into a routine u_1 that will include all the operations included in routine u_2, where u_2 is the translation of sentence S_2 that differs from S_1 only in having "cause to die" where S_1 has "kill." Many philosophers, like Austin, Quine, Ryle, and

Wittgenstein, have claimed that a phrase such as "the meaning of 'kill' " does not function as a referring expression, that there is no object designated by such a phrase. (For a useful review of these arguments, see R. T. Garner, 1975.) Our view, of course, is that there are lexical meanings; they are mental entities that can be characterized by schemata:

(138)   MEAN(W_1, W_2):   Some expression W_1 "means" some expression W_2 for someone x if S_1 and S_2 are two sentences differing only in that S_2 contains W_2 where S_1 contains W_1 and:
   (i)   COMP$(x, S_1) = u_1$
   (ii)   COMP$(x, S_2) = u_2$
   (iii) u_1 includes u_2

Finally, let us turn to truth, a concept that has exhausted many volumes and many minds; we can offer here only the merest outline of its treatment within a procedural approach. Procedurally, truth hinges on the successful outcome of a "test" instruction applied to the result of translating an indicative sentence. Even granted the availability of such procedures, however, questions remain as to whether they will always be applicable and whether their outcomes will always be consistent.

Truth is some sort of relation between sentences and states of affairs, but it can also enter into the meanings of sentences. Thus, "true" is at one and the same time a part of the language and a metalinguistic notion concerning the semantics of the language. This ambivalent role has led some logicians to despair of giving a coherent account of truth for natural languages. The trouble arises most acutely in various paradoxical sentences that give rise to semantic antinomies. A simple example, the so-called liar paradox, is "The sentence I am now uttering is false." If this assertion is true, it is false, and if it is false, it is true. The trouble may not be limited to the concept of truth. If somebody says "Don't obey this order," a similar paradox arises (G. Lakoff, 1972a). And psychologists are familiar with a theory that a critical role is played in the genesis of schizophrenia by such "double binds" combined with further commands that prevent the individual from leaving the field (Bateson et al., 1956).

There is considerable literature on semantic paradoxes since many of them have been important in the history of logic. The liar paradox, in particular, has suggested to a number of writers (including Martin, 1950; Stroll, 1954) that natural languages are fundamentally inconsistent. According to Tarski (1956), the trouble derives from three aspects of natural language. First, any sentence that occurs in the language can also be named within it; there are, in fact, a variety of ways of naming sentences. Second, every expression formed from the formula

S is a true sentence if and only if p

by replacing p with a sentence and S with the name of this sentence, is considered to be true. Third, any empirically established premise having the same meaning as

"c is not a true sentence" is identical to c

can be formulated and accepted as a true sentence. This third possibility is Tarski's way of introducing the liar paradox. A typical instance would be

(139)   Sentence (139) is not true.

Granted these conditions, Tarski shows conclusively that no formal language can be its own metalanguage without leading to semantic paradoxes. A coherent semantics is possible only if the language in which it is expressed (the metalanguage) is strictly differentiated from the language to which it applies (the object language).

In stating Tarski's conditions, we have talked, as he does, of sentences rather than statements or propositions. A critical question is accordingly whether sentencehood is a decidable property: Is there a mechanical procedure that will determine for any arbitrary string of words whether it is a sentence of the language? If there is such a procedure—and transformational generative grammar is predicated on this notion—Tarski's proof would appear to have calamitous consequences. Given the ordinary laws of logic, natural language would indeed be inconsistent.

Bar-Hillel (1966) suggests a plausible escape from this discomfiting conclusion. It is based on the assumption that a sharp distinction must be made between sentences and statements. "Statement" is being used here as a technical term. The crux of the distinction is that in attempting to make a statement a speaker may very well fail. He may fail by using a descriptive phrase that lacks reference: saying "All of John's children are asleep" when John has no children. Another way of failing, according to Bar-Hillel, is to utter sentences like "The sentence I am now uttering is false." Such a sentence does not demonstrate that English is inconsistent, since it is neither true nor false. It simply fails to make a statement. The reason for its failure is instructive.

One of the properties of the metalinguistic terms "true" and "false" in ordinary language is that they must be predicated either of clauses or of expressions that refer to clauses. There are sentences of the form "It is false that it is raining" and of the form "That claim is false." It is the second category that causes all the trouble. Whether a sentence of this form makes a statement depends on what its nominal expression refers to. In this case it depends on what "that claim" refers to. The problem can be illustrated by a chain of sentences:

> (a)   The next sentence is false.
> (b)   The next sentence is true.
> (c)   The next sentence is false.
> (d)   Russell discovered an interesting paradox.

A little thought shows that (a) is true if (d) is: granted the truth of (d), (c) is false; hence (b) is false; and thus (a) is true. But suppose the chain is

> (a)   The next sentence is false.
> (b)   The next sentence is true.
> (c)   The next sentence is false.
> (d)   Sentence (a) is false.

If (a) is true, (b) is false, and hence (c) is false; but if (c) is false, then (d) is true, and consequently (a) is false, contrary to the initial assumption. If (a) is false, (b) is true; if (b) is true, (c) is true; if (c) is true, (d) is false; and if (d) is false, (a) is true, again contrary to the initial assumption. This second chain of sentences is a stretched-out version of the liar paradox; it demonstrates that self-reference is not a necessary component of the paradox, contrary to what has often been assumed.

Note that having procedures to translate and test indicative sentences does not suffice to avoid such problems. An attempt to verify this second chain of sentences would send the system into an endless loop. We assume, therefore, that the executive system includes a rule to the effect that "test" is inappropriate—that no statement has been made and there is nothing to test—when it finds itself testing the same set of sentences over again. The presence of contradiction is incidental. For example, the following chain introduces no contradiction yet fails to make any statement:

> The next statement is true.
> The preceding statement is true.

The point about such self-referring sentences as

(140)   Sentence (140) is true.

(141)   Sentence (141) is false.

is that although they reduce the chain to its minimal length they still lead to an endless loop. (A comparable conclusion, from a very different frame of reference, has been reached by Kneale, 1971, 1972.)

Armed with this procedure to eliminate semantic paradoxes, we might maintain that sentencehood is a decidable property. But the argument shifts from sentences to statements: statementhood is not a decidable matter. That is to say, there may be no mechanical way to determine whether any arbitrary utterance of a sentence constitutes a statement, in the technical sense of the term. From a referential point of view, this situation is hardly surprising; it would be difficult to imagine an algorithm for determining whether a referential presupposition is fulfilled. The most we can hope for is a set of heuristic procedures to determine whether a noun phrase refers to anything. Moreover, there is no simple way to determine whether "The next sentence is true" makes a real statement. Whether it succeeds in making a statement depends on what the next sentence is, and whether *it* succeeds in making a statement. Indeed, we may soon be led into a maze of sentences in trying to determine the matter, and since there is no algorithm for determining whether a program is an endless loop, it is not too difficult to imagine that the maze is undecidable. Hence it seems that language is not internally inconsistent, because statementhood is not decidable. (Herzberger, 1967, argues for the consistency of language by a reductio ad absurdum based on the paradoxical sentences, thus reversing the usual claim.)

We are still left with the problem of defining "true." The most influential philosophical approach is to define truth recursively by setting up a semantical model. This is the procedure pioneered by Tarski and exploited by Carnap, Kripke, Hintikka, van Fraassen, and many others. It has been advocated as a suitable procedure for the semantics of natural languages by such theorists as Montague, Parsons, Davidson, Lewis, and Keenan. We have not adopted it because, as we argued in chapter 3, a semantical model would distract us from a number of crucial psychological problems. But there is no reason to suppose that the approach we adopt is logically incompatible with a semantical model.

Our view is that a particular sentence uttered on a particular occasion with the force of an assertion may turn out to be true or false or may fail to have a truth value. If the sentence is translated into a routine to apply certain tests, and if those tests succeed, the sentence is true. The tests may fail in two ways. The value of the "test" instruction is undefined if the system is unable to find the referent of a referring expression or if an identifying expression fails to identify. If the tests fail when appropriate values can be assigned, the sentence is false. By defining "true" in terms of the control instruction "test" we do not avoid the problems of paradox, but we feel that those problems have less to do with "test" than with the formulation of statements to which "test" can be applied.

This account ignores many details and quibbles. For example, G. Lakoff (1972b) argues that the assignment of truth is a fuzzier matter than any dichotomy or trichotomy. Certainly the outcome of a test is sometimes uncertain. In our view such uncertainty does not argue, as Lakoff claims, for an infinite number of degrees of truth. It argues, if anything, for an infinite number of degrees of uncertainty about whether a statement is true or false. Complete uncertainty, of course, arises when it is impossible to carry out a test, as in attempting to verify "There's a gorilla in that closet whenever no one is trying to find out that there is."

Our analysis of some of the verbs of communication has introduced many problems not hitherto encountered. No one is more aware than we of the tentative nature of many of the analyses and of the limited territory that we have surveyed. Of the domains that we have left untouched, perhaps the most important are the verbs of explanation and description (see Dakin, 1970) and a number of small but important sets of verbs including "promise," "congratulate," and "thank" (see Searle, 1969).

7.5   ORGANIZATION AND SCOPE OF SEMANTIC FIELDS

Despite the tentative nature of many of our analyses, certain patterns have emerged from our study of four verbal fields. We are ready now to ask whether any general principles of lexical organization apply to all verbal semantic fields. Before we can assess the importance of the similarities between the fields of verbs we have studied, we need to know how representative they are. Have we chosen a limited set of verbs outside of which our methods would fail? How much remains outside these fields? We cannot answer these questions definitively, but we will give our reasons for believing that our sample is sufficient to justify general conclusions.

The kind of organization we have found in verbal fields is more complex than that in the nominal fields discussed in chapters 4, 5, and 6. A question therefore arises as to the relation of verbal fields to the rest of the lexicon. Is there some deep difference between nominal and verbal concepts? We see two approaches to this question, one linguistic, the other psychological. Linguistically, one would like to know the relation between, say, "move" and "moving," "speak" and "speech," "pay" and "payload," "take" and "on the take." Linguists treat such relations under the general heading of morphology. We will try to indicate the kinds of issues involved in defending the position that a word expresses the same concept regardless of the constructions in which it occurs. Psychologically, the question concerns the variety of concepts we have been required to postulate. How are the conceptual operators that we have introduced for the analysis of verbs related to those needed elsewhere?

What follows is as much speculation as conclusion. The questions raised go beyond matters of fact that might be established by observation or analysis, but they relate to the general nature of the enterprise we have undertaken.

7.5.1   Organization of Verbal Semantic Fields

For each field of verbs we have considered there are one or two concepts—TRAVEL, POSSESS, SEE, UTTER, SAY—that lie at the core of every verb in the field. That is why we think of them as semantic fields. Some verbs may express a core concept directly (Dixon, 1971, 1973, would include them among the "nuclear verbs"), whereas others embed it in a complex matrix. What elaborates a core concept into the variety of patterns found in the full array of verbs in any field are a number of basic semantic operators, perhaps a dozen, that we have been at pains to analyze. The list would include HAPPEN, DO, ACT, POSSIBLE, PERMISSIBLE, and CAUSE. These are plausible candidates for universal concepts, and they serve to connect, refine, and modulate the core concept in each field.

The ramifications of a verbal semantic field arise from the combinatorial consequences of setting a core concept into different matrices of operators. The resulting field reflects the ways in which people habitually organize their thinking about the world in terms of states, events, actions, causes, intentions. The most common ways in which the meaning of a core concept can be elaborated are the following.

— Various presuppositions can be linked to the concept. It may be presupposed, for instance, that the concept does not apply until some first moment at which it is realized, or various selectional restrictions may be placed on its arguments.

— Something about the manner of whatever action or event it involves can be stipulated.

— A causal relation can be introduced, with the argument of the concept serving either as the causal actor or as the object of causal action by something else.

— An intentional component can be introduced.

These four ways of refining a core concept are illustrated with respect to three core concepts in table 7.6. But there are other ways to elaborate a central idea:

— Negation offers manifest possibilities.

— Origins or destinations (otherwise signaled by "to" and "from") can be incorporated into the verb, as in "enter" and "rob."

— Instrumentalities can be incorporated, as in "walk" and "hand."

— Objects of the action can be incorporated, as in "paint" and "butter."

— Reciprocal relations involving the same core concept can be introduced, as in verbs of exchange.

— Two core concepts from the same field can be combined, as in verbs of expression.

— Core concepts from different fields can be combined, the way "put" combines motion and possession and "find" combines perception and possession.

This last possibility is a reminder that semantic fields are not mutually exclusive. We have concentrated on verbs falling within a single field, but it is plain that many verbs lie in the intersections of semantic fields.

These, then, are the major devices we have used to relate verbs within a semantic field. The list may not be complete—examination of other verbal

Table 7.6   Illustrations of the refinement of the core concepts in three verbal semantic fields.

	Core concept		
Method of refining core-concept meaning	TRAVEL(x)	POSSESS(x, y)	SEE(x, y)
Presupposition or selectional restriction	LEAVE(x)	KEEP(x, y)	WITNESS(x, y)
Specification of manner	LURCH(x)	OWN(x, y)	GLIMPSE(x, y)
Introduction of a causal component: (a) x is the actor	MOVE(x)	TAKE(x, y)	(AT(LOOK))(x, y)
(b) someone other than x is the actor	PUSH(w, x)	RECEIVE(x, y, w)	SHOW(w, y, x)
Introduction of an intentional component	CHASE(x, y)	SELL(w, y, x)	WATCH(x, y)

fields might reveal new methods of elaboration—and we may not have represented correctly the devices listed above. But our conclusion, after working through four fields, is that the means available for differentiating a core concept into a large variety of related verbs are limited. We assume, on grounds of cognitive economy, that a person learning English as his first language masters these devices and uses them to relate the meanings of new words to meanings of familiar words. Our sample suggests that there are considerable differences among the more complex verbs but that the verbs nearest the core concept are related to one another in relatively similar ways from field to field.

7.5.2   The Variety of Verbal Semantic Fields

If the picture we have painted of semantic fields of English verbs is to be viewed seriously, we need an independent estimate of the landscape it represents. The dangers inherent in selecting a single semantic field—kin terms, for example—as the model for all lexical organization are clear. We have taken a broader view than that, but is it broad enough? Rather than make claims about the breadth of what we have analyzed, we should ask what we have omitted.

We are concerned with the lexical resources of everyday speech. The special vocabularies of modern scholarship, science, and technology have grafted all varieties of lexical conveniences onto this common heritage. If we simply counted the number of word senses we have tried to analyze and expressed it as a fraction of all the senses defined in the dictionary, the result would be pitifully small. But that is not a measure that interests us. We assume that at the heart of the sprawling and ever changing English lexicon some nuclear, widely shared set of words and concepts provides a framework for the development of special vocabularies for special uses. The omissions that seriously concern us are those in this lexical center of everyday speech.

If we had a definitive list of semantic fields in this central lexicon we could simply check off those we have attempted to treat in order to discover how much remains to be done. Lacking such a list, we must find alternative means of assessment.

Dixon (1971) has studied the North Queensland language Dyirbal, which offers advantages for semantic description because it contains a "mother-in-law language" that must be spoken when a person's mother-in-law is within hearing distance. The mother-in-law language has about a quarter as many words as the everyday language and every possible means is exploited to keep its vocabulary to a minimum, yet everything can be said in it that can be said in the everyday language. It is possible therefore to identify the nuclear verbs of Dyirbal as those that are retained in this extremely parsimonious sublanguage. Dixon's tentative classification, based on both semantic and syntactic criteria, distinguishes seven types: (a) verbs of position, including both rest and motion, (b) verbs of affect, (c) verbs of giving, (d) verbs of attention, including perception, (e) verbs of speaking and gesturing, (f) verbs dealing with other bodily activities, and (g) metaverbs of "breaking off" some state or action.

If we were to take Dixon's classification as a list of indispensable verbal fields, we could claim to have explored a significant portion of them. What we have missed are verbs of affect (which in Dyirbal include contact verbs like "hit," "pierce," "rub"), nonperceptual verbs of attention, and verbs dealing with other bodily activities (like "cry," "blow," "copulate," "cough"). (Verbs of breaking off some state or action have been considered in our discussion of aspect, 6.2.4.) By this accounting, our major omissions are verbs of special psychological interest: verbs denoting psychological states or processes of thought or affect and some behavioral verbs.

We may be misusing Dixon's work; a generalization from Dyirbal to English is presumptuous. However, there is an English equivalent to the mother-in-law language, albeit an artificial one, known as Basic English (Ogden, 1932). It consists of a somewhat idiosyncratic set of 850 words with which, Ogden claimed, anything of importance can be said. To support this claim, a variety of works, including plays by Shakespeare and extracts from the Bible, have been translated into Basic. Three of Basic's features should be noted. First, its syntax appears to be that of ordinary English. Second, most words are allowed several senses, as in ordinary English. Third, there are very few verbs in Basic—one constructs sentences like "He took a swim" instead of "He swam." This last feature might seem to make Basic inappropriate for our purposes, but we can overcome the difficulty by ignoring the syntactic categories of Basic words.

In discovering the main semantic fields in Basic, the relevant words are verbs and the nouns that can function as verbs. From a natural grouping of these words emerge a number of semantic fields that concern behavior and mentality. Human beings perceive, cogitate, and act. They perceive other persons and their acts, and they perceive things and events. Such perceptions may relate their objects temporally and spatially (causally); they often isolate particular properties of their objects (motion).

The system of core concepts and operators that we have proposed seems to embrace most of these aspects of perception. It also seems to capture most of the ways in which objects and human beings act. A specification of overt human behavior must include accounts of bodily movements and postures, and accounts of how such movements can change things, use them, make or destroy them, and so on. Although we have not exhausted the lexical resources of English for characterizing these various activities, the majority of their requisite core concepts do seem to have emerged. And we have offered an analysis of language, that very special behavior involving perception, cogitation, and overt action.

Here again what lie outside our present scope are most of the core concepts underlying cogitation. Its more intellectual aspects can be conveyed in Basic by the following terms (on which we have imposed a rudimentary classification):

$$
\text{think} \begin{cases} \text{know, doubt, believe} \\ \text{judge, compare, decide} \\ \text{imagine, picture, theorize} \\ \text{intend, plan} \\ \text{reason} \\ \text{remember} \end{cases}
$$

A more sophisticated exploitation of intellectual core concepts in causal contexts is found in other Basic words, illustrated by various disparate terms: discover, choose, teach, learn, trick. Although we have suggested a few candidates for core concepts in this intellectual domain, it is clear that this area needs further analysis.

Emotional aspects of cogitation can also be expressed in Basic. Consider the causal verbs alongside those expressing feelings directly:

$$
\text{feel} \begin{cases} \text{like, love, desire} \\ \text{fear} \\ \text{hate} \end{cases}
\qquad \text{cause to feel} \begin{cases} \text{comfort} \\ \text{please, amuse} \\ \text{interest, attract} \\ \text{surprise, shock} \\ \text{shame, disgust} \\ \text{trouble, anger} \\ \text{wound, pain} \end{cases}
$$

We have skirted the vocabulary of emotion because of the great complexity of the topic. Studies of the use of language to describe emotions exist (Davitz, 1969, 1970, for example), but not an adequate account of the semantics of emotional terms or an adequate theory of human emotions. These two inadequacies, which are probably related, make semantic analysis hazardous, but we can at least survey the extent of the problem.

There is an analogy between the language of emotion and the language of color. The resemblance is in part a matter of synesthesia (Odbert, Karwoski, and Eckerson, 1942; J. Block, 1957; Osgood, 1960). D'Andrade and Egan (1974) have determined the color and emotion associations of Tzeltal-speaking adults from highland Chiapas and of college undergraduates in the United States; they find that, within the limits of translation equivalence, color chips and emotion words show very similar patterns of association in both cultures.

There is also, to some extent, a formal resemblance (McDougall, 1921; Geach, 1957). Like colors, emotions occur with different intensities, a dimension expressed in such series as happiness, joy, ecstasy; sadness, grief, despair; surprise, astonishment, shock; annoyance, anger, rage; anxiety, fear, terror; scorn, disgust, loathing. Perhaps the most striking resemblance is that emotions, like colors, can be mixed. This suggests, as Descartes argued, that there is some set of primary or landmark emotions from which more complex feelings derive. Psychologists have been unable to agree what the primary emotions are. Although it is widely accepted that some sort of emotional solid can be constructed along the lines of a color solid, there is little agreement about its main dimensions or the relative locations of emotions within it. Schlosberg

(1954) suggests dimensions of pleasantness/unpleasantness, attention/rejection, and intensity. These three dimensions are integrated in a cone-shaped model, with a roughly circular cross section denoting the two qualitative dimensions and a vertical dimension denoting intensity. The major emotions are ranged around the circular cross section according to figure 7.1. Plutchik (1962) presents a conical model in which the emotions are arranged according to the cross section depicted in figure 7.2. Despite these formal similarities, Schlosberg and Plutchik have different conceptions of the location of emotions in their multidimensional models, and it is easy to find still other conceptions (see, for example, Millenson, 1967). There are also several incompatible accounts of the primary emotions and the consequences of blending them. Is pride, for instance, a mixture of gladness and love or anger and joy?

The psychology of emotion implicit in ordinary language suggests to us that important distinctions have been overlooked in most psychological accounts. English distinguishes between an emotion, the cause of an emotion, and the

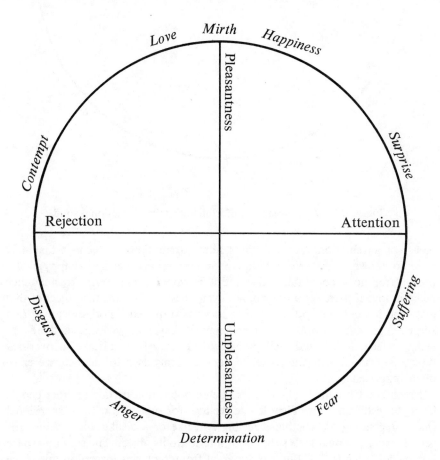

Figure 7.1   A cross section of Schlosberg's (1954) emotional solid.

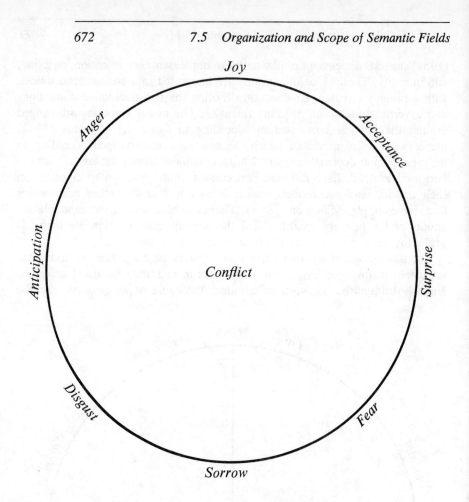

Figure 7.2   A cross section of Plutchik's (1962) emotional solid.

object of an emotion. Certain words refer to emotions or feelings that may
have no known cause or object: a person may report that he is happy or depressed for no accountable reason. But it would be nonsense to announce
being in love if there were no one, not even oneself, who was the object of that
love, and it would be odd to say that one was surprised if nothing caused that
surprise. In other words, ordinary-language psychology suggests there are
feelings, feelings *for*, and feelings *because*. It may be a mistake to overlook
these distinctions in trying to relate various terms used to characterize emotional experiences.

Krech and Crutchfield (1965) separate emotions that pertain to other people
from those that do not. They locate feelings for others in a two-dimensional
space, depending on whether a feeling is a like or a dislike and whether the
person experiencing it feels superior or inferior to its object. The resulting space
is depicted in figure 7.3. But it is apparent from the terms located in this space
that emotional concepts are expressed in a number of semantic domains. For

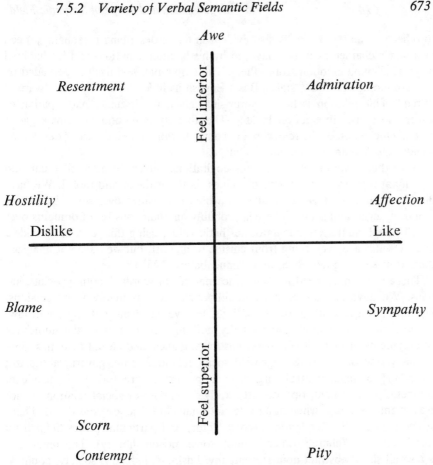

Figure 7.3 Emotions toward others. (After Krech and Crutchfield, 1965.)

example, "pity" combines an intellectual and an emotional concept: to pity someone is to know or to perceive something about him for which one feels sorry. (For a comparable analysis of "blame," see Fillmore, 1971b.) "Like," on the other hand, suggests a direct emotional bond.

Another example of emotional aspects entering a semantic field is found in the language of motivation. Apart from the central term, "need," Basic contains few explicitly motivational words—one looks in vain for "hunger" and "thirst." Yet it is clear that many states of mind with an emotional complexion can be motivating: boredom, loneliness, curiosity.* The spread of emotional colorings

*Ryle's (1949) view that such states cannot be *causes* of behavior seems to rest on an assumption that causes are always happenings. He claims that the use of dispositional terms in explanations of behavior amounts to stating a lawlike proposition. To explain a man's behavior in terms of a motive is like saying that a glass broke because it was brittle. And "brittle" means here roughly: the glass, if struck or twisted, will not dissolve or stretch or evaporate but fly into fragments. We accept this argument, but point out that such "laws" are causal assertions of the form "*x* allows *y* and not-*x* prevents *y*."

to other semantic domains is also evident in terms describing personality; much of a man's character can be conveyed by his habitual emotions and his habitual ways of eliciting emotion from others. The emotional field itself is pervaded by the terminology of bodily states; Basic English includes "cold," "pain," "warm," "tired." This relation is hardly surprising, given the intimate participation of visceral responses in emotional states. The ubiquity of emotional terms suggests that an elucidation of the relevant core concepts will be a vital part of developing an adequate semantics of natural language.

A further component of human cogitations, apart from intellectual and emotional matters, is judgment of values, both aesthetic and moral. We have discussed the notion of permissibility, which may range over several domains —moral, legal, and social. There is probably an analogous set of domains over which people make judgments of aesthetic value, using this term in its widest sense to embrace everything from cuisine to fine art, but we have not analyzed them (but see Osgood, Suci, and Tannenbaum, 1957).

There is a similar need for semantic analyses of words denoting social relations. We have considered permissibility, transactions involving possessions, kinship, and a few other social relations, but we have said nothing about law, government, and politics and virtually nothing about most of the numerous employments of men—their work, pastimes, games, and casual activities. Surprisingly few Basic words deal with social relations: rule, govern, authorize; represent; manage, control; organize; help, serve, care for; work, produce; compete; punish; fight, oppose, attack. The compass of social relations is not greatly enlarged even when other relevant nouns in Basic are considered. There are nouns denoting occupations (cook, actor) and particular places defined by social functions (church, office, school, town, prison, library). The remainder is a small set of abstract nouns: company, business, industry; society, country, nation; group, committee; power; crime; war, peace. Although the number of Basic social words is small, it is unclear whether any radically new core concepts would be needed to accommodate them.

The world view reflected in Basic English reveals a need for a number of core concepts we have not introduced here, concepts required to render a satisfactory account of the semantic fields of verbs pertaining to human cogitations, motives, and values. These fields, and the fields that represent social relations, stand most in need of semantic exploration. In spite of these gaps, however, our analyses of verbs of motion, possession, seeing, and saying seem to include a substantial fraction of the verbal concepts that are central to everyday speech. Our views of the internal organization of these fields, therefore, are based on a sufficient sample of English verbs to merit generalization.

7.5.3   Derivatives and Compounds

Our efforts to put particular verbal fields into perspective began with a consideration of their relation to other verbal fields. A natural next step is to consider their relation to the rest of the English lexicon.

What we have in mind is illustrated by the following experimental finding (Johnson-Laird, Robins, and Velicogna, 1974). One group tested could remember the meaning of a sentence like "The buyer of the fridge sold the car" without being able to recall the lexical category, noun or verb, with which the different parts of its meaning were conveyed. They tended to confuse the sentence with the nearly synonymous "The seller of the car bought the fridge" when they were confronted with an unexpected recognition test that included both items. Another group, whose instructions led them to expect the test, were much better at retaining lexical categories. Evidently the same meaning is sometimes conveyed by either the noun or the verb.

The distinction between verbs and nouns is syntactic. Our concerns are primarily semantic. Yet we have treated verbs separately, as if syntactic categories were needed in isolating semantic fields. This division has simplified our exposition, since words in the same syntactic category can be contrasted in similar grammatical environments, but is it fundamental? Many of the verbs we have analyzed can serve equally well as nouns or adjectives. Do their meanings change in important ways as their grammatical roles change? Or is there a conceptual constancy behind the different uses?

We would like to believe in conceptual constancy. It is difficult to estimate how strong an argument for constancy can be made in terms of cognitive economy—in terms of reducing the memory load for the language user—given the size, complexity, and irregularity of the English lexicon. But if a person knows a given word, that knowledge can make it easier to learn related words. Such facilitation suggests that the concept expressed by the first word may remain constant as it is transferred to related words.

Facilitation, moreover, is a basic fact of learning; it need not await the acquisition of some vocabulary of basic concepts from which to generalize. We have speculated that a young child begins to learn relatively specific uses of words; experience is required to appreciate, say, that "bring" in a question to be answered and "bring" in a command to others are instances of the same word. Such generalizations occur in much the same way for all who acquire the language. It would be inconceivable for a fluent adult user of English not to assimilate "walk," "walks," "walking," and "walked" into a common lexical concept. It is almost as inconceivable that the verbal and nominal uses of "walk" in "Let's walk" and "Let's take a walk" would not also be assimilated into a common lexical concept. But how far do these generalizations extend? The common component of "turn" in "Turn the wheel" and "It's your turn" requires a more abstract concept, but perhaps it could be found. If we extend the concept expressed by "take" to cover dishonesty ("take money"), capture ("take prisoners"), and endurance ("take punishment"), the common component becomes so general it is almost meaningless. Before we can understand how far a concept expressed by a particular verb can be generalized, we need to understand lexical generalization as a basic process in vocabulary acquisition.

One gets hold of a lexical concept first in a particular context of use and then searches for ways to generalize it appropriately to other contexts in which the same word occurs. Let us consider, therefore, a topic we have been avoiding: polysemy, the multiple senses of a single word. The problem can be illustrated by comparing uses of "move," where each context suggests a slightly different interpretation: "Move your foot," "Move the car," "The wheel moved," "It's your move," "This merchandise isn't moving," "He's on the move," "I move to adjourn," "That poem moved me," "They moved in yesterday," "He moved his bowels," "The earth moves about the sun," "The army moved forward," "The story moved rapidly," "Get a move on," "He moved heaven and earth," "Don't make a move."

A different contrastive set (see sec. 4.3) is suggested in each context. Can all these uses be assimilated into a single concept? We have made no attempt to provide a different formal schema for each slightly different sense but have assumed that a single schema, supplemented by some unspecified procedure for modulation by context, is involved in each use. And we have taken this approach in the face of psychological evidence that words with multiple meanings have multiple entries in semantic memory (Rubenstein, Garfield, and Millikan, 1970; Jastrzembski and Stanners, 1975).

The fact that a contrastive set can affect the meaning of any word is "the law of the field," emphasized by Weisgerber (1962). Presumably on any given occasion of use the contrastive set depends on both (a) the relative location of the word in the conceptual organization of the lexicon and (b) the context in which the word is used, because different contexts highlight different aspects of a single underlying concept. The formal listing of truth conditions that we have used to characterize verbal concepts seems to serve well enough to specify a general lexical location, but it is not obvious how a context of use could modulate such formulas. Perhaps the total schema of a verb has an informal as well as a formal part. On page 585 we suggested that just as we supplemented the perceptual paradigm for TABLE with functional information, so we can supplement the truth conditions for MOVE with information about typical scenarios of motion. The context of use could then modulate a representative scenario rather than the truth conditions.

As an example of how a typical scenario could be used we considered the "principle of implication." If you purchase an item of merchandise, in the normal course of events (following a typical scenario of purchasing, not of motion) the merchandise moves from the seller's location to your location; "move" picks up a sense of "sell" by the principle of implication. That is to say, in this context "move" takes on the contrastive set normally associated with "sell." The principle of implication is one example of a construal rule. Given the schema of a verb and a particular context of use, a construal rule modifies the schema to provide an interpretation of the word appropriate to that context. Another example of a construal rule is the convention we introduced in the discussion of double-purpose causative verbs (sec. 6.3), which are construed as noncausative when used intransitively.

We have not explored the variety of construal rules that would be required to account for all the modulations of meaning that lexicographers have noted. We have relied on incomplete definitions to give us the larger dimensions of lexical organization and have tried to leave open the question of how best to account for polysemy. But verbs like "move" cannot be indefinitely polysemous. We prefer the view that there is a lexical concept common to almost all these senses and that the meaning of a word can be extended in only some finite number of ways without baffling native speakers. However, important psychological questions (like the creativity of metaphorical extensions) are related to construal rules, so we should avoid making our more general argument contingent on our preference for conceptual generalization. But our bias should be obvious.

Some of the uses of "move" illustrated above cut across syntactic categories: "move" occurs in some sentences as a verb and in others as a noun. We would like to believe that the same schema underlies both uses—that construal rules can be formulated in such a way that a single schema is modified appropriately for either verbal or nominal uses. If this position could be defended it would mean that the analyses we have given apply to much more of the lexicon than we have considered explicitly.

In order to ascertain what fraction of the lexicon our analyses have touched we must consider morphological relations between words. By "morphology" linguists generally mean the study of the internal structure of words. Students of morphology traditionally distinguish processes of inflection from processes of word formation. Matthews (1974) calls these two main branches inflectional morphology and lexical morphology, but terminology in this area, as Matthews points out, is very fluid. Inflections are changes in a word to indicate case, number, gender, person, mood, voice, tense, aspect. In English, inflections are suffixes and their occurrence is determined by rules of syntax. Word formations are of two kinds, derivational and compositional. Derivatives in English are formed by affixation—by adding prefixes or suffixes. Compounds are formed by combining segments that can be used as words in their own right. For example, "see" is inflectionally related to "sees," "saw," "seen," and "seeing," derivationally related to "seeable" and "unseen," and compositionally related to "oversee" and "sightseeing." Dictionaries generally respect the difference between inflectional and lexical morphology by including inflectionally related words in a single entry and putting derivationally or compositionally related words in separate entries. But there are many exceptions, as when "ate" is entered separately as the past tense of "eat" or when a small dictionary lists "eater" under "eat."

In order to reduce the ambiguity of "word" in such discussions, some linguists use "lexeme" to refer to a lexical entry, that is, to a set of inflectionally related words. The schemata we have proposed may be regarded as associated with lexemes. Indeed, there may be more than a terminological advantage to treating a whole set of inflectionally related words as a psychological unit.

The particular inflection a word must take depends on the surface syntax of the sentence in which it occurs. For example, a speaker may know that EAT is the relation he wants to express between beans and Manuel yet not have decided whether to say "Manuel eats beans," where "eat" takes the inflection "-s," or "Beans are eaten by Manuel," where "eat" takes the inflection "-en." Halle (1973) once suggested that if all of the inflected forms of a given word were selected in the deep structure, the form appropriate in a particular surface structure could then be selected by rules of concord. It is not clear that selective conventions about concord are simpler than syntactic transformations that introduce inflections, but in either case inflections are superficial—a conclusion that fits well with our emphasis on the concept that a verb expresses rather than the inflected forms it can take. We claim, therefore, that each of our semantic analyses represents a lexeme—a set of inflectionally related words.

But what about derivationally related words? The adjective "movable" is derived from the verb "move" by addition of the suffix "-able." We have analyzed "move"; "movable" expresses the notion "capable of being moved," so the suffix might be defined in terms of "possible," which we have also discussed. Have we thus provided an analysis of "movable"? If so, what about other related words: commotion, commove, immovable, motion, motional, motionless, movability, movably, movement, mover, movie, removable, removal, remove? Can we define all these derivatives by combining our schema for "move" with schemata for affixes? It would be a strong claim, amounting to a hypothesis about how thousands of abstract concepts are related lexically to perceptible things and events. Derivational relations are complex and pose many questions for lexicology.

We have not hesitated to analyze words into semantic components, and similar analyses of derivatives should be even simpler—an appropriate analysis is often indicated in the morphology of the words themselves. In order to avoid circularity, we would need merely to ensure that none of the derivatives was used in an essential way in the analysis of its own roots. But many things that look simple turn out to be complicated when one tries to do them. Derivational relations in English are notorious for their irregularity and specificity. Without exploring them in greater detail it would be rash to claim they pose no substantial problems.

For compositionally related words, interpreting compound meanings from constituent meanings can be made to seem baffling. For example, if a bulldog is a dog that looks like a bull, a lapdog should be a dog that looks like a lap and a watchdog a dog that looks like a watch. Lees (1960) has tried to describe the generation of nominal compounds in terms of transformational grammar. He explains "pushbutton" as related to a nominalization like "button that someone pushes," whose deep structure also underlies "Someone pushes the button." "Pushbutton," according to Lees, thus illustrates a rule of composition based on the syntactic relation of verb to direct object. Lees's style of argument has been adapted and extended by others to account for derivative as well as compositional morphology, and even for semantic relations (like those between "kill" and "die") that have no morphological basis at all. The wisdom of this attempt to reduce compositional morphology to syntax has been questioned (Chomsky, 1970; Jackendoff, 1972) and we will not adopt it here.

We will argue instead that commonly used derivatives and compounds have their own entries in the mental lexicon, equal in all respects to any entries for words that they may incorporate morphologically. In most cases the decision tables that define them and their morphological constituents will have test conditions in common, as described in 4.4.3, but they are not understood in two steps, first as separate components and then as a unit. For example, "journalistic" has no human element in its semantics, although it contains "journalist," which does (Chapin, 1970); we do not first understand "journalist" and "-ic," then put those concepts together to obtain "journalistic." A compound like "White House" may share some test conditions with "white" and "house," but it involves something more that can best be represented in a separate lexical entry. The need for separate entries is clear when words like "fusion" and "fission" are compared; "fusion" is derived from "fuse" plus "-ion," but there is no root "fiss" from which "fission" could be derived. Since there must be a separate, full entry for "fission," it would be awkward to treat "fusion" differently (Jackendoff, 1975).

If each lexeme requires a full entry of its own, the generality of our analyses may seem limited. There will be a full entry for "move" and a full entry for "movable"; nothing prevents them from being as totally unrelated as "inform" and "informal." However, the mechanism of decision tables, or some equivalent, gives us a way to think about their relation, whenever there is one: some of the test conditions for MOVE are also relevant for MOVABLE, whereas none of the test conditions for INFORM are relevant for INFORMAL. It is a matter of historical accident whether the meaning of a derivative or compound preserves the same test conditions as its components or whether it has evolved some unrelated meaning. The generality of our analyses is thus left, as it should be, a matter for empirical investigation.

The trouble with this approach is that it fails to capture obvious similarities within sets of derivatives or sets of compounds. "Movable" is paralleled morphologically by other "-able" adjectives: agreeable, comparable, desirable, profitable, reasonable, serviceable. "Pushbutton" is paralleled morphologically by other verb-noun compounds: blowpipe, dragnet, firearm, flashlight, hacksaw, mincemeat, setscrew, stopwatch, turnbuckle. Such regularities are an invitation to search for rules of word formation; it seems unparsimonious to suppose that they play no role at all in the learning or use of similarly formed words. If they do play a role—if suffixes or modes of composition are seen as similar by people speaking the language—our theory should provide a way to express those similarities.

Kintsch (1974) has shown that for many reading tasks understanding takes no longer and is no less accurate for morphologically complex than for morphologically simple words. Either the semantic decomposition of a word is not an automatic and essential step in understanding it or decomposition can be performed without error or measurable delay. But Kintsch notes that semantic decomposition is necessary in some tasks; people cannot be totally ignorant of the relations that a separate, full-entry theory fails to capture, since those relations are apparently available on demand. MacKay (1974) asked people whether spoken sounds were words or not. They took longer to recognize words like "excision" than words like "refinement," where nonwords like "indusion" and "reactment" were used for the catch trials. MacKay points out that to derive "refinement," the suffix "-ment" is added to the root "refine," with no phonological modifications of either the root or the suffix being required. To derive "excision," on the other hand, several phonological changes are required in "excise": stress is shifted from the first to the second syllable, the vowel in the second syllable is changed and the glide is deleted, the final consonant is changed, and the new consonant phoneme is grouped with the third syllable of the derivative word. In order to perform the task, MacKay argues, listeners must identify both the root and the suffix; complex phonological changes would make that identification slower and more time-consuming, so the observed results indicate that phonological decomposition must be occurring. Under appropriate circumstances, therefore, it does seem possible to demonstrate that people use their implicit knowledge of derivational morphology. The natural way to represent such implicit knowledge theoretically is in the form of rules.

What are the rules of word formation? At one level are rules of pronunciation, like those tested by MacKay—rules for phonological accommodations required to link syllables together correctly. These rules have been stated precisely (Chomsky and Halle, 1968; Aronoff, 1974); some linguists have tried unsuccessfully to make the rules of word formation a part of phonology. A second level of rule relates syntactic categories. As we have noted, some linguists have tried (also unsuccessfully) to make these a part of syntax—to introduce all affixes transformationally and to account for compounds as abbreviated nominalizations. But even when these theories are rejected, it is still necessary to recognize that syntactic category is modified systematically by morphological changes. For example, the suffix "-ment" is characteristically added to a verb to change it into a noun (bewilderment, enjoyment, movement, punishment). So there must be word-formation rules like V + "ment" → N, which are very different from phonological rules (Halle, 1973).

A third kind of rule is needed for semantic relations. For example, a noun can name the act or process that a verb can predicate. "Refusal" is "the act of refusing." That is to say, "Ford refused the offer" and "There was an act such that it was Ford's refusal of the offer" have closely related truth conditions. English would be simpler if this relation, usually defined as "the act or process of ——ing," were always marked in the same way, but such is not the case. The same semantic relation can be marked by "-ment" or "-tion," as in "movement" and "motion," and "-al" is more likely to mark an adjective than a noun. So there must be rules like: "v(x, y)" is related to "x's act of V-ing y," which expresses a common semantic relation without confining it to any particular morphological relation (Jackendoff, 1974).

The first kind of rule, dealing with pronunciation, will concern us no further. The second requires more discussion, and the third is most relevant to our question of how much of the lexicon we have analyzed indirectly. We will consider the last two types of rule for derivatives first, then consider how the same distinction fares with compounds.

We will adapt a suggestion by Soboleva (1973) and maintain that the basic outlines of derivational morphology can be described in terms of operators that take a word as their argument and whose values are derived forms based on the same root. Since only the major syntactic categories—noun, verb, adjective, adverb—admit new word forms, the variety of operators required is limited. For example, if MOVE((x), y) is taken as the argument, we need some kind of morphological operator to indicate that the verb form is to be adopted, a different operator to indicate that an adjectival form is to be adopted, and still another operator for a nominal form. Three general operators, which we can designate as V, M, and N, for verb, modifier, and noun, suffice to illustrate the plan. Since this root morpheme is normally a verb, the basic form in this instance would be VMOVE. Derived forms can then be represented by compound operators: MVMOVE for the deverbal adjective "movable" and NVMOVE for the deverbal nouns "mover," "motion," "movement," and "move" itself when used as a noun. This example makes it clear that NV is a general operator that can be realized in English in a variety of forms—by adding "-er," "-tion," "-ment," or the null affix $\emptyset$ to the root verb "move." Soboleva displays such families of related derivatives in tree diagrams.

Longer derivational relations can be represented in this operator notation. For example, beginning with the root verb "edit" we can obtain "editorialize" as

edit	VEDIT
editor	NVEDIT
editorial	NNVEDIT
editorialize	VNNVEDIT

The adjective "immovable" would be MMVMOVE. The root need not be a verb: from the adjective "just" we can obtain "justifiability" as NMVMJUST; from the noun "sense" we can obtain "sensationalization" as NVMNNSENSE. Soboleva, who illustrates his proposal with Russian examples, regards the general forms as language universals whose concrete manifestations in any given language depend on the poverty or richness of derivational patterns available in that language. Complexity arises at the level of specific forms; general forms are relatively simple.

English, having both Anglo-Saxon and Latin origins, is rich in specific instances of the general forms. A mass of detailed facts about word formation in English have been assembled by Marchand (1969), who discusses the following prefixes: a-, ante-, anti-, archi-, auto-, be-, bi-, circum-, cis-, co-, counter-, crypto-, de-, demi-, di-, dis-, en-, epi-, ex-, extra-, fore-, hyper-, hypo-, in-, inter-, intra-, mal-, meta-, micro-, mid-, mis-, mono-, multi-, neo-, non-, pan-, para-, per-, peri-, poly-, post-, pre-, preter-, pro-, proto-, pseudo-, re-, retro-, semi-, step-, sub-, super-, supra-, sur-, trans-, tri-, twi-, ultra-, un-, uni-, vice-. He also treats the following suffixes: -able, -acy, -age, -al, -an, -ance, -ancy, -ant, -ard, -arian, -ary, -ate, -ation, -by, -cy, -dom, -ed, -ee, -een, -eer, -en, -er, -erel, -ery, -ese, -esque, -ess, -et, -ette, -fold, -ful, -hood, -iana, -ic, -ician, -ie, -ify, -ine, -ing, -ish, -ism, -ist, -ister, -ite, -ity, -ive, -ize, -kin, -le, -less, -let, -ling, -ly, -ment, -mo, -most, -ness, -ory, -ous, -ship, -some, -ster, -th, -ton, -ure, -ward, -y, -sy, -ty.

The list of affixes is even longer than it looks. Just as the same phonological string can be two different words (colonel, kernel) so the same phonological affix can play more than one morphological role. For example, the prefix "un-" can be really two prefixes; one converts adjectives into antonymous adjectives (unfair, unhappy) and another converts verbs into inverse verbs (undo, untie). The suffix "-er" provides a complicated example of homophonous affixes. In "taller" the "-er" is an inflection that marks a comparative adjective; in "clatter" it is a suffix that occurs frequently on words expressing sound or movement; in "speaker" it is a suffix that converts a verb into a noun. "Clatter" is not derived from "clat" plus "-er," yet the semantic similarities between chatter, clatter, flicker, flutter, glimmer, glitter, jabber, mutter, quaver, quiver, shudder, snicker, splutter, stammer, stutter, titter, seem to demand some separate recognition of this "-er" suffix. The "-er" that occurs derivatively can take either nouns or verbs as its argument: "speaker" is a deverbal noun and "lawyer" is a denominal noun. Beyond this division between deverbal and denominal "-er" derivatives there is little morphological reason to distinguish further varieties of "-er," although on semantic grounds it sometimes seems to serve different purposes: speaker, New Yorker, foreigner, old-timer, broiler. Indeed, if there are not at least two different "-er" suffixes, how do we account for the ambiguity of the following: counter, drawer, dresser, pointer? Polysemy among affixes is just as complicated as polysemy among root words.

Weaving together roots and affixes yields a complicated net of morphological relations. We can reach into the net and pick up a root, like "move," in order to study all the derivatives based on it, or we can pick up an affix, like negative "un-," and study all the roots that can take it. The set of roots to which an affix can apply may be called the base for that affix. We could simply list the base, but we would discover many similarities that would suggest obvious groupings. Those groupings can always be specified syntactically, and may be further specified semantically. Aronoff (1974) gives the following set of conditions on the morphology of the base for negative "un-":

Past participles used as adjectives	(seen, trained)
Gerundives used as adjectives	(bending, reasoning)
Deverbal adjectives ending in "-able"	(learnable, reasonable)
Adjectives ending in "-y"	(happy, worthy)
Adjectives ending in "-ly"	(seemly, timely)
Adjectives ending in "-ful"	(faithful, mindful)
Adjectives ending in "-al"	(conditional, critical)
Adjectives ending in "-like"	(ladylike, warlike)

This characterization of the base for negative "un-" is much more specific than a general observation that this affix attaches to adjectives. A full statement of derivational rules of word formation in English would include such descriptions of a base along with the syntactic and semantic effects of every affix.

The semantic rule for negative "un-" is simply stated as the negation of the meaning of the root adjective. Consider an example. Since every derivative is assumed to have its own entry, there must be an entry for UNHAPPY as well as an entry for HAPPY. We can write the schema

(142)   UNHAPPY(x) or MMHAPPY(x):   Someone x is "unhappy" if:
        (i) notHAPPY(x)

In this case the semantics is clearly compositional: the meaning of "unhappy" is the meaning of "un-" plus the meaning of "happy." It is easy to see how HAPPY and UNHAPPY could be entered in a single decision table.

The simple pattern of (142) is not always realized. Consider one example of the agentive suffix "-er":

(143)   BUYER(x) or NVBUY(x):   Someone x is a "buyer" if there is something w, an amount of money m, and someone y such that:
        (i) (FROM(FOR(BUY)))(x, w, m, y)

In this case the semantics is not compositional; "-er" serves to select a particular argument of the verb "buy." It is still reasonably obvious, however, how BUY and BUYER could be entered in the same decision table.

Whereas (143) selects one argument of the verb and presupposes the others, causative affixes can introduce new arguments. For example:

(144)   BRIGHTEN$((x), y)$ or VMBRIGHT(y):   Something x "brightens" something y if:
        (i) BECOME(y, y') & BRIGHTER(y', y)
        (ii) DO(x, S)
        (iii) CAUSE$(S, (i))$

In (144) we have replicated our general schema for double-purpose causative verbs (6.3.7)—verbs that are causative when used transitively ("He brightened the lights") and noncausative when used intransitively ("The lights brightened"). If we try to parcel out in (144) what represents "bright" and what represents "-en," nearly everything goes to "-en." Yet we cannot associate this particular semantic transformation with "-en" uniquely because it is also associated with "-ize" (legalize, materialize), "-ify" (prettify, purify), and other causative affixes (see p. 469).

One of the most common deverbal nominalizations serves to abstract the action that the verb predicates. "Refusal" has been cited as an example. How should such abstractions be represented in the schemata we have developed? The verb "refuse" presumably takes two arguments, one for the person who performs the act and one for the thing or offer that is refused. The noun "refusal," on the other hand, takes a single argument, the event so described; at this level of abstraction, neither the subject nor the object of the verb appears as an argument. The following schema shows one way to represent this abstraction:

(145)   REFUSAL(S) or NVREFUSE(x, y):   An action characterized by S is
a "refusal" if there is someone x and something y such that:
(i) ACT(x, S)
(ii) S = REFUSE(x, y)

However, (145) will occur in the same decision table with a schema like

(146)   REFUSE(x, y):   Someone x "refuses" something y if:
(i) ACT(x, S)
(ii) ALLOW(S, notACCEPT(x, y))

The act denoted by S is the same in (145i) and (146i). What the abstractive "-al" suffix indicates, therefore, is a selection of an implicit argument of the verbal root. With intransitive root verbs ("arrive," "survive") the implicit arguments are E statements for events and P statements for processes. For example, ARRIVAL(E) would be something like E = BEGIN(notTRAVEL(x))— compare (23) in 7.1.5.

According to the argument we are advancing here, a person who knows English will have separate entries in his subjective lexicon (separate rules in his lexical decision tables) for each derivative word, yet the entries will be so related that he will be able to verify easily, by searching semantic memory (by exercising the decision table containing both rules), that various morphological rules of word derivation apply. He will be able to use affixes (inflectional as well as derivational) as indicators of the syntactic category of words he hears in ordinary discourse. He will probably be able to recognize the meaning and syntactic category of novel words even though he would not have known how to derive them himself. For example, a person familiar with the causative "-ify" suffix on such VM words as "justify," "simplify," and "clarify" should understand "uglify" on first encounter—by inferring that it is related to "ugly" in the same way—even if he did not know in advance whether "uglify," "uglyize," "enugly" or none of these was an acceptable VM form. And even if he happened to be unfamiliar with "ugly," he should have a strong suspicion that "uglify" is a verb. Moreover, having heard the deadjectival verb "uglify," he would probably expect there to be a deverbal noun "uglification" following the model of such NVM forms as "justification," "simplification," and "clarification." All he would need to learn in order to take advantage of these derivational rules is which one of a limited number of specific operators serves this general purpose in the case of "ugly." What he would not know is any explicit rule of the form: "-ify" converts adjectives into verbs, or "-ify" means that something causes the adjective to become assertable. Such rules are creatures of theory; they are not stored in any lexical entry or decision table. At best they represent learning strategies for vocabulary enlargement—they may be rules for constructing a subjective lexicon, but they are not information that the subjective lexicon must contain.

The processes of word composition are less well understood than those of word derivation. There is an interesting psychological contrast between English derivatives and compounds. Derivation seems to facilitate abstract generalizations; composition seems to facilitate concrete specifications. In part this is because most of the derivational resources of English come from Latin, and Latinate words dominate legal, medical, and scientific language, where abstract generalizations abound. But even when we avoid derivational patterns inherited from Latin or Greek the difference is apparent. For example, a boy is a concrete individual and a schoolboy is a particular kind of boy; "boyish," on the other hand, is an abstract term used to denote a personality trait. The compounds "searchlight," "flashlight," "pilot light," and "traffic light" are hyponyms of "light source"; "moonlight," "candlelight," "firelight," and "sunlight" are hyponyms of "light illumination." These compounds are all more specific than their head noun. The derivative "lightness," on the other hand, abstracts an attribute of light; "lighting" is a generic term for artificial light or sources of artificial light; "lighten" introduces a causative agent or refers to a change in light; "enlighten" is related to illumination metaphorically; "enlightenment" is an abstraction made possible by the Latinate suffix "-ment." These derivatives tend to be less specific than their root. Perhaps the very specificity and concreteness of most compounds makes it difficult to formulate general rules for their formation—their interpretation seems to rely heavily on nonlinguistic knowledge about specific things, events, processes, people.

The distinction between rules that express syntactic effects of word formation and rules that express semantic effects is more difficult to maintain for compounds than for derivatives. Compositionally, there is little temptation to parallel the affixal operators—it would be odd, for example, to call "carry" a morphological operator that converts adjectives into nouns, citing "carryall" as evidence. The syntactic-semantic distinction must be formulated differently. A syntactic rule for compounds might classify them according to the syntactic categories of the component words: some are verb-noun ("pushbutton"), some are noun-verb ("sunrise"), some are noun-noun ("boyfriend"), some are adjective-noun ("madman"), some are noun-adjective ("color-blind"). A semantic rule for compounds might classify them as endocentric ("eyestrain" is a hyponym of "strain") or exocentric ("pickpocket" is not a hyponym of "pocket").

And so a syntactic-semantic distinction can be maintained. But usually a definitional approach is taken, which has the effect of combining syntactic and semantic information: "A fisherman is a man who fishes." This definition follows the formula "A V-er-N is a N that V-s." Other compounds have definitions that fit the same formula: blinker light, drummer boy, fighter plane, killer shark, lover boy, retainer fee, washerwoman. In this way a class of similar compounds is discovered.

One problem with the definitional approach concerns the criteria by which a theorist should select his formulas. Lees (1960) suggests that the definitions should be nominalizations derived syntactically from sentences underlying the compounds. "Popcorn" is from "popping corn," which is from "corn that pops," which is a nominalization of the sentence "The corn pops"; each syntactic transformation can be justified on the grounds that it is required elsewhere in the grammar of English. It is not obvious how a person encountering a compound for the first time would know which syntactic transformations to use in tracking it back to a definitional sentence, but one might hope that the variety of compositional rules would be relatively limited.

Syntactic reconstructions of a defining sentence are most questionable when the compound is noun-noun, that is, when a verb has been omitted from the hypothetical sentence relating them. In the case of "garden party," the missing predicate might be something like "occurs in"; for "whalebone" it might be "is a part of"; for "nightshirt" it might be "worn at"; and so on through a variety of verbs that must be supplied from the theorist's imagination. Is "garden party" to be thought of as ambiguous between "The party occurs in the garden," "The party is a part of the garden," "The party worn at the garden"? Or is there supposed to be some syntatic rule that associates an appropriate verb with each compound?

Lees (1970) writes that "it may be possible to associate one, or a small number of generalized verbs with certain classes of compounds by fixed grammatical rule" (p. 182). One example of what he means by a generalized verb is the semantic intersection of "energize," "drive," "power," "actuate," "propel," "impel." In a case grammar, these verbs take an Object and an Instrument case, and the Instrument is the grammatical subject. "Steam energizes/drives/powers/actuates/propels/impels the boat" underlies "steamboat"; "Wind energizes/drives/powers/actuates/propels/impels the mill" underlies "windmill"; similarly for air rifle, alcohol lamp, heat engine, hydrogen bomb, motor car, oil stove, suction pump, waterwheel. Another group of nominal compounds represents the Object and Locative cases of the generalized verb common to "live," "work," "infest," "inhabit." "The bug lives in/works in/infests/inhabits the bed" underlies "bedbug," and similarly for bank teller, boll weevil, caveman, field mouse, garage mechanic, hospital orderly, parlor maid, store clerk.

Although we have not found it necessary to introduce such grammatical cases in order to analyze the semantics of English verbs (see 6.3.2), the suggestion that a limited number of generalized verbs might underlie all the nominal compounds is an invitation to compare Lees's selection with the lexical concepts we have considered. His generalized verbs are presented in the following list, where on the left we give a lexical concept that seems to capture the generalization and on the right examples of compounds so based:

MOVE: energize, drive, power, actuate, propel, impel (steamboat)

CAUSE: cause, yield, engender, emit, produce (fingerprint)

PREVENT: repel, prevent, reject, forstall, suppress, remove (mothball)

KEEP: preserve, ensure, protect, retain, foster, secure (chicken wire)

MAKE: provide, vend, supply, afford, produce (tone arm)

MEASURE: determine, measure, establish (hourglass)

SHOW: exhibit, portray, show (flowchart)

IN: live in, work in, infest, inhabit (caveman)

(IN(KEEP)):   keep, nurture, put, raise (cowshed, greenhouse)

(IN(SELL)):   sell, deal in, service (stock market, tearoom)

(IN(USE)):   use, put (hairbrush, nosedrops)

(FROM(GET)):   get, obtain, derive (silkworm, sugarbeet)

(FROM(MAKE)):   make, prepare, concoct (coal tar, oatmeal)

These could be grouped according to the semantic fields we have analyzed.

Lees's search for a semantic rationalization of compositional variety may be incomplete or incorrect in detail, but it serves as a reminder that one of the benefits we might expect from analyses of the kind proposed here would be a firmer basis for just such explorations. Until they are further advanced, however, we will not speculate on any limited variety of ways in which entries for compounds could be grouped in decision tables for related lexemes. It is clear that a compound is not to be defined as the union of the test conditions for its component words, but exactly how it should be defined remains a problem for further study.

The claim that compound words are formed and understood according to rules can be tested empirically by inventing unusual compounds and asking people for interpretations. If every compound must be separately learned, people should be unable to agree about the meanings of unfamiliar compounds. But if meanings can be constructed according to some general rules, there should be considerable agreement on the correct meanings of novel compounds. Gleitman and Gleitman (1970) chose such relatively arbitrary triplets as "bird," "foot," and "house" and spoke them with intonations that produced twelve compounds: foot bird-house, foot-bird house, foot house-bird, foot-house bird, house foot-bird, house-foot bird, bird foot-house, bird-foot house, bird house-foot, bird-house foot, house bird-foot, house-bird foot. "A birdhouse for feet" was considered a correct interpretation of the compound "foot bird-house," whereas "the bottom of a birdhouse" was considered an error of ordering (it would have been a correct response to "bird-house foot"). To "house bird-foot" a correct response was "a disease birds get from being in the house," whereas "a foot for house-birds" was considered an error in the interpretation of the stress pattern (it would have been a correct response to "house-bird foot").

Gleitman and Gleitman tested people with different educational backgrounds and found consistent differences between groups. Judges with postgraduate education made fewer errors, both in producing and recognizing correct paraphrases, than judges with only a high school degree. Since all of the judges were competent users of English, their different performances were not attributable to differences in their knowledge of syntactic rules. On the other hand, since the most educated judges were in good agreement with one another and with the experimenters, their performance seemed to follow rules that the less educated judges did not have. Gleitman and Gleitman, who followed Lees's (1960) syntactic strategy for interpreting compounds, suggest a distinction between a core grammar that everyone knows and a penumbral grammar consisting of rules observed only by a linguistic elite. Alternatively, we would argue that everyone must know the rules for sentence formation, but that rules for word formation are an intellectual luxury—people who do not know rules for compounding can still use the language without difficulty by learning the meanings of compounds more or less independently.

We have raised these questions about derivatives and compounds in order to explore the limitations of our work. One reason for psychological interest in the limits of our analyses is that a crude parallel might be drawn between our developing theory of lexical knowledge and a child's acquisition of his native vocabulary. The grounds on which we might claim that an analysis of word W also captures the meanings of words W', W'', . . . , are the same grounds on which a psychologist might expect a child to generalize his learning of W to the learning of related words W', W'', . . . Moreover, if we had been able to confine our primitive lexical concepts to those given directly in perception, there might even have been some reason for philosophical interest in the generalizability of our analyses—empiricistic theories of language usually hold that the indispensable core of the lexicon consists of words whose meanings are acquired perceptually. This idea was one whose plausibility we set out to explore. As we discovered how much of the lexicon is based on primitive concepts that are not perceptual, we were forced to revise our program. If a person knew only words whose meanings are given perceptually and related words interpretable by generalization from the perceptual words, his vocabulary would be severely limited.

Indeed, from the present discussion of derivatives and compounds it would seem that a person who knew only the concepts, perceptual and nonperceptual, that we have analyzed would also have a limited vocabulary. We believe that, given a knowledge of grammar, he would understand the various inflected forms, and we can see how he might develop a strategy for learning derivatives, but his understanding of compounds and idioms would remain mysterious. In short, our analyses touch on far more than we have considered in any detail, but the advance from touching to grasping may be difficult. Perhaps it will be impossible to reduce all lexical concepts to a small set of primitives.

We have said that a concept is a kind of implicit theory—or that a theory is a self-consciously elaborated concept. We have no wish to underestimate the variety of theories the human mind can generate, and no hope of finding a classificatory system to deal with all of them. But the theories that are sufficiently important to be invoked repeatedly and to achieve the degree of social endorsement represented by incorporation into the lexicon of everyday speech seem to us to represent a subset particularly appropriate for psychological study. The general acceptance required for lexical incorporation is unlikely for concepts that do not reflect basic aspects of the human mind, and consequently their analysis must be pursued systematically if we are ever to understand that mysterious organ.

Conclusion

Language is complicated. Any instrument adaptable to an unforeseeable variety of social, personal, and intellectual demands has to be complicated—the more complicated the better. As users of language we can feel only gratitude for the potentially infinite diversity of linguistic expression. As students of language, however, this complexity can inspire more frustration than gratitude; it is a major obstacle for those who seek a self-conscious understanding of what language is and how it works. One wonders whether anything so variable and intricate could ever be tamed by scientific theories.

Analysis seems our best hope. Scientists sometimes overcome complexity by analyzing an unmanageable problem into manageable subproblems; the trick is to identify variables that interact strongly with one another but are independent of the rest of the system. This strategy has been applied to the study of language with some success: linguists have tried to define phonology, morphology, lexicon, grammar, and rhetoric as components of language that can be studied independently; philosophers have tried to sort their linguistic concerns into syntactic, semantic, or pragmatic kinds. A perspicacious partitioning gives the student of language a general idea of where his work fits into the larger theory and a general hope that apparently remote discoveries will not render his results invalid or irrelevant.

Such considerations suggest that analysis would also be a good strategy for psychologists interested in language. How that suggestion should be implemented has been a central question for us. It is not an easy question, for in psychology everything is related to everything else. Our answer evolved piecemeal through a series of theortical revisions.

A psychology of language should be psychological. That is to say, if we hope to create something recognizable as a psychological theory of human language, psychological methods and principles should be applied in the same way they are applied to other mental and behavioral phenomena. An immediate consequence of this condition is that language loses its singularity. It becomes one phenomenon among many, distinguished perhaps by its greater complexity, but still analyzable into stimuli, responses, and reinforcements and subject to the same principles of perception, learning, and motivation that are believed to govern all thought and behavior.

But a psychology of language should also be plausible. We began with psychological theories that reduced language to little more than a collection of habitual associations of perceived situations with descriptive vocal responses. From there we traveled a long road with many detours, delays, and dead ends —as each obstacle was encountered we revised the theory and set out anew. In the end we were propounding a different kind of analysis, an analysis into concepts and procedures for using them, rather than analysis into stimuli, responses, and reinforcements. Content and method were still psychological, but from a kind of psychology more compatible with linguistics, philosophy, and artificial intelligence. The necessary revisions were introduced on several levels at the same time. The levels are closely related, but we will try to separate them here for the purpose of recapitulation.

Let us recall a view of language and perception once popular among psychologists and philosophers. Theories of learning were believed to provide simple explanations of how words come to be associated with percepts. It was taken to be a general principle of psychology that when a response made in the presence of a discriminative stimulus is consistently followed by reinforcement, a connection is strengthened between that stimulus and that response. One needed merely to equate percepts with stimuli and words with responses in order to apply this theory to language.

Psychologists inspired by the analogy elaborated many extensions consistent with it. Associations between words were explained in terms of generalization; sentences of the form "x is a y" were viewed as conditioning devices connecting x and y; covert responses were introduced to mediate and lend flexibility to connections between words and actions; contingencies of reinforcement were used to explain language acquisition in children and language use in adults. Once language was reduced to a vast network of connections, the concept of language seemed unnecessary; it could be replaced by "verbal behavior" based on socially shared "verbal habits."

Although there are obviously associations between percepts and the words people use to label them (the word "lamp" is in some sense associated with the objects it labels) we rejected an approach via standard learning theory on the grounds of superficiality. Even if words were responses conditioned to occur in the presence of distinctive stimuli—a possibility we reject but would entertain for purposes of argument—nothing in standard learning theory is adequate to account for the type of productive creativity that characterizes human language. Generously interpreted, associationism accounts for only one aspect of language learning and use: mastery of certain substantive words in the vocabulary of one's language. Beyond that, the analogy founders on linguistic phenomena far more complex than the kinds of behavior that learning and conditioning theories were developed to explain.

To reject an approach to language based on an associative theory of learning is not to claim that language is unlearned; children must learn their native tongues. In criticizing associative learning theory as a basis for understanding human language, moreover, we did not offer any judgment on its adequacy to account for the observations that gave rise to it. It would be just as wrong to say that no theory of learning could be correct unless it explained language learning as it would be to say that no theory of language could be correct unless it explained conditioned responses. We assume that there is more than one kind of learning and that the kinds required for mastering a language are still poorly understood. What is needed is a theory of learning adequate to account for language acquisition, but such a theory is not likely to emerge until we know a great deal more about what it is that has to be acquired.

When people talk they generally intend to say something. They often say things that other people can agree or disagree with. A conditioned response, on the other hand, is a brute fact, like a tree or a sunset. It may occur or fail to occur. If it occurs, it may have some character, strength, or latency that can be measured, recorded, analyzed. What makes a response an assertion? An associative theory should provide some explanation of how the utterance of a noise like /læmp/, which is said to be a vocal response conditioned to occur automatically in the presence of certain discriminative stimuli, can come to play the role of an observational assertion "Lamp," having the force of "That is a lamp," which can, in the context of use, be judged true or false. An advocate of standard learning theory might take the following line: a child's first utterances of /læmp/ will be followed by adult utterances of /yɛs/, with pleasurable consequences for the child; when the child hears an adult utter the same noise in appropriate circumstances, he endeavors to complete the episode pleasurably once more by supplying the missing /yɛs/. Thus the child is inducted into the mysteries of assent, which subsequent learning can refine into truth. Such an account sounds plausible, perhaps, but a critical problem remains. There is no evidence that the transition from response to assertion that this theory is intended to explain ever occurs in the language learning of young children.

The issue can be avoided by not starting with the assumption that learning a label consists initially of strengthening an automatic association between a percept and a vocalization. One way to avoid it is to include judgment in the process of perception itself. This alternative assumption would be that in order to make a discriminative response to stimulation, one has to attend to and make judgments of various properties and relations offered by the perceived situation. For this reason we phrased our discussion of sensation and perception in terms of perceptual predicates expressing such judgments. We assumed that it was the outcome of such attentional-judgmental abstractions from perception, not the particular percept itself, that provided a basis for learning labels. The capacity to make a match/mismatch judgment can be built into the theory at its foundations, obviating the need to explain its development as a consequence of learning.

Our first revision, therefore, was a shift from theories about learning automatic connections between percepts and words to theories about learning rules relating perceptual judgments to assertible utterances. This revision made it possible to consider a more sophisticated class of theories based on verification. Such theories generally assume that in order for a person to understand some such sentence as "Der Schnee ist weiss" he must know an appropriate truth rule: "Der Schnee ist weiss" is true if and only if snow is white. According to this approach, the relation between perception and language is established by learning metalinguistic rules that specify how perceptual judgments can be used to verify or falsify sentences. To know the meaning of a sentence is to know how it could be verified.

Verifiability theories of meaning are not psychological theories. They hold rigorously only for formal languages like logic or mathematics, which describe timeless domains very different from the world that ordinary language is used to describe. For example, unlike "Two is the only even prime number," the sentence "The cat is on the mat" may be true in some situations and false in others. A sentence in a natural language like English may express different propositions, or make different statements, on different occasions. It is not the sentence per se that is true or false, but the proposition that the sentence expresses on a given occasion. Following this line, some theorists distinguish two steps in verification: discovering the proposition that a sentence expresses in a particular situation, and determining the truth value of that proposition. The first step can be taken as defining the problems of pragmatics, the second, semantics.

This maneuver allows a logician to set aside various complicated pragmatic aspects of ordinary language and to develop his semantic ideas in a rigorous fashion. There are still many problems to be solved, of course. For example, what are the truth conditions for propositions expressed by sentences like "John believes that the cat is on the mat"? One approach to sentences expressing propositional attitudes is via possible worlds. One may claim that "A believes that P" divides all possible worlds into two classes such that one class is compatible with everything A believes and the other is incompatible with it. Then "A believes that P" is true if and only if P is true in all possible worlds compatible with what A believes. Possible worlds carry verification into realms of imagination far removed from immediate perception, but something of the sort seems necessary in order to deal with the fact that people often make assertions about states of affairs other than the one that prevails at the moment they are speaking.

The relation of language to perception is also involved in pragmatic theory. In order to determine what proposition a speaker is asserting when he says "The cat is on the mat" on a particular occasion, a listener must be able, at the time of utterance, to identify the particular cat and the particular mat to which the speaker refers. Then he can formulate some proposition relating that cat to that mat at that time, a proposition that can then be turned over to semantic theory for verification. Identifying the correct cat and the correct mat at the correct time may involve perceptual search and recognition. Deictic terms are a major concern of pragmatic theory; their reference can be determined only from knowledge of the context in which they are used, and that knowledge often comes from perception.

How might psychology take advantage of these philosophical formulations? There seems to be a natural division of labor. Psychologists could contribute by providing an account of the procedures that a person follows in carrying out a verification. In order to verify the proposition expressed by "Der Schnee ist weiss," for example, a person must look at some snow and judge its color, or remember what it looks like, or whatever. Perceptual predicates seem an ideal foundation on which to build such an account.

This theoretical approach led us to consider the following general formulation. A person learns many rules of the form "P is true if and only if $F(x) = 1$," where $F(x)$ describes a mental computation to be performed, such as attending to x and judging whether it is F. If the result of the computation is that $F(x) = 1$, then P is true; otherwise it is not true (false or indeterminate). The psychological problem would be to characterize the mental computations that a person performs when he learns and applies such rules.

As soon as the problem was stated in this way it became clear that further theoretical revision was needed. Philosophical accounts say little or nothing about actual operations, procedures, or computations performed in verification. The relation of verifiability theory to actual verification is similar to the relation of the axioms of arithmetic to actual arithmetic computation. In order for a psychologist to offer useful suggestions about the operations involved, he must introduce a theory of mental computation. The best idea currently available as to what such a theory might look like is the theory of computation developed to describe the operation of computers.

We assumed, therefore, that $F(x)$ is a program of instructions to be executed. The program could contain such instructions as find(in a given search domain, x) and test(at time t, x satisfies the description $D(x)$). The description D could be a perceptual paradigm composed of the perceptual predicates introduced in the theory of sensation and perception. That is to say, some cognitive executor would request the perceptual system to search for, attend to, and make judgments of various combinations of perceptual predicates that identify objects or events taking various labels, where each label is associated with a particular perceptual paradigm $D(x)$. In order to develop such a procedural semantics, we introduced a small set of control instructions, each representing a complex skill that must be acquired in the course of cognitive development.

The division between pragmatics and semantics advocated by some propositional semanticists has its rough parallel in procedural semantics. Again, a two-step process is imagined: the sentence is translated into an appropriate program, and then the program may be executed. The first step can be considered analogous to compiling a program written in a higher-order language (in this case, English) into a procedural language suitable for execution by the system (in this case, the appropriate control instructions and paradigms to be tested). Once a clause is compiled, the resulting program may or may not be executed; translation is separated from execution. (In some cases it may be necessary to execute a program derived from one clause before a program can be compiled for another clause; Isard, 1975). A speaker's task is to write a program that if correctly compiled and executed will result in the intended outcome for the listener.

The revisionary impact of introducing this procedural machinery was to reduce verification to but one of many processes that the system can perform. Upon compiling a sentence, the executive system may take overt action, search for information and compose a sentence expressing it, store it for future use, generate imagery of it, use it as a subroutine in a larger problem-solving program, or take whatever other actions are required to attain its goals. The result was a much broader base for psychological theory; the cost was the introduction of other control instructions needed to supplement "find" and "test."

Having revised our hypotheses to this extent, we undertook to explore possible formulations for the part of the system that translates sentences into programs—the part that determines which computations should be performed in order for the system to (a) verify the proposition expressed by that sentence used in that context, (b) take action satisfying the request made by that sentence in that context, (c) find information answering the question posed by that sentence in that context, or whatever. It is obviously necessary for such a system to have syntactic capabilities. Since the variety of grammatical sentences is unlimited, it is inconceivable that a person associates every sentence with a particular program or set of programs. Some way to decompose sentences into phrases and words is indispensable, but we took the position that there is probably not an isolated parsing component that determines the phrase structure and transformational history of a sentence before turning it over to some other component for lexical lookup and semantic interpretation. Syntactic and semantic theories are distinct, yet they cannot be independent. In any plausible theory of language use, segmentation, parsing, lexical lookup, and similar functions must all be performed in an integrated, mutually supporting manner in order for the total system to accomplish its task of producing an executable program. We may have underestimated the complexity of the syntactic processes involved in this decomposition, but we preferred to concentrate on the lexicon and to include as much information as possible in its internal representations.

Our explorations, therefore, were directed primarily at what linguists call the lexical component of language. We began by considering copulative sentences of the form "x is a W," where translation would normally produce a simple program, $F(x)$, and execution would involve finding an x and testing whether it satisfied the description D given in F. That is to say, we began by trying to play the truth-rule game procedurally in the simplest possible instances.

This exercise led to some instructive complications. Our basic assumption was that paradigms compounded from perceptual predicates would provide descriptions adequate for labeling objects. We quickly discovered that such matters as the nonequivalence of instances, vagueness and the contribution of noncriterial features, and the importance of characteristic orientation were not explained by purely perceptual descriptions. Lists of shared perceptual predicates account reasonably well for many relations between labels for concrete objects, like hyponymy and partonymy, but we found that a labeling system needs information about functions as well as about forms of the objects to be labeled.

These explorations led to a final theoretical revision. On the one hand, a routine for identifying instances of a label has to include more than a perceptual description. On the other hand, a routine for identifying instances of a label does not exhaust all that people know about such instances. We concluded that we must associate lexical concepts with each label. Having gone that far, we assumed that every word expresses a lexical concept. A lexical concept is anything capable of being the meaning of a word. Even a deictic word, whose reference shifts with every context, expresses a lexical concept; its meaning is given by the procedures for determining its denotation in context. For most words, the lexical concept consists of two parts, a definitional part depending on a functional-perceptual schema for recognizing instances and a connotative part consisting of knowledge associated with the word, including the relation of the concept to other concepts. These connotative relations between lexical concepts provide some of the basic furniture of the mind. In short, we adopted a conceptual theory of meaning, similar in some respects to Frege's but with a more psychological conception of "concepts" and tied to procedural rather than propositional interpretations of sentences.

This revision assumes that the referential part of semantics does not exhaust all that a psychologist should mean by "meaning." Even a procedural semantics, which admits more than verification as a basic operation, should rest on a conceptual base. The meaning of a sentence is not given solely by the routine into which it can be translated in particular situations; it must also have a place in a larger system of knowledge and belief.

A semantics based wholly on either verifiability or on the compilation and execution of programs moves easily only with sentences (or sentences-in-context). Individual words are neither true nor executable; one might conclude, therefore, that a word has no meaning outside of its use in a sentence. Psychologically, however, individual words do have meanings; they are not simple vocal responses conditioned to discriminative stimuli. When one talks about the meaning of a word one is presumably offering a generalization about the semantics of a large class of sentences containing that word; one is assuming that the word makes roughly the same contribution everywhere it appears. In a conceptual theory of meaning, one can think of a sentence-in-context as expressing a concept formed by a particular arrangement of lexical concepts. Although verifiability or executability may not emerge until a sentence has been formulated, meaning is as inherent in lexical concepts as in sentential concepts. To say that an individual word has meaning, that it can make roughly the same contribution to every sentence that includes it, is to say that the lexical concept (or range of concepts) it expresses is always the same.

This revisionary pilgrimage broke off here, after we had made our way to a position that sounds much like common sense. Common sense has a bad name, however, and most of the alternatives we cut our path through can be construed as attempts to provide better accounts of language and language use. Concepts are invisible, impalpable, ill-defined abstractions that have a nasty way of being whatever a theorist needs them to be at the moment. If our position is to be seriously defended, some principled way must be found to identify what a concept is and what cognitive work it can do. Since there seems to be no humanly conceivable limit to the variety and complexity of human conceptualizations, the task would appear impossible. But perhaps a foothold could be established by beginning with lexical concepts.

Lacking a clear way to continue our description of the underlying conceptual system, we turned to analyses of the parts of it frozen by social convention into the English lexicon. Having separated percepts from words by an intervening conceptual system of inscrutable complexity, we began to take words apart one by one, disciplining our analyses with the methods of procedural representation developed along the way.

At this point a second level of theoretical revisionism was introduced. It began with the requirement that the translator compile an executable program based on the sentence it is given. The translator has at its disposal a store of routines associated with each of the words of the language, and can use them, guided by the syntactic structure of the sentence, as subroutines in compiling the program. These routines were assumed to be of the form

(1) $F(x)$: In order to determine whether something x is labeled W execute the following routine:
         (i) find(search domain, x)
         (ii) test(time, $D(x)$)

Here control instructions are stated explicitly in the labeling routine, which serves to relate the label W and the perceptual paradigm D. When W occurs in a sentence, the translator calls $F(x)$ and includes its routine in the compiled program.

When we considered the variety of programs that might call $F(x)$, however, we found that these particular control instructions are not always appropriate. For example, a speaker may already have found x and want to institute a search for the label W. In order to admit such alternative uses, we might have allowed a variety of routines associated with W and introduced a decision process to select the routine appropriate for any given use. But it seemed simpler to revise this formulation by removing the control instructions—to assume that the translator has the capability of constructing the routine needed in any particular context.

So we assumed that the lexical information includes not explicit routines but information needed for the translator to construct explicit routines. Then we could represent the rule connecting W and D as follows:

(2) $F(x)$:   Something x is a W if and only if it satisfies the perceptual paradigm $[D(x)]$.

Brackets around the description isolate it from execution; it is essentially an assertion, not a routine for testing an assertion. The translator can use the asserted information to construct an appropriate subroutine in the program it compiles for the sentence.

Consideration of the kinds of information required in order to determine the applicability of a label revealed that often a purely perceptual description is inadequate. For many labels, functional information must supplement perceptual information. We called this total, form-plus-function type of description a conceptual schema of the object to be labeled. This revision acknowledged that an identification device is a particular exploitation of a general concept:

(3)   F(x):   Something x is a W if and only if it satisfies the conceptual schema $[C(x)]$.

$C(x)$ includes both perceptual and functional criteria. The small capital F indicates that the concept F relates the label W and the schema C. Thus, with each label there is an associated lexical concept that presumably includes much more information than is required merely to identify instances of W. The schema C is an identifying expression stripped of all other conceptual knowledge not normally required for identifying instances of W. The perception of an instance and the label W are now related as alternative routes into or out of this larger store of information.

With these revisions, which leave room for syntactic information and general knowledge to be associated conceptually with W, we claimed that we were characterizing words, not mere labels. In order to test this claim, we attempted to formulate lexical concepts associated with words other than those denoting concrete objects. For example, if v(x, y) is the lexical concept associated with a transitive verb V relating two nominal expressions whose denotata are indicated by x and y, we can write

(4)   v(x,y):   Something x "V-s" something y if and only if the presuppositions of v are satisfied and the relation between x and y satisfies:
           (i) $[C(x, y)]$

The major revision that was required concerned the introductory phrase, which now incorporates phonological and syntactic information and any presuppositions characteristic of sentences using this verb. (This metalinguistic phrase might also be regarded as a placeholder for all other information included in the connotative part of the lexical concept.) The test of our claim depended on the possibility of phrasing the schema $C(x, y)$ in a plausible and intuitively revealing manner. Chapters 5, 6, and 7 explored this possibility for a variety of semantic and conceptual domains: color, kinship, space, time, cause, motion, possession, vision, and communication.

Omitted from this discussion of appropriate formulas for representing lexical concepts is any consideration of the possible intensional relations between lexical concepts. Any lexical concept might be isolated and formulated in the manner of (3) or (4), but that would tell us little or nothing about the organization of such concepts in semantic memory. The question of interest concerns the possibility of developing a coherent, mutually interdependent system of lexical concepts. A third level of theoretical revision was concerned with these organizational matters.

Lexical concepts are obviously related, unlike independent entries in a dictionary. We began with the intuitively appealing idea that they are organized into semantic fields. The field property that has received most discussion is hyponymy, which creates hierarchical structures related as genus and species. Within each level of a hierarchy, however, contrastive sets of terms can be organized in relatively complex ways. This hierarchical organization can be imposed on nouns with considerable success.

Associationistic psychology might view such intensional relations as a network of connections of differing strengths between nodes representing individual words, or senses of words. In order to incorporate the hierarchical field property, it would presumably be necessary to distinguish various kinds of connections: hyponymic, partonymic, locative. One way to construct such networks is to include explicit cross-indexing between lexical concepts; a hyponymic relation, for example, would require us to say explicitly in the entry for x that it is a species of y and to say in the entry for y what all its species are. We considered various schemes for reducing the redundancy of such cross-referencing and selected decision tables as the most convenient.

The intensional part of the theory was accordingly revised to admit two levels of organization, one for core concepts and one for lexical concepts. Central to each semantic field is some very general and important conceptual core that provides a relative location for each lexical concept in that field. This organization is reflected lexically in the schemata of individual concepts. Each schema specifies a set of conditions that must be satisfied for an appropriate use of the term. Since many of these conditions are shared by several schemata, a decision table can be based on shared conditions. Each schema (a column in the table) is represented by a pattern of outcomes for these conditions, plus an indication of which words are assertible given that pattern. The table can be entered with a pattern of conditions and the appropriate words found or it can be entered with a word and the pattern of conditions found. Many of the facilitative effects of one word on another might be explained in terms of activating whole sets of related lexical concepts by consulting the decision table of any one of them.

What characterizes a semantic field according to this view is a set of shared conditions that are simultaneously activated. The relevant conditions in turn depend on the conceptual core. If a word is satisfied by the pattern of outcomes, all its superordinate words are also satisfied, so a speaker requires an additional device to select the level of specificity appropriate to his communicative intent. But the general problem of cross-indexing related lexical concepts seems to be solved efficiently by including them in the same decision table.

As we explored a greater variety of English words, however, unexpected complications arose. Color and kin terms, which have been studied repeatedly by ethnologists and psychologists, submitted reasonably well to formulations as semantic fields, but then we encountered some important concepts—person, space, time, cause, intention (quantity would have been another if we had had the temerity to analyze it)—that did not seem to have lexical fields associated with them. The problem was not that our method of representation was inadequate—decision tables are extremely general—but that these concepts seem too important to be confined to a single semantic field. When we explored semantic fields of verbs, we found these important concepts in every field. It is probably significant that all of them can be expressed grammatically as well as lexically.

As a final revision on this third level, therefore, we had to distinguish core concepts that form the nucleus of a semantic field from those that do not. The most general core concepts seem to give rise not to semantic fields but to various elaborative concepts that differentiate and modulate a nuclear concept into a lexical field of related verbs. The structure of nominal domains is simpler, since the transitive, asymmetric relations that characterize their organization, which is frequently hierarchical, emerge as a consequence of the structure we have postulated for semantic memory.

No standard formalism was introduced to represent core concepts, though we suggested that they could be represented procedurally; they were thought of as lay theories, serving to organize a person's knowledge and beliefs, and as varying indefinitely from one realm to another. Lexical concepts must be shared by speakers of a common language, and the organization of a lexical field is derivative from this conceptual organization, yet there is room for considerable individual difference in the details of any concept. The identifying conditions that determine the extension of a concept are compatible with a variety of conceptualizations determining its intension.

Other revisionary threads might be extracted from our work, but these three, tightly interwoven, provide an adequate trace of our intellectual path. Unlike many exercises in procedural semantics that have been programmed for computer execution, we have deliberately avoided formulating the details of higher-order routines that compute appropriate identifications, determine the illocutionary force of utterances from their context, and so on. Winograd (1971) and Charniak (1973a) have provided evidence of the role of inference in understanding language. They have also illustrated the advantages of a procedural representation of general knowledge, a representation exploiting a system such as PLANNER (Hewitt, 1971).

What we have said about syntax, sentences, and significance-in-context is extremely limited, and we have failed to arrive at a satisfactory solution to the problem of presuppositions. Our approach to presuppositions relies on a computational metaphor: when a presupposition is violated, it is as though a program attempts, say, to return the head of a list from a structure that is not a list;* the computation blocks and returns an error. We have not resolved the details of how this metaphor is to be implemented.

We suggested, for the simple case of adjectival modification, how a procedural theory of selectional restrictions might exploit conceptual information given by the meanings of the adjective and its head noun. We did not explore the more difficult problems posed by verbs. It seems obvious to us that selectional restrictions associated with a verb also derive from the meaning of that verb, and perhaps they could be dealt with simply by postulating a special sort of execution of the procedure based on the verb's meaning. The fact that a verb like "chase" selects an animate subject is a simple consequence of its routine's containing an INTEND component: only animate beings are capable of intentions. Many verbs seem to inherit the selectional restrictions of the constituents occurring in their routines. In some situations we can imagine that a listener performs some sort of "protected execution" in which he tries out in his imagination a potential argument of a verb in order to determine whether it is acceptable. This process might be readily affected by the context of an utterance; it is not difficult to generate imaginary contexts in which "The car chased me down the road" would seem acceptable. The problem is to specify the mental computations involved in trying out an argument in imagination. They would seem to be related to the logical notion of a possible-world semantics—the listener is trying to determine whether it is possible for certain things to happen. What stands in need of specification is the nature of such computations. Perhaps we need a procedural equivalent to a possible-world semantics, but we have no substantial ideas how such procedures might be developed for worlds containing a richer set of possibilities than ticktacktoe (Isard and Longuet-Higgins, 1971). Perhaps, instead, we need a flexible representation of beliefs and inference rules for deriving from them, and from context, the relevant set of possibilities. We suspect that an adequate account of selectional restrictions and presuppositions must await more sophisticated theories of context, belief, and inference.

Our motivation for placing a heavy load on higher-order routines was the same as our motivation for isolating schemata from execution (by the notational device of brackets) and isolating intermediate translations from the

---

* Mark Steedman (personal communication) has written a program that handles the existential presuppositions of conjunctive and disjunctive sentences in just this way. It demonstrates an appropriate "filtering" of presuppositions (Karttunen, 1973a).

actual programs compiled for utterances (by the "instruct" instruction). It derived from the fact that our explorations were directed primarily at what linguists call the lexical component of language.

The salient feature of our ultimate position is its emphasis on the meanings of words. We assume that it makes sense to ask what the meaning of a word is. We assume that words are the meaning-conveying elements of discourse. What, then, is the meaning of a word?

Our answer turns out to be considerably more complicated than most psychologists might hope:

— The meaning of a word can tell you what is, and what is not, an entity that can be labeled with that word. It makes possible programs that incorporate perceptual paradigms applicable to objects, events, properties, and relations in the world. It incorporates basic semantic operators concerning space, time, cause, and intention. It sometimes is a direct specification of an operator or a core concept—a schema that acts as a primitive for other schemata.

— The meaning can tell you the function or purpose of the entity that the word labels. It is associated with a schema that incorporates functional information, information about what is possible.

— The meaning can lead you to all you know about an entity. It has access to encyclopedic information in long-term memory.

— The meaning can tell you about relations between what the word labels and what other words label. Its schema is integrated with schemata represented by other words, a part of a system that captures conceptual relations between words.

— The meaning of a word can tell you about what other sorts of words can occur with it in sentences. It can place syntactic and semantic constraints on other words.

Not every word incorporates all these elements of meaning, but if each element is possessed by some words, psychological theory is confronted with a large number of demands. Satisfaction of these theoretical requirements is one way to gauge the success of a theory. We could perhaps best evaluate our conceptual theory, and justify its complexity, by considering its performance on each of them. (We would find, of course, that we have scarcely touched on some of them.)

The meanings of words must be compatible with the meanings of sentences. Procedures for constructing sentences and interpreting them must dovetail with procedures representing the meanings of words. We do not know how this integration occurs; we have not tried to specify it. What we do know is that the integration is subtle. Children seem to learn their first language without noticing any cleavage between grammar and meaning; adults are often unable to divorce the two in making metalinguistic judgments; and linguists are currently unable to characterize the frontier between them with any precision. Perhaps the belief that a frontier exists is a consequence of the strategy of beginning with relations that seem most syntactic. Even linguists who would include semantic features in their theories tend in practice to concentrate first on syntactic relations and to work from them toward semantic relations. Our strategy has been to concentrate first on relations that seem most explicitly semantic. An attempt to work back toward syntactic relations is something we have barely started. The relation between meaning and syntax may look very different when it comes to be surveyed from the conceptual side of the frontier. Likewise, it would be instructive to develop a pragmatic theory of discourse. Such a theory would seek to explain relations between utterances and their contexts; it would probably be committed to units of text or discourse larger than a sentence. A view of syntax and semantics from this pragmatic standpoint might even expose the traditional divisions between them as often illusory.

A conceptual theory of meaning must be able to explain intensional relations that hold between words by virtue of their meaning. We have tried to show how such relations as hyponymy, synonymy, antonymy, and the general framework of hierarchies of contrastive terms can be accounted for within the internal structure of a semantic field. We conceive the structure of a semantic field as articulated by a series of interlinked decision tables whose shared conditions and actions embody the intuition that word meanings are interrelated. But they are more than a convenient summarizing device. They make possible an extremely flexible access to the information stored in the mental lexicon.

Great flexibility is required. Consider how a listener might attempt to verify "Smith is sitting in the chair." Most picture-verification models proposed by psychologists (Clark and Chase, 1972, Trabasso, 1972; but compare Glucksberg, Trabasso, and Wald, 1973) suggest that an internal representation of the sentence is matched against an internal representation of the picture. This matching process is often impossible when you are dealing with reality rather than a picture, because it is often impossible to know what aspects of the world to examine until you have partially understood the sentence. It is nonsense, therefore, to speak of *the* process of verifying a sentence. What you do will depend on the significance of "Smith is sitting in the chair." It may identify Smith for you; it may identify a particular chair for you; it may tell you where Smith is; it may tell you what Smith is doing with the chair; doubtless it may signify—even with a literal interpretation—many other matters. In few of these cases can you match a representation of the sentence against a representation of the world. Rather, you take part of the sentence as a guide to where you should look, or for whom or what you should look, and then compare what you see with what the rest of the sentence says. Furthermore, the sentence may function as a request or command, rather than as a description —"Smith is sitting in the chair" may mean "Warn him that it will collapse." Mere verification misses the significance of the utterance; the listener is required to act in a different way.

Whatever general course of action is appropriate—verification, action, answer—the listener must first understand at least part of the sentence before he can determine what to do; he must compile some program before he can execute it. As this example shows, the literal meaning of a sentence is not just a program. Perhaps we should say that there is no such thing as the literal meaning of a sentence, only the literal meaning that a given listener places on a given utterance of it. Or perhaps we should say that the literal meaning of a sentence (divorced from any particular context) consists of procedures that can be called in many different orders, even omitted in certain cases, by higher-order programs responsible for verifying statements, answering questions, obeying commands, storing information in episodic memory.

The moral for the mental lexicon is clear. If the meaning of a word were a fixed set of procedures or structured set of semantic markers, it would be impossible to handle utterances of a given sentence with sufficient flexibility. It would be a mistake to impose a standard order on the texts making up the representation of any lexical items. A natural way to solve this ordering problem is to represent lexical items in decision tables (or an equivalent formulation) and to think of the compiler that interprets sentences as capable of exploiting their conditions in a variety of different orders depending on the higher-order programs controlling the system at that time.

A dictionary is a poor metaphor for a person's lexical knowledge. Dictionaries define words in terms of words. Such definitions, like some semantic theories, may provide plausible accounts of intensional relations between words, but their circularity is vicious. There is no escape from the round of words. Language can apply to the nonlinguistic world, however, and this fact cannot be ignored by a theory of meaning. It is perhaps the single most important feature of language; a theory that overlooks it will provide simply a means of translating natural language into theoretical language. Although such a theory may be extremely useful as a device for formulating intensional relations, its ultimate value rests on a tacit appeal to its users' extensional intuitions.

The need to relate language to reality has been emphasized by philosophers and linguists of what might be called the extensionalist school. Inspired by nominalism and semantical models of modal logic, they tend to agree that the semantics of natural language should concern itself with the truth conditions of sentences and the extensions of linguistic expressions. Although such a goal might provide a logically secure foundation for semantics, its pursuit to the exclusion of other goals is inimical to a psychological explanation of meaning. Yet it would be a mistake to ignore the lesson of extensionalism. A semantic theory having no contact with the world, a mere translation of one set of words into another, is a ladder without rungs.

One of the main burdens of our attempt to relate language to perception was to provide an extensional basis for the meanings of words. It is worth stressing two aspects of a procedural approach. First, procedures offer a plausible solution to the problem of novel instances. If, for example, words were simply stored with a set of images, it would not be clear how one could identify an object not seen before. To talk of generalization from a set of images is merely to introduce a procedure covertly; one might as well introduce it overtly from the start. Second, procedures can be related in higher-order structures. If the

meaning of a word were merely the set of objects, events, properties, or relations that constitute its extension, that is, the set of instances accepted by the
procedure, meanings would be totally independent entities and words could be
represented by a large number of independent, idiosyncratic procedures. Such
a psychological state of affairs is barely imaginable. Words obviously relate to
each other: children do not learn their vocabulary as independent and in-
sulated items and adults do not have to search their whole vocabulary every
time they describe something. These considerations argue for the existence of
a unifying device, the sort we have tried to suggest by linked decision tables
and prototheoretical concepts.

We have tried to establish our reasons for representing the mental lexicon
in these terms. Such a representation handles the obvious intensional relations
between words and the fact that they appear to be organized into semantic
fields. It offers the necessary degree of flexibility in accessing information. And
it establishes extensional relations of words to the perceptual world.

An important prerequisite for working with decision tables, however, is a
set of primitive terms (or tests) from which to construct the procedures that
define their conditions. Most semanticists agree about the need for some set
of primitive entities. What has been little discussed is the motivation for any
particular set; theorists' intuitions have generally stood in place of reasoned
argument. No one, for instance, would propose "bachelor" and "spinster" as
primitives and define "married" as "(adult and) not a bachelor or a spinster."
One can see immediately that this would be absurd, but it is more difficult to
say why it is absurd. We have taken the view that all questions of the appropriateness of primitives—ignoring for the moment their logical consistency
or completeness—reduce to psychological criteria. The way to justify them
is by appeal to psychological evidence. Some theorists, especially those working in artificial intelligence, take the view that developing a logically adequate
set of primitives should take precedence over ensuring that they are psychologically correct. The principle is justified, although it may be easier to collect empirical evidence than to prove logical adequacy; it may be easier to show
psychologically that "bachelor" is not primitive than to show logically that
a set to which it belongs is inadequate to characterize the semantics of English.
We have tried to develop a set of primitives motivated by the psychology of
perception and conception, and we have related our choices to what we know
about children's intellectual and linguistic development.

Empirical studies suggest a further requirement for any adequate theory.
A theory of meaning must explain, or at least not run counter to, findings
from experiments on the processes of comprehension, retrieval of information
from semantic memory, judgments of similarity of meaning, verification of
sentences. We introduce this requirement last because it will place little strain
on any theory capable of meeting the preceding requirements. That is to say,
any theory that meets them will be a sophisticated affair, whereas laboratory
studies of semantic memory can usually be explained by relatively simple
theories. Adding additional assumptions to a comprehensive theory in order

to meet empirical requirements should not prove an insuperable task, but theories formulated to explain experimental data are not easily extended to meet the more general requirements considered above.

We can summarize these requirements:

—A theory of meaning should represent meanings of words and sentences in a compatible form.

—It should account for the intensional properties of linguistic expressions and for the intensional relations between them.

—It should allow for the differing significance of sentences depending on their context and for flexible access to information in lexical memory.

—It should account for the extensional relations between linguistic expressions and the world.

—It should account for the organization of words in semantic fields.

—The primitive terms of the theory should be logically adequate and psychologically motivated.

—It should be compatible with established psycholinguistic phenomena.

No existing theory meets all these requirements, but that does not mean there is nothing to be learned from current theories. Indeed, our own views rely on theories developed in psychology, linguistics, anthropology, logic, and artificial intelligence. But our temerity in proposing a new theory should indicate that we are dissatisfied with the other accounts.

The theories psychologists have largely favored, especially those offered to explain experimental findings on semantic memory (see, for example, Meyer, 1970), are in general not powerful enough to explain much more than certain intensional relations between words. A more satisfactory account of such relations may be feasible on the basis laid down by Osgood (1970), and a satisfactory dovetailing with syntactic requirements may be feasible within a "network" approach to semantics of the sort proposed by Collins and Quillian (1972) or Rumelhart, Lindsay, and Norman (1972). The focus on intensional properties and relations is also apparent in linguistic theories of semantics (such as those by Chafe, 1970; Katz, 1972) and in many artificial intelligence approaches to meaning (Schank, 1972, for example). None of these theories has offered explicit proposals to deal with extensional relations between language and the world. None allows for a sufficiently flexible access to lexical memory. And few consider a psychological motivation for the choice of primitives. Theories that give priority to extensional relations (Keenan, 1972; D. K. Lewis, 1971; Montague, 1974) tend to consider all other requirements as either secondary or irrelevant. Perhaps the most ambitious approach to meaning is Winograd's (1971) procedural semantics for natural language. His use of a microworld of blocks, pyramids, and boxes allowed him to finesse many problems, however. His lexicon is small, and both intensional and extensional relations are greatly simplified. In general, however, we have found these approaches to lean too far in either an intensional or extensional direction.

From a consideration of the relations between language and perception we were led ineluctably to a procedural approach to semantics. We have tried to add psychological substance to this approach, hitherto dominated by artificial microworlds of computer programmers. We have looked for what is psychologically primitive. We have tried to test our theory of meaning not by a few carefully selected examples but by its ramifications for a significant proportion of the lexicon. We have taken a broad view of meaning and searched for a satisfactory synthesis of ideas developed for particular aspects of the larger psycholinguistic problem. We believe that the implications of local hypotheses can be appreciated only in terms of a broader theoretical framework and that such a framework can be provided only by psychology. We hope we have taken a significant step toward this goal. Much remains to be done, but one exciting aspect of the study of language is the feeling, lacking in some areas of psychology, that problems are tractable, that work has a cumulative effect, and that even mistakes can ultimately lead to advances in knowledge.

REFERENCES
INDEXES

References

Aaronson, M., and E. E. Schaefer. 1968. Preschool preposition test: manual of instructions. Unpublished. (Described in O. G. Johnson and J. W. Bommarito, *Tests and measurements in child development: a handbook* [San Francisco: Josey-Bass, 1971], p. 75.)

Abelson, R. P. 1973. The structure of belief systems. In R. C. Schank and K. M. Colby, eds., *Computer models of thought and language.* San Francisco: Freeman.

Akmajian, A., and F. Heny. 1975. *An introduction to the principles of transformational syntax.* Cambridge, Mass.: MIT Press.

Allport, F. H. 1955. *Theories of perception and the concept of structure.* New York: Wiley.

Ames, A., Jr. 1955. *An interpretive manual: the nature of our perceptions, prehensions, and behavior.* Princeton, N.J.: Princeton University Press.

Ames, L. B. 1946. The development of the sense of time in the young child. *Journal of Genetic Psychology* 68:97–125.

Ames, L. B., and J. Learned. 1948. The development of verbalized space in the young child. *Journal of Genetic Psychology* 72:63–84.

Amidon, A., and P. Carey. 1972. Why five-year-olds cannot understand before and after. *Journal of Verbal Learning and Verbal Behavior* 11:417–423.

Anderson, J. A. 1970. Two models for memory organization using interacting traces. *Mathematical Biosciences* 8:137–160.

————1972. A simple neural network generating interactive memory. *Mathematical Biosciences* 14:197–220.

Anderson, J. M. 1971. *The grammar of case: towards a localistic theory.* Cambridge: Cambridge University Press.

Anderson, J. R. 1972. FRAN: a simulation model of free recall. In G. H. Bower, ed., *The psychology of learning and motivation,* vol. 5. New York: Academic Press.

Anderson, J. R., and G. H. Bower. 1972. Recognition and retrieval processes in free recall. *Psychological Review* 79:97–123.

————1973. *Human associative memory.* Washington, D.C.: Winston.

Anglin, J. M. 1970. *The growth of word meaning.* Cambridge, Mass.: MIT Press.

Anscombe, G. E. M. 1957. *Intention.* Oxford: Blackwell.

————1965. The intentionality of perception: a grammatical feature. In R. J. Butler, ed., *Analytical Philosophy,* 2d ser. Oxford: Blackwell.

Arbib, M. A. 1972. *The metaphorical brain: an introduction to cybernetics as artificial intelligence and brain theory.* New York: Wiley-Interscience.

Aronoff, M. H. 1974. Word-structure. Ph.D. dissertation, Massachusetts Institute of Technology.

Asch, S. E. 1958. The metaphor: a psychological inquiry. In R. Tagiuri and L. Petrullo, eds., *Person perception and interpersonal behavior.* Stanford: Stanford University Press.

Atkinson, R. C., and R. M. Shiffrin. 1965. *Mathematical models for memory and learning.* Institute for Mathematical Studies in the Social Sciences technical report 79, Stanford University.

————1968. Human memory: a proposed system and its control processes. In K. W. Spence and J. T. Spence, eds., *Advances in the psychology of learning and motivation research and theory,* vol. 2. New York: Academic Press.

Attneave, F. 1959. *Applications of information theory to psychology: a summary of basic concepts, methods, and results.* New York: Holt.

Austin, J. L. 1962a. *Sense and sensibilia.* Oxford: Oxford University Press.

————1962b. *How to do things with words.* Cambridge, Mass.: Harvard University Press.

Ayer, A. J. 1940. *The foundations of empirical knowledge.* London: Macmillan.

Bach, E. 1967. *Have* and *be* in English syntax. *Language* 43:462–485.

————1968. Nouns and noun phrases. In E. Bach and R. T. Harms, eds., *Universals in linguistic theory.* New York: Holt, Rinehart, & Winston.

Baddeley, A. D. 1966. Short-term memory for word sequences as a function of acoustic, semantic, and formal similarity. *Quarterly Journal of Experimental Psychology* 18:362–365.

Baddeley, A. D., and G. Hitch. 1974. Working memory. In G. H. Bower, ed., *Recent advances in learning and motivation,* vol. 8. New York: Academic Press.

Banfield, A. 1973. Narrative style and the grammar of direct and indirect speech. *Foundations of Language* 10:1–39.

Bar-Hillel, Y. 1966. Do natural languages contain paradoxes? *Studium Generale* 19:391–397.

Barker, R. C. 1968. *Ecological psychology: concepts and methods for studying the environment of human behavior.* Stanford: Stanford University Press.

Barlow, H. B. 1961. Possible principles underlying the transformations of sensory messages. In W. A. Rosenblith, ed., *Sensory communication.* Cambridge, Mass.: MIT Press.

Baron, N. S. 1972. The evolution of English periphrastic causatives: contributions to a general theory of linguistic variation and change. Ph.D. dissertation, Stanford University.

Barrie-Blackley, S. 1973. Six-year-old children's understanding of sentences adjoined with time adverbs. *Journal of Psycholinguistic Research* 2:153–165.

Bartlett, F. C. 1932. *Remembering: a study in experimental and social psychology.* Cambridge: Cambridge University Press.

Bateman, W. G. 1915. The naming of colors by children: the Binet test. *Pedagogical Seminary* 22:469–486.

Bateson, G., D. D. Jackson, J. Haley, and J. H. Weakland. 1956. Towards a theory of schizophrenia. *Behavioral Science* 1:251–264.

Battig, W. F., and W. E. Montague. 1969. Category norms for verbal items in fifty-six categories: a replication and extension of the Connecticut Category Norms. *Journal of Experimental Psychology Monographs* 80, no. 3, part 2, pp. 1–46.

Beaglehole, E. 1968. Property. In D. L. Sills, ed., *International encyclopedia of the social sciences,* vol. 12. New York: Macmillan and Free Press.

Beare, A. C. 1963. Color-name as a function of wavelength. *American Journal of Psychology* 76:248–256.

Becker, A. L., and D. G. Arms. 1969. Prepositions as predicates. In *Papers from the Fifth Regional Meeting of the Chicago Linguistic Society.* Chicago: University of Chicago, Department of Linguistics.

Bendix, E. H. 1966. *Componential analysis of general vocabulary: the semantic structure of a set of verbs in English, Hindi, and Japanese.* The Hague: Mouton.

————1971. The data of semantic description. In D. D. Steinberg and L. A. Jakobovits, eds., *Semantics: an interdisciplinary reader in philosophy, linguistics, and psychology.* Cambridge: Cambridge University Press.

Bennett, D. C. 1968. English prepositions: a stratificational approach. *Journal of Linguistics* 4:153–172.

————1972. Some observations concerning the locative-directional distinction. *Semiotica* 5:58–88.

————1975. *Spatial and temporal uses of English prepositions: an essay in stratificational semantics.* London: Longman.

Berlin, B., and P. Kay. 1969. *Basic color terms: their universality and evolution.* Berkeley and Los Angeles: University of California Press.

Bernstein, N. 1967. *The coordination and regulation of movements.* Oxford: Pergamon.

Bever, T. G. 1970. The comprehension and memory of sentences with temporal relations. In G. B. Flores d'Arcais and W. J. M. Levelt, eds., *Advances in psycholinguistics.* Amsterdam: North Holland.

Bever, T. G., and P. S. Rosenbaum. 1970. Some lexical structures and their empirical validity. In R. A. Jacobs and P. S. Rosenbaum, eds., *Readings in English transformational grammar.* Waltham, Mass.: Ginn.

Bierwisch, M. 1967. Some semantic universals of German adjectivals. *Foundations of Language* 3:1–36.

————1970. Semantics. In J. Lyons, ed., *New horizons in linguistics.* Baltimore: Penguin.

Binet, A., and T. Simon. 1911. *The development of intelligence in children.* Translated by E. S. Kite. Baltimore, Md.: Williams & Wilkins, 1916.

Binnick, R. I. 1968. On the nature of the "lexical item." In *Papers from the Fourth Regional Meeting of the Chicago Linguistic Society.* Chicago: University of Chicago, Department of Linguistics.

————1971. Bring and come. *Linguistic Inquiry* 2:260–265.

Black, M., and D. Metzger. 1965. Ethnographic description and the study of law. *American Anthropologist* 6, part 2, pp. 141–165.

Blank, M. 1973. *Teaching learning in the preschool: a dialogue approach.* Columbus, Ohio: Merrill.

Blank, M., and W. Bridger. 1964. Cross-modal transfer in nursery school children. *Journal of Comparative and Physiological Psychology* 58:277–282.

Block, J. 1957. Studies in the phenomenology of emotions. *Journal of Abnormal and Social Psychology* 54:358–363.

Block, N. J. 1974. Why do mirrors reverse right/left but not up/down? *Journal of Philosophy* 71:259–277.

Bloom, L. 1970. *Language and development: form and function in emerging grammars.* Cambridge, Mass.: MIT Press.

Bloomfield, L. 1933. *Language.* New York: Holt.

Bobrow, D., and B. Fraser. 1969. An augmented state transition network analysis procedure. In D. Walker and L. Norton, eds., *Proceedings of the International Joint Conference on Artificial Intelligence.* Washington, D.C.

Boring, E. G. 1929. *A history of experimental psychology.* New York: Century.

————1933. *The physical dimensions of consciousness.* New York: Century.

————1942. *Sensation and perception in the history of experimental psychology.* New York: Appleton-Century-Crofts.

Borkin, A. 1973. *To be* and not *to be.* In *Papers from the Ninth Regional Meeting of the Chicago Linguistic Society.* Chicago: Chicago Linguistic Society.

Bornstein, M. H. 1973. Color vision and color naming: a psychological hypothesis of cultural difference. *Psychological Bulletin* 80:257–285.

————1975. Qualities of color vision in infancy. *Journal of Experimental Child Psychology* 19:401–419.

Bousefield, W. A., and B. H. Cohen. 1965. Clustering in recall as a function of the number of word categories in the stimulus word list. *Journal of General Psychology* 55:95–107.

Bouwsma, O. K. 1942. Moore's theory of sense-data. In P. A. Schilpp, ed., *The philosophy of G. E. Moore.* Evanston, Ill.: Northwestern University Press.

Bower, G. H. 1972. A selective review of organizational factors in memory. In E. Tulving and W. Donaldson, eds., *Organization and memory.* New York: Academic Press.

Bower, G. H., M. C. Clark, A. M. Lesgold, and D. Winzenz. 1969. Hierarchical retrieval schemes in recall of categorized word lists. *Journal of Verbal Learning and Verbal Behavior* 8:323–343.

Bower, T. G. R. 1974. *Development in infancy.* San Francisco: Freeman.

Bowerman, M. 1974. Learning the structure of causative verbs: a study in the relationship of cognitive, semantic, and syntactic development. In *Papers and Reports on Child Language Development,* vol. 8. Stanford, Calif.: Stanford University, Committee on Linguistics.

Bowers, F. 1968. English complex sentence formation. *Journal of Linguistics* 4:83–88.

Boynton, R. M., and J. Gordon. 1965. Bezold-Brücke hue shift measured by color-naming techniques. *Journal of the Optical Society of America* 55:78–86.

Boynton, R. M., W. Shafer, and M. E. Neun. 1964. Hue-wavelength relation measured by color-naming method for three retinal locations. *Science* 146:666–668.

Bradley, N. C. 1947. The growth of the knowledge of time in children of school age. *British Journal of Psychology* 38:67–78.

Brand, M., ed. 1970. *The nature of human action*. New York: Scott, Foresman.

Bransford, J. D., and M. K. Johnson. 1972. Contextual prerequisites for understanding: some investigations of comprehension and recall. *Journal of Verbal Learning and Verbal Behavior* 11:717–726.

Bransford, J. D., and N. S. McCarrell. 1974. A sketch of a cognitive approach to comprehension: some thoughts about understanding and what it means to comprehend. In W. B. Weimer and D. S. Palermo, eds., *Cognition and the symbolic processes*. Hillsdale, N.J.: Erlbaum.

Bresnan, J. W. 1970. On complementizers: toward a syntactic theory of complement types. *Foundations of Language* 6:297–321.

Brindley, G. S., and P. A. Merton. 1960. The absence of position sense in the human eye. *Journal of Physiology* (London) 153:127–130.

Bromley, M. 1967. The linguistic relationships of Grand Valley Dani: a lexico-statistical classification. *Oceania* 37:286–308.

Brown, R. 1957. Linguistic determinism and the parts of speech. *Journal of Abnormal and Social Psychology* 55:1–5.

———1958. How shall a thing be called? *Psychological Review* 65:14–21.

———1973. *A first language: the early stages*. Cambridge, Mass.: Harvard University Press.

Brown, R., and J. Berko. 1960. Word association and the acquisition of grammar. *Child Development* 31:1–14.

Brown, R., and M. Ford. 1961. Address in American English. *Journal of Abnormal and Social Psychology* 62:375–385.

Brown, R., and A. Gilman. 1960. The pronouns of power and solidarity. In T. A. Sebeok, ed., *Style and language*. Cambridge, Mass.: MIT Press.

Brown, R., and E. H. Lenneberg. 1954. A study in language and cognition. *Journal of Abnormal and Social Psychology* 49:454–462.

Brown, R., and D. McNeill. 1966. The "tip of the tongue" phenomenon. *Journal of Verbal Learning and Verbal Behavior* 5:325–337.

Bruner, J. S. 1957. On perceptual readiness. *Psychological Review* 64:123–152.

Bryant, P. 1974. *Perception and understanding in young children: an experimental approach*. New York: Basic Books.

Bühler, K. 1934. *Sprachtheorie: die Darstellungsfunktion der Sprache*. Jena: Gustav Fischer.

Bull, W. E. 1960. *Time, tense, and the verb*. Berkeley and Los Angeles: University of California Press.

Burge, T. 1973. Reference and proper names. *Journal of Philosophy* 70:425–439.

Burks, A. W. 1951. The logic of causal propositions. *Mind* 60:363–382.

Burling, R. 1964. Cognition and componential analysis: God's truth or hocus-pocus? *American Anthropologist* 66:20–28.

Caplan, D. 1973. A note on the abstract readings of verbs of perception. *Cognition* 2:269–277.

Carelman. 1969. *Catalogue d'objets introuvables*. Paris: André Balland.

Carnap, R. 1928. *Der logische Aufbau der Welt*. Leipzig: Meiner.

———1956. *Meaning and necessity: a study in semantics and modal logic*. 2d ed. Chicago: University of Chicago Press.

Carroll, J. B., and J. B. Casagrande. 1958. The function of language classifications in behavior. In E. E. Maccoby, T. M. Newcomb, and E. L. Hartley, eds., *Readings in social psychology*. New York: Holt, Rinehart, & Winston.

Cassirer, E. 1923. *The philosophy of symbolic forms*, vol. 1, *Language*. Translated by R. Manheim. New Haven: Yale University Press, 1953.

Chafe, W. L. 1970. *The meaning and structure of language*. Chicago: University of Chicago Press.

————1973. Language and memory. *Language* 49:261–281.

Chapin, P. G. 1970. On affixation in English. In M. Bierwisch and K. E. Heidolph, eds., *Progress in linguistics*. The Hague: Mouton.

Charniak, E. 1973a. Jack and Janet in search of a theory of knowledge. *Advance papers of the Third International Joint Conference on Artificial Intelligence, August 1973*. Stanford, Calif.: Stanford Research Institute.

————1973b. Context and the reference problem. In R. Rustin, ed., *Courant computer science symposium 8: natural language processing*. New York: Algorithmics Press.

Chase, W. P. 1937. Color vision in infants. *Journal of Experimental Psychology* 20:203–222.

Chisholm, R. M. 1963. The logic of knowing. *Journal of Philosophy* 60:773–795.

Chomsky, N. 1962. A transformational approach to syntax. In A. A. Hill, ed., *Proceedings of the Third Texas Conference on Problems of Linguistic Analysis in English, 1958*. Austin: University of Texas.

————1963. Formal properties of grammars. In R. D. Luce, R. R. Bush, and E. Galanter, eds., *Handbook of mathematical psychology*, vol. 2. New York: Wiley.

————1965. *Aspects of the theory of syntax*. Cambridge, Mass.: MIT Press.

————1968. *Language and mind*. New York: Harcourt, Brace & World.

————1970. Remarks on nominalization. In R. A. Jacobs and P. S. Rosenbaum, eds., *Readings in English transformational grammar*. Waltham, Mass.: Ginn.

————1971. Deep structure, surface structure, and semantic interpretation. In D. D. Steinberg and L. A. Jakobovits, eds., *Semantics: an interdisciplinary reader in philosophy, linguistics, and psychology*. Cambridge: Cambridge University Press.

Chomsky, N., and M. Halle. 1968. *The sound pattern of English*. New York: Harper and Row.

Church, A. 1951. The need for abstract entities in semantic analysis. In *Contributions to the analysis and synthesis of knowledge. Proceedings of the American Academy of Arts and Sciences* 80 (1):100–112.

Clark, E. V. 1970. How young children describe events in time. In G. B. Flores d'Arcais and W. J. M. Levelt, eds., *Advances in psycholinguistics*. Amsterdam: North Holland.

————1971. On the acquisition of the meaning of "before" and "after." *Journal of Verbal Learning and Verbal Behavior* 10:266–275.

————1972. Some perceptual factors in the acquisition of locative terms by young children. In *Papers from the Eighth Regional Meeting of the Chicago Linguistic Society*. Chicago: Chicago Linguistic Society.

————1974a. Normal states and evaluative viewpoints. *Language* 50:316–332.

————1974b. Non-linguistic strategies and the acquisition of word meanings. *Cognition* 2:161–182.

Clark, H. H. 1970. Word associations and linguistic theory. In J. Lyons, ed., *New horizons in linguistics*. Baltimore: Penguin.

————1973. Space, time, semantics and the child. In T. E. Moore, ed., *Cognitive development and the acquisition of language*. New York: Academic Press.

Clark, H. H., and W. G. Chase. 1972. On the process of comparing sentences against pictures. *Cognitive Psychology* 3:472–517.

Clark, H. H., and E. V. Clark. 1968. Semantic distinctions and memory for complex sentences. *Quarterly Journal of Experimental Psychology* 20:129–138.

Clark, H. H., and R. A. Stafford. 1969. Memory for semantic features in the verb. *Journal of Experimental Psychology* 80:326–334.

Clowes, M. B. 1967. Perception, picture processing and computers. In N. L. Collins and D. Michie, eds., *Machine intelligence 1*. Edinburgh: Oliver & Boyd.

Cocchiarella, N. B. 1966. Tense logic: a study of temporal reference. Ph.D. dissertation, University of California, Los Angeles.

Cole, M., and S. Scribner. 1974. *Culture and thought: a psychological introduction*. New York: Wiley.

Collins, A. M., and M. R. Quillian. 1969. Retrieval time from semantic memory. *Journal of Verbal Learning and Verbal Behavior* 8:240–247.

————1972. How to make a language user. In E. Tulving and W. Donaldson, eds., *Organization and memory*. New York: Academic Press.

Conklin, H. C. 1955. Hanunóo color categories. *Southwestern Journal of Anthropology* 11:339–344.

————1962. Lexicographical treatment of folk taxonomies. *International Journal of American Linguistics* 28, no. 2, part 4, pp. 119–141.

————1964. Ethnogenealogical method. In W. H. Goodenough, ed., *Explorations in cultural anthropology: essays in honor of George Peter Murdock*. New York: McGraw-Hill.

Conrad, R. 1964. Acoustic confusions in immediate memory. *British Journal of Psychology* 55:75–84.

Cooper, G. S. 1968. A semantic analysis of English locative prepositions. Bolt, Beranek & Newman report 1587.

Court, S. R. A. 1920. Number, time and space in the first five years of a child's life. *Journal of Genetic Psychology* 27:71–89.

Craik, F. I. M., and R. S. Lockhart. 1972. Levels of processing: a framework for memory research. *Journal of Verbal Learning and Verbal Behavior* 11:671–684.

Cromer, R. F. 1968. The development of temporal references during the acquisition of language. Ph.D. dissertation, Harvard University.

————1971. The development of the ability to decenter in time. *British Journal of Psychology* 62:353–365.

Crothers, E. J. 1972. Memory structure and the recall of discourse. In J. B. Carroll and R. O. Freedle, eds., *Language comprehension and the acquisition of knowledge*. Washington, D.C.: Winston.

Crowder, R. G. 1972. Visual and auditory memory. In J. F. Kavanagh and I. G. Mattingly, eds., *Language by ear and by eye: the relationships between speech and reading*. Cambridge, Mass.: MIT Press.

Dakin, J. 1970. Explanations. *Journal of Linguistics* 6:199–214.

D'Andrade, R., and M. Egan. 1974. The colors of emotion. *American Ethnologist* 1:49–63.

Danziger, K. 1957. The child's understanding of kinship terms: a study in the development of relational concepts. *Journal of Genetic Psychology* 91:213–232.

Davey, A. 1974. The formalisation of discourse production. Ph.D. dissertation, University of Edinburgh.

Davidson, D. 1967. The logical form of action sentences. In N. Rescher, ed., *The logic of decision and action*. Pittsburgh: University of Pittsburgh Press.

———1969. On saying that. In D. Davidson and J. Hintikka, eds., *Words and objections: essays on the work of W. V. Quine*. New York: Humanities Press.

Davies, D. J. M. 1974. Representing negation in a PLANNER system. Mimeographed. Edinburgh: University of Edinburgh, School of Artificial Intelligence, Theoretical Psychology Unit.

Davies, D. J. M., and S. D. Isard. 1972. Utterances as programs. In D. Michie, ed., *Machine intelligence 7*. Edinburgh: Edinburgh University Press.

Davis, J., and M. C. Smith. 1972. Memory for unattended input. *Journal of Experimental Psychology* 96:380–388.

Davitz, J. R. 1969. *The language of emotion*. New York: Academic Press.

———1970. A dictionary and grammar of emotion. In M. D. Arnold, ed., *Feelings and emotions: the Loyola symposium*. New York: Academic Press.

Dawes, R. M. 1966. Memory and distortion of meaningful written material. *British Journal of Psychology* 57:77–86.

Day, J. P. 1966. Locke on property. *The Philosophical Quarterly* 16:207–220.

Deese, J. 1965. *The structure of associations in language and thought*. Baltimore: Johns Hopkins University Press.

Deutsch, J. A., and D. Deutsch. 1963. Attention: some theoretical considerations. *Psychological Review* 70:80–90.

De Valois, R. L. 1965. Behavioral and electrophysiological studies of primate vision. In W. D. Neff, ed., *Contributions to sensory physiology*. New York: Academic Press.

De Valois, R. L., and I. Abramov. 1966. Color vision. *Annual Review of Psychology* 17:337–362.

De Villiers, P. A., and J. G. De Villiers. 1974. On this, that, and the other: nonegocentrism in very young children. *Journal of Experimental Child Psychology* 18:438–447.

Dewey, J. 1910. *How we think*. Boston: D. C. Heath.

Dixon, R. M. W. 1970. Where have all the adjectives gone? Mimeographed.

———1971. A method of semantic description. In D. D. Steinberg and L. A. Jakobovits, eds., *Semantics: an interdisciplinary reader in philosophy, linguistics, and psychology*. Cambridge: Cambridge University Press.

———1973. The semantics of giving. In M. Gross, M. Halle, and M.-P. Schützenberger, eds., *The formal analysis of natural languages*. The Hague: Mouton.

Donnellan, K. S. 1972. Proper names and identifying descriptions. In D. Davidson and G. Harman, eds., *Semantics of natural language*. Dordrecht: Reidel.

Dorcus, R. M. 1932. Habitual word associations to colors as a possible factor in advertising. *Journal of Applied Psychology* 16:277–287.

Dore, J. 1973. The development of speech acts. Ph.D. dissertation, City University of New York.

Dowty, D. R. 1972a. On the syntax and semantics of the atomic predicate CAUSE.

In *Papers from the Eighth Regional Meeting of the Chicago Linguistic Society.*
Chicago: Chicago Linguistic Society.

———1972b. Studies in the logic of verb aspect and time reference in English.
Ph.D. dissertation, University of Texas, Austin.

Duncan, S. 1974. On the structure of speaker-auditor interaction during speaking
turns. *Language in Society* 3:161–180.

Duncker, K. 1929. Über induzierte Bewegung. *Psychologische Forschung*
12:180–259.

Dunnell, R. C. 1971. *Systematics in prehistory.* New York: Free Press.

Ekman, P., W. V. Frieson, and P. Ellsworth. 1972. *Emotion in the human face:
guidelines for research and an integration of findings.* New York: Pergamon.

Elkind, D. 1961. Children's conceptions of right and left: Piaget replication study
IV. *Journal of Genetic Psychology* 99:269–276.

———1962. Children's conceptions of brother and sister: Piaget replication study
V. *Journal of Genetic Psychology* 100:129–136.

Entwisle, D. R. 1966. *Word associations of young children.* Baltimore: Johns
Hopkins University Press.

Ervin, S. M. 1961. Changes with age in the verbal determinants of word-association.
American Journal of Psychology 74:361–372.

Ervin-Tripp, S. M. 1970. Discourse agreement: how children answer questions. In J.
R. Hayes, ed., *Cognition and the development of language.* New York: Wiley.

Evans, G. W., and R. B. Howard. 1973. Personal space. *Psychological Bulletin*
80:334–344.

Evans, R. M. 1948. *An introduction to color.* New York: Wiley.

Exner, S. 1875. Ueber das Sehen von Bewegungen und die Theorie des zusammen-
gesetzen Auges. *Sitzungsberichte Akademie Wissenschaft Wein* 72:156–190.

Falk, G. 1972. Interpretation of imperfect line data as a three-dimensional scene.
Artificial Intelligence 3:101–144.

Farrell, M. 1953. Understanding of time relations of five-, six-, and seven-year-old
children of high I.Q. *Journal of Educational Research* 46:587–594.

Feyerabend, P. K. 1962. Explanations, reduction, and empiricism. In H. Feigl and
G. Maxwell, eds., *Scientific explanation, space, and time.* Minnesota Studies in
the Philosophy of Science, vol. 3. Minneapolis: University of Minnesota Press.

Fillenbaum, S., and A. Rapoport. 1971. *Structures in the subjective lexicon.* New
York: Academic Press.

Fillmore, C. J. 1966. Deictic categories in the semantics of "come." *Foundations of
Language* 2:219–227.

———1968. The case for case. In E. Bach and R. T. Harms, eds., *Universals in
linguistic theory.* New York: Holt, Rinehart & Winston.

——— 1969. Review of Bendix, *Componential analysis of general vocabulary.*
General Linguistics 9:41–65.

———1970. The grammar of *hitting* and *breaking.* In R. A. Jacobs and P. S.
Rosenbaum, eds., *Readings in English transformational grammar.* Waltham,
Mass.: Ginn.

———1971a. Some problems for case grammar. In R. J. O'Brien, ed., *Report of
the Twenty-second Annual Round Table Meeting on Linguistics and Language
Studies.* Washington, D.C.: Georgetown University Press.

————1971b. Verbs of judging: an exercise in semantic description. In C. J. Fillmore and D. T. Langendoen, eds., *Studies in linguistic semantics.* New York: Holt, Rinehart & Winston.

————1971c. Types of lexical information. In D. D. Steinberg and L. A. Jakobovits, eds., *Semantics: an interdisciplinary reader in philosophy, linguistics, and psychology.* Cambridge: Cambridge University Press.

————1971d. Toward a theory of deixis. Paper read at Pacific Conference on Contrastive Linguistics and Language Universals, January 1971, University of Hawaii. Mimeographed.

————1973. May we come in? *Semiotica* 9:98–115.

Firbas, J. 1964. On defining the theme in Functional Sentence Analysis. *Travaux linguistiques de Prague* 1:267–280.

Flavell, J. H., A. G. Friedrichs, and J. D. Hoyt. 1970. Developmental changes in memorization processes. *Cognitive Psychology* 1:324–340.

Flickinger, A., and K. J. Rehage. 1949. Building time and space concepts. *Yearbook of the National Council of Social Studies* 20:107–116.

Fodor, J. A. 1970. Three reasons for not deriving "kill" from "cause to die." *Linguistic Inquiry* 1:429–438.

Fodor, J. A., T. G. Bever, and M. F. Garrett. 1974. *The psychology of language.* New York: McGraw-Hill.

Foss, D. J., and D. A. Harwood. 1975. Memory for sentences: implications for human associative memory. *Journal of Verbal Learning and Verbal Behavior* 14:1–16.

Fraisse, P. 1963. *The psychology of time.* New York: Harper & Row.

Frake, C. O. 1961. The diagnosis of disease among the Subanun of Mindanao. *American Anthropologist* 63:113–132.

————1962. The ethnographic study of cognitive systems. In T. Gladwin and W. C. Sturtevant, eds., *Anthropology and human behavior.* Washington, D.C.: Anthropological Society of Washington.

Frankenhaeuser, M. 1959. *Estimation of time: an experimental study.* Stockholm: Almqvist & Wiksell.

Frase, L. T. 1969. A structural analysis of the knowledge that results from thinking about text. *Journal of Educational Psychology Monograph* 60:1–16.

————1972. Maintenance and control in the acquisition of knowledge from written materials. In J. B. Carroll and R. O. Freedle, eds., *Language comprehension and the acquisition of knowledge.* Washington, D.C.: Winston.

Fraser, B. 1970. Some remarks on the action nominalization in English. In R. A. Jacobs and P. S. Rosenbaum, eds., *Readings in English transformational grammar.* Waltham, Mass.: Ginn.

————1975. Hedged performatives. In P. Cole and J. L. Morgan, eds., *Syntax and semantics,* vol. 3, *Speech acts.* New York: Academic Press.

Fredericksen, C. H. 1972. Effects of task-induced cognitive operations on comprehension and memory processes. In J. B. Carroll and R. O. Freedle, eds., *Language comprehension and the acquisition of knowledge.* Washington, D.C.: Winston.

Frege, G. 1892. Über Sinn und Bedeutung. *Zeitschrift für Philosophie und philosophische Kritik* 100:25–50. (Translated as *On sense and reference* in P. T. Geach and M. Black, eds., *Translations from the philosophical writings of Gottlob Frege* [Oxford: Blackwell, 1952].)

Friedrich, P. 1970. Shape in grammar. *Language* 46:379–407.
Frijda, N. H. 1972. Simulation of human long-term memory. *Psychological Bulletin* 77:1–31.

Galambos, R. 1974. The human auditory evoked response. In H. R. Moskowitz, B. Scharf, and J. C. Stevens, eds., *Sensation and measurement*. Dordrecht: Reidel.
Gallagher, M. 1970. Adverbs of time and tense. In *Papers from the Sixth Regional Meeting of the Chicago Linguistic Society*. Chicago: Chicago Linguistic Society.
García, E. C. 1967. Auxiliaries and the criterion of simplicity. *Language* 43:853–870.
Gardner, G. T. 1973. Evidence for independent parallel channels in tachistoscopic perception. *Cognitive Psychology* 4:130–155.
Garner, R. T. 1975. 'Meaning.' In P. Cole and J. L. Morgan, eds., *Syntax and semantics*, vol. 3, *Speech acts*. New York: Academic Press.
the verbs of possession. In D. A. Norman and D. E. Rumelhart, eds., *Explora-*
Garner, W. R. 1962. *Uncertainty and structure as psychological concepts*. New York: Wiley.
————1974. *The processing of information and structure*. Potomac, Maryland: Erlbaum.
Geach, P. 1957. *Mental acts: their content and their objects*. London: Routledge & Kegan Paul.
————1967. Intentional identity. *Journal of Philosophy* 64:627–632.
Geis, M. L. 1970. Time prepositions as underlying verbs. In *Papers from the Sixth Annual Meeting of the Chicago Linguistic Society*. Chicago: Chicago Linguistic Society.
————1975. English time and place adverbials. In *Working papers in linguistics*, no. 18. Columbus: Ohio State University, Department of Linguistics.
Gentner, D. 1975. Evidence for the psychological reality of semantic components: the verbs of possession. In D. A. Norman and D. E. Rumelhart, eds. *Explorations in cognition*. San Francisco: Freeman.
Gesell, A., and F. L. Ilg. 1943. *Infant and child in the culture of today*. New York: Harper.
Gibson, E. J. 1969. *Principles of perceptual learning and development*. New York: Appleton-Century-Crofts.
Gibson, J. J. 1950. *The perception of the visual world*. Boston: Houghton Mifflin.
————1954. The visual perception of objective motion and subjective movement. *Psychological Review* 61:304–314.
————1957. Optical motions and transformations as stimuli for visual perception. *Psychological Review* 64:288–295.
————1966. *The senses considered as perceptual systems*. Boston: Houghton Mifflin.
Gibson, J. J., P. Olum, and F. Rosenblatt. 1955. Parallax and perspective during aircraft landings. *American Journal of Psychology* 68:372–375.
Gibson, J. J., and A. D. Pick. 1963. Perception of another person's looking behavior. *American Journal of Psychology* 76:386–394.
Givón, T. 1972. Forward implications, backward presupposition, and the time axis of verbs. In J. Kimball, ed., *Syntax and semantics*, vol. 1. New York: Seminar Press.
Gladwin, T. 1970. *The East is a big bird*. Cambridge, Mass.: Harvard University Press.

Gleitman, L. R., and H. Gleitman. 1970. *Phrase and paraphrase: some innovative uses of language.* New York: Norton.

Glucksberg, S., R. M. Krauss, and E. T. Higgins. 1975. The development of referential communication skills. In F. D. Horowitz, ed., *Review of child development research*, vol. 4. Chicago: University of Chicago Press.

Glucksberg, S., R. M. Krauss, and R. Weisberg. 1966. Referential communication in nursery school children: method and some preliminary findings. *Journal of Experimental Child Psychology* 3:333–342.

Glucksberg, S., T. Trabasso, and J. Wald. 1973. Linguistic structures and mental operations. *Cognitive Psychology* 5:338–370.

Goodenough, W. H. 1956. Componential analysis and the study of meaning. *Language* 32:195–216.

———1965. Yankee kinship terminology: a problem in componential analysis. *American Anthropologist* 67, no. 5, part 2, pp. 259–287.

Goodman, N. 1951. *The structure of appearance.* Cambridge, Mass.: Harvard University Press.

———1955. *Fact, fiction, and forecast.* Cambridge, Mass.: Harvard University Press. (2d ed., 1965.)

Gordon, D., and G. Lakoff. 1971. Conversational postulates. In *Papers from the Seventh Regional Meeting of the Chicago Linguistic Society.* Chicago: Chicago Linguistic Society.

Gottschaldt, K. 1926. Ueber den Einfluss der Erfahrung auf die Wahrnehmung von Figuren. *Psychologische Forschung* 8:261–317.

Gragg, G. B. 1972. Semi-indirect discourse and related nightmares. In *Papers from the Eighth Regional Meeting of the Chicago Linguistic Society.* Chicago: Chicago Linguistic Society.

Grassman, H. 1854. On the theory of compound colors. *Philosophical Magazine* 7:254–264.

Green, B. F. 1961. Figure coherence in the kinetic depth effect. *Journal of Experimental Psychology* 62:272–282.

Green, G. M. 1974. *Semantics and syntactic regularity.* Bloomington: Indiana University Press.

Greenberg, J. H. 1949. The logical analysis of kinship. *Philosophy of Science* 16:58–64.

Greenfield, P. M., J. H. Smith, and B. Laufer. 1976. *The structure of communication in early language development.* New York: Academic Press.

Grice, H. P. 1957. Meaning. *Philosophical Review* 66:377–388.

———1967. Logic and conversation. In D. Davidson and G. Harman, eds., *The logic of grammar.* Encino, Calif.: Dickenson, 1975.

———1968. Utterer's meaning, sentence-meaning, and word-meaning. *Foundations of Language* 4:225–242.

Griffiths, A. P., ed. 1967. *Knowledge and belief.* Oxford: Oxford University Press.

Grimes, J. E. 1968. *The thread of discourse.* ERIC document ED-019669.

Gruber, J. S. 1965. Studies in lexical relations. Ph.D. dissertation, Massachusetts Institute of Technology.

———1967. Look and see. *Language* 43:937–947.

Guzmán, A. 1968. Computer recognition of three-dimensional objects. Massachusetts Institute of Technology, report MAC-TR-59.

Haas, W. A. 1971. Truth-functional and communicational bases for prescriptive discourse. In *Papers from the Seventh Regional Meeting of the Chicago Linguistic Society*. Chicago: Chicago Linguistic Society.

Halle, M. 1973. Prolegomena to a theory of world formation. *Linguistic Inquiry* 4:3–16.

Halliday, M. A. K. 1967. Notes on transitivity and theme in English, Part II. *Journal of Linguistics* 3:177–244.

Hallowell, A. I. 1943. The nature and function of property as a social institution. *Journal of Legal and Political Science* 1:115–138.

————1958. Ojibwa metaphysics of being and the perception of persons. In R. Tagiuri and L. Petrullo, eds., *Person perception and interpersonal behavior*. Stanford, Calif.: Stanford University Press.

Halsey, R. M., and A. Chapanis. 1954. Chromaticity-confusion contours in a complex viewing situation. *Journal of the Optical Society of America* 46:442–454.

Harris, C. S. 1965. Perceptual adaptation to inverted, reversed, and displaced vision. *Psychological Review* 72:419–444.

Harris, L. J., and E. A. Strommen. 1972. The role of front-back features in children's "front," "back," and "beside" placements of objects. *Merrill-Palmer Quarterly of Behavior and Development* 18:259–271.

Harris, R. J. 1974. Memory for presuppositions and implications: a case study of twelve verbs of motion and inception-termination. *Journal of Experimental Psychology* 103:594–597.

Harrison, B. 1972. *Meaning and structure*. New York: Harper & Row.

Hart, H. L. A., and A. M. Honoré. 1959. *Causation in the law*. Oxford: Clarendon Press.

Hart, J. T. 1967. Memory and the memory-monitoring process. *Journal of Verbal Learning and Verbal Behavior* 6:685–691.

Harter, M. R. 1967. Excitability cycles and cortical scanning: a review of two hypotheses of central intermittency in perception. *Psychological Bulletin* 68:47–58.

Hatch, E. 1971. The young child's comprehension of time connectives. *Child Development* 42:2111–2113.

Haviland, S. E., and E. V. Clark. 1974. "This man's father is my father's son": a study of the acquisition of English kin terms. *Journal of Child Language* 1:23–47.

Hawtrey, R. G. 1928. *Currency and credit*. New York: Longmans, Green.

Hay, J. C. 1966. Optical motions and space perception: an extension of Gibson's analysis. *Psychological Review* 73:550–565.

Hebb, D. O. 1949. *The organization of behavior*. New York: Wiley.

Heider, E. R. 1971. "Focal" color areas and the development of color names. *Developmental Psychology* 4:447–455.

————1972. Universals in color naming and memory. *Journal of Experimental Psychology* 93:10–20.

Heider, E. R., and D. C. Olivier. 1972. The structure of the color space in naming and memory for two languages. *Cognitive Psychology* 3:337–354.

Heider, F., and M. Simmel. 1944. An experimental study of apparent behavior. *American Journal of Psychology* 57:243–259.

Heinämäki, O. T. 1972. Before. In *Papers from the Eighth Regional Meeting of the Chicago Linguistic Society*. Chicago: Chicago Linguistic Society.

———1974. Semantics of English temporal connectives. Ph.D. dissertation, University of Texas, Austin.

Held, R. 1961. Exposure-history as a factor in maintaining stability of perception and coordination. *Journal of Nervous and Mental Diseases* 132:26–32.

Held, R., and A. V. Hein. 1958. Adaptation of disarranged eye-hand coordination contingent upon re-afferent stimulation. *Perceptual Motor Skills* 8:87–90.

Helson, H. 1947. Adaptation-level as frame of reference for prediction of psychophysical data. *American Journal of Psychology* 60:1–29.

———1948. Adaptation-level as a basis for a quantitative theory of frames of reference. *Psychological Review* 55:297–313.

Hering, E. 1920. *Outlines of a theory of the light sense*. Translated by L. M. Hurvich and D. Jameson. Cambridge, Mass.: Harvard University Press, 1964.

Herrnstein, R. J., and E. G. Boring, eds. 1965. *A source book in the history of psychology*. Cambridge, Mass.: Harvard University Press.

Herskovits, M. J. 1952. *Economic anthropology: the economic life of primitive peoples*. New York: Knopf.

Herzberger, H. G. 1967. The truth-conditional consistency of natural languages. *Journal of Philosophy* 64:29–35.

Hewitt, C. 1971. Description and theoretical analysis (using schemas) of PLANNER: a language for proving theorems and manipulating models in a robot. Ph.D. dissertation, Massachusetts Institute of Technology.

Hickerson, N. P. 1971. Review of *Basic Color Terms* by Berlin and Kay. *International Journal of American Linguistics* 37(4):257–270.

Hintikka, J. 1962. *Knowledge and belief: an introduction to the logic of the two notions*. Ithaca, N. Y.: Cornell University Press.

———1969. *Models for modalities: selected essays*. Dordrecht: Reidel.

———1973. *Logic, language-games, and information*. Oxford: Oxford University Press.

Hockett, C. F. 1958. *A course in modern linguistics*. New York: Macmillan.

Hoijer, H. 1945. Classificatory verb stems in the Apachean languages. *International Journal of American Linguistics* 11:13–23.

Holst, E. von. 1957. Active functions of human visual perception. Reprinted in E. von Holst, *The behavioural physiology of animals and man*, vol. 1. Translated by R. Martin. London: Methuen, 1973.

Holway, A. H., and E. G. Boring. 1941. Determinants of apparent visual size with distance variant. *American Journal of Psychology* 54:21–37.

Hopmann, M. R. 1972. Acquisition of basic color terms. Minneapolis: University of Minnesota, Institute of Child Development.

Hörmann, H. 1971. *Psycholinguistics: an introduction to research and theory*. Translated by H. H. Stern. Berlin: Springer-Verlag.

Howard, I. P., and W. B. Templeton. 1966. *Human spatial orientation*. New York: Wiley.

Hubel, D. H., and T. N. Wiesel. 1962. Receptive fields, binocular interaction and functional architecture in the cat's visual cortex. *Journal of Physiology* 160:106–154.

———1965. Receptive fields and functional architecture in two non-striate visual areas (18 and 19) of the cat. *Journal of Neurophysiology* 28:229–289.

————1968. Receptive fields and functional architecture of monkey striate cortex. *Journal of Physiology* 195:215–243.

Huddelston, R. 1969. Some observations on tense and deixis in English. *Language* 45:777–806.

Hughes, G. E., and M. J. Cresswell. 1968. *An introduction to modal logic*. London: Methuen.

Humbodlt, W. von. 1885. On the verb in American languages. *Proceedings of the American Philosophical Society* 22:332–354.

Hurtig, R. R. 1974. The relation of linguistic tense and psychological time. Ph.D. dissertation, Columbia University.

Hurvich, L. M., and D. Jameson. 1957. An opponent-process theory of color vision. *Psychological Review* 64:384–404.

Hurvich, L. M., D. Jameson, and D. H. Krantz. 1965. Theoretical treatment of selected visual problems. In R. D. Luce, R. R. Bush, and E. Galanter, eds., *Handbook of mathematical psychology*, vol. 3. New York: Wiley.

Hutchinson, L. G. 1971. Presupposition and belief-inferences. In *Papers from the Seventh Regional Meeting of the Chicago Linguistic Society*. Chicago: Chicago Linguistic Society.

Huttenlocher, J. 1967. Children's ability to orient and order objects. *Child Development* 38:1169–1176.

Huttenlocher, J., and S. Strauss. 1968. Comprehension and a statement's relation to the situation it describes. *Journal of Verbal Learning and Verbal Behavior* 7:300–304.

Indow, T., and K. Kanazawa. 1960. Multidimensional mapping of Munsell colors varying in hue, chroma, and value. *Journal of Experimental Psychology* 59:330–336.

Indow, T., and K. Ohsumi. 1971. Multidimensional mapping of sixty Munsell colors by nonmetric procedure. Paper read at Symposium on Color Metrics, International Colour Association, September 1971, Driebergen. Mimeographed.

Indow, T., and T. Uchizono. 1960. Multidimensional mapping of Munsell colors varying in hue and chroma. *Journal of Experimental Psychology* 59:321–329.

Ingram, D. 1971. Transitivity in child language. *Language* 47:888–910.

Ipsen, G. 1924. Der alte Orient und die Indogermanen. In *Stand und Aufgaben der Sprachwissenschaft: Festschrift für W. Streitberg*. Heidelberg: C. Winter.

Isard, S. D. 1975. What would you have done if . . . ? *Journal of Theoretical Linguistics* 1:233–255.

Isard, S. D., and C. Longuet-Higgins. 1971. Modal tic-tac-toe. In R. J. Bogdan and I. Niiniluoto, eds., *Logic, language, and probability*. The Fourth International Congress for Logic, Methodology, and Philosophy of Science, Bucharest, September 1971. Dordrecht: Reidel, 1973.

Istomina, Z. M. 1963. Perception and naming of color in early childhood. *Soviet Psychology and Psychiatry* 1(2):37–45.

Jackendoff, R. S. 1972. *Semantic interpretation in generative grammar*. Cambridge, Mass.: MIT Press.

————1974. A deep structure projection rule. *Linguistic Inquiry* 5:481–505.

————1975. Morphological and semantic regularities in the lexicon. *Language* 51:639–671.

Jacobs, G. H., and H. A. Gaylord. 1967. Effects of chromatic adaptation on color naming. *Vision Research* 7:645–653.

James, W. 1890. *The principles of psychology.* New York: Holt.

———1907. *Pragmatism.* New York: Longmans, Green.

Jameson, D., and L. M. Hurvich. 1955. Some quantitative aspects of an opponent-colors theory: I, chromatic responses and spectral saturation. *Journal of the Optical Society of America* 45:546–552.

———1959. Perceived color and its dependence on focal, surrounding, and preceding stimulus variables. *Journal of the Optical Society of America* 49:890–898.

Jammer, M. 1954. *Concepts of space.* Cambridge, Mass.: Harvard University Press.

Jarvella, R. J. 1971. Syntactic processing of connected speech. *Journal of Verbal Learning and Verbal Behavior* 10:409–416.

Jarvella, R. J., and J. Lubinsky. 1975. Deaf and hearing children's use of language describing temporal order among events. *Journal of Speech and Hearing Research* 18:58–73.

Jastrzembski, J. E., and R. F. Stanners. 1975. Multiple word meanings and lexical search speed. *Journal of Verbal Learning and Verbal Behavior* 14:534–537.

Jenkins, J. J., and W. A. Russell. 1960. Systematic changes in word association norms: 1910–1952. *Journal of Abnormal and Social Psychology* 60:293–304.

Johansson, G. 1950. *Configurations in event perception.* Uppsala: Almqvist & Wiksell.

———1964. Perception of motion and changing form. *Scandanavian Journal of Psychology* 5:181–208.

———1971. Visual perception of biological motion and a model for its analysis. Department of Psychology report 100, University of Uppsala.

———1972. Projective transformations as determining visual space perception. Mimeographed. Uppsala: University of Uppsala.

Johnson, M. G. 1970. A cognitive-feature model of compound free associations. *Psychological Review* 77:282–293.

Johnson-Laird, P. N. 1975. Models of deduction. In R. Falmagne, ed., *Reasoning: representation and process.* Hillsdale, N.J.: Erlbaum.

Johnson-Laird, P. N., C. Robins, and L. Velicogna. 1974. Memory for words. *Nature* 251:704–705.

Joos, M. 1964. *The English verb: form and meanings.* Madison: University of Wisconsin Press.

Jorgensen, C. C., and W. Kintsch. 1973. The role of imagery in the evaluation of sentences. *Cognitive Psychology* 4:110–116.

Julesz, B. 1960. Binocular depth perception of computer generated patterns. *Bell System Technical Journal* 39:1125–1161.

Kahneman, D. 1973. *Attention and effort.* Englewood Cliffs, N.J.: Prentice-Hall.

Kaplan, R. M. 1972. Augmented transition networks as psychological models of sentence comprehension. *Artificial Intelligence* 3:77–100.

———1974. Transient processing load in sentence comprehension. Ph.D. dissertation, Harvard University.

———1975. On process models for sentence analysis. In D. A. Norman and D. E. Rumelhart, eds., *Explorations in cognition.* San Francisco: Freeman.

Karttunen, L. 1970. On the semantics of complement sentences. In *Papers from the Sixth Regional Meeting of the Chicago Linguistic Society*. Chicago: Chicago Linguistic Society.

——1971. Implicative verbs. *Language* 47:340–358.

——1972. Possible and must. In J. P. Kimball, ed., *Syntax and semantics,* vol. 1. New York: Seminar Press.

——1973a. Presuppositions of compound sentences. *Linguistic Inquiry* 4:169–193.

——1973b. Stop—is there a presupposition, or isn't there? Memorandum of the Mathematical Social Science Board Workshop on Formal Pragmatics, August 23, 1973.

Katz, D. 1935. *The world of colour*. Translated by R. B. MacLeod and C. W. Fox. London: Kegan Paul.

Katz, J. J. 1964a. Semantic theory and the meaning of "good." *Journal of Philosophy* 61:739–766.

——1964b. Analyticity and contradiction in natural language. In J. A. Fodor and J. J. Katz, eds., *The structure of language: readings in the philosophy of language*. Englewood Cliffs, N.J.: Prentice-Hall.

——1966. *The philosophy of language*. New York: Harper & Row.

——1968. The logic of questions. In B. Van Rootselaar and J. F. Staal, eds., *Logic, methodology and philosophy of science,* vol 3. Amsterdam: North-Holland.

——1972. *Semantic theory*. New York: Harper & Row.

——1975. Propositional structure: a study of the contribution of sentence meaning to speech acts. Forthcoming.

Katz, J. J., and J. A. Fodor. 1963. The structure of a semantic theory. *Language* 39:170–210.

Katz, J. J., and P. M. Postal. 1964. *An integrated theory of linguistic descriptions*. Cambridge, Mass.: MIT Press.

Katz, N., E. Baker, and J. Macnamara. 1974. What's in a name? a study of how children learn common and proper names. *Child Development* 45:469–473.

Kay, P. 1971. Taxonomy and semantic contrast. *Language* 47:866–887.

Keenan, E. L. 1972. On semantically based grammar. *Linguistic Inquiry* 3:413–461.

Kelley, H. H. 1973. The process of causal attribution. *American Psychologist* 28:107–128.

Kenny, A. 1963. *Action, emotion, and will*. New York: Humanities Press.

Kent, G. H., and A. J. Rosanoff. 1910. A study of association in insanity. *American Journal of Insanity* 67:37–96, 317–390.

Kinchla, R. A., and L. G. Allan. 1969. A theory of visual movement perception. *Psychological Review*. 76:537–558.

Kintsch, W. 1972. Notes on the semantic structure of memory. In E. Tulving and W. Donaldson, eds., *Organization of memory*. New York: Academic Press.

——1974. *The representation of meaning in memory*. Hillsdale, N.J.: Erlbaum.

Kintz, R. T., J. A. Parker, and R. M. Boynton. 1969. Information transmission in spectral color naming. *Perception and Psychophysics* 5:241–245.

Kiparsky, P., and C. Kiparsky. 1970. Fact. In M. Bierwisch and K. E. Heidolph, eds., *Progress in linguistics*. The Hague: Mouton.

Kirsch, R. A. 1963. *Symposium on automated processing of illustrated text*. National Bureau of Standards report 8144.

———1964. Computer interpretation of English text and picture patterns. *IEEE Transactions on Electronic Computers* EC-13 (4):170–210.

Klein, G. S. 1964. Semantic power as measured through the interference of words with color naming. *American Journal of Psychology* 77:576–588.

Kling, J. W., and L. A. Riggs, eds. 1971. *Woodworth and Schlosberg's experimental psychology.* 3d ed. New York: Holt, Rinehart & Winston.

Kneale, W. C. 1971. Russell's paradox and some others. *British Journal of the Philosophy of Science* 22:321–338.

———1972. Propositions and truth in natural language. *Mind* 81:225–243.

Koffka, K. 1935. *Principles of gestalt psychology.* New York: Harcourt, Brace.

Köhler, W. 1929. *Gestalt psychology.* New York: Liveright.

Kolers, P. A. 1972. *Aspects of motion perception.* Oxford: Pergamon.

Krantz, D. H. 1972. Measurement structures and psychological laws. *Science* 175:1427–1435.

Krauss, R. 1952. *A hole is to dig.* New York: Harper & Row.

Krauss, R. M., and S. Glucksberg. 1969. The development of communication: competence as a function of age. *Child Development* 40:255–256.

Krauss, R. M., and S. Weinheimer. 1964. Changes in the length of reference phrases as a function of social interaction: a preliminary study. *Psychonomic Science* 1:113–114.

———1966. Concurrent feedback, confirmation, and the encoding of referents in verbal communication. *Journal of Personality and Social Psychology* 4:343–346.

Krech, D., and R. S. Crutchfield. 1965. *Elements of psychology.* New York: Knopf.

Kripke, S. A. 1963a. Semantical analysis of modal logic: I, normal propositional calculi. *Zeitschrift für mathematische Logik und Grundlagen der Mathematik* 9:67–96.

———1963b. Semantical considerations on modal logics. *Acta Philosophica Fennica* 16:83–94.

———1972. Naming and necessity. In D. Davidson and G. Harman, eds., *Semantics of natural language.* Dordrecht: Reidel.

Kroch, A. 1972. Lexical and inferred meanings for some time adverbs. Research Laboratory of Electronics quarterly progress report 104, Massachusetts Institute of Technology.

Kučera, H., and W. N. Francis. 1967. *Computational analysis of present-day American English.* Providence, R.I.: Brown University Press.

LaBerge, D., and S. J. Samuels. 1974. Toward a theory of automatic information processing in reading. *Cognitive Psychology* 6:293–323.

Labov, W. 1972a. The boundaries of words and their meanings. In C.–J. N. Bailey and R. W. Shuy, eds., *New ways of analyzing variation in English,* vol. 1. (Papers from conference, 1972.) Washington: Georgetown University Press, 1973.

———1972b. *Sociolinguistic patterns.* Philadelphia: University of Pennsylvania Press.

Lackner, J. R., and M. F. Garrett. 1972. Resolving ambiguity: effects of biasing context in the unattended ear. *Cognition* 1:359–372.

Lakoff, G. 1968. Instrumental adverbs and the concept of deep structure. *Foundations of Language* 4:4–29.

———1970. *Irregularity in syntax.* New York: Holt, Rinehart & Winston.

————1971a. On generative semantics. In D. D. Steinberg and L. A. Jakobovits, eds., *Semantics: an interdisciplinary reader in philosophy, linguistics and psychology.* Cambridge: Cambridge University Press.

————1971b. Linguistics and natural logic. *Synthese* 22:151–271.

————1972a. Performative antinomies. *Foundations of Language* 8:569–572.

————1972b. Hedges: a study of meaning criteria and the logic of fuzzy concepts. In *Papers from the Eighth Regional Meeting of the Chicago Linguistic Society.* Chicago: Chicago Linguistic Society.

Lakoff, G., and S. Peters. 1969. Phrasal conjunction and symmetric predicates. In D. A. Reibel and S. A. Schane, eds., *Modern studies in English: readings in transformational grammar.* Englewood Cliffs, N.J.: Prentice-Hall.

Lakoff, R. 1972. Language in context. *Language* 48:907–928.

————1973. The logic of politeness; or, minding your p's and q's. In *Papers from the Ninth Regional Meeting of the Chicago Linguistic Society.* Chicago: Chicago Linguistic Society.

Langendoen, D. T. 1970. *Essentials of English grammar.* New York: Holt, Rinehart & Winston.

Langford, C. H. 1942. Moore's notion of analysis. In P. A. Schlipp, ed., *The philosophy of G. E. Moore.* New York: Tudor.

Lantz, D., and V. Stefflre. 1964. Language and cognition revisited. *Journal of Abnormal and Social Psychology* 69:472–481.

Larkin, D., and M. H. O'Malley. 1973. Declarative sentences and the rule-of-conversation hypothesis. In *Papers from the Ninth Regional Meeting of the Chicago Linguistic Society.* Chicago: Chicago Linguistic Society.

Laurendeau, M., and A. Pinard. 1962. *Causal thinking in the child.* New York: International Universities Press.

————1970. *The development of the concept of space in the child.* New York: International Universities Press.

Lee, P. G. 1969. Subjects and agents. In *Working papers in linguistics,* vol. 3. Computer and Information Sciences Research Center technical report 69–4, Ohio State University.

Leech, G. N. 1969. *Towards a semantic description of English.* London: Longmans.

Lees, R. 1960. *The grammar of English nominalizations.* The Hague: Mouton.

————1970. Problems in the grammatical analysis of English nominal compounds. In M. Bierwisch and K. E. Heidloph, eds., *Progress in linguistics.* The Hague: Mouton.

Leeuwenberg, E. L. J. 1968. *Structural information of visual patterns: an efficient coding system in perception.* The Hague: Mouton.

————1971. A perceptual coding language for visual and auditory patterns. *American Journal of Psychology* 84:307–349.

Legrenzi, P. 1972. The description of being observed: linguistic factors and eye-contact judgments. Mimeographed. Padova: University of Padova.

Lenneberg, E. H. 1967. *Biological foundations of language.* New York: Wiley.

Leont'ev, A. A. 1973. Some problems in learning Russion as a foreign language (essays on psycholinguistics). Translated by C. Gaddy. *Soviet Psychology* 11(4):1–117.

Lévi-Strauss, C. 1966. *The savage mind.* London: Weidenfeld & Nicholson.

Lewis, C. I. 1918. *A survey of symbolic logic.* Berkeley: University of California Press.

Lewis, D. K. 1969. *Convention: a philosophical study*. Cambridge, Mass.: Harvard University Press.

———1971. General semantics. *Synthese* 22:18–67.

———1973. *Counterfactuals*. Cambridge, Mass.: Harvard University Press.

Lewis, J. L. 1970. Semantic processing of unattended messages using dichotic listening. *Journal of Experimental Psychology* 85:225–228.

Lewis, M. M. 1937. The beginning of reference to past and future in a child's speech. *British Journal of Educational Psychology* 7:39–56.

Liberman, A. M., F. S. Cooper, D. P. Shankweiler, and M. Studdert-Kennedy. 1967. Perception of the speech code. *Psychological Review* 74:431–461.

Lindsay, R. K. 1963. Inferential memory as the basis of machines which understand natural language. In E. A. Feigenbaum and J. Feldman, eds., *Computers and thought*. New York: McGraw-Hill.

Litteral, R. 1972. Rhetorical predicates and time topology in Anggor. *Foundations of Language* 8:391–410.

Long, B. S. 1975. The development of semantic features: how children learn verbs of motion. Ph.D. dissertation, Cornell University.

Lowenthal, D., and M. Riel. 1972. *Environmental structures: semantic and experiential components*. Publications in Environmental Perception, no. 8. New York: American Geographical Society.

Lynch, K. 1960. *The image of the city*. Cambridge, Mass.: The Technology Press and Harvard University Press.

Lyons, J. 1963. *Structural semantics: an analysis of part of the vocabulary of Plato*. Publications of the Philological Society. Oxford: Blackwell.

———1968. *Introduction to theoretical linguistics*. Cambridge: Cambridge University Press.

———1973. Deixis as the source of reference. *Work in progress*, vol. 6. Edinburgh: University of Edinburgh, Department of Linguistics.

McCawley, J. D. 1971. Tense and time reference in English. In C. J. Fillmore and D. T. Langendoen, eds., *Studies in linguistic semantics*. New York: Holt, Rinehart & Winston.

McDougall, W. 1921. *An introduction to social psychology*. Boston: Luce.

MacKay, D. G. 1973. Aspects of the theory of comprehension, memory, and attention. *Quarterly Journal of Experimental Psychology* 25:22–40.

———1974. Derivational processes in word perception. In S. A. Thompson and C. Lord, eds., *Approaches to the lexicon*. UCLA Papers in Syntax, no. 6. Los Angeles: University of California.

Macnamara, J. 1972. Cognitive basis of language learning in infants. *Psychological Review* 79:1–13.

McNeill, N. B. 1972. Colour and colour terminology. *Journal of Linguistics* 8:21–33.

McTaggart, J. M. E. 1927. *The nature of existence*. Cambridge: Cambridge University Press.

Maerz, A., and M. R. Paul. 1930. *Dictionary of color*. New York: McGraw-Hill.

Malcolm, N. 1963. *Knowledge and certainty: essays and lectures*. Englewood Cliffs, N.J.: Prentice-Hall.

———1971. *Problems of mind: Descartes to Wittgenstein*. New York: Harper.

Mandler, G. 1967. Organization and memory. In K. W. Spence and J. T. Spence, eds., *The psychology of learning and motivation*. New York: Academic Press.

Marchand, H. 1969. *The categories and types of present-day English word-formation: a synchronic-diachronic approach*. 2d ed. Munich: Beck.

Marshall, J. 1969. Psychological linguistics: psychological aspects of semantic structure. In A. R. Meetham, ed., *Encyclopedia of linguistics, information, and control*. London: Pergamon.

Marslen-Wilson, W. D. 1975. Sentence perception as an interactive parallel process. *Science* 189:226–228.

Martin, R. M. 1950. Some comments on truth and designation. *Analysis* 10:65.

Masangkay, Z. S., K. A. McCluskey, C. W. McIntyre, J. Sims-Knight, B. E. Vaughn, and J. H. Flavell. 1974. The early development of inferences about the visual percepts of others. *Child Development* 45:357–366.

Matthews, P. H. 1967. Review of *Aspects of the theory of syntax* by N. Chomsky. *Journal of Linguistics* 3:119–152.

————1974. *Morphology: an introduction to the theory of word-structure*. Cambridge: Cambridge University Press.

Meacham, J. A. 1972. The development of memory abilities in the individual and society. *Human Development* 15:205–228.

Meiland, J. W. 1970. *The nature of intention*. London: Methuen.

Melden, A. I. 1961. *Free action*. New York: Humanities Press.

Meyer, B. J. F. 1974. The organization of prose and its effects on recall. Ph.D. dissertation, Cornell University.

Meyer, D. E. 1970. On the representation and retrieval of stored semantic information. *Cognitive Psychology* 1:242–299.

Meyer, D. E., and R. W. Schvaneveldt. 1971. Facilitation in recognizing pairs of words: evidence of a dependence between retrieval operations. *Journal of Experimental Psychology* 90:227–234.

Meyer, D. E., R. W. Schvaneveldt, and M. G. Ruddy. 1972. Activation of lexical memory. Paper read to Psychonomic Society, November 1972. Mimeographed.

Michotte, A. 1954. *La perception de la causalité*. 2d ed. Louvain: Publications Universitaires de Louvain.

————1962. *Causalité, permanence et réalité phénoménales*. Louvain: Publications Universitaires Belgium.

Mill, J. S. 1843. *A system of logic*. New York: Longmans, Green, 1956.

Millenson, J. R. 1967. *Principles of behavioral analysis*. London: Collier-Macmillan.

Miller, G. A. 1953. What is information measurement? *American Psychologist* 8:3–11.

————1956. The magical number seven, plus or minus two: some limits on our capacity for processing information. *Psychological Review* 63:81–97.

————1969a. The organization of lexical memory: are word associations sufficient? In G. A. Talland and N. C. Waugh, eds., *The pathology of memory*. New York: Academic Press.

————1969b. A psychological method to investigate verbal concepts. *Journal of Mathematical Psychology* 6:169–191.

————1972. English verbs of motion: a case study in semantics and lexical memory. In A. W. Melton and E. Martin, eds., *Coding processes in human memory*. Washington, D.C.: Winston.

————1974a. Toward a third metaphor for psycholinguistics. In W. B. Weimer and D. S. Palermo, eds., *Cognition and the symbolic processes.* Hillsdale, N.J.: Erlbaum.

————1974b. Listen and hear. In H. R. Moskowitz, B. Scharf, and J. C. Stevens, eds., *Sensation and measurement.* Dordrecht: Reidel.

Miller, G. A., E. Galanter, and K. Pribram. 1960. *Plans and the structure of behavior.* New York: Holt, Rinehart & Winston.

Miller, G. A., and D. McNeill. 1969. Psycholinguistics. In G. Lindzey and E. Aaronson, eds., *Handbook of social psychology,* vol. 3. Reading, Mass.: Addison-Wesley.

Miller, G. A., and W. G. Taylor. 1948. The perception of repeated bursts of noise. *Journal of the Acoustical Society of America* 20:171–182.

Miller, R. L. 1968. *The linguistic relativity principle and Humboldtian ethno-linguistics.* The Hague: Mouton.

Minsky, M. 1961. Steps toward artificial intelligence. *Proceedings of the IRE* 49:8–29.

————ed. 1968. *Semantic information processing.* Cambridge, Mass.: MIT Press.

Minsky, M., and S. Papert. 1969. *Perceptrons.* Cambridge, Mass.: MIT Press.

————1972. *Artificial intelligence progress report.* Artificial Intelligence Laboratory A. I. memorandum 252, January 1, 1972, Massachusetts Institute of Technology.

Mischel, T., ed. 1969. *Human action: conceptual and empirical issues.* New York: Academic Press.

Montague, R. 1974. *Formal philosophy: selected papers.* New Haven: Yale University Press.

Moore, G. E. 1959. Proof of an external world. In *Philosophical papers,* chap. 7. London: Macmillan.

Moore, J., and A. Newell. 1974. How can Merlin understand? In L. Gregg, ed., *Knowledge and cognition.* Hillsdale, N.J.: Erlbaum.

Moran, L. J. 1966. Generality of word-association response sets. *Psychological Monographs* 80, whole no. 612.

Moravcsik, J. M. E. 1972. Review of *Towards a semantic description of English* by G. N. Leech. *Language* 48:445–454.

Morgan, J. L. 1969. On arguing about semantics. *Papers in Linguistics* 1:49–70.

Morrissey, M. D. 1973. The English perfective and "still"/"anymore." *Journal of Linguistics* 9:65–69.

Murdock, B. B., Jr. 1967. Recent developments in short-term memory. *British Journal of Psychology* 58:421–433.

Mussen, P. H., ed. 1970. *Carmichael's manual of child psychology.* 3d ed. New York: Wiley.

Nachshon, I., and S. Wapner. 1967. Effect of eye contact and physiognomy on perceived location of other person. *Journal of Personality and Social Psychology* 7:82–89.

Nakamura, H. 1966. Time in Indian and Japanese thought. In J. T. Fraser, ed., *The voices of time.* New York: Brazillier.

Neimark, E. D. 1974. Natural language concepts: additional evidence. *Child Development* 45:508–511.

Neisser, U. 1967. *Cognitive psychology.* New York: Appleton-Century-Crofts.

Nelson, K. 1973a. Some evidence for the cognitive primacy of categorization and its functional basis. *Merrill-Palmer Quarterly of Behavior and Development* 19:21–39.

————1973b. Structure and strategy in learning to talk. *Monographs of the Society for Research in Child Development*, serial no. 149, vol. 38, nos. 1–2.

————1974. Concept, word, and sentence: interrelations in acquisition and development. *Psychological Review* 81:267–285.

Neumann, J. von. 1951. The general and logical theory of automata. In L. A. Jeffress, ed., *Cerebral mechanisms in behavior: the Hixon symposium*. New York: Wiley.

Newell, A., and H. A. Simon. 1972. *Human problem solving*. Englewood Cliffs, N.J.: Prentice-Hall.

Nice, M. M. 1915. The development of a child's vocabulary in relation to environment. *Pedagogical Seminary* 22:35–64.

Nida, E. A. 1975. Componential analysis of meaning. The Hague: Mouton.

Nilsen, D. L. F. 1973. *The instrumental case in English*. The Hague: Mouton.

Norman, D. A. 1969. *Memory and attention: an introduction to human information processing*. New York: Wiley.

————1973. Memory, knowledge, and the answering of questions. In R. L. Solso, ed., *Contemporary issues in cognitive psychology: the Loyola symposium*. Washington, D.C.: Winston.

————ed. 1970. *Models of human memory*. New York: Academic Press.

Norman, D. A., and D. E. Rumelhart, eds. 1975. *Exploration in cognition*. San Francisco: Freeman.

Nye, P. W., ed. 1971. *Evaluation of mobility aids for the blind*. Washington, D.C.: National Academy of Engineering, Committee on the Interplay of Engineering with Biology and Medicine.

Oackden, E. C., and M. Sturt. 1922. The development of the knowledge of time in children. *British Journal of Psychology* 12:309–337.

Odbert, H. S., T. F. Karwoski, and A. B. Eckerson. 1942. Studies in synesthetic thinking: I, musical and verbal association of color and mood. *Journal of Genetic Psychology* 26:153–173.

Ogden, C. K. 1932. *The basic words: a detailed account of uses*. London: Kegan Paul.

Ohm, G. S. 1843. Ueber die Definition des Tones, nebst daran geknüpfter Theorie der Sirene und ähnlicher tonbildener Vorrichtungen. *Annalen der Physik und Chemie* 135:497–565.

Olson, D. R. 1970. Language and thought: aspects of a cognitive theory of semantics. *Psychological Review* 77:257–273.

————1972. Language use for communicating, instructing, and thinking. In J. B. Carroll and R. O. Freedle, eds., *Language comprehension and the acquisition of knowledge*. Washington, D.C.: Winston.

Ornstein, R. E. 1969. *On the experience of time*. Harmondsworth: Penguin.

Osgood, C. E. 1960. The cross-cultural generality of visual-verbal synesthetic tendencies. *Behavioral Science* 5:146–169.

————1970. Interpersonal verbs and interpersonal behavior. In J. L. Cowan, ed., *Studies in thought and language*. Tucson: University of Arizona Press.

————1971. Where do sentences come from? In D. D. Steinberg and L. A.

Jakobovits, eds., *Semantics: an interdisciplinary reader in philosophy, linguistics, and psychology*. Cambridge: Cambridge University Press.

Osgood, C. E., G. J. Suci, and P. H. Tannenbaum. 1957. *The measurement of meaning*. Urbana: University of Illinois Press.

Ota, A. 1963. *Tense and aspect of present-day American English*. Tokyo: Kenkyusha.

Paivio, A. 1971. *Imagery and verbal processes*. New York: Holt, Rinehart & Winston.

Paivio, A., J. C. Yuille, and S. A. Madigan. 1968. Concreteness, imagery, and meaningfulness for 925 nouns. *Journal of Experimental Psychology Monograph Supplement* 76, no. 1, part 2, pp. 1–25.

Palermo, D. S., and J. J. Jenkins. 1964. *Word association norms: grade school through college*. Minneapolis: University of Minnesota Press.

Palmer, F. R. 1965. *A linguistic study of the English verb*. London: Longmans.

Parsons, T. 1972. Some problems concerning the logic of grammatical modifiers. In D. Davidson and G. Harman, eds., *Semantics of natural language*. Dordrecht: Reidel.

Partee, B. H. 1973. The syntax and semantics of quotation. In S. R. Anderson and P. Kiparsky, eds., *A festschrift for Morris Halle*. New York: Holt, Rinehart & Winston.

Peirce, C. S. 1932. *Collected papers*, vol. 2. Cambridge, Mass.: Harvard University Press.

Perlmutter, D. M. 1970. The two verbs *begin*. In R. A. Jacobs and P. S. Rosenbaum, eds., *Readings in English transformational grammar*. Waltham, Mass.: Ginn.

Piaget, J. 1924. *Judgment and reasoning in the child*. Translated by M. Worden. New York: Harcourt, Brace & World, 1928.

———1926. *The child's conception of the world*. Translated by J. Tomlinson and A. Tomlinson. New York: Harcourt, Brace & World, 1929.

———1927a. *The child's conception of time*. Translated by A. J. Pomerans. London: Routledge & Kegan Paul, 1969.

———1927b. *The child's conception of physical causality*. Translated by M. Worden. New York: Harcourt, Brace & World, 1930.

———1937. *The construction of reality in the child*. Translated by M. Cook. New York: Basic Books, 1954.

———1947. *The psychology of intelligence*. Translated by M. Piercy and D. E. Berlyne. London: Routledge & Kegan Paul, 1950.

———1948. *Play, dreams, and imitation in childhood*. Translated by C. Gattengo and F. M. Hodgson. New York: Norton, 1951.

———1961. *The mechanisms of perception*. Translated by G. N. Seagrim. New York: Basic Books, 1969.

Piaget, J., and B. Inhelder. 1948. *The child's conception of space*. Translated by F. J. Langdon and J. L. Lunzer. London: Routledge & Kegan Paul, 1956.

Pike, K. L. 1960. *Language in relation to a unified theory of the structure of human behavior*, part 3. Glendale, Ill.: Summer Institute of Linguistics.

Pitcher, G. 1971. *A theory of perception*. Princeton, N.J.: Princeton University Press.

Plutchik, R. 1962. *The emotions: facts, theories and a new model*. New York: Random House.

Pollock, S. L. 1971. *Decision tables: theory and practice*. New York: Wiley.

Porzig, W. 1934. Wesenhafte Bedeutungsbeziehungen. *Beiträge zur Geschichte der deutschen Sprache und Literatur* 58:70–97.

Postal, P. M. 1966. On so-called "pronouns" in English. In F. P. Dinneen, ed., *Monograph series on languages and linguistics*, no. 19. Washington, D.C.: Georgetown University Press.

————1971. *Cross-over phenomena*. New York: Holt, Rinehart & Winston.

Postman, L. J., and G. Keppel, eds. 1970. *Norms of word association*. New York: Academic Press.

Potter, M. C. 1975. Meaning in visual search. *Science* 187:965–966.

Potter, M. C., and E. I. Levy. 1969. Recognition memory for a rapid series of pictures. *Journal of Experimental Psychology* 81:10–15.

Power, R. 1974. A computer model of conversation. Ph.D. dissertation, University of Edinburgh.

Powers, W. T. 1973. *Behavior: the control of perception*. Chicago: Aldine.

Preusser, D., and S. Handel. 1970. The free classification of hierarchically and categorically related stimuli. *Journal of Verbal Learning and Verbal Behavior* 9:222–231.

Pribram, K. H. 1971. *Languages of the brain: experimental paradoxes and principles in neuropsychology*. Englewood Cliffs, N.J.: Prentice-Hall.

Prior, A. N. 1967. *Past, present, and future*. Oxford: Oxford University Press.

Putnam, H. 1975. The meaning of "meaning." In K. Gunderson, ed., *Language, mind, and knowledge*. Minnesota Studies in the Philosophy of Science, vol. 7. Minneapolis: University of Minnesota Press.

Pylyshyn, Z. W. 1973a. What the mind's eye tells the mind's brain: a critique of mental imagery. *Psychological Bulletin* 80:1–24.

————1973b. The role of competence theories in cognitive psychology. *Journal of Psycholinguistic Research* 2:21–50.

Quine, W. V. 1951. *Mathematical logic*. Rev. ed. Cambridge, Mass.: Harvard University Press.

————1960. *Word and object*. Cambridge, Mass.: MIT Press.

————1973. *The roots of reference*. La Salle, Ill.: Open Court.

Radford, R. A. 1945. The economic organization of a P.O.W. camp. *Economica* November 1945, pp. 189–201.

Ramsdell, D. A. 1947. The psychology of the hard-of-hearing and the deafened adult. In H. Davis, ed., *Hearing and deafness*. New York: Murray Hill.

Rawls, J. 1971. *A theory of justice*. Cambridge, Mass.: Harvard University Press.

Reder, L. M., J. R. Anderson, and R. A. Bjork. 1974. A semantic interpretation of encoding specificity. *Journal of Experimental Psychology* 102:648–656.

Reichenbach, H. 1947. *Elements of symbolic logic*. New York: Free Press.

Rescher, N., ed. 1967. *The logic of decision and action*. Pittsburgh, Pa.: University of Pittsburgh Press.

Rescher, N., and A. Urquhart. 1971. *Temporal logic*. New York: Springer-Verlag.

Ricciuti, H. 1965. Object grouping and selective ordering behavior in infants 12–24 months old. *Merrill-Palmer Quarterly of Behavior and Development* 11:129–148.

Rips, L. J., E. J. Shoben, and E. E. Smith. 1973. Semantic distance and the verification of semantic relations. *Journal of Verbal Learning and Verbal Behavior* 12:1–20.

Rock, I. 1974. The perception of disoriented figures. *Scientific American* 230(1):78–85.

Rogers, A. 1971. Three kinds of physical perception verbs. In *Papers from the Seventh Regional Meeting of the Chicago Linguistic Society*. Chicago: Chicago Linguistic Society.

————1972. Another look at flip perception verbs. In *Papers from the Eighth Regional Meeting of the Chicago Linguistic Society*. Chicago: Chicago Linguistic Society.

Rommetveit, R. 1968. *Words, meanings, and messages.* New York: Academic Press.

Romney, A. K., and R. G. D'Andrade. 1964. Cognitive aspects of English kin terms. *American Anthropologist* 66, no. 3, part 2, pp. 146–170.

Rosch, E. 1973. On the internal structure of perceptual and semantic categories. In T. M. Moore, ed., *Cognitive development and the acquisition of language*. New York: Academic Press.

————1975. Cognitive reference points. *Cognitive Psychology* 7:532–547.

Rosenbaum, P. S. 1967. *The grammar of English predicate complement constructions.* Cambridge, Mass.: MIT Press.

Rosenblatt, F. 1962. A comparison of several perceptron models. In M. C. Yovits, G. T. Jacobi, and G. D. Goldstein, eds., *Self-organizing systems*. Washington, D.C.: Spartan.

Ross, J. R. 1967. Constraints on variables in syntax. Ph.D. dissertation, Massachusetts Institute of Technology.

————1970. On declarative sentences. In R. A. Jacobs and P. S. Rosenbaum, eds., *Readings in English transformational grammar*. Waltham, Mass.: Ginn.

————1972a. More on *begin*. *Foundations of Language* 8:574–577.

————1972b. Act. In D. Davidson and G. Harman, eds., *Semantics of natural language*. Dordrecht: Reidel.

Rubenstein, H., L. Garfield, and J. A. Millikan. 1970. Homographic entries in the internal lexicon. *Journal of Verbal Learning and Verbal Behavior* 9:487–494.

Rubenstein, H., and J. B. Goodenough. 1965. Contextual correlates of synonymy. *Communications of the ACM* 8:627–633.

Rumelhart, D. E. 1970. A multicomponent theory of the perception of briefly presented displays. *Journal of Mathematical Psychology* 7:191–218.

Rumelhart, D. E., P. H. Lindsay, and D. A. Norman. 1972. A process model for long-term memory. In E. Tulving and W. Donaldson, eds., *Organization and memory*. New York: Academic Press.

Rushton, W. A. H. 1962. Visual pigments in man. *Scientific American* 207:120–132.

Russell, B. 1905. On denoting. *Mind* 14:479–493.

————1912. *The problems of philosophy.* London: Thornton Butterworth.

Russell, W. A., and J. J. Jenkins. 1954. The complete Minnesota norms for responses to 100 words from the Kent-Rosanoff word association tests. Mimeographed. Minneapolis: University of Minnesota, Department of Psychology.

Rustin, R., ed. 1973. *Courant computer science symposium 8: natural language processing.* New York: Algorithmics Press.

Ryle, G. 1949. *The concept of mind.* New York: Barnes & Noble.

Sacks, H., E. A. Schegloff, and G. Jefferson. 1974. A simplest systematics for the organization of turn-taking for conversation. *Language* 50:696–735.

Sadock, J. M. 1971. Queclaratives. In *Papers from the Seventh Regional Meeting of the Chicago Linguistic Society.* Chicago: Chicago Linguistic Society.

Sahlins, M. 1972. *Stone age economics.* Chicago and New York: Aldine-Atherton.

Saltz, E. 1971. *The cognitive bases of human learning.* Homewood, Ill.: Dorsey.

Saltz, E., and I. E. Sigel. 1967. Concept overdiscrimination in children. *Journal of Experimental Psychology* 73:1–8.

Saltz, E., E. Soller, and I. E. Sigel. 1972. The development of natural language concepts. *Child Development* 43:1191–1202.

Sapir, E. 1944. Grading: a study in semantics. *Philosophy of Science* 11:83–116.

Savin, H. B. 1973. Meanings and concepts: a review of Jerrold J. Katz's *Semantic Theory. Cognition* 2:213–238.

Schaefer, B., J. A. Lewis, and A. Van Decar. 1971. The growth of children's semantic memory: semantic elements. *Journal of Experimental Child Psychology* 11:296–309.

Schank, R. C. 1972. Conceptual dependency: a theory of natural language understanding. *Cognitive Psychology* 3:552–631.

———1973a. The fourteen primitive actions and their inferences. Computer Science Department A.I. memorandum 183, Stanford University.

———1973b. Causality and reasoning. Istituto per gli studi Semantici e Cognitivi technical report 1, Castagnola. Mimeographed.

Schank, R. C., and K. M. Colby, eds. 1973. *Computer models of thought and language.* San Francisco: Freeman.

Schegloff, E. A. 1972. Notes on a conversational practice: formulating place. In D. Sudnow, ed., *Studies in social interaction.* New York: Free Press.

Schegloff, E. A., and H. Sacks. 1973. Opening up closings. *Semiotica* 8:289–327.

Schlosberg, H. 1954. Three dimensions of emotions. *Psychological Review* 61:81–88.

Schvaneveldt, R. W., and D. E. Meyer. 1973. Retrieval and comparison processes in semantic memory. In S. Kornblum, ed., *Attention and performance IV.* New York: Academic Press.

Scovel, T. S. 1971. A look-see at some verbs of perception. *Language Learning* 21:75–84.

Searle, J. R. 1969. *Speech acts: an essay in the philosophy of language.* Cambridge: Cambridge University Press.

Shallice, T., and E. K. Warrington. 1970. Independent functioning of verbal memory stores: a neuropsychological study. *Quarterly Journal of Experimental Psychology* 22:261–273.

Shankweiler, D. P., and M. Studdert-Kennedy. 1967. Identification of consonants and vowels presented to left and right ears. *Quarterly Journal of Experimental Psychology* 19:59–63.

Shepard, R. N. 1962. The analysis of proximities: multidimensional scaling with an unknown distance function. *Psychometrika* 27:125–139, 219–246.

Shepard, R. N., and J. Metzler. 1971. Mental rotation of three-dimensional objects. *Science* 171:701–703.

Sherif, M. 1935. A study of some social factors in perception. *Archives of Psychology,* no. 187.

Shiffrin, R. M. 1970. Memory search. In D. A. Norman, ed., *Models of human memory.* New York: Academic Press.

Sibley, F. N. 1955. Seeking, scrutinizing, and seeing. *Mind* 64:455–478.

Siegel, A. W., and S. H. White. 1974. The development of spatial representations of large-scale environments. In H. Reese, ed., *Advances in child development and behavior,* vol. 10. New York: Academic Press.

Simon, H. A. 1957. *Models of man.* New York: Wiley.

———1972. Complexity and the representation of patterned sequences of symbols. *Psychological Review* 79:369–382.

Simon, H. A., and L. Siklossy, eds. 1972. *Representation and meaning: experiments with information processing systems.* Englewood Cliffs, N.J.: Prentice-Hall.

Simpson, G. G. 1961. *Principles of animal taxonomy.* New York: Columbia University Press.

Sinclair, J. McH., I. J. Forsyth, R. M. Coulthard, and M. Ashby. 1972. The English used by teachers and pupils. Report to Social Science Research Council of Great Britain from the University of Birmingham. Mimeographed.

Skinner, B. F. 1957. *Verbal behavior.* New York: Appleton-Century-Crofts.

Slobin, D. 1971. Developmental psycholinguistics. In W. O. Dingwall, ed., *A survey of linguistic science.* College Park: University of Maryland, Linguistics Program.

Smith, C. S. 1964. Determiners and relative clauses in generative grammar of English. *Language* 40:37–52.

Smith, E. E., E. J. Shoben, and L. J. Rips. 1974. Structure and process in semantic memory: a featural model for semantic decisions. *Psychological Review* 81:214–241.

Smith, K. H., and L. E. McMahon. 1970. Understanding order information in sentences: some recent work at Bell Laboratories. In G. B. Flores d'Arcais and W. J. M. Levelt, eds., *Advances in psycholinguistics.* Amsterdam: North-Holland.

Snare, F. 1972. The concept of property. *American Philosophical Quarterly* 9:200–206.

Soboleva, P. A. 1973. Derivational structure of the Russian lexicon. In F. Kiefer, ed., *Trends in Soviet theoretical linguistics.* Dordrecht: Reidel.

Solomons, L. M., and G. Stein. 1896. Studies from the Psychological Laboratory of Harvard University: II, normal motor automatisms. *Psychological Review* 3:492–512.

Spears, A. K. 1973. Complements of *significant*-class predicates: a study in the semantics of complementation. In *Papers from the Ninth Regional Meeting of the Chicago Linguistic Society.* Chicago: Chicago Linguistic Society.

Sperling, G. 1963. A model for visual memory tasks. *Human Factors* 5:19–31.

Staal, J. F. 1967. Some semantic relations between sentoids. *Foundations of Language* 3:66–88.

Stalnaker, R. C. 1968. A theory of conditionals. In N. Rescher, ed., *Studies in logical theory.* Oxford: Oxford University Press.

———1972. Pragmatics. In D. Davidson and G. Harman, eds., *Semantics of natural language.* Dordrecht: Reidel.

Stenning, K. 1975. Understanding English articles and quantifiers. Ph.D. dissertation, Rockefeller University.

Sternheim, C. E. and R. M. Boynton. 1966. Uniqueness of perceived hues investigated with a continuous judgmental technique. *Journal of Experimental Psychology* 72:770–776.

Stevens, S. S. 1934. The volume and intensity of tones. *American Journal of Psychology* 46:397–408.

———1975. *Psychophysics: introduction to its perceptual, neural, and social prospects.* New York: Wiley.

Stevens, S. S., and H. Davis. 1938. *Hearing.* New York: Wiley.

Stevens, S. S., and J. Volkmann. 1940. The relation of pitch to frequency: a revised scale. *American Journal of Psychology* 53:329–353.

Stockwell, R. P., P. Schachter, and B. H. Partee. 1973. *The major syntactic structures of English.* New York: Holt, Rinehart & Winston.

Stone, A. A. 1972. Law, property, and liberty. *American Journal of Orthopsychiatry* 42:627–631.

Strawson, P. F. 1950. On referring. *Mind* 59:320–344.

———1952. *Introduction to logical theory.* London: Methuen.

———1958. Persons. In H. Feigl, M. Scriven, and G. Maxwell, eds., *Concepts, theories, and the mind-body problem.* Minnesota Studies in the Philosophy of Science, vol. 2. Minneapolis: University of Minnesota Press.

———1959. *Individuals: an essay in descriptive metaphysics.* London: Methuen.

———1974. *Subject and predicate in logic and grammar.* London: Methuen.

Stroll, A. 1954. Is everyday language inconsistent? *Mind* 63:219–225.

Stroop, J. R. 1938. Factors affecting speed in serial verbal reactions. *Psychological Monographs* 50(5):38–48.

Stroud, J. M. 1956. The fine structure of psychological time. In H. Quastler, ed., *Information theory in psychology.* Glencoe, Ill.: Free Press.

———1967. The fine structure of psychological time. In R. Fischer, ed., *Interdisciplinary perspectives of time. Annals of the New York Academy of Sciences* 138, art. 2.

Sudnow, D., ed. 1972. *Studies in social interaction.* Glencoe, Ill.: Free Press.

Sutherland, N. S. 1968. Outlines of a theory of visual pattern recognition in animals and man. *Proceedings of the Royal Society* B171:297–317.

———1976. Intelligent picture processing. In N. S. Sutherland, ed., *Tutorial essays in psychology,* vol. 1. Hillsdale, N.J.: Erlbaum.

Sutherland, N. S., and N. J. Mackintosh. 1971. *Mechanisms of animal discrimination learning.* New York: Academic Press.

Swartz, K., and A. E. Hall. 1972. Development of relational concepts and word definitions in children five through eleven. *Child Development* 43:239–244.

Szasz, T. A., and G. J. Alexander. 1972. Law, property, and psychiatry. *American Journal of Orthopsychiatry* 42:610–626.

Tarski, A. 1956. *Logic, semantics, metamathematics: papers from 1923 to 1938.* Translated by J. H. Woodger. Oxford: Oxford University Press.

Teller, P. 1969. Some discussion and extension of Manfred Bierwisch's work on German adjectivals. *Foundations of Language* 5:185–217.

Thomas, G. J. 1949. Equal-volume judgments of tones. *American Journal of Psychology* 62:182–201.

Thomason, R. H., and R. C. Stalnaker. 1973. A semantic theory of adverbs. *Linguistic Inquiry* 4:195–220.

Thompson, S. A. 1973. On subjectless gerunds in English. *Foundations of Language* 9:374–383.

Thomson, L. C. 1954. Sensations aroused by monochromatic stimuli and their prediction. *Optica Acta* 1:93–102.

Thorne, J. P., P. Bratley, and H. Dewar. 1968. The syntactic analysis of English by machine. In D. Michie, ed., *Machine intelligence 3*. New York: American Elsevier.

Thorpe, W. H. 1963. *Learning and instinct in animals*. 2d ed. London: Methuen.

Thurnwald, R. 1932. *Economics in primitive communities*. Oxford: Oxford University Press.

Titchener, E. B. 1910. *A text-book of psychology*. New York: Macmillan.

Tolman, E. C. 1932. *Purposive behavior in animals and men*. New York: Appleton-Century.

Trabasso, T. 1972. Mental operations in language comprehension. In J. B. Carroll and R. O. Freedle, eds., *Language comprehension and the acquisition of knowledge*. Washington, D.C.: Winston.

Travis, C. 1971. A generative theory of illocutions. In J. F. Rosenberg and C. Travis, eds., *Readings in the philosophy of language*. Englewood Cliffs, N.J.: Prentice-Hall.

Trier, J. 1934. Das sprachliche Feld. *Neue Jahrbücher für Wissenschaft und Jungenbilden* 10:428–449.

Tucker, G. R., W. E. Lambert, and A. A. Rigault. 1973. *French speakers' skill with grammatical gender: an example of rule-governed behavior*. The Hague: Mouton.

Tulving, E. 1962. Subjective organization in free recall of "unrelated" words. *Psychological Review* 69:344–354.

————1972. Episodic and semantic memory. In E. Tulving and W. Donaldson, eds., *Organization of memory*. New York: Academic Press.

Tulving, E., and W. Donaldson, eds., 1972. *Organization of Memory*. New York: Academic Press.

Tulving, E., and S. A. Madigan. 1970. Memory and verbal learning. *Annual Review of Psychology* 21:437–484.

Tulving, E., and D. M. Thompson. 1973. Encoding specificity and retrieval processes in episodic memory. *Psychological Review* 80:352–373.

Ullmann, S. 1962. *Semantics: an introduction to the science of meaning*. Oxford: Blackwell and Mott.

Urban, W. M. 1939. *Language and reality: the philosophy of language and the principles of symbolism*. London: Allen & Unwin.

Valéry, P. 1943. *Tel quel*. New York: French and European Publications.

van Fraassen, B. C. 1971. *Formal semantics and logic*. New York: Macmillan.

Vendler, Z. 1967. *Linguistics in philosophy*. Ithaca, N.Y.: Cornell University Press.

————1968. *Adjectives and nominalizations*. Papers on Formal Linguistics, no. 5. The Hague: Mouton.

————1970. Say what you think. In J. L. Cowan, ed., *Studies in thought and language*. Tucson: University of Arizona Press.

————1972. *Res cogitans: an essay in rational psychology.* Ithaca, N.Y.: Cornell University Press.

Verkuyl, H. J. 1972. *On the compositional nature of the aspects.* Dordrecht: Reidel.

Vurpillot, E. 1968. The development of scanning strategies and their relation to visual differentiation. *Journal of Experimental Child Psychology* 6:622–650.

Wagner, K. H. 1968. Verb phrase complementation: a criticism. *Journal of Linguistics* 4:89–91.

Walk, R. D., and E. J. Gibson. 1961. A comparative and analytic study of visual depth perception. *Psychological Monographs* 75, whole no. 519.

Wallace, A. F. C., and J. Atkins. 1960. The meaning of kinship terms. *American Anthropologist* 62:58–79.

Wallach, H., and D. N. O'Connel. 1953. The kinetic depth effect. *Journal of Experimental Psychology* 45:205–217.

Wallach, H., D. N. O'Connel, and U. Neisser. 1953. The memory effect of visual perception of three-dimensional form. *Journal of Experimental Psychology* 45:360–368.

Wallach, H.; A. Weisz; and P. Adams. 1956. Circles and derived figures in rotation. *American Journal of Psychology* 69:48–59.

Wanner, E., and M. Maratsos. 1975. An augmented transition network model of relative clause comprehension. Mimeographed. Cambridge, Mass.: Harvard University.

Warnock, G. J. 1967. Introduction. In G. J. Warnock, ed., *The philosophy of perception.* Oxford: Oxford University Press.

Warren, R. E. 1972. Stimulus encoding and memory. *Journal of Experimental Psychology* 94:90–100.

Warrington, E. K., V. Logue, and R. T. C. Pratt. 1971. The anatomical localization of selective impairment of auditory verbal short-term memory. *Neuropsychologia* 9:377–387.

Wason, P. C. 1961. Response to affirmative and negative binary statements. *British Journal of Psychology* 52:133–142.

Wason, P. C., and P. N. Johnson-Laird. 1972. *Psychology of reasoning: structure and content.* Cambridge, Mass.: Harvard University Press.

Wasow, T., and T. Roeper. 1972. On the subject of gerunds. *Foundations of Language* 8:44–61.

Waugh, N. C., and D. A. Norman. 1965. Primary memory. *Psychological Review* 72:89–104.

Weil, J. 1970. The relationship between time conceptualization and time language in young children. Ph.D. dissertation, City University of New York.

Weinreich, U. 1960. Lexicographic definition in descriptive semantics. In F. W. Householder and S. Saporta, eds., *Problems in lexicography* (a report of the Conference on Lexicography, November 1960, Indiana University). Bloomington: Indiana University, 1967.

————1966. Explorations in semantic theory. In T. A. Sebeok, ed., *Current trends in linguistics,* vol. 3. The Hague: Mouton.

Weisgerber, L. 1962. Von den Kräften der deutschen Sprache. 2 vols. Düsseldorf: Päd. Verlag Schwann.

Welch, L. 1940. A preliminary investigation of some aspects of the hierarchical development of concepts. *Journal of General Psychology* 22:359–378.

Werner, H. 1912. Skizze zu einer Begriffstafel auf genetischer Grundlage. *Archiv für Systematische Philosophie* 18:47–62.

Werner, H., and B. Kaplan. 1963. *Symbol formation: an organismic-developmental approach to language and the expression of thought.* New York: Wiley.

Werner, H., and S. Wapner. 1952. Toward a general theory of perception. *Psychological Review* 59:324–338.

Wertheimer, M. 1938. Numbers and numerical concepts in primitive peoples. In W. D. Ellis, ed., *A source book of gestalt psychology.* New York: Harcourt, Brace.

Wexler, K. N., and A. K. Romney. 1972. Individual variations in cognitive structures. In A. K. Romney, R. N. Shepard, and S. B. Nerlove, eds., *Multidimensional scaling: theory and applications in the behavioral sciences,* vol. 2. New York: Seminar Press.

White, B. L., P. Castle, and R. Held. 1964. Observations on the development of visually-directed reaching. *Child Development* 35:349–364.

White, C. T. 1963. Temporal numerosity and the psychological unit of duration. *Psychological Monographs* 77, 12, whole no. 575.

White, J. H. 1964. The methodology of sememic analysis with special application to the English preposition. *Mechanical Translation* 8:15–31.

Wierzbicka, A. 1972. *Semantic primitives.* Berlin: Atheneum Verlag.

Williams, J. 1976. Synaesthetic adjectives: a possible law of semantic change. *Language,* in press.

Wilson, D. 1972. Presuppositions on factives. *Linguistic Inquiry* 3:405–410.

————1975a. Presupposition, assertion, and lexical items. *Linguistic Inquiry* 6:95–114.

————1975b. *Presuppositions and non-truth-conditional semantics.* New York: Academic Press.

Wilson, G. D. 1966. Arousal properties of red versus green. *Perceptual Motor Skills* 23:947–949.

Winograd, T. 1971. Procedures as a representation for data in a computer program for understanding natural language. Artificial Intelligence report TR-17, Massachusetts Institute of Technology.

Winston, P. H. 1970. Learning structural descriptions from examples. Artificial Intelligence report TR-231, Massachusetts Institute of Technology.

————1973. Learning to identify toy block structures. In R. L. Solso, ed., *Contemporary issues in cognitive psychology: the Loyola symposium.* Washington, D.C.: Winston.

Witkin, H. A. 1959. The perception of the upright. *Scientific American* 200:50–56.

Witkin, H. A., H. B. Lewis, M. Hertzman, K. Machover, P. B. Meissner, and S. Wapner. 1954. *Personality through perception.* New York: Harper.

Wittgenstein, L. 1953. *Philosophical investigations.* Translated by G. E. M. Anscombe. New York: Macmillan.

Woodrow, H. 1951. Time perception. In S. S. Stevens, ed., *Handbook of experimental psychology.* New York: Wiley.

Woodrow, H., and F. Lowell. 1916. Children's association frequency tables. *Psychological Monographs* 22, whole no. 97.

Woods, W. A. 1967. Semantics for a question-answering system. Mathematical Linguistics and Automatic Translation report NSF-19, Harvard Computational Laboratory.

—————1970. Transition network grammars for natural language analysis. *Communications of the ACM* 13:591–606.

—————1973. An experimental parsing system for transition network grammars. In R. Rustin, ed., *Courant computer science symposium 8: natural language processing.* Englewood Cliffs, N.J.: Prentice-Hall.

Woods, W. A., and R. M. Kaplan. 1971. The lunar sciences natural language information system. Bolt, Beranek & Newman report 2265.

Woodworth, R. S. 1910. The puzzle of color vocabularies. *Psychological Bulletin* 7:325–334.

—————1938. *Experimental psychology.* New York: Holt.

Wooten, B. R. 1970. The effects of simultaneous and successive chromatic contrast on spectral hue. Ph.D. dissertation, Brown University.

Wright, G. H. von. 1963. *Norm and action.* New York: Humanities Press.

—————1968. *An essay in deontic logic and the general theory of action.* Amsterdam: North-Holland.

Wright, W. D. 1947. *Researches on normal and defective color vision.* St. Louis: Mosby.

Yamanashi, M. 1972. Lexical decomposition and implied proposition. In *Papers from the Eighth Regional Meeting of the Chicago Linguistic Society.* Chicago: Chicago Linguistic Society.

Yarbus, A. L. 1967. *Eye movements and vision.* New York: Plenum.

Yntema, D. B., and F. P. Trask. 1963. Recall as a search process. *Journal of Verbal Learning and Verbal Behavior* 2:65–74.

Young, F. W., and N. Cliff. 1971. Interactive scaling with individual subjects. Psychometric Laboratory report 94, University of North Carolina.

Zipf, G. K. 1945. The meaning-frequency relationship of words. *Journal of General Psychology* 33:251–256.

Zusne, L. 1970. *Visual perception of form.* New York: Academic Press.

Zwicky, A. M. 1971a. In a manner of speaking. *Linguistic Inquiry* 11:223–233.

—————1971b. On reported speech. In C. J. Fillmore and D. T. Langendoen, eds., *Studies in linguistic semantics.* New York: Holt, Rinehart & Winston.

Index of Names

Index of Subjects